The

Rock

Who's

Who

The

Rock

Who's

Brock Helander

Who

2nd EDITION

SCHIRMER BOOKS

AN IMPRINT OF SIMON & SCHUSTER MACMILLAN

NEW YORK

PRENTICE HALL INTERNATIONAL

LONDON / MEXICO CITY / NEW DELHI / SINGAPORE / SYDNEY / TORONTO

Schirmer Books
An Imprint of Simon & Schuster Macmillan
1633 Broadway
New York, NY 10019

Library of Congress Catalog Card Number: 96-28307

Printed in the United States of America

Printing Number
10 9 8 7 6 5 4 3 2

Design by Brady McNamara

Library of Congress Cataloging-in-Publication Data
Helander, Brock.
    The rock who's who / Brock Helander.—[2nd ed.]
        p.   cm.
    Includes bibliographical references and index.
    ISBN 0-02-871031-2 (alk. paper)
    1. Rock musicians—Biography—Dictionaries.   2. Rock Music—Bio-bibliography.
    3. Rock music—Discography.   I. Title.
    ML102.R6H5   1996
    781.66'092'2—dc20   96-28307
    [B]   CIP
                                                    MN

The paper used in this publication meets the minimum requirements of American National Standard for Information Sciences–Permanence of Paper for Printed Library Materials. ANSI Z3948-1992.

This book is dedicated to the spirit and memory of Elvis Presley and John Lennon

CONTENTS

PREFACE

This book serves as a revision and update of my book *The Rock Who's Who*, published in 1982 by Schirmer Books. This new volume is an annotated critical and historical discography of rock and soul music, encompassing major acts who have contributed significantly to the development of contemporary popular music. In choosing the musical acts to cover, I have focused on musicians and singers who were unique and innovative in their style, musicianship, and/or songwriting; who were significant and influential in the evolution of rock and soul music; who were in the forefront of developing musical trends; who accomplished unprecedented feats; who changed the look and sound of music; and who had an enduring impact on the music and recording industries and popular culture. Additionally, I have included a number of disc jockeys, music industry luminaries, and songwriting-production teams.

I have chosen to exclude white cover artists of the 1950s and most "bubblegum" groups of the 1960s. White cover artists of the 1950s co-opted the success and accomplishments of truly innovative and distinctive rhythm-and-blues acts in an exploitative and crassly commercial fashion. Bubblegum acts were specifically marketed to pubescent and prepubescent audiences in a contrived and exploitative manner, with little regard to the quality of music or lyrics.

Since the publication of *The Rock Who's Who*, the contemporary music scene has been irrevocably changed as the result of the introduction of the compact disc (CD). The compact disc has made the vinyl LP virtually obsolete, although a number of acts, Pearl Jam in particular, have sought to encourage the issuance of recorded material on LP. The initial focus of this book was going to be on CDs, but my editor, Richard Carlin, convinced me of the wisdom of including material issued on vinyl. Thus, in this book I include record albums, cassettes, and CDs that were regular releases in the United States. No foreign releases or so-called bootleg albums are listed. I have endeavored to be comprehensive in my discographies, yet some albums may have been omitted because of oversight or uncertainty as to an album's release.

Recording artists are listed in alphabetical order, by group name for groups and by last name for individual artists. Releases by former group members are generally listed with their former group. However, later recordings by the four members of the Beatles are each listed separately. If the reader experiences confusion, he or she need merely consult the index, which cross-references all artists included to the entry under which they are listed. Albums are listed in recording order rather than release order, and anthology albums are often listed separately.

In the discussion of hit singles, the gradation from biggest to smallest success is indicated in the following order: top, smash, major, moderate, and minor. Hit singles are discussed in the context of the three major chart categories: pop, rhythm and blues, and country and western.

I have tried to provide a comprehensive and definitive critical and historical discography of rock and soul music. All conclusions herein are my own. If the reader does not agree with my observations and conclusions, I hope that he or she will be provoked to think about my ideas. I hope the use of this book will provide as much pleasure to the reader as the researching and writing of it provided me.

Brock Helander
Sacramento, California

ACKNOWLEDGMENTS

First, I would like to thank my parents, Ed and Helen, and my brother Bruce for their support and encouragement during this arduous project. I would also like to thank my faithful friends who have supported and encouraged me throughout this project, particularly Mark and Judy Staneart, Gerry Helland, Susan Espey and family, Tom Partington, Dave Parker, and Kim Rogers. I would like to thank singer-songwriter Paula Joy Welter for typing the index as my deadline approached. Also, I acknowledge the editorial assistance of Robert Christgau. Further, I would like to acknowledge the assistance of Frank Kofsky, Joel Selvin, and Jeff Hughson in the development of the first edition of this book, *The Rock Who's Who*. Additionally, I would like to thank former editor Ken Stuart for signing me to my initial contract in 1979, and current editor Richard Carlin for tracking me down and signing me to my new contract. Finally, I thank the following record companies and their representatives for providing biographical and discographical information during the course of my recent research: Asylum, BMG, Elektra, Epic, Mesa/Blue Moon, Scotti Brothers, Warner/Reprise, and Windham Hill.

The primary source of release date information used in this volume is as tabulated in Joel Whitburn's *Top Pop Albums, 1955–1992* and yearly supplements to that book through 1994, as compiled from *Billboard*'s album charts. This book is published independently. Write to Record Research, P.O. Box 200, Menomonee Falls, Wisconsin 53052-0200.

USE OF THE DISCOGRAPHIES

The organization of the discographies appearing herein is illustrated by the examples below.

1	2	3	4	5
Meet the Beatles	Capitol/Apple	2047	'64	†
	Capitol	90441		LP/CD
Kink Kronikles	Reprise	(2) 6454	'72	†
	Reprise	6454		CS/CD
Traffic	United Artists	6676	'68	†
	Island	90059		LP/CS/CD†
	Island	842590		CS/CD
The Who's Tommy (excerpts from 1993 Broadway original cast musical)	RCA	61874	'93	CS/CD

From left to right, the five columns supply the following information:

Column one lists the album title. Other information is included parenthetically following the album title. Such information includes recording dates and movie soundtrack, original cast, and television recording information.

Column two lists the name of the record label on which the album was released. Albums are often reissued on a label different from the original. Thus, for example, Traffic's *Traffic* was issued on United Artists and reissued on Island.

Column three lists the record label's catalog number for the album. When an album is a multiple-record set, the number of LPs, cassettes, or compact discs is indicated parenthetically before the catalog number.

Column four lists the release year. Release date information is based on Joel Whitburn's *Top Pop Albums*, which compiles information based on *Billboard* magazine's Top Pop Albums charts. Various catalogs and, of course, the albums themselves have been used to supplement the Whitburn information. Where no information is available, the column is left open. Where two dates appear, the second is the year of release on compact disc.

Column five lists the format in which the release is or was available. Formats include LP (vinyl), CS (cassette), CD (compact disc), and CD-ROM. If no information appears in the column, then the release was an LP. A dagger (†) in this column indicates that the release was unavailable at regular retail outlets in spring 1996. These titles may be found at used record and CD stores.

KEY TO ABBREVIATIONS

Abbreviations of instruments played and positions held by personnel are listed below.

bar	baritone
bjo	banjo
brs	brass
bs	bass
drm	drums
flt	flute
gtr	guitar
har	harmonica
kybd	keyboards
mdln	mandolin
org	organ
perc	percussion
pno	piano
rds	reeds
sax	saxophone
sop	soprano
ten	tenor
trmb	trombone
trpt	trumpet
synth	synthesizer
vln	violin
voc	vocals
wdwnd	woodwinds

The
Rock
Who's
Who

ABBA

Benny Andersson (b. Dec. 16, 1946, Stockholm, Sweden), kybd, gtr, voc; **Bjorn Ulvaeus** (b. Apr. 25, 1945, Gothenburg, Sweden), gtr, voc; **Agnetha "Anna" Faltskog** (b. Apr. 5, 1950, Jonkping, Sweden), voc; **Anna-Frid "Frida" Lyngstad** (b. Nov. 15, 1945, Narvik, Norway), voc

ABBA

One of the few non-British European groups to achieve consistent success stateside, ABBA issued a series of international hits beginning in 1974 that established them as the world's number one pop group by 1977.

Formed in 1970 in Stockholm, Sweden, ABBA first gained international recognition as the winner of the Eurovision network song contest in 1974. Their winning song, "Waterloo," became a near-smash American hit from their debut album of the same name. Major hits through 1980 include "SOS," "Fernando," "Dancing Queen," "Take a Chance on Me," and, perhaps their finest offering, "The Winner Takes All." Following *Super Trouper* and their final major hit, "When All Is Said and Done," ABBA disbanded. Faltskog and Lyngstad each recorded solo albums in the early '80s, while Andersson and Ulvaeus achieved their greatest subsequent success as composers for the musical *Chess*. In the mid-'90s ABBA experienced a revival of interest in their music, when it was used in the Australian movies *Muriel's Wedding* and *Priscilla, Queen of the Desert*.

ABBA

Waterloo	Atlantic	18101	'74	†
	A&M	3643	'95	CS/CD
ABBA	Atlantic	18146	'75	CS
	Polydor/A&M	5832	'95	CS/CD
Greatest Hits	Atlantic	18189	'76	
	Atlantic	19114	'78/'84	CS/CD
Arrival	Atlantic	18207	'76	†
	Atlantic	19115	'78	†
	Polydor/A&M	1319	'95	CS/CD
The Album	Atlantic	19164	'78	†
	Polydor	1217	'95	CS/CD
Voulez-Vous	Atlantic	16000	'79	†
	Polydor	1320	'95	CS/CD
Greatest Hits, Volume 2	Atlantic	16009	'79	†
Super Trouper	Atlantic	16023	'80	†
	Polydor	0023	'95	CS/CD
The Visitors	Atlantic	19332	'80	†
	Polydor	0011	'95	CS/CD
The Singles	Atlantic	80036	'82	†
I Love ABBA	Atlantic	80142	'84	†
ABBA Live	Atlantic	81675	'86	†
Gold—Greatest Hits	Polydor	517007	'93	CS/CD
Thank You for the Music	Polydor	(4) 523472	'95	CD

Frida Lyngstad

Something's Going On	Atlantic	80018	'82	†

Agnetha Faltskog

Wrap Your Arms Around Me	Polydor	812342	'83	CD†
I Stand Alone	Atlantic	81820	'88	LP/CS/CD†

Benny Andersson, Bjorn Ulvaeus, and Tim Rice

Chess (studio cast)	RCA	5340		CS/CD
Chess (Broadway original cast)	RCA	7700	'88	CS/CD

AC/DC

Ronald Belford "Bon" Scott (b. July 9, 1946, Kirriemuir, Scotland; d. Feb. 20, 1980), voc; **Angus Young** (b. Mar. 31, 1959, Glasgow, Scotland), lead gtr; **Malcolm Young** (b. Jan. 6, 1953, Glasgow, Scotland), rhythm gtr; **Mark Evans**, bs; **Phil Rudd**, drm [Bon Scott was replaced by **Brian Johnson** (b. Oct. 5, 1947, Newcastle, England) in 1980.]

A prototypical heavy-metal band formed in Sydney, Australia, in 1974, AC/DC established themselves in Great Britain and then the United States on the basis of tireless touring, and eventually broke through with 1979's *Highway to Hell*.

Recording songs that focus on sex, violence, and the occult packaged in live-action album covers, AC/DC achieved notoriety in 1985 when Los Angeles mass murderer Richard Ramirez, known as the Night Stalker, cited recordings by the band as the source of his satanic inspiration. Fundamentalist Christians in the United States were outraged, and the band was accused of planting messages detectable only when their albums were played backward. The controversy spurred Tipper Gore of the Washington-based Parents' Music

Resource Center to call for warning labels on albums, which in turn ignited the issue of censorship in mass media.

Persevering with vocalist Brian Johnson after the alcohol-related death of Bon Scott in 1980, AC/DC garnered tremendous popularity with *Back in Black*—ostensibly the best-selling (more than nine million copies) heavy-metal album in history—and *For Those About to Rock, We Salute You*. Projecting a blue-collar charm to their young, mostly male fans, and eschewing synthesizers, AC/DC again sparked public hostility when several fans were crushed to death in a rush to the stage at a 1991 show in Salt Lake City.

AC/DC

'74 Jailbreak	Atlantic	80178	'84	CS/CD
Australian Recordings (1975–1976)	Atlantic	92449	'94	CS/CD
Dirty Deeds Done Cheap (recorded 1976)	Atlantic	16033	'81	CS/CD
High Voltage (recorded 1976)	Atco	36142	'81	†
	Atco	92413	'94	CS/CD
Let There Be Rock	Atco	36151	'77	†
	Atco	92445	'94	CS/CD
Powerage	Atlantic	19180	'78	†
	Atco	92446	'94	CS/CD
If You Want Blood, You've Got It	Atlantic	19212	'78	†
	Atco	92447	'94	CS/CD
Highway to Hell	Atlantic	19244	'79	†
	Atco	92419	'94	CS/CD
Back in Black	Atlantic	16018	'80	†
	Atco	92418	'94	CS/CD
For Those About to Rock, We Salute You	Atlantic	11111	'81	†
	Atco	92412	'94	CS/CD
Flick of the Switch	Atlantic	80100	'83	†
	Atco	92448	'94	CS/CD
Fly on the Wall	Atlantic	81263	'85	CS/CD
Who Made Who (soundtrack to film *Maximum Overdrive*)	Atlantic	81650	'86	CS/CD
Blow Up Your Video	Atlantic	81828	'88	CS/CD
The Razors Edge	Atco	91413	'90	LP/CS/CD
Live (special collector's edition)	Atco	(2) 92212	'92	CS/CD
Live	Atco	92215	'92	CS/CD
Ballbreaker	East/West	61780	'95	LP/CS/CD

AEROSMITH

Steve Tyler (b. Steve Tallarico, Mar. 26, 1948, Yonkers, NY), lead voc; **Joe Perry** (b. Sept. 10, 1950, Lawrence, MA), lead gtr; **Brad Whitford** (b. Feb. 23, 1952, Winchester, MA), rhythm gtr; **Tom Hamilton** (b. Dec. 31, 1951, Colorado Springs, CO), bs; **Joey Kramer** (b. June 21, 1950, New York, NY), drm

One of the most popular American hard-rock bands of the mid- to late '70s, Aerosmith played blues-based music reminiscent of the Rolling Stones and the Yardbirds. Comparisons to the Stones were reinforced by the interplay between taciturn lead guitarist Joe Perry and colorful lead vocalist Steve Tyler, for a time known as the Toxic Twins because of their well-publicized abuse of alcohol and drugs.

Formed in 1970 in Sunapee, New Hampshire, as Chain Reaction by Steve Tyler, Joe Perry, and Tom Hamilton, the group became Aerosmith with the 1971 addition of Brad

Whitford and Joey Kramer. By 1972 the band had caught the ear of the then-president of Columbia Records, Clive Davis, who signed the band. Playing more than two hundred concerts a year for a number of years, Aerosmith first charted in 1973 with the minor hit "Dream On." (When issued in the longer, album version at the beginning of 1976, "Dream On" became a smash hit.) The band finally broke through in 1975 with *Toys in the Attic* and its moderate hit single "Sweet Emotion." The album also contained the group favorite "Big Ten Inch Record" and yielded the classic "Walk This Way."

With the charismatic and irrepressible Steve Tyler presiding over rambunctious concerts with his screaming style of singing, by 1978 Aerosmith were established as prime purveyors of arena rock, and ultimately they influenced a new generation of hard-rock bands, such as Bon Jovi, Motley Crue, and Guns N' Roses. *Rocks*, Aerosmith's highest-charting album of the '70s, yielded the hits "Home Tonight," "Back in the Saddle," and "Last Child." The band managed a major hit with the Beatles' "Come Together" from the movie *Sgt. Pepper's Lonely Hearts Club Band*, but following *A Night in the Ruts* Perry left to form the Joe Perry Project. Brad Whitford left in 1981 to record with Derek St. Holmes; Tyler, Hamilton, and Kramer persevered with new members for several years.

In 1984 Steve Tyler, Joe Perry, and Brad Whitford reconciled their differences and re-assembled the original members, although they did not have a recording contract. Signed to Geffen Records, Aerosmith recorded the pedestrian *Done with Mirrors* and resumed touring. In 1986 the rap group Run-D.M.C. scored a smash R&B and pop hit with "Walk This Way," recorded in both audio and video form with Tyler and Perry. That success generated renewed interest in Aerosmith, and the band responded with *Permanent Vacation*, hailed by critics as a remarkable comeback and a return to the vitality of their '70s sound. The album produced three major hits: the sarcastic "Dude (Looks Like a Lady)," the ballad "Angel," and "Rag Doll." Aerosmith's 1988 tour with Guns N' Roses became one of the highest-grossing of the '80s.

Pump revealed renewed depth and emotion in Aerosmith's songwriting and sustained their comeback with the hits "Love in an Elevator," "Janie's Got a Gun" (about child abuse), "What It Takes," "The Other Side," and "Monkey on My Back" (about their collective battle with drugs). Enjoying newfound popularity with a younger generation through FM rock radio and MTV, the band continued their best-selling ways with *Get a Grip* and its attendant hits "Cryin'," "Amazing," "Crazy," and the ballad "Livin' on the Edge," plus "Eat the Rich" and "Flesh." In 1994 Aerosmith headlined the Woodstock II festival.

After their next release on Geffen the band will move to Sony Music, with whom they have signed a recording contract reportedly valued at $30 million.

Aerosmith

Aerosmith	Columbia	32005	'73	†
Get Your Wings	Columbia	32847	'74	†
	Columbia	57361		CS/CD
Toys in the Attic	Columbia	33479	'75	†
	Columbia	57362		CS/CD
Rocks	Columbia	34165	'76	†
	Columbia	57363		CS/CD
Draw the Line	Columbia	34856	'77	†
Live Bootleg	Columbia	35564	'78	†
	Columbia	57365		CS/CD
A Night in the Ruts	Columbia	36050	'79	†
	Columbia	57366		CS/CD
Greatest Hits	Columbia	36865	'80	†
	Columbia	57367		CS/CD

Rock in a Hard Place	Columbia	38061	'82	
	Columbia	57368		CS/CD
Classics Live!	Columbia	40329	'86	CS/CD†
Gems (1973–1982)	Columbia	44487	'88	CS/CD
Pandora's Box	Columbia	(3) 46209	'91	CS/CD
Done with Mirrors	Geffen	24091	'85	LP/CS/CD
Permanent Vacation	Geffen	24162	'87	LP/CS/CD
Pump	Geffen	24254	'89	CS/CD
Get a Grip	Geffen	21821	'93	CS/CD
Big Ones	Geffen	24716	'94	CS(2)/CD(1)
The Joe Perry Project				
Let the Music Do the Talking	Columbia	36388	'80	CD
I've Got the Rock 'n' Rolls Again	Columbia	37364	'81	CD
Once a Rocker, Always a Rocker	MCA	11028	'94	CD

THE ALLMAN BROTHERS BAND

Duane Allman (b. Nov. 20, 1946, Nashville, TN; d. Oct. 29, 1971, Macon, GA), first lead and slide gtr, voc; **Gregg Allman** (b. Dec. 8, 1947, Nashville, TN), kybd, gtr, voc; **Richard "Dickey" Betts** (b. Dec. 12, 1943, West Palm Beach, FL), second lead and slide gtr, dobro, voc; **Berry Oakley** (b. Apr. 4, 1948, Jacksonville, FL; d. Nov. 11, 1972, Macon, GA), bs; **Butch Trucks** (b. Jacksonville, FL), drm; **Jai Johanny "Jaimoe" Johanson** (b. July 8, 1944, Ocean Springs, MS), drm, perc

The first and probably the best of the many blues- and country-oriented bands to emerge from the South in the '70s, the Allman Brothers Band established themselves as one of the finest performing groups in the country through touring and the release of the live double-record set *At Fillmore East*. Propelled by the twin lead guitars of Dickey Betts and Duane Allman, a revered session man and perhaps rock's greatest slide guitarist, the Allman Brothers Band helped open up rock to music created outside the recording centers of New York and Los Angeles, and provided the impetus for the rise of other Southern bands such as Lynyrd Skynyrd and the Charlie Daniels and Marshall Tucker bands. They persevered despite the deaths of Duane Allman in 1971 and Berry Oakley in 1972, only to disband for separate projects in 1974. The Allman Brothers Band regrouped from 1978 to 1982 and again in 1989 for touring and recording.

Duane and Gregg Allman moved in 1958 to Florida, where they formed their first band while still in high school. In 1965 the brothers assembled the regional band the Allman Joys, which lasted two years. They subsequently formed Hourglass for two albums on Liberty, only to split up in spring 1968 as Duane pursued session work in Muscle Shoals, Alabama, backing Wilson Pickett, Aretha Franklin, and many others. After Duane's death this session work was compiled on two double-record sets entitled *An Anthology*.

The Allman Brothers Band was formed in the spring of 1969 after a jam session between Duane Allman and the members of the groups the 31st of February (which included Butch Trucks) and the Second Coming (which included Dickey Betts and Berry Oakley). Signed by Phil Walden, who subsequently formed Capricorn Records in the band's adopted hometown of Macon, Georgia, the Allman Brothers Band recorded their debut album for Atco in 1969. It included the rock classics "It's Not My Cross to Bear," "Trouble No More," and "Whipping Post."

Duane continued his session work with Boz Scaggs (on his overlooked first album), Delaney and Bonnie (*To Delaney From Bonnie*), and, most notable, Eric Clapton (Derek and the

THE ALLMAN BROTHERS BAND

Dominos' *Layla and Other Assorted Love Songs*). Duane declined Clapton's invitation to join his group, and the Allman Brothers soon recorded *Idlewild South*, which contained Betts's "In Memory of Elizabeth Reed" and Gregg's "Midnight Rider." Having established themselves as thrilling and dynamic performers, the band switched to Walden's Capricorn label for their breakthrough live double-record set *At Fillmore East*, which included an outstanding 13-minute version of "Elizabeth Reed" and an extended version of Gregg's "Whipping Post."

On October 29, 1971, Duane was killed in a motorcycle accident in Macon. The band subsequently abandoned their twin lead guitar configuration for 1972's *Eat a Peach*, which contained the minor hits "One Way Out" and "Melissa." Pianist Chuck Leavell was added in October 1972, but on November 11, 1972, Berry Oakley was fatally injured in a motorcycle accident, again in Macon. Despite the double loss, the Allman Brothers Band persevered, recruiting bassist Lamar Williams. *Brothers and Sisters*, from 1973, featured the instrumental "Jessica" and the band's only Top 10 hit, Betts's "Ramblin' Man."

Band members then pursued solo projects. Gregg Allman retained Trucks, Johanson, and Leavell for *Laid Back*, which produced a major hit single, "Midnight Rider," and a tour in 1974, the year Betts recorded and toured in support of his first solo album, *Highway Call*. Reunited for 1975's *Win, Lose or Draw*, the Allman Brothers Band fragmented in 1976 following Gregg's testimony against former road manager John "Scooter" Herring, who faced drug charges.

Subsequently Betts formed Great Southern with guitarist Dan Toler; Leavell formed Sea Level with Johanson, Williams, and guitarist Jimmy Nalls; Butch Trucks assembled Trucks; and Gregg formed his own band for 1977's *Playin' Up a Storm*. In June 1975 Gregg married Cher (of Sonny and Cher fame) and endured a stormy marriage; the poorly received 1977 duet album *Allman and Woman — Two the Hard Way*; and a dismal European tour.

In October 1978 the Allman Brothers Band reassembled, with Gregg Allman, Dickey Betts, Johanny Johanson, Butch Trucks, and Dan Toler, plus David Goldflies from Betts's Great Southern. Having resumed the double-lead-guitar format, the reconstituted Allman Brothers scored a major hit with "Crazy Love" from *Enlightened Rogues*. The group then switched to Arista Records for two albums before another breakup. Gregg Allman recorded two albums in the late '80s and reconstituted the Allman Brothers Band once again in 1989, with Betts, Trucks, Johanson, Toler, Goldflies, and others, for touring and recordings on Epic Records. Also in 1989, Chuck Leavell toured as one of the two keyboardists on the Rolling Stones' Steel Wheels tour.

The Allman Joys

Early Allman	Dial	60005	'73	†
Allman Joys	Mercury	518040	'93	CD

Hourglass

Hourglass	Liberty	7536	'67	†
	Liberty	96059	'92	CS/CD
Power of Love	Liberty	7555	'68	†
	EMI	98826	'93	CS/CD
Hourglass	United Artists	(2) 013	'73	†

Duane and Gregg Allman

Duane and Gregg Allman	Bold	33-301	'72	†

31st of February

31st of February	Vanguard	6503	'68	†

Duane Allman

An Anthology, Volume 1	Capricorn	(2) 0108	'72	†
	Polydor	(2) 831444	'87	CD
An Anthology, Volume 2	Capricorn	(2) 0139	'74	†
	Polydor	(2) 831445	'87	CD
Best	Polydor	6338	'81	†
	Polydor	827563		CS

The Allman Brothers Band

The Allman Brothers Band	Atco	33-308	'69	†
	Polydor	823653		CS/CD
Idlewild South	Atco	33-342	'70	†
	Capricorn	0197		†
	Polydor	833334	'88	CS/CD
Beginnings	Atco	(2) 805	'73	†
	Capricorn	(2) 0132		†
	Polydor	(2) 827588		CS/CD
Live at Ludlow Garage, 1970	Polydor	843260	'90	CS
	Polydor	(2) 843260	'90	CD
At Fillmore East	Capricorn	(2) 802	'71	†
	Capricorn	0131		†
	Polydor	(2) 0131		†
	Polydor	(2) 823273		CS/CD
	Mobile Fidelity	(2) 20588	'92	CD
The Fillmore Concerts	Polydor	(2) 517294	'92	CD
Eat a Peach	Capricorn	(2) 0102	'72	†
	Polydor	(2) 0102		†
	Polydor	823654		CS/CD
	Mobile Fidelity	157	'84	†
	Mobile Fidelity	10513	'88	CD
Brothers and Sisters	Capricorn	0111	'73	†
	Polydor	0111		†
	Polydor	825092		CS/CD
	Mobile Fidelity	617	'94	CD
	Mobile Fidelity	213	'95	CS
Win, Lose or Draw	Capricorn	0156	'75	†
	Polydor	827586		CS/CD

Wipe the Window, Check the Oil, Dollar Gas (1972–1975)	Capricorn	(2) 0177	'76	†
	Polydor	831595	'87	CS/CD
The Allman Brothers Band	Polydor	(2) 0196		†
Enlightened Rogues	Capricorn	0218	'79	†
	Polydor	831589	'87	CS/CD
Reach for the Sky	Arista	9535	'80	†
Brothers of the Road	Arista	9564	'81	†
Hell and High Water: The Best of the Arista Years	Arista	18724	'94	CS/CD
Best	Polydor	6339	'81	†
	Polydor	823708		CS
Dreams	Polydor	(4) 839417	'89	CS/CD
A Decade of Hits, 1969–1979	Polydor	(4) 511156	'91	CS/CD
Ramblin' Man	Polygram	843771		CS/CD
Seven Turns	Epic	46144	'90	CD†
Shades of Two Worlds	Epic	47877	'91	CS/CD
An Evening with the Allman Brothers Band	Epic	48998	'92	CS/CD
Where It All Begins	Epic	64232	'94	CS/CD
2nd Set	Epic	66795	'95	CS/CD
(The) Gregg Allman (Band)				
Laid Back	Capricorn	0116	'73	†
	Polydor	831941		CS/CD
Gregg Allman Tour	Capricorn	(2) 0141	'74	†
	Polydor	831940		CD†
Playin' Up a Storm	Capricorn	0181	'77	†
	Razor & Tie	2069	'95	CD
I'm No Angel	Epic	40531	'87	CS/CD
Just Before the Bullets Fly	Epic	44033	'88	CS/CD
Allman and Woman (Gregg Allman and Cher)				
Two the Hard Way	Warner Bros.	3120	'77	†
Dickey Betts				
Highway Call	Capricorn	0123	'74	†
Dickey Betts and Great Southern				
Dickey Betts and Great Southern	Arista	4123	'77	†
Atlanta's Burning Down	Arista	4168	'78	†
Dickey Betts Band				
Pattern Disruptive	Epic	44289	'88	CS/CD
Sea Level				
Sea Level	Capricorn	0178	'77	†
Cats on the Coast	Capricorn	0198	'78	†
On the Edge	Capricorn	0212	'78	†
Ball Room	Arista	9531	'80	†
Best of Sea Level	Polydor	843140	'90	CD

THE ANIMALS

Alan Price (b. Apr. 19, 1942, Fairfield, County Durham, England), org, pno; **Eric Burdon** (b. May 11, 1941, Newcastle upon Tyne, England), voc; **Bryan "Chas" Chandler** (b. Dec. 18, 1938, Newcastle upon Tyne, England), bs; **Hilton Valentine** (b. May 22, 1943, North

Shields, England), lead gtr; **John Steel** (b. Feb. 4, 1941, Gateshead, County Durham, England), drm

Often labeled as the greatest blues band to emerge from England in the mid-'60s, the Animals for a time rivaled both the Beatles and the Rolling Stones in stature, despite their lack of the songwriting talents that sustained the two longer-lived groups. Gaining initial recognition on the basis of Eric Burdon's raw and often compelling vocals and Alan Price's subtle arrangements and inspired organ-playing, the Animals faded within two years of Price's departure. Burdon subsequently disbanded the group for an equivocal solo career, eventually reemerging in 1970 backed by War, an American soul ensemble. In the meantime, Animals bassist Chas Chandler became the manager for Jimi Hendrix, while Price pursued a solo career that established him in England, if not America. The original Animals reunited briefly in 1977 and 1983, and Burdon toured on his own in the '90s.

Originally formed in 1958 by Alan Price as the Alan Price Combo, the group became known as the Animals sometime after Eric Burdon joined in 1962. Originating in Newcastle, England, and gaining local popularity, the band signed with manager-producer Mickie Most and moved to London in January 1964, initially scoring a top hit with the blues classic "House of the Rising Sun" (note Price's outstanding arrangement and organ work). They followed up with the major hits "I'm Crying" (by Price and Burdon), "Don't Let Me Be Misunderstood," and "We Gotta Get Out of This Place" (by Brill Building songwriters Barry Mann and Cynthia Weil), and moderate-hit versions of John Lee Hooker's "Boom Boom" and Sam Cooke's "Bring It On Home to Me."

Following Alan Price's departure for a solo career in May 1965, the Animals hit with Carole King and Gerry Goffin's "Don't Bring Me Down" and the traditional blues number "See See Rider." Eric Burdon disbanded the group in September 1966, but he retained the group's name. With a reconstituted Animals, Burdon recorded a number of second-rate psychedelic hits, such as "When I Was Young," "Monterey," and "Sky Pilot" before "retiring" in late 1968.

In the meantime, Alan Price formed the Alan Price Set, hitting with a remake of Screamin' Jay Hawkins's "I Put a Spell on You" in 1966. Their one album, *The Price Is Right*, contained some of the first Randy Newman songs ever to be recorded. Disbanding the group in 1968, Price later toured and did television shows with Georgie Fame, who had a major hit in 1965 with "Yeh Yeh." Chas Chandler "discovered" Jimi Hendrix in New York and became his first manager, and managed the English rock band Slade during the '70s.

Moving to California, Eric Burdon helped form the backup group War with members of Los Angeles's Night Shift and Danish harmonica blower Lee Oskar. Recording two albums and the smash-hit single "Spill the Wine" with Burdon for MGM, War later became a popular act in its own right. After recording an album with legendary blues shouter Jimmy Witherspoon, Burdon formed yet another band, cutting two albums for Capitol.

Alan Price reemerged with his band of three years in 1973 for the soundtrack recording of (and appearance in) the Lindsay Anderson film *O Lucky Man*, and then recorded one other album for Warner Bros. before concentrating his activities in Great Britain. By the '80s Price was well established in Great Britain as a performer and composer, writing scores for movies, television, and a stage musical.

The original Animals reunited for tours and the recording of *Before We Were So Rudely Interrupted* and *Ark* in 1977 and 1983, respectively. Eric Burdon performed the lead role of a fallen rock star in the 1982 film *Comeback*, wrote an autobiography, and recorded the solo album *Wicked Man* in 1988. He toured with ex-Doors guitarist Robbie Krieger in 1990 and keyboardist Brian Auger in 1992.

The Animals

| In the Beginning | Wand | 690 | † |

Early Animals	Pickwick	3330		†
The Animals (with Eric Burdon)	MGM	4264	'64	†
On Tour	MGM	4281	'65	†
Animal Tracks	MGM	4305	'65	†
Best	MGM	4324	'66	†
Animalization	MGM	4384	'66	†
Animalism	MGM	4414	'66	†
Best, Volume 2	MGM	4454	'67	†
Best	Abkco	4226	'73	†
	Abkco	4324		LP/CS/CD
Before We Were So Rudely Interrupted	Jet	790	'77	†
Looking Back	Accord	7193	'82	†
Ark	I.R.S.	70037	'83	†
Rip It to Shreds (live 1983)	I.R.S.	70043	'84	†
	I.R.S./A&M	0043	'89	CS/CD
Don't Bring Me Down	Polygram	837671		CS
Best of Eric Burdon and the Animals (1966–1968)	Polydor	849388	'86/'91	CS/CD
Animal Tracks: Heavy Hits	Special Music	5027	'94	CS/CD

Eric Burdon and the Animals

Eric Is Here	MGM	4433	'67	†
	One Way	31376	'95	CD
Winds of Change	MGM	4484	'67	†
Twain Shall Meet	MGM	4537	'68	†
Every One of Us	MGM	4553	'68	†
	One Way	30337	'94	CD
Love Is	MGM	(2) 4591	'68	†
	One Way	30038	'94	CD
Best	MGM	4602	'69	†

Eric Burdon and War

Eric Burdon Declares War	MGM	4663	'70	†
	Avenue	71050	'92	CS/CD
(reissued as) Spill the Wine	Lax	37109	'81	†
Black Man's Burdon	MGM	(2) 4710	'70	†
	Rhino	(2) 71193	'93	CS/CD
Love Is All Around	ABC	988	'76	†
	Rhino	71218	'93	CS/CD
Best	Avenue	71954	'95	CD

Eric Burdon and Jimmy Witherspoon

Guilty!	MGM	4791	'71	†

Eric Burdon Band

Sun Secrets	Capitol	11359	'74	†
	LAX	37110	'81	†
Stop!	Capitol	11426	'75	†
Sun Secrets/Stop!	Rhino	71219	'93	CS/CD

Eric Burdon

Animals' Greatest Hits Sung by Eric Burdon	Special Music	4919		CS/CD
Eric Burdon's Greatest Animal Hits	Pair	1209		CD
Wicked Man	GNP Crescendo	2194	'88	LP/CS/CD
The Unreleased Eric Burdon	Blue Wave	117	'92	CS/CD

Greatest Animal Hits	Avenue	71708	'94	CD
Alan Price				
The Price Is Right	Parrot	71018	'68	†
	London	71018	'73	†
O Lucky Man! (soundtrack)	Warner Bros.	2710	'73	†
Between Today and Yesterday	Warner Bros.	2783	'74	†
Alan Price	United Artists	809	'77	†
Lucky Day	Jet	35710	'79	†
Rising Sun	Jet	36510	'80	†
House of the Rising Sun	Townhouse	7126	'81	†
Hilton Valentine				
All in Your Head	Capitol	330	'70	†

PAUL ANKA

(b. July 30, 1941, Ottawa, Canada)

One of the more sophisticated performers and songwriters to come out of the rock-and-roll '50s, Paul Anka scored a number of hits with his own compositions while still a teenager. Established as a top nightclub performer by 1960, Anka pursued a successful career as a songwriter, composing more than four hundred songs, and reemerged with several huge hits in the mid-'70s.

Raised in Canada, Paul Anka first performed in public at age 12. Traveling to Hollywood in 1956, he recorded his first, albeit unsuccessful, single for Modern Records. In May 1957, at age 15, Anka auditioned a song for Don Costa of ABC-Paramount Records in New York that would become one of the biggest-selling singles (100 million records) of the '50s, "Diana." Over the next three years he hit the charts consistently with compositions that often reflected the simple, even naive, but nonetheless poignant concerns of teenagers. His best-remembered smash hits of the period include "You Are My Destiny," "Lonely Boy," "Put Your Head on My Shoulder," "Puppy Love," and "My Home Town."

Anka switched to RCA Records in 1962, but remained off the charts after 1963. He continued to perform his past hits on the nightclub circuit through 1966, when he became disillusioned with living in the past. Having written songs for others beginning with "It Doesn't Matter Anymore" for Buddy Holly in 1958, Anka concentrated on his songwriting. Subsequently his *Tonight Show* theme became one of his most profitable compositions; and his rewrite of the French ballad "Comme d'Habitude" as "My Way" in 1968 became perhaps his best-known song, and Frank Sinatra's theme song. Anka's "She's a Lady" became a smash hit for Tom Jones in 1971.

Anka reestablished himself as a recording artist in 1974 with the top hit "(You're) Having My Baby," recorded with Odia Coates, with whom he toured for several years. Other near-smash hits of the era included "One Man Woman"/"One Woman Man" (with Coates), "I Don't Like to Sleep Alone," and "Times of Your Life." Paul Anka continues to write, record, tour, and appear in the occasional television show. He has also formed his own movie production company, Paul Anka Films, in order to pursue yet another aspect of his career.

Paul Anka				
Paul Anka	ABC-Paramount	240	'58	†
My Heart Sings	ABC-Paramount	296	'59	†
Swings for Young Lovers	ABC-Paramount	347	'60	†

At the Copa	ABC-Paramount	353	'60	†
It's Christmas Everywhere	ABC-Paramount	360	'60	†
Instrumental Hits	ABC-Paramount	371	'61	†
Diana	ABC-Paramount	420	'62	†
Young, Alive and in Love	RCA	2502	'62	†
Let's Sit This One Out	RCA	2575	'62	†
Our Man Around the World	RCA	2614	'63	†
Italiano	RCA-Italian	10130	'63	†
Songs I Wish I'd Written	RCA	2744	'63	†
		2482	'77	†
Excitement on Park Avenue	RCA	2966	'64	†
Strictly Nashville	RCA	3580	'66	†
Live!	RCA	3875	'67	†
Goodnight My Love	RCA	4142	'69	†
Sincerely	RCA	4203	'69	†
Life Goes On	RCA	4250	'69	†
Paul Anka in the '70s	RCA	4309	'70	†
	RCA	66203	'93	CS/CD
Listen to Your Heart	RCA	2892	'78	†
Headlines	RCA	3382	'79	†
Both Sides of Love	RCA	3926	'81	†
Paul Anka	Buddah	5093	'72	†
Jubilation	Buddah	5114	'72	†
Anka	United Artists	314	'74	†
Feelings	United Artists	367	'75	†
	Liberty	10149	'82	†
Times of Your Life	United Artists	569	'75	†
The Painter	United Artists	653	'76	†
The Music Man	United Artists	746	'77	†
Live	Barnaby	6013	'75	†
Walk a Fine Line	Columbia	38442	'83	†
Live	Columbia	39323	'84	†

Anthologies

Sings His Big 15	ABC-Paramount	323	'60	†
Sings His Big 15, Volume 2	ABC-Paramount	390	'61	†
Sings His Big 15, Volume 3	ABC-Paramount	409	'62	†
21 Golden Hits	RCA	2691	'63	†
(rerecordings)	RCA	3808	'67/'84	CS/CD
Remember Diana	RCA	0896	'75	†
	RCA-Camden	2713		CS/CD
Lady	RCA	1054		†
She's a Lady	RCA	1098	'75	†
	Accord	7117	'81	†
	Richmond	2353		CS/CD
Sings His Favorites	RCA	1584	'76	†
Diana and Other Hits	RCA	2086	'90	CS
This Is Paul Anka	Buddah	5622	'75	†
The Essential Paul Anka	Buddah	(2) 5667	'76	†
His Best	United Artists	922	'78	†
	Liberty	46739		CS/CD†
	EMI-Manhattan	46739	'88	CS/CD

Songs I Wrote and Sing (recorded 1974–1978)	Pair	(2) 1129	'86	†
Best of Paul Anka	Pair	1204		CD
Gold—28 Original Hit Recordings	Sire	(2) 3704	'74	†
Vintage Years (1957–1961)	Sire	6043	'77	†
My Way	Camden	0616	'76	†
Puppy Love	Pickwick	3508	'76	†
Lonely Boy	Pickwick	3523	'76	†
Paul Anka	Pickwick	(2) 2087	'76	†
Very Best	Ranwood	8203	'81	LP/CS
Black Tie	Piccadilly	3403	'82	†
Teach Me Tonight	Richmond	2349		CS
Best (14 Original Hits, 1957–1961)	Rhino	70220	'86	†
30th Anniversary Anthology (1957–1978)	Rhino	(2) 71489	'89	CS/CD
Five Decades of Hits	Curb/CEMA	77467	'91	CS/CD
Sings His Big 10, Volume 1	Curb/CEMA	77557	'92	CS/CD
Sings His Big 10, Volume 2	Curb/CEMA	77558	'92	CS/CD
Classic Hits	Curb/CEMA	77566	'92	CS/CD
Live	GNP Crescendo	2175		CS/CD

THE ASSOCIATION

Gary "Jules" Alexander (b. Sept. 25, 1943, Chattanooga, TN), lead gtr, voc; **Terry Kirkman** (b. Dec. 12, 1941, Salinas, KS), brs, rds, perc, voc; **Jim Yester** (b. Nov. 24, 1939, Birmingham, AL), rhythm gtr, kybd, voc; **Russ Giguere** (b. Oct. 18, 1943, Portsmouth, NH), gtr, voc; **Brian Cole** (b. Sept. 8, 1942, Tacoma, WA; d. Aug. 2, 1972, Los Angeles, CA), bs, voc; **Ted Bluechel Jr.** (b. Dec. 2, 1942, San Pedro, CA), drm [Russ Giguere was replaced by **Richard Thompson** (b. San Diego, CA) in 1971.]

Hitting in 1966 with the psychedelic classic "Along Comes Mary," the Association is best remembered for the softer and more urbane sound of pop hits such as "Cherish," "Windy," and "Never My Love" through 1968. Like the Byrds, the Association grew out of the vibrant folk-rock scene in Los Angeles. Kirkman and Alexander had the original idea to put a group together; both had been active on the scene (Kirkman playing briefly as a duo with Frank Zappa on the local coffeehouse circuit). They brought Cole and Yester into the group to form a quartet, and then Giguere and Bluechel joined while the band was rehearsing in mid-'65. They made their first public performance in Pasadena, California.

The group signed with a small local label, Valiant, which issued their first single, "Along Comes Mary," in 1965. (Some conservative critics thought the song was drug-inspired, "Mary" being one of the names for marijuana; to modern ears the song sounds like a harmless pop love ballad.) This was followed by the group's biggest hits, all pop-flavored ballads. Warner Bros. absorbed the Valiant label to purchase the group's contract, and issued their single "Windy" in 1967 to much hype and fanfare. The group supplied the title song for the 1969 film *Goodbye Columbus*, but soon after their work fell off the charts. They took a more psychedelic-rock turn, but listeners were uninterested in hearing this sunny harmony group take on a more groovy persona.

Giguere left in 1971 and made a solo album issued also by Warner Bros. The Association suffered a crippling blow with the death of group mentor Brian Cole in 1972. The group pretty much disbanded in 1973. Ramos, Bluechel, and Yester released a single together in 1975, and the surviving members of the original group came back together in 1981. Giguere and Ramos have managed to keep the "Association" name alive with various touring groups to the present.

The Association

And Then . . . Along Comes the Association	Valiant	5002	'66	†
	Warner Bros.	1702	'69	†
Renaissance	Valiant	5004	'67	†
	Warner Bros.	1704	'69	†
Insight Out	Warner Bros.	1696	'67	†
Birthday	Warner Bros.	1733	'68	†
Greatest Hits	Warner Bros.	1767	'68	CS/CD
Goodbye Columbus (soundtrack)	Warner Bros.	1786	'69	†
The Association	Warner Bros.	1800	'69	†
"Live"	Warner Bros.	1868	'70	†
Stop Your Motor	Warner Bros.	1927	'71	†
Waterbeds in Trinidad	Columbia	31348	'72	†
Songs That Made Them Famous	Pair	1061	'84/'86	CD

Russ Giguere

Hexagram 16	Warner Bros.	1910	'71	†

B

BURT BACHARACH
(b. May 12, 1928, Kansas City, MO)

With lyricist Hal David, Burt Bacharach formed one of the most successful professional songwriting teams in rock-music history. Their dozens of hit compositions featured David's Tin Pan Alley lyrics and Bacharach's distinctive melodies, bridges and modulations, and uncommon rhythms. In arranging horn and string parts for the Drifters in the early '60s and for Dionne Warwick throughout the '60s, Bacharach helped change the sound of contemporary R&B and soul music. After a fallow period during the '70s, Bacharach reemerged in the '80s with a number of huge hits in collaboration with lyricist Carole Bayer Sager, including Dionne Warwick's "That's What Friends Are For."

Burt Bacharach studied music at McGill University in Montreal. By 1958 he had teamed with Hal David, who had been writing song lyrics since 1943. Early successful collaborations include "The Story of My Life" for country crooner Marty Robbins and "Magic Moments" for popster Perry Como. Initially the two often worked separately, and each were associated with a number of hits, such as Sarah Vaughan's "Broken-Hearted Melody" (by David and Sherman Edwards), Gene McDaniels's "Tower of Strength" (by Bacharach and Bob Hilliard), and the Shirelles' "Baby, It's You" (by Bacharach, Mack David, and Barney Williams).

In the early '60s the team collaborated on smash hits such as Gene Pitney's "Only Love Can Break a Heart," Dusty Springfield's "Wishin' and Hopin'," and Jackie DeShannon's "What the World Needs Now Is Love." From the mid- to late '60s the duo provided Dionne Warwick with at least 39 charting records, among them "Anyone Who Had a Heart," "Walk On By," "Message to Michael," "Do You Know the Way to San Jose?," and "I Say a Little Prayer."

Throughout the '60s Bacharach and David composed for films, providing the title songs to *What's New Pussycat* (by Tom Jones, 1965) and *Alfie* (by Dionne Warwick, 1967), "The Look of Love" (sung by Dusty Springfield, 1967) from *Casino Royale*, and the top hit "Raindrops Keep Falling on My Head" (by B. J. Thomas, 1969) from *Butch Cassidy and the Sundance Kid*. In the late '60s the two collaborated on the smash Broadway musical *Promises, Promises*, from which Dionne Warwick scored two hits, the title song and "I'll Never Fall in Love Again."

Although Bacharach embarked on his own recording career in 1966, he and Hal David provided smash hits for the Carpenters ("Close to You") and the Fifth Dimension ("One Less Bell to Answer") in 1970. Bacharach and Dionne Warwick also ended their professional relationship in the early '70s (although they reunited briefly for a tour in 1987). During the '70s Bacharach performed to enthusiastic audiences, both live and on television. He recorded a symphonic suite, *Woman*, with the Houston Symphony in 1979.

In 1981 Bacharach began collaborating with lyricist Carole Bayer Sager (b. Mar. 8, 1946, New York, NY). She had provided the lyrics for a number of smash-hit songs, including "Groovy Kind of Love" (sung by the Mindbenders, 1966), "Midnight Blue" and "Don't Cry Out Loud" (sung by Melissa Manchester in 1975 and 1978, respectively), "When I Need You" (sung by Leo Sayer, 1977), and "Nobody Does It Better" (sung by Carly Simon, 1977). Bacharach and Sager's first collaboration, with songwriter-singer Peter Allen and singer Christopher Cross, yielded the top hit "Best That You Can Do" as the theme to the film *Arthur* in 1981.

Bacharach and Sager married in 1982 and soon composed the hits "Making Love" for Roberta Flack and "Heartlight" with and for Neil Diamond. In 1986 they supplied the top hits "On My Own" to Patti Labelle and Michael McDonald, and "That's What Friends Are For" to Dionne Warwick with Stevie Wonder and others. The profits from "That's What Friends Are For"—more than $1.5 million—were donated to the American Foundation for AIDS Research (AMFAR). The following year Bacharach toured with Warwick, and Bacharach and Sager provided Warwick and Jeffrey Osborne with the major hit "Love Power." Bacharach and Sager divorced in 1991. In 1995 Bacharach collaborated with Elvis Costello on "God Give Me Strength" from the *Grace of My Heart* soundtrack.

Burt Bacharach

Man! His Songs	Kapp	3447	'66	†
Plays His Hits	Kapp	3577	'69	†
	MCA	65		†
Reach Out	A&M	4131	'67	†
	A&M	3102		†
Make It Easy on Yourself	A&M	4188	'69	†
Butch Cassidy and the Sundance Kid (soundtrack)	A&M	3159	'69	CD
Burt Bacharach	A&M	3501	'71	†
Living Together	A&M	3527	'74	†
Greatest Hits	A&M	3661	'74	†
	A&M	3321	'89	CS/CD
Futures	A&M	4622	'77	†
Burt Bacharach	A&M	2521	'87	CD

Burt Bacharach with the Houston Symphony

Woman	A&M	3709	'79	†

BAD COMPANY

Paul Rodgers (b. Dec. 12, 1949, in Middlesbrough, England), voc; **Mick Ralphs** (b. May 31, 1944, Hereford, England), gtr; **Raymond "Boz" Burrell** (b. 1946, Lancashire, England), bs; **Simon Kirke** (b. Aug. 27, 1949, Wales, England), drm

A third-generation British superstar rock band whose antecedents lie with Free, Mott the Hoople, and King Crimson, Bad Company quickly rose to prominence in the second half of the '70s with its loud, hard-driving music and the distinctive vocals of Paul Rodgers.

London-born guitarist Paul Kossoff played with drummer Simon Kirke in Black Cat Bones before forming Free in 1968 with bassist Andy Fraser and vocalist Paul Rodgers. Though critically acclaimed (particularly in England), the group managed only one hit, "All Right Now," before breaking up in 1971. Kossoff revived the group from 1972 to 1973, and later formed Back Street Crawler. On March 19, 1976, while en route via airplane from Los Angeles to New York to confer with executives of Atlantic Records, Paul Kossoff died of heart failure.

Formed in late 1973, Bad Company debuted in Newcastle, England, in March 1974. Like Paul Rodgers and Simon Kirke, the other two members had prior British-rock-band experience: guitarist Mick Ralphs with Mott the Hoople, and bassist Boz Burrell with King Crimson. Bad Company was the first group signed to Led Zeppelin's Swan Song label. Their debut album included the signature song "Bad Company," plus "Ready for Love," "Movin' On," and the smash-hit single "Can't Get Enough." Their 1974 tour, originally scheduled for six weeks as an opening act, was extended to three months, with the band returning to England as headliners. *Straight Shooter*, their second album, featured "Good Lovin' Gone Bad" and the major hit "Feel Like Makin' Love." After recording *Burnin' Sky* in France in 1977, Bad Company waited three years before recording *Desolation Angels*, which yielded the hit "Rock 'n' Roll Fantasy."

Paul Rodgers left Bad Company in late 1982; he performed all the chores, from playing all the instruments to producing, in recording his solo album, *Cut Loose*. He subsequently manned supergroups the Firm (with Led Zeppelin guitarist Jimmy Page) from 1984 to 1986 and the Law (with drummer Kenney Jones) in 1991. He later recorded a tribute album to Muddy Waters on Victory Records with Jeff Beck, Neal Schon, Slash, and Brian May, and toured in support of the album with Schon.

Mick Ralphs and Simon Kirke continued with Bad Company, adding vocalist Brian Howe in 1986, and guitarist Geoffrey Whitehorn and bassist Paul Cullen in 1990. That year's *Holy Water* included the hits "If You Needed Somebody" and "Walk Through Fire." In late 1992 bassist Rick Wills, formerly with Foreigner, joined the group. In 1995 Bad Company switched to EastWest Records for *Company of Strangers*.

Free

Tons of Sobs	A&M	4198	'69	†
Free	A&M	4204	'70	†
Fire and Water	A&M	4268	'70	†
	A&M	3126		CS/CD
Highway	A&M	4287	'71	†
Free Live	A&M	4306	'71	LP/CD†
Free at Last	A&M	4349	'72	
The Best of Free	A&M	3663	'75	LP/CS/CD
Modern Gold: The Anthology	A&M	8456	'93	CS/CD
Heartbreaker	Island	9324	'73	†
	Island	9217		†
	Island	842361	'92	CD
The Free Story	Island	(2) 4	'75	†

Bad Company

Bad Company	Swan Song	8410	'74	†
	Swan Song	8501		CS/CD†
	Swan Song	92441	'94	CS/CD
Straight Shooter	Swan Song	8413	'75	†
	Swan Song	8502		CS/CD
Run with the Pack	Swan Song	8415	'76	†
	Swan Song	8503		CS/CD
Burnin' Sky	Swan Song	8500	'77	CS/CD†
	Swan Song	92450	'94	CS/CD
Desolation Angels	Swan Song	92451	'79	CS/CD
Rough Diamonds	Swan Song	90001	'82	CS/CD†
	Swan Song	92452	'94	CS/CD
Best (10 from 6)	Atlantic	81625	'86	CS/CD

Fame and Fortune	Atlantic	81684	'87	CS/CD
Dangerous Age	Atlantic	81884	'88	CS/CD
Holy Water	Atco	91371	'90	CS/CD
Here Comes Trouble	Atco	91759	'92	CS/CD
Best: What You Hear Is What You Get	Atco	92307	'93	CS/CD
Company of Strangers	EastWest	61808	'95	CS/CD
Paul Rodgers				
Cut Loose	Atlantic	80121	'83/'91	CD
A Tribute to Muddy Waters	Victory	480013	'93	CS/CD
The Hendrix Set	Victory	480014	'93	CS/CD
The Firm				
The Firm	Atlantic	81239	'85	CS/CD
Mean Business	Atlantic	81628	'86	CS/CD
The Law				
The Law	Atlantic	82195	'91	CS/CD

JOAN BAEZ
(b. Jan. 9, 1941, Staten Island, NY)

One of the finest female singers to emerge from the early-'60s folk scene, Joan Baez was most probably the first folk singer of the era to achieve massive international success. One of the first solo folk singers to record best-selling albums of traditional folk material, she helped introduce Bob Dylan to a wider audience as she became one of the first folk singers to be involved with the protest movement. Associated with the protest classic "We Shall Overcome," Baez later enjoyed popularity as a song interpreter before emerging as a singer-songwriter, particularly with 1975's *Diamonds and Rust* album. Although accorded star status in Europe, she was reduced to mere celebrity status in the United States and remained without an American record label for much of the '80s. While continuing to involve herself with protest and freedom movements internationally, Joan Baez recorded her first album in years for a major label in 1992.

Joan Baez started performing in public, accompanying herself on guitar, at small clubs around Cambridge and Boston in the late '50s, and soon graduated to New York's Greenwich Village. Successful appearances at the 1959 and 1960 Newport Folk festivals followed. Baez moved to California in 1961. On Vanguard Records, her first three albums consisted of standard folk fare, primarily traditional English and American ballads. Her fourth album, *In Concert, Part 2*, featured the song that was to become the protest anthem of the '60s, "We Shall Overcome." That and subsequent albums contained her versions of songs by then-unrecognized folk artists such as Phil Ochs ("There But for Fortune") and Greenwich Village friend Bob Dylan ("Don't Think Twice," "It's All Over Now, Baby Blue," and others). Baez supported Dylan in his early career, often inviting him onstage as her surprise guest. She accompanied him on his first tour of England in 1965, immortalized in the film *Don't Look Back*. With 1967's *Joan*, Baez began recording songs by contemporary songwriters such as Tim Hardin ("If I Were a Carpenter") and Lennon and McCartney. *Any Day Now*, released in 1968, was a double-record set comprised of songs by Bob Dylan.

Covering material by songwriters such as Willie Nelson, Hoyt Axton, and John Prine, Joan Baez achieved her only major hit in 1971 with Robbie Robertson's "The Night They Drove Old Dixie Down." Having begun writing her own songs in the early '70s, she placed six of her songs on *Come from the Shadows* (her first album for A&M Records), including the undisguised "To Bobby," as well as her sister Mimi Farina's "In the Quiet Morning." Her 1975 *Diamonds and Rust* album contained her own compositions "Winds of the Old Days" and the hit title song, plus John Prine's "Hello in There" and Janis Ian's "Jesse." From 1975 to 1976 Baez toured with Bob Dylan's curious Rolling Thunder Revue, and appeared in the even more curious film made of the tour, *Renaldo and Clara*. After two final albums for A&M, she switched to Portrait Records (reissued on Epic) for *Blowin' Away* and *Honest Lullaby*.

Having founded the Institute for the Study of Non-Violence in 1965, Joan Baez confirmed her commitment to humanitarian causes with the 1979 formation of the human rights organization Humanitas International. During the '80s she toured the world in support of other human rights organizations, including Poland's Solidarity movement and Palestinian civil disobedience groups. In 1985 she sang on the Amnesty International tour and appeared at Live Aid. Her second autobiography, *And a Voice to Sing With*, was published in 1987, the year the small Gold Castle label released the first of three albums recorded by Baez, *Recently*. In 1992, in order to reinvigorate her musical career, Joan Baez ceased operation of Humanitas International and recorded her first major label release in 13 years, only to find herself without a record label in 1993.

Joan Baez

Very Early Joan (recorded live 1961–1963)	Vanguard	79446/7	'83	CS/CD
Joan Baez	Vanguard	2077	'60	LP/CS/CD
Joan Baez, Volume 2	Vanguard	2097	'61	LP/CS/CD
In Concert	Vanguard	2122	'62/'90	CS/CD
In Concert, Part 2	Vanguard	2123	'63/'90	CS/CD
The Best of Joan Baez	Squire	33001	'63	†
Joan Baez in Concert	Vanguard	(2) 113/14	'88	CD
Five	Vanguard	79160		CS/CD
Farewell Angelina	Vanguard	79200	'65	CS/CD
Noel	Vanguard	79230	'66	CS/CD
Joan	Vanguard	79240	'67	CS/CD
Baptism	Vanguard	79275	'68/'95	CS/CD
Any Day Now	Vanguard	(2) 79306/7	'68	CS
	Vanguard	79306/7		CD
David's Album	Vanguard	79308	'69/'95	CS/CD
One Day at a Time	Vanguard	79310	'70/'96	†
Blessed Are . . .	Vanguard	6570/1	'71	†
Carry It On (soundtrack)	Vanguard	79313	'71	†
Come from the Shadows	A&M	4339	'72	†
	A&M	3103		CS/CD†
Where Are You Now, My Son	A&M	4390	'73	†
Gracias a la Vida—Here's to Life	A&M	3614	'74	†
Diamonds and Rust	A&M	4527	'75	†
	A&M	3233	'84	CS/CD
From Every Stage	A&M	(2) 6506	'76	CS
	A&M	6506		CD
Gulf Winds	A&M	4603	'76	†
Blowin' Away	Epic	34697	'77/'90	CD
Honest Lullaby	Epic	35766	'79/'90	CD
Recently	Gold Castle	71304	'87	LP/CS/CD†
Diamonds and Rust in the Bullring	Gold Castle	71321	'89	LP/CS/CD†
Speaking of Dreams	Gold Castle	71324	'89	LP/CS/CD†

Play Me Backwards	Virgin	86458	'92	CS/CD
Ring Them Bells	Guardian	34989	'95	CS/CD
Anthologies				
The First Ten Years	Vanguard	(2) 6560/1	'70	CS
	Vanguard	6560/1		CD
Hits, Greatest and Others	Vanguard	79332	'73	CS/CD
Ballad Book	Vanguard	(2) 41/2	'72	CS
Ballad Book, Volume 1	Vanguard	73107		CS
Ballad Book, Volume 2	Vanguard	73115		CS
Contemporary Ballad Book	Vanguard	(2) 49/50	'74	CS
Lovesong Album	Vanguard	(2) 79/80	'76	CS
The Night They Drove Old Dixie Down	Vanguard	73119		CS
The Country Music Album	Vanguard	(2) 105/6	'79	CS
	Vanguard	105/6		CD
Rare, Live and Classic	Vanguard	(3)	'93	CD†
Selections from Rare, Live and Classic	Vanguard	705	'93	CD
Best	A&M	4668	'77	†
	A&M	3234	'84	CS/CD
Joan Baez	A&M	2506	'87	CD

HANK BALLARD
(b. Nov. 18, 1936, Detroit, MI)

As lead singer and songwriter with the Midnighters (originally known as the Royals), Hank Ballard helped bring the open sexuality of rhythm and blues into early rock and roll with the 1954 smash "Work with Me Annie." Enduring banishment from radio airplay and the release of a bowdlerized version of his "Roll with Me Henry" by white artist Georgia Gibbs, Ballard wrote and recorded the dance classic "The Twist" in 1959. However, it took Chubby Checker's soundalike cover version to make the song one of the all-time best-selling singles, launching the international dance craze of the '60s.

Discovered by bandleader Johnny Otis in 1952 while they were using the name the Royals, the group signed with Cincinnati's Federal label, a subsidiary of King, and achieved early success with Otis's ballad "Every Beat of My Heart." Hank Ballard joined in 1953, and the Royals scored a R&B smash with "Get It." Comprised of Ballard, Henry Booth, Charles Sutton, and Sonny Woods, the group changed their name to the Midnighters in April 1954, and soon had a top R&B hit with the blatantly sexual "Work with Me Annie." Although banned from radio airplay, the song sold more than a million copies. Through 1955 the Midnighters achieved major rhythm-and-blues hits with "Sexy Ways," the inevitable "Annie Had a Baby," "Annie's Aunt Fannie," and "It's Love Baby (24 Hours a Day)." Etta James recorded the "answer" to the Annie songs as "The Wallflower" (subtitled "Roll with Me Henry"), with songwriting credit going to James, Ballard, and Otis.

The Midnighters endured a number of personnel changes and became Hank Ballard and the Midnighters in 1959. Their 1959 smash R&B hit "Teardrops on Your Letter" was backed by Ballard's own "The Twist." The latter song saw little activity until Chubby Checker's version hit the charts in 1960–1961. Hank Ballard and the Midnighters achieved their biggest success with the late-'60s "Let's Go, Let's Go, Let's Go," a smash pop and top rhythm-and-blues hit. Other major pop hits through 1961 included more dance-oriented songs, "The Hoochi Coochi Coo" and "The Switcheroo," but after 1962 neither the Midnighters nor Ballard had another major hit. The group disbanded around 1968, and Ballard later toured the so-called chitlin' circuit of small black clubs before joining the James Brown Revue for several years. In the late '80s Hank Ballard once again toured. Ballard was inducted into the Rock and Roll Hall of Fame in 1990.

Hank Ballard and the Midnighters

Greatest Juke Box Hits	King	541	'56	LP/CS/CD
Hank Ballard and the Midnighters	King	581	'56/'89	LP/CS/CD
Singin' and Swingin'	King	618	'59	LP/CS/CD
The One and Only	King	674	'60/'89	LP/CS/CD
Mr. Rhythm and Blues	King	700	'60	LP/CS/CD
Spotlight on Hank Ballard	King	740	'61/'89	LP/CS/CD
Dance Along	King	759	'61	LP/CS/CD
The Twistin' Fools	King	781	'62	†
Jumpin'	King	793	'63	†
1963 Sound	King	815	'63	†
Greatest Hits	King	867	'64	†
A Star in Your Eyes	King	896		†
Those Lazy, Lazy Days	King	913		†
Glad Songs, Sad Songs	King	927		†
Hank Ballard Sings 24 Great Songs	King	981		†
20 Hits (1953–1962)	King	5003	'77	†
Finger Poppin' Time	Power Pak	276		†
	Richmond	2216		CS
20 Original Greatest Hits	Deluxe	7836		CS
What You Get When the Gettin' Gets Good	Charly	29		CD†
Work with Me Annie: The Best of Hank Ballard and the Midnighters	Rhino	71512	'93	CD
Naked in the Rain	After Hours	4137	'92	CS/CD

Hank Ballard

24 Hit Tunes	King	950	'66	LP/CS/CD
You Can't Keep a Good Man Down	King	1052	'69	†

THE BAND

Jaime Robert "Robbie" Robertson (b. July 5, 1944, Toronto, Canada), electric gtr, acoustic gtr, bs, pno, voc; **Richard Manuel** (b. Apr. 3, 1944, Stratford, Ontario, Canada; d. Mar. 4, 1986, Winter Park, FL), kybd, drm, voc; **Garth Hudson** (b. Aug. 2, 1942, London, Ontario, Canada), kybd, brs, wdwnd; **Rick Danko** (b. Dec. 9, 1943, Simcoe, Ontario, Canada), bs, voc; **Levon Helm** (b. May 26, 1943, Marvell, AK), drm, mdln, voc

One of the most popular bands in the United States from the late '60s to the mid-'70s, the Band ironically was manned by four Canadians and only one American. With only an underground reputation despite years of playing together, the Band achieved their first widespread recognition as Bob Dylan's backing rock band, later breaking through into mass popularity with the landmark *Music from Big Pink*, without benefit of the usual supporting tour. In refreshing contrast to psychedelic music, the Band featured a country-gospel sound supplemented by electric instrumentation and loose yet precise musicianship, combined with oblique vocal harmonies and incisive songwriting. Their songs frequently reflected an America of yore, as evidenced by the Robbie Robertson classic "The Night They Drove Old Dixie Down." The Band dissolved after 1978's *The Last Waltz*, and members pursued individual careers before reuniting without Robertson in the early '80s.

The Band began in the person of Levon Helm, when he and several other Arkansans moved to Canada in 1958 to back Ronnie Hawkins as the Hawks. Having pursued an unspectacular career as a country musician, Hawkins turned to rock and roll, hitting with "Forty Days" and "Mary Lou" in 1959. In 1961 Robbie Robertson took over for guitarist Fred Carter Jr.; within months, the Arkansans, except Helm, were replaced by Canadians Rick Danko, Richard Manuel, and Garth Hudson. They recorded a stunning version of "Who Do You Love," featuring Robertson's psychedelic lead work, but the group left Hawkins around 1963 to tour East Coast clubs as Levon and the Hawks, under Helm's leadership.

After the release of his first rock-oriented album, *Bringing It All Back Home*, Bob Dylan recruited the group while in New Jersey in summer 1965. Without the recalcitrant Helm, the group toured with Dylan for nearly a year, performing as his backup band, including for his infamous appearance at the Newport Folk Festival when he was booed off the stage for appearing with electric instruments. Following Dylan's much-publicized motorcycle accident, Levon Helm was summoned from Arkansas, and the group and Dylan removed to upstate New York to rehearse and record the so-called Basement Tapes. Available for years only on bootleg albums of questionable legality, some of this material was eventually released officially in 1975.

While in upstate New York the group—known simply as the Band—recorded their first album under the influence of Dylan. Released in mid-1968, *Music from Big Pink* contained one Dylan song, "I Shall Be Released," two Dylan collaborations, "Tears of Rage" (with Manuel) and "This Wheel's on Fire" (with Danko), and several excellent songs by chief songwriter Robertson, including "The Weight" and "Caledonia Mission."

Making their debut in April 1969 at Bill Graham's Winterland in San Francisco, the Band's self-titled second album was even more popular than their first and revealed a maturation of Robertson's songwriting talents. *The Band* included his classic "The Night They Drove Old Dixie Down" as well as "Across the Great Divide" and "Up on Cripple Creek." Their next album, *Stage Fright*, yielded only one minor hit, "Time to Kill," yet contained several memorable cuts, including the title song as well as "The Shape I'm In" and "Just Another Whistle Stop." In 1970 Robertson began outside musical activities, producing Jesse Winchester's debut album. The Band's *Cahoots* album contained several intriguing Robertson songs ("Smoke Signal" and "Shootout in Chinatown") and the collaborative "Life Is a Carnival." After the live *Rock of Ages*, the group recorded the amusing *Moondog Matinee*, which consisted primarily of covers of old rock-and-roll songs. In July 1973 the Band appeared before the largest crowd in rock history—some 600,000—with the Grateful Dead and the Allman Brothers, at the Watkins Glen, New York, racetrack. Recordings from the show were eventually released in 1995.

In 1974 the Band again backed their old mentor and friend Bob Dylan for his *Planet Waves* album and his first tour since 1965. From the tour came *Before the Flood*, an album combining both Dylan and Band favorites. Subsequently the Band's first recording of original material since 1971, *Northern Lights—Southern Cross*, was critically acclaimed as their best since 1969's *The Band*. Comprised entirely of Robertson songs, the album included "Acadian Driftwood," "Ophelia," and "Jupiter Hollow."

Again busy outside the group, Robbie Robertson produced Neil Diamond's *Beautiful Noise* in 1976. Later that year the Band announced their retirement after more than fifteen years on the road. Only days after recording *Islands*, their final album as a group, they made their final appearance as a group, at Bill Graham's Winterland on Thanksgiving night, 1976. Billed as the Last Waltz, this final show featured performances by a number of stars and superstars of rock, from Bob Dylan to Joni Mitchell, Eric Clapton, Neil Diamond, and Van Morrison. Both a film and an album from the show were released the following spring.

Subsequently both Rick Danko and Levon Helm recorded solo albums, Helm with the RCO All-Stars (which included Paul Butterfield and Dr. John) first, later with his own group. Helm garnered an Academy Award nomination for his supporting role as Loretta Lynn's father in *Coal Miner's Daughter*; Robbie Robertson cowrote, produced, and costarred in the less-than-successful *Carny*, with Gary Busey and Jodie Foster. In the meantime, Garth Hudson became Los Angeles's premier session accordion player and formed his own company that specialized in using digitally assisted music in scoring films such as *King of Comedy*, *Raging Bull*, and *The Color of Money*.

The Band reunited, without Robbie Robertson, for touring in 1983, augmented by the Cate Brothers Band. While on tour in Florida, Richard Manuel hanged himself in a motel bathroom on March 4, 1986. Levon Helm has continued his film work (*Smooth Talk*, *End of the Line*), whereas Robertson has recorded *Robbie Robertson* and *Storyville*. In 1993 Rick Danko, Garth Hudson, and Levon Helm reunited as the Band with three members of the Cate Brothers Band to record *Jericho* for Rhino Records and tour. In 1994 Robbie Robertson composed the music, recorded with a number of Native American musicians, for the three-part, six-hour TBS cable network miniseries *The Native Americans*. Helm wrote his autobiography, *This Wheel's On Fire*, recounting his experiences in the Band.

Ronnie Hawkins and the Hawks

Ronnie Hawkins	Roulette	25078	'59	†
Mr. Dynamo	Roulette	25102	'60	†
Folk Ballads	Roulette	25120	'60	†
Ronnie Hawkins Sings the Songs of Hank Williams	Roulette	25137	'60	†
Ronnie Hawkins with the Band	Roulette	42045	'70		
The Best of Ronnie Hawkins and the Hawks	Rhino	70966	'90	CS/CD

The Band

Music from Big Pink	Capitol	2955	'68	†
	Capitol	46069		CS/CD
	Mobile Fidelity	527	'90	CD
The Band	Capitol	132	'69	
	Capitol	16296	'84		
	Capitol	46493		CD
Stage Fright	Capitol	425	'70	†
	Capitol	16006		†
	Capitol	93593	'90	CD
Cahoots	Capitol	651	'71	†
	Capitol	16003		†
	Capitol	48420	'94	CD
Rock of Ages	Capitol	(2) 11045	'72	†
	Capitol	(2) 16008/9		†
	Capitol	(2) 93595	'90	CD
Live at Watkins Glen	Capitol	31742	'95	CD
Moondog Matinee	Capitol	11214	'73	†
	Capitol	16004		†
	Capitol	93592	'90	CD
Northern Lights—Southern Cross	Capitol	11440	'75	†
	Capitol	16005		†
	Capitol	93594		CD†
Best	Capitol	11553	'76	†
	Capitol	16331	'85	†
	Capitol	46070		CS/CD

Islands	Capitol	11602	'77	†
	Capitol	16007		†
	Capitol	93591		CD†
Anthology	Capitol	11856	'78	†
	Capitol	48419		CD†
To Kingdom Come: The Definitive Collection	Capitol	(2) 92169	'89	CD
Across the Great Divide	Capitol	(3) 89565	'94	CD
The Last Waltz	Warner Bros.	(3) 3146	'78	†
	Warner Bros.	(2) 3146	'88	CS/CD
Jericho	Rhino	71564	'93	CS/CD
The Band and Bob Dylan				
The Basement Tapes	Columbia	(2) 33682	'75	CS/CD
Planet Waves	Asylum	1003	'74	†
	Columbia	37637		CS/CD
Before the Flood	Asylum	(2) 201	'74	†
	Columbia	(2) 37661	'86	CS/CD
Levon Helm and the RCO All-Stars				
Levon Helm and the RCO All-Stars	ABC	1017	'77	†
	Mobile Fidelity	761	'92	CD
Levon Helm				
Levon Helm	ABC	1089	'78	†
	Mobile Fidelity	759	'92	CD
American Son	MCA	5120	'80	†
Levon Helm	Capitol	12201	'82	†
Rick Danko				
Rick Danko	Arista	4141	'77	†
Robbie Robertson				
The Color of Money	MCA	6189	'86	CD
Robbie Robertson	Geffen	24160	'87	CS/CD
	Mobile Fidelity	618	'94	CD
Storyville	Geffen	24303	'91	CS/CD
Robbie Robertson and the Red Road Ensemble				
The Native Americans	Capitol	28295	'94	CS/CD

JEFF BARRY AND ELLIE GREENWICH

Jeff Barry (b. Apr. 3, 1938, Brooklyn, NY); **Ellie Greenwich** (b. Oct. 23, 1940, Brooklyn, NY)

Jeff Barry and Ellie Greenwich comprised one of several New York songwriting-production teams that supplied hit compositions to producers Phil Spector and Jerry Leiber—Mike Stoller in the early '60s. Their compositions included the classics "Da Doo Ron Ron," "Be My Baby," and "Chapel of Love."

Originally intending a career as a recording artist, Jeff Barry became a professional songwriter at the beginning of the '60s. His early hit compositions include "Tell Laura I Love Her" for Ray Peterson (1960) and "Chip Chip" for Gene McDaniels (1962). In 1962 Barry met and married songwriter Ellie Greenwich. The two collaborated on a number of hits in conjunction with producer Phil Spector on his Philles label in 1963: "Da Doo Ron

Ron" and "Then He Kissed Me" for the Crystals, and "Be My Baby" and "Baby, I Love You" for the Ronettes. That year the duo also recorded an album for Jubilee Records as the Raindrops, hitting with their song "The Kind of Boy You Can't Forget."

Signed to write and produce for Jerry Leiber and Mike Stoller's Red Bird label in 1964, Jeff Barry and Ellie Greenwich composed a number of hits for several different "girl groups": "Chapel of Love" (with Phil Spector) and "People Say" for the Dixie Cups; "I Wanna Love Him So Bad" for the Jellybeans; and "Leader of the Pack" (with George "Shadow" Morton) for the Shangri-Las. Two other Barry-Greenwich songs also became hits in 1964: "Maybe I Know" sung by Lesley Gore and "Do Wah Diddy Diddy" sung by Manfred Mann.

By 1966 the couple had divorced, yet they continued to work together. When Red Bird was sold, they took fellow songwriter Neil Diamond to Bert Berns's Bang Records, where they produced the first three albums for the label. In 1966 the Barry-Greenwich composition "Hanky Panky" (a Raindrops song) became a hit for Tommy James; "River Deep—Mountain High," cowritten with Phil Spector and recorded by Ike and Tina Turner, was conspicuously unsuccessful and led to Spector's withdrawal from the music scene for several years. Subsequent production chores for Barry included the Monkees and the studio group the Archies, who had a smash hit with Barry and Andy Kim's "Sugar, Sugar" in 1969. Earlier that year, "I Can Hear Music," composed by Barry, Greenwich, and Spector, was a major hit for the Beach Boys.

Jeff Barry became a producer for A&M Records in 1971, but had little success. He composed the 1977 country hit "I Honestly Love You" for Olivia Newton-John with Peter Allen, and produced Tommy James's *Midnight Rider* and John Travolta's second album. Ellie Greenwich recorded solo albums for United Artists Records in 1968 and for Verve Records in 1973, and she continued to write songs into the '80s. In 1984 she became involved in the musical revue *Leader of the Pack*, based on her life and career, which resulted in an original cast album featuring Spector vocalist Darlene Love the following year.

The Raindrops

The Raindrops	Jubilee	5023	'63	†

Ellie Greenwich

Composes, Produces and Sings	United Artists	6648	'68	†
Let It Be Written, Let It Be Sung	Verve	65091	'73	†
	Verve/Polydor	825531	'85	†

Leader of the Pack

Original Cast	Elektra	(2) 60409	'85	†
Excerpts	Elektra	60420	'85	†

THE BEACH BOYS

Brian Wilson (b. June 20, 1942, Hawthorne, CA), kybd, bs, voc; **Dennis Wilson** (b. Dec. 4, 1944, Hawthorne, CA; d. Dec. 28, 1983, Marina Del Ray, CA), drm, voc; **Carl Wilson** (b. Dec. 21, 1946, Hawthorne, CA), lead gtr, voc; **Mike Love** (b. Mar. 15, 1941, Los Angeles, CA), lead voc, sax; **Al Jardine** (b. Sept. 3, 1942, Los Angeles, CA), rhythm gtr, voc [**Bruce Johnston** (b. June 24, 1944, Chicago, IL) joined the group in 1965.]

One of America's most popular groups in the '60s, the Beach Boys were perhaps the first white vocal-and-instrumental group to employ complex vocal arrangements to create a distinctive ensemble sound. The biggest popularizers of surf music, the Beach Boys established themselves with songs of their own creation at a time dominated by artists who recorded songs provided by professional songwriters. With Brian Wilson writing the songs,

THE BEACH BOYS

singing the falsetto parts, arranging the other voices, and producing the group's records, the Beach Boys were likely the first self-contained rock group, using studios, musicians, and technicians of their own choosing.

Brian Wilson's increasing sophistication of production, beginning with the "California Girls" single of 1965 and culminating in "Good Vibrations" and the album *Pet Sounds*, revealed a unique use of a wide range of instrumentation, styles, and sound effects rivaled at the time only by the Beatles (under George Martin) and Phil Spector. Additionally, the Beach Boys' formation in 1967 of their own label, Brother Records (with distribution handled by Capitol), was one of the first artist's custom-label deals, predating the Beatles' Apple deal by one year. Experiencing a decline in popularity and influence with Brian's recession from the group following 1971's *Surf's Up*, the Beach Boys staged a remarkable comeback with Brian's return for 1976's *15 Big Ones*, only to recede from the music scene thereafter. Debuting in a Nevada casino showroom in 1980, the current lineup is generally regarded as an oldies act.

Formed in 1961 as Kenny and the Cadets and Carl and the Passions, the Beach Boys recorded the regional hit "Surfin'" for the small local label X in 1961. They debuted in Long Beach, CA, on New Year's Eve, 1962. Between 1962 and 1965 the Beach Boys issued smash hits ad nauseam on the Southern California themes of surfing, cars and motorcycles, girls, and high school, virtually all written solely by or in collaboration with Brian Wilson. Among these hits were the title songs to *Surfin' Safari*, *Surfin' U.S.A.*, *Shut Down* (an anthology album with only two Beach Boys songs), *Surfer Girl*, and *Little Deuce Coupe*, as well as "Be True to Your School" and "Fun, Fun, Fun" from *Shut Down, Volume 2*. Beginning with "Surfer Girl," the group's releases included ballads such as the underrated "In My Room," "Don't Worry Baby," and "The Warmth of the Sun." Subsequent rockers include "I Get Around," "Wendy," "Dance, Dance, Dance," and "Help Me Rhonda."

Suffering a nervous breakdown in December 1964, Brian Wilson ceased touring with the Beach Boys. With Carl Wilson becoming the onstage leader and Al Jardine taking over Brian's falsetto parts, the group was briefly augmented by session guitarist Glen Campbell, who was replaced by Beach Boys' associate Bruce Johnston in April 1965. Johnston had previously recorded surf albums and had been a member of the Rip Chords, who scored a smash hit in 1963–1964 with "Hey Little Cobra." Relieved of his arduous touring duties, Brian continued to write for the group and, with "California Girls," introduced elaborate production techniques to the group's recordings. While the rest of the Beach Boys were on tour in mid-1965, Brian began working on his epic album, *Pet Sounds*, employing scores of studio musicians and utilizing advanced studio techniques. Although perplexed by Brian's work on the album in their absence, the returning group persevered to complete the critically acclaimed masterpiece. However, despite the lush orchestral sound and the inclusion of songs such as "Wouldn't It Be Nice," "God Only Knows," "Caroline No," and the folk song "Sloop John B.," *Pet Sounds* sold poorly compared to previous releases.

Severely disappointed, Brian Wilson nonetheless initiated work on the next album, tentatively titled *Smile*, with lyricist Van Dyke Parks. While he was deeply immersed in the project, Capitol Records issued his monumental single "Good Vibrations." Taking more than six months to record, using ninety hours of studio time, and costing $16,000 (an enormous sum to spend on one song at the time), "Good Vibrations" became the Beach Boys' only million-selling single. Meanwhile, the already troubled Brian, working against the perceived competition of producer Phil Spector and the Beatles, began behaving erratically as rumors of heavy drug use abounded. For whatever reason, *Smile* was not issued. *Smiley Smile* was released in its place on the group's recently formed custom label, Brother Records, distributed by Capitol. The album contained several songs from the abortive Brian Wilson—Van Dyke Parks collaboration, including the hit "Heroes and Villains."

The group's fascination with transcendental meditation, particularly that of Mike Love, culminated in a near-disastrous tour with the Maharishi Mahesh Yogi in 1968; the album *Friends* reflects their conversion to TM. *20/20*, their final album of new material for Capitol, featured a remake of the Phil Spector—Jeff Barry—Ellie Greenwich song "I Can Hear Music," which became a minor hit. The group switched to Warner Bros./Reprise Records in 1970, reestablishing Brother Records under that company's distributorship. The Beach Boys appeared to be emerging from their doldrums that year with their successful performance at the Big Sur Folk Festival and the release of the underrated album *Sunflower*. However, Brian's withdrawal from the group as songwriter and producer with the album *Surf's Up* and his traumatizing appearance at the Whisky a-Go-Go in 1971 left the rest of the group's members to their own devices. An old *Smile* song, "Surf's Up," and the hastily completed "Sail On Sailor" were issued, while the Beach Boys seemed to enjoy another revival with the release of older Capitol material on *Endless Summer* and *Spirit of America* in the mid-'70s.

The Beach Boys resumed touring in 1975, and during 1976 Brian Wilson rejoined the others for an hour-long television documentary that aired in August, a three-month concert tour of the United States and Canada, and *15 Big Ones*. The album, comprised half of new original material and half of remade oldies, saw Brian once again producing, though eschewing the production style pioneered with *Pet Sounds*.

Bruce Johnston provided Barry Manilow with the top hit "I Write the Songs" (said to be inspired by Brian Wilson's prolific output) in late 1975. In 1977 Johnston recorded the solo album *Going Public*, Dennis Wilson recorded *Pacific Ocean Blue*, and Mike Love recorded with both Waves and Celebration, who hit with "Almost Summer." Neither *M.I.U.* nor *L.A. (Light Album)*, recorded on the band's new Caribou label, fared particularly well. After Dennis Wilson recorded a second solo album, the Beach Boys issued *Keepin' the Summer Alive*, produced by Johnston. In 1981 Carl Wilson became the first Beach Boy to undertake a solo tour, in support of his debut solo album on Caribou.

Mike Love became the front man for the Beach Boys during the '80s, as Brian Wilson embarked on an unorthodox rehabilitation program under therapist Eugene Landy from 1983 to 1988. Dennis Wilson, the only actual surfer in the group, drowned off Marina Del Rey, California, on December 28, 1983, a victim of drug and alcohol abuse.

Since the mid-'80s, due to various lawsuits and the publication of the books *Heroes and Villains* (1986) and *Wouldn't It Be Nice* (1991), the Beach Boys and Brian Wilson have been little noticed for their music. Nonetheless, in 1988 Sire Records issued the critically acclaimed but poor-selling album *Brian Wilson*. The Beach Boys, without Brian Wilson, scored a top hit with "Kokomo," written by Mike Love, Terry Melcher, John Phillips, and Scott

McKenzie, from the soundtrack to the Tom Cruise movie *Cocktail*. Since 1991 the personal and business affairs of Brian Wilson have been managed by a court-appointed conservator. Producer Don Was directed a film documentary of Brian Wilson's life, *I Just Wasn't Made for These Times*, released in 1995; a soundtrack album consisting of remakes of old Beach Boys' songs was issued in conjunction with the film. In that same year Brian Wilson collaborated with old friend Van Dyke Parks, singing all the vocals on an album of songs written by Parks called *Orange Crate Art*.

In 1989 Brian Wilson's daughters Carnie and Wendy formed the vocal group Wilson Phillips with Chynna Phillips, the daughter of John and Michelle Phillips of the Mamas and the Papas. Their debut album produced five hits, including "Hold On," "Release Me," and "You're In Love," but the more personal *Shadows and Light* yielded only two hits. In 1993 Carnie and Wendy Wilson recorded the Christmas album *Hey Santa!* Carnie hosted her own TV talk show briefly in 1995.

The Beach Boys

Lost and Found, 1961–1962	DCC	054	'91	CS/CD
Original Surfin' Hits: Their First Recordings	Curb/Atlantic	77747	'95	CS/CD
Surfin' Safari	Capitol	1808	'62	†
	Capitol	16012	'80	†
	Capitol	29661	'94	CS/CD
Surfin' U.S.A.	Capitol	1890	'63	†
	Capitol	16015		†
	Capitol	48422	'94	CS/CD
Shut Down (two songs)	Capitol	1918	'63	†
Surfer Girl	Capitol	1981	'63	†
	Capitol	16014		†
	Capitol	29628	'94	CS/CD
Little Deuce Coupe	Capitol	1998	'63	†
	Capitol	16013		†
	Capitol	29630	'94	CS/CD
Shut Down, Volume 2	Capitol	2027	'64	†
	Capitol	29629	'94	CS/CD
All Summer Long	Capitol	2110	'64	†
	Capitol	16016		†
	Capitol	29631	'94	CS/CD
Christmas Album	Capitol	2164	'64	†
	Capitol	95084	'91	CS/CD
Live in London (recorded 1964)	Capitol	11584	'76	†
	Capitol	12011		†
	Capitol	16134		†
	Capitol	93695	'90	CS/CD†
	Capitol	29634	'94	CS/CD
Concert	Capitol	2198	'64	†
	Capitol	16154		†
	Capitol	90427	'94	CS/CD
Today!	Capitol	2269	'65	†
	Capitol	29632	'94	CS/CD
Summer Days (and Summer Nights)	Capitol	2354	'65	†
	Capitol	29633	'94	CS/CD

Party!	Capitol	2398	'65	†
	Capitol	16272	'82	†
	Capitol	29640	'94	CS/CD
Pet Sounds	Capitol	2458	'66	†
	Capitol	16156	'81	†
	Capitol	48421	'90	CS/CD
	DCC	1035		CD
Smiley Smile	Brother	9001	'67	†
	Capitol	2891	'68	†
	Capitol	16158		†
	Capitol	29635	'94	CS/CD
Wild Honey	Capitol	2859	'67	†
	Capitol	16159		†
	Capitol	29636	'94	CS/CD
Stack-o-Tracks	Capitol	2893	'68	†
	Capitol	29641	'94	CS/CD
Friends	Capitol	2895	'68	†
	Capitol	16157		†
	Capitol	29637	'94	CS/CD
20/20	Capitol	133	'69	†
	Capitol	16155		†
	Capitol	29638	'94	CS/CD
Sunflower	Reprise	6382	'70	†
	Caribou	46950	'90	CS/CD†
Surf's Up	Reprise	6453	'71	†
	Caribou	46951	'90	CS/CD†
Carl and the Passions—So Tough	Brother	2090	'72	†
	Caribou	46953		CS/CD†
Holland	Reprise	2118	'72	†
	Caribou	46952	'90	CS/CD†
In Concert	Reprise	(2) 6484	'73	†
	Caribou	46954		CS/CD†
15 Big Ones	Reprise	2251	'76	†
	Caribou	46955	'91	CS/CD†
The Beach Boys Love You	Reprise	2258	'77	†
	Caribou	46956		CS/CD†
M.I.U.	Reprise	2268	'78	†
	Caribou	46957	'91	CS/CD†
L.A. (Light Album)	Caribou	35752	'79	CS/CD†
Keepin' the Summer Alive	Caribou	36283	'80/'91	CS/CD†
The Beach Boys	Caribou	39946	'85	CS/CD†

Anthologies and Reissues

Greatest Hits, 1961–1963	ERA	805	'70	†
	Hollywood/IMG	109		CS/CD
Best	Capitol	2545	'66	†
	Capitol	91318		CS/CD
Best, Volume 2	Capitol	2706	'67	†
Deluxe Set	Capitol	(3) 2813	'67	†
Best, Volume 3	Capitol	2945	'68	†
Close Up	Capitol	253	'69	†

Good Vibrations	Capitol	442	'70	†
All Summer Long/California Girls	Capitol	(2) 500	'70	†
Fun, Fun, Fun/Dance, Dance, Dance	Capitol	701	'71	†
Endless Summer	Capitol	(2) 11307	'74	†
	Capitol	46467		CS/CD
Spirit of America	Capitol	(2) 11384	'75	†
	Capitol	(2) 46618		LP/CS/CD†
California Girls	Capitol	16017		†
Fun, Fun, Fun	Capitol	16018		†
Dance, Dance, Dance	Capitol	16019		†
Be True to Your School	Capitol	16273	'82	†
Sunshine Dream	Capitol	12220	'82	†
Rarities	Capitol	1229	'83	†
Made in the U.S.A. (1961–1986)	Capitol	12396	'86	†
	Capitol	46324	'86	CD†
Gift Set	Capitol	91341	'89	CD†
Still Cruisin'	Capitol	92639	'89	CS/CD
The Absolute Best of the Beach Boys, Volume 1	Capitol	96795	'91	CS/CD
The Absolute Best of the Beach Boys, Volume 2	Capitol	96796	'91	CS/CD
Thirty Years of the Beach Boys	Capitol	(5) 81294	'93	CD
The Greatest Hits	Capitol	29418	'95	CS/CD
Surfin' Safari/ Surfin' U.S.A.	Capitol	93691	'90	CS/CD†
Surfin' U.S.A./Surfer Girl	Mobile Fidelity	10521	'89	CD
Surfer Girl/Shutdown, Volume 2	Capitol	93692	'90	CS/CD†
Little Deuce Coupe/ All Summer Long	Capitol	93693	'90	CS/CD†
Today/Summer Days (and Summer Nights)	Capitol	93694	'90	CS/CD†
Smiley Smile/Wild Honey	Capitol	93696	'90	CS/CD†
Friends/ 20/20	Capitol	93697	'90	CS/CD†
Party/Stack-o-Tracks	Capitol	93698	'90	CS/CD†
The Beach Boys	Pickwick	3221	'70	†
Good Vibrations	Pickwick	3269	'71	†
Wow! Great Concert	Pickwick	3309	'72	†
High Water	Pickwick	(2) 2059	'73	†
Surfer Girl	Pickwick	3351	'73	†
Little Deuce Coupe	Pickwick	3562	'76	†
Best of the Beach Boys	Scepter	18004	'72	†
Pet Sounds/Carl and the Passions — So Tough	Reprise/Brother	(2) 2083	'72	†
	Warner Bros.	(2) 2083		†
Wild Honey/ 20/20	Reprise	(2) 2166	'74	†
Friends/Smiley Smile	Reprise	(2) 2167	'74	†
Pet Sounds	Reprise	2197	'74	†
Good Vibrations	Reprise	2223	'75	†
	Reprise	2280		†
Ten Years of Harmony (1970–1980)	Caribou	(2) 37445	'81/'91	LP/CD†
For All Seasons	Pair	1068	'86	†
Golden Harmonies	Pair	1084	'86	CS

Bruce Johnston

Surfin' Round the World	Columbia	8857	'63	†
Surfers Pajama Party	Del-Fi	1228	'63	†
Going Public	Columbia	34459	'77	†

Dennis Wilson

Pacific Ocean Blue	Caribou	34354	'77	CS/CD†
One of Those People	Elektra	230	'79	†

Carl Wilson

Carl Wilson	Caribou	37010	'81	†
Youngblood	Caribou	37970	'83	†

Brian Wilson

Brian Wilson	Sire	25669	'88	CS/CD†
I Just Wasn't Made for These Times	MCA	11270	'95	CS/CD

Brian Wilson and Van Dyke Parks

Orange Crate Art	Warner Bros.	44527	'95	CS/CD

Wilson Phillips

Wilson Phillips	SBK	93745	'90	CS/CD
Shadows and Light	SBK	98924	'92	CS/CD

Carnie and Wendy Wilson

Hey Santa!	Capitol	16318	'93	ǀ
	SBK	27113	'93	CS/CD

THE BEATLES

John Lennon (b. Oct. 9, 1940, Woolton, Liverpool, England; d. Dec. 8, 1980, New York, NY), rhythm gtr, pno, har, voc; **Paul McCartney** (b. June 18, 1942, Allerton, Liverpool, England), bs, pno, bjo, trpt, voc; **George Harrison** (b. Feb. 25, 1943, Wavertree, Liverpool, England), lead gtr, sitar, pno, voc; **Ringo Starr** (b. Richard Starkey, July 7, 1940, Dingle, Liverpool, England), drm, voc [Early members included **Stuart Sutcliffe** (b. June 23, 1940, Edinburgh, Scotland; d. Apr. 10, 1962, Hamburg, Germany) on bass and **Pete Best** (b. England, 1941) on drums.]

The Beatles caused and inspired many of the changes within the rock-music scene during the '60s, and also helped foster a youth culture based in large part on long hair, loud music, and drugs. The Beatles will be known as the group that institutionalized many of the advances pioneered in rock music in the late '50s, from the self-contained music group to sophisticated arrangements and production. In encompassing so many diversified forms of music (pop love songs, ballads, novelty songs, folk, country and western, rhythm and blues) within the basic rock format, the Beatles revitalized rock and roll. Their music exhibited a fresh, clean, exuberant sound, in contrast to the vapid pop ballads and dance songs pervading the popular-music scene in the early '60s. Initiating an eclecticism that was to become one of their trademarks with the album *Something New*, the Beatles went beyond the standard three-chord progression, often utilizing diminished or augmented seventh and ninth chords while devising intriguing melodies and engaging vocal harmonies.

Particularly after the album *Help!*, songwriters John Lennon and Paul McCartney brought an unprecedented lyric sophistication to rock music, writing songs of a personal and emotionally evocative nature that often contained pointed social commentary. Their frequent philosophical concerns in lyrics widened the intellectual boundaries of rock in a manner rivaled only by Bob Dylan. Beginning with *Revolver*, perhaps the most innovative rock album ever made, the Beatles introduced novel instrumental combinations into rock, explored elaborate electronic production techniques under the guidance of producer

THE BEATLES

George Martin, and sparked the use of the East Indian sitar in rock music. The landmark *Sgt. Pepper's Lonely Hearts Club Band*, regarded by many as the first fully realized concept album, may be the best-known rock album of all time; its intricate jacket design also set new standards for the developing field of album art.

Within the music industry, the Beatles were the most commercially successful musical phenomenon, be it group or individual, to invade popular music to date, becoming even bigger than Elvis Presley and eventually selling well more than a hundred million singles and a hundred million albums. Their enormous success turned the industry away from its preoccupation with individual singers performing songs written by professional songwriters toward music groups performing original material. The consistency of the Beatles' musical performances switched the focus of the consumer from singles to albums, and essentially united the hitherto separate concepts of composer and performer. The Beatles' rise enabled dozens of other British musicians to express themselves musically and achieve popularity, thereby breaking the American stranglehold on popular music. Perhaps most significant, the musical and songwriting advances pioneered by the Beatles led critics to view rock music as a valid art form in and of itself, and induced the public to perceive rock music as a total, internally coherent form of conscious experience.

In social terms, the Beatles brought public attention to psychedelic drugs, the peace movement, Indian music, and Eastern spiritualism. Moreover, they helped promote a growing youth culture and inspired many young people to begin playing music by and for themselves, making music an essential part of their lives.

The evolution of the Beatles began in 1955 when John Lennon formed a group called the Quarrymen, modeled after the popular skiffle bands of the day. Skiffle was a unique British combination of folk, rhythm and blues, and jazz; the skiffle movement promoted the idea that anyone could make music, which encouraged young pickers like Lennon to take to the stage. In June 1956, at a local church picnic where the Quarrymen performed, Lennon met Paul McCartney, who subsequently joined the group. George Harrison joined in August 1958, and by 1959 they were performing as a trio. The group's name changed several times during that year, eventually becoming the Silver Beatles. In 1960 the Silver Beatles—Lennon, McCartney, Harrison, Peter Best on drums, and Stu Sutcliffe on bass guitar—backed singer Tony Sheridan in Hamburg, Germany. In Hamburg the group completed their musical apprenticeship, playing rigorous night-long shows to unappreciative audiences; live recordings made at one of the Hamburg clubs where they performed, the Star Club, were eventually issued in 1977. In April 1961 Stu Sutcliffe left the group; he died of a brain hemorrhage in Hamburg on April 10, 1962.

The Silver Beatles returned to England and took up residence at the Cavern, a club in Liverpool, beginning in February 1961. In late 1961 record-shop owner Brian Epstein attempted to secure them a recording contract. They were initially rejected by Decca and then picked up by Parlophone, a small division of EMI (British Capitol) in early 1962. That August drummer Ringo Starr quit Rory Storme's Hurricanes and replaced Pete Best, whose talents were minimal at best. Best later recorded an album for Savage Records and served as technical advisor for the 1979 Dick Clark production *The Birth of the Beatles*, which aired on ABC-TV. In September, with George Martin producing, the Beatles, as they were now known, had their first recording session. In October their first single, "Love Me Do," was issued in Great Britain. Their second single, "Please Please Me," was released in January 1963, making the top of the charts in February. The Beatles' first British album, *Please Please Me*, issued in March, remained at the top of the British charts for six months. However, Capitol Records in the United States passed on this product, and it was released on a variety of small labels, including Swan, Tollie, and VeeJay.

In the United States the next Beatles single, "I Want to Hold Your Hand," backed with "I Saw Her Standing There," was released in January 1964, and received heavy promotion from Capitol. The song became a hit within two weeks—one of the fastest-selling singles of the '60s. The group's first U.S. tour began in February, with massive media coverage. "Beatlemania" took America by storm, beginning with the group's famous first appearance on the *Ed Sullivan Show*.

The dam burst. Nothing could stop the Beatles, and in their wake followed dozens of British groups. Indeed, Lennon and McCartney provided a number of hit songs to up-and-coming groups, including "Bad to Me" for Billy J. Kramer and the Dakotas, and "I Don't Want to See You Again" and "World Without Love" for Peter and Gordon. Lennon and McCartney's "I Wanna Be Your Man" was one of the Rolling Stones' first hit singles.

For many weeks after the release of "I Want to Hold Your Hand," the Beatles dominated the top chart position with "She Loves You" and "Can't Buy Me Love" (on Capitol), "Please Please Me" and "Do You Want to Know a Secret" (on VeeJay), and "Twist and Shout" and "Love Me Do" backed with "P.S. I Love You" (on Tollie). In March 1964 the group began work on their first film, *A Hard Day's Night*, and John Lennon published his first book, *In His Own Write*. The film premiered in July, and the Beatles's second U.S. tour began in August. In February and March 1965 they recorded and filmed their second movie, *Help!*, which opened in late July. In June Lennon published his second book, *A Spaniard in the Works*. Through mid-1965 the Beatles continued their string of hit singles with "A Hard Day's Night," "And I Love Her," "I'll Cry Instead," Carl Perkins's "Matchbox" backed with "Slow Down," "I Feel Fine" backed with "She's a Woman," "Eight Days a Week," and "Ticket to Ride."

Increasing sophistication in the lyrics of Lennon and McCartney became evident after mid-1965. The words to the singles "Help!," "Yesterday," "Nowhere Man," and "Eleanor Rigby," and songs such as "In My Life" (from *Rubber Soul*), possessed a profound emotional intensity not apparent in earlier work. Moreover, George Harrison's songwriting ability began to be showcased; *Revolver* contained the three Harrison songs "Taxman," "Love You To," and "I Want to Tell You." With the single "Rain" (the flip side of "Paperback Writer") and "Tomorrow Never Knows" (from *Revolver*), the Beatles began utilizing complex studio-production techniques in their recordings. The influence of producer-arranger George Martin became particularly strong between 1966 and 1968. Lyrically, the songs of Lennon and McCartney began a tendency toward the bizarre and surreal, often defying logical explanation. This penchant for the surreal, first evident with "Norwegian Wood" (from *Rubber Soul*), continued with "Lucy in the Sky with Diamonds" (thought by some to be an allusion to LSD) and the quintessential "A Day in the Life" (from *Sgt. Pepper*), and with the singles "Strawberry Fields Forever"/"Penny Lane" and "I Am the Walrus."

Having ceased live performances at the end of their August 1966 U.S. tour, the Beatles focused their attention on recording and, later, individual endeavors. *Sgt. Pepper's Lonely Hearts Club Band*, with advance sales of more than a million copies, was issued in June 1967.

As the music industry's first recognized concept album, the record was highly acclaimed by critics, marking perhaps the high point of the Beatles' recording career. The album included "With a Little Help from My Friends" (sung by Ringo), Harrison's self-consciously philosophical "Within You, Without You," and the quintessential '60s production, "A Day in the Life."

Individual endeavors in 1967 included the acting debuts of John Lennon and Ringo Starr in the films *How I Won the War* and *Candy*, respectively. The Beatles scripted, cast, directed, and edited the made-for-TV movie *Magical Mystery Tour*, a conspicuous failure in its poor editing and photography. The soundtrack album, released in November in the United States only, included "The Fool on the Hill," "I Am the Walrus," and "All You Need Is Love." In 1968 George Harrison composed, arranged, and recorded his own music for the soundtrack to the film *Wonderwall*. Lennon, now romantically involved with conceptual artist Yoko Ono, recorded with her the controversial album *Two Virgins*, consisting of tape montages and featuring a famous nude photograph of the pair on its cover.

In July 1968 the animated movie *Yellow Submarine* premiered. It was one of the most engaging psychedelic movies to come out in the late '60s. The soundtrack album included the title song and "All You Need Is Love." In April the Beatles had formed Apple, their own record company. "Hey Jude," released in August, was the first single on the label. The double-record set entitled *The Beatles* (also known as *The White Album*), issued in November, was the first album on Apple. Disjointed and revealing the telltale signs of a Lennon-McCartney rift, the album contained diverse songs such as "Back in the U.S.S.R." (a Beach Boys parody), the folk ballad "Blackbird," the electronic-music montage "Revolution #1," and Harrison's superlative "While My Guitar Gently Weeps" (recorded, without credit, with lead guitar by Eric Clapton).

During most of 1969 the individual Beatles worked apart. Ringo appeared in the movie *The Magic Christian*. The soundtrack album contained a solo McCartney composition, "Come and Get It," performed by Badfinger, a group newly signed to Apple. In March 1969 John Lennon married Yoko Ono and Paul McCartney married Linda Eastman. The marriages seemed to mark the informal end of the Beatles. John Lennon became the first Beatle to perform publicly outside the group, in September 1969, with the Plastic Ono Band in Toronto, featuring Clapton and longtime Beatles associate Klaus Voorman on bass.

The only Beatles album release of 1969, *Abbey Road* (named for the studio in which the group had recorded since 1962), came out in November, and included Harrison's best-known songs, "Something" and "Here Comes the Sun"; Ringo's "Octopus' Garden"; and a long side-two medley of songs, including "She Came in Through the Bathroom Window." *Abbey Road* was actually the final Beatles recording. *Let It Be*, initially produced by George Martin and later reworked by Phil Spector, was held up by remixing disputes and film-editing problems; it was eventually issued in May 1970. The album included "Let It Be," "Get Back," and "The Long and Winding Road," the band's final single release.

In early 1971 Paul McCartney sued for dissolution of the Beatles' partnership, which legally ended on December 30, 1974. Subsequent Beatles album-releases were the live sets *Live at the Star Club* (recorded in 1962) and *Live at the Hollywood Bowl* (recorded in 1964 and 1965), *Rarities*, and various anthology sets.

Throughout the '70s rumors persisted that the Beatles would reunite for recordings, but such speculation finally ended with the murder of John Lennon in New York City on December 8, 1980. The remaining three, with Linda McCartney, jointly recorded the 1981 tribute to Lennon, "All Those Years Ago," written by Harrison.

The public's fascination with the Beatles was sustained in the early '80s through the film documentary *The Compleat Beatles* (1982) and a book by longtime associate Peter Brown, *The Love You Make: An Insider's Story of the Beatles* (1983). In 1985 superstar Michael Jackson purchased the copyrights to 40,000 songs, including more than two hundred Lennon-

McCartney songs. During 1987, the 25th anniversary year of the Beatles' first recording, Capitol Records issued for the first time on CD the Beatles' first seven albums in their British versions (the U.S. versions contained one to four fewer songs), as well as their last five albums (the U.S. and British versions were identical). *Sgt. Pepper*, released in June, rapidly became the best-selling CD of all time.

In 1994 the movie *Backbeat* focused on the early days of the Beatles, and on Stu Sutcliffe in particular. Late in 1994 Apple Records issued *Live at the BBC*, 56 songs recorded for broadcast by the British broadcasting company between March 1962 and June 1965. Consisting largely of cover songs, the album quickly sold more than four million copies, demonstrating the remarkable popularity of a group that had disbanded nearly a quarter of a century earlier.

In fall 1995 the six-hour television film *Anthology* premiered, featuring two "new" songs consisting of demo recordings made by John Lennon in the late '70s that were reworked by the surviving group members and producer Jeff Lynne. Apple issued the first of three sets of outtakes, rarities, and never-before-issued tracks by the group in fall 1995, and it quickly shot to number one on the *Billboard* pop charts.

Early Beatles Recordings

The Beatles with Tony Sheridan and Their Guests (four songs)	MGM	4215	'64	†
(reissued as) This Is Where It Started	Metro	563	'66	†
Live at the Star Club	Lingasong	(2) 7001	'77	†
Live at the Star Club, 1962, Volume 1	Sony	48544	'91	CS/CD†
Live at the Star Club, 1962, Volume 2	Sony	48604	'91	CS/CD†
In the Beginning	Polydor	244504	'70	†
	Polydor	823701	'87	CD
	Polydor	825073	'87	CS
Introducing . . . The Beatles	VeeJay	1062	'64	†
Jolly What! The Beatles and Frank Ifield	VeeJay	1085	'64	†
Songs, Pictures and Stories of the Fabulous Beatles	VeeJay	1092	'64	†
The Beatles vs. The Four Seasons	VeeJay	(2) 30	'64	†
Ain't She Sweet	Atco	33109	'64	†
The Early Beatles	Capitol/Apple	2309	'65	†
	Capitol	90451		CS

Pete Best

Best of the Beatles	Savage	71	'66	†

The Beatles

NOTE: The seven album releases for the Beatles through 1966 were significantly different in Great Britain (aka U.K.) on Parlophone from those in the United States on Capitol. Capitol has chosen to release the U.K. albums on CD, except in the case of *Meet the Beatles,* an album that doesn't exist in Britain.

Meet the Beatles	Capitol/Apple	2047	'64	†
	Capitol	90441		LP/CD
Second Album	Capitol/Apple	2080	'64	†
	Capitol	90444		LP/CS
A Hard Day's Night	United Artists	6366	'64	†
(American)	Capitol	11921	'79	LP/CS
Something New	Capitol/Apple	2108	'64	†
	Capitol	90443		LP/CS
The Beatles' Story	Capitol/Apple	(2) 2222	'64	†

Beatles '65	Capitol/Apple	2228	'64	†
	Capitol	90446		LP/CS
Beatles VI	Capitol/Apple	2358	'65	†
	Capitol	90445		LP/CS
Help! (American)	Capitol/Apple	2386	'65	†
	Capitol	90454		LP/CS
Rubber Soul (American)	Capitol/Apple	2442	'65	†
	Capitol	90453		LP/CS
Yesterday . . . and Today	Capitol/Apple	2553	'66	†
	Capitol	90447		LP/CS
Revolver (American)	Capitol/Apple	2576	'66	†
	Capitol	90452		LP/CS
Hey Jude	Apple/Capitol	385	'70	†
	Capitol	90442		LP/CS
Please Please Me (U.K.)	Capitol	46435	'63/'87	LP/CS/CD
With the Beatles (U.K.)	Capitol	46436	'63/'87	LP/CS/CD
A Hard Day's Night (U.K.)	Capitol	46437	'64/'87	LP/CS/CD
Beatles for Sale (U.K.)	Capitol	46438	'64/'87	LP/CS/CD
Help! (U.K.)	Capitol	46439	'65/'87	LP/CS/CD
Rubber Soul (U.K.)	Capitol	46440	'65/'87	LP/CS/CD
Revolver (U.K.)	Capitol	46441	'66/'87	LP/CS/CD
Sgt. Pepper's Lonely Hearts Club Band	Capitol/Apple	2653	'67	†
	Capitol	46442	'87	LP/CS/CD
Magical Mystery Tour	Capitol/Apple	2835	'67	†
	Capitol	48062		LP/CS/CD
The Beatles (White Album)	Apple/Capitol	(2) 101	'68	†
	Capitol	46443	'87	LP/CS/CD
Yellow Submarine (soundtrack)	Apple/Capitol	153	'69	†
	Capitol	46445	'87	LP/CS/CD
Abbey Road	Apple/Capitol	383	'69	†
	Capitol	46446	'87	LP/CS/CD
Let It Be	Apple	34001	'70	†
	Capitol	11922	'79	†
	Capitol	46447	'87	CS/CD
Live at the BBC	Apple	(2) 31796	'94	CS/CD
Anthologies				
1962–1966	Apple/Capitol	(2) 3403	'73	†
	Capitol	(2) 90435		LP/CS
	Capitol	(2) 97036	'93	CS/CD
1967–1970	Apple/Capitol	(2) 3404	'73	†
	Capitol	(2) 90438		LP/CS
	Capitol	(2) 97039	'93	CS/CD
Rock 'n' Roll Music	Capitol	(2) 11537	'76	†
Rock 'n' Roll Music, Volume 1	Capitol	16020		LP/CS
Rock 'n' Roll Music, Volume 2	Capitol	16021		LP/CS
Live at the Hollywood Bowl	Capitol	11638		LP/CS
Love Songs	Capitol	(2) 11711		LP/CS
Rarities	Capitol	12060		LP/CS
Reel Music	Capitol	12199		LP/CS
20 Greatest Hits	Capitol	12245		LP/CS

Past Masters—Volume 1	Capitol	90043	'88	CD
Past Masters—Volume 2	Capitol	90044	'88	CD
Past Masters, Volumes 1 & 2	Capitol	(2) 91135		LP
	Capitol	91135		CS
The Ultimate Box Set	Capitol	(16) 91302	'88	LP/CS/CD
Anthology, Volume I	Apple	(2) 34445	'95	CS/CD
Anthology, Volume II	Apple	34448	'95	CS/CD

Don Was (composer)

Backbeat (soundtrack)	Virgin Movie Music	39413	'94	CS/CD

Tribute Albums

Come Together: America Salutes the Beatles	Liberty	31712	'95	LP/CS/CD
Motown Meets the Beatles	Motown	0410	'95	CS/CD

JEFF BECK
(b. June 24, 1944, Wallington, Surrey, England), ld gtr

British lead guitarist extraordinaire Jeff Beck is one of rock music's most intelligent, innovative, and respected players. One of the first electric guitarists to utilize a fuzztone device and make extensive use of feedback while playing, Beck introduced both modal and East Indian tonalities into rock (with the Yardbirds), while earning the dubious distinction of being one of the first rock musicians to destroy equipment onstage. He is also known for introducing vocalist Rod Stewart to American audiences with his first Jeff Beck Group. Moreover, with his album *Blow by Blow*, Beck helped redefine and revitalize the more challenging and ambitious sound of so-called fusion music, a '70s phenomenon not strictly classifiable as jazz or rock but containing elements of both. Taking regular extended breaks from recording throughout his career, Jeff Beck is regarded as a musician's musician.

Replacing Eric Clapton in the Yardbirds in spring 1965, Jeff Beck played lead guitar with the group through its greatest hit-making period ("Heart Full of Soul," "I'm a Man," "Over Under Sideways Down"). Leaving the Yardbirds in December 1966, he formed the first of several Jeff Beck groups in late 1967, featuring Rod Stewart, Ron Wood playing bass and harmonica, and Mickey Waller on drums. The group recorded *Truth* for Epic Records and proved enormously successful during a spring 1968 tour of the United States with its blues-oriented material. That tour introduced American audiences to Rod Stewart, who had been singing almost anonymously with various blues aggregations in Britain for years. The group expanded in October 1968 with the addition of session keyboardist Nicky Hopkins. Following *Beck-ola*, the group fragmented, with Stewart and Wood joining the Faces, and Hopkins moving to California to join Quicksilver Messenger Service.

An attempt to form a new band with Tim Bogert and Carmine Appice of Vanilla Fudge failed, and a car crash then put Beck out of commission for eighteen months. He reemerged in late 1971 with his second Jeff Beck Group, featuring keyboardist Max Middleton and drummer Cozy Powell. The group recorded two undistinguished albums before disbanding in 1972. With the demise of their second-generation band, Cactus, bassist Tim Bogert and drummer Carmine Appice rejoined Beck briefly.

After a two-year layoff, Jeff Beck returned with 1975's *Blow by Blow*, a surprising yet intriguing change of musical direction for Beck. Made with former Beatles producer George Martin, the all-instrumental album had a distinctive jazz (and occasionally disco) flavor and sold remarkably well. *Wired*, recorded with Czech jazz keyboard wizard Jan Hammer, was also well received. Beck subsequently toured with Hammer, releasing a live set from the tour in 1977. After another sabbatical, Beck returned with a new band, the album *There and Back*, and another round of touring as an all-instrumental unit.

In 1983 Jeff Beck joined Eric Clapton, Jimmy Page, and a cast of established British musicians for a brief tour in support of Ronnie Lane's Appeal for Action Research into Multiple Sclerosis. The following year, Beck played on Rod Stewart's album *Camouflage* and its smash-hit single "Infatuation"; Beck toured with Stewart before leaving due to "artistic differences." Later he toured and recorded a mini-CD as part of the '50s-style revival band the Honeydrippers, with Robert Plant, Jimmy Page, Brian Setzer, and Cozy Powell. Beck also played on Tina Turner's smash hit "Private Dancer" and Mick Jagger's *She's the Boss*. In 1985 Epic issued his first solo album in five years, *Flash*, which featured Rod Stewart performing vocals on "People Get Ready," a minor hit. Jeff Beck again took several years off, reemerging in 1989 with *Jeff Beck's Guitar Shop*, an all-instrumental album recorded with keyboardist Tony Hymas and drummer Terry Bozzio, and his first major tour in nearly a decade, this time headlining with Texas blues guitarist Stevie Ray Vaughan. In 1995 Beck toured with Carlos Santana.

The Jeff Beck Group

Truth	Epic	26413	'68	†
	Epic	47412		CD
Beck-ola	Epic	26478	'69	†
	Epic	47411		CD
Truth/Beck-ola	Epic	(2) 33779	'75	†
	Epic	33779		CD
Rough and Ready	Epic	30973	'71	CS
Jeff Beck Group	Epic	31331	'72	CS

Beck, Bogert and Appice

Beck, Bogert and Appice	Epic	32140	'73	CS/CD

Jeff Beck

Early Anthology	Accord	7141	'81	†
Blow by Blow	Epic	33409	'75	CS/CD
	Epic	53442	'93	CD
Wired	Epic	33849	'76	CS/CD
	Mobile Fidelity	531	'90	CD
Wired/Blow by Blow	Epic	38227	'86	CS
There and Back	Epic	35684	'80	CS/CD
Flash	Epic	39483	'85	CS/CD
Jeff Beck's Guitar Shop	Epic	44313	'89	CS/CD
Beckology	Epic/Legacy	(3) 48661	'91	CS/CD

Jeff Beck and Jan Hammer

Live	Epic	34433	'77	†
	Columbia/Legacy	34433		CS/CD

The Honeydrippers

Volume 1	Atlantic (mini)	90220	'84	CS/CD

Jeff Beck and the Big Town Playboys

Crazy Legs	Epic	53562	'93	CS/CD

THE BEE GEES

Barry Gibb (b. Sept. 1, 1946, Douglas on the Isle of Man, England), voc, rhythm gtr; **Robin Gibb** (b. Dec. 22, 1949, Douglas on the Isle of Man, England), voc, bs; **Maurice Gibb** (b.

Dec. 22, 1949, Douglas on the Isle of Man, England), voc; **Andy Gibb** (b. Mar. 5, 1958, Manchester, England; d. Mar. 10, 1988, Oxford, England), voc

Perhaps the most popular rock group of the mid- to late '70s, the three brothers Gibb had their first success as a late-'60s harmony group. Emerging from Australia and sustaining their early career with surreal ballads featuring strong melodies and thick harmonies (as exemplified by "Massachusetts" and "I Started a Joke"), the Bee Gees survived a midcareer crisis to become international stars on the basis of their own near-formulaic disco-style songs, beginning with 1975's "Jive Talkin'." The *Saturday Night Fever* soundtrack album, most of it written and much of it performed by the brothers, became the best-selling album in music history. Buoyed by his siblings' enormous popularity, younger brother Andy Gibb launched his own successful recording/performing career in 1977. Not touring and seldom recording during the '80s, the Bee Gees eventually scored a near-smash hit with the title song to 1989's *One*.

Barry Gibb and twin brothers Robin and Maurice began their professional careers in the mid-'50s in Manchester, England, when Barry was nine and the twins were seven. In 1958 they emigrated with their family to Australia, where they became radio and television stars as the Bee Gees. Signed to Australia's Festival Records in August 1962, the group scored a number of hits, including "Spicks and Specks," and returned to England in February 1967 with guitarist Vince Melouney and drummer Colin Peterson. They soon signed with producer-promoter Robert Stigwood, and within two months had a major hit on Atco with the haunting "New York Mining Disaster 1941," composed by Barry and Robin. The song was typical of the Bee Gees' hits over the next two years: a maudlin ballad with a strong melody, written and produced by the brothers, and characterized by Robin's vocal quaver, the brothers' wispy nasal harmonies, and lush, almost heavy-handed orchestral arrangements. With Barry playing rhythm guitar and Robin playing bass, subsequent hits include "To Love Somebody," "Holiday," "Massachusetts," "I've Gotta Get a Message to You," and perhaps their two finest compositions, "Words" and "I Started a Joke." Their 1968 tour created a rock-music milestone when the Bee Gees performed with a full orchestra.

The Bee Gees' popularity, however, faltered in 1969, when their ambitious concept album *Odessa* failed to attract much notice. Former accompanists Vince Melouney and Colin Peterson had departed in December 1968 and August 1969, respectively, and Robin had announced his intention to leave the group in March 1969. He recorded *Robin's Reign*, while Barry and Maurice recorded *Cucumber Castle*. Reuniting in August 1970, the Bee Gees staged a successful comeback with the smash hits "Lonely Days" and "How Can You Mend a Broken Heart." Nonetheless, their career languished between 1972 and 1974.

Veteran producer Arif Mardin got the Bee Gees back on track with *Main Course*. The album included two disco-style smash hits, "Jive Talkin'" and "Nights on Broadway," and established the pattern to be followed by the brothers and two new producers. *Children of the World* yielded the hits "You Should Be Dancing" and "Love So Right," and the group's first live album sold quite well. In 1977 younger brother Andy Gibb started his musical career, scoring hits with Barry's "I Just Want to Be Your Everything" and "(Love Is) Thicker than Water" on Robert Stigwood's RSO label.

Massive international success came to the Bee Gees with the *Saturday Night Fever* soundtrack. It included three top hits written by the Bee Gees, "How Deep Is Your Love," "Stayin' Alive," and "Night Fever," as well as singer Yvonne Elliman's top hit "If I Can't Have You," written and produced by the brothers. In 1978 the Bee Gees costarred with Peter Frampton and sang five songs in the contrived fairytalelike film *Sgt. Pepper's Lonely Hearts Club Band*, based on the Beatles' landmark album. In the meantime, they wrote smash hit songs for Samantha Sang ("Emotion"), Frankie Valli ("Grease"), and brother Andy ("Shadow Dancing").

In 1979 the Bee Gees issued another hit album, *Spirits Having Flown*, and three more hit singles, "Too Much Heaven," "Tragedy," and "Love You Inside Out." Brother Andy's hits continued through 1980 with "An Everlasting Love," "(Our Love) Don't Throw It All Away," "Desire," "I Can't Help It" (in duet with Olivia Newton-John), and "Time Is Time." In 1980 Barry Gibb produced and wrote the songs for Barbra Streisand's *Guilty* album, yielding a hit with "Woman in Love" and a smash hit with the title song, sung as a duet by Barry and Streisand. Barry later produced Dionne Warwick's *Heartbreaker* (1982) and Kenny Rogers's *Eyes that See in the Dark* (1983).

The Bee Gees recorded one side of the *Saturday Night Fever* film sequel, *Staying Alive*, yet were largely inactive during most of the '80s. Andy Gibb died at age 30 in Oxford, England, on March 10, 1988, of myocarditis, a rare viral infection of the heart muscle. By 1987 the Bee Gees had moved to Warner Bros. Records. They finally managed another near-smash hit in 1989 with the title song to *One*.

The Bee Gees

Rare, Precious and Beautiful (recorded 1963–1966)	Atco	33-264	'68	†
Rare, Precious and Beautiful, Volume 2 (recorded 1963–1966)	Atco	33-321	'70	†
First	Atco	33-223	'67	†
	Polydor	825220		CD†
	Polydor	833341		CS†
Horizontal	Atco	33-233	'68	†
	Polydor	833659	'87	CS/CD†
Idea	Atco	33-253	'68	†
	Polydor	833660	'87	CS/CD
Best	Atco	33-292	'69	
	RSO	874		
	Polydor	831594	'87	CD
Odessa	Atco	(2) 702	'69	†
	Polydor	825451		CD
Odessa (condensed)	RSO	3007	'76	†
Cucumber Castle	Atco	33-327	'70	†
	Polydor	833783		CD
Two Years On	Atco	33-353	'70	†
	Polydor	833785	'89	CD†
Melody (soundtrack)	Atco	33-363	'71	†
Trafalgar	Atco	7003	'71	†
	Polydor	833786	'89	CD†
To Whom It May Concern	Atco	7012	'72	†
	Polydor	833787	'92	CD
Life in a Tin Can	Atco	870	'73	†
	Polydor	833788	'92	CD
Best, Volume 2 (1969–1972)	RSO	875	'73	†
	Polydor	831960	'87	CD
Mister Natural	RSO	4800	'74	†
	Polydor	833789		CD
Main Course	RSO	4807	'75	†
	RSO	3024	'77	†
	Polydor	833790	'88	CS/CD†
	Polydor	822790	'94	CD
Children of the World	RSO	3003	'76	†
	Polydor	823658	'89	CS/CD

Gold	RSO	3006	'76	†
	Polydor	823659		CS
Here at Last . . . Live	RSO	(2) 3901	'77	†
	Polydor	833791	'90	CD
Saturday Night Fever (soundtrack)	RSO	(2) 4001	'77	†
	Polydor	(2) 800068		CD
	Polydor	(2) 825389		CS
Spirits Having Flown	RSO	3041	'79	†
	Polydor	827335	'89	CS/CD
Greatest Hits	RSO	(2) 4200	'79	†
	Polydor	(2) 800071		CD
	Polydor	(2) 825390		CS
Living Eyes	RSO	3098	'81	†
Staying Alive (soundtrack)	RSO	813269	'83	†
	Polydor	813269		CS/CD
Tales from the Brothers Gibb: A History in Song (1967–1990)	Polydor	(4) 843911	'90	CS/CD
Size Isn't Everything	Polydor	521055	'93	CS/CD
E-S-P	Warner Bros.	25541	'87	CS/CD
One	Warner Bros.	25887	'89	CS/CD†
High Civilization	Warner Bros.	26530	'91	CS/CD
Robin Gibb				
Robin's Reign	Atco	33-323	'70	†
How Old Are You?	Polydor	810896	'03	†
Secret Agent	Mirage	90170	'84	†
Andy Gibb				
Flowing Rivers	RSO	3019	'77	†
Shadow Dancing	RSO	3034	'78	†
After Dark	RSO	3069	'80	†
Greatest Hits	RSO	3091	'80	†
A Collection of His Greatest Hits	Polydor	511585	'91	CS/CD

BROOK BENTON

(b. Benjamin Peay, Sept. 9, 1931, Camden, SC; d. Apr. 9, 1988, New York, NY)

One of the first rock-and-roll artists to write his own material, Brook Benton was also among the first soul artists, employing thick string arrangements on pop ballads sung in a rich, mellifluous baritone voice. First recording in 1953, Brook Benton met songwriter Clyde Otis in the late '50s. The two wrote the smash hit "Looking Back" for Nat "King" Cole, and Benton cowrote "A Lover's Question" for Clyde McPhatter, both from 1958. Benton and Otis teamed for a number of hit recordings by Benton on Mercury Records between 1959 and 1963, including "It's Just a Matter of Time," "Endlessly," "Thank You Pretty Baby," "Kiddio," and "The Boll Weevil Song." *The Two of Us*, recorded with singer Dinah Washington and issued in 1960, yielded two huge hits with "Baby (You've Got What It Takes)" and "A Rockin' Good Way." "Hotel Happiness" in 1963 was Benton's last hit from this phase of his career; although he continued to record through the '60s, he was unable to crack the charts.

Benton managed a brief comeback with Tony Joe White's "Rainy Night in Georgia" in 1970, but was unable to follow up with another hit. Further recordings in the '70s and early '80s for a variety of labels failed to produce much interest. Benton died on April 9, 1988, of complications from spinal meningitis.

Brook Benton and Jesse Belvin

Brook Benton and Jesse Belvin	Crown	350		†

Brook Benton and Dinah Washington

The Two of Us	Mercury	60244	'60	†
	Mercury	824823	'85	CS

Brook Benton

At His Best	RCA	3573	'59	†
It's Just a Matter of Time	Mercury	60077	'59	†
Endlessly	Mercury	60146	'59	†
So Many Ways I Love You	Mercury	60225	'60	†
Songs I Love to Sing	Mercury	60602	'60	†
Golden Hits	Mercury	60607	'61	†
If You Believe	Mercury	60619	'61	†
The Boll Weevil Song	Mercury	60641	'61	†
There Goes That Song Again	Mercury	60673	'62	†
Lie to Me	Mercury	60740	'62	†
	Polygram	836687		CS
Golden Hits, Volume 2	Mercury	60774	'63	†
Best Ballads of Broadway	Mercury	60830	'63	†
Born to Sing the Blues	Mercury	60886	'64	†
On the Country Side	Mercury	60918	'64	†
This Bitter Earth	Mercury	60934	'64	†
Mother Earth	Mercury	16314	'66	†
It's Just a Matter of Time: His Greatest Hits	Mercury	822321		CS
Best	Mercury	830772	'87	CD
40 Greatest Hits	Mercury	836755	'89	CD†
The Dynamic Brook Benton Sings	Strand	1121		†
Brook Benton	Camden	564	'60	†
Soul	Harmony	7346	'65	†
Mother Nature, Father Time	RCA	3526	'65	†
That Old Feeling	RCA	3514	'66	†
My Country	RCA	3590	'66	†
Sings a Love Song	RCA	1044	'75	†
This Is Brook Benton	RCA	9597	'89	CS/CD
I Wanna Be with You	Camden	2431	'70	†
Laura, What's He Got that I Ain't Got	Reprise	6268	'67	†
Do Your Thing	Cotillion	9002	'69	†
Today	Cotillion	9018	'70	†
Home Style	Cotillion	9028	'70	†
Gospel Truth	Cotillion	058	'71	†
	Atlantic	058		†
Story Teller	Cotillion	9050	'72	†
Something for Everyone	MGM	4874	'73	†
As Long as She Needs Me	Pickwick	3217		†
Greatest Hits	Pickwick	8005		†
This Is Brook Benton	All Platinum	3015	'76	†
The Brook Benton Anthology (1959–1970)	Rhino	(2) 71497	'86	CS
Greatest Hits	Curb/CEMA	77445	'91	CS/CD

Greatest Songs	Curb/Atlantic	77741	'95	CS/CD
At His Best	Pair	1289		CS/CD
All His Best	Special Music	4825		CS/CD
Best	Dominion	7203		CD
20 Golden Hits	Deluxe	7861		CS/CD
Best of Easy Listening	Richmond	2123		CS

CHUCK BERRY
(b. Oct. 18, 1926, St. Louis, MO)

CHUCK BERRY

Chuck Berry is arguably the single most important figure, regardless of race, in the entire history of rock. As the first major rock artist to compose virtually all of his own material, Berry wrote songs that were aggressive, exuberant, and wry, and reflected the romance between rock and roll and the youth culture and its concerns (school, cars, girls, and dancing). He is often cited as rock's first folk poet. With his engaging lyrics, enticing music, and uncommonly clear diction, Berry became the first black artist to achieve mass popularity with young white audiences. Moreover, his innovative use of boogie-woogie and shuffle rhythms, his alternating chord changes on rhythm guitar, and his distinctive off-time, double-note lead guitar playing set the early standard for rock guitar and helped popularize the electric guitar. Despite his personal penchant for the blues, Chuck Berry's primary influence comes through his up-tempo rock songs. The Beatles, the Rolling Stones, and most other British groups recorded his songs during their early careers. The Beach Boys's "Surfin' U.S.A." is an obvious reworking of Berry's "Sweet Little Sixteen"; Bob Dylan's first rock hit, "Subterranean Homesick Blues," bears a remarkable resemblance to Berry's "Too Much Monkey Business." Virtually every rock group performing today has at least one Chuck Berry song in their repertoire.

Charles "Chuck" Berry began singing in a St. Louis church at age six, later taking up guitar while in high school and forming his first group in 1952. In early 1955 he traveled to Chicago and played with blues great Muddy Waters, who introduced him to Leonard Chess of Chess Records. Leonard Chess signed Berry immediately, and Berry's first single, "Maybellene," ostensibly cowritten with disc jockey Alan Freed, became a huge hit, one of rock and roll's first. Excelling on stage, his now-signature "duck walk" was fortuitously introduced into his act in New York in 1956, the year he appeared in the film *Rock, Rock, Rock*. Hits continued through 1959 with "Roll Over, Beethoven," "School Days," "Rock and Roll Music," "Sweet Little Sixteen," and the autobiographical "Johnny B. Goode."

Unfortunately, in late 1959 Chuck Berry was busted for violation of the Mann Act (transportation of an underage female across state lines), and after a sensationalized trial, he entered federal prison in February 1962. Released in 1963, he came back with "Nadine," "No Particular Place to Go," and "You Never Can Tell." His minor hit from 1964, "Promised Land," has been recorded by a wealth of artists, including Elvis Presley. After moving to Mercury Records in 1966, Berry weathered a fallow period before returning to Chess in 1969 and recording several classic albums. In 1972 he scored his first hit in many years with the childishly risqué "My Ding-a-Ling," from *The London Chuck Berry Sessions*.

Imprisoned for four months in 1979 for income-tax evasion, Chuck Berry reemerged with a new round of touring and his first album of new material in years, *Rockit*. In 1987 Berry published his autobiography and starred in the concert tribute-film documentary *Hail! Hail! Rock 'n' Roll*, featuring Keith Richards and Eric Clapton. Pianist Johnnie Johnson, the backbone of Chuck Berry's recorded sound since the early '50s, began recording for himself in the '90s, completing *Johnnie B. Bad* with Keith Richards and Eric Clapton, and *That'll Work* with the Kentucky Headhunters, as well as several other albums.

Chuck Berry

Rock, Rock, Rock (1956 soundtrack)	Chess	1425	'58	†
	Chess	31270	'86	CD
After School Sessions	Chess	1426	'58	†
	MCA	20873	'95	CS/CD
One Dozen Berrys	Chess	1432	'58	†
Chuck Berry Is On Top	Chess	1435	'59	†
	Chess	9256	'87	CS
	Chess	31260	'87	CD
Rockin' at the Hops	Chess	1448	'60	†
	Chess	9259	'87	CS/CD
New Juke Box Hits	Chess	1456	'61	†
	Chess	9171		CS/CD
More Chuck Berry	Chess	1465	'63	†
Chuck Berry On Stage	Chess	1480	'63	†
St. Louis to Liverpool	Chess	1488	'64	†
Chuck Berry in London	Chess	1495	'65	†
Fresh Berrys	Chess	1498	'65	†
Back Home	Chess	1550	'70	†
San Francisco Dues	Chess	50008	'71	†
The London Chuck Berry Sessions	Chess	60020	'72	†
	Chess	9295	'89	CS/CD
Bio	Chess	50043	'73	†
Chuck Berry	Chess	60032	'75	†
Rock 'n' Roll Rarities (recorded 1957–1965)	Chess	92521	'86	CS/CD
Missing Berries: Rarities, Volume 3	Chess	9318	'90	LP/CD
In Memphis	Mercury	61123	'67	†
Live at the Fillmore	Mercury	61138	'67	†
From St. Louis to Frisco	Mercury	61176	'68	†
Concerto in B. Goode	Mercury	61223	'69	†
St. Louis to Frisco to Memphis	Mercury	(2) 6501	'72	†
Rockit	Atco	38-118	'79	†
Attention	Phillips	6430022	'82	†
Hail! Hail! Rock 'n' Roll (soundtrack)	MCA	6217	'88	CS/CD

Anthologies

Greatest Hits	Chess	1485	'64	†
Golden Decade	Chess	(2) 1514	'67	†
Golden Decade, Volume 2	Chess	(2) 60023	'73	†
Golden Decade, Volume 3	Chess	(2) 60028	'74	†
On the Blues Side	Ace	397	'93	CD
The Chess Box	Chess	(6) 80001	'88	LP
	Chess	(3) 80001	'88	CS/CD
Golden Hits	Mercury	61103	'67	†
	Mercury	826256		CS/CD
Flashback	Pickwick	2061		†
Johnny B. Goode	Pickwick	3327		†
Sweet Little Rock and Roller	Pickwick	3345		†
Wild Berrys	Pickwick	3392		†
Greatest Hits	Archive of Folk and Jazz Music	321	'76	†
Best	Gusto	0004	'78	†
The Chuck Berry Story	Vogue	(3) 660501	'90	CD†
The Great 28	Chess	(2) 8201	'82	†
	Chess	(2) 92500		CS
	Chess	92500		CD
The Incredible Chuck Berry	RCA-Camden	5010		CS
Best of the Best of Chuck Berry	Hollywood/IMG	100		CS/CD
21 Greatest Hits	Zeta	520		CD
Live Hits	Quicksilver	1017		LP/CS

Chuck Berry and Bo Diddley

Two Great Guitars	Checker	2991	'64	†
	Chess	9170	'92	CD

Chuck Berry and Howlin' Wolf

Pop Origins	Chess	1544	'69	†

Johnnie Johnson

Johnnie B. Bad	Elektra/Nonesuch	61149	'91	CS/CD
That'll Work (with Kentucky Headhunters)	Elektra/Nonesuch	61476	'93	CS/CD
Blue Hand Johnnie	Evidence	26017	'93	CD
Blues, Ballads and Jumpin' Jazz	Fantasy/OBC	570	'94	CD
Stompin' at the Penny	Columbia/Legacy	57829	'94	CS/CD

Johnnie Johnson Band

Johnnie Be Back	MusicMasters	65131	'95	CS/CD

BLACK SABBATH

John "Ozzy" Osbourne (b. Dec. 3, 1948, Birmingham, England), lead voc; **Tony Iommi** (b. Feb. 19, 1948, Birmingham, England), lead gtr, kybd; **Terry "Geezer" Butler** (b. July 17, 1949, Birmingham, England), bs; **Bill Ward** (b. May 5, 1948, Birmingham, England), drm [Ozzy Osbourne left in 1978, to be replaced by **Ronnie James Dio** (b. July 10, 1949, Portsmouth, NH) until 1983, when Dio was replaced by **Ian Gillan** and others.]

Despite being dismissed by critics and enduring an entire career without ever registering a major hit single, Black Sabbath nonetheless established themselves as the earliest purveyors of nihilistic, belligerent, repugnant occultism within the heavy-metal format of deafening volume, plodding tempos, and anguished vocals. Fronted through the '70s by vocalist Ozzy Osbourne, an ungainly and oddly endearing rock-and-roll maniac, the group set the early standard for the sound and sentiment of heavy metal and ultimately influenced later groups such as Metallica, Megadeth, and Soundgarden. As a practitioner of rock performed for its shock value as popularized by Alice Cooper and Kiss, Osbourne enjoyed an almost incomprehensible success as a solo act in the '80s.

Originally formed in Birmingham, England, in 1968 as Earth, the band changed its name to Black Sabbath in late 1969, securing a record contract with Warner Bros. Their cheaply recorded debut album sold remarkably well, and instigated charges of satanism for songs such as "Black Sabbath" and "Wicked World." Their second album, *Paranoid*, became an acknowledged heavy-metal classic on the basis of the minor hits "Paranoid" and "Iron Man," as well as the group favorites "Fairies Wear Boots," "Hand of Doom," and "War Pigs." Debuting in the United States in the fall of 1971, Black Sabbath established themselves as a popular live band through relentless touring.

Touring and recording regularly to maintain their status as heavy-metal pioneers, Black Sabbath did not falter with the departure of Osbourne in 1978, thanks to the addition of former Rainbow vocalist Ronnie James Dio. However, beginning in the early '80s, defections impeded the group's subsequent success. Bill Ward quit in 1981, to be replaced by a succession of drummers, starting with Vinnie Appice. Dio and Appice left amidst recriminations in 1983 to form Dio; former Deep Purple vocalist Ian Gillan was the first of many vocalists to front the band during the '80s. With the 1985 departure of Geezer Butler, only Tony Iommi remained from the original lineup. The original members reunited for the July 1985 Live Aid concert in Philadelphia. By 1989 Black Sabbath had switched to I.R.S. Records, and in the summer of 1991 they regrouped with Iommi, Dio, Butler, and Appice. The group's "Time Machine" was featured in the hit 1992 movie *Wayne's World*.

Ozzy Osbourne launched his solo career amidst controversy when he bit the head off a dove at a meeting of Columbia Records executives in 1980. Recruiting young guitarist Randy Rhoads, he recorded two best-selling albums issued in 1981 that established him among heavy-metal fans. However, on March 19, 1982, Rhoads was killed near Leesburg, Florida, when the group's bus driver accidentally crashed his small plane into the mansion in which the group was staying. Osbourne's public spectacle continued as he reportedly bit the head off a bat at a concert in Des Moines and was arrested for public drunkenness in Memphis. In 1985 he was targeted by the censorship-advocating Parents' Music Resource Center for his lyrics, and sued by an irate father who charged that Osbourne's "Suicide Solution" had caused his son to kill himself. *The Ultimate Sin* became his first Top 10 album in 1986 (without the benefit of a hit single). By 1988 he had recruited guitar prodigy Zakk Wylde for touring and recording, and cleaned up at the Betty Ford Center in Rancho Mirage, California. In 1989 Osbourne assisted in the recording of Lita Ford's smash hit "Close My Eyes Forever." His 1991 album, *No More Tears*, yielded two hits with the title song and the ballad "Mama, I'm Coming Home." That year Osbourne embarked on a "No More Tours" show to support the album, ostensibly to end his career at least as a solo artist; he gave his last public performance in 1993, including four songs with a reconstituted Black Sabbath. The tour was recorded and issued as *Live and Loud*, garnering Osbourne his first Grammy nomination. Osbourne also recorded one track on a 1994 tribute album to Black Sabbath.

Black Sabbath

Black Sabbath	Warner Bros.	1871	'70	CS/CD
Paranoid	Warner Bros.	1887	'71	†
	Warner Bros.	3104		CS/CD

Master of Reality	Warner Bros.	2562	'71	CS/CD
Volume IV	Warner Bros.	2602	'72	CS/CD
Sabbath, Bloody Sabbath	Warner Bros.	2695	'74	CS/CD
Sabotage	Warner Bros.	2822	'75	CS/CD
We Sold Our Soul for Rock 'n' Roll	Warner Bros.	2923	'76	CS/CD
Technical Ecstasy	Warner Bros.	2969	'76	CS/CD
Never Say Die	Warner Bros.	3186	'78	CS/CD
Heaven and Hell	Warner Bros.	3372	'80	CS/CD
Paranoid/Heaven and Hell	Warner Bros.	25132		CS
The Mob Rules	Warner Bros.	3605	'81	CS/CD
Live Evil	Warner Bros.	23742	'83	CS/CD
Born Again	Warner Bros.	23978	'83	CS
Seventh Star	Warner Bros.	25337	'86	†
The Eternal Idol	Warner Bros.	25548	'87	CS/CD
Dehumanizer	Reprise	26965	'92	CS/CD
Headless Cross	I.R.S.	13002	'89	CS/CD
Tyr	I.R.S.	13049	'90	CS/CD
Cross Purposes	I.R.S.	13222	'94	CS/CD
Cross Purposes—Live	I.R.S.	77806	'95	CD
Forbidden	I.R.S.	30620	'95	CS/CD

Tribute Album

Nativity in Black: A Tribute to Black Sabbath	Columbia	66335	'94	CS/CD

Ozzy Osbourne

Blizzard of Ozz	Jet	36812	'81	CS/CD
Diary of a Madman	Jet	37492	'81	CS/CD
Speak of the Devil	Jet	(2) 38350	'82	†
	Jet	38350		CS/CD
Bark at the Moon	CBS Associated	38987	'83/'85	CS/CD
The Ultimate Sin	CBS Associated	40026	'86	CS/CD
No Rest for the Wicked	CBS Associated	44245	'88	CS/CD
Just Say Ozzy (mini)	CBS Associated	45451	'90	CS/CD
No More Tears	Epic Associated	46795	'91	LP/CS/CD
Live and Loud (recorded 1992)	Epic	(2) 67244	'95	CS/CD
Ozzmosis	Epic	67091	'95	CS/CD

Ozzy Osbourne and Randy Rhoads

Tribute	CBS Associated	40714	'87	CS/CD
	Epic	67240	'95	CS/CD

THE BLASTERS

Phil Alvin (b. Mar. 6, 1953, Los Angeles, CA), lead voc, rhythm gtr; **Dave Alvin** (b. Nov. 11, 1955, Los Angeles, CA), rhythm gtr; **John Bazz** (b. July 6, 1952), bs; **Bill Bateman** (b. Dec. 16, 1951, Orange, CA), drm [Later members include **Gene Taylor** (b. July 2, 1952, Tyler, TX), piano; **Lee Allen**, tenor sax; and **Steve Berlin** (b. Sept. 14, 1955, Philadelphia, PA), baritone sax.]

First recognized for their authentic, original re-creations of the sound and spirit of vintage rockabilly and rhythm and blues in the early '80s, the Blasters soon expanded their repertoire into the realm of socially conscious songs concerned with the plight of common people, leading to comparisons with Bruce Springsteen and John Mellencamp. Centered around lead vocalist Phil Alvin and songwriter Dave Alvin, one of the most talented brother duos of the '80s, the group were a fixture in the Los Angeles alternative-rock scene. The group endured after Dave Alvin departed in 1985 to join X and that band's folk- and country-style spinoff the Knitters before launching his own career as one of America's most compelling songwriters.

Formed in 1979 in Downey, California, the Blasters were initially comprised of brothers Phil and Dave Alvin, bassist John Bazz, and drummer Bill Bateman. Developing a local reputation during the waning days of punk music, the Blasters toured the United States as opening act for Queen in 1980. Rockabilly singer Shakin' Stevens scored a major British hit with Dave Alvin's "Marie Marie." The group recorded their debut album, *American Music*, for the small independent label Rollin' Rock. They added pianist Gene Taylor to rerecord the album for another Los Angeles independent label, Slash. Released as simply *The Blasters*, the album sold remarkably well after Warner Bros. picked up distribution of the label. The album featured the celebratory classic "American Music," the nostalgic but rocking "Border Radio," and "Marie Marie," all written by Dave Alvin and performed in an exciting, bare-bones style. The Blasters toured tirelessly to establish themselves as one of this country's most engaging live bands, and next recorded the EP *Over There* live in London.

The Blasters won their greatest critical acclaim with 1983's *Non Fiction*, recorded with short-time members Lee Allen (tenor saxophone) and Steve Berlin (baritone saxophone). Songs such as "Boomtown," "Fool's Paradise," and "Jubilee Train" revealed a concern for the plight of the common man; the album also included "Long White Cadillac" (later covered by Dwight Yoakam) and the ballad "Leaving." Returning to the basic quintet of the Alvins, Taylor, Bazz, and Bateman, the Blasters recorded *Hard Line*, which included the rocking "Trouble Bound," the ominous "Dark Night," the blatantly political "Common Man," John Mellencamp's "Colored Lights," and "Just Another Saturday Night," cowritten by Dave Alvin and John Doe of X.

During his free time Dave Alvin had been playing with John Doe, Exene Cervenka, and D. J. Bonebrake of X in an acoustic folk and country group called the Knitters. The group toured and then recorded *Poor Little Critter on the Road* for Slash. Alvin quit the Blasters in 1985, and the remaining quartet added guitarist Michael "Hollywood Fats" Mann, but he died of a heart attack soon after at age 32. Dave rejoined the group for their 1987 European tour, after which the group added guitarist Greg Hormel. In 1986 Phil Alvin recorded the eclectic *Un' Sung Stories* for Slash.

Dave Alvin joined X in 1985, staying on through the recording of *See How We Are*, which included his "Fourth of July." He left X in 1987 to pursue a solo career, recording *Every Night about This Time* in England. The album was picked up by Epic in the United States and released as *Romeo's Escape*. In the '90s Alvin recorded for the Oakland-based independent label Hightone, but his albums were sorely neglected despite his excellent songwriting. In 1994, with singer-songwriter Tom Russell, Alvin coproduced the Merle Haggard tribute album *Tulare Dust*, featuring artists such as Dwight Yoakam, Robert Earl Keen, Joe Ely, Marshall Crenshaw, Iris DeMent, and Katy Moffatt. Touring with Russell and Peter Case under the Tulare Dust banner, Alvin concluded the tour in April 1995 with a live version of the album performed by many of the artists at San Francisco's Fillmore Auditorium; Haggard himself closed the show.

The Blasters

American Music	Rollin' Rock	021	'80	†
The Blasters	Slash	3680	'81	†
Over There	Slash (mini)	23735	'82	†
Non Fiction	Slash	23818	'83	†

Hard Line	Slash	25093	'85	†
Collection	Slash	26451	'91	CS/CD
Phil Alvin				
Un' Sung Stories	Slash	25481	'86	CS
County Fair 2000	Hightone	8056		CS/CD
The Knitters				
Poor Little Critter on the Road	Slash	25310	'85	CS/CD
X (with Dave Alvin)				
See How We Are	Elektra	60492	'87	CS/CD
Dave Alvin				
Romeo's Escape	Epic	40921	'87	†
	Razor & Tie	2074	'95	CD
Blue Blvd	Hightone	8029	'91	CD
Museum of the Heart	Hightone	8049	'93	CS/CD
King of California	Hightone	8054	'94	CS/CD
Various Artists				
Tulare Dust: A Song-Writer's Tribute to Merle Haggard	Hightone	8058	'94	CS/CD

BLONDIE

Deborah Harry (b. July 1, 1945, Miami, FL), voc; **Chris Stein** (b. Jan. 5, 1950, Brooklyn, NY), gtr; **Jimmy Destri** (b. Apr. 13, 1954, Brooklyn, NY), kybd; **Gary Valentine**, bs; **Clem Burke** (b. Nov. 24, 1955, New York, NY), drm [Later members include **Frank Infante** on bass and guitar, and **Nigel Harrison** (b. Apr. 24, 1951, Stockport, England), bass.]

The most commercially successful group to emerge from the late-'70s New York punk scene, Blondie crafted a series of excellent pop singles between 1979 and 1982 under producer Mike Chapman. Remarkably eclectic musically, Blondie scored the first crossover hit between New Wave and disco with "Heart of Glass," promoted reggae with "The Tide Is High," and helped introduce rap with "Rapture." The group's success opened the door for tough, aggressive female vocalists such as Pat Benatar, Joan Jett, and Chrissie Hynde, and the up-front sexuality of lead vocalist Deborah Harry set the stage for the rise of Madonna.

Deborah Harry was adopted by the Harry family of Hawthorne, New Jersey, at age three months. She grew up in Hawthorne and attended Centenary College for two years before moving to Manhattan. In 1968 she recorded an album with the folk-rock group Wind in the Willows. Later Harry worked as a Playboy "bunny" and waited tables at Max's Kansas City, one of the New York clubs that served as the base for the emerging punk movement. In the early '70s she helped form the glitter-rock group the Stilettos, recruiting guitarist Chris Stein in late 1973. Harry and Stein subsequently formed Angel and the Snakes, then changed the group's name to Blondie.

Adding Farfisa organist Jimmy Destri, Blondie won a local cult following through appearances at CBGB's, another important punk club on New York's Lower East Side, and Max's Kansas City. Debuting on the West Coast as the opening act for the Ramones at Los Angeles's Whisky a-Go-Go in early 1977, Blondie recorded their first album for the small Private Stock label. Achieving hits in Great Britain, Europe, and Australia with "In the Flesh" and "Rip Her to Shreds," Blondie was picked up by Chrysalis Records, for whom they recorded *Plastic Letters* with producer Richard Gottehrer.

Original bassist Gary Valentine was replaced first by Frank Infante, and then by Englishman Nigel Harrison; Infante switched to guitar after Harrison joined the band. Under producer Mike Chapman they cut their next album, *Parallel Lines*, which established Blondie in the United States. The album included "Hanging on the Telephone" and yielded the major hits "One Way or Another" and the disco-style "Heart of Glass." Established as headliners, Blondie toured America in 1979, and next recorded the hard-rocking *Eat to the Beat*, which produced the three hits "Dreaming," "The Hardest Part," and "Atomic." In early 1980 the group scored big with "Call Me," the theme to the film *American Gigolo*, recorded under disco producer Giorgio Moroder. That year Harry demonstrated her acting ability in two movies, *Union City* with Pat Benatar and *Roadie* with Meat Loaf and others. The diverse album *Autoamerican* produced two top hits for Blondie: a remake of the Paragons' reggae song "The Tide Is High," and the early rap song "Rapture." Following Debbie Harry's debut solo album *KooKoo* and the group effort *The Hunter*, Blondie disbanded in 1983.

Debbie Harry was largely out of the public view between 1983 and 1985, save for her costarring role in the disturbing David Cronenberg film *Videodrome*, while she cared for Chris Stein, who was afflicted with the rare genetic disorder pemphigus. Harry reemerged in 1986 with the album *Rockbird*, recorded with Stein, guitarist Nile Rodgers (Chic), and producer-keyboardist Seth Justman (J. Geils Band). The album produced minor hits with "French Kissing" and the Harry-Stein composition "In Love with Love." Debbie Harry subsequently appeared in the films *Hairspray* and *Tales from the Darkside*, and in the Showtime cable-TV thriller *Intimate Stranger*; she recorded *Def, Dumb and Blonde* for Sire under producer Mike Chapman, and *Once More into the Bleach* for Chrysalis. In 1994 Harry contributed one song to the Jazz Passengers' *In Love* album and toured as the group's lead vocalist.

Wind in the Willows

Wind in the Willows	Capitol	2956	'68	†
Blondie				
Blondie	Private Stock	2023	'77	†
	Chrysalis	41165	'83	†
	Chrysalis	21165		CS/CD
Plastic Letters	Chrysalis	1166	'78	†
	Chrysalis	41166	'83	†
	Chrysalis	21166		CS/CD
Parallel Lines	Chrysalis	1192	'78	†
	Chrysalis	21192	'86	CS/CD
Eat to the Beat	Chrysalis	1225	'79	†
	Chrysalis	41225	'83	†
	Chrysalis	21225		CS/CD
Autoamerican	Chrysalis	1290	'80	†
	Chrysalis	41290	'83	†
	Chrysalis	21290		CS/CD
Best	Chrysalis	1337	'81	†
	Chrysalis	21337		CS/CD
The Hunter	Chrysalis	1384	'82	†
	Chrysalis	41384	'83	†
	Chrysalis	21384		CS/CD
Blondie and Beyond: Rarities and Oddities	Chrysalis	21990	'93	CS/CD
The Platinum Collection	Chrysalis	(2) 31100	'94	CD
Debbie Harry				
KooKoo	Chrysalis	1347	'81	†
	Chrysalis	41347	'84	†
Once More into the Bleach	Chrysalis	21658		CS/CD

Rockbird	Geffen	24123	'86	CS/CD†
Def, Dumb and Blonde	Sire	25938	'89	CS/CD
Debravation	Sire	45303		CS/CD

BLOOD, SWEAT AND TEARS

Al Kooper (b. Feb. 5, 1944, Brooklyn, NY), kybd, voc; **Steve Katz** (b. May 9, 1945, Brooklyn, NY), gtr, voc; **Jerry Weiss** (b. May 1, 1946, New York, NY), trpt, flüegelhorn; **Randy Brecker** (b. Nov. 27, 1945, Philadelphia, PA), trpt, flüegelhorn; **Fred Lipsius** (b. Nov. 19, 1944, New York, NY), alto sax, pno; **Dick Halligan** (b. Aug. 29, 1943, Troy, NY), trpt, flt, kybd; **Jim Fielder** (b. Oct. 4, 1947, Denton, TX), bs; **Bobby Colomby** (b. Dec. 20, 1944, New York, NY), drm, voc [Al Kooper, Jerry Weiss, and Randy Brecker left after the first album, to be replaced by **David Clayton-Thomas** (b. David Tomsett, Sept. 13, 1941, Surrey, England), vocals; **Lew Soloff** (b. Feb. 20, 1944, Brooklyn, NY) and **Chuck Winfield** (b. Feb. 5, 1943, Monessen, PA), trumpet and flüegelhorn; and **Jerry Hyman** (b. May 19, 1947, Brooklyn, NY), trombone and recorder.]

The first major rock group to successfully augment its sound with horns, Blood, Sweat and Tears displayed an early amalgamation of jazz and rock music. Inadvertently, Blood, Sweat and Tears helped inspire the independent development of so-called fusion music, a form pursued by Miles Davis, Herbie Hancock, and Weather Report in the '70s, as well as by rock bands such as Chicago. Following the departure of keyboardist-vocalist Al Kooper, Blood, Sweat and Tears evolved into an enormously popular, highly arranged pop band (most successfully fronted by vocalist David Clayton-Thomas) that set the standard for the blending together of rock, pop, and jazz music.

Blood, Sweat and Tears was formed in 1968 by Al Kooper, Steve Katz, and Bobby Colomby following Katz and Kooper's departure from the Blues Project. These founders recruited additional musicians Jim Fielder, Jerry Weiss, Randy Brecker, Fred Lipsius, and Dick Halligan. Although their debut album on Columbia, *Child Is Father to the Man*, failed to generate any hit singles, it contained a number of excellent Al Kooper compositions ("I Love You More than You'll Ever Know," "My Days Are Numbered," "I Can't Quit Her") as well as early versions of Harry Nilsson's "Without Her" and Randy Newman's "Just One Smile."

In mid-1968 Kooper left Blood, Sweat and Tears to accept a lucrative offer from Columbia Records to become a producer. Weiss and Brecker also left, and were replaced by Lew Soloff, Chuck Winfield, and Jerry Hyman. The lead vocalist role was taken over by David Clayton-Thomas. Clayton-Thomas had worked around Toronto for ten years, recording five Canadian gold-award records with the Bossmen. The new lineup's first album exploded onto the music scene in early 1969. In addition to including Steve Katz's beautiful "Sometimes in Winter" and a remake of Billie Holiday's "God Bless the Child," the album yielded three smash-hit singles: Laura Nyro's "And When I Die," and Clayton-Thomas's "Spinning Wheel" and "You've Made Me So Very Happy."

Blood, Sweat and Tears' next album contained two hit singles, "Hi-De-Ho" and "Lucretia MacEvil," and the elaborately arranged "Symphony/Sympathy for the Devil" and "40,000 Headmen." However, their followup album included only one moderate hit, "Go Down Gamblin'," setting the stage for a long decline. A series of defections struck Blood, Sweat and Tears, effectively crippling the group. Clayton-Thomas departed in late 1971 for an undistinguished solo career. Lipsius and Halligan also left, followed by Katz and Winfield in 1973. The group persevered with new personnel and a succession of lead vocalists: Bobby Doyle, Jerry Fisher, and Jerry La Croix.

Appearing with Blood, Sweat and Tears at Mister Kelly's in Chicago in late 1974, David Clayton-Thomas subsequently rejoined the group. By then only Bobby Colomby remained from the original group. Personnel shifts continued to plague Blood, Sweat and Tears, and on January 31, 1978, one-year member Gregory Herbert was found dead in an Amsterdam hotel room during the group's European tour. By 1980 David Clayton-Thomas was the only longtime member left in Blood, Sweat and Tears; he continues to lead a version of the band on the Las Vegas and rock-revival circuit.

Blood, Sweat and Tears

Child Is Father to the Man	Columbia	9619	'68	†
	Columbia/Legacy	64214	'94	CD
Blood, Sweat and Tears	Columbia	9720	'69	LP/CS/CD
	Mobile Fidelity	559	'92	CD
Blood, Sweat and Tears 3	Columbia	30090	'70/'86	CD
Blood, Sweat and Tears 4	Columbia	30590	'71	†
	Columbia/Legacy	66422	'96	CD
Greatest Hits	Columbia	31170	'72	CS/CD
New Blood	Columbia	31780	'72	†
No Sweat	Columbia	32180	'73	†
Mirror Image	Columbia	32929	'74	†
New City	Columbia	33484	'75	†
More than Ever	Columbia	34233	'76	†
Brand New Day	ABC	1015	'78	†
Blood, Sweat and Tears	MCA	3227	'80	†
Live and Improvised	Columbia/Legacy (2) 46918		'91	CS/CD
Greatest Hits	IMG	738		CS
Nuclear Blues (recorded 1980)	Avenue	71922	'95	CD
Live (recorded 1982)	Avenue	71287	'94	CS/CD

David Clayton-Thomas

I Got a Woman	Decca	75146	'69	†
Magnificent Sanctuary Band	Columbia	31000	'72	†
Tequila Sunrise	Columbia	31700	'72	†
Harmony Junction	RCA	0173	'73	†
Clayton	ABC/MCA	1104	'78	†

MIKE BLOOMFIELD

(b. July 28, 1944, Chicago, IL; d. Feb. 15, 1981, San Francisco, CA)

One of the first white musicians to achieve popular acclaim as a blues guitarist, Mike Bloomfield was in the forefront of the late-'60s blues revival with the Paul Butterfield Blues Band and the Electric Flag (which he cofounded with Nick Gravenites). His most famous session job was as lead guitarist on Bob Dylan's "Like a Rolling Stone" and *Highway 61 Revisited*. He also participated in the famous *Super Session* album with Al Kooper and Steven Stills, which set the stage for numerous supergroups. Bloomfield himself participated in two more super groupings, one with blues picker John Hammond Jr. and New Orleans pianist Dr. John, and the second (and his last major stab at stardom) with the group KGB, featuring bassist Rick Grech and keyboard player Barry Goldberg along with Carmine Appice on drums and vocalist Ray Kennedy. KGB cut an album for MCA in 1976, but failed to generate much interest. Discouraged by his lack of success in the rock arena, Bloomfield retired to playing primarily in the local San Francisco Bay Area blues scene while recording a number of albums of acoustic and electric blues. Bloomfield died of a drug overdose on February 15, 1981.

The Paul Butterfield Blues Band

The Paul Butterfield Blues Band	Elcktra	7294	'65	CD
East-West	Elektra	7315	'66	CD

The Electric Flag

A Long Time Comin'	Columbia	9597	'68	CD
An American Music Band	Columbia	9714	'68	†
Best	Columbia	30422	'71	†
The Band Kept Playing	Atlantic	18112	'74	†

Bloomfield, Kooper And Stills

Super Session	Columbia	9701	'68	CS/CD

Mike Bloomfield and Al Kooper

Live Adventures of Mike Bloomfield and Al Kooper	Columbia	(2) 6	'69	

Mike Bloomfield

It's Not Killing Me	Columbia	9883	'69	†
	Harmony	30395	'71	
Don't Say That I Ain't Your Man: Essential Blues, 1964–1969	Columbia/Legacy	57631	'94	CS/CD
Try It Before You Buy It	Columbia	33173	'75	†
Bloomfield	Columbia	(2) 37578	'83	†
If You Love These Blues	Guitar Player	3002	'77	†
	Kicking Mule	166		CS
Analine	Takoma	7059	'77	†
	Takoma	72759		†
Michael Bloomfield	Takoma	7063	'78	†
	Takoma	72763		†
Between the Hard Place and the Ground	Takoma	7070	'79	†
	Takoma	72770		†
	Magnum America	12	'95	CD
Cruisin' for a Bruisin'	Takoma	7091	'81	
	Takoma	72791		†
Best	Takoma	72815	'87	CD†
Count Talent and the Originals	Clouds	8805	'78	†
Living in the Fast Lane	Waterhouse	11	'81	†
	ERA	5006	'92	CS/CD
Junko Partner	Intermedia	5068		LP/CS
Blues, Gospel and Ragtime Guitar Instrumentals	Shanachie	99007	'93	CS/CD

Mike Bloomfield, John Paul Hammond, and Dr. John

Triumvirate	Columbia	32172	'73	CD

Mike Bloomfield with KGB

KGB	MCA	2166	'76	†

Mike Bloomfield and Woody Harris

Gospel Guitar Duets	Kicking Mule	164	'80	CS
Mike Bloomfield with Woody Harris	Sky Ranch	2328	'92	CD

BLUE ÖYSTER CULT

Donald "Buck Dharma" Roeser, lead gtr, voc; **Allen Lanier**, kybd, gtr, voc; **Eric Bloom**, gtr, synthesizer, voc; **Joe Bouchard** (b. Nov. 9, 1948, Watertown, NY), b, voc; and **Albert Bouchard** (b. May 24, 1947, Watertown, NY), drm, voc

Mainstays of heavy-metal music during the '70s, Blue Öyster Cult featured a deafening yet frequently melodic triple-guitar attack on songs often concerned with death and destruction. Formed as Soft White Underbelly on New York's Long Island in 1968, the group took the name Stalk Forest before becoming Blue Öyster Cult in 1971. A variety of band members passed through these early incarnations, including the rock critic R. Meltzer, who has since gone on to be one of the group's strongest champions. The final lineup included frontmen guitarist-songwriter Donald "Buck Dharma" Roeser, guitarist-keyboardist Allen Lanier, and guitarist-vocalist Eric Bloom. The band spent the early '70s touring as a support act to Alice Cooper, finally breaking through in 1976 with the album *Agents of Fortune*, which featured their only major hit, "(Don't Fear) The Reaper." A special guest on the album was Lanier's then-girlfriend, Patti Smith, the New York punk diva who contributed some vocals and songs to the effort. Blue Öyster Cult established themselves as exciting live performers, as evidenced by their best-selling live set, *On Your Feet or On Your Knees*, as well as two other live discs. The group pursued a more pop sound with the 1981 departure of drummer-songwriter Albert Bouchard. He eventually returned to the otherwise intact group in 1988 for the album *Imaginos*. The band soldiered on into the early '90s, although the Bouchard brothers Joe and Albert had jumped ship by 1994.

Blue Öyster Cult

Blue Öyster Cult	Columbia	31063	'72	CS/CD
Tyranny and Mutation	Columbia	32017	'73	CS/CD
Secret Treaties	Columbia	32858	'74	CS/CD
On Your Feet or On Your Knees	Columbia	(2) 33371	'75	†
	Columbia	33371		CD
Agents of Fortune	Columbia	34164	'76	CS/CD
Spectres	Columbia	35019	'77	CS/CD
Some Enchanted Evening	Columbia	35563	'78	CS/CD
Mirrors	Columbia	36009	'79	CS/CD
Cultosaurus Erectus	Columbia	36550	'80	CS/CD
Fire of Unknown Origin	Columbia	37389	'81	CS/CD
Extraterrestrial Live	Columbia	37946	'82	CS/CD
The Revolution by Night	Columbia	38947	'83	CD
Club Ninja	Columbia	39979	'86	CS/CD†
Imaginos	Columbia	40618	'88	CD
Career of Evil: The Metal Years (1974–1986)	Columbia	44300	'90	CS/CD
Cult Classic	Herald	008	'94	CS/CD
Workshop of the Telescopes	Columbia/Legacy	(2) 64163	'95	CD

Buck Dharma

Flat Out	Portrait	38124	'82	†

THE BLUES PROJECT

Tommy Flanders, voc; **Danny Kalb** (b. Sept. 19, 1942, Brooklyn, NY), gtr; **Andy Kulberg** (b. 1944, Buffalo, NY), bs, flt; and **Roy Blumenfeld**, drm [Tommy Flanders left after the first album, and keyboardist-vocalist **Al Kooper** (b. Feb. 5, 1944, Brooklyn, NY) and guitarist **Steve Katz** (b. May 9, 1945, Brooklyn, NY) were added.]

Along with the Chicago-based Paul Butterfield Blues Band, the Blues Project were among the first white bands to use electric instruments in playing the blues and folk music. They achieved both underground success and an aboveground reputation despite never registering a hit single. Formed by folk guitarist Danny Kalb and jazz drummer Roy Blumenfeld, the group soon added guitarist Steve Katz and the multitalented Al Kooper. Kooper contributed the underground favorites "Flute Thing" and "No Time Like the Right Time," but he and Katz left the Blues Project in 1968 to form Blood, Sweat and Tears. By 1969 original members Andy Kulberg and Roy Blumenfeld had moved to California to form Seatrain. Later joined by bluegrass veteran Peter Rowan, Seatrain was one of the first rock bands to play country-style material, as evidenced by their early recording of Lowell George's "Willin'." The Blues Project reunited in 1971 and briefly in 1973 with Al Kooper. Steve Katz helped form American Flyer with Eric Kaz, Craig Fuller, and Doug Yule in 1976.

The Blues Project

"Live" at the Cafe Au Go Go	Verve/Folkways	3000	'66	†
	Verve	8333346	'89	CS/CD
Projections	Verve/Folkways	3008	'66	†
	Verve	827918	'89	CD
"Live" at Town Hall	Verve/Forecast	3025	'67	†
	One Way	30010	'94	CD
Planned Obsolescence	Verve/Forecast	3046	'68	†
Kooper, et. al. of the Blues Project	Verve/Forecast	3069	'69		
Best	Verve/Forecast	3077	'69	†
The Blues Project	MGM	118	'70	†
Archetypes	MGM	4953	'74	†
Lazarus	Capitol	782	'71	†
The Blues Project	Capitol	11017	'72	†
Reunion at Central Park	MCA	(2) 8003	'73	†
Best: "No Time Like the Right Time"	Rhino	70165	'89	CS/CD

Danny Kalb and Stefan Grossman

Crosscurrents	Cotillion	9007	'69	†

Seatrain

Seatrain	A&M	4171	'69	†
Seatrain	Capitol	659	'71	†
	Capitol	29800	'94	CS
Marblehead Messenger	Capitol	829	'71	†
	One Way	57661		CD
Watch	Warner Bros.	2692	'73	†

American Flyer

American Flyer	United Artists	650	'76	†
Spirit of a Woman	United Artists	720	'77	†

THE BONZO DOG BAND

Vivian Stanshall (b. Mar. 21, 1943, Shillingford, Oxfordshire, England), trpt, voc; **Neil Innes** (b. Dec. 9, 1944, Danbury, Essex, England), kybd, gtr, bs, voc; **Roger Ruskin Spear** (b. June 29, 1943, Hammersmith, London), rds, sound effects; **Rodney Slater** (b. Nov. 8, 1941, Crowland, Lincolnshire, England), rds; **"Legs" Larry Smith** (b. Jan. 18, 1944, Oxford, England), drm, perc, tap dancing

One of the first groups to explore the visual, the theatrical, and the absurd within the rock format, the Bonzo Dog Band parodied '50s rock and roll, pretentious folk music, and the English music hall tradition while satirizing many aspects of contemporary life. Although virtually unrecognized in the United States, this late-'60s English group recorded a number of underground favorites, including "The Intro and The Outro," "Can Blue Men Sing the Whites," and "Mr. Apollo," and even managed a smash hit in England with "I'm the Urban Spaceman." They deflated the pretension of the Who's rock opera, *Tommy*, by recording their own very pretentious rock opera, *Keynsham*. The group broke up in 1970, reunited in 1971 for one more album, and then finally called it quits. Member Neil Innes joined Monty Python's Eric Idle for the irreverent Beatles parody album *The Rutles* in 1978.

The Bonzo Dog Doodah Band

Gorilla	Imperial	12370	'68	†
	One Way	17370		CD

The Bonzo Dog Band

Urban Spaceman	Imperial	12432	'69	†
	One Way	17430		CD
Tadpoles	Imperial	12445	'69	†
	One Way	17431		CD
Keynsham	Imperial	12457	'70	†
	One Way	17432		CD
The Beast of the Bonzoes	United Artists	5517	'71	†
Let's Make Up and Be Friendly	United Artists	5584	'72	†
	One Way	17795	'94	CD
The History of the Bonzo Dog Band	United Artists	(2) 321	'74	†
Best	Rhino	71006	'90	CD

Roger Ruskin Spear

Electric Shocks	United Artists	097	'72	†

Grimms Rockin' Duck (with Neil Innes)

Grimms Rockin' Duck	Antilles	7012	'76	†

Neil Innes and Eric Idle

Rutland Weekend Songbook	Passport	98018	'76	†

Neil Innes, Eric Idle, and Others

The Rutles	Warner Bros.	3151	'78	†
	Rhino	75760	'90	CD

BOOKER T. AND THE MGs

Booker T. Jones (b. Nov. 12, 1944, Memphis, TN), kybd, gtr, bs; **Steve Cropper** (b. Oct. 21, 1941, Willow Springs, MO), lead and rhythm gtr; **Donald "Duck" Dunn** (b. Nov. 24, 1941, Memphis, TN), bs; **Al Jackson Jr.** (b. Nov. 27, 1935, Memphis, TN; d. Oct. 1, 1975, Memphis, TN), drm

Best remembered historically as the studio band for Stax/Volt Records during the '60s, Booker T. and the MGs created the so-called Memphis Sound, illustrated in the hit recordings of Carla and Rufus Thomas, Otis Redding, and Sam and Dave, among others. Perhaps the last rock band to issue albums comprised entirely of instrumentals, the group featured a cohesive yet spare sound on hits of their own, such as "Green Onions," "Hang 'Em High," and "Time Is Tight." They were also one of the few multiracial bands, with two black men (Jones and Jackson) and two white.

In 1962 Booker T. and the MGs (for *Memphis Group*) formed as the house band for Memphis's Stax Records. Steve Cropper and Donald "Duck" Dunn had been members of the Mar-Keys since the late '50s, and both played on the group's 1961 instrumental hit "Last Night." Dunn remained with the Mar-Keys until 1964 while also playing as part of the

MGs. In the early '60s Booker T. and the MGs provided the instrumental backing for hits by Carla Thomas ("Gee Whiz") and her father Rufus Thomas ("Walking the Dog"). Their reputation as a band in their own right was established in 1962 with the smash instrumental hit "Green Onions."

Over the next seven years Booker T. and the MGs recorded independently and backed various Stax/Volt artists while individual members pursued solo projects. Booker T. Jones cowrote with artist-producer William Bell the oft-recorded blues classic "Born Under a Bad Sign." In 1966 Jones received a degree in music from Indiana University. In the meantime, Steve Cropper supervised the recordings of Otis Redding and cowrote hits by Wilson Pickett ("In the Midnight Hour"), Eddie Floyd ("Knock on Wood"), and Redding ("[Sittin' on the] Dock of the Bay"). Al Jackson produced recordings by blues guitarist Albert King. Booker T. and the MGs also served as the backing band for Sam and Dave's two biggest hits, "Hold On! I'm Coming" and "Soul Man." On their own, Booker T. and the MGs scored major hits with "Groovin'" and "Soul Limbo" and near-smashes with "Hang 'Em High" and "Time Is Tight," the latter from the soundtrack to *Uptight*, scored by Booker T. In 1969 Steve Cropper recorded the album *With a Little Help from My Friends*, as well as *Jammed Together* with Albert King and gospel patriarch "Pop" Staples.

By 1970 Booker T. and the MGs had abandoned their role as Stax house band, officially disbanding in 1972. Booker Jones moved to California and joined A&M Records as a staff producer. There he supervised recording sessions for Rita Coolidge, his wife Priscilla (Rita's sister), and Bill Withers. In the early '70s Jones recorded three albums with his wife, plus the solo album *Evergreen*. Cropper continued with session and production chores at Stax/Volt Records until 1975, when Stax/Volt folded. He then moved to Los Angeles.

The original members of Booker T. and the MGs were planning a reunion when Al Jackson was shot to death in Memphis on October 1, 1975. The band reunited, with Willie Hall (formerly of the Bar-Kays) succeeding Jackson on drums, for the album *Universal Language*. In 1977 Jones, Cropper, and Dunn recorded and toured with Levon Helm's RCO All-Stars. Also in 1977–1978, Cropper and Dunn re-created their distinctive '60s sound behind the Blues Brothers (John Belushi and Dan Aykroyd) on tours and albums, as well as in the popular 1980 movie *The Blues Brothers*. In 1988 Booker T., Steve Cropper, and Duck Dunn reunited and joined drummer Anton Fig to perform at Atlantic Records' 40th anniversary show at Madison Square Garden; that lineup subsequently stayed together for several years to perform as Booker T. and the MGs. In October 1992 Jones, Cropper, and Dunn, with session drummer Jim Keltner, served as the house band for the four-hour Bob Dylan tribute staged at Madison Square Garden. In 1994 Booker T., Cropper, and Dunn recorded their first album in seventeen years, *That's the Way It Should Be*, with session drummers.

The Mar-Keys

Last Night	Atlantic	8055	'61	†
Do the Pop-Eye	Atlantic	8062	'62	†
The Great Memphis Sound	Stax	707	'66	†
	Atlantic	82339	'91	CS/CD
Damifiknew	Stax	2025	'69	†
The Memphis Experience	Stax	2036	'71	†
Damnifiknew/The Memphis Experience	Stax	88021	'94	CD

Booker T. and the MGs/The Mar-Keys

Back to Back	Stax	720	'67	†
	Atlantic	90307	'91	CS/CD

Various Artists

The Complete Stax-Volt Singles, 1959–1968	Atlantic	(9) 82218	'91	CD

Booker T. and the MGs

Green Onions	Stax	701	'62	†
	Atlantic	7701		†
	Atlantic	82255	'91	CS/CD
Soul Dressing	Stax	705	'65	†
	Atlantic	7705		†
	Atlantic	82337	'91	CS/CD
And Now!	Stax	711	'66	†
	Atlantic	7711		†
	Rhino	70297	'92	CS/CD
In the Christmas Spirit	Stax	713	'66	†
	Atlantic	7713	'69	†
	Atlantic	82338	'91	CS/CD
Hip Hug-Her	Stax	717	'67	†
	Atlantic	7717		†
	Rhino	71013	'92	CS/CD
Doin' Our Thing	Stax	724	'68	†
	Atlantic	7724		†
	Rhino	71014	'92	CS/CD
Soul Limbo	Stax	2001	'68	†
	Stax	4113	'78	LP/CD
Uptight (soundtrack)	Stax	2006	'69	†
The Booker T. Set	Stax	2009	'69	†
	Stax	8531	'90	LP/CS/CD
McLemore Avenue	Stax	2027	'70	†
	Stax	8552	'90	LP/CS/CD
Greatest Hits	Stax	2033	'70	†
	Stax	8505		LP/CS
Melting Pot	Stax	2035	'71	†
	Stax	8521	'83/'90	LP/CS/CD
Free Ride	Stax	4104	'78	†
Best	Stax	004		CD
	Atlantic	8202	'68	†
	Atlantic	81281	'85	CS/CD
Universal Language	Asylum	1093	'77	†
Groovin'	Rhino	71234	'93	CS/CD
Very Best	Rhino	71738	'94	CS/CD
That's the Way It Should Be	Columbia	53307	'94	CS/CD

Steve Cropper

With a Little Help from My Friends	Volt	6006	'69	†
	Stax	8555	'90	LP/CS/CD
Playin' My Thang	MCA	5171	'81	†
Night After Night	MCA	5340	'82	†

Steve Cropper/Albert King/"Pop" Staples

Jammed Together	Stax	2020	'69	†
	Stax	8544	'90	LP/CS/CD

Priscilla Jones

Gypsy Queen	A&M	4297	'71	†

Booker T. and Priscilla Jones

Booker T. and Priscilla	A&M	(2) 3504	'71	†

Home Grown	A&M	4351	'72	†
Chronicles	A&M	4413	'73	†
The MGs				
The MGs	Stax	3024	'73	†
Booker T. Jones				
Evergreen	Epic	33143	'74	†
Try and Love Again	A&M	4720	'78	†
The Best of You	A&M	4798	'80	†
Booker T. Jones	A&M	4874	'81	†
The Runaway	MCA	6282	'89	LP/CS/CD
Levon Helm and the RCO All-Stars				
Levon Helm and the RCO All-Stars	ABC	1017	'77	†
	Mobile Fidelity	761	'92	CD
The Blues Brothers				
Briefcase Full of Blues	Atlantic	19217	'78	CS/CD
The Blues Brothers (soundtrack)	Atlantic	16017	'80	CS/CD
Made in America	Atlantic	16025	'80	CS/CD
Best	Atlantic	19331	'81	CS/CD
The Definitive Collection	Atlantic	82428	'92	CS/CD
Red, White and Blues	Turnstyle	14206	'92	CS/CD

DAVID BOWIE
(b. David Jones, Jan. 8, 1947, Brixton, London, England)

Rock's master of image and sound manipulation, David Bowie has pursued an erratic career based very much on image, as opposed to musical substance. His successes have totally transformed the way in which musical heroes are regarded by the consuming public, in terms of shock value, cleverness, and timeliness rather than substance or talent. Tapping musical wellsprings as diverse as folk, pop, disco, and punk, Bowie has demonstrated the uncanny ability to exploit virtually every musical trend without mastering any. Nonetheless, Bowie can be seen as a genius of performance art and astute for his choices of musical collaborators, be it Mick Ronson, Brian Eno, or Nile Rodgers.

David Bowie achieved his earliest major success at the hands of producer-guitarist Mick Ronson, with the classic *Hunky Dory*, *Ziggy Stardust*, and *Aladdin Sane* albums and tours. Bowie was thereby established as the first star of glitter rock, with its ambivalent sexuality, bizarre costuming and cosmetics, contrived theatricality, and elaborate stage lighting and presentation. This achievement helped open rock and pop to artists unafraid to display their flamboyance (Kiss, the New York Dolls), androgyny (Boy George, Michael Jackson), and openly gay sexuality (Queen). During the '70s Bowie established a vital link between music, dance, acting, mime, and street theater that presaged the development of performance art in the '80s. His electronic and synthesizer experiments of the late '70s opened the door for the synthesizer-dominated pop sound of the '80s and the ambient sound of the '90s. His 1980 album *Scary Monsters* inspired a new generation of performers such as Ultravox and Duran Duran, yet he garnered his most widespread popularity with 1983's *Let's Dance* album and Serious Moonlight tour, both in a more pop vein, thanks to the influence of producer Nile Rodgers. Abandoning more than 20 years of hits following 1990's Sound + Vision tour, David Bowie explored heavy metal with Tin Machine before reemerging in 1993 with the jazz–soul–hip-hop sound of *Black Tie White Noise*.

DAVID BOWIE

David Jones took up saxophone at age 12, later forming a number of groups, including David Jones and the Lower Third. Scoring several minor British hits in 1967, he changed his name to David Bowie to avoid confusion with Davy Jones of the Monkees. After a first album heavily influenced by the British music hall tradition, Bowie shifted to a hippie image for his first episode in science fiction, *Space Oddity*, an album not released in the United States until 1972. The title song became a smash hit in Great Britain and eventually became his first major American hit in 1973.

Nonetheless, he "retired" for 18 months to run an Arts Lab in Beckenham, South London, before reemerging with *The Man Who Sold the World*, recorded with guitarist Mick Ronson and drummer Woody Woodmansey. With the British cover (banned in the United States) depicting Bowie as a drag queen with a striking resemblance to Lauren Bacall, the album earned him the beginnings of an English following and introduced the concept of glitter rock. Switching to RCA Records, Bowie managed a moderate hit with "Changes" from *Hunky Dory*.

Arranged by Mick Ronson, *The Rise and Fall of Ziggy Stardust and the Spiders from Mars* was the first of four concept albums that brought Bowie widespread publicity and acclaim and his first recognition in the United States. With Bowie becoming rock star Ziggy Stardust, and Mick Ronson, Woody Woodmansey, and bassist Trevor Bolder becoming the Spiders from Mars, the album featured the minor hit "Starman" and Bowie classics such as "Star," "Suffragette City," and "Rock 'n' Roll Suicide." The 1972 Ziggy Stardust tour of the United States introduced American audiences to Bowie's peculiar, camp mixture of makeup, costume and set changes, and elaborate lighting and staging. The follow-up album, *Aladdin Sane*, generated a minor hit with "Jean Genie."

At this same time David Bowie composed and produced Mott the Hoople's first hit, "All the Young Dudes," and produced Lou Reed's *Transformer* and Iggy Pop's *Raw Power*. Following his final album with the Spiders from Mars and the conclusion of his British tour of 1973, Bowie announced his retirement. However, he was soon back with *Diamond Dogs*, his first album without the services of Mick Ronson, and its minor hit "Rebel Rebel."

Young Americans revealed another image shift, with Bowie embracing the sound of Philadelphia soul. With a new, sophisticated playboy look, he hit with "Young Americans" and "Fame," coauthored by John Lennon. Bowie continued his soul persona with *Station to Station* and the smash "Golden Years." Later in 1976 he revealed a talent for acting, in the title role of Nicolas Roeg's *The Man Who Fell to Earth*, portraying a space voyager stranded on Earth.

Bowie's next three studio albums featured a spare, minimalist sound created by avant-garde keyboardist Brian Eno. Although the albums failed to sell spectacularly, they influenced an entire generation of European rock bands who used electronic synthesizers and sparse arrangements in their playing. In 1980 Bowie received rave reviews for his performance on tour and on Broadway as the grossly deformed John Merrick in Bernard Pomerance's *The Elephant Man*. He recorded *Scary Monsters* without Brian Eno, but with former King Crimson guitarist Robert Fripp. The album included "Ashes to Ashes," promoted with one of the most expensive videos to date, and the minor hit "Fashion." Bowie's next major hit, "Under Pressure," was recorded with Queen.

Bowie switched to EMI America Records and enlisted Nile Rodgers and Tony Thompson of Chic for his 1983 album *Let's Dance*. The title song and hits "China Girl" and "Modern Love" featured Stevie Ray Vaughan on guitar. Playing stadiums rather than arenas, the subsequent Serious Moonlight tour established Bowie as a performing act, without the theatrical effects of earlier tours. In 1984 "Blue Jean" became a near-smash hit from *Tonight*, and the following year Bowie and Mick Jagger hit with a remake of "Dancing in the Street," with all proceeds donated to Live Aid. Bowie later acted in the 1986 film *Labyrinth* and recorded its soundtrack.

David Bowie returned to his theatrics for the 1987 Glass Spider tour, supported by guitarist Peter Frampton, who played on *Never Let Me Down* and its two major hits "Day-In Day-Out" and the title cut. In late 1988 Bowie formed Tin Machine as an integrated band under the influence of punk and heavy-metal music. However, their albums generated little interest, and in 1990 Bowie conducted his Sound + Vision tour with guitarist Adrian Belew as a recapitulation of his career to date. He eventually reemerged with his first solo album in six years, *Black Tie White Noise*, but within months his new label, Savage Records, had ceased operations. Bowie attempted to woo a younger crowd by touring in 1995 with Nine Inch Nails; the audience seemed more interested in the young rockers, though, and Bowie's new material was mostly ignored.

Early David Bowie

Early On (1964–1966)	Rhino	70526	'91	CS/CD
1966	DCC	101		CD
The World of David Bowie	Deram	18003	'67	†
	Deram	800087		CD
Images, 1966–1967	London	(2) 628/9	'73	†
Starting Point	London	50007	'77	†
	Deram	820323		CS
Love You Till Tuesday	London	820083	'84	CS

David Bowie

David Bowie	Mercury	61246	'68	†
(reissued as) Space Oddity	RCA	4813	'72/'85	CD†
	Rykodisc	10131	'90	CS/CD
The Man Who Sold the World	Mercury	61325	'70	†
	RCA	4816	'72/'85	CD†
	Rykodisc	10132	'90	CS/CD
Hunky Dory	RCA	4623	'71/'84	CD†
	Rykodisc	10133	'90	CS/CD

David Bowie and the Spiders from Mars

The Rise and Fall of Ziggy Stardust and the Spiders from Mars	RCA	4702	'72/'84	CD†
	Rykodisc	10134	'90	CS/CD
	Rykodisc	90134	'90	CD
Aladdin Sane	RCA	4852	'73/'84	CD†
	Rykodisc	10135	'90	CS/CD
Pin Ups	RCA	0291	'73/'84	CD†
	Rykodisc	10136	'90	LP/CS/CD

The Spiders from Mars

The Spiders from Mars	Pye	12125	'76	†

David Bowie

Diamond Dogs	RCA	0576	'74/'85	CD†
	Rykodisc	10137	'90	CS/CD
David Live	RCA	(2) 0771	'74	†
	Rykodisc	10138/9	'90	CS/CD
Young Americans	RCA	0998	'75/'84	CD†
	Rykodisc	0140	'91	CS
	Rykodisc	10140	'91	CD
Station to Station	RCA	1327	'76/'84	CD†
	Rykodisc	0141	'91	CS
	Rykodisc	10141	'91	CD
Changesonebowie	RCA	1732	'76	CD†
Low	RCA	2030	'77/'85	CD†
	Rykodisc	10142	'91	CS/CD
Heroes	RCA	2522	'77/'85	CD†
	Rykodisc	10143	'91	CS/CD
Stage	RCA	(2) 2913	'78	†
	Rykodisc	(2) 10144/5	'91	CD
Lodger	RCA	3254	'79/'85	CD†
	Rykodisc	10146	'91	CS/CD
Scary Monsters	RCA	3647	'80/'85	CD†
	Rykodisc	20147	'92	CD
Changestwobowie	RCA	4202	'81/'84	CD†
Christiane F. (soundtrack)	RCA	4239	'82	†
In Bertolt Brecht's "Baal"	RCA	4346	'82	†
Golden Years	RCA	4792	'83/'85	CD†
Ziggy Stardust: The Motion Picture	RCA	(2) 4862	'83	†
	RCA	4862		CS
	Rykodisc	40148	'92	CD
Fame and Fashion (All-Time Greatest Hits)	RCA	4919	'84	CD†
Let's Dance	EMI America	17093	'83	†
	EMI America	46002		CD†
	Virgin	40982	'95	CS/CD
Tonight	EMI America	17138	'84	†
	EMI America	46047		CD†
Labyrinth (soundtrack)	EMI America	17206	'86	†
	EMI America	46312	'86	CS/CD
Never Let Me Down	EMI America	17267	'87	†
	Virgin	40986	'95	CS/CD
Sound + Vision	Rykodisc	(6) 90120/21/22	'89	LP
	Rykodisc	(3) 00120/21/22	'89	CS
	Rykodisc	(3) 90120/21/22	'89	CD
Changesbowie	Rykodisc	10171	'90	CS/CD
Bowie: The Singles	Rykodisc	(2) 10218/19	'93	CS/CD
Black Tie White Noise	Savage	50212	'93	CS/CD
	Virgin	40987	'95	CD
Jump	Ion	40004	'94	CD ROM
Outside	Virgin	40711	'95	CS/CD

David Bowie/Eugene Ormandy and the Philadelphia Orchestra

David Bowie Narrates Prokofiev's "Peter and the Wolf"	RCA	2743	'78	†
Tin Machine				
Tin Machine	EMI America	91990	'89	LP/CS/CD†
	Virgin	40995	'95	CD
Tin Machine II	Victory	511216	'91	CS/CD
	Victory	511575	'91	CD
Oy Vey, Baby	Victory	480004	'92	CS/CD

JAMES BROWN

(b. May 3, 1928, Macon, GA)

JAMES BROWN

Probably the single most popular black artist (at least for a black audience) until the mid-'70s, James Brown may very well be the last vaudeville performer. His high-powered, histrionic, and intensely dramatic stage show influenced generations of performers, from Mick Jagger and Sly Stone to Michael Jackson and Prince. His classic 1962 album *Live at the Apollo* is regarded by some as the greatest in-concert album ever recorded, and was likely the first album bought in mass quantities by blacks. With his unique mixture of gospel, blues, and even jazz, and the powerful choreographed vocals of the Fabulous Flames, Brown reinvigorated soul music in the '60s. One of the first rock entertainers to gain complete control over his own career, James Brown was certainly the first black artist to achieve independence from his record company in matters of arrangements, production, and packaging.

In emphasizing polyrhythms from the late '60s to mid-'70s with his backing group the JBs (which included Maceo Parker, Fred Wesley, and William "Bootsy" Collins), Brown Africanized American R&B and originated funk music, which influenced so many groups, black and white, during the '70s, particularly after the wane of disco music. That influence extended into the '80s and '90s with the development of rap and hip-hop music, which regularly mimicked his style and sampled his early recordings. Moreover, Brown was one of the first blacks to champion black self-pride and political consciousness in the '60s, at the same time establishing himself as one of the nation's first black entrepreneurs. Without a major pop hit since the mid-'80s, James Brown has endured a rocky period of financial, legal, and health problems beginning in the late '80s.

Raised in Augusta, Georgia, James Brown took up keyboards, then drums and bass, at an early age. He formed his first group, a gospel group, in the early '50s. Changing their name to the Fabulous Flames and concentrating on R&B music, the group came to the attention of Ralph Bass of Cincinnati's King Records, who quickly signed them in January 1956 after hearing their first demonstration record. Rerecorded, the song "Please, Please, Please" became a smash R&B hit. Brown quickly became the undisputed leader of the group. Their next hit, 1958's "Try Me," filtered into the pop charts. A series of R&B hits began in 1960 with "Think," followed by "I Don't Mind," "Baby, You're Right," "Lost Someone," and "Night Train." Brown organized the James Brown Revue: dozens of singers, musicians (The JBs), and dancers, with a tightly rehearsed and choreographed stage act polished to near-perfection. They played to sell-out, box-office record audiences in black neighborhoods across the country in the early '60s. The live recording of their show at Harlem's Apollo Theater on October 24, 1962, reflects Brown's mastery of showmanship, and the resulting album is regarded as a classic.

During 1962 James Brown reluctantly recorded several songs with vocal chorus and strings, at the insistence of King Records. One of the songs, "Prisoner of Love," became a major pop hit. By 1964, however, Brown had deemphasized vocals in favor of strong, hard polyrhythms, as performed by the JBs. He brought a set of recently recorded songs to Smash Records of Chicago. One of them, "Out of Sight," became a major pop hit and Brown's first record to sell in large quantities to whites. Brown eventually returned to King with complete control over all aspects of his recording career; releases on Smash were hence restricted to instrumentals and recordings by members of the Revue, soon renamed the JBs. With the JBs as his backing band, James Brown became perhaps the earliest purveyor of funk.

Over the years, the JBs included saxophonists Maceo Parker (1964–1970, 1973–1976, and 1984–1988, the last as band director) and Pee Wee Ellis (1965–1970), guitarist Jimmy Nolan (1965–1983), trombonist Fred Wesley (1968–1970), and bassist William "Bootsy" Collins (1969–1971). In the early '70s Parker, Ellis, and Wesley recorded as Maceo and the King's Men and Maceo and the Macks. The JBs left James Brown in early 1971 and recorded a number of albums for People Records in the first half of the '70s. Parker, Wesley, and Collins all joined George Clinton's Parliament-Funkadelic aggregation in the '70s. Collins later went on to his own successful funk career, and Parker and Wesley recorded jazz albums in the '90s.

Eschewing club engagements in favor of concert auditoriums, James Brown placed a number of songs in the pop Top 10 through 1968: "Papa's Got a Brand New Bag," "I Got You (I Feel Good)," "It's a Man's, Man's, Man's World," "Cold Sweat," and "I Got the Feelin'." By the late '60s James Brown was producing the entire show for the Revue: songs, costumes, routines, choreography, and lighting. Credited with helping quell riots after the assassination of Dr. Martin Luther King Jr. by making an impassioned plea for calm in a radio interview, Brown issued one of the first anthems of black pride in 1968, "Say It Loud, I'm Black and I'm Proud." After scoring hits with "Give It Up or Turnit a-Loose" and "I Don't Want Nobody to Give Me Nothing," Brown returned to more conventional dance-music hits, including "Mother Popcorn," "Get Up, I Feel Like Being a Sex Machine," "Super Bad," and "Hot Pants." Signing with Polydor Records in 1971, he scored major pop hits for the label through 1974 with "Get on the Good Foot," "I Got Ants in My Pants," "The Payback," and "My Thang."

Diminishing popularity ensued in the late '70s, particularly with the rise of disco music. Brown even utilized the services of an outside producer for the first time for his 1979 album *The Original Disco Man*. Touring the rock club circuit for the first time in 1980, he was introduced to a new generation of fans with his appearance in the movie *The Blues Brothers*. He began playing the supper-club circuit in 1983, and experienced a revival of interest in his music with the smash pop hit "Living in America" from the movie *Rocky IV*. He switched to Scotti Brothers Records in 1986, the same year he was honored by the Rock and Roll

Hall of Fame, but was soon beset by personal, health, and financial troubles. In September 1988 he was arrested in South Carolina following a two-state car chase by police; Brown ultimately served more than two years in prison. Paroled in February 1991, James Brown has resumed touring and recording, although the wear and tear of years of road life show in his diminished voice and more limited physical abilities.

James Brown

Please, Please, Please	King	610	'59	†
	King	909		†
Try Me	King	635	'60	†
Think!	King	683	'60	†
The Always Amazing James Brown	King	743		†
Jump Around/Night Train	King	771		†
Shout and Shimmy/Good Good Twistin'	King	780	'62	†
Tour the U.S.A.	King	804	'62	†
"Live" at the Apollo	King	826	'63	†
(reissued as) Lowdown at the Apollo, Volume 1	Solid Smoke	8006	'80	†
(reissued as) Live at the Apollo: October 24, 1962	Polydor	843479	'90	CS/CD
Prisoner of Love	King	851	'63	†
Pure Dynamite!	King	883	'64	†
Unbeatable	King	919		†
Papa's Got a Brand New Bag	King	938	'65	†
	Polygram	847982	'92	CS/CD
I Got You (I Feel Good)	King	946	'66	†
Mighty Instrumentals	King	961		†
It's a Man's World	King	985	'66	†
Christmas Songs	King	1010		†
Raw Soul	King	1016	'67	†
Live at the Garden	King	1018	'67	†
Cold Sweat	King	1020	'67	†
Live at the Apollo, Volume 2	King	(2) 1022		†
(reissued as) Live at the Apollo	Polydor	823001	'87	CS/CD
	Mobile Fidelity	583	'93	CD
Live at the Apollo, Volume 2, Part 1	Rhino	70217	'85	CS
Live at the Apollo, Volume 2, Part 2	Rhino	70218	'85	CS
I Can't Stand Myself When You Touch Me	King	1030	'68	†
I Got the Feelin'	King	1031	'68	†
Nothing but Soul	King	1034	'68	†
Thinking About Little Willie John and a Whole New Thing	King	1038		†
Say It Loud, I'm Black and I'm Proud	King	1047	'69	†
Gettin' Down to It	King	1051	'69	†
Popcorn	King	1055	'69	†
It's a Mother	King	1063	'69	†
Ain't It Funky	King	1092	'70	†
It's a New Day	King	1095	'70	†
Soul on Top	King	1100	'70	†
Sex Machine	King	(2) 1115	'70	†
	Polydor	517984	'93	CS/CD
Sho Is Funky Down Here	King	1110	'71	†
Hey America—Christmas	King	1124	'71	†
Super Bad	King	1127	'71	†

Federal Years, Volume 1	Solid Smoke	8023	'84	†
Federal Years, Volume 2	Solid Smoke	8024	'84	†
Showtime	Smash	67054	'64	†
Grits and Soul	Smash	67057	'65	†
Today and Yesterday	Smash	67072	'65	†
Plays New Breed	Smash	67080	'66	†
Handful of Soul	Smash	67084	'66	†
Presenting . . . The James Brown Show	Smash	67087	'66	†
Plays the Real Thing	Smash	67093	'67	†
Sings Out of Sight	Smash	67109	'68	†
Hot Pants	Polydor	4054	'71	†
	Polydor	517985	'93	CS/CD
Revolution of the Mind	Polydor	(2) 3003	'71	†
	Polydor	517983	'93	CS/CD
Love Power Peace: Live at the Olympia, Paris, 1971	Polydor	513389	'92	CS/CD
Soul Classics, Volume 1	Polydor	5401	'72	†
There It Is	Polydor	5028	'72	†
	Polydor	517986	'93	CS/CD
Get on the Good Foot	Polydor	(2) 3004	'72	†
	Polydor	3982	'95	CS/CD
Black Caesar (soundtrack)	Polydor	6014	'73	†
	Polydor	517135	'92	CS/CD
Slaughter's Big Rip-Off (soundtrack)	Polydor	6015	'73	†
	Polydor	517136	'92	CS/CD
Soul Classics, Volume 2	Polydor	5402	'73	†
The Payback	Polydor	(2) 3007	'74	†
	Polydor	517137	'92	CS/CD
It's Hell	Polydor	(2) 9001	'74	†
	Polydor	3983	'95	CS/CD
Reality	Polydor	6039	'75	†
	Polydor	3981	'95	CS/CD
Sex Machine Today	Polydor	6042	'75	†
Everybody's Doin' the Hustle	Polydor	6054	'75	†
Hot	Polydor	6059	'76	†
Get Up Offa That Thing	Polydor	6071	'76	†
Body Heat	Polydor	6093	'77	†
Mutha's Nature	Polydor	6111	'77	†
Sex Machine Recorded Live at Home	Polydor	(2) 9004	'77	†
Jam 1980s	Polydor	6140	'78	†
Take a Look at Those Cakes	Polydor	6181	'79	†
The Original Disco Man	Polydor	6212	'79	†
People	Polydor	6258	'80	†
Live . . . Hot on the One	Polydor	(2) 6290	'80	†
Best	Polydor	6340	'81	†
Roots of a Revolution (1956–1964)	Polydor	(2) 817304	'84/'95	CD
Ain't That a Groove (1966–1969)	Polydor	821231	'84	CS†
Doin' It to Death (1969–1973)	Polydor	821232		CS
The CD of JB: Sex Machine and Other Soul Classics	Polydor	825714		CD†
Dead on the Heavy Funk (1974–1976)	Polydor	827439	'85	CS†
Solid Gold: 30 Golden Hits	Polydor	(2) 829254		†
	Polydor	829254		CS

James Brown's Funky People (recorded 1971–1975)	Polydor	829417	'86	CS/CD†
In the Jungle Groove	Polydor	(2) 829624	'86	†
	Polydor	829624	'86	CS/CD†
The CD of JB II (Cold Sweat and Other Soul Classics)	Polydor	831700	'88	CD†
James Brown's Funky People, Part II	Polydor	835857	'88	LP/CS/CD†
Motherlode	Polydor	837126	'88	LP/CS/CD†
Messing with the Blues (1957–1975)	Polydor	(2) 847258	'90	CD†
	Chronicles/Polydor	(2) 7258	'95	CD
Star Time	Polydor	(4) 849108	'91	CS/CD
20 All-Time Greatest Hits	Polydor	511326	'91	CS/CD
Soul Pride: The Instrumentals (1960–1969)	Polydor	(2) 517845	'93	CS/CD
Spank	Polygram	837726		CS
Greatest Hits (1964–1968)	Rhino	219	'86	†
	Rhino	70219		CS
Santa's Got a Brand New Bag	Rhino	70194	'88	CS/CD
Soul Syndrome	Rhino	70569	'91	CS/CD
James Brown Is Back	Hollywood/IMG	458	'91	CS/CD
Living in America	Scotti Brothers	75467	'85/'95	CS/CD
Gravity	Scotti Brothers	40380	'86	CS/CD†
	Scotti Brothers	5212	'91	CS/CD
I'm Real	Scotti Brothers	44241	'88	LP/CS/CD†
	Scotti Brothers	5213	'91	CS/CD
James Brown and Friends: Soul Session Live	Scotti Brothers	45164	'89	LP/CS/CD†
	Scotti Brothers	5214	'91	CS/CD
Love Overdue	Scotti Brothers	75225	'91	LP/CS/CD
Greatest Hits of the Fourth Decade	Scotti Brothers	75259	'92	CS/CD
Universal James	Scotti Brothers	75274	'92	CS/CD
Live at the Apollo 1995	Scotti Brothers	75480	'95	CS/CD

The JBs

Food for Thought	People	5601	'72	
Doing It to Death	People	5603	'73	†
Damn Right I Am Somebody	People	6602	'74	†
Breakin' Bread	People	6604	'75	†
Hustle with Speed	People	6606	'75	†
Funky Good Time: The Anthology (recorded 1970–1976)	Polydor	(2) 7094	'95	CS/CD

Maceo and the King's Men

Doin' Their Own Thing	House		'71	†

Maceo and the Macks

Maceo	People	6601	'74	†

Maceo Parker

For All the King's Men	4th & Broadway	4027	'90	LP/CS/CD
Roots Revisited	Verve	843751	'90	CS/CD
Mo' Roots	Verve	511068	'91	CS/CD
Southern Exposure	Novus	63175	'94	CS/CD

Fred Wesley

New Friends	Antilles	848280	'91	CS/CD
Comme Ci Comme Ça	Antilles	512002	'92	CS/CD
Swing and Be Funky	Minor Music	801027	'93	CD
Amalgamation	Minor Music	801045	'95	CD

RUTH BROWN
(b. Ruth Weston, Jan. 30, 1928, Portsmouth, VA)

The most prolific black female vocalist of the '50s, rivaling Dinah Washington for a time, Ruth Brown helped establish Atlantic Records as a major purveyor of R&B music. Atlantic's top-selling artist of the '50s, surpassing even Ray Charles, Ruth Brown helped form the link between R&B and rock and roll through her appearances on Alan Freed's pioneering stage shows.

Ruth Brown sang in her father's church choir before beginning her professional singing career in 1946 with the Lucky Millinder Band. Brought to the attention of Herb Abramson of the newly formed Atlantic Records label by Duke Ellington, Brown signed with the label in 1948, only to be hospitalized before her first recording session for nine months as the result of an automobile accident. Her eventual debut release, "So Long," became a smash R&B hit, and the first of a series of hits that lasted through 1960. Between 1950 and 1954 she scored five top R&B hits with "Teardrops from My Eyes," "5-10-15 Hours," "(Mama) He Treats Your Daughter Mean," "Oh What a Dream," and "Mambo Baby." "(Mama) He Treats Your Daughter Mean" even became a major pop hit. Other R&B hits through 1956 included "Daddy Daddy," "Wild Wild Young Men," and "As Long As I'm Moving."

In 1956 Ruth Brown began performing on Alan Freed's rock-and-roll shows, and later R&B hits such as 1957's "Lucky Lips" and 1958's "This Little Girl's Gone Rockin'" became major pop hits, thus establishing her as a rock-and-roll artist. Subsequent successes in both fields include "I Don't Know" and "Don't Deceive Me." However, in 1961 she left Atlantic for Phillips, only to retire soon after. She eventually reemerged in the '70s with new recordings. Later she appeared in the 1988 film *Hairspray*, won a Tony for her performance in the Broadway musical *Black and Blue*, and began recording jazz-style albums for the Fantasy label. She continues to perform on the cabaret circuit, mixing jazz, rock, Broadway, and R&B in her repertoire. In 1993 she was honored with induction into the Rock and Roll Hall of Fame.

Ruth Brown

Ruth Brown	Atlantic	8004	'57	†
Late Date with Ruth Brown	Atlantic	1308	'59	†
Miss Rhythm	Atlantic	8026	'59	†
Best	Atlantic	8080	'63	†
Miss Rhythm (Greatest Hits and More)	Atlantic	(2) 82061	'89	CD
Along Comes Ruth	Phillips	600028	'62	†
Ruth Brown '65	Mainstream	6044	'65	†
Softly	Mainstream	369		†
Sugar Babe	President		'76	†
Real Ruth Brown	Cobblestone	9007		†
Black Is Brown	Skye	13		†
The Soul Survives	Flair		'82	†
You Don't Know Me	Dobre	1041		†
Help a Good Girl Go Bad	DCC Jazz	602		CS/CD
Have a Good Time	Fantasy	9661	'88	LP/CS/CD
Blues on Broadway	Fantasy	9662	'89	LP/CS/CD
Fine and Mellow	Fantasy	9663	'91	CS/CD
The Songs of My Life	Fantasy	9665	'93	CD

Ruth Brown and the Millstone Singers

Gospel Time	Phillips	600055	'62	†
	Lection	839315		CS/CD

JACKSON BROWNE

(b. Oct. 9, 1948, Heidelberg, Germany)

Perhaps the most stimulating and profound male song-poet of the '70s, Jackson Browne established the singer-songwriter genre with subtle, honest songs with romantic, spiritual, or apocalyptic themes. Exhibiting a feel for both folk and rock music, his compelling sound featured multi-instrumentalist David Lindley, who introduced unusual stringed instruments, including the lap steel guitar, into rock music. A political activist since the late '70s, Browne possesses a social awareness that came to the forefront in his music with 1986's *Lives in the Balance*, addressing the then-current crisis in Nicaragua.

Born in Germany but raised in Los Angeles, Jackson Browne first sang at "hoots" in Orange County in 1966. He wrote his first song in high school and was signed to a songwriting contract by Elektra Records in September 1966, then released. Browne played folk clubs around New York during winter 1967, often accompanying Nico (of Velvet Underground fame) and Tim Buckley. Returning to Los Angeles, he served a brief tenure with the Nitty Gritty Dirt Band. Folk singer Tom Rush became the first major artist to showcase Browne's songs, recording "Shadow Dream Song" in 1967 and "These Days" in 1968. Browne's first performing success came in the fall of 1969, when he opened for Linda Ronstadt at the Troubadour Club in Los Angeles. He completed his first concert tour in 1970, opening for Laura Nyro.

By 1971 Jackson Browne had initiated his own recording career with the invaluable assistance of multi-instrumentalist David Lindley (formerly with Kaleidoscope). "Doctor My Eyes" became a smash hit from his debut album, which also contained "Jamaica Say You Will" and "Rock Me on the Water." During spring 1972 Browne toured with songstress Joni Mitchell, and later that year his song "Take It Easy" (cowritten with Glenn Frey) launched the Eagles on their spectacularly successful career. Coming nearly two years later, his second album included the minor hit "Redneck Friend" as well as his own versions of "Take It Easy" and "These Days." By 1974 Browne was touring as a headline act with a band formed around David Lindley. Browne's *Late for the Sky* album, though yielding no hit single, was his most poignant and penetrating work to date, featuring visions of death, apocalypse, and resigned hope; it contained most notably "Fountain of Sorrow," "The Late Show," "For a Dancer," and "Before the Deluge."

Another two years elapsed before the release of *The Pretender*. Although displaying a degree of melodic and rhythmic repetition, the album again included a number of honest and moving songs, from the hit "Here Comes Those Tears Again" to "The Fuse" to the title song. Browne's next, the live *Running on Empty*, displayed a wide range of moods and material. This album yielded a near-smash hit with the anthemic title song and a major hit with a remake of Maurice Williams's 1960 "Stay."

A leader of the antinuclear movement, Jackson Browne helped found MUSE (Musicians United for Safe Energy) in 1979 and was one of the major backers of the *No Nukes* concert, movie, and album. His 1980 album *Hold Out* included the major hits "Boulevard" and "That Girl Could Sing" and introduced Browne to the arena-rock crowd. Browne was involved in the production of Warren Zevon's first two albums and coproduced David Lindley's album *El Rayo X* from 1981, the year they parted company. In September 1981 Browne was one of the demonstrators arrested at California's Diablo Canyon nuclear-power plant.

In 1982 Browne scored a major hit with "Somebody's Baby" from the Sean Penn film *Fast Times at Ridgemont High*, and the following year he hit with "Tender Is the Night" and the satirical "Lawyers in Love" from his next album of the same title. In 1984 and 1985 he visited Central America to learn more about the turmoil engulfing the region. Browne subsequently became involved with Little Steven (Van Zandt of Bruce Springsteen's E Street Band) in Artists United Against Apartheid, while managing a pop hit with "You're a Friend of Mine," recorded with Clarence Clemons. The politically charged *Lives in the Balance* focused largely on his social concerns, whether foreign or domestic, and yielded two hits, "For America" and "In the Shape of a Heart."

Browne toured in 1986 and 1988, releasing another collection of socially conscious songs in 1989 on the album *World in Motion*, including "The Word Justice," "Anything Can Happen," and Little Steven's "I Am a Patriot." Following his breakup with actress Darryl Hannah in 1992, Browne recorded *I'm Alive*, an album pervaded with songs of lost love. By this time he was unable to equal his earlier chart success, although his core audience continued to buy his albums and attend his concerts.

Jackson Browne

Jackson Browne	Asylum	5051	'72	CS/CD
For Everyman	Asylum	5067	'73	CS/CD
Late for the Sky	Asylum	1017	'74	†
	Elektra	1017		CS/CD
	DCC	1036		CD
The Pretender	Asylum	1079	'76	†
	Asylum	107		†
	Elektra	107		CS/CD
	DCC	1047		CD
Running on Empty	Asylum	113	'77	†
	Elektra	113		CS/CD
Jackson Browne/Running on Empty	Elektra	60277		CS
Hold Out	Asylum	511	'80	†
	Elektra	511		CS/CD
Lawyers in Love	Asylum	60268	'83	†
	Elektra	60628	'84	CS/CD
Lives in the Balance	Asylum	60457	'86	CS/CD
World in Motion	Elektra	60830	'89	CS/CD
I'm Alive	Elektra	61524	'93	CS/CD

THE BUFFALO SPRINGFIELD

Neil Young (b. Nov. 12, 1945, Toronto, Canada), first lead gtr, voc; **Stephen Stills** (b. Jan. 3, 1945, Dallas, TX), second lead gtr, kybd, voc; **Richie Furay** (b. May 9, 1944, Yellow Springs, OH), rhythm gtr, voc; **Bruce Palmer** (b. 1946, Liverpool, Ontario, Canada), bs; **Dewey Martin** (b. Sept. 30, 1942, Chesterville, Ontario, Canada), drm [**Jim Messina** (b. Dec. 5, 1947, Maywood, CA) replaced Bruce Palmer in late 1967.]

One of the first American groups to combine electric instrumentation and drums with distinctive, incisive songwriting and intricate vocal harmonies, the Buffalo Springfield (along with the Byrds and the Mamas and Papas) left critics scrambling for a label to describe this new sound and style. Thus was invented the first hyphenated phrase to be applied to a new type of rock music: folk-rock. Although the group helped pioneer the three-guitar format, they failed to garner major commercial success during their existence, perhaps due to their inability to transfer the tension and excitement of their live shows onto recordings. The Buffalo Springfield nonetheless became rock legends, and their influence is still felt today through various aggregations and solo endeavors.

Also known as the Herd in its early days, the Buffalo Springfield formed in Los Angeles in spring 1966. Canadian Neil Young had done solo work and played with the Mynah Birds in the Detroit area before moving to Los Angeles in 1965. Stephen Stills and folk musician

Richie Furay had been members of the New York–based Au Go Go Singers. Canadian-born Bruce Palmer had been with the Mynah Birds, and fellow Canadian Dewey Martin had played with the bluegrass group the Dillards and toured with Roy Orbison.

Featured at a July 1966 Hollywood Bowl concert, the Buffalo Springfield toured with the Byrds and the Beach Boys later that year. Soon they embarked on a long engagement at Los Angeles's Whisky a-Go-Go. Signed to Atco Records, their third single, Stills's "For What It's Worth," became the group's best-selling release and launched their popular recording career. Their debut album contained seven Stills songs, including the country-flavored "Go and Say Goodbye" and "Hot Dusty Roads," and five Neil Young songs, including the beautiful love song "Do I Have to Come Right Out and Say It" and "Flying on the Ground Is Wrong," both sung by Richie Furay.

The gutsier *Buffalo Springfield Again* contained a wider range of material, from rock and roll (Young's psychedelic "Mr. Soul" and Stills's "Bluebird" and "Rock & Roll Woman") to the major production effort of Young's "Broken Arrow." Jim Messina handled part of the engineering duties along with playing some bass. Palmer soon departed, and amidst reports of dissension and group infighting, *Last Time Around* was produced by Jim Messina, who also played bass, sang, and contributed "Carefree Country Day." Other outstanding songs on the album include "On the Way Home" and "I Am a Child" by Young, "Pretty Girl Why" and "Four Days Gone" by Stills, and Furay's "Kind Woman." Clashes between Stills and Young intensified, and Young quit the group at least twice before his final departure. The Buffalo Springfield performed their last concert at Long Beach in May 1968.

Subsequently Jim Messina and Richie Furay formed one of the first country-rock bands, Poco, whereas Neil Young recorded solo before joining Stephen Stills in the supergroup Crosby, Stills, Nash and Young. Stills later recorded solo, and Messina joined Kenny Loggins, first as a producer and then as a performing partner. In the mid-'70s Furay helped form the Souther-Hillman-Furay Band, another supergroup with ex-Byrdsman Chris Hillman and noted California singer-songwriter J. D. Souther. Young has enjoyed an incredibly diverse solo career.

The Buffalo Springfield

Buffalo Springfield	Atco	33200	'67	LP/CS
Buffalo Springfield Again	Atco	33226	'67	CS/CD
Last Time Around	Atco	33256	'68	†
	Atco	90393	'92	CD
Retrospective	Atco	33283	'69	†
	Atco	38105		CS/CD
Buffalo Springfield	Atlantic	(2) 806	'73	CS
Dewey Martin				
Medicine Ball	Uni	73088	'70	†
Bruce Palmer				
The Cycle Is Complete	Verve/Forecast	3086	'71	ǀ

JIMMY BUFFETT
(b. Dec. 25, 1946, Mobile, AL)

One of the most amusing singer-songwriters to emerge in the '70s, Jimmy Buffett appealed to country and rock audiences with an intriguing variety of songs, alternately silly and sentimental, about sailing, partying, and womanizing, all portraying his unique, laid-back lifestyle. Achieving only one major hit in 25 years of recording (1977's "Margaritaville"), Buffett nonetheless established himself as one of the most popular touring acts of the '80s and '90s.

Jimmy Buffett began sidelining as a folk singer while attending the University of Southern Mississippi, from which he was graduated with a degree in history and journalism. After working in New Orleans he moved to Nashville in 1969, ultimately settling in Key West, Florida, in 1971. Recording two obscure albums for the Barnaby label, Buffett assembled the Coral Reefers as his backup band and switched to Dunhill Records (absorbed by MCA, as was his later label, ABC). He gained his first recognition with songs such as "Railroad Lady," cowritten with Jerry Jeff Walker, and "Why Don't We Get Drunk and Screw" from his debut album. His first moderate hit, the ballad "Come Monday," came in 1974.

Throughout the '70s Buffett recorded best-selling albums that featured fun ditties such as Lord Buckley's "God's Own Drunk," "My Head Hurts, My Feet Stink and I Don't Love Jesus," "Margaritaville" (his only major hit), "Livingston Saturday Night," "Cheeseburger in Paradise," "Fins," and "Volcano," and moving ballads such as "A Pirate Looks at Forty," "Havana Daydreamin'," and "Treat Her Like a Lady." He also recorded songs by excellent contemporary songwriters such as Jesse Winchester ("Defying Gravity") and Steve Goodman ("Door Number Three" and "Banana Republics"). Buffett appeared in and performed the music for the 1975 film *Rancho Deluxe*. He toured tirelessly and established himself with legions of fans who made him one of the best-drawing pop acts of the '80s and '90s.

During the '80s Buffett continued to record his own compositions, including fan favorites such as "Coconut Telegraph," "It's My Job," "Growing Older but Not Up," "Where's the Party," and "Gypsies in the Palace," as well as Rodney Crowell's "Stars on the Water" and Van Morrison's "Brown Eyed Girl." In 1989 he published a collection of short stories, *Tales from Margaritaville*, followed by the novel *Where Is Joe Merchant?* in 1992, the year he founded Margaritaville Records, distributed by MCA, for subsequent recordings.

Jimmy Buffett

Down to Earth	Barnaby	30093	'70	†
High Cumberland Jubilee	Barnaby	6014	'77	†
Before the Salt: Early Jimmy Buffett	Barnaby	(2) 6019	'79	†
A White Sports Coat and a Pink Crustacean	Dunhill	50150	'73	†
	MCA	37026		†
	MCA	1589		CS
	MCA	31090		CD
Living and Dying in 3/4 Time	Dunhill	50132	'74	†
	MCA	37025		†
	MCA	1588		CS
	MCA	31059		CD
Living and Dying in 3/4 Time/A White Sports Coat and a Pink Crustacean	MCA	(2) 6927		CS
A-1-A	Dunhill	50183	'74	†
	MCA	37027		†
	MCA	1590		CS/CD
Rancho Deluxe (soundtrack)	United Artists	466	'75	†
Havana Daydreamin'	ABC	914	'76	†
	MCA	37023		†
	MCA	1586		CS
	MCA	31093		CD
Changes in Latitudes, Changes in Attitudes	ABC/MCA	990	'77	†
	MCA	1652		CS
	MCA	31070		CD
	MCA	10951	'93	CD
Changes in Latitudes/Havana Daydreamin'	MCA	(2) 6908		CS

Son of a Son of a Sailor	ABC	1046	'78	†
	MCA	37024		|
	MCA	1587		CS
	MCA	31091		CD
You Had to Be There	ABC	(2) 1108	'78	†
	MCA	(2) 1008		†
	MCA	(2) 6005		CS/CD
Volcano	MCA	5102	'79	†
	MCA	1657		CS/CD
A-1-A/Volcano	MCA	(2) 6919		CS
Coconut Telegraph	MCA	5169	'81	†
	MCA	1664		CS
	MCA	31092		CD
Son of a Son of a Sailor/Coconut Telegraph	MCA	(2) 6917		CS
Somewhere Over China	MCA	5285	'82	†
	MCA	37241	'84	†
	MCA	1481		CS
	MCA	31168		CD
One Particular Harbor	MCA	5447	'83	†
	MCA	25061	'87	CS
	MCA	31094	'87	CD
Riddles in the Sand	MCA	5512	'84	†
	MCA	25075		CS
	MCA	31095		CD
Last Mango in Paris	MCA	5600	'85	†
	MCA	25077		CS
	MCA	31157		CD
Songs You Know by Heart (Greatest Hits)	MCA	5633	'85	CS/CD
	MCA	11169	'94	CD
Floridays	MCA	5730	'86	CS/CD
Hot Water	MCA	42093	'88	CS/CD
Off to See the Lizard	MCA	6314	'89	CS/CD
Feeding Frenzy	MCA	10022	'90	CS/CD
Boats Beaches Bars and Ballads	Margaritaville	(4) 10613	'92	CD
Before the Beach	Margaritaville	10823	'93	CS/CD
Fruitcakes	Margaritaville	11043	'94	CS
	Margaritaville	10993	'94	CD

JOHNNY BURNETTE AND THE ROCK AND ROLL TRIO

Johnny Burnette (b. Mar. 25, 1934, Memphis, TN; d. Aug. 1, 1964, Clear Lake, CA), gtr, voc; **Dorsey Burnette** (b. Dec. 28, 1932, Memphis, TN; d. Aug. 19, 1979, Canoga Park, CA), bs, voc; **Paul Burlison**, lead gtr

With brother Dorsey and electric lead guitarist Paul Burlison, Johnny Burnette founded the pioneering but largely overlooked rockabilly group Johnny Burnette and the Rock and Roll Trio in the early '50s. Although they never enjoyed national acclaim, the group provided some of the wildest rockabilly of the time and helped open the door for Elvis Presley's early success. Disbanding the group in 1957, the Burnette brothers moved to California, where they wrote hits for Ricky Nelson and launched their own solo careers.

Johnny and Dorsey Burnette began playing in bands with Memphis-born guitarist Paul Burlison while still in high school. In 1952 all three worked as electricians for Crown Electric Company, which later employed a truck driver named Elvis Presley. Officially formed in 1953, the Johnny Burnette Rock and Roll Trio auditioned for Sam Phillips's Sun Records following the local success of Presley's "That's Alright Mama." Although they were not signed, they persevered, traveling to New York in late 1955, where they won *The Ted Mack Amateur Hour* television competition three times in a row. Soon signed to Coral Records, the group recorded their first single in New York City in May 1956. The wild rockabilly classic "Tear It Up" became a regional hit in Boston and Baltimore, but failed to make the national charts. The group toured nationally and finished their first album in Nashville, recording at the Barn under producer Owen Bradley. They returned to the Nashville studio in July, recording "The Train Kept A-Rollin'." Years later the Yardbirds would rerecord the song, re-creating it virtually note for note. The group went into the studio for the third and final time in March 1957, but Dorsey Burnette soon departed. The Johnny Burnette Rock and Roll Trio officially disbanded in the fall of 1957.

Brothers Dorsey and Johnny Burnette moved to California in 1958, where they concentrated on writing songs and recording demonstration records. They provided Ricky Nelson with two of his most boisterous hits, "Waitin' in School" and "Believe What You Say," as well as "It's Late" and "Just a Little Too Much." Johnny and Dorsey also recorded separately and for several labels. The most interesting of these recordings were "Way in the Middle of the Night," "Sweet Baby Doll," and "Cincinnati Fireball." In 1960 Dorsey scored hits with "Tall Oak Tree" and "Hey Little One" on Era, while Johnny hit with "Dreamin'" and the classic "You're Sixteen." The following year, Johnny had success with "Little Boy Sad," the forlorn "Big Big World," and "God, Country and My Baby"; many of his later recordings were marred by Hollywood-style production values. On August 1, 1964, Johnny died in a boating accident on a California lake. Dorsey left the pop fold by the late '60s to pursue a country career. He had a number of moderate country-and-western hits between 1972 and August 1979, when he died of a heart attack.

Dorsey Burnette's son Billy (b. May 8, 1953, Memphis, TN) had some recording success in the early '80s and was a member of Fleetwood Mac from 1987 to 1993. Johnny Burnette's son Rocky (b. June 12, 1953, Memphis, TN) had a smash pop hit in 1980 with "Tired of Toein' the Line," but was unable to follow it up.

Johnny Burnette and the Rock and Roll Trio

Johnny Burnette and the Rock and Roll Trio	Coral	57080	'56	†
	Solid Smoke	8001	'78	†
Listen to Johnny Burnette and the Rock and Roll Trio	MCA	1513	'82	†
The Johnny Burnette Trio, Volume 2	MCA	1561		†

Johnny and Dorsey Burnette

Together Again	Solid Smoke	8005	'80	†

Johnny Burnette

Dreamin'	Liberty	7179	'60	†
Johnny Burnette	Liberty	7183	'61	†
Johnny Burnette Sings	Liberty	7190	'61	†
Roses Are Red	Liberty	7255	'62	†
Hits and Other Favorites	Liberty	7206	'63	†
	Liberty	10144		†
The Johnny Burnette Story	Liberty	7389	'66	†
Dreamin'	Sunset	5179	'67	†
Very Best	United Artists	432	'75	†
Dreamin': The Best of Johnny Burnette	Liberty	99997	'92	CS/CD

Dorsey Burnette

Tall Oak Tree	Era	102	'60	†
Best: The Era Years	Era	5021	'95	CS/CD
Dorsey Burnette Sings	Dot	25456	'63	†
Here and Now	Capitol	11094	'72	†
Dorsey Burnette	Capitol	11219	'73	†
Rock & Roll	Richmond	2134		CS

Billy Burnette

Billy Burnette	Entrance	31228	'72	†
Billy Burnette	Polydor	6187	'79	†
Billy Burnette	Columbia	36792	'80	†
Gimme You	Columbia	37460	'81	†
Coming Home	Capricorn	42007	'93	CS/CD

Rocky Burnette

The Son of Rock and Roll	EMI America	17033	'80	†
	EMI America	16254		†

JERRY BUTLER

(b. Dec. 8, 1939, Sunflower, MS)

One of the most engaging soul-music singer-songwriters to emerge in the late '50s, Jerry Butler possesses a powerful, mellifluous, baritone voice that has served as the foundation of his three-decade-long career. He achieved his initial success with the Impressions, scored a number of pop and soul hits on his own in the early '60s, and later was in the forefront of the Philadelphia sound of producer-songwriters Kenny Gamble and Leon Huff.

Raised in Chicago, Jerry Butler began singing in gospel groups as a child. He sang with Curtis Mayfield in the Northern Jubilee Gospel Singers, and during 1957 he and Mayfield joined the Roosters. By 1958 they had changed their name to the Impressions and signed with VeeJay Records. Featuring Butler's soothing baritone, the Impressions' first single, "For Your Precious Love" (coauthored by Butler), became a major pop hit.

Leaving the Impressions after the solitary hit, Butler scored a smash in late 1960 with "He Will Break Your Heart," cowritten by Butler and Mayfield. The hits continued into 1964 with "Find Another Girl," "I'm-a Telling You," Henry Mancini's "Moon River," Burt Bacharach's "Make It Easy on Yourself," and "Need to Belong." In 1964 Butler scored with "Let It Be Me," recorded with Betty Everett, and later wrote "I've Been Loving You Too Long (To Stop Now)" for and with Otis Redding.

With the demise of VeeJay Records in 1966, Butler moved to Mercury Records, where he worked with songwriter-producers Kenny Gamble and Leon Huff. The collaboration resulted in a number of major hits for Butler, including "Never Give You Up," "Hey Western Union Man," the smash "Only the Strong Survive," "Moody Woman," and "What's the Use of Breaking Up." His 1969 album *The Iceman Cometh* provided Butler with his nickname, denoting his cool, calm style.

Butler stayed with Mercury Records when Kenny Gamble and Leon Huff moved to Columbia Records in 1970. With Brenda Lee Eager he scored his last major pop hit, "Ain't Understanding Mellow," plus the soul hit "Power of Love." He subsequently switched to Motown Records, where he made the soul charts with "I Wanna Do It to You" and recorded two albums with Thelma Houston. In 1978 he reunited with Kenny Gamble and Leon Huff at Philadelphia International Records for the soul hit "(I'm Just Thinking About) Cooling Out." Less active in the '80s, Jerry Butler returned to recording with the albums *Time and*

Faith and *Simply Beautiful* in the early '90s. Butler and the Impressions were inducted into the Rock and Roll Hall of Fame in 1991.

The Impressions with Jerry Butler

For Your Precious Love	VeeJay	1075	'63	LP/CS
The Impressions/Jerry Butler	Dominion	324		CS/CD†

Jerry Butler

Jerry Butler Esquire	Abner	2001		†
	VeeJay	1027	'61	†
	VeeJay	1034		†
He Will Break Your Heart	VeeJay	1029	'61	†
Aware of Love	VeeJay	1038	'62	†
Moon River	VeeJay	1046	'63	†
Best	VeeJay	1048	'63	†
Folk Songs	VeeJay	1057	'63	†
Giving Up on Love/Need to Belong	VeeJay	1076	'63	†
More of the Best	VeeJay	1119	'64	†
Gold	VeeJay	(2) 1003	'87	†
The Iceman	VeeJay	700		CS/CD
Soul Artistry	Mercury	61105	'67	†
Mr. Dream Merchant	Mercury	61146	'68	†
Golden Hits (Live)	Mercury	61151	'68	†
The Soul Goes On	Mercury	61171	'68	†
The Iceman Cometh	Mercury	61198	'69	†
Ice on Ice	Mercury	61234	'69	†
You and Me	Mercury	61269	'70	†
Best	Mercury	61281	'70	†
	Mercury	810639		CS
Sings Assorted Sounds	Mercury	61320	'70	†
Sagittarius Movement	Mercury	61347	'71	†
Spice of Life	Mercury	(2) 7502	'72	†
Power of Love	Mercury	689	'74	†
Sweet Sixteen	Mercury	1006	'74	†
Only the Strong Survive—The Great Philadelphia Hits	Mercury	822212	'84	†
Very Best	Mercury	510967	'92	CS/CD
Iceman: The Mercury Years Anthology	Mercury	(2) 510968	'92	CS/CD
Hey Western Union Man	Polygram	838170		CS
Gift of Love	Sunset	5216	'68	†
Very Best	Buddah	4001	'69	†
Starring Jerry Butler	Tradition	2068		†
All-Time Hits	Up Front	124		†
Jerry Butler	Pickwick	3202		†
All-Time Hits	Trip	(2) 8011		†
Best	United Artists	498	'76	†
Melinda (soundtrack)	Pride	0006		
Love's on the Menu	Motown	850	'76	†
	Motown	5479	'90	CS/CD†
Suite for the Single Girl	Motown	878	'77	†
	Motown	5476	'90	CS/CD†
It All Comes Out in My Song	Motown	892	'77	†
Nothing Says I Love You Like I Love You	Philadelphia Int'l	35510	'78	†

The Best Love I Ever Had	Philadelphia Int'l	36413	'80	†
Best, 1958–1969	Rhino	70216	'85	CS
	Rhino	75881	'85	CD
Greatest Hits	Curb/CEMA	77419	'91	CS/CD
Time and Faith	Urgent!	1151	'92	CS/CD
Simply Beautiful	Valley Vue	22006	'95	CD
Jerry Butler and Betty Everett				
Delicious Together	VeeJay	1099	'64	†
Starring Jerry Butler and Betty Everett	Tradition	2073	'68	†
Together	Buddah	7507	'70	†
Jerry Butler and Gene Chandler				
One and One	Mercury	61330	'71	†
Jerry Butler and Brenda Lee Eager				
The Love We Have	Mercury	660	'73	†
Jerry Butler and Thelma Houston				
Thelma and Jerry	Motown	887	'77	†
Two to One	Motown	903		†

PAUL BUTTERFIELD

(b. Dec. 17, 1942, Chicago, IL; d. May 4, 1987, North Hollywood, CA)

Paul Butterfield formed one of the first white blues bands to achieve recognition and critical acclaim for playing the blues with rock instrumentation, thus initiating the use of the term *blues-rock*. Bringing much-deserved recognition to the contributions of black blues performers, the Paul Butterfield Blues Band laid the foundation for the blues revival of the late '60s and paved the way for blues-rock bands such as Cream and the Electric Flag. The Paul Butterfield Blues Band was the first band to bring electric instrumentation to the Newport Folk Festival, in 1965 (on their own and when accompanying Bob Dylan), and Butterfield became known as one of America's leading white blues harmonica players. They were also one of the first biracial bands to play the primarily white rock circuit, as they featured a black bassist and drummer (Jerome Arnold and Sam Lay, respectively), who had previously backed legendary blues shouter Howlin' Wolf. The band's *East-West* album was one of the first recordings to explore the fusion of Western and Eastern musical styles, and their *Pigboy Crabshaw* was one of the first to augment electric instrumentation with horns (several months before Blood, Sweat and Tears).

One of the two guitarists with the early Paul Butterfield Blues Band, Mike Bloomfield was one of the first white musicians to garner acclaim as a blues guitarist. Bloomfield later formed one of the premier blues-rock bands of the late '60s, the Electric Flag. The band's other early guitarist, Elvin Bishop, along with early members Nick Gravenites and Mark Naftalin, moved to the San Francisco Bay Area in the late '60s and helped establish a regional blues scene second only to that of Chicago.

Paul Butterfield was hanging out at Chicago black blues clubs at age 14 and had mastered blues harmonica by age 16. He attended the University of Chicago in 1963, where he studied classical flute. He formed his first blues band that same year, and by 1965 had assembled the Paul Butterfield Blues Band with guitarists Mike Bloomfield and Elvin Bishop, keyboardist Mark Naftalin, vocalist-songwriter Nick Gravenites, bassist Jerome Arnold, and drummer Sam Lay. Mike Bloomfield had learned blues guitar in the early '60s while hanging around black blues clubs, and he eventually became a respected session musician.

Elvin Bishop (b. Oct. 21, 1942, Tulsa, OK) had moved to Chicago in 1960 to pursue his education at the University of Chicago, where he met Paul Butterfield.

Signed to Elektra Records by Paul Rothchild, the Paul Butterfield Blues Band shocked the audience at 1965's Newport Folk Festival by playing electrified instruments. Their debut album featured rock instrumentation on standard blues fare, thus pioneering blues-rock. Their second effort, *East-West*, included more blues standards plus the exotic 13-minute title cut, which mixed Indian influences with the rock format. In 1967 Bloomfield and Gravenites departed to form the Electric Flag, but the band was history by 1968. Butterfield, Bishop, and Gravenites regrouped, adding a three-piece horn section (including future tenor star David Sanborn) for the album *The Resurrection of Pigboy Crabshaw*, one of the first instances of horns augmenting a rock band. In 1968 both Gravenites and Bishop had left the band, to move to the San Francisco Bay Area. Butterfield persevered with a series of guitarists, bassists, and drummers, eventually disbanding the group in the fall of 1972.

Butterfield then formed Paul Butterfield's Better Days with guitarist Amos Garrett and folk-blues guitarist Geoff Muldaur. The group had a more acoustic-based sound than Butterfield's previous band; they failed to live up to expectations, at least on record, and broke up in 1974. Butterfield went on to produce some solo albums through the mid-'80s on a sporadic basis; many featured rather tepid pop arrangements, including Butterfield playing synthesizer rather than his trademark harmonica and eschewing blues altogether. Paul Butterfield died in 1987 after a long battle with drugs and alcohol.

Nick Gravenites, Elvin Bishop, and Mark Naftalin had all moved to the San Francisco Bay Area by 1968. Gravenites recorded two albums with Big Brother and the Holding Company (without Janis Joplin) in the early '70s, scored several soundtracks, and produced albums by the Quicksilver Messenger Service and Mike Bloomfield. He continues to play the blues around the Bay Area. Elvin Bishop recorded two albums for Bill Graham's short-lived Fillmore label before switching to Epic in 1972 and Capricorn in 1974. His Capricorn debut, *Let It Flow*, featured favorites like "Stealin' Watermelons" and the minor hit "Travelin' Shoes." His biggest success came in 1976 with the smash hit "Fooled Around and Fell in Love," sung by Mickey Thomas, who later joined the Jefferson Starship. Playing West Coast engagements during the '80s, Bishop ultimately returned to recording in 1988 with the Chicago-based blues label Alligator Records. Mark Naftalin pursued session work, recording more than 70 albums with others and involved himself in the Bay Area blues scene, producing music and radio shows into the '90s.

The Paul Butterfield Blues Band

The Paul Butterfield Blues Band	Elektra	7294	'65	CD
East-West	Elektra	7315	'66	CD
The Resurrection of Pigboy Crabshaw	Elektra	74015	'67/'89	CD
In My Own Dream	Elektra	74025	'68	†
Keep on Moving	Elektra	74053	'69	†
Live	Elektra	(2) 2001	'70	†
Sometimes I Feel Like Smiling	Elektra	75013	'71	†
Golden Butter	Elektra	(2) 2005	'72	†
Better Days	Bearsville	2119	'73	†
	Rhino	70877	'87	CS/CD
It All Comes Back (with Better Days)	Bearsville	2170	'73	†
	Rhino	70878	'87	CS/CD
Put It in Your Ear	Bearsville	6960	'76	†
	Rhino	70879	'87	CS
North South	Warner Bros.	6995	'81	†
	Rhino	70880	'87	CS

The Legendary Paul Butterfield Rides Again	Amherst	3305	'86	LP
	Amherst	53305	'86	CS
	Amherst	93305	'86	CD

Sam Lay

In Bluesland	Blue Thumb	14	'70	†
Shuffle Master	Appaloosa	6106	'93	CS/CD

Elvin Bishop

Elvin Bishop	Fillmore	30001	'69	†
	Columbia	30001		†
Feel It!	Fillmore	30239	'70	†
Rock My Soul	Epic	31563	'72	†
Best: Crabshaw Rising	Epic	33693	'75	LP/CS
Tulsa Shuffle: The Best of Elvin Bishop	Columbia/Legacy	57630	'94	CS/CD
Let It Flow	Capricorn	0134	'74	†
	Polygram	839142		CS
Juke Joint Jump	Capricorn	0151	'75	†
Struttin' My Stuff	Capricorn	0165	'75	†
Hometown Boy Makes Good!	Capricorn	0176	'76	†
Live! Raisin' Hell	Capricorn	(2) 0185	'77	†
Sure Feels Good: The Best	Polydor	513307	'92	CS/CD
Big Fun	Alligator	4767	'88	LP/CS/CD
Don't Let the Bossman Get You Down!	Alligator	4791	'91	LP/CS/CD
Ace in the Hole	Alligator	4833	'95	CS/CD

THE BYRDS

Jim (later Roger) McGuinn (b. July 13, 1942, Chicago, IL), lead electric 12-string gtr, voc; **Gene Clark** (b. Nov. 17, 1941, Tipton, MO; d. May 24, 1991, Sherman Oaks, CA), gtr, har, voc; **David Crosby** (b. Aug. 14, 1941, Los Angeles, CA), rhythm gtr, voc; **Chris Hillman** (b. Dec. 4, 1942, Los Angeles, CA), bs, mdln, voc; **Mike Clarke** (b. June 3, 1944, New York, NY; d. Dec. 19, 1993, Treasure Island, FL), drm [Gene Clark left in March 1966; David Crosby left in October 1967. **Gram Parsons** (b. Nov. 5, 1946, Winter Haven, FL; d. Sept. 19, 1973, Joshua Tree, CA) was a member in 1968. Other later members include guitarist-vocalist **Clarence White** (b. June 6, 1944, Lewiston, ME; d. July 14, 1973), bassists **John York** and **Skip Battin**, and drummers **Kevin Kelly** and **Gene Parsons**.]

The group that revolutionized the American popular-music scene with their unique blend of folk and rock styles, the Byrds presented the first substantial challenge to the popularity of the Beatles and other British groups in the mid-'60s. Their recording of Bob Dylan's "Mr. Tambourine Man" marked the first time his still-acoustic music had been adapted to rock and launched a new sound on the contemporary music scene that critics dubbed folk-rock. Ostensibly their recording inspired Dylan to take up electric guitar.

The Byrds' 1966 hit "Eight Miles High" was probably the first recorded psychedelic song and introduced Roger McGuinn's chiming 12-string electric guitar playing into rock (a sound later emulated by Tom Petty and R.E.M.). The song was also one of the first to be banned from radio airplay due to its supposed reference to drugs.

Anchored by the excellent songwriting of Roger McGuinn, David Crosby, Gene Clark, and Chris Hillman, the Byrds were an inspiration to the singer-songwriter movement that proved so popular in the '70s. Moreover, the attention to melody and harmony among the

THE BYRDS

members, particularly David Crosby, opened rock to the gentle sophistication later explored by groups such as Crosby, Stills and Nash.

The Byrds' 1968 *Sweetheart of the Rodeo* album, one of the first recorded in Nashville by an established rock group, introduced Gram Parsons to rock audiences and initiated yet another new sound, this time labeled country-rock by critics. The Byrds subsequently became the first rock act to play the Grand Ole Opry, and Parsons went on to form the Flying Burrito Brothers with fellow Byrd Chris Hillman. Although not commercially successful, this album and those of the Flying Burrito Brothers laid the foundation for dozens of bands that explored country and rock during the '70s. Indeed, Chris Hillman's most recent success with the Desert Rose Band has been exclusively in the country field.

The Byrds formed in Los Angeles in the summer of 1964. They had all been professional musicians for some years, mostly working the folk circuit. Jim McGuinn had made his debut at the Gate of Horn in Chicago in the late '50s, and he later worked as a folk guitarist, backing the Limeliters and Judy Collins. He performed as a solo folk artist in Greenwich Village and played with the Chad Mitchell Trio for two years. After working with Bobby Darin in New York, he returned to solo work in early 1964. Gene Clark had been a member of the New Christy Minstrels, while Crosby had been a member of Les Baxter's Balladeers and a folk singer of five years' experience. Chris Hillman had fronted his own bluegrass band, the Hillmen, in 1963–1964.

During 1964, with the assistance of producer Jim Dickinson, the group recorded a demonstration tape at World Pacific Studios. Initially signed to Elektra Records as the Beefeaters (a name inspired by the Beatles), the group's first single, "Please Let Me Love You," flopped. They subsequently signed with Columbia Records in September 1964, thus becoming the first rock act signed by this mainstream label. In preparing their first album, the Byrds recorded Bob Dylan's "Mr. Tambourine Man" at the urging of Dickinson. Ironically, only McGuinn actually played an instrument on the recording, his electric 12-string. With McGuinn singing lead and Crosby and Clark providing harmonies, the instrumentation was done by Los Angeles studio stalwarts pianist Leon Russell, guitarist Larry Knechtel, and drummer Hal Blaine. The single, issued in March 1965, became a top hit and launched the Byrds into instant international prominence. Debuting that month at the popular club Ciro's in Los Angeles, the original group remained far more effective recording than performing.

All of the Byrds actually played on the debut album, with the exception of the songs "Mr. Tambourine Man" and "I Knew I'd Want You." The album contained four Dylan songs, including the moderate hit "All I Really Want to Do," Gene Clark's classic "I'll Feel a Whole Lot Better," and Jackie DeShannon's "Don't Doubt Yourself, Babe." Their second album yielded a top hit with "Turn! Turn! Turn!" (adapted from the biblical Book of Ecclesiastes by folksinger Pete Seeger) and contained two more Dylan songs and Clark's "Set You Free This Time," a minor hit.

Conflicts in the group soon became apparent as Crosby and McGuinn frequently disagreed on the Byrds's direction, often coming to actual blows. However, the first defection was Gene Clark in March 1966; he suffered from depression and a fear of flying, and found touring difficult. He soon recorded with the Gosdin Brothers (Vern and Rex), who had previously played with Hillman in the group the Hillmen, before joining bluegrass musician Doug Dillard in Dillard and Clark. Their debut, recorded with future Flying Burrito Brother and Eagle Bernie Leadon, featured the Clark-Leadon composition "Train Leaves Here This Mornin'." Fiddler Byron Berline joined for the second album.

Having lost a singer and their principal songwriter, the Byrds realigned, with Hillman taking up vocals and McGuinn and Crosby writing more songs. At the same time, the group started experimenting with a more sophisticated sound, McGuinn immersing himself in the music of jazz saxophonist John Coltrane. The result was the hit single "Eight Miles High," recorded shortly before Gene Clark's departure. With three-part harmony and an almost imperceptible melody, the song featured McGuinn playing his electric 12-string modally (rather than in a major or minor scale). Probably the first recorded "psychedelic" song, with its reference to the LSD experience, "Eight Miles High" had the dubious distinction of being the first '60s single to be banned from airplay. The eclectic album *Fifth Dimension* also included several psychedelic songs as well as standard folk fare, the moderate hit "Mr. Spaceman," and the bluesy "Hey Joe."

The Byrds' increasing musical sophistication was evident with the release of *Younger Than Yesterday*. Although marred by two overdone production numbers, the album yielded two hits with Dylan's "My Back Pages" and McGuinn and Hillman's bitterly satiric "So You Want to Be a Rock 'n' Roll Star." It contained Crosby's beautiful "Everybody's Been Burned," two McGuinn-Crosby collaborations, "Why" and "Renaissance Faire," and four Hillman songs, including the country-flavored "Time Between." By mid-1967 the rift between McGuinn and Crosby had become irreparable. When Crosby refused to sing two Gerry Goffin–Carole King compositions, he was summarily paid off and fired in October. Crosby later produced Joni Mitchell's debut album and helped form Crosby, Stills and Nash. The group was now officially a trio.

Recorded with the assistance of outside musicians, most notably Clarence White of the Kentucky Colonels, *The Notorious Byrd Brothers* was critically hailed and marked the beginning of a trend toward simplicity rather than sophistication in the Byrds' music. The album contained the two disputed Goffin-King songs, "Wasn't Born to Follow" and "Goin' Back," a minor hit, and McGuinn and Hillman's "Change Is Now." Drummer Mike Clarke departed in November 1967, to be replaced by Hillman's cousin Kevin Kelly.

Singer-songwriter-guitarist Gram Parsons (formerly the leader of the early country-rock group the International Submarine Band) was added to the group, lending them a country-music orientation. Their next album, *Sweetheart of the Rodeo*, openly embraced country-and-western music and was hailed as the first country-rock album. However, the album was years ahead of its time and proved a commercial flop. It yielded a minor hit with Dylan's "You Ain't Going Nowhere" and included two Parsons's songs, "Hickory Wind" and "One Hundred Years from Now."

The Byrds subsequently began to deteriorate. Gram Parsons quit in mid-1968, followed in October by Chris Hillman. The two soon formed the Flying Burrito Brothers with Chris Ethridge. McGuinn, now using the name Roger and the only original member left, put a new group together with Clarence White, bassist-vocalist John York, and drummer-vocalist

Gene Parsons (no relation to Gram). *Dr. Byrds and Mr. Hyde* proved unspectacular, yet the Byrds' nosedive into obscurity was arrested briefly by the surprise popularity of the Peter Fonda–Dennis Hopper film *Easy Rider*. The best-selling soundtrack album contained three songs sung by McGuinn, including the minor hit "The Ballad of Easy Rider." The obvious follow-up album, *The Ballad of Easy Rider*, yielded the Byrds' final hit, "Jesus Is Just All Right."

John York left next, to be replaced by Skip Battin. Years earlier, Battin had been half of the duo Skip and Flip, who hit with a remake of Marvin and Johnny's "Cherry Pie" in 1960. (*Untitled*), half live and half studio material, included "Truck Stop Girl" (written by Lowell George and Bill Payne of Little Feat) and several McGuinn–Jaques Levy collaborations, most notably "Lover of the Bayou" and "Chestnut Mare." Defections continued, and finally, in 1973, McGuinn disbanded the Byrds. The original Byrds reassembled briefly for 1973's rather crassly commercial reunion album, which featured McGuinn's "Born to Rock 'n' Roll."

During the '70s Chris Hillman, Gene Clark, and Roger McGuinn each recorded solo albums, all of which are unavailable on CD, save McGuinn's overlooked *Cardiff Rose*. That album contained two previously unrecorded songs, Joni Mitchell's "Dreamland" and Bob Dylan's "Up to Me." Hillman formed a short-lived supergroup with J. D. Souther and Richie Furay, recording one album for Asylum to little success. In 1975 and 1976 McGuinn toured with Dylan's Rolling Thunder Revue. During 1977 McGuinn formed a new band, Thunderbyrd. That spring Chris Hillman's band toured Europe with Gene Clark's band and McGuinn's Thunderbyrd, leading to a jam session among the three at London's Hammersmith Odeon. Clark also joined McGuinn onstage at the Troubadour in Los Angeles, and they later toured as a duo, becoming a trio when Hillman joined. The three, playing acoustic guitars, opened the Canadian leg of Eric Clapton's Slowhand tour. In late 1978 the three recorded the highly polished *McGuinn, Clark and Hillman* album for Capitol Records and managed a moderate hit with "Don't Write Her Off." Clark soon defected again, continuing to suffer from emotional problems, and the duo of McGuinn and Hillman recorded one more record.

Chris Hillman recorded two country-style albums for the small Sugar Hill label in the early '80s. In 1987 he formed the Desert Rose Band with Herb Pedersen and John Jorgenson and enjoyed considerable success in the country field. Gene Clark toured with John York and others as the Byrds from 1985 to 1987. In the late '80s he recorded *So Rebellious a Lover* with singer Carla Olson, but on May 24, 1991, he was found dead in his home in Sherman Oaks, California. The release by Columbia of a large boxed set of Byrds recordings reunited McGuinn, Crosby, and Hillman to record a couple of bonus tracks for it. Roger McGuinn reemerged as a solo artist in 1991 with *Back from Rio*, recorded with the assistance of Elvis Costello and Tom Petty (a rabid Byrds fan). That same year the Byrds were honored by the Rock and Roll Hall of Fame.

The Hillmen

The Hillmen	Together	1012	'69	†
	Sugar Hill	3719	'95	LP/CS

The Byrds

Preflyte	Together	1001	'68	†
	Columbia	32183	'73	†
In the Beginning	Rhino	70244	'88	CS/CD
Mr. Tambourine Man	Columbia	9712	'65	CS/CD
Turn! Turn! Turn!	Columbia	9254	'65	CS/CD
Mr. Tambourine Man/Turn! Turn! Turn!	Columbia	(2) 33645	'75	†
Fifth Dimension	Columbia	9349	'66	CD

Younger Than Yesterday	Columbia	9442	'67	CD
Greatest Hits	Columbia	9516	'67	CD
	Columbia	00268		CS
The Original Singles (1965–1967)	Columbia	37335	'81	CS/CD
Notorious Byrd Brothers	Columbia	9575	'68	CD
Sweetheart of the Rodeo	Columbia	9670	'68	CS/CD
Dr. Byrds and Mr. Hyde	Columbia	9755	'69/'91	CD
Ballad of Easy Rider	Columbia	9942	'69/'91	CD
(Untitled)	Columbia	(2) 30127	'70	†
	Columbia	30127		CD
Byrdmaniax	Columbia	30640	'71/'93	CD
Farther Along	Columbia	31050	'71	†
Best (Greatest Hits, Volume 2)	Columbia	31795	'72/'87	CS/CD
The Byrds Play Dylan	Columbia	36293	'79	†
The Byrds	Columbia	(4) 46773	'90	CS/CD
20 Essential Tracks from the Boxed Set: 1965–1990	Columbia/Legacy	47884	'92	CS/CD
Clark, Hillman, Crosby, McGuinn, Clarke	Asylum	5058	'73	†
Very Best	Pair	1040	'86	†

Dillard and Clark

The Fantastic Expedition of Dillard and Clark	A&M	4158	'68	†
Through the Morning, Through the Night	A&M	4203	'70	†
The Fantastic Expedition of Dillard and Clark/ Through the Morning, Through the Night	Mobile Fidelity	791		CD

Gene Clark

Early L.A. Sessions	Columbia	31123	'72	†
Gene Clark with the Gosdin Brothers	Columbia	9418	'67	†
Echoes	Columbia/Legacy	48523	'91	CS/CD
Gene Clark	A&M	4292	'71	†
No Other	Asylum	1016	'74	†
Two Sides to Every Story	RSO	3011	'77	†

Gene Clark And Carla Olson

So Rebellious a Lover	Rhino	70832	'87	†
	Razor & Tie	1992	'92	CD

Chris Hillman

Cherokee	ABC	719	'71	†
Slippin' Away	Asylum	1062	'76	†
Clear Sailin'	Asylum	1104	'77	†
Morning Sky	Sugar Hill	3729	'83/'91	LP/CS/CD
Desert Rose	Sugar Hill	3743	'84	LP/CS/CD

The Desert Rose Band

The Desert Rose Band	MCA	5991	'87	CS/CD†
	Curb/CEMA	77570	'92	CS/CD
Running	Curb/MCA	42169	'88	CS/CD†
	Curb/CEMA	77573	'92	CS/CD
Pages of Life	Curb/MCA	42332	'90	LP/CS/CD†
	Curb/CEMA	77567	'92	CS/CD
One Dozen Roses—Greatest Hits	MCA	10018	'91	CS/CD
	Curb/CEMA	77571	'92	CS/CD

True Love	MCA	10407	'91	CS/CD†
	Curb/CEMA	77572	92	CS/CD
Traditional	Curb/CEMA	77602	'93	CS/CD

Skip Battin

Skip Battin	Signpost	8408	'73	†

Gene Parsons

Early Years, Volume 1	Sierra	4215		LP/CS
Kindling	Warner Bros.	2687	'73	†
Melodies	Sierra	8703	'80	†
	Sierra	4217		LP/CS
	Sierra	6010		CD
The Kindling Collection	Sierra	6007	'94	CD

Gene Parsons And Meridian Green

Birds of a Feather	Sierra	4223		LP/CS
	Sierra	6004		CD

Roger McGuinn

Roger McGuinn	Columbia	31946	'73	†
Peace on You	Columbia	32956	'74	†
Roger McGuinn and Band	Columbia	33541	'75	†
Cardiff Rose	Columbia	34154	'76/'92	CD
Thunderbyrd	Columbia	34656	'77	†
Born to Rock & Roll	Columbia/Legacy	47494	'91	CD
Back from Rio	Arista	8648	'91	LP/CS/CD

McGuinn, Clark and Hillman

McGuinn, Clark and Hillman	Capitol	11910	'79	†
	Capitol	16280	'83	†
	Capitol	96355	'91	CS/CD†
City	Capitol	12043	'80	†

McGuinn and Hillman

McGuinn and Hillman	Capitol	12108	'80	†

C

J. J. CALE

(b. Jean Jacques Cale, Dec. 5, 1938, Oklahoma City, OK)

Perhaps best remembered as the composer of songs successfully recorded by others, J. J. Cale wrote "Magnolia" (Poco), "They Call Me the Breeze" (Lynyrd Skynyrd), and "After Midnight" and "Cocaine" (Eric Clapton). Developing a devoted cult following for his songwriting, laid-back vocal style, and subtle guitar playing, J. J. Cale achieved his greatest recorded success with his debut album, *Naturally*, which yielded the moderate hits "After Midnight" and "Crazy Mama." Cale's haunting, sensuous guitar style influenced both Clapton and Dire Straits's Mark Knopfler.

Cale spent his high school years in Tulsa, Oklahoma, where he met pianist Leon Russell and drummer Carl Radle. The trio first went to Los Angeles in 1964, where they met folk rockers Delancy and Bonnie, with whom Cale played for a while; he returned to Tulsa in 1967. Russell meanwhile became an L.A. session musician, and founded Shelter Records with producer Denny Cordell in 1969. Radle gave Cordell Cale's demo tape, and Cale was among the first signings to the label. He released *Naturally* on Shelter in 1972, followed by a few more albums through the '70s. He signed to Mercury in the early '80s, and then semiretired, continuing to tour but not recording again until the early '90s. In 1994 he returned to a major label with an album for Virgin records. He has also worked as a producer for two of John Hammond Jr.'s albums of traditional blues recorded in the early '90s.

Leather Coated Minds

Trip Down Sunset Strip	Viva	36003	'67	†

J. J. Cale

Naturally	Shelter	8908	'72	†
	Shelter	2122	'74		
	Shelter	52009		†
	Mercury	830042	'87	CD
Really	Shelter	8912	'72	†
	Shelter	52012		†
	Mercury	810314	'90	CD
Okie	Shelter	2107	'74	†
	Shelter	52015		†
	Mercury	842102	'90	CD
Troubadour	Shelter	52002	'76	†
	Mercury	810001		CD
Five	MCA	3163	'79	†
	Mercury	810313	'90	CD

87

Shades	MCA	5158	'81	†
	Mercury	800105	'91	CD
Grasshopper	Mercury	4038	'82	†
	Mercury	800038		CD
#8	Mercury	811152	'83/'91	CD
Special Edition	Mercury	818633	'84	CD
Travel-Log	Silvertone	1306	'90	CS/CD
Closer to You	Virgin	39610	'94	CS/CD

CANNED HEAT

Bob "The Bear" Hite (b. Feb. 26, 1945, Torrance, CA; d. Apr. 5, 1981), voc, har; **Alan "Blind Owl" Wilson** (b. July 4, 1943, Boston, MA; d. Sept. 3, 1970, Los Angeles, CA), gtr, har, voc; **Henry Vestine** (b. Dec. 25, 1944, Washington, D.C.), gtr; **Larry Taylor** (b. Samuel Taylor, June 26, 1942, New York, NY), bs; **Frank Cook**, drm [Frank Cook was replaced by **Adolpho "Fito" de la Parra** (b. Feb. 8, 1946, Mexico City, Mexico) in 1968; Henry Vestine was replaced by guitarist **Harvey Mandel** (b. Mar. 11, 1945, Detroit, MI) in 1969. Mandel and Taylor defected in 1970 and were replaced by the returning Vestine and Antonio de la Barreda on bass.]

CANNED HEAT

A late-'60s American blues-and-boogie band, Canned Heat created its own distinctive style without the use of horns. Rather than favoring electric-blues standards, the group performed more obscure country-blues material. Achieving their greatest success in the late '60s, the group played both the Monterey and Woodstock music festivals, and scored hits with "On the Road Again," "Going Up the Country," and Wilbert Harrison's "Let's Work Together." Other recorded favorites included "Rollin' and Tumblin'" and "Amphetamine Annie." The band became famous for their long, onstage jam sessions, which would often lapse into endless improvisations with only the most slender relation to the song itself.

The group never really recovered from the drug-overdose death of founding member Alan "Blind Owl" Wilson, who besides being nearly blind had long suffered from depression. Harvey Mandel (who replaced Henry Vestine for a while) and bassist Larry Taylor left to join British bluester John Mayall's band. Canned Heat regrouped with Vestine and a new bass player to record *Hooker 'n' Heat* with blues legend John Lee Hooker; the group also backed blues legends Clarence "Gatemouth" Brown and Memphis Slim on European-only albums in the early '70s. They soldiered on with various lineups through the '80s, but were dealt another devestating blow when blues enthusiast and cofounder Bob "The Bear" Hite died of a drug-related heart attack on April 5, 1981. Still, they managed a comeback with the album *Reheated* in 1990, although with little commercial success. Mandel, Taylor, and Vestine appeared on the 1994 album *Internal Combustion*.

Canned Heat

Live at Topanga	Wand	693		†
	Pickwick	3364		†
Canned Heat	Liberty	7526	'67	†
Boogie with Canned Heat	Liberty	7541	'68	†
	Pickwick	3614	'78	†
	Liberty	10105	'80	†
Livin' the Blues	Liberty	27200	'68	†
	United Artists	9955	'71	†
Hallelujah	Liberty	7618	'69	†
Cookbook (Best)	Liberty	11000	'69	†
	Liberty	10106	'81	†
Future Blues	Liberty	11002	'70	†
Vintage Canned Heat	Janus	3009	'70	†
Collage	Sunset	5298	'71	†
Live in Europe	United Artists	5509	'71	†
Historical Figures and Ancient Heads	United Artists	5557	'72	†
The New Age	United Artists	049	'73	†
Very Best	United Artists	431	'75	†
One More River to Cross	Atlantic	7289	'74	†
Canned Heat	Springboard Int'l	4026	'75	†
Human Condition	Takoma	7066	'79	†
Captured Live	Accord	12179	'81	†
Best	EMI America	48377	'87	CS/CD

Canned Heat and John Lee Hooker

Hooker 'n' Heat	Liberty	(2) 35002	'71	|
	EMI America	(2) 97896	'91	CD

CAPTAIN BEEFHEART

(b. Don Van Vliet, Jan. 15, 1941, Glendale, CA)

An early associate of both Frank Zappa and Ry Cooder, Captain Beefheart, along with his backup group His Magic Band, played a curious mix of delta blues, rock and roll, and avant-garde jazz that may still be years ahead of its time. The band's unique sound, passed over by all but the most progressive of fans, was characterized by Beefheart's incredible voice (growling and gravely, with a range of more than four octaves), intricate arrangements, enigmatic lyrics (generally written by Beefheart), and early use of the Theremin, an electronic instrument. Perhaps best known for the 1969 album *Trout Mask Replica*, Captain Beefheart and His Magic Band are an acknowledged influence on New Wave music.

Don Van Vliet moved to the desert town of Lancaster at age 13 and became friends with Frank Zappa in high school. Playing harmonica and saxophone, Van Vliet performed with several R&B bands before forming Captain Beefheart and His Magic Band in 1964. Gaining a reputation in area desert towns, the group recorded Bo Diddley's "Diddy Wah Diddy" for A&M Records, and the single became a regional hit. However, their material for a first album was rejected by A&M as "too negative," and Van Vliet retreated to Lancaster. In 1965 he brought the material to Buddah Records, which released it as *Safe as Milk*. Winning considerable critical acclaim in the United States and Europe, the album spurred a successful tour of Europe in early 1966.

With the departure of lead guitarist Ry Cooder, Captain Beefheart and His Magic Band were paralyzed, since the lead guitar parts, complex and erratic, were personally taught by Van Vliet to Cooder over a long period of time. Nonetheless, sessions for their next album began in April 1968. The album was ultimately released in altered form, and the disappointed Van Vliet subsequently accepted Frank Zappa's offer to make a new album, free of all artistic restrictions, for Zappa's new label, Straight Records. Following Van Vliet's lead, the members of the reorganized Magic Band took on bizarre names: guitarist-flutist Bill Harkleroad became Zoot Horn Rollo; guitarist Jimmy Simmons became Antennae Jimmy Semens; and bassist Mark Boston became Rockette Morton. Joining them was an unidentified drummer (John French, known as Drumbo) and the Mascara Snake on vocals and clarinet. *Trout Mask Replica*, produced by Frank Zappa, was hailed as one of the most advanced concepts in rock music, but it proved a commercial failure.

Following another Zappa-sponsored recording, *Lick My Decals Off, Baby*, Beefheart switched to Reprise Records and, in 1971, made one of the group's infrequent tours of the United States, to play before befuddled fans. Art Tripp (known also as Ed Marimba) was added on drums and marimba for *The Spotlight Kid* and *Clear Spot*. Moving to Mercury Records, the band recorded the softer and more accessible *Unconditionally Guaranteed*. After *Bluejeans and Moonbeams*, Beefheart and His Magic Band parted company.

On May 20 and 21, 1975, Captain Beefheart recorded *Bongo Fury* with Frank Zappa and the Mothers at the Armadillo World Headquarters in Austin, Texas. By 1976 Beefheart had assembled a new Magic Band for occasional club appearances. During 1977 and 1978 the group successfully toured Europe and played sold-out engagements at New York's Bottom Line and Hollywood's Roxy. Subsequent album releases were *Shiny Beast (Bat Chain Puller)*, *Doc at the Radar Station* (hailed as perhaps the best of Beefheart's career), and *Ice Cream for Crow*. An accomplished artist for many years, Don Van Vliet retired from music in 1986 to pursue painting as a full-time profession. In early 1989 he had his first museum showing, at the San Francisco Museum of Modern Art.

Captain Beefheart and His Magic Band

Safe as Milk	Buddah	5001	'65	†
	Buddah	5063	'69	†
	One Way	29088		CD
Mirror Man	Buddah	5077	'71	†
	One Way	22166		CD
Strictly Personal	Blue Thumb	1	'68	†
Trout Mask Replica	Straight	(2) 1053	'69	†
	Reprise	(2) 2027	'70	LP
	Reprise	52027		CS
	Reprise	2027		CD
Lick My Decals Off, Baby	Reprise	6420	'70	†
	Bizarre/Straight	70364	'91	CS/CD
The Spotlight Kid	Reprise	2050	'72	†
Clear Spot	Reprise	2115	'72	†
The Spotlight Kid/Clear Spot	Reprise	26249	'91	CD
Unconditionally Guaranteed	Mercury	709	'74	†
	Blue Plate	1633		CD
Bluejeans and Moonbeams	Mercury	1018	'74	†
	Blue Plate	1631		CD

Captain Beefheart

Shiny Beast (Bat Chain Puller)	Warner Bros.	3256	'78	†
	Bizarre/Straight	70365	'91	CS/CD
Doc at the Radar Station	Virgin	13148	'80	†
	Blue Plate	1824	'92	CD
Ice Cream for Crow	Virgin/Epic	38274	'82	†
	Blue Plate	1632		CD
Captain Beefheart at His	Special Music Best	4922		CS/CD
The Best Beefheart	Pair	1232		CD†

Captain Beefheart/Frank Zappa/The Mothers

Bongo Fury	DiscReet	2234	'75	†
	Barking Pumpkin/ Capitol	74220	'89	†
	Rykodisc	74220		CS
	Rykodisc	10097	'89	CD

THE CARPENTERS

Karen Carpenter (b. Mar. 2, 1950, New Haven, CT; d. Feb. 4, 1983, Downey, CA), voc, drm; **Richard Carpenter** (b. Oct. 15, 1946, New Haven, CT), kybd, voc

One of the most popular easy-listening acts of the '70s, the Carpenters scored an impressive string of hits with the compositions of songwriters such as Burt Bacharach, Paul Williams, Leon Russell, Carole King, and Neil Sedaka. Featuring the full, resonant, yet spiritless alto voice of Karen Carpenter and the delicate harmony of brother Richard, the duo ultimately had more Top 20 singles than even the Everly Brothers and sold more than 80 million records. A longtime sufferer of anorexia nervosa, Karen died in 1983 at age 32 of heart failure due to the condition.

Karen and Richard Carpenter moved with their family to Downey, California, in 1963. Richard began playing piano at age nine and completed his musical education at California State University, Long Beach, whereas Karen took up drums while in high school. They formed the Carpenter Trio with bassist Wes Jacobs in 1965, winning a Battle of the Bands contest at the Hollywood Bowl in 1966. Although signed to RCA Records, no recordings were ever released, and the trio disbanded.

By the late '60s Karen and Richard had formed a duo to pursue their interest in vocal harmonies and were signed to A&M Records by Herb Alpert on the strength of a demonstration tape. Their first hit came in 1970, with Burt Bacharach's "Close to You." Subsequent early-'70s hits included "For All We Know," two Paul Williams–Roger Nichols compositions, "We've Only Just Begun" and "Rainy Days and Mondays," and Leon Russell and Bonnie Bramlett's "Superstar." *A Song for You* provided six hits: "Bless the Beasts and the Children," "Hurting Each Other," Carole King's "It's Going to Take Some Time," "Goodbye to Love," "Top of the World," and the Williams-Nichols composition "I Won't Last a Day Without You." Other major hits through 1976 were "Sing," "Yesterday Once More," "Only Yesterday," Neil Sedaka's "Solitaire," and "I Need to Be in Love." Although the Carpenters' popularity waned in the late '70s, they managed a major hit in 1981 with "Touch Me When We're Dancing."

While working on *Voice of the Heart*, Karen Carpenter died at her parents' Downey home of heart failure due to anorexia nervosa on February 4, 1983, at age 32. The Karen Carpenter Memorial Foundation was formed to aid in the research of anorexia, and a music scholarship fund in her name was established at California State University, Long Beach. Richard worked as a staff producer at A&M. The 1988 made-for-TV movie *The Karen*

Carpenter Story portrayed her life and death. The posthumusly released album *Lovelines* contained 10 previously unreleased songs, including 4 by Karen from a never-completed solo album. In 1994 A&M issued a Carpenters tribute album, with their songs being covered by contemporary acts such as Sonic Youth, the Cranberries, Sheryl Crow, Matthew Sweet, and Babes in Toyland.

The Carpenters

Ticket to Ride	A&M	4205	'69	CD†
Close to You	A&M	4271	'70	†
	A&M	3184	'70	CS/CD
The Carpenters	A&M	3502	'71	CD
A Song for You	A&M	3511	'72	CS/CD
	Mobile Fidelity	525		CD
Now and Then	A&M	3519	'73	CS/CD
The Singles: 1969–1973	A&M	3601	'73	CS/CD
Horizon	A&M	4530	'75	CD
A Kind of Hush	A&M	4581	'76	†
	A&M	3197		CD
Passage	A&M	4703	'77	†
	A&M	3199		CS/CD†
A Christmas Portrait	A&M	4726	'78	†
	A&M	5171		CS
	A&M	5173	'87	CD
Made in America	A&M	3723	'81	CD†
Voice of the Heart	A&M	4954	'83	CD
An Old-Fashioned Christmas	A&M	3720	'85	†
	A&M	5172		CS
Yesterday Once More	A&M	(2) 6601	'85	CS/CD
The Carpenters	A&M	(2) 6750		CD
Lovelines	A&M	3931	'89	CD
From the Top: The Ultimate Retrospective	A&M	(4) 6875	'91	CD

Tribute Album

If I Were a Carpenter	A&M	0704	'94	LP
	A&M	0258	'94	CS/CD

JOHNNY CASH

(b. Feb. 26, 1932, Kingsland, AR)

One of the first rockabilly stars—along with Sun Records stablemates Carl Perkins, Jerry Lee Lewis, and Elvis Presley—Johnny Cash recorded folk-oriented material in the early '60s before becoming a mainstream country star. Cash brought an unprecedented social consciousness to country music with 1964's "Ballad of Ira Hayes" from *Bitter Tears*, his monumental tribute to the American Indian. His cameo appearance on Bob Dylan's *Nashville Skyline* album helped introduce him to a rock audience. Perhaps the first international country star, Johnny Cash may have done more to popularize country music than anyone since Hank Williams. Indeed, his nationally broadcast television series (1969–1971) was instrumental in widening the audience for country music. In addition, he was instrumental in introducing Bob Dylan and Kris Kristofferson to broader public acceptance; he appeared with and recorded the songs of each of them early in their careers. Cash scored his most recent success with Kris Kristofferson, Willie Nelson, and Waylon Jennings in the Highwaymen, and in 1994 he achieved his first album chart-entry in 18 years, with *American Recordings*, which also won a Grammy for best contemporary folk album that year. He was inducted into the Rock and Roll Hall of Fame in 1992.

Johnny Cash grew up in Dyess, Arkansas, where he had moved at age three. Following his discharge from the Air Force in July 1954, he traveled to Memphis, where he met guitarist Luther Perkins and bassist Marshall Grant. With Cash playing guitar and singing in a deep baritone voice of exceptionally low and narrow range, the three practiced together, eventually auditioning for Sam Phillips of Sun Records in March 1955. Signed to Sun as Johnny Cash and the Tennessee Two, their first single, "Cry, Cry, Cry," became a moderate country hit. Their first big pop hit came in 1956 with Cash's own "I Walk the Line." Subsequent pop hits on Sun included "Ballad of a Teenage Queen," "Guess Things Happen That Way," and "The Ways of a Woman in Love." In 1957 the group appeared on the *Louisiana Hayride* and *Grand Ole Opry* radio shows, and the following year they became Johnny Cash and the Tennessee Three with the addition of W. S. Holland, one of country music's first drummers.

Cash was unhappy with the teen-pop material Sun was giving him to record, though, feeling it did not suit his style. He began actively looking for a new company to pick up his contract. In August 1958 Johnny Cash and the Tennessee Three switched to Columbia Records and soon hit with "Don't Take Your Guns to Town." Moving to California, Cash started working with June Carter, of the legendary Carter Family, in 1961. He began feeling the strain of constant touring, and the collapse of his first marriage along with the death of friend Johnny Horton were serious personal blows. As a consequence, Cash started taking amphetamines and tranquilizers to cope with his hectic life. In 1963 he scored his first major pop hit on Columbia with "Ring of Fire."

Cash was soon hanging out on the periphery of the Greenwich Village folk-music scene, and his next hit, "Understand Your Man," had a distinctive folk feel to it. In 1964 he appeared with Bob Dylan at the Newport Folk Festival. During this time Cash recorded a number of folk songs, including Peter LaFarge's "Ballad of Ira Hayes" and Dylan's "Don't Think Twice, It's All Right" and, with June Carter, "It Ain't Me, Babe," another country and pop hit. He also made a number of theme albums, including songs of the American Indian and of working men, an unusual move for a country performer at this time.

Despite increasing popular success, Johnny Cash's life seemed to deteriorate. In October 1965 he was arrested at El Paso International Airport in possession of hundreds of stimulants and tranquilizers. After being found near death in a small Georgia town in 1967, Cash decided to reform. With June Carter providing moral support, he cleaned up his act. The couple scored a smash country hit with "Jackson" in 1968, the year they married. In 1970 they hit the pop charts with Tim Hardin's "If I Were a Carpenter."

Although guitarist Luther Perkins died accidentally in 1968, Johnny Cash persevered, replacing him with Bob Wooten. A series of successful television appearances had begun in 1967, and his 1968 live album, *Johnny Cash at Folsom Prison*, revitalized his career and made him an international country star. The album yielded a pop and country hit with "Folsom Prison Blues" (a remake of Cash's 1956 country hit). In early 1969 Cash scored a top country and moderate pop hit with Carl Perkins's "Daddy Sang Bass." Cash's penchant for novelty songs, as evidenced by 1959's "I Got Stripes" and 1966's "The One on the Right Is on the Left," culminated in his biggest pop hit, Shel Silverstein's "A Boy Named Sue," from *Johnny Cash at San Quentin*, another best-seller.

The 1969 debut show for his ABC network television series featured a film of Cash and Bob Dylan recording "Girl from the North Country." The song later appeared on Dylan's first country album, *Nashville Skyline*. Later shows featured artists such as Gordon Lightfoot, Kris Kristofferson, Waylon Jennings, and Joni Mitchell. During the 1969 Newport Folk Festival, Cash introduced Kristofferson, later recording Kristofferson's "Sunday Morning Coming Down" and bolstering his early career. Cash demonstrated his social consciousness again in the early '70s with the hits "What Is Truth" and "Man in Black." He also narrated and coproduced the soundtrack to the Christian epic *Gospel Road*, and assisted in the production of *The Trail of Tears*, a dramatization of the tragedy of the Cherokee Indians, broadcast on public television (PBS).

Cash scored another pop novelty hit with "One Piece at a Time" in 1976, and hit the country charts in 1978 with "There Ain't No Good Chain Gangs," recorded with Waylon Jennings. His last major country hit came in 1981 with "The Baron." Future country star Marty Stuart was a member of Cash's band from 1979 to 1985. In 1985 Cash joined Waylon Jennings, Willie Nelson, and Kris Kristofferson to tour and record as the Highwaymen. They hit the top of the country charts with Jimmy Webb's "The Highwayman." The following year Cash reunited with old Sun Records alumni Carl Perkins, Jerry Lee Lewis, and Roy Orbison for *Class of '55*, contributing "I Will Rock & Roll With You." However, that same year Cash was dropped from the Columbia Records roster, after almost 30 years with the label. He subsequently signed with Mercury Records, switching to American Records in 1993. In 1990 he joined Jennings, Nelson, and Kristofferson as the Highwaymen for another album and a round of touring. In 1993 Cash sang "The Wanderer" with U2, included on their *Zooropa* album, and the following year he recorded the moody, acoustic *American Recordings* album, produced by Rick Rubin, best known for his work with Run-D.M.C., Public Enemy, and the Red Hot Chili Peppers. In 1995 Cash once again joined the Highwaymen to tour and record for Liberty Records the album *The Road Goes On Forever*, which included Steve Earle's "The Devil's Right Hand," Stephen Bruton's "It Is What It Is," Billy Joe and Eddie Shaver's "Live Forever," and Robert Earl Keen's title song.

Over the years Johnny Cash has appeared in films (1971's *A Gunfight* with Kirk Douglas), on television (1986's *Stagecoach* with the other Highwaymen, 1988's *Davy Crockett*), and he's even written a novel (1986's *Man in White*). Despite health problems (he had a double-bypass heart operation in 1988), Johnny Cash continued to tour with his wife June and son John Carter Cash.

Johnny Cash on Sun Records

Johnny Cash with His Hot and Blue Guitar	Sun	1220		†
Sings the Songs That Made Him Famous	Sun	1235		†
Greatest!	Sun	1240		†
Sings Hank Williams	Sun	1245		†
Now Here's Johnny Cash	Sun	1255		†
All Aboard the Blue Train	Sun	1270		†
Original Sun Sound	Sun	1275		†
Original Golden Hits, Volume 1	Sun	100	'69	†
Original Golden Hits, Volume 2	Sun	101	'69	†
Story Songs of Trains and Rivers	Sun	104	'69	†
Get Rhythm	Sun	105	'69	†
Showtime	Sun	106	'69	†
The Singing Storyteller	Sun	115	'70	†
Living Legend	Sun	118	'70	†
Rough Cut King of Country Music	Sun	122	'70	†
The Man, the World, His Music	Sun	126	'71	†
Original Golden Hits, Volume 3	Sun	127	'72	†
I Walk the Line	Sun	139		†
Folsom Prison Blues	Sun	140		†
Blue Train	Sun	141		†
Greatest Hits	Sun	142		†
Superbilly (1955–1958)	Sun	1002	'78	†

The Original	Sun	1006		†
Sun Story, Volume 1	Sunnyvale	901	'77	†
The Sun Years	Rhino	70950	'90	CS/CD

Johnny Cash and Jerry Lee Lewis

Sunday Down South	Sun	119		†
Sing Hank Williams	Sun	125		†
Country Boy	Charly	18		CD†
Up Through the Years (1955–1957)	Bear Family	15247		CD†

Johnny Cash on Columbia

The Fabulous Johnny Cash	Columbia	1253	'58	†
	Columbia	8122	'59	†
	Sony	8122		CS/CD†
	K-tel	75024	'95	CS/CD
Hymns by Johnny Cash	Columbia	8125	'59	†
Songs of Our Soil	Columbia	8148	'59	†
Ride This Train	Columbia	8255	'60	†
	Sony	8255		CS/CD†
	K tel	75026	'95	CS/CD
Now, There Was a Song!	Columbia	8254	'60	†
	Columbia/Legacy	66506	'94	CD
Hymns from the Heart	Columbia	8522	'62	†
The Sound of Johnny Cash	Columbia	8602	'62	†
Blood, Sweat and Tears	Columbia	8730	'63	†
	Columbia/Legacy	66508	'94	CD
Ring of Fire	Columbia	8853	'63	†
Christmas Spirit	Columbia	8917	'63	†
I Walk the Line	Columbia	8990	'64	†
Bitter Tears	Columbia	9048	'64		
	Columbia/Legacy	66507	'94	CD
Orange Blossom Special	Columbia	9109	'65	†
Ballads of the True West	Columbia	(2) 838	'65	†
Mean as Hell	Columbia	9246	'66	†
Everybody Loves a Nut	Columbia	9292	'66	†
That's What You Get for Lovin' Me	Columbia	9337	'66	†
From Sea to Shining Sea	Columbia	9447	'68	†
Greatest Hits	Columbia	9478		CD
	Columbia	00264		CS
At Folsom Prison	Columbia	9639	'68	†
The Holy Land	Columbia	9726	'69	†
At San Quentin	Columbia	9827	'69	CS
At Folsom Prison and San Quentin	Columbia	(2) 33639	'75	†
	Columbia	33639	'75	CS/CD
Hello, I'm Johnny Cash	Columbia	9943	'70	†
The World of Johnny Cash	Columbia	(2) 29	'70	†
The Johnny Cash Show	Columbia	30100	'70	†
I Walk the Line (soundtrack)	Columbia	30397	'70	†
Man in Black	Columbia	30550	'71	†
Greatest Hits, Volume 2	Columbia	30887		CS
A Thing Called Love	Columbia	31332	'72	†
America: A 200-Year Salute in Story and Song	Columbia	31645	'72	†

Any Old Wind That Blows	Columbia	32091	'73	†
Gospel Road (soundtrack)	Columbia	(2) 32253	'73	†
	Priority	(2) 32253	'82	†
That Ragged Old Flag	Columbia	32917	'74	†
Five Feet High and Rising	Columbia	32951	'74	†
The Junkie and the Juicehead Minus Me	Columbia	33086	'74	†
Sings Precious Memories	Columbia	33087	'75	CS
	Priority	33087	'84	†
John R. Cash	Columbia	33370	'75	†
Look at Them Beans	Columbia	33814	'75	†
Strawberry Cake	Columbia	34088	'76	†
One Piece at a Time	Columbia	34193	'76	†
Last Gunfighter Ballad	Columbia	34314	'77	†
The Rambler	Columbia	34833	'77	†
I Would Like to See You Again	Columbia	35313	'78	†
Greatest Hits, Volume 3	Columbia	35637	'78	†
Gone Girl	Columbia	35646	'78	†
Silver	Columbia	36086	'79	†
A Believer Sings the Truth	Cachet	9001	'79	†
	Priority	38074	'82	†
	Columbia	38074		CS
Rockabilly Blues	Columbia	36779	'80	†
Classic Christmas	Columbia	36866	'80	†
The Baron	Columbia	37179	'81	†
Encore	Columbia	37355	'81	†
The Adventures of Johnny Cash	Columbia	38094	'82	†
Biggest Hits	Columbia	38317	'82	CS/CD
Johnny 99	Columbia	38696	'83	†
Columbia Records, 1958–1986	Columbia	40637	'87	CS/CD
Patriot (recorded 1964–1976)	Columbia	45384	'90	CS/CD
The Essential Johnny Cash (1955–1983)	Columbia	(3) 47991	'92	CS/CD

Johnny Cash Budget Releases

Johnny Cash	Harmony	11342	'69	†
Walls of a Prison	Harmony	30138	'70	†
Johnny Cash Songbook	Harmony	31602	'72	†
Ballad of the American Indians	Harmony	32388	'73	†
Folsom Prison Blues	Hilltop	6116	'72	†
	Pickwick	6114		†
I Walk the Line/Rock Island Line	Pickwick	(2) 2045		†
Johnny Cash	Pickwick	(2) 2052		†
I Walk the Line	Pickwick	6097		†
Rock Island Line	Pickwick	6101		†
Big River	Pickwick	6118		†
Country Gold	Power Pak	246		†
Johnny Cash	Archive of Folk and Jazz Music	278		†
Classic Cash	Pair	(2) 1107	'86	†
This Is Johnny Cash	RCA-Camden	3014		CS

Johnny Cash and June Carter

Carryin' On	Columbia	9528	'67	†

Johnny Cash and His Woman	Columbia	32443	'73	†
The Johnny Cash Family	Columbia	31754	'72	†
Super Hits	Columbia	66773	'94	CS/CD
Give My Love to Rose	Harmony	31256	'72	†

The Tennessee Three

The Sound Behind Johnny Cash	Columbia	30220	'71	†

Recent Johnny Cash Releases

Believe in Him	Word	8333	'86	†
Johnny Cash Is Coming to Town	Mercury	832031	'87	LP/CS/CD†
Classic Cash	Mercury	834526	'88	CS/CD
Water from the Wells of Home	Mercury	834778	'88	LP/CS/CD†
Boom Chick a Boom	Mercury	842155	'90	CS/CD†
The Mystery of Life	Mercury	848051	'91	CS/CD
Wanted Man	Mercury	522709	'94	CS/CD
Greatest Hits	CSI	40105	'91	CD
Best	Curb/CEMA	77494	'91	CS/CD
American Recordings	American	45520	'94	CS/CD

Johnny Cash, Jerry Lee Lewis, and Carl Perkins

The Survivors	Columbia	37961	'82	LP/CS
	Razor & Tie	2077	'95	CS/CD

Johnny Cash and Waylon Jennings

Heroes	Columbia	40347	'86	LP/CS
	Razor & Tie	2078	'95	CS/CD

Johnny Cash, Jerry Lee Lewis, Roy Orbison, and Carl Perkins

Class of '55	America/Smash	830002	'86	LP/CS/CD

The Highwaymen

Highwayman	Columbia	40056	'85	CS/CD
Highwayman 2	Columbia	45240	'90	CS/CD
The Road Goes On Forever	Liberty	28091	'95	CS/CD

ROSANNE CASH

(b. May 24, 1955, Memphis, TN)

Married to singer-songwriter Rodney Crowell from 1979 to 1992, Rosanne Cash began achieving success in the early '80s as a purveyor of highly personal, country-style material played in a rock, almost New Wave style. Garnering the most public attention for a female country singer since Emmylou Harris, Cash pioneered this "new country" woman's sound and style, and opened the door for other intelligent songwriters such as Mary-Chapin Carpenter and Shawn Colvin.

Rosanne Cash, Johnny Cash's daughter by Vivian Liberto, moved to Ventura, California, with her mother in 1966, when her parents divorced. After high school she toured with her father's road show for three years with stepsisters Rosey Nix and Carlene Carter. She attended Vanderbilt University and studied for six months in Lee Strasberg's noted drama school in Hollywood. She met Rodney Crowell in 1977, married him in 1979, and made her first recordings (with Crowell producing) in Germany that year. Signed to Columbia Records, her first album, *Right or Wrong*, launched her recording career, producing three major country hits with "No Memories Hangin' Around" (in duet with Bobby Bare),

"Couldn't Do Nothin' Right," and "Take Me, Take Me." With Crowell as her producer, Cash became fully established as a country artist with *Seven Year Ache*. The album yielded three top country hits with her title song (also a major pop hit), Leroy Preston's "My Baby Thinks He's a Train," and her "Blue Moon with Heartache."

After 1982's *Somewhere in the Stars*, which featured the country hits "Ain't No Money," "I Wonder," and "It Hasn't Happened Yet," Rosanne Cash underwent treatment for cocaine addiction, and her marriage nearly ended. This led to an almost three-year exile from recording. She rebounded with 1985's *Rhythm and Romance*, largely produced by David Malloy. The album contained four country hits: "I Don't Know Why You Don't Want Me" (cowritten by Cash and Crowell), "Never Be You" (written by Tom Petty and Benmont Tench), "Hold On," and "Second to No One." *King's Record Shop*, again produced by Crowell, was more issue-oriented and yielded four more top country hits: "The Way We Make a Broken Heart" (by John Hiatt), "Tennessee Flat Top Box" (a major hit for her father in 1962), "If You Change Your Mind" (by Cash and Hank DeVito), and "Runaway Train" (by John Stewart). She also had a top country hit in 1988 with "It's Such a Small World," a duet with Crowell.

Rosanne Cash transcended the country field with 1990's introspective *Interiors*, which she wrote and produced. Hailed by some as the album of her career, it did not produce any pop hits, yet it did establish her in the front ranks of intelligent female singer-songwriters. Following her divorce from Rodney Crowell in spring 1992, Cash recorded *The Wheel*, a semiconfessional album that featured "Seventh Avenue," "Roses in the Fire," and "The Truth About You."

Rosanne Cash

Right or Wrong	Columbia	36155	'80	CS/CD
Seven Year Ache	Columbia	36965	'81	CS/CD
Somewhere in the Stars	Columbia	37570	'82	CS/CD
Rhythm and Romance	Columbia	39463	'85	CS/CD
King's Record Shop	Columbia	40777	'87	CS/CD
Hits, 1979–1989	Columbia	45054	'89	CS/CD
Interiors	Columbia	46079	'90	CS/CD
The Wheel	Columbia	52729	'93	CD
Retrospective	Columbia	67321	'95	CS/CD
10-Song Demo	Captiol	32390	'95	CS/CD

RAY CHARLES

(b. Ray Charles Robinson, Sept. 23, 1930, Albany, GA)

A multitalented, blind, black musician, Ray Charles pioneered soul music, which became enormously popular among both black and white audiences beginning in the late '50s. In secularizing certain aspects of gospel music (chord changes, song structures, call-and-response techniques, and vocal screams, wails, and moans) and adding blues-based lyrics to the mix, he essentially invented a new genre of popular music. Along with musicians such as Horace Silver, Ray Charles was instrumental in leading many jazz musicians away from the abstracted and relatively inaccessible music of bebop as practiced by Charlie Parker, John Coltrane, and Dizzy Gillespie back to the roots of soul and funk.

Ray Charles's gospel-based vocal style influenced virtually all the soul singers of the '60s, as well as many of the white English singers that emerged in the '60s (Mick Jagger, Eric Burdon, Joe Cocker, and Rod Stewart). In using the electric piano on his first major pop hit, "What'd I Say," Charles introduced the instrument to jazz and rock musics. Moreover, the vocal work of his female backup group, the Raeletts, set the standard for black vo-

RAY CHARLES

cal groups that was so successfully exploited by Motown Records in the '60s. Also, in applying his gospel-oriented style to country-and-western material in the early '60s, Ray Charles became the first black artist to score hits in the country field *and* the first male black singer to make a major impact on the white adult market.

Ray Charles grew up in Greenville, Florida, and was blinded by glaucoma at age six. From 1937 to 1945 he attended the St. Augustine (Florida) School for the Blind, where he learned piano and, later, clarinet and alto saxophone, plus composing and arranging. Orphaned at 15, Charles struck out on his own, performing in bands around the South and later touring with blues artist Lowell Fulson. In 1948 he moved to Seattle and formed the Maxim Trio (also known as the McSon Trio and the Maxine Trio), a group grounded in the style of Nat "King" Cole and Charles Brown. As the Maxine Trio, they scored a major R&B hit in 1949 with "Confession Blues" on the Downbeat label. In 1951 and 1952 Charles had R&B hits with "Baby Let Me Hold Your Hand" and "Kiss Me Baby" on the small Los Angeles–based Swingtime label.

Around 1952 the New York–based Atlantic label bought Ray Charles's recording contract, and shedding his Nat "King" Cole stylization and adapting gospel-music techniques to blues lyrics, he soon hit with "It Should Have Been Me." In early 1955 his new sound hit in both the popular and R&B fields with his own composition "I've Got a Woman." Using topflight studio musicians such as saxophonist David "Fathead" Newman and the vocal backup group the Raeletts, Charles scored consistently on the R&B charts through the late '50s with songs such as "A Fool for You," "Drown in My Own Tears," and "Hallelujah I Love Her So." He also became popular with jazz fans, recording two highly acclaimed records with Modern Jazz Quartet vibraphonist Milt Jackson and performing a startling set at the 1958 Newport Jazz Festival. In 1959 Ray Charles finally established himself as a popular recording artist with the release of his own top R&B and smash pop composition "What'd I Say."

Sensing that Atlantic was still basically an R&B organization, Ray Charles switched to ABC-Paramount Records in late 1959. With an unusual arrangement that allowed him complete control over his own recordings, Charles recorded pop, country, and R&B for ABC while cutting jazz for its subsidiary label, Impulse. Through 1961 he scored with the top pop hits "Georgia on My Mind" and "Hit the Road Jack" and the major pop hits "Ruby" and "Unchain My Heart." He also recorded *Genius + Soul = Jazz* for Impulse, with arrangements by Quincy Jones played by the Count Basie Band. Yielding a near-smash hit with the instrumental "One Mint Julep," this album and one recorded with Betty Carter for ABC-Paramount brought him an increasing measure of popularity with jazz fans, black and white.

By 1962 Ray Charles was utilizing 40-piece orchestras and large vocal choruses for his recordings. With this full, commercial sound, his *Modern Sounds in Country and Western* album became phenomenally popular, producing the smash hits "I Can't Stop Loving You" backed with "Born to Lose," and "You Don't Know Me." Within a year *Volume II* of country-and-western material was released with the near-smash hits "You Are My Sunshine" backed with "Your Cheating Heart," and "Take These Chains from My Heart." Through 1966 Charles scored major pop hits with "Busted," "That Lucky Old Sun," "Crying Time," "Together Again," and "Let's Go Get Stoned." He later hit with the Beatles' "Yesterday" and "Eleanor Rigby."

Ray Charles formed his own independent Crossover label in 1973 and returned to Atlantic in 1977, moving to Columbia in the '80s, where he primarily recorded in a country vein. During 1976 he recorded *Porgy and Bess* with English songstress Cleo Laine for RCA Records. Charles achieved a major country hit with "Born to Love Me" in 1982, and later recorded duets with country stars on *Friendship*. The album yielded five major country hits, including "We Didn't See a Thing" (with George Jones), "Seven Spanish Angels" (with Willie Nelson), and "Two Old Cats Like Us" (with Hank Williams Jr.). In late 1989 Charles had his first major pop hit in more than 20 years, appearing on the Quincy Jones recording "I'll Be Good to You" in a duet with Chaka Khan.

During the '90s Ray Charles has appeared in a series of stylish commercials for Pepsi and was the subject of a PBS documentary. He continues to work about eight months a year, touring with a large orchestra. He lives in Los Angeles, where he was involved with RPM International, a corporation that includes Crossover Records, the music-publishing companies Tangerine and Racer Music, and RPM Studios, where he records. In 1990 Charles began recording for Warner Bros. Records, where he returned to a more pop vein, particularly on 1993's *My World* with Eric Clapton, Billy Preston, Mavis Staples, and June Pointer.

Ray Charles has been awarded numerous honors, including his 1986 induction as one of the first members into the Rock and Roll Hall of Fame. He won a Kennedy Center Honor in the same year, and a 1993 National Medal of the Arts award.

Early Ray Charles

Birth of a Legend	Ebony	(2) 8001/2	'92	CD
With Arbee Stidham, Lil Son Jackson and James Wayne	Mainstream	310	'71	†
Ray Charles	Archive of Folk and Jazz Music	244	'70	†
Ray Charles, Volume 2	Archive of Folk and Jazz Music	292	'74	†
14 Hits: The Early Years	King	5011	'77	†
14 Original Great Hits	Deluxe	7844		CS
Sings 28 Great Songs	Deluxe	7859	CS	
The Early Years (1947–1951)	Zeta	707	'89	CD†
	EPM	15707	'89	CD
The Early Years	Tomato	(2) 71656	'94	CD

Ray Charles on Atlantic in the '50s and '60s

Hallelujah I Love Her So	Atlantic	8006	'57	†
The Great Ray Charles	Atlantic	1259	'57	CS
The Great Ray Charles (includes entire above album and six cuts from The Genius of Ray Charles, below)	DCC	81731		CD
Ray Charles at Newport	Atlantic	1289	'58	†
Yes Indeed!	Atlantic	8025	'58	†
What'd I Say	Atlantic	8029	'59	†
The Real Ray Charles (compilation of above two)	Pair	1139	'86	CS
The Genius of Ray Charles	Atlantic	1312	'59	CS/CD
Ray Charles in Person	Atlantic	8039	'60	†

The Genius After Hours	Atlantic	1369	'61	†
	Atlantic	90464	'86	CS
The Genius Sings the Blues	Atlantic	8052	'61	†
The Greatest Ray Charles	Atlantic	8054	'61	CS
The Ray Charles Story, Volume I	Atlantic	8063	'62	†
The Ray Charles Story, Volume II	Atlantic	8064	'62	†
The Ray Charles Story, Volumes I and II	Atlantic	(2) 900	'62	†
The Ray Charles Story, Volume III	Atlantic	8083	'63	†
The Ray Charles Story, Volume IV	Atlantic	8094	'64	†
Great Hits of Ray Charles	Atlantic	7101	'64	†
Best	Atlantic	1543		CS/CD
Memories of a Middle-Aged Movie Fan	Atco	33-263	'68	†
Live	Atlantic	(2) 503	'73	†
	Atlantic	503		CS
A Life in Music	Atlantic	(5) 3700		LP/CS
Ray Charles Live	Atlantic	81732		CD
The Birth Of Soul—The Complete Atlantic Rhythm & Blues Recordings, 1952–1959	Atlantic	(3) 82310	'91	CS/CD

Ray Charles and Milt Jackson

Soul Brothers	Atlantic	1279	'58	CS
Soul Meeting	Atlantic	1360	'62	CS
Soul Brothers/Soul Meeting	Atlantic	(2) 81951	'89	CD

Ray Charles on ABC

The Genius Hits the Road	ABC	335	'60	†
Dedicated to You	ABC	355	'61	†
Genius + Soul = Jazz	Impulse	2	'61	†
	DCC	038	'88	CS/CD
	Sandstone	33073	'92	CD
Rock + Soul = Genius (recorded 1961)	Jazz Music Yesterday	1009	'91	CD
Modern Sounds in Country and Western	ABC	410	'62	†
	Rhino	70099	'88	CS/CD
Greatest Hits	ABC	415	'62	†
Modern Sounds in Country and Western, Volume II	ABC	435	'62	†
Ingredients in a Recipe for Soul	ABC	465	'63	†
	DCC	047		CS/CD
	DCC	1027		CD
	Sandstone	33074	'92	CD
Sweet and Sour Tears	ABC	480	'64	†
Have a Smile with Me	ABC	495	'64	†
Live in Concert	ABC	500	'65	†
Together Again	ABC	520	'65	†
Crying Time	ABC	544	'66	†
Ray's Moods	ABC	550	'66	†
A Man and His Soul	ABC	(2) 590	'67	†
Invites You to Listen	ABC	595	'67	†
A Portrait of Ray	ABC	625	'68	†
I'm All Yours	ABC	675	'69	†
Doing His Thing	ABC	695	'69	†
Love Country Style	ABC	707	'70	†

Volcanic Action of My Soul	ABC	726	'71	†
25th Anniversary Salute	ABC	(3) 731	'71	†
Cryin' Time	ABC	744	'71	†
A Message from the People	ABC	755	'72	†
Through the Eyes of Love	ABC	765	'72	†
All-Time Greats	ABC	(2) 781/2	'73	†
My Kind of Jazz	Tangerine/ABC	1512	'70	†
Jazz Number II	Tangerine/ABC	1516	'73	†

Ray Charles and Betty Carter

Ray Charles and Betty Carter	ABC	385	'61	†
	DCC	039	'88	CS/CD

Ray Charles: Recent Recordings

Come Live with Me	Crossover	9000	'74	†
Renaissance	Crossover	9005	'75	†
My Kind of Jazz, Part 3	Crossover	9007	'75	†
True to Life	Atlantic	19142	'77	†
Love and Peace	Atlantic	19199	'78	†
Ain't It So	Atlantic	19251	'79	†
Brother Ray Is at It Again	Atlantic	19281	'80	†
Wish You Were Here Tonight	Columbia	38293		†
Do I Ever Cross Your Mind	Columbia	38990		†
Friendship	CBS	39415	'85	CD†
The Spirit of Christmas	Columbia	40125		LP/CS
From the Pages of My Mind	Columbia	40338	'86	CS
Just Between Us	Columbia	40703	'89	CS/CD
Seven Spanish Angels and Other Hits (1982–1986)	Columbia	45062	'89	CS/CD
Would You Believe?	Warner Bros.	26343	'90	LP/CS/CD
My World	Warner Bros.	26735	'93	CS/CD

Compilations

Original Ray Charles	Hollywood	504	'62	†
Fabulous Artistry	Hollywood	505	'63	†
Great Ray Charles	Premier	2004	'62	†
Fabulous Ray Charles	Premier	2005	'62	†
Ray Charles	Design	145	'62	†
Ray Charles	Time Volumes	(2) 2/4	'63	†
Incomparable Ray Charles	Strand	1086	'63	†
Greatest Hits, Volume I	DCC	036		CD
Greatest Hits, Volume II	DCC	037		CD
Greatest Hits, Volumes I and II	DCC	(2) 36/37		CD
Greatest Country and Western Hits	DCC	040	'88	CS/CD
Anthology	Rhino	75759	'88	CD
Greatest Hits, Volume 1	Rhino	70097	'88	CS
Greatest Hits, Volume 2	Rhino	70098	'88	CS
Blues + Jazz	Rhino	(2) 71607	'94	CD
Classics	Rhino	71874	'95	CS/CD
Ray Charles	Bella Musica	89904	'90	CD†
Greatest Hits	CSI	40141	'91	CD
His Greatest Hits	Sandstone	(2) 33079	'92	CD
The Session, Volume 2	Royal Collection	83154	'92	CD
Best of Easy Listening	Richmond	2154		CS

Goin' Down Slow	Intermedia	5013		LP/CS
20 Golden Pieces of Ray Charles	Bulldog	2012		LP/CS

Ray Charles and Cleo Laine

Porgy and Bess	RCA	(2) 1831	'76	†

CHIC

Nile Rodgers (b. Sept. 19, 1952, New York, NY), gtr; **Bernard Edwards** (b. Oct. 31, 1952, Greenville, NC), kybd, bs, voc; **Tony Thompson** (b. Nov. 15, 1954, Queens, NY), drm [Vocalists included **Norma Jean Wright** and **Luci Martin**; Wright was replaced by **Alfa Anderson** in 1978.]

The most commercially successful black disco group of the late '70s, Chic featured the lean, funky bass-playing of Bernard Edwards—perhaps the most imitated bassist since Larry Graham of Sly and the Family Stone—and the sophisticated lead guitar playing of Nile Rodgers. As the writers, arrangers, and producers, Edwards and Rodgers provided Chic with a playful, glistening sound flavored with strings and jazzy ornamentation. In addition, the rhythm track to Chic's "Good Times" served as the foundation to the early rap hit "Rapper's Delight" by the Sugarhill Gang. As a producer Rogers later created one of the most engaging and successful sounds of the '80s, on albums by a wide range of performers, including Diana Ross's *Diana*, David Bowie's *Let's Dance*, and Madonna's *Like a Virgin*.

Bernard Edwards lived in New York since age 10 and Nile Rodgers grew up in Greenwich Village and Hollywood. As a guitarist, Rodgers played a wide variety of styles, from folk to classical to jazz. Jimi Hendrix was a major influence. Rodgers was a member of the house band at the Apollo Theater in the early '70s and a session and nightclub musician from 1971 to 1977. Rodgers was introduced to Edwards in 1970, and in 1972 the two formed the Big Apple Band with drummer Tony Thompson to back up the vocal group New York City, who scored a major pop hit with "I'm Doin' Fine Now" in 1973. After years of studio and tour work, the three formed Chic in early 1977 with female vocalists Norma Jean Wright and Luci Martin. They soon hit with the silly "Dance, Dance, Dance (Yowsah, Yowsah, Yowsah)" on Buddah, and switched to Atlantic in fall 1977.

Wright left in 1978, to be replaced by Alfa Anderson. Chic then scored a top R&B and pop hit with "Le Freak." Still dismissed as purveyors of superficial disco music, Rodgers and Edwards achieved a measure of recognition for their distinctive sound with the Chic hits "I Want Your Love" and "Good Times" (which served as the basis for several early rap songs) and their production of Sister Sledge's "We Are Family." Although subsequent recordings by Chic were far less successful commercially, Rodgers soon found great success as a producer, beginning with the recording of Diana Ross's 1980 *Diana*, the best-selling album of her career.

Chic broke up in 1983, and Nile Rodgers and Bernard Edwards each recorded solo albums. Rodgers successfully applied his production talents to David Bowie's comeback album *Let's Dance* (1983), Madonna's *Like a Virgin* (1984), and Mick Jagger's *She's the Boss*. In 1984 Rodgers joined Robert Plant, Jimmy Page, and Jeff Beck in the supergroup the Honeydrippers, hitting with a remake of Phil Phillips's 1959 smash "Sea of Love." In 1985, with Bernard Edwards as producer, Tony Thompson recorded with Robert Palmer and John and Andy Taylor (of Duran Duran) as the Power Station, scoring near-smashes with "Some Like It Hot" and "Get It On." Edwards produced and provided the bass for Robert Palmer's top 1986 hit "Addicted to Love." In 1992 Edwards and Rodgers briefly regrouped as Chic with vocalists Sylvester Logan Sharp and Jenn Thomas on Warner Bros. Records.

Chic

Chic	Atlantic	19153	'77	†
	Atlantic	80407	'92	CD
C'est Chic	Atlantic	19209	'78	†
	Atlantic	81552		CD
Risqué	Atlantic	16003	'79	†
	Atlantic	80406	'92	CD
Greatest Hits	Atlantic	16011	'79	†
Real People	Atlantic	16016	'80	†
	Atlantic	80420	'92	CD
Take It Off	Atlantic	19323	'82	†
	Atlantic	80421	'92	CD
Tongue in Chic	Atlantic	80031	'82	†
Believer	Atlantic	80107	'83	†
Dance, Dance, Dance—The Best of Chic	Atlantic	82333	'91	CS/CD
The Best of Chic, Volume 2	Rhino	71085	'92	CS/CD
Everybody Dance	Rhino	71851	'95	CS/CD
Chicism	Warner Bros.	26394	'92	CS/CD

Nile Rodgers

Adventures in the Land of the Good Groove	Mirage	90073	'83	†
B Movie Matinee	Warner Bros.	25290	'85	†

The Honeydrippers

Volume 1	Es Paranza (mini)	90220	'84	†
	Atlantic (mini-CD)	90220		CS/CD

The Power Station

The Power Station	Capitol	12380	'85	†
	Capitol	46127		CS/CD

CHICAGO

Robert Lamm (b. Oct. 13, 1944, Brooklyn, NY), kybd, voc; **Terry Kath** (b. Jan. 31, 1946, Chicago, IL; d. Jan. 23, 1978, Los Angeles, CA), gtr; **Peter Cetera** (b. Sept. 13, 1944, Chicago, IL), bs, gtr, voc; **James Pankow** (b. Aug. 20, 1947, Chicago, IL), trmb; **Lee Loughnane** (b. Oct. 21, 1946, Chicago, IL), trpt, perc, voc; **Walt Parazaider** (b. Mar. 14, 1945, Chicago, IL), rds; **Danny Seraphine** (b. Aug. 28, 1948, Chicago, IL), drm [Keyboardist-vocalist **Bill Champlin** joined in 1982.]

A big-band rock group that initially featured compelling jazz-style improvisation, Chicago quickly degenerated into purveyors of melodic but inconsequential ballads and pop songs. Initially formed in Chicago in 1967 as the Big Thing, Chicago was manned by keyboardist Robert Lamm, guitarist Terry Kath, trumpeter Lee Loughnane, trombonist James Pankow, reed player Walt Parazaider, bassist Peter Cetera, and drummer Danny Seraphine. All had extensive musical training except Kath and Cetera. With Cetera as lead vocalist and Lamm, Cetera, and Pankow serving as principal songwriters, the group changed their name to Chicago Transit Authority (later simply Chicago) and moved to Los Angeles.

Their debut album featured two long and exciting jams on "Beginnings" and Stevie Winwood's "I'm a Man" and the hits "Does Anybody Really Know What Time It Is?" and "Questions 67 and 68." However, by their second album, save perhaps "25 or 6 to 4," Chicago had adapted a formula of recording tuneful but superficial easy-listening songs. Smash hits

CHICAGO

through 1977 included "Saturday in the Park," "Feelin' Stronger Every Day," "Just You and Me," "Call on Me," "Old Days," "If You Leave Me Now," and "Baby, What a Big Surprise."

On January 23, 1978, Terry Kath died of an accidental self-inflicted gunshot wound, and Chicago seemed to lose its momentum. Guitarist Donnie Dacus was recruited for the album *Hot Streets*, but was soon dismissed. The group eventually staged a remarkable comeback with *Chicago XVI* and *XVII*, with their newest member, singer-songwriter-keyboardist Bill Champlin, the erstwhile leader of Northern California's Sons of Champlin Subsequent smash hits through 1989 included "Hard to Say I'm Sorry," "Hard Habit to Break," "You're the Inspiration," "Will You Still Love Me?," "I Don't Wanna Live without Your Love," "Look Away," and "What Kind of Man Would I Be?" Peter Cetera left the group in 1985 for a successful solo career that produced smash hits "Glory of Love," "The Next Time I Fall," "One Good Woman," and "After All," recorded with Cher. He was replaced by bassist Jason Scheff. Danny Seraphine left the group in 1989.

Chicago

Live in Toronto	Special Music	4818		CS/CD
Chicago Transit Authority	Columbia	8	'69	†
	Columbia	00008	'89	CS/CD
Chicago II	Columbia	(2) 24	'70	†
	Columbia	00024		CS/CD
Chicago III	Columbia	(2) 30110	'71	†
	Columbia	30110	'86	CD
Live at Carnegie Hall	Columbia	(4) 30865	'71	†
At Carnegie Hall, Volumes 1–4	Columbia	(3) 30865		CD
Chicago V	Columbia	31102	'72	CS/CD
Chicago VI	Columbia	32400	'73	CS/CD
Chicago VII	Columbia	(2) 32810	'74	†
	Columbia	32810	'86	CD
Chicago VIII	Columbia	33100	'75	CD
Greatest Hits, Volume 1	Columbia	33900	'75	CS/CD
Chicago X	Columbia	34200	'76	CD
Chicago XI	Columbia	34860	'77	CS/CD
Hot Streets	Columbia	35512	'78	†
Chicago (XIII)	Columbia	36105	'79/'90	CS/CD
Chicago XIV	Columbia	36517	'80	†

Greatest Hits, Volume 2	Columbia	37682	'81	CS/CD
If You Leave Me Now	Columbia	38590	'83	CS/CD
Take Me Back to Chicago	Columbia	39579	'85	CD
Group Portrait	Columbia/Legacy (4) 47416		'91	CS/CD
Chicago 16	Full Moon/Asylum	23689	'82	CS/CD
Chicago 17	Full Moon/Asylum	25060	'84	CS/CD
Chicago 18	Warner Bros.	25509	'86	CS/CD
19	Reprise	25714	'88	CS/CD
Greatest Hits, 1982–1989	Reprise	26080	'89	CS/CD
Twenty 1	Reprise	26391	'91	CS/CD
Night and Day	Giant	24615	'95	CS/CD
Live	Richmond	2188		CS

Peter Cetera

Peter Cetera	Full Moon	3624	'82	†
Solitude/Solitaire	Warner Bros.	25474	'86	CS/CD
One More Story	Warner Bros.	25704	'88	CS/CD
World Falling Down	Warner Bros.	26894	'92	CS/CD
One Clear Voice	River North/PGD	1110	'95	CS/CD

ERIC CLAPTON
(b. Eric Clapp, Mar. 30, 1945, Ripley, Surrey, England)

Rock music's first guitar hero and the world's most famous guitarist, Eric Clapton was one of the two finest lead guitarists to emerge during the '60s (Jimi Hendrix, of course, is the other). As a member of three of the most influential English blues groups of the '60s (The Yardbirds, John Mayall's Bluesbreakers, and Cream), Clapton set the standard for the "clean" school of lead playing with his tasty, precise, yet fluid guitar work. Cream, rock music's first supergroup and first powerhouse vocal and instrumental trio, made virtuoso playing an art form within rock and sparked the late-'60s blues revival.

The short-lived Blind Faith continued the improvisatory tradition, as did Clapton's first group, Derek and the Dominos. Indeed, *Layla and Other Assorted Love Songs* was a remarkably focused and intense work, uniting two of rock's most revered guitarists, Clapton and Duane Allman. Clapton's subsequent solo work emphasized his modest songwriting and vocal talents. However, his hit recording of Bob Marley's "I Shot the Sheriff" introduced reggae to a wider audience, and "Lay Down Sally" and "Promises" expanded his audience into the country field. Recently he has scored astounding successes with his acoustic *Unplugged* album, taken from the MTV series, and his album of covers of blues standards, *From the Cradle*.

Eric Clapton took up guitar at 15, later playing in a number of bands such as the Roosters and Casey Jones and the Engineers before joining, in October 1963, the Metropolis Blues Quartet, which later changed its name to the Yardbirds. Clapton stayed on through March 1965, but he became increasingly disturbed by the growing pop direction of the group. Seeking to remain a blues purist, Clapton sought out musicians dedicated to the traditional sound of the blues, joining John Mayall's Bluesbreakers in April 1965. While with the Bluesbreakers, he received extensive adulation as England's premier lead guitarist.

Clapton left the Bluesbreakers in July 1966 to form Cream, rock's first supergroup, with bassist Jack Bruce and drummer Peter "Ginger" Baker. Cream revolutionized rock music with their patented improvisational jams and pioneered the power trio (guitar-bass-drums) format. With internal strains becoming increasingly apparent by mid-1968, Cream announced their intention to disband, performing their final concert at London's Royal

Albert Hall in December. Almost immediately, Clapton helped form another supergroup, Blind Faith, with Cream alumni Ginger Baker, Traffic's Stevie Winwood, and Family's Rick Grech. Unable to live up to the overly enthusiastic expectations of the rock community, Blind Faith completed one English and one American tour and recorded one album before disbanding at the end of 1969. The interesting, if flawed, album featured Winwood's "Sea of Joy" and "Can't Find My Way Back Home" and Clapton's "In the Presence of the Lord."

Clapton next participated in a number of sessions for other artists before joining the Delaney and Bonnie and Friends tour of 1970. Their studio album produced a major hit with Dave Mason's "Only You Know and I Know." Many of these "friends" later assisted Clapton in recording his first solo album, *Clapton*. They included Delaney and Bonnie, Leon Russell, Rita Coolidge, Steve Stills, organist Bobby Whitlock, bassist Carl Radle, drummer Jim Gordon, saxophonist Bobby Keys, and trumpeter Jim Price. The album yielded a major hit with J. J. Cale's "After Midnight" and featured outstanding lead guitar work on "Blues Power" and "Let It Rain."

In May 1970 Eric Clapton formed Derek and the Dominos on the U.S. West Coast with Whitlock, Radle, Gordon, and the Allman Brothers' Duane Allman. Recorded between August 26 and October 2 at Miami's Criteria Studio, *Layla and Other Assorted Love Songs* was a stunning album of tortured love and traditional blues. The album contained excellent ensemble playing on extended versions of the originals "Anyday," "Keep on Growing," and "Why Does Love Got to Be So Sad" (by Clapton and Whitlock), "Layla" (by Clapton and Gordon), Clapton's "Bell Bottom Blues," and the blues standards "Have You Ever Loved a Woman" and "Key to the Highway," plus Jimi Hendrix's "Little Wing." In 1971 Derek and the Dominoes toured without Allman; live recordings from the tour were issued in 1973. However, the group disbanded and Clapton, disillusioned by the death of Duane Allman and the failure of the "Layla" single (it became a near-smash hit when rereleased in 1972), went into near-retirement; a growing addiction to heroin also contributed to his withdrawal from performance. Clapton performed only twice (at George Harrison's Concert for Bangladesh in August 1971 and at Leon Russell's Rainbow Theater engagement in December 1971) before finally being coaxed into reemerging by the Who's Pete Townshend at the Rainbow Theater in January 1973.

Clapton's first album of new material in several years, *461 Ocean Boulevard*, released in 1974, showcased his modest vocal talents, relegating his guitar playing to a support role. The album yielded one of Clapton's biggest hit singles with his cover of Bob Marley's "I Shot the Sheriff," plus the major hit remake of Johnny Otis's "Willy and the Hand Jive." That year he also began attempts to clear up his alcohol and heroin habits and moved in with George Harrison's ex-wife Patti (the object of "Layla"), whom he married in 1979.

Clapton toured the United States again in 1974 and 1975, and live recordings from the tour were issued as *E.C. Was Here*. He began concentrating on his songwriting, and 1976's *No Reason to Cry* produced a major hit with his own "Hello Old Friend." *Slowhand* included J. J. Cale's "Cocaine" and yielded a smash pop hit (and major country hit) with "Lay Down Sally," and a major hit with the love song "Wonderful Tonight." Subsequent major hits through 1985 included "Promises," "I Can't Stand It," "I've Got a Rock 'n' Roll Heart," and "Forever Man." During the '80s Clapton toured regularly, usually accompanied by an outstanding second guitarist, such as Albert Lee, Tim Renwick, or Mark Knopfler.

Eric Clapton's relationship with Patti Harrison ended in 1986 and the couple divorced in 1988. He finally overcame his alcohol and heroin addictions in 1987 and has been in a recovery program ever since. Surrounded by tragedy most of his life, as evidenced by the deaths of Duane Allman, Yardbirds lead vocalist Keith Relf, and Domino Carl Radle (in 1971, 1976, and 1980, respectively), the murder of Cream producer Felix Pappalardi in 1983, and the institutionalization of Domino Jim Gordon in 1984, Clapton further suffered the loss of Stevie Ray Vaughan in a helicopter crash minutes after the two had performed together in August 1990. Then, on March 20, 1991, his son Conor (by Italian actress Lori Del Santo) fell to his death from the 53rd floor of the Galleria Condominium in New York. Grief-stricken, Clapton ultimately reemerged in early 1992 with the poignant smash hit "Tears in Heaven," written for his son, and an inspiring appearance on MTV's *Unplugged*. The album from the show later yielded a surprise hit with a slowed-down acoustic version of "Layla," which amazingly sold more than seven million copies. Cream reunited in 1993 when the trio was inducted into the Rock and Roll Hall of Fame. In 1994 Clapton recorded the best-selling *From the Cradle*, an album of traditional blues that included covers of songs by Willie Dixon, Elmore James, and Muddy Waters, and conducted a blues-only tour of arenas and halls. In May 1995 Eric Clapton appeared in a 90-minute PBS television special that focused on the blues. Recorded at the Fillmore in San Francisco, the special was produced by filmmaker Martin Scorsese.

Eric Clapton with John Mayall's Bluesbreakers

Bluesbreakers	London	492	'67	†
	London	50009	'78	†
	Deram	800086		CS/CD
	Mobile Fidelity	616	'94	CD

Blind Faith

Blind Faith	Atco	33-304	'69	†
	RSO	3016	'77	†
	Polydor	825094		CS/CD
	Mobile Fidelity	507	'89	CD

Eric Clapton with Delaney and Bonnie

On Tour with Eric Clapton	Atco	33326	'70	CS/CD

Derek and the Dominos

Layla and Other Assorted Love Songs	Atco	(2) 704	'70	†
	Polydor	(2) 3501		†
	RSO	(2) 3801	'77	†
	Polydor	847090	'91	CS/CD
	Mobile Fidelity	585	'93	CD
The Layla Sessions	Polydor	(3) 847083	'90	CS/CD
In Concert	RSO	(2) 8800	'73	†
	Polydor	(2) 831416		CS/CD†
Live at the Fillmore	Polydor	(2) 521682	'94	CS/CD

The Rainbow Concert

Eric Clapton's Rainbow Concert	RSO	877	'73	†
	Polydor	831320	'87	CS/CD

Eric Clapton

Eric Clapton	Atco	33-329	'70	†
	RSO	3008	'77	†
	Polydor	825093		CS/CD
History of Eric Clapton	Atco	(2) 803	'72	†
Eric Clapton at His Best	Polydor	(2) 3503	'72	†
Clapton	Polydor	5526	'73	†
461 Ocean Boulevard	RSO	4801	'74	†
	Polydor	811697		CS/CD
	Mobile Fidelity	594	'93	CD

There's One in Every Crowd	RSO	4806	'75	†
	Polydor	829649	'87	CS/CD
E.C. Was Here	RSO	4809	'75	†
	Polydor	831519	'87	CS/CD
No Reason to Cry	RSO	3004	'76	†
	Polydor	813582	'87	CS/CD
Slowhand	RSO	3030	'77	†
	Polydor	823276		CS/CD
	Mobile Fidelity	553	'91	CD
Backless	RSO	3039	'78	†
	Polydor	813581	'86	CS/CD
Just One Night	RSO	(2) 4202	'80	†
	Polydor	825391		CS
	Polydor	(2) 800093		CD
	Mobile Fidelity	(2) 608	'94	CD
Another Ticket	RSO	3095	'81	†
	Polydor	827579		CS/CD
Time Pieces/Best of Eric Clapton	RSO	3099	'82	†
	Polydor	825382	'88	CS
	Polydor	800014	'88	CD
Time Pieces/Live in the '70s	Polydor	811835	'88	CS/CD
Crossroads	Polydor	(4) 835261	'88	CS/CD
The Cream of Clapton	Polydor	527116	'95	CS/CD
Money and Cigarettes	Warner Bros.	23773	'83	CS/CD
Behind the Sun	Warner Bros.	25166	'85	CS/CD
August	Warner Bros.	25476	'86	CS/CD
Homeboy (soundtrack)	Virgin	91241	'89	CS/CD
Journeyman	Reprise	26074	'89	CS/CD
24 Nights	Reprise	(2) 26420	'91	CS/CD
Rush (soundtrack)	Reprise	26794	'92	CS/CD
Unplugged	Duck	45024	'92	CS/CD
From the Cradle	Duck	45735	'94	CS/CD

THE DAVE CLARK FIVE

Dave Clark (b. Dec. 15, 1942, Tottenham, London, England), drm; **Mike Smith** (b. Dec. 12, 1943, Edmonton, London, England), lead voc, kybd; **Lenny Davidson** (b. May 30, 1944, Enfield, Middlesex, England), gtr; **Denny Payton** (b. Aug. 1, 1943, Walthamstow, London, England), horns; **Rick Huxley** (b. Aug. 5, 1942, Dartford, Kent, England), gtr, bs

Dave Clark, Mike Smith, and Lenny Davidson were the principal songwriters of the Dave Clark Five, one of the first and best of the so-called British Invasion bands to hit it big in the United States. Between 1964 and 1966 they scored major hits with the original rockers "Glad All Over," "Bits and Pieces," "Can't You See That She's Mine," "Anyway You Want It" and "Catch Us If You Can," and the original ballads "Because" and "Everybody Knows (I Still Love You)." The group appeared in the 1965 film *Having a Wild Weekend*, and had their last major U.S. hit in 1967 with "You Got What It Takes." The Dave Clark Five disbanded in 1973.

The group was originally formed by members of the Tottenham, London, local soccer league, who hoped to raise money to be able to compete in a soccer match on the Continent. The astute (and incidentally good-looking) Clark, who had worked previously as a movie stuntman, became the group's de facto business manager and leader; he also quickly mastered the drums. With a tougher sound than the Beatles, they quickly hit the charts with a series of ballsy, R&B-influenced numbers, beginning with the raucous "Glad All Over." A unique component of the group's sound was Denny Payton's sax solos, an unusual instrument for British combos that tended to copy the Beatles's two guitars-bass-drums lineup. Pushing the drums forward in the mix (as on the introduction to the chorus of "Glad All Over") made the group's music punchier and very danceable. Lead vocalist Mike Smith was obviously influenced by American R&B; he had an engaging vocal style that wed the cheeky, sunny quality of British singers with Ray Charles–style gospel shouting.

The group had no trouble capturing the American charts following their initial British success. They appeared on *The Ed Sullivan Show* following the Beatles, and made an impressive 18 guest appearances on the program. More hits followed through 1967 stateside and 1970 in Britain; then the group partially disbanded. Smith and Clark continued to perform as Dave Clark and Friends until 1973, primarily trading off the group's previous hits. Smith continued to work through the mid-'70s and more sporadically through the '80s; he made a comeback album in 1990. Clark, meanwhile, became a music-industry executive. His musical *Time* was a minor 1986 hit on the London stage.

Dave Clark Five

Glad All Over	Epic	26093	'64	†
Return!	Epic	26104	'64	†
American Tour	Epic	26117	'64	†
Coast to Coast	Epic	26128	'65	†
Weekend in London	Epic	26139	'65	†
Having a Wild Weekend (soundtrack)	Epic	26162	'65	†
I Like It Like That	Epic	26178	'65	†
Greatest Hits	Epic	26185	'66	†
Try Too Hard	Epic	26198	'66	†
Satisfied with You	Epic	26212	'66	†
More Greatest Hits	Epic	26221	'66	†
5 by 5	Epic	26236	'67	†
You Got What It Takes	Epic	26312	'67	†
Everybody Knows	Epic	26354	'68	†
The Dave Clark Five	Epic	30434	'71	†
Glad All Over (All-Time Greatest Hits)	Epic	(2) 33459	'75	
The History of the Dave Clark Five	Hollywood	61482	'93	CS/CD

DICK CLARK

(b. Nov. 30, 1929, Mount Vernon, NY)

As host of the first network television series devoted to rock and roll and the longest-running musical show in television history, *American Bandstand*, Dick Clark made rock music palatable to the mainstream American public and helped promote the careers of most of the rock-and-roll artists of the '50s, both the talents and the no-talents. Presenting a sanitized, even emasculated form of rock and roll, the show nonetheless influenced the dance and fashion trends of the day and opened the door for other music ventures on television, from *Soul Train* to MTV. Escaping most of the ill effects of the payola scandal of 1959, despite his heavy involvement with record labels and music-publishing companies, Dick Clark prospered after the furor whereas others (most notably deejay Alan Freed) were totally ruined by the investigation.

Dick Clark majored in business administration at Syracuse University, where he served as a disc jockey on the campus radio station. After graduation in 1951 he worked as a news anchor on WKTV in Utica before moving to Philadelphia in 1952 to become a radio announcer at WFIL, the local ABC affiliate. By July 1956 WFIL-TV's dance-and-music show *Bandstand* (originally created by disc jockey Bob Horn in 1952) had become the city's top-rated daytime show. Clark took over as host of *Bandstand* and subsequently persuaded officials of ABC-TV to broadcast the show over the entire network as *American Bandstand* on weekday afternoons. The format generally included one or two guest stars synchronizing their lip movements (known as lip-syncing) to their recorded songs, teenagers dancing to records, and small-talk and record ratings by members of the audience. Debuting on ABC on August 5, 1957, *American Bandstand* became enormously popular, and a number of Philadelphia teenagers who regularly appeared as dancers became household celebrities. The show provided the first national exposure for Jerry Lee Lewis, Buddy Holly, and Chubby Checker, among many others.

During the late '50s Dick Clark became a full partner in Philadelphia-based record labels such as Jamie and Swan, while promoting local talents such as Fabian, Frankie Avalon, and Bobby Rydell (many of whom were groomed to be teen stars based on their looks) on *American Bandstand*. Called before the Senate investigating committee probing payola (pay-for-play) activities among disc jockeys, Clark admitted to accepting a fur stole and expensive jewelry from a record-company president. He was admonished for this single transgression only, despite the fact that songs and artists in which he had a considerable interest were frequently featured on *American Bandstand*. Clark had apparently divested himself of his music-business holdings before appearing to testify.

In 1964 Dick Clark moved *American Bandstand* to Los Angeles, where he hosted *Where the Action Is* with house band Paul Revere and the Raiders in the late '60s. During the '70s he expanded his media exploits through his Burbank-based Dick Clark Productions, producing television shows and specials. He hosted the game show *The $25,000 Pyramid* from 1973, the American Music Awards from 1974, the Academy of Country Music Awards from 1978, and (with Ed McMahon) *TV's Bloopers and Practical Jokes* from 1984. He also hosts the syndicated radio shows *Rock, Roll and Remember* and *Countdown America* and is the founder and director of the Unistar Radio Network, which supplies programs to more than 1,800 radio stations. Furthermore, his company has produced the film *Remo Williams* (1985) and made-for-TV movies, including *Elvis* and *The Birth of the Beatles*. *American Bandstand* left ABC for syndication in 1987, and in 1989 Clark stepped down as host. The show lasted only six months on the USA cable network with a different host. In 1993 Dick Clark was one of few nonmusicians inducted into the Rock and Roll Hall of Fame; that same year he began hosting the game show *Scattergories*.

Dick Clark

Dance with Dick Clark, Volume 1	ABC-Paramount	258		†
Dance with Dick Clark, Volume 2	ABC-Paramount	288	'59	†
20 Years of Rock 'n' Roll	Buddah	(2) 5133	'73	†
Dick Clark's 21 All-Time Hits, Volume 1	Original Sound	8891		CS/CD
Volume 2	Original Sound	8892		CS/CD
Volume 3	Original Sound	8894		CS/CD
Volume 4	Original Sound	8895		CS/CD
Dick Clark's 21 All-Time Hits, Double Pack, Volumes 1–2	Original Sound	(2) 9319		CD
Dick Clark's 21 All-Time Hits, Double Pack, Volumes 3–4	Original Sound	(2) 9320		CD
Dick Clark's 21 All-Time Hits	Original Sound	(4) 1234		CS/CD

THE CLASH

Joe Strummer (b. John Mellor, Aug. 21, 1952, Ankara, Turkey), voc, rhythm gtr; **Mick Jones** (b. June 26, 1953, Brixton, London, England), voc, lead gtr; **Paul Simonon** (b. Dec. 15, 1956, London, England), bs [Early guitarist **Keith Levene** left after the group's first tour. The group's drummers were **Tory "Terry" Chimes**, **Nicky "Topper" Headon** (b. May 30, 1955, Bromley, England), and **Pete Howard**. Mick Jones left in 1983, to be replaced by guitarists **Vince White** and **Nick Sheppard**.]

The first British punk band to capture the attention of American audiences, the Clash persevered with their assured, overtly political music while the Sex Pistols quickly self-destructed as a consequence of their defeatist nihilism. Along with Elvis Costello, the Clash were the prime innovators to emerge from punk and displayed a remarkable eclecticism (unlike their contemporaries), exploring reggae and rockabilly, as well as rock, from their very start. Ironically, while establishing themselves in Great Britain with disenfranchised working-class youth in the late '70s, the Clash broke through in the United States to middle-class audiences with their 1982 hits "Should I Stay or Should I Go" and "Rock the Casbah." Hailed for both their debut album and *London Calling*, the Clash ultimately disintegrated in the mid-'80s.

Formed in May 1976 by musicians from the 101ers and London SS, the Clash toured Great Britain and the United States on the Sex Pistols' ill-fated Anarchy in the U.K. tour that December. Early guitarist Keith Levene, who later surfaced in Public Image Ltd. with former Sex Pistols vocalist Johnny "Rotten" Lydon, left the band after the first tour, when the band added drummer Terry Chimes. Signed to Columbia Records in February 1977, the Clash's debut album was judged too crude to be issued in the United States. It was eventually released, in altered form, on Epic in 1979. Hailed as the definitive punk album, *The Clash* included the rebellious "White Riot," "London's Burning," and "Hate and War," and featured musical attacks on unemployment ("Career Opportunities"), record companies ("Complete Control"), and cultural imperialism ("I'm So Bored with the U.S.A."), plus their signature song, "I Fought the Law."

With Nicky "Topper" Headon taking over on drums and Joe Strummer and Mick Jones acting as the group's primary songwriters, the Clash recorded their next album (and American debut), *Give 'Em Enough Rope*, with Blue Öyster Cult producer Sandy Pearlman. The album contained their first British hit single, "Tommy Gun," and included "All the Young Punks," "Guns on the Roof," "English Civil War," "Safe European Home," and "Stay Free." They debuted as headliners in the United States in February 1979 and subsequently recorded *London Calling*. The album featured explorations of reggae ("Revolution Rock" and "Wrong 'Em Boyo") and rockabilly ("Brand New Cadillac"), and included "London Calling," "Lost in the Supermarket," the ballad "Lover's Rock," and their first major American hit, "Train in Vain (Stand By Me)."

Established in America as the only extant British punk band, the Clash next recorded the sprawling 36-song *Sandinista* album. Their biggest hits came off their next album, 1982's *Combat Rock*: the moderate hit "Should I Stay or Should I Go" and the near-smash "Rock the Casbah," written by drummer Topper Headon. The Clash opened for the Who's Farewell tour in late 1982. Headon soon left the band due to ongoing problems with drug addiction; he was replaced by original drummer Chimes, and then in 1983 by Pete Howard. At the pinnacle of their popularity, Strummer and Simonon fired Mick Jones in late 1983. By 1984 only Strummer and Simonon remained from the original group; they managed to record one final album, *Cut the Crap*, before disbanding in 1986.

Joe Strummer turned to acting (*Straight to Hell*) and production, and later recorded *Earthquake Music* and toured with the Pogues, while Mick Jones formed Big Audio Dynamite with New Wave filmmaker-keyboardist Don Letts. The group broke up in 1989; Jones subsequently assembled Big Audio Dynamite II with entirely new members, scoring a moderate hit with "Rush" in 1991. By then Paul Simonon had formed Havana 3 A.M. with Sex Pistols' guitarist Steve Jones.

The Clash

Crucial Music: 1977 Revisited	Relativity	1036		CS/CD
The Clash	Epic	36060	'79	CS/CD
Give 'Em Enough Rope	Epic	35543	'79	CS/CD
London Calling	Epic	(2) 36328	'80	†
	Epic	36328		CS/CD
Black Market Clash	Epic	36846	'80	†
	Epic	38540		LP/CS
Sandinista!	Epic	(2) 37037	'81	CS/CD
Combat Rock	Epic	37689	'82/'85	CS/CD
Cut the Crap	Epic	40017	'88	CS
	Epic/Legacy	66419	'94	CD
The Story of the Clash, Volume 1	Epic	(2) 44035	'88	CS/CD
Clash on Broadway	Epic/Legacy	(3) 46991	'91	CS/CD
Crucial Music: The Clash Collection	Relativity	1022		CS/CD

Joe Strummer

Earthquake Weather	Epic	45372	'89	CS/CD†

Joe Strummer and the Latino Rockabilly War

Permanent Record (soundtrack)	Epic	40879	'88	LP/CS/CD

Big Audio Dynamite

This Is Big Audio Dynamite	Columbia	40220	'85	CS/CD
No. 10 Upping St.	Columbia	40445	'86	†
	Columbia	40705		CS/CD
Tighten Up, Volume '88	Columbia	44074	'88	CS/CD
Megatop Phoenix	Columbia	45212	'89	CS/CD
Planet Bad Greatest Hits	Columbia	67350	'95	CS/CD
Punk	Radioactive	11280	'95	CS/CD

Big Audio Dynamite II

The Globe	Columbia	46147	'91	LP/CS/CD

Havana 3 A.M.

Havana 3 A.M.	I.R.S.	13069	'91	CS/CD

JIMMY CLIFF

(b. James Chambers, Apr. 1, 1948, Somerton, Jamaica)

Established in the Caribbean, Latin America, and Europe as a reggae artist by the late '60s, Jimmy Cliff introduced reggae to a mainstream American audience with the 1973 film *The Harder They Come*. He starred in the movie and provided the enduring songs "Sitting in Limbo" and "The Harder They Come" to the soundtrack. Along with Bob Marley and Peter Tosh, Cliff was a prime purveyor of reggae music, and although his albums have been criticized as pop-oriented, he did provide authentic reggae in concert.

Jimmy Cliff moved to Kingston, Jamaica, after his primary-school graduation. He recorded his first single in Jamaica in 1958, and scored his first local hit with "Hurricane Hattie" in 1961. Cliff toured the United States as part of a ska revue in 1964, and subsequently signed with Island Records and moved to England. Established in Europe, the Caribbean, and Latin America by 1965, he returned to Jamaica in 1968 and scored his first major American hit with "Wonderful World, Beautiful People" in 1970. Reggae finally broke big in the United States in 1973 with the release of the film *The Harder They Come,* starring Cliff. The soundtrack album included three Cliff originals, "You Can Get It If You Really Want," "Sitting in Limbo," and "The Harder They Come," Cliff's version of Bob Marley's "Many Rivers to Cross," plus the Melodians' "Rivers of Babylon," the Slickers' "Johnny Too Bad," and the Maytals' "Pressure Drop."

By the late '70s Jimmy Cliff's recorded music was moving in a pop direction, but his tours provided authentic roots music. Recording for Columbia in the '80s, he costarred with Robin Williams in the 1986 movie *Club Paradise* and toured with Stevie Winwood that year. Switching to JRS Records for 1992's *Breakout*, Jimmy Cliff tours six months per year, performing to his most enthusiastic audiences in Brazil and Africa.

Jimmy Cliff

Can't Get Enough of It	Veep	16536	'69	†
Wonderful World, Beautiful People	A&M	4251	'70	†
	A&M	3189		CS/CD
The Harder They Come (soundtrack)	Mango	7400	'73	†
	Island/Mango	9202	'75	†
	Mango	539202		LP/CS/CD
Struggling Man	Island	9343	'74	†
	Island/Mango	9235		†
Reggae Greats	Mango	539794		CS/CD
Unlimited	Reprise	2147	'73	†
Music Maker	Reprise	2188	'74	†
Follow My Mind	Reprise	2218	'75	†
In Concert: The Best of Jimmy Cliff	Reprise	2256	'76	CS/CD
Give Thanx	Warner Bros.	3240	'78	CS
I Am the Living	MCA	5153	'80	†
	MCA	813		CS
Give the People What They Want	MCA	5217	'81	†
	MCA	820		CS
Special	Columbia	38099	'82	CS/CD
The Power and the Glory	Columbia	38986	'83/'85	CS/CD
Cliff Hanger	Columbia	40002	'85	CS/CD
Club Paradise (soundtrack)	Columbia	40404	'86/'88	CS
Hanging Fire	Columbia	40845	'88	CS/CD
Breakout	JRS	35808	'92	CS/CD

GEORGE CLINTON

(b. July 22, 1940, Plainfied, OH)

The Parliaments were led by George Clinton as an R&B vocal group during the '50s and '60s, but lost the use of their name in the late '60s. They regrouped as the rock-oriented Funkadelic, incorporating the innovations of Sly Stone and Jimi Hendrix. Funkadelic continued to record on a separate label once Clinton regained use of the Parliament name (now without the *s*). Augmented by bassist William "Bootsy" Collins and horn players Maceo Parker and Fred Wesley from James Brown's JBs, Parliament recorded a series of bizarre, oddly conceptual albums of so-called funk music, perhaps the last vestige of R&B

music not overwhelmed by the rise of mindless disco music. Appealing primarily to African-American teenagers and promoting humanitarian ideals such as equality and self-determination through an off-the-wall synthesis of ghetto jargon, science fiction fantasies, parodied psychedelia, and spiritual values—Parliament finally broke through to mainstream success with 1976's *Mothership Connection* album and tour.

George Clinton subsequently concentrated on the Funkadelic side of the group, achieving enormous success with 1978's *One Nation Under a Groove*. He also recorded various members of the Parliament-Funkadelic "family" such as Walter "Junie" Morrison, the Horny Horns, Parlet, and the Brides of Funkenstein; he formed his own label, Uncle Jam, for recordings by the Sweat Band and the P-Funk All-Stars. Former member William "Bootsy" Collins launched his own career with Bootsy's Rubber Band, as did Roger Troutman with his family band Zapp.

Recording sporadically on his own in the '80s, George Clinton served as inspiration to the hip-hop movement, and saw many of his hit songs sampled by rap acts. He ultimately joined Prince's Paisley Park label for *The Cinderella Theory*, hailed as his comeback, and enjoyed renewed popularity as a result of his appearances with the Red Hot Chili Peppers at the Grammy Awards in 1993 and his participation in the Lollapalooza tour of 1994.

In 1955 George Clinton formed the Detroit R&B vocal group the Parliaments with Raymond Davis, Calvin Simon, Clarence "Fuzzy" Haskins, and Grady Thomas. They first recorded for ABC in 1956, and subsequently recorded for a number of different labels before signing with Motown in 1964. They eventually scored a major pop and smash R&B hit with "(I Wanna) Testify" on Revilot in 1967, but the company soon folded and Motown claimed the rights to the Parliament name. Nevertheless, they managed to record *Osmium* for Holland-Dozier-Holland's Invictus label before losing the rights to the name.

George Clinton, assuming the persona of Dr. Funkenstein, augmented Parliament with guitarists Eddie Hazel and Lucius Ross, keyboardist Bernie Worrell, drummer Ramon Fullwood, and vocalist Ray Davis, and the group took the name of Funkadelic. Signed to the Detroit-based Westbound label in 1969, Funkadelic recorded a series of albums that attempted to bridge the gap between '60s rock and contemporary R&B styles. Through 1976 Funkadelic scored a series of minor-to-moderate R&B hits, highlighted by "I'll Bet You," "I Wanna Know if It's Good to You?," and "On the Verge of Getting It On," while recording modest-selling albums such as *Maggot Brain*, *America Eats Its Young*, *Cosmic Slop*, and *Tales of Kidd Funkadelic* for Westbound.

With Clinton regaining the use of the Parliament name by 1974, the group signed with Casablanca Records, recording bizarre yet entertaining albums backed by Funkadelic that included the near-smash R&B hit "Up for the Down Stroke." The astounding success of the classic "Tear the Roof Off the Sucker (Give Up the Funk)" single (a major pop and smash R&B hit) and best-selling *Mothership Connection* album finally brought the group mainstream success in 1976. By then the members of Parliament-Funkadelic included veteran guitarists Bernie Worrell, Eddie Hazel, and Ray Davis, horn players Maceo Parker and Fred Wesley, and bassist William "Bootsy" Collins, all former members of James Brown's band, plus former Ohio Players keyboardist Walter Morrison. A weird conceptual album blending brilliant if erratic music and Clinton's funk monologues regarding science fiction and psychedelic and spiritual fantasies, *Mothership Connection* was supported by a sell-out tour that incorporated odd costumes and massive stage props, including a spaceship dubbed the Mothership.

The success of *Mothership Connection* paved the way for subsequent best-selling albums by Parliament, including *Funkentelechy vs. The Placebo Syndrome*, which yielded a major pop and top R&B hit with "Flash Light." Subsequent R&B hits for Parliament through 1980 included the top hit "Aqua Boogie" and the near-smashes "Theme from the Black Hole" and "Agony of DeFeet." By 1977 Funkadelic had switched to Warner Bros. Records, where they scored a top R&B and major pop hit with the title song to the classic *One Nation Under a*

Groove album. Toward the end of 1979 Funkadelic scored a top R&B hit with "(Not Just) Knee Deep—Part 1" from *Uncle Jam Wants You*.

The members of Parliament-Funkadelic began taking on solo projects in 1975. Junie Morrison recorded three albums for Westbound before switching to Columbia by 1980; he later recorded for Island. Bootsy's Rubber Band, headed by Bootsy Collins, began recording for Warner Bros. in 1976. The group produced a smash R&B hit with "The Pinocchio Theory" in 1977, and a top R&B hit with "Bootzilla" in 1978. An offshoot of Bootsy's Rubber Band, the Sweat Band (with Maceo Parker), recorded an album for Clinton's newly formed Uncle Jam label in 1980, the year Collins began recording on his own for Warner Bros. In 1982 he had a major R&B hit with "Body Slam!" He eventually switched to Columbia Records for 1988's *What's Bootsy Doin'?* and formed the New Rubber Band and Zillatron in the '90s.

In 1977 Fred Wesley and the Horny Horns (again with Maceo Parker) recorded an album for Atlantic, and Eddie Hazel recorded one for Warner Bros. Also in 1977, three of the original Parliaments, Clarence Haskins, Calvin Simon, and Grady Thomas, left Parliament-Funkadelic to eventually record an album for LAX records as Funkadelic. In 1978 the vocal trio Parlet, with Mahalia Franklin and Shirley Hayden, began recording for Casablanca, and the Brides of Funkenstein, with Lynn Mabry, Dawn Silva, Ron Banks, and Larry Demps, recorded the first of two albums for Atlantic, producing the smash R&B hit "Disco to Go." Bernie Worrell recorded an album for Arista in 1979, and in 1980 Roger Troutman formed Zapp with his brothers Lester, Tony, and Larry. Through 1983 they achieved R&B smashes with "More Bounce to the Ounce—Part 1," "Dance Floor (Part 1)," "Doo Wa Ditty (Blow That Thing)," and "I Can Make You Dance (Part 1)." Roger began recording on his own in 1981, scoring a top R&B hit with "I Heard It Through the Grapevine," which featured his use of the voice-box device. In 1986 Zapp hit the R&B charts with "Computer Love," and in 1987 Roger topped the R&B charts with "I Want to Be Your Man."

In 1980 George Clinton withdrew from his high profile in the popular-music world. He recorded on his own for Capitol Records during the '80s, scoring a top R&B hit with "Atomic Dog" from *Computer Games* in 1983. Around 1982 he formed the P-Funk All-Stars, whose album *Urban Dancefloor Guerrillas* came to be regarded as a funk masterpiece. He also produced albums by Jimmy Giles and the Tac-Heads, the Brides of Motown, and the Red Hot Chili Peppers' second album. Bernie Worrell assisted in the recording of the Talking Heads' celebrated 1980 *Remain in Light* album, and joined the group's 1983 tour that produced the excellent concert film *Stop Making Sense*. By 1988 George Clinton had switched to Prince's Paisley Park label for *The Cinderella Theory*, lauded as his comeback. In 1989 he toured with a new edition of his P-Funk All-Stars.

During the '90s Bernie Worrell returned to recording after a stint with the Talking Heads, and Fred Wesley and Maceo Parker established themselves as jazz artists. Roger Troutman returned with 1991's *Bridging the Gap* after a four-year absence, and George Clinton recorded *Hey Man, Smell My Finger* with veterans Bootsy Collins, Bernie Worrell, and Maceo Parker, plus Prince and rappers Ice Cube and Dr. Dre. Clinton's renewed career got a boost from his appearance with the Red Hot Chili Peppers at the Grammy Awards in 1993 and his successful performances with the P-Funk All-Stars on the Lollapalooza '94 tour.

Parliament

Osmium	Invictus	7302	'71	†
Up for the Down Stroke	Casablanca	9003	'74	†
	Casablanca	7002		†
	Casablanca	842619	'90	CS/CD
Chocolate City	Casablanca	7014	'75	†
	Casablanca	836700	'90	CS/CD

Mothership Connection	Casablanca	7022	'76	†
	Casablanca	824502	'85	CS/CD
The Clones of Dr. Funkenstein	Casablanca	7034	'76	†
	Casablanca	842620	'90	CS/CD
P-Funk Earth Tour	Casablanca	(2) 7053	'77	†
	Casablanca	834941	'91	CS/CD
Funkentelechy vs. The Placebo Syndrome	Casablanca	7084	'77	†
	Casablanca	824501		CS/CD
Motor Booty Affair	Casablanca	7125	'78	†
	Casablanca	842621	'90	CS/CD
Gloryhallastoopid (Pin the Tale on the Funky)	Casablanca	7195	'79	†
	Casablanca	842622	'90	CS/CD
Trombipulation	Casablanca	7249	'81	†
	Casablanca	842623	'90	CS/CD
Greatest Hits (The Bomb)	Casablanca	822637	'84	CS/CD
The Best of Parliament: Give Up the Funk	Casablanca	526995	'95	CS/CD
Tear the Roof Off (1974–1980)	Mercury	(2) 514417	'93	CS/CD

Funkadelic

Funkadelic	Westbound	2000	'70	†
	Westbound	216	'75	†
	Westbound	010		LP/CD
Free Your Mind and Your Ass Will Follow	Westbound	2001	'70	†
	Westbound	217	'75	†
	Westbound	012		LP/CD
Maggot Brain	Westbound	2007	'71	†
	Westbound	218	'75	†
	Westbound	002		LP/CD
America Eats Its Young	Westbound	(2) 2020	'72	†
	Westbound	(2) 221	'75	†
	Westbound	(2) 029		LP
	Westbound	029		CS
Cosmic Slop	Westbound	2022	'73	†
	Westbound	223		†
	Westbound	035		LP/CS/CD
Standing on the Verge of Getting It On	Westbound	1001	'74	†
	Westbound	208	'75	†
	Westbound	040		LP/CS/CD
Greatest Hits	Westbound	1004	'75	†
Let's Take It to the Stage	Westbound	215	'75	†
	Westbound	044		LP/CS/CD
Tales of Kidd Funkadelic	Westbound	227	'76	†
Best of the Early Years, Volume 1	Westbound	303	'77	†
Music for Your Mother—Funkadelic 45s	Westbound	(2) 055		LP/CS/CD
Hardcore Jollies	Warner Bros.	2973	'76	†
One Nation Under a Groove	Warner Bros.	3209	'78	†
Uncle Jam Wants You	Warner Bros.	3371	'79	†
The Electric Spanking of War Babies	Warner Bros.	3482	'81	†
Who's a Funkadelic	Avenue	71087	'92	CS/CD

George Clinton

The George Clinton Band Arrives	ABC	831	'74	†

Computer Games	Capitol	12246	'82	†
	Capitol	16463	'87	†
	Capitol	96266	'91	CS/CD
You Shouldn't-Nuf Bit Fish	Capitol	12308	'84	†
	Capitol	96357	'91	CS/CD†
Some of My Best Jokes Are Friends	Capitol	12417	'85	†
	Capitol	96356	'91	CS/CD†
R&B Skeletons in the Closet	Capitol	12481	'86	†
	Capitol	96267	'91	CS/CD†
The Best of George Clinton	Capitol	48424	'87	CD†
George Clinton Presents Our Gang Funky	MCA	42048	'89	LP/CS/CD†
The Cinderella Theory	Paisley Park	25994	'89	CS/CD
Hey Man, Smell My Finger	Paisley Park	25518	'93	CS/CD
Bootsy's Rubber Band				
Stretchin' Out in Bootsy's Rubber Band	Warner Bros.	2920	'76	†
Ahh . . . The Name Is Bootsy, Baby!	Warner Bros.	2972	'77	†
Bootsy? Player of the Year	Warner Bros.	3093	'78	†
This Boot Is Made for Funkin'	Warner Bros.	3295	'79	†
Jungle Bass	4th & Broadway	4023	'90	LP/CS/CD
The Sweat Band				
The Sweat Band	Uncle Jam	37087	'80	†
William "Bootsy" Collins				
Ultra Wave	Warner Bros.	3433	'80	†
The One Giveth, the Count Taketh Away	Warner Bros.	3667	'82	†
Back in the Day: The Best of Bootsy	Warner Bros.	26581	'94	CS/CD
What's Bootsy Doin'?	Columbia	44107	'88	CS/CD
Keepin' Dah Funk Alive 4 1995	Rykodisc	(2) 90323	'95	CD
Bootsy's New Rubber Band				
Blasters of the Universe	Rykodisc	(2) 90307/8	'94	CD
Zillatron				
Lord of the Harvest	Black Arc	10301	'94	CD
Walter "Junie" Morrison				
When We Do	Westbound	200	'75	†
Freeze	Westbound	214	'76	†
Suzie Super Groupie	Westbound	228	'76	†
Bread Alone	Columbia	36585	'80	†
	Sony Music	36585		CS/CD†
Junie 5	Columbia	37133	'81	†
Evacuate Your Seats	Island	90191	'84	†
Fred Wesley and the Horny Horns				
A Blow for Me, a Toot for You	Atlantic	18214	'77	†
Fred Wesley				
New Friends	Antilles	848280	'91	CS/CD
Comme Ci Comme Ça	Antilles	512002	'92	CS/CD
Swing and Be Funky	Minor Music	801027	'93	CD
Amalgamation	Minor Music	801045	'95	CD
Maceo Parker				
For All the King's Men	4th & Broadway	4027		LP/CS/CD

Roots Revisited	Verve	843751	'90	CS/CD
Mo' Roots	Verve	511068	'91	CS/CD
Life on Planet Groove	Verve	517197	'92	CS/CD
Southern Exposure	Novus	63175	'94	CS/CD
Eddie Hazel				
Games, Dames, and Other Thangs	Warner Bros.	3058	'77	†
Parlet				
Pleasure	Casablanca	7094	'78	†
Invasion of the Body Snatchers	Casablanca	7146		†
Play Me or Trade Me	Casablanca	7224		†
The Best of Parlet, Featuring Parliament	Casablanca	522455	'94	CS/CD
Brides Of Funkenstein				
Funk or Walk	Atlantic	19201	'78	†
Never Buy Texas from a Cowboy	Atlantic	19261	'80	†
Bernie Worrell				
All the Woo in the World	Arista	4209	'79	†
Funk of Ages	Gramavision	79460	'90	CD
Blacktronic Science	Gramavision	79474	'93	CS/CD
Zapp				
Zapp	Warner Bros.	3463	'80	LP/CS/CD
Zapp II	Warner Bros.	23583	'82	CS/CD
Zapp III	Warner Bros.	23875	'83	†
The New Zapp IV U	Warner Bros.	25327	'85	CS/CD
Zapp V	Reprise	25807	'89	CS/CD
Roger Troutman				
The Many Facets of Roger	Warner Bros.	3594	'81	†
The Saga Continues	Warner Bros.	23875	'84	†
Unlimited	Reprise	25496	'87	CS/CD
Bridging the Gap	Reprise	26524	'91	CS/CD
Zapp and Roger				
All the Greatest Hits	Reprise	45143	'93	CD
The Sweat Band				
The Sweat Band	Uncle Jam	36857	'80	†
Funkadelic (Former Members)				
Connections and Disconnections	LAX	37087	'81	†
P-Funk All-Stars				
Urban Dancefloor Guerrillas	Uncle Jam	39168	'84	CS/CD
	CBS Associated	39168	'89	CD†
Live	Westbound	(2) 031		LP/CD
	Westbound	031		CS

THE CLOVERS

John "Buddy" Bailey (b. Dec. 27, 1931, Washington, D.C.), lead ten voc; **Matthew McQuarter** (b. 1924, Washington, D.C.), second ten voc; **Harold "Hal" Lucas** (b. Aug. 27, 1932; d. Jan. 6, 1994, Washington, D.C.), bar voc; **Harold Winley** (b. May 13, 1933, Washington, D.C.), bs voc; **Bill Harris** (d. Dec. 10, 1988), gtr

The most popular R&B vocal group of the first half of the '50s, the Clovers were one of the first such groups to be acknowledged as rock-and-roll artists, playing on Alan Freed's shows in 1954. Recording the classics "Blue Velvet," "Devil or Angel," and "Your Cash Ain't Nothin' but Trash" (later covered by white artists), the Clovers featured the accompaniment of some of the finest saxophone players in New York, and utilized twin lead tenor vocalists beginning in 1954, years before the Temptations adopted the practice.

Formed in 1946 in Washington, D.C., by Harold "Hal" Lucas, the group called themselves the Four Clovers after John "Buddy" Bailey joined the group. When Bill Harris joined in 1949, they officially became the Clovers. Signed to Atlantic Records after one single for Rainbow, the Clovers scored a string of top and smash R&B hits beginning in 1951 with "Don't You Know I Love You." Featuring saxophone accompaniment on up-tempo blues-based songs and the occasional ballad, they scored smash R&B hits with "Fool, Fool, Fool," "One Mint Julep" (covered by Ray Charles in 1961) backed with "Middle of the Night," "Ting-a-Ling" backed with "Wonder Where My Baby's Gone," "Hey Miss Fannie" (considered by some to be the first rock-and-roll record) backed with "I Played the Fool," and "Crawlin'." In 1952 Charlie White became the new lead while Bailey served a stint in the Army. White was featured on the hits "Good Lovin'," "Comin' On," and "Lovey Dovey" (covered by Buddy Knox in 1961) backed with "Little Mama."

In early 1954 the Clovers performed on Alan Freed's first rock-and-roll show. By April Charlie White had left, to be replaced by Billy Mitchell. When Bailey returned in the fall of 1954, the group began featuring twin lead tenors, Bailey and Hal Lucas. Subsequent R&B hits include "I've Got My Eyes on You" backed with the classic "Your Cash Ain't Nothin' but Trash" (covered by Steve Miller in 1974), "Blue Velvet" (covered by Bobby Vinton in 1963), "Nip Sip," and "Devil or Angel" (covered by Bobby Vee in 1960) backed with "Hey, Baby Doll." The Clovers scored their first major pop hit in 1956 with "Love, Love, Love," but their Atlantic contract expired in July 1957. They managed one final hit with "Love Potion No. 9" in late 1959. By the '70s at least two groups were touring as the Clovers, one led by Harold Winley, another by Hal Lucas. Bill Harris died of pancreatic cancer on December 10, 1988; Hal Lucas died of cancer on January 6, 1994.

The Clovers

The Clovers	Atlantic	1248		†
	Atlantic	8009	'57	†
Dance Party	Atlantic	8034	'59	†
Down in the Alley—The Best of the Clovers	Atlantic	82312	'91	CS/CD
In Clover	United Artists	6033		†
Love Potion Number Nine	United Artists	6099	'59	†
The Best of the Clovers: Love Potion No. 9	EMI	96336	'91	CS/CD

THE COASTERS

Carl Gardner (b. Apr. 29, 1928, Tyler, TX), lead voc; **Bobby Nunn** (b. June 25, 1925, Birmingham, AL; d. Nov. 5, 1986, Los Angeles, CA), bs voc; **Leon Hughes** (b. 1938), ten voc; **Billy Guy** (b. June 20, 1936, Hollywood, CA), lead and ten voc; **Adolph Jacobs**, gtr [Later members include **Young Jessie**, **Cornelius "Cornell" Gunter** (b. Nov. 14, 1936, Los Angeles, CA; d. Feb. 26, 1990), **Will "Dub" Jones**, and **Earl "Speedo" Carroll** (b. Nov. 2, 1937, New York, NY).]

Rock and roll's first consistently successful comedy-vocal group, the Coasters provided a number of wry and satirical songs of adolescent pathos under the direction of the premier '50s songwriting-production team, Jerry Leiber and Mike Stoller. One of the first R&B vocal groups to achieve widespread popularity with white youth, the Coasters' recordings featured the lusty saxophone playing of King Curtis, who helped establish the instrument as the third most important in rock and roll, behind guitar and piano.

The Coasters evolved out of the Robins, an R&B vocal group formed in Los Angeles in 1947. In early 1950 the group scored an R&B hit with "If It's So, Baby" with the Johnny Otis Band, and backed Esther Phillips on her top R&B hit "Double Crossing Blues." Songwriters Jerry Leiber and Mike Stoller began recording the group after the duo formed Spark Records in late 1953. The Robins enjoyed regional success with the classic "Riot in Cell Block Number 9," and had their first national hit with "Smokey Joe's Cafe" when the song was reissued on Atco in late 1955.

In 1955 Leiber and Stoller signed what was likely the first independent production deal with the Atco subsidiary of the New York–based Atlantic label. Atlantic acquired the Spark catalog, and the producers attempted to coax the Robins into joining them at the new label. Not all were willing, so Leiber and Stoller convinced Bobby Nunn and Carl Gardner to form a new group, the Coasters, with Leon Hughes, Billy Guy, and Adolph Jacobs. Their first single, "Down in Mexico," became a major R&B hit; their third single, "Youngblood"/"Searchin'," became a smash pop hit for the group and their songwriter-producers. Featured was the ribald saxophone playing of King Curtis, whose dynamic sound would grace virtually all their recordings.

Moving to New York in the fall of 1957, the Coasters replaced Leon Hughes first with Young Jessie, then with Cornelius Gunter; Will "Dub" Jones of the Cadets ("Stranded in the Jungle") replaced the retiring Bobby Nunn in early 1958. Through 1959 the group scored smash hits with "Yakety Yak," "Charlie Brown," "Along Came Jones," and "Poison Ivy," the songs most closely associated with the group. "Run Red Run"/"What About Us" and "Wake Me, Shake Me" proved only moderate successes, and the funky "Shoppin' for Clothes," featuring an unusually lewd saxophone break by King Curtis, fared even less well. The Coasters achieved their last major hit with "Little Egypt" in 1961, the year Earl "Speedo" Carroll of the Cadillacs ("Speedo") replaced Cornell Gunter.

The Coasters performed on various shows during the rock-and-roll revival of the early '70s. Several editions of the Coasters toured during the '80s, sometimes as many as four. The various leaders were Carl Gardner, Bobby Nunn, Leon Hughes, and Cornelius Gunter. Bobby Nunn died on November 5, 1986, of a heart attack in Los Angeles. The Coasters were inducted into the Rock and Roll Hall of Fame in 1987.

The Coasters

The Coasters	Atco	33-101	'58	†
Greatest Hits	Atco	33-111	'59	†
	Atco	33111		CS/CD
One by One	Atco	33-123	'60	†
Coast Along with the Coasters	Atco	33-135	'62	†
Greatest Recordings/The Early Years	Atco	33-371	'71	†
	Atco	33371		CS
It Ain't Sanitary	Trip	8028	'72	†
On Broadway	King	1146	'73	†
Greatest Hits	Power Pak	310	'78	†
Greatest Hits	Pair	1306	'91	CS/CD
50 Coastin' Hits	Rhino	(2) 71090	'92	CS/CD
Very Best	Rhino	71597	'94	CS/CD
The Ultimate Coasters	Warner	27604		CD
20 Greatest Hits	Deluxe	7786		CS/CD
Greatest Hits	Hollywood/IMG	282		CS/CD

EDDIE COCHRAN

(b. Oct. 3, 1938, Oklahoma City, OK; d. Apr. 17, 1960, Chippenham, Wiltshire, England)

One of rock music's first legends due to his early accidental death, Eddie Cochran was a distinguished guitarist and one of the first white rock-and-rollers. He helped pioneer the studio technique of overdubbing, particularly on his oft-covered classic 1958 smash, "Summertime Blues." Cochran's contribution to early rock was acknowledged by his 1987 induction into the Rock and Roll Hall of Fame.

Eddie Cochran moved with his family to Albert Lea, Minnesota, as an infant, and then to California when he was 11, settling in Bell Gardens in 1953. He began playing guitar at 12 and joined country singer Hank Cochran (no relation) as his backup guitarist in 1954. They toured and recorded as the Cochran Brothers until 1956. Switching to rock and roll after seeing Elvis Presley in Dallas in late 1955, Eddie Cochran met songwriter Jerry Capehart, who secured him a contract with Liberty Records. Cochran appeared with Gene Vincent and Little Richard in the 1957 film *The Girl Can't Help It*, performing the classic "Twenty Flight Rock." His first Liberty single, the tame "Sittin' in the Balcony," was a major hit in early 1957, but his next hit didn't come until the summer of 1958, when the classic "Summertime Blues" became a near-smash. For the recording, Cochran overdubbed his voice (some say), or his voice and all of the instruments (according to others). He toured tirelessly, yet his next single, the raucous "C'mon Everybody," proved only a moderate hit.

Like Gene Vincent, Cochran was far more popular in England, and in February 1960 he embarked on his only European tour. Upon completing the tour, while on his way to London airport, Eddie Cochran was killed in an auto crash in Chippenham, Wiltshire. Seriously injured in the crash were Gene Vincent and songwriting girlfriend Sharon Sheeley (author of Rick Nelson's "Poor Little Fool" and coauthor of Cochran's "Somethin' Else").

Eddie Cochran

Singin' to My Baby	Liberty	3061	'57	†
	Liberty	10137	'81	†
Eddie Cochran	Liberty	3172	'60	†
Never To Be Forgotten	Liberty	3220	'63	†
Singin' to My Baby/Never To Be Forgotten	EMI	80240	'93	CD
Summertime Blues	Sunset	1123	'58	†
Eddie Cochran	Sunset	5123	'69	†
Legendary Masters, Volume IV	United Artists	(2) 9959	'71	
(reissued as) Eddie Cochran	EMI	92809		CS/CD
Very Best (15th Anniversary Album)	United Artists	428	'75	†
The Early Years	Ace	237	'88	LP/CD
Greatest Hits	Curb/CEMA	77371	'90	CS/CD

JOE COCKER

(b. John Cocker, May 20, 1944, Sheffield, Yorkshire, England)

An English R&B vocal stylist whose jerky body movements brought him notoriety during the late '60s and early '70s, Joe Cocker achieved his biggest successes with his 1969 appearance at the Woodstock Festival and his 1970 Mad Dogs and Englishmen tour with Leon Russell and Rita Coolidge.

Joe Cocker formed his first band, The Cavaliers, in 1959. A day laborer with the gas company, Cocker continued to perform on a local, amateur basis. By 1963 he was the lead vocalist of Vance Arnold (his then-stage name) and the Avengers; the group toured with the

JOE COCKER

Hollies and the Rolling Stones. Cocker was offered a solo contract with Decca Records in 1964, resulting in a cover of the Beatles's "I'll Cry Instead," which did nothing on the charts. Returning to his work with the gas company, Cocker formed a new band with keyboardist and musical mentor Chris Stainton in 1965, later called the Grease Band. They scored a minor English hit in 1968 with Stainton's "Marjorine." The follow-up, a slow blues version of Lennon and McCartney's "With a Little Help from My Friends," became a top British and minor American hit. The song was culled from Cocker's debut album, which featured the band along with guest musicians such as Jimmy Page and Stevie Winwood; the album also included a driving version of Dave Mason's "Feelin' Alright."

In 1969 Cocker and Stainton gathered the Grease Band for a successful U.S. tour that culminated in Cocker's much-heralded appearance at Woodstock. During the tour he met session keyboardist Leon Russell, who later produced and played on *Joe Cocker!*, which yielded a minor hit with Russell's "Delta Lady" and a moderate hit with Lennon and McCartney's "She Came in Through the Bathroom Window." Russell subsequently assembled a 43-piece revue dubbed Mad Dogs and Englishmen, with a full horn section and vocal chorus (that included Rita Coolidge), for an enormously successful tour. The double record set of recordings from the tour eventually produced three hit singles: "The Letter," "Cry Me a River," and "Feelin' Alright." The tour launched the popular careers of Leon Russell and Rita Coolidge and marked the high point of Cocker's career.

Joe Cocker, from late 1972, yielded two major hits, "High Time We Went" and "Midnight Rider," and two minor hits, "Woman to Woman" and "Pardon Me Sir." Cocker's 1974 album, *I Can Stand a Little Rain*, was a virtual disaster, and he didn't hit again until 1975's "You Are So Beautiful," cowritten by Billy Preston. The mid-'70s were a tough time for Cocker personally, who suffered from alcoholism and drug abuse, and his performances became erratic at best. Dumped by A&M, Cocker switched in 1978 to Elektra and in 1982 to Island, where he scored a top hit with Jennifer Warnes on the love theme from the film *An Officer and a Gentleman*, "Where We Belong." By this time he had finally cleaned up his act, although he would never again achieve the popularity he had in the early '70s. By 1984 he had moved to Capitol, where he eventually had a major hit with "When the Night Comes." In 1994 Joe Cocker moved to 550 Music for the album *Have a Little Faith*.

Joe Cocker

With a Little Help from My Friends	A&M	4182	'69	†
	A&M	3106		CS/CD
Joe Cocker!	A&M	4224	'69	†
	A&M	3326	'89	CD
Mad Dogs and Englishmen	A&M	(2) 6002	'70	CD
	A&M	6002		CS
Joe Cocker	A&M	4368	'72	†
I Can Stand a Little Rain	A&M	3633	'74	†
	A&M	3175		CD†
Jamaica Say You Will	A&M	4529	'75	†
Stingray	A&M	4574	'76	†
Greatest Hits	A&M	4670	'77	†
	A&M	3257	'84	CS/CD
Joe Cocker	A&M	2503		CS/CD
Box Set	A&M	0018	'92	CD
Luxury You Can Afford	Asylum	145	'78	†
Sheffield Steel	Island	9750	'82	†
	Island	842476	'92	CD
	Mobile Fidelity	631	'95	CD
One More Time	Island	90096	'83	†
Civilized Man	Capitol	12335	'84	LP/CS/CD†
	Capitol	46038		CS/CD
Cocker	Capitol	12394	'86	LP/CS/CD†
	Capitol	46268		CS/CD
Unchain My Heart	Capitol	48285	'87	CS/CD
One Night of Sin	Capitol	92861	'89	CS/CD
Joe Cocker Live!	Capitol	93416	'90	CS/CD
Night Calls	Capitol	97801	'92	CS/CD
Best	Capitol	81243	'93	CS/CD
Have a Little Faith	550 Music	66460	'94	CS/CD

LEONARD COHEN
(b. Sept. 21, 1934, Montreal, Canada)

A Canadian-born poet and novelist who has recorded as a singer-songwriter, Leonard Cohen was one of the most powerful song-poets to emerge in the '60s. Despite the limited musical effectiveness of his gruffy, monotonic voice and sparse musical settings, his poetics, legitimately described as brooding and gloomy, even depressing, more than compensate, inasmuch as his lyrics ultimately succeed through the underlying intensity of their humanity. One of the first artists to bring a spiritual and poetic sensibility to rock music, Cohen endured years as a cult figure before emerging as a contemporary force with 1988's *I'm Your Man*.

Leonard Cohen studied English literature at McGill and Columbia universities and published his first book of poetry in 1956. During the '60s he published a number of books of poetry as well as two novels, *The Favorite Game* (1963) and *Beautiful Losers* (1966). The second became standard college literary fare and sold more than 300,000 copies.

Taught the classics of music as a child, Leonard Cohen began playing guitar and singing at 15 and performed with a barn-dance group called the Buckskin Boys during his late teens. He started writing songs around 1964, but received little popular acclaim until Judy Collins recorded one of his most romantic compositions, "Suzanne," for her 1966 *In My Life* album. Launching his performing career that year, Cohen built a musical reputation through appearances at the Newport Folk Festival and New York's Central Park (with Collins) in 1967. Signed to Columbia Records, his debut album included "Suzanne," the alienated "Stranger Song," the sorrowful "Hey, That's No Way to Say Goodbye," and the compassionate "Sisters of Mercy." The latter three songs had appeared on Collins's *Wildflower* album. In 1969 Cohen successfully toured North America and Europe and issued *Songs from a Room*, which contained "The Story of Isaac," "Tonight Will Be Fine," and the oft-recorded classic "Bird on a Wire." Retiring from public performance at the end of 1970, he released *Songs of Love and Hate* the following year. It contained "Famous Blue Raincoat," "Joan of Arc," "Dress Rehearsal Rag," "Diamonds in the Mine," and "Love Calls You by Your Name." He also provided the songs for the soundtrack to the 1971 Robert Altman film *McCabe and Mrs. Miller*.

Leonard Cohen withdrew from the spotlight in the early '70s, recording only sporadically over the next decade. He continued to write, publishing another volume of poetry, *The Energy of Slaves*, in 1972. An album of new material, *New Skin for the Old Ceremony*, was issued in 1974, and he toured again in 1975. Cohen collaborated with songwriter-producer Phil Spector for the less-than-successful *Death of a Ladies Man* in 1977, followed by a return to form on *Recent Songs* in 1979.

In 1986 longtime associate Jennifer Warnes recorded an entire album of Leonard Cohen songs, *Famous Blue Raincoat*. The album sold quite well and revived interest in his material. Already well established in Europe, Cohen's 1988 *I'm Your Man* sold spectacularly in Europe and reawakened interest in his songs in North America. Hailed as a masterpiece, the album contained a number of haunting, compelling songs, such as "First We Take Manhattan," "Ain't No Cure for Love," and "Take This Waltz." The less impressive follow-up, *The Future*, included "Democracy," "Light as a Breeze," and "Waiting for a Miracle." Contemporary alternative artists such as R.E.M., Nick Cave, and the Pixies paid tribute to Cohen with the 1991 tribute album *I'm Your Fan*. In 1993 the book *Stranger Music: Selected Poems and Songs* assembled his poems, prose, and lyrics. A live concert album was issued in 1994.

Leonard Cohen

Songs of Leonard Cohen	Columbia	9533	'68	CS/CD
Songs from a Room	Columbia	9767	'69/'90	CD
Songs of Love and Hate	Columbia	30103	'71	CS
Live Songs	Columbia	31724	'73	†
New Skin for the Old Ceremony	Columbia	33167	'74	†
Best	Columbia	34077	'76	CS/CD
Death of a Ladies Man	Warner Bros.	3125	'77	†
	Columbia	44286	'88	CD
Recent Songs	Columbia	36264	'79	CD
I'm Your Man	Columbia	44191	'88	CS/CD
The Future	Columbia	53226	'92	CS/CD
Cohen Live—Leonard Cohen in Concert	Columbia	66327	'94	CS/CD

Jennifer Warnes

Famous Blue Raincoat: The Songs of Leonard Cohen	Cypress	0100	'86	LP/CS/CD†
	Private Music	82092	'91	CS/CD

Tribute Albums

I'm Your Fan—The Songs of Leonard Cohen	Atlantic	82349	'91	CS/CD
Tower of Song: The Songs of Leonard Cohen	A&M	0259	'95	CS/CD

JUDY COLLINS

(b. May 1, 1939, Seattle, WA)

As a guitarist, pianist, and singer with a clear soprano voice, Judy Collins, along with Joan Baez, set the standard for female folk artists in the early to mid-'60s. Popular as a protest singer in her early career, Collins demonstrated impeccable taste in her selection of material, popularizing the songs of then-obscure songwriters such as Gordon Lightfoot, Joni Mitchell, Randy Newman, and Leonard Cohen. Her hit recordings of Cohen's "Suzanne" and Mitchell's "Both Sides Now" were largely responsible for their subsequent careers. By the late '60s she began writing her own songs, and with the mid-'70s success of her cover version of Stephen Sondheim's "Send in the Clowns," Collins became a contemporary pop star.

Judy Collins moved as a child first to Los Angeles, then to Denver, Colorado, with her family. She began classical piano lessons at age five, and studied for eight years under female symphony conductor Antonia Brico. Making her classical piano debut at 13, she took up guitar at 15 and began singing in Boulder, Colorado, folk clubs at 19. At the beginning of the '60s Collins moved to New York, where she immersed herself in the burgeoning Greenwich Village folk music scene. Signed to Elektra Records in 1961, she recorded two albums of standard folk fare before recording protest songs such as "Masters of War" and "Deportees." She subsequently began recording the songs of young Village songwriters. Her *Concert* album contained Tom Paxton's "The Last Thing on My Mind," and her *Fifth Album* included Richard Farina's "Pack Up Your Sorrows," Eric Andersen's "Thirsty Boots," Gordon Lightfoot's "Early Morning Rain," as well as three Bob Dylan songs.

With *In My Life* Collins broke away from the folk-singer role and established herself as a performer of a wide range of contemporary material. The album contained Dylan's "Tom Thumb's Blues," Farina's "Hard Lovin' Loser" (her first, albeit minor, hit), Randy Newman's "I Think It's Gonna Rain Today," and two Leonard Cohen songs. The popularity of one of those songs, "Suzanne," effectively launched the musical career of Cohen. *Wildflowers*, her next album, featured lush arrangements by classical composer Joshua Rifkin and included two of her own songs plus two more Cohen songs, and two songs by Joni Mitchell. One of these, "Both Sides Now," became Collins's first major hit and spurred Mitchell's career. *Who Knows Where the Time Goes* continued the presentation of outstanding contemporary material with the inclusion of Cohen's "Bird on a Wire," Robin Williamson's "The First Boy (Girl) I Loved," Ian Tyson's "Someday Soon," and Sandy Denny's title song.

After *Whales and Nightingales*, which yielded her second major hit with the traditional gospel song "Amazing Grace," and two other albums, Judy Collins withdrew from music to produce and codirect a documentary film on the life of her former piano teacher, Antonia Brico. The film, entitled *Antonia: A Portrait of the Woman*, premiered in September 1974 and garnered an Academy Award in 1975.

Collins moved fully into the pop field with her recording of Stephen Sondheim's "Send in the Clowns," a moderate hit in 1975 and a major hit upon rerelease in 1977. She achieved a minor hit with "Hard Time for Lovers" in 1979, the year she debuted in the Las Vegas casino milieu. She performed six months a year, appearing with symphony orchestras and at concerts and supper clubs around the country. Following 1984's *Home Again*, Elektra Records dropped Collins from its roster. She subsequently recorded two albums for the small Gold Castle label, including *Trust Your Heart*, which also served as the title to her autobiography. In 1990 Judy Collins switched to Columbia for *Fires of Eden*, moving to Geffen for 1993's *Judy Sings Dylan*. In 1995, in an unusual arrangement, Collins issued her first novel, *Shameless,* a piece of romantic fiction, along with an album of songs designed to accompany the reading of the book.

Judy Collins

| A Maid of Constant Sorrow | Elektra | 7209 | '61 | † |

Golden Apples of the Sun	Elektra	7222	'62	†
#3	Elcktra	7243	'63	I
Concert	Elektra	7280	'64	†
Fifth Album	Elektra	7300	'65	CD
In My Life	Elektra	7320	'66	†
	Elektra	74027		CS/CD
Wildflowers	Elektra	74012	'67	CS/CD
Who Knows Where the Time Goes	Elektra	74033	'68	CS/CD
Recollections	Elektra	74055	'69	†
	Elektra	61350	'92	CD
Whales and Nightingales	Elektra	75010	'70	CS/CD
Living	Elektra	75014	'71	CD
Colors of the Day	Elektra	75030	'72	CS/CD
True Stories and Other Dreams	Elektra	75053	'73	CS/CD
Judith	Elektra	1032	'75	†
	Elektra	111		CS/CD
Bread and Roses	Elektra	1076	'76	CS/CD
So Early in the Spring: The First Fifteen Years	Elektra	(2) 6002	'77	†
	Elektra	6002		CS
Hard Time for Lovers	Elektra	171	'79	CS/CD
Running for My Life	Elektra	253	'80	CS/CD
Times of Our Lives	Elektra	60001	'82	CS/CD
Home Again	Elektra	60304	'84	CS/CD
False True Lovers	Folkways	3564	'67	†
Trust Your Heart	Gold Castle	71302	'87	LP/CS/CD†
Sanity and Grace	Gold Castle	71318	'89	LP/CS/CD†
Fires of Eden	Columbia	46102	'90	CS/CD
Judy Sings Dylan: Just Like a Woman	Geffen	24612	'93	CS/CD
Come Rejoice! A Judy Collins Christmas	Mesa	79085	'94	CS/CD
Shameless	Mesa	92584	'95	CS/CD

Judy Collins and Richard Stoltzman

Innervoices	RCA	7888	'89	CS/CD

COMMANDER CODY AND HIS LOST PLANET AIRMEN

Commander Cody (b. George Frayne IV, July 19, 1944, Boise, ID), kybd, voc; **Billy C. Far-low** (b. Decatur, AL), lead voc, har; **Bill Kirchen** (b. Jan. 29, 1948, Ann Arbor, MI), lead gtr, voc; **Bobby Black**, pedal steel gtr, voc; **Andy Stein** (b. Aug. 31, 1948, New York, NY), vln, sax; **John Tichy** (b. St. Louis, MO), gtr; **Bruce Barlow** (b. Dec. 3, 1948, Oxnard, CA), bs, voc; **Lance Dickerson** (b. Oct. 15, 1948, Livonia, MI), drm, voc

A '70s American band that was instrumental in turning hippies on to country music, Commander Cody and His Lost Planet Airmen played a refreshing mixture of rock-and-roll classics, country-and-western standards, and engaging originals. Initially formed in Ann Arbor, Michigan, in 1967 through the merger of the bands of George Frayne, also known as Commander Cody, and Billy C. Farlow, Commander Cody and His Lost Planet Airmen moved to Berkeley, California, in 1968 and added fiddle and steel guitar. Building a devoted local following, the group signed with Paramount Records in 1971. Their debut album, *Lost in the Ozone*, yielded a minor hit with "Beat Me Daddy Eight to the Bar" and a near-smash with a remake of 1960's "Hot Rod Lincoln." It also included the favorites "Seeds and Stems

(Again)" and the title track. The band's *Hot Licks* album contained other nuggets such as "Looking at the World Through a Windshield" and "Mama Hated Diesels."

After *Live from Deep in the Heart of Texas* the band switched to Warner Bros. for three albums before breaking up in 1976. Recording two albums for Arista in the late '70s, Commander Cody eventually returned with *Let's Rock* for the small San Francisco–based Blind Pig label in 1986. Cody continued to lead a group under the Lost Planet Airmen moniker on the oldies circuit, and has achieved some success as a painter. Bill Kirchen formed his own group, The Moonlighters, in the late '70s, and subsequently worked with British retrorocker, Nick Lowe, touring with him in 1995.

Commander Cody and His Lost Planet Airmen

Lost in the Ozone	Paramount	6017	'71	†
	MCA	1633		CS
	MCA	31185		CD
Hot Licks, Cold Steel and Trucker's Favorites	Paramount	6031	'72	†
	MCA	31186		CD
Country Casanova	Paramount	6054	'73	†
	MCA	661	'89	CD
Live from Deep in the Heart of Texas	Paramount	1017	'74	†
	MCA	659	'90	CD
Too Much Fun: The Best of Commander Cody and His Lost Planet Airmen	MCA	10092	'92	CD
Commander Cody and His Lost Planet Airmen	Warner Bros.	2847	'75	†
Tales from the Ozone	Warner Bros.	2883	'75	†
We've Got a Live One Here	Warner Bros.	(2) 2939	'76	†
Sleazy Roadside Stories	Relix	2028		CS/CD
The Moonlighters				
The Moonlighters	Amherst	1009	'77	†
The Commander Cody Band				
Rock and Roll Again	Arista	4125	'77	†
Commander Cody				
Flying Dreams	Arista	4183	'78	†
Let's Rock	Blind Pig	2086	'86	LP/CS
Aces High	Relix	2041		CS/CD

RY COODER
(b. Mar. 15, 1947, Los Angeles, CA)

Arguably the best all-around guitarist in rock music, Ry Cooder has played innumerable sessions and recorded a series of modest-selling albums that explored a diverse set of material, from folk to blues, from country to gospel and rock, as well as Dixieland and Tex-Mex and Hawaiian music. An outstanding bottleneck guitarist, Cooder won his first widespread acclaim as lead guitarist with Little Village, along with fellow musical iconoclasts Nick Lowe and John Hiatt.

Ry Cooder took up guitar at age 10 and began frequenting Los Angeles's Ash Groove folk club as a teenager. Self-taught on mandolin, banjo, and bottleneck guitar, Cooder briefly worked with singer-songwriter Jackie De Shannon in 1963 and formed the Rising Sons with Taj Mahal and Jesse Ed Davis in 1965. The group recorded one single for Columbia before breaking up. Cooder subsequently joined Captain Beefheart, recording on his album *Safe as Milk* and performing on one tour before pursuing session work with Taj Mahal, Neil Young, Paul Revere and the Raiders, the Rolling Stones, Longbranch Penny-whistle (with J. D. Souther and future Eagle Glenn Frey), Randy Newman, and Gordon Lightfoot, among others.

Signed to Reprise Records, Ry Cooder initiated his solo recording career with a self-named debut album. Through 1972 he recorded two more solo albums and worked on the debut albums of Little Feat, Rita Coolidge, and Crazy Horse. He also assisted the Rolling Stones with the recordings of the soundtrack *Performance*, *Sticky Fingers*, and *Jammin' with Edward*. Cooder began working with gospel singer Bobby King, who guested on Cooder's classic album *Paradise and Lunch*, which featured "Mexican Divorce," "If Walls Could Talk," and "Jesus on the Mainline." Terry Evans joined Bobby King for gospel backups for *Chicken Skin Music*, which included Cooder's idols Hawaiian guitarist Gabby Pahinui on two songs and Tex-Mex accordionist Flaco Jimenez on three others. Cooder's session work continued with Randy Newman, Arlo Guthrie, Maria Muldaur, John Sebastian, and Gabby Pahinui.

Cooder made a series of radical changes in style, beginning with his album *Jazz*, which explored Dixieland. The follow-up *Bop Till You Drop* celebrated early rock and roll. It was probably Cooder's best-seller, featuring another guitar god, David Lindley, and including the favorites "Little Sister," "The Very Thing That Makes You Rich," and "Down in Hollywood," cowritten by Cooder. Cooder returned to an eclectic mixture of material on his next two albums, *Borderline*, which featured John Hiatt's "The Way We Make a Broken Heart" and Cooder's title song, and *The Slide Area*, which included two songs written by Cooder and session drummer Jim Keltner (most notably "I'm Drinking Again") and three others cowritten by Cooder.

During the '80s Ry Cooder found a new outlet for his talents: composing, arranging, and performing soundtracks for films, including *The Long Riders* (1980), *The Border* (1982), *Paris, Texas* and *Alamo Bay* (1985), *Blue City* and *Crossroads* (1986), and *Johnny Handsome* (1989). In 1983 he guested on Eric Clapton's *Money and Cigarettes* album and subsequent tour, inspiring some of Clapton's best guitar playing in a number of years. In 1987 Cooder joined Nick Lowe and Jim Keltner in the recording of John Hiatt's breakthrough album, *Bring the Family*. The following year backup gospel singers Bobby King and Terry Evans began recording for Rounder Records. After more than 25 years of recording, Ry Cooder finally received a modicum of recognition with the group, tour, and album *Little Village*, a collaborative effort recorded with Hiatt, Lowe, and Keltner. However, the band soon dissolved due to the clash of egos among the individual members. Cooder next recorded the outstanding *Talking Timbuktu* with Ali Farka Touré from the African nation of Mali, a unique cross-cultural exploration.

The Rising Sons

The Rising Sons Featuring Taj Mahal and Ry Cooder	Columbia/Legacy	52828	'92	CS/CD

Ry Cooder

Ry Cooder	Reprise	6402	'70	†
	Warner Bros.	27510	'95	CD
Into the Purple Valley	Reprise	2052	'71	CS/CD
Boomer's Story	Reprise	2117	'72	†
	Reprise	26398	'91	CD
Paradise and Lunch	Reprise	2179	'74	CS/CD
Chicken Skin Music	Reprise	2254	'76	CS/CD
Showtime	Warner Bros.	3059	'77	†
Jazz	Warner Bros.	3197	'78	CS/CD
Bop Till You Drop	Warner Bros.	3358	'79	CS/CD
Borderline	Warner Bros.	3489	'80	CS/CD

The Slide Area	Warner Bros.	3651	'82	CS/CD
Get Rhythm	Warner Bros.	25639	'87	CS/CD
Ry Cooder Soundtracks				
Paris, Texas	Warner Bros.	25270	'85	LP/CS/CD
Blue City	Warner Bros.	25386	'86	LP/CS
Crossroads	Warner Bros.	25399	'86	CS/CD
Johnny Handsome	Warner Bros.	25996	'89	CS/CD
Trespass	Sire	26978	'92	LP/CS/CD
Geronimo	Columbia	57760	'93	CS/CD
Music by Ry Cooder	Warner Bros.	(2) 45987	'95	CS/CD
Bobby King and Terry Evans				
Live and Let Live!	Rounder	2089	'88	LP/CS/CD
Rhythm, Blues, Soul and Grooves	Rounder	2101	'90	LP/CS/CD
Terry Evans				
Blues for Thought	Pointblank/Charisma	39064	'94	CS/CD
Puttin' It Down	Audioquest	1038	'95	CD
Little Village				
Little Village	Reprise	26713	'92	CS/CD
Ali Farka Touré with Ry Cooder				
Talking Timbuktu	Hannibal	1381	'94	CS/CD

SAM COOKE

(b. Jan. 2, 1931, Clarksdale, MS [although some claim Jan. 2, 1935, Chicago, IL]; d. Dec. 11, 1964, Los Angeles, CA)

One of the most popular and influential black singers to emerge in the late '50s, Sam Cooke was one of the first African-American recording artists to successfully synthesize a blend of gospel and pop musics. Eschewing the harsher shouting style of Ray Charles and emphasizing his high, clear, sensual tenor voice, Cooke helped establish the soul sound that influenced singers from Smokey Robinson to Otis Redding, Aretha Franklin to Al Green, and British singers such as Mick Jagger and Rod Stewart. Along with James Brown, Sam Cooke was one of the first black artists to write his own songs and gain total control over his recording career (he even founded two record labels), and he demonstrated an early sense of social consciousness with the song "A Change Is Gonna Come."

Raised in Chicago, the son of Reverend Charles Cooke, Sam Cooke was a member of a family gospel quartet known as the Singing Children by age nine. While still in high school he performed with one of his brothers in the gospel group the Highway Q.C.s, where his vocals soon attracted attention among more seasoned groups, including the Chicago-based Soul Stirrers, one of the best-known groups on the gospel circuit. Cooke was invited to join the Soul Stirrers as lead vocalist around 1950, remaining with them until 1956 (to be replaced by Johnnie Taylor, who later enjoyed his own secular career, topped by 1968's "Who's Making Love"). Cooke made his first successful recordings with the Stirrers and established a fanatical following thanks to the many live performances that the group made.

After leaving the Stirrers, Cooke briefly manned the Pilgrim Travelers with Lou Rawls while also embarking on a solo career. In 1956 Cooke began recording pop material for Specialty Records, initially as Dale Cook (to avoid alienating the gospel audience who might be upset by his tackling secular material). In late 1957 he scored a top R&B and pop hit on Keen Records with "You Send Me," written by his brother Charles "L.C." Cooke.

Subsequent major hits through 1960 included "I'll Come Running Back to You" on Specialty and "You Were Made for Me," "Win Your Love for Me," "Everybody Loves to Cha Cha Cha," the classic "Only Sixteen," and "Wonderful World" on Keen.

In 1959 Sam Cooke formed his own record labels SAR and Derby Records and accepted a lucrative offer to join RCA Records. Initially recorded with cloying pop arrangements featuring strings and horns, he scored a series of hits between 1960 and 1964, including the smashes "Chain Gang," "Twistin' the Night Away," and "Another Saturday Night." Other hits of the period were "Cupid," "Bring It on Home to Me" backed with "Having a Party," "Nothing Can Change This Love," "Send Me Some Lovin'," "(Ain't That) Good News," and "Good Times." Hits on his own labels included "Soothe Me" by the Sims Twins (1961), "Meet Me at the Twistin' Place" by Johnnie Morisette (1962), and "Lookin' for a Love" by the Valentinos (1962; covered by the J. Geils Band in 1972) on SAR, and "When a Boy Falls in Love" by Mel Carter (1963) on Derby. Cooke became a fixture on the supper-club/Las Vegas circuit, and his performances suffered both in his choice of material and their annoying popish accompaniments, as shown on his 1964 *Live at the Copa* album; a far more representative set, *Feel It! Live at the Harlem Square Club, 1963*, was eventually released in 1985, showing that at the right venue Cooke could still give a dynamic performance.

Sam Cooke's career was secure by 1964, with much promise for the future, but on December 11 of that year he was shot to death in Los Angeles. The circumstances of his death are shrouded in mystery. Although the case was settled as a "justifiable homicide," questions linger about the real details of Cooke's killing. Posthumously, his "Shake" (covered by Otis Redding in 1967) became a near-smash hit in 1965, followed by his most enduring composition, "A Change Is Gonna Come," only a few days later. In 1985 RCA issued the excellent live set *Live at the Harlem Square Club*, and in 1994 Abkco issued gospel and soul recordings made in the early '60s for Cooke's SAR Records. Cooke was among the first inductees into the Rock and Roll Hall of Fame in 1986; the Soul Stirrers were inducted three years later.

Sam Cooke and the Soul Stirrers

In the Beginning	Ace	280		CD
Sam Cooke and the Soul Stirrers	Specialty	2106	'59	LP/CS
The Gospel Soul of Sam Cooke, Volume 1	Specialty	2116	'70	LP/CS
The Gospel Soul of Sam Cooke, Volume 2	Specialty	2128	'71	LP/CS
The Original Soul Stirrers	Specialty	2137	'71	LP/CS
That's Heaven to Me	Specialty	2146	'72	LP/CS
Sam Cooke and the Soul Stirrers	Specialty	7009	'91	CD
Jesus Gave Me Water	Specialty	7031	'93	CD
Heaven Is My Home	Specialty	7040	'93	CD
The Last Mile of the Way	Specialty	7052	'94	CD

Sam Cooke

Two Sides of Sam Cooke	Specialty	2119	'69	LP/CS/CD
Sam Cooke Sings	Keen	2001	'58	†
Encore	Keen	2003		†
Tribute to the Lady	Keen	2004		†
Hit Kit	Keen	86101		†
I Thank God	Keen	86103		†
Wonderful World	Keen	86106	'61	†
Sam's Songs	Famous	502		†
Only Sixteen	Famous	505		†
So Wonderful	Famous	508		†
You Send Me	Famous	509		†
Right On	Cherie	1001		†

Cooke's Tour	RCA	2221	'60	†
Hits of the '50s	RCA	2236	'60	†
Sam Cooke	RCA	2293	'61	†
My Kind of Blues	RCA	2392	'61	†
Twistin' the Night Away	RCA	2555	'62	†
Best	RCA	2625	'62	†
	RCA	3863		LP/CS/CD
Mister Soul	RCA	2673	'63	†
Night Beat	RCA	2709	'63	†
	Abkco	1124	'95	LP/CS/CD
Feel It! Live at the Harlem Square Club, 1963	RCA	5181	'85	CS/CD
At the Copa	RCA	2970	'64	†
	RCA	2658	'78	†
	Abkco	2970	'88	LP/CS/CD
Shake	RCA	3367	'65	†
Best, Volume 2	RCA	3373	'65	†
Try a Little Love	RCA	3435	'65	†
The Unforgettable Sam Cooke	RCA	3517	'66	†
The Man Who Invented Soul	RCA	3991	'68	†
This Is Sam Cooke	RCA	(2) 6027	'70	†
Interprets Billie Holiday	RCA	0899	'75	†
The Man and His Music	RCA	(2) 7127	'86	LP/CS
	RCA	7127	'86	CD
One and Only	Camden	2264	'68	CS
Sam Cooke	Camden	2433	'70	†
The Unforgettable Sam Cooke	Camden	2610	'73	CS
You Send Me	Camden	0445	'75	†
Golden Sound	Trip	(2) 8030	'73	†
Sings the Billie Holiday Story	Up Front	160	'73	†
You Send Me	Pair	1006	'86	CD
An Original	Pair	1186		CD
SAR Records				
Sam Cooke's SAR Records Story	Abkco	(2) 2231	'94	CD

RITA COOLIDGE
(b. May 1, 1944, Nashville, TN)

A vocalist-pianist who emerged from session work, Rita Coolidge toured with Delaney and Bonnie and Joe Cocker's infamous Mad Dogs and Englishmen tour before launching a solo career as a cover artist. Known as the Delta Lady (Leon Russell wrote the song for her), Coolidge collaborated with and was married to Kris Kristofferson from 1973 to 1980.

Rita Coolidge and her sisters Priscilla and Linda grew up in Lafayette, Tennessee. The sisters began performing in high school, and Priscilla and Rita moved to Los Angeles in 1968. Priscilla later married Booker T. Jones, while Rita met producer Leon Russell and folk-rock singers Delaney and Bonnie. Over the next two years she recorded with Delaney and Bonnie, Russell, Joe Cocker, Eric Clapton, Steve Stills, and Dave Mason as a backup vocalist. She toured several times with Delaney and Bonnie and became a member of the Mad Dogs and Englishmen—Joe Cocker tour of the United States and Europe. On that tour she performed the Delaney Bramlett—Leon Russell composition "Superstar," later popularized by the Carpenters. Signed to A&M Records in late 1970, Coolidge recorded a number of excellent songs by Marc Benno on her early albums, including "Second Story Window," "(I Always Called Them) Mountains," "Nice Feelin'," and "Inside of Me." In 1973 she married and toured and recorded with Kris Kristofferson. Their *Full Moon* album contained a number of fine compositions such as "I Never Had It So Good," "Take Time to Love," and "Loving Arms," a minor hit. They later recorded *Breakaway* (1974) and *Natural Act* (1979).

Rita Coolidge achieved her greatest success with her *Anytime . . . Anywhere* album, scoring three hits with Jackie Wilson's "Higher and Higher," Boz Scaggs's "We're All Alone," and the Motown classic "The Way You Do the Things You Do." Later hits included 1979's "I'd Rather Leave While I'm in Love" and 1983's "All Time High," but by the late '80s she was without a record label. For a while Coolidge pursued a country career, after her laid-back vocal style became passé on the pop/rock charts. In 1992 Rita Coolidge returned to recording with *Love Sessions* for Critique/Caliber. The album included a duet with Lee Greenwood, "Heart Don't Fail Me Now," which was used as the love theme for the CBS television soap opera *As the World Turns*, and "Cherokee," a tribute to her half-Cherokee father, sung with her sister Priscilla.

Rita Coolidge

Rita Coolidge	A&M	4291	'71	†
	A&M	3107		†
Nice Feelin'	A&M	4325	'71	†
	A&M	3130		†
The Lady's Not for Sale	A&M	4370	'72	†
Fall into Spring	A&M	3627	'74	†
It's Only Love	A&M	4531	'75	†
Anytime . . . Anywhere	A&M	4616	'77	†
Love Me Again	A&M	4699	'78	†
Satisfied	A&M	4781	'79	†
Greatest Hits	A&M	4836	'81	†
	A&M	3238	'84	CS/CD
Heartbreak Radio	A&M	3727	'81	†
Never Let You Go	A&M	4914	'83	†
Inside the Fire	A&M	5003	'84	†
Rita Coolidge	A&M	2504		CD
Love Sessions	Critique/Caliber	15410	'92	CS/CD

Rita Coolidge and Kris Kristofferson

Full Moon	A&M	4403	'73	†
Natural Act	A&M	4690	'79	†
Breakaway	Monument/Columbia	33278	'74	†
	Monument	47065	'91	CS/CD

ALICE COOPER

Alice Cooper (b. Vincent Furnier, Feb. 4, 1948, Detroit, MI), lead voc; **Glen Buxton** (b. June 17, 1947, Washington, D.C.), lead gtr; **Michael Bruce** (b. Nov. 21, 1948, CA), gtr, kybd; **Dennis Dunaway** (b. Mar. 15, 1946, Cottage Grove, OR), bs; **Neal Smith** (b. Jan. 10, 1946, Washington, D.C.), drm

Both the name of the '70s rock group and the pseudonym of its protagonist-vocalist, Alice Cooper established their reputation through the onstage simulation of acts of violence. Group leader Cooper, often dressed in clothes intended to suggest bisexuality and transvestism, acted out such fantasies as necrophilia, infanticide, and execution. Initially rejected

ALICE COOPER

en masse by audiences, the group cultivated a perverse and repulsive image, and profited from sensationalized adverse publicity. Thus Alice Cooper became the first rock act to achieve widespread popularity *because of* a carefully perpetrated distasteful image, predating the wave of late-'70s punk groups and antedated by groups such as Iggy Pop and the Stooges. Moreover, Alice Cooper was one of the first rock acts to utilize extravagant stage sets, and group leader Cooper was one of the first to use garish makeup, both practices taken up by groups from Kiss to Gwar. The group did produce a number of classic rock songs with "Eighteen," "School's Out," "Elected," and "No More Mr. Nice Guy." Protagonist Cooper disbanded the group in 1974 and assembled a new group for his classic *Welcome to My Nightmare* tour of 1975. Out of action for much of the '80s, Alice Cooper staged a remarkable comeback with his 1989 *Trash* album and tour. He also made a humorous appearance in the 1992 film *Wayne's World*, in which he parodied his badder-than-bad image.

Group protagonist Vincent Furnier traveled extensively with his family in early childhood, eventually settling in Phoenix, Arizona, in the early '60s. In 1964, while still in high school, he formed his first band, the Earwigs, with friends Glen Buxton and Dennis Dunaway. By fall 1965 the group had changed its name to the Spiders and added Michael Bruce. Playing local engagements in 1966, the band next adopted the name the Nazz and added Neal Smith.

Making forays into Los Angeles in search of club dates and a recording contract, the group again changed its name when they discovered that a Philadelphia band led by Todd Rundgren was also using the name the Nazz. Vincent Furnier became Alice Cooper and the group as a whole took on the name. They achieved their first notoriety in Los Angeles by performing at a memorial birthday party for the controversial comedian Lenny Bruce. Thousands of people left the show shortly after the band took the stage, but two important individuals stayed: Frank Zappa and Shep Gordon. Zappa signed Alice Cooper to his new label, Straight Records, and Gordon became the group's manager. They moved to Los Angeles in 1968, but their first two albums were virtually ignored.

Alice Cooper moved to Detroit in 1969, and during 1970 the group began playing engagements across the country. Switching to Warner Bros. Records, the group scored their first major hit with the alienated "Eighteen." Receiving intense publicity for their outrageous stage act, the group achieved a near-smash with 1972's "School's Out." *Billion Dollar Babies* in 1973 yielded the hits "Elected," "Hello, Hurray," and "No More Mr. Nice Guy." Their subsequent tour was one of the biggest moneymakers of its time.

Unable to match the Billion Dollar Babies tour, Cooper disbanded the group in 1974, replacing them with musicians who had earlier backed Lou Reed. Cooper switched to Atlantic Records for 1975's *Welcome to My Nightmare*, which formed the basis for an hour-long television special and perhaps the definitive tour of his career. The album yielded a major hit with the uncharacteristic ballad "Only Women (Bleed)." Cooper returned to Warner Bros., scoring other mid-'70s hits including the ballads "I Never Cry" and "You and Me." In 1978 Cooper served a stint in a psychiatric hospital for treatment for chronic alcoholism, and the experience served as the basis for his *From the Inside* album of the same year, and his Madhouse Rock tour.

Weary from years of touring and inundated by the wave of disco groups then popular, Alice Cooper withdrew from the music scene in 1980. He eventually reemerged in 1986 with a new band and a new record label, MCA. The comeback failed, but in 1989 he proved successful, scoring a near-smash with "Poison" from *Trash*, his best-selling album in more than a decade.

Alice Cooper

Live at the Whisky	Bizarre/Straight	70369	'92	CS/CD
Pretties for You	Straight	1051	'69	†
	Warner Bros.	1840	'70	†
	Bizarre/Straight	70351	'91	CS/CD
Easy Action	Straight	1845	'70	†
	Bizarre/Straight	70350	'91	CS/CD
Love It to Death	Warner Bros.	1883	'71	CS/CD
Killer	Warner Bros.	2567	'71	CS/CD
School's Out	Warner Bros.	2623	'72	CS/CD
Billion Dollar Babies	Warner Bros.	2685	'73	CS/CD
Muscle of Love	Warner Bros.	2748	'73	†
	Metal Blade/WB	26447	'90	CS/CD
Greatest Hits	Warner Bros.	2803	'74	†
	Warner Bros.	3107		CS/CD
Welcome to My Nightmare	Atlantic	18130	'75	†
	Atlantic	19157		CS/CD
Alice Cooper Goes to Hell	Warner Bros.	2896	'76	CS/CD
Lace and Whiskey	Warner Bros.	3027	'77	†
	Metal Blade/WB	26446	'90	CS/CD
The Alice Cooper Show	Warner Bros.	3138	'77	CS/CD
From the Inside	Warner Bros.	3263	'78	†
	Metal Blade/WB	26445	'90	CS/CD
Flush the Fashion	Warner Bros.	3436	'80	†
Special Forces	Warner Bros.	3581	'81	†
Zipper Catches Skin	Warner Bros.	23719	'82	†
Da Da	Warner Bros.	23969	'83	†
Constrictor	MCA	5761	'86	CS
Raise Your Fist and Yell	MCA	42091	'87	CS/CD
Prince of Darkness	MCA	42315	'89	CS/CD
Trash	Epic	45137	'89	LP/CS/CD
Hey Stoopid	Epic	46786	'91	LP/CS/CD
The Last Temptation	Epic	52771	'94	CS/CD
The Last Temptation: Comic Book Version	Epic	66196	'94	CS/CD
A Man Called Alice	Pair	1163		CS

Billion Dollar Babies

Battle Axe	Polydor	6100	'77	†

ELVIS COSTELLO

(b. Declan McManus, Aug. 25, 1954, Liverpool, England)

Along with the Clash, Elvis Costello was the British punk or New Wave act that persevered long enough to achieve both acclaim and notoriety in the United States. Certainly the most prolific songwriter of the New Wave movement, perhaps even the most productive song-writer of his generation regardless of genre, Costello was also the most lyrically intelligent and musical ambitious singer-songwriter to emerge in the late '70s. His biting, incisive, and literate songs and his basic, unadorned rock music served as a stark and refreshing contrast to both the overproduced, pretentious music of British compatriots such as Genesis and Pink Floyd, and the mindless, contrived dance music of disco.

Initially favoring vituperative, sarcastic, and angry songs (witness his stunning *My Aim Is True*), Costello developed into a profound and compassionate songwriter by the early '80s without abandoning his fire and rage. His early caustic, aloof manner in performance evolved into a sincere, almost congenial style that ingratiated him to fans. Although criticized for his perceived lack of vocal range, he possessed one of the most emotionally evocative voices performing in rock.

Remarkably eclectic from the very beginning—utilizing the sound of reggae, soul, country, jazz, and even pop in his music—Costello produced the most diverse catalog of songs imaginable. He even recorded an album of country standards in the early '80s, and in the early '90s an album for voice and classical string quartet.

Elvis Costello grew up in a musical household. His father, Ross McManus, was a big-band singer. Playing guitar and writing songs as a youth, he took the name Elvis Costello to perform as a country act in pubs around London. He was the first artist to submit a demonstration tape to England's Stiff Records, a small, independent label formed in 1976 to record punk music. His debut album, recorded with the northern California-based country-rock group Clover under producer Nick Lowe, was released in Great Britain in the spring of 1977. That fall Costello completed his first British tour with the Attractions, comprised of keyboardist Steve Nieve, bassist Bruce Thomas, and drummer Pete Thomas (no relation).

When the cofounders of Stiff Records split up in late 1977, Elvis Costello switched to Columbia Records. The company issued the brilliant album *My Aim Is True* on the verge of his American debut in San Francisco. The first New Wave album to sell well in the United States, it featured a number of compelling songs, such as "Watching the Detectives," "Red Shoes," "Mystery Dance," "I'm Not Angry," and "Waiting for the End of the World," plus the uncharacteristic love ballad "Alison." The latter song was recorded by Linda Ronstadt for her 1978 *Living in the U.S.A.* album, giving a further boost to Costello's career.

Without a hit single, Elvis Costello quickly achieved an underground following with his early American tours. His enigmatic reputation was bolstered by *This Year's Model*, recorded with the Attractions under producer Nick Lowe. The album included "No Action," "Pump It Up," "Lipstick Vogue," and "Radio Radio." Costello's early 1979 American tour was equivocal at best, frequently alienating curious American rock artists, promoters, and audiences alike. A strange incident in Columbus, Ohio, when an apparently drunken Costello attacked singers Steve Stills and Bonnie Bramlett and reportedly made racist remarks about Ray Charles, was widely covered in the press, doing little to help his career. Nonetheless, *Armed Forces* became a best-seller, featuring "Accidents Will Happen," "Party Girl," and Nick Lowe's "(What's So Funny About) Peace, Love and Understanding," a minor hit.

Costello continued to pump out albums, with two releases in 1980. *Get Happy!!* included 20 songs, and was quickly followed by *Taking Liberties*, which contained B-sides to singles and previously unreleased recordings such as "Girls Talk" (a minor hit for Dave Edmunds in 1979), "Talking in the Dark" (recorded by Linda Ronstadt), and "Stranger in the

House" (recorded by country star George Jones). *Trust*, released in 1981, included "Clubland," "Pretty Words," and "Different Finger." It was followed by an entirely new style on *Almost Blue*, recorded in Nashville and produced by country veteran Owen Bradley, revealing Costello's country music bent with performances of country standards by Hank Williams, Merle Haggard, and George Jones, and two Gram Parsons songs.

Costello returned to his own songwriting on 1982's *Imperial Bedroom*, regarded by many as his masterpiece. Exploring the anguish of love in a variety of styles, the album featured "The Long Honeymoon," "Human Hands," "Pidgin English," and the moving ballad "Almost Blue." A U.S. tour followed, as did two more albums: *Punch the Clock* included the antiwar "Shipbuilding" and yielded Costello's first (moderate) hit with "Everyday I Write the Book," while *Goodbye Cruel World* produced a minor hit with "The Only Flame in Town."

In spring 1984 Elvis Costello toured America again, this time as a solo artist performing primarily acoustic music. Without the din of the Attractions his lyrics were far easier to appreciate, and he revealed a warm and lighter side, unlike his tours of the '70s. Dominated by country ballads, *King of America* was recorded without the Attractions (save one song), and Costello played acoustic guitar for producer T-Bone Burnett. The Attractions and producer Nick Lowe were back for *Blood and Chocolate*, which included "I Hope You're Happy Now," "Honey, Are You Straight or Are You Blind?," and the ballad "I Want You."

In May 1986 Elvis Costello married Cait O'Riordan, bassist of the Pogues, which she left late in the year. In 1987 the Attractions split up, and for a time Costello was without a record label. Signed to Warner Bros., he reemerged in 1989 with *Spike*, his best-selling album in years. Recorded with Paul McCartney, Roger McGuinn, coproducer T-Bone Burnett, and the Dirty Dozen Brass Band, the album featured "Baby Plays Around," "God's Comic," and Costello's first major hit single, "Veronica," cowritten with McCartney. At the same time, McCartney scored a major hit with "My Brave Face," cowritten with Costello. Costello toured again in 1989, with the Rude 5, who included guitarist Marc Ribot (who worked with Tom Waits), ace session keyboardist Larry Knechtel, bassist Jerry Scheff (who worked with Elvis Presley), and Attractions drummer Pete Thomas. The Rude 5 helped Costello record *Mighty Like a Rose* in Los Angeles. It included "Broken" (written by O'Riordan), "So Like Candy," and "Playboy to a Man" (cowritten with McCartney), plus "The Other Side of Summer" and "Hurry Down Doomsday."

In 1992 Elvis Costello made perhaps the boldest move of his career, recording *The Juliet Letters* with the Brodsky Quartet, a respected British classical string quartet. Sharing songwriting credit with the Quartet on more than half the songs, Costello bore sole responsibility for the vocals. The album, comprised largely of ballads, featured "Taking My Life in Your Hands" and "I Almost Had a Weakness." In 1994 Costello reassembled the Attractions to make the album *Brutal Youth* and for their first tour in eight years. Taking another right turn, Costello then issued an album of cover songs, *Kojak Variety*, ranging from Mose Allison's "Everybody's Crying Mercy" to Randy Newman's "I've Been Wrong Before" and Jesse Winchester's "Payday."

Elvis Costello

Beginning in 1990, Rykodisc began reissuing Elvis Costello's early albums with additional studio and live tracks, so the Rykodisc recordings do not correspond exactly to the original U.S. issues.

My Aim Is True	Columbia	35037	'77	CS/CD†
	Rykodisc	20271	'93	CS/CD
This Year's Model	Columbia	35331	'78	CS/CD†
	Rykodisc	10272	'93	CS/CD
Armed Forces	Columbia	35709	'79	CS/CD
	Rykodisc	20273	'93	CS/CD

Get Happy!!	Columbia	36347	'80	CS/CD†
	Rykodisc	20275	'94	CS/CD
Taking Liberties	Columbia	36839	'80	CS/CD†
Trust	Columbia	37051	'81	CS/CD†
	Rykodisc	20276	'94	CS/CD
Almost Blue	Columbia	37562	'81	CS/CD†
	Rykodisc	20277	'94	CD
Imperial Bedroom	Columbia	38157	'82	CS/CD
	Rykodisc	20278	'94	CD
Punch the Clock	Columbia	38897	'83	CS/CD†
	Rykodisc	20279	'95	CS/CD
Goodbye Cruel World	Columbia	39429	'84	CS/CD†
	Rykodisc	20280	'95	CS/CD
The Best of Elvis Costello and the Attractions, 1977–1984	Columbia	40101	'85	CS/CD†
King of America	Columbia	40173	'86	CS/CD
	Rykodisc	20281	'95	CS/CD
Blood and Chocolate	Columbia	40518	'86	CS/CD
	Rykodisc	20282	'95	CD
Girls, Girls, Girls	Columbia	(2) 46897	'90	CS/CD
Spike	Warner Bros.	25848	'89	CS/CD
Mighty Like a Rose	Warner Bros.	26575	'91	CS/CD
	Warner Bros.	26593	'91	CD
Brutal Youth	Warner Bros.	45535	'94	CS/CD
Kojak Variety	Warner Bros.	45903	'95	CS/CD
All This Useless Beauty	Warner Bros.	46198	'96	LP/CS/CD
2 1/2 Years	Rykodisc	(4) 90271/4	'93	CD
The Very Best of Elvis	Rykodisc	40283	'94	CD
Elvis Costello and the Brodsky Quartet				
The Juliet Letters	Warner Bros.	45180	'93	CS/CD

COUNTRY JOE AND THE FISH

"Country" Joe McDonald (b. Jan. 1, 1942, El Monte, CA), voc, gtr, har; **Barry Melton** (b. 1947, Brooklyn, NY), gtr; **David Cohen** (b. 1942, Brooklyn, NY), kybd; **Bruce Barthol** (b. 1947, Berkeley, CA), bs; **"Chicken" Hirsh** (b. 1940, CA), drm

The most overtly political band to emerge from the psychedelic San Francisco scene of the mid- to late '60s, Country Joe and the Fish are best remembered for their "Fish Cheer," the antiwar song "I-Feel-Like-I'm-Fixin'-to-Die Rag," and their appearance at the Woodstock Festival in 1969, immortalized in the subsequent film and record set. After the group's breakup in 1970, Country Joe McDonald pursued a solo career on the Vanguard and Fantasy record labels before becoming show business's most outspoken activist for Vietnam veterans.

Born into a left-wing family, Joe McDonald taught himself guitar as a youth, later serving in the Navy for four years and attending college. In 1962 he moved to Berkeley, where he met Barry Melton in 1965. They formed the folk-style jug band Country Joe and the Fish and issued the political newspaper *Ragbaby* that included a recording of the group's "I-Feel-Like-I'm-Fixin'-to-Die Rag." Playing up and down the West Coast, the group issued another EP in July 1966 that included "Bass Strings," "Love," and "Section 43." Signed to Vanguard Records, the group recorded *Electric Music for the Mind and Body*, which included "Section 43," "Grace" (written for Grace Slick), and the minor hit "Not So Sweet Martha

Lorraine." Their second album introduced "The Fish Cheer" and "I-Feel-Like-I'm-Fixin'-to-Die Rag" to a national audience and included "Janis," written by McDonald for Janis Joplin. Subsequent albums included favorites such as "Rock and Soul Music" and "Here I Go Again," but the group didn't stir the nation's attention until their heralded appearance at the Woodstock Festival in August 1969. Nonetheless, they broke up in 1970.

Through 1975 Country Joe McDonald recorded folk, protest, and country albums for Vanguard Records while establishing himself as a performer in Europe. He switched to Fantasy Records in 1975 and even managed a minor hit with "Breakfast for Two." Involved with the Save the Whales movement in the late '70s, McDonald formed his own record label, Rag Baby, and took up the cause of Vietnam veterans in the '80s. He eventually reemerged in 1991 with his first record in more than 12 years on a label other than his own with *Superstitious Blues* on Rykodisc.

Barry Melton became a lawyer in 1982. During the '80s and into the '90s he manned the Dinosaurs with veteran Bay Area musicians such as John Cipollina (Quicksilver), Peter Albin (Big Brother), and Spencer Dryden (Jefferson Airplane). In 1994 he became a deputy public defender in Mendocino County, California. Late that year the original members of Country Joe and the Fish reunited briefly.

Country Joe and the Fish

Collector's Items: The First Three EPs	One Way	30990	'94	CD
Electric Music for the Mind and Body	Vanguard	79244	'67	CS/CD
I Feel Like I'm Fixin' to Die	Vanguard	79266	'67	CS/CD
Together	Vanguard	79277	'68	CS/CD
Here We Are Again	Vanguard	79299	'69	†
Greatest Hits	Vanguard	6545	'70	†
C. J. Fish	Vanguard	6555	'70/'94	CS/CD
Life and Times—From Haight-Ashbury to Woodstock	Vanguard	(2) 27/8	'71	CS/CD
The Collected Country Joe and the Fish (1965–1970)	Vanguard	111	'87	CS/CD
Reunion	Fantasy	9530	'77	†

Barry Melton

Bright Sun Is Shining	Vanguard	6551	'70	†
Melton, Levy and the Dey Brothers	Columbia	31279	'72	†
We Are Like the Ocean	Music Is Medicine	9007	'78	†
Level with Me	Music Is Medicine	9014	'80	†

Country Joe Mcdonald

The Early Years	Piccadilly	3309	'80	†
Thinking of Woody Guthrie	Vanguard	6546	'70	†
Tonight I'm Singing Just for You	Vanguard	6557	'70	†
	One Way	31000	'95	CD
Quiet Days in Clichy (soundtrack)	Vanguard	79303	'71	†
Hold On It's Coming	Vanguard	79314	'71	│
War, War, War	Vanguard	79315	'71	†
	One Way	30995	'95	CD
Incredible! Live!	Vanguard	79316	'72	†
Paris Sessions	Vanguard	79328	'73	†
Country Joe	Vanguard	79348	'75	†
Essential	Vanguard	(2) 85/6	'76	†
The Best of Country Joe McDonald: The Vanguard Years (1969–1975)	Vanguard	(2) 119/20	'90	CS/CD
Paradise with an Ocean View	Fantasy	9495	'75/'94	CD
Love Is a Fire	Fantasy	9511	'76	†

Goodbye Blues	Fantasy	9525	'77	†
Rock 'n' Roll Music from Planet Earth	Fantasy	9544	'78	†
Leisure Suite	Fantasy	9586	'80	†
Classics	Fantasy	7709		CD
Child's Play	Rag Baby	1018	'83	LP
Superstitious Blues	Rykodisc	10201	'91	CS/CD
Vietnam Experience	One Way	30991	'95	CD
Peace on Earth	One Way	31369	'95	CD
Classics	Big Beat	108		CD

ROBERT CRAY

(b. Aug. 1, 1953, Columbus, GA)

Along with George Thorogood and the Vaughan brothers Stevie Ray and Jimmie (Fabulous Thunderbirds), Robert Cray both revitalized and popularized guitar-based blues music in the '80s. With his rich tenor voice, economical yet fluid guitar style, and original material, Cray broke through into mass popularity with 1986's *Strong Persuader* album, the best-selling blues album since the blues revival of the late '60s and perhaps the best-selling blues recording in history.

Robert Cray moved often with his Army family, eventually settling in Tacoma, Washington. He studied classical piano as a child, and took up guitar at age 12. In 1969 he met bassist Richard Cousins and formed his first group, One Way Street, performing locally. Around 1974 the two moved to Eugene, Oregon, and formed the Robert Cray Band. Playing local honky-tonks through 1976 and then touring tirelessly up and down the West Coast, the band gained its first recognition at the San Francisco Blues Festival in 1977. Between 1976 and 1978 Cray and Cousins toured in support of Cray's guitar idol, Albert Collins. Signed to Tomato Records, the group recorded their debut album, *Who's Been Talkin'* (reissued as *Too Many Cooks*) in 1978, but Tomato soon went out of business and the album wasn't released until 1980.

Playing 250 engagements a year, the Robert Cray Band recorded *Bad Influence* for the small, independent Bay Area label Hightone in 1983. The album, recorded with saxophonists Mike Vannice and Warren Rand, revealed the group's penchant for the sound of Memphis's Stax/Volt Records. It was hailed as the first major stylistic advance for the blues in years and brought the group's first recognition. By 1985's *False Accusations* Vannice and Rand had left the band and keyboardist Peter Boe had been added. The album included "Last Time (I Get Burned Like This)" and "Playin' in the Dirt." Cray's first national recognition came with *Showdown!*, recorded with blues guitarists Albert Collins and Johnny Copeland and released on the small Chicago-based Alligator label in 1986.

A new contract with Polygram (Mercury) Records gave Hightone complete control over the production of *Strong Persuader*, the Robert Cray Band's breakthrough album. The album yielded a major hit with "Smoking Gun" and a minor hit with "Right Next Door (Because of Me)," and became the best-selling blues album since B. B. King's *Completely Well*— and perhaps the best-selling blues recording of all time. In 1986 Eric Clapton recorded Cray's "Bad Influence" for his *August* album, and the Robert Cray Band toured in support of Clapton in 1987. *Don't Be Afraid of the Dark* was recorded with saxophonist David Sanborn, and in 1989 Cray assisted in the recording of John Lee Hooker's comeback album *The Healer* along with Bonnie Raitt, George Thorogood, and Carlos Santana, among others.

Cray subsequently regrouped his band, retaining Richard Cousins and bringing in guitarist Tim Kaihatsu, keyboardist Jimmy Pugh, and drummer Kevin Hayes for *Midnight Stroll*, which featured the Memphis Horns, Wayne Jackson (trumpet) and Andrew Love (saxophone). The Robert Cray Band cut their touring schedule to about a hundred dates in 1992, recording *I Was Warned* with new bassist Karl Sevareid under producer Dennis Walker, who cowrote 7 of the album's 10 songs. Tim Kaihatsu was dismissed before the band's next album, *Shame + a Sin. Some Rainy Morning* followed in 1995.

The Robert Cray Band

Too Many Cooks	Tomato	70381	'80/'91	CS/CD
Bad Influence	Hightone	8001	'83	LP/CS/CD
False Accusations	Hightone	8005	'85	LP/CS/CD
Strong Persuader	Mercury/Hightone	830568	'86	CS/CD
	Mobile Fidelity	564	'93	CD
Don't Be Afraid of the Dark	Mercury	834923	'88	CS/CD
Midnight Stroll	Mercury	846652	'90	CS/CD
I Was Warned	Mercury	512721	'92	CS/CD
Shame + a Sin	Mercury	518237	'93	CS/CD
Some Rainy Morning	Mercury	526867	'95	CS/CD

Robert Cray, Albert Collins, and Johnny Copeland

Showdown	Alligator	4743	'86	LP/CS/CD

CREAM

Eric Clapton (b. Eric Clapp, Mar. 30, 1945, Rippley, Surrey, England), lead gtr, voc; **Jack Bruce** (b. May 14, 1943, Glasgow, Scotland), bs, kybd, har, voc; **Peter "Ginger" Baker** (b. Aug. 19, 1939, Lewisham, London), drm, voc

Possibly the second most influential British group of the '60s, Cream was the first rock band to improvise extensively and perform extended pieces, thus elevating virtuoso instrumental playing within rock to an art form. Whereas the Beatles revolutionized rock by shifting the consuming public's attention from singles to albums on the basis of the consistency of their songwriting, Cream reinforced that shift through their instrumental prowess.

Although all three members of Cream demonstrated exceptional talent on their respective instruments, Jack Bruce was the real musical pioneer. Bruce established the use of the repeated musical figure, or ostinato (the so-called heavy riff), on bass, around which he played lead lines, thus liberating the instrument from its strictly rhythmic role. Ginger Baker instituted the long drum solo into rock, a phenomenon that became almost obligatory, particularly in performance. Eric Clapton unwittingly created the cult of the superstar guitarist, a role that was to follow him for years after the dissolution of Cream.

In openly acknowledging their debt to many obscure black American bluesmen (Robert Johnson, in particular), Cream helped inspire the blues revival of 1968. As the first rock group to utilize the power-trio format, they established the viability of the three-man instrumental lineup, a configuration used by the Jimi Hendrix Experience, Grand Funk Railroad, and many others. Ostensibly the first supergroup, though neither Bruce nor Baker was particularly well known in the United States, Cream also sparked the fusion of jazz and rock musics, a movement that was to revitalize jazz in the '70s.

Cream was formed in the summer of 1966 by lead guitarist Eric Clapton, bassist Jack Bruce, and drummer Peter "Ginger" Baker. Clapton had previously played with the Yardbirds and John Mayall's Bluesbreakers, whereas Baker had played with blues revivalist Alexis Korner and Graham Bond, and Bruce with Bond, Mayall, and Manfred Mann. Signed almost immediately by Atlantic Records, Cream's first album, *Fresh Cream*, was issued in early 1967. Although the album contained little of the improvisation that characterized the group in performance, it did include the British hit "I Feel Free," written by Bruce and lyricist Peter Brown, and the first version of Baker's "Toad" that would evolve into a concert tour de force.

Undeniably more exciting in concert than on records, Cream soon completed enormously successful tours of Great Britain and the United States. Produced by Felix Pappalardi, their second album, *Disraeli Gears*, established Cream's improvisational format. Rather than playing a song straight through, Clapton, Bruce, and Baker would set up the basic riff to a song, then take off into individual improvisatory jams. The album consisted of standard blues fare plus original songs composed by Bruce and Clapton, frequently in collaboration with Peter Brown. In fact, Brown was a frequent coauthor with Bruce of much of Cream's original material. "Sunshine of Your Love," written by Clapton, Bruce, and Brown, was a moderate hit from the album, later to become a major hit when rereleased in the summer of 1968. Other outstanding cuts included "Strange Brew" (written by Clapton, Pappalardi, and Pappalardi's wife-to-be, Gail Collins), "Tales of Brave Ulysses," "Take It Back," and "Swlabr."

Wheels of Fire, again produced by Felix Pappalardi, was a double-record set, one from the studio and one recorded live at the Fillmore Auditorium in San Francisco. Among the extended live pieces were Robert Johnson's "Crossroads" (a major hit), Willie Dixon's "Spoonful," and "Toad," on which Baker soloed for more than ten minutes. Pappalardi played on the studio record, which contained Booker T. Jones's "Born Under a Bad Sign," and "Politician" and "White Room" (a near-smash hit), both written by Bruce and Brown. By mid-1968 internal strains within the group became increasingly evident and, coupled with the limited amount of mutually acceptable material, led Cream to announce their intention to disband. After a farewell tour of America in October and November and a final album, *Goodbye* (which included "Badge," written by Clapton and George Harrison), Cream made their final appearance at London's Royal Albert Hall on November 26, 1968.

Almost immediately Eric Clapton and Ginger Baker formed the supergroup Blind Faith with Traffic's Stevie Winwood (keyboards) and Family's Rick Grech (bass). Completing one British and one American tour, the group recorded one interesting, if flawed, album. Clashes between Winwood and Baker tore the group apart, and Blind Faith disbanded at the end of 1969. Clapton subsequently pursued session work and a solo career (see Eric Clapton entry).

Jack Bruce, the odd man out in the formation of Blind Faith, briefly toured with keyboardist Mike Mandel, guitarist Larry Coryell, and drummer Mitch Mitchell before pursuing a solo career in conjunction with lyricist Peter Brown, recording two albums for Atco and two albums for RSO during the '70s. (Material from these albums and 1978's unreleased *Jet Set Jewel* were issued on 1989's *Willpower* album.) Bruce also joined Tony Williams's Lifetime, a jazz-rock fusion band that featured former Miles Davis drummer Tony Williams, organist Larry Young, and guitarist extraordinaire John McLaughlin, for touring and the albums *Emergency* and *Turn It Over*.

Producer-bassist Felix Pappalardi, who had worked with Joan Baez and Ian and Sylvia and produced the Youngblood's first two albums, was assigned by Atlantic Records to produce the New York group the Vagrants in 1968. Although recordings proved unsuccessful, Pappalardi was sufficiently impressed by the group's lead guitarist Leslie West to produce his debut solo album. In 1969 Pappalardi and West formed Mountain with keyboardist Steve Knight and drummer Corky Laing. They scored a major hit in 1970 with "Mississippi Queen," but disbanded in 1972. West and Laing then joined former Cream bassist Jack Bruce for West, Bruce, and Laing. That group broke up in 1973, and West and Pappalardi briefly reformed Mountain in 1974. Pappalardi later organized and produced the Japanese heavy-metal group Creation around 1975. On April 17, 1983, Felix Pappalardi was shot to death by his wife Gail in their New York apartment.

At the beginning of 1970 drummer Ginger Baker formed Ginger Baker's Air Force with Stevie Winwood, Rick Grech, Chris Wood, Denny Laine, Graham Bond, and a host of others. Baker later pursued an interest in African music, building a recording studio in Nigeria, which opened in January 1973 (Paul McCartney's *Band on the Run* was recorded there), and recording with Fela Kuti. From late 1974 until 1976 he manned the Baker-Gurvitz Army with Gurvitz brothers Adrian and Paul. Baker was out of the limelight during the '80s, eventually reemerging in 1991 with *Middle Passage* (recorded with jazz artist Bill Laswell and former George Clinton/Talking Heads keyboardist Bernie Worrell), and the hard-rock group Masters of Reality.

In addition to his solo albums, Jack Bruce recorded with a number of jazz artists during the '70s, including Carla Bley and Mike Mantler, while playing sessions for Lou Reed, John McLaughlin, and Frank Zappa. In the early '80s he recorded with erstwhile Procol Harum lead guitarist Robin Trower and his drummer Bill Lordan (*B.L.T.*) and Trower (*Truce*); *No Stopping Anytime*, from 1989, compiled these recordings. Jack Bruce recorded *A Question of Time* for Epic in 1989 and *Somethinels* for Creative Music in 1993. In 1994 Ginger Baker recorded with Bill Frisell and Charlie Haden as the Ginger Baker Trio and formed BBM with Jack Bruce and Gary Moore for the album *Around the Next Dream*.

Cream was inducted into the Rock and Roll Hall of Fame in 1993, and the group reformed for the ceremony, performing three of their hits.

Cream

Fresh Cream	Atco	33-206	'67	†
	RSO	3009	'77	†
	Polydor	827576		CS/CD
	DCC	1022		CD
Disraeli Gears	Atco	33-232	'67	†
	RSO	3010	'77	†
	Polydor	823636	'84	CS/CD
	Mobile Fidelity	562	'92	CD
Wheels of Fire	Atco	(2) 700	'68	†
	RSO	(2) 3802	'77	†
	Polydor	(2) 827578	'86	CS/CD
	DCC	(2) 1020		CD
Goodbye	Atco	7001	'69	†
	RSO	3013	'77	†
	Polydor	823660		CS/CD
Best	Atco	33-291	'69	†
Live Cream, Volume 1	Atco	33-328	'70	†
	RSO	3014	'77	†
	Polydor	827577		CD
Live Cream, Volume 2	Atco	7005	'72	†
	RSO	3015	'77	†
	Polydor	823661		CS/CD
Live Cream/Live Cream, Volume II	Mobile Fidelity	(2) 625	'95	CD
Heavy Cream	Polydor	(2) 3502	'72	†
Off the Top	Polydor	5529	'73	†
Strange Brew: The Very Best of Cream	Polydor	811639	'83	CS/CD
Very Best	Polydor	3752	'95	CS/CD

Blind Faith

Blind Faith	Atco	33-304	'69	†
	RSO	3016	'77	†
	Polydor	825094		CS/CD
	Mobile Fidelity	507	'89	CD

Ginger Baker

Ginger Baker's Air Force	Atco	(2) 703	'70	†
	Polydor	837349	'89	CD†
Ginger Baker's Air Force—2	Atco	33-343	'70	†
Stratavarious	Atco	7013	'72	†
Fela Ransome-Kuti and Africa '70 with Ginger Baker—Live!	Signpost	8401	'72	†
At His Best	Polydor	(2) 3504	'72	†
11 Sides of Baker	Sire	7532	'77	†
Middle Passage	Axiom	846753	'91	CS/CD
Horses and Trees	Celluloid	6126		CS/CD

Baker-Gurvitz Army

Baker-Gurvitz Army	Janus	7015	'75	†
Elysian Encounters	Atco	36-123	'75	†
Hearts on Fire	Atco	36-137	'76	†

Masters of Reality

Masters of Reality	Delicious Vinyl/Island	842904	'90	CS/CD
Sunrise on the Sufferbus	Chrysalis	21976	'93	CS/CD

The Ginger Baker Trio

Going Back Home	Atlantic	82652	'94	CS/CD

Jack Bruce

At His Best	Polydor	(2) 3505	'72	†
Songs for a Tailor	Atco	33-306	'69	†
	Polydor	835242	'88	CD†
Harmony Row	Atco	33-365	'71	†
	Polydor	835243	'88	CD†
Things We Like	Polydor	835244	'88	CD†
Out of the Storm	RSO	4805	'74	†
	Polydor	835284	'88	CD†
How's Tricks	RSO	3021	'77	†
	Polydor	835285	'88	CD†
I've Always Wanted to Do This	Epic	36827	'80	†
A Question of Time	Epic	45729	'89	CS/CD†
Willpower: A Twenty Year Retrospective	Polydor	(2) 837806	'89	†
	Polydor	837806	'89	CS/CD†
	Polydor	527116	'95	CS/CD
Somethinels	Creative Music	1001	'93	CS/CD

Tony Williams's Lifetime (with Jack Bruce)

Emergency	Polydor	30001	'69	†
	Polydor	849068		CD
Turn It Over	Polydor	244021	'70	†
Once in a Lifetime	Verve	(2) 2541	'83	†

Mountain (Felix Pappalardi, Leslie West, Corky Laing)

Mountain	Windfall	4500	'69/'96	†
Mountain Climbing	Windfall	4501	'70	†
	Columbia/Legacy	47361	'92	CS/CD
Nantucket Sleighride	Windfall	5500	'71	†
	Columbia/Legacy	47362	'92	CS/CD
Flowers of Evil	Windfall	5501	'71/'96	†
The Road Goes Ever On	Windfall	5502	'72	†

Best	Windfall	32079	'73	†
	Columbia	32079		CS/CD
Twin Peaks	Windfall	32818	'74	†
	Columbia	32818		CD
Avalanche	Windfall	33088	'74	†
West, Bruce, and Laing				
Why Dontcha	Windfall	31929	'72	†
	Columbia	31929	'89	CD
Whatever Turns You On	Windfall/Columbia	32216	'73	†
Live 'n' Kickin'	Windfall/Columbia	32899	'74	†
Carla Bley (with Jack Bruce)				
Escalator Over the Hill	JCOA	(3) 3	'73	†
	ECM/Watt	839310		CD†
Jack Bruce, Bill Lordan, and Robin Trower				
B.L.T.	Chrysalis	1324	'81	†
	Chrysalis	21324	'91	CS/CD†
Jack Bruce and Robin Trower				
Truce	Chrysalis	1352	'82	†
	Chrysalis	21352		CS
No Stopping Anytime	Chrysalis	21704	'89	CS/CD†
	One Way	17609		CD
BBM (Jack Bruce, Ginger Baker, and Gary Moore)				
Around the Next Dream	Virgin	39728	'94	CS/CD

CREEDENCE CLEARWATER REVIVAL

John Fogerty (b. May 28, 1945, Berkeley, CA), lead gtr, lead voc, kybd, har; **Tom Fogerty** (b. Nov. 9, 1941, Berkeley, CA; d. Sept. 6, 1990, Scottsdale, AZ), rhythm gtr, pno, voc; **Stu Cook** (b. Apr. 24, 1945, Oakland, CA), bs, pno; **Doug Clifford** (b. Apr. 24, 1945, Palo Alto, CA), drm

Perhaps the most popular American rock band of the late '60s, Creedence Clearwater Revival was the greatest American singles band of the era, scoring nine smash hits and six two-sided hits between 1969 and 1971. Leader John Fogerty's narrative-style rock-and-roll songs often explored Americana, much like the Band, and proved a refreshing contrast to the British, soft rock, and psychedelic music then dominating popular music. The group was honored in 1993 by the Rock and Roll Hall of Fame.

After Creedence Clearwater Revival broke up in 1972, the various members pursued a variety of other musical projects that proved marginally successful at best. John Fogerty ultimately staged one of the most astounding comebacks of the '80s, exceeded perhaps by only Tina Turner, with *Centerfield*; but the momentum soon dissipated. Stu Cook enjoyed considerable popularity in the late '80s as bassist of the country-rock group Southern Pacific, which ironically achieved their successes in the country field only.

The evolution of Creedence Clearwater Revival began in 1959, when three El Cerrito, California, junior high school students formed the Blue Velvets. John Fogerty, Stu Cook, and Doug Clifford were later joined by John's older brother Tom. Playing local engagements for years, the band recorded unsuccessfully for the Kristy and Orchestra labels before securing a recording contract with Berkeley's Fantasy Records in 1964. With a name change to the Golliwogs, the group released a series of unsuccessful singles between 1965 and 1967. Producer Saul Zaentz took over Fantasy in 1967 and the group changed their name to Creedence Clearwater Revival.

Creedence Clearwater Revival's self-titled debut album, released in the middle of 1968, contained a mixture of rock standards and John Fogerty originals. The first single release, a reworking of Dale Hawkins's "Suzie Q," became a major hit and launched the band on its successful career as a singles band. *Bayou Country* produced the smash-hit classic "Proud Mary" and included "Born on the Bayou." *Green River* contained the ballad "Wrote a Song for Everyone" and yielded two smash two-sided hits: "Bad Moon Rising" backed with "Lodi," and "Green River" backed by "Commotion." The hits continued with "Down on the Corner"/"Fortunate Son" and three two-sided smash hits from the album *Cosmo's Factory*, "Travelin' Band"/"Who'll Stop the Rain," "Up Around the Bend"/"Run Through the Jungle," and "Lookin' Out My Back Door"/"Long As I See the Light." "Have You Ever Seen the Rain"/"Hey Tonight" became a near-smash hit in early 1971.

John Fogerty's creative dominance of the group led to dissension among the other members, with Tom Fogerty leaving in February 1971. The remaining trio subsequently toured and recorded *Mardi Gras*, which yielded the hit singles "Sweet Hitchhiker" and "Someday Never Comes." In October 1972 Creedence Clearwater Revival disbanded.

During the '70s the members of Creedence Clearwater Revival pursued a variety of projects. Tom Fogerty recorded five solo albums and two albums with the group Ruby. On September 6, 1990, he died of respiratory failure. Doug Clifford recorded a solo album and two albums with the Don Harrison Band, which included Stu Cook. Only John Fogerty enjoyed any measure of success. He played all instruments and sang all parts on 1973's *Blue Ridge Rangers*, an album comprised primarily of country material. The album yielded two hits with Hank Williams's "Jambalaya" and "Hearts of Stone." He later recorded an album for Asylum Records that produced the minor hit "Almost Saturday Night."

Embroiled in lawsuits with the group's accountants and Fantasy Records for years, John Fogerty eventually reemerged in 1985. He again played all instruments on *Centerfield*, which contained the hits "The Old Man Down the Road," "Rock and Roll Girls," and the baseball classic "Centerfield." He toured in 1985–1986 for the first time in 14 years, but his follow-up album *Eye of the Zombie* sold only moderately.

Stu Cook joined the country-rock band Southern Pacific in 1984 after their debut album, which had yielded the country-only hits "Thing About You" (written by Tom Petty), "Perfect Stranger," and "Reno Bound." The group included John McFee (gtr, pedal steel gtr, fiddle) and Keith Knudsen (drm), both formerly with the Doobie Brothers. Featuring intricate, multipart harmonies, Southern Pacific scored major country-only hits with "A Girl like Emmylou" and "Midnight Highway," and the country smashes "New Shade of Blue," "Honey I Dare You," and "Any Way the Wind Blows" through 1989. The group disbanded in 1991.

The Golliwogs

Pre-Creedence	Fantasy	9474	'75	†
Creedence Clearwater Revival				
Creedence Clearwater Revival	Fantasy	8382	'68	†
	Fantasy	4512		LP/CS/CD
Bayou Country	Fantasy	8387	'69	CD
	Fantasy	4513		LP/CS
	DCC	1038		CD
Green River	Fantasy	8393	'69	†
	Fantasy	4514		LP/CS/CD
Willy and the Poor Boys	Fantasy	8397	'69	†
	Fantasy	4515		LP/CS/CD

The Concert (recorded 1970)	Fantasy	4501	'80	LP/CS/CD
Cosmo's Factory	Fantasy	8402	'70	†
	Fantasy	4516		LP/CS/CD
	DCC	1031		CD
Pendulum	Fantasy	8410	'70	†
	Fantasy	4517		LP/CS/CD
Mardi Gras	Fantasy	9404	'72	†
	Fantasy	4518		LP/CS/CD
Creedence Gold	Fantasy	9418	'72	LP/CS/CD
More Creedence Gold	Fantasy	9430	'73	LP/CS/CD
Live in Europe	Fantasy	(2) 79001	'73	†
	Fantasy	(2) CCR1		†
	Fantasy	4526		LP/CS/CD
Chronicle	Fantasy	(2) CCR2	'76	LP/CS
	Fantasy	CCR2		CD
1968/1969	Fantasy	(2) 68	'78	LP/CS
1969	Fantasy	(2) 69	'78	LP/CS
1970	Fantasy	(2) 70	'78	LP/CS
Chooglin'	Fantasy	9621		LP/CS
Creedence Country	Fantasy	4509		LP/CS
The Movie Album	Fantasy	4522	'85	LP/CS
Chronicle, Volume 2	Fantasy	(2) CCR3	'87	LP/CS
	Fantasy	CCR3	'87	CD
Tom Fogerty				
Tom Fogerty	Fantasy	9407	'72	†
Excalibur	Fantasy	9413	'73	†
Zephyr National	Fantasy	9448	'74	†
Myopia	Fantasy	9469	'74	†
Deal It Out	Fantasy	9611	'81	†
Ruby (with Tom Fogerty)				
Ruby	PBR International	7001	'77	†
Rock and Roll Madness	PBR International	7004	'78	†
Tom Fogerty/Kevin Oda				
Sidekicks	Fantasy	9664	'93	CD
Doug Clifford				
Cosmo	Fantasy	9411	'72	†
The Don Harrison Band (with Doug Clifford and Stu Cook)				
The Don Harrison Band	Atlantic	18171	'76	†
Red Hot	Atlantic	18208	'77	†
Southern Pacific (with Stu Cook)				
Killbilly Hill	Warner Bros.	25409	'86	CS
Zuma	Warner Bros.	25609	'88	CS/CD†
Country Line	Warner Bros.	25895	'90	CS/CD
Greatest Hits	Warner Bros.	26582	'91	CS/CD
John Fogerty				
Blue Ridge Rangers	Fantasy	9415	'73	†
	Fantasy	4502		LP/CS/CD
John Fogerty	Asylum	1046	'75	CS

Hoodoo	Asylum	1081	'76	†
Centerfield	Warner Bros.	25203	'85	CS/CD
Eye of the Zombie	Warner Bros.	25449	'86	CS/CD

JIM CROCE

(b. Jan. 10, 1943, Philadelphia, PA; d. Sept. 20, 1973, near Natchitoches, LA)

One of America's finest singer-songwriters of the early '70s, known for his amusing character songs and gentle love songs, Jim Croce died in an airplane crash just as he was beginning to receive much-deserved recognition. His son, A. J. Croce, has recently begun his own recording career.

Raised in Philadelphia, Jim Croce began playing music professionally at Villanova University in 1964. Recording an album on his own Croce label in 1966, he moved to New York, where he played coffeehouses on the advice of college friend Tommy West. Signed to Capitol Records, he recorded an album with his wife Ingrid before returning to Pennsylvania. Joined by lead guitarist Maury Muehleisen, Croce recorded a demonstration tape under producers Tommy West and Terry Cashman that lead to a recording contract with ABC Records.

Jim Croce's debut album for ABC yielded two major hits, "You Don't Mess Around with Jim" and "Operator (That's Not the Way It Feels)," and included the love song "Time in a Bottle," which became a top hit when it was issued in late 1973. Croce was established as a singer-songwriter with his second ABC album, *Life and Times*, which produced the moderate hit "One Less Set of Footsteps" and the top hit "Bad, Bad Leroy Brown." Croce and Muehleisen were killed on September 20, 1973, when their chartered plane crashed on takeoff near Natchitoches, Louisiana. *I Got a Name*, released posthumously, yielded three hits: "I Got a Name," "I'll Have to Say I Love You in a Song," and "Workin' at the Car Wash Blues."

Born in 1971 near Philadelphia, Adrian James "A. J." Croce began playing piano at six and started playing professionally at 12. Raised in San Diego, he performed for years at his mother Ingrid's nightclub, Croce's, before winning a recording contract with Private Music in 1993.

Jim and Ingrid Croce

Jim and Ingrid Croce	Capitol	315	'69	†
Another Day, Another Town	Pickwick	3332	'76	†

Maury Muehleisen

Gingerbread	Capitol	644	'70	†

Jim Croce

You Don't Mess Around with Jim	ABC	756	'72	†
	Lifesong	34993	'77	†
Life and Times	ABC	769	'73	†
	Lifesong	35008	'77	†
I Got a Name	ABC	797	'73	†
	Lifesong	35009	'77	†
Photographs and Memories: His Greatest Hits	ABC	835	'74	†
	Lifesong	35010	'77	†
	21 Records/Atco	90467	'85	LP/CS/CD
The Faces I've Been	Lifesong	(2) 900	'75	†

Time in a Bottle: Jim Croce's Greatest Love Songs	Lifesong	6007	'77	†
	Lifesong	35000	'77	†
	21 Records/Atco	90469	'85	LP/CS/CD
Bad, Bad Leroy Brown: Jim Croce's Greatest Character Songs	Lifesong	35571	'78	†
Down the Highway	21 Records/Atco	90468	'85/'92	LP/CS/CD
Jim Croce Live: The Final Tour	Saja	91326	'90	CS/CD
The 50th Anniversary Collection	Saja	(2) 92205	'92	CS/CD

A. J. Croce

A. J. Croce	Private Music	82108	'93	CS/CD
That's Me in the Bar	Private Music	82127	'95	CS/CD

CROSBY, STILLS, NASH (AND YOUNG)

David Crosby (b. David Van Cortland, Aug. 14, 1941, Los Angeles, CA), gtr, voc; **Stephen Stills** (b. Jan. 3, 1945, Dallas, TX), gtr, kybd, voc; **Graham Nash** (b. Feb. 2, 1942, Blackpool, Lancashire, England), gtr, voc; **Neil Young** (b. Nov. 12, 1945, Toronto, Canada), gtr, voc

Quintessential vocal-harmony, acoustic-guitar songwriting trio of the late '60s and early '70s, Crosby, Stills and Nash combined their considerable talents to produce an outstanding album of gentle melodic songs before adding the harder-edged sound of Neil Young. Relying more on their voices than their instruments, the quartet retained its own distinctive musical personality and became the darlings of the hippie movement with songs alternately mystical, communal, political, and romantic. More an aggregation of three (and four) individuals than a group, Crosby, Stills, Nash (and Young) formed one of rock's first supergroups. They were among the first rock groups to embrace political and environmental causes, as evidenced by Young's "Ohio" and Nash's involvement with the antinuclear movement. During the '70s each member pursued separate recording projects while regrouping as Crosby and Nash and Crosby, Stills and Nash. However, during the first half of the '80s Crosby was embroiled in personal and legal difficulties stemming from his addiction to cocaine that made him one of rock's most tragic figures of the era. He eventually dealt with his drug and legal problems and reemerged in the late '80s with a solo album and further work with Nash and Stills (and sometimes Young).

Ex-Byrd David Crosby and ex–Buffalo Springfield Stephen Stills met Graham Nash of the Hollies in 1968. An informal jam session in Los Angeles so impressed the three that they decided to form a group as soon as Nash could sever relations with the English group. Nash performed his last engagement with the Hollies on December 8, 1968, and the three began recording for Atlantic Records in 1969. Their debut album, *Crosby, Stills and Nash*, yielded two moderate hits with Nash's "Marrakesh Express" and Stills's "Suite: Judy Blue Eyes," written for Judy Collins. With Crosby on rhythm guitar and Stills overdubbing lead guitar, organ, and bass, the album featured precise three-part harmonies. Included were two excellent Crosby songs, "Long Time Gone" and "Guinnevere," Nash's "Lady of the Island," Stills's "Helplessly Hoping," and the mystical "Wooden Ships," composed by Crosby, Stills, and (uncredited) Paul Kantner.

In an effort to fill out the acoustic sound, ex–Buffalo Springfield Neil Young, already pursuing a successful solo career, was invited to join the group. They debuted at New York's Fillmore East less than a month before the quartet's celebrated appearance at the Woodstock Festival in August 1969. By the end of the year, however, the good vibes that had produced the magnificent results on the first album were dashed, as Stills broke up with Judy Collins, Nash broke up with Joni Mitchell, and Crosby's girlfriend Christine Hinton was killed in an auto crash. Young admirably took up the slack for *Déjà Vu*, the group's most successful album. It featured three hits: an electric version of Joni Mitchell's "Woodstock" and two Nash songs, "Teach Your Children" and "Our House." The album also contained Crosby's title song and the hippie lament "Almost Cut My Hair," Stills's "4 and 20," and Young's three-part production effort "Country Girl." By fall 1970 the group had split in four directions, but not before issuing Young's brilliant "Ohio," an outraged response to the Kent State student murders of May 1970. Nash subsequently compiled the double-record live set *Four Way Street*, which included Young classics "On the Way Home," "Cowgirl in the Sand," and "Southern Man" and two beautiful Crosby songs, "Triad" and "The Lee Shore."

Stephen Stills had already recorded one side of the *Super Session* album with Al Kooper. His debut solo album, comprised entirely of his own songs, yielded his only major hit with "Love the One You're With" and the moderate hit "Sit Yourself Down." The album also contained "We Are Not Helpless" and the inebriated "Black Queen," plus the instrumental "Old Times, Good Times" (featuring Jimi Hendrix) and "Go Back Home" (with Eric Clapton on second lead guitar). Stills's second solo album included "Sugar Babe" and "Singin' Call" and yielded moderate hits with "Change Partners" and "Marianne." Conducting his first major solo tour in July 1971, Stills subsequently formed Manassas in October with former Byrd and Flying Burrito Brother Chris Hillman and pedal steel guitarist Al Perkins. The group recorded two albums before disintegrating in September 1973.

In the meantime, David Crosby recorded his debut solo album, the aptly titled *If I Could Only Remember My Name*. Featuring several songs comprised of wordless vocal harmonies, the album contained Crosby's "Laughing" and "Traction in the Rain," as well as Nash, Young and Crosby's "Music Is Love" and the conspiratorial "What Are Their Names." Graham Nash's debut solo album, *Songs for Beginners*, produced moderate hits with the political songs "Chicago" and "Military Madness," and included Nash's "Better Days" and the old Hollies' song "I Used to Be a King." In 1972 Crosby and Nash teamed for touring and an album that yielded a moderate hit with "Immigration Man." Nash recorded a second solo album in 1973, and Crosby, Stills, Nash and Young conducted a summer-long tour in 1974. Crosby and Nash subsequently recorded *Wind on the Water* and *Whistling Down the Wire*, while Stills recorded three albums for Columbia through 1978. During 1976 Stills and Neil Young formed the short-lived Stills-Young Band for one album on Reprise and an aborted tour. Crosby, Stills and Nash regrouped for touring and 1977's *CSN*, which included Stills's "Dark Star" and the near-smash "Just a Song Before I Go" (by Nash). Nash was a founding director of the anti–nuclear power Musicians United for Safe Energy (MUSE) and organizer of the No Nukes concerts of September 1979, where the group performed; their work subsequently appeared on the concert album and film.

Five years of legal problems began for David Crosby in 1980. Nonetheless, Crosby, Stills and Nash regrouped in 1982 for touring and the album *Daylight Again*, which yielded the near-smash hit "Wasted on the Way" and the major hit "Southern Cross." The three continued to tour and record, while Stills recorded *Right by You* and Nash *Innocent Eyes*. However, David Crosby was arrested several times on drug and weapons charges in the early '80s, leading to his imprisonment in Texas in 1985 and 1986. Breaking his addiction to cocaine while in prison, he was paroled in September 1986 and exonerated of charges in November 1987. Pulling his life back together, Crosby married longtime girlfriend Jan Dance in May 1987 and published the autobiography *Long Time Gone* in 1988. He subsequently recorded *American Dream* with Stills, Nash, and Young and *Oh Yes I Can* solo for A&M Records. During the '90s Crosby, Stills, and Nash recorded and toured, including 1992's all-acoustic tour, and Crosby recorded *Thousand Roads*, which included "Yvette in English," cowritten with Joni Mitchell, and "Hero," a moderate hit cowritten with Phil Collins. Returning the favor, Crosby sang harmony on Collins's protest song "Another Day in Paradise." In late 1994 David Crosby underwent a liver transplant operation.

Crosby, Stills and Nash

Crosby, Stills and Nash	Atlantic	8229	'69	†
	Atlantic	19117		CS/CD†
	Atlantic	82522	'94	CD
	Atlantic	82651	'94	CS/CD
CSN	Atlantic	19104	'77	CS/CD†
	Atlantic	82659	'94	CS/CD
Replay	Atlantic	16026	'81	†
	Atlantic	82679	'94	CS/CD
Daylight Again	Atlantic	19360	'82	CS/CD†
	Atlantic	82672	'94	CS/CD
Live It Up	Atlantic	82107	'90	LP/CS/CD
Crosby, Stills and Nash	Atlantic	(4) 82319	'91	CS/CD
After the Storm	Atlantic	82654	'94	CS/CD

Crosby, Stills, Nash and Young

Déjà Vu	Atlantic	7200	'70	†
	Atlantic	19118		CS/CD†
	Atlantic	82649	'94	CS/CD
4 Way Street	Atlantic	(2) 902	'71	†
	Atlantic	(2) 82406	'92	CD
	Atlantic	(2) 82408	'92	CS/CD
So Far	Atlantic	18100	'74	†
	Atlantic	19119		CS/CD†
	Atlantic	82648	'94	CS/CD
American Dream	Atlantic	81888	'88	CS/CD

Stephen Stills, Al Kooper, and Mike Bloomfield

Super Session	Columbia	9701	'68	CS/CD

Stephen Stills

Stephen Stills	Atlantic	7202	'70	CS/CD
Stephen Stills 2	Atlantic	7206	'71/'92	CD
Manassas	Atlantic	(2) 903	'72	CS
	Atlantic	903		CD
Down the Road (with Manassas)	Atlantic	7250	'73	CD
Live	Atlantic	18156	'75	CS/CD
Best	Atlantic	18201	'77	†
Right by You	Atlantic	80177	'84	CD
Stills	Columbia	33575	'75/'93	CD
Illegal Stills	Columbia	34148	'76/'90	CD
Thoroughfare Gap	Columbia	35380	'78	†

The Stills-Young Band

Long May You Run	Reprise	2253	'76	CS/CD

David Crosby

If I Could Only Remember	Atlantic	7203	'71	CS/CD
Oh Yes I Can	A&M	5232	'89	LP/CS/CD†
Thousand Roads	Atlantic	82484	'93	CS/CD
It's All Coming Back to Me Now	Atlantic	82620	'95	CS/CD

Graham Nash

Songs for Beginners	Atlantic	7204	'71	CS/CD
Wild Tales	Atlantic	7288	'73/'88	CD
Earth and Sky	Capitol	12014	'80	†

Graham Nash and David Crosby

Graham Nash/David Crosby	Atlantic	7220	'72	†
Live	Atlantic	19150		CS
Best	Atlantic	19203		CS
Wind on the Water	ABC	902	'75	†
	MCA	37007		†
	MCA	31251		CD
Whistling Down the Wire	ABC	956	'76	†
Live	ABC	1042	'77	†
Best	ABC	1102	'78	†
	MCA	37008		†

RODNEY CROWELL

(b. Aug. 7, 1950, Houston, TX)

The first of the new wave of country-rock singer-songwriter-guitarists to emerge in the '80s, Rodney Crowell gained his earliest recognition as leader of Emmylou Harris's Hot Band in the late '70s. Recognized as a songwriter and producer by the early '80s, Crowell utilized both rock and country instrumentation and arrangements on his own recordings of songs either joyously amusing or profoundly honest, insightful, and emotive. He inspired country-style singer-songwriter-guitarists such as Jimmie Dale Gilmore and Robert Earl Keen, advanced the careers of others such as Guy Clark, produced much of the best work of his then-wife Rosanne Cash, and eventually broke through in the country field with 1988's *Diamonds and Dirt*.

Rodney Crowell began playing in his father's weekend honky-tonk band around age 11. In 1972 he moved to Nashville, where he met songwriters Guy Clark, Townes Van Zandt, and Steve Young. In 1974 Crowell moved to Los Angeles to join Emmylou Harris's Hot Band with electric guitarist James Burton (and later Albert Lee), pedal steel guitarist Hank DeVito, pianist Glen D. Hardin, and bassist Emory Gordy. He toured and recorded with Harris through 1977, contributing compositions such as "'Til I Gain Control Again," "Tulsa Queen," "Leaving Louisiana in the Broad Daylight," "I Ain't Living Long Like This," "Even Cowgirls Get the Blues," and "Amarillo" (cowritten with Harris). During the late '70s Jerry Jeff Walker recorded his "Song for the Life" and Bobby Bare recorded his "On a Real Good Night." Crowell also produced albums by Bare and Guy Clark. In 1977 he met singer Rosanne Cash; he married her two years later. The two worked together on Cash's solo albums (and recorded a number of duets) through much of the '80s.

Rodney Crowell's 1978 debut album for Warner Bros. contained a number of these songs, but other artists made hits out of them: The Oak Ridge Boys and Waylon Jennings scored top country hits with "Leaving Louisiana in the Broad Daylight" and "I Ain't Living Long Like This," respectively, and the Nitty Gritty Dirt Band scored a major pop hit with "American Dream," all in 1980. Crowell garnered a cult following with *But What Will the Neighbors Think*, which included his "It's Only Rock 'n' Roll," "On a Real Good Night," and "Ashes by Now" (a moderate pop hit), plus Guy Clark's "Heartbroke" and Hank DeVito's "Queen of Hearts." *Rodney Crowell*, from 1981, featured his "Stars on the Water," "Victim or a Fool," "'Til I Gain Control Again," and "Shame on the Moon." In 1983 Bob Seger scored a major country and smash pop hit with "Shame on the Moon," but Crowell's next album was rejected by Warner Bros.

Crowell switched to Columbia for *Street Language*, which yielded the minor country hits "When I'm Free Again," "She Loves the Jerk," and "Looking for You." Finally, in 1988 he was established as a country recording artist with *Diamonds and Dirt*, which produced five hit singles, including the top country hits "It's Such a Small World" (in duet with Rosanne Cash), "I Couldn't Leave You If I Tried," "She's Crazy for Leaving" (cowritten with Guy Clark), and "After All This Time." Still, Crowell remained primarily a fringe figure in country music, with a more eccentric, personal outlook than the hunks in hats who dominated the charts. *Keys to the Highway* featured "Soul Searchin'," "The Faith Is Mine," and "Tell Me the Truth" and was followed in 1992 with *Life Is Messy*, which reflected the breakup of his marriage to Rosanne Cash. He left Columbia in 1994 and has since issued an album on MCA.

Rodney Crowell

Ain't Living Long Like This	Warner Bros.	3228	'78	†
But What Will the Neighbors Think	Warner Bros.	3407	'80	†
Rodney Crowell	Warner Bros.	3587	'81	†
The Rodney Crowell Collection	Warner Bros.	25965	'89	CS/CD
Street Language	Columbia	40116	'86	CS/CD
Diamonds and Dirt	Columbia	44076	'88	LP/CS/CD
Keys to the Highway	Columbia	45242	'90	CS/CD
Life Is Messy	Columbia	47985	'92	CS/CD
Greatest Hits	Columbia	57580	'93	CS/CD
Jewel of the South	MCA	11223	'95	CS/CD

THE CRYSTALS

Barbara Alston (b. 1943, Brooklyn, NY); **Delores "Dee Dee" Kennibrew** (b. Delores Henry, 1945, Brooklyn, NY); **Mary Thomas** (b. 1946, Brooklyn, NY); **Pattie Wright** (b. 1945, Brooklyn, NY); **Merna Girard** (b. 1943, Brooklyn, NY); **Darlene Love** (b. Darlene Wright, July 26, 1938, Los Angeles, CA) [Merna Girard was replaced by **La La Brooks** (b. 1946, Brooklyn, NY) in 1962.]

Producer Phil Spector's first "girl group," the Crystals recorded his first million-selling single ("He's a Rebel") and were the object of his increasingly adventuresome productions in the early '60s before he turned his attention to the Ronettes and the Righteous Brothers. Darlene Love, the actual lead vocalist on "He's a Rebel," was lead vocalist for Bob B. Soxx and the Blue Jeans and performed background vocals for Dionne Warwick during the '70s, eventually initiating her own career in the '80s, most notably in the musical *Leader of the Pack*.

Formed in Brooklyn in 1961 by teenagers Barbara Alston, Delores "Dee Dee" Kennibrew, Mary Thomas, Pattie Wright, and Merna Girard, the Crystals were discovered by producer Phil Spector and were the first signing to his Philles label. With Barbara Alston on lead vocals, the group soon scored major hits with Spector's "There's No Other (Like My Baby)" and "Uptown," written by Barry Mann and Cynthia Weil. La La Brooks replaced Girard in 1962, but the group's next two hits, the classic "He's a Rebel" (written by Gene Pitney) and "He's Sure the Boy I Love," were actually recorded by the Blossoms, who consisted of lead vocalist Darlene Wright, Fanita James, and Gloria Jones. Subsequent smash hits for the Crystals included the classic "Da Doo Ron Ron" and "Then He Kissed Me," both written by Spector, Ellie Greenwich, and Jeff Barry. Their next singles failed to sell significantly, and by 1965 the Crystals were recording for United Artists Records.

Darlene Wright took the name Love at the behest of Phil Spector in 1963. With Bobby Sheen and Fanita James, she recorded as Bob B. Soxx and the Blue Jeans, who had already had a near-smash hit with "Zip-A-Dee-Doo-Dah." The group subsequently hit with "Why Do Lovers Break Each Other's Heart?" and "Not Too Young to Get Married." Darlene Love also had solo hits with "(Today I Met) The Boy I'm Gonna Marry" and "Wait Til My Bobby Gets Home."

Throughout the '70s Darlene Love worked as backup vocalist to Dionne Warwick, later backing Aretha Franklin. In 1981 she began pursuing her own career, touring with background vocalist Gloria Jones and appearing in the Tony-nominated 1985 Broadway musical *Leader of the Pack*, based on the songs of Ellie Greenwich. However, the original cast recording of the musical, live recordings of Love issued on Rhino in 1985, and her 1988 Columbia album were all quickly deleted. In 1992 Darlene Love recorded *Bringing It Home* with Lani Groves for the specialty Shanachie label.

The Crystals

Twist Uptown	Philles	4000	'62	†
He's a Rebel	Philles	4001	'63	†
Greatest Hits	Philles	4003	'63	†
Best	Abkco	7214		CS/CD
He's a Rebel (recorded 1986)	Jango	777	'87	LP/CS/CD†

Bob B. Soxx and the Blue Jeans

Zip-a-Dee-Doo-Dah	Philles	4002	'63	†

Darlene Love

Live	Rhino	855	'85	†
Paint Another Picture	Columbia	40605	'88	†
Best	Abkco	7213		CS/CD

Leader of the Pack

Original Cast	Elektra	(2) 60409	'85	†
Excerpts	Elektra	60420	'85	†

Darlene Love and Lani Groves

Bringing it Home	Shanachie	9003	'92	CS/CD

CHARLIE DANIELS
(b. Oct. 28, 1936, Wilmington, NC)

A respected session musician in the late '60s, Charlie Daniels modeled his early band on the Allman Brothers, utilizing twin lead guitars and twin drums. Achieving initial success with hippie-redneck songs such as "Uneasy Rider" and "Long Haired Country Boy," Daniels was recognized as a popular country fiddler with the 1979 classic "The Devil Went Down to Georgia." By the '80s the Charlie Daniels Band was solidly established in the country field.

Charlie Daniels took up guitar at age 15, later learning fiddle and playing in the bluegrass band the Misty Mountain Boys. From 1958 to 1967 he was the leader of the Jaguars, who regularly toured the South. In 1967 he went to Nashville, where he played sessions for Bob Dylan's *Nashville Skyline*, *Self Portrait*, and *New Morning* albums. He also played on three Leonard Cohen albums, and produced four albums for the Youngbloods. In 1971 he formed the Charlie Daniels Band with keyboardist-vocalist Joel "Tex" DiGregorio. Initially recording under his own name, he recorded one album for Capitol Records before switching to Kama Sutra for the near-smash pop hit "Uneasy Rider." In 1974 the band recorded *Fire on the Mountain*, which yielded two hit singles with "The South's Gonna Do It" and "Long Haired Country Boy." By 1975 the band's lineup had stabilized with Daniels, DiGregorio, guitarist-vocalist Tom Crain, and bassist Charlie Hayward. The band twice played the Grand Ole Opry as well as President Jimmy Carter's inaugural ball.

In 1976 the Charlie Daniels Band switched to Epic Records, eventually scoring a top country and smash pop hit with the fiddle classic "The Devil Went Down to Georgia." During the early '80s the band scored pop hits with "In America," "The Legend of Wooley Swamp" and "Still in Saigon," but their subsequent success was confined to the country field. "Drinking My Baby Goodbye," "Boogie Woogie Fiddle Country Blues," and "Simple Man" became near-smash country hits in 1986, 1988, and 1990, respectively.

The Charlie Daniels Band

The Charlie Daniels Band	Capitol	790	'71	†
	Capitol	11414	'75	†
	Capitol	16039		†
TeJohn, Grease and Wolfman	Kama Sutra	2060	'72	†
	Epic	34665	'78	†
Honey in the Rock	Kama Sutra	2071	'73	†
(reissued as) Uneasy Rider	Epic	34369	'76	†
Way Down Yonder	Kama Sutra		'74	†
(reissued as) Whiskey	Epic	34664	'77	†
Fire on the Mountain	Kama Sutra	2603	'74	†
	Epic	34365	'76/'85	CS/CD

Nightrider	Kama Sutra	2607	'75	†
	Epic	34402	'76	CS
Essential	Kama Sutra	(2) 2612	'76	†
Saddletramp	Epic	34150	'76	CS/CD
High Lonesome	Epic	34377	'76	†
	Epic/Legacy	34377		CS/CD
Midnight Wind	Epic	34970	'77	†
Million Mile Reflections	Epic	35751	'79	CS/CD
Full Moon	Epic	36571	'80	CS/CD
Million Mile Reflections/Full Moon	Epic	38563		CS
Windows	Epic	37694	'82	CS
A Decade of Hits	Epic	38795	'83	CS/CD
Me and the Boys	Epic	39878	'85	CS/CD
Powder Keg	Epic	40760	'87	CS
Homesick Heroes	Epic	44324	'88	CS/CD
Simple Man	Epic	45316	'89	CS/CD
Charlie Daniels				
Renegade	Epic	46835	'91	CS/CD
Greatest Fiddlin' Licks	Epic	52401	'92	CS/CD
Super Hits	Epic	64182	'94	CS/CD
America, I Believe in You	Liberty	80477	'93	CS/CD
The Door	Sparrow	51428	'94	CS/CD
Same Ol' Me	Capitol Nashville	32008	'95	CS/CD
Back to Back	K-tel	3099	'92	CS/CD
At His Best	IMG	708		CS

BOBBY DARIN

(b. Walden Robert Cassotto, May 14, 1936, Bronx, NY; d. Dec. 20, 1973, Los Angeles, CA)

A rock-and-roll artist in the late '50s, Bobby Darin moved into the pop mainstream with the definitive version of "Mack the Knife" in 1959. He later explored both country and folk music and formed his own record label, Direction, before ending his career at Motown Records. A childhood victim of rheumatic fever, Darin was not expected to live beyond 25, yet he persevered until 1973, when he died at age 37.

Bobby Darin contracted rheumatic fever at age eight and suffered health problems throughout his life. He learned to play drums, piano, and guitar as a child and studied drama for a time at Hunter College in New York. Changing his name to enter show business, Darin recorded briefly for Decca Records before switching to the Atco subsidiary of Atlantic Records in 1957. He eventually broke through in mid-1958 with his own composition "Splish Splash," quickly followed by "Queen of the Hop." He also recorded his composition "Early in the Morning" for Brunswick under the name the Ding Dongs. The song later became a major hit on Atco under the name the Rinky-Dinks, and then became a hit for Buddy Holly.

Bobby Darin broadened his base of popularity during 1959 with the smash hit "Dream Lover" and the top hit "Mack the Knife," based on Kurt Weill's 1928 "Moritat," from *The Threepenny Opera*. His shift to the pop mainstream was completed with a live album recorded at the Copacabana and the album *Two of a Kind*, recorded with singer-lyricist Johnny Mercer. Subsequent hits through 1962 included "Beyond the Sea," "Artificial Flowers," "Irresistible You" backed with "Multiplication," and the smash "Things." Signed to Capitol Records to replace departed Frank Sinatra, Darin scored smash hits with the country-style "You're the Reason I'm Living" and "18 Yellow Roses" in 1963.

His popularity thereafter faded dramatically, but he later rebounded on Atlantic with a near-smash hit version of Tim Hardin's folk song "If I Were a Carpenter" in 1966. He formed Direction Records in 1968 and recorded for the label before moving to Motown in 1971, where he managed his last minor hit with "Happy," the love theme from the movie *Lady Sings the Blues*. On December 20, 1973, Bobby Darin died in Los Angeles of heart failure while undergoing an operation. Darin gained a spot in the Rock and Roll Hall of Fame in 1990.

Bobby Darin

Bobby Darin	Atco	33-102	'58	†
That's All	Atco	33-104	'59	†
This Is Darin	Atco	33-115	'60	†
At the Copa	Atco	33-122	'60	†
	Bainbridge	6220		LP/CS
For Teenagers Only	Atco	1001	'60	†
It's You or No One	Atco	33-124		†
25th Day of December	Atco	33-125		†
	Atco	91772	'91	CS/CD
Two of a Kind (with Johnny Mercer)	Atco	33-126	'61	†
	Atco	90484	'86	CS/CD
The Bobby Darin Story	Atco	33-131	'61	†
	Atco	33131		CS/CD
Love Swings	Atco	33-134	'61	†
Twist with Bobby Darin	Atco	33 138	'62	†
Sings Ray Charles	Atco	33-140	'62	†
Things and Other Things	Atco	33-146	'62	†
Winners	Atco	33-167	'64	†
Splish Splash—The Best of Bobby Darin, Volume One	Atco	91794	'91	CS/CD
Splish Splash—The Best of Bobby Darin, Volume Two	Atco	91795	'91	CS/CD
Oh! Look at Me Now	Capitol	1791	'62	†
Earthy	Capitol	1826	'63	†
You're The Reason I'm Living	Capitol	1866	'63	†
18 Yellow Roses	Capitol	1942	'63	†
Golden Folk Hits	Capitol	2007	'64	†
From Hello Dolly to Goodbye Charlie	Capitol	2194	'64	†
Venice Blue	Capitol	2322	'65	†
Best	Capitol	2571	'66	†
Bobby Darin	Capitol	91625	'89	CS/CD
Spotlight on Bobby Darin	Capitol	28512	'94	CS/CD
The Shadow of Your Smile	Atlantic	8121	'66	‖
In a Broadway Bag	Atlantic	8126		†
If I Were a Carpenter	Atlantic	8135	'67	†
Inside Out	Atlantic	8142	'67	†
Doctor Doolittle	Atlantic	8154	'67	†
Bobby Darin	Atlantic	82626	'94	CS/CD
That's All	Atlantic	82627	'94	CS/CD
Bobby Darin	Direction	1936	'68	†
Commitment	Direction	1937	'69	†
Bobby Darin	Motown	753	'72	†

1936–1973	Motown	813	'74	†
	Motown	5185	'89	CS/CD
Live at the Desert Inn	Motown	9070	'87	CD†
Best	Curb/CEMA	77325	'90	CS/CD
The Ultimate Bobby Darin	Warner	27606		CD
As Long as I'm Singin'	Jass	9		LP/CS
	Jass	4		CD
As Long as I'm Singin': Rare'n Darin #1	r 'n' d	1301		LP/CS/CD

DEEP PURPLE

Ritchie Blackmore (b. Apr. 14, 1945, Weston-super-Mare, England), lead gtr; **Jon Lord** (b. June 9, 1941, Leicester, England), org; **Rod Evans** (b. 1945, Edinburgh, Scotland), voc; **Nick Simper** (b. 1946, London, England), bs; **Ian Paice** (b. June 29, 1948), drm [Later members included vocalists **Ian Gillan** (b. Aug. 19, 1945, Hounslow, England) and **David Coverdale** (b. Sept. 22, 1949, Saltburn, England); bassists **Roger Glover** (b. Nov. 30, 1945, Brecon, Wales) and **Glenn Hughes** (b. Penkridge, England); and guitarist **Tommy Bolin** (b. Sioux City, IA, 1951; d. Dec. 4, 1976, Miami, FL). Rainbow included vocalist **Ronnie James Dio** (b. Ronald Padavona, July 10, 1949, Portsmouth, NH).]

Formed in the late '60s, Deep Purple was a seminal high-decibel English rock band that defined heavy-metal music in the early '70s. Recording the heavy-metal classics "Hush" and "Smoke on the Water" and the symphonic *Concerto for Group and Orchestra*, Deep Purple disintegrated in 1976. Guitarist Ritchie Blackmore (Rainbow) and latter-day vocalist David Coverdale (Whitesnake) later pursued their own careers, as did Rainbow vocalist Ronnie James Dio. Deep Purple's original lineup reunited in 1984.

Ritchie Blackmore took up guitar at 11 and was playing English sessions by age 17. He played with Screaming Lord Sutch for several years before moving to Hamburg, Germany, where he formed Deep Purple in March 1968 with Jon Lord, Rod Evans, Nick Simper, and Ian Paice. Lord had played for four years with the Artwoods; Simper had been a member of Johnny Kidd and the Pirates; Evans and Paice came from the group Maze. Deep Purple's first single, a loud version of Joe South's "Hush," became a smash British and American hit in the summer of 1968, soon followed by a moderate hit version of Neil Diamond's "Kentucky Woman."

Recording three albums for Tetragrammaton, Deep Purple regrouped in July 1969 with Blackmore, Lord, Paice, and two members of Episode Six, vocalist Ian Gillan and bassist Roger Glover. This lineup of Deep Purple recorded a concerto for rock band and symphony orchestra composed by Jon Lord for Warner Bros. before breaking through into mass popularity with 1972's *Machine Head* and its smash hit, the heavy-metal classic "Smoke on the Water." After the live set *Made in Japan*, Gillan and Glover quit the band, to be replaced by vocalist David Coverdale and bassist Glenn Hughes. This version of Deep Purple recorded the best-selling *Burn* and *Stormbringer* albums, but Blackmore quit the group in May 1975. He was replaced on lead guitar by American Tommy Bolin, but Deep Purple broke up in July 1976.

Original vocalist Rod Evans formed Captain Beyond, recording two albums with the group in the early '70s. During the '70s Roger Glover, Ian Gillan, and Tommy Bolin recorded solo albums. Bolin died in Miami of a drug overdose on December 4, 1976. Ritchie Blackmore formed the heavy-metal band Rainbow with four members of Elf, including vocalist Ronnie James Dio. Achieving their greatest success with their first two albums, Rainbow endured numerous personnel changes, adding drummer Cozy Powell in

September 1975 and Roger Glover in April 1979. In January 1978 vocalist David Coverdale formed the heavy metal band Whitesnake with keyboardist Jon Lord, later adding Deep Purple drummer Ian Paice.

Ronnie James Dio replaced Ozzy Osbourne in Black Sabbath in 1978, staying on until 1983, when he formed Dio. He was replaced by vocalist Joe Lynn Turner in Rainbow, but that group broke up in 1984 when Blackmore, Lord, Gillan, Glover, and Paice re-formed Deep Purple. The revitalized group achieved their biggest success with *Perfect Strangers*, but Gillan left in 1989 to form Garth Rockett and the Moonshiners. By 1990 Joe Lynn Turner had joined Blackmore, Lord, Glover, and Paice in Deep Purple. In the meantime, David Coverdale assembled an entirely new band as Whitesnake. In 1993 Geffen Records issued *Coverdale/Page*, recorded by David Coverdale and Jimmy Page of Led Zeppelin.

Deep Purple

Shades of Deep Purple	Tetragrammaton	102	'68	†
Book of Taliesyn	Tetragrammaton	107	'68	†
Deep Purple	Tetragrammaton	119	'69	†
	Tetragrammaton	5005		†
Deep Purple/The Royal Philharmonic Orchestra	Warner Bros.	1860	'70	†
Deep Purple in Rock	Warner Bros.	1877	'70	CS/CD
Fireball	Warner Bros.	2564	'71	†
	Deep Purple	2564		CS/CD
Machine Head	Warner Bros.	2607	'72	†
	Warner Bros.	3100		CS/CD
Purple Passages	Warner Bros.	(2) 2644	'72	
Who Do We Think We Are?	Warner Bros.	2678	'73	†
	Deep Purple	2678		CS/CD
Machine Head/Who Do We Think We Are?	Warner Bros.	25134		CS
Made in Japan	Warner Bros.	(2) 2701	'73	†
	Deep Purple	2701		CS/CD
Burn	Warner Bros.	2766	'74	†
	Deep Purple	2766		CS/CD
Stormbringer	Warner Bros.	2832	'74	†
	Metal Blade/WB	26456	'90	CS/CD
Come Taste the Band	Warner Bros.	2895	'75	†
	Metal Blade/WB	26454	'90	CS/CD
Made in Europe	Warner Bros.	2995	'76	†
	Metal Blade/WB	26455	'90	CS/CD
When We Rock, We Rock and When We Roll, We Roll	Warner Bros.	3223	'78	†
	Deep Purple	3233		CS/CD
Deepest Purple: The Very Best of Deep Purple	Warner Bros.	3486	'80	†
	Deep Purple	3486		CS/CD
In Concert	Portrait	(2) 38050	'82	†
Perfect Strangers	Mercury	824003	'84	CS
	Mercury	823777		CD
The House of Blue Light	Mercury	831318	'87	†
Nobody's Perfect	Mercury	835897	'88	CS/CD
Knocking at Your Back Door: The Best of Deep Purple in the 80's	Mercury	513430	'91	CS/CD
Slaves and Masters	RCA	2421	'90	LP/CS/CD
The Battle Rages On	Giant	24517	'93	CS/CD

Roger Glover

The Butterfly Ball	UK	56000	'76	†

Elements	Polydor	6137	'78	†
Mask	21 Records	821063	'84	†
Ian Gillan				
Child in Time	Oyster	1602	'76	†
Scarabus	Island	9511	'78	†
	Antilles	7066		†
	Metal Blade/WB	26333	'90	CS/CD†
Glory Road	Virgin	13146	'80	†
	Metal Blade/WB	26326	'90	CS/CD†
Clean Air	Metal Blade/WB	26325	'90	CS/CD†
Live at Budokan	Metal Blade/WB	26327	'90	CS/CD†
Mr. Universe	Metal Blade/WB	26328	'90	CS/CD†
Double Trouble	Metal Blade/WB	26330	'90	CS/CD†
Future Shock	Metal Blade/WB	26331	'90	CS/CD†
Magic	Metal Blade/WB	26332	'90	CS/CD†
Ian Gillan and Roger Glover				
Accidentally on Purpose	Virgin	90953	'88	LP/CS/CD†
Tony Ashton and Jon Lord				
First of the Big Bands	Warner Bros.	2778	'74	†
	Windsong UK	33	'93	CD
Paice, Ashton and Lord				
Malice in Wonderland	Warner Bros.	3038	'77	†
Paice, Ashton and Lord	Windsong UK	25	'93	CD
Tommy Bolin				
Teaser	Nemperor	436	'75	†
Private Eyes	Columbia	34329	'76	CS/CD
The Ultimate Tommy Bolin	Geffen	(2) 24248	'89	CS/CD
Elf				
Elf	Epic	31789	'72/'91	CD
L.A. 59	MGM	4974	'74	†
Trying to Burn the Sun	MGM	4994	'75	†
Ritchie Blackmore's Rainbow				
Ritchie Blackmore's Rainbow	Polydor	6049	'75	†
	Polydor	825089		CS/CD
Rainbow Rising	Oyster	1601	'76	†
	Polydor	823655		CS/CD
Rainbow				
On Stage	Oyster	(2) 1801	'77	†
	Polydor	823656		CS/CD
Long Live Rock 'n' Roll	Polydor	6143	'78	†
	Polydor	825090		CS/CD
Down to Earth	Polydor	6221	'79	†
	Polydor	823705		CD
Difficult to Cure	Polydor	6316	'81	†
	Polydor	800018		CD
Jealous Lover	Polydor	502	'81	†
Straight Between the Eyes	Mercury	4041	'82	†
	Polydor	825387		CS
	Polydor	800028		CD

Bent Out of Shape	Mercury	815305	'83	CS/CD
Final Vinyl	Mercury	827987	'86	CS/CD
Dio				
Holy Diver	Warner Bros.	23836	'83	CS/CD
The Last in Line	Warner Bros.	25100	'84	CS/CD
Sacred Heart	Warner Bros.	25292	'85	CS/CD
Intermission	Warner Bros.	25443	'86	CS
Dream Evil	Warner Bros.	25612	'87	CS/CD
Lock Up the Wolves	Reprise	26212	'90	CS/CD
Strange Highways	Reprise	45527	'94	CS/CD
Whitesnake				
Saints and Sinners	Geffen	24173	'88	CS/CD
Snakebite	United Artists	915	'78	†
	Geffen	24174	'88	CS/CD
Trouble	United Artists	937	'79	†
	Geffen	24175	'88	CS/CD†
Love Hunter	United Artists	981	'79	†
	Geffen	24176	'88	CS/CD†
Ready an' Willing	Mirage	19276	'80	†
Live . . . In the Heart of the City	Mirage	19292	'80	†
	Geffen	24168	'87	CS/CD
Come an' Get It	Atlantic	16043	'81	†
	Geffen	24167	'87	CS/CD
Slide It In	Geffen	4018	'84	CS/CD
Whitesnake	Geffen	24099	'87	CS/CD
Slip of the Tongue	Geffen	24249	'89	CS/CD
Greatest Hits	Geffen	24620	'94	CS/CD
David Coverdale and Jimmy Page				
Coverdale/Page	Geffen	24487	'93	CS/CD

RICK DERRINGER

Rick Zehringer (b. Aug. 5, 1947, Celina, OH); **Randy Zehringer** (b. 1951, Union City, IN)

Rick Zehringer and his brother Randy were the leaders of the pop-rock group the McCoys, famous for their top hit "Hang on Sloopy" and the smash hit "Fever" in 1965. The group was formed by the brothers along with bassist Dennis Kelly in Union City, Indiana, when they were in high school. They performed under a variety of names, taking the McCoys moniker after organist Randy Hobbs joined them. Discovered by pop promoter Bert Berns, who ran Bang Records, they were originally promoted as a light pop-rock group. However, they fell in with the trendy Scene club in New York, and found a new manager with its owner, Steve Paul, who introduced them to more psychedelic sounds. The McCoys failed to make it as a hipper band, but Paul did bring the band together with a young Texas guitarist named Johnny Winter. Rick Zehringer, now renamed Derringer, produced Winter's first album, and remained closely associated with him through the beginning of his career.

In the '70s Derringer played and recorded with Johnny Winter, and produced and played with brother Edgar Winter, manning the Edgar Winter Group from 1974 to 1976. On his own, Derringer achieved a major hit in 1974 with "Rock and Roll Hoochie Koo." However, his next solo outing was less successful; Derringer then formed a self-named band, which stayed together through the '70s and produced four albums, with little successs. During the '80s he switched to production work, producing numerous artists, including "Weird Al" Yankovic, who had his biggest hit in 1984 with "Eat It," a parody of Michael Jackson's "Beat It." Derringer returned as a solo artist in the early '90s for the specialty Shrapnel label, recording traditional electric-blues material.

The McCoys

Hang On Sloopy	Bang	212	'65	†
You Make Me Feel So Good	Bang	213	'66	†
Infinite McCoys	Mercury	61163	'68	†
Human Ball	Mercury	61207	'69	†
Outside Stuff	Mercury	(2) 7506	'74	†
The Psychedelic Years	One Way	30642	'94	CD

Rick Derringer and Johnny Winter

Johnny Winter And	Columbia	30221	'70	CS
Johnny Winter And Live	Columbia	30475	'71	CS/CD
Johnny Winter And/Alive	Columbia	(2) 33651		CS
John Dawson Winter III	Blue Sky	33292	'74	†

Rick Derringer and Edgar Winter

White Trash	Epic	30512	'71	CS/CD
Road Work	Epic	(2) 31249	'72	†
	Epic	31249	'87	CS/CD
They Only Come Out at Night	Epic	31584	'72	CS/CD
Jasmine Night Dreams	Blue Sky	33483	'75	†
Edgar Winter Group with Rick Derringer	Blue Sky	33798	'75	†

Rick Derringer

All American Boy	Blue Sky	32481	'73/'85	CS/CD
Spring Fever	Blue Sky	33423	'75	†
Back to the Blues	Shrapnel	2008	'93	CS/CD
Electra Blues	Shrapnel	2023	'94	CS/CD

Derringer

Derringer	Blue Sky	34181	'76	†
	Epic Associated	34181	'92	CD
Sweet Evil	Blue Sky	34470	'77	†
Live	Blue Sky	34848	'77	†
If I Weren't So Romantic, I'd Shoot You	Blue Sky	35075	'78	†
Guitars and Women	Blue Sky	36092	'79	†
Face to Face	Blue Sky	36551	'80	†

NEIL DIAMOND

(b. Noah Kaminsky, Jan. 24, 1941, Brooklyn, NY)

A prolific songwriter in the Tin Pan Alley tradition since the mid-'60s, Neil Diamond enjoyed enormous success in the first half of the '70s, becoming one of the best-selling artists of the era. Criticized for his tame, safe lyrics, pompous, melodramatic music, and the contrived grandeur of his live performances, Diamond nonetheless garnered one of the most devoted and loyal followings of any contemporary pop artist. Rebounding musically with three smash hits from the 1980 movie *The Jazz Singer*, Neil Diamond scored his last major hit with 1982's "Heartlight," yet he was the top-grossing solo performer of the 1986 concert season and the top-grossing American performer of the 1993 concert season.

Diamond began writing songs as a child and later took up guitar, playing Greenwich Village coffeehouses in the early '60s. Making his first recording for the Duel label in 1961, he was hired and fired by a series of New York music-publishing companies before being "discovered" by Brill Building songwriters Jeff Barry and Ellie Greenwich. After Diamond wrote "Solitary Man" and "Cherry, Cherry" at his first session, Barry brought him to Jerry Wexler of Atlantic Records, who subsequently turned him over to Bert Berns of Bang Records.

"Solitary Man" became only a minor hit for Neil Diamond in mid-1966, but "Cherry, Cherry" became a near-smash within a few months. The string of hit singles for Bang continued through 1967 with "I Got the Feelin' (Oh No No)," "You Got to Me," "Girl, You'll Be a Woman Soon," "I Thank the Lord for the Night Time," and "Kentucky Woman." In 1966 Diamond signed with MCA's Uni label and moved to Los Angeles, where he wrote for the Monkees' television show, penning their smash hits "I'm a Believer" and "A Little Bit Me, A Little Bit You." His own hits on the Uni label through 1972 included "Brother Love's Traveling Salvation Show," the smashes "Sweet Caroline," "Holly Holy," and "I Am . . . I Said," the top hits "Cracklin' Rosie" and "Song Sung Blue," plus "He Ain't Heavy . . . He's My Brother," "Stones," and "Play Me."

In the fall of 1972 Diamond announced a sabbatical from touring that was to last more than three years. In 1973 he signed with Columbia Records for $5 million, then the biggest single-artist deal in recording history. His debut album, accompanying the film adaptation of the best-selling book *Jonathan Livingston Seagull*, became the best-selling soundtrack album in history, only to be surpassed by 1977's *Saturday Night Fever*. *Serenade* yielded the smash hit "Longfellow Serenade," and the Band's Robbie Robertson was brought in to produce *Beautiful Noise* (Diamond performed at the Band's famous "Last Waltz" final concert). Diamond returned to live performance in 1976 and recorded *Love at the Greek* at the Greek Theatre in Los Angeles. His 1978 top-hit duet with Barbra Streisand, "You Don't Bring Me Flowers," was soon followed by the major hit "Forever in Blue Jeans."

Although universally panned, the movie *The Jazz Singer* (a remake of the Al Jolson classic) did produce three smash hits for Neil Diamond: "Love on the Rocks," "Hello Again," and the glibly patriotic "America." Since 1982's smash "Heartlight," written with Burt Bacharach and Carole Bayer Sager, Diamond has achieved no major hits, and his last pop-chart entry came in 1986. Nonetheless, his tours have been enormously successful. In 1986 he was the top-grossing solo performer of the year, and in 1993 only U2 out-grossed him.

Neil Diamond

The Feel of Neil Diamond	Bang	214	'66	†
Just for You	Bang	217	'67	†
Greatest Hits	Bang	219	'68	†
Shilo/Solitary Man	Bang	221	'70	†
Do It!	Bang	224	'71	†
Double Gold	Bang	(2) 227	'73	†
Classics: The Early Years (1966–1967)	Columbia	38792	'83	CS/CD
Velvet Gloves and Spit	Uni	73030	'69	†
	MCA	2010		†
	MCA	37056		†
Sweet Caroline—Brother Love's Traveling Salvation Show	Uni	73047	'69	†
	MCA	2011		†
	MCA	37057		†
	MCA	1604		CS
	MCA	31050		CD

Touching You, Touching Me	Uni	73071	'69	†
	MCA	2006		†
	MCA	37058		†
	MCA	1605		CS
	MCA	31052		CD
Sweet Caroline/Touching You, Touching Me	MCA	(2) 6922		CS
Gold	Uni	73084	'70	†
	MCA	2007		†
	MCA	1683		CS/CD
Tap Root Manuscript	Uni	73092	'70	†
	MCA	2013		†
	MCA	1671		CS
	MCA	31071		CD
Stones	Uni	93106	'71	†
	MCA	2008		†
	MCA	1670		CS
	MCA	31049		CD
Moods	Uni	93136	'72	†
	MCA	2005		†
	MCA	1669		CS
	MCA	31061		CD
Stones/Moods	MCA	(2) 6934		CS
Rainbow	MCA	2103	'73	†
	MCA	37059		†
	MCA	1606		CS/CD
Rainbow/Velvet Gloves and Spit	MCA	(2) 6905		CS
Hot August Night	MCA	(2) 8000	'72	†
	MCA	(2) 6896		CS/CD
	Mobile Fidelity	00584	'93	CD
His 12 Greatest Hits	MCA	2106	'74	†
	MCA	1489		LP/CS
	MCA	37252		CD
And the Singer Sings His Songs	MCA	2227	'76	†
	MCA	37060		†
	MCA	1607		CS/CD
Love Songs	MCA	5239	'81	†
	MCA	1490		CS/CD
Glory Road, 1968–1972	MCA	(2) 10502	'92	CS/CD
Neil Diamond 12 Greatest Hits	MCA	10955	'93	CD
Jonathan Livingston Seagull (soundtrack)	Columbia	32550	'73	CS/CD
Serenade	Columbia	32919	'74	CS/CD
Beautiful Noise	Columbia	33965	'76/'85	CS/CD
Love at the Greek	Columbia	(2) 34404	'77	†
	Columbia	34404		CD
I'm Glad You're Here with Me Tonight	Columbia	34990	'77	CS/CD
You Don't Bring Me Flowers	Columbia	35625	'78	CS/CD
September Morn	Columbia	36121	'80	
The Jazz Singer (soundtrack)	Capitol	12120	'80	†
	Capitol	46026	'96	CS/CD
On the Way to the Sky	Columbia	37628	'81	CS/CD
12 Greatest Hits, Volume 2	CBS	38068	'82	CS/CD

Heartlight	Columbia	38359	'82	CS/CD
Primitive	Columbia	39199	'04	CS/CD
Headed for the Future	Columbia	40368	'86	CS/CD
Hot August Night II	Columbia	40990	'87	CS/CD
The Best Years of Our Lives	Columbia	45025	'89	CS/CD
Lovescape	Columbia	48610	'91	LP/CS/CD
The Greatest Hits, 1966–1992	Columbia	(2) 52703	'92	CS/CD
The Christmas Album	Columbia	52914	'92	CS/CD
Up on the Roof: From the Brill Building Songs	Columbia	57529	'93	CS/CD
Live in America	Columbia	(2) 66321	'94	CS/CD
The Christmas Album, Volume II	Columbia	66465	'94	CS/CD

BO DIDDLEY

(b. Ellas McDaniel, Dec. 30, 1928, McComb, MS)

Bo Diddley

Best remembered for his percussive shave-and-a-haircut guitar-playing style that influenced the Yardbirds and the Rolling Stones, Bo Diddley was one of rock and roll's first electric guitarist-singers. Combining crude energy, compulsive rhythms, and an open sense of sexuality, Diddley composed the oft-covered classics "I'm a Man," "Who Do You Love," and "Mona."

Bo Diddley moved to Chicago with his adopted family in 1934; he got his distinctive nickname while still in grammar school. Taking up guitar as a teenager, he debuted at the 708 Club in 1951. He signed with Chess Records in 1955, recording on the sister label, Checker. His first single, "Bo Diddley"/"I'm a Man," became a top R&B hit that year, followed by "Diddley Daddy" and "Pretty Thing." He finally broke through into the pop field in 1959 with "Say Man," trading insults with maraca player Jerome Green (Green could also be heard on "Hey Bo Diddley" and "Bring It to Jerome"). In the early '60s he hit with "Road Runner" and "You Can't Judge a Book by the Cover." He later teamed with Chuck Berry for the album *Two Great Guitars*, Muddy Waters and Little Walter for *Super Blues*, and Muddy Waters and Howlin' Wolf for *Super, Super Blues Band*. His influence on '60s British groups became apparent when the Yardbirds hit with his "I'm a Man" and the Rolling Stones recorded his "Mona."

Not surprising, Diddley was inducted into the Rock and Roll Hall of Fame in 1987 for his contributions to the rock rhythm. In 1989 he returned to recording with *Breaking Through the B.S.* on Triple X Records. In 1992 Rhino Records issued the tribute set *Bo Diddley Beats*, assembling recordings by Buddy Holly, Dee Clark, the Miracles, and others.

Bo Diddley

Bo Diddley	Checker	1431	'58	†
	Chess	9194	'87	CS
Go Bo Diddley	Checker	1436		†
	Checker	3006	'68	†
Bo Diddley/Go Bo Diddley (recorded 1955–1958)	Chess	5904		CD
Have Guitar, Will Travel	Checker	2974		†
In the Spotlight	Checker	2976	'60	†
	Chess	9264	'87	CS/CD
Bo Diddley Is a Gunslinger	Checker	2977	'60	†
	Chess	9285	'89	CS/CD
Bo Diddley Is a Lover	Checker	2980		†
Bo Diddley's a Twister	Checker	2982		†
(reissued as) Roadrunner	Checker	2982		†
Bo Diddley	Checker	2984	'62	†
Bo Diddley and Company	Checker	2985		†
Surfin' with Bo Diddley	Checker	2987		†
Bo Diddley's Beach Party	Checker	2988	'63	†
16 All-Time Greatest Hits	Checker	2989	'64	†
Hey Good Lookin'	Checker	2992	'65	†
500 Per Cent More Man	Checker	2996	'66	†
The Originator	Checker	3001		†
Boss Man	Checker	3007	'68	†
Black Gladiator	Checker	3013		†
Another Dimension	Chess	50001	'71	†
Where It All Began	Chess	50016		†
The London Bo Diddley Sessions	Chess	50029	'73	†
	Chess	9296	'89	CS/CD
Got My Own Bag of Tricks	Chess	60005	'72	†
Big Bad Bo	Chess	50047	'74	†
20th Anniversary of Rock 'n' Roll	RCA	1229	'76	†
His Greatest Sides, Volume 1	Chess	9106		LP/CS
The Chess Box	Chess	(3) 19502	'90	CS
	Chess	(2) 19502	'90	CD
Rare and Well Done	Chess	9331	'91	CS/CD
Breaking Through the B.S.	Triple X		'89	†
This Should Not Be	Triple X	51130	'93	CS/CD
Bo's Blues	Ace	396	'93	CD
Bo Knows Bo	MCA	20872	'95	CS/CD

Bo Diddley and Chuck Berry

Two Great Guitars	Checker	2991	'64	†
	Chess	9170		CS

Bo Diddley, Muddy Waters, and Little Walter

Super Blues	Checker	3008	'67	†
	Chess	9168		CS/CD

Bo Diddley, Muddy Waters, and Howlin' Wolf

The Super Super Blues Band	Checker	3010	'68	†
	Chess	9169		CS

Tribute Album

Bo Diddley Beats	Rhino	70291	'92	CS/CD

DION AND THE BELMONTS

Dion DiMucci (b. July 18, 1939, Bronx, NY), lead voc; **Angelo D'Aleo** (b. Feb. 3, 1940, Bronx, NY), first ten; **Fred Milano** (b. Aug. 22, 1939, Bronx, NY), second ten; **Carlo Mastrangelo** (b. Oct. 5, 1938, Bronx, NY), bs voc

DION AND THE BELMONTS

The most popular white doo-wop vocal group to emerge from the New York a cappella street-corner scene of the '50s, Dion and the Belmonts paved the way for the Four Seasons and influenced a generation of rock singers, from Paul Simon to Lou Reed. Launching a solo career in 1960, Dion hit with gutsy, conflict-ridden, even antagonistic and arrogant songs that bore sharp contrast to the pop fluff of the early '60s. Dion played the coffeehouse circuit after scoring a smash hit with the classic tribute song "Abraham, Martin and John" in 1968. He also reunited with the Belmonts occasionally, most notably in 1967 and 1972, for special concerts and recordings. He subsequently recorded Christian music for more than 10 years before reemerging in the late '80s with the album *Yo Frankie*.

Dion DiMucci began making public appearances playing acoustic guitar around age 11. He first recorded as Dion and the Timberlanes in 1957, forming Dion and the Belmonts in 1958. Signing with Laurie Records, the group soon hit with "I Wonder Why" and "No One Knows." D'Aleo served in the Navy in 1959 while the group scored smash hits with Doc Pomus and Mort Shuman's "A Teenager in Love" and the Rodgers and Hart classic "Where or When."

Dion left the group to pursue a solo career in October 1960, and the Belmonts, rejoined by Angelo D'Aleo, recorded for their own Sabina label, achieving moderate hits with "Tell Me Why" and "Come On, Little Angel." Dion quickly hit with "Lonely Teenager," followed in 1961 by the top hit "Runaround Sue," cowritten with Ernie Maresca. Backed by the Del Satins, Dion subsequently scored smash hits through 1963 with "The Wanderer" (written by Maresca), his own "Little Diane," and "Lovers Who Wander" and "Donna the Prima Donna" (cowritten with Maresca), as well as the major hits "Love Came to Me," "Sandy," and "This Little Girl." Recording for Columbia Records between 1963 and 1966, Dion saw his pop career crumble; he dabbled in many styles, even recording traditional blues under the influence of producer John Hammond. He reunited with the Belmonts for 1967's *Together Again*.

In 1968 Dion returned to Laurie, where he achieved his best-remembered smash hit with Dick Holler's ode to assassinated leaders, "Abraham, Martin and John." He subsequently toured the college-and-coffeehouse circuit playing acoustic guitar; during this time he recorded an unlikely acoustic version of Jimi Hendrix's "Purple Haze" and more standard folk fare like Joni Mitchell's "Both Sides Now." By 1970 he had switched to Warner Bros. Records, with little success. He reunited with the Belmonts again in 1972, and recorded *Born to Be with You* under producer extraordinaire Phil Spector in 1974. However, the album was released in England only, and by 1978 Dion was recording modern Christian music.

Dion returned to rock and roll in June 1987 with a series of sold-out concerts at Radio City Music Hall. He published his autobiography, *The Wanderer*, in 1988, and with the assistance of Paul Simon, Lou Reed, and Canadian Bryan Adams recorded *Yo Frankie* under producer Dave Edmunds, managing a minor hit with "And the Night Stood Still." A year later he was honored by the Rock and Roll Hall of Fame. In 1990 Dion toured with Edmunds, Graham Parker, and Kim Wilson of the Fabulous Thunderbirds.

Dion and the Belmonts

Presenting	Laurie	1002	'60	†
	Collectables	5025	'84	LP/CS
	Ace	966		CD
When You Wish Upon a Star	Laurie	2006	'60	†
	Collectables	5026	'84	LP/CS
By Special Request: Together on Record	Laurie	2016	'66	†
Everything You Always Wanted to Hear by Dion and the Belmonts	Laurie	4002		CS
60 Greatest Hits of Dion and the Belmonts	Laurie	(3) 6000		LP/CS
Together Again	ABC	599	'67	†
Greatest Hits	Columbia	31942	'73/'87	CS/CD
Reunion: Live at Madison Square Garden, 1972	Warner Bros.	2664	'73	†
	Rhino	70228	'87	CS/CD
Doo-Wop	Pickwick	3521	'76	†
Best	Pair	1142	'86	CS
20 Golden Classics	Collectables	5041		LP/CS
The Wanderer	3C Records	105		CD
The Fabulous Dion and the Belmonts	Ace	002		CS/CD

The Belmonts

Carnival of Hits	Sabina	5001	'62	†
Summer Love	Dot	25949	'69	†
Cigars, Accapella, and Candy	Buddah	5123	'73	†
Cheek to Cheek	Strawberry	6001	'78	†
The Laurie, Sabina and United Artists Sides, Volume 1	Ace	580	'95	CD

Dion

Alone with Dion	Laurie	2004		†
	Ace	115		†
Runaround Sue	Laurie	2009	'61	†
	Collectables	5027		LP/CS
	The Right Stuff	27304	'93	CS/CD
Lovers Who Wander	Laurie	2012	'62	†
	Ace	163		†
	The Right Stuff	27305	'93	CS/CD
Sings His Greatest Hits	Laurie	2013	'62	†
Love Came to Me	Laurie	2015		†
Dion Sings to Sandy	Laurie	2017	'63	†
15 Million Sellers	Laurie	2019		†
More Greatest Hits	Laurie	2022		†

Dion	Laurie	2047	'68	†
	The Right Stuff	29667	'94	CS/CD
(reissued as) Abraham, Martin and John	Ace	204	'87	†
Dion Sings the Hits of the 50s and 60s	Laurie	4013		CS
Ruby Baby	Columbia	8810	'63	†
	Columbia	35577	'79	†
Donna the Prima Donna	Columbia	8907	'63	†
	Columbia	35995	'79	†
Wonder Where I'm Bound	Columbia	9773	'69	†
Bronx Blues: The Columbia Recordings	Columbia/Legacy	46972	'91	CD
Sit Down Old Friend	Warner Bros.	1826	'70	†
You're Not Alone	Warner Bros.	1872	'71	†
Sanctuary	Warner Bros.	1945	'71	†
Suite for Late Summer	Warner Bros.	2642	'72	†
Streetheart	Warner Bros.	2954	'76	†
The Return of the Wanderer	Lifesong	35356	'78	†
	DCC	049		CS/CD
24 Original Classics	Arista	(2) 8206	'84	†
Yo Frankie	Arista	8549	'89	CS/CD
Hits	Ace	176		LP/CD
Runaround Sue: The Best	Ace	915		CD
The Fabulous Dion	Ace	008		CS/CD
Dion at His Best: Classic Old and Gold, Volume 3	3C Records	102		CD
Dion at His Best: Classic Old and Gold, Volume 4	3C Records	103		CD
Christian Music by Dion				
Inside Job	DaySpring	4022	'80	†
I Put Away My Idols	DaySpring	4109	'83	†
	DaySpring	8111	'85	†
Seasons	DaySpring	8112	'85	†
Kingdom in the Streets	Word	8285	'85	†
Velvet and Steel	Word	8372	'87	†
	Word/Epic	47798	'91	CS/CD

DIRE STRAITS

Mark Knopfler (b. Aug. 12, 1949, Glasgow, Scotland), lead gtr, voc; **David Knopfler** (b. Dec. 27, 1951, Glasgow, Scotland), rhythm gtr, voc; **John Illsley** (b. June 24, 1949, Leicester, England), bs, voc; **Pick Withers**, drm

In a time dominated by punk and disco musics and '70s supergroups, Dire Straits emerged in 1979 with the unique and distinctive "Sultans of Swing" single. During the '80s lead guitarist Mark Knopfler established himself as the most celebrated British guitarist since Eric Clapton with his fluid, sinewy guitar playing. Also featuring his laconic vocals and ironic songwriting, Dire Straits ushered in the compact-disc era with 1985's *Brothers in Arms*, which set new standards for rock-album production. Pursuing soundtrack, session, and production work throughout the '80s, Knopfler assembled an oversize nine-piece unit for '90s tours and recordings by Dire Straits.

Mark Knopfler moved to Newcastle with his family at age 9, taking piano and violin lessons from his father as a child. He left home at 17 to attend journalism school, later working as a reporter and music critic for the *Yorkshire Evening Post* from 1968 to 1970. He received a degree in English literature from Leeds College in 1973, and worked as a lecturer at Loughton College from 1973 to 1977 while manning weekend pub bands such as Brewer's Droop and Cafe Racers. In 1977 he settled in Deptford, South London, where he formed Dire Straits with brother David, bassist John Illsley, and drummer Pick Withers. Recording a demonstration tape that included "Sultans of Swing," the group signed with Warner Bros. after rock critic Charlie Gillette played the song on Radio London. Their debut album initially succeeded outside Great Britain, yielding the smash American pop hit with its title song.

Dire Straits toured in support of Talking Heads in early 1978, and conducted a successful American tour in early 1979. Later that year Mark Knopfler and Pick Withers aided Bob Dylan in the recording of his *Slow Train Coming* album. Dire Straits' *Communiqué*, produced by Jerry Wexler and Barry Beckett, saw the further development of Mark Knopfler's incisive songwriting, but in 1980 David Knopfler left the group for a solo career. He was replaced by Hal Lindes, and the band added keyboardist Alan Clark for the tougher *Making Movies* album, recorded in New York with E Street Band keyboardist Roy Bittan under producer Jimmy Iovine. The album included "Expresso Love," "Romeo and Juliet," and "Tunnel of Love" and yielded a minor hit with "Skateaway." The group toured extensively between October 1980 and July 1981, but Pick Withers left the group in 1982. Dire Straits added drummer Terry Williams for *Love Over Gold*, which contained the title song as well as "Private Investigations," the 14-minute "Telegraph Road," and the minor hit "Industrial Disease."

During the '80s Mark Knopfler began pursuing a number of outside projects. He played sessions for Steely Dan (*Gaucho*), Van Morrison (*Beautiful Vision*), and Bryan Ferry (*Boys and Girls*), and produced and performed on Bob Dylan's *Infidels*. He recorded the soundtracks to *Local Hero* and *Cal*, and wrote "Private Dancer," a smash hit for Tina Turner in 1985.

With the dawning of the compact disc era, Dire Straits became favorites of rock music fans with their classic 1985 album *Brothers in Arms*, recorded with second guitarist Guy Fletcher. A sonic delight, the album topped the charts, eventually sold 20 million copies, and yielded the major hit "So Far Away," the near-smash "Walk of Life," and the controversial top hit "Money for Nothing," which poked fun at rock-video stars.

Following Dire Straits' arduous world tour that included an appearance at Live Aid, Mark Knopfler withdrew to spend time with his family and pursue other projects. He recorded the soundtracks to 1987's *The Princess Bride* and 1989's *Last Exit to Brooklyn*, and produced Randy Newman's *Land of Dreams*. He toured with Eric Clapton in 1988, and recorded *Neck and Neck* with veteran Nashville guitarist Chet Atkins. In 1990 Knopfler formed the short-lived Notting Hillbillies with Guy Fletcher, Brendan Croker, and Steve Phillips for one British tour and the ironically titled album *Missing . . . Presumed Having a Good Time*.

In 1991 Mark Knopfler reassembled Dire Straits with original member John Illsley, later members Alan Clark and Guy Fletcher, guitarist Phil Palmer, pedal steel guitarist Paul Franklin, and others for *On Every Street* and a massive world tour. David Knopfler reemerged in the mid-'90s on Mesa Records.

Dire Straits

Dire Straits	Warner Bros.	3266	'78	CS/CD
Communiqué	Warner Bros.	3330	'79	CS/CD
Making Movies	Warner Bros.	3480	'80	CS/CD
Dire Straits/Making Movies	Warner Bros.	25135		CS
Love Over Gold	Warner Bros.	23728	'82	CS/CD
Twisting by the Pool (mini)	Warner Bros.	29800	'83	†
Dire Straits Live—Alchemy	Warner Bros.	(2) 25085	'84	CS/CD
Brothers in Arms	Warner Bros.	25264	'85	CS/CD
Money for Nothing	Warner Bros.	25794	'88	CS/CD

On Every Street	Warner Bros.	26680	'91	LP/CS/CD
On the Night	Warner Bros.	45259	'93	CS/CD
Mark Knopfler				
Local Hero (soundtrack)	Warner Bros.	23827	'83	CS/CD
Cal (soundtrack)	Vertigo	822769	'84/'87	CD
The Princess Bride (soundtrack)	Warner Bros.	25610	'87	CS/CD
Last Exit to Brooklyn (soundtrack)	Warner Bros.	25986	'89	CS/CD
The Notting Hillbillies				
Missing . . . Presumed Having a Good Time	Warner Bros.	26147	'90	CS/CD
Chet Atkins and Mark Knopfler				
Neck and Neck	Columbia	45307	'90	CS/CD
David Knopfler				
The Giver	Mesa	79076	'94	CS/CD
Small Mercies	Mesa	92548	'95	CS/CD

DR. JOHN
(b. Malcolm "Mac" Rebbenack, Nov. 21, 1941, New Orleans, LA)

First recognized for his exotic 1968 *Gris-Gris* album, which combined elements of voodoo and psychedelic rock, Dr. John has been a stalwart of the New Orleans music scene, first as a sessions musician, and later as a recording artist in his own right. Like the Meters, their successors the Neville Brothers, and pianist-songwriter-producer Allen Toussaint, Dr. John helped preserve and promote the distinctive sound of New Orleans's R&B, funk, and Mardi Gras music. As a pianist he has maintained the tradition of New Orleans piano players such as Professor Longhair and Huey "Piano" Smith on the albums *Gumbo* and *Goin' Back to New Orleans.*

Malcolm "Mac" Rebbenack started guitar lessons at age 12. He dropped out of school at 15 to become a professional musician, playing sessions as a guitarist at Cosimo Matassa's J&M Studios and touring as a backup musician. He worked his way up to writer and arranger and eventually played French Quarter dives on his own. After being shot in the hand in 1961, he stopped playing guitar and began concentrating on piano under the tutelage of Professor Longhair, who had a smash R&B hit in 1950 with "Bald Head." During the mid-'60s Dr. John moved to Los Angeles for session work with Sonny and Cher, Phil Spector, and producer-arranger Harold Battiste; during this time he formed a succession of bands.

In Los Angeles Mac Rebbenack took on the name Doctor John Creaux the Night Tripper for his astounding *Gris-Gris* album. Recorded with Harold Battiste and singer-pianist Jesse Hill (known for the '60s hit "Ooh Poo Pah Doo"), the album was suffused with hypnotic arcane chants and esoteric lyrics. It featured the entrancing eight-minute "I Walk on Gilded Splinters." Touring in wildly colorful attire with band and dancing girls, Dr. John was firmly established as a cult attraction.

After two more voodoo-infused albums and *The Sun, Moon and Herbs*, recorded in England with Mick Jagger and Eric Clapton, Dr. John returned to his New Orleans R&B roots with *Gumbo*. It included a Huey "Piano" Smith medley and the minor hit "Iko Iko," popularized by the Dixie Cups in 1965. Dr. John scored his biggest success in 1973 with *In the Right Place*, produced by veteran Allen Toussaint with backing by the Meters. It yielded the near-smash hit "Right Place, Wrong Time" and the moderate hit "Such a Night." That year he also recorded as a member of the supergroup Triumvirate, with Mike Bloomfield and John Paul Hammond.

During the '70s and '80s Dr. John played sessions for Aretha Franklin, James Taylor, and Emmylou Harris, among others, and worked on Rickie Lee Jones's debut album. He also recorded two albums of solo piano for the Clean Cuts label, made television and radio commercials, and contributed to soundtracks such as 1988's *Bull Durham*. In 1989 he recorded for a major label for the first time in more than 10 years. *In a Sentimental Mood* was comprised of pop standards such as "Accentuate the Positive" and "Makin' Whoopee!," the latter in duet with Rickie Lee Jones. Dr. John returned to his musical roots with 1992's *Goin' Back to New Orleans*. By 1994 he had switched to MCA/GRP Records for *Television*, and then recorded *Afterglow* for the revived Blue Thumb label, distributed by GRP.

Dr. John

Dr. John and His New Orleans Congregation	Ace	2020		†
Gris-Gris	Atco	33-234	'68	†
	Alligator	3904	'87	CS
Babylon	Atco	33-270	'69	†
Remedies	Atco	33-316	'70	†
The Sun, Moon and Herbs	Atco	33-362	'71	†
Gumbo	Atco	7006	'72	CD
In the Right Place	Atco	7018	'73/'90	CD
The Right Place/Gumbo	Mobile Fidelity	619	'94	CD
Desitively Bonnaroo	Atco	7043	'74	†
Anytime, Anyplace	Barometer	67001	'74	†
Hollywood Be Thy Name	United Artists	552	'75	†
Zu Zu Man	Trip	9518		†
Superpak	Trip	(2) 3507	'76	†
Night Tripper at His Best	Power Pak	263		†
One Night Late	Karate	5404	'78	†
City Lights	Horizon	732	'78	†
Tango Palace	Horizon	740	'79	†
Love Potion	Accord	7118	'81	†
Plays Mac Rebbenack	Clean Cuts	705	'82/'88	LP/CS/CD
The Brightest Smile in Town	Clean Cuts	707	'83	LP/CS/CD
In a Sentimental Mood	Warner Bros.	25889	'89	CS/CD
Goin' Back to New Orleans	Warner Bros.	26940	'92	CS/CD
The Ultimate Dr. John at His Best	Warner	27612		CD
	Special Music	4814		†
Mos's Scocious	Rhino	(2) 71450	'93	CS/CD
Television	MCA/GRP	4024	'94	CS/CD
Very Best	Rhino	71924	'95	CS/CD
Afterglow	Blue Thumb	7000	'95	CS/CD
Dr. John, Mike Bloomfield, and John Paul Hammond				
Triumvirate	Columbia	32172	'73	CD
Dr. John and Chris Barber				
On a Mardi Gras Day	Great Southern	11024	'91	LP

FATS DOMINO
(b. Antoine Domino, Feb. 26, 1928, New Orleans, LA)

The second-most popular of the '50s rock-and-rollers (after Elvis), Fats Domino successfully made the transition from R&B to rock and roll with his pleasant, upbeat songs and

FATS DOMINO

gentle, engaging piano style. An established R&B artist for years before breaking into the pop field with "Ain't That a Shame" in 1955, Domino was aided immeasurably by bandleader-trumpeter David Bartholomew and tenor saxophonist Herb Hardesty, who both played on virtually all of his hits. The most famous New Orleans–born musician since Louis Armstrong, Domino helped focus attention on the music of the city, and inspired other Southern black singers such as Little Richard and Lloyd Price to record. Of all the survivors of '50s rock and roll, only Fats Domino and Jerry Lee Lewis have retained their old drive and style.

"Fats" Domino started playing piano at 6, debuting professionally at 10. At 14 he dropped out of school to perform in local nightclubs. In the mid-'40s he joined the band of trumpeter David Bartholomew, who recommended him to Imperial Records' owner Lew Chudd in 1949. Signed to the label, Domino began a 10-year string of smash hits recorded with cowriter-arranger-producer Bartholomew and tenor saxophonist Herb Hardesty in 1950 with "The Fat Man." He produced smash R&B hits with songs such as "Every Night About This Time," "Goin' Home," "Goin' to the River," "Please Don't Leave Me," and "Something's Wrong" before breaking through into the pop market in 1955 with "Ain't That a Shame." Through 1960 he scored smash pop and R&B hits with "I'm in Love Again," "Blueberry Hill," "Blue Monday," "I'm Walkin'," "It's You I Love," "Whole Lotta Loving," "I Want to Walk You Home," "Be My Guest," and "Walking to New Orleans." Major pop hits of the era included "My Blue Heaven," "Valley of Tears," "I'm Ready," "I'm Gonna Be a Wheel Someday," and "My Girl Josephine," an early example of the rhythm adopted by reggae.

Although his popularity faded in the early '60s, Fats Domino managed major hits through 1962 with "What a Price," "It Keeps Rainin'," "Let the Four Winds Blow," "What a Party," and the Hank Williams classics "Jambalaya" and "You Win Again." In 1963 he signed with ABC-Paramount Records for two years, subsequently switching to Mercury. Established as a popular performer in Las Vegas by 1965, Domino moved to Reprise Records for his final pop hit in 1968 with a cover of the Beatles' "Lady Madonna." In 1980 he achieved a modest country hit with "Whiskey Heaven" from the movie *Any Which Way You Can*; he continues to perform on the oldies circuit. Fats Domino was among the inaugural group of artists inducted into the Rock and Roll Hall of Fame in 1986.

Fats Domino

Fats Domino	Archive of Folk and Jazz Music	280	'74	†
Fats Domino, Volume 2	Archive of Folk and Jazz Music	330	'77	†

Rock and Rollin' with Fats Domino	Imperial	9004	'56	†
Rock and Rollin'	Imperial	9009	'56	†
This Is Fats Domino!	Imperial	9028	'57	†
Here Stands Fats Domino	Imperial	9038	'57	†
This Is Fats	Imperial	9040	'57	†
Fabulous Mr. D	Imperial	9055	'58	†
	Liberty	10136	'81	†
Swings 12,000,000 Records	Imperial	9065	'59	†
	Liberty	10135	'81	†
Million Record Hits	Imperial	9103	'60	†
A Lot of Dominos	Imperial	12066	'60	†
I Miss You	Imperial	9138	'61	†
Let the Four Winds Blow	Imperial	12073	'61	†
What a Party	Imperial	9164	'61	†
Twistin' the Stomp	Imperial	9170	'62	†
Million Sellers by Fats	Imperial	9195	'62	†
	United Artists	1027	'80	†
Just Domino	Imperial	9208	'62	†
Walking to New Orleans	Imperial	9227	'63	†
Let's Dance with Domino	Imperial	9239	'63	†
Here He Comes Again	Imperial	9248	'63	†
Legendary Masters	United Artists	9958	'72	†
30 Hits—The Fats Domino	United Artists	104		†
Superpak	United Artists	(2) 122	'73	†
Very Best	United Artists	233	'74	†
Play It Again, Fats	United Artists	380	'75	†
My Blue Heaven: The Best of Fats Domino	EMI	92808	'90	CS/CD
They Call Me the Fat Man: The Legendary Imperial Recordings	EMI	(4) 96784	'91	CD
Here Comes Fats Domino	ABC-Paramount	455	'63	†
Fats on Fire	ABC-Paramount	479	'64	†
Getaway with Fats Domino	ABC-Paramount	510	'66	†
'65	Mercury	61039	'65	†
Southland U.S.A.	Mercury	61065	'66	†
Fats Is Back	Reprise	6304	'68	†
Fats	Reprise	6439	'71	†
Live in Montreux (recorded 1973)	Atlantic	81751	'87	CS
Fats Domino	Sunset	5103	'66	†
Stompin' Fats Domino	Sunset	5158	'67	†
Trouble in Mind	Sunset	5200	'69	†
Ain't That a Shame	Sunset	5299	'71	†
Fats Domino	Grand Award	267	'68	
Fats Domino	Pickwick	2031		†
Blueberry Hill	Pickwick	3111	'69	†
My Blue Heaven	Pickwick	3295	'72	†
Fats's Hits	Pickwick	5005		†
When I'm Walking	Harmony	11343	'69	†
	Columbia	35996	'79/'87	CD†
Getaway with Fats	Ace	90		†
Boogie Woogie Baby	Ace	140		
His Greatest Hits	Silver Eagle	6170	'88	CS/CD†
Whole Lotta Rock 'n' Roll	Pair	1123		CD†

The Best of Fats	Pair	1268	'90	CD
20 Hits	Fest	4400	'91	CS/CD
18 Hits	Fest	4402		CS/CD
All-Time Greatest Hits	Curb/CEMA	77378	'91	CS/CD
Best of Fats Domino, Live, Volume 1	Curb/CEMA	77538	'92	CS/CD
Best of Fats Domino, Live, Volume 2	Curb/CEMA	77539	'92	CS/CD
Antoine "Fats" Domino	Tomato	(2) 70391	'92	CS/CD
The Fat Man	SMS	2	'95	CD
Greatest Hits	Special Music	4817		CS/CD
Live in Concert	K-tel	619		CD†
16 Great Hits	Zeta	518		CD
Live Hits	Quicksilver	1016		LP/CS
So Long	Polygram	838642		CS

TOM DONAHUE

(b. May 21, 1928, South Bend, IN; d. Apr. 28, 1975, San Francisco, CA)

As disc jockey at San Francisco FM radio station KMPX, "Big Daddy" Tom Donahue created America's first alternative to banal AM radio programming in 1967. By playing album cuts rather than Top 40 singles, reintroducing live music broadcasts, and utilizing the airwaves as a true public service to its listeners, Donahue founded underground radio. The popularity of KMPX and its successor KSAN-FM (with Donahue as program director) showed that radio audiences would gratefully accept a nonfrenetic approach to recorded musical presentation that eschewed limited playlists, the use of offensive and inane commercials, and the abhorrence of controversy, while promoting public access to the air waves. The stations' success inspired the formation of underground FM radio stations across the country, virtually forced AM radio stations to revise their programming, and encouraged the development of album-oriented-rock (AOR) radio, a format which continues to dominate to this day, though with tighter playlists. Album-oriented rock also helped expand the audience for artists not recording singles; informed consumers of these artists; and ultimately changed the music industry's focus from singles to albums.

Tom Donahue first worked as a disc jockey during the late '40s in Charleston, West Virginia. He later worked at Washington, D.C.'s WINX and Philadelphia's WIBG before being hired by San Francisco radio station KYA in 1961. Known as Big Daddy for his 400-pound girth, Donahue and fellow disc jockey Bobby Mitchell formed Autumn Records in early 1964, hiring Sylvester Stewart (Sly Stone) as its only producer. Autumn issued the earliest hits of San Francisco's first major group, the Beau Brummels, and recorded Grace Slick's first group, the Great Society. Donahue and Mitchell also presented rock concerts in the Bay Area at least two years before Bill Graham, including the Beatles' final public performance, on August 29, 1966.

On April 7, 1967, Tom Donahue took over the 8 P.M.–to–midnight shift at FM radio station KMPX. The station allowed Donahue to play album cuts, broadcast live music, make public announcements of a political or general interest nature, and generally get involved with the community at large and its concerns. KMPX soon became the nation's first full-time, album-cut playing, reasonably intelligent FM radio station. The format proved enormously popular and was adopted by FM radio stations across the country, thus liberating contemporary music fans from the banality and myopia of AM radio programming. After a bitter strike against KMPX management, Donahue and nearly the entire staff defected to KSAN-FM on his 40th birthday, May 21, 1968. KSAN-FM was virtually unchallenged as the area's top progressive-rock station for years, and Donahue became the station's general manager in 1972. On the verge of becoming the general manager and part-owner of the recently sold KMPX station, Big Daddy Tom Donahue died of a heart attack on April 28, 1975, at age 46.

Tom Donahue

The Golden Age of Underground Radio with Tom Donahue (1968–1972)	DCC	045		CS/CD

DONOVAN

(b. Donovan Leitch, May 10, 1946, Glasgow, Scotland)

Initially appearing in the mid-'60s as an English (actually Scottish) folk artist strongly resembling America's Bob Dylan, Donovan later embraced beneficent psychedelia and naive spiritualism for a series of self-penned hit singles and best-selling albums during the late '60s.

Donovan moved to London at age 10 and took up guitar as a teenager. Performing on BBC-TV's "Ready, Steady, Go" in early 1965, he signed with Hickory Records, recording an album of folk-style music, *Catch the Wind*, and hitting with the title cut, "Colours," and Buffy Sainte-Marie's "Universal Soldier." Abandoning the Dylan-like image, he switched to Epic Records for a number of psychedelic, quasi-mystical hits through the late '60s. His debut Epic album, *Sunshine Superman*, yielded a top hit with the title cut and featured perhaps his finest composition, the ominous "Season of the Witch." *Mellow Yellow* produced a smash hit with the title song and included the haunting "Young Girl Blues."

Donovan was among the British popsters who studied with the Maharishi Mahesh Yogi (including the Beatles and various others), and he took to heart the message of transcendental meditation, as was reflected in his increasingly subdued hits "Epistle to Dippy," "There Is a Mountain," and "Wear Your Love Like Heaven." The album *Hurdy Gurdy Man* produced one mellow hit, "Jennifer Juniper," and one hard-driving hit with the title cut. *Barabajagal* yielded three hits with "Goo Goo Barabajagal" (recorded with the Jeff Beck Group), "To Susan on the West Coast Waiting," and the inane "Atlantis." Several minor hits ensued, but most of his '70s albums failed to sell and by 1978 Donovan was without a major label affiliation. In 1983 he attempted a comeback under producer Jerry Wexler, but the resulting album, *Lady of the Stars*, failed to do much business and Donovan again faded from the scene. Donovan's son was a brief sensation as an actor, model, and singer in the early '90s, while his daughter, Ione Skye, is a recognized actress.

Donovan

Catch the Wind	Hickory	123	'65	†
	Garland	016	'65	†
	Sandstone	33077	'92	CD
Fairy Tales	Hickory	127	'65	†
The Real Donovan	Hickory	135	'66	†
Like It Is, Was and Evermore Shall Be	Hickory	143	'67	†
Best	Hickory	149	'69	†
Sunshine Superman	Epic	26217	'66/'90	CD
Mellow Yellow	Epic	26239	'67	†
A Gift from a Flower to a Garden	Epic	(2) 171	'67	†
Wear Your Love Like Heaven	Epic	26349	'67	†
For Little Ones	Epic	26350	'67	†
In Concert	Epic	26386	'68	†
Sunshine Superman/In Concert	Epic	(2) 33734	'75	†
Hurdy Gurdy Man	Epic	26420	'68/'86	CD

Greatest Hits	Epic	26439	'69	CS/CD
Barabajagal	Epic	26481	'69/'87	CD
Barabajagal/Hurdy Gurdy Man	Epic	(2) 33731	'75	†
Open Road	Epic	30125	'70	†
World-Physical/Spiritual	Epic	(2) 31210	'72	†
Cosmic Wheels	Epic	32156	'73	†
Essence to Essence	Epic	32800	'74	†
7-Tease	Epic	33245	'74	†
Slow Down World	Epic	33945	'76	†
Troubadour: The Definitive Collection, 1964–1976	Epic/Legacy	(2) 46986	'92	CS/CD
Donovan P. Leitch	Janus	(2) 3022	'70	†
History of British Pop	Pye	502	'76	†
History of British Pop, Volume 2	Pye	507	'76	†
Donovan	Arista	4143	'77	†
Lady of the Stars	Allegiance	72857	'87	LP/CS/CD†
The Classic Live	Great Northern	61007	'91	CS/CD

THE DOOBIE BROTHERS

Tom Johnston (b. Visalia, CA), lead voc, gtr, kybd; **Patrick Simmons** (b. Jan. 23, 1950, Aberdeen, WA), gtr, voc; **Tiran Porter** (b. Los Angeles, CA), bs, voc; **John Hartman** (b. Mar. 18, 1950, Falls Church, VA), drm; **Mike Hossack** (b. Sept. 18, 1950, Paterson, NY), drm [Mike Hossack was replaced in 1974 by drummer-vocalist **Keith Knudsen** (b. Oct. 18, 1952, Ames, IA). Guitarist **Jeff "Skunk" Baxter** (b. Dec. 13, 1948, Washington, D.C.) was added in 1974. Keyboardist-vocalist **Michael McDonald** (b. Dec. 2, 1952, St. Louis, MO) joined in 1975. Later members include **John McFee** (b. Nov. 18, 1953, Santa Cruz, CA), rhythm and pedal steel guitar, dobro, and violin; **Cornelius Bumpus** (b. Jan. 13, 1952), keyboards, and saxophone; **Chet McCracken** (b. July 17, 1952, Seattle, WA), drums; and **Bobby LaKind** (b. 1945; d. Dec. 24, 1992, Los Angeles), percussion.]

One of the most popular American bands of the '70s, the Doobie Brothers initially recorded hard-driving guitar-based rock albums and hit singles, utilizing a double-lead-guitar format. Transformed into a sophisticated keyboard-based white R&B band with the addition of Michael McDonald in 1975, the Doobie Brothers became one of America's top live acts by 1978. Disbanding in 1982, the band returned to its earlier sound upon reuniting (without McDonald) in 1988, as McDonald pursued a solo career. Meanwhile former members John McFee and Keith Knudsen enjoyed success in the country field with Southern Pacific.

In 1969 drummer John Hartman moved from West Virginia to San Jose, California, ostensibly to join the re-formed Moby Grape. The plan failed to materialize, but Moby Grape guitarist Skip Spence introduced Hartman to guitarist-songwriter Tom Johnston. The two subsequently formed Pud with bassist Greg Murphy, who was soon replaced by David Shogren. The group became a quartet with the addition of guitarist Patrick Simmons and adopted the name the Doobie Brothers (*doobie* was hippie slang for a joint) for engagements around the San Francisco Bay Area. Signed to Warner Bros. Records, the group recorded an overlooked album before replacing Shogren with Tiran Porter and adding a second drummer, Mike Hossack.

Using the double-guitar, double-drums format popularized by the Allman Brothers, the Doobie Brothers recorded *Toulouse Street*, which yielded the major hit "Listen to the Music" (written by Tom Johnston) and the moderate hit "Jesus Is Just Alright," as well as the favorite album track "Rockin' Down the Highway." Their next album, *The Captain and Me*, produced

THE DOOBIE BROTHERS

two major hits with "Long Train Runnin'" and "China Grove," both written by Johnston. By early 1974 Mike Hossack had been replaced by drummer-vocalist Keith Knudsen. Former Steely Dan and session guitarist Jeff "Skunk" Baxter, who had toured and recorded with the band for six months on a part-time basis, joined the group full-time just as Patrick Simmons's "Black Water" was becoming a top hit at the end of 1974. The group's first album with Skunk Baxter as a full-time member of the band, *Stampede*, featured three hits: "Take Me in Your Arms (Rock Me)," a minor hit for Kim Weston in 1965; "Sweet Maxine"; and "I Cheat the Hangman." Nonetheless, Baxter continued session and tour work with James Taylor, Elton John, and Hoyt Axton.

Near the beginning of the Doobie Brothers' spring tour of 1975, Tom Johnston collapsed and returned home to recover from health problems. He rejoined the band intermittently, but ultimately left officially in January 1977. With their chief songwriter disabled, the group enlisted former Steely Dan keyboardist-vocalist Michael McDonald in fall 1975. His "Takin' It to the Streets" and "It Keeps You Runnin'" became hits for them in 1976. With two former members of Steely Dan in the group, the Doobie Brothers began exploring a more sophisticated, jazz-oriented sound. In 1979 the R&B-influenced *Minute by Minute* album yielded the top hit "What a Fool Believes" (cowritten by McDonald and Kenny Loggins), and the major hit title track and "Dependin' on You." Also during that year, John Hartman left and Jeff Baxter dropped out to return to studio work. The Doobie Brothers realigned with McDonald, Simmons, Porter, Knudsen, and new members John McFee, Cornelius Bumpus, and Chet McCracken. This lineup's *One Step Closer* produced the smash hit "Real Love," cowritten by McDonald, and the major hit "One Step Closer," written by McFee, Knudsen, and Carlene Carter. The group broke up following their farewell tour of September 1982.

Of all the Doobies, Michael McDonald had the most successful career on his own. During the late '70s he cowrote with Carly Simon her smash hit "You Belong to Me"; he provided harmony vocals for Lauren Wood's major hit "Please Don't Leave"; and he cowrote with Kenny Loggins his near-smash "This Is It." In 1980 McDonald provided backing vocals for Christopher Cross's first (smash) hit, "Ride Like the Wind," and dueted with Nicolette Larson on her moderate hit "Let Me Go, Love." He launched his solo career in 1982 with *If That's What It Takes* and the smash "I Keep Forgettin' (Every Time You're Near)," and debuted in the Las Vegas casino milieu in 1983. In the mid-'80s McDonald scored a top hit with "On My Own" in duet with Patti Labelle, and a smash hit on his own with "Sweet Freedom" from the movie *Running Scared*. McDonald's hit-making days dried up in the '90s, however; he produced two solo albums, 1990's *Take It to Heart* and 1993's *Blink of an Eye*, both of which were commercial disasters, although he did manage one hit in duet with Aretha Franklin on her "Ever Changing Times" in 1992. Also in the early '90s, he reunited with

Steely Dan gurus Donald Fagen and Walter Becker to perform as part of the New York Rock and Soul Revue.

Other group members have worked as both solo acts and in other groups. Tom Johnston scored a moderate hit in 1979 with "Savannah Nights," and Patrick Simmons managed a moderate hit with "So Wrong" in 1983. In 1985 John McFee and Keith Knudsen formed the country-rock band Southern Pacific with vocalist Tim Goodman and keyboardist Kurt Howell. The group soon achieved major country hits with "Thing About You" (written by Tom Petty) and "Perfect Stranger." They were joined by former Creedence Clearwater Revival bassist Stu Cook after their first album. Southern Pacific scored a smash country hit with "Reno Bound" (cowritten by McFee) in 1986, the year David Jenkins, formerly of Pablo Cruise, replaced Goodman. In 1988 the group had three country smash hits, "New Shade of Blue," "Honey I Dare You," and "Any Way the Wind Blows." Jenkins left in 1989, and the group disbanded in 1991.

In 1987 the Doobie Brothers reunited for a brief, ecstatically received tour, playing mostly benefits. All former members participated, except David Shogren and bassist Willie Weeks. Early the next year the group reconvened with Tom Johnston, Patrick Simmons, Tiran Porter, John Hartman, Mike Hossack, and Bobby LaKind, a percussionist who had started out as a member of the Doobie Brothers' lighting crew. Their *Cycles* album yielded a near-smash with "The Doctor," but 1991's *Brotherhood* proved far less successful. On December 24, 1992, Bobby LaKind died in Los Angeles of cancer. In summer 1994 Johnston, Simmons, Hossack, Knudsen, and McFee toured under the Doobie banner.

The Doobie Brothers

The Doobie Brothers	Warner Bros.	1919	'71	†
	Warner Bros.	26215	'95	CS/CD
Toulouse Street	Warner Bros.	2634	'72	CS/CD
The Captain and Me	Warner Bros.	2694	'73	CS/CD
What Were Once Vices Are Now Habits	Warner Bros.	2750	'74	CS/CD
Stampede	Warner Bros.	2835	'75	CS/CD
Takin' It to the Streets	Warner Bros.	2899	'76	CS/CD
Best	Warner Bros.	2978	'76	†
	Warner Bros.	3112		CS/CD
Livin' on the Fault Line	Warner Bros.	3045	'77	CS/CD
Minute by Minute	Warner Bros.	3193	'78	CS/CD
One Step Closer	Warner Bros.	3452	'80	†
	Warner Bros.	26628	'91	CD
Best, Volume 2	Warner Bros.	3612	'81	†
	Warner Bros.	23612	'95	CD
Farewell Tour	Warner Bros.	(2) 23772	'83	†
Best, Volumes 1 & 2	Warner Bros.	23945		CS
Cycles	Capitol	90371	'89	LP/CS/CD†
Brotherhood	Capitol	94623	'91	CS/CD†

Tom Johnston

Everything You've Heard Is True	Warner Bros.	3304	'79	†
Still Feels Good	Warner Bros.	3527	'81	†

Michael McDonald

That Was Then: The Early Recordings of Michael McDonald	Arista	2008	'83	†
If That's What It Takes	Warner Bros.	23703	'82	CS/CD
No Lookin' Back	Warner Bros.	25291	'85	CS/CD
	Warner Bros.	25534		CS
Take It to Heart	Reprise	25979	'90	CS/CD

Blink of an Eye	Reprise	45293	'93	CS/CD
Patrick Simmons				
Arcade	Elektra	60225	'83	†
Southern Pacific				
Southern Pacific	Warner Bros.	25206	'85	CS
Killbilly Hill	Warner Bros.	25409	'86	CS
Zuma	Warner Bros.	25609	'88	CS/CD
Country Line	Warner Bros.	25895	'90	CS/CD
Greatest Hits	Warner Bros.	26582	'91	CS/CD

THE DOORS

Jim Morrison (b. Dec. 8, 1943, Melbourne, FL; d. July 3, 1971, Paris, France), lead voc; **Ray Manzarek** (b. Feb. 12, 1935, Chicago, IL), kybd, voc; **Robbie Krieger** (b. Jan. 8, 1946, Los Angeles, CA), gtr; **John Densmore** (b. Dec. 1, 1945, Los Angeles, CA), drm

One of the first groups to achieve underground popularity by means of extensive FM radio airplay, the Doors were also one of the first rock groups to have an extended album cut edited down for release as a single ("Light My Fire"). An excellent improvisatory group, the Doors' sound was grounded in the keyboard playing of Ray Manzarek, who provided the bass line for the music and became one of the few rock keyboardists to be recognized for his individual style. Fronted by vocalist Jim Morrison, who contributed powerful pieces of surreal poetry often preoccupied with sex and death, the Doors explored the dark and forbidding side of life years before heavy-metal and punk artists came to the fore.

In acting out his poetry with carefully orchestrated performances in concert, Jim Morrison and the Doors became perhaps the first rock group to consciously inject serious and often compelling theatrics into their act. As a result, the Doors were one of the first rock bands to be analyzed and critiqued in terms of rock music, lyrics, and performance as art. Furthermore, like Bob Dylan and John Lennon, Morrison was able to use his musical success as a springboard for recognition as a literary poet.

As Morrison's later performances turned into self-indulgent spectacle, he set the stage for the mythologizing of his persona that occurred after his unexpected death in 1971. Much like actor James Dean, Morrison's image and talent became magnified after his death and evoked the fascination of fans too young to have viewed them firsthand. Morrison's mystery and notoriety were renewed in the early '80s with the publication of his biography, and in the early '90s with the movie *The Doors*.

Jim Morrison was born into a naval family and eventually enrolled in the theater arts department of UCLA in 1964, majoring in film. Ray Manzarek met him in 1965 while also attending film classes at UCLA. The two appproached jazz drummer John Densmore about forming a music group, and the Doors' lineup was completed with the addition of Densmore's acquaintance Robbie Krieger. After several months of rehearsal, the Doors were hired to play at Los Angeles's Whisky a-Go-Go for four months. Signed to Elektra Records, the group recorded their debut album in 1966. A stunning blend of rock and aural theater, *The Doors* was an instant success through widespread FM radio airplay, thus becoming one of the first rock albums popularized by the alternative media. The album contained Morrison's psychosexual epic "The End" and sported a number of hard-driving rock songs such as "Break on Through," "Back Door Man," "Take It As It Comes," and Krieger's "Light My Fire." Shortened from its original seven-minute length for release as a single, "Light My Fire" became a top hit in 1967 and broadened the Doors' base of popularity beyond the underground.

Exhibiting more sophisticated musical arrangements, *Strange Days* contained another extended Morrison piece, the 11-minute "When the Music's Over"; the potent rock song "My Eyes Have Seen You"; and the haunting title cut and "Unhappy Girl." "People Are Strange" and "Love Me Two Times" were the hits from the album. *Waiting for the Sun* included the printed words to the epic Morrison poem "The Celebration of the Lizard" and featured "Not to Touch the Earth," Krieger's puerile top hit "Hello, I Love You," and the moderate hit "Unknown Soldier." Morrison's anarchistic "Five to One" bore stark contrast to the album's otherwise shallow ballads.

In the meantime, given Morrison's penchant for drama in performance, the Doors became an enormous concert attraction by the end of 1968. As audiences grew larger, Morrison increased the theatricality, but his performances became erratic in 1969, culminating in his arrest for indecent exposure in Miami that March. Many subsequent concerts turned into outrageous fiascoes due to Morrison's onstage antics, often inspired by his increasing dependence on alcohol and drugs.

The Soft Parade was dominated by Krieger's juvenile lyrics and produced only one major hit, "Touch Me." The Doors returned with "Roadhouse Blues" and "You Make Me Real" from *Morrison Hotel*. Following the album's release, the Doors completed a successful tour largely free of untoward incidents. *L.A. Woman*, the final Doors album with Jim Morrison, included the excellent title song and yielded two hits with "Love Her Madly" and "Riders on the Storm."

In March 1971 a disillusioned and weary Morrison, beset by legal problems and years of alcohol and drug abuse, moved to Paris, France, for rest and recuperation, intent on devoting himself to his poetry. He died under mysterious circumstances on July 3, 1971, and was buried in Père-Lachaise cemetery. News of his death was withheld until after his burial, and speculation began that he died of a heroin overdose, although the cause of death was listed as a heart attack (no autopsy was performed). The three remaining Doors persevered for two albums before disbanding in 1973.

Ray Manzarek recorded two obscure albums for Mercury before forming Nite City with vocalist Noah James for one album on 20th Century. Robbie Krieger and John Densmore formed the Butts Band for two albums on Blue Thumb. Krieger later recorded the jazz-rock album *Robbie Krieger and Friends* before working with the Los Angeles band X, Iggy Pop, and Philip Glass. In 1989 he recorded the all-instrumental album *No Habla* for the I.R.S. label, and he toured with Eric Burdon in 1990. In the late '80s Manzarek collaborated with poet Michael McClure.

In 1978 Robbie Krieger, Ray Manzarek, and John Densmore edited more than 20 hours of Jim Morrison's recited poetry for *An American Prayer*, for which they provided the musical backdrop. The opening sequence to Francis Coppola's epic 1979 Vietnam War film *Apocalypse Now* used the Doors' "The End." Interest in the career of Jim Morrison and the Doors was fully revived in 1980 with the publication of the Morrison biography *No One Here Gets Out Alive* by longtime Doors associate Danny Sugarman (with Jerry Hopkins) and the release of *The Doors Greatest Hits*, which stayed on the album charts for nearly two years. Volumes of Jim Morrison's poetry were published in 1988 and 1990, and another surge of interest in the group took place with the release of the Oliver Stone movie *The Doors* in 1991. The Doors entered the Rock and Roll Hall of Fame in 1993, the 50th anniversary year of Morrison's birth (the occasion was also marked by a large, impromptu gathering at Morrison's grave site; his tombstone had been stolen three years earlier).

The Doors

The Doors		Elektra	74007	'67	CS/CD
		DCC	1023		CD

Strange Days	Elektra	74014	'67	CS/CD
	DCC	1026		CD
Live at the Hollywood Bowl (recorded July 5, 1968)	Elektra	60741	'87	†
Waiting for the Sun	Elektra	74024	'68	CS/CD
	DCC	1045		CD
Live in Europe 1968	Vision	(2) 50298	'91	CS
	Vision	(2) 50299	'91	CD
The Doors/Waiting for the Sun	Elektra	60156		CS
The Soft Parade	Elektra	75005	'69	CS/CD
Morrison Hotel	Elektra	75007	'70	CS/CD
Absolutely Live	Elektra	(2) 9002	'70	†
13	Elektra	74079	'70	†
L.A. Woman	Elektra	75011	'71	CS/CD
	DCC	1034		CD
Strange Days/L.A. Woman	Elektra	60274		CS
Other Voices	Elektra	75017	'71	†
Weird Scenes Inside the Gold Mine	Elektra	(2) 6001	'71	†
Full Circle	Elektra	75038	'72	†
Best	Elektra	5035	'73	†
An American Prayer	Elektra	502	'78	CS
	Elektra	61812	'95	LP/CS/CD
Greatest Hits	Elektra	515	'80/'91	CS
Alive She Cried	Elektra	60269	'83/'84	CD
Classics	Elektra	60417	'85	CS
Best	Elektra	(2) 60345	'87	CS/CD
The Doors (soundtrack)	Elektra	61047	'91	CS/CD
In Concert	Elektra	(2) 61082	'91	CS/CD

The Butts Band

The Butts Band	Blue Thumb	63	'74	†
Hear and Now	Blue Thumb	6018	'75	†

Ray Manzarek

The Golden Scarab	Mercury	703	'74	†
	Mercury	512445	'92	CD
The Whole Thing Started with Rock and Roll	Mercury	1014	'75	†
Carmina Burina	A&M	4945	'83	LP/CS/CD†

Nite City

Nite City	20th Century	528	'77	†

Robbie Krieger

Robbie Krieger and Friends	Blue Note	664	'77	†
	World Pacific	96101	'91	CD†
Door Jams (recorded 1977–1985)	I.R.S./MCA	82014	'89	CS/CD†
No Habla	I.R.S./MCA	82004	'89	LP/CS/CD†
	I.R.S.	13004		CS/CD†
RKO Live	One Way	31371	'95	CD

THE DRIFTERS

Ben E. King (b. Benjamin Nelson, Sept. 23, 1938, Henderson, NC), lead bar; **Charles Thomas**, ten; **Doc Green** (b. Oct. 8, 1934; d. Mar. 10, 1989, New York, NY), bar; **Ellsbury Hobbs**, bs voc [Later members include **Rudy Lewis** (d. 1964) and **Johnny Moore**.]

Not to be confused with the Drifters led by Clyde McPhatter and later Johnny Moore between 1953 and 1958, this "new" Drifters initially featured Ben E. King on lead vocals. This and subsequent groupings of the Drifters created an early soul sound, with gospel-style singing, pop-oriented material, and lush orchestral backgrounds. Although they were not the first R&B vocal group to utilize strings for recordings (that claim probably goes to the Orioles with 1953's "Crying in the Chapel"), the Drifters did popularize the format, a format subsequently adopted by many R&B and soul acts.

The original Drifters were formed in 1953 around lead vocalist Clyde McPhatter. He departed the group in late 1954, to be replaced by Johnny Moore, who sang lead vocals on the R&B smash hits "Adorable," "Ruby Baby," and "Fools Fall in Love." Manager George Treadwell, owner of the Drifters name, fired the group in June 1958 and recruited the (Five) Crowns as the "new" Drifters. Lead baritone Ben E. King coauthored the Drifters' first hit single, "There Goes My Baby," with manager Treadwell. The recording, a top R&B and smash pop hit in 1959, was produced by legendary songwriter-producers Jerry Leiber and Mike Stoller, who produced many of their subsequent hits. "Dance with Me," cowritten by Treadwell, was the next in a series of smash R&B and major pop hits essentially aimed at white audiences. Brill Building professional songwriters "Doc" Pomus and Mort Shuman provided the Drifters with their next four hits: "(If You Cry) True Love, True Love," "This Magic Moment," "Save the Last Dance for Me" (a top R&B and pop hit), and "I Count the Tears."

In May 1960 Ben E. King left the Drifters to pursue a solo career. His first hit came with "Spanish Harlem," written by Jerry Leiber and then-apprentice producer Phil Spector. Later R&B and pop hits included the smash "Stand By Me" (cowritten by King), "Amor," "Don't Play That Song," and "I (Who Have Nothing)."

In the meantime, the Drifters were enjoying their greatest hit-making period with Rudy Lewis on lead vocals. Through 1963 the group scored major pop hits with Carole King and Gerry Goffin's "Some Kind of Wonderful," "Please Stay," "Sweets for My Sweet," "When My Little Girl Is Smiling," the Goffin-King classic "Up on the Roof," and two Barry Mann—Cynthia Weil compositions, "On Broadway" and "I'll Take You Home." Rudy Lewis died in the summer of 1964 and was replaced by original Drifter Johnny Moore for the group's final pop hits in 1964, "Under the Boardwalk" and "Saturday Night at the Movies." The Drifters continued to record into the early '70s. Several different groupings of the Drifters perform today, one fronted by Charles Thomas and Ellsbury Hobbs.

Ben E. King reemerged in 1974 with the smash funk hit "Supernatural Thing." He later recorded with the Average White Band and enjoyed renewed popularity (and a near-smash hit) with the title song to the 1986 movie *Stand By Me*. The Drifters entered the Rock and Roll Hall of Fame in 1988.

The Drifters

Rockin' and Drifitin'	Atlantic	8022	'58	†
Greatest Hits	Atlantic	8041	'60	†
Save the Last Dance for Me	Atlantic	8059	'62	†
Up on the Roof	Atlantic	8073	'63	†
Our Biggest Hits	Atlantic	8093	'64	†
Under the Boardwalk	Atlantic	8099	'64	†

The Good Life	Atlantic	8103	'65	†
I'll Take You Where the Music's Playing	Atlantic	8113	'65	†
Golden Hits	Atlantic	8153	'67	CS/CD
1959–1965: All Time Greatest Hits and More	Atlantic	(2) 81931		CS/CD
The Drifters Now	Bell	219		†
Best	Arista	4111	'77	†
Greatest Hits	Dominion	3000	'91	CS/CD
Bringing You Their Best	Pair	1305	'91	CS/CD
Very Best	Rhino	71211	'93	CS/CD
Up on the Roof, On Broadway and Under the Boardwalk	Rhino	71230	'93	CS/CD
Greatest Hits	Hollywood/IMG	119		CS/CD
16 Greatest Hits	Deluxe	7818		CS/CD
	Deluxe	7898		CS

Ben E. King

Spanish Harlem	Atco	33-133	'61	†
Sings for Soulful Lovers	Atco	33-137	'62	†
Don't Play That Song	Atco	33-142	'62	†
Greatest Hits	Atco	33-165	'64	†
7 Letters	Atco	33-174	'65	†
Rough Edges	Maxwell	88001	'70	†
Beginning of It All	Mandala	3007	'72	†
Supernatural	Atlantic	18132	'75	†
I Had a Love	Atlantic	18169	'76	†
Let Me In Your Life	Atlantic	19200	'78	†
Music Trance	Atlantic	19269	'80	†
Street Tough	Atlantic	19300	'81	†
Stand By Me/The Ultimate Collection	Atlantic	80213	'87	CD
Stand By Me ("Best")	Atlantic	81716	'87	CS
Save the Last Dance for Me	EMI Manhattan	46904	'88	LP/CS/CD†
What's Important to Me	Ichiban	1133	'92	CS/CD
Anthology	Rhino	71215	'93	CS/CD
Best	Curb/CEMA	77594	'93	CS/CD

Ben E. King and the Average White Band

Benny and Us	Atlantic	19105	'77	†

BOB DYLAN

(b. Robert Zimmerman, May 24, 1941, Duluth, MN)

Certainly the single most important figure in contemporary music during the '60s, Bob Dylan was the first and most significant song-poet to emerge from the folk-music scene, inspiring a whole generation of folk artists (and later rock artists) to explore the power of popular songwriting. Having successfully made the transition from traditional folk music to penetrating, highly political, socially conscious protest music, Dylan revitalized folk music and songwriting with his highly personal, intense song poetics permeated with acute literary and philosophical references.

Seemingly one step ahead of his audience at critical intellectual and musical junctures, Bob Dylan somehow managed to avoid becoming typecast by fans and critics alike at progressive stages of his career to maintain his status as contemporary music's most independent, elusive, and enigmatic figure. First a folk singer, Dylan alienated his fans when he

BOB DYLAN

went electric and entered the world of rock and roll. Just when the rock audience was beginning to embrace him, he made another U-turn and recorded one of the first country-rock albums, *Nashville Skyline*. The '70s saw Dylan become a mainstream singer-songwriter; but after being "born again" late in the decade, he recorded several Christian-themed albums. Although less creative as a songwriter in the '80s and '90s, Dylan continues to follow his own vision.

In popular music before Dylan, professional songwriters provided music to good-looking, pleasant-voiced singers— music aimed at a particular market, whether it be teen pop, country, or easy listening. Dylan was among the first artists to prove that a songwriter, no matter how "untalented" he or she might be as a singer or instrumentalist, could be the best interpreter of his or her own material. Thanks largely to Dylan, rock became a medium of self-expression with the goal of creating important, meaningful music (which, by the way, might find a commercial audience). Through his widespread popularity, Dylan encouraged a number of artists to use their marginally adequate singing voices on recordings, most notably Jimi Hendrix, Neil Young, and Bruce Springsteen. To date, the entire body of Dylan's work has been sung in a harsh, strident, adenoidal voice lacking polished musical nuance.

Robert Zimmerman moved with his family to Hibbing, Minnesota, when he was 6. Taking up guitar around age 12, he later formed several rock groups while still in high school. After graduation, he attended the University of Minnesota for several months, dropping out in December 1960 to travel to New York to visit his early idol Woody Guthrie, who was hospitalized with Huntington's disease. Dylan began performing at Greenwich Village folk clubs in early 1961, debuting at Gerde's Folk City that April. First noticed by *New York Times* critic Robert Shelton that September, Dylan was signed to Columbia Records by noted pop jazz producer John Hammond in October. His first album featured traditional folk and blues songs, such as "Man of Constant Sorrow" and "House of the Rising Sun," as well as Eric Von Schmidt's "Baby, Let Me Follow You Down" and the original "Song to Woody."

Dylan's second album, *The Freewheelin' Bob Dylan*, contained all his own material and effectively established him as a songwriter, at least in folk circles. The songs included a number of potent protest and antiwar songs, such as "Masters of War," "A Hard Rain's a-Gonna Fall," and "Blowin' in the Wind." In 1963 the folk group Peter, Paul and Mary popularized two songs from the album, "Blowin' in the Wind" and "Don't Think Twice, It's All Right."

The Times They Are a-Changin' featured several songs concerning the treatment of blacks in America ("The Lonesome Death of Hattie Carroll" and "Only a Pawn in Their Game"), the antiwar "With God on Our Side," and the title song, adopted by the youth-protest movement as a political anthem. The more personal *Another Side* includes a number of songs later recorded by others in the so-called folk-rock mold: "It Ain't Me Babe" (The Turtles), "All I Really Want to Do" (The Byrds and Cher), and "Chimes of Freedom" and "My Back Pages" (The Byrds).

Bob Dylan left the folk and protest movements behind with 1965's *Bringing It All Back Home*. Half acoustic and half electric, the album contained a number of songs written in a stream-of-consciousness style, pervaded with incisive, evocative, and surreal images, such as "Gates of Eden" and "Subterranean Homesick Blues," his first (albeit moderate) hit. Other inclusions were the provocative "It's Alright Ma (I'm Only Bleeding)" and "It's All Over Now, Baby Blue," and the underrated love songs "She Belongs to Me" and "Love Minus Zero/No Limit." The Byrds soon recorded "Mr. Tambourine Man" as the first folk-rock song. By now an international celebrity, Dylan was being hailed by critics as the spokesman of his disillusioned and alienated generation.

Already dismayed by the electric, rock sound of "Subterranean Homesick Blues," folk fans and critics were positively shocked by the album *Highway 61 Revisited*, the single "Like a Rolling Stone," and Dylan's performance at the Newport Folk Festival backed by the electrified Paul Butterfield Blues Band. The album, recorded with electric guitarist Mike Bloomfield and keyboardist Al Kooper, created an unmistakable sound and featured some of Dylan's most startling songwriting efforts. Filled with surreal images, stimulating existential observations, and evocative song-poetry, the album contained a number of classics of '60s songwriting: "Ballad of a Thin Man," "Queen Jane Approximately," and the tour de force "Desolation Row." Indeed, the album was remarkably consistent in its high level of songwriting and performance. Rather than focusing on a single song, Dylan effectively made the entire album the unit of his expression. The quintessential "Like a Rolling Stone," arguably his finest composition, became Dylan's first smash-hit single and established his credibility with the new rock audience. "Positively 4th Street" soon became a smash hit, followed by the minor hit "Can You Please Crawl Out Your Window?"

During summer 1965 Bob Dylan contacted a Canadian group known as Levon and the Hawks, then touring the U.S. East Coast. Between fall 1965 and summer 1966 the group, later known simply as the Band, toured with Dylan, but without their recalcitrant drummer and leader, Levon Helm.

In fall 1966 Columbia issued one of the first nonanthology double-record sets in rock history for Dylan, *Blonde on Blonde*. Considered by many as Dylan's most fully realized album, the recording was made with outstanding Nashville session musicians such as Wayne Moss, Charlie McCoy, Kenny Buttrey, and Hargus "Pig" Robbins, as well as Al Kooper and the Band's Robbie Robertson. An immensely wide-ranging album in terms of the songwriting, *Blonde on Blonde* yielded four hits: "Rainy Day Women #12 & 35" (a smash), "I Want You," "Just Like a Woman," and "Leopard-Skin Pill-Box Hat." Another strikingly consistent set in terms of musical performance and lyrical invention, the album included the desolate "Visions of Johanna," the vituperative "Most Likely You'll Go Your Way and I'll Go Mine," and the sidelong "Sad-Eyed Lady of the Lowlands," ostensibly composed in the studio as the musicians waited.

On July 29, 1966, Bob Dylan was seriously injured in a motorcycle accident. He subsequently retreated to upstate New York to recuperate amidst a variety of wild and irresponsible rumors. He summoned the members of the Band, and rehearsed and recorded with them during his public absence. The recordings, made between June and September 1967, were somehow pirated and released on bootleg albums. Among the material were a number of previously unrecorded Dylan songs, such as "Million Dollar Bash," "Lo and Behold!," and "Please, Mrs. Henry." Several of the songs were later recorded by other groups: "Too Much of Nothing" by Peter, Paul and Mary, and "You Ain't Goin' Nowhere" and "Nothing

Was Delivered" by the Byrds on their *Sweetheart of the Rodeo* album. Thanks to their association with Dylan, the Band was signed to Capitol Records and released their own debut album, featuring other songs written during this period, including "Tears of Rage" and "This Wheel's on Fire." The Dylan/Band rehearsal recordings were eventually officially released in 1975 in part as *The Basement Tapes*.

Bob Dylan reemerged in early 1968 with *John Wesley Harding*, although he was not to tour again until 1974. This album also befuddled many of his fans. The harsh, strident voice was replaced by a mellow, pleasing voice, and the songs contained little of the vituperation and anger of his previous albums. Instead the songs were concerned with resignation, regeneration, and resurrection, and an almost religious wariness. Moreover, the songs exhibited little of the rock-and-roll raunch evident earlier. Recorded with only Nashville session players Charlie McCoy on bass and Kenny Buttrey on drums, the album yielded no hit singles yet featured a number of profoundly moving existential pieces, including "All Along the Watchtower," later recorded in its definitive version by Jimi Hendrix. The album's final two songs, "Down Along the Cove" and "I'll Be Your Baby Tonight," introduced another stylistic shift fully realized with 1969's *Nashville Skyline*—a move into a country-pop sound.

Recorded with the same basic personnel as used earlier (Buttrey and McCoy as well as Pete Drake and Charlie Daniels), *Nashville Skyline* once again turned confused critics' and fans' heads in dismay. Attacked as sentimental and simplistic, the album included a duet with Johnny Cash on the early Dylan song "Girl from the North Country" and a number of songs written in an almost Tin Pan Alley mold. "Lay Lady Lay" became a near-smash hit from the album, which also included "I Threw It All Away" and "Tonight I'll Be Staying Here with You."

The disjointed *Self Portrait* contained a variety of material, including live recordings with the Band ("Like a Rolling Stone" and "The Mighty Quinn") and cover versions of songs written by Paul Simon and Gordon Lightfoot. Universally panned, the album was hastily followed by *New Morning*, which contained ditties such as "If Dogs Run Free," "Time Passes Slowly," and "If Not for You." For several years after *New Morning* Dylan was largely out of the public eye. He appeared at George Harrison's August 1971 Concert for Bangladesh, performing a well-received set of his '60s hits accompanied by his own guitar and harmonica, backed by Harrison on acoustic guitar and Ringo Starr on tambourine. His only recordings of the period were five songs for *Greatest Hits, Volume II* and the singles "Watching the River Flow" and "George Jackson." In 1973 he appeared in a small role in the film *Pat Garrett and Billy the Kid*, for which he wrote and performed the soundtrack music. The album yielded a major hit with the classic "Knockin' on Heaven's Door." Embroiled in a dispute with Dylan, Columbia Records retaliated by capitalizing on this success and releasing *Dylan*, which featured cover versions of songs such as Jerry Jeff Walker's "Mr. Bojangles" and Joni Mitchell's "Big Yellow Taxi" drawn from earlier sessions.

Dylan returned to touring and recording, reuniting with the Band for the album *Planet Waves*. Again Dylan received a critical drubbing, although some of the songs, such as "Going, Going, Gone," "Something There Is About You," and "Forever Young," were finely crafted. In January and February 1974 he toured for the first time in eight years, again with the Band. The tour was an instant sellout and yielded the double-record set *Before the Flood*. A year later Dylan convincingly reestablished himself as a powerful songwriter with *Blood on the Tracks*. The album included diverse material, from the vituperative "Idiot Wind" to a number of moving songs such as "Tangled Up in Blue," "Simple Twist of Fate," and "Shelter from the Storm," as well as the epic Western tale "Lily, Rosemary and the Jack of Hearts."

In an effort to reestablish grassroots contact with his audience, Bob Dylan assembled the Rolling Thunder Revue for engagements in the Northeast. Participants varied greatly, with appearances by Roger McGuinn, Joan Baez, Ramblin' Jack Elliott, Ronnie Hawkins, Mick Ronson, and others. Although it continued into 1976, the tour culminated in a December 8, 1975, benefit performance at Madison Square Garden for ex-boxer Rubin "Hurricane" Carter, who was alleged to have been unjustly convicted of three New Jersey murders in 1974. Dylan's next album, *Desire*, stirred controversy with its song "Hurricane," which sought to bring attention to Carter's plight. Perhaps his best-selling album, *Desire* features seven songs written by Dylan in collaboration with Jacques Levy.

In early 1978 Bob Dylan released the 3-hour, 52-minute movie *Renaldo and Clara*, shot during the Rolling Thunder Revue tour. Written, produced, directed, and coedited by Dylan, the film assembled 56 songs from the tour within a series of confusing and widely careening parables revolving around Renaldo (Dylan), Clara (then-wife Sara), the Woman in White (Joan Baez), and Dylan (Ronnie Hawkins). Greeted by disparaging reviews, the film was later withdrawn for re-editing. Beginning in February of that year, Dylan made his first concert appearances outside the United States in more than 11 years in Japan, Australia, New Zealand, and western Europe. The tour produced *Bob Dylan at Budokan*. At midyear the erratic *Street Legal* was issued to mixed reviews, and his subsequent three-month U.S./Canadian tour was the subject of negative criticism.

Dylan shocked friends and fans alike with his next startling announcement, that he had converted to Christianity. In fall 1979 Columbia issued the best-selling *Slow Train Coming* recorded with Dire Straits guitarist Mark Knopfler. Comprised of essentially Christian material, the album yielded a major hit with "Gotta Serve Somebody"; it also contained "When You Gonna Wake Up," "Gonna Change My Way of Thinking," and "When He Returns." *Saved* sold less well, but included two intriguing nonreligious songs, "What Can I Do for You" and "Solid Rock."

Following *Shot of Love*, Bob Dylan did not record for two years. When released in 1983, *Infidels* was hailed as a powerful comeback and his best album since *Blood on the Tracks*. Coproduced by Dylan and Dire Straits guitarist Mark Knopfler, the album announced his movement away from Christian-only material. It included pointed songs such as "Man of Peace," "Neighborhood Bully," and "Union Sundown," as well as the gentle "Don't Fall Apart on Me" and the rousing "Sweetheart Like You," a minor hit. Dylan toured Europe with Santana in 1984, and during 1985 he appeared at the Live Aid and Farm Aid benefits and joined in the recording of the benefit singles "We Are the World" and "Sun City." *Empire Burlesque* was received equivocally, but the retrospective boxed-set *Biograph* was greeted enthusiastically, especially by Dylan collectors. The set contained 53 songs recorded between 1962 and 1981, including 18 previously unreleased tracks and 3 hard-to-find singles, plus a fascinating 36-page booklet written by Cameron Crowe. This was among the first boxed sets, and its success set the stage for hundreds more, particularly in the CD era.

In 1986 Dylan conducted his first major American tour in seven years, backed by Tom Petty and the Heartbreakers, the most skilled band he had played with since the Band. Petty and the Heartbreakers also helped record his *Knocked Out Loaded* album, which included "Got My Mind Made Up," cowritten with Petty, and "Under Your Spell," cowritten with Carole Bayer Sager. In the latter part of the year Dylan acted in the movie *Hearts of Fire*, but the film was released in Europe only in 1987 and panned upon U.S. release in 1990. During summer 1987 he played six stadium shows with the Grateful Dead that yielded *Dylan and the Dead* in 1989. His 1988 tour was neither well attended nor well received, and that year's album, *Down in the Groove*, failed to sell, despite the assistance of Eric Clapton, Mark Knopfler, and Jerry Garcia. Dylan appeared on *Folkways: A Vision Shared—A Tribute to Woody Guthrie and Leadbelly*, recording a rousing version of Guthrie's "Pretty Boy Floyd." Also in 1988 he participated in the playful Traveling Wilburys project along with George Harrison, Jeff Lynne, Tom Petty, and Roy Orbison, contributing "Tweeter and the Monkey Man" and "Congratulations" to their first album; a second Traveling Wilburys set was released in 1990.

In an effort to thwart long-active bootleggers, Columbia issued *The Bootleg Series—Volumes 1–3* in 1991. The three-CD set contained 58 songs never before officially released, including "Quit Your Lowdown Ways," "She's Your Lover Now," and "Seven Days." Later in the year Rhino released *I Shall Be Unreleased: The Songs of Bob Dylan*, with selections by Rod Stewart, Joan Baez, Rick Nelson, and Roger McGuinn, among others. In October 1992, Columbia Records Celebrates the Music of Bob Dylan was staged at New York's Madison Square Garden, to celebrate his 30th anniversary on the label (and his 50th birthday). Musicians who played one or more Dylan songs included Neil Young, George Harrison, Eric Clapton, Tom Petty, Willie Nelson, and Tracy Chapman. Also in that year, Dylan recorded *Good As I Been to You* by himself, a set of traditional folk songs with just his guitar and harmonica accompaniment; a second collection appeared under the title *World Gone Wrong* in 1993. He appeared at the Woodstock II concert-festival in August 1994, and in December he performed on *MTV Unplugged* with his band. Recordings from the show were released as a highly acclaimed album in 1995. Dylan is the subject of the 1995 CD-ROM *Bob Dylan: Highway 61 Interactive*, which included several rare early recordings and a brief clip from his 1965 Newport Folk Festival performance.

Bob Dylan has received numerous awards, from a Grammy lifetime achievement award to his induction into the Rock and Roll Hall of Fame in 1988.

Bob Dylan

Bob Dylan	Columbia	8579	'62	CS/CD
The Freewheelin' Bob Dylan	Columbia	8786	'63	CS/CD
The Times They Are a-Changin'	Columbia	8905	'64	CS/CD
Bob Dylan/The Times They Are a-Changin'	Columbia	38221	'86	CS
Another Side of Bob Dylan	Columbia	8993	'64	†
	Columbia	53200	'92	CS/CD
Bringing It All Back Home	Columbia	9128	'65	CS/CD
Highway 61 Revisited	Columbia	9189	'65	CS/CD
	DCC	1021		CD
Blonde on Blonde	Columbia	(2) 841	'66	|
	Columbia	00841		CS/CD
Greatest Hits	Columbia	9463	'67	CS/CD
John Wesley Harding	Columbia	9604	'68	CS/CD
Nashville Skyline	Columbia	9825	'69	CS/CD
Self-Portrait	Columbia	30050	'70	CS/CD
New Morning	Columbia	30290	'70	CS/CD
Greatest Hits, Volume 2	Columbia	(2) 31120	'71	CD
	Columbia	31120	'71	CS
Pat Garrett and Billy the Kid (soundtrack)	Columbia	32460	'73	CS/CD
Dylan	Columbia	32747	'73	CS
Blood on the Tracks	Columbia	33235	'75/'84	CS/CD
Desire	Columbia	33893	'76	CS/CD
Hard Rain	Columbia	34349	'76	CS/CD
Street Legal	Columbia	35453	'78	CS/CD
Bob Dylan at Budokan	Columbia	(2) 36067	'79	CD
	Columbia	36067	'79	CS
Slow Train Coming	Columbia	36120	'79	CS/CD
Saved	Columbia	36553	'80/'90	CS/CD
Shot of Love	Columbia	37496	'81	CS/CD
Infidels	Columbia	38819	'83	CS/CD
Real Live	Columbia	39944	'84/'85	CS/CD
Empire Burlesque	Columbia	40110	'85	CS/CD
Biograph (1961–1981)	Columbia	(3) 38830	'85	CS/CD

Knocked Out Loaded	Columbia	40439	'86	CS/CD
Hearts of Fire (soundtrack)	Columbia	40870	'87	CS/CD
Down in the Groove	Columbia	40957	'88	CS/CD
Oh, Mercy!	Columbia	45281	'89	CS/CD
Under the Red Sky	Columbia	46794	'90	CS/CD
The Bootleg Series, Volumes 1–3 (Rare and Unreleased), 1961–1991	Columbia	(3) 47382	'91	CS/CD
Good As I Been to You	Columbia	53200	'92	CS/CD
World Gone Wrong	Columbia	57590	'93	CS/CD
Greatest Hits, Volume 3	Columbia	66783	'94	CS/CD
MTV Unplugged	Columbia	67000	'95	CS/CD
Bob Dylan and the Band				
The Basement Tapes (recorded 1967)	Columbia	(2) 33682	'75	CS/CD
Planet Waves	Columbia	37637	'74	CS/CD
Before the Flood	Columbia	(2) 37661	'74	CS/CD
Bob Dylan and the Grateful Dead				
Dylan and the Dead (recorded 1987)	Columbia	45056	'89	CS/CD
The Traveling Wilburys				
Volume One	Wilbury	25796	'88	CS/CD
Volume 3	Wilbury	26324	'90	CS/CD
Tribute Albums				
I Shall Be Unreleased: The Songs of Bob Dylan	Rhino	70518	'91	CS/CD
The 30th Anniversary Concert Celebration	Columbia	(3) 53230	'93	LP

THE EAGLES

Glenn Frey (b. Nov. 6, 1948, Detroit, MI), gtr, kybd, voc; **Don Henley** (b. July 22, 1947, Gilmer, TX), drm, voc; **Bernie Leadon** (b. July 19, 1947, Minneapolis, MN), gtr, bjo, mdln, slide and steel gtrs, voc; **Randy Meisner** (b. Mar. 8, 1946, Scottsbluff, NE), bs, voc [In January 1974 the group added **Don Felder** (b. Sept. 21, 1947, Gainesville, FL) on guitar, banjo, and pedal steel guitar. Bernie Leadon left in December 1975, to be replaced by **Joe Walsh** (b. Nov. 20, 1947, Wichita, KS) on guitar and vocals. Randy Meisner left in September 1977, to be replaced by **Timothy B. Schmit** (b. Oct. 30, 1947, Sacramento, CA).]

THE EAGLES

The most popular American rock band of the '70s, the Eagles used rock instrumentation to create a distinctive country sound based on easily identifiable melodies, strong vocal harmonies, and engaging lyrics. As a singles band the Eagles approached the consistency of Creedence Clearwater Revival; as an album band they featured the incisive and affecting songwriting of Don Henley and Glenn Frey, proclaimed as the most successful and prolific rock songwriting pair of the '70s. Their second album, *Desperado*, had a certain conceptual consistency with its theme of outlaws of the old and new West, yet the group benefited greatly when joined by guitarist Joe Walsh, who added much-needed instrumental punch to their otherwise tame sound. *Hotel California* became the group's masterpiece, with its tough sound, gutsy singing, and powerful lyrics exploring existential and social concerns. However, the album was so successful that the group began disintegrating while attempting to record an equally significant and moving follow-up.

All former members of the Eagles recorded solo albums following the dissolution of the group, but only Don Henley was able to establish a distinctive musical identity. With *Building the Perfect Beast* and *The End of the Innocence*, his songwriting became more mature, provocative, and profound. The Eagles reunited in 1994 for their Hell Freezes Over tour and album.

Glenn Frey took piano lessons as a child and played Detroit clubs with his first band, the Subterraneans, often with Bob Seger. He relocated to California, and along with Detroit-born singer-songwriter J. D. Souther formed the duo Longbranch-Pennywhistle, recording an album for Amos Records in Los Angeles. Don Henley grew up in Linden, Texas, and played in bands during and after high school. He attended four years of college, but did not graduate, electing to move to Los Angeles with his band Shiloh, who also recorded an album for Amos. Randy Meisner had been an original member of Poco before playing in Rick Nelson's Stone Canyon Band from 1969 to 1971. Bernie Leadon had recorded single albums with Hearts and Flowers and Dillard and Clark before recording two albums with the Flying Burrito Brothers. Frey, Henley, Meisner, and Leadon worked as Linda Ronstadt's backing band in 1970 before forming the Eagles a year later.

Signed to Asylum Records, the Eagles recorded their first album in London. "Take It Easy," written by Frey and Jackson Browne, was the group's first big hit, followed by Henley and Leadon's "Witchy Woman" and Jack Tempchin's "Peaceful Easy Feeling." The debut album also contained "Train Leaves Here This Morning," written by Leadon and Gene Clark, originally included on the first Dillard and Clark album. *Desperado*, also recorded in London, was somewhat of a concept album, based on the theme of the rock band as old-and new-West outlaws. The album yielded only two minor hits with Henley and Frey's classic "Desperado" and David Blue's "Outlaw Man." During 1973 the Eagles successfully toured the United States, but they displayed little instrumental punch.

While recording *On the Border* in early 1974 the Eagles added session musician Don Felder to fill out their sound. Felder had recorded one album with the jazz band Flow. *On the Border* contained three songs written by outside writers—Paul Craft's "Midnight Flyer," Tom Waits's "Ol' 55," and Jack Tempchin's "Already Gone" (a moderate hit)—and included the Eagles' first top hit, the tender and delicate "Best of My Love."

The Eagles' popularity was established with 1975's *One of These Nights*. The album produced the top hit title song and the smash "Lyin' Eyes" (both written by Henley and Frey), and the smash "Take It to the Limit" (written by Meisner, Henley, and Frey). During that year the band toured internationally in support of the album, but by year's end Leadon had departed. Guitarist-vocalist Joe Walsh, formerly with the James Gang and also a solo recording artist, was added to provide a more dynamic, rough-edged quality to the group's sound.

Joe Walsh's contribution was immediately evident on the group's masterwork *Hotel California*. The album's first (top) hit, "New Kid in Town" (by Henley, Frey, and J. D. Souther) resembled the group's earlier hits, but the top hit "Hotel California" (by Felder, Henley, and Frey) and the major hit "Life in the Fast Lane" (by Henley, Frey, and Walsh) exhibited the verve of Walsh's lead-guitar playing. The album also revealed the growing maturity of Henley and Frey's songwriting with "Wasted Time" and "The Last Resort," the latter expressing a deep if pessimistic concern with the environment.

During 1977 the Eagles toured successfully the United States, Great Britain, and Europe. In September Randy Meisner left the group, to be replaced by former Poco bassist-vocalist Tim Schmit. In late 1978 the Eagles scored a major hit with "Please Come Home for Christmas" as they struggled to complete work on the follow-up to *Hotel California*. Finally issued in late 1979, *The Long Run* yielded the top hit "Heartache Tonight" (by Henley, Frey, J. D. Souther, and Bob Seger) and the near-smashes "The Long Run" (by Henley and Frey) and "I Can't Tell You Why" (by Schmit, Henley, and Frey), the latter with lead vocals by Schmit. In September 1980 Glenn Frey informed Don Henley that he was making a solo album, essentially ending the group, although no official announcement was ever made. They managed to put together the double-record set *Eagles Live*, which produced a major hit with Steve Young's "Seven Bridges Road."

Bernie Leadon was the first former Eagle to record an album away from the group. *Natural Progressions*, recorded with guitarist-vocalist Michael Georgiades, was issued in 1977. In 1987 Leadon was a member of the Nitty Gritty Dirt Band. Randy Meisner recorded three albums through 1982, scoring major hits with "Deep Inside My Heart" and "Hearts on Fire" from *One More Song*, and "Never Been in Love." Don Felder managed a moderate hit in 1981 with "Heavy Metal (Takin' a Ride)" from the animated movie *Heavy Metal*, contributed "Never Surrender" to the soundtrack for the 1982 movie *Fast Times at Ridgemont High*, and recorded a solo album in 1983. Timothy Schmit achieved a minor hit with "So Much in Love" (also from *Fast Times At Ridgemont High*) and a major hit with "Boys Night Out" in 1987; he recorded three albums, including 1990's *Tell Me the Truth*. During the '80s Joe Walsh recorded four albums, hitting with "A Life of Illusion" in 1981 and "Space Age Whiz Kids" in 1983. In 1991 Pyramid Records issued his *Ordinary Average Guy*.

The two principal songwriters of the Eagles, Glenn Frey and Don Henley, were the most active of the former members during the '80s. Frey collaborated with Jack Tempchin on six songs for his album *No Fun Aloud*, which yielded major to moderate hits with "I Found Somebody," "The One You Love," and "All Those Lies." The album also included "Partytown" and Bob Seger's "That Girl." *The Allnighter* produced a major hit with "Sexy Girl." In 1985 Frey scored a smash hit with "The Heat Is On" from the movie *Beverly Hills Cop*, and a major hit with "Smuggler's Blues" and smash hit with "You Belong to the City," both from the television show *Miami Vice*. He made his acting debut in *Miami Vice* and later appeared in seven episodes of *Wiseguy*. He hit again with "True Love" in 1988 and "Part of Me, Part of You" (from the movie *Thelma and Louise*) in 1991. In 1993 Frey starred in the short-lived CBS private detective series *South of Sunset*; it was canceled after only one episode!

Commercially and artistically, Don Henley was the most successful of the former Eagles in the '80s. In late 1981 he scored a smash hit with Stevie Nicks on "Leather and Lace" from her *Bella Donna* album. Henley's 1982 *I Can't Stand Still* was recorded with former James Taylor and Jackson Browne guitarist Danny "Kootch" Kortchmar, who cowrote the smash hit "Dirty Laundry." The album also included "Johnny Can't Read" and "I Can't Stand Still" (minor hits), and "Nobody's Business" and "You Better Hang Up." With the mature and finely crafted *Building the Perfect Beast*, Henley established his own musical identity and broke through commercially. The album yielded four hits with the nostalgic smash "The Boys of Summer," the near-smash "All She Wants to Do Is Dance," and the major hits "Not Enough Love in the World" and "Sunset Grill." "Drivin' with Your Eyes Closed" and "You're Not Drinking Enough" were also on the album.

Don Henley's 1989 album *The End of the Innocence* remained on the charts for nearly three years and produced five hit singles in a year and a half: the moving title ballad, cowritten with Bruce Hornsby; the major hits "The Last Worthless Evening" and, perhaps his finest composition since "Desperado," "The Heart of the Matter"; and the minor hits "How Bad Do You Want It?" and "New York Minute." Touring in 1989 and 1990, Henley scored another smash in 1992 with "Sometimes Love Just Ain't Enough" with Patty Smyth, the lead singer of Scandal. Henley issued a greatest-hits package in 1995, *Actual Miles*, including a new song, "In the Garden of Allah."

In late 1993 Giant Records issued the Eagles tribute album *Common Thread*, with contemporary country artists such as Travis Tritt and Alan Jackson covering Eagles songs. The album proved enormously successful and encouraged the Eagles to reunite. In April 1994 Don Henley, Glenn Frey, Don Felder, Timothy Schmit, and Joe Walsh taped an MTV reunion special backed by a 30-piece orchestra that yielded *Hell Freezes Over* late in the year. In addition to the live cuts, the album included four new songs recorded in the studio, including Henley and Frey's acerbic "Get Over It," a moderate pop hit, and Schmit and Paul Carrack's "Love Will Keep Us Alive," a top easy-listening hit. The Eagles began touring again in May 1994, but the tour was interrupted in October by Frey's surgery for intestinal problems before it resumed in January 1995.

Longbranch/Pennywhistle (with Glenn Frey)

Longbranch/Pennywhistle	Amos	7007	'69	†

Shiloh (with Don Henley)

Shiloh	Amos	7015	'70	†

Hearts and Flowers (with Bernie Leadon)

Of Horses, Kids and Forgotten Women	Capitol	2868	'68	†

Flow (with Don Felder)

Flow	CTI	1003	'70	†

The Eagles

The Eagles	Asylum	5054	'72	CS/CD
Desperado	Asylum	5068	'73	CS/CD
The Eagles/Desperado	Asylum	60155		CS
On the Border	Asylum	1004	'74	CS/CD
One of These Nights	Asylum	1039	'75	CS/CD
On the Border/One of These Nights	Asylum	60154		CS
Greatest Hits, 1971–1975	Asylum	1052	'76	†
	Asylum	105		CS/CD
	DCC	1039		CD
Hotel California	Asylum	1084	'76	†
	Asylum	103		CS/CD
	DCC	1024		CD
The Long Run	Asylum	508	'79	CS/CD
Hotel California/The Long Run	Asylum	60275		CS
Eagles Live	Asylum	(2) 705	'80	CS/CD
Greatest His, Volume 2	Asylum	60205	'82	CS/CD
Hell Freezes Over	Geffen	24725	'94	CS/CD

Tribute Album

Common Thread: The Songs of the Eagles	Giant	24531	'93	CS/CD

The Bernie Leadon–Michael Georgiades Band

Natural Progressions	Asylum	1107	'77	†

Randy Meisner

Randy Meisner	Elektra	140	'78	†
One More Song	Epic	36748	'80/'91	CD

Glenn Frey

No Fun Aloud	Asylum	60129	'82	CS
The Allnighter	MCA	5501	'84	†
	MCA	31158	'85	CD
	MCA	39307		CS
Soul Searchin'	MCA	6239	'88	CS/CD
Strange Weather	MCA	10599	'92	CS/CD
Glenn Frey Live	MCA	10826	'93	CS/CS
Solo Collection	MCA	11227	'95	CS/CD

Don Henley

I Can't Stand Still	Asylum	60048	'82	CS/CD

Building the Perfect Beast	Geffen	24026	'84/'85	CS/CD
The End of Innocence	Geffen	24217	'89	CS/CD
Actual Miles: Don Henley's Greatest Hits	Geffen	24834	'95	CS/CD
Timothy B. Schmit				
Tell Me the Truth	MCA	6420	'90	CS/CD

EARTH, WIND AND FIRE

Maurice White (b. Dec. 19, 1941, Memphis, TN), drm, voc; **Verdine White** (b. July 25, 1951, IL), bs, voc; **Philip Bailey** (b. May 8, 1951, Denver, CO), voc, perc; **Andrew Woolfolk** (b. Oct. 11, 1950, TX), horns; **Ralph Johnson** (b. July 4, 1951, CA), perc [**Larry Dunn** (b. Lawrence Dunhill, June 19, 1953, CO), keyboards, and **Al McKay** (b. Feb. 2, 1948, LA), guitar and percussion, were added by 1974.]

The most successful black crossover band of the '70s, Earth, Wind and Fire featured the songwriting of leader-producer-vocalist Maurice White and the stunning falsetto of colead vocalist Philip Bailey surrounded by punchy horn playing and exquisite vocal harmonies. Purveyors of dance tunes and gentle ballads, Earth, Wind and Fire promoted spiritual brotherhood through music and enjoyed extensive popularity beginning with their 1975 album *That's the Way of the World*. Disbanded from 1984 to 1987 for solo projects by White and Bailey, the group did not approach the level of their early success upon reuniting.

Originally conceived as a cooperative musical ensemble by Maurice White in Los Angeles, Earth, Wind and Fire recorded two albums for Warner Bros. before switching to Columbia in 1972. Maurice White had been raised in Chicago and served as a session drummer at Chess Records for three years. Beginning in 1967 he toured with popular jazz pianist Ramsey Lewis for three years before forming the Salty Peppers with his brother, bassist Verdine White. With the core of the White brothers plus percussionist-vocalist Philip Bailey, Earth, Wind and Fire added horn player Andrew Woolfolk and percussionist Ralph Johnson after their Columbia debut. Their third Columbia album, 1974's *Open Our Eyes*, yielded smash R&B hits with "Kalimba Story" and "Mighty Mighty," also a major pop hit, as was "Devotion."

Earth, Wind and Fire began establishing themselves as a major crossover act with 1975's *That's the Way of the World*. The album included the top R&B and pop hit "Shining Star," and the title song, a smash hit in both fields. Their next three, best-selling albums conveyed a sense of spiritual brotherhood through lyrics and music while producing a number of crossover hits. *Gratitude* was comprised mostly of live material and yielded a top R&B and smash pop hit with the studio-recorded "Sing a Song." *Spirit* contained the major pop and smash R&B hits "Getaway" and "Saturday Night," while *All 'n All* included the major hits "Serpentine Fire" (a top R&B hit) and "Fantasy." In 1978 Earth, Wind and Fire scored a smash crossover hit with the Beatles' "Got to Get You into My Life" from the *Sgt. Pepper* movie. They continued the pattern through 1981 with "September," "Boogie Wonderland" (with the Emotions), the classic "After the Love Has Gone," and "Let's Groove." "Fall in Love with Me" and "Magnetic" became the hits from *Electric Universe*, but in 1984 Earth, Wind and Fire disbanded.

During the '80s Maurice White produced albums for Ramsey Lewis, Jennifer Holliday, Deniece Williams, and Barbra Streisand (*Emotion*) and recorded his debut solo album. Philip Bailey recorded both religious and pop albums, scoring a smash pop and R&B hit in 1984–1985 with "Easy Lover," in duet with Phil Collins.

In 1987 Earth, Wind and Fire reunited with Maurice and Verdine White, Philip Bailey, Andrew Woolfolk, and Ralph Johnson. However, *Touch the World* yielded only minor pop hits with "System of Survival" and "Thinking of You," although both were smash R&B hits. In 1993 the group scored a moderate pop hit with "Sunday Morning" on Reprise. By 1995 only Philip Bailey and Verdine White remained from the original members for touring, although Maurice White continued to record with the group in the studio.

Earth, Wind and Fire

Earth, Wind and Fire	Warner Bros.	1905	'71	†
The Need of Love	Warner Bros.	1958	'71	†
Another Time	Warner Bros.	(2) 2798	'74	†
Last Days and Times	Columbia	31702	'72	CS/CD
Head to the Sky	Columbia	32194	'73	CS/CD
Open Our Eyes	Columbia	32712	'74	CS/CD
That's the Way of the World	Columbia	33280	'75	CS/CD
Gratitude	Columbia	33694	'75	CS/CD
Spirit	Columbia	34241	'76	CS/CD
All 'n All	Columbia	34905	'77	CS/CD
	Columbia/Legacy	57189	'93	CD
Best, Volume 1	Columbia	35647	'78	CS/CD
I Am	Columbia	35730	'79	CS/CD
Faces	Columbia	36795	'80	CS/CD
Raise!	Columbia	37548	'81	CS/CD
Powerlight	Columbia	38367	'83	CS/CD
Electric Universe	Columbia	38980	'83	CS
Touch The World	Columbia	40596	'87	CS
Best, Volume 2	Columbia	45013	'88	CS/CD
Heritage	Columbia	45268	'90	CS/CD
The Eternal Dance	Columbia	(3) 52439	'92	CS/CD
Millennium	Reprise	45274	'93	CS/CD
Singasong	IMG	709		CS

Philip Bailey

Continuation	Columbia	38725	'83	†
Chinese Wall	Columbia	39542	'84	CS/CD
Inside Out	Columbia	40209	'86	†
Philip Bailey	Zoo	11051	'94	CS/CD

Religious Albums by Philip Bailey

The Wonders of His Love	Myrrh	8102	'84	†
Triumph	Horizon	0754	'86	†
Family Affair	Word/Epic	47756	'91	CS/CD
The Best of Philip Bailey: A Gospel Collection	Word/Epic	77004	'91	LP/CS/CD

Maurice White

Maurice White	Columbia	39883	'85	CS/CD†

DUANE EDDY

(b. Apr. 26, 1938, Corning, NY)

Rock and roll's best-selling instrumentalist, Duane Eddy scored a series of hits between 1958 and 1963 featuring a deep "twangy" sound produced by playing the guitar's bass strings. As with many early rock-and-rollers, Eddy retained his popularity much longer in England, and consequently influenced a number of British guitarists, including Eric Clapton, George Harrison, and Mark Knopfler.

Duane Eddy started playing guitar at age 5 and moved with his family to the Phoenix, Arizona, area at 13. He left high school at 16 to perform locally, meeting multi-instrumentalist Al Casey in 1955. While performing with Casey's group, Eddy devised the technique of playing his guitar's bass strings to produce a low, reverberant "twangy" sound. In 1957 he met disc jockey Lee Hazlewood, who wrote songs, published music, produced records, and ran a recording studio. Eddy recorded "Movin' and Groovin'," a song cowritten by Hazlewood, with studio musicians dubbed the Rebels. Forwarded to Dick Clark, the song won Eddy a recording contract with Jamie Records.

Eddy's next single, the smash instrumental hit "Rebel Rouser," also written by Eddy and Hazlewood, launched his pop career. Recording with studio aces such as Al Casey, pianist Larry Knechtel, and saxophonists Plas Johnson, Jim Horn, and Steve Douglas, he scored a series of major pop instrumental hits on Jamie through 1960 with "Ramrod," "Cannonball," "The Lonely One," the classic "Forty Miles of Bad Road," the smash "Because They're Young," and "Peter Gunn." Eddy made a cameo appearance in the film *Because They're Young*, and the title instrumental featured one of the first uses of horns and strings on an instrumental rock single.

By 1962 Duane Eddy had switched to RCA Records, where he scored hits with "The Ballad of Paladin" and two songs recorded with the intrusive female chorus dubbed the Rebelettes (actually Darlene Love and the Blossoms), "(Dance with the) Guitar Man" and "Boss Guitar." Eddy continued to record through the '60s, with little subsequent success. The '70s were spent in the background of the music business; Eddy backed B. J. Thomas's 1972 hit "Rock and Roll Lullaby," and scored a British-only hit with "Play Me Like You Play Your Guitar" in 1975, and a country-only hit in 1977 with "You Are My Sunshine," backed by Waylon Jennings and Willie Nelson.

Duane Eddy returned to live performance in 1983, backed by Ry Cooder. He moved to Nashville in 1985 and the following year managed a moderate hit with a remake of "Peter Gunn," recorded with the British band the Art of Noise. During 1987 he recorded *Duane Eddy* for Capitol with guests George Harrison, Paul McCartney, John Fogerty, and Jeff Lynne and session guitarists Steve Cropper, David Lindley, James Burton, and Ry Cooder, but the album was quickly deleted. However, Eddy's early recordings began to find a new audience, thanks to 1993's *Twang Thang*, released by Rhino Records, and Eddy's 1994 induction into the Rock and Roll Hall of Fame.

Duane Eddy

Have Twangy Guitar, Will Travel	Jamie	3000	'59	†
	Motown	5431	'89	CS/CD†
Especially for You	Jamie	3006	'59	†
The Twang's the Thang	Jamie	3009	'60	†
Plays Songs of Our Heritage	Jamie	3011			
$1,000,000 Worth of Twang	Jamie	3014	'60	†
	Motown	5424	'89	CS/CD†
Have Twangy Guitar, Will Travel/$1,000,000 Worth of Twang	Motown	9068		CD†
Girls! Girls! Girls!	Jamie	3019	'61	†
$1,000,000 Worth of Twang—Volume 2	Jamie	3021		†
Twisting with Duane Eddy	Jamie	3022		†
Surfin' with Duane Eddy	Jamie	3024		†
Duane Eddy with the Rebels—In Person	Jamie	3025		†
16 Greatest Hits	Jamie	3026		†
Twistin' 'n' Twangin'	RCA	2525	'62	†
Twangy Guitar—Silky Strings	RCA	2576	'62	†
Dance with the Guitar Man	RCA	2648	'63	†

"Twang" a Country Song	RCA	2681	'63	†
Twangin' Up a Storm	RCA	2700	'63	†
Lonely Guitar	RCA	2798	'64	†
Water Skiing	RCA	2918	'64	†
Twangin' the Golden Hits	RCA	2993	'65	†
Twangsville	RCA	3432	'65	†
Best	RCA	3477	'66	†
(reissued as) Pure Gold	RCA	2671	'78	†
A-Go-Go	Colpix	490	'65	†
Goes Bob Dylan	Colpix	494	'66	†
The Biggest Twang of All	Reprise	6218	'66	†
The Roaring Twangies	Reprise	6240	'67	†
The Vintage Years	Sire	(2) 3707	'75	†
Compact Command	Motown	9068	'87	CD†
Duane Eddy	Capitol	12567	'87	LP/CS†
	Capitol	46897	'87	CD†
Twang Thang	Rhino	71223	'93	CS/CD

ELECTRIC LIGHT ORCHESTRA (ELO)

Roy Wood (b. Nov. 8, 1946, Birmingham, England), gtr, voc; **Jeff Lynne** (b. Dec. 30, 1947, Birmingham, England), gtr, voc; **Bev Bevan** (b. Nov. 25, 1945, Birmingham, England), drm [Roy Wood left after the first album and keyboardist **Richard Tandy** (b. Mar. 26, 1948, Birmingham, England) was added.]

THE MOVE. Roy Wood and Bev Bevan; **Carl Wayne** (b. Aug. 18, 1944, Birmingham, England), voc; **Trevor Burton** (b. Mar. 9, 1949, Birmingham, England), gtr, voc; and **Ace Kefford** (b. Dec. 10, 1946). [Later members include bassist **Rick Price** (b. June 10, 1944) and Jeff Lynne.]

Formed out of the Move, an enigmatic and controversial '60s British singles band, the Electric Light Orchestra realized Roy Wood's conception of an electric rock band augmented by a classical string section. Ironically, Wood left after only one album, ceding leadership of the group to Jeff Lynne. Despite the fact that the string section produced little more than gratuitous four- and eight-bar introductions and a lush orchestral sound, the Electric Light Orchestra was hailed as one of the most successful progressive-rock groups of the '70s. Certainly one of the world's top concert attractions by the late '70s, the Electric Light Orchestra toured America in 1978 with a massive stage structure and laser light show, a testament to technology and the public's apparent demand for extravagant stage presentation. After the group's demise, during the late '80s Jeff Lynne established himself as a producer and member of the supergroup the Traveling Wilburys.

Formed in late 1965 by a number of musicians from the Birmingham area, the Move quickly drew the attention of the London underground with their dramatic and often violent stage presentations. Roy Wood had previously manned Gerry Levene and the Avengers with Graeme Edge (later with the Moody Blues) and Mike Sheridan and the Nightriders. Trevor Burton had played guitar with Danny King and the Mayfair Set, while Bev Bevan had drummed with Denny Laine and the Diplomats and Carl Wayne and the Vikings, which included vocalist Wayne and bassist Ace Kefford. With Wood composing virtually all the Move's material, the band scored a series of British hits with "Night of Fear," "I Can Hear the Grass Grow," "Flowers in the Rain," "Fire Brigade," and "Blackberry Way." Gaining notoriety for smashing TV sets and pianos on stage, the Move remained virtually unknown in the United States for years. Personnel changes started in 1968, and by 1970 guitarist-vocalist Jeff Lynne was brought in for the avowed reason of forming an outfit that would combine classical strings and rock instrumentation. Lynne had played with the Idle Race for four years, recording one album with the group. By the time of the Move's first (minor) American hit, Lynne's "Do Ya," the group had disbanded.

Formed in 1971 by Roy Wood, Jeff Lynne, and Bev Bevan, the Electric Light Orchestra signed with United Artists and recorded the critically acclaimed *No Answer*, which yielded a British hit with Lynne's "10538 Overture." However, by 1972 Wood had lost interest in the project and left the group to form Wizzard with onetime Move bassist Rick Price. During the '70s Wood recorded two albums with Wizzard and three solo albums.

The true beginning of the Electric Light Orchestra came with the album *ELO II*. Jeff Lynne assumed the role of producer, arranger, composer, lead vocalist, and lead guitarist, and added keyboardist Richard Tandy, a bassist, and three former members of the London Symphony Orchestra (two cellists and a violinist). *ELO II* secured the band's position at the forefront of progressive rock and yielded their first albeit minor American hit with a re-make of Chuck Berry's "Roll Over, Beethoven." The band completed its first American tour in the summer of 1973, in support of their next album, *On the Third Day*, which produced two minor American hits, "Showdown" and "Daybreaker." *Eldorado* yielded a near-smash hit with the Bee Gees—sounding "Can't Get It Out of My Head."

When their next album, *Face the Music*, was released in 1975, the Electric Light Orchestra's lineup had stabilized with Lynne, Tandy, Bevan, bassist-vocalist Kelly Groucutt, cellists Hugh McDowell and Melvyn Gale, and violinist Mik Kaminski. The album featured the major hits "Evil Woman" and "Strange Magic," whereas 1976's *A New World Record* produced the hits "Livin' Thing," "Telephone Line," and a remake of the Move's "Do Ya." *Out of the Blue* contained Lynne's first extended piece since *Eldorado*, the side-long "Concerto for a Rainy Day," and the hits "Turn to Stone" and "Sweet Talkin' Woman."

For their 1978 American tour the Electric Light Orchestra assembled one of the most spectacular and grandiose stage presentations in the history of rock music. For approximately half of the tour's shows, the band utilized a 5-ton, 60-foot-wide fiberglass structure resembling a spaceship. The top half of the structure ascended to reveal the band inside. Complete with synchronized lasers, the production stood as a remarkable tribute to technology and showmanship.

In 1978 the Electric Light Orchestra switched to Columbia Records, with all previous and subsequent albums through 1983 released on the Jet subsidiary. Their Jet debut, *Discovery*, was recorded with a 42-piece German Orchestra and a 30-voice all-male choir, yielding two smash hits, "Shine a Little Love" and "Don't Bring Me Down," and two moderate hits, "Confusion" and "Last Train to London." In 1980 the group recorded most of the music for the movie *Xanadu*, starring Gene Kelly and Olivia Newton-John. The soundtrack album produced two Electric Light Orchestra hits with "I'm Alive" and "All Over the World," and a near-smash hit with the title song, recorded with Newton-John. Adopting the moniker ELO for a time, the group scored major hits with the rockabilly style "Hold on Tight" in 1981 and "Rock 'n' Roll Is King" in 1983, but then the band dissolved.

Jeff Lynne managed a minor solo hit with "Video" from the 1984 movie *Electric Dreams*. The Electric Light Orchestra (Lynne, Tandy, and Bevan) reemerged in 1986 with *Balance of Power* and the hit "Calling America" on CBS Associated. During the late '80s Lynne produced albums for George Harrison (*Cloud Nine*) and Tom Petty (*Full Moon Fever*) and worked on albums by Duane Eddy, Del Shannon, and Roy Orbison. In 1988 and again in 1990 he recorded with the supergroup the Traveling Wilburys. A playful exercise, the group's members all took fictitious names, such as Nelson (George Harrison), Lucky (Bob Dylan), Lefty (Roy Orbison), Charlie T. Jr. (Tom Petty), and Otis (Lynne); for *Volume 3* the Wilburys were Spike (Harrison), Boo (Dylan), Muddy (Petty), and Clayton (Lynne). In the '90s Lynne recorded *Armchair Theatre* for Reprise, which disappeared on the charts, and produced Tom Petty and the Heartbreakers' *Into the Great Wide Open*. In 1991 Bev Bevan formed Electric Light Orchesta Part Two; one year later they enlisted the aid of the Moscow Symphony Orchestra to stage a live show of their greatest hits, subsequently released on record.

The Idle Race (with Jeff Lynne)

The Birthday Party	Liberty	7603	'69	†

The Move

The Move	A&M			†
Shazam	A&M	4259	'70	†
	A&M	3181	'82	†
Looking On	Capitol	658	'71	†
Message from the Country	Capitol	811	'71	†
	One Way	57476		CD
Split Ends	United Artists	5666	'73	†
Best	A&M	(2) 3625	'74	†
Best	EMI	96060	'94	CD

Roy Wood

Wizzard's Brew	United Artists	042	'73	†
Boulders	United Artists	168	'73	†
Introducing Eddy and the Falcons	United Artists	219	'74	†
Mustard	United Artists	575	'76	†
Super Active Wizzo	Warner Bros.	3065	'77	†
On the Road	Warner Bros.	3247	'81	†
One Man Band	Townhouse	7127	'81	†

The Electric Light Orchestra

No Answer	United Artists	5573	'72	†
	Jet	35524	'78	CS/CD
ELO II	United Artists	040	'73	†
	Jet	35533	'78	CD
On the Third Day	United Artists	188	'73	†
	Jet	35525	'78	CD
Eldorado	United Artists	339	'74	†
	Jet	35526	'78	CS/CD
	DCC	1041		CD
Face the Music	United Artists	546	'75	†
	Jet	35527	'78	CS/CD
Olé ELO	United Artists	630	'76	†
	Jet	35528	'78/'88	CS/CD
A New World Record	United Artists	679	'76	†
	Jet	35529	'78	CS/CD
Out of the Blue	Jet/United Artists	(2) 823	'77	†
	Jet	(2) 35530	'78	†
	Jet	35530		CS/CD
Discovery	Jet	35769	'79	CS/CD
Greatest Hits	Jet	36310	'79	CS/CD
A Box of Their Best	Jet	(4) 36966	'80	†
Time	Jet	37371	'81	CS/CD
Secret Messages	Jet	38490	'83	CS/CD
Balance of Power	CBS	40048	'86	CD

Afterglow	Epic Associated	(3) 46090	'90	CS/CD
Moment of Truth	Curb/Atlantic	77692	'95	CS/CD
ELO and Olivia Newton-John				
Xanadu (soundtrack)	MCA	6100	'80	CS
The Traveling Wilburys (with Jeff Lynne)				
Volume One	Wilbury	25796	'88	CS/CD
Volume 3	Wilbury	26324	'90	CS/CD
Jeff Lynne				
Armchair Theatre	Reprise	26184	'90	CS/CD
Electric Light Orchestra Part Two				
ELO Part Two	Scotti Brothers	75222	'91	CS/CD
ELO's Greatest Hits Live	Scotti Brothers	75269	'92	CS/CD

EMERSON, LAKE AND PALMER

Keith Emerson (b. Nov. 2, 1944, Todmorden, England), kybd; **Greg Lake** (b. Nov. 10, 1948, Bournemouth, Dorset, England), bs, gtr, voc; **Carl Palmer** (b. Mar. 20, 1947, Birmingham, England), drm

One of the first British rock bands to provide classical music within the rock format during the late '60s was the Nice. After their debut album, they were perhaps the first rock group to explore the trio format utilizing keyboards rather than electric guitar as the primary musical focus. Disbanding by 1970, the Nice were superseded by Emerson, Lake and Palmer, one of the first supergroups of the '70s. Emerson, Lake and Palmer continued the progressive, keyboard-based power-trio format, and Emerson effectively introduced the synthesizer into rock music. One of the biggest American concert attractions by the mid-'70s, Emerson, Lake and Palmer were one of the first rock bands to tour with a truly quadraphonic sound system (in 1974) and perhaps the first to attempt to tour with a full symphony orchestra (in 1977). Disbanding in 1979, the group eventually reunited in 1992.

Originally formed to back soul singer Pat Arnold, the Nice began touring on their own in October 1967. Signed to Andrew Oldham's Immediate label, the Nice's debut album featured Emerson's rousing "Rondo" (based on Dave Brubeck's "Blue Rondo à la Turk"). With the departure of David O'List (b. Dec. 13, 1948, Chiswick, London, England), the group's primary singer and songwriter, Emerson became the musical and visual focus of the Nice. His flamboyant stage act, which included stabbing and assaulting his electric organ, brought the group widespread notoriety in Great Britain and Europe. As a keyboard-based power trio—Emerson; Lee Jackson (b. Jan. 8, 1943, Newcastle upon Tyne, England) on bass, guitar, and vocals; and Brian "Blinky" Davison (b. May 25, 1942, Leicester, England) on drums—the group recorded *Ars Longa Vita Brevis*, which showcased the title composition performed in four movements with coda. By 1970 the group was on the verge of an American breakthrough but elected to disband. Ironically, the Nice soon entered the American album charts with *Five Bridges Suite*, perhaps their finest work.

In late 1969 in San Francisco, Keith Emerson, still with the Nice, met guitarist-bassist-vocalist Greg Lake, a founding member of King Crimson. With the demise of the Nice, they formed Emerson, Lake and Palmer with drummer Carl Palmer, a former member of the Crazy World of Arthur Brown (1968's smash "Fire") and Atomic Rooster. With Emerson exploring the sound of the synthesizer, the group debuted at the 1970 Isle of Wight Festival, garnering a reputation for their furious stage act and virtuoso abilities. Their first two albums were best-sellers, with the debut yielding a minor hit, the somber ballad

"Lucky Man." Their third album was an ambitious live recording based on Modest Mussorgsky's classical composition *Pictures at an Exhibition*. The follow-up, *Trilogy*, contained Aaron Copland's "Hoedown," Maurice Ravel's "Bolero," and the subtle and intricate "In the Beginning," a moderate hit.

In 1974 Emerson, Lake and Palmer recorded *Brain Salad Surgery* for their own Manticore label. To support the album, they completed a spectacular American tour, transporting 36 tons of equipment. Emerson played six Moog synthesizers, two organs, a Steinway, and an electric piano. Each of Palmer's drums had its own synthesizer, and his equipment included two timpani, two gongs, chimes, and a large church bell. In addition, the tour used the first truly quadraphonic sound system. The live set *Welcome Back, My Friends, to the Show That Never Ends* was issued following the tour.

The group took a two-year hiatus following the tour, eventually releasing the double-record set *Works, Volume 1*, in 1977. Each member used one side for a solo effort, with all three playing together on the final side. The haunting "C'est La Vie," composed by Lake, became a minor hit from the album. That May the group embarked on a comeback tour of America with a 57-piece orchestra and 6-person vocal choir. The cost, estimated at $250,000 per week, proved prohibitive and the orchestra was dismissed after 15 concerts. Late 1978's *Love Beach* was greeted hostily and in 1979 Emerson, Lake and Palmer disbanded.

In the early '80s Keith Emerson recorded the soundtrack to the movie *Nighthawks* and Greg Lake recorded solo albums. In spring 1981 Carl Palmer joined in the formation of the supergroup Asia with guitarist Steve Howe (Yes), keyboardist Geoff Downes (Yes), and bassist-vocalist John Wetton (King Crimson). They recorded two best-selling albums, scoring a smash hit with "Heat of the Moment" and major hits with "Only Time Will Tell" and "Don't Cry." In 1986 Emerson and Lake recruited drummer Cozy Powell (Jeff Beck Group, Rainbow, Whitesnake) for touring and the album *Emerson, Lake and Powell*. Palmer left Asia around 1986 and formed 3 with Emerson and California session musician Robert Berry in 1988. Emerson, Lake and Palmer ultimately reunited in 1992 for *Black Moon* and another round of touring.

The Nice

The Thoughts of Emerlist Davjack	Immediate	1252004	'68	†
	Immediate	52425	'92	CS/CD†
Ars Longa Vita Brevis	Immediate	1252020	'69	
	Immediate	47890	'91	CD
The Nice	Immediate	1252022	'69	†
	Immediate	47347	'91	CD
Five Bridges Suite	Mercury	61295	'70	†
	Mercury	830291		†
Elegy	Mercury	61324	'71	†
	Mercury	830292		†
Elegy/Five Bridges Suite (highlights)	Mercury	830457	'87	CD
Keith Emerson with the Nice	Mercury	(2) 6500	'72	†
Autumn to Spring	Charisma	1	'73	†
Immediate Story, Volume 1	Sire	(2) 3710	'76	†

Emerson, Lake and Palmer

Emerson, Lake and Palmer	Cotillion	9040	'71	†
	Atlantic	19120		LP/CS/CD†
	Victory	480016	'93	CS/CD

Tarkus	Cotillion	9900	'71	†
	Atlantic	19121		LP/CS/CD†
	Victory	480017	'93	CD
	Mobile Fidelity	598	'94	CD
	Mobile Fidelity	203	'94	LP
Pictures at an Exhibition	Cotillion	66666	'72	†
	Atlantic	19122		LP/CS/CD†
	Victory	480020	'93	CD
Trilogy	Cotillion	9903	'72	†
	Atlantic	19123		LP/CS/CD†
	Victory	480019		CS/CD
	Mobile Fidelity	621	'95	CD
Brain Salad Surgery	Manticore	66669	'73	†
	Atlantic	19124		LP/CS/CD†
	Victory	480015	'93	CD
	Victory	480020	'94	CS/CD
Welcome Back, My Friends . . .	Manticore	(3) 200	'74	†
	Victory	(2) 484001	'93	CD
Works, Volume 1	Atlantic	(2) 7000	'77	LP/CS/CD†
	Victory	(2) 484002	'93	CD
Works, Volume 2	Atlantic	19147	'77	LP/CS/CD†
	Victory	480025	'93	CD
Works Live	Victory	484003	'93	CD
Love Beach	Atlantic	19211	'78	†
	Victory	480028	'93	CD
In Concert	Atlantic	19255	'79	CS/CD†
Best	Atlantic	19283	'80	CS/CD†
	Victory	480036	'94	CS/CD
The Atlantic Years	Atlantic	(2) 82403	'92	CS/CD†
Black Moon	Victory	480003	'92	CS/CD
Live at Royal Albert Hall by Appointment	Victory	480011	'93	CS/CD
The Return of the Manticore	Victory	(4) 484004	'93	CD
In the Hot Seat	Victory	480034	'94	CS/CD
Keith Emerson				
Nighthawks (soundtrack)	MCA	5196	'81	†
Greg Lake				
Greg Lake	Chrysalis	1357	'81	†
Manoeuvres	Chrysalis	41392	'83	†
Asia (with Carl Palmer)				
Asia	Geffen	2008	'82	CS/CD
Alpha	Geffen	4008	'83	CS/CD
Astra	Geffen	24072	'85	LP/CS/CD†
	MCA	20851	'95	CS/CD
Then and Now	Geffen	24298	'90	CS/CD
Aqua	Pyramid/Rhino	71833	'94	CD
Asia Live in Moscow	Rhino	70377	'92	CS/CD
Emerson, Lake and Powell				
Emerson, Lake and Powell	Polydor	829297	'86	CS/CD
. . . To the Power of Three	Geffen	24181	'88	LP/CS/CD†

THE EVERLY BROTHERS

Don Everly (b. Feb. 1, 1937, Brownie, KY); **Phil Everly** (b. Jan. 19, 1939, Brownie, KY, although some say Chicago, IL)

The most popular vocal duo from the rock-and-roll '50s, the Everly Brothers introduced country harmonies into rock music, with Don usually singing tenor lead and Phil supplying high harmony. Their precise, assured harmonies influenced a whole generation of rock singers, from the Beatles and Hollies to the Beach Boys and Byrds, from Simon and Garfunkel to the Eagles. Aided immeasurably by the songwriting team of Felice and Boudleaux Bryant, and the guitar playing and production of Chet Atkins, the Everly Brothers recorded songs concerned with teenage subjects such as parents, school, and young love. Yet their appeal was so widespread that "Bye Bye Love," "Bird Dog," "Devoted to You," and "('Til) I Kissed You" became three-way crossover hits, i.e., hits in the pop, country, *and* R&B fields. "Wake Up Little Susie" and "All I Have to Do Is Dream" topped all three charts. Without the assistance of the Bryants and Atkins, the Everly Brothers maintained their hit-making ways from 1960 to 1962 at Warner Bros. They continued to tour until 1973, when they broke up acrimoniously. They eventually settled their differences and reunited in 1983.

Don and Phil Everly were taught the guitar at an early age. Their parents, Ike and Margaret, were touring musicians and hosted a weekly radio show on KMA in Shenandoah, Iowa. The brothers began appearing on the *Everly Family Show* when Don was eight and Phil six. During summers they toured the country circuit with their parents. In 1955 Ike and Margaret quit show business and the brothers moved to Nashville, where they recorded briefly for Columbia Records. They also met the songwriting team of Felice and Boudleaux Bryant and Chet Atkins, who was to produce many of their early records.

Signed to Cadence Records, the Everly Brothers scored their first hit in 1957 with "Bye Bye Love," written by the Bryants. Subsequent smash hits on Cadence include "Wake Up Little Susie" and "Problems" (by the Bryants), and "All I Have to Do Is Dream" and "Bird Dog" (by Boudleaux). Ray Charles's "This Little Girl of Mine," Roy Orbison's "Claudette," and Boudleaux's "Devoted to You" were major hits through 1958. The Everly Brothers toured Great Britain for the first time that year and resumed their string of hits with "Take a Message to Mary" backed with "Poor Jenny" (both by the Bryants), Don's "('Til) I Kissed You" (recorded with the Crickets), the tender ballad "Let It Be Me" (their first recording with strings), and Phil's "When Will I Be Loved."

In 1960 the Everly Brothers were the first artists signed to the newly formed Warner Bros. label. Without the services of the songwriting Bryants and producer Atkins, they nonetheless continued to score hits with their own "Cathy's Clown," "So Sad" backed with "Lucille," and "Walk Right Back"/"Ebony Eyes." Their last major hits came in 1962 with "Crying in the Rain" (written by Carole King and Howie Greenfield) and "That's Old Fashioned." The two subsequently joined the Marine Corps Reserve, serving six months active duty, but their relationship seemed to deteriorate, particularly after Phil suffered a nervous breakdown during their 1963 tour of Great Britain. Nonetheless, they managed a moderate hit with their own "Gone, Gone, Gone" in 1964, a British smash with "The Price of Love" in 1965, and a moderate hit with the country-rock flavored "Bowling Green" in 1967.

The Everly Brothers continued to tour and won critical acclaim for 1968's *Roots* and 1972's *Stories We Could Tell*, but on July 14, 1973, Phil smashed his guitar and stormed off stage at Knotts Berry Farm in Buena Park, California, effectively ending their 28-year career. Both pursued solo careers and recorded solo albums. Don scored his biggest solo hit in the country field with "Yesterday Just Passed My Way Again" in 1976. During the '70s Phil performed on albums by John Sebastian, Dion, Warren Zevon (his debut), and J. D. Souther. In 1983 Phil had a moderate country hit with "Who's Gonna Keep Me Warm" and a major British hit with "She Means Nothing to Me," recorded with Cliff Richard.

Don and Phil Everly ended their bitter separation in September 1983 with concerts at London's Royal Albert Hall. The following year they recorded *EB '84* with producer Dave Edmunds, guitarist Albert Lee, and keyboardist Pete Wingfield (1975's "Eighteen with a Bullet"). The album produced a country and pop hit with Paul McCartney's "On the Wings of a Nightingale," written especially for the two. The brothers toured with Lee and Wingfield in 1984 and 1986 and recorded *Born Yesterday* under Edmunds, followed in 1988 by *Some Hearts*, recorded with Brian and Dennis Wilson of the Beach Boys. The Everly Brothers were among the first into the Rock and Roll Hall of Fame, inducted in 1986. In 1992 Don Everly's son Edan recorded *Dead Flowers* with his band Edan for Hollywood Records. Boxed sets of the Everly Brothers' early recordings have been issued through the '90s on Rhino, Mercury, and Warner Bros.

The Everly Brothers

The Everly Brothers	Cadence	3003	'58	†
	Rhino	70211		CS/CD
Songs Our Daddy Taught Us	Cadence	3016	'58	†
Us	Rhino	70212		CS/CD
Best	Cadence	3025	'59	†
The Fabulous Style of the Everly Brothers	Cadence	25040	'60	†
	Rhino	70213		CS/CD
The Everly Brothers/The Fabulous Style of the Everly Brothers	Ace	932		CD
Folk Songs	Cadence	25059		†
15 Everly Hits	Cadence	25062		†
All They Had to Do Was	Rhino	70214	'85	CS/CD
The Best of the Everly Brothers (1957–1960)	Rhino	70173	'87	CS
Cadence Classics: Their 20 Greatest Hits	Rhino	5258		CD
It's Everly Time	Warner Bros.	1381	'60	†
A Date with the Everly Brothers	Warner Bros.	1395	'60	†
Top Vocal Duet	Warner Bros.	1418	'61	†
Instant Party	Warner Bros.	1430	'62	†
Golden Hits	Warner Bros.	1471	'62	CS/CD
Christmas with the Everly Brothers	Warner Bros.	1483		†
Sing Great Country Hits	Warner Bros.	1513	'63	†
Very Best	Warner Bros.	1554	'64	
Rock 'n' Soul	Warner Bros.	1578	'65	†
Gone, Gone, Gone	Warner Bros.	1585	'65	†
Beat 'n' Soul	Warner Bros.	1605	'65	†
In Our Image	Warner Bros.	1620	'66	†
Two Yanks in England	Warner Bros.	1646	'66	†
Hit Sound	Warner Bros.	1676	'67	†
The Everly Brothers Sing	Warner Bros.	1708	'67	†
Roots	Warner Bros.	1752	'68	†
	Warner Bros.	26927	'95	CD
The Everly Brothers Show	Warner Bros.	1858		†
Walk Right Back: The Everly Brothers on Warner Brothers	Warner Bros.	(2) 45164	'93	CS/CD
Stories We Could Tell	RCA	4620	'72	†
Pass the Chicken and Listen	RCA	4781	'72	†
The Reunion Concert (recorded 1983)	Mercury	824479	'84	CD
EB '84	Mercury	822431	'84	LP/CS/CD†
	Razor & Tie	2040	'95	CD

Home Again	RCA	5401	'85	†
Born Yesterday	Mercury	826142	'86	LP/CS/CD†
Some Hearts	Mercury	823520	'88	LP/CS/CD†
The Mercury Years	Mercury	514905	'93	CS/CD

Anthologies

Wake Up, Little Susie	Harmony	11304	'69	†
	LaserLight	419	'94	CS/CD
Chained to a Memory	Harmony	11388	'70	†
Original Greatest Hits	Barnaby	(2) 350	'70	†
End of an Era	Barnaby	(2) 30260	'71	†
History of the Everly Brothers	Barnaby	(2) 15008	'73	†
Greatest Hits	Barnaby	(2) 6006	'74	†
Greatest Hits, Volume 1	Barnaby	4004	'79	†
Greatest Hits, Volume 2	Barnaby	4005	'79	†
Greatest Hits, Volume 3	Barnaby	4006	'79	†
24 Original Classics	Arista	(2) 8207	'84	CS/CD†
Living Legends	Pair	(2) 1063	'86	CS†
Rip It Up	Ace	64		LP†
Pure Harmony	Ace	118		LP
Rip It Up/Pure Harmony	Ace	804		CS†
In the Studio	Ace	159		LP
Greatest Hits	Ace	903	'86	CD
Songs Our Daddy Taught Us	Ace	75		CD
Greatest Recordings	Ace	194	'87	LP/CS
The Fabulous Everly Brothers	Ace	006		CS/CD
All-Time Greatest Hits	Curb/CEMA	77311	'90	CS/CD
Rare Solo Classics	Curb/CEMA	77472	'91	CS/CD
All I Have to Do Is Dream	LaserLight	418	'94	CD
Bye Bye Love	LaserLight	420	'94	CS/CD
Heartaches and Harmonies	Rhino	(4) 71779	'94	CD
Golden Hits	Hollywood/IMG	439		CS/CD
Rockin' in Harmony	Crown	002		LP/CS†

Don Everly

Don Everly	Ode	77005	'71	†
Sunset Towers	Ode	77023	'74	†
Brother Juke-Box	Hickory	44003	'77	†

Phil Everly

Star-Spangled Springer	RCA	0092	'73	†
Phil's Diner	Pye	12104	'75	†
Mystic Line	Pye	12121	'75	†
Living Alone	Elektra	213	'79	†

Edan (with Edan Everly)

Dead Flowers	Hollywood	61329	'92	CS/CD

FAIRPORT CONVENTION

Richard Thompson (b. Apr. 3, 1949, London, England), gtr, voc; **Simon Nicol** (b. Oct. 13, 1950, Muswell Hill, London, England), gtr, bjo, dulcimer, bs, viola, voc; **Ashley "Tyger" Hutchings** (b. Jan. 26, 1945, Muswell Hill, London, England), bs, gtr, voc; **Judy Dyble** (b. Feb. 13, 1949, London, England), pno, voc; **Martin Lamble** (b. Aug. 28, 1949, St. Johns Wood, London, England; d. May 12, 1969), drm [**Ian Matthews** (b. Iain Matthews MacDonald, June 16, 1946, Scunthorpe, Lincolnshire, England), guitar and vocals, joined in 1967. Judy Dyble left in March 1968, to be replaced by **Sandy Denny** (b. Alexandra Denny, Jan. 6, 1941, Wimbledon, London, England; d. Apr. 21, 1978) on guitar, keyboards, and vocals. Violinist **Dave Swarbrick** (b. Apr. 5, 1941, New Malden, Surrey, England) and keyboardist-drummer **Dave Mattacks** (b. Mar. 13, 1948, Edgware, Middlesex, England) joined in 1969; Tyger Hutchings left in late 1969, to be replaced by bassist **Dave Pegg** (b. Nov. 2, 1948, England); Sandy Denny also left in late 1969 and was not replaced, although she returned in 1974. Richard Thompson left in 1970; Simon Nicol left in 1972, to be replaced by **Trevor Lucas** (b. Dec. 25, 1943, Bungaree, Australia; d. Feb. 4, 1989, Sydney, Australia) and then **Jerry Donahue** (b. Sept. 24, 1946, New York, NY). Dave Mattacks left in 1975, to be replaced by **Bruce Rowland** (b. England) on drums; Denny, Lucas, and Donahue left in 1976. The band re-formed in 1977 with Dave Swarbrick, Nicol, Dave Pegg, and Rowland; it "officially" disbanded in 1979, save for annual reunions. Band again re-formed as a trio (Nicol, Pegg, Mattacks) in 1983, soon joined by violinist **Ric Sanders** (b. England) and **Martin Allcock** (b. Jan. 5, 1957, Manchester, England) on guitar, bouzouki, mandolin, and keyboards.]

Although sorely neglected in the United States, Fairport Convention was perhaps the first British folk-rock group, combining traditional British folk music, compelling original songs, and rock instrumentation. During her tenure with Fairport Convention, Sandy Denny was established as one of the top British female vocalists and won recognition as an outstanding songwriter, primarily on the strength of "Who Knows Where the Time Goes," popularized by Judy Collins. Mainstay Dave Swarbrick was one of the first musicians to play violin as a lead instrument within the rock format.

A seminal British group, Fairport Convention introduced Sandy Denny, Ian Matthews, and Richard Thompson to a wider audience. Richard Thompson became established as a cult figure after his stint with Fairport Convention, recognized by critics and his devoted following as an excellent songwriter and an innovative guitarist (some claim he is one of only a handful of original and creative guitarists working in rock today). Acclaimed for his recordings with onetime wife Linda (particularly the 1982 album *Shoot Out the Lights*) and subsequent solo recordings, Richard Thompson eventually began receiving wide recognition during the '80s.

Officially formed in 1967, Fairport Convention's initial lineup was Richard Thompson, Simon Nicol, Ashley "Tyger" Hutchings, Judy Dyble, and Martin Lamble. Richard Thompson had taken up guitar by age 11, turned professional by 14, and turned to folk and traditional British musics by his late teens. Around 1965 he began playing with Nicol and Hutchings. Soon augmented by Ian Matthews, Fairport Convention recorded one British album before the departure of vocalist Judy Dyble in March 1968. She was replaced by Sandy Denny, a member of the Strawbs before that group recorded its first album. Featuring Denny's stunning contralto voice, the group's first American album, *Fairport Convention*, included Denny's "Fotheringay," Thompson's "Meet on the Ledge," and a moving version of Bob Dylan's "I'll Keep It with Mine," as well as the then-obscure Joni Mitchell song "Eastern Rain." Martin Lamble was killed in an accident involving the group's van in August 1969, and Ian Matthews left the group before the release of *Unhalfbricking*. For that album, Fairport Convention was assisted by virtuoso violinist Dave Swarbrick, who soon joined on a permanent basis. The album contained Thompson's "Genesis Hall" and an 11-minute version of the traditional folk song "A Sailor's Life," in addition to Denny's best-known composition, "Who Knows Where the Time Goes," and their first major British hit, Bob Dylan's "If You Gotta Go, Go Now," sung by Denny in French.

Liege & Lief, which included the traditional "Matty Groves" and "Tam Lin" as well as Denny and Hutchings's "Come All Ye" and Thompson's "Farewell, Farewell," won Fairport Convention their first substantial recognition. A concept album based on traditional British folk music, it inspired dozens of other bands to adopt the folk-rock style. However, both Denny and Hutchings left the group in late 1969, Denny because she wanted to write and perform her own material, Hutchings because he wanted to explore traditional music even deeper. Hutchings formed Steeleye Span with vocalist Maddy Prior; he left that group in 1971, and has since headed the Albion Band, with various personnel (including from time to time Mattacks and Nicol). Denny formed the short-lived Fotheringay with vocalist-guitarist Trevor Lucas and drummer Gerry Conway, both former members of Eclection, before embarking on a solo career. Bassist Dave Pegg was brought in for Fairport Convention's *Full House*, recorded without a recognized vocalist. Personnel changes continued to plague the group, as Richard Thompson quit the band in January 1971 to work with Matthews and Denny and later record solo. After two more Fairport Convention albums, Nicol and Mattacks dropped out.

In the meantime, Ian Matthews had formed Matthews's Southern Comfort, eventually scoring a major American and smash British hit with a thinly sung version of Joni Mitchell's "Woodstock." He left the group abruptly in November 1970 and recorded seven solo albums through 1978, scoring a major hit with "Shake It"; he also recorded one album with the short-lived Plainsong. Matthews eventually reemerged in 1988 with *Walking a Changing Line*, an album of songs by Jules Shear, the author of Cyndi Lauper's smash 1984 hit "All Through the Night." In the '90s, as Iain Matthews, he reemerged for recordings on Mesa and Watermelon.

Fotheringay, formed in March 1970 by Sandy Denny, Trevor Lucas, and Gerry Conway, recorded one album, which featured the Denny-Lucas composition "Peace in the End." Through 1974 Denny recorded three solo albums, including the excellent *Like an Old-Fashioned Waltz*, as well as the '50s nostalgia romp *Rock On*, recorded in 1972 with many members of the Fairport-Fotheringay community calling themselves the Bunch. Denny continued to work closely with Lucas, who had become her husband, and along with lead guitarist Jerry Donahue the trio rejoined Fairport Convention in the mid-'70s to record and tour. In 1977 Sandy Denny recorded her last solo album, the highly produced *Rendezvous*; on April 21, 1978, she died of a cerebral hemorrhage following a fall.

Dave Swarbrick and Dave Pegg assembled a "new" Fairport Convention in August 1972, recording five albums through 1976. Neither *Rosie* nor *Rising for the Moon*, recorded with

Sandy Denny, sparked much interest, and after *Gottle o' Geer*, Fairport Convention dissolved in 1979. Dave Pegg joined Jethro Tull as bassist that year. Beginning in 1980, Pegg organized a Fairport Convention reunion concert every summer, eventually leading to the recording of *Gladys' Leap*, with Pegg, Simon Nicol, and Dave Mattacks. Their 1987 reunion concert was issued as *In Real Time*, and during that year Fairport Convention made its first full tour of the United States since 1975 in support of Jethro Tull, with Pegg playing bass for both bands. With the addition of Martin Allcock (formerly of the Bully Wee Band) on a number of string instruments and jazz-rock violinist Ric Sanders (formerly of Soft Machine and the Albion Band), the group stabilized as a quintet, recording several albums through the mid-'90s.

Richard Thompson launched his solo recording career in 1972 with the quirky *Henry the Human Fly*, recorded with mezzo-soprano vocalist Linda Peters. The couple soon married and recorded the stunning but overlooked 1974 British-only album *I Want to See the Bright Lights Tonight* (it was eventually released in the United States as half of the double-record set *Live [More or Less]*). Through 1982 Richard and Linda Thompson recorded five more British albums (three apparently released in the United States), culminating in *Shoot Out the Lights*. Hailed as one of the best albums of the year, *Shoot Out the Lights* was recorded with Fairport veterans Simon Nicol, Dave Pegg, and Dave Mattacks. It contained Linda's heartrending "Walking on a Wire," the desperate "Man in Need," the rocker "Back Street Slide," the ballad "Just the Motion," and the compelling title track, with Richard's inspired lead-guitar playing throughout. The couple made their debut American tour in support of the album, but it was fraught with mutual hostility and on- and off-stage shouting matches. The couple divorced, and Linda Thompson recorded a solo album, *One Clear Moment*, in 1985.

Richard Thompson began his solo recording career with Nicol, Mattacks, and Pegg, plus horns and an accordion. *Hand of Kindness* was Thompson's first American album-chart entry. It included "Poisoned Heart and a Twisted Memory," "Both Ends Burning," "Tear Stained Letter" (a near-smash country hit for Jo-El Sonnier in 1988), and the jaunty "Two Left Feet." Thompson's first album on a major label since his days with Fairport Convention, *Across a Crowded Room* contained more songs of embittered love, such as "She Twists the Knife Again" and "When the Spell Is Broken," plus the socially conscious "Walking in a Wasted Land." In 1985, 1986, and 1988, Thompson toured with rhythm guitarist Clive Gregson and vocalist Christine Collister, who later launched their own duo career. *Daring Adventures* included "How Will I Ever Be Simple Again," "Long Dead Love," and the rocker "Valerie," plus the concert favorite "Al Bowlly's in Heaven." In 1987 Thompson recorded the avant-garde album *Live, Love, Larf and Loaf* with multi-instrumentalist Fred Frith, guitarist Henry Kaiser, and drummer John French, followed in 1990 by *Invisible Means*.

Switching to Capitol Records, Richard Thompson recorded *Amnesia*, regarded by some as his best album since *Shoot Out the Lights*. It contained "I Still Dream," "Don't Tempt Me," "Reckless Kind," and the upbeat "Turning of the Tide." He has since recorded *Rumor and Sigh* and *Mirror Blue*, the latter sporting a more acoustic guitar–oriented sound. Thompson has been working with producer-multikeyboardist Mitchell Froom, who has given his music a more dense, heavily produced sound. In 1993 and 1994 he toured as an acoustic duo with bassist Danny Thompson, formerly of the British folk-rock group Pentangle. In 1994 Green Linnet and Capitol Records each issued a compilation album of various artists performing the songs of Richard Thompson.

Dave Swarbrick, who has suffered increasingly from hearing problems due to his long years of playing with Fairport, formed in the late '80s the acoustic quartet Whippersnapper, featuring violinist Chris Leslie. Since then he has toured America twice, with old friend guitarist Martin Carthy; the pair recorded several albums together in the '60s and one studio and one live album in the early '90s.

Sandy Denny and the Strawbs

Sandy Denny and the Strawbs	Hannibal	1361	'91	CS/CD

Fairport Convention

Fairport Convention	Cotillion	9024	'70	†
	Polydor	835230	'90	CD
Fairport Convention	A&M	4185	'69	†
Unhalfbricking	A&M	4206	'70	†
	Hannibal	4418		CS/CD
Liege & Lief	A&M	4257	'70	CD
Full House	A&M	4265	'70	†
	Hannibal	4417		CS/CD
Angel Delight	A&M	4319	'71	†
"Babbacombe Lee"	A&M	4333	'72	†
Rosie	A&M	4386	'73	†
Nine	A&M	3603	'74	†
Fairport Chronicles	A&M	(2) 3530	'76	†
	A&M	(2) 6016		†
A Movable Feast	Island	9285	'74	†
Rising for the Moon	Island	9313	'75	†
Gottle o' Geer	Island	9389	'76	†
	Antilles	7054		LP
House Full	Hannibal	1319	'86/'90	CS/CD
Heyday	Hannibal	1329		CS/CD
What We Did on Our Holidays	Hannibal	4430		CS/CD
Gladys' Leap	Varrick	023	'86	LP/CS/CD
Expletive Delighted!	Varrick	029	'87	CS/CD
In Real Time	Island	842856	'88	CD
Jewel in the Crown	Green Linnet	3103	'95	CS/CD

Matthews' Southern Comfort

Matthews' Southern Comfort	Decca	75191		†
2nd Spring	Decca	75242	'70	†
Later That Same Year	Decca	75264	'71	†
Best	MCA	10519	'92	CD

Ian (Iain) Matthews

If You Saw Thro' My Eyes	Vertigo	1002	'71	†
Tigers Will Survive	Vertigo	1010	'72	†
Valley Hi	Elektra	75061	'73	†
Some Days You Eat the Bear . . . and Some Days the Bear Eats You	Elektra	75078	'74	†
Go for Broke	Columbia	34102	'76	†
Hit and Run	Columbia	34671	'77	†
Stealin' Home	Mushroom	5012	'78	†
Walking a Changing Line: The Songs of Jules Shear	Windham Hill	1070	'88	CS/CD
Skeleton Keys	Mesa	79054	'93	CS/CD
The Dark Side	Watermelon	1025	'94	CS/CD

Plainsong (with Ian Matthews)

In Search of Amelia Earhart	Elektra	75044	'72	†
Dark Room	Mesa	79065	'93	CS/CD

Eclection (with Trevor Lucas and Gerry Conway)

Eclection	Elektra	74023	'68	†

Fotheringay

Fotheringay	A&M	4269	'70	†
	Hannibal	4426		CS/CD

The Bunch

Rock On	A&M	4354	'72	†
	Carthage	4424		†
	Hannibal	4424		CS

Sandy Denny

The North Star Grassman and the Ravens	A&M	4317	'71	†
	Carthage	4429		†
	Hannibal	4429		CS/CD
Sandy	A&M	4371	'72	†
Like an Old-Fashioned Waltz	Island	9340	'74	†
	Island	9258		†
	Carthage	4425		†
	Hannibal	4425		CS/CD
Rendezvous	Island	9433	'77	†
	Carthage	4423		†
	Hannibal	4423		CS/CD
Best	Hannibal	1328		CS/CD
Who Knows Where the Time Goes	Hannibal	(3) 5301		CD

Richard and Linda Thompson

I Want to See the Bright Lights Tonight	Carthage	4407	'74	LP/CS/CD†
	Hannibal	4407		CS/CD
Hokey Pokey	Island	9305	'75	†
	Carthage	4408		LP/CS/CD†
Pour Down Like Silver	Carthage	4404	'76	LP/CS/CD†
	Hannibal	4404		CS/CD
At First Light	Chrysalis	1177	'78	†
	Carthage	4412		†
	Hannibal	4412		CS/CD
Shoot Out the Lights	Hannibal	1303	'82	CS/CD

Richard Thompson

Henry the Human Fly	Reprise	2112	'72	†
	Carthage	4405		LP/CS/CD†
	Hannibal	4405		CS/CD
Guitar, Vocal	Carthage	4413	'76	LP/CS/CD†
Live (More or Less)	Island	(2) 9421	'77	†
Strict Tempo!	Carthage	4409	'81	LP/CS/CD†
	Hannibal	4409		CD
Hand of Kindness	Hannibal	1313	'83	CS/CD
Small Town Romance	Hannibal	1316	'84	LP/CS/CD†
Watching the Dark: The History of Richard Thompson	Hannibal	(3) 5303	'93	CD
Across a Crowded Room	Polydor	825421	'85	CD
Daring Adventures	Polydor	829728	'86	CS/CD
Amnesia	Capitol	48845	'88	CS/CD
Rumor and Sigh	Capitol	95713	'91	CS/CD
Mirror Blue	Capitol	81492	'94	CS/CD
You? Me? Us?	Capitol	(2) 33704	'96	CS/CD

Richard Thompson Tribute Albums

The World Is a Wonderful Place: The Songs of Richard Thompson	Green Linnet	3086	'94	CS/CD
Beat the Retreat: Songs by Richard Thompson	Capitol	95929	'94	LP/CS/CD

John French, Fred Frith, Henry Kaiser, and Richard Thompson

Live, Love, Larf and Loaf	Rhino	70831	'87	CS
Invisible Means	Windham Hill	1094	'90	CS/CD

Dave Swarbrick

Swarbrick	TransAtlantic	337	'80	†
	Kicking Mule	337		LP

Dave Swarbrick and Martin Carthy

Martin Carthy and Dave Swarbrick	Antilles	7041		LP
Life and Limb	Green Linnet	3052	'91	CS/CD
Skin and Bone	Green Linnet	3075	'93	CS/CD

Linda Thompson

One Clear Moment	Warner Bros.	25164	'85	†

RICHARD AND MIMI FARIÑA

Richard Fariña (b. c. 1937, Brooklyn, NY; d. Apr. 30, 1966, near Carmel, CA), dulcimer, voc; **Mimi Fariña** (b. Mimi Baez, Apr. 30, 1945, New York, NY), gtr, voc

Prominent members of the Greenwich Village folk music scene in the '60s, Richard and Mimi Fariña recorded two excellent albums of Richard's songs, including "One-Way Ticket," "Reno Nevada," "Bold Marauder," "Hard-Loving Loser," and "Reflections in a Crystal Wind," and the classic "Pack Up Your Sorrows," plus the protest songs "Mainline Prosperity Blues" and "House Un-American Blues Activity Dream." Richard Fariña was second only to Bob Dylan in the quality and variety of his output, and his music was quite influential on the folk-music scene. He died tragically in a motorcycle accident near Carmel, California, on April 30, 1966, shortly after the publication of his classic underground novel, *Been Down So Long It Looks Like Up to Me*.

Mimi Fariña subsequently sang briefly with a folk-rock band and joined the San Francisco improvisational comedy group the Committee for one year. In 1971 she recorded an album with Tom Jans that included "In the Quiet Morning (For Janis Joplin)," popularized by her sister Joan Baez in 1972. In 1974 Mimi Fariña formed the nonprofit Bread and Roses organization in California's Marin County to provide entertainment for shut-ins at local prisons, halfway houses, drug rehabilitation centers, and hospitals. The success of Bread and Roses inspired groups in other communities across the country to set up similar organizations. To fund the group's ongoing expenses Mimi Fariña staged benefit concerts of acoustic music from 1977 to 1982 at Berkeley's Greek Theatre, as one of the few all-acoustic music festivals of its time. Participants included Paul Simon, Joni Mitchell, and Peter, Paul and Mary. The festivals were resumed in 1989, when Kris Kristofferson and David Crosby and Graham Nash performed. Participants in 1990 included Jackson Browne, Boz Scaggs, and Michelle Shocked.

Richard and Mimi Fariña

Celebrations for a Grey Day	Vanguard	79174	'65/'95	CS/CD
Reflections in a Crystal Wind	Vanguard	79204	'66/'95	CS/CD
Memories	Vanguard	79263	'69	†
Best	Vanguard	(2) 21/22	'71/'89	CS/CD

Mimi Fariña and Tom Jans				
Take Heart	A&M	4310	'71	†
Bread and Roses				
The Bread and Roses Festival of Acoustic Music (recorded 1977)	Fantasy	(2) 79009	'79/'90	CS/CD
The Bread and Roses Festival of Acoustic Music, Volume 2	Fantasy	(2) 79011	'81	LP
The Bread and Roses Festival of Acoustic Music, Greek Theatre, U.C. Berkeley	Big Beat	103		CD
Mimi Fariña				
Solo	Philo	1102	'86	LP/CS/CD

THE FIFTH DIMENSION

Lamonte McLemore (b. Sept. 17, 1939, St. Louis, MO); **Marilyn McCoo** (b. Sept. 30, 1943, Jersey City, NJ); **Billy Davis Jr.** (b. June 26, 1939, St. Louis, MO); **Florence LaRue** (b. Feb. 4, 1944, Philadelphia, PA); **Ron Townson** (b. Jan. 20, 1941, St. Louis, MO)

One of the more popular black vocal groups of the late '60s and early '70s, the Fifth Dimension featured lush, warm harmonies on pop material such as Jimmy Webb's "Up, Up and Away" and Laura Nyro's "Wedding Bell Blues" and "Stoned Soul Picnic." Without a major hit after 1972, the Fifth Dimension established themselves on the supper-club circuit, while early members Marilyn McCoo and Billy Davis Jr. enjoyed popularity in 1976–1977.

Lamonte McLemore formed the vocal group the Hi-Fi's in Los Angeles during the mid-'60s with Marilyn McCoo and two others. McCoo was raised in Los Angeles and began performing at age 12. The Hi-Fi's toured with Ray Charles, then broke up, leading McLemore and McCoo to form a new group with Florence LaRue, Ron Townson, and McLemore's cousin, Billy Davis Jr. Davis had formed his first group while still in high school, and later served with the Emeralds and the St. Louis Gospel Singers. Initially known as the Versatiles, the group signed with Johnny Rivers's Soul City Records in 1966, changing their name to the Fifth Dimension by year's end.

The Fifth Dimension achieved a major pop hit with John Phillips's "Go Where You Wanna Go" at the beginning of 1967, followed at midyear by a near-smash with Jimmy Webb's "Up, Up and Away," a tame recording somehow identified with psychedelic music. During 1968 the group scored a smash pop and R&B hit with Laura Nyro's "Stoned Soul Picnic" and major pop hits with Nyro's "Sweet Blindness" and Nicholas Ashford and Valerie Simpson's "California Soul." The following year they had top pop hits with the medley "Aquarius/Let the Sun Shine In," from the Broadway musical *Hair*, and Nyro's "Wedding Bell Blues," and major pop hits with Neil Sedaka's "Workin' on a Groovy Thing," and "Blowing Away." The Fifth Dimension managed a major hit with Nyro's "Save the Country" in 1970, followed by the pop and R&B smash "One Less Bell to Answer," written by Burt Bacharach and Hal David. After the near-smash 1972 hits "(Last Night) I Didn't Get to Sleep at All" and "If I Could Reach You," the group never achieved more than a moderate hit, winning only one chart entry after 1973.

Married in 1969, Marilyn McCoo and Billy Davis Jr. left the Fifth Dimension in November 1975. They had a top pop and R&B hit with "You Don't Have to Be a Star (To Be in My Show)" and a near-smash hit in both fields with "Your Love," and hosted their own summer variety television show in 1977. McCoo went solo in 1978, launching her own supper-club career while hosting the television show "Solid Gold" from 1981 to 1984. She later appeared in the soap opera *Days of Our Lives*, and in 1991 she recorded an album of contemporary gospel music, *The Me Nobody Knows*.

Following the departure of McCoo and Davis, the Fifth Dimension endured a series of personnel changes. Lamonte McLemore, Florence LaRue, and Ron Townson served as the group's mainstays as they established themselves on the nightclub circuit.

The Fifth Dimension

Up, Up and Away	Soul City	92000	'67	†
The Magic Garden	Soul City	92001	'67	†
Stoned Soul Picnic	Soul City	92002	'68	†
The Age of Aquarius	Soul City	92005	'69	†
Greatest Hits	Soul City	33900	'70	†
The July 5th Album	Soul City	33901	'70	†
Portrait	Bell	6045	'70	†
Love's Lines, Angles and Rhymes	Bell	6060	'71	†
Live!	Bell	(2) 9000	'71	†
Reflections	Bell	6065	'71	†
Individually and Collectively	Bell	6073	'72	†
Greatest Hits on Earth	Bell	1106	'72	†
	Arista	4002		†
	Arista	8335		CS/CD
Living Together, Growing Together	Bell	1116	'73	†
Soul and Inspiration	Bell	1315	'75	†
Earthbound	ABC	897	'75	†
Star Dancing	Motown	896	'78	†
High on Sunshine	Motown	914	'79	†
The Glory Days	Pair	(2) 1108	'86	CS†
The Fifth Dimension Anthology (1967–1973)	Rhino	71104	'86	CS
16 Greats	Fest	4403		CS
The Fifth Dimension Is in the House	Columbia	64375	'95	CS/CD

Marilyn McCoo and Billy Davis Jr.

I Hope We Get to Love on Time	ABC	952	'76/'96	CD
Two of Us	ABC	1026	'77	†
Marilyn and Billy	Columbia	35603	'78	†

Marilyn McCoo

The Me Nobody Knows	Warner Bros.	26667	'91	CS/CD

ROBERTA FLACK

(b. Feb. 10, 1939, Asheville, NC)

A multitalented musician, Roberta Flack eventually established herself as a black female vocalist at a time when soul music was dominated by male vocal groups and male solo artists. Scoring a number of smash crossover pop and R&B hits in the early '70s, Flack advanced the career of Donny Hathaway by recording several duets with him, and sustained her own career into the '90s.

Raised in Arlington, Virginia, Roberta Flack started piano lessons at age 9, graduated from high school at 15, and attended Howard University on a full music scholarship, receiving her degree at 19. From 1962 to 1968 she performed at a posh Washington, D.C., nightclub called the Tivoli Club, accompanying opera singers and filling in between performances. "Discovered" by jazz pianist Les McCann at Mr. Henry's in 1968, Flack signed with Atlantic Records, recording two albums before achieving her first hit in 1971 with Carole King's "You've Got a Friend."

Roberta Flack scored her first top pop and easy-listening and smash R&B hit with Ewan McColl's folk song "The First Time Ever I Saw Your Face" (originally from her debut 1969 album) in 1972 after the song was included in the Clint Eastwood movie *Play Misty for Me*. That year she collaborated with former classmate Donny Hathaway, and the duo achieved a top R&B and easy-listening and smash pop hit with "Where Is the Love." She subsequently had top pop and smash R&B hits with "Killing Me Softly with His Song" (ostensibly inspired by Don McLean) and Gene McDaniels's "Feel Like Makin' Love," and a major hit with Janis Ian's "Jesse."

Taking time off from touring and recording, Roberta Flack was back in 1978 with the pop and R&B smash "The Closer I Get to You" (another duet with Hathaway), and the major hit "If Ever I See You Again," composed by Joe Brooks, the author of "You Light Up My Life." "You Are My Heaven," recorded with Hathaway, became a near-smash R&B hit a year after his death from a fall from the 15th floor of the Essex Hotel in New York City on January 13, 1979. Flack recorded two duet albums with Peabo Bryson in the early '80s, hitting with him on "Make the World Stand Still" in 1980 and "Tonight I Celebrate My Love" in 1983. She also worked on the soundtrack to the 1981 movie *Bustin' Loose*.

Roberta Flack maintained a low profile during the mid-'80s, reemerging in 1988 with *Oasis* and its smash R&B title song. In 1991 she scored a near-smash pop hit with reggae singer Maxi Priest on "Set the Night to Music" from her album of the same name. In 1994 Flack recorded *Roberta* with jazz instrumentalists Randy Brecker and Steve Jordan.

Roberta Flack

First Take	Atlantic	8230	'69	CS/CD
Chapter Two	Atlantic	1569	'70	CS/CD
Quiet Fire	Atlantic	1594	'71	CS/CD
Killing Me Softly	Atlantic	7271	'73	†
	Atlantic	19154		CS/CD
Feel Like Makin' Love	Atlantic	18131	'75	†
	Atlantic	80333	'92	CD
Blue Lights in the Basement	Atlantic	19149	'77	CD
Roberta Flack	Atlantic	19186	'78	†
Rest	Atlantic	19317	'81	CS/CD
I'm the One	Atlantic	19354	'82	CS/CD
Oasis	Atlantic	81916	'88	CS/CD
Set the Night to Music	Atlantic	82321	'91	CS/CD
Softly with These Songs: The Best of Roberta Flack	Atlantic	(2) 82498	'93	CS/CD
Roberta	Atlantic	82597	'94	CS/CD
Bustin' Loose (soundtrack)	MCA	5141	'81	†

Roberta Flack and Donny Hathaway

Roberta Flack and Donny Hathaway	Atlantic	7216	'72	CS/CD
Roberta Flack Featuring Donny Hathaway	Atlantic	16103	'80	CS

Roberta Flack and Peabo Bryson

Live and More	Atlantic	(2) 7004	'80	†
	Atlantic	7004		CS
Born to Love	Columbia	12284	'83	CS

FLEETWOOD MAC

Mick Fleetwood (b. June 24, 1942, London, England), drm; **John McVie** (b. Nov. 26, 1945, London, England), bs; **Peter Green** (b. Peter Greenbaum, Oct. 29, 1946, Bethnal

Green, London, England), gtr, voc; **Jeremy Spencer** (b. July 4, 1948, West Hartlepool, England), gtr, voc [Guitarist-vocalist **Danny Kirwan** (b. May 13, 1950, London) was added in August 1968. Peter Green departed in May 1970. In August 1970 keyboardist-vocalist **Christine McVie** (b. Christine Perfect, July 12, 1943, Birmingham, England) joined. Jeremy Spencer left in February 1971. **Bob Welch** (b. July 31, 1946, Los Angeles, CA), lead guitar and vocals, joined in April 1971 and left at the end of 1974. In January 1975, **Lindsey Buckingham** (b. Oct. 3, 1947, Palo Alto, CA), guitar and vocals, and **Stephanie "Stevie" Nicks** (b. May 26, 1948, Phoenix, AZ), vocals, joined. Buckingham left in 1987, to be replaced by **Billy Burnette** (b. May 8, 1953, Memphis, TN) and **Rick Vito** (b. Oct. 13, 1949, Darby, PA). Nicks and Burnette left in 1992 and were replaced by **Bekka Bramlett** (b. Apr. 19, 1968, Westwood, CA), vocals, and **Dave Mason** (b. May 10, 1946, Worcester, England), guitar and vocals. Burnette returned in 1994, the year Christine McVie left.]

FLEETWOOD MAC WITH BUCKINGHAM AND NICKS

Undergoing numerous personnel and stylistic changes for more than 25 years, Fleetwood Mac was one of the longest-lived of the British groups of the '60s, surpassed in terms of longevity by only the Rolling Stones. Formed by three former members of John Mayall's Bluesbreakers in 1967, Fleetwood Mac initially pursued a successful British career as a blues band during the late '60s blues revival. For a time sporting a three-guitar front line of Peter Green, Jeremy Spencer, and Danny Kirwan, the band gradually left the blues behind with the departure of cofounder Green in 1969. Subsequently creating a softer, more harmonious sound with the addition of singer-songwriters Christine McVie, Stevie Nicks, and guitarist Lindsey Buckingham, Fleetwood Mac broke through in the United States with the seminal album *Rumours* in 1977. The band went on to be one of the biggest-selling of all rock groups, although internal frictions led to the group's splintering for solo careers.

Fleetwood Mac was formed in July 1967 by two former members of John Mayall's Bluesbreakers, Peter Green and Mick Fleetwood, with Jeremy Spencer and Bob Brunning. Green had joined Mayall following Eric Clapton's departure to form Cream in mid-1966, and he appeared on Mayall's *A Hard Road* album. Green had previously been a member of Peter B's Looners and Shotgun Express, as had Mick Fleetwood. Fleetwood, a drummer since age 13, had shared drumming duties with Aynsley Dunbar in Mayall's group during 1966 and 1967. In September former Mayall bassist John McVie replaced Brunning in Mayall's band, and the nucleus of Fleetwood Mac was in place.

Originally known as Peter Green's Fleetwood Mac, the group debuted at the British National Jazz and Blues Festival on August 12, 1967, and soon signed with Mike Vernon's

Blue Horizon label. Issued on Epic in the United States, their debut album included songs by Elmore James, Howlin' Wolf, and Sonny Boy Williamson, as well as blues-based originals by Green and Spencer. Only marginally successful in the United States, the album proved surprisingly popular in Great Britain. The group soon scored their first British-only hit with Green's instrumental "Albatross." In August 1968 Green brought in a third guitarist-vocalist, Danny Kirwan; Fleetwood Mac's second American album, *English Rose*, contained songs by all three guitarists, including Green's "Black Magic Woman," popularized by Santana in 1970. Green's "Man of the World" became the group's second British hit in 1969, the year the group recorded two albums in Chicago with blues greats Otis Spann and Willie Dixon.

Switching to Reprise Records, Fleetwood Mac recorded *Then Play On* without Jeremy Spencer. Leaving much of the blues influence behind, the album featured a number of pop-style songs by Green. His "Oh Well" became a minor American hit in early 1970, but surprisingly he announced his departure from the group in May. He subsequently recorded an album for Reprise, only to drop out of sight for many years, eventually reemerging in the late '70s on Sail Records. At the time of his exit Peter Green was considered one of Great Britain's premier blues-based guitarists, rivaled by only Eric Clapton in terms of aptitude and stature.

Fleetwood Mac's first album without Peter Green, *Kiln House*, confirmed the group's move toward a softer, more harmonic, pop-oriented sound. Containing widely divergent material, the album included Spencer's Western parody "Blood on the Floor," Kirwan's rousing "Tell Me All the Things You Do," "Station Man," and "Jewel-Eyed Judy," featuring lead vocals by Kirwan. The album became the group's first substantial success in the United States, and expanded their popularity beyond the cult following that had attended their American tours since 1968. For the album, Fleetwood Mac was assisted by John McVie's wife Christine. Married in August 1968, the former Christine Perfect had been a member of another British blues-revival band, Chicken Shack, playing piano and singing on the group's British-only 1969 hit "I'd Rather Go Blind." She also recorded a solo album that was reissued in 1976 as *The Legendary Christine Perfect Album*. She officially joined Fleetwood Mac in August 1970, shortly before the release of *Kiln House*. In February 1971, during Christine's first American tour with Fleetwood Mac, Jeremy Spencer abruptly left the group in Los Angeles.

Fleetwood Mac, now comprised of Kirwan, Fleetwood, and the McVies, held auditions for Spencer's replacement, eventually choosing lead guitarist–singer–songwriter Bob Welch, who joined in April 1971. Welch, a veteran of both the Los Angeles and Las Vegas club scenes, had been a member of the R&B band the Seven Sons. With the departures of original guitarists Peter Green and Jeremy Spencer, Fleetwood Mac switched to ballads and softer rock songs with *Future Games*, Christine McVie and Bob Welch's debut recording with the group. The follow-up, *Bare Trees*, included Kirwan's "Dust" and the title song as well as Christine's "Spare Me a Little" and Welch's "Sentimental Lady." In October 1972 Danny Kirwan left Fleetwood Mac, eventually recording three albums for DJM Records.

Experiencing several personnel changes over the next few years, Fleetwood Mac recorded *Penguin* and *Mystery to Me*, which sold surprisingly well in the United States. *Heroes Are Hard to Find*, regarded as Fleetwood Mac's first album as a transplanted Los Angeles band, yielded an underground hit with Welch's "Bermuda Triangle." A protracted series of legal and financial problems beset Fleetwood Mac, as their manager, claiming control of the group name, assembled a group of unknowns to tour America as Fleetwood Mac. The matter was litigated as the real Fleetwood Mac moved to Los Angeles, where Mick Fleetwood assumed the group's management. Eventually vindicated by the courts, the real Fleetwood Mac suffered the departure of Bob Welch at the end of 1974.

Reduced to a trio, Fleetwood Mac recruited Stevie Nicks and Lindsey Buckingham. Nicks had been raised in California, settling in the San Francisco Bay Area after dropping out of San Jose State College. In 1968 she joined a band named Fritz, whose bassist and second vocalist was Buckingham. The two persevered with the group until 1971, then moved to Los Angeles, where they recorded a duet album for Polydor Records. The two had come to the attention of Fleetwood Mac through producer Keith Olsen before Welch's departure. With Buckingham and Nicks joining the group in January 1975, the new lineup recorded *Fleetwood Mac*. Once again featuring three independent singer-songwriters, Fleetwood Mac became the quintessential British-California rock band. The album yielded three major hits, Christine's "Over My Head" and "Say You Love Me" and Nicks's "Rhiannon," and contained Christine's "Warm Ways" and Nicks's "Landslide." Spurred by the visual and musical focus provided by Christine McVie and Stevie Nicks, the subsequent six-month tour made Fleetwood Mac a massively popular concert attraction and established the group as one of the prime purveyors of pop-oriented, harmonically rich, and extravagantly produced music.

The self-produced follow-up to *Fleetwood Mac*, *Rumours*, capitalized on the group's burgeoning popularity as the two couples, John and Christine McVie and Lindsey Buckingham and Stevie Nicks, were splitting up. The album produced four hits—Buckingham's "Go Your Own Way," Nicks's top hit "Dreams," and Christine's "Don't Stop" and "You Make Loving Fun"—and eventually sold 20 million copies. Their popularity as a concert attraction was enhanced by a 10-month, 10-country world tour in support of the album.

During 1977 Bob Welch initiated a solo career under the auspices of Mick Fleetwood. For his debut album, *French Kiss*, Welch played all instruments except drums and sang all vocal parts. A remake of "Sentimental Lady" became a near-smash hit, followed by the major hit "Ebony Eyes" and the moderate hit "Hot Love, Cold World." Welch toured with Fleetwood Mac to promote *French Kiss*; he later recorded four more albums, scoring a major hit in 1979 with "Precious Love." Other solo projects recorded between 1979 and 1981, including Jeremy Spencer's *Flee*, Peter Green's *In the Sky* and *Little Dreamer*, and Mick Fleetwood's *The Visitor*, recorded in Africa, were less successful and quickly deleted.

Fleetwood Mac's *Tusk*, recorded over a two-year period at the cost of more than $1 million, was issued in late 1979. Overlong and disjointed, the album marked the creative ascendancy of Lindsey Buckingham, whose odd, near-smash hit title cut was recorded with the U.S.C. Trojan Marching Band. *Tusk* also yielded a near-smash hit with Nicks's "Sara" and a major hit with "Think About Me." The group completed an exhaustive American tour in late 1979 and a nine-month world tour in 1980.

During 1981 both Stevie Nicks and Lindsey Buckingham launched solo recording careers. Buckingham scored a near-smash hit with "Trouble," while Nicks achieved four hits from her solo debut album, *Bella Donna*, including the smashes "Stop Draggin' My Heart Around" (recorded with Tom Petty and the Heartbreakers) and "Leather and Lace" (recorded with Don Henley), and the near-smash "Edge of Seventeen." Nicks toured with a top-notch band of session players in 1981 and 1983, and had smash hits with "Stand Back" and "Talk to Me" in 1983 and 1985, respectively. Buckingham recorded *Go Insane* in 1984, hitting with the title song. Christine's 1984 *Christine McVie* album produced the hits "Got a Hold on Me" and "Love Will Show Us How," cowritten by guitarist Todd Sharp.

Following 1982's *Mirage*, its hits "Hold Me" and "Love in Store" (by Christine) and "Gypsy," and the subsequent tour, Fleetwood Mac was generally inactive as a group. The members reassembled for 1987's *Tango in the Night*, which produced the smash hits "Big Love" and "Little Lies" and the major hits "Seven Wonders" and "Everywhere." On the eve of the tour in support of the album, Lindsey Buckingham abruptly quit the group. Guitarist-vocalist Billy Burnette (Dorsey Burnette's son), a member of Mick Fleetwood's side band the Zoo for many years, was added for the tour, as was guitarist-vocalist Rick Vito, a veteran of the touring bands of Jackson Browne and Bob Seger. As full-fledged members, the two recorded *Behind the Mask* with Fleetwood Mac and performed on their subsequent tour. The album failed to produce any major hits. With their final performance in Los Angeles on December 7, 1990, Christine McVie and Stevie Nicks vowed to never tour with the group again. The two did record several new songs for 1992's *25 Years — The Chain*, but by then Rick Vito had also left the group. During the '90s Mick Fleetwood recorded an album of his own, as did Lindsey Buckingham, who toured with his own band in 1993. In 1993 the *Rumours*-era edition of Fleetwood Mac reunited to perform at President Bill Clinton's Inauguration. Stevie Nicks's first album since leaving Fleetwood Mac, 1994's *Street Angel*, featured "Maybe Love Will Change Your Mind." By 1994 a new Fleetwood Mac had emerged, with singer Bekka Bramlett (the daughter of Delaney and Bonnie Bramlett) and old Traffic hand Dave Mason on board; Billy Burnette also rejoined the group for touring.

Early Fleetwood Mac

The Original Fleetwood Mac (recorded 1967)	Sire	6045	'77	†
Fleetwood Mac	Epic	26402	'68	†
English Rose	Epic	26446	'69	†
English Rose/Fleetwood Mac	Epic	(2) 33740	'75	†
Black Magic Woman	Epic	(2) 30632	'71	†
Vintage Years: Best	Sire	(2) 3706	'75	†
	Sire	(2) 6006		†
Blues Jam in Chicago, Volume 1	Blue Horizon	4803	'69	†
Blues Jam in Chicago, Volume 2	Blue Horizon	4805	'69	†
Fleetwood Mac in Chicago	Blue Horizon	(2) 3801	'70	†
(reissue of above two)	Sire	(2) 3715	'76	†
	Sire	(2) 6009		†
	Blue Horizon	(2) 45283	'94	CS/CD
Jumping at Shadows	Varrick	020	'86	CS
Early Treasures	Pair	1208		CD
The Early Years	Special Music	4918		CS/CD

Chicken Shack

40 Blue Fingers Freshly Packed and Ready to Serve	Epic	26414	'69	†
O.K. Ken?	Blue Horizon	7705	'69	†

Christine McVie

The Legendary Christine Perfect Album	Sire	7522	'76	†
	Sire	6022		†
Christine McVie	Warner Bros.	25059	'84	†

Peter Green

End of the Game	Reprise	6436	'71	†
In The Skies	Sail	0110	'79	†
Little Dreamer	Sail	0112	'80	†

Jeremy Spencer

Jeremy Spencer and the Children of God	Columbia	31990	'72	†
Flee	Atlantic	19236	'79	†

Fleetwood Mac

Then Play On	Reprise	6368	'69	CS/CD
Kiln House	Reprise	6408	'70	CS/CD
Future Games	Reprise	6465	'71	CS/CD
Bare Trees	Reprise	2080	'72	†
	Reprise	2278		CS/CD
Penguin	Reprise	2138	'73/'90	CD

Mystery to Me	Reprise	2158	'73	†
	Reprise	2279		†
	Reprise	25982	'90	CD
Heroes Are Hard to Find	Reprise	2196	'74/'87	CD

Danny Kirwan

Second Chapter	DJM	1	'75	†
Danny Kirwan	DJM	9	'77	†
Hello There, Big Boy	DJM	22	'79	†

Paris (with Bob Welch)

Paris	Capitol	11464	'76	†
Big Town, 2061	Capitol	11560	'76	†

Bob Welch

French Kiss	Capitol	11663	'77	†
	Capitol	16125		†
	Capitol	91850	'89	CD†
Three Hearts	Capitol	11907	'79	†
	Capitol	16126		†
The Other One	Capitol	12017	'79	†
	Capitol	16127		†
Man Overboard	Capitol	12107	'80	†
Bob Welch	RCA	4107	'81	†
Eye Contact	RCA	4659	'83	†
Best	Rhino	70597	'91	CS/CD
Greatest Hits	Capitol	77684	'94	CS/CD

Lindsey Buckingham and Stevie Nicks

Buckingham/Nicks	Polydor	5058	'73	†

Later Fleetwood Mac

Fleetwood Mac	Reprise	2225	'75	†
	Reprise	2281		CS/CD
Rumours	Warner Bros.	3010	'77/'84	CS/CD
Fleetwood Mac/Rumours	Warner Bros.	23705		CS
Tusk	Warner Bros.	(2) 3350	'79	†
	Warner Bros.	3350		CS
	Warner Bros.	2694		CD
Live	Warner Bros.	(2) 3500	'80	CS/CD
Mirage	Warner Bros.	23607	'82/'84	CS/CD
Tango in the Night	Warner Bros.	25471	'87	CS/CD
Greatest Hits	Warner Bros.	25801	'88	CS/CD
Behind the Mask	Warner Bros.	26111	'90	CS/CD
	Warner Bros.	26206	'90	CD
25 Years — The Chain	Warner Bros.	(4) 45129	'92	CS/CD
Time	Warner Bros.	45920	'95	CS/CD

Mick Fleetwood

The Visitor	RCA	4080	'81	†
I'm Not Me	RCA	4652	'83	†

Stevie Nicks

Bella Donna	Modern	38139	'81	CS/CD
The Wild Heart	Modern	90084	'83	CS/CD

Rock a Little	Modern	90479	'85	CS/CD
The Other Side of the Mirror	Modern	91245	'89	CS/CD
Timespace: The Best of Stevie Nicks	Modern	91711	'91	CS/CD
Street Angel	Modern	92246	'94	CS/CD
Lindsey Buckingham				
Law & Order	Asylum	561	'81/'84	CS/CD
Go Insane	Elektra	60363	'84	CS/CD
Out of the Cradle	Reprise	26182	'92	CS/CD
John McVie				
John McVie's "Gotta Band"	Warner Bros.	26909	'92	CS/CD

THE FLYING BURRITO BROTHERS

Gram Parsons (b. Ingram Cecil Connor III, Nov. 5, 1946, Winter Haven, FL; d. Sept. 19, 1973, Joshua Tree, CA), rhythm gtr, kybd, voc; **Chris Hillman** (b. Dec. 4, 1942, Los Ange-les, CA), gtr, mdln, voc; **"Sneaky" Pete Kleinow** (b. c. 1935, South Bend, IN), pedal steel gtr; **Chris Ethridge**, bs, pno; **Michael Clarke** (b. June 3, 1944, New York, NY; d. Dec. 19, 1933, Treasure Island, FL), drm [Chris Ethridge left after one album, to be replaced by gui-tarist-vocalist **Bernie Leadon** (b. July 19, 1947, Minneapolis, MN); **Al Perkins**, pedal steel guitar, replaced Leadon in 1971. Gram Parsons left in 1970, to be replaced by **Rick Roberts** (b. Aug. 31, 1949, Clearwater, FL) on guitar and vocals.]

Although virtually unrecognized in their own time, the Flying Burrito Brothers, particu-larly in the person of Gram Parsons, exerted a tremendous influence on rock music in the late '60s and early '70s. Artistically they successfully combined rock and country instru-mentation, rock amplification, and plaintive country-style lyrics, opening the way for the eventual success of country-rock bands such as Poco and the Eagles. Although the Byrds' *Sweetheart of the Rodeo* album (with Flying Burrito Brothers founders Chris Hillman and Gram Parsons) was generally regarded as the first major country-rock album, some claim Parsons's International Submarine Band album *Safe at Home* deserves that accolade. More-over, the songwriting of Parsons inspired Emmylou Harris and later encouraged the devel-opment of a whole generation of country-style rockers, from Rodney Crowell to Elvis Costello.

Gram Parsons, however, may be better known to the public for his early death at age 26 than for his contributions to the development of country-rock. Indeed, he never enjoyed even a minor hit in any field, despite recording two albums with the Flying Burrito Broth-ers and two solo albums. Parsons's replacement in the Flying Burrito Brothers, Rick Roberts, similarly received little recognition with the group, eventually achieving his suc-cess with Firefall in the second half of the '70s. Chris Hillman ultimately established him-self in the late '80s with the Desert Rose Band, but like Emmylou Harris, Rodney Crowell, and Southern Pacific, their success was largely limited to the country field.

Gram Parsons grew up in Waycross, Georgia, and obtained his first guitar while in his early teens. After playing with several Georgia bands, he formed the folk-style quartet the Shilos in New York's Greenwich Village and toured the East Coast college and coffeehouse circuit between 1963 and 1965. Early recordings with the Shilos were eventually issued in 1979 as *Gram Parsons: The Early Years* on Sierra Records. After briefly studying theology at Harvard University, Parsons formed perhaps the first country-rock band, the International Submarine Band, in 1965 in the Cambridge area. The group recorded two obscure singles before realigning with a new bassist and drummer for *Safe at Home*, recorded for country producer Lee Hazlewood's LHI label.

In 1968 Gram Parsons joined the Byrds for their celebrated *Sweetheart of the Rodeo* album. Hailed as the first country-rock record, the album included two Parsons's songs, "Hickory Wind" and "One Hundred Years from Now." Leaving the Byrds after only three months, Parsons was soon followed by Chris Hillman. In late 1968 the two formed the Flying Burrito Brothers with "Sneaky" Pete Kleinow and Chris Ethridge.

Signed to A&M Records, the Flying Burrito Brothers' debut album, *The Gilded Palace of Sin*, was issued in 1969. Picturing the members in elaborate country-and-western-style Nudie suits (Parsons's suit prominently featured marijuana leaves), the album contained some of Parsons's finest songwriting efforts, including "Sin City" and "Juanita" (coauthored by Hillman) and "Hot Burrito #1" (coauthored by Ethridge), with lead vocals by Parsons. During 1969 Ethridge exited for session work and was replaced by future Eagle Bernie Leadon, formerly with Dillard and Clark, with Hillman switching to bass. Ex-Byrd Michael Clarke became the group's drummer that year. *Burrito Deluxe* featured a fine countrified version of Mick Jagger and Keith Richards's "Wild Horses," as well as a number of songs written or cowritten by Parsons, including "High Fashion Queen" and "Lazy Days."

Gram Parsons left the Flying Burrito Brothers shortly before the release of *Burrito Deluxe*; he was replaced by Rick Roberts, who led the group through a variety of incarnations into 1972. "Sneaky" Pete Kleinow and Bernie Leadon both departed in 1971, and by October the group was reconstituted with Roberts, Hillman, Clarke, pedal steel guitarist Al Perkins, and three members of the bluegrass group Country Gazette (guitarist Kenny Wertz, banjo player Alan Munde, and fiddler Byron Berline). This grouping recorded the live *Last of the Red Hot Burritos*, but before a late 1971 tour, Hillman, Perkins, and Clarke dropped out. Following the tour, undertaken as the Hot Burrito Revue with Country Gazette, the group disbanded.

By 1972 Gram Parsons was recording again, with vocalist Emmylou Harris, Byron Berline, Al Perkins, and guitarist extraordinaire James Burton. His first solo album, *GP*, included "Kiss the Children," cowritten by Parsons and Rick Grech, a former member of Blind Faith. *Grievous Angel*, also recorded with Emmylou Harris and Al Perkins, contained another Parsons-Grech collaboration, "Las Vegas"; Parsons's originals "Return of the Grievous Angel" and "Brass Buttons"; and "In My Hour of Darkness," cowritten with Emmylou Harris. Several months before the release of the album, Gram Parsons died from apparent multiple-drug use at age 26 on September 19, 1973, at Joshua Tree, California. Never fully recognized during his own lifetime, Gram Parsons found life in the work of Emmylou Harris, whose popularity, ironically, was primarily in the country field.

During 1974 the Flying Burrito Brothers re-formed with "Sneaky" Pete Kleinow, Chris Ethridge, Louisiana fiddler Gib Guilbeau, Joel Scott Hill, and former Byrds drummer Gene Parsons (no relation). After one album Ethridge departed. With guitarist Greg Harris, the group scored a minor country hit in 1980, "White Line Fever," but by 1985 mainstay Guilbeau had disbanded the Flying Burrito Brothers.

After two early-'70s albums for A&M, Rick Roberts formed Firefall in Boulder, Colorado, with guitarists Larry Burnett and Jock Bartley, bassist Mark Andes (Spirit), and drummer Mike Clarke. Signed to Atlantic Records, Firefall's eponymous debut yielded two moderate hits, "Cinderella" and "Livin' Ain't Livin'" and the near-smash "You Are the Woman," the latter two written by Roberts. Subsequent major hits in 1977–1978 were "Just Remember I Love You" and "Strange Way," both by Roberts. After 1983's "Always," Firefall fell off the charts.

In October 1971 Chris Hillman helped form Steve Stills's Manassas with Al Perkins and Stills's touring veterans Paul Harris, Calvin "Fuzzy" Samuels, and Dallas Taylor. The group recorded two albums, but disintegrated in September 1973 when Hillman, Perkins, and Harris left. At the behest of David Geffen, the head of Asylum Records, they helped form the Souther-Hillman-Furay Band with John David Souther and Richie Furay. Souther had been an early associate of Glenn Frey and Jackson Browne, had contributed three of his songs to Linda Ronstadt's *Don't Cry Now* album, and had coauthored three songs on the Eagles' album *On the Border*, including "The Best of My Love." Furay had been a member of the Buffalo Springfield and Poco. Intended as a supergroup in the tradition of Crosby, Stills and Nash, they instead managed only one (major) hit, Furay's "Fallin' in Love," through two albums, and they disbanded in late 1975.

During the '70s Chris Hillman recorded three solo albums, one before and two after Souther-Hillman-Furay. In 1978 he joined former Byrds Gene Clark and Roger McGuinn for touring and two albums, and he recorded an album with McGuinn in 1980. During the early '80s Hillman recorded two albums for the small Sugar Hill label before forming the Desert Rose Band with longtime associate Herb Pedersen in 1987. Favoring country and bluegrass, the Desert Rose Band scored four country-only hits from their debut album: the major hit "Ashes of Love" and the smashes "Love Reunited," "One Step Forward," and "He's Back and I'm Blue." Subsequent smash country hits included "Summer Wind," "I Still Believe in You," "She Don't Love Nobody," and "Start All Over Again." In 1992 the Desert Rose Band recorded *Traditional* with Alison Krause and Emmylou Harris.

The Shilos

Gram Parsons: The Early Years	Sierra	8702	'79	†
	Sierra	4215		†

The International Submarine Band

Safe at Home	LHI	12001	'68	†
	Rhino	069	'85	†

The Byrds (with Gram Parsons and Chris Hillman)

Sweetheart of the Rodeo	Columbia	9670	'68	CS/CD

The Flying Burrito Brothers

The Gilded Palace of Sin	A&M	4175	'69	†
	A&M	3122		†
Burrito Deluxe	A&M	4258	'70	†
The Flying Burrito Brothers	A&M	4295	'71	†
Last of the Red Hot Burritos	A&M	4343	'72	CD†
Hot Burritos	A&M	8070		†
Close Up the Honky Tonks	A&M	(2) 3631	'74	†
Farther Along: The Best of the Flying Burrito Brothers	A&M	5216	'88	CS/CD
Flying Again	Columbia	33817	'75	†
Airborne	Columbia	34222	'76	†
Live from Tokyo	Regency	79001	'80	LP
The Flying Burrito Brothers	Mobile Fidelity	772	'91	CD
Eye of a Hurricane	One Way	30330	'94	CD
Cabin Fever	Relix	2008		CS/CD
Live from Europe	Relix	2022		CS/CD
Close Encounters to the West Coast	Relix	2044		CS/CD
Sin City	Relix	2052		CS/CD

Gram Parsons

GP	Reprise	2123	'73	†
Grievous Angel	Reprise	2171	'74	†
GP/Grievous Angel	Reprise	26108	'90	CD

Gram Parsons and the Flying Burrito Brothers

Sleepless Nights	A&M	4578	'76	†

Gram Parsons and the Fallen Angels

Live 1973	Sierra	1973	'82	†
	Sierra	4222		LP/CS
Live 1973—Original Unedited Broadcast Recording	Sierra	6003		CD

Gram Parsons Tribute Album

Conmemoritivo: A Tribute to Gram Parsons	Rhino	71269	'93	CS/CD

Rick Roberts

Windmills	A&M	4372	'72	†
She Is a Song	A&M	4404	'73	†

Firefall

Firefall	Atlantic	18174	'76	†
	Atlantic	19125		CS
	Rhino	70379	'92	CS/CD
Luna Sea	Atlantic	19101	'77	†
	Rhino	71925	'95	CD
Elan	Atlantic	19183	'78	†
	Rhino	71926	'95	CD
Undertow	Atlantic	16006	'80	†
	Rhino	71927	'95	CD
Clouds Across the Sun	Atlantic	16024	'81	†
Best	Atlantic	19316	'81	CS
Break of Dawn	Atlantic	80017	'83	†
Mirror of the World	Atlantic	80120	'83	†
Greatest Hits	Rhino	71055	'92	CS/CD
You Are the Woman	Rhino	71231	'93	CS/CD

McGuinn, Clark and Hillman

McGuinn, Clark and Hillman	Capitol	11910	'79	†
	Capitol	16280	'83	†
	Capitol	96355	'91	CS/CD†
The City	Capitol	12043	'80	†
	One Way	18503	'96	CD

McGuinn and Hillman

McGuinn and Hillman	Capitol	12108	'80	†
	One Way	18498	'96	CD

Chris Hillman

Cherokee	ABC	719	'71	†
Slippin' Away	Asylum	1062	'76	†
Clear Sailin'	Asylum	1104	'77	†
Morning Sky	Sugar Hill	3729	'83/'91	LP/CS/CD
Desert Rose	Sugar Hill	3743	'84	LP/CS/CD

The Desert Rose Band

The Desert Rose Band	MCA	5991	'87	CS/CD†
	Curb/CEMA	77570	'92	CS/CD
Running	Curb/MCA	42169	'88	CS/CD†
	Curb/CEMA	77573	'92	CS/CD
Pages of Life	Curb/MCA	42332	'90	LP/CS/CD†
	Curb/CEMA	77567	'92	CS/CD

One Dozen Roses — Greatest Hits	MCA	10018	'91	CS/CD
	Curb/CEMA	77571	'92	CS/CD
True Love	MCA	10407	'91	CS/CD†
	Curb/CEMA	77572	'92	CS/CD
Traditional	Curb/CEMA	77602	'93	CS/CD

FOREIGNER

Lou Gramm (b. Lou Grammatico, May 2, 1950, Rochester, NY), lead voc; **Mick Jones** (b. Dec. 27, 1944, London, England), lead gtr, kybd, voc; **Ian McDonald** (b. June 25, 1946, London, England), gtr, kybd, voc; **Al Greenwood** (b. Oct. 20, 1951, New York, NY), kybd, synth; **Ed Gagliardi** (b. Feb. 13, 1952, New York, NY), bs, voc; **Dennis Elliott** (b. Aug. 18, 1950, London, England), drm [In 1979 Ed Gagliardi was replaced by bassist **Rick Wills** and Ian McDonald and Al Greenwood were fired from the band.]

A late-'70s hard-rock band initially comprised of former members of the British groups King Crimson and Spooky Tooth and the American band Black Sheep, Foreigner helped pioneer the heavy-rock style that led to the success of groups such as Journey, Styx, and REO Speedwagon. Mixing superficial lyrics by Mick Jones and Lou Gramm, heavy guitar riffs, and swirling synthesizer chords played at sluggish tempos, Foreigner provided the sound that later dominated album-oriented radio in the '80s.

Foreigner was formed in New York in early 1976 by Britons Mick Jones and Ian McDonald and American vocalist Lou Gramm, with Al Greenwood, Ed Gagliardi, and Dennis Elliott. Mick Jones had served as a session musician and songwriter and had been a member of Spooky Tooth. McDonald had been a member of King Crimson, appearing on the group's sensational debut album, *In the Court of the Crimson King*. In the early '70s Lou Gramm cofounded the band Black Sheep, who eventually recorded two albums for Capitol Records. Al Greenwood had played in a group called Storm, whereas Dennis Elliott was a session drummer who had played on Ian Hunter's debut solo album. Ed Gagliardi was the last to join Foreigner.

Foreigner rehearsed for several months before signing with Atlantic Records and recording their debut album. The album remained on the album charts for more than two years and yielded two smash hits, "Feels Like the First Time" and "Cold as Ice," as well as the major hit "Long, Long Way from Home." Touring the United States in 1977 and 1978, Foreigner's next album, *Double Vision*, also produced three hits, the smashes "Hot Blooded" and the title track, and the major hit "Blue Morning, Blue Day." In April 1979 Ed Gagliardi was replaced by Rick Wills, a former member of Peter Frampton's Camel and Steve Marriott's re-formed Small Faces. Their next release, *Head Games*, included three hits, "Dirty White Boys," "Head Games," and the sexist "Women."

In September 1979 Ian McDonald and Al Greenwood were dismissed from Foreigner, and the remaining four (Gramm, Jones, Wills, and Elliott) recorded perhaps their finest album, *4*. The album contained five hits, including the smashes "Urgent" (with saxophone solo by Junior Walker) and "Waiting for a Girl Like You" (an uncharacteristic ballad) and the major hits "Juke Box Hero" and "Break It Up." Foreigner then took a three-year break from touring and recording, coming back in 1985 with *Agent Provocateur* and its hits, the top ballad "I Want to Know What Love Is" and the major hit "That Was Yesterday."

During the late '80s Lou Gramm recorded two solo albums, scoring smash hits with "Midnight Blue" in 1987 and "Just Between You and Me" in 1989. Foreigner's *Inside Information* produced two smash hits with "Say You Will" and "I Don't Want to Live Without You." Jones recorded a solo album in 1989, and Gramm left Foreigner in 1991 to form Shadow King. Replaced by Johnny Edwards, Gramm returned to the group in mid-1992, while

Rick Wills left to join Bad Company and Elliott quit. By 1995 guitarist Mick Jones had returned to Foreigner.

McDonald and Giles

McDonald and Giles	Cotillion	9042	'71	†

Black Sheep

Black Sheep	Capitol	11369	'75	†
Encouraging Words	Capitol	11447	'75	†

Foreigner

Foreigner	Atlantic	18215	'77	†
	Atlantic	19109		CS/CD
Double Vision	Atlantic	19999	'78	CS/CD
Head Games	Atlantic	29999	'79	CS/CD
4	Atlantic	16999	'81	CS/CD
	Atlantic	82545	'94	CD
Foreigner Records	Atlantic	80999	'82/'84	CS/CD
Agent Provocateur	Atlantic	81999	'85	CS/CD
Inside Information	Atlantic	81808	'87	CS/CD
Unusual Heat	Atlantic	82999	'91	CS/CD
The Very Best . . . and Beyond	Atlantic	89999	'92	CS/CD
Classic Hits Live	Atlantic	82525	'93	CS/CD

Lou Gramm

Ready or Not	Atlantic	81728	'87	CD
Long Hard Look	Atlantic	81915	'89	LP/CS/CD†

Shadow King

Shadow King	Atlantic	82324	'91	LP/CS/CD†

Mick Jones

Mick Jones	Atlantic	81991	'89	LP/CS/CD†

THE FOUR SEASONS

Frankie Valli (b. Francis Castelluccio, May 3, 1937, Newark, NJ), lead voc; **Bob Gaudio** (b. Nov. 17, 1942, Bronx, NY), kybd, voc; **Tommy De Vito** (b. June 19, 1935, Bellville, NJ), gtr, voc; **Nick Massi** (b. Nicholas Macioci, Sept. 19, 1935, Newark, NJ), bs, voc

The most successful East Coast white vocal group of the '60s, exceeding the popularity of their stylistic predecessors Dion and the Belmonts, the Four Seasons scored a series of smash hit singles between 1962 and 1967 featuring the shrill piercing falsetto lead voice of Frankie Valli. One of the few American white groups other than the Beach Boys to challenge the Beatles, the Four Seasons became so popular that they were able to launch Valli on a successful simultaneous solo recording career in 1966. The Four Seasons and Frankie Valli enjoyed renewed success in the mid-'70s, but have since been relegated to the oldies revival circuit.

The evolution of the Four Seasons began in 1955 in Newark, New Jersey, with the formation of the Varietones by drummer Frankie Valli, guitarist brothers Nick and Tommy De-Vito, and bassist Hank Majewski. Changing their name to the Four Lovers in 1956, the group signed with RCA Victor Records and scored a minor hit with "You Are the Apple of My Eye." They subsequently languished on the lounge circuit for several years. In the meantime, another New Jersey group, originally formed in 1957, achieved a major hit as the

Royal Teens with the novelty song "Short Shorts" in early 1958. Among the members were songwriter-keyboardist Bob Gaudio and, for a brief time in 1959, Al Kooper.

In 1959 Bob Gaudio replaced Nick DeVito in the Four Lovers, and in 1960 Hank Majewski was replaced by Nick Massi. With a name change to the Four Seasons in 1961, the group recorded the unsuccessful single "Bermuda" for George Goldner's Gone label before signing with VeeJay Records with the help of writer-producer Bob Crewe. With Gaudio and Crewe splitting the songwriting duties, the Four Seasons scored a top pop and R&B hit with "Sherry" in late summer 1962. "Big Girls Don't Cry" and "Walk Like a Man" became top pop and smash R&B hits, followed by the pop-only hits "Candy Girl" (a smash), "Stay," and "Alone." Near the end of 1964 VeeJay assembled early recordings by the Beatles and hits by the Four Seasons for the album *The Beatles versus the Four Seasons*, today one of the most valuable of all rock collectors' items.

By 1964 the Four Seasons had switched to Philips Records, where the hits continued with the smashes "Dawn (Go Away)," "Ronnie," "Save It for Me," "Let's Hang On!," "Working My Way Back to You," and the top-hit classic "Rag Doll." The Four Seasons' sound was so popular that the group was able to score a major hit as the Wonder Who with a dreadful version of Bob Dylan's "Don't Think Twice." They also recorded the album *The Four Seasons Sing Big Hits by Burt Bacharach . . . Hal David . . . Bob Dylan*, certainly one of the worst albums of the '60s, had enough to make even the most casual Dylan fan cringe.

In 1966–1967 the Four Seasons hit with "I've Got You Under My Skin," "Tell It to the Rain," and "C'mon Marianne," as Frankie Valli initiated his solo recording career, scoring a smash hit with "Can't Take My Eyes off You." In 1968 the Four Seasons attempted to be socially conscious with a concept album, *The Genuine Imitation Life Gazette*, but the album sold poorly. Personnel changes started in 1965 when Bob Crewe ceased producing the group, handing the chore off to Bob Gaudio. By 1971 only Frankie Valli remained of the original members.

During the early '70s the Four Seasons recorded for Mowest and Warner Bros., while Frankie Valli recorded for Motown and Private Stock. Between 1974 and 1976 Valli scored smash hits with "My Eyes Adored You" and "Swearin' to God" on Private Stock, while the Four Seasons achieved smashes with "Who Loves You" and "December, 1963 (Oh, What a Night)" on Warner/Curb. The Four Seasons had no more major hits, and Frankie Valli scored his last major hit (a top hit!) with the title song to the 1978 movie *Grease*. The Four Seasons were inducted into the Rock and Roll Hall of Fame in 1990.

The Four Lovers

Joyride	RCA	1317		†

The Royal Teens

Short Shorts: Golden Classics	Collectable	5094		LP/CS/CD

The Four Seasons on Veejay

Sherry	VeeJay	1053	'62	†
Four Seasons Greetings	VeeJay	1055		†
Big Girls Don't Cry	VeeJay	1056	'63	†
Ain't That a Shame	VeeJay	1059	'63	†
Golden Hits	VeeJay	1065	'63	†
Stay and Other Great Hits (reissued as *Folk-Nanny*)	VeeJay	1082	'64	†
More Golden Hits	VeeJay	1088	'64	†
Girls, Girls, Girls, We Love Girls	VeeJay	1121		†
Recorded Live On Stage	VeeJay	1154		†

The Four Seasons and the Beatles

The Beatles versus The Four Seasons	VeeJay	(2) 30	'64	†

The Four Seasons

Dawn (Go Away)	Philips	600124	'64	†
Born to Wander	Philips	600129	'64	†
Rag Doll	Philips	600146	'64	†
The Four Seasons Entertain You	Philips	600164	'65	†
Sing Big Hits by Burt Bacharach . . . Hal David . . . Bob Dylan	Philips	600193	'65	†
	Rhino	70248	'88	CS/CD
Gold Vault of Hits	Philips	600196	'65	†
Working My Way Back to You	Philips	600201	'66	†
	Rhino	70247	'88	CS/CD
Second Vault of Golden Hits	Philips	600221	'66	†
Lookin' Back	Philips	600222	'66	†
The Four Seasons' Christmas Album	Philips	600223	'66	†
	Rhino	70234	'88	CS/CD
New Gold Hits	Philips	600243	'67	†
Edisione D'Oro (Gold Edition)— 29 Golden Hits	Philips	(2) 6501	'68	†
The Genuine Imitation Life Gazette	Philips	600290	'68	†
	Rhino	70249	'88	CS/CD
Half and Half	Philips	600341	'70	†
Chameleon	Mowest	108	'72	†
Who Loves You	Warner Bros.	2900	'75	†
Helicon	Warner Bros.	3016	'77	†

Frankie Valli and the Four Seasons

Reunited Live	Warner/Curb	(2) 3497	'81	†

Anthologies

The Four Seasons Story	Private Stock	(2) 7000	'75	†
Brotherhood of Man	Pickwick	3223		†
24 Original Classics	Arista	(2) 8208	'84	†
25th Anniversary Collection	Rhino	(3) 72998	'87	CD
Anthology	Rhino	(2) 71490	'88	CS
	Rhino	71490	'88	CD
Rarities, Volume 1	Rhino	70973	'90	CS/CD
Rarities, Volume 2	Rhino	70974	'90	CS/CD
Greatest Hits, Volume 1	Rhino	70594	'91	CS/CD
Greatest Hits, Volume 2	Rhino	70595	'91	CS/CD
20 Greatest Hits: Live	Curb/CEMA	77319	'90	CD
Greatest Hits	Curb/CEMA	77304	'91	CS/CD
Hope + Glory	Curb/CEMA	77546	'92	CS/CD
The Dance Album	Curb/CEMA	77634	'93	CS/CD
Oh What a Night	Curb/Atlantic	77693	'95	CS/CD

Original Classics Collection Series

Volume 1: Sherry and 11 Other Hits	Curb/Atlantic	77695	'95	CS/CD
Volume 2: Big Girls Don't Cry and 12 Other Hits	Curb/Atlantic	77696	'95	CS/CD
Volume 3: Ain't That a Shame and 11 Other Hits	Curb/Atlantic	77697	'95	CS/CD
Volume 4: Dawn (Go Away) and 11 Other Hits	Curb/Atlantic	77698	'95	CS/CD
Volume 5: Rag Doll and 10 Other Hits	Curb/Atlantic	77699	'95	CS/CD
Volume 6: Let's Hang On and 11 Other Hits	Curb/Atlantic	77711	'95	CS/CD
Volume 7: New Gold Hits	Curb/Atlantic	77712	'95	CS/CD
Volume 8: Who Loves You	Curb/Atlantic	77713	'95	CS/CD

Frankie Valli

Solo	Philips	600247	'67	†
Timeless	Philips	600274	'68	†
Inside You	Motown	852	'75	†
Closeup	Private Stock	2000	'75	†
Gold	Private Stock	2001	'75	†
Our Day Will Come	Private Stock	2006	'75	†
Valli	Private Stock	2017	'77	†
Lady Put the Light Out	Private Stock	7002	'78	†
Hits	Private Stock	7012	'78	†
Frankie Valli . . . Is the Word	Warner Bros.	3233	'78	†
Very Best	MCA	3198	'79	†
Heaven Above Me	MCA	5134	'80	†
Motown Superstar Series, Volume 4	Motown	5104	'81	CS/CD†

THE FOUR TOPS

Levi Stubbs (b. Levi Stubbles, ca. 1938, Detroit, MI); **Abdul "Duke" Fakir** (b. Dec. 26, 1935, Detroit, MI); **Renaldo "Obie" Benson** (b. ca. 1937, Detroit, MI); **Lawrence Payton Jr.** (b. c. 1938, Detroit, MI)

THE FOUR TOPS

Performing with their original members for more than 40 years, the Four Tops scored a series of major pop and smash R&B hits at Motown Records between 1964 and 1967, almost all written by the songwriting production team of Brian Holland, Lamont Dozier, and Eddie Holland. Featuring the soulful voice of lead vocalist Levi Stubbs, the Four Tops were acclaimed for their polished close-harmony singing, precise choreography, and complex stage routines. Perhaps the most popular Motown act in Great Britain, they were overshadowed by the Supremes in the United States. Enduring the departure of Holland-Dozier-Holland (H-D-H) from Motown in 1968, the Four Tops recorded for a number of different labels beginning in 1972, achieving major pop hits in 1972–1973 and 1981.

Born and raised in Detroit, the members of the Four Tops began singing together as high school students and later performed in local nightclubs. Known as the Four Aims since their formation in 1953, the group changed the name to the Four Tops upon signing with Chess Records in 1956. Their sole single for the label failed to sell, and they subsequently recorded for Red Top, Columbia, and Riverside. Signing with the infant Motown Records aggregation in March 1963, the Four Tops initially recorded for the company's short-lived jazz-oriented Workshop label.

Switching to the parent label Motown, the Four Tops scored a major R&B and pop hit in 1964 with "Baby I Need Your Loving," written by Holland-Dozier-Holland. Their next major hit came with William Stevenson's "Ask the Lonely," one of their few hits not written by H-D-H. After the top pop and R&B hit classic "I Can't Help Myself (Sugar Pie, Honey Bunch)," they achieved smash R&B and major pop hits with "It's the Same Old Song," "Something About You," and "Shake Me, Wake Me (When It's Over)." After the top pop and R&B hit "Reach Out, I'll Be There," the Four Tops achieved smash crossover hits with "Standing in the Shadows of Love" and "Bernadette." Major R&B and moderate pop hits ensued with "Seven Rooms of Gloom" and "You Keep Running Away," but by 1968 the group was reduced to covering the Left Banke's "Walk Away Renee" and Tim Hardin's "If I Were a Carpenter." The Holland-Dozier-Holland team left Motown in 1968, and the Four Tops did not achieve another major pop hit until 1970, when they scored with a remake of "It's All in the Game," Smokey Robinson and Frank Wilson's "Still Water (Love)," and "River Deep—Mountain High," recorded with the Supremes. Renaldo "Obie" Benson coauthored Marvin Gaye's smash "What's Going On," one of the first social-protest songs released by Motown. Following 1972's R&B near-smash "(It's the Way) Nature Planned It," the Four Tops left Motown for ABC-Dunhill Records.

On their new label, the Tops continued to produce, scoring major pop and smash R&B hits with "Keeper of the Castle," "Ain't No Woman (Like the One I've Got)," and "Are You Man Enough" from the movie *Shaft in Africa*. Subsequent R&B smashes through 1976 included "Sweet Understanding Love," "One Chain Don't Make No Prison," and "Midnight Flower" for Dunhill, and "Catfish" for ABC. The Four Tops scored another top R&B and near-smash pop hit with "When She Was My Girl" in 1981 on Casablanca. Levi Stubbs was the voice of the voracious plant Audrey II in the 1986 musical movie *Little Shop of Horrors*. Following their sensational appearance with the Temptations at the 20th anniversary celebration of Motown Records, the Four Tops briefly re-signed with their old label, yet their next moderate hit came with "Indestructible" on Arista Records in 1988. In 1990 they were inducted into the Rock and Roll Hall of Fame.

The Four Tops

The Four Tops	Motown	622	'65	†
	Motown	5122	'89	CS/CD
Second Album	Motown	634	'65	†
	Motown	5264	'89	CS/CD†
The Four Tops/Second Album	Motown	8127	'86	CD†
On Top	Motown	647	'66	†
	Motown	5444		CS/CD
Live!	Motown	654	'66	†
	Motown	5258		CS/CD
On Broadway	Motown	657	'67	†
Reach Out	Motown	660	'67	†
	Motown	5149	'89	CS/CD
Reach Out/The Four Tops	Motown	(2) 6075		CS†
Greatest Hits	Motown	662	'67	†
	Motown	5209		CS/CD
Yesterday's Dream	Motown	669	'68	†
Now	Motown	675	'69	†
	Motown	5466	'90	CS/CD

Soul Spin	Motown	695	'69	†
Still Waters Run Deep	Motown	704	'70	†
	Motown	5224	'89	CS/CD
Motown Legends	Motown	5363		CS†
Reach Out/Still Waters Run Deep	Motown	8007	'86	CD†
Changing Times	Motown	721	'70	†
	Motown	5478	'90	CS/CD†
Until You Love Someone: More of the Best (1965–1970)	Rhino	71183	'93	CS/CD
Greatest Hits, Volume 2	Motown	740	'71	†
Nature Planned It	Motown	748	'72	†
	Motown	5446	'89	CS/CD†
Best	Motown	(2) 764	'73	†
Anthology	Motown	(3) 809	'74	LP/CS
	Motown	(2) 809		CD
Motown Superstar Series, Volume 14	Motown	5114		CS
Compact Command Performances (19 Greatest Hits)	Motown	9042		CD†
Great Songs and Performances That Inspired the Motown 25th Anniversary TV Show	Motown	5314		CS/CD
Keeper of the Castle	Dunhill	50129	'72	†
	Motown	5428	'89	CS/CD
Main Street People	Dunhill	50144	'73	†
Meeting of the Minds	Dunhill	50166	'74	†
Live and In Concert	Dunhill	50188	'74	†
I Can't Help Myself	Pickwick	3381	'75	†
Night Lights Harmony	ABC	862	'75	†
Catfish	ABC	968	'76	†
Best (1972–1976)	MCA	27019	'82	CS/CD
The Show Must Go On	ABC	1014	'77		
At the Top	ABC/MCA	1092	'78	†
Tonight	Casablanca	7258	'81	†
One More Mountain	Casablanca	7266	'82		
Back Where I Belong	Motown	6066	'83	†
Magic	Motown	6130	'85	†
Indestructible	Arista	8492	'88	LP/CS/CD†
When She Was My Girl	Casablanca	514127	'92	CS/CD
Motown Legends	Esx	8528	'95	CS/CD

The Four Tops and the Supremes

The Magnificent Seven	Motown	717	'70	†
	Motown	5123		CS/CD†
The Return of the Magnificent Seven	Motown	736	'71	†
Dynamite	Motown	745	'72	†
The Best of the Supremes and the Four Tops	Motown	5491	'91	CS/CD

PETER FRAMPTON
(b. Apr. 22, 1950, Beckenham, Kent, England)

Gaining initial recognition in the late '60s with the British band the Herd, guitarist Peter Frampton was introduced to American audiences during his membership in Humble Pie. Acknowledged as an early hard-rock romanticist for his early-'70s recordings, Frampton broke through with the totally unexpected success of 1976's *Frampton Comes Alive!*, which prominently featured his use of the voice-box, a synthesizer-type device that seemed to make words emanate from his guitar. The album became both the best-selling live album and the best-selling double-record set in music history, eventually selling more than 15 million copies worldwide. However, his career faded quickly after the followup album, due perhaps to his unfortunate appearance in the inane *Sgt. Pepper's Lonely Hearts Club Band* movie with the Bee Gees, and a serious automobile accident in 1978.

Peter Frampton got his first guitar at age 8 and debuted professionally at 12. By 16 he was a member of the Herd, who scored several British hits and recorded one album for Fontana Records. In late 1968 Frampton left the Herd to form Humble Pie with ex–Small Face guitarist-vocalist Steve Marriott, ex–Spooky Tooth bassist Greg Ridley, and drummer Jerry Shirley. After two albums for Andrew Oldham's Immediate label, Humble Pie began displaying a harder and louder sound at A&M Records, thus thwarting Frampton's gentler, more romantic style. He quit the group before their breakthrough with the live set *Rockin' at the Fillmore.*

Peter Frampton then pursued session work, assisting in the recording of George Harrison's *All Things Must Pass* and Harry Nilsson's *Son of Schmilsson*. He recorded his debut solo album in 1972, and formed Frampton's Camel for one album and an American tour before disbanding the group in 1974. His first album to sell in significant quantities in the United States, 1975's *Frampton*, contained the unsuccessful singles "Show Me the Way" and "Baby, I Love Your Way."

Peter Frampton finally broke through in the United States with the live double-record set *Frampton Comes Alive!*, recorded at San Francisco's Winterland on June 14, 1975. Compiling much of his earlier material, the album yielded the smash hit "Show Me the Way" and the near-smashes "Baby, I Love Your Way" and "Do You Feel Like We Do" and included "All I Want to Be (Is by Your Side)." "Do You Feel Like We Do" featured Frampton using a so-called voice-box, a device which sent the electric guitar signal through a tube in his mouth, making the guitar "sing" synthesized words. The album took critics totally by surprise and stayed on the album charts for nearly two years, eventually selling 15 million copies. Frampton instantly (if temporarily) became a superstar, playing to stadium audiences throughout the summer of 1976 and into 1977.

Peter Frampton's follow-up album, *I'm in You*, produced a smash hit with the title song, but subsequent singles fared progressively less well. During 1977 and 1978 he worked on the $12 million Robert Stigwood film production of *Sgt. Pepper's Lonely Hearts Club Band*. Costarring with the Bee Gees, Frampton filled the role of Billy Shears in this abysmal fairy-tale-like musical featuring 29 Beatles songs. Poorly received by critics and the public alike, the movie was quickly relegated to the cheap-movie-house circuit. To add injury to insult, Frampton was severely hurt in an automobile accident on June 29, 1978, in the Bahamas that necessitated an extended period of recuperation.

Peter Frampton's career never regained its momentum. Albums sold progressively less well and he played small venues rather than baseball stadiums on tour. After a four-year hiatus he returned in 1986 with another album and a tour opening for Stevie Nicks. He performed as guest guitarist on David Bowie's 1987 *Never Let Me Down* album and the following Glass Spider tour. In 1989 he recorded another unsuccessful album. Frampton began collaborating again with Steve Marriott, in 1991, but Marriott died in a house fire that April 20th. Peter Frampton toured again in 1992 and 1995.

The Herd

Lookin' Through You	Fontana	67579	'68	†
The Herd Featuring Peter Frampton	Fontana	522746	'94	CS/CD

Peter Frampton

Wind of Change	A&M	4348	'72	†
	A&M	3133		†
Frampton's Camel	A&M	4389	'73	†
	A&M	3138		†
Somethin's Happening	A&M	3619	'74	†
Frampton	A&M	4512	'75	†
Frampton Comes Alive!	A&M	(2) 3703	'76	†
	A&M	(2) 6505		CS/CD
I'm in You	A&M	4704	'77	†
Where Should I Be	A&M	3710	'79	†
Breaking All the Rules	A&M	3722	'81	†
The Art of Control	A&M	4905	'82	†
Premonition	Atlantic	81290	'86	LP/CS/CD†
When All the Pieces Fit	Atlantic	82030	'89	LP/CS/CD†
Peter Frampton	A&M	2510		CD
Shine On: A Collection	A&M	(2) 0015	'92	CD

CONNIE FRANCIS

(b. Concetta Franconero, Dec. 12, 1938, Newark, NJ)

America's top-selling female recording artist of the late '50s and early '60s, Connie Francis recorded popular up-tempo songs and heart-rending ballads during a time dominated by male acts. Rivaled at the time by only Brenda Lee, Francis charted more than 50 singles, a record eventually broken by Aretha Franklin. Moving firmly into the pop field in the '60s, Connie Francis proved herself a survivor, eventually returning to touring and recording in the late '80s after years of psychological problems brought on by her rape after a performance in 1974.

Concetta Franconero began accordion lessons at age three and sang at local functions as a child. In 1950 she won first place on the national television show *Talent Scouts*, hosted by Arthur Godfrey, who suggested that she change her name to Connie Francis. From 1950 to 1954 she performed weekly on the TV variety program *Startime*. Signed to MGM Records in 1955, Francis recorded 10 unsuccessful singles for the label before breaking through with the smash hit "Who's Sorry Now" in 1958. Originally popularized in 1923, the song was followed by the major hit "Stupid Cupid," written by Neil Sedaka and Howard Greenfield. Through 1964 she scored hits with standards such as "My Happiness," "Among My Souvenirs," "Mama," and "Together" and softly rocking contemporary songs such as "Lipstick on Your Collar," "Everybody's Somebody's Fool," and "My Heart Has a Mind of Its Own" (both top hits) and "Vacation." She also achieved hits with tearful ballads such as "Many Tears Ago," "Breakin' in a Brand New Broken Heart," "Don't Break the Heart that Loves You," and "Second Hand Love." During the first half of the '60s she worked in four films, including *Where the Boys Are* and *Follow the Boys*, which featured her hit title songs.

Since 1960 Connie Francis had recorded albums of Italian, Spanish, Latin, and Jewish favorites that endeared her to the easy-listening audience. She turned to those fans to sustain her career as she faded from the charts after the advent of the Beatles. Francis recorded albums throughout the '60s (including folk and country albums, even an album with Hank Williams Jr.) and toured into the '70s.

However, after a performance at the Westbury Music Fair in New York on November 8, 1974, Francis was raped. She performed sporadically thereafter, enduring psychiatric treatment and confinement, a temporarily damaged voice, and the Mafia-style slaying of her brother. She made a much-publicized return appearance at Westbury in 1981, but her father had her committed, against her will, to a psychiatric hospital in 1983. Francis published her memoirs, *Who's Sorry Now*, in 1984, and eventually she regained her health. She returned to performing in 1989, adopting as her theme song the poignant "If I Never Sing Another Song." In 1992 Connie Francis's *Tourist in Paradise* was released on Liberty Records. The German label Bear Family issued a comprehensive box of her early recordings in 1993.

Connie Francis

Who's Sorry Now	MGM	3686	'58	†
Exciting Connie Francis	MGM	3761	'59	†
My Thanks to You	MGM	3776	'59	†
Italian Favorites	MGM	3791	'59	†
Christmas in My Heart	MGM	3792	'59	†
	Mercury	823561		†
	Polydor	823561	'87	CS/CD
Greatest Hits	MGM	3793	'59	†
Rock 'n' Roll Million Sellers	MGM	3794	'59	†
Country and Western Golden Hits	MGM	3795	'60	†
Spanish and Latin American Favorites	MGM	3853	'60	†
Jewish Favorites	MGM	3869	'60	†
More Italian Favorites	MGM	3871	'60	†
Songs to a Swingin' Band	MGM	3893	'61	†
At the Copa	MGM	3913	'61	†
More Greatest Hits	MGM	3942	'61	†
Never on Sunday	MGM	3965	'61	†
Folk Song Favorites	MGM	3969	'61	†
Irish Favorites	MGM	4013	'62	†
Do the Twist	MGM	4022	'62	†
Fun Songs	MGM	4023	'62	†
Award Winning Motion Picture Hits	MGM	4048	'62	†
Connie Francis Sings	MGM	4049	'62	†
Country Music Connie Style	MGM	4079	'62	†
More Italian Hits	MGM	4102	'63	†
Follow the Boys	MGM	4123	'63	†
Greatest American Waltzes	MGM	4145	'63	†
Mala Femmena (Evil Woman)	MGM	4161	'63	†
Very Best	MGM	4167	'63	†
German Favorites	MGM	4124	'64	†
In the Summer of His Years	MGM	4210	'64	†
Looking for Love	MGM	4229	'64	†
A New Kind of Connie	MGM	4253	'64	†
Rocksides (1957–1964)	Polydor	(2) 831698	'88	LP/CS/CD†
Sings for Mama	MGM	4294	'65	†
All-Time International Hits	MGM	4298	'65	†
Connie Francis	Metro	519	'65	†
Folk Favorites	Metro	538	'65	†
When the Boys Meet the Girls	MGM	4334	'66	†
Jealous Heart	MGM	4355	'66	†
At the Sahara in Las Vegas	MGM	4411	'67	†
Love Italian Style	MGM	4448	'67	†
Happiness	MGM	4472	'67	†

My Heart Cries for You	MGM	4487	'67	†
Incomparable	Metro	603	'67	†
Hawaii	MGM	4522	'68	†
Connie and Clyde	MGM	4573	'68	†
Sings Burt Bacharach/Hal David	MGM	4585	'68	†
Wedding Cake	MGM	4637	'69	†
Songs of Les Reed	MGM	4655	'70	†
Greatest Golden Groovie Goodies	MGM	109	'70	†
Spanish and Latin American Favorites	MGM	10014	'71	†
I'm Me Again	MGM	5406	'81	†
Tourist in Paradise	Liberty	96498	'92	CS/CD

Connie Francis and Hank Williams Jr.

Great Country Favorites	MGM	4251	'65	†

Anthologies

In Portuguese and Italian	Polydor	827365		†
Very Best	Polydor	827569		CS/CD
Greatest Hits	Polydor	827582		CS
Greatest Italian Hits	Polydor	827584		CS
Very Best, Volume II	Polydor	831699	'88	CS/CD
Greatest Hits	Dominion	3346	'94	CS/CD
De Coleccion	Polydor	527226	'95	CS/CD
At Her Best	RCA-Camden	1167		CS
Solid Gold	Pair	1167		CS
Where the Hits Are	Malaco	2003		LP/CS/CD
White Sox, Pink Lipsticks . . . and Stupid Cupid	Bear Family		'93	†

ARETHA FRANKLIN

(b. Mar. 25, 1942, Memphis, TN)

The most exciting, inspiring, and influential female soul singer of the late '60s, Aretha Franklin started her career as a gospel singer touring with her father C. L. Franklin's evangelistic troupe as a teenager. Her secular career, launched in 1960, languished for a number of years at Columbia Records, where her undeniably powerful and emotive vocal style was constricted by inappropriate material, production, and arrangements. She ultimately found sympathetic treatment in the late '60s under veteran producer Jerry Wexler at Atlantic Records, where she recorded a series of classic pop and R&B hits and best-selling albums, including *I Never Loved a Man the Way I Love You* and *Lady Soul*. Acclaimed at that time as the most popular female artist in rock music, Franklin endured a fallow period before coming back in the early '70s with the astonishing *Live at Fillmore West* and gospel *Amazing Grace* albums. Subsequently recording a number of uneven albums under a variety of producers, she reemerged in the mid-'80s with the rocking *Who's Zoomin' Who?*

Born the daughter of well-known evangelist preacher Cecil "C. L." Franklin, Aretha Franklin was raised in Buffalo and Detroit, where she began singing in her father's New Bethel Baptist Church Choir at age 8. By 14 she was a featured vocalist on his evangelistic tour, performing on the gospel circuit for four years and recording *The Gospel Sound of Aretha Franklin* (rereleased as *Aretha Gospel*) on the Chess Records subsidiary Checker at age 16.

In 1960, with the encouragement of her father and Teddy Wilson bassist Major "Mule" Holly, Aretha Franklin auditioned for Columbia Records' John Hammond, who immediately signed her. She toured the upper echelon of the so-called chitlin' circuit as Hammond

ARETHA FRANKLIN

guided her in the direction of classic jazz and blues singers such as Bessie Smith and Billie Holiday. She managed major R&B hits with "Today I Sing the Blues" and "Won't Be Long" from her debut album, and "Operation Heartbreak," and a moderate pop hit with "Rock-a-Bye Your Baby with a Dixie Melody," but subsequent recordings of Tin Pan Alley—style material using glossy pop arrangements met with little success. Of her Columbia albums, her tribute to Dinah Washington, *Unforgettable*, was perhaps her best.

In November 1966 Aretha Franklin switched to Atlantic Records, where she was personally supervised by veteran producer Jerry Wexler. Her first Atlantic single, "I Never Loved a Man (The Way I Love You)," recorded in Muscle Shoals, Alabama, with Franklin on piano and King Curtis on saxophone, became a top R&B and near-smash pop hit. Her debut album also contained favorites such as "Do Right Woman—Do Right Man" and "Dr. Feelgood" and yielded the top pop and R&B hit classic "Respect," written by Otis Redding. After the smash pop and R&B hit "Baby I Love You," *Lady Soul*, perhaps her finest album ever, produced four crossover hits: the smashes "(You Make Me Feel Like) A Natural Woman" (by Carole King and Gerry Goffin), "Chain of Fools" (by Don Covay), and "(Sweet, Sweet Baby) Since You've Been Gone" (coauthored by Franklin), and the major hit "Ain't No Way," written by her sister Carolyn Franklin.

In the late '60s Aretha Franklin's sisters Carolyn (b. 1945; d. Apr. 25, 1988, Bloomfield Hills, MI) and Erma (b. 1939) inaugurated their own recording careers. Carolyn had written "Baby Baby Baby" (a minor R&B hit for Anna King and Bobby Byrd in 1964) and "Don't Wait Too Long" (a major R&B hit for Bettye Swann in 1965), as well as Aretha's "Ain't No Way." She managed two moderate R&B hits in 1969–1970. Erma scored a smash R&B hit in 1967 with "Piece of My Heart," arranged by Carolyn. The song was later popularized by Janis Joplin.

Aretha Franklin achieved four crossover smashes from *Aretha Now* with her own "Think," "The House That Jack Built," Burt Bacharach and Hal David's "I Say a Little Prayer," and Don Covay and Steve Cropper's "See Saw." In 1969 she had major pop and smash R&B hits with Robbie Robertson's "The Weight," "I Can't See Myself Leaving You," Lennon and McCartney's "Eleanor Rigby," and "Call Me." In 1970 she hit with "Spirit in the Dark" and Ben E. King's "Don't Play That Song," disbanding her 16-piece band that fall in favor of a tighter combo of session players directed by saxophonist King Curtis. This unit recorded the astounding *Live at Fillmore West*, which featured an appearance by surprise guest Ray Charles and yielded a smash crossover hit with Simon and Garfunkel's "Bridge Over Troubled Water." Following the smash "Spanish Harlem," Franklin registered four hits from *Young, Gifted and Black*, including the smashes "Rock Steady" and "Day Dreaming."

In early 1972 Aretha Franklin returned to her gospel roots, recording the double-record set *Amazing Grace* at the New Temple Missionary Baptist Church in Watts, California, with perennial gospel favorite Reverend James Cleveland and his Southern California Community Choir. The album was a surprise success, becoming possibly the best-selling gospel album of all time. Smash R&B hits for Franklin continued with "All the King's Horses," "Master of Eyes," Carolyn Franklin's "Angel," Stevie Wonder's "Until You Come Back to Me," "I'm in Love," "Ain't Nothing Like the Real Thing," and "Without Love," but only "Until You Come Back to Me" became a pop smash.

In 1976 Aretha Franklin worked with songwriter-producer Curtis Mayfield on the soundtrack to the movie *Sparkle*, which produced a top R&B and smash pop hit with "Something He Can Feel" and the R&B near-smash "Look into Your Heart." Subsequent albums for Atlantic sold less well, and by 1980 Franklin had switched to Arista Records for the R&B smashes "United Together" and "Love All the Hurt Away," the latter recorded with pop-jazz guitarist-vocalist George Benson. In the early '80s Franklin scored a major pop and top R&B hit with "Jump to It," written and produced by Luther Vandross.

Aretha Franklin reestablished her popularity with the pop audience with 1985's *Who's Zoomin' Who?* It yielded the crossover smashes "Freeway of Love" and the title track, and the major pop hits "Sisters Are Doin' It for Themselves" (recorded with the Eurythmics) and "Another Night." Major pop hits continued in 1986 with "Jumpin' Jack Flash" and "Jimmy Lee," and 1987's duet with George Michael on "I Knew You Were Waiting (For Me)" became a top pop and smash R&B hit; that same year she became the first woman inducted into the Rock and Roll Hall of Fame. But 1987 also saw her gospel album, *One Lord, One Faith, One Baptism*, fail to match the success of *Amazing Grace*, and 1988 was a sad year for Franklin, marked by the deaths of her songwriting sister Carolyn, of cancer, and her brother, Cecil, who had served as her manager. Scoring pop hits in 1989 with "Through the Storm," recorded with Elton John, and "It Isn't, It Wasn't, It Ain't Never Gonna Be," recorded with Whitney Houston, Franklin stopped touring in the '90s, but she continued to record and appear on television. In 1994 Aretha Franklin scored a smash R&B and major pop hit with "Willing to Forgive" and "A Deeper Love" from the *Sister Act 2* soundtrack. She announced the formation of her own record label, World Class Records, in 1995.

Reverend C. L. and Aretha Franklin

Never Grow Old	Chess	91538		CS

Aretha Franklin

The Gospel Sound of Aretha Franklin	Checker	10009	'64	
(reissued as) Aretha Gospel	Chess	91521	'91	LP/CS/CD
Aretha (with Ray Bryant Trio)	Columbia	8412	'61	†
(reissued as) The First 12 Sides	Columbia	31953	'73/'88	CS/CD
Electrifying	Columbia	8561	'62	†
Tender, Moving, Swinging	Columbia	8676	'62	†
Laughing on the Outside	Columbia	8879	'63	†
Unforgettable	Columbia	8963	'64	†
Runnin' Out of Fools	Columbia	9081	'64	†
Yeah!!!	Columbia	9151	'65	†
Aretha Sings the Blues (recorded 1961–1965)	Columbia	40105	'85	CS/CD
Aretha After Hours (recorded 1962–1965)	Columbia	40708	'87	CS/CD
Soul Sister	Columbia	9321	'66	†
Take It Like You Give It	Columbia	9429	'67	†

Greatest Hits	Columbia	9473	'67	†
Take a Look	Columbia	9554	'67	†
In the Beginning: The World of Aretha Franklin (1960–1967)	Columbia	(2) 31355	'72	†
Greatest Hits, Volume 2	Columbia	9601	'68	†
Aretha Franklin	Columbia	(2) 4	'68	†
Soft and Beautiful	Columbia	9776	'69	†
Today I Sing the Blues	Columbia	9956	'70	†
The Legendary Queen of Soul	Columbia	(2) 37377	'81	†
Sweet Bitter Love	Columbia	38042	'82	CS/CD
Jazz to Soul	Columbia	(2) 48515	'92	CS/CD
I Never Loved a Man the Way I Love You	Atlantic	8139	'67	LP/CS/CD†
	Rhino	8139		CS/CD
	Rhino	71934	'95	CD
	Mobile Fidelity	574	'93	CD
Aretha Arrives	Atlantic	8150	'67	†
	Rhino	71274	'93	CS/CD
Lady Soul	Atlantic	8176	'68	LP/CS/CD†
	Rhino	8176	'88	CS/CD
	Rhino	71933	'95	CD
Aretha Now	Atlantic	8186	'68	†
	Rhino	71273	'93	CS/CD
Aretha Now/Lady Soul	Mobile Fidelity	623	'95	CD
Aretha in Paris	Atlantic	8207	'68	†
	Rhino	71852	'94	CD
Soul '69	Atlantic	8212	'69	†
	Rhino	71523	'93	CD
Aretha's Gold	Atlantic	8227	'69	†
	Atlantic	81445		CD†
	Rhino	8227		CS/CD
This Girl's in Love with You	Atlantic	8248	'70	†
	Rhino	71524	'93	CD
Spirit in the Dark	Atlantic	8265	'70	†
	Rhino	71525	'93	CD
Aretha's Greatest Hits	Atlantic	8295	'71	†
Live at Fillmore West	Atlantic	7205	'71	†
	Rhino	71526	'93	CD
Young, Gifted and Black	Atlantic	7213	'72	†
	Rhino	71527	'93	CD
Amazing Grace	Atlantic	(2) 906	'72	LP/CS/CD†
	Rhino	(2) 906		CS/CD
Hey, Now, Hey (The Other Side of the Sky)	Atlantic	7265	'73	†
	Rhino	71853	'94	CD
Aretha's Jazz (reissue of *Soul '69* and *Hey, Now, Hey*)	Atlantic	81230		CS/CD
Let Me in Your Life	Atlantic	7292	'74	†
	Rhino	71854	'94	CD
With Everything I Feel in Me	Atlantic	18116	'74	†
You	Atlantic	18151	'75	†
Sparkle	Atlantic	18176	'76	†
	Rhino	71148	'92	CS/CD
Sweet Passion	Atlantic	19102	'77	†
Almighty Fire	Atlantic	19161	'78	†

La Diva	Atlantic	19248	'79	†
Best	Atlantic	81280	'85	LP/CS/CD†
	Rhino	81280		CS/CD
30 Greatest Hits	Atlantic	(2) 81668	'86	LP/CS/CD†
	Rhino	(2) 81668		CS/CD
Aretha	Arista	9538	'79	†
	Arista	8556	'88	CS/CD
Love All the Hurt Away	Arista	9552	'81	†
Jump To It	Arista	9602	'82	†
Get It Right	Arista	8019	'83	†
Who's Zoomin' Who?	Arista	8286	'85	CS/CD
Aretha Franklin	Arista	8442	'86	CD†
One Lord, One Faith, One Baptism	Arista	(2) 8497	'87	LP/CS/CD†
Through the Storm	Arista	8572	'89	LP/CS/CD†
What You See Is What You Get	Arista	8628	'91	CS/CD
Anthologies				
Queen of Soul	Harmony	11274	'68	†
Once in a Lifetime	Harmony	11349	'69	†
2 Sides of Love	Harmony	11418	'70	†
Greatest Hits, 1960–1965	Harmony	30606	'71	†
Queen of Soul	Rhino	(4) 71063	'92	CS/CD
Chain of Fools	Rhino	71429		CS/CD
Very Best, Volume 1	Rhino	71598	'94	CS/CD
Very Best, Volume 2	Rhino	71599	'94	CS/CD

ALAN FREED

(b. Dec. 15, 1922, Johnstown, PA; d. Jan. 20, 1965, Palm Springs, CA)

One of the most important popularizers of rock and roll during the '50s, Alan Freed was the first disc jockey and concert producer of rock and roll. Often credited with popularizing the term *rock and roll* in 1951, ostensibly to avoid the stigma attached to R&B and so-called race music, Freed opened the door to white acceptance of black music as a disc jockey, eschewing white cover versions in favor of the R&B originals. A staunch defender of rock and roll and R&B when these musics were under attack, Alan Freed began producing rock-and-roll concerts in 1952. Indulging in the questionable but almost standard practice of taking unsubstantiated songwriting credits and accepting money to play certain records, Freed was ruined by the so-called payola investigation of 1959–1960. He was made the scapegoat of the entire scandal, as others, most notably the more-established and less-daring Dick Clark, escaped virtually unscathed. Dying ignominiously and impoverished in 1965, Alan Freed received a modicum of recognition as a result of the fictionalized 1978 movie *American Hot Wax*; he was among the first inductees into the Rock and Roll Hall of Fame, a rare honor for a nonmusician.

Alan Freed grew up in Salem, Ohio, performing his first radio work while attending Ohio State College. Following jobs as announcer at WKST and disc jockey at WAKR, he moved to Cleveland's WJW in 1951. Prompted by record shop owner Leo Mintz, he began playing black R&B records there. Calling the music "rock and roll" to avoid any racial stigma, the songs proved unexpectedly popular with white youth, and as a consequence Freed started producing rock-and-roll concerts. His first, staged in Cleveland in March 1952, was oversold and subsequently canceled, leading to rock and roll's first riot. In September 1954 Freed moved to New York's WINS, where his rock-and-roll show helped make the station the city's most popular among white audiences. During the mid-'50s he began taking partial songwriting credit for songs such as the Moonglows' "Sincerely" and Chuck Berry's "Maybellene," as a form of payback for his playing the songs on the air (and thus making them hits). Freed's concert-promotion activities culminated in the establishment of box-office records at New York's Paramount Theater in 1957. He also appeared in some of the earliest rock-and-roll movies, including 1956's *Rock Around the Clock*.

Alan Freed's decline began in March 1958, when a stabbing and a number of beatings occurred at one of his concerts in Boston. Rock-and-roll shows were subsequently banned in several cities, and Freed was charged with inciting to riot and unlawful destruction of property, charges that were finally dismissed 17 months later. He quit WINS and switched to New York's WABC, only to be fired in November 1959 for refusing "on principle" to sign statements denying his acceptance of bribes for playing records. Experiencing the brunt of the anti-rock-and-roll movement, Freed was indicted in 1960 for accepting $30,000 in payola; he eventually pleaded guilty, in March 1963, to taking $2,700 from two companies. Run out of New York, he worked briefly at KDAY in Los Angeles. Charged with income-tax evasion in 1964, Freed died in obscurity on January 20, 1965, at age 42, in Palm Springs, California. Some belated recognition of his contributions to rock and roll came with the 1978 release of the Paramount Pictures movie *American Hot Wax*, a fictionalized "week in the life of rock and roll," with Alan Freed as its central character.

Alan Freed

Rock 'n' Roll Radio (recorded live 1956)	Radiola	1087		CS/CD
Rock 'n' Roll Dance Party, Volume 1	Coral	57063	'56	†
Rock 'n' Roll Dance Party, Volume 2	Coral	57115	'57	†
TV Record Hop	Coral	57177	'57	†
Rock Around the Block	Coral	57213	'58	†
The Alan Freed Rock & Roll Show	Brunswick	54043	'59	†
Alan Freed's Memory Lane	End	314	'62	†

THE FUGS

Ed Sanders (b. Kansas City, MO), voc, gtr; **Tuli Kupferberg** (b. New York, NY), voc; **Ken Weaver** (b. Galveston, TX), drm; various others

Organized by two Beat-generation poets, the Fugs sought to stir '60s audiences with outrageous and iconoclastic poetry, satire and outright obscenity in their songs, which were concerned with sex, drugs, and politics. One of the earliest rock satire groups and certainly the first underground group, the Fugs' pioneering efforts paved the way for the premeditated offensiveness of Frank Zappa's Mothers of Invention, Iggy Pop and the Stooges, Alice Cooper, and the late-'70s punk-rockers, and the silliness of Flo and Eddie and Cheech and Chong.

Conceived by Beat poets Ed Sanders and Tuli Kupferberg near the end of 1964, the Fugs also included poet-drummer Ken Weaver and a host of guitarists, bassists, keyboard players, and other musicians (including Steve Weber and Peter Stampfel of another New York satiric folk-rock band, the Holy Modal Rounders, and playwright Sam Shepard). Kansas City–raised Sanders, a former classical languages major at New York University, published *Poem from Jail* in 1963, and served as editor-publisher of *Fuck You: A Magazine of the Arts*, a publication so obscene that it could neither be sent through the mail nor sold, but rather was given away to friends and sympathetic readers. He was as well the owner-manager of the Peace Eye Bookstore on New York's Lower East Side. Missourian Kupferberg, an avowed anarchist, had published *Snow Job; Poems: 1946–1959* in 1959.

Debuting at Greenwich Village's Folklore Center, the ever-changing Fugs later occupied the Players Theater on MacDougal Street, logging some 900 consecutive performances there. Their first album, on the small Broadside label (later leased to the even-smaller ESP), included songs such as "Slum Goddess," "I Couldn't Get High," "Boobs a Lot," and "Nothing." Their second album contained Sanders's "Group Grope" and "Dirty Old Man," Kupferberg's antiwar "Kill for Peace," and the uncommonly lyrical "Morning, Morning," composed by Kupferberg and recorded by Richie Havens on his *Mixed Bag* album. *The Virgin Fugs* sported Fugs classics such as "Caca Rock," "Coca Cola Douche," and "New Amphetamine Shriek."

Seemingly on the verge of a major breakthrough with their signing to the major label Reprise, the Fugs managed only modest sales, although the backup band gained a more professional sound with the addition of guitarist Danny "Kooch" Kortchmar, later a well-known session guitarist and producer-songwriter for Don Henley and Billy Joel. The Fugs' second album for Reprise featured "Johnny Pissoff Meets the Red Angel," "Burial Waltz," and "National Haiku Contest." By late 1969 the Fugs had disbanded. Ken Weaver returned to the Southwest, whereas Sanders recorded two obscure albums for Reprise. Tuli Kupferberg recorded one album before compiling the book *Listen to the Mockingbird: Satiric Songs to Tunes You Know*, published in 1973. Ed Sanders returned to writing with 1971's *The Family*, chronicling the story of the Charlie Manson commune, and *Tales of Beatnik Glory*, published in 1975. He resurfaced in 1979 with the irreverent two-hour "Karen Silkwood Cantata," performed at the Creative Musical Studio near Woodstock, New York. Kupferberg has made an industry out of writing irreverent how-to manuals on a wide variety of subjects (*1,001 Ways to Make Love*, etc.). Sanders and Kupferberg reemerged on the New Rose label in the mid-'80s and the Gazell label in the '90s, performing with a new band of Fugs.

The Fugs

Ballads of Contemporary Protest, Point of Views, and General Dissatisfaction	Broadside	304	'66	†
(reissued as) The Fugs' First Album	ESP	1018	'66	†
	Fantasy	9669	'94	CD
(also reissued as) Slum Goddess	ESP	1018		LP
The Fugs	ESP	1028	'66	†
(reissued as) The Fugs' Second Album	Fantasy	9668	'94	CD
(also reissued as) Kill for Peace	ESP	1028		LP
The Virgin Fugs	ESP	1038	'68	
Tenderness Junction	Reprise	6280	'68	†
It Crawled into My Hand, Honest	Reprise	6305	'68	†
Belle of Avenue A	Reprise	6359	'69	†
Golden Filth	Reprise	6396	'70	†
Rounder's Score	ESP	2018	'75	†
Best of the Fugs	Adelphi	4116		LP/CS
No More Slavery/Live Tracks	New Rose	79		CD†
Songs from a Portable Forest	Gazell	2003		CS/CD
The Fugs	Fugs	121	'93	CD
Refuse to Be Burnt Out	Fugs	139	'95	CD

Tuli Kupferberg

No Deposit, No Return	ESP	1035		†

Ed Sanders

Sanders' Truckstop	Reprise	6374	'70	†
Beer Cans on the Moon	Reprise	2105	'72	†
Songs in Ancient Greek	Olufsen	5073	'92	CD

G

MARVIN GAYE
(b. Marvin Gay Jr., Apr. 2, 1939, Washington, D.C.; d. Apr. 1, 1984, Los Angeles, CA)

MARVIN GAYE

In a career that spanned the entire history of R&B, from '50s doo-wop to '80s soul, Marvin Gaye helped define the Motown sound. Recording some of the label's most personal and engaging songs, Gaye made a graceful transition from early gospel-style recordings to a pop-oriented sound that emphasized his smooth, sensual tenor voice. The top sex symbol among black male singers throughout his career, he was one of soul music's most charismatic figures, and one of its most important stylists, influencing both black and white male vocalists. Gaye was the first Motown star to assert his independence from the label, self-producing and writing much of the seminal social-protest album *What's Going On?* in 1971. He was also among the first to frankly address sexual topics, beginning with 1973's *Let's Get It On.* A fallow period followed, although he managed a comeback with the frankly sexual *Midnight Love* album in 1982–1983. In 1984, however, Marvin Gaye's career was ended by gunshots triggered by his father.

Raised in his native Washington, D.C., Marvin Gaye first sang solos with his father's church choir at age three. During high school he studied piano while also learning to play drums. In the mid-'50s he was a member of the local vocal group the Rainbows, whose membership included Don Covay and Billy Stewart. Gaye made his first recordings in 1957 as a member of the Marquees, who were drafted to replace the original members of the Moonglows in 1958. Spotted performing with the group in 1961 by Berry Gordy

Jr., Gaye was signed to the fledging family of Motown labels. He initially served as a session drummer and later toured with the Miracles for six months.

Marvin Gaye started recording solo for the Motown subsidiary Tamla label in 1961, scoring his first near-smash R&B and moderate pop hit with "Stubborn Kind of Fellow," recorded with Martha and the Vandellas in late 1962. A string of major hits in both the R&B and pop fields followed with "Hitch Hike" and "Pride and Joy" (which he cowrote) and Holland-Dozier-Holland's "Can I Get a Witness." A more pop-oriented sound emerged in 1964 for the crossover hits "Try It Baby" (by Berry Gordy Jr.) and "You're a Wonderful One," the overlooked "Baby, Don't Do It," and the smash "How Sweet It Is to Be Loved by You," all written by H-D-H.

Marvin Gaye began a series of recordings with Motown-organization female singers in 1964 with Mary Wells. Their duet album produced the major two-sided hit "What's the Matter with You, Baby"/"Once Upon a Time." Gaye and Kim Weston had a minor hit in late 1964 with "What Good Am I Without You" and a smash crossover hit in 1967 with "It Takes Two."

Established as a singles artist by 1965, Marvin Gaye continued his hit-making ways with "I'll Be Doggone" and "Ain't That Peculiar," both cowritten by Smokey Robinson, and the definitive top-hit version of Barrett Strong and Norman Whitfield's "I Heard It Through the Grapevine," recorded a year earlier by Gladys Knight and the Pips. Subsequent crossover hits included "Too Busy Thinking About My Baby" and "That's the Way Love Is."

In 1967 Marvin Gaye began teaming with Tammi Terrell, recording three albums with her through 1969. Their smash R&B and pop hits of the period include four Nicholas Ashford–Valerie Simpson compositions—"Ain't No Mountain High Enough," "Your Precious Love," "Ain't Nothing Like the Real Thing," and "You're All I Need to Get By"—as well as "If I Could Build My World Around You." However, Gaye ceased touring after Terrell collapsed in his arms on stage in 1969. She died on March 16, 1970, of a brain tumor.

After a protracted period of seclusion, Marvin Gaye reemerged to demand more independence from the Motown organization. Eschewing the rigid singles format, he recorded and produced *What's Going On*, one of the first concept albums in the R&B format. The album, which revealed Gaye's growing concern with inner-city decay, ecology, and spiritual poverty, was reluctantly released in mid-1971. With all songs either written or cowritten by Gaye, the album ironically became one of Motown's best-selling albums, yielding top R&B and smash pop singles with "What's Going On," "Mercy, Mercy Me (The Ecology)," and "Inner City Blues (Make Me Wanna Holler)." Gaye's success inspired Stevie Wonder to seek more control over his work for Motown. Gaye followed up the stunning success of *What's Going On* with the largely instrumental soundtrack to the movie *Trouble Man*, which yielded a smash crossover hit with the title song.

In 1973 Marvin Gaye cowrote, coproduced, and recorded *Let's Get It On*, his most popular album. A dramatic contrast to his previous effort, the album shunned social commentary in favor of sensual, romantic material. The title song became a top R&B and pop hit, and the album also yielded the two-sided hit "Come Get to This"/"You Sure Love to Ball." Later that year Gaye teamed with Diana Ross for an album and the hits "You're a Special Part of Me" (an R&B smash), "My Mistake (Was to Love You)," and "Don't Knock My Love."

In early 1974 Marvin Gaye returned to live performance at the Oakland (California) Coliseum, which resulted in *Marvin Gaye Live!* Subsequent '70s successes included the top R&B hits "I Want You" and "Got to Give It Up (Part I)," also a top pop hit. During 1979, bankrupt and the subject of divorce proceedings, Marvin Gaye issued the embittered double-record set *Here, My Dear*, with royalties assigned to his ex-wife, Anna (also Berry Gordy Jr.'s sister).

Marvin Gaye moved to Europe in 1980, eventually settling in Belgium. He negotiated his release from his Motown contract and signed with Columbia Records in 1982. His debut for the label, *Midnight Love*, was recorded in Belgium and became a best-seller, yielding a top R&B and smash pop hit with the reggae-infused "Sexual Healing." He returned to the United States to tour in support of the album in 1983, but on April 1, 1984, while in the midst of recording material for a new album, he was shot to death by his father at his parents' home in Los Angeles. The posthumous *Dream of a Lifetime* produced a R&B-only smash with "Sanctified Lady." In 1987 Marvin Gaye was inducted into the Rock and Roll Hall of Fame. Gaye's daughter Nona, from his second marriage, began recording in the early '90s.

Marvin Gaye

Soulful Moods of Marvin Gaye	Tamla	221	'62	†
	Motown	530370	'94	CS/CD
That Stubborn Kinda Fellow	Tamla	239	'63	†
	Motown	5218	'89	CD†
Live on Stage	Tamla	242	'63	†
When I'm Alone I Cry	Tamla	251	'64	†
	Motown	530356	'94	CS/CD
How Sweet It Is to Be Loved by You	Tamla	258	'65	†
	Motown	5419	'89	CD†
Hello Broadway	Tamla	259	'65	†
	Motown	5493	'91	CS/CD†
A Tribute to the Great Nat King Cole	Tamla	261	'66	†
	Motown	5216	'89	CS/CD
Moods of Marvin Gaye	Tamla	266	'66	†
	Motown	5296	'89	CS/CD
In the Groove	Tamla	285	'68	†
(reissued as) I Heard It Through the Grapevine	Motown	5395	'89	CS/CD
M.P.G.	Tamla	292	'69	†
	Motown	5125	'89	CD†
That's the Way Love Is	Tamla	299	'69	†
	Motown	5422	'89	CD†
What's Going On	Tamla	310	'71	†
	Motown	9036		CD†
	Motown	5339		CS/CD†
	Motown	530022	'94	CS/CD
Trouble Man (soundtrack)	Tamla	322	'72	†
	Motown	5241	'89	CS/CD
Let's Get It On	Tamla	329	'73	†
	Motown	9006		CD†
	Motown	5192	'89	CS/CD
Marvin Gaye Live!	Tamla	333	'74	
	Motown	9004		CD†
	Motown	5181		LP/CS/CD
I Want You	Tamla	342	'76	†
	Motown	5292	'89	CS/CD
Live at the London Palladium	Tamla	(2) 352	'77	†
	Tamla	6191		CD†
	Motown	(2) 5259		LP/CS
	Motown	5259		CD
Here, My Dear	Tamla	(2) 364	'79	†
	Motown	6310	'94	CS/CD
Love Man	Tamla	369	'80	†

In Our Lifetime: The Final Motown Sessions	Tamla	374	'81	†
	Motown	6379	'94	CS/CD
The Last Concert Tour	Giant	24436	'91	CS/CD
Midnight Love	Columbia	38197	'82/'85	CS/CD
Dream of a Lifetime	Columbia	39916	'85	CS/CD
Romantically Yours	Columbia	40208	'86	CS/CD

Reissues (two LPs on one CD)

I Heard It Through the Grapevine/I Want You	Motown	8110	'86	CD†
Let's Get It On/What's Going On	Motown	8113	'86	CD†
Trouble Man (ST)/M.P.G.	Motown	8136	'86	CD†
That Stubborn Kinda Fellow/How Sweet It Is to Be Loved by You	Motown	8157		CD†
Moods of Marvin Gaye/That's the Way Love Is	Motown	8161		CD†

Anthologies

Greatest Hits	Tamla	252	'64	†
	Tamla	348	'76	†
	Motown	9005		CD†
	Motown	5191		CS/CD
Greatest Hits, Volume 2	Tamla	278	'67	†
Marvin Gaye and His Girls	Tamla	293	'69	†
	Motown	5246	'90	CS/CD
Super Hits	Tamla	300	'70	†
	Motown	5301		LP/CS/CD
Anthology	Motown	(3) 791	'74	LP/CS
	Motown	(2) 791		CD
Every Great Motown Hit of Marvin Gaye	Motown	6058	'83	CS/CD
Motown Superstar Series, Volume 15	Motown	115	'84	†
Great Songs and Performances	Motown	5311	'84	CS/CD
Marvin Gaye and His Women: Classic Duets	Motown	9053		CD†
Motown Legends	Motown	9084		CD†
	Motown	5359		CS/CD†
Compact Command Performance, Volume 1 (15 Greatest Hits)	Motown	6069		CD†
Compact Command Performance, Volume 2	Motown	6201	'86	CD†
Motown Remembers Marvin Gaye (1963–1972)	Motown	6172	'86	LP/CS†
A Musical Testament, 1964–1984	Motown	(2) 6255	'88	LP/CS
	Motown	6255	'88	CD
The Marvin Gaye Collection	Motown	(4) 6311	'90	CS/CD
The Marvin Gaye Classics Collection	Motown	(4) 530320	'94	CS/CD
The Norman Whitfield Sessions	Motown	530355	'94	CS/CD
The Master, 1961–1984	Motown	(4) 0492	'95	CS/CD
Seek and Ye Shall Find: More of the Best	Rhino	71182	'93	CS/CD
Motown Legends	Esx	8515	'95	CS/CD
Adults Only	IMG	704		CS

Tribute Album

Inner City Blues: The Music of Marvin Gaye	Motown	0452	'95	CS/CD

Marvin Gaye and Mary Wells

Marvin and Mary Together	Motown	613	'64	†
	Motown	5260		CS/CD

Marvin Gaye and Kim Weston

It Takes Two	Tamla	270	'66	†

Marvin Gaye and Tammi Terrell

United	Tamla	277	'67	†
	Motown	9009		CD†
	Motown	5200		CS/CD
You're All I Need to Get By	Tamla	284	'68	†
	Motown	5142	'89	CS/CD
United/You're All I Need to Get By	Motown	8147		CD†
Easy	Tamla	294	'69	†
	Motown	5394	'90	CS/CD†
Greatest Hits	Tamla	302	'70	†
	Motown	9089		CD†
	Motown	5225		CS/CD
Motown Superstar Series, Volume 2	Motown	5102		CS†

Marvin Gaye and Diana Ross

Diana and Marvin	Motown	803	'73	†
	Motown	5124	'87	CS/CD

Nona Gaye

Love for the Future	Third Shore	92181	'92	CS/CD

THE J. GEILS BAND

Jerome "J." Geils (b. Feb. 20, 1946, New York, NY), lead gtr; **Peter Wolf** (b. Peter Blankfield, Mar. 7, 1946, Bronx, NY), lead voc; **Seth Justman** (b. Jan. 27, 1951, Washington, D.C.), kybd; **Magic Dick** (b. Richard Salwitz, May 13, 1945, New London, CT), har; **Danny Klein** (b. May 13, 1946, Worcester, MA), bs; **Stephen Bladd** (b. July 31, 1942, Boston, MA), drm

A hard-driving '70s rock and blues band from the Boston region, the J. Geils Band won a reputation as a performing band by touring almost constantly for more than a decade. Eventually breaking through as a recording band in the early '80s, the J. Geils Band retained their original lineup for 15 years, until the departure of lead vocalist and front man Peter Wolf in 1983.

Formed in 1967 by the merger of two Boston bands, the J. Geils Blues Band and the Hallucinations, the J. Geils Band was completed with the addition of Seth Justman shortly after the group signed with Atlantic Records in 1968. Featuring blues and R&B covers, the J. Geils Band's overlooked debut album includes the underground favorite "First I Look at the Purse" (a hit for the Contours in 1965), whereas their second album, *The Morning After*, yielded their first moderate hit with "Looking for a Love" (a hit for the Valentinos in 1962). As the band continually crisscrossed the United States in search of a wider audience, they recorded the live *Full House* set. After the moderate hit "Give It to Me" from the best-selling *Bloodshot* album, the J. Geils Band scored their first near-smash hit with "Must of Got Lost" in late 1974. After three more albums and several minor hits for Atlantic, the band switched to EMI-America.

The J. Geils Band's debut for their new label, *Sanctuary*, sold quite well, yielding the moderate hit "One Last Kiss." The group added layered synthesizer parts to their sound for *Love Stinks*, which produced two moderate hits with "Come Back" and the title tune. They finally broke through in late 1981 with the top album *Freeze Frame*, for which Seth Justman wrote or cowrote with Peter Wolf all the songs. The album contained three hits: the top "Centerfold," the smash title song, and the moderately successful "Angel in Blue." However, tensions between Wolf and Justman led, in October 1983, to Wolf leaving the group. The

J. Geils Band managed only minor hits through 1985, while Wolf scored major hits as a solo artist with "Lights Out" in 1984 and "Come as You Are" in 1987 on EMI-America. By 1990 he had switched to MCA Records for *Up to No Good!* In 1993 Wolf reunited with Magic Dick to form Bluestime to perform traditional blues and original numbers, releasing an album a year later on the specialty Rounder label.

The J. Geils Band

The J. Geils Band	Atlantic	8275	'71	CD
The Morning After	Atlantic	8297	'71	CD
Full House	Atlantic	7241	'72	CS/CD
Bloodshot	Atlantic	7260	'73	CS/CD
Ladies Invited	Atlantic	7286	'73	CD
Nightmares	Atlantic	18107	'74	CS/CD
Hot Line	Atlantic	18147	'75	CD
Blow Your Face Out	Atlantic	(2) 507	'76	†
	Rhino	71278	'93	CS/CD
Monkey Island	Atlantic	19103	'77	CS/CD
Best	Atlantic	19234	'79	CS/CD
Best, Volume 2	Atlantic	19284	'80	†
Sanctuary	EMI-America	17006	'78	†
	Capitol	16316	'86	†
Love Stinks	EMI-America	17016	'80	†
	Capitol	16375	'86	†
	EMI-America	92703	'86	CS/CD
Freeze Frame	EMI-America	17062	'81	†
	Capitol	16374	'86	†
	EMI-America	46014	'86	CS/CD
Showtime!	EMI-America	17087	'82	†
	Capitol	16373	'86	†
You're Gettin' Even While I'm Gettin' Odd	EMI-America	17137	'84	†
Flashback	Capitol	46551	'87	CD†
	EMI-America	46551	'87	CS/CD
Anthology: Houseparty	Rhino	71164	'93	CS/CD
Must of Got Lost	Rhino	71875	'95	CS/CD

Peter Wolf

Lights Out	EMI-America	17121	'84	†
	EMI-America	46046		CD†
Come as You Are	EMI-America	17230	'87	†
	EMI-America	46563	'87	CD†
Up to No Good	MCA	6349	'90	LP/CS/CD†

Bluestime

Bluestime	Rounder	3134	'94	†

BOB GELDOF

(b. Oct. 5, 1954, Dun Langhaire, Ireland)

Spearheading interest in young Irish rock and subsumed under the label *punk*, the Boomtown Rats won substantial success in Britain and Europe in the late '70s, but they were virtually ignored in the United States. The band's songwriter, lead vocalist, and performing focal point, Bob Geldof later endeavored to raise money for African famine relief, first with the Band Aid single "Do They Know It's Christmas?" (purportedly the best-selling single ever in England), and later with the massive Live Aid concert staged in London and Philadelphia. Geldof's efforts reawakened the music scene to social concerns and served as an inspiration for other musical benefits such as Farm Aid. Spending two years administering the distribution of the contributions, Bob Geldof launched a solo career in the late '80s that fared little better than that of the Boomtown Rats.

Bob Geldof formed the Nightlife Thugs in 1975 after a stint as music reporter and editor with the *Georgia Straight* in Vancouver, British Columbia. The group soon evolved into the Boomtown Rats, with Geldof, Gerry Cott, Garry Roberts, Johnnie Fingers, Pete Briquette, and Simon Crowe. Establishing themselves in Ireland, the Boomtown Rats moved to London in 1976 and signed with Ensign Records. Conducting their first full-scale tour of England in 1977, the band recorded their debut album in Germany. "Looking After No. 1" became the first of a series of major British hits that included "She's So Modern" and "Rat Trap," from their second album, and the controversial "I Don't Like Mondays," their first and only (minor) American hit. With Geldof as songwriter and lead vocalist, the group garnered a reputation in Britain and Europe for their brash and cynical songs and arrogant stage presence. However, the group's albums after *A Tonic for the Troops* were less well-received, and their American record company, Columbia, dropped the band in late 1985, leading to their dissolution in 1986.

After viewing a BBC television documentary on the famine in Ethiopia in 1984, Bob Geldof contacted Midge Ure of Ultravox and began booking an array of British rock stars to record a single to raise money to remedy the situation. Recruiting Sting, Boy George, Phil Collins, and members of U2, Ultravox, and Duran Duran, among others, the assemblage recorded "Do They Know It's Christmas?," written by Geldof and Ure, in November 1984. Released under the name Band Aid, the song became a major American hit and top British hit, selling more than seven million copies worldwide. The project inspired the ad-hoc group USA (United Support of Artists) for Africa in the United States, with superstars such as Bruce Springsteen, Bob Dylan, Paul Simon, Stevie Wonder, Michael Jackson, Prince, Lionel Richie, and Tina Turner recording the top hit "We Are the World," written by Jackson and Richie.

In 1985 Bob Geldof visited Africa and soon began organizing a huge simultaneous benefit concert linking London and Philadelphia. Staged on July 13, 1985, Live Aid was broadcast worldwide to an audience estimated to approach one billion viewers. Performers included Bob Dylan, Madonna, Crosby, Stills and Nash, Eric Clapton, Jimmy Page and Robert Plant, U2, the Who, Elvis Costello, and David Bowie. The concert ultimately raised more than $100 million for famine relief, a project overseen by Geldof for the next two years. He became an international celebrity, met with leaders of many nations, and was knighted by Queen Elizabeth II in 1986 and nominated for the Nobel Peace Prize in 1986 and 1987.

Never exploiting his fame for personal gain, Bob Geldof wrote his autobiography, *Is That All?*, published in 1986, and returned to music with his solo debut album, *Deep in the Heart of Nowhere*, and its minor American hit "This Is the World Calling." He recorded a follow-up album two years later and then lay low for a while, returning to tour America for the first time in 12 years in support of 1993's *The Happy Club*.

The Boomtown Rats

The Boomtown Rats	Mercury	1188	'77	†
A Tonic for the Troops	Columbia	37750	'79	CS/CD†
The Fine Art of Surfacing	Columbia	36248	'79	CS/CD†
Mondo Bongo	Columbia	37062	'81	†
	Columbia/Legacy	37062	'91	CD†
V Deep	Columbia	38915	'82	†

In the Long Grass	Columbia	39335	'84	†
Best (1977–1982)	Columbia	40615	'87	LP/CS/CD†
Bob Geldof				
Deep in the Heart of Nowhere	Atlantic	81687	'86	LP/CS/CD†
The Happy Club	Polydor	519132	'93	CS/CD

GENESIS

Peter Gabriel (b. Feb. 13, 1950, London, England), lead voc; **Tony Banks** (b. Mar. 27, 1951, East Heathly, Sussex, England), kybd, voc; **Steve Hackett** (b. Feb. 12, 1950, London, England), lead and 12-string gtrs; **Mike Rutherford** (b. Oct. 2, 1950, Guildford, England), bs, 12-string gtr, voc; **Anthony Phillips** (b. Dec. 1951, Putney, England), gtr; **Chris Stewart**, drm [Chris Stewart left almost immediately, to be replaced by **John Silver** in 1968, **John Mayhew** in 1969, and finally **Phil Collins** (b. Jan. 30, 1951, London, England) on drums and vocals in 1970; guitarist Steve Hackett replaced Anthony Phillips in the same year. Peter Gabriel left in June 1975; Hackett left in 1977.]

GENESIS

Seminal British progressive-rock group of the late '60s and '70s, Genesis favored a variety of keyboards and synthesizers in producing its sophisticated, richly textured music that set the style for other progressive-rock groups of the '70s, such as Emerson, Lake and Palmer and Yes. Formed as a songwriters' collective, the group emphasized the songs rather than virtuoso musicianship. Building their reputation on the flamboyance and theatrics of lead vocalist Peter Gabriel, Genesis attempted to break through in America as a headline group rather than a supporting act in 1972. By 1975 the group had established itself with their early tour de force *The Lamb Lies Down on Broadway*, an elaborate album combining a story line with surreal lyrics; some critics hailed it as the definitive concept album. The band employed progressively more ambitious stage presentations for subsequent tours.

With Peter Gabriel's departure in 1975, Genesis began moving in a mainstream direction, with drummer Phil Collins taking over the lead vocal chores. Leaving behind their progressive pretensions with the 1977 departure of guitarist Steve Hackett, Genesis became an enormously popular touring and recording act in the '80s, bolstered by the uncanny pop success of Phil Collins as a solo artist. Despite being criticized as boring, unimaginative, and repetitious, Genesis became one of the most popular and profitable rock groups in the world, and Collins likewise achieved huge success as a singles artist.

Meanwhile Gabriel has continued to produce provocative, personal music, achieving his greatest success with 1986's *So* and the hit song "Sledgehammer" and its innovative music video. Most recently he has become a champion of world music, founding the World Music Arts and Dance (WOMAD) festival.

Genesis was formed in January 1967 as a songwriters' collective by four students at England's Charterhouse School: Peter Gabriel, Tony Banks, Mike Rutherford, and Anthony Phillips. After sending a tape to producer-songwriter Jonathon King (1965's "Everyone's Gone to the Moon"), the group recorded their debut album, *In the Beginning* (rereleased as *From Genesis to Revelation*), for Mercury Records with King as producer. The group was released from its recording contract after a year and was joined by drummer John Mayhew in 1969. This lineup of Genesis recorded *Trespass* for the ABC subsidiary Impulse (released on Charisma in Great Britain). Phillips and Mayhew left the group in 1970, and Phil Collins was recruited to play drums and sing backup vocals. He had been a child actor, appearing as the Artful Dodger in the London production of *Oliver*, and had taken up drums at age 10. He had begun playing sessions at 14, and played with Flaming Youth in 1969. Several months later guitarist Steve Hackett joined Genesis.

For *Nursery Cryme*, on Charisma Records, Genesis featured extensive use of the mellotron (an early synthesizer). The album contained two Genesis favorites, "Musical Box" and "Return of the Giant Hogweed," and garnered rave reviews in Britain. The band then began experimenting with visuals and theatrics in performance that later became the group's early trademark. Peter Gabriel became the visual focus of Genesis, utilizing mime, costuming, and lengthy song introductions on stage. *Foxtrot* included Genesis favorites "Watcher of the Skies" and the 23-minute "Supper's Ready," which featured spectacular lighting and elaborate costuming by Gabriel in performance. In an effort to generate a following beyond its cult status in America, the group debuted in the United States as a headlining act in December 1972.

Genesis's first breakthrough into the American market came with 1973's *Selling England by the Pound*. Featuring songwriting developments on the themes of myth, legend, and fantasy, plus Banks's synthesizer work and several songs in odd time signatures, the album contained the group's first British hit, "I Know What I Like." With their reputation secure as a major British band by 1974, Genesis switched to Atlantic Records for the double-record concept album *The Lamb Lies Down on Broadway*. Written in its entirety by Peter Gabriel, the album traced the surreal contemporary adventures of its hero, Rael, in the harsh New York City environment. The subsequent British and American tours virtually duplicated the album in performance, with Gabriel portraying Rael through a series of odd costume changes.

In June 1975 Peter Gabriel, sensing a loss of creative momentum and weary from years of touring and recording, left Genesis. Inasmuch as Gabriel had been (incorrectly) assumed to be the band's musical leader and chief songwriter, critics began predicting its demise. Phil Collins took over on lead vocals for subsequent recordings. *A Trick of the Tail* proved surprisingly successful, as did *Wind and Wuthering*, which yielded their first (minor) American hit, "Your Own Special Way." In order to free Collins from his drumming duties, Genesis recruited former King Crimson and Yes drummer Bill Bruford for their 1976 tours. For their 1977 worldwide tour they used all new sound and lighting equipment, enlisting American drummer Chester Thompson. The 1976 and 1977 tours were documented on *Seconds Out*.

Phil Collins began working outside Genesis in 1976, recording six albums with the jazz fusion group Brand X through 1980. Former member Anthony Phillips launched a solo career in 1976, and in 1977 Steve Hackett dropped out of Genesis to pursue a solo career. He recorded six albums through 1983 and formed GTR with vocalist Max Bacon and former Asia and Yes guitarist Steve Howe in 1986.

Reduced to a trio after Hackett's departure, Genesis recorded the appropriately titled *And Then There Were Three*, with Rutherford playing all guitar and bass parts. Revealing a mainstream pop sound, the album yielded a major hit single with "Follow You, Follow Me." Genesis next recorded *Duke* and the best-selling *Abacab*, which produced major hits with "Misunderstanding" and "Abacab," respectively. Augmented by drummer Chester Thompson and new American guitarist Darryl Stuermer for tours, Genesis next released the double-record set *Three Sides Live*. All three members of the core band (Collins-Rutherford-Banks) have maintained their commitment to the group while pursuing various solo and other band projects from this period forward.

Phil Collins began recording as a solo artist in 1981, soon hitting with "I Missed Again" and "In the Air Tonight." He scored a near-smash in 1982–1983 with a remake of the Supremes's "You Can't Hurry Love." His success seemed to bolster the career of Genesis, and 1983's *Genesis* yielded four hits, including the smash "That's All." Genesis toured in 1984, and thereafter Collins and Genesis alternated producing smash hits. Through 1986 Collins had three smash hits with "Easy Lover" (in duet with Philip Bailey), "Don't Lose My Number," and "Take Me Home," and top hits with "Against All Odds" (from the movie of the same name), "One More Night," "Sussudio," and "Separate Lives" (in duet with Marilyn Martin from the movie *White Nights*). Genesis scored five smash hits in 1986–1987 with "Invisible Touch" (a top hit), "Throwing It All Away," "Land of Confusion," "Tonight, Tonight, Tonight," and "In Too Deep" from *Invisible Night*. Collins starred in the 1988 movie *Buster*, which yielded top hits for Collins with a remake of the Mindbenders' "Groovy Kind of Love" and "Two Hearts."

During the '90s Genesis scored major hits with "No Son of Mine," "I Can't Dance," "Hold On My Heart," "Jesus Knows Me," and "Never a Time" from *We Can't Dance*. The American stadium tour in support of the album yielded the two-part live set *The Way We Walk* (the first volume, "The Shorts," celebrated their recent hits, while the second, "The Longs," featured re-creations of their more ambitious '70s progressive tunes). Phil Collins recorded the socially conscious album *. . . But Seriously*, which yielded pop and easy-listening hits with the top "Another Day in Paradise," the smashes "I Wish It Would Rain Down," "Do You Remember?," and "Something Happened on the Way to Heaven," and the major "Hang In Long Enough." He scored a major hits in 1993–1994 with "Both Sides of the Story" and "Everyday."

Peter Gabriel returned to recording with three solo albums—released in 1977, 1978, and 1980—all, oddly, with the same name, *Peter Gabriel*. Exploring electronic instrumentation and Third World music on these albums, Gabriel was at the forefront of rock's avantgarde with his imaginative, complex arrangements and performance artist persona in concert. He scored his first minor American hit in 1977 with "Solsbury Hill," and the third *Peter Gabriel* album included the moderate hit "Games Without Frontiers," with backing vocals by Kate Bush, and "Biko," his tribute to South African activist Steve Biko, who died in prison in 1977.

In 1982 Peter Gabriel founded the World Music Arts and Dance organization in England, to promote contemporary non-Western music, or "world music." Over the years, the organization has presented more than 60 festivals in 12 countries, featuring acts from Jamaica, Africa, India, and Russia. That year the brooding, dense *Security* produced Gabriel's first major hit, "Shock the Monkey." He toured in 1983 and recorded five instrumental versions of previously released songs for the soundtrack to the movie *Birdy*. He finally made his commercial breakthrough in 1986 with the accessible *So* album, which yielded four hits: the top hit "Sledgehammer," the major hit "In Your Eyes," the near-smash hit "Big Time," and the minor hit "Don't Give Up," recorded with Kate Bush.

In 1986 Gabriel performed on the Amnesty International tour, and he later conducted his own international tour of arenas, introducing Senegal's most popular musician, Youssou N'Dour, to a new audience. He subsequently formed Real World Records for releases by Third World artists, and scored and recorded the music for the controversial 1989 Martin

Scorsese movie *The Last Temptation of Christ* using musicians from Africa, India, Pakistan, and the Middle East. Gabriel managed moderate hits in 1992–1993 with "Digging in the Dirt" and "Steam," and introduced his impressive CD-ROM *Peter Gabriel's Secret World* in late 1993.

In 1985 Mike Rutherford formed Mike and the Mechanics with vocalists Paul Young (b. June 17, 1947, Manchester, England) and Paul Carrack (b. Apr. 22, 1951, Sheffield, England), keyboardist Adrian Lee (b. Sept. 9, 1947, London, England), and drummer Peter Van Hooke (b. June 4, 1950, London, England). Young had been lead vocalist with Sad Cafe, and Carrack had sung on Ace's smash 1975 hit "How Long" and Squeeze's moderate 1981 hit "Tempted." Mike and the Mechanics scored smash hits with "Silent Running (On Dangerous Ground)" and "All I Need Is a Miracle," and they toured the United States in 1986. They toured again in 1989, in support of *Living Years* and its top-hit title song.

Genesis

In the Beginning	Mercury	61175	'68	†
	London	50006	'77	†
	London	820322		†
(reissued as) From Genesis to Revelation	London	643	'74	†
	DCC	051		CS/CD
And Then There Was	London	820496	'87	CD†
Trespass	Impulse	9205	'70	†
	ABC/MCA	816		†
	MCA	1653	'93	CS/CD
Nursery Cryme	Charisma	1052	'71	†
	Atlantic	80030		CS/CD†
	Atlantic	82673	'94	CS/CD
Foxtrot	Charisma	1058	'72	†
	Atlantic	81848	'88	LP/CS/CD†
	Atlantic	82674	'94	CS/CD
Best (reissue of above two)	Buddah	(2) 5659	'76	†
Nursery Cryme/Foxtrot	Charisma	(2) 2701	'79	†
Selling England by the Pound	Charisma	6060	'73	†
	Atlantic	19277		LP/CS/CD†
	Atlantic	82675	'94	CS/CD
Genesis Live	Charisma	1666	'74	†
	Atlantic	81855	'88	LP/CS/CD†
	Atlantic	82676	'94	CS/CD
The Lamb Lies Down on Broadway	Atlantic	(2) 401	'74	LP/CS/CD†
	Atlantic	(2) 82677	'94	CS/CD
A Trick of the Tail	Atco	36-129	'76	†
	Atco	38101		CS/CD†
	Atco	82688	'94	CS/CD
Wind and Wuthering	Atco	36-144	'77	†
	Atco	38100		LP/CS/CD†
	Atco	82690	'94	CS/CD
Seconds Out	Atlantic	(2) 9002	'77	CS/CD†
	Atco	(2) 82689	'94	CS/CD
. . . And Then There Were Three	Atlantic	19173	'78	LP/CS/CD†
	Atco	82691	'94	CS/CD
Duke	Atlantic	16014	'80	CS/CD†
	Atco	82692	'94	CS/CD

Abacab	Atlantic	19313	'81	CS/CD†
	Atlantic	82521	'94	CD
	Atco	82693	'94	CS/CD
Three Sides Live	Atlantic	(2) 2000	'82	CS/CD†
	Atco	(2) 82694	'94	CS/CD
Genesis	Atlantic	80116	'83	CS/CD
Invisible Touch	Atlantic	81641	'86	CS/CD
We Can't Dance	Atlantic	82344	'91	CS/CD
Live/The Way We Walk—Volume One: The Shorts	Atlantic	82452	'92	CS/CD
The Way We Walk—Volume Two: The Longs	Atlantic	82461	'93	CS/CD

The London Symphony Orchestra

We Know What We Like: The Music of Genesis	RCA	6242	'87	LP/CS/CD†
	RCA	56242	'93	CS/CD

Steve Hackett

Voyage of the Acolyte	Chrysalis	1112	'76	†
	Chrysalis	4112	'83	†
	Blue Plate	1863	'91	CD
Please Don't Touch	Chrysalis	1176	'78	†
	Chrysalis	41176	'83	†
	Blue Plate	1861	'91	CD
Spectral Mornings	Chrysalis	1223	'79	†
	Blue Plate	1862	'91	CD
Defector	Charisma	3103	'80	†
	Blue Plate	1859	'91	CD
Cured	Epic	37362	'81	†
	Blue Plate	1858		CD
Highly Strung	Epic	38515	'83	†
	Blue Plate	1860		CD
Time Lapse	Blue Plate	1839	'92	CS/CD
Momentum	Herald	009	'94	CD
Till We Have Faces	Herald	010	'94	CD
Bay of Kings	Herald	011	'94	CD
Blues with a Feeling	Herald	13	'95	CD

GTR (with Steve Hackett)

GTR	Arista	8400	'86	†

Brand X (with Phil Collins)

Unorthodox Behaviour	Passport	9819	'76		
	Blue Plate	1387		CD
Moroccan Roll	Passport	9822	'77	†
	Blue Plate	1392		CD
Livestock	Passport	9824	'77	†
	Blue Plate	1388		CD
Masques	Passport	9829	'78	†
	Blue Plate	1391		CD
Product	Passport	9840	'79	†
	Blue Plate	1390		CD
Do They Hurt?	Passport	9845	'80	†
	Blue Plate	1389		CD

Anthony Phillips

The Geese and the Ghost	Passport	98020	'77	†
Wise After the Event	Passport	9828	'78	†
Sides	Passport	9834	'80	†
Private Parts and Pieces, Part III—Antiques	Blue Plate	1827	'92	CD
1984	Blue Plate	1840	'92	CD
Slow Dance	Caroline	1709	'91	CD
Private Parts and Pieces, Volume 8	Venture/Caroline	1883	'93	CD

Peter Gabriel

Peter Gabriel	Atco	36147	'77	CS/CD
Peter Gabriel	Atlantic	19181	'78	CS/CD
Revisited	Atlantic	82429	'92	CS/CD
Peter Gabriel	Mercury	3848	'80	†
Security	Geffen	2011	'82/'84	CS/CD
Peter Gabriel	Geffen	2035	'83	CS/CD
Plays Live	Geffen	4012	'83	CS/CD
Birdy (soundtrack)	Geffen	24070	'85	CS/CD
So	Geffen	24088	'86	CS/CD
Passion: Music from the Last Temptation of Christ	Geffen	24206	'89	CS/CD
Shaking the Tree: 16 Golden Greats	Geffen	24326	'90	CS/CD
Us	Geffen	24473	'92	CS/CD
Secret World Live	Geffen	(2) 24722	'94	CS/CD
Xplora	Interplay	CXPLORM	'93	CD-ROM

Tony Banks

A Curious Feeling	Charisma	2207	'79	†
	Blue Plate	1823	'92	CD
The Fugitive	Atlantic	80071	'83	†
The Wicked Lady (soundtrack)	Atlantic	80073	'84	†
Soundtracks	Atlantic	81680	'86	CS/CD
Still	Giant	24441	'92	CS/CD

Phil Collins

Face Value	Atlantic	16029	'81/'84	CS/CD
	Atlantic	82520	'94	CD
Hello, I Must Be Going!	Atlantic	80035	'82/'84	CS/CD
No Jacket Required	Atlantic	81240	'85	CS/CD
12"ers	Atlantic	81847	'88	CD
. . . But Seriously	Atlantic	82050	'89	LP/CS/CD
Serious Hits . . . Live!	Atlantic	82157	'90	LP/CS/CD
Both Sides	Atlantic	82550	'93	CS/CD

Mike Rutherford

Smallcreep's Day	Passport	9843	'80	†
Acting Very Strange	Atlantic	80015	'82/'91	CD

Mike and the Mechanics

Mike + The Mechanics	Atlantic	81287	'85	CS/CD
Living Years	Atlantic	81923	'88	CS/CD
Word of Mouth	Atlantic	82233	'91	CS/CD
Beggar on a Beach of Gold	Atlantic	82738	'95	CS/CD

STEVE GOODMAN

(b. July 25, 1948, Chicago, IL; d. Sept. 20, 1984, Seattle, WA)

Much like cohort John Prine, Steve Goodman emerged from the Chicago folk scene in the early '70s and wrote engaging songs alternately poignant and humorous. Best known as the author of the railroad classic "City of New Orleans," popularized by Arlo Guthrie in 1972, Goodman also composed the country smash "You Never Even Call Me by My Name" and the talking-blues, baseball classic "A Dying Cub Fan's Last Request." An energetic and enthusiastic performer, projecting an impish sense of humor on stage, Goodman developed one of the most appreciative and loyal underground followings in popular music. He died of leukemia in 1984 at age 36.

Steve Goodman took up guitar at age 13 and performed at folk festivals during the late '60s. Ostensibly "discovered" with John Prine simultaneously by Kris Kristofferson and Paul Anka, Goodman soon signed with Buddah Records. His two albums for the label failed to sell significantly, yet they contained excellent compositions such as "City of New Orleans," "You Never Even Call Me by My Name," "Would You Like to Learn to Dance," and "Somebody Else's Troubles." In 1972 Arlo Guthrie's recording of "City of New Orleans" became a major pop hit (revived as a top country hit by Willie Nelson in 1984), and David Allan Coe's recording of "You Never Even Call Me by My Name" became a smash country hit in 1975.

Switching to Asylum Records in 1975, Steve Goodman recorded five albums for the label through 1980. Joan Baez, Johnny Cash, and Nicolette Larson recorded his songs. Goodman cowrote "Door Number Three" with Jimmy Buffett, who recorded Goodman's "Banana Republics" for his best-selling *Changes in Latitudes* album. During the '80s Goodman recorded for his own Red Pajamas label, finally issuing the unforgettable baseball song "A Dying Cub Fan's Last Request" on *Affordable Art*. Diagnosed with leukemia in 1969, Steve Goodman died in Seattle on September 20, 1984, from complications arising from a bone marrow transplant operation to treat the disease.

Steve Goodman

Steve Goodman	Buddah	5096	'72	†
	One Way	28559		CD
Somebody Else's Trouble	Buddah	5121	'72	†
	One Way	28560		CD
The Essential Steve Goodman	Buddah	(2) 5665	'76	†
The Original Steve Goodman	Special Music	4923		CS/CD
Jessie's Jig and Other Favorites	Asylum	1037	'75	†
Words We Can Dance To	Asylum	1061	'76	†
Say It in Private	Asylum	1118	'77	†
High and Outside	Asylum	174	'79	†
Hot Spot	Asylum	297	'80	†
Best of the Asylum Years, Volume 1	Red Pajamas	006	'89	CS/CD
Best of the Asylum Years, Volume 2	Red Pajamas	007		CS/CD
Artistic Hair	Red Pajamas	001	'83	CS/CD
Affordable Art	Red Pajamas	002	'84	CS/CD
Santa Ana Winds	Red Pajamas	003	'84	CS/CD
Unfinished Business	Red Pajamas	005		CS/CD
Memorial Collection	Red Pajamas	(5) 008		CS
	Red Pajamas	(6) 008		CD
City of New Orleans	Pair	1233		CD

Tribute Album

Tribute to Steve Goodman	Red Pajamas	(2) 004	'85	CS/CD

BERRY GORDY JR.

(b. Nov. 28, 1929, Detroit, MI)

Founder and owner of the Motown family of record labels, Berry Gordy Jr. established Motown Records as one of the most important independent record labels in the early '60s. Assembling an industrious staff of songwriters and producers, and building one of the most impressive rosters of artists in the history of pop music, Motown Records became the largest and most successful independent record company in the United States by 1964. Aided immeasurably by William "Smokey" Robinson and the Brian Holland–Lamont Dozier–Eddie Holland songwriting-production team, Motown created a sophisticated commercial blend of gospel and pop musics that was recognized as distinct from raunchier R&B. The new sound proved enormously popular with both black and white audiences, rivaled the Beatles in the extent of its appeal, and encouraged the ascendancy of black vocal groups throughout the '60s. Indeed, the company's success was so widespread that it became the largest black-owned company in America.

Berry Gordy Jr. dropped out of high school to become a featherweight boxer. Upon his discharge from the army in 1953, he set up a record store that soon went bankrupt. Subsequently working on a Ford Motor Company assembly line, Gordy began writing songs during the mid-'50s. His first song sale, to Decca, was "Reet Petite," Jackie Wilson's first, albeit minor, pop hit in 1957. His earliest major songwriting success came with "Lonely Teardrops," a top R&B and smash pop hit in 1958 for Wilson. Gordy began producing records for Eddie Holland and Marv Johnson, who scored a smash R&B and pop hit with Gordy's "You Got What It Takes" in 1959.

Encouraged by songwriter-friend William "Smokey" Robinson, Berry Gordy Jr. borrowed money from his family to found Tammie Records, soon changed to Tamla Records. The label's first significant success occurred as distributor of Barrett Strong's "Money," released on his sister's Anna label. Later in 1960, "Shop Around," cowritten by Gordy and Robinson, became Tamla's first smash hit for Robinson's Miracles, establishing the label as an important independent. Eddie Holland's brother Brian subsequently collaborated on early hits by the Marvelettes, and Robinson worked with Mary Wells for a series of hits in 1962 on the newly formed Motown label. Before year's end the Contours hit with the raucous "Do You Love Me," written by Gordy, on yet another label, Gordy.

As the Motown family of labels developed local Detroit talent, Brian and Eddie Holland teamed with songwriter Lamont Dozier in 1963 to create a distinctive pop sound that appealed to white as well as to black audiences. Initially working with the rather raw-sounding Martha and the Vandellas, Holland-Dozier-Holland (H-D-H) achieved massive songwriting and production success with the Supremes from 1964 to 1967. The team also wrote and produced major hits for Marvin Gaye, the Four Tops, and Martha and the Vandellas. In the meantime, Smokey Robinson was writing hits for Mary Wells, the Temptations, Marvin Gaye, and his own Miracles. Gordy concentrated his attentions on Diana Ross, whom he elevated to leader of the Supremes, seeking to establish her as a major pop star by personally supervising every stage of her career.

Recognized by 1964 as the largest independent record company through its success in the singles market, Motown diversified into an entertainment complex. The previously established Jobete Music Company handled song publishing and copyrighting, whereas Hitsville, U.S.A., controlled the company's recording studios, and International Talent Management trained artists in matters of deportment. Gordy's unprecedented concern with career management, coupled with the rigorous discipline imposed on artists, alienated some of his acts and led to the company's first defection in 1964 by Mary Wells. Nonetheless, Motown became respectable, as acts originally aimed at teen audiences were groomed for the adult pop market. Thus acts were introduced into the American supper-club and prime-time television fields while the company was establishing itself internationally. A high degree of sameness in the sound of Motown acts was recognizable after 1966, leading to challenges by Atlantic and Stax/Volt artists in the pop and R&B/soul fields. During 1967, to create a higher degree of visibility for several of its singers, Motown renamed three of its acts: the Supremes became Diana Ross and the Supremes; the Miracles, Smokey Robinson and the Miracles; and Martha and the Vandellas, Martha Reeves and the Vandellas. The label also experimented with "psychedelic soul" for the Temptations under producer-songwriter Norman Whitfield.

Enduring the departure of the Holland-Dozier-Holland team in 1968, Berry Gordy Jr. concentrated on the career of Diana Ross as a solo act beginning in 1970. Maintaining the company's success with the astounding popularity of the teen-oriented Jackson Five, Gordy moved the operation to Hollywood in 1971 and established Motown Industries, expanding his activities to a Broadway musical and films. Bolstered by the success of Marvin Gaye and Stevie Wonder as album-oriented singer-songwriters (on their albums *What's Going On* and *Music of My Mind*, respectively), Motown was nonetheless challenged in the pop and soul fields by Kenny Gamble and Leon Huff's Philadelphia International label by 1973, particularly by the O'Jays.

During the first half of the '70s, Diana Ross was established as Motown's first all-around entertainer through her work in supper clubs and films, particularly with 1972's *Lady Sings the Blues*, as well as through recordings. Other films, including *Mahogany* and *The Wiz*, proved flops between 1975 and 1978. Moreover, Motown suffered a series of defections in the '70s. Martha Reeves began recording solo for other labels in 1974, and the Four Tops switched to ABC/Dunhill. Gladys Knight and the Pips recorded for Buddah beginning in 1974, and in 1975 the Jackson Five moved to Epic, as did Michael Jackson in 1978. The Miracles (without Smokey Robinson) switched to Columbia in 1977 and the Temptations went to Atlantic. Nonetheless, Motown maintained its position as an important independent label with the recordings of Diana Ross, Marvin Gaye, Stevie Wonder, and the Commodores.

During the '80s Motown struggled to retain its prominence in popular music. Diana Ross moved to RCA in 1981, and Marvin Gaye signed with Columbia in 1982. The Temptations returned in 1980 and the Four Tops were back during the mid-'80s, later switching to Arista. The Gordy label introduced the popular DeBarge family in 1983. The company staged a successful 25th Anniversary celebration in 1983, later broadcast on ABC-TV, and Motown Productions produced "Lonesome Dove," one of the highest-rated miniseries of the decade, for CBS-TV in 1989. However, many former employees, including Eddie Holland and members of the Vandellas and Marvelettes, sued Motown, alleging failure to pay royalties.

In June 1988 Berry Gordy Jr. sold Motown Records to MCA and Boston Ventures for $61 million. That same year Gordy became one of the few nonperforming members of the Rock and Roll Hall of Fame. Boston Ventures later bought out MCA's interest and sold Motown Records to the Dutch-based Polygram conglomerate for $325 million in August 1993. In late 1994 Warner Books published Gordy's self-serving biography, *To Be Loved*.

BILL GRAHAM

(b. Wolfgang Grajonca, Jan. 8, 1931, Berlin, Germany; d. Oct. 25, 1991, near Vallejo, CA)

Rock music's most famous and influential concert producer from the mid-'60s through the '80s, Bill Graham established rock's first and most famous hall, San Francisco's Fillmore Auditorium, in 1966. In terms of its historical importance to a specific type of popular music, the Fillmore can be compared only to New York's Apollo Theater (R&B) and Nashville's

Ryman Auditorium (the longtime home of country's Grand Ole Opry). With the openings of Fillmore West in San Francisco and Fillmore East in New York City in 1968, Bill Graham advanced the ballroom rock-concert scene that flourished until the early '70s. Thereafter he was at the forefront of concert producers promoting concerts at large arenas, outdoor stadiums, and parks. Effectively establishing the standards for rock concert production and promotion, whether in small halls, ballrooms, or outdoor arenas, Bill Graham was also actively involved in staging benefit concerts for a wide variety of causes throughout his career. He supervised massive tours for the likes of Bob Dylan, the Rolling Stones, and the Who, staged the first major rock concert in the Soviet Union, in 1987, and produced and acted in films. Bill Graham was killed after a northern California concert on October 25, 1991, when his helicopter slammed into a utility tower.

Wolfgang Grajonca escaped the Nazi persecution of Jews as a child, fleeing first to France, then, in 1941, to the United States, where he was raised in the Bronx by a foster family. He formally changed his name to Bill Graham in 1949, when granted U.S. citizenship. He later served in the U.S. Army in the Korean War and graduated from New York's City College with a degree in business administration before moving to California. By 1960 he was an executive with the Allis-Chalmers farm equipment company in San Francisco. In 1965 he quit his position to take over management of the radical street-theater improvisational group the Mime Troupe.

On November 6, 1965, Bill Graham staged a benefit concert for the Mime Troupe at San Francisco's Longshoremen's Hall with various Bay Area musicians. On December 10 he promoted another benefit concert at the 1,100-seat Fillmore Auditorium in one of San Francisco's black ghettos with the Jefferson Airplane, the Great Society (with Grace Slick), and the Warlocks (later the Grateful Dead). The financial and artistic success of the benefits, along with his subsequent production of the now-legendary Trips Festival at the Longshoremen's Hall in January 1966, led Graham to the regular presentation of rock shows at the Fillmore Auditorium. Booking three different acts for weekend shows at the Fillmore into 1968, Bill Graham displayed an eclecticism that exposed rock fans to jazz, gospel, blues, and even comedy. Along with competitor Chet Helms, who operated the Avalon Ballroom, Graham helped introduce and popularize both light shows and psychedelic poster art during his tenure at the Fillmore. In booking virtually every major rock act except the Beatles, Graham helped launch the careers of hundreds of rock bands in the '60s while fostering the growth and development of San Francisco bands such as the Jefferson Airplane, the Grateful Dead, and Santana. By year's end he was also presenting concerts at the 5,400-seat Winterland Arena and managing, if briefly, the Jefferson Airplane. The concerts became astoundingly successful and featured both little-known local talent and big-name outside acts.

Bill Graham presented his last show at the Fillmore Auditorium in July 1968. He opened Fillmore East in New York City in March 1968 and assumed management of the Carousel Ballroom on San Francisco's Market Street in August. The old dance hall, which he renamed Fillmore West, had been run by the Jefferson Airplane and Grateful Dead since early in the year. Over the next three years Graham presented virtually every major rock act at the Fillmores while giving little-known acts a chance to perform and booking a number of nonrock acts such as Miles Davis, Lenny Bruce, and the Staple Singers.

Graham's success with the Fillmores encouraged the establishment of similar venues across the country and marked the heyday of concert rock. He opened a talent-booking agency in October 1968, and formed Fillmore and San Francisco Records in February 1969, recording Cold Blood and Elvin Bishop before dissolving the labels at the beginning of 1972. The Woodstock Festival of August 1969 presaged the demise of the ballroom concert scene, as audiences became larger and expenses increased. As ballrooms across the country folded in 1970 and 1971, Graham announced his intention to close the Fillmores.

By July 1971 both Fillmore East and Fillmore West had been closed. Graham "retired" for a time, but was back in 1972, producing the Rolling Stones' tour. He booked acts into the Winterland Arena and produced the massive Watkins Glen Pop Festival in upstate New York in 1973, the largest gathering of its kind. In 1974 he staged the Band's celebrated Last Waltz, and produced George Harrison's tour, Bob Dylan's comeback tour, and the reunion of Crosby, Stills, Nash and Young. By 1978 the Winterland venue had also become obsolete, giving way to impersonal and lucrative festivals and stadium concerts. On New Year's Eve 1978–1979 the New Riders of the Purple Sage, the Blues Brothers, and the Grateful Dead played the final performance at Winterland, a hall once castigated as overly large and acoustically unsound, but now sorely missed.

Bill Graham became the master of arena-concert production, supervising the Rolling Stones' 1981 world tour and presenting the US Festival near San Bernardino in 1982. He reopened San Francisco's most successful nightclub, the Old Waldorf, as Wolfgang's in 1983. Withdrawing from the day-to-day operation of his organization, Graham appeared in small roles in the films *Apocalypse Now*, *The Cotton Club*, and *Gardens of Stone* during the '80s. His organization financed outdoor amphitheaters in Sacramento (Cal Expo) and Palo Alto (Shoreline), which opened in 1983 and 1987, respectively. In 1985 he presided over the daylong Live Aid benefit in Philadelphia, and later personally supervised the Amnesty International tours of 1986 and 1988. In 1987 Graham presented the first rock concert in Russia, at Moscow's Izmajlovo Stadium, with Santana, the Doobie Brothers, James Taylor, and Bonnie Raitt. Personal setbacks included fires which destroyed his warehouse offices in 1985 and Wolfgang's in 1987.

In March 1988 the nightclub wing of the Bill Graham organization began presenting shows at the refurbished Fillmore Auditorium once again, but the hall was closed after October 1989's Loma Prieta earthquake. Graham presented three simultaneous benefit concerts for victims of the quake. He also made the final legal arrangements for and produced the Oliver Stone movie *The Doors*, and he performed the role of Lucky Luciano in the movie *Bugsy*, starring Warren Beatty. In 1990 he helped produce the Gathering of the Tribes concert, which inspired 1991's important Lollapalooza tour. However, on October 25, 1991, Graham, companion Melissa Gold, and longtime pilot Steve Kahn were killed in a fiery helicopter crash near Vallejo, California.

In fitting tribute to the life and memory of Bill Graham, the Fillmore Auditorium reopened on April 27, 1994, after more than $1 million in renovations. Mixing widely varying types of music, as Graham had in the early days of the Fillmore, the announced acts were American Music Club, Ry Cooder and David Lindley, and Smashing Pumpkins, with impromptu performances by Linda Perry and Joe Satriani.

Anthologies

Live at Bill Graham's Fillmore West	Columbia	9893	'69	†
Fillmore: The Last Days	Fillmore	(3) 31390	'72	†
	Epic/Legacy	(2) 31390	'91	CD

GRAND FUNK RAILROAD

Mark Farner (b. Sept. 29, 1948, Flint, MI), kybd, gtr, voc, har; **Mel Schacher** (b. Apr. 3, 1951, Owosso, MI), bs, voc; **Don Brewer** (b. Sept. 3, 1948, Flint, MI), drm, voc [Keyboardist **Craig Frost** (b. Apr. 20, 1948, Flint, MI) was added in 1973.]

Blisteringly loud American hard-rock band of the '70s, the power trio Grand Funk Railroad recorded a series of best-selling albums and hit singles, including the top hits "We're an American Band" and "The Loco-Motion" and the smash hits "Some Kind of Wonderful" and

"Bad Time." The original group evolved out of the group Terry Knight and the Pack, who scored a hit with "I (Who Have Nothing)" in 1966. Terry Knight became manager, molding their image and sound until 1972, when the group, which included Mark Farner and Don Brewer, sought to end their relationship. A series of suits and countersuits resulted, ending in a cash settlement to pay Knight off. Grand Funk Railroad managed their success despite minimal radio airplay and a scathingly hostile critical reception. Grand Funk Railroad has the dubious distinction of being one of the first rock bands to attain massive popularity through promotion and constant touring rather than talent. In 1970 they broke the Beatles' record by selling out two shows at New York's Shea Stadium in 72 hours. Disbanding in 1976, the band regrouped briefly in 1981. During the '80s Craig Frost and Don Brewer manned Bob Seger's Silver Bullet Band. Mark Farner was "born again" in the '80s, and his song "Isn't It Amazing" was a gospel hit in 1988.

Terry Knight and the Pack

Terry Knight and the Pack	Lucky Eleven	8000	'66	†
The Best of Mark Farner, Terry Knight and Donnie Brewer	Lucky Eleven	8001		†
Reflections	Cameo	2007		†
Mark, Don and Terry—1966–1967	Abkco	4217	'72	†

Grand Funk Railroad

On Time	Capitol	307	'69	†
	Capitol	16178		†
Grand Funk	Capitol	406	'70	†
	Capitol	16177		†
Closer to Home	Capitol	471	'70	†
	Capitol	16176		†
	Capitol	48429	'95	CD
Live Album	Capitol	633	'70	†
	Capitol	91899	'95	CD
Survival	Capitol	764	'71	†
	Capitol	94202	'95	CD
E Pluribus Funk	Capitol	853	'71	†
	Capitol	31928	'95	CD
Mark, Don and Mel, 1969–1971	Capitol	11042	'72	LP/CS
Phoenix	Capitol	11099	'72	†
We're an American Band	Capitol	11207	'73	†
	Capitol	31929	'95	CD
Shinin' On	Capitol	11278	'74	†
All the Girls in the World Beware!!!	Capitol	11356	'74	†
Caught in the Act	Capitol	(2) 11445	'75	†
	Capitol	48430		CD†
	Capitol	48430	'95	CS/CD
Born to Die	Capitol	11482	'76	†
Grand Funk Hits	Capitol	11579	'76	†
	Capitol	12010	'79	†
	Capitol	16138		†
	Capitol	46623		CD†
Grand Funk Railroad	Capitol	90608	'91	CS/CD
Good Singin', Good Playin'	MCA	2216	'76	†
Grand Funk Railroad Lives	Full Moon	3625	'81	†
What's Funk	Full Moon	23750	'83	†
More of the Best	Rhino	70530	'91	CS/CD

Great! Grand Funk Railroad	Pair	1178		CD
Mark Farner				
Mark Farner	Atlantic	18232	'77	†
No Frills	Atlantic	19196	'78	†

THE GRATEFUL DEAD

Jerome "Jerry" Garcia (b. Aug. 1, 1942, San Francisco, CA; d. Aug. 9, 1995, Forest Knolls, CA), lead gtr, voc; **Bob Weir** (b. Oct. 16, 1947, San Francisco, CA), rhythm gtr, voc; **Ron "Pig Pen" McKernan** (b. Sept. 8, 1945, San Bruno, CA; d. Mar. 8, 1973), har; **Phil Lesh** (b. Mar. 15, 1940, Berkeley, CA), b; **Bill Kreutzmann** (b. June 7, 1946, Palo Alto, CA), drm [The band's full-time lyricist beginning in 1969 was **Robert Hunter**. Drummer **Mickey Hart** (b. ca. 1950, Long Island, NY), joined in 1967, after their first album. Other members included keyboardists **Tom Constanten**, **Keith Godchaux** (b. July 9, 1948, San Francisco, CA; d. July 23, 1980, Ross, CA), **Brent Mydland** (b. ca. 1953, d. July 26, 1990), and **Vince Welnick**, and vocalist **Donna Godchaux** (b. Aug. 22, 1947, San Francisco, CA).]

THE GRATEFUL DEAD

One of America's best-loved bands since its inception during the heyday of psychedelia in San Francisco, the Grateful Dead was challenged in terms of longevity by only the Rolling Stones. As a band, the Grateful Dead staunchly maintained an anticommercial, anti-show-business stance that nonetheless produced several durable and popular albums and even a near-smash hit single, 1987's "Touch of Grey," from their best-selling album *In the Dark*. Essentially a live band that performed marathon shows of up to five hours, often starting sluggishly and ending spectacularly, the Grateful Dead introduced more free-form music into the body of rock than any other group, based on the often extraordinary lead-guitar playing of Jerry Garcia and the virtuoso bass playing of Phil Lesh.

Building an underground reputation by playing regularly and often for free, the Grateful Dead favored live performance as most other area bands signed recording contracts. A true people's band, actually living in the Haight-Ashbury district during the hippie era, the Grateful Dead approached rock music on their own terms, dividing funds communally and supporting a massive "family" entourage while eschewing the trappings of the rock stars they nonetheless became. Over the years their live performances and iconoclastic attitude won them the most staunchly devoted and fiercely loyal following in all of rock music, perhaps in all of music in any style. These fanatics—known as Deadheads—revered the group as fountainheads and mainstays of the hippie values of humanity, brotherhood, unity, and even spirituality.

Jerry Garcia grew up in San Francisco and Menlo Park, obtaining his first guitar, an electric model, at age 15. Dropping out of high school, he served a brief stint in the Army before returning to the Palo Alto area and forming a duo with Robert Hunter to play local coffeehouses. Garcia took up banjo in 1960 and formed the Wildwood Boys with Hunter and David Nelson (later of the New Riders of the Purple Sage). Garcia, Hunter, and Nelson were later members of the Hart Valley Drifters, who won an amateur bluegrass contest at the Monterey Folk Festival in 1963. Garcia next helped form Mother McCree's Uptown Jug Champions, a jug band, with harmonica player Ron "Pig Pen" McKernan, guitarist Bob Weir, John "Marmaduke" Dawson (also later with the New Riders), and Bob Matthews.

In 1965 the jug band went electric and Pig Pen switched to organ. By June the group had evolved into the blues band the Warlocks, with Garcia, Weir, Pig Pen, drummer Bill Kreutzmann, and bassist Phil Lesh, a classically trained trumpeter and composer of 12-tone and electronic music. The Warlocks played at Bill Graham's first rock event at the Fillmore Auditorium in late 1965, and later at the Trips Festival, and at author Ken Kesey's infamous Acid Tests, chronicled in Tom Wolfe's *The Electric Kool-Aid Acid Test*. Performing frequently, often for free, in San Francisco's Golden Gate Park with the Jefferson Airplane and other Bay Area bands, the Warlocks became the Grateful Dead around the time the group moved into 710 Ashbury Street, in the heart of San Francisco's Haight-Ashbury district, in June 1966.

Concentrating on live performances, the Grateful Dead eventually signed with Warner Bros. Records. Their eponymous debut album featured Pig Pen's gruff lead vocals on blues-based material such as "Good Morning, Little School Girl" and "Morning Dew." During summer 1967 keyboardist Tom Constanten joined the group, as did percussionist-drummer Mickey Hart, thus freeing Lesh from his strictly rhythmic function on bass. The Grateful Dead's second album, *Anthem of the Sun*, released almost 18 months after the first, was again blues oriented.

During 1969 keyboardist Constanten departed and the group recruited Robert Hunter as full-time nonperforming lyricist. *Aoxomoxoa* contained several band favorites, such as "St. Stephen" and "China Cat Sunflower," with lyrics by Hunter. Also recorded that year was the live set *Live Dead*, which included a 23-minute rendition of "Dark Star" and a rousing version of "Turn on Your Lovelight."

In 1970 the Grateful Dead dropped their blues- and improvisatory-based approach for a country-flavored, vocally rich, and much simplified sound that resulted in what many regard as the group's finest two albums, *Workingman's Dead* and *American Beauty*. Indeed, these two albums featured some of Robert Hunter's most striking efforts as a songwriter. *Workingman's Dead* contained the group's first (albeit minor) hit, "Uncle John's Band," as well as "Easy Wind," "Casey Jones," and "New Speedway Boogie," their "official" statement about the December 1969 debacle at Altamont Speedway with the Rolling Stones, where they were slated to perform. *American Beauty*, recorded with the assistance of the New Riders of the Purple Sage and featuring Garcia on pedal steel guitar, included Grateful Dead classics such as Pig Pen's "Operator," Weir and Hunter's "Sugar Magnolia," and the Hunter-Garcia collaborations "Candyman," "'Till the Morning Comes," and "Truckin'," the group's second minor hit and one of their anthem songs. Their next Warner Bros. album, entitled simply *The Grateful Dead*, was a live set. Often regarded as one of the Dead's finest live recordings, the album contained the band favorites "Bertha," "Wharf Rat" and "Playing in the Band," as well as Merle Haggard's "Mama Tried," John Phillips's "Me and My Uncle," and Chuck Berry's "Johnny B. Goode."

By 1970 the remarkably diffuse outside activities of the members of the group had begun. While performing and recording with keyboardist Howard Wales, former Creedence Clearwater Revival member Tom Fogerty, and funk keyboardist Merl Saunders, Jerry Garcia played sessions for Crosby, Stills, Nash and Young and the Jefferson Airplane. Garcia also began playing pedal steel guitar and banjo with Dave Torbert and former associates David

Nelson and John "Marmaduke" Dawson in the countrified New Riders of the Purple Sage that spring. He remained with the New Riders into 1971, appearing on their debut Columbia album. The album included "I Don't Know You," "Whatcha Gonna Do," "Henry," "Dirty Business," and "All I Ever Wanted," all written by Dawson. The New Riders continued to record for Columbia, without Garcia, through 1975. Their *Adventures of Panama Red* featured Peter Rowan's title song and "Lonesome L.A. Cowboy," and Robert Hunter's "Kick in the Head." With Dawson as the group's mainstay, the New Riders toured and recorded albums into the '90s.

During 1971 Pig Pen fell ill and seldom toured with the Grateful Dead. He was replaced by keyboardist-vocalist Keith Godchaux by year's end. By the time of the group's first major European tour in the spring of 1972, Mickey Hart had left the group and Pig Pen had rejoined.

In 1972 Jerry Garcia, Bob Weir, and Mickey Hart each issued solo albums. Garcia played all instruments except drums on *Garcia*, which included "Sugaree" (a minor hit), "Deal," and "The Wheel," with songs credited to Garcia, Hunter, and drummer Bill Kreutzmann. Weir's *Ace* was recorded with Garcia, Lesh, Kreutzmann, keyboardist Keith Godchaux, and Godchaux's vocalist wife, Donna. It contained "Walk in the Sunshine" and "Mexicali Blues," written by Weir and John Barlow, Weir's own "One More Saturday Night," and the classic Weir-Hunter collaboration "Playing in the Band." Hart's *Rolling Thunder* was recorded with Garcia, Grace Slick, and Steve Stills.

The two-month European tour of 1972, with Keith and Donna Godchaux as full-time members, yielded the multirecord set *Europe '72*. The album served as a live compendium of the songs of the Grateful Dead. In addition to featuring songs such as "China Cat Sunflower," "Sugar Magnolia," and "Truckin'," the album introduced "Jack Straw," "Tennessee Jed," "Ramble On Rose," and "Brown-Eyed Woman." The album proved a best-seller, remaining on the album charts for nearly six months. However, founding member Ron "Pig Pen" McKernan died of liver failure on March 8, 1973, at age 27.

In July 1973 the Grateful Dead financed the establishment of their own label, Grateful Dead Records. In order to market their albums, and to stay in better touch with their fans, they set up an office that quickly became one of the most effective operations in communicating with fans ever established by a rock band. The label's first release was the Dead's next album, *Wake of the Flood*, which contained more Hunter-Garcia songs, such as "Row Jimmy" and "Mississippi Half-Step." The following January, Round Records was founded for outside recordings by members of the group. By May, Round Records had issued Garcia's second solo album, with Peter Rowan's "Mississippi Moon" and Doctor John's "What Goes Around," and Robert Hunter's first solo effort, *Tales of the Great Rum Runners*, which included "It Must Have Been the Roses" and "Keys to the Rain." During 1973 and 1974 the bluegrass aggregation Old and in the Way played around the San Francisco Bay Area. Comprised of Jerry Garcia (bjo), Peter Rowan (gtr), David Grisman (mdln), Vassar Clements (fdl), and John Kahn (bs), the group recorded *Old and in the Way* for Round Records in fall 1973. A modern bluegrass classic, the album included Peter Rowan's "Land of the Navajo," "Midnight Moonlight," and "Panama Red."

From March to October 1974 the Grateful Dead utilized a massive $400,000 state-of-the-art sound system that emitted a loud, clear, and clean sound, rather than the usual distorted, bone-crushing noise normally associated with such a powerful system. That June the group issued *Live from Mars Hotel*, which featured "U.S. Blues" and the Dead classic "Ship of Fools." Following a European tour, the Grateful Dead played five consecutive nights at San Francisco's Winterland in October before retiring from live performance for more than a year. Recorded remote, the shows later yielded the poorly mixed album *Steal Your Face*. Filmed by seven camera crews, this concert stand was captured, edited, and eventually released in film form in June 1977 as *The Grateful Dead Movie*.

In 1975 Round Records issued *Keith and Donna* (by the Godchauxs), *Seastones* (by Phil Lesh and composer—synthesizer wizard Ned Lagin), and Robert Hunter's *Tiger Rose*. Bob Weir assisted in the recording of the debut Round album by Kingfish, formed by Dave Torbert, a former member of the New Riders of the Purple Sage. Also in 1976, Round issued Garcia's third solo album, *Reflections*, and *Diga* by the Diga Rhythm Band, featuring Mickey Hart and tabla player Zakir Hussain.

In June 1975 the Grateful Dead signed an agreement with United Artists for worldwide distribution of both Round and Grateful Dead records. Following the return of percussionist Mickey Hart, the Grateful Dead recorded *Blues for Allah*, a decidedly jazz-oriented venture that included the minor hit "The Music Never Stopped" by Weir and John Barlow, and the Hunter-Garcia-Kreutzmann collaboration "Franklin's Tower." In 1977 the Grateful Dead switched to Arista Records, employing for the first time an outside producer, Keith Olsen of *Fleetwood Mac* fame, for *Terrapin Station*. Prominently featuring horns, strings, and vocal choruses, the album included "Estimated Prophet," "Samson and Delilah," and the extended cut "Terrapin."

Bob Weir's *Heaven Help the Fool*, produced by Olsen and recorded with guitarist Bobby Cochran and keyboardist Brent Mydland, was issued on Arista in early 1978, yielding the minor hit "Bombs Away." Soon after, the Jerry Garcia Group's *Cats Under the Stars* was released on Arista, again showcasing the lyrics of Robert Hunter. In September the Grateful Dead spent $500,000 to ship 25 tons of equipment to Egypt so they could play at the foot of the Great Pyramids in a benefit performance for the Egyptian Department of Antiquities and the Faith and Hope Society, a charitable organization. Before year's end, the group's *Shakedown Street* was issued. Produced by Lowell George of Little Feat, the album evinced a sophisticated, almost disco-fied sound. Their next album, *Go to Heaven*, was produced by Gary Lyons and yielded a minor hit with the Garcia-Hunter composition "Alabama Getaway."

In March 1979 Keith and Donna Godchaux left the Grateful Dead to pursue solo projects. Keith was replaced by keyboardist Brent Mydland, a former touring and recording partner of Bob Weir. He debuted with the Grateful Dead in April. Keith Godchaux died on July 23, 1980, in Ross, California, of injuries suffered in a motorcycle accident two days prior. Meanwhile Mickey Hart scored, in part, the music for the epic yet equivocal 1979 Vietnam War movie *Apocalypse Now*. Other recordings that were not used in the film (featuring exotic percussion instruments from Hart's extensive collection) surfaced in late 1980 as *The Rhythm Devils Play River Music*. By early 1981 Bob Weir had formed Bobby and the Midnites with guitarist Bobby Cochran, Dead keyboardist Brent Mydland, and fusion drummer Billy Cobham, among others, for a brief tour and eponymous album on Arista Records. The Grateful Dead issued two live sets in 1981, the acoustic *Reckoning* and the electric *Dead Set*.

The Grateful Dead concentrated on live performances during the '80s. By the mid-'80s they had become one of the top-grossing touring rock acts, and had expanded their audience to a new, youthful generation of fans. During this time Jerry Garcia recorded *Run for the Roses*, Bob Weir recorded a second album with Bobby and the Midnites, and Mickey Hart recorded *Dafos* with Airto Moreira, Flora Purim, and Batucaje. For a time Robert Hunter performed in the Dinosaurs with Barry Melton, John Cipollina, Peter Albin, and Spencer Dryden, all veterans of psychedelic San Francisco bands. In July 1986 Jerry Garcia nearly died after collapsing in a diabetic coma. The Grateful Dead resumed touring in December, and Garcia and friends staged a three-week run at New York's Lunt-Fontaine Theater in October 1987 under the banner Garcia on Broadway.

The Grateful Dead emerged spectacularly in 1987. Their first studio album in seven years, *In the Dark*, was hailed as perhaps their best work since *Workingman's Dead* and *American Beauty*. It contained Weir's "Throwing Stones" and Mydland's "Tons of Steels" and yielded their first major hit (a near-smash, in fact) with "Touch of Grey." They performed with Bob Dylan at six concerts in July, and recordings from the shows were issued in early 1989. Later that year *Rolling Stone* magazine declared them the single most successful touring band in rock history.

In 1984 the Grateful Dead set up the nonprofit philanthropic Rex Foundation to oversee contributions to environmental lobbies, social causes, and private ventures. By 1993 the organization had distributed more than $4 million. The group's September 24, 1988, concert at Madison Square Garden in New York heralded their lifetime commitment to the issue of rain-forest preservation, raising $500,000 for Cultural Survival, Greenpeace, and the Rainforest Action Network. In 1993 the Grateful Dead contributed about one-half of the cost of a liver transplant for legendary poster artist Stanley Mouse, who with Alton Kelley created the Grateful Dead skull-and-roses logo.

On July 26, 1990, keyboardist Brent Mydland was found dead of a drug overdose in his Lafayette, California, home. He was replaced temporarily by singer-keyboardist Bruce Hornsby and permanently by Vince Welnick of the Tubes in August.

Honored in 1991 with *Deadicated*, a benefit album of their songs by artists such as Los Lobos, Midnight Oil, Elvis Costello, Jane's Addiction, Doctor John, and Lyle Lovett, the Grateful Dead became the top concert attraction of 1991 and 1993, with U2 intervening. In 1992 the Grateful Dead canceled an 18-date East Coast tour when Jerry Garcia was reported to be suffering "exhaustion." He subsequently adopted a new vegetarian diet and initiated weight-loss and exercise programs that improved his health significantly.

During the '80s Mickey Hart had immersed himself in the music of non-Western cultures and initiated a study of the myth and meaning of drumming. As a result he presented and recorded the chants of Gyuto Tibetan Buddhist Monks in 1985. In 1988 he released six discs of exotic music on Rykodisc as *The World*. The recordings included Sudanese folk music, traditional Jewish music, the music of Egypt and India, and Nigerian drum master Batunde Olatunji. In the '90s Hart's drum studies produced two books, *Drumming at the Edge of Magic*, a chronicle of his personal quest, and *Planet Drum*, a collection of world drum lore and legend. Each of the books had a companion CD, released on Rykodisc.

During the '90s Jerry Garcia recorded *Blues from the Rainforest* with keyboardist Merl Saunders, accompanied David Grisman on Beat wordsmith Ken Nordine's *Devout Catalyst*, and performed and recorded with mandolinist David Grisman and his own band while continuing to perform with the Grateful Dead. In 1994 the band was inducted into the Rock and Roll Hall of Fame in recognition of its many years of influential music-making. Garcia died unexpectedly on August 9, 1995, in a Forest Knolls, California, treatment facility at age 53, bringing his musical and spiritual legacy and that of the Grateful Dead to increased public awareness and analysis. The band ended months of speculation in December 1995 when they announced they would not continue performing or recording without Garcia.

The Grateful Dead

The Grateful Dead	Warner Bros.	1689	'67	CS/CD
Anthem of the Sun	Warner Bros.	1749	'68	LP/CS/CD
Aoxomoxoa	Warner Bros.	1790	'69	LP/CS/CD
Workingman's Dead	Warner Bros.	1869	'70	LP/CS/CD
American Beauty	Warner Bros.	1893	'70	CS/CD
American Beauty/Workingman's Dead	Warner Bros.	23706		CS
Best—Skeletons from the Closet	Warner Bros.	2764	'74	CS/CD
Best—What a Long Strange Trip It's Been	Warner Bros.	(2) 3091	'77	†
	Warner Bros.	3091		CS/CD
Wake of the Flood	Grateful Dead	01	'73	†
	Grateful Dead	4002		CS/CD

From Mars Hotel	Grateful Dead	102	'74	†
	Grateful Dead	4007		CS/CD
Blues for Allah	Grateful Dead	494	'75	†
	Grateful Dead	4001		CS/CD
Terrapin Station	Arista	7001	'77	†
	Arista	8065		CD
	Arista	8329		LP/CS
Shakedown Street	Arista	4198	'78	†
	Arista	8228		CD
	Arista	8321		LP/CS
Go to Heaven	Arista	9508	'80	†
	Arista	8181		CD
	Arista	8332		LP/CS
In the Dark	Arista	8452	'87	LP/CS/CD
Dead Zone: The Grateful Dead CD Collection, 1977–1987	Arista	(6) 8530	'87	CD†
Built to Last	Arista	8575	'89	LP/CS/CD
Dead in a Deck (limited edition of *Built to Last*)	Arista	8575	'89	CS/CD

Recorded Live

Live Dead (recorded 1969)	Warner Bros.	1830	'69	LP/CS/CD
The Grateful Dead	Warner Bros.	(2) 1935	'71	†
	Warner Bros.	1935		CS/CD
Europe '72	Warner Bros.	(3) 2668	'72	CS
	Warner Bros.	(2) 2668		CD
History of the Grateful Dead—Bear's Choice (recorded 1970)	Warner Bros.	2721	'73	CS/CD
Steal Your Face (recorded 1980)	Grateful Dead	(2) 620	'76	†
	Grateful Dead	(2) 4006		CS/CD
One from the Vault (recorded 1975)	Grateful Dead	(2) 4013	'91	CS/CD
Infrared Roses	Grateful Dead	4014	'91	CS/CD
Two from the Vault (recorded 1968)	Grateful Dead	(2) 4016	'92	CS/CD
Reckoning (recorded 1980)	Arista	8604	'81	†
	Arista	8523	'90	CD
Dead Set (recorded 1980)	Arista	(2) 8606	'81	†
	Arista	(2) 8112		LP/CS/CD
Without a Net (recorded 1989)	Arista	(3) 8634	'90	LP
	Arista	(2) 8634	'90	CS/CD
Hundred Year Hall	Arista	14020	'95	CS/CD
Dick's Picks, Volume 1	Arista	(2) 14018	'95	CS/CD

Anthologies

Vintage Grateful Dead	Sunflower	5001	'70	†
Historic Dead	Sunflower	5004	'71	†
History	Pride	0016		†
Reckoning	Pair	(2) 1053	'86	CS

The Grateful Dead and Bob Dylan

Dylan and the Dead (recorded 1987)	Columbia	45056	'89	CS/CD

New Riders of the Purple Sage

N.R.P.S.	Columbia	30888	'71	CD
Powerglide	Columbia	31284	'72	†
Gypsy Cowboy	Columbia	31930	'72	†
The Adventures of Panama Red	Columbia	32450	'73	CS/CD

Home, Home on the Road	Columbia	32870	'74	†
Brujo	Columbia	33145	'74	†
Oh, What a Mighty Time	Columbia	33688	'75	†
Best	Columbia	34367	'76	CS/CD
New Riders	MCA	2196	'76	†
	One Way	22108		CD
Who Are These Guys?	MCA	2248	'77	†
	One Way	22109		CD
Marin County Line	MCA	2397	'77	†
	MCA	632		†
	One Way	22107		CD
Feelin' All Right	A&M	4818	'81	†
Live (recorded 1982)	Avenue	71289	'95	CD
Before Time Began	Relix	2024		CS/CD
Vintage New Riders of the Purple Sage	Relix	2025		CS/CD
Midnight Moonlight	Relix	2050		CS/CD

Jerry Garcia and Howard Wales

Hooteroll?	Douglas	30859	'71	†
	Rykodisc	10052	'88	CS/CD
	Ryko Analogue	0052	'88	LP/CS

Jerry Garcia

Garcia	Warner Bros.	2582	'72	†
	Grateful Dead	4003		CS/CD
Compliments of Garcia	Round	102	'74	†
	Grateful Dead	4009	'90	CS/CD
Reflections	Round	565	'76	†
	Grateful Dead	4008	'90	CS/CD
Almost Acoustic	Grateful Dead	4005		CS/CD
Cats Under the Stars	Arista	4160	'78	†
	Arista	8535	'88	CS/CD
Run for the Roses	Arista	9603	'82	†
	Arista	8557	'88	CS/CD
Jerry Garcia Band	Arista	(2) 18690	'91	CS/CD

Jerry Garcia and Merl Saunders

Live at the Keystone	Fantasy	(2) 79002	'73	LP
	Fantasy	79002		CS
Live at the Keystone, Volume 1 (recorded 1973)	Fantasy	4535	'88	LP/CS
	Fantasy	7701	'88	CD
Live at the Keystone, Volume 2 (recorded 1973)	Fantasy	4536	'88	LP/CS
	Fantasy	7702	'88	CD
Keystone Encores, Volume 1 (recorded 1973)	Fantasy	4533	'88	LP/CS
	Fantasy	7703	'88	CD
Keystone Encores, Volume 2 (recorded 1973)	Fantasy	4534		LP/CS
Blues from the Rainforest	Grateful Dead	3901	'91	CS/CD

Old and in the Way

Old and in the Way	Round	103	'75	†
	Rykodisc	10009		CD
	Sugar Hill	3746	'93	CS/CD

Jerry Garcia and David Grisman

Garcia/Grisman	Acoustic Disc	2	'91	CS/CD

Jerry Garcia, David Grisman, and Ken Nordine

Devout Catalyst	Grateful Dead	4015		CS/CD

Bob Weir

Ace	Warner Bros.	2627	'72	†
	Grateful Dead	4004		CS/CD†
	Arista	14004	'95	CS/CD
Kingfish	Round	564	'76	†
	Grateful Dead	4010	'90	CS/CD
	Arista	14010	'95	CS/CD
Heaven Help the Fool	Arista	4155	'78	†
	Arista	8165	'88	CS/CD

Bobby and the Midnites (with Bob Weir)

Bobby and the Midnites	Arista	9568	'81	†
	Arista	8558	'88	CS/CD
Where the Beat Meets the Street	Columbia	39276	'84	†

Kingfish (with Bob Weir)

Kingfish	Kingfish	564	'76	†
	Grateful Dead	4010	'90	CS/CD
Live 'n' Kickin'	Jet/United Artists	732	'77	†
Trident	Jet/Columbia	35479	'78	†
Live at the Roxy	Townhouse	7128	'81	†
Kingfish	Relix	2005		CS/CD
Alive in '85	Relix	2016		CS/CD

Mickey Hart

Rolling Thunder	Warner Bros.	2635	'72	†
	Grateful Dead	4011	'90	CS/CD
Diga (with the Diga Rhythm Band)	Round	600	'76	†
Music to Be Born By	Rykodisc	20112		CS/CD
At the Edge	Rykodisc	10124	'90	CS/CD
Planet Drum	Rykodisc	10206	'91	CS/CD

The Rhythm Devils (with Mickey Hart)

Play River Music	Passport	9844	'80	†
The Apocalypse Now Sessions	Rykodisc	10109		CS/CD

Mickey Hart, Airto, and Flora Purim

Dalos	Rykodisc	10108		CS/CD

Robert Hunter

Tales of the Great Rum Runners	Round	101	'74	†
	Rykodisc	10158	'90	CS/CD
Tiger Rose	Round	105	'75	†
	Rykodisc	10115	'89	CS/CD
Jack O' Roses	Relix		'81	†
Promontory Rider	Relix	2002		CS/CD
Amagamalin Street	Relix	2003		CS/CD
Rock Columbia	Relix	2019		CS/CD
Liberty	Relix	2029		CS/CD
A Box of Rain: Live 1990	Rykodisc	10214	'91	CS/CD

Sentinel (poetry)	Rykodisc	20265	'93	CD
Keith and Donna Godchaux				
Keith and Donna	Round	104	'75	†
Seastones (with Phil Lesh)				
Seastones	Round	106	'75	†
Dead Tribute Album				
Deadicated: A Tribute to the Grateful Dead	Arista	8669	'91	CS/CD

AL GREEN

(b. Al Greene, Apr. 13, 1946, Forrest City, AR)

One of the premier soul singers of the first half of the '70s, Al Green attained his R&B and pop successes on the basis of his affecting songwriting and high, sensual voice, and the production and arrangements of Memphis's Willie Mitchell. Pursuing a career as a preacher and gospel singer since the late '70s, Green became one of gospel music's most popular artists in the '80s and '90s, and has occasionally returned to secular music.

Al Green began singing with the family gospel group The Greene Brothers when he was 9 years old, remaining with them until he was 16. He toured with the group, making his first recordings with them for Fargo Records in 1960. His father was dismayed when he heard the young singer listening to Jackie Wilson's music, and he dismissed Al from the group. By now living in Grand Rapids, Michigan, Al Green quickly formed his own pop group, The Creations, active from 1964 to 1967. Under the new name the Soul Mates, with Lee Virgins and brother Robert in 1967–1968, the group scored a smash R&B and moderate pop hit with "Back Up Train" on Hot Line Records.

Spotted by bandleader-producer Willie Mitchell in Midland, Texas, in 1969, Al Green signed with the Memphis-based Hi label. After several major R&B-only hits in 1970, he initiated a series of pop and R&B smashes with his own "Tired of Being Alone" in 1971. Writing his own material, either alone or in collaboration with Mitchell and Al Jackson (of Booker T. and the MGs), Green topped both the pop and R&B charts with "Let's Stay Together." *I'm Still in Love with You*, his most popular album, yielded two crossover smashes, "Look What You've Done to Me" and the title track. Subsequent crossover smashes through 1974 include "You Ought to Be with Me," "Call Me (Come Back Home)," "Here I Am (Come and Take Me)," "Livin' for You," "Sha-La-La (Make Me Happy)," and "L-O-V-E (Love)." R&B smashes continued through 1976 with "Let's Get Married," "Oh Me, Oh My (Dreams in My Arms)," "Full of Fire," and "Keep Me Cryin'."

In 1974 Green was attacked by a former girlfriend, who poured hot grits on the star and then killed herself; this incident apparently inspired his conversion to Christianity. On December 17, 1976, Green opened the Full Gospel Tabernacle, his own church in Memphis. However, he did not turn his back entirely on secular music; in 1977 he broke with Willie Mitchell, to produce his next recording, *The Belle Album*, which featured the hit "Belle." Two years later a second incident, a fall from stage that could have left him seriously injured, convinced Green that he must abandon his secular career. In the '80s he recorded gospel albums and was eventually embraced by churchgoing record buyers, becoming one of gospel music's best-selling black male artists. Performing on the gospel circuit, Al Green returned to the pop charts in late 1988 with the near-smash hit "Put a Little Love in Your Heart," recorded with Annie Lennox of the Eurythmics. A 1992 secular album recorded in Memphis has yet to be released in the United States. In 1995 Al Green was inducted into the Rock and Roll Hall of Fame.

Al Greene

Back Up Train	Hot Line	1500	'68	†

Al Green

Al Green (recorded 1967–1968)	Bell	6076	'72	†
Green Is Blues	Hi	32055	'69	†
	The Right Stuff	66710	'93	CS/CD
Al Green Gets Next to You	Hi	32062	'71	†
	The Right Stuff	66709	'93	CS/CD
Let's Stay Together	Hi	32070	'72	†
	Motown	5290	'89	CS/CD†
	The Right Stuff	27121	'93	LP/CS/CD
I'm Still in Love with You	Hi	32074	'72	†
	Motown	5284	'89	LP/CS/CD†
	The Right Stuff	27627	'93	LP/CS/CD
Call Me	Hi	32077	'73	†
	Motown	5286	'89	CS/CD†
	The Right Stuff	28538	'94	CS/CD
Livin' for You	Hi	32082	'73	†
	Motown	5304	'89	CS/CD†
	The Right Stuff	29791	'94	CS/CD
Call Me/Livin' for You	Motown	8140	'86	CD†
Al Green Explores Your Mind	Hi	32087	'74	†
	Motown	5287		CS/CD†
Greatest Hits, Volume 1	Hi	32089	'75	†
	Motown	5283		CS/CD†
Al Green Is Love	Hi	32092	'75	†
	Motown	5432	'89	CD†
Full of Fire	Hi	32097	'76	†
	Motown	5285	'89	CS/CD†
Al Green Is Love/Full of Fire	Motown	8148		CD
Have a Good Time	Hi	32103	'76	†
Greatest Hits, Volume 2	Hi	32105	'77	†
	Motown	5291		CS/CD†
The Belle Album	Hi (Cream)	6004	'77	†
	Motown	5318		CS/CD
	The Right Stuff	30579	'95	CS/CD
Tired of Being Alone	Hi (Cream)	8000	'77	†
Can't Get Next to You	Hi (Cream)	8001	'77	†
Let's Stay Together	Hi (Cream)	8007	'78	†
Truth 'n' Time	Hi (Cream)	6009	'78	†
	Motown	5317		CS/CD†
Compact Command Performances (14 Greatest Hits)	Motown	6111		CD†
Tokyo Live	Motown	(2) 5302		CS†
	Motown	5302		CD†
	The Right Stuff	31975	'95	CS/CD
Love Ritual (recorded 1968–1976)	London	710	'78	†
	MCA	42308		LP/CS/CD†
Your Heart's in Good Hands	MCA	11350	'95	CS/CD

Gospel Albums

The Lord Will Make a Way	Myrrh	8113	'80	LP/CS†

Higher Plane	Myrrh	8114		LP/CS†
I'll Rise Again	Myrrh	6747	'83	†
	Word/Epic	47754	'91	CS/CD†
Precious Lord	Myrrh	8115		LP/CS†
	Myrrh	8116		LP/CS†
	Word/Epic	47805	'85/'92	CS/CD†
Christian Album	Myrrh	8117		LP/CS†
Trust in God	Myrrh	6783	'84	†
	Myrrh	8118		LP/CS†
Full Gospel Tabernacle Choir	Myrrh	8209		LP/CS†
He Is the Light	A&M	5102	'85	LP/CS/CD†
Soul Survivor	A&M	5150	'87/'95	CS/CD
I Get Joy	A&M	5228	'89	LP/CS/CD†
Al Green Sings the Gospel	Motown	5319		CS/CD
One in a Million	Word/Epic	77000	'91	CS/CD
Love Is Reality	Word/Epic	48860	'92	CS/CD
From My Soul	Arrival	709		CS/CD†
Gospel Soul	Arrival	3127	'93	CS/CD

THE GUESS WHO/BACHMAN-TURNER OVERDRIVE

THE GUESS WHO. Burton Cummings (b. Dec. 31, 1947, Winnipeg, Manitoba, Canada), lead voc, kybd, rhythm gtr; **Randy Bachman** (b. Sept. 27, 1943, Winnipeg, Manitoba, Canada), lead gtr; **Jim Kale** (b. Aug. 11, 1943, Winnipeg, Manitoba, Canada), bs; **Garry Peterson** (b. May 26, 1945, Winnipeg, Manitoba, Canada) [The band experienced many personnel changes, beginning in 1970.]

BACHMAN-TURNER OVERDRIVE. Randy Bachman, voc, lead gtr; **Tim Bachman** (b. Winnipeg, Manitoba, Canada), rhythm gtr; **Robbie Bachman** (b. Feb. 18, 1953, Winnipeg, Manitoba, Canada), drm; **C. Fred Turner** (b. Oct. 16, 1943, Winnipeg, Manitoba, Canada), bs, voc [Tim Bachman left in 1973, to be replaced by **Blair Thornton** (b. July 23, 1950).]

A popular North American singles band of the late '60s and early '70s, the Guess Who were the first Canadian band to achieve international success. Superseded by the harder-rocking Bachman-Turner Overdrive (BTO) in the mid-'70s, the Guess Who disbanded in 1975 when lead vocalist Burton Cummings left to pursued a solo career. BTO leader Randy Bachman later formed Ironhorse, and the Guess Who and Bachman-Turner Overdrive regrouped in the '80s.

The Guess Who began their evolution in Winnipeg, Manitoba, Canada, in 1963, when Chad Allan (born Allan Kobel), Randy Bachman, Bob Ashley, Jim Kale, and Garry Peterson formed the Reflections. They also recorded as Chad Allan and the Expressions, scoring a major hit with "Shakin' All Over" in 1965. In 1966 Ashley and Allan dropped out, Allan being replaced by Burton Cummings, and the group became the Guess Who. During 1967 the Guess Who appeared on the Canadian television show *Where It's At*, and they recorded more than a dozen Canadian singles through 1968. They secured U.S. distribution of their recordings with RCA Records in 1969, and soon scored a smash hit with the Bachman-Cummings composition "These Eyes" from their debut RCA album. Their second RCA album, *Canned Wheat*, yielded the two-sided hit "Laughing"/"Undun" and the smash hit "No Time," another Bachman-Cummings collaboration.

The Guess Who became international stars with 1970's *American Woman* album and the top-hit two-sided single "American Woman"/"No Sugar Tonight." Despite Randy Bachman's subsequent departure, the Guess Who continued to score major hits through 1971, with "Hand Me Down World," "Share the Land," "Albert Flasher," and "Rain Dance." Experiencing a number of personnel changes, the Guess Who achieved two final hits in 1974, "Clap for the Wolfman" (a smash) and "Dancin' Fool." The group disbanded at the end of 1975. Burton Cummings pursued a solo career in the late '70s, managing a near-smash hit with "Stand Tall" in 1976. In 1979 Jim Kale reconstituted the group for a single album and subsequent touring.

After leaving the Guess Who Randy Bachman formed Brave Belt with Chad Allan. After a sole album with Allan, Brave Belt regrouped with Bachman, his brothers Tim and Robbie, and C. Fred Turner. In 1973 the group became Bachman-Turner Overdrive, with Blair Thornton replacing Tim Bachman. Signed to Mercury Records, the group scored major hits with "Let It Ride" and "Takin' Care of Business" and a top hit in 1974 with "You Ain't Seen Nothing Yet." The hits continued in 1975 with "Roll On Down the Highway" and "Hey You." Randy Bachman departed in 1977, and the group continued to chart into 1979. Randy formed Ironhorse, who achieved a modest hit with "Sweet Lui-Louise" in 1979. Randy and Tim Bachman regrouped with Fred Turner in 1984.

The Guess Who

Shakin' All Over	Scepter	533	'66	†
	MGM	4645	'69	†
Sown and Grown in Canada	Wand	691	'71	†
The Guess Who Play the Guess Who	P.I.P.	6806	'71	†
Wheatfield Soul	RCA	4141	'69/'89	CS/CD
	RCA	1171	'75	†
Canned Wheat Packed by the Guess Who	RCA	4157	'69/'89	CS/CD†
	RCA	0983	'75	†
American Woman	RCA	4266	'70	CD
	RCA	3673		CS
Share the Land	RCA	4359	'70	†
	RCA	54359	'94	CS/CD
Best	RCA	1004	'71	†
	RCA	3662	'80	CD
	RCA	7623		CS
So Long, Bannatyne	RCA	4574	'71	†
Rockin'	RCA	4602	'72	†
	RCA	2683	'78	†
Live at the Paramount	RCA	4779	'72/'90	CS/CD
Artificial Paradise	RCA	4830	'73	†
Number 10	RCA	0130	'73	†
Best, Volume 2	RCA	0269	'73	†
Road Food	RCA	0405	'74	†
Flavours	RCA	0636	'75	†
Power in the Music	RCA	0995	'75	†
The Way We Were	RCA	1778	'76	†
The Greatest of the Guess Who	RCA	2253	'77	†
	RCA	3746	'88	CD
	RCA	7622	'88	CS
American Woman, These Eyes and Other Hits	RCA	2076	'90	CS/CD
Track Record: The Guess Who Collection	RCA	(2) 61077	'91	CS/CD
These Eyes	RCA	61133	'92	CS/CD
	RCA	61152	'92	CD
The Guess Who at Their Best	RCA	66200	'93	CS/CD

Shakin' All Over	Springboard Int'l	4022	'75	†
The Guess Who	Pickwick	3246		†
All This for a Song	Hilltak	19227	'79	†
	Lacindy	22010	'94	CD

Randy Bachman

Axe	RCA	4348	'70	†
Survivor	Polydor	6141	'78	†

Brave Belt

Brave Belt	Reprise	6447	'71	†
Brave Belt II	Reprise	2057	'72	†
Bachman-Turner-Bachman as Brave Belt	Reprise	2210	'75	†

Bachman-Turner Overdrive

Bachman-Turner Overdrive	Mercury	673	'73	†
	Mercury	838196	'89	CD
Bachman-Turner Overdrive II	Mercury	696	'73	†
	Mercury	822504	'89	CD
Not Fragile	Mercury	1004	'74	†
	Mercury	830178		CS/CD
Four Wheel Drive	Mercury	1027	'75	†
	Mercury	830970	'89	CD
Head On	Mercury	1067	'75	†
	Mercury	838197	'89	CD†
Best of B.T.O. (So Far)	Mercury	1101	'76	†
	Mercury	822786		CS
Freeways	Mercury	3700	'77	†
	Mercury	838199	'89	CD†
Street Action	Mercury	3713	'78	†
Rock 'n' Roll Nights	Mercury	3748	'79	†
Greatest Hits	Mercury	830039	'86	CD
The Anthology	Mercury	(2) 514902	'93	CS/CD
You Ain't Seen Nothin' Yet	Polygram	838165	'92	CS/CD
Bachman-Turner Overdrive	Compleat	1010	'84	†
BTO Live! Live! Live!	MCA/Curb	5760	'86	†
All-Time Greatest Hits: Live	MCA/Curb	10808	'90	CD†
	Curb/CEMA	77328	'90	CD
Best Of: Live	Curb/CEMA	77653	'94	CS/CD

Ironhorse

Ironhorse	Scotti Brothers	7103	'79	†

GUNS N' ROSES

Axl Rose (b. William Bailey, Feb. 7, 1962, Lafayette, IN), lead voc; **Slash** (b. Saul Hudson, July 23, 1965, Stoke-on-Trent, Staffordshire, England), lead gtr; **Izzy Stradlin** (b. Jeffrey Isbell, Apr. 8, 1962, Lafayette, IN), rhythm gtr; **Michael "Duff" McKagan** (b. Feb. 5, 1964, Seattle, WA), bs; **Steven Adler** (b. 1965, OH), drm [Steven Adler left in 1990, to be replaced by **Matt Sorum** (b. Nov. 19, 1960, Long Beach, CA); keyboardist **Dizzy Reed** (b. Darren Reed, June 18, 1963, Hinsdale, IL) also joined at this time. In November 1991 Izzy Stradlin left, to be replaced by **Gilby Clarke** (b. Aug. 17, 1962, Cleveland, OH).]

Perhaps the most controversial rock band since the Sex Pistols and certainly the most controversial to emerge in the late '80s, Guns N' Roses produced angry, belligerent songs focused largely on the decadent side of life and its attendant rage, fear, and insecurity. Featuring the abrasive vocals of Axl Rose, rock's most notorious and volatile male performer of the '90s, Guns N' Roses gained massive popularity with best-selling albums and insolent concert performances that sometimes led to riots. Along with Metallica, with whom they toured in 1992, Guns N' Roses challenged established heavy-metal bands such as Van Halen and reinvigorated the staid metal scene.

Axl Rose met guitarist Izzy Stradlin in 1984 in Los Angeles, where they formed a band variously known as Rose, Hollywood Rose, and LA Guns. In 1985 Guns N' Roses was formed by Rose and Stradlin; two members of Road Crew, Steven Adler and Slash; and Seattle-born Michael "Duff" McKagan. In 1986 Guns N' Roses recorded a four-song EP for the independent Uzi/Suicide label entitled *Live Like a Suicide*. Subsequently signed to Geffen Records, the group scored their first (top) hit with "Sweet Child o' Mine" in 1988, achieving their earliest notoriety as the opening act for Aerosmith's 1988 tour. Their debut album, *Appetite for Destruction*, stayed on the album charts for nearly three years and yielded the smash hits "Welcome to the Jungle" (used in the Clint Eastwood movie *Dead Pool*) and "Paradise City" and the minor hit "Nightrain." *G N'R Lies*, their next release, compiled the *Live Like a Suicide* EP and four songs recorded in 1988, producing the smash hit "Patience" while including "Used to Love Her" and the controversial "One in a Million."

Mired in personal and professional difficulties for a time (the band members were admitted alcohol and drug abusers), Guns N' Roses resumed recording in 1990, but Adler was dismissed, to be replaced by former Cult drummer Matt Sorum, and keyboardist Dizzy Reed was added. "You Could Be Mine," from the Arnold Schwarzenegger movie *Terminator 2*, became a major hit in 1991. In late 1991 Guns N' Roses issued the dark, sprawling albums *Use Your Illusion I* and *II* simultaneously. The ballads "Don't Cry" and "November Rain" and a remake of Paul McCartney's "Live and Let Die" became the hits from *Use Your Illusion I*, which contained "Don't Damn Me," the 10-minute "Coma," and the psychedelic "The Garden" (with Alice Cooper). *Use Your Illusion II* included the minor hit "Yesterdays," "Estranged," a version of Bob Dylan's "Knockin' on Heaven's Door" (used in the Tom Cruise movie *Days of Thunder*), and the antiwar "Civil War." In November 1991 Izzy Stradlin left Guns N' Roses and was replaced by Gilby Clarke of Kills for Thrills. In 1992 Guns N' Roses toured North America with the rival heavy-metal band Metallica.

In 1993 Guns N' Roses toured without their usual backing musicians, Izzy Stradlin returning for five overseas engagements in place of the injured Gilby Clarke. Their late 1993 album, *The Spaghetti Incident*, perhaps their finest work, contained covers of punk songs such as the New York Dolls' "Human Being," the Stooges' "Raw Power," Fear's "I Don't Care About You," and Johnny Thunders's "You Can't Put Your Arms Around a Memory," plus mass-murderer Charles Manson's "Look at Your Game, Girl" and the Skyliners' "Since I Don't Have You."

In 1992 Izzy Stradlin assembled his own band, The Ju Ju Hounds, with Georgia Satellites guitarist Rick Richards, recording an album for Geffen Records and touring in support of Keith Richards's X-Pensive Winos in early 1993. In 1994 Gilby Clarke recorded *Pawnshop Guitars* with Axl Rose, Slash, Duff McKagan, Matt Sorum, and others for Virgin Records. Slash later recorded and toured with Snakepit, which included Clarke, Sorum, Jellyfish vocalist Eric Dover, and Alice in Chains bassist Mike Inez.

Guns N' Roses

Appetite for Destruction	Geffen	24148	'87	LP/CS/CD
Appetite for Destruction (edited version)	Geffen	24211		CS/CD
G N' R Lies	Geffen	24198	'88	LP/CS/CD

Use Your Illusion I	Geffen	24415	'91	LP/CS/CD
Use Your Illusion II	Geffen	24420	'91	LP/CS/CD
The Spaghetti Incident	Geffen	24617	'93	LP/CS/CD

Izzy Stradlin and the Ju Ju Hounds

Izzy Stradlin and the Ju Ju Hounds	Geffen	24490	'92	CS/CD

Gilby Clarke

Pawnshop Guitars	Virgin	39567	'94	CS/CD

Slash's Snakepit

It's Five O'Clock Somewhere	Geffen	24730	'95	CS/CD

BILL HALEY

(b. July 6, 1925, Highland Park, MI; d. Feb. 9, 1981, Harlingen, TX)

Bill Haley and the Comets fused elements of country music, Western swing, and black R&B to produce some of the earliest rock-and-roll song hits. His "Crazy, Man, Crazy," from 1953, was regarded as the first rock-and-roll record to make the pop charts, and "Dim, Dim the Lights (I Want Some Atmosphere)," from 1955, was the first rock-and-roll song to make the R&B charts. When rereleased as the opening song to the 1955 film *Blackboard Jungle*, "Rock Around the Clock" became an astounding success, eventually selling nearly 40 million copies and establishing Haley as the first international rock-and-roll star. His backup band, originally called the Saddlemen but renamed the Comets in 1953, featured the saxophone playing of Rudy Pompilli and the lead guitar of Fran Beecher. Haley's spit-curled, boyish (if pudgy) looks belied his years, and teen fans were dismayed when they discovered their idol was older than they had originally thought. His career was eclipsed by Elvis and younger rockers in the '50s. Haley continued to record and perform sporadically through the '70s, maintaining popularity in Europe well after his career in the States had ended. He died in obscurity in Harlingen, Texas, of a heart attack on February 9, 1981. Bill Haley's role as a rock veteran was acknowledged in 1987, when he was among the second year's inductees into the Rock and Roll Hall of Fame.

Bill Haley and the Comets

Rock with Bill Haley and the Comets	Essex	202		†
Rock Around the Joint! The Original Essex Recordings, 1951–1954	Schoolkids's	1529	'95	CD
Bill Haley and the Comets	Decca	8225	'56	†
	Decca	78225	'62	†
He Digs Rock and Roll	Decca	8315		†
	Decca	78315		†
Rock and Roll Stage Show	Decca	8345	'56	†
	Decca	78345		†
Rockin' the Oldies	Decca	8569	'57	†
	Decca	78569		†
Rockin' Around the World	Decca	8692		†
	Decca	78692		†
Rockin' the Joint	Decca	8775	'58	†
	Decca	78775		†
Bill Haley's Chicks	Decca	78821	'59	†
Strictly Instrumental	Decca	78964	'59	†
Greatest Hits!	Decca	75027	'68	†
	MCA	161		CS/CD

Golden Hits	Decca	(2) 7211	'73	†
From the Original Master Tapes	MCA	5539		CD
Bill Haley and the Comets	Warner Bros.	1378	'60	†
Haley's Juke Box	Warner Bros.	1391	'60	†
Rock 'n' Roll Revival	Warner Bros.	1831	'70	†
Bill Haley and the Comets	Vocalion	3696	'63	†
Scrapbook	Kama Sutra	2014	'70	†
The King of Rock and Roll	Alshire	5202	'70	†
Razzle Dazzle	Janus	(2) 7003	'71	†
Travelin' Band	Janus	3035	'72	†
Bill Haley and the Comets	Pickwick	3256		†
Rock and Roll Revival	Pickwick	3280		†
Rock and Roll	GNP Crescendo	2077	'74	LP/CS
Rock Around the Country	GNP Crescendo	2097	'76	LP
Rockin' & Rollin'	Accord	7125	'81	†
Rock Around the Clock	Special Music	4917		CS

HALL AND OATES

Daryl Hall (b. Oct. 11, 1948, Philadelphia, PA); **John Oates** (b. Apr. 7, 1949, New York, NY)

Veteran Philadelphia-soul session musicians of the late '60s, Daryl Hall and John Oates formed their singer-songwriter duo in the early '70s, recording several overlooked R&B-inflected albums for Atlantic Records. Breaking through with "Sara Smile" in 1976 on RCA, the duo scored a series of catchy but superficial hit songs in the '80s, which eventually led to their surpassing the Everly Brothers as the most-charted duo of rock. Although only "I Can't Go for That (No Can Do)" and "One on One" became smash R&B hits, Hall and Oates placed more singles on the black charts than any other white act.

Daryl Hall and John Oates met in 1967 at Temple University in Philadelphia. Both had early musical training, Hall in voice and classical piano, Oates on accordion and, later, guitar. Hall sang and recorded with the Temptones in 1966–1967. Hall and Oates each worked sessions at Sigma Sound in Philadelphia under songwriter-producers Kenny Gamble and Leon Huff, playing with soul groups such as the Delfonics and the Stylistics. The two began writing songs together and formed the group Gulliver, cutting one album for Elektra Records before breaking up in 1970.

Hall and Oates began performing as a duo, eventually signing with Atlantic Records in 1972. Their debut album was overlooked, but their second, *Abandoned Luncheonette*, yielded a minor hit with "She's Gone." The song became a top R&B hit for Tavares in 1974, the year Hall and Oates recorded their final Atlantic album, *War Babies*. Switching to RCA Records in April 1975, Hall and Oates scored a smash pop and major R&B hit with Hall's "Sara Smile" at the beginning of 1976. Spurred by its success, Atlantic rereleased "She's Gone," and the single became a near-smash hit. Daryl Hall recorded the controversial and esoteric *Sacred Songs* with Robert Fripp in 1977. That year the duo scored a top pop hit with "Rich Girl" and a major hit with "Back Together Again." Subsequent major hits included "It's a Laugh" in 1978 and "Wait for Me" in 1979.

Daryl Hall and John Oates established themselves with *Voices* in 1980. It stayed on the album charts for nearly two years and yielded four hit singles, including the top hit "Kiss on My List," the smash "You Make My Dreams," and a remake of the Righteous Brothers' "You've Lost That Lovin' Feeling." The follow-up, *Private Eyes*, also produced four hits, including the top hits "Private Eyes" and "I Can't Go for That (No Can Do)" (also a top R&B, easy-listening, and dance hit!) and the near-smash "Did It in a Minute." H_2O, perhaps their best-selling album, included the top hit "Maneater" and the near-smashes "Family Man" and "One on One" (an R&B near-smash). The anthology set *Rock 'n' Soul, Part 1* included two new songs, "Say It Isn't So" and "Adult Education," which became smash hits. *Big Bam Boom* continued Hall and Oates's hit-making ways with "Out of Touch" and "Method of Love."

Following 1985's *Live at the Apollo*, recorded with former Temptations David Ruffin and Eddie Kendrick, Hall and Oates ceased working together. Oates produced the Canadian group the Parachute Club and cowrote "Electric Blue," a near-smash for the Australian group Icehouse. Hall recorded *Three Hearts in the Happy Ending Machine*, which yielded three hits, including the smash "Dreamtime" and "Somebody Like You." The duo reunited in 1988 for *Ooh Yeah!* on Arista Records. It yielded three hits: the smash "Everything Your Heart Desires" (their last R&B hit), "Missed Opportunity," and "Downtown Life." "So Close" became Daryl Hall and John Oates's final major pop hit in 1990.

Gulliver

Gulliver	Elektra	74070	'70	†

Daryl Hall and John Oates

Past Times Behind (recorded 1969–1972)	Chelsea	547	'77	†
	Mobile Fidelity	879	'88	CD
The Early Years	Intermedia	5040		LP/CS
Whole Oates	Atlantic	7242	'72	CD
Abandoned Luncheonette	Atlantic	7269	'73	†
	Atlantic	19139		CS/CD
War Babies	Atlantic	18109	'74	CS
No Goodbyes	Atlantic	18213	'77	CS
Daryl Hall and John Oates	RCA	1144	'75	†
	RCA	3836		CS
	RCA	51144	'94	CS/CD
Bigger than Both of Us	RCA	1467	'76/'90	CS/CD
	RCA	3866		†
Beauty on a Back Street	RCA	2300	'77	†
	RCA	4230	'82	†
Livetime	RCA	2802	'78	†
	RCA	4722	'83	†
Along the Red Ledge	RCA	2804	'78	†
	RCA	4231	'82	†
X-Static	RCA	3494	'79	†
	RCA	4303	'82	†
Voices	RCA	3646	'80	CS/CD
	Mobile Fidelity	530		CD
Private Eyes	RCA	4028	'81	CS/CD
H_2O	RCA	4383	'82/'84	CS/CD
Rock 'n' Soul, Part 1	RCA	4858	'83	CS/CD
Big Bam Boom	RCA	5309	'84	†
	RCA	5336		CD
Live at the Apollo	RCA	7035	'85	CS/CD
Soulful Sounds	RCA	61132	'92	CS/CD
	RCA	61151	'92	CD
Best	RCA	66204	'95	CS/CD
Ooh Yeah!	Arista	8539	'88	CS/CD
Change of Season	Arista	8614	'90	LP/CS/CD
Deep River Blues	Richmond	2299		CS

Daryl Hall

Sacred Songs	RCA	3573	'80	†
Three Hearts in the Happy Ending Machine	RCA	7196	'86	LP/CS/CD†
Soul Alone	Epic	53937	'93	†

EMMYLOU HARRIS
(b. Apr. 2, 1947, Birmingham, AL)

Emerging from the remnants of the East Coast folk scene in the late '60s, Emmylou Harris was introduced to traditional country music by Gram Parsons, with whom she toured and recorded as a backup vocalist. Virtually a full collaborator on his final album, *Grievous Angel*, Harris established herself as a prime purveyor of country music with a rock sound during the '70s. Essentially a song interpreter, her success was based largely on her astute selection of material and the excellence of her bands, which have included James Burton, Rodney Crowell, Ricky Skaggs, and Sam Bush. Introducing Crowell and Skaggs to a wider audience, Emmylou Harris bolstered the late-'80s movement toward simple production and uncluttered instrumentation among country performers such as Dwight Yoakam, Lyle Lovett, and k. d. lang.

Emmylou Harris moved with her family to the Washington, D.C., area from her native Alabama, and obtained her first guitar at age 16. She initiated her musical career in 1967, performing around Washington and New York in folk clubs. Signed to Jubilee Records in 1969, her debut album was virtually ignored upon release in 1970. Retiring for a time and unsuccessfully attempting a breakthrough in Nashville during the latter half of 1970, Harris was "discovered" at the Cellar Door in Washington by members of the Flying Burrito Brothers. She was asked to join the group before its second incarnation dissolved. Introduced to Gram Parsons in late 1971, Harris was summoned to Los Angeles to sing backup on his debut solo album, *GP*. She toured with Parsons in spring 1973 as a member of his Fallen Angels band, and worked on his landmark *Grievous Angel* album, which included their collaboration "In My Hour of Darkness." However, Gram Parsons died unexpectedly on September 19, 1973.

Emmylou Harris signed with Warner Bros. in mid-1974, recording two albums for the label's subsidiary Reprise. Her debut for the label, *Pieces of the Sky*, contained standard country-and-western material, such as the country smash (and minor pop hit) "If I Could Only Win Your Love" (by the Louvin Brothers), Merle Haggard's "The Bottle Let Me Down," and "Queen of the Silver Dollar," as well as Lennon and McCartney's "For No One" and the original "Boulder to Birmingham," cowritten with Bill Danoff. In 1975 Harris formed her Hot Band with songwriter Rodney Crowell (rhythm gtr), James Burton (lead gtr), Glen D. Hardin (kybd), Hank DeVito (pedal steel), Emory Gordy (b), and John Ware (drm). *Elite Hotel* included three Gram Parsons's songs ("Wheels," "Sin City," and "Ooh, Las Vegas") and yielded three country smashes with Buck Owens's "Together Again," Don Gibson's "Sweet Dreams," and "One of These Days." Other inclusions were "Amarillo," cowritten by Harris and Crowell; the minor pop hit "Here, There and Everywhere"; and "Feelin' Single — Seein' Double."

After a triumphant tour of Europe and Britain in 1976, Emmylou Harris recorded *Luxury Liner*, replacing guitarist James Burton with Briton Albert Lee. The album contained Gram Parsons's title song as well as Townes Van Zandt's "Pancho and Lefty" and two near-smash country hits with Kitty Wells's "Making Believe" and Chuck Berry's "C'est la Vie." *Quarter Moon in a Ten-Cent Town*, recorded with the Hot Band, included three country hits — Dolly Parton's "To Daddy," Delbert McClinton's "Two More Bottles of Wine," and "Easy

From Now On"—plus two Jesse Winchester songs and Rodney Crowell's "Ain't Living Long Like This" and "Leaving Louisiana in the Broad Daylight."

In February 1978 Emmylou Harris began work on an album with Dolly Parton and Linda Ronstadt, but the project, with its promise of the first female country supergroup, was later abandoned. Harris next recorded the bluegrass-flavored *Blue Kentucky Girl* with the Hot Band and multi-instrumentalist Ricky Skaggs. The album contained the country smashes "Save the Last Dance for Me," the title cut, and "Beneath Still Waters," as well as Gram Parsons's "Hickory Wind," Rodney Crowell's "Even Cowgirls Get the Blues," and Willie Nelson's "Sister's Coming Home." The follow-up bluegrass-style *Roses in the Snow*, again recorded with Skaggs, yielded near-smash country hits with "Wayfaring Stranger" and Paul Simon's "The Boxer." Harris subsequently scored a smash country (and minor pop) hit with "That Lovin' You Feelin' Again" in duet with Roy Orbison; recorded the Christmas album *Light of the Stable*; and registered another pop and country hit with a remake of the Chordettes's 1954 hit "Mister Sandman," recorded with Parton and Ronstadt. Other early-'80s country smashes were "Tennessee Rose" with vocal backing by the Whites, and "Born to Run" from *Cimarron*. Harris's last major solo album success came with the live set *Last Date* (now deleted), which included the smash country hits "(Lost His Love) On Our Last Date" and "I'm Movin' On."

Emmylou Harris's subsequent '80s albums fared less well than previous releases. These included the rock-and-roll set *White Shoes* and the song cycle *The Ballad of Sally Rose*, cowritten with new husband Paul Kennerley. Moving to Nashville in 1984, Harris assembled a new edition of the Hot Band with lead guitarist Frank Reckard, pedal steel guitarist Steve Fishell, and rhythm guitarist–vocalist Barry Tashian for touring.

In 1986 Linda Ronstadt, Dolly Parton, and Emmylou Harris finally recorded their album, *Trio*, with a stellar backup cast that included Albert Lee, David Lindley, and Mark O'Connor. A best-seller, the album stayed on the charts for nearly a year, yielding smash country hits with "To Know Him Is to Love Him," "Those Memories of You," Linda Thompson's "Telling Me Lies," and Parton's "Wildflowers." Harris subsequently scored smash country hits with "We Believe in Happy Endings," in duet with Earl Thomas Conley, and "Heartbreak Hill," from the album *Bluebird*. *Duets* assembled her recorded duets with the likes of Gram Parsons, Roy Orbison, Neil Young, Ricky Skaggs, and Willie Nelson.

In 1990 Emmylou Harris debuted her new backing band, the Nash Ramblers, on tour. Members included former New Grass Revival leader Sam Bush (mdln, fdl), Al Perkins (dobro), Jon Randall Stewart (gtr), and Roy Huskey Jr. (b). On April 30, 1991, Harris and the group recorded at Nashville's Ryman Auditorium, the original home of the Grand Ole Opry. The resulting album and cable television show (on the Nashville Network) included songs by Bill Monroe, plus Steve Earle's "Guitar Town," Bruce Springsteen's "Mansion on the Hill," and John Fogerty's "Lodi."

Emmylou Harris was inducted into the Grand Ole Opry in 1992 and recorded *Cowgirl's Prayer* for Asylum in 1993. The following year she recorded *Songs of the West* with Linda Ronstadt, Dolly Parton, Rodney Crowell, Willie Nelson, and others for Warner Bros. A major change in direction came in 1995, when she joined with producer Daniel Lanois, famous for his atmospheric production work with the Neville Brothers, Bob Dylan, and U2. They produced the album *Wreckin' Ball*, featuring a more hard-edged accompaniment, including Lanois on guitar, and Harris taking on a rougher vocal style; the title cut by Neil Young attracted some radio play. Harris and Lanois subsequently toured as a duo.

Gram Parsons (with Emmylou Harris)

GP	Reprise	2123	'73	†
Grievous Angel	Reprise	2171	'74	†
GP/Grievous Angel	Reprise	26108	'90	CD

Gram Parsons and the Fallen Angels (with Emmylou Harris)

Live 1973	Sierra	1973	'82	†
	Sierra	4222		LP/CS
Live 1973—Original Unedited Broadcast	Sierra	6003		CD

Emmylou Harris

Gliding Bird	Jubilee	12052	'70	†
Pieces of the Sky	Reprise	2213	'75	†
	Reprise	2284		CS/CD
Elite Hotel	Reprise	2236	'76	†
	Reprise	2286		CS/CD
Luxury Liner	Warner Bros.	2998	'77	†
	Warner Bros.	3115		CS/CD
Quarter Moon in a Ten-Cent Town	Warner Bros.	3141	'78	CS/CD
Profile: The Best of Emmylou Harris	Warner Bros.	3258	'78/'84	CS/CD
Blue Kentucky Girl	Warner Bros.	3318	'79	CS/CD
Roses in the Snow	Warner Bros.	3422	'80	CS/CD
Light of the Stable—The Christmas Album	Warner Bros.	3484	'80	†
	Warner Bros.	23484		CS
Evangeline	Warner Bros.	3508	'81	†
Cimarron	Warner Bros.	3603	'81	CS
Last Date	Warner Bros.	23740	'82	†
White Shoes	Warner Bros.	23961	'83	CS/CD
Profile II: The Best of Emmylou Harris	Warner Bros.	25161	'84	CS/CD
The Ballad of Sally Rose	Warner Bros.	25205	'85	CS/CD
Thirteen	Warner Bros.	25352	'86	CS
Angel Band	Warner Bros.	25585	'87	CS/CD
Bluebird	Reprise	25776	'89	CS/CD
Duets	Reprise	25791	'90	CS/CD
Brand New Dance	Reprise	26309	'90	CS/CD
Cowgirl's Prayer	Asylum	61541	'93	CS/CD
Songs of the West	Warner Bros.	45725	'94	CS/CD
Wrecking Ball	Asylum	61854	'95	CS/CD

Emmylou Harris, Dolly Parton, and Linda Ronstadt

Trio	Warner Bros.	25491	'87	CS/CD

Emmylou Harris and the Nash Ramblers

At the Ryman	Reprise	26664	'92	CS/CD

GEORGE HARRISON
(b. Feb. 25, 1943, Wavertree, Liverpool, England)

Neither the most prolific nor the most successful of the former Beatles, George Harrison was the group member most involved in Eastern music and mysticism. One of the first rock artists to express spiritual and humanitarian concerns in his music, Harrison's first post-Beatles album, *All Things Must Pass*, was hailed as one of the rock masterpieces of the '70s, despite its occasional lapses into didacticism and pedantry. His humanitarian impulses produced the benefit show Concert for Bangladesh, the forerunner of mid-'80s benefits such as Live Aid. In 1974 he formed his own record company, Dark Horse, and became the first former Beatle to tour America. In 1978 Harrison and his personal manager formed

Hand Made Film Productions, which became a respected force in the British film industry. A return to performing in 1987 with a new solo album, and the formation of the mock supergroup the Traveling Wilburys, brought Harrison renewed attention at the decade's end.

George Harrison took up guitar and formed his first group, the Rebels, at age 13. In 1958 he joined Paul McCartney and John Lennon in the skiffle group the Quarrymen, but they disbanded around the end of 1959. Harrison, McCartney, and Lennon then formed the Moondogs, later changing their name to the Silver Beatles. Regularly performing at the Cavern Club in Liverpool after January 1961 and making occasional forays into Hamburg, Germany, the Beatles' lineup was completed with the August 1962 addition of drummer Ringo Starr. Harrison, overshadowed by songwriters Lennon and McCartney, made his songwriting debut with "Don't Bother Me" from *Meet the Beatles* (1964; issued as *With the Beatles* in the United Kingdom and on CD in the U.S./U.K.). Later Beatles songs written by Harrison included "If I Needed Someone," "Taxman," "Within You, Without You," the classic "While My Guitar Gently Weeps," "Something" (his first number one hit with the Beatles), and "Here Comes the Sun." During his tenure with the Beatles, Harrison recorded *Wonderwall Music*, an Eastern-sounding instrumental album, and the experimental *Electronic Sound* album, one of the few releases on the short-lived Zapple label.

Although Paul McCartney did not sue for dissolution of the Beatles until December 1970, George Harrison was essentially independent of the group by the May 1970 release of *Let It Be*. His debut solo album, *All Things Must Pass*, was coproduced by Phil Spector and recorded with Eric Clapton and Billy Preston. An instant best-seller, the album yielded the top hit "My Sweet Lord" (backed with "Isn't It a Pity") and the near-smash "What Is Life," as well as "Wah-Wah," "If Not for You," "Beware of Darkness," and "Apple Scruffs."

Concerned with the famine overwhelming Bangladesh, Harrison organized two benefit performances staged in New York's Madison Square Garden on August 1, 1971. Enlisting the services of Ringo Starr, Billy Preston, and Leon Russell (among others), Harrison was able to coax both Bob Dylan and Eric Clapton (both in semiretirement) into performing at the charity show. The resulting multirecord set, *Concert for Bangladesh*, accrued hundreds of thousands of dollars for relief of the heinous situation in Bangladesh (although it took years of legal haggling for the money to be finally released).

In the meantime, George Harrison took nearly two years to complete his second solo album, *Living in the Material World*. Finally released in mid-1973, the album was critically lambasted despite yielding the top hit "Give Me Love (Give Me Peace on Earth)." Also included were the title song as well as "Try Some Buy Some" and the satiric "Sue Me, Sue You Blues," inspired by the bickering among the former Beatles. Meanwhile, Harrison himself faced a lawsuit because of the remarkable similarities between his "My Sweet Lord" and the Chiffons' 1963 top hit "He's So Fine" (the melody is clearly the same).

In June 1974 Harrison announced the formation of Dark Horse Records. The label's first signing was longtime friend Ravi Shankar, the sitar player. During November 1974 Harrison became the first former Beatle to tour the United States, with Shankar. However, the tour was met by scathing reviews, due in large part to voice problems and a muddled sound mix. The soon-released *Dark Horse* took another critical drubbing, although it contained two hits, "Dark Horse" and "Ding Dong, Ding Dong," and a rewritten version of the Everly Brothers' "Bye Bye, Love," an apparent indictment of Eric Clapton's cuckolding of Harrison. (Clapton had become involved with Harrison's then-wife, Patti Boyd, inspiring the song "Layla"; the Harrisons were divorced, and Clapton married Boyd.)

Following *Extra Texture* and its hit "You," George Harrison released *Thirty-Three & 1/3*, which produced the major hits "This Song," which refers to the plagiarism suit regarding "He's So Fine," and "Crackerbox Palace." Also in 1976, Capitol issued *The Best of George Harrison*, which included seven of his hits recorded by the Beatles. In March 1978 he appeared in a small part in the television special *The Rutles: All You Need Is Cash*, Monty Python alumnus Eric Idle's Beatles parody. During that year Harrison formed Hand Made Film Productions with his personal manager, Denis O'Brien. The company produced the irreverent and controversial Monty Python film *Life of Brian*, released in 1979. Subsequent film projects included 1981's *Time Bandits*, with Pythons Terry Gilliam and Michael Palin, and 1982's *The Missionary*, with Palin.

In 1981 George Harrison scored a smash hit with the tribute to the slain John Lennon, "All These Years Ago," recorded with Ringo Starr and Paul and Linda McCartney. Following 1982's uninspired *Gone Troppo*, Harrison remained largely out of sight. Hand Made Films produced the wry 1985 film *A Private Function*, the 1986 flop *Shanghai Surprise* (with Madonna and then-husband Sean Penn), and the critically acclaimed *Mona Lisa* (1986) and *Withnail and I* (1987). Harrison reemerged musically in 1987 with *Cloud Nine*, coproduced by Jeff Lynne; it had a top hit with "Got My Mind Set on You," originally recorded by R&B singer James Ray in 1962, and a major hit, "When We Was Fab," which was reminiscent (in its lyrics and in its arrangement, complete with sitar) of the Beatles. In 1988 and again in 1990, Harrison recorded as one of the Traveling Wilburys with Bob Dylan, Jeff Lynne, and Tom Petty (and Roy Orbison in 1988); the group had a hit with Harrison's "Handle with Care." In late 1991 George Harrison toured Japan with Eric Clapton and his band, resulting in *Live in Japan*. In 1995 the three living former Beatles reunited to promote their *Anthology* TV/CD/video package, and recorded two new songs based on demo tapes by John Lennon that prominently featured George Harrison's guitar work and harmony vocals.

George Harrison

Wonderwall Music	Apple	3350	'68	†
	Apple	98706	'92	CS/CD
Electronic Sound	Zapple	3358	'69	†
All Things Must Pass	Apple/Capitol	(3) 639	'70	†
	Capitol	(3) 46688		LP/CS
	Capitol	(2) 46688		CD
Living in the Material World	Apple/Capitol	3410	'73	†
	Capitol	16216		†
	Apple	94110	'92	CS/CD
Dark Horse	Apple/Capitol	3418	'74	†
	Capitol	16055		†
	Apple	98079	'92	CS/CD
Extra Texture	Apple/Capitol	3420	'75	†
	Capitol	16217		†
	Apple	98080	'92	CS/CD
The Best of George Harrison	Capitol	11578	'76	CS
	Capitol	46682		CD
33 & 1/3	Dark Horse	3005	'76	†
	Dark Horse	26612	'91	CD
George Harrison	Dark Horse	3255	'79	†
	Dark Horse	26613	'91	CD
Somewhere in England	Dark Horse	3492	'81	†
	Dark Horse	26614	'91	CD
Gone Troppo	Dark Horse	23734	'82	†
	Dark Horse	26615	'91	CD
Cloud Nine	Dark Horse	25643	'87	CS/CD
The Best of Dark Horse, 1976–1989	Dark Horse	25726	'89	CS/CD
Live in Japan	Dark Horse	(2) 26964	'92	CS/CD

George Harrison and Friends

The Concert for Bangladesh	Apple	(3) 3385	'72	†
	Capitol	(2) 93265	'91	CD
	Columbia/Legacy	(2) 48616	'91	CS

The Traveling Wilburys

Volume One	Wilbury	25796	'88	CS/CD
Volume 3	Wilbury	26324	'90	CS/CD

ISAAC HAYES

(b. Aug. 20, 1942, Covington, TN)

Session musician to Otis Redding and other Stax/Volt artists, and coauthor (with David Porter) of '60s soul classics such as "Hold On! I'm Comin'" and "Soul Man," Isaac Hayes established himself as a recording artist with 1969's *Hot Buttered Soul*. The album established the "rap" introduction format to songs later exploited by Barry White, and popularized the sensual, romantic side of soul later plied by White and Marvin Gaye; it broke soul music's preoccupation with the three-minute song and infused it with an unprecedented level of musical sophistication and complexity. Hayes's 1971 album *Shaft* established both the scratch guitar rhythm and wah-wah bass in soul music, and was the first of a spate of massively successful soundtrack albums to '70s black-oriented movies.

Isaac "Ike" Hayes began singing with the Morning Stars vocal group after moving to Memphis with his family. He later took up piano and saxophone, and worked as a session musician, songwriter, and producer at Stax/Volt Records after meeting Floyd Newman of the Mar-Keys. Otis Redding's longtime keyboard accompanist, Hayes played organ on Redding's first major pop hit, "I've Been Loving You Too Long (To Stop Now)." In collaboration with David Porter, Hayes wrote "I Got to Love Somebody's Baby" for Johnnie Taylor and "B-A-B-Y" for Carla Thomas. The team also wrote three smash soul and major pop hits for Sam and Dave: "Hold On! I'm Comin'," "Soul Man," and "I Thank You."

Initiating his own recording career in 1967 on Enterprise Records, Isaac Hayes scored a smash success with 1969's *Hot Buttered Soul*. The album featured "rap" song introductions, elaborately orchestrated arrangements, and lengthy song renditions that became standard soul music practices (and eventually clichés) while yielding the two-sided pop and soul hit "Walk on By"/"By the Time I Get to Phoenix." The best-selling follow-up, *The Isaac Hayes Movement*, included the major soul and moderate pop hit "I Stand Accused." In 1971 he achieved a smash soul and major pop hit with "Never Can Say Goodbye."

Isaac Hayes arranged, performed, and wrote, in part, the soundtrack to the immensely popular 1971 movie *Shaft*. Released a year before Curtis Mayfield's *Super Fly*, *Shaft* was the first of a series of best-selling soundtracks to black-oriented movies. Of the 15 tracks, only 3 featured vocals; "Theme from Shaft" became a smash soul and pop hit, and "Do Your Thing" became a smash soul and major pop hit.

Assuming the persona of Black Moses, replete with shaven head, gold chains, and an entourage of beautiful women, Isaac Hayes was soon established on the supper-club circuit, as evidenced by *Live at the Sahara Tahoe*. He scored a smash soul and major pop hit with "Joy—Pt. 1" in 1974, the year he composed the score for the movies *Tough Guys* and *Truck Turner*; he starred in both films. Forming Hot Buttered Soul (HBS) Records under the affiliation of ABC Records in 1975 for five albums, including a live duet set with Dionne Warwick, Hayes later switched to Polydor for his last major pop hit, a remake of Roy Hamilton's "Don't Let Go," and five albums, including *Royal Rappin's*, recorded with Millie Jackson. Moving to Columbia Records in the mid-'80s, Isaac Hayes scored a near-smash soul hit with "Ike's Rap" in 1986. Isaac Hayes eventually returned to the studio for two 1995 albums for Pointblank Records, *Branded* and the instrumental *Raw and Refined*.

Isaac Hayes

In the Beginning	Atlantic	1599	'72	†
Presenting Isaac Hayes	Enterprise	13-100	'68	†
	Stax	8596	'95	CD
Hot Buttered Soul	Enterprise	1001	'69	†
	Stax	4114	'78	LP/CS/CD
The Isaac Hayes Movement	Enterprise	1010	'70	†
	Stax	4129	'80	LP/CS/CD
To Be Continued . . .	Enterprise	1014	'70	†
	Stax	4133		LP/CS/CD
Shaft (soundtrack)	Enterprise	(2) 5002	'71	†
	Stax	(2) 88002	'78	LP/CS
Black Moses	Enterprise	(2) 5003	'71	†
	Stax	(2) 88006		CD
Excerpts from "Black Moses"	Stax	8509		LP/CS
Live at the Sahara Tahoe	Enterprise	(2) 5005	'73	†
	Stax	(2) 88004		LP/CD
	Stax	88004		CS
Joy	Enterprise	5007	'73	†
	Stax	8530		LP/CS/CD
Tough Guys (soundtrack)	Enterprise	7504	'74	†
Truck Turner (soundtrack)	Enterprise	(2) 7507	'74	†
Tough Guys/Truck Turner (soundtracks)	Stax	(2) 88014	'93	CD
The Best of Isaac Hayes	Enterprise	7510	'75	†
Hotbed	Stax	4102	'78	LP/CS
Enterprise: His Greatest Hits	Stax	(2) 88003	'80	LP
	Stax	88003	'80	CS
Greatest Hit Singles	Stax	8515	'82	LP/CS/CD
The Best of Isaac Hayes, Volume 1	Stax	60001		CD
The Best of Isaac Hayes, Volume 2	Stax	60002		CD
Chocolate Chip	Hot Buttered Soul	874	'75	†
Groove-a-Thon	Hot Buttered Soul	925	'76	†
Juicy Fruit (Disco Freak)	Hot Buttered Soul	953	'76	†
New Horizon	Polydor	6120	'77	†
For the Sake of Love	Polydor	6164	'78	†
Don't Let Go	Polydor	6224	'79	†
	Polygram	843770		CS
And Once Again	Polydor	6269	'80	†
Lifetime Thing	Polydor	6329	'81	†
U-Turn	Columbia	40316	'86	CS/CD†
Love Attack	Columbia	40941	'88	CS/CD
Branded	Pointblank/Virgin	40335	'95	CS/CD
Raw and Refined	Pointblank/Virgin	40336	'95	CS/CD

Isaac Hayes and Dionne Warwick

A Man and a Woman	ABC	(2) 996	'77	†
	MCA	(2) 10012	'80	†

Isaac Hayes and Millie Jackson

Royal Rappin's					
	Polydor	6229	'79		†
	Westbound	059			CD

JIMI HENDRIX

THE JIMI HENDRIX EXPERIENCE. Jimi Hendrix (b. James Marshall Hendrix, Nov. 27, 1942, Seattle, WA; d. Sept. 18, 1970, London, England), lead gtr, lead voc; **Noel Redding** (b. Dec. 25, 1945, Folkstone, England), bs, background voc; **John "Mitch" Mitchell** (b. July 9, 1946, London, England), drm

JIMI HENDRIX

One of the two superstar rock guitarists of the '60s, Jimi Hendrix is revered by many as *the* master virtuoso of the electric guitar. Undoubtedly the most adventurous and daring electric guitarist of the '60s, Hendrix is regarded by some as rock's single most important instrumentalist and perhaps the most influential guitarist ever.

Hendrix enormously expanded the possibilities of the electric guitar, masterfully manipulating devices such as the wah-wah pedal, fuzz-box, and delay mechanism to produce sounds sometimes gentle and melodic, but more often loud and psychedelic, even extraterrestrial and aquatic. His masterful and imaginative use of studio techniques with equipment that would be regarded as primitive by today's standards vastly extended the potential of recorded electric music. His carefully controlled use of distortion and feedback laid the foundation for *all* the heavy-metal guitarists that followed, and inspired jazz musicians, such as Miles Davis, to adopt certain elements of rock music, leading to the development of so-called fusion music.

A left-handed guitarist, Jimi Hendrix astoundingly played a right-handed guitar upside down and backward, rather than using a left-handed guitar. Perhaps rock music's most outstanding and flamboyant showman during his days with the Jimi Hendrix Experience, he performed old bluesmen's showstopping techniques, such as playing the guitar behind his back or head, playing the guitar with his teeth, and aggressively caressing, humping, and attacking his guitar with such sexual lewdness as to become instantly notorious. As rock music's first black superstar, he was the first black musician to shatter the recording industry's preoccupation with blacks as singles artists and establish himself as an album artist.

James Hendrix obtained his first acoustic guitar at age 11, graduating to electric guitar at 12. Playing in a number of Seattle-area bands by 14, he dropped out of high school at 16 and eventually joined the Army in 1963. While serving he became a paratrooper and met and jammed with bassist Billy Cox. Discharged after slightly more than a year because of a back injury sustained in a parachute jump, Hendrix subsequently toured the South's chitlin' circuit, backing artists such as B. B. King, Sam Cooke, and Jackie Wilson. He then worked for Little Richard and Ike and Tina Turner before moving to New York in 1964 to back the Isley Brothers and King Curtis and recording with Curtis Knight and Lonnie Youngblood. The following year he formed his own group, Jimmy James and the Blue Flames, for engagements around Greenwich Village. "Discovered" there by former Animals bassist Bryan "Chas" Chandler, Hendrix went to England at Chandler's behest in September 1966, forming the Jimi Hendrix Experience with two English musicians, Noel Redding and Mitch Mitchell.

The Jimi Hendrix Experience became an immediate success in Great Britain, scoring major hits with "Hey Joe," "Purple Haze," and "The Wind Cries Mary" in early 1967. Commencing their first British tour in March, the group's debut album, *Are You Experienced?*, containing all three singles, was riding high on the British charts when they debuted in the United States at the Monterey Pop Festival in June. The widely heralded performance included Hendrix's covers of Dylan's "Like a Rolling Stone" and the awe-inspiring finale, "Wild Thing," which culminated in Hendrix torching his lighter-fluid-drenched guitar. Word of Hendrix's spectacular, flamboyant Monterey performance spread rapidly, and *Are You Experienced?*, upon American release on Reprise Records in August, became an instant best-seller, remaining on the album charts for more than two years, although it yielded only minor hit singles with the classics "Purple Haze" and "Foxey Lady." Following an abortive tour with the Monkees (a mismatch if ever there was one), Hendrix returned to England.

The Jimi Hendrix Experience's *Axis: Bold as Love*, released stateside in early 1968, became another immediate best-seller, producing the minor hit "Up from the Skies" and containing the masterful "Little Wing," the gentle "One Rainy Wish," and the ominous "If 6 Was 9," later used in the breakthrough Peter Fonda–Dennis Hopper movie *Easy Rider*. *Electric Ladyland*, the Experience's final album and the crowning achievement of their brief recording career, yielded the group's only major hit, Dylan's "All Along the Watchtower," in its definitive version. Included on the double-record set were the vituperative "Crosstown Traffic," the lilting "Rainy Day, Dream Away," the challenging "1983," and the extended jam "Voodoo Chile," featuring Steve Winwood on organ.

Tours by the Experience in 1968 saw Hendrix retreating from his role as psychedelic, flash guitarist-showman, much to the chagrin of inflexible fans. In November the Jimi Hendrix Experience announced their intention to disband, although contractual obligations kept the group together into 1969. Noel Redding formed Fat Mattress in 1969, Road in 1971, and the Noel Redding Band in 1975. Mitch Mitchell continued to play with Hendrix on-and-off until Hendrix's death, briefly becoming a member of Ramatam with former Iron Butterfly guitarist Mike Pinera in 1972.

During 1969 Jimi Hendrix began building his own studio, Electric Ladyland, in New York City, while seldom performing publicly. He eventually logged more than six hundred hours of studio tapes with various participants, including jazz musicians such as John McLaughlin. In August Hendrix, backed by Mitch Mitchell and Army buddy Billy Cox, played the Woodstock Festival. The performance closed with a stunning version of "The Star-Spangled Banner," replete with the sounds of rockets and bombs that accurately portrayed the violence of both past and contemporary American cultures, which appropriately segued into "Purple Haze" (later included on the first *Woodstock* album).

On New Year's Eve, 1969–1970, the all-black Band of Gypsys (Hendrix, Cox, and drummer Buddy Miles) debuted at Bill Graham's Fillmore East. The performance, recorded and later released in album form, included Miles's "(Them) Changes" and Hendrix's 12-minute-plus "Machine Gun." However, the group never really worked out, perhaps due to Buddy Miles's overbearing drumming style.

Jimi Hendrix was soon recording his next album, a double-record set tentatively entitled *First Rays of the New Rising Sun*, with Mitch Mitchell and Billy Cox. During the spring and summer of 1970, Hendrix toured with them, opening his Electric Ladyland studio shortly before their August appearance at the Isle of Wight. On September 18, 1970, Jimi Hendrix died of "inhalation of vomit due to barbiturate intoxication" in London at age 27. His death served to amplify his reputation and legend, and he became, along with Jim Morrison, Elvis Presley, and John Lennon, one of the most exploited and mythologized of all dead rock stars.

Much of the material from *First Rays of the New Rising Sun* was ultimately released on *The Cry of Love* and *Rainbow Bridge*, and reissued on *Voodoo Soup* in 1995. *The Cry of Love* featured Buddy Miles on "Ezy Rider" and Noel Redding on "My Friend" and included two excellent but overlooked slow blues songs, "Drifting" and "Angel." *Rainbow Bridge* contained "Dolly Dagger," "Pali Gap," and the live "Hear My Train a Comin'." *Hendrix in the West* assembled live recordings such as Chuck Berry's "Johnny B. Goode" and the Hendrix originals "Red House," "Little Wing," and "Voodoo Chile." *War Heroes* contained nearly completed recordings by Hendrix, including "Izabella" and "Stepping Stone." *Soundtrack Recordings from the Film "Jimi Hendrix"* compiled live performances and interviews.

In 1974 the estate of Jimi Hendrix hired producer Alan Douglas to sort through the tape archives left by Jimi Hendrix. For *Crash Landing* and *Midnight Lightning*, Douglas erased the original sidemen and grafted on Los Angeles session players, while *Nine to the Universe* was taken from the jam sessions recorded in 1969–1970. Subsequent album releases included the live compilation *The Jimi Hendrix Concerts*, the complete *Jimi Plays Monterey*, *Radio One* (live recordings made for the BBC in 1967), and the four-CD anthology of alternate takes, demonstration records, live performances, and interviews, *Lifelines*. In 1993 Reprise issued the tribute album *Stone Free*, on which various contemporary artists, from Ice-T to Eric Clapton, the Pretenders to Nigel Kennedy, recorded versions of Jimi Hendrix's songs. Hendrix's recordings, from his first work backing Little Richard and the Isley Brothers through almost everything he put on tape on his own, have been packaged and repackaged in a bewildering number of versions, on LP, CD, and cassette, a testimony to his continued popularity. In 1992 Jimi Hendrix was inducted into the Rock and Roll Hall of Fame.

Jimi Hendrix and Little Richard

Roots of Rock	Archive of Folk and Jazz Music	296	'74	†
Together	Pickwick	3347		†

Jimi Hendrix with the Isley Brothers

In the Beginning	T-Neck	3007	'71	†

Jimi Hendrix and Curtis Knight

Get That Feeling	Capitol	2856	'67	†
Flashing	Capitol	2894	'68	†
Get That Feeling/Flashing	Capitol	(2) 659	'71	†

Jimi Hendrix and Lonnie Youngblood

Together	Maple	6004	'71	†

The Jimi Hendrix Experience/Otis Redding

At Monterey	Reprise	2029	'70	†

The Jimi Hendrix Experience

Are You Experienced?	Reprise	6261	'67	LP/CS/CD†
	MCA	10893	'93	CS/CD
Axis: Bold as Love	Reprise	6281	'68	LP/CS/CD†
	MCA	10894	'93	CS/CD
Electric Ladyland	Reprise	(2) 6307	'68	†
	Reprise	6307		CS/CD†
	MCA	10895	'93	CS/CD
Smash Hits	Reprise	2276	'69	LP/CS/CD†
The Ultimate Experience	MCA	10829	'93	CS/CD
The Experience Collection	MCA	(4) 10936	'93	CS/CD

Fat Mattress (with Noel Redding)

Fat Mattress	Atco	33-309	'69	†
Fat Mattress II	Atco	33-347	'71	†

The Noel Redding Band

Clonkakilty Cowboys	RCA	1237	'75	†
Blowin'	RCA	1863	'76	†

Ramatam (with Mitch Mitchell)

Ramatam	Atlantic	7236	'72	†

Band of Gypsys

Band of Gypsys	Capitol	472	'70	†
	Capitol	16319		†
	Capitol	96414	'95	LP/CS/CD
Band of Gypsys 2	Capitol	12416	'86	†

Live Recordings by Jimi Hendrix (in release order)

Hendrix in the West	Reprise	2049	'72	†
The Jimi Hendrix Concerts	Reprise	(2) 22306	'82	†
Jimi Plays Monterey (recorded June 18, 1967)	Reprise	25358	'86	LP/CS/CD†
In Concert	Springboard Int'l	4031		†
Live at Winterland (recorded October 1968)	Rykodisc	20038	'87	CS/CD
	Rykodisc	90038	'88	CD
The Last Experience Concert	Zeta	517		CD
Woodstock (recorded August 1969)	MCA	11063	'94	CS/CD

Posthumous Releases

The Cry of Love	Reprise	2034	'71	LP/CS/CD†
Rainbow Bridge	Reprise	2040	'71	†
War Heroes	Reprise	2103	'72	†
Soundtrack Recordings from the Film "Jimi Hendrix"	Reprise	(2) 6481	'73	†
Crash Landing	Reprise	2204	'75	LP/CS/CD|
Midnight Lightning	Reprise	2229	'75	†
The Essential Jimi Hendrix	Reprise	(2) 2245	'78	†
The Essential Jimi Hendrix, Volume II	Reprise	2293	'79	†
The Essential Jimi Hendrix, Volume 1 and 2	Reprise	(2) 26035		CD†
Nine to the Universe	Warner Bros.	2299	'80	†
Kiss the Sky	Reprise	25119	'84/'85	LP/CS/CD†
Lifelines: The Jimi Hendrix Story	Reprise	(4) 26435	'91	CS/CD†
Stages	Reprise	(4) 26732	'91	CS/CD†
Blues	MCA	11060	'94	CS/CD
Voodoo Soup	MCA	11236	'95	CS/CD

Anthologies

In the Beginning	Shout	502	'72	†
Rare Hendrix	Trip	9500	'72	†
Roots of Hendrix	Trip	9501	'73	†
The Genius of Jimi Hendrix	Trip	9523	'74	†
Superpak	Trip	(2) 3509	'76	†
Very Best	United Artists	505	'76	†
Jimi	Pickwick	3528	'76	†
Before London	Accord	7101	'81	†
Free Spirit	Accord	7112	'81	†
Cosmic Feeling	Accord	7139	'81	†
Radio One (recorded 1967)	Rykodisc	20078	'88	CS/CD
Rock and Roll	Richmond	2153		CS

Tribute Album

Stone Free: A Tribute to Jimi Hendrix	Reprise	45438	'93	CS/CD

HERMAN'S HERMITS

Peter "Herman" Noone (b. Nov. 5, 1947, Manchester, England), voc, pno, gtr; **Keith Hopwood** (b. Oct. 26, 1946, Manchester, England), rhythm gtr; **Derek "Lek" Leckenby** (b. May 14, 1946, Leeds, England; d. June 4, 1994), lead gtr; **Karl Green** (b. July 31, 1947, Salford, England), bs; **Barry Whitwam** (b. July 21, 1946, Manchester, England), drm

Following on the heels of the Beatles, Herman's Hermits enjoyed greater popularity in the United States than in Great Britain, with their novelty songs, covers, and teen-oriented material. Showing greater sophistication in their song selection in the later '60s ("Dandy," "No Milk Today"), Herman's Hermits broke up in 1971, although a group continued to tour under that name without lead vocalist Peter Noone, who pursued a varied entertainment career on his own.

Formed in 1962 by Peter Noone as the Heartbeats, Peter became Herman and the group became his Hermits at the behest of producer Mickie Most. The group actually played their instruments on the first (major) hit from late 1964, Carole King and Gerry Goffin's "I'm Into Something Good." Future Led Zeppelin members Jimmy Page and John Paul Jones handled much of the subsequent guitar and bass work. In 1965 Herman's Hermits scored smash hits with "Can't You Hear My Heartbeat," remakes of the Rays's "Silhouettes" and Sam Cooke's "Wonderful World," the ditties "Mrs. Brown You've Got a Lovely Daughter" and "I'm Henry VIII, I Am," and "Just a Little Bit Better." In 1966 the group starred in the movie *Hold On!*, which yielded the smash hits "A Must to Avoid" and "Leaning on a Lamp Post." That year they also scored smash hits with "Listen People," from the Connie Francis movie *When the Boys Meet the Girls*, and "Dandy," written by the Kinks' Ray Davies.

Following the 1967 smash "There's a Kind of Hush" (backed with "No Milk Today"), Herman's Hermits managed only major hits through 1968, with "Don't Go into the Rain (You're Going to Melt)" and "I Can Take or Leave Your Loving." The group persevered until 1971, when Noone began a solo career. In 1973 original members Green, Leckenby, and Whitwam reconstituted Herman's Hermits. Leckenby died of non-Hodgkin's lymphoma on June 4, 1994.

Peter Noone subsequently appeared in an English television comedy show for three years before moving to the south of France, where he recorded a number of hit French singles. He later moved to Los Angeles and became a studio musician. In 1980 Noone recorded an album with the Tremblers for Johnston Records, for whom he recorded a solo album in 1982. He played Frederic in *The Pirates of Penzance* on Broadway later that year and launched a five-year comeback plan in 1986. Beginning in 1989, Peter Noone hosted a music-video show, *My Generation*, on cable channel VH-1. He recut "I'm Into Something Good" for the hit film *The Naked Gun* in 1992.

Herman's Hermits

Introducing Herman's Hermits	MGM	4282	'65	†
On Tour	MGM	4295	'65	†
Best	MGM	4315	'65	†
Hold On!	MGM	4342	'66	†
Both Sides of Herman's Hermits	MGM	4386	'66	†
Best, Volume II	MGM	4416	'66	†
There's a Kind of Hush All Over the World	MGM	4438	'67	†
Blaze	MGM	4478	'67	†
Best, Volume III	MGM	4505	'67	†
Mrs. Brown, You've Got a Lovely Daughter	MGM	4548	'68	†
Their Greatest Hits	Abkco	4227	'73/'88	LP/CS/CD
Greatest Hits	Hollywood/IMG	386		CS/CD

The Tremblers

Twice Nightly	Johnston	36532	'80	†

Peter Noone

One of the Glory Boys	Johnston	37369	'82	†

JOHN HIATT

(b. 1952, Indianapolis, IN)

Along with Graham Parker, John Hiatt was one of the most overlooked and underappreciated singer-songwriters to begin recording in the '70s. His often acerbic songs fall into both country and R&B stylings; and although his 1987 *Bring the Family* album finally brought him critical acclaim, he has yet to find a wide audience as a performer.

John Hiatt picked up guitar at age 11, and as a teenager played in Indianapolis-area R&B bands such as the White Ducks in the late '60s. In 1970 he moved to Nashville, where he worked as a songwriter for Tree Publishing beginning in 1971. His compositions included 1974's major pop hit "Sure As I'm Sittin' Here" for Three Dog Night and "Heavy Tears," recorded by Conway Twitty. He signed with Epic Records and recorded two albums for the label before touring solo, moving to Los Angeles, and switching to MCA for *Slug Line* and *Two-Bit Monsters*, his first albums to garner any attention. The Neville Brothers recorded his "Washable Ink" in 1978, and Dave Edmunds recorded his "Something Happens" in 1981.

In the early '80s John Hiatt recorded with Ry Cooder, contributing "The Way We Make a Broken Heart" to *Borderline* and adding guitar and vocals to *The Slide Area*. He also recorded three albums for Geffen Records, including *Riding with the King*, before suffering the suicide of his estranged wife. He subsequently cleaned up after years of alcohol and drug abuse and retreated to Nashville. During this time Rosanne Cash recorded his "Pink Bedroom," Nick Lowe his "She Don't Love Nobody," and Rodney Crowell his "She Loves the Jerk."

John Hiatt finally made his breakthrough with 1987's *Bring the Family*, recorded with Ry Cooder, Nick Lowe on bass, and session drummer Jim Keltner. The album included "Memphis in the Meantime," "Have a Little Faith in Me," "Learning How to Love You," and "Thing

Called Love"; the last song was Bonnie Raitt's first comeback hit in 1988. The follow-up, *Slow Turning*, was recorded with Hiatt's then-touring band, the Goners, and featured "Icy Blue Heart" (recorded by Emmylou Harris in 1989), "Is Anybody Out There?," the rocker "Tennessee Plates," and the oft-covered "Drive South." In 1987 Rosanne Cash scored a top country hit with his "The Way We Make a Broken Heart," and the Jeff Healey Band had a smash pop hit with his "Angel Eyes" in 1989. That year Geffen issued a compilation of his recordings made between 1979 and 1985.

Despite critical acclaim for his compelling, highly personal songwriting and distinctive, expressive voice, 1990's *Stolen Moments* also failed to produce any hit singles for John Hiatt. The album contained "Real Fine Love," "Bring Back Your Love to Me," "Rest of the Dream," and "Through Your Hands." In 1991 Hiatt joined Ry Cooder, Nick Lowe, and Jim Keltner in the collective band Little Village. The group's sole album, with Hiatt on lead vocals for 6 of the 11 songs, sold respectably, but did not really establish any of the participants as major stars.

In 1993 Rhino Records issued an album of other artists performing Hiatt's songs, while Hiatt recorded *Perfectly Good Guitar*. Rocking more than his previous three albums, it included the title cut, "Something Wild," the romantic "Straight Outta Time," and the controversial "Wreck of the Barbie Ferrari." Hiatt completed his years at A&M with a live album recorded with the same band who accompanied him on *Perfectly Good Guitar*, featuring many of his better recent songs.

Hiatt moved to Capitol Records in 1995 to issue *Walk On*. This collection of songs about a failed marriage included the title track, "Cry Love" (issued as a single), and "Dust on a Country Road."

John Hiatt

Hanging Around the Observatory	Epic	32688	'74	†
	Epic/Legacy	32688	'91	CD
Overcoats	Epic	33190	'75/'91	CD
Slug Line	MCA	3088	'79	†
	MCA	748		†
	MCA	31358	'90	CD
Two-Bit Monster	MCA	5123	'80	†
	MCA	741		†
	MCA	31359	'90	CD
All of a Sudden	Geffen	2009	'82	†
Riding with the King	Geffen	4017	'83	CS/CD
Warming Up the Ice Age	Geffen	24055	'85	CS/CD
Y'all Caught?: The Ones that Got Away, 1979–1985	Geffen	24247	'89	CS/CD
Bring the Family	A&M	5158	'87	CS/CD
	Mobile Fidelity	603	'94	CD
	Mobile Fidelity	210	'94	LP
Slow Turning	A&M	5206	'88	CS/CD
Stolen Moments	A&M	5310	'90	CS/CD
Perfectly Good Guitar	A&M	0135	'93	CS/CD
Hiatt Comes Alive at Budokan	A&M	540284	'94	CS/CD
Walk On	Capitol	33416	'95	CS/CD

Little Village

Little Village	Reprise	26713	'92	CS/CD

Tribute Album

Love Gets Strange: The Songs of John Hiatt	Rhino	71267	'93	CS/CD

DAN HICKS

Dan Hicks (b. Dec. 9, 1941, Little Rock, AR); **Sid Page** (b. 1947, Portland, OR)

Evolving out of the Charlatans, perhaps the first San Francisco hippie band, Dan Hicks and his Hot Licks recorded four albums between 1969 and 1973 that effectively combined elements of vocal jazz, Western swing, and jug-band music in an acoustic setting. Featuring the outstanding fiddle work of Sid Page and the precise vocal harmonies of two female singers (known as the Lickettes), the band was fronted by singer-songwriter-guitarist Dan Hicks, whose wry, amusing songs include "How Can I Miss You When You Won't Go Away," "Canned Music," "I Scare Myself," "By Hook or by Crook," and "Moody Richard (The Innocent Bystander)." Although the group never produced a hit single, Dan Hicks and His Hot Licks later inspired nostalgia acts such as Manhattan Transfer, the Pointer Sisters, and Bette Midler. The group disbanded in 1973, with Hicks reemerging in the '80s with His Acoustic Warriors for engagements largely on the West Coast. In 1984 Sid Page recorded the jazz album *Odyssey* with David Shelander. Dan Hicks eventually returned to recording for 1994's *Shootin' Straight*.

The Charlatans

The Charlatans	Philips	600309	'69	†
	One Way	31442	'95	CD

Dan Hicks and His Hot Licks

Original Recordings	Epic	26464	'69	†
	Sony	26464		CS/CD†
Where's the Money	Blue Thumb	29	'71	†
	MCA	31337	'89	CD
Striking It Rich!	Blue Thumb	36	'72	†
	MCA	31187		CD
Last Train to Hicksville	Blue Thumb	51	'73	†
	MCA	31188		CD
Dan Hicks and His Hot Licks	K-tel	75053		CS/CD

Dan Hicks

It Happened One Bite	Warner Bros.	3158	'78	†

Dan Hicks and His Acoustic Warriors

Shootin' Straight	On the Spot	62118	'94	CS/CD

Sid Page and David Shelander

Odyssey	Bainbridge	6257	'84	CD

HOLLAND-DOZIER-HOLLAND

Eddie Holland (b. Oct. 30, 1939, Detroit, MI); **Lamont Dozier** (b. June 16, 1941, Detroit, MI); **Brian Holland** (b. Feb. 15, 1941, Detroit, MI)

Motown Records' premier songwriting-production team, rivaled only by William "Smokey" Robinson in the early '60s and Norman Whitfield–Barrett Strong in the late '60s, Eddie Holland, Lamont Dozier, and Brian Holland were largely responsible for the Motown Sound. Utilizing an excellent team of session musicians and sophisticated studio equipment, Holland-Dozier-Holland (hereafter referred to as H-D-H) composed and produced more than 25 Top 10 hits for Motown that registered popularity with black and white audiences and thrust soul into the forefront of American popular music in the '60s. Severing relations with Motown in 1968, H-D-H continued their hit-making ways on their own labels Invictus and Hot Wax in the early '70s. Recently Lamont Dozier has been active as a songwriter and recording artist.

Lamont Dozier began singing as a child in his grandmother's church choir. He wrote his first song at age 10 and made his recording debut with the Romeos at 15. In 1958 he met Berry Gordy Jr., and he recorded as Lamont Anthony for Gordy's Anna Records in 1961. Eddie Holland dropped out of college to work for Gordy and later scored one of Motown's first hits, "Jamie," in 1962. Brother Brian Holland collaborated on two early hits for the Marvelettes, "Please Mr. Postman" and "Playboy."

In 1963 Brian and Eddie Holland and Lamont Dozier teamed up as a songwriting-production unit. Between 1963 and the end of 1967, H-D-H wrote and produced the majority of Motown's hit singles, with Brian and Lamont providing the music and Eddie the lyrics. Their hit crossover songs included "Heat Wave," "Quicksand," and "Nowhere to Run" for Martha and the Vandellas, "Mickey's Monkey" for the Miracles, and "How Sweet It Is (To Be Loved by You)" for Marvin Gaye.

Much of H-D-H's finest material was provided to the Four Tops and the Supremes. Their song hits for the Four Tops included "Baby I Need Your Loving," "I Can't Help Myself," "It's the Same Old Song," "Reach Out, I'll Be There," "Standing in the Shadows of Love," and "Bernadette." H-D-H's biggest success came with the Supremes, regarded by many as Motown's premier act. The team wrote and produced at least 10 top pop and smash soul hits for the Supremes, as well as numerous major hits. These included "Where Did Our Love Go," "Baby Love," "Come See About Me," "Stop! In the Name of Love," "Back in My Arms Again," "I Hear a Symphony," "My World Is Empty Without You," "Love Is Like an Itching in My Heart," "You Can't Hurry Love," "You Keep Me Hangin' On," "Love Is Here and Now You're Gone," and "The Happening" (with Frank DeVol). H-D-H extended their string of hits for the group as Diana Ross and the Supremes in 1967 with "Reflections" and "In and Out of Love." In addition, Eddie Holland collaborated with Norman Whitfield in 1966 on several major hits for the Temptations, including "Ain't Too Proud to Beg," "Beauty Is Only Skin Deep," and "(I Know) I'm Losing You."

However, in 1968 Brian Holland, Lamont Dozier, and Eddie Holland bitterly quit Motown to form their own record labels, Invictus and Hot Wax. A series of lawsuits ensued between Motown and H-D-H, and the team was enjoined from writing songs after May 1969. Nonetheless, they produced a number of hits in the early '70s. Invictus crossover hits included "Give Me Just a Little More," "Pay to the Piper," "Chairman of the Board," and "Finder's Keepers" by the Chairmen of the Board, and "Band of Gold," "Deeper and Deeper," and the controversial "Bring the Boys Home" by Freda Payne. Crossover hits on Hot Wax included "Somebody's Been Sleeping" by 100 Proof Aged in Soul, and "Girls It Ain't Easy," "Want Ads," "Stick-Up," "One Monkey Don't Stop No Show," and "The Day I Found Myself" by Honey Cone.

Following an out-of-court settlement of the Motown/H-D-H lawsuits in early 1972, Brian Holland and Lamont Dozier returned to active recording, scoring major soul and minor pop hits with "Why Can't We Be Lovers" and "Don't Leave Me Starvin' for Your Love" on Invictus. In 1973 Dozier left the Hollands to pursue a solo recording career, achieving smash soul and major pop hits with "Trying to Hold On to My Woman" and "Fish Ain't Biting," and a soul smash with "Let Me Start Tonight" on ABC Records in 1974. Dozier later switched to Warner Bros. Records, then Columbia. During the mid- to late '80s, Lamont Dozier was busy writing songs for Simply Red, Boz Scaggs, and Eric Clapton, and the soundtrack to the Phil Collins movie *Buster*. In 1991 he recorded *Inside Seduction* for Atlantic Records.

Eddie Holland

| Eddie Holland | Motown | 604 | '63 | † |

Lamont Dozier

Out Here on My Own	ABC	804	'74	†
Black Bach	ABC	839	'74	†
Love and Beauty	Invictus	33134	'74	†
Right There	Warner Bros.	2929	'76	†
Peddlin' Music on the Side	Warner Bros.	3039	'77	†
Bittersweet	Warner Bros.	3282	'78	†
Working on You	Columbia	37129	'81	†
Inside Seduction	Atlantic	82228	'91	CS/CD

THE HOLLIES

Allan Clarke (b. Apr. 5, 1942, Salford, Lancashire, England), lead voc; **Graham Nash** (b. Feb. 2, 1942, Blackpool, Lancashire, England), harmony voc, gtr; **Tony Hicks** (b. Dec. 16, 1945, Nelson, Lancashire, England), lead gtr, voc, bjo; **Eric Haydock** (b. Sept. 16, 1944, Burnley, Lancashire, England), bs; **Bobby Elliott** (b. Dec. 8, 1942, Burnley, England), drm [Eric Haydock was replaced by **Bernie Calvert** (b. Sept. 16, 1943, Burnley, England) in 1966, and **Terry Sylvester** (b. Jan. 8, 1945, Liverpool, England) took over for Graham Nash in 1968.]

One of the most popular British singles groups to emerge in the wake of the Beatles, the Hollies achieved their mid-'60s success on the basis of Allan Clarke's distinctive lead vocals, the whining, high-pitched and sometimes harsh harmonies of Graham Nash and Tony Hicks, and the songwriting of Graham Gouldman and the Clarke-Hicks-Nash team. Never able to make serious inroads as an album group, essentially restricted to pop material, the Hollies persevered after the 1968 departure of Nash to score smash hits with "He Ain't Heavy, He's My Brother," "Long Cool Woman (In a Black Dress)," and "The Air That I Breathe." Clarke, Nash, Hicks, and Elliott reunited briefly in 1983.

Allan Clarke and Graham Nash became friends in elementary school and later sang together as the Two Teens, Ricky and Dane, and the Guytones. They added other members and became the Fourtones and then the Deltas. In 1962 the two teamed with Tony Hicks and two others. By 1963, with one replacement, the group had become the Hollies, with Clarke, Nash, Hicks, Eric Haydock, and Bobby Elliott. Signed to Parlophone Records (Imperial in the United States) in early 1963, the Hollies scored British hits with "Searchin'" and "Stay" before scoring their first (minor) American hit with "Just One Look" in 1964. Although "I'm Alive" became a top British hit in 1965, the group did not have even a moderate American hit until "Look Through Any Window," written by Graham Gouldman. The group toured the United States for the first time in spring 1965, replacing Haydock with Bernie Calvert in early 1966. Years earlier, Calvert had been a member of the Dolphins with Tony Hicks and Bobby Elliott.

The Hollies' most successful years were 1966 and 1967. After scoring a smash hit with Graham Gouldman's "Bus Stop," they hit with "Stop! Stop! Stop!," "On a Carousel," "Pay You Back with Interest," and "Carrie Anne," all Clarke-Hicks-Nash collaborations, the last on Epic Records. An attempt to make inroads in the album market with *Dear Eloise/King Midas in Reverse* failed, and Nash, unhappy with the prospect of recording an album of Bob Dylan songs, left the group in late 1968 to join David Crosby and Steve Stills in the supergroup Crosby, Stills and Nash. Nash was replaced by vocalist–rhythm guitarist Terry Sylvester, a former member of the Swinging Blue Jeans (1964's "Hippy Hippy Shake").

In 1969–1970 the rather maudlin ballad "He Ain't Heavy, He's My Brother" became a near-smash hit for the Hollies. In October 1971 the group fired Allan Clarke, who pursued a neglected solo career. Nonetheless, he was the lead vocalist on the 1972's smash hit "Long Cool Woman (In a Black Dress)" from *Distant Light*, which also produced a major hit with "Long Dark Road." *Greatest Hits*, released in 1973, included the group's hits on both the Imperial and Epic labels. Clarke was back for 1974's *The Hollies*, which contained the smash hit "The Air That I Breathe." The group continued to record for Epic through 1978. In 1983 Hollies mainstays Tony Hicks and Bobby Elliott reunited briefly with Allan Clarke and Graham Nash for *What Goes Around* and a major hit with the old Supremes' number "Stop in the Name of Love." Clarke, Hicks, Elliott, Sylvester, and Haydock have continued to tour on the oldies circuit under the Hollies name, and have made a few recordings, most notably 1993's "The Woman I Love," a minor British hit.

The Hollies

Here I Go Again	Imperial	12265	'65	†
Hear! Here!	Imperial	12299	'66	†
Beat Group	Imperial	12312	'66	†
Bus Stop	Imperial	12330	'66	†
Stop! Stop! Stop!	Imperial	12339	'67	†
Evolution	Epic	26315	'67	†
Dear Eloise/King Midas in Reverse	Epic	26344	'68	†
Words and Music By Bob Dylan	Epic	26447	'69	†
He Ain't Heavy, He's My Brother	Epic	26538	'70	†
	Columbia	13092	'76	†
Moving Finger	Epic	30255	'71	†
Distant Light	Epic	30958	'72/'91	CD
Romany	Epic	31992	'73	†
The Hollies	Epic	32574	'74	†
	Columbia/Legacy	32574	'91	CD
Another Night	Epic	33387	'75	†
Clarke, Hicks, Sylvester, Elliott, Calvert	Epic	34714	'77	†
Crazy Steal	Epic	35334	'78	†
What Goes Around	Atlantic	80076	'83	†

Anthologies

Greatest Hits	Imperial	12350	'67	†
Greatest Hits	Epic	32061	'73	CS/CD
Epic Anthology: From the Original Master Tapes	Epic	46161	'90	CS/CD
Very Best	United Artists	329	'75	†
The Hollies' Greatest	Capitol	16056	'80	†
Hottest Hits	Pair	(2) 1041	'86	†
More Great Hits (1963–1968)	EMI-America	16397	'86	†
The Best of the Hollies	EMI-America	10329	'87	†
	EMI	92882		CS/CD†
Later Hits	EMI-America	16482	'87	†
Best, Volume I	EMI-Manhattan	46584	'88	CS/CD†
Best, Volume II	EMI-Manhattan	48831	'88	CS/CD†
The 30th Anniversary Collection	EMI	(3) 99917	'93	CD
All-Time Greatest Hits	Curb/CEMA	77377	'90	CS/CD
Magic Touch	IMG	706		CS

Allan Clarke

My Real Name Is 'Arold	Epic	31757	'72	†
I've Got Time	Asylum	1056	'76	†
I Wasn't Born Yesterday	Atlantic	19175	'78	†

Legendary Heroes	Curb	267	'80	†
Terry Sylvester				
Terry Sylvester	Epic	33076	'74	†

BUDDY HOLLY

(b. Charles Hardin Holley, Sept. 7, 1936, Lubbock, TX; d. Feb. 2, 1959, near Mason City, IA)

THE CRICKETS. Buddy Holly, gtr, voc; **Niki Sullivan**, gtr; **Joe Mauldin**, stand-up bs;
Jerry Allison (b. Aug. 31, 1939, Hillsboro, TX), drm

BUDDY HOLLY

One of the two great singer-song-writer-guitarists of the '50s (the other being Chuck Berry), Buddy Holly was probably the first rock artist to concern himself with virtually every aspect of his music, including arranging and record production. Coming from a country-and-western background, Holly was one of the first white musicians to apply the heavy backbeat of black R&B to country and pop material. With the Crickets, he originated the standard lineup for the rock band (lead and rhythm guitars, bass, and drums) and set the precedent for the self-contained rock band. One of the earliest innovators of rock and roll, Holly pioneered the studio techniques of overdubbing and double tracking under producer Norman Petty. Later utilizing vocal choirs and a studio orchestra, Holly became one of the originators of the modern pop song within the rock tradition. Probably the first rock-and-roll legend, due to his early accidental death, Buddy Holly and his legacy inspired numerous contemporary artists, and he lives on in the work of many (Linda Ronstadt in particular), despite a career that lasted just two years.

Buddy Holly took up violin and piano at age 11, soon switching to acoustic guitar. He met guitarist Bob Montgomery, with whom he became a popular local duo, in the seventh grade. The two played western and bop music on radio station KDAV in Lubbock between 1953 and 1955, recording a number of songs later released on the album *Holly in the Hills*. Spotted opening for Bill Haley and the Comets in Lubbock, Holly was soon signed to Decca Records. Three times during 1956 he traveled to Nashville to record under veteran producer Owen Bradley, the second time accompanied by the Three Tunes: guitarist Sonny Curtis, bassist Don Guess, and drummer Jerry Allison. These recordings, issued in 1958 as *That'll Be the Day*, included an early version of "That'll Be the Day," as well as "Rock Around with Ollie Vee" and "Midnight Shift." However, none of Decca's 1956 singles releases became hits.

Subsequently released from his contract by Decca, Buddy Holly started recording at producer Norman Petty's studio in Clovis, New Mexico, in February 1957 with rhythm guitarist Niki Sullivan, bassist Larry Welborn, and Three Tunes drummer Jerry Allison. The session yielded another version of the Holly-Allison collaboration "That'll Be the Day" that found its way to Bob Thiele after being rejected by Roulette Records. Thiele released the song on Brunswick Records under the name the Crickets and quickly signed the group. By September the song had become a smash pop, R&B, and British hit.

In April 1957 the Crickets came together with Sullivan, Allison, and stand-up bassist Joe B. Mauldin. Norman Petty took over the career of Buddy Holly and the Crickets as manager, producer, session leader, and occasional keyboardist, negotiating separate contracts for the Crickets with Brunswick and for Holly with Coral Records. Holly soon scored a pop and R&B hit with the classic rock song "Peggy Sue" (backed with "Everyday"), while the Crickets had major crossover hits with "Oh, Boy!" (backed with "Not Fade Away") and "Maybe Baby." The debut Crickets album, *The "Chirping" Crickets*, was released at the end of 1957, but Sullivan left the group in December. Reduced to a trio, Holly was obliged to play both lead and rhythm guitar on tours of the United States and, in early 1958, Australia and England.

During 1958, pop-only hits included "Think It Over" for the Crickets and "Rave On" and Bobby Darin's "Early in the Morning" for Buddy Holly. "Early in the Morning" was recorded in New York without the Crickets, but with vocal choir and saxophonist Stan "The Man" Taylor. However, "It's So Easy" and "Heartbeat," recorded with guitarist Tommy Allsup, fared poorly, and by October the Crickets had split from Holly and Holly had left Norman Petty. Holly married Maria Elena Santiago in August and moved to New York, where he recorded "True Love Ways," "Raining in My Heart," and Paul Anka's "It Doesn't Matter Anymore" under producer Dick Jacobs, utilizing Jacobs's orchestra. Holly then embarked on a tour of the Midwest with guitarist Allsup, drummer Charlie Bunch, and guitarist-turned-bassist Waylon Jennings. Following a concert at Clear Lake, Iowa, on February 2, 1959, Buddy Holly, then 22, Ritchie Valens ("Donna," "La Bamba"), and J. P. "Big Bopper" Richardson ("Chantilly Lace") died when their chartered plane crashed shortly after take-off. Jennings had been bumped from the plane, and Dion and the Belmonts, also on the tour, had made alternate travel arrangements.

"It Doesn't Matter Anymore" (backed with "Raining in My Heart") soon became a major hit for Buddy Holly. Norman Petty assembled a variety of Buddy Holly albums and singles from old tapes, overdubbing various instrumentation. The Crickets stayed together through 1965, recording one album for Coral and three for Liberty, including one with Bobby Vee. Sonny Curtis wrote "I Fought the Law," a near-smash hit for the Bobby Fuller Four in 1966, and cowrote with Jerry Allison "More Than I Can Say," a smash hit for Leo Sayer in 1980. Curtis recorded into the '80s, scoring major country hits with "Love Is All Around" in 1980 and "Good Ol' Girls" in 1981. Bob Montgomery proved successful as a songwriter ("Misty Blue") and an independent producer for Johnny Darrell and Bobby Goldsboro. Waylon Jennings struggled as a country-and-western artist through the '70s, finally achieving recognition as an "outlaw" country musician in 1976. Norman Petty died on August 15, 1984, in Lubbock after a long illness.

During the '60s Buddy Holly's legacy was kept alive, as the Rolling Stones debuted in the American charts with "Not Fade Away," Peter and Gordon hit with "True Love Ways," and the Bobby Fuller Four scored a major hit with Holly's "Love's Made a Fool of You." The Beatles freely acknowledged Holly's influence on their songwriting, and Paul McCartney became a promoter of Holly's songs in the '80s after he purchased the rights to the catalog. In the latter half of the '70s Linda Ronstadt recorded a number of Holly's songs, hitting with "That'll Be the Day" and "It's So Easy." In May 1978 *The Buddy Holly Story*, starring Gary Busey, was released, becoming a surprise film hit and sparking revitalized interest in

Holly. *Buddy*, a stage musical based on the life and songs of Buddy Holly, debuted in London in October 1989 and toured the United States in 1990.

Buddy Holly and Bob Montgomery

Holly in the Hills	Coral	757463	'65	†
Buddy Holly and the Crickets				
The "Chirping" Crickets	Brunswick	54038	'57	†
	MCA	31182	'88	CS/CD
(reissued as) Buddy Holly and the Crickets	Coral	757405	'62	†
Buddy Holly				
That'll Be the Day	Decca	8707	'58	†
(reissued as) The Great Buddy Holly	Vocalion	73811	'67	†
	Coral/MCA	20101		†
	MCA	31037		CD†
Buddy Holly	Coral	57210	'58	†
	MCA	25239	'89	LP/CS/CD†
The Buddy Holly Story	Coral	57279	'59	†
The Buddy Holly Story, Volume 2	Coral	57326	'60	†
Reminiscing	Coral	757426	'63	†
Buddy Holly Showcase	Coral	757450	'64	†
The Best of Buddy Holly	Coral	8	'66	†
Greatest Hits	Coral	757492	'67	†
Giant	Coral	757504	'69	†
Good Rockin'	Vocalion	73293	'71	†
Buddy Holly: A Rock 'n' Roll Collection	Decca	(2) 7207	'72	†
	MCA	(2) 4009		†
20 Golden Greats	MCA	3040	'78	†
	MCA	1484		CS/CD
Buddy Holly Complete	MCA	(6) 80000	'81	†
(reissued as) The Complete Buddy Holly	MCA	(6) 80000		CS
From the Original Master Tapes	MCA	5540		CD
Legend	MCA	(2) 4184		CS
Best	MCA	20290		†
For the First Time Anywhere	MCA	27059	'87	LP/CS†
	MCA	31048	'87	CD†
Buddy Holly	Bella Musica	89919	'90	CD†
Soundtrack Albums				
The Buddy Holly Story	Epic	35412	'78/'87	CS/CD
Buddy: The Buddy Holly Story	Relativity/	1048		CS/CD
(1989 London first night original cast)	First Night			
Tribute Album				
Every Day Is a Holly Day	Emergo	9465	'89	LP/CS/CD†
The Crickets				
In the Style with the Crickets	Coral	757320	'61	†
Bobby Vee Meets the Crickets	Liberty	7228	'62	†
Somethin' Else	Liberty	7272	'63	†
California Sun	Liberty	7351	'64	†
The Liberty Years	EMI	95845	'91	CS/CD
Rockin' 50s Rock and Roll	Barnaby	30268	'71	†
Remnants	Mercury	695	'74	†

WHITNEY HOUSTON
(b. Aug. 9, 1963, Newark, NJ)

In a carefully orchestrated career, Whitney Houston was established simultaneously in the R&B, pop, and easy-listening fields with her 1985 self-named release. The album sold 18 million copies worldwide, making it the biggest-selling debut album ever and challenging Carole King's *Tapestry* as best-selling album ever by a female vocalist. Her second album, *Whitney*, became the first album by a female singer to debut at the top of the charts; she was the biggest pop music vocalist of the time, and the top-selling female recording artist in the world. However, despite possessing an exquisite, technically precise, three-octave voice, Houston was criticized for both her song selection and her emotional conviction as a recording artist. In 1992 she starred with Kevin Costner in the surprise hit movie *The Bodyguard*, and the film's soundtrack, featuring six songs sung by Houston, became one of the best-selling soundtracks ever, yielding five hits.

The daughter of gospel/soul singer Cissy Houston, Whitney Houston began singing in her mother's New Hope Baptist Church choir in Newark at age 4, debuting as a soloist at 11. She toured with her mother, lead singer of the Sweet Inspirations, as a teenager, singing "The Greatest Love of All" as a soloist. She also recorded commercial jingles and provided background vocals for the likes of Chaka Khan and Lou Rawls. In 1979 she began a modeling career, appearing in the magazines *Glamour*, *Seventeen*, and *Cosmopolitan*.

Whitney Houston was signed to Arista Records by president Clive Davis in April 1983 after being showcased to industry executives at a special concert in a Manhattan nightclub. She scored her first smash soul and moderate pop hit in 1984 with "Hold Me," in duet with Teddy Pendergrass. Her eponymous debut album, released in 1985, was an instant best-seller, staying on the album charts for more than three years and yielding smash pop, R&B, and easy-listening hits with "You Give Good Love," "Saving All My Love for You," "How Will I Know," and "The Greatest Love of All." She toured in 1986 and 1987, but her concerts were not particularly well-received by critics, who found her performances bland and emotionally vapid. Nonetheless, her next album, *Whitney*, produced five smash crossover hits with "I Wanna Dance with Somebody (Who Loves Me)," "Didn't We Almost Have It All," "So Emotional," "Where Do Broken Hearts Go," and "Love Will Save the Day." She scored a smash pop hit with "One Moment in Time," used as the theme for NBC-TV's broadcast of the 1988 Summer Olympics, and she achieved a moderate pop hit in duet with Aretha Franklin on "It Isn't, It Wasn't, It Ain't Never Gonna Be" in 1989.

Plagued by rumors regarding her personal affairs and attacked as a prima donna who was "too white" to be an R&B artist, Whitney Houston did not release another album until 1990, more than three years after *Whitney*. *I'm Your Baby Tonight* yielded the three-way crossover smashes title tune and "All the Man That I Need" (originally recorded by Sister Sledge in 1982), the near-smash "Miracle," and the major hit "My Name Is Not Susan." She even managed a major pop hit in 1991 with "The Star-Spangled Banner," recorded "live" at Super Bowl XXV, although it was later revealed the performance was "partly prerecorded." She starred in her first solo concert on television (HBO) in March 1991, welcoming home troops from the Persian Gulf, and subsequently toured North America.

In 1992 Whitney Houston starred as a misunderstood, maligned female vocalist in the surprise hit film *The Bodyguard* with Kevin Costner. The soundtrack album contained 12 songs, including 6 performed by Houston, 5 of which became hits: Dolly Parton's "I Will Always Love You" (which topped all three charts and was one of the fastest-selling singles in history), Nicholas Ashford and Valerie Simpson's "I'm Every Woman," "I Have Nothing," "Run to You," and "Queen of the Night."

On July 18, 1992, Whitney Houston married singer Bobby Brown, a former member of New Edition. The couple hit in late 1993 with "Something in Common," from Brown's

Remixes N the Key of B. Whitney Houston toured in 1993 and again in 1994, subsequently shifting her attention to movie projects. In 1995 she scored another surprise box-office hit with the film *Waiting to Exhale*, while her performance of the title song "Waiting to Exhale (The Shoop-Shoop Song)" was another major hit. Rumors of marital trouble continued to plague her throughout that year.

Whitney Houston

Whitney Houston	Arista	8212	'85	LP/CS/CD
Whitney	Arista	8405	'87	LP/CS/CD
I'm Your Baby Tonight	Arista	8616	'90	LP/CS/CD
The Bodyguard (soundtrack)	Arista	18699	'92	CS/CD

I

JANIS IAN

(b. Janis Eddy Fink, Apr. 7, 1951, New York, NY)

In and out of the music business since age 14, singer-songwriter Janis Ian is best remembered for 1967's socially conscious hit "Society's Child" and 1975's song of adolescent angst, "At Seventeen." Starting as a folksinger in 1965, Ian dropped out of music between 1968 and 1971, ultimately reemerging with the best-selling album *Between the Lines*. The author of Roberta Flack's 1973 major pop and soul hit ballad "Jesse," Ian was again largely absent from the music scene during the first half of the '80s. She resumed touring in 1986 and moved to Nashville in 1988, where she collaborated with country songwriter Kye Fleming. Ian returned with 1993's *Breaking the Silence*, which served to announce her "coming out" as a lesbian.

Janis Ian

Janis Ian	Verve	3017	'67	†
For All the Seasons of Your Mind	Verve	3024	'67	†
The Secret Life of J. Eddy Fink	Verve	3048	'68	†
Who Really Cares	Verve	3063	'71	†
Society's Child: The Verve Recordings	Chronicles/Polydor	7591	'95	CD
Present Company	Capitol	683	'71	†
	One Way	17962	'94	CD
Stars	Columbia	32857	'74	†
Between the Lines	Columbia	33394	'75	CS/CD
Aftertones	Columbia	33919	'76	†
Miracle Row	Columbia	34440	'77	†
Janis Ian	Columbia	35325	'78	†
Night Rains	Columbia	36139	'79	†
Restless Eyes	Columbia	37360	'81	†
Breaking the Silence	Morgan Creek	20023	'93	CS/CD

ICE-T

(b. Tracy Marrow, c. late '50s, Newark, NJ)

BODY COUNT. Ice-T, voc; **Ernie-C** (Eric Cunningham) and **D-Roc** (Dennis Miles), gtrs; **Moose Man** (Lloyd Roberts), bs; **Beat Master V** (Victor Wilson), drm

One of the most outspoken purveyors of rap music from the West Coast, Ice-T helped develop and popularize the style know as gangsta rap, with its menacing, violent, and often misogynist depiction of crime and street-life in South Central Los Angeles. Ice-T helped open the door for N.W.A., Ice Cube, and other gangsta rappers of the '90s. While winning popularity with black youths trapped in the ghetto lifestyle, Ice-T successfully garnered perhaps the biggest following of any rap act among white youth, whom he consciously sought to educate about the realities of an existence most of them had never known. In 1992 Ice-T formed and joined the speed-metal band Body Count for touring and recording, but the resulting album sparked a national controversy because of the lyrics to the song "Cop Killer."

Tracy Marrow wrote rhymes for Los Angeles gangs in the '70s and became a street criminal in South Central Los Angeles in the early '80s after serving in the military for four years. As Ice-T, he recorded "The Coldest Rap" for a local label in 1982 and made his film debut in *Breakin'* in 1984. Signed to Sire Records, Ice T's debut album featured "Make It Funky," "Somebody Gotta Do It (Pimpin' Ain't Easy)," and "Squeeze the Trigger," and became a surprise best-seller. In 1988 he performed the frightful theme to the controversial movie *Colors*, recorded the album *Power*, with "I'm Your Pusher" and "Radio Suckers," and formed his own Rhyme Syndicate label, recording acts such as Hijack and Lord Finesse. As Ice-T the Iceberg he recorded *Freedom of Speech . . . Just Watch What You Say* in 1989. The album included "Girl Tried to Kill Me," "Hit the Deck," "Lethal Weapon," and "Shut Up, Be Happy." In 1991 he starred with Denzel Washington in the film *Ricochet*, and as a police officer in the Mario Van Peebles drug-and-crime film *New Jack City*; he also contributed to the soundtrack. He proclaimed himself the "Original Gangster" with an album of the same name that contained "Bitches 2," "Body Count," "Straight Up Nigga," and "Home of the Bodybag." The album yielded a minor pop hit with "New Jack Hustler (Nino's Theme)."

In 1992 Ice-T formed Body Count with longtime associate Ernie-C. Favoring a frantic, hard-driving form of heavy metal known as speed metal, Body Count almost immediately found themselves in the eye of a virulent controversy over the lyrics to "Cop Killer" from their debut album. Police associations protested that the song advocated killing police officers, and political luminaries such as George Bush and Dan Quayle attacked Ice-T and his label's distributor, Time-Warner, Inc. The album, which otherwise included the antidrug "Winner Loses," the virulent "There Goes the Neighborhood," the sexist "KKK Bitch," and the hateful "Mama's Gotta Die Tonight," was later reissued without "Cop Killer." Ice-T appeared in the 1992 movie *Trespass* and, at year's end he voluntarily ended his association (and that of Body Count) with Time-Warner and Sire Records. The band moved to Virgin Records for 1994's *Born Dead*, with "Surviving the Game," the antidrug diatribe "Street Lobotomy," and the domestic-violence revenge fantasy "Who Are You?" Nonetheless, the free-speech controversy continued, as Time-Warner sold its interest in Interscope Records in 1995. The label had distributed Snoop Doggy Dogg's recordings and recorded Tupac Shakur and Nine Inch Nails, acts attacked as tasteless, sexist, and nihilistic. In 1995 Ice-T appeared in the odd but amusing cartoonlike movie *Tank Girl*.

Ice-T

Rhyme Pays	Sire	25602	'87	CS/CD
Power	Sire	25765	'88	CS/CD
Freedom of Speech . . . Just Watch What You Say	Sire	26028	'89	CS/CD
O.G.—Original Gangster	Sire	26492	'91	CS/CD
Home Invasion	Rhyme Syndicate	53858	'93	LP/CS/CD
The Classic Collection	Rhino	71170	'93	CS/CD

Body Count

Body Count	Sire	26878	'92	CS/CD†
	Sire	45139	'92	CS/CD
Born Dead	Virgin	39802	'94	LP/CS/CD

IRON BUTTERFLY

Doug Ingle (b. Sept. 9, 1946, Omaha, NE), voc, kybd; **Erik Braunn** (b. Aug. 11, 1950, Boston, MA), gtr; **Lee Dorman** (b. Sept. 15, 1945, St. Louis, MO), bs; **Ron Bushy** (b. Sept. 23, 1945, Washington, D.C.), drm

One of the first American heavy-metal bands, Iron Butterfly burst onto the music scene in 1968 with Doug Ingle's 17-minute epic "In-a-Gadda-Da-Vida," one of the longest album cuts in rock music at the time. *In-a-Gadda-Da-Vida* remained on the album charts for nearly three years and sustained the group's career until they disbanded in 1971. (The personnel list above reflects the lineup as of the time of their best-known recording.) Iron Butterfly also re-formed briefly in 1975. Considered an important group in their day, they are now more or less forgotten.

Iron Butterfly

Heavy	Atco	33227	'68	†
	Rhino	71521	'93	CD
In-a-Gadda-Da-Vida	Atco	33250	'68	CS/CD
Ball	Atco	33280	'69/'91	CD
Live	Atco	33318	'70	CD
Metamorphosis	Atco	33339	'70	†
	Rhino	71522	'93	CD
The Best of Iron Butterfly/Evolution	Atco	33369	'71	†
Scorching Beauty	MCA	465	'75	†
Sun and Steel	MCA	2164	'75	†
Rare Flight	Pair	1065	'86	CD
Light and Heavy: The Best of Iron Butterfly	Rhino	71166	'93	CS/CD

THE ISLEY BROTHERS

Ronald Isley (b. May 21, 1941, Cincinnati, OH); **O'Kelly Isley** (b. Dec. 25, 1937, Cincinnati, OH; d. Mar. 31, 1986); **Rudolph Isley** (b. Apr. 1, 1939, Cincinnati, OH) [In September 1969 they were joined by **Ernie Isley** (b. Mar. 7, 1952), lead guitar and drums; **Marvin Isley**, bass and percussion; and **Chris Jasper**, keyboards.]

The long-lived R&B/soul vocal group the Isley Brothers recorded for a variety of labels following their 1959 hit classic "Shout," enjoying success over the years with R&B, rock, and disco-style music. After a stint with Motown Records, the brothers gained a large measure of control over their recordings at T-Neck Records beginning in 1969, thus becoming one of the first black acts to achieve independence from major record companies. Joined by younger brothers Ernie and Marvin and brother-in-law Chris Jasper that year, the group became a self-contained band for smash soul hits and several best-selling albums through 1983. The new members began recording separately from Isley brothers Ronald and Rudolph in 1984, with Ernie, Marvin, and Ronald reuniting as the Isley Brothers in 1990.

Isley brothers Ronald and O'Kelly began performing as gospel singers backed by mother Sallye Isley in the mid-'40s. Joined by brothers Vernon and Rudolph, the quartet sang at churches in Cincinnati and later toured churches throughout the Midwest. Reduced to a trio by the accidental death of Vernon at age 11, the Isley Brothers moved to New York in 1956, recording unsuccessful singles for the Teenage, Cindy, Gone, and Mark X labels. Debuting at the Howard Theater in Washington, D.C., the brothers were later showcased at New York's Apollo Theater and signed to RCA Victor Records. In 1959 they scored a mod-

THE ISLEY BROTHERS

erate pop hit with their own composition, "Shout."

Following one album for RCA, the Isley Brothers recorded for Atlantic Records under producers Jerry Leiber and Mike Stoller before joining Florence Greenberg's Scepter Records subsidiary Wand for the smash R&B and major pop hit classic "Twist and Shout" (later a hit for the Beatles). In 1963 they moved to United Artists Records, later touring the chitlin' circuit with then-unknown guitarist Jimi Hendrix in their backup band.

In 1964 the Isley Brothers formed their own production company, T-Neck (named after their adopted hometown, Teaneck, New Jersey), but a solitary release by the company, distributed by Atlantic, fared poorly. By late 1965 the brothers had moved to Motown Records, where they achieved a near-smash R&B and major pop hit with "This Old Heart of Mine (Is Weak for You)." Recording two albums for Tamla, they subsequently managed only minor pop and moderate R&B hits for the label.

By 1969 the Isley Brothers had revived T-Neck, working out a distribution deal with Buddah Records. Their first release on T-Neck, "It's Your Thing," became a smash R&B and pop hit early that year. The three vocalizing Isley brothers were joined by younger brothers Ernie and Marvin and brother-in-law Chris Jasper in September 1969 to form a self-contained band. Hits through the early '70s included the R&B smashes "I Turned You On" and Steve Stills's "Love the One You're With" (both major pop hits), and "Lay-Away" and "Pop That Thang."

The Isley Brothers switched distributorship of T-Neck to Columbia in 1973, firmly establishing themselves as album artists with *3 + 3*, which yielded the pop and R&B smash "That Lady," featuring Ernie's phase-shifter lead-guitar work, and the R&B smashes "What It Comes Down To" and "Summer Breeze." Following the R&B smashes "Live It Up" and "Midnight Sky," the Isley Brothers scored their biggest album success with *The Heat Is On*, which produced the top R&B and smash pop hit "Fight the Power" and major hit "For the Love of You."

Although the Isley Brothers did not score any more major pop hits, they continued to achieve R&B smashes through 1983, with "Who Loves You Better," "The Pride," "Livin' in the Life," "Take Me to Your Next Phase," "I Wanna Be with You," "Don't Say Goodnight (It's Time for Love)," "Between the Sheets," and "Choosey Lover." In 1984 Ernie and Marvin Isley and Chris Jasper began recording as Isley, Jasper, Isley, scoring a top R&B hit with "Caravan of Love" in 1985. Reduced to a duo with the death of O'Kelly Isley from a heart attack on March 31, 1986, Ronald and Rudolph Isley achieved a smash R&B hit with "Smooth

Sailin' Tonight" on Warner Bros. Records in 1987. In late 1990 Ernie, Marvin, and Ronald Isley reunited as the Isley Brothers.

The Isley Brothers

The Isley Brothers and Marvin and Johnny	Crown	5352		†
Shout	RCA	2156	'59	†
Shout! The Complete Victor Sessions	RCA	9901		CS/CD
Twist and Shout	Wand	653	'62	†
Take Some Time Out	Scepter	552		†
Twisting and Shouting	United Artists	6313	'64	†
The Complete UA Sessions	EMI	95203	'91	CS/CD
This Old Heart of Mine	Tamla	269	'66	†
	Motown	5128	'89	CS/CD
Soul on the Rocks	Tamla	275	'68	†
	Motown	5425	'89	CD
This Old Heart of Mine/Soul on the Rocks	Motown	8156		CD†
Greatest Hits and Rare	Motown	5483	'91	CS/CD
In the Beginning (with Jimi Hendrix)	T-Neck	3007	'71	†
It's Our Thing	T-Neck	3001	'69	†
Brothers Isley	T-Neck	3002	'69	†
Live at Yankee Stadium	T-Neck	3004	'69	†
Get Into Something	T-Neck	3006	'71	†
Givin' It Back	T-Neck	3008	'71	†
Brother, Brother, Brother	T-Neck	3009	'72	†
Live	T-Neck	3010	'73	†
3 + 3	T-Neck	32453	'73	CS/CD
Live It Up	T-Neck	33070	'74	†
The Heat Is On	T-Neck	33536	'75	CS/CD
Harvest for the World	T-Neck	33809	'76/'87	CS
Go for Your Guns	T-Neck	34432	'77	CS/CD
Showdown	T-Neck	34930	'78	CS
Winner Takes All	T-Neck	36077	'79/'86	CS/CD
Go All the Way	T-Neck	36305	'80	CS
Grand Slam	T-Neck	37080	'81	CS
Inside You	T-Neck	37553	'81	†
The Real Deal	T-Neck	38047	'82	†
Between the Sheets	T-Neck	38674	'83/'85	CS/CD
Masterpiece	Warner Bros.	25347	'85	†
Smooth Sailin'	Warner Bros.	25586	'87	CS/CD
The Isley Brothers Live	Elektra	61538	'93	CS/CD
Beautiful Ballads	Philadelphia Int'l	57860	'94	CS/CD

Anthologies

Do Their Thing	Sunset	5257	'69	†
Doin' Their Thing	Tamla	287	'70	†
Motown Superstar Series, Volume 6	Motown	5106		†
This Old Heart of Mine	Pickwick	3398		†
Rock On, Brother	Camden	0126	'73	†
Country/Rock Around the Clock	Camden	0861	'75	†
Best	Buddah	(2) 5652	'76	†
Very Best	United Artists	500	'76	†
Greatest His	T-Neck	3011	'73	†

Forever Gold	T-Neck	34452	'77	†
Timeless	T-Neck	35650	'78	†
Greatest Hits, Volume 1	T-Neck	39240	'84	CS/CD
This Old Heart of Mine: Isley Brothers Greatest Hits	Curb/CEMA	77333	'90	CS/CD
The Isley Brothers Story, Volume 1: Rockin' Soul, 1959–1968	Rhino	70908	'91	CS/CD
The Isley Brothers Story, Volume 2: T-Neck Years, 1969–1985	Rhino	(2) 70909	'91	CS/CD
Soul Kings, Volume 1	SMS	56	'95	CD
At Their Best	Special Music	4804		CS/CD
Shout	Collectables	5103		LP/CS/CD
16 Greatest Hits	Deluxe	7899		CS
Shout and Twist With Rudolph, Ronald and O'Kelly	Ace	928		CD

The Isley Brothers featuring Ronald Isley

Spend the Night	Warner Bros.	25940	'89	CS/CD
Tracks of Life	Warner Bros.	26620	'92	CS/CD

Isley, Jasper, Isley

Broadway's Closer to Sunset Boulevard	T-Neck	39873	'84	†
Caravan of Love	Columbia	40118	'85	CS/CD
Different Drummer	CBS Associated	40409	'87	CS/CD†

Ernie Isley

High Wire	Elektra	60902	'90	CS/CD

J

THE JACKSON FAMILY

Maureen "Rebbie" (b. May 29, 1950, Gary, IN); **Sigmund "Jackie"** (b. May 4, 1951, Gary, IN); **Toriano "Tito"** (b. Oct. 15, 1953, Gary, IN); **Jermaine** (b. Dec. 11, 1954, Gary, IN); **La Toya** (b. May 29, 1956, Gary, IN), **Marlon** (b. March 12, 1957, Gary, IN); **Michael** (b. Aug. 29, 1958, Gary, IN), **Randy** (b. Steven Randall, Oct. 29, 1961, Gary, IN), **Janet** (b. May 16, 1966, Gary, IN) [The Jackson Five/The Jacksons were Michael, lead vocals; Jackie, vocals and guitar; Marlon, guitar and vocals; Jermaine, bass and vocals; and Tito, guitar and vocals. Randy, vocals and keyboards, replaced Jermaine in 1976; Jermaine rejoined in 1984; Michael left in 1986.]

THE JACKSONS

The last major act introduced by the Motown Records organization, the Jackson Five enjoyed enormous crossover success with youthful black and white audiences in the first half of the '70s as purveyors of best-selling singles of innocent pop-style love and dance songs. Although he initially shared lead vocals with brother Jackie, Michael Jackson quickly took center stage with the Jackson Five, thanks to his boyish charm and exuberance and dance moves incorporated from James Brown and Jackie Wilson.

Challenged by white "family" groups such as the Osmonds and the Partridge Family, the Jackson Five quickly launched the solo careers of Michael and Jermaine Jackson, with Michael faring the better. Moving to Epic Records in 1976 without Jermaine, the Jackson Five became the Jacksons for several crossover hits through 1984.

The Jackson family were encouraged in their musical careers by their guitar-playing father, who had played in a local group before his marriage. The older sons formed a trio in the early '60s and were quickly joined by Michael and Marlon to form the original Jackson Five. The group played locally and even began to undertake limited tours as an opening act for other R&B groups. They were invited to try out for Motown Records in 1969, and their filmed audition, showing a very young Michael performing James Brown—esque dance moves, clinched the deal with Berry Gordy. He relocated the group to Los Angeles (where the label was now headquartered), and in classic Motown fashion began reshaping their image, dressing them in the latest "mod" fashions (large floppy hats, flowered shirts, exaggerated bell-bottoms, and boots). They hit it big almost immediately in January 1970 with "I Want You Back," followed quickly by the top pop and R&B hits "ABC," "The Love You Save," and "I'll Be There"; "Mama's Pearl" and "Never Can Say Goodbye" were smash hits in both fields, and "Maybe Tomorrow" and "Sugar Daddy" became smash R&B and major pop hits. The group was so popular that a cartoon series was launched in 1971 featuring animated Jacksons, to appeal to the kiddie market.

Motown also tried to market the individual Jacksons as pop stars in their own right. In late 1971 Michael Jackson's solo career was launched with the crossover smash "Got to Be There," followed in 1972 by a remake of Bobby Day's "Rockin' Robin," "I Wanna Be Where You Are," and "Ben," the title song to a movie about a trained rat. Jermaine's solo career started in 1972, but his success was largely limited to a smash remake of Shep and the Limelites "Daddy's Home" in early 1973. Jackie Jackson's solo debut on Motown from 1973 failed to produce any hits.

The Jackson Five continued to score major pop and smash R&B hits for Motown through 1973 with a remake of "Little Bitty Pretty One," "Lookin' Through the Windows," "Corner of the Sky," "Hallelujah Day," and "Get It Together." "Dancing Machine" became a top R&B and smash pop hit in 1974, followed by the R&B smashes "Whatever You Got, I Want," "I Am Love (Parts I and II)" (a major pop hit), and "Forever Came Today." In 1975 Michael scored the R&B smashes "We're Almost There" and "Just a Little Bit of You" (a major pop hit), yet he would not achieve another hit until leaving Motown.

In 1976 the Jackson Five switched to Epic Records, but Jermaine, who had married Berry Gordy's daughter Hazel in 1973, left the group and continued to record for Motown through 1982, scoring his biggest successes with 1980's "Let's Get Serious" and 1982's "Let Me Tickle Your Fancy." Adding brother Randy, the group was legally forced to abandon the name Jackson Five, becoming simply the Jacksons, after Motown sued for breach of contract. Their enormous success continued through 1980, highlighted by the pop and R&B smashes "Enjoy Yourself" and "Shake Your Body (Down to the Ground)," and the major pop and R&B smashes "Show You the Way to Go," "Lovely One," and "Heartbreak Hotel." In 1978 Michael Jackson costarred with longtime friend Diana Ross in the movie remake of *The Wizard of Oz*, *The Wiz*, which yielded his last Motown hit, "Ease on Down the Road," in duet with Ross.

In 1979 Michael Jackson also moved to Epic Records, where his debut, *Off the Wall*, became a phenomenal success, staying on the album charts for more than three years and selling more than six million copies. The album yielded two top pop and R&B hits, "Don't Stop 'Til You Get Enough" and "Rock with You," and two major pop hits, "Off the Wall" (an R&B smash) and "She's Out of My Life." LaToya Jackson, who had sung backup with the Jackson Five, started her solo career on Polydor Records in 1980, switching to Private I Records in 1984, where she scored her only significant success with "Heart Don't Lie," a major R&B hit. She is estranged from the rest of the family, and has been the most vocally critical of her parents and siblings. LaToya has provoked scandal by posing nude for *Playboy*, as well as through her well-publicized brawls with her husband, who manages her career.

Thanks to the production of Quincy Jones and a carefully orchestrated and sequenced promotional campaign, Michael Jackson's *Thriller* became the best-selling album of all time, eventually moving nearly 50 million copies worldwide. The first single, "The Girl Is

Mine," a duet with Paul McCartney, became a top R&B and easy-listening and smash pop hit. The second, "Billie Jean," became a top pop and R&B hit, in large part due to frequent airplay of its promotional video on MTV, the first by a black artist to receive such extensive exposure. The third, "Beat It," was heavily promoted as a video by MTV and featured the dynamic lead-guitar playing of heavy-metal icon Eddie Van Halen. Subsequently, "Wanna Be Startin' Somethin'" and "Thriller" became smash pop and R&B hits, "Human Nature" became a smash pop and major R&B hit, and "P.Y.T. (Pretty Young Thing)" became a major pop hit. In the meantime, a second duet with McCartney, "Say Say Say" from McCartney's *Pipes of Peace* album, became a top pop and smash R&B hit.

The year 1984 was the most successful year in the career of many of the other members of the Jackson family. Jermaine scored major pop and R&B hits with "Dynamite" and "Do What You Do" on Arista Records. Rebbie, who had worked with the Jacksons from 1974 to 1977, achieved a major pop and smash R&B hit with "Centipede" on Columbia Records. Jermaine rejoined his other brothers in the Jacksons for their hugely successful *Victory* album and tour. The album yielded a pop and R&B smash, "State of Shock," with lead vocals by Michael and Mick Jagger, and a major pop and R&B hit, "Torture," with lead vocals by Michael and Jermaine. By 1986 Michael had left the Jacksons, and the group endured into the '90s with little success. Marlon's 1987 debut solo album on Capitol yielded the R&B smash "Don't Go."

The youngest Jackson, Janet, had debuted with the Jackson Five at the MGM Grand in Las Vegas in 1973 at age seven. In the late '70s Janet Jackson inaugurated her acting career on television, appearing in the series *Good Times*, *A New Kind of Family*, and *Different Strokes* through 1982. That year she launched her solo recording career on A&M Records, scoring near-smash R&B hits with "Young Love" in 1982 and "Don't Stand Another Chance" in 1984. Her recordings were dismissed as superficial pop until she linked up with producer-songwriters Jimmy Jam and Terry Lewis for 1986's *Control*. As a coming-of-age album, *Control* explored the vagaries and aspirations of young womanhood. It sold eight million copies, establishing Janet as a potent force with a largely teenage audience. The album yielded six hits: five top R&B hits (four pop smashes) with "What Have You Done for Me Lately," "Nasty," "Control," "Let's Wait Awhile," and "The Pleasure Principle," and the top pop and smash R&B hit "When I Think of You." Like brother Michael, Janet produced heavily choreographed videos to promote these songs, which received heavy exposure on MTV.

After cowriting with Lionel Richie and performing on the "We Are the World" single in 1985 and starring in the 15-minute movie *Captain Eo*, shown exclusively at Disneyland and Disney World, Michael Jackson recorded another album under producer Quincy Jones. *Bad* was released in August 1987. The album sold nearly 20 million copies worldwide in its first year and yielded an astonishing seven hits, including four top pop and R&B hits: "I Just Can't Stop Loving You" (also a top easy-listening hit) with Siedah Garrett on backing vocals, "Bad," "The Way You Make Me Feel," and "Man in the Mirror." "Dirty Diana," recorded with Billy Idol's guitarist Steve Stevens, became a top pop and smash R&B hit, and "Another Part of Me" and "Smooth Criminal" were smash R&B and major pop hits through 1988. Again, Michael produced a series of memorable videos to promote the songs, working with distinguished directors such as Martin Scorcese on "Bad." Between September 1987 and January 1989 Michael Jackson conducted his first solo tour, playing venues around the world.

In 1989 Janet Jackson recorded *Rhythm Nation 1814* with songwriter-producers Jam and Lewis once again. The album evinced a vague yet developing sense of social consciousness to the work of the team, and the album yielded seven hits, including the top pop and R&B hits "Miss You Much" and "Escapade." "Rhythm Nation" became a smash pop and top R&B hit, while "Black Cat" and "Love Will Never Do (Without You)" became top pop and smash R&B hits. "Alright" and "Come Back to Me" (a top easy-listening hit) proved smash hits in both fields. Janet Jackson conducted a nine-month tour, her first, in support of the album, but her shows were viewed more as cultural events than musical presentations, given the spectacular staging and large cast employed.

In March 1991 Michael Jackson re-signed with the parent company of Epic Records, Sony Corporation. The 15-year contract was reportedly worth in the neighborhood of $1 billion. His first album thereafter, *Dangerous*, was met with mixed reviews, but nonetheless produced seven hit singles. "Black or White," recorded with Guns N' Roses guitarist Slash, became a top pop hit, while "Remember the Time" and "In the Closet" became smash pop and top R&B hits. "Jam," recorded with rapper Heavy D, "Heal the World" and "Who Is It" proved major crossover hits. "Will You Be There," also featured in the movie *Free Willy*, became a smash crossover hit.

In March 1991 Janet Jackson signed a contract with Virgin Records worth an estimated $32 million. After scoring a top R&B and smash pop hit with Luther Vandross on "The Best Things in Life Are Free," from the movie *Mo' Money*, she recorded her debut for Virgin, *janet.*, again with Jimmy Jam and Terry Lewis. Focusing on romance and sex and frequently "sampling" the work of other black artists, the album produced a series of smash hits through 1994, including the top pop and R&B hit debut "That's the Way Love Goes." The other smash crossover hits were "If," "Again" (featured in the movie *Poetic Justice*), "Because of Love," "Anytime, Anyplace," and "You Want This." Jackson made her movie debut in the well received (although commercially unsuccessful) film *Poetic Justice* with Tupac Shakur in July 1993 and toured once again in 1994. Despite her enormous success, Janet Jackson had not demonstrated any musical talent independent of the Jam-Lewis songwriting-production team.

In early 1993 Michael Jackson made a technologically stunning appearance during the halftime show at Super Bowl XXVII and took part in a rare television interview with Oprah Winfrey reportedly watched by 90 million viewers. However, in July, a 13-year-old boy alleged that he had been molested by Jackson. As the news dominated the front pages of newspapers worldwide, Jackson launched his next tour in August, only to cancel it in November and slip into seclusion as the press speculated about his whereabouts. He eventually surfaced in Southern California, on December 22, to tell an international television audience that the accusations were "totally false." The next month he settled out of court with the boy and his family for an estimated $20 million, although the case remained open. In the meantime, Jackson secretly married Elvis Presley's daughter, Lisa Marie, on May 26, 1994.

In 1995 Michael Jackson attempted to resume his musical career with the release of the double-CD set *HIStory—Past, Present and Future, Book 1*. Comprised of 15 remastered "greatest hits" and 15 new songs, the album was promoted by a $30 million campaign by Epic Records. Although his duet with sister Janet on "Scream" became an instant hit, the promotional film for *HIStory* was likened to Leni Riefenstahl's Nazi propaganda film, *Triumph of the Will*. Allegations of anti-Semitism were made about the lyrics to "They Don't Care about Us," and some took exception with Jackson's use of four-letter words on an album directed at youngsters. In June, Jackson and wife Lisa Marie were interviewed live on ABC's *Prime Time Live* by Diane Sawyer. Despite the fact that the interview was seen by an audience estimated at 60 million, the appearance failed to slow the collapse of Jackson's career. Soon after, the couple separated. *HIStory* sold only around 2 million copies (not 20 million, as predicted), and by October the album was already being discounted by major record stores. Jackson further faltered when a planned concert at New York's Beacon Theater, to be presented live on HBO, was canceled after the star collapsed; follow-up medical tests revealed that he was suffering from dehydration and perhaps heart and kidney disease. Jackson again retreated into seclusion, with the future of his career in some doubt.

The Jackson Five

Diana Ross Presents the Jackson Five	Motown	700	'70	†
	Motown	5129	'86	CS/CD

ABC	Motown	709	'70	†
	Motown	5152	'89	CS/CD
ABC/Diana Ross Presents the Jackson Five	Motown	8019	'86	CD†
Jackson Five Christmas Album	Motown	713	'70	†
	Motown	9080		CD†
	Motown	5250		CS/CD
Third Album	Motown	718	'70	†
	Motown	5157	'89	CS/CD
Maybe Tomorrow	Motown	735	'71	†
	Motown	5228	'89	CD
Maybe Tomorrow/Third Album	Motown	8011	'86	CD†
Goin' Back to Indiana	Motown	742	'71	†
Greatest Hits	Motown	741	'72	†
	Motown	9010		CD†
	Motown	5201		CS/CD
Lookin' Through the Windows	Motown	750	'72	†
Skywriter	Motown	761	'73	†
	Motown	5469	'90	CS/CD
Get It Together	Motown	783	'73	†
Dancing Machine	Motown	780	'74	†
Moving Violation	Motown	829	'75	†
Joyful Jukebox Music	Motown	865	'76	†
Anthology	Motown	(3) 868	'76	LP/CS
	Motown	(2) 868		CD
	Motown	6194		CD†
Motown Superstar Series, Volume 12	Motown	5112		†
The Great Love Songs	Motown	5346		†
Motown Legends	Motown	5365		†
14 Greatest Hits	Motown	6099	'84	†
Compact Command Performance (18 Greatest Hits)	Motown	9040		CD†
Great Songs and Performances	Motown	5312		CS/CD
The Jacksons: An American Dream (TV miniseries)	Motown	6356	'92	CS/CD
Soulsations! The 25th Anniversary Collection	Motown	0489	'95	CS/CD
The Ultimate Collection	Motown	0558	'95	CS/CD

The Jacksons

The Jacksons	Epic	34229	'76	CS/CD
Goin' Places	Epic	34835	'77	CS/CD
Destiny	Epic	35552	'78	CS/CD
Triumph	Epic	36424	'80	CS/CD
The Jacksons Live	Epic	(2) 37545	'81	†
	Epic	37545		CS/CD
Victory	Epic	38946	'84	CD
2300 Jackson Street	Epic	40911	'89	CS/CD†
Greatest Hits	Epic	67282	'95	CS/CD

Michael Jackson

Got to Be There	Motown	747	'72	†
	Motown	5416	'89	CS/CD
Ben	Motown	755	'72	†
	Motown	5153	'89	CS/CD
Ben/Got to Be There	Motown	8000	'86	CD†

Music and Me	Motown	767	'73	†
Farewell My Summer Love 1984 (recorded 1973)	Motown	6101	'84	†
Forever, Michael	Motown	825	'75	†
Best	Motown	851	'75	†
	Motown	9079		CD†
	Motown	5194		CS/CD
One Day in Your Life	Motown	956	'81	†
(recorded 1973–1975)	Motown	5352		CS
Motown Superstar Series, Volume 7	Motown	5107		†
Motown Legends	Motown	5369		†
Looking Back to Yesterday: A Young Michael	Motown	5384		CS/CD†
Anthology	Motown	(2) 6195	'86	CD†
	Motown	(2) 0480	'95	CS/CD
The Original Soul of Michael Jackson	Motown	6250		CS/CD
Off the Wall	Epic	35745	'79	CS/CD
Thriller	Epic	38112	'82	LP/CS/CD
Bad	Epic	40600	'87	LP/CS/CD
Dangerous	Epic	(2) 45400	'91	LP
	Epic	45400	'91	CS/CD
HIStory—Past, Present and Future, Book 1	Epic	(3) 59000	'95	LP
	Epic	(2) 59000	'95	CS/CD

Michael Jackson and the Jackson Five

14 Greatest Hits	Motown	6099	'84	†

Jermaine Jackson

Jermaine	Motown	752	'72	†
Come Into My Life	Motown	775	'73	†
My Name Is Jermaine	Motown	842	'76	†
Feel the Fire	Motown	888	'77	†
Frontiers	Motown	898	'78	†
Let's Get Serious	Motown	928	'80	†
	Motown	5354		CS
Jermaine	Motown	948	'80	†
I Like Your Style	Motown	952	'81	†
Let Me Tickle Your Fancy	Motown	6017	'82	†
Motown Superstar Series, Volume 17	Motown	5117		†
Greatest Hits and Rare Classics	Motown	5484	'91	CS/CD
Jermaine Jackson	Arista	8203	'84	†
Precious Moments	Arista	8277	'86	†
Don't Take It Personal	Arista	8493	'89	†
Jermaine Jackson	La Face	26001	'91	CS/CD

Jackie Jackson

Jackie Jackson	Motown	785	'73	†
Be the One	Polydor	837766	'89	LP/CS/CD†

Rebbie Jackson

Centipede	Columbia	39238	'84	†

Marlon Jackson

Baby Tonight	Capitol	46942	'87	†

LaToya Jackson

LaToya Jackson	Polydor	6291	'80	†

My Special Love	Polydor	6328	'81	†
Heart Don't Lie	Private I	39361	'84	†
LaToya	RCA	8502	'89	LP/CS/CD†
Janet Jackson				
Janet Jackson	A&M	4907	'82	CS/CD
Dream Street	A&M	4962	'84	CS/CD
Control	A&M	5106	'86	†
	A&M	3905		CS/CD
Janet Jackson's Rhythm Nation 1814	A&M	3920	'89	CS/CD
Design of a Decade	A&M	540399	'95	LP/CS/CD
janet.	Virgin	87825	'93	CS/CD
	Virgin	39195	'93	CD

JAN AND DEAN

Jan Berry (b. Apr. 3, 1941, Los Angeles, CA); **Dean Torrance** (b. Mar. 10, 1940, Los Angeles, CA)

Early-'60s purveyors of innocuous fun songs concerned with surfing, cars, girls, and high school, Jan and Dean were second only to the Beach Boys in the promotion of these Southern California themes. In fact, the Beach Boys' Brian Wilson wrote several of their biggest hits, including "Surf City" and "The New Girl in School." Scoring a series of hit singles between 1963 and 1965, Jan and Dean later recorded folk and Beatles songs. However, in April 1966 Jan was nearly killed in a Los Angeles auto wreck that left him in a coma for nearly a year. He eventually recovered, although permanent damage was sustained; the duo ceased recording, and Dean pursued a career as a graphic artist.

Jan Berry and Dean Torrance met in junior high school. Fascinated with the doo-wop sound of the late '50s, the two formed the group the Barons (which included future Beach Boy Bruce Johnston), and then a vocal trio with Arnie Ginsburg, recording "Jennie Lee" in Jan's garage. While Dean was serving in the Army Reserve, Jan signed with Doris Day's Arwin label, which released the song as performed by "Jan and Arnie." The song became a near-smash hit in 1958. When Ginsburg joined the Navy, Jan and Dean signed with Herb Alpert's Dore label. They scored a near-smash with the novelty song "Baby Talk" in 1959. However, the duo's next major hit didn't come until 1961, when "Heart and Soul" was released on Challenge Records.

By early 1962 Jan and Dean had signed with Liberty Records. Beginning in early 1963 the team scored a series of major hits, starting with Brian Wilson's "Linda." Wilson's "Surf City" became a top hit for the two in the summer of 1963, followed by "Honolulu Lulu," "Drag City," "Dead Man's Curve," the smash "The Little Old Lady (From Pasadena)," "Ride the Wild Surf," and Wilson's "Sidewalk Surfin'," a precursor of the skateboard rage. Subsequent hits included "You Really Know How to Hurt a Guy" and "Popsicle." Dean Torrance sat in on the Beach Boys' *Party* sessions, resulting in his (uncredited) lead vocals on the 1966 number one hit single off the album, "Barbara Ann." When the surf craze died down, the duo switched to covering folk and Beatles material.

On April 19, 1966, Jan Berry was nearly killed when his Corvette Stingray, allegedly traveling at 90 miles per hour, struck a parked truck. In a coma for nearly a year, Jan spent much of the next 10 years undergoing intensive physical therapy for a condition that included paralysis of his right side and impaired speech, hearing, vision, and memory. In the meantime, Dean opened Kittyhawk Graphics, where he designed album covers. Jan ultimately returned to the studio in 1970, later performing with Dean at Hollywood's 1973 "Surfer's Stomp Reunion." After the airing of the biographical *Dead Man's Curve* special on CBS-TV in February 1978, Jan and Dean reunited for performances with the Beach Boys that year.

Jan and Dean

Jan and Dean	Dore	101		†
The Heart and Soul of Jan and Dean	Design	181		†
Jan and Dean Take Linda Surfin'	Liberty	7294	'63	†
Surf City (and Other Swingin' Cities)	Liberty	7314	'63	†
Drag City	Liberty	7339	'64	†
Dead Man's Curve/The New Girl in School	Liberty	7361	'64	†
Ride the Wild Surf	Liberty	7368	'64	†
The Little Old Lady from Pasadena	Liberty	7377	'64	†
	Liberty	10151		†
Ride the Wild Surf/Little Old Lady from Pasadena	Liberty	80055	'92	CS/CD
Command Performance—"Live" in Person	Liberty	7403	'65	†
Folk 'n' Roll	Liberty	7431	'66	†
Filet of Soul	Liberty	7441	'66	†
Jan and Dean Meet Batman	Liberty	7444	'66	†
Save for a Rainy Day	Columbia	9461	'67	†

Anthologies

Golden Hits	Liberty	7248	'62	†
Golden Hits, Volume 2	Liberty	7417	'65	†
Golden Hits, Volume 3	Liberty	7460	'66	†
Best	Liberty	10115	'81	†
Jan and Dean	Sunset	5156	'67	†
Legendary Masters	United Artists	(2) 9961	'71	†
Gotta Take That One Last Ride	United Artists	(2) 341	'74	†
Very Best, Volume 1	United Artists	443	'75	†
Very Best, Volume 2	United Artists	515	'76	†
Dead Man's Curve	United Artists	999	'79	†
	United Artists	10011		†
California Gold	Pair	(2) 1071		†
I Gotta Drive	EMI-America	16398	'86	†
A Surfer's Dream	EMI-America	16399	'86	†
Best	EMI-America	10339	'87	†
	EMI	46885	'87	†
Surf City: The Best of Jan and Dean	EMI	92772	'90	CS/CD
All-Time Greatest Hits	Curb/CEMA	77374	'91	CS/CD
Surf City	Dominion	665		CS/CD†
Best	Special Music	4906		CS
The Jan and Dean Story	Hollywood/IMG	379		CS/CD

THE JEFFERSON AIRPLANE/STARSHIP/HOT TUNA

THE JEFFERSON AIRPLANE. Marty Balin (b. Martyn Jerel Buchwald, Jan. 30, 1943, Cincinnati, OH), voc; **Signe Tole** (b. Sept. 15, 1941, Seattle, WA), voc; **Paul Kantner** (b. Mar. 12, 1942, San Francisco, CA), rhythm gtr, voc; **Jorma Kaukonen** (b. Dec. 23, 1940, Washington, D.C.), lead gtr; **Jack Casady** (b. Apr. 13, 1944, Washington, D.C.), bs; **Alexander "Skip" Spence** (b. Apr. 18, 1946, Windsor, Ontario, Canada), drm [Signe Tole and Skip Spence left in 1966, to be replaced by **Grace Slick** (b. Grace Wing, Oct. 30, 1939,

Chicago, IL) and **Spencer Dryden** (b. Apr. 7, 1943, New York, NY). Later members include drummers **Joe E. Covington** and **John Barbata**, and electric violinist **"Papa" John Creach** (b. May 28, 1917, Beaver Falls, PA; d. Feb. 22, 1994, Los Angeles, CA).]

HOT TUNA. Jorma Kaukonen, gtr, and **Jack Casady**, bs; various supporting musicians

JEFFERSON STARSHIP. Paul Kantner, gtr, voc; **Grace Slick**, voc; **"Papa" John Creach**, vln; **David Freiberg** (b. Aug. 24, 1938, Boston, MA), kybd, bs, voc; **Craig Chaquico** (b. Sept. 26, 1954, Sacramento, CA), gtr; **Pete Sears** (b. England), kybd, voc; **John Barbata**, drm [Vocalist **Marty Balin** joined in 1975. By 1979 the Jefferson Starship was comprised of **Mickey Thomas** (b. Cairo, GA), vocals; Paul Kantner, David Freiberg, Craig Chaquico, Pete Sears, and drummer **Aynsley Dunbar** (b. Jan. 10, 1946, Liverpool, England).]

STARSHIP. Grace Slick, Mickey Thomas, Craig Chaquico, Pete Sears, and drummer **Donny Baldwin**.

THE JEFFERSON AIRPLANE

Although not the first band of San Francisco's hippie era (that claim probably belongs to the Charlatans), the Jefferson Airplane was the first '60s San Francisco group to secure a major-label recording contract. Anchored by lead guitarist Jorma Kaukonen and bassist Jack Casady, two of rock's most neglected instrumentalists, the Jefferson Airplane became transformed into San Francisco's most visible and popular psychedelic act with the addition of vocalist Grace Slick. As with the Grateful Dead, San Francisco's other enduring major group, the Jefferson Airplane was a remarkably democratic band (at least initially), quickly establishing itself with the local counterculture community. The original band began to disintegrate in 1971, with the departure of Marty Balin, and endured a long period of personnel changes. Despite these upheavals, the band managed to score major pop hits in 1975 on Balin's return, and again in 1985 with vocalist Mickey Thomas, although in both cases they were unable to build on this momentum.

Marty Balin was performing in the San Francisco area with the folk group the Town Criers in 1964. During 1965 he assembled a group of musicians, including guitarists Paul Kantner and Jorma Kaukonen and vocalist Signe Tole. Named the Jefferson Airplane, the group debuted at the Matrix on August 13, 1965, performing a blend of rock and folk music. Paul Kantner had been living in Los Angeles with David Crosby and David Freiberg before returning to the Bay Area. He met Kaukonen in Santa Cruz and, later, Balin while performing on 12-string guitar and banjo at the Drinking Gourd. The group's original rhythm section was soon replaced by Alexander "Skip" Spence, a rhythm guitarist converted to drummer, and bassist Jack Casady, a high school friend of Kaukonen's. On October 16, 1965, the Jefferson Airplane performed a dance concert at San Francisco's Longshoremen's

Hall, the precursor of the local concert scene developed by producer Bill Graham that subsequently spread across the nation.

Signed to RCA Records, thus becoming the first of many Bay Area bands to secure a major-label recording contract, the Jefferson Airplane recorded their debut album in Hollywood. Dominated by Marty Balin's songwriting and smooth, rich voice, *Jefferson Airplane Takes Off* featured the distinctive vocal harmonies of Balin, Kantner, and Signe Anderson (now married). The modest-selling album contained an early version of one of the anthem's of the emerging hippie movement, "Let's Get Together," and Balin's dynamic love song "It's No Secret." Both Anderson and Spence left the Jefferson Airplane in 1966, she to have a baby and he to form Moby Grape. Drummer Spencer Dryden and vocalist Grace Slick were recruited as replacements. Grace Slick, a former model, had been a member of the recently dissolved band the Great Society, which had been performing locally since 1965. The group also included Slick's drummer-husband Jerry Slick and his brother Darby Slick. Recordings made by the Great Society for Columbia were eventually issued in 1968, following the success of the Jefferson Airplane.

Surrealistic Pillow, Grace Slick's first album with the Jefferson Airplane, contained two songs she had performed with the Great Society, Darby Slick's "Somebody to Love" and her own "White Rabbit." The latter became somewhat of a cause célèbre, as it was widely critized for (purportedly) celebrating the drug experience (although Slick claimed that it was innocently based on Lewis Carroll's *Alice in Wonderland*). Both songs became smash hits in 1967, and the album effectively launched the San Francisco Sound. It also included two beautiful romantic ballads by Balin, "Comin' Back to Me" and "Today" (coauthored by Kantner), as well as Balin's frenetic "3/5 of a Mile in 10 Seconds" and surreal "Plastic Fantastic Lover." Slick's piercing soprano voice, more rough and powerful than Anderson's, complemented Balin's high sensual tenor, and her flamboyant stage demeanor soon made her the visual and musical focus of the Jefferson Airplane. In fact, her presence began to overwhelm Balin, as evidenced by *After Bathing at Baxter's*. The album contained only one Balin song, "Young Girl Sunday Blues" (coauthored by Kantner), and included psychedelic instrumental ruminations by Casady and Kaukonen such as "Spare Chaynge," Kantner's "The Ballad of You and Me and Pooneil" (a moderate hit), and Slick's "Two Heads," as well as two mellower Kantner compositions, "Won't You Try" and "Saturday Afternoon."

Marty Balin contributed more to *Crown of Creation*, but most attention was directed at Kantner's title song, Slick's surreal "Lather" and "Greasy Heart," and David Crosby's previously unrecorded "Triad." During 1968 the Jefferson Airplane toured Europe for the first time, issuing the live set *Bless Its Pointed Little Head* in early 1969. *Volunteers* was again dominated by Slick and Kantner. Although the standout cut was Balin and Kantner's radical political title song, the album featured Kantner's "We Can Be Together" and David Crosby, Stephen Stills, and Paul Kantner's mystical "Wooden Ships," a forerunner of the science fiction fantasies that Kantner would soon pursue.

A chaotic period of solo and joint projects and personnel changes soon engulfed the Jefferson Airplane. Jorma Kaukonen and Jack Casady had been performing together as the blues-oriented Hot Tuna since 1969, often opening shows for the Jefferson Airplane. The first of many Hot Tuna albums appeared in mid-1970, some months after Spencer Dryden quit the parent group, to be replaced by surf drummer Joe E. Covington. In October, at the urging of Covington, black electric violinist "Papa" John Creach joined the Jefferson Airplane, subsequently performing and recording with both the Airplane and Hot Tuna. In December the bombastic *Blows Against the Empire* was released under the name of Paul Kantner and the Jefferson Starship. Recorded by Kantner, Slick, Casady, and Covington, with the assistance of Jerry Garcia, David Crosby, Graham Nash, David Freiberg, and Jorma's brother Peter Kaukonen, the album featured a number of Kantner science fiction songs, the most accessible of which, "Have You Seen the Stars Tonite," was cowritten by Crosby. Conspicuously absent was Marty Balin, although he was listed as coauthor of two songs.

By spring 1971 Marty Balin had left the Jefferson Airplane. By that September the group had formed their own independent label, Grunt Records, with manufacturing and distribution handled by RCA. The label's first album release, *Bark*, credited to the Jefferson Airplane, yielded a minor hit with Covington's ditty "Pretty As You Feel." Other Grunt releases included "Papa" John Creach's first solo album and *Sunfighter*, credited to Paul Kantner and Grace Slick. The album was recorded with members of the Airplane plus Garcia, Nash, and Crosby, as well as two members of the Grunt Records group Steelwind, leader Jack Traylor and 16-year-old guitarist Craig Chaquico. By March 1972 Covington had left the Airplane, to be replaced by session veteran John Barbata. That summer the Jefferson Airplane conducted a major American tour with Barbata and bassist-keyboardist-vocalist David Freiberg, a former member of Quicksilver Messenger Service. In August Jack Casady and Jorma Kaukonen left the Jefferson Airplane to pursue Hot Tuna full time. Subsequent Jefferson Airplane releases included the live set *Thirty Seconds Over Winterland* and *Early Flight*, recordings from 1965–1970 that included Signe Anderson's vocal on "High Flying Bird."

During 1973 Marty Balin performed and recorded with the Marin County bar band Bodacious D.F. Their overlooked RCA album featured Balin's fine lead vocal on leader Vic Smith's "Drivin' Me Crazy." By mid-1974 Balin was ready to work with the band again. Meanwhile, the Airplane (now called Jefferson Starship) had added keyboardist-vocalist Peter Sears and lead guitarist Craig Chaquico for the album *Dragonfly*. It contained Slick and Sears's "Hyperdrive," and yielded a minor hit with Slick and Kantner's "Ride the Tiger." However, the feature cut was Marty Balin and Paul Kantner's "Caroline," with lead vocals by Balin.

Marty Balin rejoined the Jefferson Starship for their spring 1975 tour and stayed with the group for more than three years. The group's best-selling album ever, *Red Octopus*, yielded a smash hit with "Miracles," composed and sung by Balin, and exposed the group to a new wide audience. The album also included the minor hit "Play on Love" and "Tumblin'," written by Balin, Freiberg, and Grateful Dead lyricist Robert Hunter. "Papa" John Creach subsequently left the group for an inauspicious solo recording career. He died in Los Angeles of natural causes on February 22, 1994. The Jefferson Starship next recorded *Spitfire*, which contained "Cruisin'" (written by Charlie Hickox of Bodacious D.F.) and the major hit "With Your Love," cowritten by Balin. The follow-up, *Earth*, produced four hit singles, including the near smashes "Count On Me" (written by Jesse Barish) and "Runaway."

During summer 1978 the Jefferson Starship toured Europe for the first time in more than 10 years. However, Grace Slick's performances became erratic as she battled with alcoholism. A scheduled appearance in Frankfurt, Germany, was hastily canceled due to her inability to perform, leading to a riot in which virtually all of the group's equipment was destroyed. Following a poor performance two nights later in Hamburg, Slick returned to the United States, not to perform with the group again until January 1981.

In October 1978 drummer John Barbata was critically injured in a northern California automobile accident. He was replaced by well-traveled English drummer Aynsley Dunbar. The Jefferson Starship was reconstituted in 1979 with former Elvin Bishop vocalist Mickey Thomas ("Fooled Around and Fell in Love"), Kantner, Freiberg, Chaquico, Sears, and Dunbar. The hard-rock *Freedom at Point Zero* produced a major hit with "Jane" and the minor hit "Girl with the Hungry Eyes." After recording two solo albums, Grace Slick returned to the Jefferson Starship for the major hits "Find Your Way Back," "Be My Lady," and "No Way Out" through 1984. Meanwhile, Marty Balin had left the group to pursue a solo career. In 1981 he scored a smash hit with "Hearts" and a major hit with "Atlanta Lady" from *Balin* on EMI America Records. He recorded another solo album in 1983.

In 1984 Paul Kantner departed the Jefferson Starship acrimoniously. Through lawsuits, he forced the group to rename itself simply Starship. Soliciting songs from outside writers and pursuing a blatantly commercial direction, the Starship regrouped with Slick, Thomas, Chaquico, Sears, and drummer Donny Baldwin, who had replaced Aynsley Dunbar in 1982. The new lineup's debut album, *Knee Deep in the Hoopla*, yielded four hits, including the top hits "We Built This City," cowritten by Elton John associate Bernie Taupin, and "Sara." The group scored another top hit in 1987 with "Nothing's Gonna Stop Us Now," from the movie *Mannequin*, followed by the near-smash "It's Not Over ('Til It's Over)." Pete Sears left Starship in 1987, followed by Grace Slick in 1988 and Donny Baldwin in late 1989. Their last major hit came in 1989 with "It's Not Enough." Eventually reduced to Craig Chaquico and Mickey Thomas, the group finally disbanded in 1990. Since 1992 Thomas has been performing around the Lake Tahoe region with a set of musicians as Mickey Thomas's Starship. In the '90s Craig Chaquico recorded two instrumental acoustic albums for Higher Octave Music.

Jorma Kaukonen and Jack Casady persevered as Hot Tuna until 1978. Casady then performed and recorded with the San Francisco heavy-metal band SVT until 1982. He and Kaukonen reunited for a tour as Hot Tuna in 1983, ultimately regrouping in 1986 as an acoustic duo, recording *Pair a Dice Found* for Epic Records in 1990.

In 1985 Paul Kantner, Marty Balin, and Jack Casady formed a new group with guitarist Slick Aguilar and keyboardist Tim Gorman, among others. Signed to Arista Records, the Kantner-Balin-Casady Band recorded one album for the label in 1986, scoring a minor hit with "It's Not You, It's Not Me." They completed a national tour in 1987, but disbanded in 1988. The following year Kantner, Balin, and Casady regrouped with Grace Slick and Jorma Kaukonen, augmented by Gorman and drummer Kenny Aronoff, as the Jefferson Airplane. They recorded a modest-selling album and toured that year. Since 1991 Paul Kantner has performed with Gorman as Paul Kantner's Wooden Ships. Beginning in 1992 the two also performed in Paul Kantner's Jefferson Starship—The Next Generation with Jack Casady, "Papa" John Creach, drummer Prairie Prince, and female vocalists Darby Gould, Diana Mangano, and Signe Anderson, the original Jefferson Airplane vocalist. Marty Balin joined the aggregation in 1993, and Creach died in 1994. Grace Slick came back on board in 1995 for the album *Deep Space/Virgin Sky*.

Grace Slick and the Great Society

Conspicuous Only in Its Absence	Columbia	9624	'68	†
How It Was—Collector's Item, Volume 2	Columbia	9702	'68	
Collector's Item	Columbia	(2) 30459	'71	†
	Columbia	30459	'90	CD

The Jefferson Airplane

Early Flight	Grunt	0437	'74	†
	RCA	0437		CS/CD
Jefferson Airplane Takes Off	RCA	3584	'66/'89	CS/CD
	RCA	3739		†
Surrealistic Pillow	RCA	3766	'67	CD
	RCA	3738		LP/CS
	RCA	66598	'95	CD
After Bathing at Baxter's	RCA	1511	'67	†
	RCA	4545	'89	CS/CD
Crown of Creation	RCA	4058	'68	CS/CD
	RCA	3797		†
	Mobile Fidelity	523		CD
	Mobile Fidelity	148	'91	LP
Bless Its Pointed Little Head	RCA	4133	'69/'89	CS/CD
	RCA	3798		†

Volunteers	RCA	4238	'69	CD
	RCA	3867		CS
	Mobile Fidelity	540	'90	CD
The Worst of the Jefferson Airplane	RCA	4459	'70	CD
	RCA	3661		CS
Bark	Grunt	1001	'71	†
	Grunt	4386	'82	†
Long John Silver	Grunt	1007	'72	†
Thirty Seconds Over Winterland	Grunt	0147	'73	CS/CD
Flight Log (1966–1976)	Grunt	(2) 1255	'77	†
2400 Fulton Street—An Anthology	RCA	(2) 5724	'87	CS/CD
White Rabbit and Other Hits	RCA	2078	'90	CS/CD
The Jefferson Airplane Love You	RCA	(3) 61110	'92	CS/CD
The Best of the Jefferson Airplane	RCA	66197	'93	CS/CD
Time Machine	Pair	1090	'86	CD
Rock & Roll	Richmond	2176		CS
Jefferson Airplane	Epic	45271	'89	CS/CD

Paul Kantner and the Jefferson Starship

Blows Against the Empire	RCA	4448	'70	†
	RCA	3868	'88	CS/CD

Paul Kantner and Grace Slick

Sunfighter	Grunt	1002	'71	†
	RCA	4385	'82	†

Paul Kantner, Grace Slick, and David Freiberg

Baron von Tollbooth and the Chrome Nun	Grunt	0148	'73	†
	RCA	3799		†

Joe E. Covington's Fat Fandango

Your Heart Is My Heart	Grunt	0149	'73	†

Hot Tuna

Hot Tuna	RCA	4353	'70	†
	RCA	3864		CS/CD
Electric—Recorded Live (First Pull Up, Then Pull Down)	RCA	4550	'71	†
	RCA	3865		†
Burgers	Grunt	1004	'72	†
	Grunt	2591		†
	RCA	2591		CS/CD
	Grunt	3951		†
Phosphorescent Rat	Grunt	0348	'74	†
	RCA	0348	'89	CS/CD
America's Choice	Grunt	0820	'75	†
	RCA	0820	'90	CS/CD
Yellow Fever	Grunt	1238	'75	†
	RCA	1238	'90	CS/CD
Hoppkorv	Grunt	1920	'76	†
	Grunt	3950		†
Double Dose	Grunt	(2) 2545	'78	†
Final Vinyl	Grunt	3357	'79	†
Keep on Truckin' and Other Hits	RCA	2164	'90	CS
Pair a Dice Found	Epic	46831	'90	CD

Splashdown	Relix	2004		CS/CD
Historic Hot Tuna	Relix	2011		CS/CD
Live at Sweetwater	Relix	2058		CS/CD

Jorma Kaukonen and Tom Hobson
Quah	Grunt	0209	'74	†
	Grunt	3747		†
	Relix	2027		CS/CD

Jorma Kaukonen
Jorma	RCA	3446	'79	†
Magic	Relix	2007		CS/CD
Too Hot to Handle	Relix	2012		CS/CD

Jorma Kaukonen and Vital Parts
Barbeque King	RCA	3725	'81	†

SVT
No Regrets	MSI	2002	'81	†

Bodacious D.F. (with Marty Balin)
Bodacious D.F.	RCA	0206	'73	†
	RCA	4243	'82	†

Marty Balin
Rock Justice (original cast)	EMI-America	17036	'80	†
Balin	EMI-America	17054	'81	†
Lucky	EMI-America	17088	'83	†
Balince—A Collection	Rhino	70968	'90	CD

The KBC Band (Kantner, Balin, Casady)
The KBC Band	Arista	8440	'86	LP/CS/CD†

Grace Slick
Manhole	Grunt	0347	'74	†
	Grunt	3736		†
Dreams	RCA	3544	'80	†
Welcome to the Wrecking Ball	RCA	3851	'81	†
Software	RCA	4791	'84	†

The Jefferson Starship
Dragonfly	Grunt	0717	'74	†
	RCA	3796	'88	CS/CD
Red Octopus	Grunt	0999	'75	†
	RCA	0999		CD
	RCA	3660		CS
Spitfire	Grunt	1557	'76	†
	Grunt	3953		†
Earth	Grunt	2515	'78	†
Gold	Grunt/RCA	3247	'79	†
	RCA	3247	'91	CS/CD
Freedom at Point Zero	Grunt	3452	'79	†
	RCA	3452		CD
	RCA	5161	'84	CS
Modern Times	Grunt	3848	'81	†
	RCA	3848		CS

Winds of Change	Grunt	4372	'82	†
	RCA	4372		CS/CD
Nuclear Furniture	Grunt	4921	'84	†
	RCA	4921		CD
The Jefferson Starship at Their Best	RCA	66231	'93	CS/CD
Paul Kantner				
The Planet Earth Rock & Roll Orchestra	RCA	4320	'83	†
Starship				
Knee Deep in the Hoopla	Grunt	5488	'85	†
	RCA	5488		CS/CD
No Protection	Grunt	6413	'87	CS/CD
Love Among the Cannibals	RCA	9693	'89	LP/CS/CD†
Greatest Hits (Ten Years and Change)	RCA	2423	'91	CS/CD
Craig Chaquico				
Acoustic Highway	Higher Octave	7050	'93	CS/CD
Acoustic Planet	Higher Octave	7070	'94	CS/CD
Jefferson Starship—The Next Generation				
Deep Space/Virgin Sky			'95	†

WAYLON JENNINGS
(b. June 15, 1937, Littlefield, TX)

Along with Willie Nelson, Waylon Jennings led the '70s "outlaw" country-music movement that eschewed the sophisticated orchestral production favored in Nashville since the advent of rock and roll. After years as a relatively obscure country artist, Jennings was granted a measure of artistic independence for 1972's *Ladies Love Outlaws*, perhaps the first mainstream country-and-western album to feature simple songs unmarred by elaborate arrangements. The anthology album *The Outlaws*, with songs performed by Jennings and Nelson among others, effectively established this new approach. Gaining acceptance in both the rock and pop fields, Waylon Jennings and Willie Nelson helped promote the rise of country music since the late '70s.

Waylon Jennings took up guitar as a teenager, later moving to Lubbock, where he hosted his own show on radio station KLLL and met Buddy Holly, who produced Jennings's first recording, a cover of the Cajun classic "Jole Blon," in 1958. Performing on Holly's final 1959 tour playing electric bass, Jennings was ostensibly "bumped" from his seat on the ill-fated plane that crashed the night of February 2 in rural Iowa, killing Holly, J. P. "Big Bopper" Richardson, and Ritchie Valens.

Waylon Jennings subsequently returned to Lubbock to resume work as a disc jockey. In the early '60s he moved to Phoenix, where he formed his backing group the Waylors and performed regularly at JD's Club. After early recordings later released on Vocalion and A&M, he was signed to RCA Records by Chet Atkins in 1965. Moving to Nashville the following year, Jennings pursued a modest career as a country-and-western artist. His smash country hits during the '60s included "(That's What You Get) For Lovin' Me," "Only Daddy That'll Walk the Line," and "Brown-Eyed Handsome Man." Touring 300 days a year, Jennings's first (minor) pop hit came in 1969 with his cover of "MacArthur Park," followed the next year by "The Taker," cowritten by Kris Kristofferson.

In the early '70s Waylon Jennings negotiated a record contract with RCA that allowed him to pick his own musicians and produce his own recordings. *Ladies Love Outlaws* heralded a trend in country music toward exciting, raw, and more personalized music. *Honky Tonk Heroes*, comprised primarily of songs by Billy Joe Shaver, even made the popular-album charts in 1973. Jennings's smash country hits through 1975 included "Good Hearted Woman," "I'm a Ramblin' Man," "Rainy Day Woman," and (the somewhat ironic) "Are You Sure Hank Done It This Way."

The 1976 RCA anthology album *The Outlaws* effectively established the "outlaw" country-music movement. Assembling recordings by Jennings, Jessi Colter, Willie Nelson, and Tompall Glaser, the album became a surprise best-seller, yielding a major pop hit with the Jennings-Nelson duet "Good Hearted Woman" and a smash country hit with the Jennings-Colter duet "Suspicious Minds." The album also included Colter's "I'm Looking for Blue Eyes," and Jennings's versions of "Honky Tonk Heroes" and "My Heroes Have Always Been Cowboys."

Established with rock and pop fans as well as the country-and-western audience, Waylon Jennings scored a major pop and top country hit with "Luckenbach, Texas (Back to the Basics of Love)" in duet with Willie Nelson from the album *Ol' Waylon*. The 1978 duet set with Willie Nelson, *Waylon and Willie*, produced the moderate pop and top country hit "Mamas Don't Let Your Babies Grow Up to Be Cowboys" and the top country hit "The Wurlitzer Prize," by Jennings. Other '70s country smashes for Jennings included "There Ain't No Good Chain Gangs" (with Johnny Cash), "I've Always Been Crazy," "Don't You Think This Outlaw Bit's Done Got Out of Hand," and "Amanda."

In 1980 Waylon Jennings scored top country hits with Rodney Crowell's "I Ain't Living Long Like This" and "Theme from 'The Dukes of Hazzard' (Good Ol' Boys)," his last major pop hit. In the early '80s he recorded a duet album with Jessi Colter and a second with Willie Nelson, *WW II*. He continued to achieve smash country hits on RCA through 1985, when he joined Nelson, Johnny Cash, and Kris Kristofferson for *The Highwayman* and its top country hit title song, composed by Jimmy Webb.

In 1986 Waylon Jennings recorded *Heroes* with Johnny Cash and switched to MCA Records for *Will the Wolf Survive*, featuring an engaging version of Los Lobos' title song. He reunited with Nelson, Cash, and Kristofferson for a second album and tour as the Highwaymen in 1990. Waylon Jennings moved to Epic Records for 1990's *The Eagle* and 1992's *Too Dumb for New York, Too Ugly for L.A.*, recording another duet set with Willie Nelson, *Clean Shirt*, for the label in 1991. He returned to RCA for 1994's *Waymore's Blues (Part II)* and reunited with the Highwaymen for 1995's *The Road Goes On Forever* on Liberty Records.

Waylon Jennings

In the Beginning	Bulldog	1052		LP/CS
Waylon Jennings	Vocalion	/3873	'69	†
Don't Think Twice	A&M	4238	'70	†
Folk-Country	RCA	3523	'66	†
Leavin' Town	RCA	3620	'66	†
Nashville Rebel	RCA	3736	'66	†
Ol' Harlan	RCA	3660	'67	†
Love of the Common People	RCA	3825	'67	†
Hangin' On	RCA	3918	'68	†
Jewels	RCA	4085	'69	†
Just to Satisfy You	RCA	4137	'69	†
Country Folk	RCA	4180	'69	†
Waylon	RCA	4260	'70	†
Singer of Sad Songs	RCA	4418	'70	†
The Taker/Tulsa	RCA	4487	'71	†
Cedartown, Georgia	RCA	4567	'71	†

Good-Hearted Woman	RCA	4647	'72	†
	RCA	3737		†
Ladies Love Outlaws	RCA	4751	'72	†
Lonesome, On'ry and Mean	RCA	4854	'73	†
Honky Tonk Heroes	RCA	0240	'73	†
	RCA	3897		†
	RCA-Nashville	50240	'94	CS/CD
The Taker/Tulsa and Honky Tonk Heroes	Mobile Fidelity	779	'90	CD
This Time	RCA	0539	'74	†
	RCA	3942		†
The Ramblin' Man	RCA	0734	'74	†
	RCA	4073		†
Dreaming My Dreams	RCA	1062	'75	†
	RCA	4072		†
Are You Ready for the Country	RCA	1816	'76	†
	RCA	3663	'80	†
Live (1974)	RCA	1108	'76	†
	RCA	4163	'81	†
Ol' Waylon	RCA	2317	'77	CD†
	RCA	5126	'84	†
I've Always Been Crazy	RCA	2979	'78	†
What Goes Around Comes Around	RCA	3493	'79	†
Music Man	RCA	3602	'80	†
Black on Black	RCA	4247	'82	†
It's Only Rock & Roll	RCA	4673	'83	†
Waylon and Company	RCA	4826	'83/'85	CD†
	RCA	5433	'85	†
Never Could Toe the Mark	RCA	5017	'84	†
Turn the Page	RCA	5428	'85	†
Sweet Mother Texas	RCA	7184	'86	†
Will the Wolf Survive	MCA	31102	'86	CD†
	MCA	5688		CS
Hangin' Tough	MCA	31298	'87	CS/CD†
A Man Called Hoss	MCA	42038	'88	LP/CD/CS
Full Circle	MCA	42222	'88	LP/CS/CD†
The Eagle	Epic	46104	'90	CS/CD
Too Dumb for New York, Too Ugly for L.A.	Epic	48982	'92	CS/CD
Waymore's Blues (Part II)	RCA-Nashville	66409	'94	CS/CD

Anthologies

The One and Only Waylon Jennings	RCA-Camden	2183	'67	CS
Heartaches by the Number	RCA-Camden	2556	'72	CS
Ruby, Don't Take Your Love to Town	RCA-Camden	2608	'73	CS
Only Daddy That'll Walk the Line	RCA-Camden	0306	'74	†
The Early Years (1965–1968)	RCA	9561	'89	CS/CD
Only the Greatest	RCA	4023	'68	†
Best	RCA	4341	'70	†
	RCA	4828	'84	†
	RCA	9510		†
Greatest Hits	RCA	3378	'79	LP/CS/CD†
	RCA	8506		CS/CD

Greatest Hits, Volume 2	RCA	5325	'84	CS/CD
Collector's Series	RCA	5473	'85	†
	RCA-Nashville	58400		CS/CD
Waylon: The Best	RCA	5620	'87	LP/CS/CD†
Best	RCA	6327		CS/CD
Are You Sure Hank Done It This Way	RCA	61139	'92	CS/CD
	RCA	61156	'92	CD
Only Daddy That'll Walk the Line: The RCA Years	RCA-Nashville	(2) 66299	'93	CS/CD
Waylon!	Pair	(2) 1005	'86	CS†
A Couple More Years	Pair	(2) 1033	'86	CS†
Honky Tonk Hero	Pair	(2) 1110	'86	CS†
New Classic Waylon	MCA	42287	'89	CS/CD

Waylon Jennings, Willie Nelson, Jessi Colter, and Tompall Glaser

The Outlaws	RCA	1321	'76	†
	RCA	5976		CS/CD

Waylon Jennings and Willie Nelson

Waylon and Willie	RCA	2686	'78	†
	RCA	5134	'84	†
	RCA	8401		CS
	RCA	58401	'95	CD
WW II	RCA	4455	'82	†
	RCA	5138	'84	†
	RCA	56329		CS/CD
Take It to the Limit	Columbia	38562	'83/'87	CD
Clean Shirt	Epic	47462	'91	CS/CD

Waylon Jennings and Jessi Colter

Leather and Lace	RCA	3931	'81	†

The Highwaymen

Highwayman	Columbia	40056	'85	CS/CD
Highwayman 2	Columbia	45240	'90	CS/CD
The Road Goes On Forever	Liberty	28091	'95	CS/CD

Waylon Jennings and Johnny Cash

Heroes	Columbia	40347	'86	LP/CS
	Razor & Tie	2078	'95	CS/CD

JETHRO TULL

Ian Anderson (b. Aug. 10, 1947, Edinburgh, Scotland), flt, gtr, sax, lead voc; **Mick Abrahams** (b. Apr. 7, 1943, Luton, Bedfordshire, England), gtr; **Glenn Cornick** (b. Apr. 24, 1947, Barrow-in-Furness, England), bs; **Clive Bunker** (b. Dec. 12, 1946, Blackpool, England), drm [Mick Abrahams left in early 1969, to be replaced by **Martin Barre** (b. Nov. 17, 1946). Glenn Cornick left in 1971, to be replaced by **Jeffrey Hammond-Hammond** (b. July 30, 1946, Blackpool, England). Keyboardist **John Evan** (b. Mar. 28, 1948, Blackpool, England) joined in 1971. Clive Bunker left in late 1971, to be replaced by **Barriemore Barlow** (b. Sept. 10, 1949, Blackpool, England). Hammond-Hammond left in December 1975, to be replaced by **John Glascock** (d. Nov. 17, 1979). Glascock was replaced by **Dave Pegg** (b. Nov. 2, 1947, Birmingham, England) in 1979.]

Starting out as a blues-oriented British band, Jethro Tull evolved into one of the earliest "progressive" bands, opening the way for numerous similarly labeled British and European bands of the early '70s. Generally more popular in the United States than in their native country, Jethro Tull became firmly established as an album band with a series of concept albums, beginning with *Aqualung* and continuing with the best-selling *Thick as a Brick*. Featuring Ian Anderson's jazz-style flute playing and manic stage presence in performance, Jethro Tull subsequently became increasingly theatrical in concert, culminating in the critically scorned but enormously popular *A Passion Play* album and tour. Sustaining popularity through the '70s, Jethro Tull's slide into obscurity in the '80s was arrested by 1987's *Crest of a Knave*. By then the band as such was an open door to various musicians, serving primarily as accompanists for Anderson's musical vision.

During 1966 and 1967, future Jethro Tull members Ian Anderson, John Evan, Glenn Cornick, Barriemore Barlow, and Jeffrey Hammond-Hammond were at various times members of the John Evan Band. Performing around Blackpool in northern England, the band traveled to London in 1967 to establish themselves on the club circuit. As the other members gradually drifted off, Cornick and Anderson persevered, forming Jethro Tull before year's end with Mick Abrahams and Clive Bunker, Abrahams and Anderson being the principle songwriters.

An immediate success on the club circuit, Jethro Tull was well received at the 1968 National Jazz and Blues Festival. Signed to Island Records (Reprise in the United States), the group's blues-oriented debut album *This Was* sold modestly. However, in early 1969 Abrahams departed to form Blodwyn Pig. Briefly replaced by future Black Sabbath guitarist Tommy Iommi, Abrahams's permanent replacement was guitarist Martin Barre.

Ian Anderson effectively took over as Jethro Tull's leader, abandoning Abrahams's penchant for blues-based material in favor of highly melodic folk and classically influenced songs often featuring wry, offbeat lyrics. *Stand Up*, regarded by some as Jethro Tull's classic album, contained group favorites such as "Bouree" (adapted from J. S. Bach), "Look into the Sun," and "We Used to Know."

By 1970 Jethro Tull had established itself as one of the top concert attractions in the United States through regular tours, perhaps to the detriment of their British popularity. Following that year's album, *Benefit*, Glenn Cornick left the group to form Wild Turkey in 1971. He resurfaced in Bob Welch's power trio Paris in 1975. He was replaced on bass by Jeffrey Hammond-Hammond, formerly of the John Evan Band. Moreover, Evan himself joined on keyboards during the year, debuting on the group's first concept album, *Aqualung*. Although attacked by some critics as bombastic and pretentious, the album sold well in both Great Britain and the United States and included Tull favorites such as "Cross-Eyed Mary," "Locomotive Breath," and "Aqualung."

Clive Bunker departed Jethro Tull in late 1971 to form Jude and later resurface with the reformed Blodwyn Pig. He was replaced on drums by Barriemore Barlow, another veteran of the John Evan Band. Extensive touring of the United States continued in 1971 and 1972. Their next release, *Thick as a Brick*, essentially an album-long ballad without individual cuts, sold spectacularly, staying on the American album charts for nearly a year.

Living in the Past assembled live performances and early songs unreleased in the United States for Jethro Tull's new label, Chrysalis, yielding the group's first major American hit with the title track, which was a British hit from 1969. The group's final concept album, *A Passion Play*, was critically lambasted by virtually every rock critic, and it sold poorly in Britain but massively in the United States. The subsequent American tour featuring the theatrically oriented performance of the album was greeted by record-breaking, sellout crowds.

Nonetheless, apparently road weary and disillusioned by hostile press reviews, Jethro Tull announced their retirement from live performance in August 1973. The group retreated to Switzerland, where they recorded *War Child* as the soundtrack to a movie. The movie was eventually abandoned as too costly, but the album yielded the group's second (and last) major hit, "Bungle in the Jungle." Jethro Tull resumed touring in late 1974 to sell-out crowds. In December 1975 Jeffrey Hammond-Hammond left the group, to be replaced by bassist John Glascock. By 1977 keyboardist David Palmer, the orchestrator of all Jethro Tull albums except *Benefit*, had joined the group. In fall 1979 Dave Pegg of Fairport Convention replaced the ailing Glascock on bass. On November 17, 1979, Glascock died in a London hospital at age 27.

During 1980 Ian Anderson dismissed Barriemore Barlow, John Evan, and David Palmer. Jethro Tull pursued a synthesizer-based sound for the first half of the '80s with two different keyboardists and four different drummers. In the meantime, Ian Anderson recorded a solo album, *Walk into Light*, and rerecorded a number of Jethro Tull classics with the London Symphony Orchestra, released as *A Classic Case*. Reduced to the trio of Ian Anderson, Martin Barre, and Dave Pegg by 1987, the group recorded their best-selling album in years, *The Crest of a Knave*. They also toured for the first time in three years, accompanied by keyboardist Don Airey and drummer Doane Perry, with Fairport Convention as the opening act. By 1989 Martin Allcock (a member of the re-formed Fairport Convention) had replaced Airey on keyboards. Jethro Tull's May 1992 world tour produced *A Little Light Music*, featuring Anderson, Barre, Pegg, and Fairport drummer Dave Mattacks. In 1995 Anderson released *Divinities: Twelve Dances with God*, a classical-music work, on Angel/EMI.

Early Jethro Tull

This Was	Reprise	6336	'69	†
	Chrysalis	1041		†
	Chrysalis	41041	'83	†
	Chrysalis	21041		CS/CD
Stand Up	Reprise	6360	'69	†
	Chrysalis	1042		†
	Chrysalis	41042	'83	†
	Chrysalis	21042		CS/CD
	Mobile Fidelity	524		CD
Benefit	Reprise	6400	'70	†
	Chrysalis	1043		†
	Chrysalis	41043	'83	†
	Chrysalis	21043		CS/CD

Blodwyn Pig (with Mick Abrahams)

Ahead Rings Out	A&M	4210	'69	†
	A&M	3180	'82	†
Getting to This	A&M	4243	'70	†

Mick Abrahams

Mick Abrahams	A&M	4312	'71	†

Wild Turkey (with Glenn Cornick)

Battle Hymn	Reprise	2070	'72	†

Jethro Tull

Aqualung	Reprise	2035	'71	†
	Chrysalis	1044		†
	Chrysalis	21044	'84	CS/CD
Thick as a Brick	Reprise	2072	'72	†
	Chrysalis	1003		†
	Chrysalis	21003	'86	CS/CD
	Mobile Fidelity	510		CD

Living in the Past	Chrysalis	(2) 1035	'72	†
	Chrysalis	21035		CS/CD
A Passion Play	Chrysalis	1040	'73	†
	Chrysalis	41040	'83	†
	Chrysalis	21040		CS/CD
War Child	Chrysalis	1067	'74	†
	Chrysalis	41067	'83	†
	Chrysalis	21067		CS/CD
M.U.: The Best of Jethro Tull	Chrysalis	1078	'75	†
	Chrysalis	21078		CS/CD
Minstrel in the Gallery	Chrysalis	1082	'75	†
	Chrysalis	41082	'83	†
	Chrysalis	21082		CS/CD
Too Old to Rock 'n' Roll . . . Too Young to Die	Chrysalis	1111	'76	†
	Chrysalis	41111	'83	†
	Chrysalis	21111		CS/CD
Songs from the Wood	Chrysalis	1132	'77	†
	Chrysalis	41132	'83	†
	Chrysalis	21132		CS/CD
Repeat: The Best of Jethro Tull, Volume 2	Chrysalis	1135	'77	†
	Chrysalis	41135	'83	†
	Chrysalis	21135	'86	CS/CD
Heavy Horses	Chrysalis	1175	'78	†
	Chrysalis	41175	'83	†
	Chrysalis	21175		CS/CD
Bursting Out	Chrysalis	1201	'78	†
	Chrysalis	41201	'83	†
	Chrysalis	21201		CS/CD
Stormwatch	Chrysalis	1238	'79	†
	Chrysalis	41238	'83	†
	Chrysalis	21238		CS/CD
"A"	Chrysalis	1301	'80	†
	Chrysalis	21301		CS/CD
The Broadsword and the Beast	Chrysalis	1380	'82	†
	Chrysalis	21380	'86	CS/CD
Under Wraps	Chrysalis	41461	'84	†
	Chrysalis	21461		CS/CD
Original Master	Chrysalis	41515	'85	†
	Chrysalis	21515	'88	CS/CD
The Crest of a Knave	Chrysalis	21590	'87	CS/CD
20 Years of Jethro Tull: The Definitive Collection	Chrysalis	(3) 21653	'88	CD
20 Years of Jethro Tull (selections)	Chrysalis	21655	'89	CS/CD
Rock Island	Chrysalis	21708	'89	CS/CD
Catfish Rising	Chrysalis	21863	'91	CS/CD
A Little Light Music	Chrysalis	21954	'92	CS/CD
Jethro Tull: 25th Anniversary Box Set	Chrysalis	(4) 26004	'93	CD
The Best of Jethro Tull: The Anniversary Collection	Chrysalis	(2) 26015	'93	CD
Roots to Branches	Chrysalis	35418	'95	CS/CD
Ian Anderson				
Walk into Light	Chrysalis	41443	'83	†
	Chrysalis	21443	'86	CS/CD

Divinities: Twelve Dances with God	Angel	55262	'95	CS/CD
The London Symphony Orchestra				
A Classic Case: The Music of Jethro Tull	RCA	9505	'86	LP/CS†
	RCA	7067	'86	CD†
	RCA	62510	'94	CS/CD

BILLY JOEL

(b. May 9, 1949, Hicksville, Long Island, NY)

Classically trained pianist Billy Joel persevered through several New York rock bands and solo albums before emerging as a pop-style singer-songwriter with 1974's autobiographical "Piano Man." Unable to sustain public interest in his career, Joel continued to write and record highly melodic, imaginatively arranged ballads, eventually breaking through into mass popularity with 1977's *The Stranger*. Although favorably compared to the other surviving '70s pop-rock singer-songwriter, Elton John, Billy Joel was also likened to Neil Diamond and Barry Manilow for his superficial, facile songs and cloying, haughty style. Still, he achieved great success on the pop charts through the '80s despite being the bane of rock critics everywhere.

Billy Joel grew up in the working-class community of Hicksville, on New York's Long Island, initiating a dozen years of classical piano training at age four. Raised by his mother after his parents's divorce at age seven, Joel formed his first band, the Echoes, in 1964. The group evolved into the Lost Souls, which was superseded by the Hassles by 1968. Signed to United Artists Records, the group recorded two albums before disbanding. Joel subsequently formed the rock duo Attila with Hassles drummer Jon Small, recording one album for Epic Records.

Signed to Family Productions in 1971, Billy Joel recorded his first album of all-original material, *Cold Spring Harbor*, for Epic, but the poorly produced album failed to generate any interest despite six months of touring to promote it. A live broadcast by Joel and his band in Philadelphia nonetheless produced a regional favorite with "Captain Jack," which was played regularly on radio station WMMR-FM for months. Joel, embroiled in legal disputes with Family Productions, moved to Los Angeles, where he took up residence at the Executive Room piano bar, performing as "Bill Martin" (this experience inspired his first hit, "Piano Man").

On the strength of "Captain Jack," Billy Joel was signed to Columbia Records in spring 1973. The blatantly autobiographical title song to *Piano Man* became a major hit, but interest in Joel waned. After a moderate hit with "The Entertainer" from *Streetlife Serenade*, Joel switched management and moved to upstate New York, forming a new band with drummer Larry DeVitto. *Turnstiles*, issued in 1976, sold poorly, yet contained Joel's classic "New York State of Mind" (covered by Barbra Streisand on her 1977 album *Superman*) and the Phil Spector–style "Say Goodbye to Hollywood."

Subsequently touring for nearly a year, Billy Joel initiated a decade-long relationship with producer Phil Ramone, well known in the industry for his work with Paul Simon and Phoebe Snow. They first collaborated on 1978's *The Stranger*, which remained on the album charts for more than two years and established Joel as a contemporary singer-songwriter. It yielded four hits: the smash "Just the Way You Are," and the major "Movin' Out (Anthony's Song)," "Only the Good Die Young" (which raised the ire of the Catholic Church), and "She's Always a Woman." His next album, *52nd Street*, produced three hits, the smash personal anthem "My Life," "Big Shot," and "Honesty"; it also included the Spector-style "Until the Night."

Projecting a tougher image, Billy Joel's *Glass Houses* yielded four hits, with the facile "It's Still Rock and Roll to Me" (a top hit), "You May Be Right" (a near-smash), "Don't Ask Me Why," and "Sometimes a Fantasy." Following *Songs in the Attic*, 1980 tour recordings of older material, *The Nylon Curtain* exhibited a sense of social consciousness, containing the seven-minute Vietnam portrait "Goodnight Saigon" and yielding major hits with "Pressure" and "Allentown."

Billy Joel reaffirmed his mass popularity with the diverse *An Innocent Man*. Purposely re-creating different pop styles, including '50s doo-wop and '60s soft rock, the album was perhaps Joel's most popular and successful. It produced four top easy-listening crossover hits with "Tell Her About It" (a top pop hit), "An Innocent Man," "The Longest Time," and "Leave Me a Tender Moment Alone," the pop smash "Uptown Girl," and the major pop hit "Keeping the Faith." In 1985 Joel married supermodel Christie Brinkley and scored a near-smash with "You're Only Human (Second Wind)," the royalties to which he donated to the National Committee for Youth Suicide Prevention. The following year he toured for the first time in three years and issued *The Bridge*, which produced major hits with "Modern Woman," "A Matter of Trust," and "This Is the Time"; it also included a duet with Ray Charles, "Baby Grand." Joel's 1987 international tour included stops in Moscow and Leningrad that resulted in two films, the HBO concert movie *Live from Leningrad* and the documentary *A Matter of Trust*, and a live album.

Billy Joel coproduced 1989's *Storm Front* with Foreigner's Mick Jones. The album yielded five hits, including the top hit "We Didn't Start the Fire" and the smash "I Go to Extremes." Joel toured in 1989–1990 and again in 1993. His next album, *River of Dreams*, produced by guitarist Danny Kortchmar (who had previously worked with James Taylor and Don Henley), entered the charts at Number One, a first for the singer. It produced the pop smash title song and the major hit "All About Soul," recorded with Color Me Badd, while containing "The Great Wall of China" and "No Man's Land." Joel and Brinkley were divorced in 1994.

The Hassles

The Hassles	United Artists	6631	'68	†
	Liberty	10138	'81	†
	EMI	98828	'92	CS/CD†
Hour of the Wolf	United Artists	6699	'69	†
	Liberty	10139	'81	†

Attila

Attila	Epic	30030	'70	†

Billy Joel

Cold Spring Harbor	Family Productions	2700	'72	†
	Columbia	38984	'84	CS/CD
Piano Man	Columbia	32544	'73	CS/CD
Streetlife Serenade	Columbia	33146	'74	CS/CD
Piano Man/Streetlife Serenade	Columbia	38216	'86	CS
Turnstiles	Columbia	33848	'76	CS/CD
The Stranger	Columbia	34987	'77	CS/CD
52nd Street	Columbia	35609	'78/'85	CS/CD
Glass Houses	Columbia	36384	'80	CS/CD
Songs in the Attic	Columbia	37461	'81	CS/CD
The Nylon Curtain	Columbia	38200	'82	CS/CD
An Innocent Man	Columbia	38837	'83	CS/CD
Greatest Hits, Volumes 1 and 2	Columbia	40121	'85	CS
	Columbia	(2) 40121	'85	LP/CD

The Bridge	Columbia	40402	'86	CS/CD
In Concert: KOHUEPT	Columbia	40996	'87	CS/CD
Storm Front	Columbia	44366	'89	CS/CD
River of Dreams	Columbia	53003	'93	CS/CD

ELTON JOHN

Elton John (b. Reginald Dwight, Mar. 25, 1947, Pinner, Middlesex, England); **Bernie Taupin** (b. May 22, 1950, Sleaford, Lincolnshire, England)

ELTON JOHN

In collaboration with lyricist Bernie Taupin, Elton John composed some of the most popular songs of the '70s, characterized by Taupin's vaguely romantic, nostalgic, and often esoteric words and John's highly melodic music and ever-present hook, or catchy repetitive motif. With Bernie Taupin and Elton John established as poignant songwriters by 1971, and with John established as a virtual rock institution by 1972, Elton John elicited perhaps the broadest appeal of any rock performer (rivaled only by Paul McCartney) with his penchant for showmanship and catchy melodies and his command of a variety of musical styles. Although critically reproached as lacking evocative emotional commitment or a defined musical character, and regarded as a consolidator rather than as an innovator of musical styles, Elton John nevertheless bridged the gap between pop and rock with enormous success, particularly in the United States. Although suffering a delcine in popularity in the early to mid-'80s, John has since returned to his former prominence on the charts and as a performer with a somewhat more subducd style. He has also become an active fundraiser in the war against AIDS.

Reginald Dwight began playing piano at age 4, winning a scholarship to the Royal Academy of Music in London at age 11. He later performed in a succession of local bands before joining Bluesology as a teenager. Taken over by "Long" John Baldry as his backing group by 1967, Bluesology backed visiting American black acts such as Major Lance, Patti Labelle and the Bluebelles, and Billy Stewart. After the smash British 1967 hit "Let the Heartaches Begin" by Baldry, Bluesology disbanded and Reginald Dwight became Elton John.

Unsuccessfully auditioning for Liberty Records, Elton John was put in touch with lyricist Bernie Taupin, and the two were signed to a three-year songwriting contract with Dick James Music. As the team had little luck writing commercial material, John recorded an anonymous series of budget albums covering current hits. Urged by publicist Steve Brown to follow their own muse, Taupin and John assembled new material and recorded an album, *Empty Sky* (eventually released in the United States in 1975), but both the album and John's first single, "Lady Samantha," sold minimally in Great Britain. Subsequently employing arranger Paul Buckmaster and producer Gus Dudgeon, John recorded *Elton John*, but the album's first single, "Border Song," became only a minor hit in Britain and the United States. John soon recruited drummer Nigel Olsson and bassist Dee Murray, former members of the Spencer Davis Group, for a promotional tour of Britain's college circuit.

Undaunted by initial failures, Elton John's American record company Uni (later absorbed by the parent company, MCA) launched a massive publicity campaign to hype John's American debut at the Troubadour in Los Angeles in August 1970. The tactic worked exceedingly well, and shows there, in New York, and in Philadelphia were greeted by ecstatic reviews. By late 1970 the second single from *Elton John*, "Your Song" (one of the duo's finest compositions), had become a near-smash American hit, and the album, which also included "Take Me to the Pilot," remained on the charts for nearly a year.

Tumbleweed Connection, revealing Bernie Taupin's fascination with the American Old West, contained "Burn Down the Mission" and "Country Comfort," already covered by Rod Stewart, yet yielded no hit singles. During 1971 two Elton John albums were issued in rapid succession: the soundtrack to *Friends* (on Paramount) and the live *11-17-70* (on Uni). *Madman Across the Water*, recorded with Nigel Olsson, Dee Murray, and guitarist Davey Johnstone, produced the major hit "Levon" and the moderate hit "Tiny Dancer," but was greeted harshly by British critics.

Over the next two years, Elton John enjoyed what was generally regarded as the artistic high point of his career. In early 1972 he and his band (Olsson, Murray, and Johnstone) traveled to France to record *Honky Chateau*, eschewing elaborate string arrangements in favor of Johnstone's guitar. "Rocket Man" and "Honky Cat" became smash hits from the album. *Don't Shoot Me, I'm the Piano Player* yielded the derivative top hit "Crocodile Rock" and the poignant smash hit "Daniel," another of the duo's finest compositions. The double-record set *Goodbye Yellow Brick Road* remained on the album charts nearly two years, containing the Marilyn Monroe tribute "Candle in the Wind" and "Funeral for a Friend," and featuring three smash hit singles, "Saturday Night's Alright for Fighting," "Bennie and the Jets," and the title song. *Caribou*, recorded in the United States, contained two more smash hits, "Don't Let the Sun Go Down on Me" and "The Bitch Is Back," and was followed by two more smash hits, a cover of the Beatles' "Lucy in the Sky with Diamonds" and "Philadelphia Freedom."

John was (in)famous for his elaborate stage shows through this period. Exhibiting a flair for outrageous showmanship, wearing wild and often silly costumes, and performing in a flamboyant and flashy fashion, he was compared to Little Richard and Jerry Lee Lewis, and, perhaps more accurately, Liberace. Often identified with the so-called glitter-rock movement, John nonetheless retained an ironic sense of tastefulness that avoided the garish and disconcerting image attached to David Bowie and others of the genre.

In 1973 Elton John and manager John Reid formed Rocket Records. In late 1974 Kiki Dee and American singer-songwriter Neil Sedaka had huge hits on the label, Dee with "I've Got the Music in Me" and Sedaka with "Laughter in the Rain." Sedaka's revitalized career with Rocket lasted through late 1976 (with "Bad Blood" and a slow version of his 1962 hit "Breaking Up Is Hard to Do"), when he switched to Elektra Records. Dee had a smash hit in duet with John on "Don't Go Breakin' My Heart" in 1976. In June 1974 Elton John concluded negotiations on a new recording contract with MCA Records valued at $8 million, the largest such deal in rock history until Stevie Wonder's $13 million contract with Motown in August 1975. John appeared as the Pinball Wizard in Ken Russell's bizarre film version of the Who's *Tommy* in 1975. *Captain Fantastic and the Brown Dirt Cowboy*, which dealt with the early career of John and Taupin, featured the smash hit "Someone Saved My Life Tonight."

During spring 1975 bassist Dee Murray and drummer Nigel Olsson left the Elton John Band. Olsson later scored a major hit with "Dancin' Shoes" and a moderate hit with "Little Bit of Soap" in 1978–1979. With holdover guitarist Davey Johnstone, the band brought in drummer Roger Pope, debuting at Wembley Stadium in June. *Rock of the Westies* produced the two-sided hit "Grow Some Funk of Your Own"/"I Feel Like a Bullet (In the Gun of Robert Ford)," and was followed by the live album *Here and There*. In August 1976 John announced that he was disbanding his group and retiring from live performance. *Blue Moves*, John's final album with producer Gus Dudgeon and collaborator Bernie Taupin, yielded the smash hit "Sorry Seems to Be the Hardest Word" and the moderate hit "Bite Your Lip (Get Up and Dance!)."

Elton John's next album, 1978's critically attacked *A Single Man*, recorded with lyricist Gary Osborne, yielded only one major hit, "Part-Time Love." In February 1979 John returned to live performances, accompanied only by percussionist Ray Cooper, culminating in several appearances in Russia that May. During the year, John recorded with Philadelphia International producer Thom Bell, scoring a near-smash hit with "Mama Can't Buy You Love." He also recorded the inane disco-fied *Victim of Love* under songwriter-producer Pete Bellotte. Late that year John toured the United States for the first time in three years, playing remarkably subdued concerts in medium-size halls, accompanied by only percussionist Cooper. During 1980 John scored a smash hit with "Little Jeannie," toured again with Dee Murray and Nigel Olsson, and signed to the newly formed Geffen Records.

Under producer Chris Thomas, Elton John recorded four albums for Geffen. The first two yielded the major hits "Nobody Wins"; the John Lennon tribute "Empty Garden (Hey Hey Johnny)," with lyrics by Taupin; and "Blue Eyes," with lyrics by Gary Osborne. John again toured with Johnstone, Murray, and Olsson in 1982 and 1984, retaining Johnstone into the '90s. Dee Murray died on January 5, 1992, in Nashville after suffering a stroke while fighting cancer. The defiant "I'm Still Standing" announced John's return to form. John returned to collaborating solely with Bernie Taupin on *Too Low for Zero* (for the first time since *Blue Moves*), resulting in the major hit "Kiss the Bride" and the smash "I Guess That's Why They Call It the Blues." *Breaking Hearts* produced three hits, including the smash "Sad Songs (Say So Much)." Elton John's *Ice on Fire* yielded two hit duets with George Michael, "Wrap Her Up" and the smash "Nikita." John joined Dionne Warwick, Gladys Knight, and Stevie Wonder for the top pop and R&B hit "That's What Friends Are For" in 1985 in support of AMFAR (for AIDS research). *Leather Jackets* marked a low point for John in the '80s, yet he toured from September 1985 to June 1987, undergoing throat surgery in January 1987. The tour wrapped up with successful appearances in China.

Elton John returned to MCA for *Live in Australia*, recorded with the Melbourne Symphony Orchestra, which produced a smash hit with a live version of "Candle in the Wind." By 1988 he had given up his elaborate stage costumes and flamboyant stage demeanor in concert, while for the first time employing electric piano. *Reg Strikes Back*, recorded in England under Chris Thomas, yielded the smash "I Don't Wanna Go On with You Like This" and the major hit "A Word in Spanish." After the major hit "Through the Storm," recorded with Aretha Franklin, John scored three hits from *Sleeping with the Past*, including "Healing Hands" and "Sacrifice."

In 1991 Elton John had a top hit with "Don't Let the Sun Go Down on Me," recorded live in London with George Michael, from the tribute album to John and Taupin, *Two Rooms*. The socially aware album *The One*, recorded under producer Chris Thomas, yielded three hits: the title song (a near-smash), the poignant "The Last Song," and "Simple Life." In November 1992 Elton John and Bernie Taupin signed a $39 million songwriting contract with Warner Chappell Music. At the same time, John established the Elton John AIDS Foundation in Atlanta.

In 1994 Elton John scored a smash pop and top easy-listening hit with "Can You Feel the Love Tonight," and a major pop and smash easy listening hit with "Circle of Life," from the popular animated movie *The Lion King*. He was also inducted into the Rock and Roll Hall of Fame. In early 1995 Polygram Records bought out Elton John's remaining MCA contract to revive his Rocket label for *Made in England*, featuring the hit single "Believe."

Elton John

Empty Sky (recorded 1969)	MCA	2130	'75	†
	MCA	3008		†
	MCA	620		†
	MCA	31000		CD†
	Polydor	832017	'92	CS/CD
Elton John	Uni	73090	'70	†
	MCA	2012		†
	MCA	3000		†
	MCA	37067		†
	MCA	31105		CD†
	Polydor	827689	'92	CS/CD
Tumbleweed Connection	Uni	73096	'71	†
	MCA	2014		†
	MCA	3001		†
	MCA	31103		CD†
	Polydor	829248	'92	CS/CD
	Mobile Fidelity	543	'91	CD
Friends (soundtrack)	Paramount	6004	'71	†
	Pickwick	3598	'78	†
11-17-70	Uni	93105	'71	†
	MCA	2015		†
	MCA	3002		†
	MCA	619		LP/CS/CD†
	Polydor	512738	'92	CS/CD
Madman Across the Water	Uni	93120	'71	†
	MCA	2016		†
	MCA	3003		†
	MCA	31190		CD†
	Polydor	825487	'92	CS/CD
	Mobile Fidelity	516		CD
Tumbleweed Connection/Madman Across the Water	MCA	(2) 6935		CS
Honky Chateau	Uni	93135	'72	†
	MCA	2017		†
	MCA	3004		†
	MCA	37064		†
	MCA	31104		CD†
	Polydor	829249	'92	CS/CD
	Mobile Fidelity	536	'90	CD
Don't Shoot Me, I'm Only the Piano Player	MCA	2100	'73	†
	MCA	3005		†
	MCA	31077		CD†
	Polydor	827690	'92	CS/CD

Honky Chateau/Don't Shoot Me, I'm Only the Piano Player	MCA	(2) 6915		CS
Goodbye Yellow Brick Road	MCA	(2) 10003	'73	†
	MCA	6894		CS/CD†
	Polydor	821747	'92	CS/CD
	Mobile Fidelity	10526		CD
Your Songs (1970–1973)	MCA	37266	'86	CS
	MCA	31016	'86	CD
Caribou	MCA	2116	'74	†
	MCA	3006		†
	MCA	37065		†
	MCA	31189		CD†
	Polydor	825488	'92	CS/CD
Greatest Hits	MCA	2128	'74	†
	MCA	3007		†
	MCA	37215		CD†
	Polydor	512532	'92	CS/CD
Here and There (recorded 1974)	MCA	2197	'76	†
	MCA	3010		†
	MCA	622		LP/CS/CD†
	Polydor	512739	'92	CS/CD
Captain Fantastic and the Brown Dirt Cowboy	MCA	2142	'75	†
	MCA	3009		†
	MCA	37066		†
	MCA	31078		CD†
	Polydor	821746	'92	CS/CD
Rock of the Westies	MCA	2163	'75	†
	MCA	3011		†
	MCA	621		†
	MCA	31001		CD†
	Polydor	832018	'92	CS/CD
Blue Moves	MCA	(2) 11004	'76	†
	MCA	(2) 6011		CS
	MCA	6011		CD
Greatest Hits, Volume 2	MCA	3027	'77	†
	MCA	37216		CD†
	Polydor	512533	'92	CS/CD
Rare Masters	Polydor	514138	'92	CS/CD
The Thom Bell Sessions (recorded 1977)	MCA	39115	'89	CS/CD
A Single Man	MCA	3065	'78	†
	MCA	37068		†
	MCA	1615		CS
	MCA	31181		CD
Victim of Love	MCA	5104	'79	†
	MCA	771	'82	†
21 at 33	MCA	5121	'80	†
	MCA	772		CS
	MCA	31054		CD
The Fox	Geffen	2002	'81	†
	MCA	10497	'92	CS/CD
Jump Up!	Geffen	2013	'82	†
	MCA	10499	'92	CS/CD

Too Low for Zero	Geffen	4006	'83	†
	MCA	10485	'92	CS/CD
Breaking Hearts	Geffen	24031	'84	†
	MCA	10501	'92	CS/CD
Ice on Fire	Geffen	24077	'85	†
	MCA	10500	'92	CS/CD
Leather Jackets	Geffen	24114	'86	LP/CS/CD†
	MCA	10498	'92	CS/CD
Greatest Hits, Volume 3 (1979–1987)	Geffen	24153	'87	LP/CS/CD†
Live in Australia	MCA	(2) 8022	'87	LP/CS/CD
Reg Strikes Back	MCA	6240	'88	CS/CD
Sleeping with the Past	MCA	6321	'89	CS/CD
To Be Continued	MCA	(4) 10110	'90	CS/CD
The One	MCA	10614	'92	CS/CD
Greatest Hits, 1976–1986	MCA	10693	'92	CS/CD
Duets	MCA	10926	'93	CS/CD
Made in England	Rocket/Island	6185	'95	CD
Nigel Olsson				
Drum Orchestra and Chorus	Uni	73113	'71	†
Nigel Olsson	Rocket	2158	'75	†
Nigel Olsson	Columbia	35048	'78	†
Nigel	Bang	35792	'79	†
Changing Tides	Bang	36491	'80	†
Bernie Taupin				
Bernie Taupin	Elektra	75020	'72	†
He Who Rides the Tiger	Asylum	263	'80	†
Words and Music	RCA	4700		†
Tribe	RCA	5922	'87	LP/CS/CD†
Davey Johnstone				
Smiling Faces	MCA	340	'73	†

JANIS JOPLIN

(b. Jan. 19, 1943, Port Arthur, TX; d. Oct. 4, 1970, Hollywood, CA)

BIG BROTHER AND THE HOLDING COMPANY. Janis Joplin, lead voc; **Sam Andrew** (b. Dec. 18, 1941, Taft, CA), gtr; **James Gurley** (b. Dec. 22, 1939, Detroit, MI), gtr; **Peter Albin** (b. June 6, 1944, San Francisco, CA), bs; **David Getz** (b. Jan. 24, 1940, Brooklyn, NY), drm

Perhaps the first female superstar of rock music, Janis Joplin is regarded by some as the greatest white female blues singer of all time. She certainly redefined the role of the white female vocalist with her gutsy, physically and emotionally wrenching, and virtually sexual delivery, opening the way for female "shouters" in rock music. Along with the Jefferson Airplane and the Grateful Dead, Joplin's first group, Big Brother and the Holding Company, formed the nucleus of San Francisco's burgeoning counterculture music scene of the mid- to late '60s. Big Brother and the Holding Company exploded out of the August 1967 Monterey Pop Festival into international prominence, with Joplin emerging as one of the most powerful personalities of the era and essentially becoming a legend in her own time. The group recorded the classic album *Cheap Thrills* before Joplin's departure in late 1968. Sub-

JANIS JOPLIN

sequently recording and performing with backup bands, Joplin died from a heroin overdose on October 4, 1970, at age 27. Meanwhile, Big Brother struggled on without her but was unable to regain its former glory.

Raised in Port Arthur, Texas, Janis Joplin had discovered the blues by age 17. She began singing locally in 1961, primarily at Ken Threadgill's Austin bar. She traveled to San Francisco in 1965, performing at folk clubs and bars before returning to Texas, where she planned to attend the University of Texas at Austin. Meanwhile, during that same year musicians Sam Andrew, Peter Albin, James Gurley, and later David Getz were hanging out at Chet Helms's Haight-Ashbury residence in San Francisco. They subsequently formed Big Brother and the Holding Company. While organizing dances at the Avalon Ballroom, Helms became the group's manager; he had met Joplin during her 1965 trip to San Francisco, and successfully recruited her to return to the Bay Area in spring 1966 to be vocalist for the band. Backed by screeching "psychedelic" guitars, Joplin sang, almost shouted, in the style of blues singers such as Bessie Smith, investing her performances with intense, agitated passion. Debuting at the Avalon Ballroom in June 1966, Big Brother and the Holding Company signed a recording contract with the small Chicago-based Mainstream label, which released the group's poorly produced debut album in September 1967.

Big Brother and the Holding Company were launched into international prominence with their celebrated appearance at the Monterey Pop Festival in August 1967. Their soon-released Mainstream album featured Janis Joplin's stunning performances of "Women Is Losers" and "Down on Me," as well as the whole band's overlooked "Blindman." Signed to a management contract with Albert Grossman (then Bob Dylan's manager) in January 1968, the group switched to Columbia Records for their only other album with Joplin, *Cheap Thrills*. "Piece of My Heart" became a near-smash from the album, which included "Big Mama" Thornton's "Ball and Chain," Janis's own "Turtle Blues," and a moving rendition of George Gershwin's "Summertime." With Joplin garnering the bulk of the media attention, rumors of the group's breakup began to spread in November and were confirmed on December 1 with Joplin's final appearance with the band at Chet Helms's Family Dog.

Retaining guitarist Sam Andrew, Janis Joplin formed a new band, alternately known as Squeeze and the Janis Joplin Revue, with organist Bill King, bassist Brad Campbell, drummer Ron Markowitz, and a horn section. Debuting equivocally at the Memphis Sound Party on December 18, 1968, the group soon suffered a variety of personnel changes. After recording *Kozmic Blues* with the group, Joplin performed her final concert with this band on December 29, 1969, at Madison Square Garden. In April 1970 she again appeared with Big Brother and the Holding Company, reconstituted by Sam Andrew and blues singer-songwriter Nick Gravenites, at Fillmore West. Big Brother (without Janis Joplin) subsequently recorded two albums for Columbia, the first featuring Gravenites's tongue-in-cheek ode to

Merle Haggard, "I'll Change Your Flat Tire, Merle." The group reunited for a time in the late '80s.

Forming a new band, Full-Tilt Boogie, in May, Janis Joplin debuted the group at Freedom Hall in Louisville, Kentucky, on June 12, 1970. The members included guitarist John Till (a latter-day member of her prior band) and bassist Brad Campbell. By September they had nearly finished recording their album, but on October 4, 1970, Janis Joplin was found dead in her Hollywood hotel, the victim of a heroin overdose. Released posthumously, the album, *Pearl*, yielded a top hit with Kris Kristofferson's "Me and Bobby McGee" and included "Cry Baby," the silly ditty "Mercedes Benz," and one of her theme songs, "Get It While You Can."

Columbia later released the live set *Joplin in Concert*, recorded with Big Brother and Full-Tilt Boogie; *Janis*, a soundtrack album to the 1975 film documentary film of the same name; and *Farewell Song*. The 1979 Bette Midler movie *The Rose* was inspired by the life of Janis Joplin. Joplin was inducted into the Rock and Roll Hall of Fame in 1995.

Big Brother and the Holding Company

Big Brother and the Holding Company	Mainstream	6099	'67	†
	Columbia	30631	'71	†
Cheap Thrills	Columbia	9700	'68	CD
	Columbia	00488		CS
Be a Brother	Columbia	30222	'70	†
How Hard It Is	Columbia	30738	'71	†

Janis Joplin

I Got Dem Ol' Kozmic Blues Again Mama	Columbia	9913	'69	CD
	Columbia	00748		CS
Pearl	Columbia	30322	'71	CS/CD
Pearl/Cheap Thrills	CBS	38219	'86	CS
Joplin in Concert	Columbia	31160	'72	CS/CD
Greatest Hits	Columbia	32168	'73	CS/CD
Janis (soundtrack)	Columbia	(2) 33345	'75	†
	Columbia	33345		CS
Farewell Song	Columbia	37569	'82	CS/CD
Janis Joplin	Columbia/Legacy	(3) 48845	'93	CS/CD

K

B. B. KING

(b. Riley B. King, Sept. 16, 1925, near Itta Bena, MS)

The single most popular, successful, and influential black bluesman, B. B. King has served as an international ambassador for the blues since his first widespread recognition in the late '60s. One of the world's most soulful guitar soloists, B. B. King developed a style of playing featuring his trademark arpeggios and bent-note improvisations that influenced virtually every guitarist in the rock and blues fields, an influence acknowledged by white guitarists during the late '60s, most notably by Eric Clapton and Mike Bloomfield. With his style popularized by these and other white guitarists, his tour with the Rolling Stones in 1969, and the conspicuous success of "The Thrill Is Gone" in 1970, B. B. King became the first and only blues singer and guitarist to graduate into extensive mainstream popularity. Elevated to the exclusive Nevada casino and supper club circuit by the '70s, B. B. King was the first black bluesman to tour Russia in 1979, and the first blues artist inducted into the Rock and Roll Hall of Fame, in 1987.

B. B. King grew up on a farm near Indianola, Mississippi, and sang in local gospel choirs. He acquired his first guitar while in his early teens, and he formed his first group, the Elkhorn Singers, for performances in local black clubs. Drafted in 1943, King moved to Memphis in 1947 after his discharge. There he moved in with a cousin, country-blues artist Bukka White, and later secured a 10-minute afternoon show on radio station WDIA. King subsequently formed the Beale Streeters, whose members at various times included Bobby "Blue" Bland and Johnny Ace. King became known as the Beale Street Blues Boy, later shortened to B. B.

After initial recordings for the small Nashville-based Bullet label in 1949, B. B. King was signed to the Los Angeles–based Modern/RPM label by Ike Turner. Scoring his first top R&B hit with "Three O'Clock Blues" in 1952, King formed a band that included a small horn section (a regular feature of his bands) and began relentlessly touring the so-called chitlin' circuit of small black clubs. Smash R&B hits on RPM through 1957 include "You Know I Love You," "Woke Up This Morning," "Please Love Me," "You Upset Me," "Every Day I Have the Blues" (his signature song), "Bad Luck," and "On My Word of Honor." With the discontinuation of the RPM label in 1959, King recorded singles on Kent, with albums issued on Crown and reissued on United and Custom. R&B hits on Kent included "Please Accept My Love," "Sweet Sixteen," and "Partin' Time."

In 1961 B. B. King signed with ABC Records, recording for both ABC and its subsidiary Bluesway. "Rock Me Baby" became his first moderate pop hit in 1964. Although early albums did not sell particularly well, *Live at the Regal*, from 1965, came to be regarded as one of his finest albums. "Don't Answer the Door" was a smash R&B hit in late 1966, and "Paying the Cost to Be the Boss" became a near-smash R&B and moderate pop hit in 1968. By then King had successfully appeared at the Fillmore West and East and received laudatory comments concerning his playing from white guitarists such as Eric Clapton and Mike

Bloomfield. *Lucille* became King's first album-chart entry, and he was soon introduced to a new, international audience with his tour in support of the Rolling Stones in 1969. He became fully established with white audiences after the album *Completely Well* and its near-smash crossover hit "The Thrill Is Gone."

Established on the supper-club and Nevada-casino circuits by the early '70s, B. B. King began recording exclusively for ABC following 1970's *Indianola Mississippi Seeds*. He recorded a series of modest-selling albums, including 1973's *To Know You Is to Love You*, which produced major crossover hits with the title song, cowritten by Stevie Wonder, and "I Like to Live the Love." King also enjoyed considerable commercial success in collaboration with Bobby "Blue" Bland on 1974's *Together for the First Time: Live*. By 1979 King had switched to MCA Records. In February and March of 1979 he performed about 20 shows in Russia, becoming the first black bluesman to tour that country.

B. B. King continued to tour 300 days a year and record for MCA in the '80s and '90s. Noteworthy albums include *There Must Be a Better World Somewhere* and *Live at San Quentin*. He achieved a major R&B hit with "Into the Night" in 1985, and a minor pop hit in 1989 with "When Love Comes to Town," recorded with the Irish rock band U2.

B.B. King

Original Folk Blues, 1949–1950	United	7788		†
Singin' the Blues	Crown	5020		†
	United	7726		†
The Blues	Crown	5063		†
	United	7732		†
Singin' the Blues/The Blues	Flair	86296	'93	CD
	Ace	320		CS/CD
B. B. King Wails	Crown	5115		†
	Crown	147		†
(reissued as) I Love You So	United	7711		†
	Custom	1049		†
B. B. King Sings Spirituals	Crown	5119		†
	Crown	152		†
	United	7723		†
	Custom	1059		†
The Great B. B. King	Crown	5143		†
	United	7728		†
King of the Blues	Crown	5157		†
	Crown	195		†
	United	7730		†
My Kind of Blues	Crown	5188		†
	United	7724		†
Blues for Me	Crown	5230		†
	United	7708		†
	Custom	1046		†
Easy Listening Blues	Crown	5286		†
	United	7705		†
Blues in My Heart	Crown	5309		†
	Custom	1040		†
The Soul of B. B. King	Crown	5359		†
	United	7714		†
	Custom	1052		†
	Kent	539		†

Swing Low, Sweet Chariot	United	7721	'70	†
Rock Me, Baby—14 Great Hits	United	7733		†
Let Me Love You	United	7734		†
Live! B. B. King On Stage	United	7736		†
The Jungle	United	7742		†
Boss of the Blues	United	7750		†
The Incredible Soul of B. B. King	United	7756		†
Turn On with B. B. King	United	7763		†
Greatest Hits, Volume 1	United	7766		†
Better than Ever	United	7771		†
Live	United	7772		†
The Original Sweet Sixteen	United	7773		†
Mr. Blues	ABC	456	'63	†
Live at the Regal	ABC	509	'65	†
	MCA	724	'71	†
	Pickwick	3593	'78	†
	Ace	86		LP
	MCA	27006		CS
	MCA	31106		CD
	Mobile Fidelity	548	'91	CD
Confessin' the Blues	ABC	528	'65	†
Blues Is King	Bluesway	6001	'67	†
	ABC	704		†
	MCA	31368	'90	CD
Blues on Top of Blues	Bluesway	6011	'68	†
	ABC	709			
Lucille	Bluesway	6016	'68	†
	ABC	712		†
	MCA	10518	'92	CS/CD
Live and Well	Bluesway	6031	'69	†
	ABC/MCA	819		†
	MCA	27008		CS
	MCA	31191		CD
Completely Well	Bluesway	6037	'69	†
	ABC/MCA	868		†
	MCA	27009		CS
	MCA	31039		CD
	MCA	11207	'95	CD
Indianola Mississippi Seeds	ABC	713	'70	†
	MCA	31343	'89	CS/CD
Live at Cook County Jail	ABC	723	'71	†
	MCA	27005		CS
	MCA	31080		CD
In London	ABC	730	'71	†
	MCA	10843	'93	CD
L.A. Midnight	ABC	743	'72	†
Guess Who	ABC	759	'72	†
	MCA	10351	'91	CS/CD
To Know You Is to Love You	ABC	794	'73	†
	MCA	10414	'91	CS/CD
Lucille Talks Back	ABC	898	'75	†

King Size	ABC	977	'77	†
Midnight Believer	ABC/MCA	1061	'78	†
	MCA	27011		CS/CD
Take It Home	MCA	3151	'79	†
Live "Now Appearing" at Ole Miss	MCA	(2) 8016	'80	CS/CD
There Must Be a Better World Somewhere	MCA	5162	'81	†
	MCA	27034	'84	CS/CD
Love Me Tender	MCA	5307	'82	†
	MCA	886		CS/CD
Blues 'n' Jazz	MCA	5413	'83	†
	MCA	27119		CS/CD
Six Silver Strings	MCA	5616	'85	CS/CD
Blues 'n' Jazz/The Electric B. B.	MCA	5881	'87	CD†
The King of the Blues: 1989	MCA	42183	'89	CS/CD
Live at San Quentin	MCA	6455	'90	CS/CD
There Is Always One More Time	MCA	10295	'91	CS/CD
Blues Summit	MCA	10710	'93	CS/CD
B. B. King in London	MCA	10843	'94	CD
Got My Mojo Working	MCA	20541	'94	CS/CD
Live at the Apollo	GRP	9637	'91	CS/CD
Heart and Soul: A Collection of Blues Ballads	Pointblank/Virgin	40072	'95	CD

Anthologies

Best	Galaxy	8202	'63	†
16 Greatest Hits	Galaxy	8208		†
Electric B. B.—His Best	Bluesway	6022	'69	†
	ABC/MCA	813		†
	MCA	27007		CS/CD
Back in the Alley	Bluesway	6050	'73	†
	ABC/MCA	878		†
	MCA	27010		CS/CD
Paying the Cost to Be the Boss	Pickwick	3385	'75	†
The Best of B. B. King	MCA	27074		CS
	MCA	31040		CD
Great Moments with B. B. King	MCA	(2) 4124		CS
	MCA	4124		CD
The King of the Blues	MCA	(4) 10677	'92	CS/CD
The Best of B. B. King	Ace	30		LP
The Memphis Masters	Ace	50		LP
King of the Blues Guitar	Ace	152		LP
Spotlight on Lucille	Ace	187	'87	CD
The Best of B. B. King, Volume 1	Ace	198	'87	CS
	Ace	908	'87	CD
The Best of B. B. King, Volume 2	Ace	199	'87	LP/CS/CD
My Sweet Little Angel	Ace	300		LP/CD
	Virgin	39103	'93	CD
Heart and Soul	Ace	376		CD
The Best of B. B. King/The Memphis Masters	Ace	801		CS
Do the Boogie (Early 50s Classics)	Ace	916		CD
The Fabulous B. B. King	Ace	004		CS/CD

Spotlight on Lucille	Flair	91693	'92	CD†
	Flair	86231		CD
The Best of B. B. King, Volume 1	Flair	91691	'92	CD†
	Flair	86230		CD
The Fabulous B. B. King	Flair	29653	'94	CD
B. B. King's Early 50s	Flair	39654	'94	CD

B. B. King and Bobby "Blue" Bland

Together for the First Time: Live	Dunhill	(2) 50190	'74	†
	MCA	(2) 4160	'82	LP/CS
	MCA	4160		CD
Together Again	Impulse	9317	'76	†
	MCA	27012		CS/CD

CAROLE KING

(b. Carol Klein, Feb. 9, 1942, Brooklyn, NY)

In collaboration with Gerry Goffin, Carole King wrote an astounding series of best-selling songs while working as a professional songwriter at New York's famed Brill Building during the '60s. Prolific writers, Goffin (b. Feb. 11, 1939, Queens, NY) and King wrote nearly as many hits as did Beatles Lennon and McCartney, scoring more than 70 chart entries by 1970, including the top hits "Will You Love Me Tomorrow," "Take Good Care of My Baby," "Go Away, Little Girl," and "The Loco-Motion." With the King-Goffin team breaking up in 1967, Carole King embarked on a solo career in 1970. Her second album, *Tapestry*, sold spectacularly and heralded the rise of the singer-songwriter, becoming the best-selling female solo album of all time during its nearly six-year reign on the album charts. Not surprising, *Tapestry* overshadowed King's subsequent recording career. Although she largely withdrew from public view in the mid-'70s, Carole King continued to record into the '90s.

Carole King began singing and taking piano lessons at age 4. She formed the female vocal group the Co-Sines at 14 and met songwriter Gerry Goffin in 1958 while attending Queens College. Signed as a staff songwriter to Al Nevins and Don Kirshner's Aldon Music at 17, she soon married Goffin and initiated their collaborative songwriting career at New York's Brill Building. First brought to the attention of the American record-buying public as the subject of Neil Sedaka's 1959 hit "Oh! Carol," King and Goffin scored their first hit, in late 1960, with "Will You Love Me Tomorrow," recorded by the Shirelles.

Through 1963 Gerry Goffin and Carole King wrote a series of hits recorded by a variety of artists. These included "Some Kind of Wonderful," "When My Little Girl Is Smiling," and the smash "Up on the Roof" for the Drifters; "Sharing You" and the top hit "Take Good Care of My Baby" for Bobby Vee; "Crying in the Rain," written with Howie Greenfield, for the Everly Brothers; "Her Royal Majesty" for James Darren; "Point of No Return" for Gene McDaniels; the smash "One Fine Day" for the Chiffons; "Hey Girl" for Freddie Scott; and "I Can't Stay Mad at You" for Skeeter Davis. In 1963 Goffin and King provided Steve Lawrence and Eydie Gorme with a number of hits, beginning with the top hit "Go Away, Little Girl" for Lawrence. The team also contributed hits to two British groups during the mid-'60s: "I'm Into Something Good" for Herman's Hermits in 1964, and "Don't Bring Me Down" for the Animals in 1966. The duo collaborated with Phil Spector on "Just Once in My Life" for the Righteous Brothers in 1965.

In 1962 Don Kirshner formed Dimension Records, and Gerry Goffin learned production and Carole King arranging, working in the studio as well as composing songs for the label. Dimension's first release, "The Loco-Motion," written by Goffin and King and recorded by Little Eva, became a top hit. Carole King's version of "It Might as Well Rain Until September," originally written for Bobby Vee, was Dimension's second hit, followed by Little Eva's "Keep Your Hands Off My Baby" and two songs recorded by the Cookies, "Chains" and "Don't Say Nothin' (Bad About My Baby)," all written by Goffin-King.

During the mid-'60s Goffin and King formed their own record label, Tomorrow, but singles by King and the Myddle Class failed to reach the charts. In 1967 they contributed hit songs to Kirshner's Monkees ("Pleasant Valley Sunday") and to Aretha Franklin ("A Natural Woman"), while providing the Byrds with "Goin' Back" and "Wasn't Born to Follow," the latter featured in the film *Easy Rider*.

Carole King subsequently broke up the songwriting team, divorcing Goffin in 1968 and marrying the bass player from the Myddle Class, Charles Larkey. King moved to Los Angeles, where she formed the City with Larkey and guitarist Danny Kortchmar and recorded one album, *Now That Everything's Been Said*, for Lou Adler's Ode Records. Although the album failed to sell, it did include "Wasn't Born to Follow" and Goffin-King's "Hi-De-Ho," a major hit for Blood, Sweat and Tears in 1970.

By 1970 Carole King had initiated a solo career, playing piano on James Taylor's *Sweet Baby James* and recording her debut solo album, *Writer*, with Larkey, Kortchmar, and Taylor. The album contained the Goffin-King songs "Up on the Roof," "Goin' Back," and "No Easy Way Down," but sold only modestly. In 1971 King recorded the enormously successful album *Tapestry*. As James Taylor's version of King's "You've Got a Friend" was climbing the charts, so was her own double-sided top hit, "It's Too Late"/"I Feel the Earth Move." The album later yielded another major two-sided hit with "So Far Away"/"Smackwater Jack," while including "Way Over Yonder" and two Goffin-King compositions, "Will You Love Me Tomorrow" and "A Natural Woman." This collection of mature, sophisticated songs (in contrast to the prior teen melodramas she had written) appealed to virtually every sector of the record-buying public, eventually selling 22 million copies and remaining on the album charts for nearly six years.

Carole King's next two albums, *Carole King Music* and *Rhymes and Reasons*, became bestsellers, each yielding a major hit single ("Sweet Seasons" and "Been to Canaan," respectively), but somehow they lacked *Tapestry*'s magic. *Fantasy* was somewhat more socially conscious, producing moderate hits with "Believe in Humanity" and "Corazon," but *Wrap Around Joy*, with most lyrics supplied by David Palmer, was decidedly jazz-oriented. The album's smash hit "Jazzman" featured an exciting saxophone solo by Tom Scott and was followed by "Nightingale." After *Really Rosie*, the soundtrack from an animated television show based on the children's books of Maurice Sendak and using Sendak's lyrics, King recorded *Thoroughbred* with the vocal assistance of Graham Nash, David Crosby, and James Taylor. The album included four Goffin-King songs and yielded a major hit with "Only Love Is Real."

At the end of 1976 Carole King severed relations with Lou Adler's Ode Records, switching to Capitol for the moderate hit "Hard Rock Cafe." By then separated from Charles Larkey, she collaborated with Rick Evers on recordings. King later married Evers and moved to Idaho, but on March 21, 1978, Evers died from a cocaine overdose in Los Angeles. Subsequent albums for Capitol sold only modestly; only 1980's *Pearls*, a collection of King's versions of the Goffin-King classics of the '60s, yielded a major hit, with "One Fine Day."

Essentially withdrawing from public, Carole King recorded two albums for Atlantic and made a brief benefit tour for presidential hopeful Gary Hart in 1984. Working for protection of the wilderness since 1984, King provided the title song to *The Care Bears Movie*, acted in several movies and television shows, and starred in the play *Getting Out*. Following an album for Capitol in 1989, Carole King recorded *Colour of Your Dreams* on her label in

1993; a concert album, featuring daughter Sherry on backup vocals, appeared a year later. Gerry Goffin and Carole King's daughter, Louise, started her modest recording career in the late-'70s. Goffin-King were inducted into the Rock and Roll Hall of Fame in 1990.

The City

Now That Everything's Been Said	Ode	1244012	'69	†

Gerry Goffin

It Ain't Exactly Entertainment	Adelphi	(2) 4102	'73	†

Carole King

Writer: Carole King	Ode	77006	'70	†
	Ode	34944	'78	†
	Columbia/Legacy	34944	'91	CD
Tapestry	Ode	77009	'71	†
	Ode	34946	'78	CS/CD
Carole King Music	Ode	77013	'71	†
	Ode	34949	'78	†
	Columbia/Legacy	34949	'91	CD
Rhymes and Reasons	Ode	77016	'72	†
	Ode	34950	'78	†
	Columbia/Legacy	34950	'91	CD
Fantasy	Ode	77018	'73	†
	Ode	34962	'78	†
	Columbia/Legacy	34962	'91	CD
Wrap Around Joy	Ode	77024	'74	†
	Ode	34953	'78	†
	Columbia/Legacy	34953	'91	CD
Really Rosie (television soundtrack)	Ode	77027	'75	†
	Ode	34955	'78	CS
Thoroughbred	Ode	77034	'76	†
	Ode	34963	'78	†
	Columbia/Legacy	34963	'91	CD
Her Greatest Hits (1972–1978)	Ode	34967	'78	CS/CD
A Natural Woman: The Ode Collection, 1968–1976	Epic	(2) 48833	'94	CS/CD
Simple Things	Capitol	11667	'77	†
	Capitol	16057		†
Welcome Home	Capitol	11785	'77	†
	Capitol	16058	'78	†
Touch the Sky	Capitol	11953	'79	†
	Capitol	16059		†
Pearls—The Songs of Goffin and King	Capitol	12073	'80	†
One to One	Atlantic	19344	'82	†
Speeding Time	Atlantic	80118	'83	LP/CS/CD
City Streets	Capitol	90885	'89	CS/CD
Colour of Your Dreams	Kings X/Rhythm Safari		'93	
Carole King: In Concert	Kings X/Rhythm Safari		'94	

Tribute Album

Tapestry Revisited: A Tribute to Carole King	Atlantic	92604	'95	CS/CD

Louise Goffin

Kid Blue	Asylum	203	'79	†
This Is the Place	Warner Bros.	25692	'88	LP/CS/CD†

KING CRIMSON

Robert Fripp (b. 1946 Wimbourne, Dorset, England), gtr; **Ian McDonald** (b. June 25, 1946, London, England), rds, wdwnd, kybd, mellotron, voc; **Greg Lake** (b. Nov. 10, 1948, Bournemouth, Dorset, England), bs, lead voc; **Mike Giles** (b. Mar. 1, 1942, Bournemouth, England), drm, voc; **Pete Sinfield**, lyrics [Later members include **Raymond "Boz" Burrell** (b. 1946, Lancashire, England) and **John Wetton** (b. June 12, 1950, Derby, England) on bass and vocals; **Bill Bruford** (b. May 17, 1949, Sevenoaks, Kent, England), drums; **Adrian Belew** (b. Robert Steven Belew, Dec. 23, 1949, Covington, KY), guitar and vocals; and **Tony Levin** (b. Anthony Levin, June 6, 1946, Boston, MA), bass.]

KING CRIMSON

Seminal British "progressive" band of the late '60s and '70s, King Crimson attained superstar status in England and Europe but remained essentially a cult band in the United States. Showcasing the doom-laden lyrics of Pete Sinfield and the guitar and mellotron playing of Robert Fripp, King Crimson's debut album, *In the Court of the Crimson King*, became a progressive-rock classic. Virtually reconstituted thereafter, King Crimson and Fripp endured a chaotic series of personnel changes for six more studio albums, including *Larks' Tongues in Aspic* and *Red*. Onetime members of King Crimson include Greg Lake (later with Emerson, Lake and Palmer), Ian McDonald (later with Foreigner), Boz Burrell (later with Bad Company), and John Wetton (later with Uriah Heep, U.K., and Asia). Guitarist extraordinaire Fripp recorded several influential albums with synthesizer player Brian Eno and on his own, before reconvening King Crimson in the early '80s with guitarist Adrian Belew while recording two instrumental albums with guitarist Andy Summers of the Police.

Robert Fripp started playing the guitar at age 11 and worked with his first music group when 14. In Bournemouth he helped form Giles, Giles and Fripp in 1967 with the Giles brothers Mike and Peter, on drums and bass, respectively. They never played in public. Their sole album for Deram failed to attract any attention, and by fall 1968 the group had disbanded.

Mike Giles and Robert Fripp began rehearsing a new band called King Crimson in January 1969, and debuted in London that April. With Pete Sinfield providing the lyrics (and manning the light show), the group's underground reputation was enhanced by a July appearance in Hyde Park at a free Rolling Stones concert. King Crimson's debut album, *In the Court of the Crimson King*, was greeted with near-unanimous critical acclaim and featured five extended pieces, including "Epitaph," "21st Century Schizoid Man," and the title song, a minor hit.

However, after King Crimson's first tour of the United States, Giles and McDonald left the group in December 1969, later to record an album together for Cotillion. Reduced to a trio, King Crimson began recording their second album, only to see Greg Lake depart to join

Emerson, Lake and Palmer during those sessions. *In the Wake of Poseidon* was completed with Gordon Haskell (bs, lead voc), Mel Collins (rds), and the Giles brothers, with Fripp taking over on mellotron. Despite its remarkable resemblance to the debut album, it sold quite well.

By late 1970 Mel Collins and Gordon Haskell had become permanent members of King Crimson, as had drummer Andy McCulloch. Nonetheless, Haskell quit shortly before the final sessions for *Lizard*, later to record a solo album for Atco. Ian Wallace replaced McCulloch, and Fripp recruited bassist Boz Burrell for *Islands*. Again, after a second American tour in early 1972, King Crimson disintegrated. Collins, Wallace, and Burrell left to join blues singer Alexis Korner, and Fripp dismissed lyricist Pete Sinfield, who later recorded a solo album for Manticore.

After a several-month layoff, Robert Fripp reconstituted King Crimson with avant-garde percussionist Jamie Muir, violin and mellotron player David Cross, lead vocalist-bassist John Wetton (from Family), and drummer Bill Bruford (from Yes). This aggregation recorded 1973's *Larks' Tongues in Aspic*, regarded as one of their finer later albums, but Muir dropped out after the first tour. *Starless and Bible Black* was recorded in 1974 by the remaining quartet, which followed that same year with *Red*, recorded without Cross but with the assistance of Mel Collins and Ian McDonald. Fripp dissolved King Crimson around October 1974.

Boz Burrell joined in the formation of Bad Company in late 1973. Ian McDonald helped form Foreigner in early 1976. Bill Bruford recorded a series of albums in the late '70s and early '80s. John Wetton joined Uriah Heep for a year, later formed U.K. with Eddie Jobson and Terry Bozzio, and eventually surfaced in the supergroup Asia. Asia scored major hits in 1982–1983 with "Heat of the Moment" and "Don't Cry."

Robert Fripp subsequently recorded two esoteric albums with Roxy Music synthesizer player Brian Eno. Eno and Fripp devised a system of musical performance, called Frippertronics, that utilized two tape recorders and solo guitar, which Fripp employed for his 1979 American "antitour." He launched his solo recording career that year with the amazing *Exposure* album, later recording with Daryl Hall, his own League of Gentlemen, and Andy Summers of the Police on two all-instrumental albums. He also played on David Bowie's *Scary Monsters* album, produced Peter Gabriel and the Roches, and served as session guitarist for Blondie and Talking Heads.

In 1981 Fripp reconvened King Crimson with vocalist-guitarist Adrian Belew, bassist Tony Levin, and drummer Bill Bruford for three album and two American tours, but the group disbanded by 1984. Belew later manned the Bears, from 1985 to 1988, and recorded solo, scoring a minor hit with "Oh Daddy" in 1989. Bill Bruford rejoined Yes bandmates for a 1989 album and later formed Earthworks. In the '90s Fripp assembled a large group of guitar players for recordings as the League of Crafty Guitarists. By 1994 King Crimson had reunited with Fripp, Belew, Levin, and Bruford, plus two others, for the concept album *THRAK* and a 1995 tour.

Giles, Giles and Fripp

The Cheerful Insanity of Of Giles, Giles and Fripp	Deram	18019	'68	†
	Deram	820965	'93	CD

King Crimson

In the Court of the Crimson King	Atlantic	8245	'69	†
	Atlantic	19155		†
	Editions EG	1502		LP/CS/CD
In the Wake of Poseidon	Atlantic	8266	'70	†
	Editions EG	1503		CS/CD
Lizard	Atlantic	8278	'71	†
	Editions EG	1504		CS/CD
3 Pack (reissue of above three)	Blue Plate	(3) 1760	'94	CD

Islands	Atlantic	7212	'72	†
	Editions EG	1505		CS/CD
Larks' Tongues in Aspic	Atlantic	7263	'73	†
	Editions EG	1506		LP/CS/CD
Starless and Bible Black	Atlantic	7298	'74	†
	Editions EG	1507		CS/CD
Red	Atlantic	18110	'74	†
	Editions EG	1508		LP/CS/CD
U.S.A.	Atlantic	18136	'75	†
Discipline	Warner Bros.	3629	'81	†
	EG	49	'91	CS/CD
Beat	Warner Bros.	23692	'82	†
	EG	51	'91	CS/CD
Three of a Perfect Pair	Warner Bros.	25071	'84	†
	EG	55	'91	CS/CD
The Abbreviated King Crimson	EG	1467	'91	CD
The Essential King Crimson: Frame by Frame	EG	(4) 1595	'91	CD
The Great Deceiver	EG	(4) 1597	'92	CD
The Compact King Crimson	Editions EG	1509		CS/CD
The Concise King Crimson	Blue Plate	1887	'93	CS/CD
THRAK	Virgin	40313	'95	CS/CD
B'Boom Official Live Bootleg	Discipline	9503	'95	CD
McDonald and Giles				
McDonald and Giles	Cotillion	9042	'71	†
Gordon Haskell				
It Is and It Isn't	Atco	33-378	'71	†
Pete Sinfield				
Still	Manticore	66667	'73	†
Robert Fripp and Brian Eno				
No Pussyfooting	Island	16	'75	†
	Antilles	7001		†
	Editions EG	1522		CD
Evening Star	Antilles	7018	'76	†
	Editions EG	103	'81	†
	Editions EG	1560		CD
The Essential Fripp and Eno	Venture/Caroline	1886	'94	CS/CD
Robert Fripp				
Exposure	Polydor	6149	'79	†
	Editions EG	1557		CS/CD
God Save the Queen/Under Heavy Manners	Polydor	4266	'80	†
The League of Gentlemen	Polydor	6317	'81	†
Let the Power Fall	Editions EG	1558	'88	CD
A Blessing of Tears	Discipline	9506	'95	CD
Daryl Hall with Robert Fripp				
Sacred Songs	RCA	3573	'80	†
	RCA	4554		†
Robert Fripp and the League of Gentlemen				
God Save the King	Editions EG	1559	'81	CS/CD

Robert Fripp and Andy Summers

I Advance Masked	A&M	4913	'82/'92	CD
Bewitched	A&M	5011	'84/'92	CD

Robert Fripp and the League of Crafty Guitarists

Live!	Editions EG	1562		CS/CD
Show of Hands	Editions EG	2102	'91	CS/CD
Intergalactic Boogie Express	Discipline	9502	'95	CD

U.K. (with John Wetton)

U.K.	Polydor	6146	'78	†
	Editions EG	1555		CD
Danger Money	Polydor	6194	'79	†
	Editions EG	1585	'90	CD
Night After Night	Polydor	6234	'79	†
	Editions EG	1586	'90	CD

John Wetton

Kings Road (1972–1980)	Editions EG	1554		CS/CD

Asia (with John Wetton)

Asia	Geffen	2008	'82	CS/CD
Alpha	Geffen	4008	'83	CS/CD
Astra	Geffen	24072	'85	†
	MCA	20851	'95	CS/CD
Then and Now	Geffen	24298	'90	CS/CD
Asia Live in Moscow	Rhino	70377	'92	CS/CD
Aqua	Pyramid/Rhino	71833	'94	CD

Bill Bruford

Earthworks	Editions EG	1523	'90	CS/CD
Feels Good to Me	Polydor	6149	'78	†
	Editions EG	1524	'90	CD
One of a Kind	Polydor	6205	'79	†
	Editions EG	1525	'90	CD
Gradually Going Tornado	Polydor	6261	'80	†
	Editions EG	1526	'90	CD
Master Strokes	Editions EG	1527	'90	CS/CD
The Bruford Tapes	Editions EG	106	'81	†
	Editions EG	1528	'90	CD
Dig	Editions EG	1500	'90	LP/CS/CD
Earthworks Live!	Venture/Caroline	1893	'94	CD

Anderson, Bruford, Wakeman, Howe

Anderson, Bruford, Wakeman, Howe	Arista	8590	'89/'90	CS/CD†

Bill Bruford and Patrick Moraz

Flags	Editions EG	1565	'90	CD

Bill Bruford Earthworks

All Heaven Broke Loose	Editions EG	2103	'91	CS/CD
Stamping Ground	Editions EG	2107	'93	CS/CD

Adrian Belew

Lone Rhino	Island	9751	'82	†
	Island	842844		†

Twang Bar King	Island	90108	'83	†
	Island	842845		†
Desire Caught by the Tail	Island	842843	'86	CD
Desire of the Rhino King	Island	510518	'91	CS/CD
Mr. Music Head	Atlantic	81959	'89	CS/CD
Young Lions	Atlantic	82099	'90	LP/CS/CD
Inner Revolution	Atlantic	82370	'92	CS/CD
Here	Caroline	1748	'94	CS/CD
The Bears (with Adrian Belew)				
The Bears	I.R.S./MCA	42011	'87	LP/CS/CD†
Rise and Shine	I.R.S.	42139	'88	LP/CS/CD†

KING CURTIS
(b. Curtis Ousley, Feb. 7, 1934, Fort Worth, TX; d. Aug. 13, 1971, New York, NY)

Along with David "Fathead" Newman and Steve Douglas, King Curtis helped make the saxophone the third most important instrument (after guitar and piano) in R&B and rock and roll as a session player during the late '50s and early '60s. Best known for his exciting and raunchy saxophone solos behind the Coasters (on, for example, "Shoppin' for Clothes" and "Yakety Yak"), Curtis was the only saxophonist of the era to become widely known outside the recording studio. By 1971 he had recorded with more than 125 artists, from Sam Cooke and Wilson Pickett to Eric Clapton, from Bobby Darin and the Shirelles to Delaney and Bonnie.

Curtis Ousley was an adopted child who showed early musical prowess, taking up the saxophone at age 12. He was influenced by jazz players like Lester Young and R&B popster Louis Jordan, and was active in high school bands. Curtis was offered musical scholarships at several colleges, but he opted instead to tour with Lionel Hampton, ending up in New York City by the time he was 18 years old. He quickly became an in-demand session blower for numerous R&B labels. Curtis's distinctive "honking" sound became his musical signature; particularly on the Coasters' hit comic recordings, he virtually became an additional member of the group. A staff musician with Atlantic and Atco Records beginning in 1958, Curtis later produced albums by Sam Moore, Roberta Flack, and Donny Hathaway. He was also a successful bandleader and recording artist, scoring major instrumental hits with his 1962 debut single, "Soul Twist"; 1964's "Spanish Harlem"; and 1967's "Memphis Soul Stew." Aretha Franklin invited Curtis to assemble a backup band for her live performances and recordings, and he became her musical director. However, shortly thereafter King Curtis was stabbed to death following an argument outside of his New York City home on August 13, 1971.

King Curtis				
Have Tenor Sax, Will Blow	Atco	33-113	'59	†
That Lovin' Feeling	Atco	33-189	'66	†
"Live" at Small's Paradise	Atco	33-198	'67	†
The Great Memphis Hit	Atco	33-211	'67	†
King Size Soul	Atco	33-231	'67	†
Sweet Soul	Atco	33-247	'68	†
Best	Atco	33-266	'68	†
Instant Groove	Atco	33-293	'69	†
Get Ready	Atco	33-338	'70	†
"Live" at the Fillmore West	Atco	33-359	'71	†
Everybody's Talkin'	Atco	33-385	'72	†

New Scene	New Jazz	8237	'60	†
	Fantasy/OJC	198		LP
Azure	Everest	1121	'61	†
Trouble in Mind	Tru-Sound	15001	'62	†
	Fantasy/OBC	512	'92	LP/CS/CD
Old Gold	Tru-Sound	15006	'62	†
It's Party Time	Tru-Sound	15008	'62	†
	Ace	262		LP
Doing the Dixie Twist	Tru-Sound	15009	'63	†
Old Gold/Doing the Dixie Twist	Ace	614	'95	CD
Night Train (recorded 1961–1962)	Prestige	24153	'95	CD
Soul Meeting (with Nat Adderley and Wynton Kelly)	Prestige	7222	'62	†
	Prestige	7833	'71	†
	Prestige	24033	'94	CD
Best	Prestige	7709	'68	†
Best-One More Time	Prestige	7775	'70	†
King Soul (with Nat Adderley)	Prestige	7789	'70	†
Jazz Groove	Prestige	(2) 24033	'73	†
Country Soul	Capitol	1756	'62	†
Soul Serenade	Capitol	2095	'64	ǀ
	Capitol	11798	'78	ǀ
The Hits Made Famous by Sam Cooke	Capitol	2341	'65	†
Best	Capitol	2858	'68	†
	Capitol	11963	'79	†
Sax in Motion	Camden	2242	'68	†
Watermelon man	Pickwick	3293	'72	†
Soul Time	Up Front	157	'73	†
Soul Twist	Collectables	5119	'89	LP/CS/CD
Golden Classics: Enjoy	Collectables	5156		LP/CS/CD
Instant Soul: The Legendary King Curtis	Razor & Tie	2054	'94	CS/CD
King Curtis and the Shirelles				
Give a Twist Party	Scepter	505		†
Eternally Soul	Scepter	569	'70	†
King Curtis and "Champion" Jack Dupree				
Blues at Montreux	Atlantic	1637	'73	†
	Atlantic	81389	'92	CD

THE KINGSTON TRIO

Bob Shane (b. Feb. 1, 1934, Hilo, HI), gtr, bjo, voc; **Dave Guard** (b. Nov. 19, 1934, Honolulu, HI; d. Mar. 22, 1991, Rollinsford, NH), gtr, bjo, voc; **Nick Reynolds** (b. July 27, 1933, San Diego, CA), gtr, voc [Dave Guard left in May 1961, to be replaced by **John Stewart** (b. Sept. 5, 1939, San Diego, CA). Bob Shane reconstituted the group in 1972.]

The most successful folk group to emerge in the late '50s, the Kingston Trio projected a clean-cut college image that enabled them to avoid the politically suspect stigma attached to early-'50s folk artists such as Woody Guthrie and the Weavers. In bringing their good-time acoustic music into the wider arenas of AM radio, television, and pop music, the Kingston Trio made folk music commercially viable and opened the way for the early-'60s folk movement, including individual artists and groups like Peter, Paul and Mary, Joan

Baez, Judy Collins, Bob Dylan, and dozens of others. Disbanding in 1967, the Kingston Trio was resurrected by Bob Shane in the '70s. Second-generation member John Stewart subsequently managed a modest performing and recording career that featured his often poignant and compelling songwriting.

Collegians Bob Shane, Dave Guard, and Nick Reynolds formed the Kingston Trio in San Francisco, California, in 1957. All three played guitar and sang, with Guard and Shane doubling on banjo. Playing local coffeehouses and clubs, most notably the Purple Onion, where they performed for eight months, the Kingston Trio signed with Capitol Records in 1958. Their first and ultimately biggest success came with the top pop hit "Tom Dooley," which was also a near-smash R&B hit. By 1960 they had scored major hits with the silly "Tijuana Jail" and "M.T.A.," and "Worried Man." Their early albums sold spectacularly, with their debut album, *The Kingston Trio*, staying on the charts nearly four years, and three of their next four albums remaining on the charts for more than two years.

Dave Guard left the Kingston Trio in May 1961 to form the Whiskeyhill Singers with Judy Henske. He later moved to Australia, where he hosted a television program, before returning to the United States in 1968. He also authored two children's books and recorded the recent *Up and In*. He died at his home in Rollinsford, New Hampshire, on March 22, 1991, of lymphoma. He was replaced by John Stewart, the founder of the folk group the Cumberland Three.

The Kingston Trio's hits continued through 1963 with Pete Seeger's "Where Have All the Flowers Gone," Dave Guard's "Scotch and Soda" (only a minor hit, but standard lounge fare today), Hoyt Axton's "Greenback Dollar," and "Reverend Mr. Black." In 1964 they switched to Decca Records but failed to achieve even a minor hit.

In 1967 the Kingston Trio disbanded, but in 1972 Bob Shane reconstituted the group with singer-guitarist Roger Gambill and banjoist George Grove. They performed on the college and supper-club circuits, but Gambill died in Atlanta, Georgia, on March 20, 1985, at age 42 after suffering a heart attack and stroke. He was replaced by Bob Haworth of the Brothers Four until the early '90s, when Nick Reynolds rejoined the group.

John Stewart subsequently pursued his own career, recording with Scott Engel, then Buffy Ford. In 1967 the Monkees scored a top hit with his "Daydream Believer," revived as a smash country hit by Anne Murray in 1980. His recordings for Capitol, including the critically acclaimed *California Bloodlines* (with "July, You're a Woman" and "Lonesome Picker") failed to sell, as did the overlooked *Lonesome Picker Rides Again* (with "All the Brave Horses" and "Touch of the Sun") for Warner Bros. and *Cannons in the Rain* (with "All Time Woman" and the minor hit "Armstrong") for RCA. John Stewart achieved his biggest success in 1979 with *Bombs Away, Dream Babies* on RSO Records. The album features the smash hit "Gold" and major hit "Midnight Wind," recorded with Stevie Nicks and Lindsey Buckingham of Fleetwood Mac, and the moderate hit "Lost Her in the Sun."

Stewart's follow-up album sold only modestly, leading him to form his own record company, Homecoming, in the '80s. Albums for the label include *The Trio Years*—rerecordings of songs written for the Kingston Trio—and the poignant *The Last Campaign*, rerecordings of songs composed during and after Bobby Kennedy's 1968 presidential campaign. In 1987 Stewart recorded *Punch the Big Guy* for Cypress with Rosanne Cash, who scored a top country hit with his "Runaway Train" in 1988. In 1992 John Stewart recorded *Bullets in the Hour Glass* for the specialty Shanachie label; a retrospective LP on the same label followed in 1995.

Early Kingston Trio

The Kingston Trio	Capitol	996	'58	†
	Capitol	92710	'90	CS/CD
(reissued as) Tom Dooley	Capitol	16185		†

From the hungry i	Capitol	1107	'59	†
	Capitol	11968		†
The Kingston Trio/From the hungry i	Capitol	96748	'92	CS/CD
Stereo Concert	Capitol	1183	'59	†
At Large	Capitol	1199	'59	†
(reissued as) Scarlet Ribbons	Capitol	16186		†
Tom Dooley/Scarlet Ribbons	Capitol	(2) 513	'70	†
Here We Go Again!	Capitol	1258	'59	†
At Large/Here We Go Again	Capitol	96749	'92	CS/CD
Sold Out	Capitol	1352	'60	†
String Along	Capitol	1407	'60	†
Sold Out/String Along	Capitol	96835	'92	CS/CD
The Last Month of the Year	Capitol	1446	'60	†
	Capitol	93116	'89	CS/CD†
Make Way	Capitol	1474	'61	†
Goin' Places	Capitol	1564	'61	†
Make Way/Goin' Places	Capitol	96836	'92	CS/CD

Dave Guard and the Whiskey Hill Singers

Dave Guard and the Whiskey Hill Singers	Capitol	1728	'62	†

Dave Guard

Up and In	Ball Bearing	1989	'89	CS/CD

The Cumberland Three

Folk Scene	Roulette	25121	'60	†
Civil War Almanac—Volume 1 (Yankees)	Roulette	25132	'60	†
Civil War Almanac—Volume 2 (Rebels)	Roulette	25133	'60	†

The Kingston Trio

Close-Up	Capitol	1642	'61	†
College Concert	Capitol	1658	'62	†
Something Special	Capitol	1747	'62	†
New Frontier	Capitol	1809	'62	†
#16	Capitol	1871	'63	†
Sunny Side!	Capitol	1935	'63	†
Sing a Song with the Kingston Trio	Capitol	2005	'63	†
Time to Think	Capitol	2011	'64	†
Back in Town	Capitol	2081	'64	†
Nick-Bob-John	Decca	74613	'65	†
	Folk Era	5271	'92	CS/CD
Stay Awhile	Decca	74656	'65	†
	Folk Era	5382	'93	CS/CD
Somethin' Else	Decca	74694	'65	†
Children of the Morning	Decca	74758	'66	†
Live at the Crazy Horse	Silverwolf	1001		CD

Anthologies

Encores	Capitol	1612	'61	†
Best	Capitol	1705	'62	†
	Capitol	16183		†
Folk Era	Capitol	2180	'64	†
Best, Volume 2	Capitol	2280	'65	†
	Capitol	16184		†

Best, Volume 3	Capitol	2614	'66	†
Very Best	Capitol	46624		CD†
The Capitol Years	Capitol	(4) 28498	'95	CD
Once Upon a Time	Tetragrammaton	5101	'69	†
Tom Dooley	Pickwick	3260	'71	†
The Kingston Trio	Pickwick	3297	'72	†
Where Have All the Flowers Gone	Pickwick	3323	'72	†
Aspen Gold	DBX	2014	'84	†
Best of the Best	Pro Acoustic	702	'86	CS/CD
Early American Heroes	Pair	(2) 1067	'86	CS/CD
Made in the U.S.A.	Pair	1221		CS/CD
American Troubadours	Pair	1240		CD
Rediscover	Folk Era	2001		CS
Hidden Treasures	Folk Era	2036		LP/CS
Stereo Concert Plus!	Folk Era	2037	'87	CS/CD
Treasure Chest	Folk Era	2052		CD
Tune Up	Folk Era	2060	'89	CD
An Evening with the Kingston Trio	Folk Era	2064	'89	CS/CD
Tom Dooley	CSI	40050	'91	CD
Greatest Hits	Curb/CEMA	77385	'91	CS/CD
Greatest Hits	Special Music	4803		CS/CD
Everybody's Talking	MTA	4134		CS

John Stewart and Scott Engel

I Only Came to Dance with You	Tower	5026	'66	†

John Stewart and Buffy Ford

John Stewart and Buffy Ford	Capitol	2975	'68	†
(reissued as) Signals Through the Glass	Capitol	2975	'75	†
	Capitol	11988		†
	Capitol	16152		†

John Stewart

California Bloodlines	Capitol	203	'69	†
	Capitol	11987	'79	†
	Capitol	16150		†
Willard	Capitol	540	'70	†
	Capitol	11989	'79	†
	Capitol	16151		†
John Stewart	Capitol	80091	'93	CS/CD
The Lonesome Picker Rides Again	Warner Bros.	1948	'71	†
Sunstorm	Warner Bros.	2611	'72	†
Cannons in the Rain	RCA	4827	'73	†
	RCA	3731		†
The Phoenix Concerts	RCA	(2) 0265	'74	†
Wingless Angels	RCA	0816	'75	†
In Concert	RCA	3513	'80	†
Fire in the Wind	Polydor	3027	'77	†
Bombs Away, Dream Babies	RSO	3051	'79	†
	Razor & Tie	2034	'94	CD
Dream Babies Go Hollywood	RSO	3074	'80	†
Blondes	Allegiance	72851	'83	†
Trancas	Affordable Dreams	0001	'84	CS/CD

Centennial	Homecoming	0200	'84	CS
The Last Campaign	Homecoming	0300	'85	LP/CS
Secret Tapes	Homecoming	0450	'86	CS
The Trio Years	Homecoming	0500	'86	CS
Secret Tapes II	Homecoming	0650	'88	CS
Neon Beach: Live	Homecoming	00700	'91	CS
Deep in the Noon	Homecoming	0750		CS/CD
Punch the Big Guy	Cypress	0105	'87	LP/CS/CD†
	Shanachie	8009	'93	LP/CS/CD
Bullets in the Hour Glass	Shanachie	8005	'92	CS/CD
Airdream Believer: A Retrospective	Shanachie	8015	'95	CS/CD
Chilly Winds	Folk Era	14010	'93	CD

THE KINKS

Ray Davies (b. June 21, 1944, Muswell Hill, London, England), lead voc, gtr; **Dave Davies** (b. Feb. 3, 1947, Muswell Hill, England), lead and rhythm gtr, kybd, voc; **Peter Quaife** (b. Dec. 27, 1943, Tavistock, Devon, England), bs, voc; **Mick Avory** (b. Feb. 15, 1944, Hampton Court, England), drm [Peter Quaife left in March 1969, to be replaced by **John Dalton** (b. May 21, 1943, England). Various personnel changes began in 1977.]

THE KINKS

One of the longest-lived groups of the '60s British invasion groups (exceeded only by the Rolling Stones), the Kinks have endured a remarkably erratic career of hit and flop singles, concept albums, and record-company changes under leader Ray Davies and his brother Dave. After some initial hit singles, including the upbeat "You Really Got Me" and the sophisticated social satire of "Dedicated Follower of Fashion," the group became a popular album-oriented band, recording a number of landmark concept albums, including the popular *Lola Versus Powerman and the Moneygoround.* After a period of lesser success, the band returned to touring in the early '80s, when several New Wave bands professed their admiration for the group and their early hit songs.

Ray Davies began playing with the Dave Hunt Band in the early '60s, while brother Dave played in the Bo Weevils with Peter Quaife before forming the Ravens to play the local debutante circuit in 1962. Ray coerced his way into the Ravens around December 1963, and the group was renamed the Kinks and "discovered" by producer Shel Talmy, who secured them a recording contract with Pye Records (Reprise in the United States).

The Kinks' first two singles barely sold, but the third, "You Really Got Me," became a smash British and American hit. The like-sounding "All Day and All of the Night" was a smash hit in early 1965, followed by the slower-paced smash "Tired of Waiting" and "Set Me Free," a major hit. Other early recordings include "Everybody's Gonna Be Happy," "Something Better Beginning," and "See My Friend." They toured the United States in late 1965, but because they missed a single engagement they were banned from performing again until 1969 by the American Federation of Musicians.

The moderate hit "Who'll Be the Next in Line" echoed the Kinks' early raunchy sound, but "A Well Respected Man" marked the beginning of a new phase of astute satire in Ray Davies's songwriting. "Dedicated Follower of Fashion" poked fun at Carnaby Street fops, but the follow-up, "Sunny Afternoon," was decidedly mellow and melodic, even compassionate. Their 1967 album *Face to Face* included Ray's "Dandy," a smash hit for Herman's Hermits.

After *Something Else*, the Kinks' final album under producer Shel Talmy, Ray Davies produced their next two albums, including the neglected concept album *Village Green Preservation Society*, and scored the soundtracks to the movies *The Virgin Soldiers* and *Percy*. Dave Davies managed a smash British-only hit with "Death of a Clown" in 1967, and the Kinks scored smash British hits through 1968 with "Dead End Street," "Waterloo Sunset," "Autumn Almanac," and "Days." However, their albums and singles sold poorly in the United States, in part due to the performance ban. In March 1969 Peter Quaife left the group, to be replaced on bass by John Dalton.

The Kinks' ambitious, critically acclaimed, historically conscious classic concept album *Arthur (or The Decline and Fall of the British Empire)* sold modestly at best, despite the inclusion of "Shangri La" and "Victoria," a minor hit. The Kinks resumed touring the United States in late 1969, with their usual sloppy stage presentation occasionally marred by open hostility between Ray and Dave Davies. Augmented by keyboardist John Gosling beginning in May 1970, the Kinks finally reestablished themselves in 1971 with *Lola Versus Powerman and the Moneygoround*, an acerbic look at the pop music industry and their situation within it. Songs include "Get Back in Line," "Top of the Pops," the moderate hit "Apeman," and the near-smash "Lola," apparently the first rock song to openly deal with transvestism.

By 1971 the Kinks had switched to RCA Records. Their RCA debut, the decidedly countrified *Muswell Hillbillies*, sold only modestly, despite the inclusion of Kinks favorites such as "Alcohol," "Acute Schizophrenia Paranoid Blues," and "20th Century Man." The follow-up, *Everybody's in Show-Biz*, included "Sitting in My Hotel" and the excellent "Celluloid Heroes."

Ray Davies and the Kinks next embarked on a program of ambitious concept albums, complete with on-tour theatrical presentations. The character of Mr. Flash from *The Village Green Preservation Society* was resurrected, but *Preservation*, originally released in two separate "acts," sold poorly. During 1974 Ray and Dave Davies formed Konk Records as an outlet for productions outside the group, but recordings by Claire Hamill and Cafe Society proved unsuccessful. The Kinks' next two albums, *Soap Opera* and *Schoolboys in Disgrace*, sold rather well despite yielding no hit singles, but concurrent tours featuring theatrical performances of each album's material seemed to perplex rather than amuse American audiences.

During the late '70s personnel changes plagued the Kinks, though the Davies brothers and Mick Avory remained as constants. By 1977 they had switched to Arista Records and abandoned the concept-album format, recording *Sleepwalker* as a mere collection of unrelated songs. The album, their best-selling in years, yielded the group's first, albeit minor, hit in six years with the title song. *Misfits* produced a major hit with "A Rock 'n' Roll Fantasy," and *Low Budget* included the underground favorite "A Gallon of Gas" and the moderate hit "(I Wish I Could Fly Like) Superman."

Following the minor hits "Destroyer" and "Better Things," the Kinks scored a smash hit with 1983's "Come Dancing" from *State of Confusion*. Subsequent hits include "Don't Forget to Dance" and "Do It Again." The 1985 made-for-British-TV movie *Return to Waterloo* marked the debut of Ray Davies as a film director/writer. He also appeared in the 1986 movie *Absolute Beginners* and wrote the music and lyrics for *80 Days*, a musical based on Jules Vernes's *Around the World in Eighty Days*, performed in 1988 at the La Jolla Playhouse in Southern California.

With Ray and Dave Davies as the only original members left, the Kinks switched to MCA Records in 1986. *Think Visual* featured Dave's "Rock 'n' Roll Cities," whereas 1989's *U.K. Jive* included the ballad "Now and Then" and "Aggravation." The Kinks were inducted into the Rock and Roll Hall of Fame in 1990, and three years later the group toured America in support of their album *Phobia*. Kinks fans were amused by the album's first single, "Hatred (A Duet)," which reflected on Ray and Dave's long-running love-hate relationship. In 1994 Ray published an autobiographical novel, *X-Ray: The Unauthorized Biography*.

The Kinks

You Really Got Me	Reprise	6143	'64	†
	Rhino	70315	'88	CS/CD
Kinks-Size	Reprise	6158	'65	†
	Rhino	70317	'88	CS
Kinda Kinks	Reprise	6173	'65	†
	Rhino	70316	'88	CS/CD
Kinks Kinkdom	Reprise	6184	'65	†
	Rhino	70318	'88	CS
Kink Kontroversy	Reprise	6197	'66	†
Face to Face	Reprise	6228	'67	†
"Live" Kinks	Reprise	6260	'67	CD
Something Else	Reprise	6279	'68	CD
Four More Respected Gentlemen	Reprise	6309	'68	†
Village Green Preservation Society	Reprise	6327	'69	CD
Arthur (Or the Decline and Fall of the British Empire)	Reprise	6366	'69	CD
Lola Versus Powerman and the Moneygoround	Reprise	6423	'70	CS/CD
Muswell Hillbillies	RCA	4644	'71	†
	Rhino	70934	'90	CS/CD
Everybody's in Show-Biz	RCA	6065	'72	†
	Rhino	70935	'90	CS/CD
Preservation, Act I	RCA	5002	'73	†
Preservation, Act II	RCA	(2) 5040	'74	†
Preservation: A Play in Two Acts	Rhino	(2) 70523	'91	CS/CD
Soap Opera	RCA	5081	'75	†
	RCA	3750		†
	Rhino	70936	'90	CS/CD
Schoolboys in Disgrace	RCA	5102	'75	†
	RCA	3749		†
	Rhino	70937	'90	CS/CD
Sleepwalker	Arista	4106	'77	†
	Arista	8068		CD†
Misfits	Arista	4167	'78	†
	Arista	8069		CD†
Low Budget	Arista	4240	'79	†
	Arista	8050	'85	CD†
One for the Road	Arista	(2) 8401	'80	†
	Arista	(2) 8041		CS
	Arista	8041		CD

Give the People What They	Arista	9567	'81	†
	Arista	8224		CD†
State of Confusion	Arista	8018	'83	†
Word of Mouth	Arista	8264	'84	†
Think Visual	MCA	5822	'86	CS/CD†
Live: The Road	MCA	42107	'88	CS/CD
U.K. Jive	MCA	6337	'89	LP/CS/CD†
Phobia	Columbia	48724	'93	CS/CD
Anthologies				
Greatest Hits	Reprise	6217	'66	†
	Rhino	70086	'89	CS/CD
Kink Kronikles	Reprise	(2) 6454	'72	†
	Reprise	6454		CS/CD
Celluloid Heroes—The Kinks' Greatest	RCA	1743	'76	†
	RCA	3869		†
Second time Around	RCA	3520	'80	†
	RCA	4719		†
History of British Pop, Volume 1	Pye	505	'76	†
History of British Pop, Volume 2	Pye	509	'76	†
Another Compleat Collection	Compleat	(2) 2003	'84	†
Come Dancing with the Kinks (Best of, 1977–1986)	Arista	8428	'86	CS/CD
Kinkdom-Size Kinks	Rhino	75769	'88	CD
Tired of Waiting for You	Rhino	71849	'95	CD
Lost and Found (1986–1989)	MCA	10338	'91	CS/CD
Dave Davies				
AFL1-3603	RCA	3603	'80	†
Glamour	RCA	4036	'81	†
Chosen People	Warner Bros.	23917	'83	†
Tribute Album				
Kinky Music—The Larry Page Orchestra Plays Music of the Kinks	Rhino	058	'83	†

KISS

Paul "Ace" Frehley (b. Apr. 27, 1951, Bronx, NY), lead gtr; **Paul Stanley** (b. Paul Stanley Eisen, Jan. 20, 1952, Queens, NY), gtr; **Gene Simmons** (b. Gene Klein, Aug. 25, 1949, Haifa, Israel), bs; **Peter Criss** (b. Peter Crisscoula, Dec. 20, 1947, New York, NY), drm [Drummer **Eric Carr** (b. July 12, 1950, Brooklyn, NY; d. Nov. 24, 1991, New York, NY) replaced Peter Criss in 1981, and **Vinnie Vincent** replaced Ace Frehley in 1982, leaving in 1984. Various others came and went through the '80s.]

Popular American touring and album band of the late '70s, Kiss combined elements of both glitter rock and heavy metal. Established through an extensive media campaign by their record company Casablanca and near-constant touring, Kiss wore garish costuming and makeup, utilized spectacular onstage special effects, and played barely competent, overloud guitar-based music. Universally attacked by critics, Kiss nonetheless endeared themselves to legions of prepubescent fans (much to the chagrin of their parents) with gimmicks such as blood-spitting, fire-breathing, explosions, dry-ice fogs, and rocket-firing guitars in performance.

The group was originally formed by Simmons and Stanley, who had previously worked together in a New York–based rock band in 1970. Through advertisements in rock magazines, they enlisted drummer Criss and guitarist Frehley, while Bill Aucoin, a local TV producer, brought them to the attention of Casablanca Records. Their first three albums, released in 1974–1975, did little to endear them to critics or fans, but the band continued to tour and build an audience. Aucoin is purported to have underwritten their second major tour in 1975 on his American Express card; the gambit apparently paid off, because their first Top 20 hit, "Rock and Roll All Nite," came later that year. Criss wrote a ballad, "Beth," that hit for the normally ballsy rockers in 1976. Their fans, now known as the Kiss Army, took to emulating their stage costumery and makeup, and the group's popularity inspired two successful Marvel Comics publications and an animated TV special. In late 1978 Kiss became the first rock band whose members simultaneously issued solo albums, backed by the largest advertising-promotion budget in music history ($2.5 million). Their last major hit was 1979's "I Was Made for Loving You"; Criss left the group a year later to pursue a solo career. In 1981 the group, now with drummer Eric Carr, recorded a concept album, *The Elder*, featuring songs coauthored by Lou Reed, but it was a failure. A return to their usual style on *Creatures of the Night* failed to reignite their earlier success.

To support a mythology perpetrated by numerous fanzines, Kiss did not appear in public without their full-face greasepaint makeup until 1983, when they reverted to a mundane yet silly and vulgar hard-rock band. Nonetheless, all of their albums since then have gone gold or platinum, and it is said that the group had sold a mind-boggling 70 million albums by the early '90s. A virtual rock industry unto themselves, Kiss merchandising includes T-shirts, comic books, jewelry, and films. In the mid-'80s second-generation member Vinnie Vincent assembled the Vinnie Vincent Invasion, while Ace Frehley formed Frehley's Comet. Carr died of cancer in 1991. In 1994 Mercury issued the tribute album *Kiss My Ass*, with recordings of Kiss songs by Garth Brooks, Lenny Kravitz, and Anthrax, among others.

Kiss

Kiss	Casablanca	9001	'74	†
	Casablanca	7001		†
	Casablanca	824146		CS/CD
Hotter Than Hell	Casablanca	7006	'74	†
	Casablanca	824147		CS/CD
Dressed to Kill	Casablanca	7016	'75	†
	Casablanca	824148		CS/CD
The Originals (reissue of above three)	Casablanca	(3) 7032	'76	†
Alive!	Casablanca	(2) 7020	'75	
	Casablanca	(2) 822780		CS/CD
Destroyer	Casablanca	7025	'76	†
	Casablanca	824149		CS/CD
Rock and Roll Over	Casablanca	7037	'76	†
	Casablanca	824150		CS/CD
Love Gun	Casablanca	7057	'77	†
	Casablanca	824151		CS/CD
Alive II	Casablanca	(2) 7076	'77	†
	Casablanca	(2) 822781		CS/CD
Double Platinum	Casablanca	7100	'78	†
	Casablanca	824155		CS/CD
Dynasty	Casablanca	7152	'79	†
	Casablanca	812770		CS/CD
Unmasked	Casablanca	7225	'80	†
	Casablanca	800041		CD

Music from "The Elder"	Casablanca	7261	'82	†
	Casablanca	824153		CS/CD
Creatures of the Night	Casablanca	7270	'82	†
	Mercury	824154		CS/CD
Lick It Up	Mercury	814297	'83	CS/CD
Animalize	Mercury	822495	'84	CS/CD
Asylum	Mercury	826099	'85	CS/CD
Crazy Nights	Mercury	832626	'87	CS/CD
Smashes, Thrashes and Hits	Mercury	836427	'88	CS/CD
Hot in the Shade	Mercury	838913	'89	CS/CD
Revenge	Mercury	848037	'92	CS/CD
Alive III	Mercury	514777	'93	CS/CD
Tribute Album				
Kiss My Ass	Mercury	522123	'94	LP/CS/CD
Kiss My A** (censored version)	Mercury	522393	'94	CS/CD
Gene Simmons				
Gene Simmons	Casablanca	7120	'78	†
	Casablanca	826239		CS/CD
Paul Stanley				
Paul Stanley	Casablanca	7123	'78	†
	Casablanca	826915		CS/CD
Peter Criss				
Peter Criss	Casablanca	7122	'78	†
	Casablanca	826917	'88	CS/CD
By Myself	Casablanca	7240	'80	†
Ace Frehley				
Ace Frehley	Casablanca	7121	'78	†
	Casablanca	826196	'88	CS/CD
Trouble Walkin'	Megaforce/Atlantic	82042	'89	LP/CS/CD†
Frehley's Comet				
Frehley's Comet	Megaforce/Atlantic	81749	'87	CS/CD
Live + 1	Megaforce/Atlantic	81826	'88	LP/CS/CD†
Second Sighting	Megaforce/Atlantic	81862	'88	CS/CD†
Vinnie Vincent Invasion				
Vinnie Vincent Invasion	Chrysalis	21529	'86	CS/CD†
All Systems Go	Chrysalis	21626	'88	CS/CD†

GLADYS KNIGHT AND THE PIPS

Gladys Knight (b. May 28, 1944, Atlanta, GA); **Merald "Bubba" Knight** (b. Sept. 4, 1942, Atlanta, GA); **William Guest** (b. June 2, 1941, Atlanta, GA); **Edward Patten** (b. Aug. 2, 1939, Atlanta, GA)

One of the longest-lived family acts in rock music, Gladys Knight and the Pips have been together for more than 40 years, scoring smash R&B and major pop hits on six different labels. With the Pips functioning as an integral part of the group, Gladys Knight and the Pips featured the precise choreography of Cholly Atkins even before they (and he) joined the Motown organization. Despite the fact that Gladys Knight was favorably compared to

GLADYS KNIGHT AND THE PIPS

Aretha Franklin, she and the Pips were treated as a second-line act at Motown, leading to their switch to Buddah Records in 1973. Developing a reputation as *the best* female-led soul group of the mid-'70s, Gladys Knight and the Pips became one of the few former Motown acts to retain (and even increase) their popularity and success after leaving the organization. Established as television and cabaret performers by 1974, Gladys Knight and the Pips recorded and toured the exclusive casino and supper-club circuit into the late '80s, after which Knight performed and recorded solo.

Gladys Knight began singing with the gospel group the Morris Brown Choir in her native Atlanta, Georgia, at age four, later touring with the group throughout the South. At age seven she won $2,000 on Ted Mack's *The Original Amateur Hour* television show, thereafter touring with Mack for a year. In 1952 Gladys joined several close relatives to sing informally at brother Merald's birthday party. Thus was born the first incarnation of the Pips, with Gladys, Brenda, and Merald "Bubba" Knight, and their cousins, Eleanor and William Guest.

The Pips began playing local engagements, then toured the nation with Jackie Wilson and Sam Cooke in 1957. Initial recordings for Brunswick proved unsuccessful. Eleanor and Brenda dropped out of the group in 1959, to be replaced by another cousin, Edward Patten, and Langston George. Finally, in 1961 the group scored their first hit (a top R&B and smash pop hit) with the Johnny Otis ballad "Every Beat of My Heart" on Vee Jay as the Pips and on Fury as Gladys Knight and the Pips. They hit with "Letter Full of Tears" on Fury in 1962, but the company soon went out of business. Gladys Knight returned to Atlanta for a year while the Pips did session work. Langston George left, and Knight rejoined the group in 1963, signing with Maxx Records, achieving a moderate pop and R&B hit with "Giving Up" in 1964.

The first signing to Motown's Soul label in 1965, Gladys Knight and the Pips languished with the company for several years before scoring a R&B smash and moderate pop hit in 1967 with "Everybody Needs Love." Later that year, under producer Norman Whitfield, the group had a top R&B and smash pop hit with "I Heard It through the Grapevine," only to see Marvin Gaye score an even bigger hit with the song a year later. Subsequent smash R&B and major pop hits on Soul include "The End of the Road," "The Nitty Gritty," "Friendship Train," and "You Need Love Like I Do (Don't You)." The group adopted a more mellow sound for later soul hits such as "If I Were Your Woman" (a pop near-smash), "I Don't Want to Do Wrong," "Make Me the Woman That You Go Home To," "Neither One of Us (Wants to Be the First to Say Goodbye)" (a pop smash), and Gladys's own "Daddy Could Swear, I Declare" through 1973.

Gladys Knight and the Pips' *Neither One of Us* album became a bestseller, but despite their consistent recording success and growing status as a live act, they felt they were not being treated as a front-line act by Motown, leading to their defection to Buddah Records in March 1973. Their debut Buddah album, *Imagination*, stayed on the album charts for more than a year and yielded three top R&B and smash pop hits with Tony Joe White's "Midnight Train to Georgia," Barry Goldberg and Gerry Goffin's "I've Got to Use My Imagination," and "Best Thing That Ever Happened to Me." The soundtrack to the movie *Claudine*, recorded under songwriter-producer Curtis Mayfield, included the pop and R&B smash "On and On." Subsequent major pop and smash R&B hits on Buddah included "I Feel a Song (In My Heart)," "The Way We Were"/"Try to Remember," and "Part Time Love." The R&B smashes "Love Finds Its Own Way," "Money," and "Baby Don't Change Your Mind" became only minor pop hits. With the group recording the soundtrack, Gladys Knight made her acting debut with then-husband Barry Hankerson in *Pipe Dreams* in 1976, but the project left the group in difficult financial straits for years.

In 1978 Gladys Knight signed with Columbia Records as a solo, whereas the Pips— "Bubba" Knight, William Guest, and Edward Patten—began recording for Casablanca Records. Allowed to work in clubs but prevented from recording together for more than two years by legal disputes, Gladys Knight and the Pips reunited for the Nicholas Ashford–Valerie Simpson–produced *About Love* and *Touch* albums for Columbia. They scored R&B smashes with "Landlord," "Save the Overtime (For Me)," and "You're Number One (In My Book)," but none of the songs was more than a minor pop hit. Gladys Knight joined Dionne Warwick, Elton John, and Stevie Wonder to record the top pop and R&B hit "That's What Friends Are For" in 1985, the year she starred with Flip Wilson in the short-lived CBS television situation comedy *Charlie and Company*. In 1986 she appeared in the HBO cable-television special *Sisters in the Name of Love* with Dionne Warwick and Patti Labelle.

By 1987 Gladys Knight and the Pips had switched to MCA Records, where they managed R&B smashes with "Love Overboard" (a major pop hit) and "Lovin' on Next to Nothin'." In 1989 Gladys Knight began performing solo engagements, later recording *Good Woman* and *Just for You* for MCA. Gladys Knight and the Pips were inducted into the Rock and Roll Hall of Fame in 1996.

Gladys Knight and the Pips

Letter Full of Tears	Fury	1003		†
Tastiest Hits	Bell	6013	'68	†
In the Beginning	Bell	1323	'75	†
Every Beat of My Heart	Accord	7103	'81	†
Letter Full of Tears	Accord	7105	'81	†
It's Showtime	Accord	7188	'82	†
Everybody Needs Love	Soul	706	'67	†
	Motown	5126	'89	CD†
Feelin' Bluesy	Soul	707	'68	†
	Motown	5467	'90	CS/CD†
Silk and Soul	Soul	711	'69	†
	Motown	5458	'90	CS/CD†
Nitty Gritty	Soul	713	'69	†
	Motown	5148	'89	CD†
All in a Knight's Work	Soul	730		†
If I Were Your Woman	Soul	731	'71	†
	Motown	5388	'89	CS/CD
Everybody Needs Love/If I Were Your Woman	Motown	8031	'86	CD†

Standing Ovation	Soul	736	'72	†
	Motown	5470	'90	CS/CD†
Neither One of Us	Soul	737	'73	†
	Motown	5193	'89	CS/CD
All I Need Is Time	Soul	739	'73	†
	Motown	5396		CD†
All I Need Is Time/Neither One of Us	Motown	8008	'86	CD†
Knight Time	Soul	741	'74	†
A Little Knight Music	Soul	744	'75	†
Imagination	Buddah	5141	'73	†
	Buddah	3304	'90	CS†
Claudine (soundtrack)	Buddah	5602	'74	†
I Feel a Song	Buddah	5612	'74	†
Second Anniversary	Buddah	5639	'75	†
Pipe Dreams (soundtrack)	Buddah	5676	'76	†
Bless This House	Buddah	5651	'77	†
Still Together	Buddah	5689	'77	†
The One and Only	Buddah	5701	'78	†
About Love	Columbia	36387	'80	†
Touch	Columbia	37086	'81/'93	CD
That Special Time of Year	Columbia	38114		LP/CS
Visions	Columbia	38205	'83	CS/CD†
Life	Columbia	39423	'85	†
All Our Love	MCA	42004	'87	LP/CS/CD†

Anthologies

Every Beat of My Heart: The Greatest Hits	VeeJay/Chameleon	74796	'89	LP/CS/CD†
Golden Classics: Full of Tears	Letter Collectables	5154		LP/CS/CD
Greatest Hits	Soul	723	'70	†
Anthology	Motown	(2) 792	'74	†
	Motown	(2) 6200		CD†
	Motown	0483	'95	CS/CD
Motown Superstar Series, Volume 13	Motown	5113		CS/CD
	Motown	9000		CD†
All The Great Hits	Motown	5303		LP/CS/CD
Motown Legends	Motown	5366		†
Compact Command Performance (17 Greatest Hits)	Motown	9044		CD†
All the Great Hits	Motown	9086		CD†
Gladys Knight and the Pips	Up Front	130		†
Best	Buddah	5653	'76	†
Every Beat of My Heart	Pickwick	3348		†
It Hurts Me So	Pickwick	3374		†
I Heard It Through the Grapevine	Pickwick	3534	'76	†
Very Best	United Artists	503	'76	†
Best: The Columbia Years	Columbia	40878	'88	CS/CD
Soul Survivors: Best (1973–1988)	Rhino	70756	'90	CS/CD
Greatest Hits	Curb/CEMA	77321	'90	CS/CD
Best	Pair	(2) 1198		CS/CD
Very Best	Special Music	4909		CS/CD
Very Best, Volume II	Special Music	4924		CS/CD

The Pips

At Last . . . The Pips	Casablanca	7081	'78	†
Callin'	Casablanca	7113	'78	†

Gladys Knight

Miss Gladys Knight	Buddah	5714	'78	†
Gladys Knight	Columbia	35704	'79	†
Good Woman	MCA	10329	'91	CS/CD
Just for You	MCA	10946	'94	CS/CD

KOOL AND THE GANG

Robert "Kool" Bell (b. Oct. 8, 1950, Youngstown, OH), bs; **Ronald Bell** (b. Nov. 1, 1951, Youngstown, OH), ten sax; **Robert "Spike" Mickens** (b. Jersey City, NJ), trpt; **Dennis "Dee Tee" Thomas** (b. Feb. 9, 1951, Jersey City, NJ), sax, flt; **Charles "Claydes" Smith** (b. Sept. 6, 1948, Jersey City, NJ), lead gtr; **Ricky West**, kybd; **George "Funky" Brown** (b. Jan. 5, 1949, Jersey City, NJ), drm [Vocalist **James "J.T." Taylor** (b. Aug. 16, 1953, Laurens, SC) was added in 1979.]

Starting out in the mid-'60s as the jazz-oriented Jazziacs, Kool and the Gang evolved into a popular early-'70s funk band with crossover hits such as "Jungle Boogie" and "Hollywood Swinging," only to be swept aside by the disco craze of the later '70s. Employing disco producer Eumir Deodato in the early '80s, Kool and the Gang established themselves as purveyors of both dance and ballad hits with the addition of vocalist James "J.T." Taylor. Thereby expanding their audience to the easy-listening crowd, Kool and the Gang and vocalist Taylor fared far less well after Taylor's departure in 1988.

Bassist Robert "Kool" Bell formed the jazz quartet the Jazziacs in 1964 in Jersey City, New Jersey, for engagements around Greenwich Village, playing with artists such as Richie Havens and Pharoah Sanders at the Cafe Wha. The other members were tenor saxophonist and brother Ronald Bell, trumpeter Robert Mickens, and saxophonist-flutist Dennis Thomas. Playing sessions in New York from 1964 to 1968, the band was joined by lead guitarist Charles "Claydes" Smith, keyboardist Ricky West, and drummer George Brown. Moving toward soul and funk as the Soul Town Revue and the New Dimensions, the band changed their name to Kool and the Gang around 1968. Signed to De-Lite Records, the band soon achieved modest instrumental hits with "Kool and the Gang" and "The Gangs Back Again." They broke through with 1973's *Wild and Peaceful*, which yielded their first major pop (and smash R&B) hit with "Funky Stuff" and the crossover smashes "Jungle Boogie" and "Hollywood Swinging." Subsequently Kool and the Gang were largely relegated to the R&B field, where they scored smash hits with "Higher Plane," "Rhyme Tyme People," "Spirit of the Boogie," the instrumental "Caribbean Festival," and "Love and Understanding (Come Together)." Seemingly overwhelmed by the tamer and stylized sound of disco music, Kool and the Gang managed a minor pop and smash R&B hit with "Open Sesame" in 1976, and the song was later included on the soundtrack to *Saturday Night Fever*.

Languishing for several years and enduring the departure of Ricky West, Kool and the Gang added vocalist James "J.T." Taylor, whose smooth tenor voice could effectively handle ballads, thus allowing the group to expand its repertoire beyond dance hits. On *Ladies's Night*, the group employed, for the first time, an outside producer, Eumir Deodato, and the album yielded smash R&B, pop, and easy-listening hits with the title cut and "Too Hot." Retaining Deodato as their producer through 1982, Kool and the Gang scored a top pop, R&B, and easy-listening hit with "Celebration," adopted as the theme of hostages returning from Iran and featured as the theme song for the television broadcast of Superbowl XV (and since played to death at weddings and bar mitzvahs across the land). For the attendant album *Celebrate!*, the group was augmented by keyboardist Curtis Williams, trombonist Clifford Adams, and trumpeter Michael Ray.

Kool and the Gang's next album, *Something Special*, remained on the album charts for more than a year, producing a top R&B and easy-listening (and major pop) hit with the ballad "Take My Heart" and the pop and R&B smash "Get Down On It." The group had hits with "Big Fun" and "Let's Go Dancin'(Ooh La, La, La)" in 1982 and were soon established on the lucrative casino circuit. Robert and Ronald Bell returned to producing the group's albums with *In the Heart*, which yielded the crossover smashes "Joanna" and "Tonight."Their next album, *Emergency*, provided four hits: "Misled," "Fresh," "Cherish," and the title track. *Forever*, on Mercury Records, also produced four hits, including the crossover smashes "Victory" and "Stone Love."

By 1987 Ronald Bell had quit touring with Kool and the Gang and brother Robert had invested in a resort on the island of Boulay, off the west coast of Africa. In 1988 James "J.T." Taylor left the group, to be replaced by three singers. Neither Taylor nor Kool and the Gang have experienced much success since.

Kool and the Gang

Kool and the Gang	De-Lite	2003		†
Live at the Sex Machine	De-Lite	2008	'71	†
Best	De-Lite	2009	'71	†
Live at P.J.'s	De-Lite	2010	'72	†
Good Times	De-Lite	2012	'73	†
Wild and Peaceful	De-Lite	2013	'73	†
Kool Jazz	De Lite	4001	'74	†
Light Of Worlds	De-Lite	2014	'74	†
Greatest Hits!	De-Lite	2015	'75	†
Spirit of the Boogie	De-Lite	2016	'75	†
Love and Understanding	De-Lite	2018	'76	†
Open Sesame	De-Lite	2025	'76	†
The Force	De-Lite	9501	'78	†
Spin Their Top Hits	De-Lite	9507	'78	†
	De-Lite	822536		CS/CD
Everybody's Dancin'	De-Lite	9509	'78	†
Ladies's Night	De-Lite	9513	'79	†
	De-Lite	822537		LP/CS/CD†
Celebrate	De-Lite	9518	'80	†
	De-Lite	822538		CS/CD
Something Special	De-Lite	8502	'81	l
	De-Lite	822534		LP/CS/CD†
As One	De-Lite	8505	'82	†
	De-Lite	822535		LP/CS/CD†
In the Heart	De-Lite	8508	'83	†
	De-Lite	814351	'84	LP/CS/CD†
Emergency	De-Lite	822943	'84/'85	CS/CD
Forever	Mercury	830398	'86	LP/CS/CD†
Everything's Kool and the Gang: Greatest Hits and More	Mercury	834780	'88	CS/CD
Sweat	Mercury	838233	'89	LP/CS/CD†
Best (1969–1976)	Mercury	514822	'93	CS/CD
Celebration: Best, 1979–1987	Mercury	522458	'94	CS/CD
Twice as Kool	Polydor	2		†

Celebration	Polygram	846494		CS
James "J.T." Taylor				
Master of the Game	MCA	6347	'90	LP/CS/CD†
Feel the Need	MCA	10304	'91	LP/CS/CD†
Baby I'm Back	MCA	10959	'93	CS/CD

KRIS KRISTOFFERSON
(b. June 22, 1936, Brownsville, TX)

Reinvigorating a staid Nashville country-and-western music scene in the early '70s with his potent songwriting, Kris Kristofferson helped broaden the appeal of country music. In drawing critical attention from folk and rock critics and fans, he helped open the way for a new generation of country songwriters such as Billy Joe Shaver, Jerry Jeff Walker, Guy Clark, and Rodney Crowell. Composing the classics "Sunday Mornin' Comin' Down," "Help Me Make It Through the Night," and "Me and Bobby McGee," Kristofferson also enjoyed considerable success in the '70s with then-wife Rita Coolidge. However, his subsequent musical career suffered as he sought to establish himself as an actor and, more recently, became committed to the cause of human rights. Nonetheless, Kristofferson enjoyed considerable success in the '80s and '90s as a member of the Highwaymen, with Johnny Cash, Willie Nelson, and Waylon Jennings.

Kris Kristofferson moved frequently with his military family before eventually settling in California. A creative-writing major at Pomona College, he won a Rhodes scholarship to Oxford University in England upon graduation in 1958. A successful short-story writer, Kristofferson began pursuing songwriting as a sideline under the name Kris Carson while in England. Remaining at Oxford for less than two years, he then joined the Army and served as a helicopter pilot in Germany, where he played service clubs. Turning down an offer to teach literature at West Point, he was discharged after four and a half years and moved to Nashville in 1965. There he worked as a bartender and as a janitor at Columbia Records, where he met Johnny Cash. He eventually signed a songwriting contract with Fred Foster, providing Roger Miller with the major country hit "Me and Bobby McGee" and Ray Stevens with the minor country hit "Sunday Mornin' Comin' Down" in 1969.

Kristofferson recorded his debut album on Foster's Monument label in 1970, but it was overlooked by the record-buying public, despite the inclusion of "Me and Bobby McGee," "Sunday Mornin' Comin' Down," "For the Good Times," "Help Me Make It Through the Night," the satirical "Best of All Possible Worlds," and "To Beat the Devil," dedicated to Johnny Cash and his wife, June Carter. However, a number of country-and-western artists took notice, recording his songs. Veteran Ray Price scored a top country and major pop hit with "For the Good Times" in 1970, followed by the country smash "I'd Rather Be Sorry" in 1971. Mentor Johnny Cash had a top country hit with "Sunday Mornin' Comin' Down" and Sammi Smith had a top country and near-smash pop hit with "Help Me Make It Through the Night."

Making his first major club appearance at the Troubadour in Los Angeles in June 1970, Kris Kristofferson performed on Johnny Cash's ABC television show a number of times during the year. His popularity was soon broadened when Janis Joplin achieved a top pop hit with "Me and Bobby McGee" in early 1971. *The Silver-Tongued Devil and I* yielded Kristofferson's first major pop hit with "Loving Her Was Easier (Than Anything I'll Ever Do Again)," and included "The Taker," "The Pilgrim—Chapter 33," and the tender "When I Loved Her." *Jesus Was a Capricorn* contained the wry title song (dedicated to John Prine) as well as "Nobody Wins" and the major pop and top country hit "Why Me."

Kris Kristofferson initiated his acting career in 1972's *Cisco Pike*. In 1973 he costarred in *Pat Garrett and Billy the Kid* with veteran James Coburn (and Bob Dylan), and in August he married Rita Coolidge. The couple scored a minor pop and country hit with Tom Jans's "Loving Arms" for A&M, and later recorded an album for Monument Records. Kristofferson's own albums fared progressively less well as he worked on movies such as the highly acclaimed *Alice Doesn't Live Here Anymore* and *The Sailor That Fell from Grace with the Sea*. In 1976 he costarred with Barbra Streisand in an updated remake of the 1937 classic *A Star Is Born*, and the soundtrack album became a best-seller, featuring three solo songs by Kristofferson, including the minor pop hit "Watch Closely Now," two duets, and Streisand's top pop and easy-listening hit "Love Theme from *A Star Is Born* (Evergreen)." Other film roles of the '70s include *Semi-Tough* (with Burt Reynolds and Jill Clayburgh), the made-for-TV movie *Freedom Road* (with Muhammad Ali), and the western (and infamous failure) *Heaven's Gate*. Kristofferson and Rita Coolidge divorced in 1980.

Kris Kristofferson switched to Columbia Records in 1977, managing minor country hits in the early '80s with "Prove It to You One More Time Again" and "Nobody Loves Anybody Anymore." During the first half of the '80s, Kristofferson starred in a series of largely forgettable movies, with the exception of *Songwriter* with Willie Nelson, acclaimed as one of the most astute movies about the country-music business since *Nashville*. In 1985 he teamed with Nelson, Johnny Cash, and Waylon Jennings for *Highwayman*, its top country hit "Highwayman" (written by Jimmy Webb), and its major country hit "Desperadoes Waiting for a Train" (written by Guy Clark). The following year he starred in the popular *Blood and Orchids* miniseries on CBS-TV and acted in the controversial miniseries *Amerika*. The show produced protests from the Soviet Union and the United Nations before its airing in early 1987. Although it proved to be a failure, the show stirred Kristofferson's growing interest in international human rights, as evidenced by the material on *Repossessed*, his first album in more than five years. It produced a minor country hit, "They Killed Him"—a tribute to Jesus Christ, Gandhi, and Martin Luther King—and contained other politically oriented songs such as "Shipwrecked in the Eighties." He subsequently visited the Soviet Union and Nicaragua, denounced American policy in Central America, and campaigned for Jesse Jackson.

In 1990 Kris Kristofferson reunited with Willie Nelson, Waylon Jennings, and Johnny Cash for an album and tour as the Highwaymen. *Singer/Songwriter*, from 1991, contained a disc of his recordings and a disc of his songs recorded by others. In 1992 Kristofferson returned to Monument for *Live at the Philharmonic*, recorded with Willie Nelson and Rita Coolidge. By 1995 Kris Kristofferson had reunited with the other Highwaymen to tour in support of *The Road Goes On Forever* on their new label, Liberty.

Kris Kristofferson

Kristofferson	Monument	18139	'70	†
(reissued as) Me and Bobby McGee	Monument/Columbia	30817	'71	†
	Monument	44351	'88	CS/CD
The Silver-Tongued Devil and I	Monument/Columbia	30679	'71	†
	Monument	44532	'88	CS/CD
Border Lord	Monument/Columbia	31302	'72	†
	One Way	26172	'95	CS
Jesus Was a Capricorn	Monument/Columbia	31909	'72	†
	Monument	47064	'91	CS/CD
Spooky Lady's Sideshow	Monument/Columbia	32914	'74	†
	One Way	26173	'95	CD
Who's to Bless and Who's to Blame	Monument/Columbia	33379	'75	†
Surreal Thing	Monument/Columbia	34254	'76	†

Songs of Kristofferson (All-Time Greatest Hits)	Columbia	34687	'77	†
	Monument	38392	'83	†
	Monument	44355	'88	CS/CD
Easter Island	Columbia	35310	'78	†
Shake Hands with the Devil	Columbia	36135	'79	†
	One Way	26177	'95	CD
To the Bone	Columbia	36885	'81	†
	One Way	26178	'95	CD
My Songs	Pair	1078	'86	CD
Repossessed	Mercury	830406	'86	†
Third World Warrior	Mercury	834629	'89	LP/CS/CD†
Singer/Songwriter	Sony	(2) 48621	'91	CS/CD
Live at the Philharmonic	Monument	52415	'92	CS/CD
Kris Kristofferson and Rita Coolidge				
Full Moon	A&M	4403	'73	†
Breakaway	Monument/Columbia	33278	'74	†
	Monument	47065	'91	CS/CD
Natural Act	A&M	4690	'79	†
Kris Kristofferson and Barbra Streisand				
A Star Is Born (soundtrack)	Columbia	34403	'76	†
	Columbia	57375	'93	CS/CD
Kris Kristofferson, Willie Nelson, Dolly Parton, and Brenda Lee				
The Winning Hand	Monument	(2) 38389	'83	†
	Sony	75067	'95	CS/CD
Kris Kristofferson and Willie Nelson				
Music from *Songwriter*	Columbia	39531	'84	CS
The Highwaymen				
Highwayman	Columbia	40056	'85	CS/CD
Highwayman 2	Columbia	45240	'90	CS/CD
The Road Goes On Forever	Liberty	28091	'95	CS/CD

L

LABELLE

Patti Labelle (b. Patricia Louise Holt, May 24, 1944, Philadelphia, PA); **Nona Hendryx** (b. Aug. 18, 1945, Trenton, NJ); **Sarah Dash** (b. Aug. 18, 1943, Trenton, NJ); **Cindy Birdsong** (b. Dec. 15, 1939, Camden, NJ)

Philadelphia-based "girl group" singers of the '60s, Patti Labelle and the Bluebelles were formed by Labelle and Cindy Birdsong, who had sung previously with the Ordettes, and Nona Hendryx and Sarah Dash, who had previously worked with the Del Capris. They were credited with scoring a major hit in 1962 with "I Sold My Heart to the Junkman," although the song was actually recorded by the Starlets. The group had two other minor hits in 1964, then were reduced to a trio in 1967 when Birdsong left to join the Supremes. In 1971, as a black female vocal trio comprised of Patti Labelle, Nona Hendryx, and Sarah Dash, they were transformed into Labelle under the auspices of British television producer Vicki Wickham. Probably the first and perhaps the only major black female glitter-rock group, Labelle wore outlandish space-age costumes and projected a blatant, kinky sense of sexuality, developing a cult following among homosexuals. The first rock group to perform at New York's Metropolitan Opera House (in 1974), Labelle finally broke through in 1975 with the top hit "Lady Marmalade," a sexually charged and controversial single banned by many radio stations. With the group's breakup in 1977, all three members launched solo careers, with Patti Labelle establishing herself as a powerful vocalist and engaging onstage personality in the '80s. Among her pop hits of the '80s were "New Attitude," "Oh, People," and the top hit duet with Michael McDonald "On My Own."

Patti Labelle and the Bluebelles

The Apollo Presents the Bluebelles	Newtown	631		†
(reissued as) At the Apollo	Collectables	5092	'95	CS
Sleigh Bells, Jingle Bells and Bluebelles	Newtown	632		†
On Stage	Cameo	7043	'64	†
Over the Rainbow	Atlantic	8119	'66	†
Dreamer	Atlantic	8147	'67	†
Over the Rainbow: The Atlantic Years	Soul Classics	2501	'94	CS/CD
At the Apollo	Up Front	129		†
Greatest Hits	Trip	8000	'71	†
Superpak	Trip	(2) 3508	'76	†
Very Best	United Artists	504	'76	†

Labelle

Labelle	Warner Bros.	1943	'71	†
Moonshadow	Warner Bros.	2618	'72	†

369

Pressure Cookin'	RCA	0205	'73	†
	RCA	4176	'82	†
Nightbirds	Epic	33075	'74	CS/CD
Phoenix	Epic	33579	'75	†
Chameleon	Epic	34189	'76/'85	CS/CD

Patti Labelle

The Early Years	Ace	441		CD
Patti Labelle	Epic	34847	'77/'85	CS/CD
Tasty	Epic	35335	'78	†
It's Alright with Me	Epic	35772	'78	†
Released	Epic	36381	'80	†
Best	Epic	36997	'82/'85	CS/CD
The Spirit's In It	Philadelphia Int'l	37380	'81	†
	The Right Stuff	27629	'93	CS/CD
I'm in Love Again	Philadelphia Int'l	38539	'84	†
	The Right Stuff	66690	'93	CS/CD
Patti	Philadelphia Int'l	40020	'85	†
Winner in You	MCA	5737	'86	CS
	MCA	31159	'86	CD†
Be Yourself	MCA	6292	'89	CS/CD
Burnin'	MCA	10439	'91	CS/CD
Live!	MCA	10691	'92	CS/CD
Gems	MCA	10870	'94	CS/CD

Nona Hendryx

Nona Hendryx	Epic	34683	'77	†
Nona	RCA	4565	'83	†
The Art of Defense	RCA	4999	'84	†
The Heat	RCA	5465	'85	†
Female Trouble	EMI-America	17248	'87	†
	EMI-America	46550	'87	CD†
SkinDiver	Private Music	2055	'89	LP/CS/CD

Sarah Dash

Sarah Dash	Kirshner	35477	'78	†
Oo-La-La, Sarah Dash	Kirshner	36207	'80	†
Close Enough	Kirshner	37659	'81	†
You're All I Need	EMI-Manhattan	90036	'88	LP/CS/CD†

LED ZEPPELIN

Robert Plant (b. Aug. 20, 1948, West Bromwich, Staffordshire, England), lead voc; **Jimmy Page** (b. Jan. 9, 1944, London, England), lead gtr, mdln, pedal steel gtr, bjo; **John Paul Jones** (b. John Baldwin, Jan. 3, 1946, Sidcup, Kent, England), bs, kybd; **John Bonham** (b. May 31, 1947, Birmingham, England; d. Sept. 25, 1980, Windsor, England), drm

The prototypical British heavy-metal band of the '70s, Led Zeppelin evolved out of one of the most seminal and influential of all British groups, the Yardbirds. Their "Stairway to Heaven" was one of the first underground, FM radio "hits," and has become an acknowledged rock classic for its innovative arrangement. Vocalist Robert Plant established the style for heavy-metal vocalists with his screaming, shrieking, histrionic vocal manner; in fact Plant remained one of rock's most recognizable vocalists even after Led Zeppelin's

LED ZEPPELIN'S ROBERT PLANT

demise. In addition, drummer John Bonham became one of the most imitated rock drummers of the '70s, with his thunderous, flamboyant style of play.

Jimmy Page took up guitar in his early teens, later playing with Neil Christian and the Crusaders before attending art college for two years. Upon returning to music, he quickly became a much-sought-after session guitarist, allegedly playing on more than half of all the records released in Great Britain between 1963 and 1965. Early session credits include the Who's "Can't Explain"; Them's "Gloria," "Here Comes the Night," and "Baby, Please Don't Go"; and unspecified recordings by the Kinks (disputed by Ray Davies), the Rolling Stones, and Herman's Hermits. Page turned down an offer to join the Yardbirds as Eric Clapton's replacement in 1965, the year Page served as house producer-arranger for Andrew Oldham's Immediate label.

In mid-1966 Jimmy Page finally joined the Yardbirds, replacing departed bass player Paul Samwell-Smith, later to play twin lead guitars with Jeff Beck after Chris Dreja switched to bass. Yardbirds recordings with Beck and Page include "The Train Kept a-Rollin'" from *Rave Up*, "Stroll On" from the soundtrack to the movie *Blow-Up*, and "Happenings Ten Years Time Ago." Jeff Beck left the Yardbirds at the end of 1966, and Page continued as the group's lead guitarist for another 18 months. Finally, in July 1968 the Yardbirds broke up, and Page and Dreja unsuccessfully attempted to continue as the New Yardbirds with vocalist-guitarist Terry Reid and drummer Paul Francis. Reid, unavailable to join the group, suggested that Robert Plant from the Birmingham group the Band of Joy be recruited as lead vocalist. Plant in turn recommended former Band of Joy drummer John Bonham. Dreja later dropped out to pursue a career as a photographer, and session bassist-keyboardist John Paul Jones was brought in as his replacement. Essentially formed in October 1968, Led Zeppelin quickly recorded their debut album for Atlantic Records, soon fulfilling the Yardbirds' remaining concert obligations. In the meantime, Page played sessions with Jeff Beck ("Beck's Bolero"), Donovan (*Hurdy Gurdy Man*), and Joe Cocker (*With a Little Help from My Friends*).

Led Zeppelin's debut album became an instant best-seller, remaining on the album charts for nearly two years. The album featured their first American singles-chart entry, "Good Times Bad Times," and the classics "Dazed and Confused" and "Communication Breakdown." In 1969 the group completed their first American tour in support of Vanilla Fudge, then returned as a headline act. Shortly thereafter, a whole school of heavy-metal rock developed in the wake of Led Zeppelin. *Led Zeppelin II* included the smash-hit classic

"Whole Lotta Love," as well as "Living Loving Maid (She's Just a Woman)" and "Ramble On."

Concentrating their activities on the United States (they never released a single in Great Britain), Led Zeppelin was conducting its fifth American tour by March 1970. *Led Zeppelin III* yielded the major hit "Immigrant Song," but *Led Zeppelin IV* was the album that finally brought the group critical recognition. In addition to containing the hits "Black Dog" and "Rock and Roll," the album included one of the definitive production arrangements of the '70s, "Stairway to Heaven," which built from a subtle acoustic guitar and vocal to a thundering climax, ending with a gentle acoustic guitar-vocal reprise. *Led Zeppelin IV* stayed on the album charts for nearly five years.

During summer 1972 Led Zeppelin again toured America, outdrawing the Rolling Stones in a number of cities. *Houses of the Holy*, which remained on the album charts for almost two years, was the first Led Zeppelin album to utilize string arrangements (by Page), yielding a major hit with "D'yer Mak'er." The group's 1973 American tour was an instant sellout, and they broke both the single-artist concert attendance and gross-income records with their Tampa, Florida, show. With the rock press finally acknowledging their enormous popularity, Led Zeppelin formed Swan Song Records with manager Peter Grant in 1974, a year during which they were relatively inactive.

In early 1975 *Physical Graffiti* was issued, yielding the moderate hit "Trampled Under Foot," but lead vocalist Robert Plant was seriously injured in an automobile accident in Greece on August 4, 1975, necessitating a layoff of more than a year. *Presence* sold quite well without the benefit of either a tour or a single. The film (and soundtrack album) *The Song Remains the Same*, taken primarily from a 1973 concert at Madison Square Garden, was released as the group's first live album and movie.

During 1977 Led Zeppelin again toured the United States, playing marathon three-hour sets to sellout crowds; but an ugly incident between shows at the Oakland Coliseum (in which three members of promoter Bill Graham's support crew were allegedly beaten up) served to reinforce the notion that Led Zeppelin had become arrogant, insensitive, and smug. The group subsequently maintained a low profile and eventually reemerged in 1979 with *In Through the Out Door* and the major hit "Fool in the Rain." That fall Led Zeppelin's first British appearance in four years at the Knebworth Festival was reviewed as perfunctory at best, obsolete at worst. On September 25, 1980, drummer John Bonham was found dead in the Windsor home of Jimmy Page, the victim of inhalation of vomit after a drinking spree. On December 4, Led Zeppelin announced that it was disbanding.

By 1982 Robert Plant was collaborating with guitarist Robbie Blount, recording three solo albums with him through 1985. Plant toured with Blount and drummer Phil Collins (of Genesis) in 1983, scoring a major hit with the oddly titled love song "Big Log" and a moderate hit with "In the Mood" from *The Principle of Moments*, the first album to be released on Plant's own Es Paranza label. In 1984 Plant helped form the short-lived supergroup the Honeydrippers with guitarists Jimmy Page, Jeff Beck, and Nile Rodgers, recording R&B material on the minialbum *Volume One* for Es Paranza. The recording yielded a smash hit with "Sea of Love" and a major hit with "Rockin' at Midnight."

In 1982 Jimmy Page recorded the largely instrumental soundtrack to the movie *Death Wish II*. Following benefit performances for Ronnie Lane's Appeal for Action Research into Multiple Sclerosis in late 1983 with former Bad Company vocalist Paul Rodgers, Page and Rodgers formed the Firm, a rather crass commercial venture, in July 1984. The group remained together until 1986, touring twice, scoring a major hit with "Radioactive" in 1985, and recording two albums.

In 1988 Jimmy Page recorded *Outrider* and toured with vocalist John Miles and drummer Jason Bonham, John Bonham's son, whereas Robert Plant reconstituted his band and began collaborating with keyboardist Phil Johnstone. Plant's *Now and Zen* produced a major hit with "Tall Cool One" (which sampled several Led Zeppelin guitar riffs) and the minor hit "Ship of Fools." Following 1990's *Manic Nirvana*, Plant expanded his band for 1993's *Fate of Nations*, a remarkably mature and engaging album that finally established him as a solo artist of some import.

In the later half of the '80s Led Zeppelin reunited briefly twice, once in July 1985 with drummers Phil Collins and Tony Thompson for the Live Aid concert in Philadelphia, and again in May 1988 with Jason Bonham for Atlantic Records' 40th Anniversary celebration. In 1989 Jason Bonham formed Bonham, recording two albums for WTG Records. Jimmy Page and onetime Deep Purple vocalist David Coverdale recorded *Coverdale/Page*, released in 1993. In May 1994 Jimmy Page and Robert Plant teamed up to perform at a tribute concert to English bluesman Alexis Korner. The following August Plant and Page performed with Egyptian and Moroccan musicians for what became the MTV special *Unledded* (broadcast in October) and the album *No Quarter*. The two, accompanied by several other rock musicians and a Middle Eastern ensemble, toured in support of the album in 1995. That same year Atlantic Records issued the Led Zeppelin tribute album *Encomium*, recorded by Sheryl Crow, Stone Temple Pilots, and Hootie and the Blowfish, among others, and the group was inducted into the Rock and Roll Hall of Fame.

Led Zeppelin

Led Zeppelin	Atlantic	8216	'69	†
	Atlantic	19126		LP/CS/CD†
	Atlantic	82632	'94	CS/CD
Led Zeppelin II	Atlantic	8236	'69	†
	Atlantic	19127		LP/CS/CD†
	Atlantic	82633	'94	CS/CD
Led Zeppelin III	Atlantic	7201	'70	†
	Atlantic	19128		LP/CS/CD†
	Atlantic	82678	'94	CS/CD
Led Zeppelin IV (Zoso)	Atlantic	7208	'71	†
	Atlantic	19129		LP/CS/CD
Houses of the Holy	Atlantic	7255	'73	†
	Atlantic	19130		LP/CS/CD
Led Zeppelin	Atlantic	(6) 82144	'90	LP
	Atlantic	(4) 82144	'90	CS/CD
Remasters	Atlantic	(3) 823/1	'92	CS/CD
Boxed Set[2]	Atlantic	(2) 82477	'93	CD
Led Zeppelin: The Complete Studio Recordings	Atlantic	(10) 82526		CD
Physical Graffiti	Swan Song	(2) 200	'75	†
	Swan Song	(2) 92442	'94	CS/CD
Presence	Swan Song	8416	'76	†
	Swan Song	92439	'94	CS/CD
The Song Remains the Same (soundtrack)	Swan Song	(2) 201	'76	LP/CS/CD
In Through the Out Door	Swan Song	16002	'79	LP/CS/CD†
	Swan Song	92443	'94	CS/CD
Coda	Swan Song	90051	'82	LP/CS/CD†
	Swan Song	92444	'94	CS/CD

Tribute Album

Encomium: A Tribute to Led Zeppelin	Atlantic	82731	'95	CS/CD

Robert Plant

Pictures at Eleven	Swan Song	8512	'82	CS/CD
The Principle of Moments	Swan Song	90101	'83	CS/CD

Shaken 'n' Stirred	Es Paranza	90265	'85	CS/CD
Little by Little (collectors edition)	Es Paranza	90485	'85	CS
Now and Zen	Es Paranza	90863	'88	CS/CD
Manic Nirvana	Es Paranza	91336	'90	LP/CS/CD
	Es Paranza	91361		CD
Fate of Nations	Es Paranza	92264	'93	CS/CD
The Honeydrippers				
Volume One	Es Paranza (mini)	90220	'84/'85	CS/CD
The Firm				
The Firm	Atlantic	81239	'85	CS/CD
Mean Business	Atlantic	81628	'86	CS/CD
Jimmy Page				
The Early Years	Immediate	52428	'92	CS/CD†
Death Wish II (soundtrack)	Swan Song	8511	'82	†
Outrider	Geffen	24188	'88	CS/CD
Coverdale/Page				
Coverdale/Page	Geffen	24487	'93	CS/CD
Jimmy Page and Robert Plant				
No Quarter	Atlantic	(2) 82706	'94	LP
	Atlantic	82796	'94	CS/CD
Bonham				
The Disregard of Timekeeping	WTG	45009	'89	CS/CD
Mad Hatter	WTG	46856	'92	CS/CD†
	WTG	52853	'92	CS/CD

BRENDA LEE

(b. Brenda Mae Tarpley, Dec. 11, 1944, Lithonia, GA)

Possessing a powerful voice equally adept at fleshing out mournful ballads as belting hard-rock songs, Brenda Lee was one of the most popular female vocalists of the late '50s and early '60s, rivaled only by the tamer-sounding Connie Francis. Among Lee's 20 major pop hits are the classics "Sweet Nothin's," "I'm Sorry," "That's All You Gotta Do," "I Want to Be Wanted," and "All Alone Am I," plus the Christmas standard "Rockin' Around the Christmas Tree." Scoring her last major pop hit with "Coming on Strong" in 1966, Lee successfully made the transition to country music in the '70s.

Brenda Lee began singing at age four, winning an Atlanta television station's children's talent contest at age six and subsequently performing on the local television show *TV Wranglers* for three years. Introduced to country music veteran Red Foley in 1955, she later appeared on his television show *Ozark Jubilee*. Signed to Decca Records in 1956, Lee had her first moderate pop hit in early 1957 with "One Step at a Time," followed by "Dynamite." She soon became known as "Little Miss Dynamite" for her powerful voice and diminutive stature.

Brenda Lee scored her first smash pop hit in 1960 with the seductive "Sweet Nothin's." That song and the top hit "I'm Sorry" were written by rockabilly artist Ronnie Self. The flip side of "I'm Sorry," "That's All You Gotta Do," written by Jerry Reed, also became a smash hit. Her two 1960 albums became best-sellers as her success continued with the top hit "I Want to Be Wanted," "Rockin' Around the Christmas Tree," and the smashes "Emotions," "You Can Depend on Me," "Dum Dum" (written by Jackie DeShannon), and "Fool #1." Smash hits continued through 1963 with "Break It to Me Gently," "Everybody Loves Me but

You" (also written by Ronnie Self), "All Alone Am I," and "Losing You." Subsequent major hits through 1966 included "My Whole World Is Falling Down," "As Usual," "Is It True," "Too Many Rivers," and "Coming on Strong."

The moderate pop hit "Johnny One Time" marked Lee's reentry into the country field. By 1973 Decca had been absorbed by MCA Records, and country smashes for Lee on MCA during the '70s included Kris Kristofferson's "Nobody Wins," "Sunday Sunrise," "Wrong Ideas," "Big Four Poster Bed," "Rock On Baby," "He's My Rock," and "Tell Me What It's Like." Following the 1980 country smashes "The Cowgirl and the Dandy" and "Broken Trust," Lee continued to have country hits through 1985, most notably with "Hallelujah, I Love Her So," in duet with George Jones. She was one of the female country stars who appeared as guests on k. d. lang's album *Shadowlands* in 1988. Reestablished on the casino circuit in the '80s, Brenda Lee moved to Warner Bros. Records in 1991.

Brenda Lee

Grandma, What Great Songs You Sang	Decca	78873	'59	†
Brenda Lee	Decca	74039	'60	†
This Is . . . Brenda Lee	Decca	74082	'60	†
Emotions	Decca	74104	'61	†
All the Way	Decca	74176	'61	†
Sincerely	Decca	74216	'62	†
That's All, Brenda	Decca	74326	'62	†
All Alone Am I	Decca	74370	'63	†
Let Me Sing	Decca	74439	'63	†
By Request	Decca	74509	'64	†
Merry Christmas from Brenda Lee	Decca	74583	'64	†
	MCA	232		†
	MCA	15021		†
Top Teen Hits	Decca	74626	'65	†
Versatile	Decca	74661	'65	†
Too Many Rivers	Decca	74684	'65	†
Bye Bye, Blues	Decca	74755	'66	†
Ten Golden Years	Decca	74757	'66	†
	MCA	107		†
Coming On Strong	Decca	74825	'66	†
Reflections in Blue	Decca	74941	'67	†
Johnny One Time	Decca	75111	'69	†
Memphis Portrait	Decca	75232	'70	†
Here's Brenda Lee	Vocalion	73795	'67	†
Let It Be Me	Vocalion	73890		†
	Coral	20044		†
Brenda	MCA	305	'73	†
The Brenda Lee Story	MCA	(2) 4012	'73	CS
	MCA	4012		CD
New Sunrise	MCA	373	'74	†
Now	MCA	433	'75	†
Sincerely, Brenda Lee	MCA	477	'75	†
L.A. Sessions	MCA	2233	'76	†
Even Better	MCA	3211	'80	†
Take Me Back	MCA	5143	'80	†
Only When I Laugh	MCA	5278	'81	†
Greatest Country Hits	MCA	5342	'82	†
	MCA	894		CS

Anthology, Volumes One and Two	MCA	(2) 10384	'91	CD
	MCA	(2) 10405/6	'91	CS
Brenda Lee	Warner Bros.	26439	'91	CS/CD
A Brenda Lee Christmas	Warner Bros.	26660	'91	CS/CD
Greatest Hits *Live*	K-tel	3077	'92	CS/CD
Brenda Lee and Pete Fountain				
For the First Time	Decca	74955	'68	†
Brenda Lee, Kris Kristofferson, Willie Nelson, and Dolly Parton				
The Winning Hand	Monument	(2) 38389	'83	†
	Sony	75067	'95	CS/CD

JERRY LEIBER AND MIKE STOLLER

Jerry Leiber (b. Apr. 25, 1933, Baltimore, MD); Mike Stoller (b. Mar. 13, 1933, New York, NY)

The single most significant, influential, and popular songwriting-production team of the '50s and early '60s, Jerry Leiber and Mike Stoller became the first independent producers in the history of rock music in 1955. Reconstituting the Robins as the Coasters for Atlantic Records, Leiber and Stoller provided that group with some of the first songs in rock music to incorporate satire and social comment. Later writing and producing some of Elvis Presley's finest post—Sun Records recordings, the duo was put in charge of the reconstituted Drifters in the late '50s. Their smash 1959 hit, "There Goes My Baby," established a precedent in black music through the use of Latin rhythms and quasi-classical strings behind Ben E. King's gospel-style lead vocal. That and subsequent recordings by the Drifters and Ben E. King proved so successful that virtually every subsequent black vocal group utilized strings in recording. In 1964 Leiber and Stoller joined record executive George Goldner in the formation of Red Bird Records, where they used professional songwriting teams such as Jeff Barry and Ellie Greenwich and Carole King and Gerry Goffin and popularized the "girl group" sound.

Jerry Leiber met Mike Stoller in Los Angeles in 1949. They soon teamed to write and produce songs for blues artists such as Amos Milburn and Jimmy Witherspoon. Their first R&B hit composition was "Hard Times" by Charles Brown in 1952, followed the next year by "Hound Dog" by Willie Mae "Big Mama" Thornton. In 1953 Leiber and Stoller formed their own label, Spark Records, for recordings by the Robins, such as "Smokey Joe's Cafe" and "Riot in Cell Block #9."

Signed to the New York—based Atlantic label as independent producers in 1955, Leiber and Stoller convinced Carl Gardner and Bobby Nunn of the otherwise recalcitrant Robins to form a new group for recordings on Atlantic's Atco subsidiary. The group was dubbed the Coasters, and between 1955 and 1961 Leiber and Stoller provided them with a series of hit songs that often incorporated wry humor, satire, and social comment. "Searchin'," from 1957, became their first pop smash. Subsequent hit recordings by the Coasters, virtually all composed by Leiber and Stoller, included "Young Blood," "Yakety Yak," "Charlie Brown," "Along Came Jones," "Poison Ivy," and "Little Egypt."

In 1955 Leiber and Stoller furnished the Cheers with the near-smash "Black Denim Trousers and Motorcycle Boots." Elvis Presley scored smash hits with their "Hound Dog" and "Love Me" in 1956, after which the team was contracted to supply songs for Presley's movies. The duo wrote the title songs to *Jailhouse Rock*, *Loving You*, and *King Creole*, while providing other hit songs such as "Treat Me Nice" and "Don't." Their songs "Kansas City" and "Love Potion #9" became pop hits for Wilbert Harrison and the Clovers, respectively, in 1959.

In the late '50s the duo was put in charge of Atlantic's reconstituted Drifters. For "There Goes My Baby," the two used Latin rhythms and a string section to back lead vocalist Ben E. King's stunning gospel-style voice. The song, a smash crossover hit, effectively established the use of such eclectic ingredients (the strings in particular) in the recording of black vocal groups and ushered in soul music. The team's "Dance with Me" became a major hit for the Drifters in 1959, and they later provided Ben E. King with crossover hits such as "Spanish Harlem" (their most recorded song) and the classic "Stand By Me" once he went solo. Apprentice producer Phil Spector, coauthor with Leiber of "Spanish Harlem," was obviously inspired by the production-arrangement technique of the team, as evidenced by his own hit productions during the first half of the '60s. In 1963 the Drifters scored a near-smash hit with the moving "On Broadway," cowritten by Leiber, Stoller, Barry Mann, and Cynthia Weil.

In 1964 Leiber and Stoller met record-company owner George Goldner and the three formed Red Bird and Blue Cat Records, utilizing the songwriting services of Jeff Barry and Ellie Greenwich, George "Shadow" Morton, and Gerry Goffin and Carole King. Red Bird hits included "Chapel of Love," "People Say," and "Iko Iko" by The Dixie Cups, and "Remember (Walkin' in the Sand)," "Leader of the Pack," and "Give Him a Great Big Kiss" by the Shangri-Las. By 1966, weary of their largely administrative duties, Leiber and Stoller sold out to Goldner.

Jerry Leiber and Mike Stoller moved to Columbia Records, but productions for the Coasters and others were poorly handled, leading the duo to terminate their agreement with the label. They subsequently retired from the studio for three years, investing in music-publishing firms such as Starday/King in 1970. In the meantime, several of their songs became hits, including "D. W. Washburn" for the Monkees in 1968 and "Is That All There Is?" for Peggy Lee in 1969.

Generally inactive during the early '70s, Jerry Leiber and Mike Stoller returned to the studio in 1973 to produce albums for Stealers Wheel (including the smash hit "Stuck in the Middle with You"), the Coasters, and T-Bone Walker. They subsequently produced albums for Peggy Lee, Elkie Brooks, and *Procol's Ninth* for Procol Harum. In 1978 the odd set *Other Songs by Leiber and Stoller*, performed by mezzo-soprano Joan Morris, was issued on Nonesuch Records. In 1987 they were inducted into the Rock and Roll Hall of Fame for their contribution to the growth of the music. In 1991 Rhino Records released a compilation album of Leiber-Stoller songs as *There's a Riot Goin' On*.

Jerry Leiber Beat Band

Scooby Doo	Kapp	1127	'59	†

Leiber-Stoller Big Band

Yakety Yak	Atlantic	8047	'61	†

Jerry Leiber and Mike Stoller

There's a Riot Goin' On: The Rock and Roll Classics of Leiber and Stoller	Rhino	70593	'91	CS/CD
Smokey Joe's Cafe: The Songs of Leiber and Stoller (original cast)	Atlantic Theatre	(2) 82765	'95	CS/CD

JOHN LENNON
(b. Oct. 9, 1940, Woolton, Liverpool, England; d. Dec. 8, 1980, New York, NY)

The first Beatle to perform and record outside the group while it was still nominally intact, John Lennon was certainly the most charismatic, controversial, and unorthodox of the group's members. After leaving the Beatles Lennon often worked with his new wife, Yoko Ono (b. Feb. 18, 1933, Tokyo, Japan), a performance artist in her own right. The duo often recorded together, or released parallel albums that would comment on each other's work.

Lennon retired from active music-making in 1975 to become a househusband to his son, Sean (b. Oct. 9, 1975, New York, NY); he and Ono were just returning to active recording when he was assassinated in December 1980. Son Julian Lennon (b. Apr. 8, 1963, Liverpool, England), from his first marriage, enjoyed brief success as a recording artist in 1985; son Sean Ono Lennon has recently emerged as Yoko Ono's newest collaborator.

During 1966, while the Beatles were still intact, John Lennon met Japanese avant-garde artist Yoko Ono, when she had a solo art show in London. In 1968 the couple recorded *Two Virgins*, an album of tape collages that they assembled at Lennon's home; the cover featured a photo of the nude couple, which sparked consternation among record retailers. In 1969 they recorded *Life with the Lions* (for the short-lived Zapple label) and, following their March 20 wedding, *Wedding Album*. After the wedding, John and Yoko continued their controversial ways with their bed-in for peace in Amsterdam. "Give Peace a Chance," recorded with the loosely aggregated Plastic Ono Band in a Montreal hotel suite, became a major hit in July and was soon adopted by the antiwar movement as one of its anthems. That September Lennon, Ono, and the Plastic Ono Band—Eric Clapton (gtr), Klaus Voorman (bs), and Alan White (drm)—played a rock festival in Toronto, producing a live album and a moderate hit with the ominous "Cold Turkey."

In February 1970 "Instant Karma (We All Shine On)," recorded with George Harrison and Billy Preston under producer Phil Spector, became a smash hit for John Lennon. He and Yoko later underwent primal-scream therapy under radical psychologist Dr. Arthur Janov that produced, at least in part, the intense, raw emotionalism of *John Lennon/Plastic Ono Band*. The album included such highly personal songs as "Mother" and "Isolation," as well as the litany "God" and the caustic sociopolitical song "Working Class Hero," banned by some radio stations for its use of obscenity. In the meantime, Yoko Ono recorded the album *Plastic Ono Band*. She recorded three more albums for Apple in the early '70s, plus 1974's unreleased *A Story*, which eventually surfaced on 1992's *Onobox*.

Moving to New York, John and Yoko achieved a major hit with "Power to the People" in spring 1971. Lennon next recorded the relatively gentle and accessible *Imagine* album, essentially his first solo album. An instant best-seller, the album yielded a smash hit with the idealistic title song and contained the poignant "Jealous Guy," the satirical "Crippled Inside," and the vitriolic attack on Paul McCartney, "How Do You Sleep." At Christmastime John and Yoko scored a smash hit with "Happy Xmas (War Is Over)," recorded with the Plastic Ono Band and the Harlem Community Choir.

Subsequently embroiled in legal proceedings by the U.S. Immigration and Naturalization Service, which sought to deport him (ultimately resolved in Lennon's favor in 1976), John Lennon, Yoko Ono, and the Plastic Ono Band recorded a double-record set, *Sometime in New York City*, with the New York–based band Elephant's Memory. The politically charged album—featuring songs concerning the Attica Prison riots and Northern Ireland—and the profeminist anthem "Woman Is the Nigger of the World" (a minor hit) were critically attacked and sold modestly at best. Between August 1973 and January 1975 Lennon and Ono were estranged, and Lennon was better known for his drunken escapades in Los Angeles than for his recorded works. His *Mind Games* album was not well-received critically but nonetheless became a best-seller, yielding a major hit with the title song. The follow-up, *Walls and Bridges*, fared better, producing the top hit "Whatever Gets You Through the Night" and the near-smash "#9 Dream." Lennon next recorded an album of remakes of early rock hits, *Rock 'n' Roll*, such as "Stand By Me" and "Peggy Sue," again working with producer Phil Spector. It was followed by the anthology set *Shaved Fish*. John Lennon and Yoko Ono subsequently reunited and retired from the music business, as Lennon served as househusband to his wife and newborn son Sean. Ono managed their business affairs.

During 1980 John Lennon began writing again, returning to the studio in August with Yoko Ono and a group of hand-picked session players to record *Double Fantasy*. Comprised of seven Lennon and seven Ono songs, the album and its first single, Lennon's "(Just Like) Starting Over," were instant top hits. The album also included the smash hit "Woman," Lennon's revealing "Watching the Wheels" (a near-smash), and the touching "Beautiful Boy." The couple continued to work in the studio, but on December 8, 1980, Lennon was shot to death outside the luxury apartment building the Dakota in Manhattan after returning from recording one night. Covered by the media in a manner usually reserved for world statesmen, Lennon's death forever quelled rumors of a Beatles reunion and ended the career of one of this century's most respected and profound artists.

A number of recordings by John Lennon were issued after his death. *Milk and Honey*, recorded in 1980, contained six songs by Yoko Ono and six by Lennon, including the smash hit "Nobody Told Me," and "I'm Stepping Out," "I Don't Wanna Face It," and "Grow Old with Me." *Live in New York City* was comprised of Lennon's final performance, August 30, 1972, at Madison Square Garden (also issued on video), and *Menlove Avenue* was assembled from outtakes from the *Rock 'n' Roll* and *Walls and Bridges* sessions. *Imagine* was taken from the 1988 film documentary of the same name.

Lennon's life continues to be honored and celebrated through the '80s and '90s. In 1984 a favorite section of Central Park was renamed Strawberry Fields in his honor. On October 9, 1990, Lennon's life was celebrated in a brief ceremony at the United Nations in New York, after which his song "Imagine" was broadcast on more than a thousand radio stations in more than 130 countries to an estimated audience of one billion people. In 1991 Yoko Ono, Sean Ono Lennon, and Lenny Kravitz assembled an all-star cast to record Lennon's "Give Peace a Chance," with new lyrics by Sean and Kravitz. The performers included Peter Gabriel, Bonnie Raitt, Steve Van Zandt, Iggy Pop, Randy Newman, Tom Petty, and Frank Zappa's three children. The recording, issued on Virgin as performed by the Peace Choir, became a minor hit. In 1994 Lennon was inducted individually into the Rock and Roll Hall of Fame (the Beatles were inducted as a group six years earlier).

Yoko Ono recorded several albums after John Lennon's death, including 1981's *Season of Glass* and 1982's *It's Alright (I See Rainbows)*. In 1984 Polydor Records issued *Every Man Has a Woman*, on which artists such as Elvis Costello, Rosanne Cash, and Harry Nilsson performed songs written by Ono. Following 1985's *Starpeace*, Yoko Ono toured in 1986. Rykodisc compiled selections of her recordings, from 1969's *Life with the Lions* to *Starpeace*, on the six-CD box set *Onobox* in 1992, followed by *Walking on Thin Ice*, which contained 19 songs from *Onobox*. In 1994 Capitol Records released the original cast recording of Yoko Ono's off-Broadway play *New York Rock*, loosely based on her life with Lennon. A year later a new album, recorded with son Sean's band, was well-received critically if not commercially.

John Lennon's son by Cynthia Powell, Julian Lennon, launched his own musical career in 1984 with *Valotte*. Julian was largely raised by his mother after his parents' divorce in 1968. His father had given him a guitar at age 11, and he later formed his first rock group with guitarist Justin Clayton as a teenager. In 1983 he secluded himself in Valotte, France, to write and compose. Signed to Charisma Records (Atlantic in the United States) on the strength of demonstration tapes, Julian Lennon recorded *Valotte* under veteran producer Phil Ramone. The album yielded the near-smash "Valotte," the smash hit "Too Late for Goodbyes," the major hit "Say You're Wrong," and the minor hit "Jesse." He toured America in 1985 and launched a world tour in 1986 in support of *The Secret Value of Daydreaming*, which included the moderate hit "Stick Around." Subsequent recordings by Julian Lennon have fared progressively less well.

John Lennon and Yoko Ono

Unfinished Music #1: Two Virgins	Apple	5001	'68	†
Unfinished Music #2: Life with the Lions	Zapple	3357	'69	†
Wedding Album	Apple	(2) 3361	'69	†

Double Fantasy	Geffen	2001	'80	†
	Capitol	91425	'89	LP/CS/CD
	Mobile Fidelity	600	'94	CD
Milk and Honey	Polydor	817160	'84	CS/CD
The John Lennon Collection (1969–1980)	Geffen	2023	'82	†
	Capitol	91516	'90	CD
John Lennon/Plastic Ono Band				
Live Peace in Toronto, 1969	Apple	3362	'69	†
	Capitol	12239	'82	†
	Capitol	90428	'95	CD
Plastic Ono Band	Apple/Capitol	3372	'70	†
	Capitol	46770		LP/CS/CD
Sometime in New York	Apple/Capitol	(2) 3392	'72	†
	Capitol	93850	'90	CD
John Lennon				
Imagine	Apple/Capitol	3379	'71	†
	Capitol	46641	'86	LP/CS/CD
Mind Games	Apple/Capitol	3414	'73	†
	Capitol	16068		†
	Capitol	46769		CS/CD
Walls and Bridges	Apple/Capitol	3416	'74	†
	Capitol	46768		LP/CS/CD
Rock 'n' Roll	Apple/Capitol	3419	'75	†
	Capitol	16069		†
	Capitol	46707		CD
Menlove Avenue (recorded 1974–1975)	Capitol	12533		LP/CS
	Capitol	46576	'86	CD
Shaved Fish	Apple/Capitol	3421	'75	†
	Capitol	46642		LP/CS/CD
Live in New York City	Capitol	12451	'86	LP/CS
	Capitol	46196	'86	CD
Imagine—The Motion Picture (soundtrack)	Capitol	90803	'88	CS/CD
Lennon	Capitol	(4) 95220	'90	CS/CD
Tribute Album				
A Tribute to John Lennon	Hollywood/PGD	62015	'95	CS/CD
Yoko Ono/Plastic Ono Band				
Plastic Ono Band	Apple	3373	'70	†
Fly	Apple	(2) 3380	'71	†
Yoko Ono				
Approximately Infinite Universe	Apple	(2) 3399	'73	†
Feeling the Space	Apple	3412	'73	†
Season of Glass	Geffen	2004	'81	†
It's Alright (I See Rainbows)	Polydor	6364	'82	†
	Polydor	823289		†
Starpeace	Polydor	827530	'85	†
Onobox	Rykodisc	(6) 10224-9	'92	CD
Walking on Thin Ice (excerpts from Onobox)	Rykodisc	20230	'92	CS/CD
New York Rock (original score)	Capitol	29843	'94	CS/CD
Rising	Capitol	35817	'95	CS/CD

Yoko Ono Tribute Album				
Every Man Has a Woman	Polydor	823490	'84	LP/CS/CD†
Jullan Lennon				
Valotte	Atlantic	80184	'84/'85	CS/CD
The Secret Value of Daydreaming	Atlantic	81640	'86	LP/CS/CD†
Mr. Jordan	Atlantic	81928	'89	LP/CS/CD†
Help Yourself	Atlantic	82280	'91	CS/CD

JERRY LEE LEWIS

(b. Sept. 29, 1935, Ferriday, LA)

The premier white piano and vocal stylist of the rock-and-roll '50s, Jerry Lee Lewis performed one of the most dynamic stage shows of the era while projecting an aura of arrogant self-confidence. His inimitable piano style, self-taught and virtually unaltered over the course of his career, featured endless glissandos and furious hammering and banging of the instrument, often with his elbows and feet. Recording rock-and-roll classics such as "Whole Lotta Shakin' Going On" and "Great Balls of Fire," Lewis never attained the stature of Elvis Presley or Chuck Berry. Moreover, Lewis suffered a crippling blow to his career through adverse publicity surrounding his marriage to his 13-year-old cousin that led to the cancellation of his first English tour in 1958. Eventually reestablished as a country artist a decade later with hits such as "Another Place Another Time" and "What's Made Milwaukee Famous," Jerry Lee Lewis continues to tour in the '90s, despite suffering from a series of personal tragedies and health problems.

JERRY LEE LEWIS

Jerry Lee Lewis began playing at age 8, and he made his first public appearance at a local Ford dealership in 1949 at age 14. Performing locally on weekends for four years, he built a solid regional following. In February 1956 Lewis traveled to Memphis to audition for Sun Records, recording some demonstration tapes for Sun engineer (and later producer) Jack Clement in the absence of owner Sam Phillips. Returning to Memphis a month later, he discovered that Phillips liked the recordings, resulting in a recording contract. His first single, "Crazy Arms," became a moderate country hit, but his second, "Whole Lotta Shakin' Going On," became a smash country, R&B, and pop hit, bolstered by his appearance on the Steve Allen television show. "Great Balls of Fire" became a smash hit in all three fields in late 1957, as did "Breathless" and "High School Confidential."

In May 1958 Jerry Lee Lewis arrived in England for his first British tour, but it was canceled by the fifth day after the British press revealed, in rather lurid terms, that he was traveling with his 13-year-old second-cousin wife, Myra. Back home, he managed a minor pop hit with "Break-Up," but subsequent records were banned by many radio stations and Lewis was unable to score even a moderate hit until 1961 with his own version of Ray Charles's "What'd I Say." Nonetheless, he continued to record for Sun until 1963.

In 1963 Jerry Lee Lewis switched to the Smash subsidiary of Mercury Records, but commercial success eluded him as he crisscrossed the country playing fairs, package shows, gymnasiums, and roadhouses. Finally, in 1968 he scored the first of a series of major country hits with "Another Place Another Time," followed by the classic "What's Made Milwaukee Famous (Has Made a Loser Out of Me)." Subsequent country-only hits on Smash included "She Still Comes Around (To Love What's Left of Me)," "To Make Love Sweeter for You," "One Has My Name (The Other Has My Heart)" (a top country hit for Jimmy Wakely in 1948), "She Even Woke Me Up to Say Goodbye," and "Once More with Feeling."

In 1970 Jerry Lee Lewis moved to Smash's parent label, Mercury, for country hits such as "There Must Be More to Love Than This," "Touching Home," "Would You Take Another Chance on Me" backed with Kris Kristofferson's "Me and Bobby McGee" (a moderate pop hit), "Sometimes a Memory Ain't Enough," and "He Can't Fill My Shoes." In 1973 he recorded his best-selling album *The Session* in London with guitarists Peter Frampton, Rory Gallagher, and Albert and Alvin Lee. Lewis's late-'70s country hits included "Let's Put It Back Together Again" and the classic "Middle Age Crazy." In 1979 Lewis switched to Elektra Records, where he scored a major country hit with the autobiographical "Rockin' My Life Away" and a smash country hit (his last) with "Thirty-Nine and Holding."

In the early '80s Jerry Lee Lewis recorded for MCA Records. During that decade he endured emergency surgery for a perforated stomach, the deaths of wives number four and five, and protracted tax disputes with the Internal Revenue Service. In 1986 he was among the original inductees into the Rock and Roll Hall of Fame. The 1989 movie *Great Balls of Fire*, starring Dennis Quaid, portrayed the early years of his career, and the soundtrack album included eight newly recorded versions of his classics. In the '90s Lewis opened the nightclub Jerry Lee Lewis's Spot in Memphis, and opened his home to tourists in order to pay off his tax debt. In 1995 Sire Records released Jerry Lee Lewis's first full studio album in more than 10 years, *Young Blood*, recorded with guitarists James Burton and Al Anderson.

Jerry Lee Lewis on Sun

Jerry Lee Lewis	Sun	1230		†
	Rhino	70656	'89	CS/CD
Jerry Lee's Greatest	Sun	1265		†
	Rhino	70657	'89	CS/CD
Original Golden Hits, Volume 1	Sun	102	'69	†
Original Golden Hits, Volume 2	Sun	103	'69	†
Rockin' Rhythm and Blues	Sun	107		†
Golden Cream of Country	Sun	108		†
Taste of Country	Sun	114		†
Memphis Rock and Roll	Sun	116		†
Ole Tyme Country Music	Sun	121		†
Monsters	Sun	124	'75	†
Original Golden Hits, Volume 3	Sun	128		†
Golden Rock and Roll	Sun	1000	'78	†
Duets	Sun	1011	'79	†
The Original	Sun	1005	'79	†

From the Vaults of Sun	Power Pak	247		†
Sun Story, Volume 5	Sunnyvale	905	'77	†
Original Sun Greatest Hits	Rhino	70255	'89	CS/CD
Wild One: Rare Tracks From Jerry Lee Lewis (recorded 1957–1963)	Rhino	70899	'89	CS/CD
Ferriday Fireball	Charly	1	'89	CD†

Jerry Lee Lewis and Johnny Cash

| Sunday Down South | Sun | 119 | | † |
| Sing Hank Williams | Sun | 125 | | † |

Jerry Lee Lewis, Charlie Rich, and Carl Perkins

| Jerry Lee Lewis and Friends | Sun | 1018 | '80 | † |

Jerry Lee Lewis

Live at the Star Club, Hamburg, 1964	Rhino	70268	'92	CS/CD
Greatest Live Show on Earth	Smash	67056	'64	†
	Smash	830528	'87	†
The Return of Rock!	Smash	67063	'65	†
	Mercury	16340	'67	†
Country Songs for City Folks	Smash	67071	'65	†
Memphis Beat	Smash	67079	'66	†
By Request	Smash	67086	'66	†
Soul My Way	Smash	67097	'67	†
Another Place, Another Time	Smash	67104	'68	†
She Still Comes Around (To Love What's Left of Me)	Smash	67112	'69	†
The Country Music Hall of Fame, Volume 1	Smash	67117	'69	†
The Country Music Hall of Fame, Volume 2	Smash	67118	'69	†
She Even Woke Me Up to Say Goodbye	Smash	67128	'70	†
Live at the International, Las Vegas	Mercury	61278	'70	†
In Loving Memories	Mercury	61318	'71	†
There Must Be More to Love than This	Mercury	61323	'71	†
Touching Home	Mercury	61343	'71	†
Would You Take Another Chance on Me?	Mercury	61346	'71	†
	Mercury	830399	'87	†
This Old Piano	Mercury	61366	'73	†
The "Killer" Rocks On	Mercury	637	'72	|
	Mercury	826262	'87	†
Session in London	Mercury	(2) 803	'73	†
Sometimes a Memory Ain't Enough	Mercury	677	'73	†
Southern Roots	Mercury	690	'74	†
I-40 Country	Mercury	710	'74	†
Boogie Woogie Country Man	Mercury	1030	'75	†
Odd Man In	Mercury	1064	'76	†
Country Class	Mercury	1109	'76	†
Country Memories	Mercury	5004	'77	†
Keeps Rockin'	Mercury	5010	'78	†
Jerry Lee Lewis	Elektra	184	'79	†
When Two Worlds Collide	Elektra	254	'80	†
Killer Country	Elektra	291	'80	†
My Fingers Do the Talkin'	MCA	5387	'83	†
I Am What I Am	MCA	5478	'84	†
Great Balls of Fire (soundtrack)	Polydor	839516	'89	CS/CD
The Complete Palomino Club Recordings	Tomato	(2) 70385	'91	CD

Rockin' My Life Away	Tomato	70392	'92	CS/CD
Heartbreak	Tomato	70697	'92	CS/CD
Rocket 88	Tomato	70698	'92	CS/CD
Young Blood	Sire	61795	'95	CS/CD

Anthologies

Golden Hits	Smash	67040	'64	†
	Smash	7001	'79	†
Best	Smash	67131	'70	†
The Golden Rock Hits of Jerry Lee Lewis	Smash	826251	'87	LP/CS/CD
Best, Volume 2	Mercury	5006	'78	†
	Mercury	822789		†
Killer: The Mercury Years, Volume One: 1963–1968	Mercury	836935	'89	CS/CD
Killer: The Mercury Years, Volume Two: 1969–1972	Mercury	836938	'89	CS/CD
Killer: The Mercury Years, Volume Three: 1973–1977	Mercury	836941	'89	CS/CD
Killer Country	Mercury	526542	'95	CS/CD
Jerry Lee Lewis	Pickwick	2055		†
Drinkin' Wine Spo-Dee O Dee	Pickwick	2344		†
High Heel Sneakers	Pickwick	3224		†
Roll Over, Beethoven	Pickwick	6110		†
Rural Route #1	Pickwick	6120		†
I Walk the Line	Accord	7133	'81	†
I'm On Fire	Polydor	826139	'85	†
Milestones (recorded 1956–1977)	Rhino	(2) 1499	'85	†
	Rhino	71499	'89	CS
All Killer, No Filler: The Anthology	Rhino	(2) 71216	'93	CS/CD
Solid Gold	Pair	1132	'86	CS
Great Balls of Fire	Grudge	4513	'89	CS/CD†
Jerry Lee Lewis	Bella Musica	89916	'90	CD†
Best	Curb/CEMA	77446	'91	CS/CD
Greatest Hits	Koch Prasent	399538	'91	CD
Rockin' My Life Away: The Jerry Lee Lewis Collection	Warner Bros.	26689	'91	CS/CD
Great Balls of Fire	CSI	75312	'92	CD
Whole Lotta Shakin'	CSI	75322	'92	CD
At His Best	RCA-Camden	5009		CS
You Win Again	Polygram	836689		CS
Greatest Hits Live	Special Music	4811		CD
Live at the Vapors Club	Ace	326		CD
Honky Tonk Rock 'n' Roll Piano Man	Ace	332		CD
Pretty Much Country	Ace	348		CD
A Private Party	Live Gold	(2) 70007/8		CD
20 Classic Jerry Lee Lewis Hits	Original Sound	8880		CS/CD

Jerry Lee Lewis and Linda Gail Lewis

Together	Smash	67126	'69	†

Jerry Lee Lewis, Johnny Cash, and Carl Perkins

The Survivors	Columbia	37961	'82	LP/CS
	Razor & Tie	2077	'95	CS/CD

Jerry Lee Lewis, Johnny Cash, Roy Orbison, and Carl Perkins

Class of '55	Columbia	830002	'86	LP/CS/CD

GORDON LIGHTFOOT

(b. Nov. 17, 1938, Orillia, Ontario, Canada)

A prolific folk-style singer-songwriter, Gordon Lightfoot was first known in the United States as the composer of "For Lovin' Me" and "Early Morning Rain," recorded by Ian and Sylvia and Peter, Paul and Mary in the '60s. Finally established in his own right in the United States with 1970's *Sit Down Young Stranger* (reissued as *If You Could Read My Mind*, after the title hit), Lightfoot enjoyed considerable success in the mid-'70s, only to fade from popularity during the '80s. The author of some five hundred compositions, Gordon Lightfoot has seen his songs covered by a wide variety of artists, including Bob Dylan, Elvis Presley, Barbra Streisand, and Waylon Jennings.

Gordon Lightfoot started piano lessons at age 8 and taught himself guitar while in high school. Writing his first song at 17, he studied composition at Westlake College in Los Angeles before returning to Toronto to play bars, clubs, and coffeehouses. In 1963 he hosted a country-music television show in England, later returning to Canada to work on the CBC television series *Country Hoedown*. He recorded for Chateau and ABC-Paramount and performed with Jim Whalen as the Two Tones in the mid-'60s. Fellow Canadians Ian and Sylvia (Tyson) were the first to record any of Lightfoot's songs, but Peter, Paul and Mary were the act that first scored hits with his "For Lovin' Me" and "Early Morning Rain," in 1965.

Signed to United Artists Records, Gordon Lightfoot recorded four albums for the label before registering a chart entry with 1969's *Sunday Concert*. Quickly recognized in Canada, he remained virtually unknown in the United States through the late '60s, despite his having recorded a number of his own excellent compositions such as "The Way I Feel," "Ribbon of Darkness," "Canadian Railroad Trilogy," "The Last Time I Saw Her," and "Did She Mention My Name?"

Switching to Warner Bros.' Reprise label at the end of 1969, Gordon Lightfoot's debut for the label yielded the smash hit "If You Could Read My Mind" while containing other outstanding songs such as "Approaching Lavender," "Saturday Clothes," and "Sit Down Young Stranger." Following several modest-selling albums, Lightfoot established himself with 1973's *Sundown*, which featured "The Watchman's Gone" and the poignant "Too Late for Praying" and produced the top title hit and near-smash "Carefree Highway." "Rainy Day People" became a major hit in 1975, followed by the dirgelike smash "The Wreck of the Edmund Fitzgerald." Lightfoot hit with "The Circle Is Small (I Can See It in Your Eyes)" in 1978 on Warner Bros., for whom he continued to record into the mid-'80s. His popularity faded during the '80s, but he eventually reemerged in 1993 with *Waiting for You*.

Gordon Lightfoot

Lightfoot		United Artists	6487	'66	†
		Liberty	10044		†
The Way I Feel		United Artists	6587	'67	†
		Liberty	10042		†
Did She Mention My Name?		United Artists	6649	'68	†
		Liberty	10041		†
Back Here on Earth		United Artists	6672	'69	†
		Liberty	10040		†
Sunday Concert		United Artists	6714	'69	†
		Liberty	10039		†
Best		United Artists	6754	'70	†
		Liberty	10038		†
		EMI	48396		CS/CD

Classic Lightfoot—Best, Volume 2	United Artists	5510	'71	†
Best, Volume 3	United Artists	189		†
Very Best	United Artists	243	'74	†
	United Artists	381	'75	†
Very Best, Volume 2	United Artists	445		†
The United Artists Collection	EMI	(2) 27015	'93	CD
Sit Down Young Stranger	Reprise	6392	'70	†
(reissued as) If You Could Read My Mind	Reprise	6392		CS/CD
Summer Side of Life	Reprise	2037	'71	†
	Reprise	45686	'94	CD
Don Quixote	Reprise	2056	'72	†
	Reprise	45687	'94	CD
Old Dan's Record	Reprise	2116	'72	†
Sundown	Reprise	2177	'73	CS/CD
Cold on the Shoulder	Reprise	2206	'75	†
	Reprise	45688	'94	CD
Gord's Gold	Reprise	(2) 2237	'75	CS
	Reprise	2237		CD
Summertime Dream	Reprise	2246	'76	CS/CD
Endless Wire	Warner Bros.	3149	'78	†
	Reprise	45685	'94	CD
Dream Street Rose	Warner Bros.	3426	'80	†
Shadows	Warner Bros.	3633	'82	†
Salute	Warner Bros.	23901	'83	†
East of Midnight	Warner Bros.	25482	'86	CS/CD
Gord's Gold, Volume II	Warner Bros.	25784	'89	CS/CD
Songbook	Pair	1081	'86	CS/CD
Best	Curb/CEMA	77428	'91	CS/CD
Waiting for You	Reprise	45208	'93	CS/CD

LITTLE ANTHONY AND THE IMPERIALS

"Little" Anthony Gourdine (b. Jerome Anthony Gourdine, Jan. 8, 1940, Brooklyn, NY), lead voc; **Clarence Collins** (b. Mar. 17, 1941, Brooklyn, NY), bar voc; **Ernest Wright** (b. Aug. 24, 1941, Brooklyn, NY), second ten voc; **Tracy Lord**, first ten voc; **Nat Rogers** (b. Glouster Rogers), bs voc [**Sammy Strain** (b. Dec. 9, 1941) joined in 1964.]

Popular Brooklyn-based R&B vocal group of the late '50s and '60s, Little Anthony and the Imperials were lead by "Little" Anthony Gourdine, who began his recording career in 1955 with the Duponts. Evolving out of the Chesters, who formed in 1957, Little Anthony and the Imperials took their name in 1958, soon scoring with the R&B and pop smash classic "Tears on My Pillow" for End Records. Later hitting with the novelty song "Shimmy, Shimmy, Ko-Ko-Bop" in 1960, the group enjoyed considerable success in 1964–1965 on DCP Records under producer-songwriter Teddy Randazzo. He wrote or cowrote their major pop and R&B hits "I'm on the Outside (Looking In)," the classic "Goin' Out of My Head" (a smash in both fields), "Hurt So Bad," and "Take Me Back." Little Anthony and the Imperials disbanded in 1975, and Anthony Gourdine has since pursued a career as a lounge entertainer and gospel recording artist. The group reunited with Anthony, Wright, Collins, and Strain for a onetime oldies show at Madison Square Garden in 1992, decided to hit the oldies circuit a year later, and continues to perform.

The Imperials

We Are the Imperials	End	302		†
Shades of the 40's	End	311		†

Little Anthony and the Imperials

I'm on the Outside (Looking In)	DCP	6801	'64	†
	Veep	16510	'67	†
Goin' Out of My Head	DCP	6808	'65	†
	Veep	16511	'67	†
Best	DCP	6809	'66	†
	Veep	16512	'67	†
Payin' Our Dues	Veep	16513	'66	†
Reflections	Veep	16514	'67	†
Movie Grabbers	Veep	16516	'67	†
Best, Volume 2	Veep	16519	'68	†
Hits	Pickwick	3029	'66	†
Greatest Hits	Roulette	25294	'66	†
Forever Yours	Roulette	42007	'69	†
Out of Sight, Out of Mind	United Artists	6720	'69	†
	Liberty	10117	'80	†
Very Best	United Artists	255	'74	†
	United Artists	382	'75	†
On a New Street	Avco	11012	'74	†
Best	Liberty	10133	'81	†
	Liberty	91475		CD†
Best	Rhino	70919	'89	CS/CD
Shimmy, Shimmy Ko-Ko-Bop	Rhino	72158	'95	CS/CD
Best	RCA-Camden	5021		CS/CD

Little Anthony

Little Anthony	Sunset	5287	'70	†
Daylight	Song Bird	3245	'80	†

LITTLE FEAT

Lowell George (b. Apr. 13, 1945, Hollywood, CA; d. June 29, 1979, Arlington, VA), gtr, voc; **Bill Payne** (b. Mar. 12, 1949, Waco, TX), kybd, perc, voc; **Roy Estrada**, bs; **Richie Hayward**, drm, voc [Roy Estrada left in 1972; **Paul Barrere** (b. July 3, 1948, Burbank, CA) on guitar and vocals, **Ken Gradney** (b. New Orleans, LA) on bass, and **Sam Clayton** on percussion and vocals joined.]

Quickly recognized by musicians and critics in the early '70s as the best "unknown" band in America, Little Feat was led during the '70s by Lowell George, often regarded as one of the most underrated singers, songwriters, and guitarists of the era. Considered one of rock music's finest slide-guitar players, George wrote such classics as "Willin'," "Truck Stop Girl," and "Dixie Chicken" for Little Feat. Breaking through with 1974's *Feats Don't Fail Me Now*, Little Feat enjoyed considerable success as an album act until George's departure and death in 1979. The group re-formed in 1988 for the best-selling album *Let It Roll*.

Lowell George made his show-business debut on television's *Ted Mack Amateur Hour* at age 6. Taking up guitar at 11, he haunted Southern California coffeehouses and clubs before forming his first rock band, the Factory, with drummer Richie Hayward around 1966. When that group broke up, George played for a time with the Standells ("Dirty Water"),

LITTLE FEAT

the Seeds ("Pushin' Too Hard"), and the Mothers of Invention. In late 1969 he formed Little Feat with former Mothers bassist Roy Estrada, keyboardist Bill Payne, and Hayward, who in the meantime had been a member of the Fraternity of Man ("Don't Bogart That Joint").

Signed to Warner Bros. on the strength of Lowell George's songwriting, Little Feat's debut album featured an acoustic version of George's oft-covered truck-driving classic "Willin'," and "Truck Stop Girl," cowritten with Payne. Although embraced by musicians and critics alike, the album failed to sell, as did *Sailin' Shoes*, regarded by many as the group's finest album. It included an electrified version of "Willin'" and George songs such as "Trouble," "Easy to Slip," and "Teenage Nervous Breakdown." Estrada left to join Captain Beefheart, and the group added guitarist Paul Barrere, bassist Ken Gradney, and percussionist Sam Clayton. *Dixie Chicken*, produced by George, proved another commercial failure, despite the inclusion of the barroom classic title song, yet it did reveal the ascendancy of Payne and Barrere as songwriters and George as singer and musician.

Having earlier produced albums for Bonnie Raitt and others, Lowell George pursued session work as Little Feat broke up for a time. They regrouped for 1974's *Feats Don't Fail Me Now*, their commercial breakthrough. The album featured Payne's "Oh Atlanta" and George's "Rock and Roll Doctor" and the title song. Successfully touring America and Europe in support of the album, Little Feat next recorded *The Last Record Album*, which contained "Mercenary Territory" and "Long Distance Love." *Time Loves a Hero*, from 1977, featured George's "Rocket in My Pocket" and Terry Allen's "New Delhi Freight Train." The live set *Waiting for Columbus* became the group's best-selling album of the Lowell George era. George produced the Grateful Dead's *Shakedown Street*, and then left the group in April 1979.

Lowell George's debut solo album, *Thanks, I'll Eat It Here*, failed to sell significantly, and while on tour with a new band to promote the album, George died of drug-related heart failure in Arlington, Virginia, on June 29, 1979, at age 34. Paul Barrere and Bill Payne completed the overdubs and mixing of Little Feat's next album, *Down on the Farm*, which featured "Straight from the Heart" and "Front Page News," written by Payne and George.

During the '80s Barrere recorded two solo albums for Mirage and played and recorded with the Bluesbusters, while Payne toured for five years with James Taylor. Little Feat eventually regrouped in 1988 with Barrere, Payne, Richie Hayward, Ken Gradney, and Sam Clayton, plus guitarist Fred Tackett and vocalist Craig Fuller (Pure Prairie League, American Flyer). *Let It Roll* sold remarkably well, staying on the album charts nearly eight months, yet by 1991 the group was recording for the small Morgan Creek label. In 1994 Shaun Murphy replaced Craig Fuller as lead vocalist in Little Feat, who recorded 1995's *Ain't Had Enough Fun* for Zoo Records.

Little Feat

Little Feat	Warner Bros.	1890	'71	CS/CD
Sailin' Shoes	Warner Bros.	2600	'72	CS/CD
Dixie Chicken	Warner Bros.	2686	'73	CS/CD

Feats Don't Fail Me Now	Warner Bros.	2784	'74	CS/CD
The Last Record Album	Warner Bros.	2884	'75	CS/CD
Time Loves a Hero	Warner Bros.	3015	'77	CS/CD
Waiting for Columbus	Warner Bros.	(2) 3140	'78	†
	Warner Bros.	3140		CS/CD
Down on the Farm	Warner Bros.	3345	'79	CS/CD
Hoy-Hoy!	Warner Bros.	3538	'81	CS/CD
Let It Roll	Warner Bros.	25750	'88	CS/CD
Representing the Mambo	Warner Bros.	26163	'90	CS/CD
Shake Me Up	Morgan Creek	20005	'91	CS/CD
Ain't Had Enough	Zoo	11097	'95	CS/CD

Lowell George

Thanks, I'll Eat It Here	Warner Bros.	3194	'79	†
	Warner Bros.	26755	'93	CD

Lowell George and the Factory

Lightning-Rod Man	Rhino	71563	'93	CS/CD

Paul Barrere

On My Own Two Feat	Mirage	90070	'83	†
Real Lies	Mirage	90138	'84	†
If the Phone Don't Ring	Zoo	11096	'95	CS/CD

LITTLE RICHARD
(b. Richard Wayne Penniman, Dec. 5, 1932, Macon, GA)

The on-again, off-again, self-styled, and self-proclaimed King of Rock and Roll, Little Richard was probably the first rock artist to achieve widespread popularity on the basis of a frantic and furious presence in recording and performance. Along with Chuck Berry, Little Richard was one of the most important early composers of rock and roll, and his classic 1956 hit "Tutti Frutti" was one of the first important rock-and-roll hits by a black performer (coming shortly after Chuck Berry's "Maybellene"). His wild and boisterous stage act influenced everyone from Jerry Lee Lewis and James Brown to Mick Jagger and Jimi Hendrix, and his shouting gospel-style vocals were emulated by artists such as Otis Redding and Joe Tex and can be seen as a harbinger of the vocal style of hard-rock singers from Robert Plant on. Moreover, his use of outrageous costumes and makeup were later emulated by the likes of David Bowie, Boy George, and Prince, making him perhaps the first androgynous rock star, and his intensely sexual persona, with its thinly veiled homosexuality, predated the open homosexuality of Bowie, Boy George, and Queen by more than a decade. One of rock and roll's most erratic and unpredictable characters, Little Richard has from time to time denounced the music and retreated into Christian fundamentalism, only to return to pop performing in the '70s and again in the late '80s.

Little Richard was singing on the streets of Macon by age 7. He became the lead singer in a local church choir at 14, and later joined a traveling medicine show. He won an Atlanta talent contest in 1951 that led to a recording contract with RCA, but his blues-based recordings (which surfaced on Camden Records in 1958) failed to sell. He switched to the Houston-based Peacock label for recordings in 1953, again with little success, and worked with the Tempo Toppers from 1953 to 1955.

In 1955 Little Richard sent a demonstration record to Art Rupe of the Los Angeles–based Specialty label that resulted in a new recording contract. Initial sessions

LITTLE RICHARD

recorded under producer Robert "Bumps" Blackwell at Cosimo Matassa's J&M Studios in New Orleans (where he was to record most of his hits) yielded the smash R&B and major pop hit classic "Tutti Frutti." Following the top R&B and smash pop hit "Long Tall Sally" (backed with "Slippin' and Slidin'"), Little Richard achieved a major crossover hit with "Rip It Up" (backed by "Ready Teddy") and a R&B near-smash with "She's Got It" (recorded in Los Angeles). In 1956–1957 he appeared in the early rock-and-roll films *Don't Knock the Rock*, *The Girl Can't Help It* (performing its hit title song), and *Mister Rock 'n' Roll*. The hits continued in 1957 with "Lucille" (backed by the unusually soulful "Send Me Some Lovin'"), "Jenny, Jenny," and "Keep a Knockin'" (recorded in Washington, D.C.).

"Good Golly, Miss Molly" became Little Richard's last major hit in early 1958, but earlier, while touring Australia, he announced his intention to leave rock and roll behind in favor of the ministry. He subsequently enrolled in Alabama's Oakwood College to study theology and was ordained a minister in 1961. During this time he recorded several gospel albums, including *It's Real*, ultimately returning to rock and roll around 1964, when he managed a minor crossover hit with "Bama Lama Bama Loo" on Specialty. He later recorded for VeeJay, Modern, and Okeh Records. During this period Jimi Hendrix was briefly Little Richard's guitar accompanist on the road.

Enjoying renewed popularity with the rock-and-roll revival of the late '60s, Little Richard signed with Reprise Records in 1970 and scored a moderate pop and R&B hit with "Freedom Blues." Around 1975 he again abandoned rock and roll to tour the Seventh Day Adventist circuit as an evangelist. In 1984 he published his memoirs, *The Life and Times of Little Richard*, but in October 1985 he was seriously injured in an automobile accident in West Hollywood. In 1986 he appeared in the hit comedy movie *Down and Out in Beverly Hills* (which included his first moderate hit in 16 years, "Great Gosh A'Mighty") and recorded *Lifetime Friend* for Warner Bros.; that same year, he was among the first inductees into the Rock and Roll Hall of Fame. He has continued to act in television and the movies. In the '90s Little Richard toured again and recorded the children's album *Shake It All About* for Walt Disney Records.

Little Richard on Specialty

Here's Little Richard	Specialty	2100	'57	LP/CS
Little Richard, Volume 2	Specialty	2103	'57	LP/CS
The Fabulous Little Richard	Specialty	2104	'58	LP/CS
His Original Specialty Albums on 3 CDs (reissue of above 3)	Ace	(3) 2		CD
His Biggest Hits	Specialty	2111	'63	LP/CS
Grooviest 17 Original Hits	Specialty	2113	'68	LP/CS
Well, Alright!	Specialty	2136	'70	LP/CS
The Essential Little Richard	Specialty	2154	'89	CD
The Specialty Sessions	Specialty	(5) 8508	'90	LP
	Specialty	(3) 8508	'90	CD

The Georgia Peach	Specialty	7012	'91	CD
The Specialty Sessions	Ace	(8) 1		LP
	Ace	(6) 1		CD

More Little Richard

Little Richard	Camden	420	'58	†
(reissued as) Original	RCA-Camden	420		CS
Recorded Live	United	7775		†
	Kent/Modern	1000		†
Wild and Frantic Little Richard	United	7777		†
	Kent/Modern	1003		†
Right Now	United	7791		†
Little Richard Is Back	VeeJay	1107	'64	†
Explosive	Okeh	14117	'67	†
Greatest Hits Live (recorded 1967)	Epic	40389	'86	CS/CD
Little Richard	Buddah	7501	'70	†
Every Hour with Little Richard	Camden	2430	'70	†
The Rill Thing	Reprise	6406	'70	†
The King of Rock and Roll	Reprise	6462	'71	†
Second Coming	Reprise	2107	'72	†
Lifetime Friend	Warner Bros.	25529	'86	†

Little Richard and Jimi Hendrix

Roots of Rock	Archive of Folk and Jazz Music	296	'74	†
Together	Pickwick	3347		†

Anthologies

His Greatest Hits	VeeJay	1124	'64	†
Greatest Hits	Okeh	14121	'67	†
Little Richard	Kama Sutra	2023	'70	†
Cast a Long Shadow	Epic	30428	'71	†
Greatest Hits	Trip	(2) 8013	'71	†
Big Hits	GNP Crescendo	9033	'75	LP/CS/CD
Very Best	United Artists	497	'76	†
Tutti Frutti	Accord	7123	'81	†
Compact Command Performance	Motown	9066	'86	CD†
18 Greatest Hits	Rhino	75899	'86	CD
Shut Up!: A Collection of Rare Tracks, 1951–1964	Rhino	70236	'88	CS
20 Classic Cuts	Ace	195	'87	LP/CS/CD
His Greatest Recordings	Ace	109		LP/CD
Rip It Up	VeeJay/Chameleon	74797	'89	LP/CS/CD†
Little Richard's Grand Slam and Other Greatest Hits	Grudge	4519	'89	CS/CD†
Greatest Songs	Curb/Atlantic	77739	'95	CS/CD
His Best	Dominion	784		CS/CD
Mega-Mix	Dominion	3457	'95	CS/CD
Good Golly Miss Molly	SMS	1	'95	CD
16 Great Hits	Zeta	519		CD
20 Greatest Hits	Deluxe	7797		CS/CD
His All-Time Greats	Special Music	4908		CS

Gospel Recordings

It's Real	Mercury	60656	'61	†
	Lection	839406		LP/CS/CD
King of the Gospel Singers	Mercury	16288	'64	†
Little Richard Sings Spirituals	United	7723		†
Little Richard Sings Freedom Songs	Crown	5362		†
Clap Your Hands	Spin O Rama	119		†
Coming Home	Coral	757446	'63	†
Little Richard Sings the Gospel	MCA	20852	'95	CS/CD

Little Richard Children's Album

Shake It All About	Walt Disney	60849	'92	CS/CD

LOGGINS AND MESSINA

Kenny Loggins (b. Jan. 7, 1948, Everett, WA), gtr, voc; **Jim Messina** (b. Dec. 5, 1947, Maywood, CA), gtr, bs, voc

Initially formed in 1971 as an informal arrangement of Kenny Loggins with producer Jim Messina, the duo's *Sittin' In* album proved so popular that they formed a road band to tour and record as Loggins and Messina. Messina was a veteran record engineer, producer, and former member of two of America's early country-rock bands, the Buffalo Springfield and Poco, whereas Loggins was a professional songwriter. With Messina providing the harder-edged songs and Loggins gentle, melodic classics such as "Danny's Song" and "A Love Song," Loggins and Messina enjoyed considerable success as an album act until their breakup in 1976. As a solo act Loggins became one of the most popular singer-songwriters of the '80s, establishing himself with both FM radio and easy-listening audiences.

Jim Messina formed several surf bands while still in high school and later recorded an obscure surf-and-dragster album in 1964. After high school he moved to Hollywood, where he learned the fundamentals of studio engineering at Harmony Recorders and Sunset Sound. Messina was introduced to the burgeoning local folk-rock scene when David Crosby asked him to record Joni Mitchell's first demonstration tape. Word of Messina's prowess as an engineer made its way to Neil Young, who enlisted Messina for "Hung Upside Down" and "Broken Arrow" from *Buffalo Springfield Again*. With the departure of Bruce Palmer, Messina was recruited to play bass for the Buffalo Springfield, and to engineer and produce *Last Time Around*, to which he contributed "Carefree Country Day."

The stormy career of the Buffalo Springfield ended in summer '68, and members Messina and Richie Furay formed Poco, with Messina staying on for the group's first three albums. Leaving Poco in November 1970, Messina became a staff producer at Columbia Records. The following month he met songwriter Kenny Loggins. Loggins had grown up in the Los Angeles suburb of Alhambra and started singing as a child. He took up guitar in high school and performed in the bands Gator Creek and Second Helping, later dropping out of Pasadena City College to concentrate on songwriting. Serving as a staff writer for ABC/Wingate, Loggins saw one of his compositions, "House at Pooh Corner," become a minor hit for the Nitty Gritty Dirt Band in early 1971.

Jim Messina was assigned to produce Kenny Loggins's debut solo album for Columbia, but Messina suggested that they record it together, with Messina informally *Sittin' In*. The album yielded the minor hit "Vahevala" and contained excellent songs by both artists, including Messina's "Nobody but You" and "Peace of Mind," and Loggins's "House at Pooh Corner" and the gently celebratory "Danny's Song," a near-smash hit for Anne Murray in early 1973. *Sittin' In* sold so well (staying on the album charts more than two years) that

Loggins and Messina decided to join forces, officially inaugurating their duo career with *Loggins and Messina*. That album included the smash hit "Your Mama Can't Dance" (cowritten by the two), the major hit "Thinking of You" (by Messina), and the duo's "Angry Eyes."

Touring regularly, Loggins and Messina eventually played more than seven hundred engagements in five years. *Full Sail* produced their last major hit, "My Music," and contained Loggins's "Love Song" and Messina's "You Need a Man." After *Mother Lode*, which yielded minor hits with "Changes" and "Growin'," and *Native Sons*, Loggins and Messina agreed to part company, completing their farewell tour in September 1976. Columbia soon issued the anthology set *The Best of Friends*.

Jim Messina eventually recorded three solo albums. Kenny Loggins quickly recorded his solo debut album, *Celebrate Me Home*, for Columbia. The album yielded a minor hit with "I Believe in Love," and Loggins toured as opening act to Fleetwood Mac in 1977. He performed at a wide variety of venues, including auditoriums, supper clubs, and casinos, in support of 1978's *Nightwatch*, which produced a smash hit with "Whenever I Call You Friend," cowritten with Melissa Manchester and sung as a rather incongruous duet with Fleetwood Mac's Stevie Nicks. *Keep the Fire* yielded a moderate hit with the title song and a near-smash with "This Is It," with Michael McDonald on backing vocal.

During the '80s Kenny Loggins initiated a highly successful career as a soundtrack performer with the near-smash "I'm Alright" from the movie *Caddyshack*. Following the major hits "Don't Fight It" (cowritten and sung with Journey's Steve Perry), "Heart to Heart" (with backing vocals by Michael McDonald), and "Welcome to Heartlight," Loggins scored two hits from the movie *Footloose*, the top hit title song and the major hit "I'm Free (Heaven Helps the Man)." The Tom Cruise movie *Top Gun* included the Loggins's smash "Danger Zone," whereas Sylvester Stallone's *Over the Top* produced the major hit "Meet Me Halfway," and *Caddyshack II* the near-smash "Nobody's Fool." The latter two hits were also included on *Back to Avalon*, which yielded minor hits with "I'm Gonna Miss You" and "Tell Her," a remake of the Exciters' 1963 hit "Tell Him."

Loggins's 1991 album *Leap of Faith* produced hits with "Real Thing," "If You Believe," and "Conviction of the Heart," an environmental song featured in campaigns in American public schools and used by the National Park Service. Kenny Loggins's *From the Redwoods—An Acoustic Afternoon* was recorded with Michael McDonald and Shanice, and his 1994 album *Return to Pooh Corner* produced a major easy listening hit with the title song.

Jim Messina and the Jesters

Jim Messina and the Jesters	Thimble	3		†
The Dragsters	Audio Fidelity	7037		†

Kenny Loggins and Jim Messina

Sittin' In	Columbia	31044	'72	CS/CD
	Mobile Fidelity	829		CD†
Loggins and Messina	Columbia	31748	'72	CS/CD
Full Sail	Columbia	32540	'73	CS/CD
On Stage	Columbia	32848	'74	CS
Mother Lode	Columbia	33175	'74	CD
So Fine	Columbia	33810	'75	CS
Native Sons	Columbia	33578	'76	CS/CD
The Best of Friends	Columbia	34388	'76	CS/CD
Finale	Columbia	(2) 34167	'77	†

Kenny Loggins

Celebrate Me Home	Columbia	34655	'77	CS/CD
Nightwatch	Columbia	35387	'78	CS/CD
Keep the Fire	Columbia	36172	'79	CS/CD

Alive	Columbia	(2) 36738	'80	CS/CD
High Adventure	Columbia	38127	'82	CS/CD
Vox Humana	Columbia	39174	'85	CS/CD
Back to Avalon	Columbia	40535	'88	CS/CD
Leap of Faith	Columbia	46140	'91	CS/CD
From the Redwoods—An Acoustic Afternoon	Columbia	57391	'93	CS/CD
Return to Pooh Corner	Sony Wonder	57672	'94	CS/CD

Jim Messina

Oasis	Columbia	36140	'79/'91	CD†
Messina	Warner Bros.	3559	'81	†
	Warner Bros.	26557	'91	CD
One More Mile	Warner Bros.	23825	'83	†
	Warner Bros.	26560	'91	CD

LOS LOBOS

David Hidalgo (b. Oct. 6, 1954, Los Angeles, CA), lead voc, gtr, accordion, lap steel, vln, hidalguera; **Cesar Rosas** (b. Sept. 26, 1954, Los Angeles, CA), lead voc, gtr, bajo sexto, vihuela, mdln; **Conrad Lozano** (b. Mar 21, 1951, Los Angeles, CA), bs, guitarrón, voc; **Luis "Louie" Perez** (b. Jan. 29, 1953, Los Angeles, CA), drm [Saxophonist **Steve Berlin** (b. Sept. 14, 1955, Philadelphia, PA) joined in 1983.]

Along with X, one of the most challenging rock bands to emerge from the early-'80s punk scene in Los Angeles, the Mexican-American group Los Lobos has recorded several intriguing, eclectic albums that ranged from R&B to country, from rock and roll to blues, from *norteña* ("Tex-Mex") to *corridas* (ballads) and traditional Mexican folk music, using both rock and traditional instruments. Achieving a musical mélange comparable to only the Meters and the Grateful Dead, Los Lobos broke through commercially with 1987's cover of Ritchie Valens's "La Bamba," the first Spanish-sung song to top the pop charts. Along with Ruben Blades, Los Lobos became one of the few contemporary Hispanic acts to be recognized by the English-speaking pop audience, yet their brilliant and engaging 1992 *Kiko* album remained a decidedly underground hit, despite widespread critical acclaim.

Formed in East Los Angeles in November 1973 by Mexican-American graduates of Garfield High, Los Lobos performed traditional Mexican folk music on acoustic instruments for nearly eight years before taking up electric instruments in 1981. Then they started writing songs (principally by Hidalgo and Perez) and playing local colleges, community events, and clubs. Having recorded two albums of Mexican folk music on their own New Vista Productions label, Los Lobos sent a demonstration tape to Phil Alvin of the Blasters. They received their first break by opening for the Blasters at the Whisky a Go-Go, and Alvin later convinced the punk-rock label Slash to sign the group. Their first recording, a seven-song EP entitled *And a Time to Dance* was coproduced by the Blasters' Steve Berlin and T-Bone Burnett and released in 1983, the year saxophonist Berlin joined the group. The EP included the traditional folk song "Anselma," which won a Grammy Award. Opening for acts such as The Clash and Public Image Ltd., Los Lobos garnered excellent reviews for their exciting, wide-ranging performances.

Los Lobos's first full-length album, *How Will the Wolf Survive?*, won outstanding critical reviews—called one of the best albums of the year—and featured the minor hit title song (covered by Waylon Jennings in 1986) and "A Matter of Time" (both written by Hidalgo and Perez), and a cover of the 1951 Peppermint Harris R&B hit "I Got Loaded." Los Lobos performed at a wide variety of venues in support of the album, and various members recorded with Ry Cooder, Paul Simon, Elvis Costello, and the Fabulous Thunderbirds in 1986. Their

1987 album *By the Light of the Moon* included the socially conscious "One Time One Night" (a minor country hit) and "Is That All There Is?" by Hidalgo and Perez and Rosas's "Set Me Free (Rosa Lee)."

During 1987, at the behest of the family of Ritchie Valens, Los Lobos recorded eight songs for the film biography of Valens, *La Bamba*. The best-selling soundtrack album yielded two hits for Los Lobos, with cover versions of Valens's "La Bamba" and "Come On, Let's Go." Typecast by some as an oldies band, Los Lobos sought to dispel the notion by recording *La Pistola y el Corazon* (The Pistol and the Heart), an entire album of traditional Mexican and South American folk songs sung in Spanish and performed on acoustic instruments. The album won the group another Grammy award.

Los Lobos began recording their next album, *The Neighborhood*, in 1989. Released in 1990, the album included "Take My Hand," Hidalgo's "Emily," and Rosas's "I Walk Alone." Their next, *Kiko*, was hailed as a masterpiece, yet it failed to sell in large quantities. The rich, haunting, mature album featured the ominous title song as well as "Dream in Blue," "Saint Behind the Glass," "That Train Don't Stop Here," and Rojas's "Wake Up Dolores." Performing and recording with the side group the Latin Playboys, Hidalgo and Perez contributed six original songs to the La Jolla Playhouse production of Bertolt Brecht's *Good Woman of Szechuan* in 1994. In 1995 Music for Little People Records, distributed by Warner Bros., issued Los Lobos's children's album, *Papa's Dream*.

Los Lobos

And a Time to Dance (mini)	Slash	23963	'83	CS
How Will the Wolf Survive?	Slash	25177	'84	CS/CD
By the Light of the Moon	Slash	25523	'87	CS/CD
La Bamba (soundtrack)	Slash	25605	'87	CS/CD
La Pistola y el Corazon	Slash	25790	'88	CS/CD
The Neighborhood	Slash	20131	'00	CS/CD
Kiko	Slash	26786	'92	CS/CD
Just Another Band from East L.A.: A Collection	Slash	(2) 45367	'93	CS/CD
Colossal Head	Warner Bros.	46172	'96	CS/CD
Children's Album				
Papa's Dream	Music for Little People	42562	'95	CS/CD
The Latin Playboys				
The Latin Playboys	Slash	45543	'94	CS/CD

LOVE

Arthur Lee (b. 1945, Memphis, TN), gtr, voc; **Bryan Maclean** (b. 1947, Los Angeles, CA), gtr, voc; **John Echols** (b. 1945, Memphis, TN), gtr; **Ken Forssi** (b. 1943, Cleveland, OH), bs; **Alban Pfisterer** (b. 1947, Switzerland), drm [Many personnel changes, save Arthur Lee, beginning in 1968.]

One of the first rock acts signed to the Elektra label, Los Angeles—based Love inspired a serious underground following in the United States and Great Britain.

The group was spearheaded by Memphis-born guitarist-lyricist-vocalist Arthur Lee, who moved with his family to Los Angeles when he was five years old. Lee's first band, the LAGS, was modeled after the popular R&B instrumental band Booker T. and the MGs and featured future-Love member John Echols on bass. Lee formed a new group, the Grassroots, but changed its name after realizing another pop group was already recording under that moniker; the new name he chose was Love. Their debut 1966 album included a sprightly rock version of Burt Bacharach and Hal David's "My Little Red Book" and an early version of the rock classic "Hey Joe." *Da Capo*, issued a year later, featured the classic "Seven and Seven Is" (the group's only moderate hit) and "Revelation," one of the first side-long album cuts in rock music. *Forever Changes*, released in 1968, was one of the definitive production-arrangements of the era. Enhanced by biting surreal lyrics (primarily by rhythm guitarist Arthur Lee) that made it one of the premier existentially oriented albums of rock history, it is one of the overlooked classics of '60s rock. Never a particularly stable group, Love was reconstituted by Lee for *Four Sail*, noteworthy for its powerhouse musicianship. Love's final studio album, *False Start*, included a dynamic performance by Jimi Hendrix on "The Everlasting First" (left over from an album recorded by Lee with Hendrix that never was released due to legal difficulties). Following the group's breakup in 1971, Arthur Lee recorded two perplexing solo albums before dropping out of sight in the mid-'70s. A new Love appeared in 1974 and again in 1979, and Lee has since toured as both a solo artist and with various musicians under the Love banner, most recently in 1994.

Love

Love	Elektra	74001	'66	CD
Da Capo	Elektra	74005	'67	CD
Forever Changes	Elektra	74013	'67	CS/CD
Four Sail	Elektra	74049	'69	†
Revisited	Elektra	74058	'70	†
	Elektra	4058		CS
Out Here	Blue Thumb	(2) 9000	'69	†
	One Way	22030	'90	CD
False Start	Blue Thumb	8822	'70	†
	One Way	22029	'90	CD
Studio/Live	One Way	22036		CD
Best (1966–1969)	Rhino	800	'80	†
	Rhino	70175	'87	CS
Love Story (recorded 1966–1972)	Rhino	(2) 78005	'95	CD
Out There	Big Beat	69		CD

Arthur Lee

Vindicator	A&M	4356	'72	†
Reel-to-Real	RSO	4804	'74	†
Arthur Lee	Rhino	020	'81	†

THE LOVIN' SPOONFUL

John Sebastian (b. Mar. 17, 1944, Greenwich Village, NY), gtr, autoharp, pno, har, voc; **Zalman Yanovsky** (b. Dec. 19, 1944, Toronto, Ontario, Canada), lead gtr, voc; **Steve Boone** (b. Sept. 23, 1943, Camp Lejeune, NC), bs, pno, voc; **Joe Butler** (b. Jan. 19, 1943, Glen Cove, Long Island, NY), drm, voc [**Jerry Yester** replaced Zalman Yanovsky in 1967.]

One of the prime movers in the New York folk-rock movement of the mid-'60s, the Lovin' Spoonful created a distinctive mixture of acoustic-based folk, blues, and rock music that appropriately became known as good-time music. Featuring a zany and extroverted stage act, the group put as much emphasis on their instrumental playing as they did on their harmony signing to produce their fresh, exuberant, uncluttered sound. A major key to the success of the Lovin' Spoonful was John Sebastian's gentle pop-style songwriting, which dealt with romantic themes maturely and realistically. Scoring a series of major hits between 1965 and 1967, including the classics "Do You Believe in Magic," "Summer in the City," and

"Darling Be Home Soon," the group disbanded in 1968. John Sebastian established himself with the so-called counterculture with his celebrated appearance at the Woodstock Festival in 1969 and his excellent *John B. Sebastian* album. Achieving his last major hit with "Welcome Back" in 1976, Sebastian worked largely in film and television until reemerging in 1993 with *Tar Beach*, his first album in 17 years.

John Sebastian was born the son of a renowned classical harmonica player. Taking up harmonica as a child, and guitar at age 12, he later added piano and autoharp to his instrumental repertoire. Playing early recording sessions for Tim Hardin and Jesse Colin Young, Sebastian joined the Even Dozen Jug band in 1963. That band included Maria Muldaur ("Midnight at the Oasis"), Stefan Grossman, and Steve Katz, later with the Blues Project and Blood, Sweat and Tears.

In 1964 Canadian-born Zalman Yanovsky was a member of the short-lived New York–based Mugwumps with singer-songwriter Jim Hendricks, and Denny Doherty and Cass Elliot, who later became half of the Mamas and the Papas. Yanovsky and Sebastian met during recording sessions for the Mugwumps (their sole album was released in 1967 after the various members had become successful in other groups). Encouraged by producer Erik Jacobsen, John Sebastian formed the Lovin' Spoonful in 1965 to record his songs with Yanovsky, Steve Boone, and Joe Butler.

Signed to Kama Sutra Records, the Lovin' Spoonful recorded their debut album in 1965. *Do You Believe in Magic* sported a fresh, clean, friendly sound on traditional folk and blues songs and Sebastian originals such as "Younger Girl," and the near-smash hits "Do You Believe in Magic" and "Did You Ever Have to Make Up Your Mind." *Daydream* yielded a smash hit with the title song and contained a number of fine songs such as "Didn't Want to Have to Do It" and "You Didn't Have to Be So Nice." Between soundtrack albums for Woody Allen's *What's Up Tiger Lily?* and Francis Ford Coppola's *You're a Big Boy Now*, the Lovin' Spoonful issued *Hums*, generally regarded as their most fully realized album. Producing a top hit with the classic summertime song "Summer in the City," the album also contained the near-smashes "Rain on the Roof" and "Nashville Cats." Subsequent hits included "Darling Be Home Soon," one of Sebastian's strongest and most endearing songs, and "Six O'Clock."

However, in late 1966 several members of the Lovin' Spoonful were busted on drug charges in San Francisco, and Yanovsky, threatened with deportation, apparently incriminated at least one area resident. He left the group in ignominy in July 1967, and the Lovin' Spoonful's image was permanently tarnished. Jerry Yester was recruited for *Everything Playing*, which contained "Six O'Clock," "She Is Still a Mystery," and "Younger Generation," but by fall 1968 John Sebastian had departed the group. Steve Boone also left, and Joe Butler reconstituted the group for one final album before dissolving the group in summer 1969.

In August 1969 John Sebastian established himself with members of the counterculture with his renowned, stoned-out appearance at the Woodstock Festival. However, he had become embroiled in legal disputes among his former manager, MGM Records (the distributor of Kama Sutra), and his new label, Reprise. The release of his debut solo album was delayed for a time, and in fact both MGM *and* Reprise issued *John B. Sebastian* in early 1970. Recorded with the assistance of Crosby, Stills and Nash (who had offered him a chair in their supergroup), the album contained several good-time up-tempo songs; two gentle love songs, "She's a Lady" and "Magical Connection"; and two songs of communal good will, "How Have You Been" and "I Had a Dream." He subsequently recorded *The Four of Us* and *Tarzana Kid* for Reprise. The latter album did not even make the album charts, despite the inclusion of Jimmy Cliff's "Sitting in Limbo," Lowell George's "Dixie Chicken," and Sebastian's own "Stories We Could Tell," recorded by the Everly Brothers in 1972. In 1976 Sebastian scored a top pop and easy-listening hit with "Welcome Back" from the ABC-TV situation comedy *Welcome Back, Kotter*.

For the next decade John Sebastian toured the concert and festival circuit, playing about a hundred engagements a year. He worked on the animated movies *Charlotte's Web* and *The Care Bears Movie*, and briefly reunited the Lovin' Spoonful for Paul Simon's movie *One-Trick Pony*. He later hosted the series *The Golden Age of Rock 'n' Roll* on cable's Arts and Entertainment network, and recorded instructional harmonica and autoharp tapes for Happy Traum's Homespun Tapes. By 1993 he had joined Shanachie Records, with the help of labelmate Stefan Grossman, for *Tar Beach*.

The Even Dozen Jug Band

The Even Dozen Jug Band	Elektra	7246	'63	†

The Mugwumps

The Mugwumps	Warner Bros.	1697	'67	†

The Lovin' Spoonful

Do You Believe in Magic	Kama Sutra	8050	'65	†
Daydream	Kama Sutra	8051	'66	†
What's Up Tiger Lily? (soundtrack)	Kama Sutra	8053	'66	†
Hums of the Lovin' Spoonful	Kama Sutra	8054	'66	†
You're a Big Boy Now (soundtrack)	Kama Sutra	8058	'67	†
Everything Is Playing	Kama Sutra	8061	'67	†
Revelation: Revolution '69	Kama Sutra	8073	'68	†

Anthologies

Best	Kama Sutra	8056	'67	†
Best, Volume 2	Kama Sutra	8064	'68	†
24 Karat Hits	Kama Sutra	(2) 750	'68	†
John Sebastian Song Book	Kama Sutra	2011	'70	†
Very Best	Kama Sutra	2013	'70	†
Once Upon a Time	Kama Sutra	2029	'71	†
The Best	Kama Sutra	(2) 2608	'76	†
The Lovin' Spoonful	Buddah	49500	'95	CS/CD
Distant Echoes	Accord	7196	'82	†
Best, Volume 2	Rhino	114	'84	†
Anthology	Rhino	70944	'90	CS/CD
Best	Rhino	71024	'94	CS/CD
All the Best	Special Music	4916		CS/CD
Best	Pair	(2) 1200		CD
Greatest Hits	Hollywood/IMG	115		CS/CD
Rock and Roll	Richmond	2205		CS
Daydream	One Way	22165		CD

Zalman Yanovsky

Alive and Well In Argentina	Kama Sutra	2030	'69	†

John Sebastian

John B. Sebastian	MGM	4654	'70	†
	Reprise	6379	'70	†
Live	MGM	4720	'70	†
Real Live John Sebastian	Reprise	2036	'71	†
The Four of Us	Reprise	2041	'71	†
Tarzana Kid	Reprise	2187	'74	†
Welcome Back	Reprise	2249	'76	†
Best: 1969–1976	Rhino	70170	'89	CS/CD
Tar Beach	Shanachie	8006	'93	CS/CD

LYNYRD SKYNYRD

Ronnie Van Zant (b. Jan. 15, 1949, Jacksonville, FL; d. Oct. 20, 1977, near Gillsburg, MS), lead voc, songwriting; **Gary Rossington**, gtr; **Allen Collins** (b. ca. 1952; d. Jan. 23, 1990, Jacksonville, FL), gtr; **Ed King**, gtr; **Billy Powell**, kybd; **Leon Wilkeson**, bs; **Bob Burns**, drm [**Artimus Pyle** replaced Bob Burns in 1974; Ed King left in 1975. Brother-and-sister team guitarist **Steve** and vocalist **Cassie Gaines** (both d. Oct. 20, 1977, near Gillsburg, MS) joined in 1976.]

Lynyrd Skynyrd

Perhaps the most popular Southern-rock band of the '70s, superseding progenitors the Allman Brothers, Lynyrd Skynyrd helped reclaim blues-based rock from British groups like Cream and Led Zeppelin. Often propelled by a *three*-guitar front line (a format otherwise utilized by only the Peter Green—era Fleetwood Mac) and featuring the strong vocal presence and prolific songwriting of leader Ronnie Van Zant, Lynyrd Skynyrd established themselves as a dynamic touring act by opening for the Who's 1973 Quadrophenia tour. Scoring a number of aggressive hits between 1974 and 1977, Lynyrd Skynyrd may be best remembered for the jam-style FM radio classic "Free Bird." However, the group disbanded in late 1977 after Van Zant and two other band members were killed in an airplane crash on October 20, 1977. During the '80s guitarist Gary Rossington persevered with the Rossington-Collins and Rossington bands. In 1987 many band members regrouped with Rossington and Ronnie Van Zant's brother Johnny for a tribute tour that eventually led to a new version of Lynyrd Skynyrd in 1991.

Vocalist Ronnie Van Zant and guitarists Gary Rossington and Allen Collins formed My Backyard, the first of a series of rock bands, in 1965. Experiencing numerous personnel and name changes, the band toured the Southern club circuit for seven years. In 1970 the group adopted the name Lynyrd Skynyrd, and by 1972 the band's membership had stabilized with Van Zant, Rossington, Collins, guitarist Ed King, keyboardist Billy Powell, bassist Leon Wilkeson, and drummer Bob Burns. (King had cowritten the 1967 psychedelic top hit "Incense and Peppermint" for his group the Strawberry Alarm Clock.)

By 1972 Lynyrd Skynyrd were making occasional forays into Atlanta, Georgia, where they were "discovered" by producer/keyboardist Al Kooper. He signed the band to MCA Records and produced their debut album, usually referred to as *Pronounced Leh-nerd Skin-nerd*. Supported by a rigorous touring schedule and major promotional campaign by MCA, the album featured "Gimme Three Steps" and the underground favorites "Simple Man" and "Free Bird," all cowritten by Van Zant. "Free Bird" became a major hit when released as a single in late 1974.

Opening for the Who's late-1973 American tour supporting their album *Quadrophenia*, Lynyrd Skynyrd were exposed to their largest audiences to date, performing creditably. The

Al Kooper—produced *Second Helping* contained "Workin' for MCA" and J. J. Cale's "Call Me the Breeze," and yielded a near-smash with the Southern anthem "Sweet Home Alabama," ostensibly a reply to Neil Young's "Southern Man." Touring exhaustively, Lynyrd Skynyrd's so-called Torture Tour of 1975 resulted in the departures of Ed King and Bob Burns. Kooper's final production for the band and King's final album with the band, *Nuthin' Fancy*, introduced drummer Artimus Pyle and included "I'm a Country Boy" and "Whiskey Rock-a-Roller," producing a major hit with the gun ode "Saturday Night Special."

Lynyrd Skynyrd continued with a two-guitar front line augmented by the female backing group the Honkettes, consisting of Cassie Gaines, Leslie Hawkins, and Joe Billingsley, in early 1976. *Gimme Back My Bullets*, produced by Tom Dowd, fared less well than Kooper's productions, and Cassie Gaines's guitarist-brother joined the group in June 1976. The live set *One More for the Road* produced a moderate hit with "Free Bird." After a touring respite, Lynyrd Skynyrd were back on the road in fall 1977, but on October 20, 1977, their chartered plane crashed near Gillsburg, Mississippi, when it ran out of fuel, killing Ronnie Van Zant and Steve and Cassie Gaines and injuring the others. *Street Survivors*, issued only three days before the crash, featured a ghastly cover (showing band members engulfed in flames) that was quickly withdrawn by MCA as being in poor taste. The album contained "I Know a Little," "I Never Dreamed," and the ominously ironic "That Smell," as well as the major hit "What's Your Name" and the minor hit "You Got That Right." As band members recovered, convalesced, and attempted to return to a normal lifestyle, MCA issued *Skynyrd's First . . . and Last*, recorded in 1970 and 1971, before the band had secured a recording contract.

In fall 1979, four surviving members of Lynyrd Skynyrd—Gary Rossington, Allen Collins, Billy Powell, and Leon Wilkeson—reunited as the Rossington-Collins Band, augmented by guitarist Barry Harwood, vocalist Dale Krantz Rossington (Gary's wife), and drummer Derek Hess. Formally debuting in June 1980, the group scored a minor hit with "Don't Misunderstand Me," only to disband in 1982. Collins subsequently formed the Allen Collins Band with Powell, Wilkeson, Harwood, and Hess. Collins was paralyzed in an automobile crash in 1986 and died of pneumonia on January 23, 1990, at age 37.

Gary Rossington and Ronnie Van Zant's vocalist brother Johnny reassembled members of Lynyrd Skynyrd for a tribute tour in 1987, including Ed King, new guitarist Randall Hall, Powell, Wilkeson, and Pyle, plus Honkettes Dale Krantz Rossington and Carol Bristow. In 1988 Rossington formed the Rossington Band with wife Dale for a single MCA album. In 1991 Lynyrd Skynyrd officially regrouped with Rossington, Johnny Van Zant, King, Hall, Powell, Wilkeson, and Pyle for touring, and for recording *Lynyrd Skynyrd 1991* and *The Last Rebel* for Atlantic, and the acoustic *Endangered Species* for Capricorn.

Lynyrd Skynyrd

Skynyrd's First . . . and Last	MCA	3047	'78	†
	MCA	37071		†
	MCA	1618		CS
	MCA	31005		CD
Pronounced Leh-nerd Skin-nerd	MCA/Sounds of the South	363	'73	†
	MCA	3019		†
	MCA	1685		CS/CD
	MCA	10953	'93	CD
Second Helping	MCA/Sounds of the South	413	'74	†
	MCA	3020		†
	MCA	1686		CS/CD
	Mobile Fidelity	556	'92	CD

Pronounced Leh-nerd Skin-nerd/Second Helping	MCA	(2) 6937		CS
Nuthin' Fancy	MCA	2137	'75	†
	MCA	3021		†
	MCA	37069		†
	MCA	1616		CS
	MCA	31003		CD
Gimme Back My Bullets	MCA	2170	'76	†
	MCA	3022		†
	MCA	37070		†
	MCA	1617		CS
	MCA	31004		CD
Nuthin' Fancy/Gimme Back My Bullets	MCA	(2) 6902		CS
One More for the Road	MCA	(2) 6001	'76	†
	MCA	(2) 8011		†
	MCA	(2) 6897		CS
	MCA	6897		CD
Street Survivors	MCA	3029	'77	†
	MCA	1687		CS/CD
	MCA	11171	'94	CD
Skynyrd's First . . . and Last/Street Survivors	MCA	(2) 6938		CS
Gold and Platinum	MCA	(2) 11008	'79	†
	MCA	(2) 6898		LP/CS/CD
The Best of the Rest	MCA	5370	'82	†
	MCA	1448	'85	CS
	MCA	31006	'85	CD
Legend	MCA	42084	'87	CS/CD
Southern by the Grace of God: The Lynyrd Skynyrd Tribute Tour, 1987	MCA	(2) 8027	'88	CS
	MCA	8027	'88	CD
Skynyrd's Innyrds	MCA	42293	'89	CS/CD
Lynyrd Skynyrd Box Set	MCA	(3) 10390	'91	CS/CD
Lynyrd Skynyrd, 1991	Atlantic	82258	'91	CS/CD
The Last Rebel	Atlantic	82447	'93	CS/CD
Endangered Species	Capricorn	42028	'94	CS/CD

Tribute Album

Skynyrd Frynds	MCA Nashville	11097	'94	CS/CD

The Rossington-Collins Band

Anytime, Anyplace, Anywhere	MCA	5130	'80	†
	MCA	31220		CD
This Is the Way	MCA	5207	'81	†
Anytime, Anyplace, Anywhere/This Is the Way	MCA	(2) 6944		CS

The Rossington Band

Love Your Man	MCA	42166	'88	LP/CS/CD†

MADONNA

(b. Madonna Louise Ciccone, August 16, 1958, Bay City, MI)

Personifying the '80s emphasis on artifice and attitude over content and commitment, Madonna was the first music act to achieve mainstream popularity thanks to regular and frequent exposure of her music videos on cable television's MTV network. Her lavish videos, usually produced by movie directors, and her carefree party sound, clearly derived from disco music, reinforced the rise of a fashionable club scene based on dancing and dress, and opened the door for the success of video-dance artists such as Paula Abdul. Although exhibiting only a modicum of talent for singing, songwriting, and dancing, Madonna became the most conspicuous and commercially successful recording act of the '80s and '90s.

Madonna initially appealed largely to an impressionable adolescent female audience. Inspiring a fashion trend based on lace, bare midriffs, and undergarments worn as outerwear, Madonna titillated, intrigued, and outraged adults and critics unused to a strong, if superficial, female personality. Her regular changes in physical appearance invited comparisons to the periodic image shifts of David Bowie, and her puerile, voyeuristic sense of sexuality was compared with that of Prince. Additionally, Madonna projected a set of seemingly contradictory images (slut/goddess, boy-toy/dominatrix, narcissist/romantic) that confounded the media and enticed fans outside of music to follow her exploits. Madonna repeatedly fostered public controversy, whether calculated or incidental, while transcending the confines of pop music and transforming herself into an international celebrity.

Madonna dropped out of the University of Michigan's dance department to move to New York in 1978, where she briefly worked with the Alvin Ailey Dance Company. She later met Dan Gilroy in France, forming the club band the Breakfast Club with him on their return to New York. She subsequently formed Emmy with drummer Steve Bray, and was "discovered" by nightclub disc jockey Mark Kamins, who produced her club hit "Everybody" in 1982. Signed to Sire Records, Madonna scored her first major hit with "Holiday," written and produced by John "Jellybean" Benitez. Her debut album, which remained on the album charts for more than three years, also yielded a near-smash hit, "Borderline," and the smash "Lucky Star."

In late 1984 Madonna broke through with her *Like a Virgin*, which stayed on the album charts for more than two years and sold seven million copies in the United States. The title song, written by Tom Kelly and Billy Steinberg, became a top pop and near-smash R&B hit. It was promoted through the first of a series of engaging and provocative videos popularized by the cable television network MTV. The album, produced by Chic's Nile Rodgers, featured scratchy guitar, swirling keyboards, and infectious dance rhythms, yielding smash hits with "Material Girl," "Angel," and "Dress You Up." The album and videos quickly established Madonna's image as an aggressive, spoiled, and slightly decadent chanteuse. She appeared in a cameo role in the 1985 movie *Vision Quest*; the soundtrack album produced her top hit "Crazy for You." Madonna broke through as an actress later that year in the film *Desperately Seeking Susan*, portraying an amoral, unconventional, hard-living rebel opposite Rosanna Arquette.

International celebrity quickly followed, as Madonna appeared on the cover of *Time* magazine in May 1985, performed at Live Aid in July, and married actor Sean Penn in August. Her public exposure and offbeat reputation were enhanced with the publication of nude photographs in *Playboy* and *Penthouse* magazines and the rerelease of her 1980 sleaze movie *A Certain Sacrifice*. Madonna's *True Blue* album yielded a top pop and easy-listening hit with "Live to Tell"; top pop hits with "Open Your Heart" and the simplistic yet controversial "Papa Don't Preach"; and the smashes "True Blue" and "La Isla Bonita," another top easy-listening hit. However, her next two endeavors, the films *Shanghai Surprise* (with husband Sean Penn) and *Who's That Girl*, failed critically and commercially, although the *Who's That Girl* soundtrack featured four new Madonna songs, including the top hit title song and the smash hit "Causing a Commotion." In late 1987 seven extended remixes of her dance hits were released as *You Can Dance*.

Madonna's tour in support of *Who's That Girl* showcased carefully prepared staging and choreography. She remained in the public eye through cover appearances on *Life* and *Vanity Fair*, introducing her new image as a glamour queen. In January 1989 Madonna signed a $5 million deal to globally promote Pepsi Cola with an elaborate two-minute commercial, but the advertisement, based on the video for the song "Like a Prayer," was withdrawn within two months of its debut in March. Viewers had apparently confused the commercial with the top hit single and video "Like a Prayer," which portrayed Catholic beliefs in what some viewed as a sacrilegious light. The resulting publicity helped make the album of the same name, coproduced with new collaborator Patrick Leonard, an international best-seller.

Ostensibly showing a more honest and mature side of Madonna, *Like a Prayer* represented a bid for critical acceptance among young adults rather than teenagers. The album included two songs concerned with the tenets of the Catholic religion, "Like a Prayer" and "Act of Contrition," and three songs concerned with family relationships: "Till Death Do Us Part," "Promises to Try," and "Oh Father," a major hit. Featuring a sultry duet with Prince on "Love Song," the album yielded smash hits with "Express Yourself" and "Cherish" (a top easy-listening hit), and a major hit with "Keep It Together." Madonna's performances in David Mamet's Broadway play *Speed the Plow* had drawn favorable reviews in May, but the movie *Bloodhounds of Broadway*, based on characters created by Damon Runyon, quickly failed at the box office upon release at year's end.

The year 1990 proved to be the most successful year of Madonna's career. Her "Vogue" dance video/single capitalized on the Manhattan posing-style dance trend and became a top hit. From April through August she conducted her worldwide Blond Ambition tour, which featured extravagant costuming, spectacular staging, and tight choreography. Madonna costarred with Warren Beatty in the popular movie *Dick Tracy* and released the album *I'm Breathless: Music from and Inspired by the Film Dick Tracy*, which contained "Vogue" and "Hanky Panky," a near-smash hit, as well as three songs written by Broadway master Stephen Sondheim: "Move," "Sooner or Later," and, in duet with Mandy Patinkin, "What You Can Lose." Near year's end the rap-style song "Justify My Love," cowritten with Lenny Kravitz, became a top hit, but the attendant video became the first by a major artist to be banned from airplay by MTV. Produced by Madonna and Shep Pettibone, "Justify My Love" and the near-smash "Rescue Me" were included on the anthology *The Immaculate Collection*; the album remained on the album charts for more than two years.

However, several Italian Catholic organizations subsequently sought to ban Madonna's performances as vulgar and blasphemous. The banishment of her "Justify My Love" video became international news when ABC-TV interviewed her and played the video on *Nightline*.

Additionally, one of her remixes of "Justify My Love," "The Beast Within," was attacked as anti-Semitic by the Simon Wiesenthal Center in Los Angeles.

Appearing on the covers of *Glamour*, *Entertainment Weekly*, and, later, *Vanity Fair*, Madonna granted the gay-oriented magazine *Advocate* a lengthy candid interview in May 1991. That same month the tour documentary *Truth or Dare*, taken from her Blond Ambition tour, opened to brisk business in limited release, despite attacks that the film was unabashedly narcissistic, flagrantly exhibitionist, and artificially spontaneous.

In April 1992 Madonna signed a seven-year agreement with Time-Warner, the parent company of Sire Records. Worth a reported $60 million, the deal enabled her to establish her own multimedia entertainment company, named Maverick. One of the most lucrative contracts offered to a pop star, the deal was unprecedented in its value and magnitude for a female performer. In September she appeared topless at a Paris fashion show, and the following month she appeared nude in *Vanity Fair* as part of a massive campaign to promote her *Erotica* album and *Sex* picture book, her first efforts for Maverick. Returning to her disco sound and embracing the style of rap music, the album was comprised largely of songs written by Madonna and producer Pettibone. It included her celebration of oral sex, "Where Life Begins," and yielded the smash hit "Erotica," the near-smash "Deeper and Deeper," the major hit "Rain," and the moderate hit "Bad Girl." The tawdry, amateurish book *Sex* featured Madonna posing with a variety of sex partners in an apparent explication of her sexual fantasies.

Both *Erotica* and *Sex* were greeted by a harsh critical backlash, a situation exacerbated by the early 1993 release of the grim movie *Body of Evidence*, which was regarded by at least one critic as one of the worst movies ever made; in less than six months the film was available on videocassette. Madonna subsequently toured internationally with her Girlie Show tour in the fall. Performances featured scantily clad and topless dancers, sometimes simulating sexual acts, and provoked controversy in Puerto Rico and Germany. In March 1994 Madonna appeared on the *David Letterman* late-night television show, shocking viewers and her host with her frequent use of four-letter words. She later appeared in the equivocal film *Dangerous*, with Harvey Keitel.

Madonna deemphasized the feigned eroticism of her music with 1994's R&B-styled *Bedtime Stories*, cut with coproducer Shep Pettibone. The album yielded a smash hit with "Secret" and a top hit with "Take a Bow." In November the Fox cable network broadcast a biographical movie based on her early career. In 1995 Madonna canceled her tour in support of *Bedtime Stories* to work on the film musical *Evita*, based on the life of Eva Perón, the wife of Argentine dictator Juan Perón.

Madonna

The Early Years	Receiver	118	'95	CD
Madonna	Sire	23867	'83/'84	CS/CD
Like a Virgin	Sire	25157	'84/'85	CS/CD
True Blue	Warner Bros.	25442	'86	CS/CD
Who's That Girl (soundtrack)	Sire	25611	'87	CS/CD
You Can Dance	Sire	25535	'87	CS/CD
Like a Prayer	Sire	25844	'89	CS/CD
I'm Breathless	Sire	26209	'90	CS/CD
The Immaculate Collection	Sire	(2) 26440	'90	LP
	Sire	26440	'90	CS/CD
The Royal Box	Sire	26464	'91	CS/CD
Erotica	Maverick	45031	'92	CD
	Maverick	45154	'92	CS/CD
Bedtime Stories	Maverick	45767	'94	CS/CD
Something to Remember	Maverick	46100	'95	CS/CD

THE MAMAS AND THE PAPAS

John Phillips (b. Aug. 30, variously reported as 1935 and 1941, Paris Island, SC), gtr, bar voc; **Denny Doherty** (b. Nov. 29, 1941, Halifax, Nova Scotia, Canada), ten voc; **Cass Elliot** (b. Ellen Cohen, Sept. 19, 1941, Baltimore, MD; d. July 29, 1974, London, England), contralto voc; **Michelle Phillips** (b. Holly Michelle Gilliam, June 4, 1945, Long Beach, CA), sop voc

THE MAMAS AND THE PAPAS

Early purveyors of gentle, harmonically sophisticated Los Angeles folk-rock, the Mamas and the Papas were one of the earliest hippie groups, sporting brightly colored, odd-looking attire *before* the crunch of San Francisco's psychedelic rock. Although most of the members emerged from a folk-music background, the Mamas and the Papas's success was due in part to the slick pop-style production of manager Lou Adler. Featuring the excellent songwriting and intricate vocal arrangements of leader John Phillips, lustrous vocal harmonies, and the outstanding playing of some of Los Angeles's finest studio musicians, the group enjoyed considerable success between 1965 and 1968. Moreover, Phillips and Adler organized the 1967 Monterey Pop Festival, perhaps the first-ever rock-music festival and certainly one of the most significant, launching the American careers of Jimi Hendrix, The Who, and Janis Joplin, among others. Following the group's breakup, Mama Cass Elliot initiated a modest solo career as a cabaret entertainer, and her Laurel Canyon home served as a center of musical and social activities that saw Crosby, Stills and Nash first join voices. Michelle Phillips later pursued an unspectacular career as an actress. In the '80s John Phillips regrouped the Mamas and the Papas with original member Denny Doherty, daughter MacKenzie, and Spanky and Our Gang vocalist Spanky McFarlane as a lounge act.

John Phillips began performing in Greenwich Village folk clubs during the late '50s with groups such as the Smoothies, which included Scott McKenzie. In 1961 Phillips, McKenzie, and Dick Weissman formed the folk trio the Journeymen, debuting at Gerde's Folk City that spring and ultimately recording three albums for Capitol Records. A year later in San Francisco, Phillips met aspiring model Michelle Gilliam, and the couple soon married. Denny Doherty recorded two albums for Epic while a member of the folk group the Halifax Three. Cass Elliot, her first husband James Hendricks, and Tim Rose formed the Big Three in New York around 1963, recording two albums for FM Records. By summer 1964 the Mugwumps had evolved, with Elliot, Hendricks, Doherty, and future Lovin'

Spoonful member Zalman Yanovsky, and the group recorded one album, which was eventually released in 1967.

With the dissolution of the Mugwumps, Denny Doherty joined John and Michelle Phillips in the Virgin Islands. Subsequently joined by Cass Elliot in New York, the four worked on perfecting their vocal harmonies for five months (Michelle had been singing less than three months) during 1965 before moving to Los Angeles. There Barry McGuire put them in touch with producer Lou Adler, who signed the group as the Mamas and the Papas to his newly formed Dunhill label.

The Mamas and the Papas recorded their debut album with studio musicians Larry Knechtel (kybd), Joe Osborn (bs), and Hal Blaine (drm), with Adler providing slick pop-style production. The album, *If You Can Believe Your Eyes and Ears*, quickly yielded smash hits with John and Michelle's "California Dreamin'" and John's "Monday, Monday," and contained John's "Go Where You Wanna Go" and Lennon and McCartney's "I Call Your Name." Their second album, *The Mamas and the Papas*, produced smash hits with John and Denny's "I Saw Her Again" and John's "Words of Love"; it also included John's "No Salt on Her Tail," "Dancing Bear," and "Strange Young Girls," and John and Michelle's "Trip Stumble and Fall." *Deliver* included the smash hits "Dedicated to the One I Love" (a 1961 smash for the Shirelles) and John and Michelle's group autobiography "Creeque Alley," and the major hit "Look Through My Window" by John.

In 1967 John Phillips and Lou Adler organized the Monterey International Pop Festival, perhaps the first rock music festival of the late '60s. Coinciding with the smash success of Phillips's insipid "San Francisco (Be Sure to Wear Some Flowers in Your Hair)" as recorded by former associate Scott McKenzie, the festival (and subsequent D. A. Pennebaker film) launched the American careers of Jimi Hendrix, The Who, and Janis Joplin. *The Papas and the Mamas* produced a major hit with John's "Twelve Thirty" and a minor hit with his excellent "Safe in My Garden." "Glad to Be Unhappy" became the group's last major hit; by mid-1968 the Mamas and the Papas had broken up.

Cass Elliot quickly recorded her debut solo album for Dunhill, which yielded the major hit "Dream a Little Dream of Me," but she did not score another hit until 1969, when "It's Getting Better" and "Make Your Own Kind of Music" proved moderately successful. Pursuing a career as a nightclub and television entertainer, Elliot later recorded an ill-received but underrated album with Dave Mason, who was coming off the huge success of his debut solo album, *Alone Together*. John Phillips managed a moderate hit with "Mississippi" in the summer of 1970, the year he and Michelle divorced. The Mamas and the Papas reunited briefly in 1971 for a single album on Dunhill.

After successfully completing a two-week engagement at the Palladium Theater in London, Cass Elliot succumbed to a heart attack on July 29, 1974, at age 32. In the meantime, John Phillips composed the music for the flop Broadway musical *Man on the Moon*, produced by Andy Warhol. Michelle Phillips launched a career as an actress with 1973's *Dillinger* and later recorded a solo album for A&M Records. Years later she was a featured player in television's nighttime soap opera *Knots Landing*. John Phillips, mired in drug addiction during the last half of the '70s, was arrested on serious drug charges in New York in July 1980, fined, and sentenced to 30 days in jail. In 1982 he reformed the Mamas and the Papas as a lounge act with Denny Doherty, daughter MacKenzie Phillips (best known for her role in the television situation comedy "One Day at a Time," 1975–1983), and Spanky McFarlane, onetime lead vocalist for Spanky and Our Gang, who scored major hits in 1967–1968 with "Sunday Will Never Be the Same," "Lazy Day," and "Like to Get to Know You." John Phillips shared songwriting credit with Scott McKenzie, Terry Melcher, and Beach Boy Mike Love on the Beach Boys' top 1988 hit, "Kokomo."

In 1989 John and Michelle's daughter Chynna Phillips formed the vocal group Wilson Phillips with Beach Boy Brian Wilson's daughters Carnie and Wendy. Their debut album produced five hits, including the top hits "Hold On," "Release Me," and "You're in Love," but their more personal *Shadows and Light* yielded only two hits. The group dissolved, and in 1995 Chynna Phillips released her first solo album, after marrying film actor William Baldwin.

The Journeymen (with John Phillips)

The Journeymen	Capitol	1629	'61	†
	Capitol	98536	'92	CS/CD
Coming Attractions—Live!	Capitol	1770	'62	†
New Directions in Folk Music	Capitol	1951	'63	†

The Halifax Three (with Denny Doherty)

The Halifax Three	Epic	26038	'63	†
San Francisco Bay Blues	Epic	26060	'63	†

The Big Three (with Cass Elliot)

The Big Three	FM	307	'63	†
Live at the Recording Studio	FM	311	'64	†
The Big Three Featuring Cass Elliot	Roulette	42000	'69	†
Distant Reflections	Accord	7180	'82	†

The Mugwumps (with Cass Elliot and Denny Doherty)

The Mugwumps	Warner Bros.	1697	'67	†

The Mamas and the Papas

If You Can Believe Your Eyes and Ears	Dunhill	50006	'66	†
	MCA	31042		CS/CD
The Mamas and the Papas	Dunhill	50010	'66	†
Dolivor	Dunhill	50014	'67	†
	MCA	31044	'87	CD
Monterey International Pop Festival	Dunhill	50100	'71	†
	One Way	22033		CD
The Papas and the Mamas	Dunhill	50031	'68	†
	MCA	31335	'87	CD
People Like Us	Dunhill	50106	'71	†

Anthologies

Book of Songs	Dunhill	50022	'67	†
Farewell to the First Golden Era	Dunhill	50025	'67	†
	MCA	709		CS
Golden Era, Volume 2	Dunhill	50038	'68	†
16 Greatest Hits	Dunhill	50064	'69	†
	MCA	1647		CS
Anthology—A Gathering of Flowers	Dunhill	50073	'70	†
20 Golden Hits	Dunhill	50145	'73	†
California Dreamin'	Pickwick	3357		†
Monday, Monday	Pickwick	3380	'75	†
Biggest Hits	Pickwick	(2) 2076	'75	†
Best	MCA	(2) 6019	'82	LP/CS
Creeque Alley/The History of the Mamas and the Papas	MCA	(2) 10195	'91	CD
16 of Their Greatest Hits	MCA	5701		CD
Words of Love	Pair	1322		CD

Cass Elliot

Dream a Little Dream	Dunhill	50040	'68	†

Bubblegum, Lemonade, and Something for Mama	Dunhill	50055	'69	†
Make Your Own Kind of Music	Dunhill	50071	'69	†
Mama's Big Ones (Her Greatest Hits)	Dunhill	50093	'70	†
	MCA	719		CS
	MCA	31147		CD
Cass Elliot	RCA	4619	'72	†
The Road Is No Place for a Lady	RCA	4753	'72	†
Don't Call Me Mama Anymore	RCA	0303	'73	†
Her Best Music	Pickwick	(2) 2075	'75	†
Dream a Little Dream	Pickwick	3359		†
Cass Elliot and Dave Mason				
Dave Mason and Cass Elliot	Blue Thumb	8825	'71	†
John Phillips				
John Phillips	Dunhill	50077	'70	†
Denny Doherty				
Watcha Gonna Do	Dunhill	50096	'71	†
Waiting for a Sign	Ember	1036	'74	†
Michelle Phillips				
Victim of Romance	A&M	4651	'77	†
Wilson Phillips				
Wilson Phillips	SBK	93745	'90	CS/CD
Shadows and Light	SBK	98924	'92	CS/CD
Chynna Phillips				
Naked and Sacred	EMI	35705	'95	CS/CD

BARRY MANN/CYNTHIA WEIL

Barry Mann (b. Barry Iberman, Feb. 9, 1939, Brooklyn, NY)

Another of the brilliant professional songwriting teams employed at New York's Brill Building during the '60s, Barry Mann and wife Cynthia Weil wrote dozens of hit songs for a variety of acts. Their songwriting credits included "On Broadway" for the Drifters, "You've Lost That Lovin' Feelin'" and "(You're My) Soul and Inspiration" for the Righteous Brothers, "Kicks" and "Hungry" for Paul Revere and the Raiders, and "Here You Come Again" for Dolly Parton.

Barry Mann abandoned his architecture studies to become a songwriter in 1958. Achieving his first hit in collaboration with Mike Anthony in early 1959 with "She Say (Oom Dooby Doom)" as performed by the Diamonds, he was hired as a staff songwriter by Al Nevins and Don Kirshner at New York's famed Brill Building music operation. Teaming with several other writers on a number of early-'60s hits, Mann cowrote "Footsteps" for Steve Lawrence, "I Love How You Love Me" for the Paris Sisters, and the maudlin "Patches" for Dickey Lee. Encouraged by Don Kirshner, Mann recorded an album of his own for ABC Records in 1961 that yielded a near-smash hit with the novelty song "Who Put the Bomp (In the Bomp, Bomp, Bomp)," cowritten with Gerry Goffin.

Barry Mann's greatest success came in collaboration with Cynthia Weil, whom he married in 1961. Their early hit compositions included "Uptown" and "He's Sure the Boy I Love" for the Crystals, both from 1962. Hit Mann-Weil compositions from 1963 include "My Dad" for Paul Petersen, "Blame It on the Bossa Nova" for Eydie Gorme, and "Only in America" for Jay and the Americans. Subsequent hit compositions were "I'm Gonna be Strong" for

Gene Pitney, "Saturday Night at the Movies" for the Drifters, and "We Gotta Get Out of This Place" for the Animals. In late 1964 the duo worked with songwriter-producer extraordinaire Phil Spector on "Walking in the Rain" for the Ronettes and the classic "You've Lost That Lovin' Feelin'" for the Righteous Brothers. During 1966 they provided the Righteous Brothers with "(You're My) Soul and Inspiration" and Paul Revere and the Raiders with "Kicks" and "Hungry." Other hit compositions with which they were associated through 1970 were Max Frost and the Troopers' "Shapes of Things to Come," Cass Elliot's "It's Getting Better" and "Make Your Own Kind of Music," and B. J. Thomas's "I Just Can't Help Believing."

Around 1970 Barry Mann and Cynthia Weil moved to the West Coast, where Mann unsuccessfully attempted to launch a solo recording career. Another attempt in 1975 yielded the minor hit "The Princess and the Punk." Later hits that Barry Mann and/or Cynthia Weil were associated with include "Here You Come Again" for Dolly Parton and "Sometimes When We Touch" for Dan Hill, both from 1977.

Barry Mann

Who Put the Bomp	ABC	399	'61	†
Lay It All Out	New Design	30876	'72	†
Survivor	RCA	0860	'75	†
Barry Mann	Casablanca	7228	'80	†

MANFRED MANN

Manfred Mann (b. Michael Lubowitz, Oct. 21, 1940, Johannesburg, South Africa), kybd; **Paul Jones** (b. Paul Pond, Feb. 24, 1942, Portsmouth, Hampshire, England), voc; **Michael Vickers** (b. Apr. 18, 1941, Southampton, Hampshire, England), gtr; **Tom McGuinness** (b. Dec. 2, 1941, London, England), bs; **Mike Hugg** (b. Aug. 11, 1942, Andover, Hampshire, England), drm [Michael Vickers left in 1965, to be replaced briefly by **Jack Bruce** (b. May 13, 1943, Glasgow, Scotland), and six months later by **Klaus Voorman**; Paul Jones was replaced by **Mike D'Abo**.]

The third British group to achieve a top American hit (the R&B-styled "Do Wah Diddy Diddy"), Manfred Mann scored more than a dozen British hits, yet only four major American hits (including "Sha La La" and one of the earliest versions of Bob Dylan's "Mighty Quinn") before disbanding in 1969.

The man Manfred Mann met Mike Hugg in London in the early '60s; they were originally interested in playing traditional blues and jazz, and at one point led an eight-piece ensemble. By 1963 they had formed a five-piece band and were performing under the name Manfred Mann. Their first big U.K. hit was 1964's "5-4-3-2-1," which was popularized as the theme for the "Ready Steady Go" teen-pop TV program. "Do Wah Diddy Diddy" from 1965 was a smash in the United Kingdom and established the group in the United States, but Vickers quit the band after its success, to be replaced in quick succession by blues-jazz bassist Jack Bruce (who left Manfred Mann to form Cream) and then German-born Klaus Voorman; Paul Jones left to pursue a solo acting and recording career, and was replaced by vocalist Mike D'Abo, who sang lead on the group's final big hit, "The Mighty Quinn," in 1968.

Mann and Hugg longed to return to their jazz roots, and they disbanded the pop group in 1969 to pursue this dream with a new ensemble, Chapter Three. An ambitious project that featured a large horn section, the group recorded two albums before Hugg left to pursue film work. Mann then formed Manfred Mann's Earth Band, a more hard-rocking ensemble. Formed in 1971, it took the group five years before it had a sizable U.S. hit with a cover of Bruce Springsteen's "Blinded by the Light" from the best-selling album *The Roaring Silence* in 1976. The group's final, minor hit was 1984's "Runner."

Manfred Mann

Manfred Mann Album	Ascot	16015	'64	†
Five Faces of Manfred Mann	Ascot	16018	'65	†
My Little Red Book of Winners	Ascot	16021	'65	†
Mann Made	Ascot	16024	'66	†
Pretty Flamingo	United Artists	6549	'66	†
Greatest Hits	United Artists	6551	'66	†
Up the Junction (soundtrack)	Mercury	61159	'68	†
The Mighty Quinn	Mercury	61168	'68	†
Second Chapter: Best of the Fontana (i.e., Mercury) Years	Fontana	522665	'94	CS/CD
Best	Janus	3064	'74	†
Greatest Hits	Capitol	11688	'77	†
Best	Capitol	16073		†
Best	EMI	96096	'92	CS/CD

Paul Jones

Sings Songs from *Privilege* and Others	Capitol	2795	'67	†
Crucifix in a Horseshoe	London	605	'70	†

Manfred Mann's Chapter Three

Manfred Mann's Chapter Three	Polydor	244013	'70	†

Manfred Mann's Earth Band

Manfred Mann's Earth Band	Polydor	5015	'72	†
Glorified, Magnified	Polydor	5031	'72	†
Get Your Rocks Off	Polydor	5050	'73	†
Solar Fire	Polydor	6019	'74	†
The Good Earth	Warner Bros.	2826	'74	†
Nightingales and Bombers	Warner Bros.	2877	'75	†
The Roaring Silence	Warner Bros.	2965	'76	†
	Warner Bros.	3055		CS
Watch	Warner Bros.	3157	'78	†
Angel Station	Warner Bros.	3302	'79	†
Somewhere in Afrika	Arista	8194	'83	†

Manfred Mann

Chance	Warner Bros.	3498	'81	†

BOB MARLEY

(b. Robert Nesta Marley, April 6, 1945, Rhoden Hall, Jamaica; d. May 11, 1981, Miami, FL)

THE WAILERS. Vocalist-guitarist **Bob Marley**; **Peter Tosh** (b. Winston Hubert Macintosh, Oct. 9, 1944, Westmoreland, Jamaica; d. Sept. 11, 1987, Kingston, Jamaica), voc, gtr; **Neville O'Reilly "Bunny" Livingstone** (b. Apr. 10, 1947, Kingston, Jamaica), voc, perc; **Junior Braithwaite**, voc; **Beverly Kelso**, voc; **Aston "Family Man" Barrett** (b. Nov. 22, 1946, Kingston, Jamaica), bs; **Carlton Lloyd "Carly" Barrett** (b. Dec. 17, 1950, Kingston, Jamaica; d. Apr. 17, 1987, Kingston, Jamaica), drm; **Al Anderson** (b. Montclair, NJ), gtr; **Alvin Patterson** (b. Jamaica), perc

THE I-THREES. Rita Marley, **Judy Mowatt,** and **Marcia Griffiths** (all b. Jamaica)

ZIGGY MARLEY (b. David Marley, Oct. 17, 1968, Kingston, Jamaica)

The most important purveyors of authentic reggae music (Jimmy Cliff's music was rather pop-oriented), Bob Marley and the Wailers were popular recording artists in Jamaica for years before securing a contract with the internationally distributed Island label in 1972. Established with the landmark *Burnin'* and *Catch a Fire* albums, the Wailers became the first reggae band to gain worldwide recognition and Bob Marley, as chief songwriter and lead vocalist, emerged as the first (and possibly only) artist from the Third World to achieve international stardom. Although their albums contained some highly personal songs, they were largely preoccupied with political repression, social injustice, and the tenets of the Rastafarian religion (which included the sacramental use of marijuana). Original members Peter Tosh and "Bunny" Livingstone left the Wailers in 1974 for their own careers, as the female vocal trio the I-Threes augmented Bob Marley and the Wailers beginning in 1975. The group achieved its biggest success with 1976's *Rastaman Vibration*. However, Marley's death in 1981 effectively coincided with the end of the first wave of reggae's popularity.

Bob Marley began recording in his native land in 1961. By 1964 he had joined fellow Jamaicans Peter Tosh and "Bunny" Livingstone in the formation of the Wailing Rudeboys. The group became the Wailin' Wailers (with Junior Braithwaite and Beverly Kelso) and later simply the Wailers for a series of recordings for small Jamaican labels, scoring their first big island hit in 1965 with "Simmer Down." Extensive local success continued into the early '70s as the group recorded for producers such as Leslie Kong and Lee Perry. They added drummer Carlton Barrett and his bass-playing brother Aston "Family Man" Barrett around 1970, issuing four Jamaican albums by 1972. Johnny Nash used the Wailers to back his top pop hit "I Can See Clearly Now" in 1972, and Marley provided Nash with the 1972 British and 1973 American hit "Stir It Up."

Signed to Chris Blackwell's Island label in 1972, the Wailers recorded their critically acclaimed debut, *Catch A Fire*, but the album failed to sell in the United States, despite the inclusion of "Stir It Up," "No More Trouble," and Tosh's militant "400 Years." Following quiet tours of Great Britain and the United States, the Wailers recorded *Burnin'*, which was similarly overlooked, despite containing Tosh's "Get Up, Stand Up" and "One Foundation" and Marley's "I Shot the Sheriff." Eric Clapton scored a top hit with a tame version of "I Shot the Sheriff" in the summer of 1974, but by then both Tosh and Livingstone had left the Wailers.

Bob Marley and the Wailers, as they became known, finally broke through with 1975's *Natty Dread*, recorded with lead guitarist Al Anderson and the Barrett brothers. In addition to the title song the album included "Rebel Music," "Them Belly Full (But We Hungry)," "Lively Up Yourself," and the touching "No Woman, No Cry," regarded as one of Marley's finest personal songs. Successful tours of America and Britain in 1975 raised Marley to the status of cult figure as the rock press declared reggae the up-and-coming music of the '70s.

In 1975 Bob Marley and the Wailers were augmented by the female vocal trio the I-Threes, which consisted of Marley's wife Rita, Judy Mowatt, and Marcia Griffiths. Griffiths started her career in the early '60s, scoring her first top Jamaican hit with "Feel Like Jumping" in 1968. Judy Mowatt had her own career as early as 1970. In 1976 the group's *Rastaman Vibration* became a best-seller. Yielding their only (minor) hit with "Roots, Rock, Reggae," the album also contained "Positive Vibration," "Rat Race," and "War."

Following an assassination attempt on December 3, 1976, Bob Marley went into self-imposed exile. His *Exodus* album included favorites such as "Jamming," "Exodus," and "Waiting in Vain," and the inspirational medley "One Love/People Get Ready," and sold quite well. However, *Kaya*, comprised entirely of love songs, sold only modestly. Bob Marley returned to the concert stage on April 22, 1978, for the One Love Peace Concert in Kingston, Jamaica. He induced political rivals Michael Manley and Edward Seaga to publicly shake hands during a time dominated by political turmoil and ghetto gang riots. In 1980 Marley performed at the independence ceremony in Zimbabwe and won a United Nations Peace Medal. Following *Survival* and *Uprising*, Bob Marley took ill with brain cancer. He died in Miami, Florida, on May 11, 1981, at age 36. He was inducted into the Rock and Roll Hall of Fame in 1994.

In the meantime, Peter Tosh launched a solo career on Columbia with *Legalize It* and *Equal Rights*. The debut album contained "Whatcha Gonna Do" and the classic title song, which advocated the legalization of marijuana. In 1978 Tosh became the first non–Rolling Stones act to record for Rolling Stones Records, and that summer he toured as the band's opening act. His debut album for the label included the minor hit "(You Got to Walk and) Don't Look Back," recorded in duet with Mick Jagger and originally written for the Temptations by Smokey Robinson. By 1981 Tosh had switched to EMI for *Wanted Dread and Alive* and *Mama Africa*, which contained the antiapartheid title song as well as "Where You Gonna Run" and a minor hit version of Chuck Berry's "Johnny B. Goode." He continued to record through 1987, but on September 11, 1987, he was fatally shot in his Kingston home during a robbery.

"Bunny" Livingstone, born Neville O'Reilly Livingstone, took the name "Bunny Wailer" for recordings on Mango and later Shanachie. His debut, *Blackheart Man*, was considered a reggae classic yet failed to make the American charts. His popularity may have suffered due to his refusal to make public appearances until the '80s.

Marcia Griffiths was recording on her own by 1978. She recorded extensively in the '80s and scored a minor hit with "Electric Boogie" in late 1989. Judy Mowatt, who's 1979 *Black Woman* came to be regarded as a reggae classic, also recorded solo in the '80s. Rita Marley, Bob's wife, recorded on her own, beginning in 1982.

Bob Marley's son David, born in 1968, began his musical career as Ziggy Marley in 1979 when his father brought him into the studio to record "Children Playing in the Streets," backed by Marley children Sharon (Rita's oldest daughter), Cedella, and Stephen. As a family group the four performed on special occasions. Ziggy began writing songs and, as the Melody Makers, the quartet recorded several albums for EMI. Switching to Virgin Records, the group recorded 1988's best-selling *Conscious Party*, which included the moderate hit "Tomorrow People," "Dreams of Home," and "Have You Ever Been to Hell." Their follow-up, *One Bright Day*, sold quite well, and with *Jahmekya*, Ziggy unveiled his modern hybrid of dance music and reggae. Despite his youth, some critics began to hail Ziggy Marley as the rightful heir to his father's legacy.

The Wailers

Catch a Fire	Island	9329	'73	†
	Island	9241	'75	†
	Island	90030		LP/CS/CD†
	Tuff Gong/Island	846201	'90	LP/CS/CD
Burnin'	Island	9338	'73	†
	Island	9256	'74	†
	Island	90031		LP/CS/CD†
	Tuff Gong/Island	846200	'90	LP/CS/CD
Talkin' Blues (recorded 1973)	Tuff Gong/Island	848243	'91	LP/CS/CD
Reggae Greats	Mango	539795		CS/CD
One Love	Heartbeat	111/112	'92	CS/CD
Bob Marley and the Wailers				
Birth of a Legend	Calla	(2) 1240	'76	†
Birth of a Legend	Calla	34759	'77	†
	Columbia	34759		CS
Roots Music	Calla	37460	'77	†
	Columbia	37460		
Natty Dread	Island	9281	'75	†
	Island	90037		LP/CS/CD†
	Tuff Gong/Island	846204	'90	LP/CS/CD

Rastaman Vibration	Island	9383	'76	†
	Island	90033		LP/CS/CD†
	Tuff Gong/Island	846205	'90	LP/CS/CD
Live!	Island	9376	'76	†
	Island	90032		LP/CS/CD†
	Tuff Gong/Island	846203	'90	LP/CS/CD
Exodus	Island	9498	'77	†
	Island	90034		LP/CS/CD†
	Tuff Gong/Island	846208	'90	LP/CS/CD
	Mobile Fidelity	628	'95	CD
Kaya	Island	9517	'78	†
	Island	90035		LP/CS/CD†
	Tuff Gong/Island	846209	'90	LP/CS/CD
Babylon by Bus	Island	(2) 11	'78	†
	Island	(2) 90029		LP/CS†
	Island	90029		CD†
	Tuff Gong/Island	846197	'90	CD
	Tuff Gong/Island	(2) 846197	'90	LP/CS
Survival	Island	9542	'79	†
	Island	90088		LP/CS/CD†
	Tuff Gong/Island	846202	'90	LP/CS/CD
Uprising	Island	9596	'80	†
	Island	90036		LP/CS/CD†
	Tuff Gong/Island	846211	'90	LP/CS/CD
Confrontation	Island	90085	'83	LP/CS/CD†
	Tuff Gong/Island	846207	'90	LP/CS/CD
Legend (The Best of Bob Marley and the Wailers)	Island	90169	'84	LP/CS/CD†
	Tuff Gong/Island	846210	'90	CS/CD
Rebel Music	Island	90520	'86	LP/CS/CD†
	Tuff Gong/Island	846206	'90	LP/CS/CD
Natural Mystic: The Legend Lives On	Tuff Gong/Island	524103	'95	LP/CS/CD

Anthologies

Jamaican Storm	Accord	7211	'82	†
The Mighty Bob Marley	Pair	1245		CS/CD
More of the Mighty Bob Marley	Pair	1285	'90	CS/CD
Birth of a Legend	Epic Associated	46796	'90	CS/CD
Bob Marley	Bella Musica	89923	'90	CD†
Saga, Volume 1	Forlane	19026		CD
Saga, Volume 2	Forlane	19041	'91	CD
Reaction	Pickwick	072	'93	CD
Bob Marley at His Best	Special Music	4808		CS/CD
Reggae Magic	Special Music	4822		CS/CD
Reggae Roots	Garland	001		CD
Early Music	Columbia	34760		CS

Bob Marley

Chances Are (recorded 1968–1972)	Cotillion	5228	'81	CS/CD
Songs of Freedom	Tuff Gong/Island	(4) 512280	'92	CS/CD

Tribute Album

A Tribute to Bob Marley: The Riddim of a Legend	Relativity	1234	'95	CS/CD

Peter Tosh

Legalize It	Columbia	34253	'76	CS/CD
Equal Rights	Columbia	34670	'77	CS/CD
Bush Doctor	Rolling Stones	39109	'78	†
Mystic Man	Rolling Stones	39111	'79	†
Wanted Dread and Alive	EMI	17055	'81	†
	EMI	91670		CS/CD
Mama Africa	EMI	17095	'83	†
	EMI	91671		CS/CD
Captured Live	EMI	17126	'84	†
	EMI	91672		CS/CD
No Nuclear War	EMI	46700	'87	CS/CD
The Toughest	Capitol	90201	'88	CS/CD

Bunny Wailer

Blackheart Man	Island/Mango	9415	'76	†
	Mango	539415		CS/CD
Protest	Island/Mango	9512	'77	†
	Mango	539512		CS/CD
Sings the Wailers	Mango	9629	'81	†
	Mango	539629		CS/CD
Roots, Radics, Rockers, Reggae	Shanachie	43013	'83	CS/CD
Peace Talks/Rockers	Shanachie		'84	†
Marketplace	Shanachie	43071	'85/'91	CS/CD
Rootsman Skanking	Shanachie	43043		CS/CD
Rule Dance Hall	Shanachie	43050	'86	CS/CD
Liberation	Shanachie	43059	'89	CS/CD
Time Will Tell: A Tribute to Bob Marley	Shanachie	43072	'90	CS/CD†
Gumption	Shanachie	43079	'90	CS/CD
Bunny Wailer in Concert	Shanachie	45009	'93	CS/CD
Crucial!	Shanachie	45014	'94	CS/CD
Retrospective (recorded 1977–1993)	Shanachie	45021	'95	CS/CD
Live	Solomonic	9	'84	CS
Just Be Nice	RAS	3121	'93	CS/CD
Hall of Fame: Bunny Wailer's Tribute to Bob Marley's 50th Anniversary	RAS	(2) 3502	'95	CS/CD

The Wailers Band

I.D.	Atlantic	81960	'89	CS/CD

Marcia Griffiths

Sweet Bitter Love			'74	†
Naturally	Shanachie	44014	'78/'92	CS/CD
Rock My Soul			'84	†
I Love Music			'86	†
Marcia	RAS	3047	'88	LP/CS/CD
Carousel	Island	842334	'90	CS/CD
Steppin'	Shanachie	44007	'91	CS/CD
Indomitable			'93	CS/CD

Judy Mowatt

Black Woman	Shanachie	43011	'79	CS/CD
Only a Woman	Shanachie	43007	'82	CS/CD

Working Wonders	Shanachie	43028	'86	CS/CD
Love Is Overdue	Shanachie	43044		CS/CD
Look at Love	Shanachie	43087	'91	CS/CD

Rita Marley

Who Feels It Knows It	Shanachie	43003	'82	CS/CD
Harambe	Shanachie	43010		CS/CD
We Must Carry On	Shanachie	43082	'91	CS/CD
Awake Zion	Rykodisc	10204		

Ziggy Marley and the Melody Makers

Play the Game Right	EMI	92705	'85	CS/CD†
Hey World	EMI	92706	'86	CS/CD
The Time Has Come (Best)	EMI	90952	'88	CS/CD
Conscious Party	Virgin	90878	'88	LP/CS/CD†
	Virgin	86038		CS/CD
One Bright Day	Virgin	91256	'89	LP/CS/CD†
	Virgin	86118		CS/CD
Jahmekya	Virgin	91626	'91	CS/CD†
	Virgin	86217		CS/CD
Joy and Blues	Virgin	87961	'93	CS/CD
Free Like We Want 2 B	Elektra	61702	'95	LP/CS/CD

THE MARSHALL TUCKER BAND

Doug Gray (b. May 2, 1948, Spartanburg, SC), lead voc; **Toy Caldwell** (b. 1948, Spartanburg, SC, d. Feb. 25, 1993, Moore, SC), lead gtr, steel gtr, voc; **Tommy Caldwell** (b. 1950, Spartanburg, SC; d. Apr. 28, 1980, Spartanburg, SC), bs, voc; **George McCorkle**, rhythm gtr; **Jerry Eubanks** (b. Mar 9, 1950, Spartanburg, SC), sax, flt; **Paul Riddle**, drm [Tommy Caldwell died in 1980 and was replaced by **Franklin Wilkie**; the band reformed in 1983 with Doug Gray and Jerry Eubanks enlisting new members **Rusty Milner** (b. June 2, 1958, Spartanburg, SC), guitar, and **Tim Lawter** (b. Dec. 10, 1958, Spartanburg, SC), bass and guitar, along with various supporting musicians.]

Another hard-working Southern rock band of the '70s, the Marshall Tucker Band helped bridge the gap between rock and country music with a mellow sound that featured the flute and saxophone playing of Jerry Eubanks. Established as a live band through years of touring, the Marshall Tucker Band was a popular album band, recording excellent songs such as "Can't You See," "Searchin' for a Rainbow," "Fire on the Mountain," and "Last of the Singing Cowboys," while scoring only one major pop hit, "Heard It in a Love Song."

The band centered around the musical Caldwell brothers and their Spartanburg, South Carolina, friends. Teenager Toy Caldwell formed a band with friend George McCorkle called the Rants; his brother Tommy played with Doug Gray in the New Generation. Both local bands were active through the mid-'60s, when various members were drafted into the Army. Toy returned to Spartanburg in 1969 and formed the Toy Factory; by 1971 brother Tommy, old buddy McCorkle, and Paul Riddle were on board and the band had a new name, the Marshall Tucker Band (Marshall Tucker owned the hall where the guys rehearsed).

The band's first album was released in 1973, and a year later they were touring as opening act for the Allman Brothers (both groups recorded for Capricorn). Although several songs received wide airplay on FM and alternative radio, the band didn't score a major hit until 1977 with "Heard It in a Love Song." That same year they played Jimmy Carter's inauguration. In 1979 the group left Capricorn for Warner Bros.

Bassist Tommy Caldwell died on April 28, 1980, from injuries sustained in an auto accident in Spartanburg six days earlier. He was replaced by former Rants and Toy Factory bassist Franklin Wilkie. The band released *Dedicated* in 1981 in memory of Tommy. Lead guitarist Toy Caldwell left the group in 1983, as did McCorkle and Riddle; Toy eventually launched a solo career in 1992, only to die on February 25, 1993. Enduring many personnel changes, the Marshall Tucker Band was subsequently fronted by originals Jerry Eubanks and lead vocalist Doug Gray. By the early '90s the band was focusing on country material.

The Marshall Tucker Band

The Marshall Tucker Band	Capricorn	0112	'73	†
	Warner Bros.	3606	'81	†
	AJK Music	618		CS/CD
A New Life	Capricorn	0124	'74	†
	Warner Bros.	3662	'82	†
	AJK Music	636		CS/CD
Where We All Belong	Capricorn	(2) 0145	'74	†
	Warner Bros.	(2) 3608	'81	†
	AJK Music	677		CS/CD
Searchin' for a Rainbow	Capricorn	0161	'75	†
	Warner Bros.	3609	'81	†
	AJK Music	702		CS/CD
Long Hard Ride	Capricorn	0170	'76	†
	Warner Bros.	3663	'82	†
	AJK Music	727		CS/CD
Carolina Dreams	Capricorn	0180	'77	†
	Warner Bros.	3610	'81	†
	AJK Music	780		CS/CD
Together Forever	Capricorn	0205	'78	†
	Warner Bros.	3664	'82	†
	AJK Music	668		CS/CD
Greatest Hits	Capricorn	0214	'78	†
	Warner Bros.	3611	'81	†
	AJK Music	799		LP/CS/CS
Running Like the Wind	Warner Bros.	3317	'79	†
Tenth	Warner Bros.	3410	'80	†
Dedicated	Warner Bros.	3525	'81	†
Tuckerized	Warner Bros.	3684	'82	†
Just Us	Warner Bros.	23803	'83	†
Greetings from South Carolina	Warner Bros.	23997	'84	†
Still Holdin' On	Mercury	832794	'88	LP/CS/CD†
Back to Back	K-tel	3099	'92	CS/CD
Best	ERA	5027	'94	CS/CD

Toy Caldwell

Toy Caldwell	Cabin Fever		'92	†

MARTHA AND THE VANDELLAS

Martha Reeves (b. July 18, 1941, AL); **Rosalind Ashford** (b. Sept. 2, 1943, Detroit, MI); **Annette Beard** [Annette Beard was replaced in 1963 by **Betty Kelly** (b. Sept. 16, 1944, Detroit, MI)

An early Motown female vocal trio, Martha and the Vandellas achieved two smash pop and R&B hits with "Heat Wave" and "Quicksand" before the ascendancy of the Supremes, who came to be regarded as the label's most important female act. Showcasing a raucous R&B style distinct from that of the less-exuberant Supremes, Martha and the Vandellas scored numerous crossover hit singles with songs composed by Holland-Dozier-Holland between 1963 and 1967. The group maintained until late 1972, when Martha Reeves left Motown for an inauspicious solo career.

Martha Reeves had been a member of the Del-Phis and recorded for Checkmate before obtaining employment as a secretary at Motown Records. Recording the occasional demonstration tape as part of her job, she first came to the attention of Berry Gordy Jr. as a substitute for an absent artist at a recording session. With high-school friends Rosalind Ashford and Annette Beard, she backed Marvin Gaye's recording of "Stubborn Kind of Fellow," his first hit from 1962. Signed to the newly formed Gordy label as Martha and the Vandellas, the group scored their first major pop and near-smash R&B hit in spring 1963 with the rather tame "Come and Get These Memories."

Subsequently utilizing a harder-edged, brassy style propelled by Martha's dynamic lead vocals, Martha and the Vandellas achieved a smash pop and top R&B hit with Holland-Dozier-Holland's classic "Heat Wave" that summer. Annette Beard soon left the group, to be replaced by Betty Kelly, formerly with the Velvelettes. The group continued having smash crossover hits with the raw-sounding "Quicksand," "Dancing in the Street," and "Nowhere to Run" through early 1965. By then, Gordy was concentrating on the career development of the Supremes, Gordy's favorite act, yet Martha and the Vandellas achieved major pop and smash R&B hits with the less raunchy "My Baby Loves Me," "I'm Ready for Love," "Jimmy Mack" (a top R&B hit), and "Honey Chile" through 1967.

However, Martha Reeves and the Vandellas, as they were billed beginning in 1967, never had another major hit. The group disbanded for two years, reforming in 1971 and later recording *Black Magic*, which produced three moderate R&B hits. In late 1972 Martha Reeves launched a solo career, but her recordings for MCA, Arista, and Fantasy through 1980 failed to sell. Reeves continues to tour and record both as a solo artist and with various Vandellas. The group was inducted into the Rock and Roll Hall of Fame in 1995.

Martha and the Vandellas

Come and Get These Memories	Gordy	902	'63	†
	Motown	530366	'94	CS/CD
Heat Wave	Gordy	907	'63	†
	Motown	5145	'89	CS/CD
Dance Party	Gordy	915	'65	†
	Motown	5433	'89	CD†
Heat Wave/Dance Party	Motown	8149		CD†
Greatest Hits	Gordy	917	'66	†
	Motown	5204		CS/CD
Watch Out	Gordy	920	'66	†
	Motown	5265	'90	CS/CD†
Live!	Gordy	925	'67	†
Anthology	Motown	(2) 778	'74	CS

Dancing in the Streets	Pickwick	3386	'75	†
Compact Command Performance	Motown	9057	'86	CD†
Motown Superstar Series, Volume 11	Motown	5111		CS
Martha Reeves and the Vandellas				
Ridin' High	Gordy	926	'68	†
Sugar and Spice	Gordy	944	'70	†
Natural Resources	Gordy	952	'70	†
Black Magic	Gordy	958	'72	†
	Motown	5477	'90	CS/CD†
Motown Milestones	Motown	0405	'95	CS/CD
Martha Reeves				
Martha Reeves	MCA	414	'74	†
The Rest of My Life	Arista	4105	'76	†
We Meet Again	Fantasy	9549	'78	†
Gotta Keep Moving	Fantasy	9591	'80	†

JOHN MAYALL

(b. Nov. 29, 1943, Macclesfield, Cheshire, England)

THE BLUESBREAKERS. So many musicians have passed through this loosely defined band over the years that it is impossible to list every contributor; in addition, many came in and out of the band, often within the same year, making any listing less than ideal. Nonetheless, here are the bare bones of the prime English lineups.

John Mayall, kybd, har, voc, gtr; **Bernie Watson**, gtr; **John McVie** (b. Nov. 26, 1945, London, England), bs; **Peter Ward**, drm [Bernie Watson was replaced by **Roger Dean** by 1964; **Hughie Flint** replaced Peter Ward in 1964. **Eric Clapton** (b. Mar. 30, 1945, Ripley, England) replaced Dean in 1965; **Peter Green** (b. Peter Greenbaum, Oct. 29, 1946, London, England) in turn replaced Clapton, and **Jack Bruce** (b. May 14, 1943, Glasgow, Scotland) briefly replaced John McVie later that year, but then McVie returned. By 1966 Hughie Flint was gone, replaced by **Aynsley Dunbar** (b. Jan. 10, 1946, Lancaster, England) on drums; a year later **Mick Fleetwood** (b. June 24, 1947, Redruth, England) took over. In late 1967 Fleetwood and Peter Green left, followed by McVie soon after; **Mick Taylor** (b. Jan. 17, 1948, Welwyn Garden City, England) came in on guitar, and **Keef Hartley** (b. Mar. 8, 1944, Preston, England) on drums, and various musicians on bass, along with sax players **Chris Mercer** and **Rip Kant**. Mayall settled in California in 1968, and the original, classic Bluesbreakers period was over. Various Bluesbreaker musicians have continued to perform, including various alumni of many different incarnations of the band, through the early '90s.]

Often labeled the grandfather of British blues, John Mayall was instrumental in sparking the blues revival of the late '60s. A staunch defender and champion of neglected and exploited black American bluesmen, Mayall himself might have remained overlooked (as were Alexis Korner and Graham Bond) had not future superstar Eric Clapton been a member of his Bluesbreakers.

Supplying a loose, noncommercial format within which his band members could explore their proclivities for the blues, John Mayall provided the training ground for many of Britain's leading instrumentalists. Among Mayall's former band members were lead guitarists Eric Clapton, Peter Green (founder of the original Fleetwood Mac), and Mick Taylor (a member of the Rolling Stones from 1969 to 1974); bassists John McVie (Fleetwood Mac) and Jack Bruce (Cream); and drummers Aynsley Dunbar (The Mothers of Invention, Journey, The Jefferson Starship), Mick Fleetwood (Fleetwood Mac), Hughie Flint, Keef Hartley, and Jon Hiseman.

John Mayall became fascinated with the blues at age 13 and eventually learned to play guitar, keyboards, and harmonica. Forming his first group, The Powerhouse Four, while in college during the mid-'50s, he assembled the semiprofessional Bluesbreakers in March 1962. At the urging of Alexis Korner he moved to London in 1963. Turning professional that February, the Bluesbreakers included bassist John McVie. By the time of Mayall's first British album the band was comprised of Mayall, McVie, guitarist Roger Dean, and drummer Hughie Flint. During spring 1965, former Yardbird Eric Clapton replaced Dean, and McVie and Jack Bruce shared bass chores through June 1966. This aggregation recorded the classic *Bluesbreakers* album, one of the most compelling blues albums ever made in Great Britain.

When Flint left and Bruce and Clapton departed to form Cream, Mayall recruited guitarist Peter Green and drummers Aynsley Dunbar and Mick Fleetwood for *A Hard Road*, often regarded as Mayall's finest album. By spring 1967 Peter Green had left the Bluesbreakers to form Fleetwood Mac. Mayall subsequently recorded *Crusade* with John McVie, guitarist Mick Taylor, drummer Keef Hartley, and two saxophonists. He recorded *The Blues Alone* as a solo album, accompanied only by Hartley. By August 1967 McVie had left to join Fleetwood Mac, and Mayall reconstituted the Bluebreakers with Taylor, Hartley, saxophonists Chris Mercer and Dick Heckstall-Smith, bassist Tony Reeves, and drummer Jon Hiseman for *Bare Wires*. Unlike past albums, *Bare Wires* contained only Mayall compositions. Next Mayall moved to Los Angeles, where he recorded *Blues from Laurel Canyon* with Mick Taylor, who dropped out in 1969 to join the Rolling Stones.

During 1968 drummer Keef Hartley formed the Keef Hartley Band, and although the group developed a strong British following, they never made serious inroads in the United States. He later formed the short-lived Dog Soldier in late 1974. Also in 1968, Jon Hiseman departed to form Colosseum with Dick Heckstall-Smith and Tony Reeves, among others. Again, the band was moderately successful in Great Britain but almost totally ignored in the United States; it disbanded in autumn 1971. Later members include vocalist Chris Farlowe, later in Atomic Rooster with Carl Palmer, and guitarist Dave Clempson, who subsequently joined Humble Pie.

With the departure of Mick Taylor, John Mayall decided to abandon the loud electric format in favor of a revolutionary, acoustic, drummerless aggregation with bassist Steve Thompson, guitarist Jon Mark, and tenor saxophonist-flutist Johnny Almond. This grouping recorded *Turning Point*, which included the favorites "Room to Move," featuring Mayall's compelling harmonica solo, and the nine-minute-long "California." Following one more album, Jon Mark and Johnny Almond left Mayall. In 1971 the two teamed up for seven albums through 1981, recording extended pieces such as "The Ghetto," "Solitude," the classic "The City," and "New York State of Mind," even scoring a minor hit with "One Way Sunday."

In 1970 John Mayall made yet another stylistic shift by employing American musicians Don "Sugarcane" Harris (vln), Harvey Mandel (gtr), and Larry Taylor (bs) for the jazz-oriented *U.S.A. Union*. The album, probably Mayall's best-selling album, has been deleted, as has virtually all of Mayall's '70s recordings for Polydor, Blue Thumb, ABC, and DJM. *Back to the Roots* (1971) was recorded with various alumni, including Clapton, Green, Mick Taylor, Dunbar, Hartley, and Hiseman, and was later remixed, rerecorded, and released by Mayall as *Archives to '80s*. In 1985 Mayall recorded *Behind the Iron Curtain* in Szeged, Hungary, for GNP Crescendo, moving to Island Records in 1988. In the '90s John Mayall recorded for Silvertone Records, returning to his blues roots for 1993's *Wake Up Call*.

John Mayall and Eric Clapton

Bluesbreakers				
	London	492	'67	†
	London	50009	'78	†
	Deram	800086		CS/CD
	Mobile Fidelity	616	'94	CD

John Mayall's Bluesbreakers

A Hard Road	London	502	'67	†
	Deram	820474	'87	CD
Crusade	London	529	'68	†
	Deram	820537	'87	CD
Bare Wires	London	537	'68	†
	Deram	820538	'88	CD†
London Blues (1964–1969)	Deram	(2) 844302	'92	CD
Diary of a Band	London	570	'70	†
	Deram	844029	'94	CD
Live in Europe	London	589	'71	†
(reissued as) Diary of a Band, Volume Two	Deram	844030	'94	CD
The 1982 Reunion Concert	One Way	30008		CD
Cross Country Blues	One Way	30009		CD
Behind the Iron Curtain	GNP Crescendo	2184	'86	LP/CS/CD
Chicago Line	Island	842869	'88	CS/CD
A Sense of Place	Island	842795	'90	CS/CD

John Mayall and Others

Raw Blues	London	543	'68	†
	Polydor	820479	'88	CS/CD

John Mayall

The Blues Alone	London	534	'68	†
	Deram	820535	'88	CD
Blues from Laurel Canyon	London	545	'69	†
	Deram	820539	'90	CD
Looking Back	London	562	'69	†
	Deram	820331		CD
Through the Years	London	(2) 600/1	'71	†
	Deram	844028	'91	CD
Primal Solos	London	50003	'77	†
	Deram	820320		CD
The Turning Point	Polydor	244004	'69	†
	Deram	823305		CS/CD
Empty Rooms	Polydor	244010	'70	†
U.S.A. Union	Polydor	244022	'70	†
Back to the Roots	Polydor	(2) 253002	'71	†
(revised edition released as) Archives to '80s	Deram	837127	'88	CS/CD
Memories	Polydor	5012	'71	†
Jazz Blues Fusion	Polydor	5027	'72	†
Moving On	Polydor	5036	'72	†
Ten Years Are Gone	Polydor	(2) 3005	'73	†
Best	Polydor	(2) 3006	'74	†
The Latest Edition	Polydor	6030	'74	†
Room to Move (1969–1974)	Polydor	(2) 517291	'92	CD
New Year, New Band, New Company	Blue Thumb	6019	'75	†
	One Way	22072		CD
Notice to Appear	ABC	926	'76	†
	One Way	22070		CD
A Banquet of Blues	ABC	958	'76	†
	One Way	22075		CD

Lots of People	ABC	992	'77	†
	One Way	22073		CD
A Hard Core Package	ABC/MCA	1039	'77	†
	One Way	22071		CD
The Last of the British Blues	ABC/MCA	1086	'78	†
	One Way	22074		CD
Bottom Line	DJM	23	'79	†
No More Interviews	DJM	29	'79	†
Roadshow Blues Band	Accord	7209	'82	†
John Mayall Plays John Mayall	Polydor	820536	'88	CD†
Wake Up Call	Silvertone	41518	'93	CS/CD
Spinning Coin	Silvertone	41541	'95	CS/CD

Keef Hartley Band

Halfbreed	Deram	18024	'69	†
The Battle of Northwest Six	Deram	18035	'70	†
The Time Is Near	Deram	18047	'70	†
Overdog	Deram	18057	'71	†
The Seventy-Second Brave	Deram	18065	'72	†
Lancashire Hustler	Deram	18070	'73	†

Dog Soldier (with Keef Hartley)

Dog Soldier	United Artists	405	'75	†

Colosseum (with Jon Hiseman)

Those Who Are About to Die, Salute You	Dunhill	50062	'70	†
Grass Is Green	Dunhill	50079	'70	†
Daughter of Time	Dunhill	50101	'71	†
Live	Warner Bros.	(2) 1942	'71	†

Colosseum II

Electric Savage	MCA	2294	'77	†

Johnny Almond

Music Machine	Deram	18030	'69	†
Hollywood Blues	Deram	18037	'70	†

Mark-Almond

Mark-Almond	Blue Thumb	27	'71	†
Mark-Almond II	Blue Thumb	32	'71	†
Best	Blue Thumb	50	'73	†
	Rhino	70571	'91	CS/CD
Rising	Columbia	31917	'72	†
'73	Columbia	32486	'73	†
'73/Rising	Columbia	(2) 33648	'75	†
To the Heart	ABC/MCA	945	'76	†
	One Way	22084		CD
Other People's Rooms	Horizon	730	'79	†
Best . . . Live	Pacific Arts	142	'81	†

Jon Mark

Songs for a Friend	Columbia	33339	'75	†
The Standing Stones of Callanish	Kuckuck	11082	'88	LP/CS/CD

CURTIS MAYFIELD

(b. June 3, 1942, Chicago, IL)

THE IMPRESSIONS. Curtis Mayfield; **Jerry Butler** (b. Dec. 8, 1939, Sunflower, MS); **Arthur Brooks** (b. Chattanooga, TN); **Richard Brooks** (b. Chattanooga); **Sam Gooden** (b. Sept. 2, 1939, Chattanooga, TN), bs voc [Jerry Butler left in 1958. Tenor **Fred Cash** (b. Oct. 8, 1940, Chattanooga, TN) joined in 1961. Arthur and Richard Brooks left in 1962. Curtis Mayfield left in 1970, to be replaced by **Leroy Hutson**.]

CURTIS MAYFIELD

Creative genius behind the success of the Impressions, one of the most popular non-Motown soul acts of the '60s, Curtis Mayfield, along with James Brown, was one of the first black songwriters to combine gospel vocal stylizations with politically aware, socially conscious lyrics, as evidenced by the hits "We're a Winner," "This Is My Country," and "Choice of Colors." Forming his own label, Curtom, in 1968 and leaving the Impressions for a solo career in 1970, Mayfield scored a smash success in 1972 with his soundtrack to the movie *Superfly*. The soundtrack, often considered one of the finest examples of orchestral soul music, was hailed for its honest and compassionate treatment of the ghetto experience. While continuing to record solo albums during the '70s, Mayfield concentrated on writing and producing soundtracks for the films *Claudine*, *Let's Do It Again*, and *Sparkle*. On the verge of reemerging with the soundtrack to *The Return of Superfly*, Curtis Mayfield was paralyzed from the neck down when a lighting rig fell on him in Brooklyn on August 13, 1990.

Curtis Mayfield met Jerry Butler at age nine at his grandmother's Traveling Souls Spiritualist Church on Chicago's west side. The two later sang in the gospel group the Northern Jubilee Singers. In 1957 Butler and Mayfield joined the transplanted Chattanooga-based vocal group the Roosters, comprised of brothers Arthur and Richard Brooks and bass singer Sam Gooden. Under manager Eddie Thomas, the group became the Impressions, scoring a smash R&B and near-smash pop hit in 1958 with "For Your Precious Love," erroneously credited to Jerry Butler and the Impressions. Butler soon left the Impressions for a successful solo career, taking with him Mayfield as guitarist and songwriter. Mayfield cowrote Butler's hits "He Will Break Your Heart," "Find Another Girl," and "I'm a Telling You."

In 1961 the Impressions reassembled with Mayfield, the Brooks brothers, Gooden, and tenor Fred Cash, the fourth member of the original Roosters. With Mayfield providing the high-tenor lead vocal, the Impressions soon scored a smash R&B and major pop hit with "Gypsy Woman" on ABC-Paramount. In 1962 the Brooks brothers left the Impressions, and the group continued as a trio. In fall 1963 the Impressions began an impressive string of crossover hits, virtually all written by Mayfield, including the smash "It's All Right." Subsequent hits through 1965 include "Talking About My Baby," "I'm So Proud," "Keep on Pushing," "You Must Believe Me," "Amen," "People Get Ready," and "Woman's Got Soul." Also, in 1963–1964 Mayfield provided hits to Gene Chandler ("Just Be True") and Major Lance ("Monkey Time" and "Um, Um, Um, Um, Um, Um").

The Impressions' popularity subsequently waned for a time, but by 1968 they were back with the prideful "We're a Winner." During that year, Mayfield formed his own record label, Curtom, for recordings by the Impressions. The group's first two Curtom albums, *This Is My Country* and *Young Mod's Forgotten Story*, contained a number of socially conscious, black-oriented songs such as "Mighty, Mighty (Spade and Whitey)" and the crossover hits "This Is My Country" and "Choice of Colors."

In 1970 Curtis Mayfield left the Impressions for a solo career as he continued to record and produce the group for Curtom. Adding Leroy Hutson, the Impressions scored major R&B hits through 1975: "Check Out Your Mind," a major pop hit; "(Baby) Turn On to Me"; "Finally Got Myself Together (I'm a Changed Man)," another major pop hit; "Sooner or Later"; and "Same Thing It Took." Many of these recordings were compiled on *Lasting Impressions*. Mayfield's debut solo album, *Curtis*, yielded a smash R&B and major pop hit with "(Don't Worry) If There's a Hell Below, We're All Going to Go." However, his biggest success came in 1972 with the soundtrack to the black-oriented movie *Superfly*. The album produced two smash crossover hits with "Freddie's Dead" and "Superfly" and included "Pusherman," remaining on the album charts for nearly a year.

Following 1973's *Back to the World*, Curtis Mayfield's albums sold modestly at best. He composed and produced the film score to the 1974 movie *Claudine*, performed by Gladys Knight and the Pips. His *There's No Place Like America Today* was critically acclaimed and yielded a smash R&B hit with "So In Love," his last pop-chart entry. In 1975 he scored and wrote the soundtrack to the film *Let's Do It Again*, performed by the Staple Singers, and the title song became a top pop and R&B hit. His next soundtrack album, *Sparkle*, was performed by Aretha Franklin and produced a top R&B and major pop hit with "Something He Can Feel." In 1977 Mayfield scored the soundtracks to *A Piece of the Action*, performed by Mavis Staples, and *Short Eyes*, in which he appeared.

In 1980 Curtis Mayfield moved his home base to Atlanta, Georgia. He continued to record in the '80s while producing Gene Chandler and gospel artist Kevin Yancy. In 1990 Mayfield scored the soundtrack to *The Return of Superfly*, which included four Mayfield tunes and rap songs performed by Ice-T, Eazy-E of N.W.A., and Tone Loc; but on August 13 of that year, Mayfield was critically injured, suffering paralysis from the neck down after a stage-lighting rig fell on him in Brooklyn. In 1993 Shanachie Records issued the tribute album *People Get Ready*, with artists such as Jerry Butler, Bunny Wailer, and Huey Lewis performing his songs. In 1994 Warner Bros. released the tribute album *A Tribute to Curtis Mayfield*, which includes performances by Eric Clapton, Whitney Houston, Bruce Springsteen, Stevie Winwood, and Aretha Franklin, among others.

Early Impressions

In the Beginning	Checker	3014		†
For Your Precious Love	VeeJay	1075	'63	LP/CS
Vintage Years	Sire	(2) 3717	'77	†

The Impressions

The Impressions	ABC	450	'63	†
	Kent	005		†
Never Ending Impressions	ABC	468	'64	†
	Kent	008		†

Keep On Pushing	ABC	493	'64	†
	Kent	009		†
People Get Ready	ABC	505	'65	†
	Kent	012		†
Greatest Hits	ABC	515	'65	†
	MCA	1500	'82	CS
	MCA	31338	'89	CD
One by One	ABC	523	'65	†
Ridin' High	ABC	545	'66	†
The Fabulous Impressions	ABC	606	'67	†
We're a Winner	ABC	635	'68	†
Best	ABC	654	'68	†
This Is My Country	Curtom	8001	'68	†
The Young Mod's Forgotten Story	Curtom	8003	'69	†
	Curtom	2013	'92	CS/CD
Versatile	ABC	668	'69	†
Best Impressions—Curtis, Sam, Fred	Curtom	8004	'70	†
Check Out Your Mind	Curtom	8006	'70	†
16 Greatest Hits	ABC	727	'71	†
	Pickwick	3602	'78	†
Times Have Changed	Curtom	8012	'72	†
Preacher Man	Curtom	8016	'73	†
Finally Got Myself Together	Curtom	8019	'74	†
Three the Hard Way (soundtrack)	Curtom	8602	'74	†
Sooner or Later	Curtom	0103	'75	†
First Impressions	Curtom	5003	'75	†
Loving Power	Curtom	5009	'76	†
Lasting Impressions	Curtom	2006		LP/CS/CD
It's About Time	Cotillion	9912	'76	†
Come to My Party	20th Century-Fox	596	'79	†
Fan the Fire	20th Century-Fox	624	'81	†
Chartbusters	Pickwick	3502		†
The Anthology, 1961–1977	MCA	(2) 10664	'92	CS/CD
It's All Right	MCA	22175	'95	CD
The Definitive Impressions	Kent	923		CD

Leroy Hutson

Love, Oh, Love	Curtom	8017	'73	†
	Curtom	5020	'78	†
Leroy Hutson	Curtom	5002	'75	†
Feel the Spirit	Curtom	5010	'76	†
Hutson II	Curtom	5011	'76	†
Closer to the Source	Curtom	5018	'78	†
Unforgettable	RSO	3062	'80	†
Paradise	Elektra	60141	'82	†

Curtis Mayfield

His Early Years with the Impressions	ABC	(2) 780	'73	†
Curtis	Curtom	8005	'70	†
Curtis Live!	Curtom	(2) 8008	'71	†
Roots	Curtom	8009	'71	†

Superfly (soundtrack)	Curtom	8014	'72	†
	Curtom	2002		LP/CS/CD
Back to the World	Curtom	8015	'73	†
Curtis in Chicago Live	Curtom	8018	'73	†
Sweet Exorcist	Curtom	8601	'74	†
Got to Find a Place	Curtom	8604	'74	†
There's No Place like America Today	Curtom	5001	'75	†
	Curtom	2003		LP/CS/CD
Give, Get, Take and Have	Curtom	5007	'76	†
	Curtom	2011	'92	CS/CD
Never Say You Can't Survive	Curtom	5013	'77	†
	Curtom	2010	'92	CS/CD
Short Eyes	Curtom	5017	'77	†
Do It All Night	Curtom	5022	'78	†
Heartbeat	RSO	3053	'79	†
Something to Believe In	RSO	3077	'80	†
	Curtom	2005		LP/CS/CD
Live in Europe	Curtom	(2) 2901	'87	LP/CS/CD
Take It to the Streets	Curtom	2008	'90	LP/CS/CD
Of All Time (Classic Collection)	Curtom	(2) 2902		LP/CS/CD

Curtis Mayfield/The Staple Singers

Let's Do It Again (soundtrack)	Curtom	5005	'75	†

Curtis Mayfield and Linda Clifford

The Right Combination	RSO	3084	'80	†

Curtis Mayfield and Others

The Return of Superfly	Capitol	94244	'90	CS/CD†

Tribute Albums

People Get Ready: A Tribute to Curtis Mayfield	Shanachie	9004	'93	CS/CD
A Tribute to Curtis Mayfield	Warner Bros.	45500	'94	CS/CD

PAUL McCARTNEY
(b. June 18, 1942, Allerton, Liverpool, England)

Often regarded as the Beatle who stabilized the group's appeal with audiences of all ages, Paul McCartney was responsible for writing most of the group's original material, in conjunction with John Lennon. The primary author of Beatles hits such as "Michelle" and "Hey Jude," McCartney composed the classic "Yesterday," which has been recorded by more than 2,500 artists and played more than six million times, making it the most frequently performed pop song in history. Moreover, McCartney was the most proficient musician and technically accomplished vocalist in the Beatles.

Paul McCartney's first solo project outside of the Beatles was the soundtrack to the movie *Family Way*, released in 1967. He later met American photographer Linda Eastman and married her on March 12, 1969, by which time the Beatles were already suffering from internal tensions. The film of the Beatles' final album release, *Let It Be*, aptly revealed McCartney's attempt to dominate the group. The four were soon embroiled in personal and business disputes, as McCartney objected to the near-simultaneous release of *Let It Be* and his first solo album, *McCartney*, and the others sought to employ Allen Klein as financial advisor while McCartney sought the appointment of his father-in-law, Lee Eastman. In April

1970 the breakup of the Beatles was announced, and on December 31, 1970, McCartney sued Klein and Apple Records for legal dissolution of the group's corporate empire.

McCartney, recorded with Linda providing harmonies and Paul playing all instruments, contained ditties by Paul such as "Every Night," "That Would Be Something," "Man, We Was Lonely," and, the one substantial song, "Maybe I'm Amazed." *McCartney* topped the album charts and remained there for nearly a year. Following the smash-hit single "Another Day," Paul and Linda McCartney recorded *Ram* with New York session players. The album included "Heart of the Country" and yielded the top hit "Uncle Albert / Admiral Halsey."

In August 1971 Paul McCartney formed his recording and touring band, Wings, with wife Linda, guitarist Denny Laine, and drummer Danny Seiwell. Session musician Seiwell had played on the *Ram* album, whereas Laine had been an original member of the Moody Blues and lead vocalist on the Moodys' first blues-inflected hit, "Go Now." *Wild Life* was generally considered to be McCartney's weakest effort, failing to yield even a minor hit. Joined in January 1972 by guitarist Henry McCullough, the band scored major hits with the singles-only releases "Give Ireland Back to the Irish," McCartney's feeble attempt at political consciousness; the inane "Mary Had a Little Lamb"; and "Hi, Hi, Hi." *Red Rose Speedway* did little to establish his artistic credibility, although it did yield the top pop and easy-listening hit "My Love."

In 1973 Paul McCartney and Wings recorded the title song to the James Bond movie *Live and Let Die*, and the single became a top hit. It served as a prototype to the clever pop-style songs—replete with reprises, codas, changing time signatures, and multiple musical themes—that McCartney crafted so successfully on the subsequent album, *Band on the Run*. During 1973 Wings appeared in a British and American television special, successfully toured Europe, and scored a major hit with "Helen Wheels." However, by July Henry McCullough and Danny Seiwell had dropped out of the group.

The McCartneys and Denny Laine traveled to Lagos, Nigeria, to record their next album, *Band on the Run*, at Ginger Baker's new ARC Studio. Often regarded as McCartney's finest post-Beatles work and certainly his most consistent, the album brought the group their first critical praise and yielded the smash hits "Jet" and the title track; it also contains "Let Me Roll It," "Helen Wheels," and the ditty "Mamunia." Remaining on the album charts for more than two years and selling more than six million copies, the album effectively established McCartney as a pop-style songwriter-arranger.

Wings added Scottish guitarist Jimmy McCulloch, formerly with Thunderclap Newman and Stone the Crows, in May 1974 for the Nashville-recorded pop hits "Junior's Farm" (a smash) and "Sally G.," also a minor country hit. Drummer Joe English joined in February 1975 for the group's next album, *Venus and Mars Are Alright Tonight*, recorded primarily at Allen Toussaint's Sea Saint Studio in New Orleans. The album produced the top hit "Listen to What the Man Said," the moderate hit "Letting Go," and the major hit "Venus and Mars Rock Show." Between fall 1975 and summer 1976 Wings successfully completed their first worldwide tour, and *Wings at the Speed of Sound* was issued in spring. Considered the band's first team effort, the album included McCulloch's "Wino Junko," Laine's "Time to Hide," and Linda's first effort as a lead vocalist, "Cook of the House," as well as Paul's smash pop and easy-listening hits "Let 'Em In" and "Silly Love Songs," the latter a gentle swipe at critics who had regularly attacked him for his inconsequential ditties.

The United States segment of the Wings tour, called Wings Over America, produced a live multirecord set that yielded the major hit "Maybe I'm Amazed." Otherwise largely inactive during 1977, Wings scored a smash British hit with the singles release "Mull Of Kintyre" (ostensibly the biggest-selling single in British history), whereas the flip side, "Girls School," became a moderate American hit. *London Town*, Wings's final album of new material for Capitol Records, was recorded primarily on a chartered yacht in the Virgin Islands and produced during 1978 the hits "With a Little Luck," "I've Had Enough," and the title song. Following the album's completion, Jimmy McCulloch and Joe English left Wings, to be replaced by session musicians.

By early 1979 Paul McCartney had signed a long-term contract with Columbia Records rumored to be the most lucrative ever in the history of popular music. Wings scored a smash hit on Columbia with the disco-style "Goodnight Tonight" and their debut Columbia album, *Back to the Egg*, yielded major hits with "Getting Closer" and "Arrow Through Me." Scheduled to make his first appearance in Japan since playing there with the Beatles in 1966, McCartney was busted upon arrival on January 16, 1980, for possession of nearly a half-pound of marijuana. Perhaps the most highly publicized drug bust in pop-music history, McCartney was deported after spending several days in jail. He subsequently wrote, engineered, produced, played, and sang all parts of his second "solo" album, *McCartney II*, with its hit, "Comin' Up." In April 1981 Wings officially disbanded.

For his next two albums McCartney utilized the services of George Martin, the Beatles' former producer. *Tug of War* included "Here Today" (a tribute to slain Beatle John Lennon) and yielded the top pop and easy-listening hit "Ebony and Ivory," sung in duet with Stevie Wonder, and the major hit "Take It Away." McCartney and Michael Jackson scored a smash pop, R&B, and easy-listening hit with "The Girl Is Mine" in late 1982, and McCartney's next album, *Pipes of Peace*, yielded another top pop hit for the duo with "Say Say Say" and a major hit for McCartney alone with "So Bad." McCartney's next project, his first solo feature film, *Give My Regards to Broad Street*, was a barely watchable flop, despite the inclusion of musicians Ringo Starr, Dave Edmunds, and John Paul Jones and actor Sir Ralph Richardson. The soundtrack album featured 13 rerecordings of Beatles and McCartney hits and included the smash hit "No More Lonely Nights."

In 1985 Paul McCartney returned to Capitol Records, quickly hitting with the title song to the Chevy Chase–Dan Aykroyd movie *Spies Like Us*. Eric Stewart, formerly with 10cc, collaborated on many of the songs from McCartney's debut Capitol album, as he had on *Tug of War*. *Press to Play*, however, produced only one hit, "Press." In September 1987 McCartney recorded his most spirited album in years for the Russian label Melodiya. Released exclusively in the Soviet Union in 1988, the album contained remade oldies and was eventually released outside that country in 1991.

In 1989 Paul McCartney and Elvis Costello collaborated on two songs for Costello's album *Spike*, the major hit "Veronica" and "Pads, Paws and Claws." McCartney's next effort, *Flowers in the Dirt*, included four songs coauthored by Costello: "Don't Be Careless Love," "That Day Is Done," "You Want Her Too," and the major hit "My Brave Face." McCartney subsequently conducted his first tour in 13 years with the recording band, comprised of the McCartneys, lead guitarist Robbie McIntosh (of the Pretenders), guitarist-bassist Hamish Stuart (of the Average White Band), keyboardist Paul "Wix" Wickens, and drummer Chris Whitten. Mixing Beatles, Wings, and McCartney favorites with more recent songs, the tour helped reestablish McCartney as a pop artist and produced the live 1990 set *Tripping the Live Fantastic*, released in both double (30 songs) and single (17 songs) CD versions.

In early 1991, with Blair Cunningham replacing Chris Whitten, McCartney and band performed on MTV's *Unplugged* program. The album from the performance was the first album released from the popular, ongoing series. Later that year McCartney debuted his *Liverpool Oratorio* at Liverpool Cathedral, with mezzo-soprano Kiri Te Kanawa and a cast of more than three hundred. Written over a three-year period with American film and theater composer Carl Davis, it was politely received and later performed at Carnegie Hall. Paul McCartney toured with his band again in 1993 in support of *Off the Ground*. In 1995 another classical piece composed by McCartney, "A Leaf," for solo piano, was debuted in London at a benefit concert for the Royal College of Music. McCartney reunited with ex-Beatles Ringo Starr and George Harrison in late 1995 for a video/TV program/record package on the group's history, recording two singles using demo tapes made by John Lennon in the late '70s, "Free as a Bird" and "Real Love," both with new lyrics by McCartney and overdubbed vocals and instruments by the trio.

Paul McCartney

Family Way (soundtrack)	London	82007	'67	†
	Philips	528922	'95	CS/CD
McCartney	Apple/Capitol	3363	'79	†
	Columbia	36478	'80	†
	Capitol	46611	'87	CS/CD
	DCC	1029		CD
McCartney II	Columbia	36511	'80	†
	Capitol	52024	'88	CS/CD
Tug of War	Columbia	37462	'82	†
	Capitol	46057		CS/CD
Pipes of Peace	Columbia	39149	'83	†
	Capitol	46018	'89	CS/CD
Give My Regards to Broad Street	Columbia	39613	'84	†
	Capitol	46043	'91	CS/CD
Press to Play	Capitol	12475	'86	CS
	Capitol	46269	'86	CD
All the Best (1970–1986)	Capitol	(2) 48287	'87	CS
	Capitol	48287	'87	CD
Choba B CCCP (released in U.S.S.R. in 1988)	Capitol	97615	'91	CS/CD
Flowers in the Dirt	Capitol	91653	'89	CS/CD
Gift Set	Capitol	92213		CD†
World Tour Pack	Capitol	93631		CD†
Tripping the Live Fantastic	Capitol	(2) 94778	'90	CS/CD
Tripping the Live Fantastic—"Highlights"	Capitol	95379	'90	CS/CD†
Unplugged	Capitol	96413	'91	CS/CD†
Off the Ground	Capitol	80362	'93	CS/CD
Paul Is Live	Capitol	27704	'93	CS/CD

Paul and Linda McCartney

Ram	Apple/Capitol	3375	'71	†
	Columbia	36479	'80	†
	Capitol	46612	'87	CS/CD
	DCC	1037		CD

Paul McCartney and Wings

Wild Life	Apple/Capitol	3386	'71	†
	Columbia	36480	'80	†
	Capitol	52017	'89	CS/CD
Red Rose Speedway	Apple/Capitol	3409	'73	†
	Columbia	36481	'80	†
	Capitol	52026	'88	CS/CD
Band on the Run	Apple/Capitol	3415	'73	†
	Columbia	36482	'80	†
	Capitol	46675	'87	CS/CD
	DCC	1030		CD
Venus and Mars Are Alright Tonight!	Capitol	11419	'75	†
	Columbia	36801		†
	Capitol	46984	'88	CS/CD
Wings at the Speed of Sound	Capitol	11525	'76	†
	Columbia	37409		†
	Capitol	48199	'89	CS/CD

Wings Over America	Capitol	(3) 11593	'76		†
	Capitol	(2) 46715	'89		CS/CD
London Town	Capitol	11777	'78		†
	Capitol	48198	'89		CS/CD
Greatest Hits	Capitol	11905	'78		†
	Capitol	46056			CS/CD
Back to the Egg	Columbia	36057	'79		†
	Capitol	48200	'89		CS/CD
Paul McCartney and Carl Davis					
Liverpool Oratorio	Angel	54371	'91		CS/CD

JOHN McLAUGHLIN
(b. Jan. 4, 1942, Yorkshire, England)

THE MAHAVISHNU ORCHESTRA. John McLaughlin, gtr; **Jan Hammer** (b. Apr. 17, 1948, Prague, Czechoslovakia), kybd; **Jerry Goodman**, vln; **Rick Laird** (b. Feb. 5, 1941, Dublin, Ireland), bs; **Billy Cobham** (b. May 16, 1944, Panama), drm

One of the more important guitarists of the '70s, John McLaughlin first gained public recognition by playing on jazz trumpeter Miles Davis's seminal jazz-rock fusion albums *In a Silent Way* and *Bitches Brew*. Quickly recognized as a virtuoso guitarist—a reputation enhanced by his playing in the Tony Williams Lifetime and his own Mahavishnu Orchestra—McLaughlin's technically amazing, incredibly rapid, and harmonically intriguing guitar stylizations influenced a generation of jazz and rock guitarists, including some of rock's more sophisticated heavy-metal guitarists. Moreover, the Mahavishnu Orchestra was one of the first fusion groups to enjoy both critical and commercial success, particularly with *The Inner Mounting Flame* and *Birds of Fire*, regarded as two of the few masterpieces of the genre. McLaughlin was also one of the first guitarists to use a guitar synthesizer, and his later experimentations with Eastern music presaged the development of "world" music.

John McLaughlin started classical piano lessons at age 9 and took up guitar at 11. Forming his first band at 15 while still in school, he later was a member of the Graham Bond Organization with Jack Bruce and Ginger Baker; he also served brief tenures with Brian Auger and Georgie Fame. McLaughlin's first solo album, *Extrapolation*, from 1969 (although apparently not released in the United States until 1972), made little commercial impact, yet it established him with musicians by means of his extraordinarily fast and technically dazzling guitar playing.

Extrapolation brought John McLaughlin to the attention of jazz drummer Tony Williams. McLaughlin subsequently recorded *In a Silent Way* with Williams and jazz great Miles Davis, and *Bitches Brew* with Davis, electric pianist Chick Corea, and others. These two albums launched so-called fusion music into international popularity and introduced McLaughlin to American audiences. He next recorded with drummer Tony Williams in the Tony Williams Lifetime, which included, for a time, former Cream bassist Jack Bruce. John McLaughlin subsequently traveled to France to record *Devotion*, regarded as his only rock record. Converting to the philosophy of Bengal mystic Sri Chinmoy during 1970, he recorded *My Goal's Beyond*, a meditation album of solo acoustic pieces and group improvisations, with American violinist Jerry Goodman (a former member of the Flock) and powerhouse drummer Billy Cobham.

In 1971 John McLaughlin formed the Mahavishnu Orchestra with Goodman, Cobham, Czechoslovakian keyboardist Jan Hammer, and bassist Rick Laird. Their debut album,

The Inner Mounting Flame, garnered excellent critical reviews for its technically adroit and emotionally moving music, but the follow-up, *Birds of Fire* (with Hammer using the synthesizer for the first time), was the album that established McLaughlin among rock fans and became the group's best-selling album. He next recorded the "jam" album *Love Devotion Surrender* with fellow Sri Chinmoy devotee Carlos Santana. McLaughlin disbanded the first edition of the Mahavishnu Orchestra after the live set *Between Nothingness and Eternity*, recorded in New York's Central Park in August 1973. In 1974 he formed a new group under the Mahavishnu Orchestra name with French violinist Jean-Luc Ponty for the ambitious *Apocalypse* album, recorded with the London Symphony Orchestra conducted by Michael Tilson Thomas under former Beatles producer George Martin. However, neither that album nor *Visions of the Emerald Beyond* reversed the critical tendency to dismiss the Mahavishnu Orchestra. By the end of 1975 the group had disbanded.

No longer a disciple of Sri Chinmoy by 1976, John McLaughlin and Indian violinist L. Shankar formed Shakti with tabla player Zakir Hussain and two other Indian musicians to pursue acoustically McLaughlin's interest in Indian musical forms. In 1978 McLaughlin recorded *Electric Guitarist* with Carlos Santana, Chick Corea, Jerry Goodman, Jack Bruce, Stanley Clarke, Tony Williams, and Billy Cobham. Following the short-lived One Truth Band with L. Shankar, McLaughlin recorded *Friday Night in San Francisco* with jazz guitarist Al Di Meola and flamenco guitarist Paco De Lucia on acoustic instruments, followed in 1983 by the trio's *Passion, Grace and Fire*.

During the mid-'80s John McLaughlin switched almost exclusively to the guitar synthesizer. He formed Mahavishnu in 1984 with keyboardist Mitchell Forman and saxophonist Bill Evans and others for touring and 1986's *Adventures in Radioland*. Returning to guitar, he joined Zakir Hussain and Jan Gabarek for 1987's *Making Music*. In the early '90s McLaughlin recorded his *Concerto for Guitar and Orchestra*, *"The Mediterranean Concerto,"* with the London Symphony Orchestra conducted by Michael Tilson Thomas, and *Que Alegria* with bassist Kai Eckhardt and percussionist Trilock Gurto.

John McLaughlin with Miles Davis

In a Silent Way	Columbia	9875	'69	†
	Columbia Jazz	40580	'87	CS/CD
Bitches Brew	Columbia	(2) 26	'70	†
	Columbia Jazz	40577	'87	CS/CD

John McLaughlin with Tony Williams Lifetime

Emergency	Polydor	(2) 244017/8	'70	†
	Polydor	(2) 253001		†
	Polydor	849068		CD
Turn It Over	Polydor	244021	'70	†
Once in a Lifetime	Verve	(2) 2541	'83	†

John McLaughlin

Extrapolation (recorded 1969)	Polydor	5510	'72	†
	Polydor	6074	'76	†
	Verve	841598		CD
Devotion	Douglas	4	'70	†
	Douglas	31568		†
	Douglas	32446		†
	Celluloid	5010		CS/CD
	Metrotone	72565	'92	CS/CD

My Goal's Beyond	Douglas	30766	'71	†
	Douglas	6003	'76	†
	Vogue	600263		CD
	Elektra Musician	60031	'82	CS
	Rykodisc	10051	'87	CS/CD
	Ryko Analogue	0051	'88	LP/CS
Where Fortune Smiles (recorded 1971)	One Way	29312		CD
Electric Guitarist	Columbia	35326	'78	†
	Columbia Jazz	46110	'90	CS/CD
Best	Columbia	36355	'80	†
Belo Horizonte	Warner Bros.	3619	'81	†
Music Spoken Here	Warner Bros.	23723	'82	†
Concerto for Guitar and Orchestra, "The Mediterranean Concerto"	CBS	45578	'90	CS/CD
Live at Royal Festival	JMT	834436	'90	CS/CD
Que Alegria	Verve	837280	'92	CS/CD
Time Remembered: John McLaughlin Plays Bill Evans	Verve	519861	'93	CS/CD
The Free Spirits Featuring John McLaughlin: Tokyo Live	Verve	521870	'94	CS/CD
After the Rain	Verve	527467	'95	CS/CD

The Mahavishnu Orchestra

The Inner Mounting Flame	Columbia	31067	'71	CS/CD
Birds of Fire	Columbia	31996	'73	CS
Between Nothingness and Eternity	Columbia	32766	'73/'87	CD
Apocalypse	Columbia	32957	'74	†
	Columbia Jazz	46111	'90	CS/CD
Visions of the Emerald Beyond	Columbia	33411	'75	†
	Columbia Jazz	46867	'91	CS/CD
Inner Worlds	Columbia	33908	'76	†
	Columbia Jazz	52923	'94	CD
Best	Columbia	36394	'80	CS

John McLaughlin and Carlos Santana

Love Devotion Surrender	Columbia	32034	'73	CS/CD

Shakti

Shakti	Columbia	34162	'76	†
	Columbia Jazz	46868	'91	CS/CD
A Handful of Beauty	Columbia	34372	'77	†
Natural Elements	Columbia	34980	'77	†

John McLaughlin and the One Truth Band

Electric Dreams	Columbia	35785	'79	†
	Columbia/Legacy	48892	'92	CS/CD

John McLaughlin/Al Di Meola/Paco De Lucia

Friday Night in San Francisco	Columbia	37152	'81	†
	Columbia	53926	'93	CD
Passion, Grace and Fire	Columbia	38645	'83	†

John McLaughlin and Mahavishnu

Adventures in Radioland	Relativity	8081	'86	CS/CD†
	Verve	519397	'93	CD

John McLaughlin with Zakir Hussain

Making Music	ECM	831544	'87	CS/CD†
	ECM	21349		CS/CD

CLYDE McPHATTER

(b. Clyde Lensley McPhatter, Nov. 15, 1931, Durham, NC; d. June 13, 1972, Teaneck, NJ)

THE ORIGINAL DRIFTERS. Clyde McPhatter, lead and first ten voc; **Bill Pinckney** (b. Aug. 15, 1925, Sumter, SC), second ten voc; **Andrew "Bubba" Thrasher** (b. Wetumpka, AL), bar voc; **Gerhart "Gay" Thrasher** (b. Wetumpka, AL), bs voc

CLYDE McPHATTER

Probably the most important and influential vocalist of the R&B '50s, Clyde McPhatter recorded dozens of hits as lead vocalist for Billy Ward's Dominoes, with his own Drifters, and as a solo act. His distinctive high tenor voice and gospel-styled phrasing, supported by smooth harmonies, set the standard for vocalists throughout the '50s and laid the groundwork for the development of soul music in the '60s. Best remembered for the classic "Money Honey," recorded with the Drifters, and his solo hits "A Lover's Question" and "Lover Please," McPhatter was reduced to the status of an oldies act by the late '60s. He died on June 13, 1972.

Born to a Baptist preacher father, Clyde McPhatter began singing in his father's choir at age five. He later moved to the New York area with his family, turning professional at age 14 with the gospel group the Mount Lebanon Singers. In 1950 McPhatter met pianist-arranger Billy Ward and joined Ward's Dominoes as lead tenor. Signed by King/Federal in late 1950, the Dominoes soon scored an R&B smash with "Do Something for Me." Their next hit, the lascivious top R&B hit "Sixty Minute Man," with lead vocals by bass singer Bill Brown, was one of the first R&B vocal-group songs to become a major pop hit. Subsequent R&B hits for the Dominoes include the top hit "Have Mercy Baby," with lead vocals by McPhatter.

After training Jackie Wilson as his replacement, Clyde McPhatter left the Dominoes to form his own Drifters in May 1953. The lineup stabilized with McPhatter, brothers Gerhart and Andrew "Bubba" Thrasher, and Bill Pinckney. The Drifters conducted their first successful recording session for Atlantic Records in August 1953, producing the top R&B hit and instant classic "Money Honey." Smash R&B hits continued with "Such a Night," "Honey Love" (another major pop hit), "Bip Bam," a stunning harmony version of "White Christmas" (with lead vocals by Pinckney and McPhatter), and "What'Cha Gonna Do." However, in 1954 McPhatter was drafted into the Air Force and replaced in the group by "Little" David Baughn and later Johnny Moore, who sang lead on the R&B hits "Adorable" and "Ruby Baby" in 1955–1956. Frequent personnel changes ensued, and the original Drifters broke up in June 1958. Manager George Treadwell, owner of the Drifters name, drafted all new members for subsequent hit recordings, such as "There Goes My Baby" and "Save the Last Dance for Me," which blended pop and gospel musical styles with sophisticated arrangements and orchestrations (see separate Drifters entry).

While on leave from the Air Force, Clyde McPhatter recorded "Seven Days" solo, and the single became a smash R&B and moderate pop hit in early 1956. Upon discharge later that year, he pursued a solo career on Atlantic Records, scoring a top R&B and major pop hit with "Treasure of Love" that spring. Touring with Bill Haley in 1956 and the Fats Domino Caravan in 1957, McPhatter achieved R&B/pop hits with "Without Love (There Is Nothing)," "Just to Hold My Hand," "Long, Lonely Nights," and "Come What May." His biggest hit, a pop smash, came in late 1958 with Brook Benton's "A Lover's Question."

Switching to MGM Records in 1959, Clyde McPhatter suffered through inappropriate nongospel arrangements with the label and subsequently signed with Mercury Records, working with producer Clyde Otis in 1960. That summer he achieved a major pop and near-smash R&B hit with "Ta Ta," but his next success didn't come until early 1962, when he scored a near-smash pop-only hit with Billy Swann's "Lover Please." His remake of "Little Bitty Pretty One" soon became a major pop-only hit, but it proved to be his last. He recorded his last Mercury album in 1965 and later recorded several unsuccessful singles for small labels. McPhatter went to England in 1968 to perform in small clubs, and upon his return Clyde Otis helped him secure a recording contract with Decca Records. However, his comeback album, *Welcome Home*, failed to endear him to the record-buying public. Subsequently relegated to small clubs and the rock-and-roll revival circuit, Clyde McPhatter died on June 13, 1972, at age 38, of complications arising from heart, liver, and kidney ailments. He was inducted into the Rock and Roll Hall of Fame in 1987, a year before the Drifters.

Billy Ward and the Dominoes

Billy Ward with Clyde McPhatter	King	548	'58	†
Clyde McPhatter with Billy Ward and His Dominoes	King	550	'58	LP/CS/CD
Billy Ward and the Dominoes Featuring Clyde McPhatter and Jackie Wilson	King	733	'61	LP/CS/CD
18 Hits	King	5006	'77	†

Clyde McPhatter and the Drifters

Clyde McPhatter and the Drifters	Atlantic	8003	'57	†
The Greatest Recordings/The Early Years	Atco	33375	'71	
Let the Boogie Woogie Roll: Greatest Hits, 1953–1958	Atlantic	(2) 81927	'89	CS/CD

Clyde McPhatter

Love Ballads	Atlantic	8024	'58	†
Clyde	Atlantic	8031	'59	†
Best	Atlantic	8077	'63	†
Deep Sea Ball—The Best of Clyde McPhatter	Atlantic	82314	'91	CS/CD
Let's Start Over Again	MGM	3775	'59	†
Greatest Hits	MGM	3866	'60	†
Ta Ta	Mercury	60262	'60	†
Golden Blues Hits	Mercury	60655	'61	†
Lover Please	Mercury	60711	'62	†
Rhythm and Soul	Mercury	60750	'63	†
Greatest Hits	Mercury	60783	'63	†
Songs of the Big City	Mercury	60902	'64	†
Live at the Apollo	Mercury	60915	'64	†
May I Sing for You	Mercury	16224	'65	†
Welcome Home	Decca	75231	'70	†
Greatest Hits	Curb/CEMA	77417	'91	CS/CD

METALLICA

James [Alan] Hetfield (b. Aug. 3, 1963, Los Angeles, CA), rhythm gtr, voc; **Kirk Hammett** (b. Nov. 18, 1962, San Francisco, CA), lead gtr; **Cliff[ord Lee] Burton** (b. Feb. 10, 1962, U.S.; d. Sept. 27, 1986, Sweden), bs; **Lars Ulrich** (b. Dec. 26, 1963, Copenhagen, Denmark), drm [Cliff Burton was replaced by **Jason Newsted** (b. Mar. 4, 1963, Battle Creek, MI)

Pioneers of the heavy-metal school of rock known variously as speed or thrash metal, distinguished by its speedy guitar playing and rapid tempos, Metallica achieved their earliest popularity through word-of-mouth communication. Revitalizing heavy-metal music without the pretense and image-pandering of glitter-rock groups while eschewing both the superficial and sexist party themes and pseudo-mythological concerns of their antecedents, Metallica won recognition for their sophisticated yet deafening arrangements and intelligent yet harrowing lyrics. Gradually expanding the band's commercial success without radio, video, or advertising support (drawing comparisons to the Grateful Dead), Metallica have consistently maintained their artistic integrity and fierce commitment to their music. Lauded for their socially conscious themes and brutal honesty, particularly on their album *Master of Puppets*, Metallica were the hit of the 1988 Monsters of Rock tour nominally headlined by Van Halen. Adopting a more thoughtful, mellower approach for their best-selling *Metallica* album, Metallica are one of the most popular American heavy-metal bands of the '90s.

The evolution of Metallica began when Danish drummer Lars Ulrich recorded a demonstration tape with guitarist James Hetfield in Los Angeles in October 1981. Their first lead guitarist was replaced by Dave Mustaine in January 1982, and bassist Cliff Burton joined at the end of the year. Gaining their first recognition by playing small clubs in Los Angeles and later San Francisco, Metallica moved to Queens, New York, where Kirk Hammett replaced Mustaine, who later formed Megadeth in Southern California.

With Ulrich and Hetfield as principal songwriters, Metallica recorded their debut album, *Kill 'Em All*, in May 1983. Published and copyrighted by the band and released on the Megaforce label, the album featured earsplitting, rapid-tempo songs often characterized by sudden mood and tempo changes that drew the attention of youthful head-bangers. Their second album, *Ride the Lightning*, also on Megaforce, included "Fight Fire with Fire" and "Creeping Death," and remained on the album charts for nearly a year. Elektra Records soon picked up distribution of Metallica's albums and signed the band. Their debut for the label, *Master of Puppets*, drew praise for its stark social commentary and broke the band into the mass market. The album featured "Battery"; "Leper Messiah," which took to task television evangelists; and the title song, which decried drug addiction.

While touring Sweden, Cliff Burton was killed on September 27, 1986, at age 24, when the group's van crashed on an icy road near Ljungby. He was quickly replace by Jason Newsted, of the Phoenix-based band Flotsam and Jetsam. In 1987 the band assembled a collection of cover tunes that was issued as *The $5.98 EP: Garage Days Re-Revisited*. In summer 1988, Metallica toured with the Monsters of Rock tour, along with Van Halen, The Scorpions, Dokken, and Kingdom Come. By tour's end they had become the hit of the tour, eclipsing even the headliners. Their diverse album . . . *And Justice for All* featured "The Frayed Ends of Sanity," the socially-conscious "Blackened," and "The Shortest Straw" and yielded their first moderate hit, the ghastly yet moving "One." The album became a best-seller.

Touring for much of 1989, Metallica next recorded the chart-topping album *Metallica*. It exhibited a more thoughtful, slower, almost gentle approach, producing five hits: "Enter Sandman," accompanied by their first video; "The Unforgiven"; the soothing "Nothing Else Matters"; the anthemic "Wherever I May Roam"; and "Sad but True." Metallica subsequently toured as single-act headliners between summer 1991 and summer 1993, playing more than three hundred engagements. In summer 1992 they conducted a seven-week tour with Guns N' Roses in one of the most anticipated tours of the year. Their *Live Sh*t* was drawn from a series of Mexico City concerts.

Metallica

Kill 'Em All	Megaforce	069	'83	†
	Elektra	60766		CS/CD
Ride the Lightning	Megaforce	769	'84	†
	Elektra	60396	'84	CS/CD
Master of Puppets	Elektra	60439	'86	CS/CD
. . . And Justice for All	Elektra	60812	'88	CS/CD
Metallica	Elektra	61113	'91	LP/CS/CD
Live Sh*t: Binge and Purge	Elektra	(2) 61594	'93	CS
	Elektra	(3) 61594	'93	CD

BETTE MIDLER

(b. Dec. 1, 1945, Paterson, NJ; also given as Honolulu, HI)

An artist of remarkably wide-ranging talents as song stylist, comedienne, and cabaret performer, Bette Midler perfected the persona of the Divine Miss M during a long-running engagement at New York's notorious club Continental Baths. Projecting the image of a streetwise, all-around entertainer through her flamboyance, uninhibited use of gutter comedy, and command of a variety of musical styles, Midler burst into prominence in the early '70s through television appearances, live performances, and two best-selling albums. Since then she has made her mark as a film and television actress, and as a solo star on Broadway, while continuing to perform and tour.

Bette Midler was raised in Honolulu, Hawaii, where she studied drama in college for a year before securing a minor role in the 1966 movie *Hawaii*. Traveling to the mainland with earnings from the film role, Midler moved to New York, where she worked a variety of mundane jobs while securing roles in several off-Broadway productions and singing in clubs and restaurants for experience. She landed a part in the chorus of *Fiddler on the Roof* and stayed with the show for three years, eventually working her way up to the central role of Tzeitel (Tevye's daughter).

In 1970 Bette Midler decided to concentrate on the singing aspect of her career by devising a cabaret-style show that proved enormously popular at New York's Continental Baths, a group-games club largely frequented by homosexuals and transvestites. Playing piano and performing widely eclectic material, she developed the persona of the Divine Miss M, a streetwise, foul-mouthed, flamboyant singer and comedienne. She was backed by the female vocal trio the Harlettes, whose original members included Melissa Manchester and Katey Sagal (later of television's *Married . . . With Children*). Her Saturday night performances became *the* cult attraction of New York, and led to national notoriety.

Introduced to a larger audience through regular television appearances in 1972, Bette Midler signed with Atlantic Records, where her debut album, naturally titled *The Divine Miss M*, became an instant best-seller and led to successful engagements at exclusive clubs across the country. The album, considered her definitive recorded work, yielded a major hit with a remake of "Do You Want to Dance" and a near-smash with the old Andrews Sisters' song "Boogie Woogie Bugle Boy"; it also contained her theme, the bittersweet "Friends," and John Prine's poignant "Hello in There," Leon Russell's "Superstar," and remakes of "The Chapel of Love" and "Leader of the Pack."

Headlining lavish New Year's Eve shows at Philharmonic Hall in 1972 and 1973, Midler successfully toured throughout the United States in 1973, accompanied by the Harlettes and musical director Barry Manilow, who produced Midler's first two albums. Her second, self-titled release became a best-seller despite yielding no major hit single; it contained such diverse material as "I Shall Be Released," "In the Mood," and "Uptown/Da Doo Run Run."

Bette Midler took 1974 off, as Barry Manilow left early in the year to pursue his own successful pop career. During 1975 she returned to live performance with a cross-country tour that concluded with her *Clams on the Half-Shell Revue* on Broadway, which broke box-office records. However, 1976's *Songs for the New Depression* was greeted with negative critical reviews, sold only modestly, and failed to produce even a minor hit. Midler's next album, *Live at Last*, fared even less well. In 1977 her *Broken Blossom* was issued, and she appeared in her first television special on NBC, *Ol' Red Hair Is Back*. Spending much of 1978 working on her first feature film, Midler also recorded *Thighs and Whispers*, which yielded the moderate hit "Married Men."

Bette Midler's film debut, *The Rose*, was a great success and revived her flagging career. She won excellent critical reviews and an Academy Award nomination for her intense and sensitive portrayal of a tough but vulnerable rock star seemingly unable to escape from a maelstrom of liquor, drugs, and sex that leads to her self-destruction (the story was loosely based on the life and times of blues rocker Janis Joplin). The soundtrack album, which featured "When a Man Loves a Woman," "Stay with Me," and the smash hit "The Rose," stayed on the album charts for nearly a year.

However, Midler was unable to build on this success, and the early '80s found her career back in the doldrums. In 1980 she released a book, *A View from a Broad*, which chronicled her world tour, and the R-rated film *Divine Madness* attempted to create, with equivocal success, the humor, compassion, and manic spontaneity of her live performances. Her 1982 film *Jinxed* proved a dismal failure, and the album *No Frills* sold only modestly while producing minor hits with Marshall Crenshaw's "Favorite Waste of Time" and the Rolling Stones' "Beast of Burden." Touring for the first time in three years in 1982–1983, Midler next recorded the all-comedy album *Mud Will Be Flung Tonight!*, another less-than-successful effort.

Midler returned to form with a series of film roles in the mid-'80s that established her as a talented comedian. In 1986 she had the starring role as a spoiled Beverly Hills matron in *Down and Out in Beverly Hills*, with Nick Nolte and Richard Dreyfuss, followed by a similar role in *Ruthless People*, with Danny DeVito. However, the identical-twin comedy, 1988's *Big Business* with Lily Tomlin, was greeted by mixed reviews. She followed this with the two-hanky weeper *Beaches*, with Barbara Hershey. Its best-selling soundtrack remained on the album charts for more than three years. It yielded a top hit with the love song "Wind Beneath My Wings" and included "Under the Boardwalk," "The Glory of Love," and Randy Newman's "I Think It's Gonna Rain Today." Her follow-up studio album, *Some People's Lives*, produced the smash hit "From a Distance," a ballad similar in style to "Wind." Midler's movie career took another nosedive with the musical *For the Boys*, although the soundtrack managed to sell despite the film's poor box-office performance.

Bette Midler returned to touring in 1993 with her Experience the Divine tour that included a record-breaking run at New York's Radio City Music Hall. She also appeared on CBS-TV in her highly rated version of the musical *Gypsy*, which yielded a soundtrack album. In late 1995 she released a new studio album.

Bette Midler

The Divine Miss M	Atlantic	7238	'72	CS/CD
Bette Midler	Atlantic	7270	'73	CS/CD
Songs for the New Depression	Atlantic	18155	'76	CS/CD

Live at Last	Atlantic	(2) 9000	'77	CS
	Atlantic	(2) 81461		CD
Broken Blossom	Atlantic	19151	'77	†
	Atlantic	80410	'93	CD
Thighs and Whispers	Atlantic	16004	'79	CS/CD
The Rose (soundtrack)	Atlantic	16010	'79	CS/CD
Divine Madness	Atlantic	16022	'80	CS/CD
No Frills	Atlantic	80070	'83	CS/CD
Mud Will Be Flung Tonight!	Atlantic	81291	'85	CS/CD
Beaches (soundtrack)	Atlantic	81933	'89	LP/CS/CD
Some People's Lives	Atlantic	82129	'90	LP/CS/CD
For the Boys	Atlantic	82329	'91	CS/CD†
The Divine Collection	Atlantic	82497	'93	CS/CD
Gypsy (television soundtrack)	Atlantic	82551	'93	CS/CD
Bette of Roses	Atlantic	82823	'95	CS/CD

MIDNIGHT OIL

Peter Garrett (b. Sydney, Australia), lead voc; **Jim Moginie** (b. Sydney, Australia), gtr; **Martin Rotsey** (b. Syndey, Australia), gtr; **Andrew "Bear" James**, bs; **Rob Hirst** (b. Sydney, Australia), drm, background voc [Andrew James was replaced by **Peter Gifford** in 1980, who in turn was replaced by **Dwayne "Bones" Hillman** (b. New Zealand) in 1990.]

Along with Air Supply and Men at Work, Midnight Oil were an Australian band that broke through into the American market and consciousness in the early '80s. Fiercely independent and insisting on total control over their product and publicity, Midnight Oil were established in their own country through a compelling combination of forceful rock music and acute awareness of political, social, and environmental issues. Launched into the international arena with 1982's *10, 9, 8, 7, 6, 5, 4, 3, 2, 1*, Midnight Oil were compared to the Clash for their successful fusion of music and politics. Considered by some to be one of rock's great contemporary bands, regardless of national origin, Midnight Oil scored their biggest success with 1988's "Beds Are Burning" single and *Diesel and Dust* album.

The original nucleus of Midnight Oil—Jim Moginie, Andrew James, and Rob Hirst—began playing together in 1971. By 1972 they had formed Farm, eventually advertising for a lead singer in 1976. They found vocalist Peter Garrett, who had earned a law degree from the University of New South Wales, added Martin Rotsey, and became Midnight Oil later that year. Finding an audience through pub engagements in Sydney, Melbourne, and Adelaide, Midnight Oil formed their own independent label, Powderworks, and set up an independent distribution network. Issuing their debut album in 1978, Midnight Oil first won a reputation for political activism that November by playing a concert to protest Australia's policy on uranium mining. They later played benefits for Save the Whales and Greenpeace, and recorded two more albums and the EP *Bird Noises* while establishing themselves in Australia. In 1980 Peter Gifford replaced Andrew James on bass.

In 1982 Midnight Oil signed with Columbia Records, and their debut for the label, *10, 9, 8, 7, 6, 5, 4, 3, 2, 1*, garnered their first recognition beyond the island continent. With Garrett, Moginie, and Hirst as principal songwriters, the album revealed an acute awareness of Australian and South Pacific social and environmental issues, underpinned by an aggressive rock sound. The album contained outspoken songs such as "Only the Strong," "The Power and the Passion," "Scream in Blue," and "Short Memory." In 1984 Peter Garrett ran for the Australian federal Senate from the state of New South Wales on the single-issue Nuclear Disarmament Party ticket and nearly won the seat.

Midnight Oil's next album, *Red Sails in the Sunset*, came to be regarded as the group's finest album. It included "Minutes to Midnight," "When the Generals Talk," and "Who Can Stand in the Way." Champions of native aboriginal rights, Midnight Oil played remote aboriginal settlements on their Black Fella While Fella tour of July 1986, observing firsthand the consequences of government policies on the island's natives. Midnight Oil's next album, *Diesel and Dust*, was well received and remained on the American album charts for more than a year. It yielded the major hit "Beds Are Burning" (which advocated the return of Australia to the aborigines) and the moderate hit "The Dead Heart," written for the movie *Uhuru-An Anangu Story*. Other topical songs include "Put Down the Weapons" and "Warakuma."

Midnight Oil toured internationally in 1988, and two years later replaced Peter Gifford with Dwayne Hillman. *Blue Sky Mining* continued to tackle Australian issues with the title song and "Stars of Warburton," and took a more global view with "One Country" and "Antarctica." That year Midnight Oil performed in front of the Exxon Building in New York City to protest the Exxon Valdez oil spill. The band took 1991 off, although they did contribute "Wharf Rat" to *Deadicated* (the Grateful Dead tribute album), and Garrett served as president of the Australian Conservation Foundation and became a board member of Greenpeace. The 1992 live set *Scream in Blue Live* again drew critical praise, inspiring some critics to call it the best live rock album in years. Their next studio album, *Earth and Sun and Moon*, was released in 1993 and commercially less successful than previous works.

Midnight Oil

Midnight Oil	Columbia	46133	'78/'90	CS/CD
Head Injuries	Columbia	46134	'79/'90	CS/CD
Bird Noises (mini)	Columbia	46136	'80/'90	CS/CD
Place Without a Postcard	Columbia	46145	'81/'90	CS/CD
10, 9, 8, 7, 6, 5, 4, 3, 2, 1	Columbia	38996	'82/'88	CS/CD
Red Sails in the Sunset	Columbia	39987	'85	CS/CD
Species Diseases (mini)	Columbia	46135	'85/'90	CS/CD
Diesel and Dust	Columbia	40967	'88	CS/CD
Blue Sky Mining	Columbia	45398	'90	CS/CD
Scream in Blue Live	Columbia	52731	'92	CS/CD
Earth and Sun and Moon	Columbia	53793	'93	CS/CD

STEVE MILLER

(b. Oct. 5, 1943, Milwaukee, WI)

THE STEVE MILLER BAND. Steve Miller, gtr, voc, songwriting; **James "Curly" Cooke**, gtr; **Jim Peterman**, org; **Lonnie Turner** (b. Feb. 24, 1947, Berkeley, CA), bs; **Tim Davis**, drm [**Boz Scaggs** (b. William Royce Scaggs, June 8, 1944, OH) replaced Curly Cooke in 1967–1968. Various musicians have been employed by Miller since the early '70s.]

Mistakenly identified with the psychedelic movement emerging from San Francisco in the late '60s, the Steve Miller Band signed with Capitol Records for a huge advance and recorded two albums, often regarded as classics of the era, featuring sophisticated production, elaborate sound effects, and the singing, guitar playing, and songwriting of Boz Scaggs. The Steve Miller Band retained their reputation as an album band after Scaggs's departure, despite a series of personnel changes, to emerge wildly successful with *The Joker*, *Fly Like an Eagle*, and *Book of Dreams*. Their popularity was largely based on Miller's ability to manufacture consummate but inconsequential recordings of his facile, uninvolving songs.

Following 1982's *Abracadabra*, Miller recorded only occasionally, while his mid-'70s hits were often revived on so-called classic-rock radio.

Steve Miller moved as an infant with his family to Dallas, Texas, where he grew up. He took up guitar at age 5 and formed his first blues band, The Marksmen, at age 12 with friend Boz Scaggs. Enrolling at the University of Wisconsin—Madison in 1961, Miller assembled the white soul group the Ardells (later the Fabulous Night Trains), again with Scaggs, and played locally for more than three years. Miller left college to move to Chicago, where he played with black bluesmen such as Muddy Waters and Buddy Guy and white blues players such as Paul Butterfield, Mike Bloomfield, and Barry Goldberg; Scaggs, meanwhile, traveled to Europe and played around Scandinavia as a folk singer. The Miller-Goldberg Band was formed and signed to Epic, but Miller soon quit and returned to Dallas before moving to San Francisco in 1966. There he formed the Steve Miller Blues Band with Curly Cooke, Jim Peterman, Lonnie Turner, and Tim Davis.

The group backed Chuck Berry on his *Live at the Fillmore* album. Miller, besieged by contract offers, carefully and slowly conducted negotiations, eventually signing with Capitol Records on highly favorable terms, which included a $60,000 advance. In September 1967 Curly Cooke dropped out of the group, by then known as simply the Steve Miller Band, and Miller summoned Boz Scaggs from Europe. This grouping went to England to record their debut album, *Children of the Future*. Although it was only minimally associated with psychedelic music and progressive rock, as some reviewers claimed, it was nonetheless well received critically. Slickly produced, the album featured Miller's title song and Scaggs's "Baby's Callin' Me Home" and "Steppin' Stone." The band quickly recorded the follow-up, *Sailor*, employing carefully produced sound effects throughout. The album contained Miller's "Song for Our Ancestors," "Living in the U.S.A." (a minor hit), and "Quicksilver Girls," as well as Scaggs's "Overdrive" and one of Miller's theme songs, "Gangster of Love."

Boz Scaggs left the Steve Miller Band in August 1968, followed soon after by Jim Peterman. Subsequently featuring himself more on stage and in recordings, Miller recruited a new keyboardist for *Brave New World* (with "Space Cowboy") and *Your Saving Grace*. After one more album, only Miller was left from the original recording band.

Steve Miller's next two albums sold poorly, but 1973's *The Joker*, recorded with a returned Lonnie Turner, yielded a top hit with its trite and self-indulgent title song. Off the concert trail for more than a year, the band reconvened with Turner, drummer Gary Mallaber, and others for *Fly Like an Eagle* and *Book of Dreams*. The former yielded the near-smash hit "Take the Money and Run" and the smashes "Rock'n Me" and "Fly Like an Eagle"; the latter produced three major hits with "Jet Airliner," "Jungle Love," and "Swingtown." Relatively inactive for a time, the Steve Miller Band reemerged in 1981 with *Circle of Love*, which included the trite, side-long "Macho City" and the major hit "Heart Like a Wheel." *Abracadabra* brought him his last Number One in 1982, the title song.

Exhausted from touring, Steve Miller retreated to Seattle and later Idaho. He recorded two albums in the mid-'80s before returning to touring in 1988 in support of *Born 2 B Blue*, with a small jazz ensemble accompanying him, including Ben Sidran, famed vibraphonist Milt Jackson, and Phil Woods on sax. A major change in direction for Miller, the album featured four Jimmy Reed songs and other standards such as "God Bless the Child." Enjoying increased popularity as his mid-'70s hits became staples of the classic-rock radio format, Steve Miller signed with Polygram Records after being courted by the label for two years. His debut for Polydor, 1993's *Wide River*, produced a minor hit with the title song.

Steve Miller					
Children of the Future		Capitol	2920	'68	†
		Capitol	91245	'94	CD

Sailor	Capitol	2984	'68	†
	Capitol	94449		CD
Brave New World	Capitol	184	'69	†
	Capitol	16078		†
	Capitol	91246		CD
Your Saving Grace	Capitol	331	'69	†
	Capitol	16079		†
	Capitol	94448	'94	CD
Number Five	Capitol	436	'70	†
	Capitol	29686	'94	CD
Children of the Future/Living in the U.S.A.	Capitol	(2) 717	'71	†
Rock Love	Capitol	748	'71	†
Recall the Beginning . . . A Journey from Eden	Capitol	11022	'72	†
Anthology	Capitol	(2) 11114	'72	CS
	Capitol	94488		CD
The Joker	Capitol	11235	'73	†
	Capitol	94445		CS/CD
The Best of Steve Miller, 1968–1973	Capitol	95271	'91	CS/CD
Fly Like an Eagle	Capitol	11497	'76	†
	Capitol	16339	'85	†
	Capitol	46475		CS/CD
	DCC	1033		CD
Book of Dreams	Capitol	11630	'77	†
	Capitol	16323	'85	†
	Capitol	46476		CS/CD
Greatest Hits: 1974–1978	Capitol	11872	'78	†
	Capitol	16321	'85	†
	Capitol	46101		CS/CD
Circle of Love	Capitol	12121	'81	†
	Capitol	94446	'94	CD
Abracadabra	Capitol	12216	'82	CS
	Capitol	46102		CD
Steve Miller Band—Live!	Capitol	12263	'83	†
	Capitol	91315		CS/CD
Italian X-Rays	Capitol	12339	'84	†
	Capitol	94447	'94	CD
Living in the 20th Century	Capitol	12445	'86	†
	Capitol	46326	'86	CD
Born 2 B Blue	Capitol	48303	'88	CD
Gift Set	Capitol	92214		CD†
Steve Miller Band Box Set	Capitol	(3) 89826	'94	CD
Wide River	Polydor	519441	'93	LP/CS/CD

JONI MITCHELL
(b. Roberta Joan Anderson, Nov. 7, 1943, Fort McLeod, Alberta, Canada)

Gaining her first recognition in the late '60s as the composer of the folk-rock classics "Circle Game" and "Both Sides Now" (as recorded by Tom Rush and Judy Collins, respectively), Joni Mitchell developed a devoted following with her first two folk-style albums. With her distinctive dulcimer and guitar playing and expressive, clear, and full-bodied soprano voice, Mitchell touched myriads of popular-music fans with her intensely personal, often confessional style of songwriting. In the '70s Mitchell's career took her through a variety of styles, always pushing the envelope of the confessional singer-songwriter style. After flirting with jazz she returned to a more rock-oriented sound in the '80s and '90s, although with less commercial success.

Joni Mitchell grew up in Saskatoon, Saskatchewan, where she took up informal singing at age nine and developed an interest in the visual arts. Taking up baritone ukulele during her teens and later learning guitar, she performed in Calgary, Alberta's best-known coffeehouse, The Depression, while attending the Alberta Institute of Art. She subsequently decided to pursue folk-style music professionally and moved to Toronto, where she played at clubs in the city's famed Yorktown district. There she met and eventually married folk singer Chuck Mitchell. They moved to Detroit in 1966 and later toured the East Coast club circuit. By 1967, however, the couple had divorced, and Joni moved to New York City, where she played folk clubs and struck up friendships with Judy Collins and Tom Rush, among others.

Signed to Reprise Records, Joni Mitchell gained her first recognition as a songwriter by means of Tom Rush's recording of her "Circle Game" and "Urge for Going" on his 1968 *Circle Game* album, and through Judy Collins's near-smash hit recording of her "Both Sides Now" that same year. Mitchell soon moved to California, and her debut album, sometimes referred to as *Song to a Seagull*, was produced in a thin and understated manner by David Crosby. Although the album sold minimally, it featured her own cover art and was entirely comprised of her own compositions, including the poignant and brilliantly sung "Michael from Mountains," "I Had a King," and "Cactus Tree."

Joni Mitchell's second album, *Clouds*, sported her colorful self-portrait and effectively established her in the forefront of the '70s female singer-songwriter movement. The album contained her celebratory "Chelsea Morning," the ominous "The Fiddle and the Drum," and her version of "Both Sides Now," as well as moving personal songs such as "I Don't Know Where I Stand" and "Songs to Aging Children Come." Often using obscure yet sophisticated tunings on her stringed instruments, Mitchell employed a sense of harmony that went beyond the limits of both pop and rock. Her songwriting—more accurately described as song-poetry—explored the themes of romantic love, the independence achieved through love's loss, and the guarded optimism of the youthful humanitarian ethic in such fiercely personal and incisively honest terms as to be embarrassing were it not for their underlying poignancy. Her next album, *Ladies of the Canyon*, again featured her art on the jacket. Bolstered commercially by the success of Crosby, Stills, Nash and Young's version of her classic "Woodstock," the album introduced her use of the piano and included her own electrifying version of "Woodstock" (far and away superior to CSNY's rock version); the oft-recorded "Circle Game"; and her first minor hit, the wry ecology song "Big Yellow Taxi." Containing wide-ranging music and varied emotional nuances, the album also included "For Free," a joyous look back at her precommercial days; the gentle autobiographical title cut; and "Willy," written about former lover Graham Nash.

Joni Mitchell's final album for Reprise, *Blue*, showed her flowering as an arranger and continued her string of best-selling, highly personal, and exquisitely performed releases. Among the songs included are "All I Want," "California," "This Flight Tonight," "A Case of You" (her second minor hit), "Carey," and the disturbing "The Last Time I Saw Richard." Switching to Asylum Records, she recorded *For the Roses*. The album revealed jazz influences and included her first major hit, "You Turn Me On, I'm a Radio," as well as "Cold Blue Steel and Sweet Fire," "See You Sometime," and "Blonde in the Bleachers." *Court and Spark*, recorded with members of Tom Scott's jazz-style group L.A. Express, became her most popular album, remaining on the album charts for well over a year. The album yielded three hits with "Raised on Robbery," "Help Me" (a near-smash), and "Free Man in Paris"; it also contained "People's Parties" as well as the romantic title song and a version of Lambert, Hendricks and Ross's "Twisted." Touring for the first time in several years during 1974 with Scott and the L.A. Express, her live *Miles of Aisles* compiled much of her finest material and produced a major hit with its version of "Big Yellow Taxi."

With 1975's *The Hissing of Summer Lawns*, Joni Mitchell began to move beyond the restrictive role of pop-style singer-songwriter. Eschewing the confessional style in favor of songs both musically and lyrically ambitious and complex, Mitchell suffered critical disparagement for the album in the rock and pop press. Maintaining an even more reduced personal profile, she recorded *Hejira* with jazz artists such as Jaco Pastorius and Larry Carlton. Regarded by some jazz critics as a masterpiece, this album encompasses a variety of musical textures and nuances, on songs such as "Coyote," "Black Crow," and "Furry Sings the Blues." With 1977's *Don Juan's Reckless Daughter*, Mitchell firmly broke with her pop-music past, recording the album with Pastorius, Latin percussionist Airto, and several members of the fusion group Weather Report. Inspiring critics to coin yet another hyphenated label, folk-jazz, the album featured the side-long "Paprika Plains," recorded with full symphony orchestra.

"Paprika Plains," heard by ailing jazz bassist and composer Charles Mingus, so fascinated him that in spring 1978 he contacted Mitchell regarding the possibility of working together. She consented and Mingus soon turned over to her six tunes to which she was to supply lyrics, plus the Mingus standard "Goodbye Pork Pie Hat." Mitchell worked on the collaboration for more than 18 months, but it was not completed until after Mingus's death on January 5, 1979. Recorded with Wayne Shorter, Jaco Pastorius, and Herbie Hancock, the resulting album was greeted by equivocal reviews. The album contained "Goodbye Pork Pie Hat," three of the six specially written tunes, and Mitchell's own tribute to Mingus, "God Must Be a Boogie Man." She subsequently toured for the first time in four years with Pastorius, percussionist Don Alias, guitarist Pat Metheny, and others.

Maintaining a low profile in the '80s, Joni Mitchell switched to Geffen Records for 1982's *Wild Things Run Fast*, in which she returned to standard song forms. The album yielded a moderate hit with a cover version of "(You're So Square) Baby, I Don't Care," recorded by Elvis Presley for his 1957 movie *Jailhouse Rock*. In 1985 she recorded *Dog Eat Dog* with English synthesizer wizard Thomas Dolby. The album was highly topical, decrying television evangelists ("Tax Free"), capitalism (the title track), nuclear holocaust ("Fiction"), and consumerism. Her orientation toward contemporary issues continued with 1988's *Chalk Mark in a Rain Storm* with "The Beat of Black Wings" and "Snakes and Ladders." In the early '90s she recorded *Night Ride Home*, which was also issued in a limited edition featuring four reproductions of her collages, while pursuing her interests as a painter, photographer, and poet. In 1994 Joni Mitchell returned to Reprise Records for *Turbulent Indigo*.

Joni Mitchell

Joni Mitchell	Reprise	6293	'68	CS/CD
Clouds	Reprise	6341	'69	CS/CD
Ladies of the Canyon	Reprise	6376	'70	CS/CD
Blue	Reprise	2038	'71	LP/CS/CD
For the Roses	Asylum	5057	'72	CS/CD
Court and Spark	Asylum	1001	'74	†
	Elektra	1001		CS/CD
	DCC	1025		CD
For the Roses/Court and Spark	Elektra	60276		CS
Miles of Aisles	Asylum	(2) 202	'74	†
	Elektra	(2) 202		CS
	Elektra	202		CD

The Hissing of Summer Lawns	Asylum	1051	'75	†
	Elektra	1051		CS/CD
Hejira	Asylum	1087	'76	†
	Elektra	1087		CS/CD
Don Juan's Reckless Daughter	Asylum	(2) 701	'77	†
	Elektra	(2) 701		CS
	Elektra	701		CD
Mingus	Asylum	505	'79	†
	Elektra	505		CS/CD
Shadows and Light	Asylum	(2) 704		CS
Wild Things Run Fast	Geffen	2019	'82/91	CS/CD
	Mobile Fidelity	570	'92	CD
Dog Eat Dog	Geffen	24074	'85/'91	CS/CD
Chalk Mark in a Rain Storm	Geffen	24172	'88	CS/CD
Night Ride Home	Geffen	24302	'91	CS/CD
	Geffen	24388	'91	CD
Turbulent Indigo	Reprise	45786	'94	CS/CD

MOBY GRAPE

Alexander "Skip" Spence (b. Apr. 18, 1946, Windsor, Ontario, Canada), gtr; **Jerry Miller** (b. July 10, 1943, Tacoma, WA), lead gtr; **Peter Lewis** (b. July 15, 1945, Los Angeles, CA), gtr; **Bob Mosley** (b. Dec. 4, 1942, Paradise Valley, CA), bs; **Don Stevenson** (b. Oct. 15, 1942, Seattle, WA), drm

Often labeled as a legendary rock band, Moby Grape emerged from San Francisco in the late '60s. Featuring a three-guitar lineup and intriguing vocal harmonies, Moby Grape was considered to be one of the earliest purveyors of country-rock. The band's reputation was sullied, however, by the aggressive promotion undertaken by their label, Columbia Records, for their first album, and they soon dissolved.

The nucleus of the group was formed from the remnants of an earlier San Francisco band, the Frantics, whose members included Miller, Mosley, and Stevenson. They enlisted singer/guitarist Peter Lewis, who had previously led his own band, Peter and the Wolves, while Skip Spence had previously worked as drummer for the original Jefferson Airplane.

Moby Grape's debut 1967 album was considered a masterpiece. The album included the haunting "Sitting by the Window," the countrified "8:05," and the minor hit "Omaha." Overall, 10 of the album's 13 songs were released simultaneously as singles, confusing deejays who might have helped promote the band and its music. A second album, aptly titled *Wow*, came with a bonus disc, *Grape Jam*, that featured then-superstar picker Mike Bloomfield and keyboardist Al Kooper. This album also sank on the charts, and the group disbanded, to reform as a quartet without Spence in 1969, producing the final album of the original band. That same year, Spence recorded *Oar* in Nashville, playing all instruments and performing all composing, arranging, and production chores. Spence's solo career was cut short by ongoing mental health problems, although by the early '90s he had recovered enough to perform on occasion with the band.

Since 1973 the group's recordings were generally unavailable due to litigation by former manager Matthew Katz, who retained the Moby Grape name. Nonetheless, the group reunited a number of times during the '70s, '80s, and '90s under a variety of names, with little success. Finally, in 1993 Columbia/Legacy issued a two-CD compilation set of Moby Grape's recordings.

Moby Grape

Moby Grape	Columbia	9498	'67		†
Wow/Grape Jam	Columbia	(2) 3	'68		†
	Columbia	9613			†
Wow	Columbia	9613			†
Grape Jam	Columbia	1	'69		†
	Columbia	9696	'69		†
Truly Fine Citizen	Columbia	9912	'69		†
Omaha	Harmony	30392	'71		†
20 Granite Creek	Reprise	6460	'71		†
Great Grape	Columbia	31098	'72		†
Live Grape	Escape	1	'78		†
Best	Columbia/Legacy	(2) 53041	'93		CS/CD

Skip Spence

Oar	Columbia	9831	'69		†
	Sony	9831			CS/CD

Bob Mosley

Bob Mosley	Reprise	2068	'72		†

THE MONKEES

Michael Nesmith (b. Dec. 30, 1942, Houston, TX), gtr, voc; **Davy Jones** (b. Dec. 30, 1945, Manchester, England), tambourine, voc; **Peter Tork** (b. Peter Torkelson, Feb. 13, 1944, Washington, D.C.), bs, voc; **Michael "Mickey" Dolenz** (b. Mar. 8, 1945, Tarzana, CA), drm, voc

A crassly manufactured American group of the late '60s, the Monkees were essentially actors hired to portray musicians for an NBC-TV situation comedy series modeled on the Beatles' successful films and recordings. Don Kirshner, head of the Brill Building professional songwriting "factory," masterminded the concept, using his staff to provide many of the Monkees' hits. Eventually allowed to play their own instruments with their third album, the Monkees appealed to pubescent and prepubescent fans, making them one of the first teenybopper groups and opening the way for the Partridge Family, the Osmonds, and the Jackson Five during the '70s. After the group's breakup in 1969, Michael Nesmith, the group's only true musician, recorded some of the earliest country-rock with his First National Band. He later formed his own Pacific Arts Records in 1977, and pioneered the production of music videos for the label in the early '80s. The concept was later popularized by the enormously successful cable network MTV.

The Monkees were created by NBC television in spring 1966 to portray musicians in the network's situation comedy series blatantly based on the zany antics performed by the Beatles in the movies *A Hard Day's Night* and *Help*. The principals were chosen from hundreds of applicants that included Stephen Stills and Charles Manson. Mickey Dolenz had been a child actor, appearing in the TV series *Circus Boy* under the name Mickey Braddock from 1956 to 1958; he later was lead singer of the Missing Links. Davy Jones had been a racehorse jockey and appeared in the London musicals *Oliver* and *Pickwick* before unsuccessfully attempting a solo singing career. Both Peter Tork and Michael Nesmith had performed music professionally. Tork had played Greenwich Village coffeehouses, whereas Nesmith had done session work for Stax/Volt.

The television series *The Monkees* debuted in September 1966, with Don Kirshner as musical supervisor. His songwriting staff provided the group with many of their hits, start-

THE MONKEES

ing with Tommy Boyce and Bobby Hart's top hit "Last Train to Clarksville." The series proved enormously successful, and subsequent hits (on which the group *did not* play instruments) included the smashes "I'm a Believer" and "A Little Bit Me, A Little Bit You," written by Neil Diamond. The members, led by Nesmith, were finally allowed to play their own instruments beginning with *Headquarters*. The Monkees' fourth album yielded a smash hit with Carole King and Gerry Goffin's wry "Pleasant Valley Sunday." To prove their ability to play their instruments, the group toured the United States in 1968, briefly having Jimi Hendrix as their opening act. After the top hit "Daydream Believer" (written by John Stewart), the smash "Valleri" (by Boyce and Hart), and the major hit "D. W. Washburn" (by Jerry Leiber and Mike Stoller), the group achieved only minor hits through 1970. Peter Tork quit the Monkees following the film and soundtrack album *Head* (scripted by Jack Nicholson and Bob Rafelson, who went on to produce the classic *Five Easy Pieces*), and the remaining trio recorded one more album before disbanding in 1969. Dolenz and Jones resurfaced in 1975–1976 with songwriters Boyce and Hart for one album and an American tour.

Of the four Monkees only Michael Nesmith was able to establish himself as a solo artist. In 1967 he provided Linda Ronstadt and the Stone Poneys with their first and only major hit, "Different Drum." After producing and conducting an instrumental album of his own songs for the Dot label, he signed with RCA and formed the First National Band, along with steel guitarist Orville "Red" Rhodes; the group is often regarded as one of the finest country-rock bands to emerge from Los Angeles. The group recorded two albums and scored a major hit in 1970 with Nesmith's "Joanne." They subsequently fell into disarray during the recording of their third album, which was completed with legendary guitarist James Burton and keyboardist Glen D. Hardin, who were later members of Emmylou Harris's Hot Band. Nesmith later formed the short-lived Second National Band and recorded *And the Hits Just Keep On Comin'*, often regarded as his finest work.

During 1972 Michael Nesmith founded his own label, Countryside, under the auspices of Elektra Records, but it was abandoned when David Geffen succeeded to the presidency of Elektra. After recording a final album for RCA with Rhodes, Nesmith allowed his contract to expire, purchased his old master recordings, and formed Pacific Arts Records in Carmel, California, in 1977. He recorded several albums for the label in the late '70s, and expanded the company's operation into the production of videos. His award-winning 1981 video *Elephant Parts* was one of the first to be specifically aimed at the home VCR market, and his *Pop Clips*, for cable's Nickelodeon network, provided the prototype for MTV a year before the music network was launched. He further expanded into feature-length movies with 1983's *Timerider*, scoring his biggest film success with the cult favorite *Repo Man* in 1984. Other film, television, and video projects followed, although none proved particularly successful.

In 1986 Davy Jones, Peter Tork, and Mickey Dolenz reunited as the Monkees for a surprisingly successful national tour. Spurred by MTV's airing of the group's television show and the reissue of their first six albums (including *Head*) on Rhino Records, the group was introduced to a new generation and enjoyed renewed popularity. Dolenz and Tork even scored a major hit with "That Was Then, This Is Now." In 1987 the three toured again and recorded all new songs for Rhino on *Pool It!*, which produced the minor hit "Heart and Soul." Rhino later issued compilations of Michael Nesmith's recordings, and Mickey Dolenz recorded two children's albums in the '90s. In the '90s Nesmith returned to recording with Rio Records, which also issued a compilation of Nesmith's recordings with the First National Band.

David Jones

David Jones	Colpix	493	'65	†

The Monkees

The Monkees	Colgems	101	'66	†
	Arista	8524	'88	CS/CD†
	Rhino	71790	'94	CS/CD
More of the Monkees	Colgems	102	'67	†
	Arista	8525	'88	CS/CD†
	Rhino	71791	'94	CS/CD
Monkees's Headquarters	Colgems	103	'67	†
	Arista	8602	'89	CS/CD†
	Rhino	71792	'95	CS/CD
Live 1967	Rhino	70139	'87	CS/CD
Pisces, Aquarius, Capricorn and Jones, Ltd.	Colgems	104	'67	†
	Arista	8603	'89	CS/CD†
	Rhino	71796	'95	CS/CD
The Birds, the Bees and the Monkees	Colgems	109	'68	†
	Rhino	144	'85	†
	Rhino	71794	'94	CS/CD
Head (soundtrack)	Colgems	5008	'68	†
	Rhino	145	'85	†
	Rhino	71795	'94	CS/CD
Instant Replay	Colgems	113	'69	†
	Rhino	71796	'95	CS/CD
Greatest Hits	Colgems	115	'69	†
	Arista	4089	'76	†
	Arista	8313		CS/CD
The Monkees Present	Colgems	117	'69	†
	Rhino	147	'85	†
	Rhino	71797	'94	CS/CD
Changes	Colgems	119	'70	†
	Rhino	71798	'94	CS/CD
Barrel Full	Colgems	(2) 1001	'71	†
More Greatest Hits	Arista	8334		CS/CD
Monkee Flips	Rhino	113	'84	†
Missing Links	Rhino	70150	'87	CS/CD
Pool It!	Rhino	70706	'87	LP/CS/CD†
	Rhino	72154	'95	CS/CD

Missing Links, Volume 2	Rhino	70903	'90	CS/CD
Listen to the Band	Rhino	(4) 70566	'91	CS/CD

Davy Jones

Davy Jones	Bell	6067	'72	†

Dolenz, Jones, Boyce and Hart

Dolenz, Jones, Boyce and Hart	Capitol	11513	'76	†

Mike Nesmith and the First National Band

Magnetic South	RCA	4371	'70	†
Loose Salute	RCA	4415	'70	†
Nevada Fighter	RCA	4497	'71	†
Michael Nesmith and the First National Band	Rio	(2) 5066	'93	CS/CD

Michael Nesmith and the Second National Band

Tantamount to Treason	RCA	4563	'72	†

Michael Nesmith

The Wichita Train Whistle Sings	Dot	25861	'68	†
	Pacific Arts	113		†
And the Hits Just Keep On Comin'	RCA	4695	'72	†
	Pacific Arts	9439	'77	†
	Pacific Arts	116		†
Pretty Much Your Standard Ranch Trash	RCA	0164	'73		
	Pacific Arts	9440	'77	†
	Pacific Arts	117		†
The Prison	Pacific Arts	9428		†
	Pacific Arts	101		†
	Rio	5076	'94	CS/CD
Compilation	Pacific Arts	9425	'77	†
	Pacific Arts	106		†
From a Radio Engine to a Photon Wing	Pacific Arts	9486	'77	†
	Pacific Arts	107		†
Live at the Palais	Pacific Arts	118	'78	†
Infinite Rider on the Big Dogma	Pacific Arts	130	'79	†
The Newer Stuff	Rhino	70168	'89	CS/CD
The Older Stuff: The Best of Michael Nesmith (1970–1973)	Rhino	70763	'91	CS/CD
Tropical Campfires	Rio	5000	'92	CS/CD
The Garden	Rio	5075	'94	CS/CD

Children's Records

Mickey Dolenz Puts Your Kid to Sleep	Rhino	70413	'91	CS/CD
Broadway Mickey	Kid Rhino	71676	'94	CS/CD

THE MOODY BLUES

Denny Laine (b. Brian Haynes, Oct. 29, 1944, Birmingham, England), gtr, voc; **Mike Pinder** (b. Dec. 27, 1941, Birmingham, England), kybd, gtr; **Clint Warwick** (b. June 25, 1949, Birmingham, England), bs; **Ray Thomas** (b. Dec. 29, 1942, Stourport-on-Severn, England), bs; **Graeme Edge** (b. Mar. 30, 1944, Rochester, Kent, England), drm [Denny Laine and Clint Warwick left in 1966, to be replaced by **Justin Hayward** (b. Oct. 14, 1946, Swindon, Wiltshire, England) on lead vocals, lead guitar, keyboards, and sitar; and **John Lodge** (b.

July 20, 1945, Birmingham) on bass and vocals. In 1978 Mike Pinder was replaced by
Patrick Moraz (b. June 24, 1948, Morges, Switzerland) on keyboards.]

Initially formed as a British R&B band in the mid-'60s, the Moody Blues regrouped in the late '60s to record the landmark *Days of Future Passed* album with the London Symphony Orchestra. The album was hailed for its fusion of rock and classical music and led to the invention of the term *progressive rock* to describe subsequent experimentation by rock groups with classical instrumentation and/or compositions. Thus the Moody Blues paved the way for groups such as Genesis, Yes, Emerson, Lake and Palmer, and the Electric Light Orchestra, and served to encourage other groups such as Deep Purple to record with full orchestras. *Days of Future Passed* was also one of the first so-called concept albums, and its success prompted the proliferation of others. The album is also noteworthy for its introduction and popularization of the mellotron, then an advanced keyboard-synthesizer instrument capable of producing prerecorded sounds of nonkeyboard instruments.

The Moody Blues were formed in 1964 in Birmingham, England, by Denny Laine, Mike Pinder, Clint Warwick, Ray Thomas, and Graeme Edge. Only Laine was well known as a musician, having led Denny Laine and the Diplomats between 1962 and 1964. The Moody Blues debuted at London's famed Marquee Club and were quickly signed to British Decca (London/Deram in the United States). The group's second single, the blues-style "Go Now!," became a smash British and major American hit in early 1965, but the initial lineup never again achieved another even moderate hit. In 1966 both Laine and Warwick left; Laine eventually joined Paul McCartney's Wings in 1971.

Suffering declining popularity, the Moody Blues added Justin Hayward and John Lodge. Nearly disbanding, the group obtained a mellotron and embarked on a totally new musical direction. The lineup's debut album, *Days of Future Passed*, eschewed their blues backgrounds and was hailed for both pioneering a new form—the concept album—and its adventurous fusion of rock and classical musics. Recorded with the London Symphony Orchestra and produced by Tony Clarke, the album yielded a major hit with "Tuesday Afternoon" and included the classic "Nights in White Satin," a smash hit upon rerelease in 1972. It remained on the album charts for more than two years. For their next album, *In Search of the Lost Chord*, the Moody Blues made extensive use of the mellotron and played more than 30 different instruments to produce their characteristic lavish sound without an orchestra. The album contained the cosmic favorites "Legend of a Mind" and "Om" and produced a minor hit with the rocking "Ride My See-Saw."

Issued in 1969, *On the Threshold of a Dream* yielded the minor hit "Never Comes the Day" and remained on the charts for more than two years. That year the group formed Threshold Records, and the label's first album release, *To Our Children's Children's Children*, contained band favorites such as "Higher and Higher" and "I Never Thought I'd Live to Be a Hundred/Million." *A Question of Balance* yielded a major hit with "Question" in 1970, followed by "The Story in Your Eyes" from *Every Good Boy Deserves Favour*.

Their next album, *Seventh Sojourn*, produced two major hits, "Isn't Life Strange" and "I'm Just a Singer (In a Rock and Roll Band)," but after a worldwide tour in 1973 the members of the Moody Blues settled down to a variety of outside projects. The first and most successful of these, Justin Hayward and John Lodge's *Blue Jays*, yielded two minor hits with "I Dreamed Last Night" and "Blue Guitar." Other projects included solo albums by Thomas, Pinder, Hayward, and Lodge, and two albums by Edge with Adrian Gurvitz.

In July 1977 the five announced their intention to reunite for yet another album. Following the release of *Octave*, which produced minor hits with "Steppin' in a Slide Zone" and "Driftwood," the Moody Blues conducted a successful worldwide tour with Patrick Moraz, formerly of Yes, substituting for Michael Pinder. Moraz later joined the band on a permanent basis. The group was fully reestablished with 1981's *Long Distance Voyager* and its two major hits, "Gemini Dream" and "The Voice." In 1986 *The Other Side of Life*, featuring guitar synthesizers and electronic drums, yielded their first near-smash hit in years, "Your Wildest Dreams." The Moody Blues subsequently retired their Threshold label, conducted a world tour in 1986, and switched to Polydor for *Sur La Mer* and its moderate hit "I Know You're Out There Somewhere." Patrick Moraz left the Moody Blues in early 1992, and in 1994 the group toured America performing with local symphony orchestras. Polydor's five-CD set *Time Traveler* compiled studio recordings from *Days of Future Passed* through *Keys to the Kingdom*, as well as Justin Hayward and John Lodge's *Blue Jays*.

The Moody Blues

Number 1	London	428	'65	†
In the Beginning	Deram	18051	'71	†
Early Blues	Compleat	(2) 672008	'85	†
Days of Future Passed	Deram	18012	'68	†
	Threshold	820006		CS/CD
	Mobile Fidelity	512	'89	CD
In Search of the Lost Chord	Deram	18017	'68	†
	Threshold	820168		CS/CD
	Mobile Fidelity	576	'93	CD
On the Threshold of a Dream	Deram	18025	'69	†
	Threshold	820170		CS/CD
	Mobile Fidelity	612	'94	CD
	Mobile Fidelity	215	'95	LP
In Search of the Lost Chord	2-4-1 Series	810100		CS
To Our Children's Children's Children	Threshold	1	'70	†
	Threshold	820364		CS/CD
A Question of Balance	Threshold	3	'70	†
	Threshold	820211		CS/CD
A Question of Balance/To Our Children's Children's Children	2-4-1 Series	810101		CS
Every Good Boys Deserves Favour	Threshold	5	'71	†
	Threshold	820160		CS/CD
	Mobile Fidelity	643	'95	CD
Seventh Sojourn	Threshold	7	'72	†
	Threshold	820159		CS/CD
This Is the Moody Blues	Threshold	(2) 12/13	'74	†
	Threshold	820007		CS
	Threshold	(2) 820007		CD
Caught Live Plus Five	London	(2) 690/1	'77	†
	Threshold	820161		CS
Octave	London	708	'78	†
	Threshold	820329		CS/CD
Long Distance Voyager	Threshold	2901	'81	†
	Threshold	820105		CS/CD
The Present	Threshold	2902	'83	†
	Threshold	810119		CS/CD
Voices in the Sky (Best)	Threshold	820155	'85	LP/CS/CD†
The Magnificent Moodies	Threshold	820758		CD†
The Other Side of Life	Threshold	829179	'86	CS/CD
Greatest Hits (1967–1988)	Threshold	840659	'89	CS/CD
Prelude	Polydor	820517	'87	CD†
Sur la Mer	Polydor	835756	'88	CS/CD

Keys to the Kingdom	Polydor	849433	'91	CS/CD
A Night at Red Rock with the Colorado Symphony Orchestra	Polydor	517977	'93	CS/CD
Time Traveler	Polydor	(5) 516436	'94	CD
Graeme Edge Band with Adrian Gurvitz				
Kick Off Your Muddy Boots	Threshold	15	'75	†
Paradise Ballroom	London	686	'77	†
Ray Thomas				
From Mighty Oaks	Threshold	16	'75	†
Hopes, Wishes and Dreams	Threshold	17	'76	†
Michael Pinder				
The Promise	Threshold	18	'76	†
Justin Hayward and John Lodge				
Blue Jays	Threshold	15	'75	†
	London	820491	'87	CD
Justin Hayward				
Songwriter	Deram	18073	'77	†
	Deram	820492		CD†
Nightflight	Deram	4801	'80	†
	Polydor	820555	'90	CD
John Lodge				
Natural Avenue	London	683	'77	†
	London	820464	'87	CD†

VAN MORRISON

(b. George Ivan, Aug. 31, 1945, in Belfast, Ireland)

THEM. Van Morrison, voc, sax, har; **Billy Harrison**, gtr; **Jackie McAuley**, org; **Alan Henderson**, bs; **Ronnie Millings**, drm

First as lead singer of the Irish R&B band Them, then as a solo artist, Van Morrison has had a long and varied career performing his own blend of rock, blues, jazz, and folk. An eccentric figure on the rock scene, like Neil Young and Bob Dylan, Morrison has been able to continue to produce music—of varying quality—on his own terms, without selling out to commercial pressures.

Born into a musical family, Van Morrison picked up guitar and saxophone as a child and was singing in local bands at age 11. In 1960, at 15, he dropped out of school to pursue a career in music. He initially played and sang with Deanie Sands and the Javelins, and joined the R&B band the Monarchs in 1961 for engagements throughout Great Britain and Europe.

Around 1964 Van Morrison formed Them in Belfast, and the group soon secured a regular engagement at a local R&B club, attracting a considerable following. Signed to British Decca (Parrot in the United States), Them traveled to London to record, scoring their first major British and American hit with producer-songwriter Bert Berns's "Here Comes the Night" in spring 1965. The group's debut album also included their second hit, "Mystic Eyes," and Morrison's rock classic "Gloria," twice a minor hit, the second time backed with "Baby, Please Don't Go," which featured studio guitarist Jimmy Page playing lead. They next recorded *Them Again* and conducted their first and only tour of the United States. Upon returning to Britain in June 1966, Van Morrison quit the band. Them recruited a new lead vocalist, but then disbanded late in the year.

Invited to the United States by record producer Bert Berns, Van Morrison initially settled in Boston and began recording for Berns's Bang Records. In summer 1967 Morrison achieved his first major solo hit with his own "Brown-Eyed Girl," and by fall Bang had assembled *Blowin' Your Mind* from songs originally recorded as singles, much to Morrison's chagrin. Nonetheless, the album did contain two songs that served as precursors to his landmark album *Astral Weeks*, "T.B. Sheets" and "Who Drove the Red Sports Car." Berns died of a heart attack on December 31, 1967, and Morrison played East Coast clubs as a member of a trio for six months, until his recording contract was bought out by Warner Bros. Records.

Van Morrison's debut album for Warner Bros., *Astral Weeks*, recorded in 48 hours with a veteran jazz rhythm section, was issued before the end of 1968. Greeted by critical acclaim but poor sales, the album featured an impressionistic kind of lyricism that was at once evocative, intelligent, and undeniably compelling. Propelled by Morrison's unique vocal style and distinctive stream-of-consciousness lyrics, the album showcased his stirring "Cypress Avenue" and "Madame George" and contained "Ballerina" and "Slim Slo Slider." His next effort, *Moondance*, appeared more than a year later. Produced by Morrison, the album sported a diversity of mature original material. It yielded a moderate hit with "Come Running" and included the Morrison favorites "These Dreams of You," "Stoned Me," "Crazy Love," "Caravan," "Into the Mystic" (often regarded as one of the most finely crafted songs in rock history), and the title cut.

Established as an album artist, Van Morrison moved to Woodstock, New York, and quickly recorded *His Band and Street Choir*. The album produced two major hits, "Domino" and "Blue Money," and contained "I've Been Working," "Gypsy Queen," and "Call Me Up in Dreamland." In spring 1971 Morrison moved to northern California's Marin County; he dismissed his band and street choir, recording the countrified *Tupelo Honey* with guitarist Ronnie Montrose. Coproduced by Morrison, the album yielded the major hit "Wild Night" and included favorites such as "Old Woodstock," "I Wanna Roo You," and "Moonshine Whiskey."

Saint Dominic's Preview, ostensibly the first album over which Morrison exercised total artistic control, continued his best-selling ways while producing only two minor hits, "Jackie Wilson Said" and "Redwood Tree"; it included the stunning "Listen to the Lion." *Hard Nose the Highway* sold quite well without producing even a minor hit. Morrison then embarked on his first full-scale tour of Europe and America with the Caledonia Soul Orchestra, which resulted in the live double-record set *It's Too Late to Stop Now*.

However, in 1974 Van Morrison disbanded his group and recorded *Veedon Fleece* before "retiring" for nearly three years, including more than a year's exile in England. Eventually reemerging in 1977 with the appropriately titled *A Period of Transition*, recorded with Doctor John, Morrison took on rock impresario Bill Graham as his manager in 1978. He staged a dramatic comeback with *Wavelength*, thought to be his finest album in years, and conducted his first American tour in more than four years. The album produced his final albeit moderate hit with the title song. In 1979 Morrison recorded *Into the Music* and again toured. With 1980's *Common One*, Van Morrison began exploring new dimensions in his music as his songs began to become even more personal and esoteric.

Touring infrequently during the '80s, Van Morrison switched to Mercury Records for 1985's *A Sense of Wonder*. He returned to Ireland and later recorded the enchanting *Irish Heartbeat* album with the Chieftains, Ireland's top Celtic music group. The album featured eight traditional folk songs arranged by Morrison and Chieftains leader Paddy Moloney, plus new versions of the previously released "Irish Heartbeat" and "Celtic Ray." Moving to Polydor for 1991's *Hymns to the Silence*, one of the most engaging albums of his career, Morrison returned to his blues roots with 1993's *Too Long in Exile*. He later recorded *A Night in San Francisco* with John Lee Hooker, Junior Wells, and Georgie Fame, and *Days Like This* with his daughter Shana. Van Morrison again surprised critics and fans with his early-1996 release, a collection of jazz standards recorded at the famous London nightclub, Ronnie Scott's.

Them

Them	Parrot	71005	'65	†
	Deram	820563		CS/CD†
Them Again	Parrot	71008	'66	†
	Deram	820564	'90	CS/CD†
Them Featuring Van Morrison	Parrot	(2) 71053/4	'72	†
	Deram	810165		CS/CD
Now and Them	Tower	5104	'68	†
Time Out! Time In! For Them	Tower	5116	'68	†
Them	Happy Tiger	1004		†
Them in Reality	Happy Tiger	1012	'70	†
Backtracking	London	639	'74	†
Story of Them	London	50001	'77	†

Van Morrison

Blowin' Your Mind	Bang	218	'67	†
Best	Bang	222	'70	†
T.B. Sheets	Bang	400	'74	†
	Columbia	46093	'90	CS/CD
Bang Masters	Epic/Legacy	47041	'91	CS/CD
Astral Weeks	Warner Bros.	1768	'68	LP/CS/CD
Moondance	Warner Bros.	1835	'70	†
	Warner Bros.	3103	'84	CS/CD
His Band and Street Choir	Warner Bros.	1884	'70	CS/CD
Tupelo Honey	Warner Bros.	1950	'71/'88	CS/CD
Saint Dominic's Preview	Warner Bros.	2633	'72/'88	CS/CD
Hard Nose the Highway	Warner Bros.	2712	'73/'88	CS/CD
It's Too Late to Stop Now	Warner Bros.	(2) 2760	'74/'88	CS/CD
Veedon Fleece	Warner Bros.	2805	'74/'88	CS/CD
A Period of Transition	Warner Bros.	2987	'77/'88	CS/CD
Wavelength	Warner Bros.	3212	'78/'88	CS/CD
Into the Music	Warner Bros.	3390	'79	†
	Warner Bros.	26248	'90	CD
Common One	Warner Bros.	3462	'80	†
	Warner Bros.	26399	'91	CD
Beautiful Vision	Warner Bros.	3652	'82	CS/CD
Inarticulate Speech of the Heart	Warner Bros.	23802	'83	CS/CD
A Sense of Wonder	Mercury	822895	'85	CS/CD
Live at the Grand Opera House, Belfast	Mercury	818336	'85	CS/CD
No Guru, No Method, No Teacher	Mercury	830077	'86	CS/CD
Poetic Champions Compose	Mercury	832585	'87	CS/CD
Avalon Sunset	Mercury	839262	'89	CS/CD
Best	Mercury	841970	'90	CS/CD
Enlightenment	Mercury	847100	'90	CS/CD
Hymns to the Silence	Polydor	849026	'91	CS/CD
	Polydor	(2) 511546	'91	CD
Best, Volume 2	Polydor	517760	'93	CS/CD
Too Long in Exile	Polydor	519219	'93	LP/CS/CD
A Night in San Francisco (recorded live, December 1993)	Polydor	(2) 521290	'94	CD

Days Like This	Polydor	7307	'95	CS/CD
Van Morrison and Georgie Fame and Friends				
How Long Has This Been Going On?	Verve	529136	'96	CD
Van Morrison and the Chieftains				
Irish Heartbeat	Mercury	834496	'88	CS/CD

MOTT THE HOOPLE

Ian Hunter (b. June 3, 1946, Shrewsbury, England), lead voc, pno, gtr; **Mick Ralphs** (b. May 31, 1944, Hereford, England), gtr, voc; **Verden Allen** (b. May 26, 1944, Hereford, England), org; **Pete "Overend" Watts** (b. May 13, 1947, Birmingham, England), bs, voc; **Dale "Buffin" Griffin** (b. Oct. 24, 1948, Ross-on-Wye, England), drm, voc [Verden Allen and Mick Ralphs left in 1973. Guitarist **Luther "James" Grosvenor** (aka Ariel Bender, b. Dec. 12, 1949, Evesham, England) was added, but left in 1974, to be replaced by **Mick Ronson** (b. ca. 1946, Hull, Yorkshire, England; d. Apr. 30, 1993, London, England).]

MOTT THE HOOPLE

Seminal British rock band of the early-'70s, Mott the Hoople featured the songwriting and singing of Ian Hunter and the guitar playing of Mick Ralphs, who later formed the enormously popular Bad Company. One of the pioneering glitter-rock groups, they enjoyed their greatest success in the early '70s before internal pressures led the group to dissolve.

In the mid-'60s Pete "Overend" Watts and Dale "Buffin" Griffin formed the group Silence in their native Herefordshire, later adding Mick Ralphs and Verden Allen. Recruiting vocalist Ian Hunter in London in 1969, the group changed their name to Mott the Hoople in June at the suggestion of manager Guy Stevens, who secured them a recording contract with Island Records (Atlantic in the United States). With Ian Hunter serving as principal songwriter as well as the visual and aural focus of the group, Mott the Hoople recorded their debut album in late 1969, but it barely made the U.S. charts upon release. *Mad Shadows* showcased Hunter's rather forceful approach on a collection of gloomy songs, whereas *Wildlife* featured Ralphs's lighter style. However, neither of these albums, nor *Brain Capers*, which included "Sweet Angeline," registered much impact.

Disbanding briefly in March 1972, Mott the Hoople re-formed later that year with the encouragement of glitter-rock star David Bowie, who produced the band's debut album for Columbia and wrote the group's only major American hit, "All the Young Dudes." With Hunter assuming leadership of the group, Verden Allen quit in January 1973, followed in July by Mick Ralphs, who subsequently joined the highly successful group Bad Company.

Adding former Spooky Tooth guitarist Luther Grosvenor (using the name Ariel Bender), Mott the Hoople conducted a headlining glitter-rock tour of the United States in August 1973. Their album *Mott* was well received critically, at least in the United States, and yielded major British hits with "Honaloochie Boogie" and "All the Way from Memphis"; it also contained "Ballad of Mott the Hoople." *The Hoople* included the group's final, albeit minor, American hit, "The Golden Age of Rock 'n' Roll," as well as "Roll Away the Stone."

In August 1974 Luther Grosvenor left Mott the Hoople, to be replaced by guitarist Mick Ronson. Ronson had produced and played on albums for David Bowie and had been instrumental in forming his Spiders from Mars band, providing the major musical force behind Bowie's *The Man Who Sold the World*, *Hunky Dory*, *Ziggy Stardust*, *Aladdin Sane*, and *Pin Ups* albums. He also had coproduced and played on Lou Reed's "Walk on the Wild Side" single. His tenure with Mott the Hoople, however, was brief. In December both Ronson and Hunter left amid unbecoming rumors and public recriminations. The group reassembled as simply Mott, with Watts, Griffin, and others for two albums before disbanding in November 1976. With vocalist John Fiddler, the remaining members reemerged as British Lions in 1977.

Ian Hunter subsequently moved to New York and began working with Mick Ronson, recording *Ian Hunter* with him and touring as the Hunter-Ronson Show in 1975. The two later separated; Ronson joined Bob Dylan's late-1975 Rolling Thunder Revue, and Hunter recorded *All-American Alien Boy*. In 1976 Hunter produced Roger McGuinn's acclaimed album *Cardiff Rose*, and had his own, minor hit, "Just Another Night," in 1979. Hunter and Ronson reunited for 1989's album *Y U I Orta*. Ronson also produced Morrisey's 1992 album *Your Arsenal*, but on April 30, 1993, he died in London from cancer at age 46. Released posthumously, Ronson's *Heaven 'n Hull* was recorded with Chrissie Hynde, David Bowie, John Mellencamp, and Queen.

Mott the Hoople

Mott the Hoople	Atlantic	8258	'70	CD
Mad Shadows	Atlantic	8272	'70	CD
Wildlife	Atlantic	8284	'71	CD
Brain Capers	Atlantic	8304	'72	CD
Rock and Roll Queen	Atlantic	7297	'74	CD
All the Young Dudes	Columbia	31750	'72	CS/CD
Mott	Columbia	32425	'73	CD
The Hoople	Columbia	32871	'74/'90	CD
Live	Columbia	33282	'74/'89	CD
Greatest Hits	Columbia	34368	'76	CS/CD
The Ballad of Mott: A Retrospective	Columbia/Legacy (2)	46973	'93	CS/CD
Backsliding Fearlessly: The Early Years	Rhino	71639	'94	CD

Mott

Drive On	Columbia	33705	'75	†
Shouting and Pointing	Columbia	34236	'76	†

Mick Ronson

Slaughter on Tenth Avenue	RCA	0353	'74	†
Play, Don't Worry	RCA	0681	'75	†
Heaven 'n Hull	Epic	53796	'94	CS/CD

Ian Hunter

Ian Hunter	Columbia	33480	'75/'90	CD
All-American Alien Boy	Columbia	34142	'76/'90	CD†
Overnight Angels	Columbia	34721	'77	†

Shades of Ian Hunter: The Ballad of Ian Hunter and Mott the Hoople	Columbia	(2) 36251	'79	†
All of the Good Ones Are Taken	Columbia	38628	'83	†
You're Never Alone with a Schizophrenic	Chrysalis	1214	'79	†
Live: Welcome to the Club	Chrysalis	(2) 1269	'80	†
Short Back 'n' Sides	Chrysalis	1326	'81	†
Shades of Ian Hunter	Chrysalis	21670	'88	CS/CD

Ian Hunter and Mick Ronson

Y U I Orta	Mercury	838973	'89	CS/CD

N

RICK NELSON

(b. Eric Hilliard Nelson, May 8, 1940, Teaneck, NJ; d. Dec. 31, 1985, near De Kalb, TX)

One of the most popular rock-and-roll artists of the late '50s and early '60s, Rick Nelson was the first artist to benefit from regular television exposure of his songs—on his parents' *The Adventures of Ozzie and Harriet*, one of the longest-running comedies in TV history. Much like the Everly Brothers, he helped make rock and roll both more palatable and popular by effectively combining gentle ballads, a lively rockabilly sound, and pop-style material that appealed to parents as well as their teenage children. Giving early exposure to the songs of Gene Pitney and the Burnette Brothers, Nelson was accompanied on his early recordings by James Burton, one of the most exciting guitarists of the era. Although his style lacked the urgency of Elvis Presley or Little Richard, his recordings showed far more emotional depth than teen idols such as Fabian and Frankie Avalon, with which he was mistakenly lumped. Overwhelmed by the British Invasion of the '60s, Rick Nelson began exploring country music in the late '60s and became one of the pioneers of country-rock with his Stone Canyon Band. Refusing to become an oldies act, as evidenced by his 1972 smash "Garden Party," he was among the first artists to record the works of Tim Hardin, Eric Andersen, and Randy Newman. Touring arduously during the '70s and '80s, Rick Nelson returned to his rockabilly sound around 1984, only to die in an airplane mishap at the end of 1985.

Born into a show-business family, Eric "Ricky" Nelson joined the cast of his parents' *Adventures of Ozzie and Harriet* radio show in March 1949 at the age of eight. The show moved to television in 1952, where it ran for a remarkable 14 years. Having studied clarinet and taken up drums, Ricky later learned guitar, and began singing in 1956. Signed to Verve Records that year, Ricky scored a smash pop and R&B hit with his first release, a version of Fats Domino's "I'm Walking" (fronted by "A Teenager's Romance"), after performing the song at the end of the television show on April 10, 1957.

Soon signing a five-year contract with Imperial Records, Ricky Nelson released the gently rocking smash pop and R&B hit "Be Bop Baby" in October 1957, soon followed by the pop, R&B, and country-and-western smash "Stood Up," backed by Johnny and Dorsey Burnette's "Waitin' in School." Accompanied by bassist Joe Osborne, and James Burton, one of the most exciting and dynamic guitar players of the time, Nelson scored three-way crossover smash hits with the Burnette Brothers' "Believe What You Say" backed by Hank Williams's "My Bucket's Got a Hole in It," and "Poor Little Fool" (written by Eddie Cochran's girlfriend Sharon Sheeley). In 1958 Nelson costarred in the classic western movie *Rio Bravo* with John Wayne and Dean Martin. His subsequent near-smash pop hits include "Lonesome Town"/"I Got a Feeling," "Never Be Anyone Else but You" backed by

Dorsey Burnette's "It's Late," and the Burnettes' "Just a Little Too Much" backed by "Sweeter Than You." Major hits in 1960 include "I Wanna Be Loved," "Young Emotions," "I'm Not Afraid," and "You Are the Only One."

Following the top hit "Travelin' Man," backed by the near-smash "Hello Mary Lou" (written by Gene Pitney), Ricky Nelson foreshortened his first name to Rick. The hits continued into 1963 with "A Wonder Like You"/"Everlovin'," the smash "Young World," the autobiographical "Teen Age Idol," and "It's Up to You." In 1963 he switched to Decca Records, where his hits include "String Along" and the standards "Fools Rush In," "For You," and "The Very Thought of You."

Overwhelmed by the myriad British acts that dominated rock music beginning in 1964, Rick Nelson began exploring country music with 1966's *Bright Lights and Country Music*, scoring a minor country hit with "Take a City Bride" in 1967. Recording the songs of contemporary songwriters, his *In Concert* album included Bob Dylan's "I Shall Be Released" and "If You Gotta Go, Go Now," and Eric Andersen's "Violets of Dawn," and yielded a moderate pop hit with Dylan's "She Belongs to Me." Additionally, he recorded an entire album of his own songs, *Rick Sings Nelson*.

In 1969 Rick Nelson formed the Stone Canyon Band with bassist Randy Meisner (later a founding member of the Eagles and Poco) and pedal steel guitarist Tom Brumley. Although the band suffered frequent personnel changes (Brumley remained until the late '70s), the group endured into the '80s to provide excellent accompaniment for Nelson's country-rock sound. They recorded the smash 1972 hit "Garden Party," which related Nelson's feelings after being booed for performing contemporary material at an oldies show. His subsequent recordings didn't do very well, and he was dropped by Decca/MCA by the mid-'70s.

Touring up to 200 days a year, Nelson conducted recording sessions in Memphis in 1979 and joined Capitol for 1981's *Playing to Win*. Around 1984 he returned to his rockabilly style, touring with James Burton, but on December 31, 1985, he was killed along with six others, including guitarist Bobby Neal, when his plane crashed near De Kalb, Texas. Two years after his death, Rick Nelson was inducted into the Rock and Roll Hall of Fame.

Several of Rick Nelson's children pursued show-business careers. His daughter, Tracy, became an actress and appeared in the television series *The Father Dowling Mysteries*. His twin sons Gunnar and Matthew (born Sept. 20, 1967) began performing in Los Angeles clubs in the mid-'80s, forming their self-named group with Matthew on bass and Gunnar on guitar and both sharing vocal chores, along with Brett Garsed on lead guitar, Joey Cathcart on rhythm, keyboardist Paul Mirkovich, and Bobby Rock on drums. Their best-selling debut album, *After the Rain*, yielded four hits, including the top "(Can't Live Without Your) Love and Affection" along with the smash-hit title song. Their 1995 album, *Because They Can*, fared less well on the charts.

Ricky Nelson

Ricky	Imperial	9048	'57	†
	Imperial	12392		†
Ricky Nelson	Imperial	9050	'58	†
	Imperial	12393		†
(reissued as) Ricky	United Artists	1004	'80	†
Ricky Sings Again	Imperial	9061	'59	†
	Imperial	12090		†
	Liberty	10134	'81	†
Songs by Ricky	Imperial	12030	'59	†
More Songs by Ricky	Imperial	12059	'60	†

Rick Nelson

Rick Is 21	Imperial	12071	'61	†

Album 7 by Rick	Imperial	12082	'62	†
For Your Sweet Love	Decca	74419	'63	†
Rick Nelson Sings "For You"	Decca	74479	'63	†
	MCA	31363	'90	CD
The Very Thought of You	Decca	74559	'64	†
Spotlight on Rick	Decca	74608	'64	†
Best Always	Decca	74660	'65	†
Love and Kisses	Decca	74678	'65	†
Bright Lights and Country Music	Decca	74779	'66	†
Country Fever	Decca	74837	'67	†
Another Side of Rick	Decca	74944	'67	†
Perspective	Decca	75014	'68	†
In Concert	Decca	75162	'70	†
	MCA	3	'73	†
(reissued as) In Concert: The Troubadour, 1969	MCA	25983	'87	CS/CD
Rick Sings Nelson	Decca	75236	'70	†
	MCA	20		†
Rudy the Fifth	Decca	75297	'71	†
	MCA	37		†
Garden Party	Decca	75391	'72	†
	MCA	62		†
	MCA	31364	'90	CD
Windfall	MCA	383	'74	†
Intakes	Epic	34420	'77	†
Playing to Win	Capitol	12109	'81	†
Live, 1983–1985	Rhino	71114	'89	CS/CD
All My Best (rerecordings)	Silver Eagle	6163	'88	LP/CS/CD†
Anthologies				
Best Sellers	Imperial	9218	'63	†
	Imperial	12218		†
It's Up to You	Imperial	9223	'63	†
	Imperial	12223		†
Million Sellers by Rick Nelson	Imperial	9232	'63	†
	Imperial	12232		†
A Long Vacation	Imperial	9244	'63	†
	Imperial	12244		†
Rick Nelson Sings for You	Imperial	9251	'64	†
	Imperial	12251		†
Rick Nelson	Sunset	5118	'66	†
I Need You	Sunset	5205	'69	†
Legendary Masters	United Artists	(2) 9960	'72	†
	Liberty	9960		†
	EMI	92771	'90	CS/CD
Very Best	United Artists	330	'75	†
Ricky Nelson Sings Again	Liberty	10134		†
Souvenirs	Liberty	10205		†
Teenage Idol	Liberty	10253		
Rick Nelson Country	MCA	(2) 4004	'73	†
The Decca Years	MCA	1517	'82	†
Best (1963–1975)	MCA	10098	'90	CS/CD

Rockin' with Ricky	Ace	85		†
Greatest Hits	Rhino	215	'85	†
	Rhino	70215		CS
Best	EMI America	46588	'87	CS/CD†
Best, Volume 2	EMI	95219	'91	CS/CD
Greatest Hits	Curb/CEMA	77372	'90	CS/CD
Best	Curb/CEMA	77484	'91	CS/CD
Nelson				
After the Rain	DGC	24290	'90	CS/CD
Because They Can	DGC	24525	'95	

WILLIE NELSON

(b. William Hugh Nelson, Apr. 30, 1933, Abbott, TX)

Willie Nelson began his career as a prolific songwriter. His early hits included "Crazy" cut by Patsy Cline and Faron Young's "Hello Walls," both released in 1961. After a frustrating period trying to establish himself as a performer in Nashville, Nelson returned to his native Texas in the early '70s, where he spearheaded the growing "outlaw" country movement, in protest to the highly commercial Nashville sound. With *Phases and Stages* and *Red Headed Stranger*, Nelson pioneered the country-rock concept album, and with *Stardust* he proved himself an able interpreter of pop standards. By the late '70s he was established as a superstar performer both on stage and in films. Although his career was slowed by problems with the IRS in the late '80s, Nelson has continued to record and perform, both as a solo artist and with fellow Nashvillians Johnny Cash, Waylon Jennings, and Kris Kristofferson as the Highwaymen.

Willie Nelson was abandoned by his parents at age six and raised by his grandparents. He took up guitar and began writing poems and songs as a child. Debuting professionally with a polka band at age 10, Nelson formed his own group at 13. He served in the Air Force during the Korean War and later worked as a disc jockey in Waco, San Antonio, and Houston, Texas, where he performed regularly at the Esquire Club. A prolific songwriter, Nelson wrote the classic "Night Life" in 1959, but he sold it in 1961 for $150. In 1960 he moved to Nashville and began frequenting Tootsie's Orchid Lounge. "Discovered" by country artist Hank Cochran, he joined Pamper Music as a songwriter and was hired as touring bassist by Pamper co-owner and established country artist Ray Price. Nelson's first success as a songwriter came in early 1960 with "Wake Me When It's Over," a minor pop hit for Andy Williams, and "Family Bible," Claude Gray's first country hit.

During 1961 a number of Willie Nelson's songs became major pop hits, including "Hello Walls" by Faron Young and "Crazy" by Patsy Cline (both smash country hits), and "Funny How Time Slips Away" by Jimmy Elledge. Signed to Liberty Records in 1962 on the strength of his songwriting, Nelson scored a near-smash country hit that year with "Touch Me." Two other modest hits followed, and in late 1963 Ray Price and Rusty Draper achieved a moderate country hit and a minor pop hit, respectively, with Nelson's "Night Life," and Roy Orbison hit in the pop field with his "Pretty Paper." Switching to RCA Records in 1965, Nelson had a number of moderate country hits during the '60s, including "The Party's Over," "Little Things," "Bring Me Sunshine," and "Once More with Feeling." In 1967, at no small personal and professional risk, he introduced black country singer Charley Pride on his tours of honky-tonks.

Nashville's '60s "countrypolitan" sound, replete with strings, horns, and vocal choruses, subjugated artists to depersonalized, formulaic music. Unhappy in the recording studio,

Willie Nelson retreated to Austin, Texas, after his Nashville home burned down in late 1969. There he wrote the material for his last Nashville album, *Yesterday's Wine*. The album yielded only a minor country hit with "Yesterday's Wine"/"Me and Paul," the latter song concerned with the travails of Nelson and his longtime drummer, Paul English. In 1972 Nelson permanently moved to Austin and initiated his celebrated Fourth of July picnics that drew tens of thousands of fans and essentially launched the so-called outlaw (or progressive country) music. Acts such as Waylon Jennings, Kris Kristofferson, and Leon Russell performed to a curiously diverse audience of rednecks and hippies.

Willie Nelson switched to Atlantic Records, where he recorded *Shotgun Willie* and *Phases and Stages*, sometimes considered his finest albums, under veteran producer Jerry Wexler. Subsequently moving to Columbia Records, Nelson was allowed to produce and arrange his own albums, beginning with his Columbia debut, *Red Headed Stranger*. The album sold more than two million copies and remained on the album charts for nearly a year. It yielded a major pop hit with "Blue Eyes Crying in the Rain," which led to a succession of crossover hits by other country artists and encouraged rising interest in country music. The RCA Records 1976 anthology set *The Outlaws* provided this developing, more personalized, and less artificial style with its label and also sold more than two million copies. Containing songs performed by Nelson, Waylon Jennings, his wife Jessi Colter, and Tompall Glaser, the album included Nelson's "Me and Paul" and "Yesterday's Wine," and the Nelson-Jennings duet on the pair's "Good Hearted Woman," a major pop hit as well as a top country hit.

Nelson's *The Sound in Your Mind* album showcased the harmonica playing of Mickey Raphael and contained a medley of "Funny How Time Slips Away"/"Crazy"/"Night Life"; Steve Fromholtz's touching "I'd Have to Be Crazy"; and the top country hit "If You've Got the Money, I've Got the Time," written by '50s country artist Lefty Frizzell. *To Lefty from Willie* contained Nelson's recordings of other songs by Frizzell. Having scored a major pop and top country hit in collaboration with Waylon Jennings on "Luckenbach, Texas (Back to the Basics of Love)" in 1977, Nelson recorded a duo album with Jennings that yielded a moderate pop and top country hit with "Mamas Don't Let Your Babies Grow Up to Be Cowboys" in 1978.

Willie Nelson next recorded *Stardust* under producer Booker T. Jones (of Booker T and the MGs fame), and the album broke country music conventions by containing only Tin Pan Alley standards, of which "Georgia on My Mind," "Blues Skies," and "All of Me" became smash country hits. After the live double-record set *Willie and Family Live*, Nelson recorded *One for the Road* with old friend Leon Russell, and the album yielded a top country hit with "Heartbreak Hotel." Nelson subsequently recorded an entire album of Kristofferson songs, and the Christmas album *Pretty Paper* before launching his acting career in 1978's *The Electric Horseman* with Robert Redford and Jane Fonda. His soundtrack album produced a top country and moderate pop hit with "My Heroes Have Always Been Cowboys." In 1980 he recorded an album with old boss Ray Price (which provided a smash country hit with Bob Wills's "Faded Love") and starred in the movie *Honeysuckle Rose*, opposite Dyan Cannon, as a traveling Texas country musician not unlike himself. The soundtrack album included four new songs and produced two top country hits with "On the Road Again" (a major pop hit) and "Angel Flying Too Close to the Ground."

In 1982 *Always on My Mind* became one of Willie Nelson's best-selling albums ever, staying on the album charts for nearly two years. The album yielded three country smashes with the title tune (a pop smash), "Let It Be Me," and "Last Thing I Needed First Thing This Morning." He also scored a top country hit with Waylon Jennings on "Just to Satisfy You," costarred with Gary Busey in the overlooked Western movie *Barbarosa*, and recorded another album with Waylon Jennings, *WW II*. The year 1983 brought his solo album, *Take It to the Limit*, and *Pancho and Lefty*, recorded with Merle Haggard; the latter produced a smash country hit with Haggard's "Reasons to Quit" and a top country hit with Townes Van Zandt's title song, and it stayed on the album charts for a year.

In 1984 Willie Nelson recorded *City of New Orleans*, which yielded a top country hit with Steve Goodman's title song, and costarred with Kris Kristofferson in *Songwriter*, one of the most clever and intelligent movies about the country-music business since *Nashville*. Nelson and others, including Neil Young, organized the first Farm Aid benefit in 1985, raising around $9 million for various farm and service organizations while bringing attention to the plight of the American family farmer. That year he joined Kristofferson, Waylon Jennings, and Johnny Cash for a tour and album as the Highwaymen, achieving a top country hit with Jimmy Webb's title song. Nelson later released *Half Nelson*, which featured his duets with a variety of artists, including Julio Iglesias ("To All The Girls I've Loved Before") and Ray Charles ("Seven Spanish Angels"). After scoring a top country hit with "Living in the Promiseland" and costarring with Kristofferson, Jennings, and Cash in the CBS-TV remake of the classic Western *Stagecoach* in 1986, Nelson produced and starred in the movie *Red Headed Stranger*, based on his 1975 album, but the film suffered from limited distribution.

Nelson continued to record in the late '80s, scoring a top country hit with "Nothing I Can Do About It Now" and a near-smash country hit with "There You Are" in 1989. In 1990 he reunited with Kristofferson, Jennings, and Cash as the Highwaymen for another album and round of touring. Embroiled in tax disputes with the Internal Revenue Service for a decade, Nelson saw his properties seized by the government agency in late 1990 and subsequently auctioned off. Longtime friend Darrell Royal, former football coach at the University of Texas, purchased his Pedernales Recording studio, country club, and golf course. In 1991 Nelson made the ironically titled *Who'll Buy My Memories? (The IRS Tapes)*, with just his voice and guitar performing his most famous songs, available through an 800 telephone number, with 75 percent of the net earnings going toward paying off his tax liability. He celebrated his 60th birthday with a TV special and a new album, *Across the Borderline*, cut with pop producer Don Was; the album featured the minor hit, Paul Simon's "An American Song." After the expiration of his Columbia contract, he released *Moonlight Becomes You* on the Houston-based independent label Justice. Finally, in August 1994 Nelson's debt to the IRS was paid off. Willie Nelson recorded *Healing Hands of Time* for Liberty and reunited with the other Highwaymen for *The Road Goes On Forever*, featuring Robert Earl Keen's title song.

Early Willie Nelson

And Then I Wrote	Liberty	7239		†
	Liberty	32464	'95	CS/CD
Here's Willie Nelson	Liberty	7308		†
Country Willie	United Artists	410	'76	†
	United Artists	10013		†
	Liberty	10013		†
	EMI-Manhattan	48399	'88	CD†
Best	United Artists	086	'76	†
	United Artists	10118		†
	Liberty	10118		†
	EMI	48398	'88	CS/CD
	EMI-Manhattan	48398		CD†
The Best of Willie Nelson	Liberty	48398	'94	CS/CD
The Early Years: The Complete Liberty Recordings Plus More	Liberty	(2) 28077	'94	CD
His Own Songs	RCA	3418	'65	†
Country Favorites	RCA	3528	'66	†
Country Music Concert	RCA	3659	'66	†
Make Way	RCA	3748	'67	†

Title	Label	Number	Year	Format
The Party's Over	RCA	3858	'67	†
Texas in My Soul	RCA	3937	'68	†
Good Times	RCA	4057	'68	†
My Own Peculiar Way	RCA	4111	'69	†
Both Sides Now	RCA	4294	'70	†
Laying My Burdens Down	RCA	4404	'70	†
Willie Nelson and Family	RCA	4489	'71	†
Yesterday's Wine	RCA	4568	'71	†
	RCA	1102	'75	†
	RCA	3800		
The Words Don't Fit the Picture	RCA	4653	'72	†
The Willie Way	RCA	4760	'72	†
What Can You Do to Me Now	RCA	1234	'75	†
	RCA	3958		†
Live (I Gotta Get Drunk)	RCA	1487	'76	†
Before His Time	RCA	2210	'77	†
	RCA	3671	'80	†
	RCA	4165	'81	†
Sweet Memories	RCA	3243	'79	†
	RCA	55975		CS/CD
Minstrel Man	RCA	4045	'81	†
Best	RCA	4420	'82	†
	RCA	5143	'84	†
	RCA	6335		CS
My Own Way	RCA	4819	'83	†
	RCA	5438		†
Don't You Ever Get Tired of Hurting Me	RCA	5174	'84	†
Collector's Series	RCA	5470	'85	†
Willie	RCA	5988	'86	CS/CD
All-Time Greatest Hits, Volume 1	RCA	8556	'89	CS/CD
Compilation	RCA	9549		†
The Best of Willie Nelson	RCA	56335	'92	CD
The Best of Willie	RCA-Nashville	66406	'94	CD
The Essential Series: Willie Nelson	RCA	66590	'95	CS/CD
Columbus Stockade Blues	RCA-Camden	2444	'70	CS
Country Winners	Camden	0326	'73	†
Spotlight	Camden	0705	'74	†
Nite Life (Early Hits and Rare Tracks)	Rhino	70987	'90	CS/CD
A Classic and Unreleased Collection	Rhino	(3) 71462	'95	CS/CD
The Early Years	Scotti Brothers	75437	'94	CS/CD

Willie Nelson, Waylon Jennings, Jessi Colter, and Tompall Glaser

Title	Label	Number	Year	Format
The Outlaws	RCA	1321	'76	†
	RCA	5076		CS/CD

Willie Nelson

Title	Label	Number	Year	Format
Shotgun Willie	Atlantic	7262	'73	CS/CD
The Troublemaker	Atlantic	7275	'74	†
Phases and Stages	Atlantic	7291	'74	†
	Atlantic	82192	'91	CS/CD
Phases and Stages/Shotgun Willie	Mobile Fidelity	581	'93	CD
Red Headed Stranger	Columbia	33482	'75	CS/CD

The Sound in Your Mind	Columbia	34092	'76	CS/CD
Red Headed Stranger/The Sound in Your Mind	Columbia	38217		CS
The Troublemaker	Columbia	34112	'76	CS
To Lefty from Willie	Columbia	34695	'77	CS/CD
Stardust	Columbia	35305	'78	CS/CD
Willie and Family Live	Columbia	(2) 35642	'78/'87	CD
	Columbia	35642		CS
Sings Kristofferson	Columbia	36188	'79	CS/CD
Pretty Paper	Columbia	36189	'79	LP/CS/CD
The Electric Horseman (soundtrack)	Columbia	36327	'80/'87	CS
Honeysuckle Rose (soundtrack)	Columbia	36752	'80	CD
Somewhere Over the Rainbow	Columbia	36883	'81	CS/CD
Always On My Mind	Columbia	37951	'82	CS/CD
Tougher than Leather	Columbia	38248	'83	CS/CD
Without a Song	Columbia	39110	'83	CD
City of New Orleans	Columbia	39145	'84	CS/CD
Half Nelson	Columbia	39990	'85	CS/CD
Partners	Columbia	39894	'86	CS/CD
Me and Paul	Columbia	40008		CS
The Promiseland	Columbia	40327	'86	CS/CD†
Island in the Sea	Columbia	40487	'87	CS
What a Wonderful World	Columbia	44331	'88	CS/CD
A Horse Called Music	Columbia	45046	'89	CS/CD
Born for Trouble	Columbia	45492	'90	CS/CD
Who'll Buy My Memories?	Sony	(2) 52981	'92	CD
Across the Borderline	Columbia	52752	'93	
Moonlight Becomes You	Justice	1601	'94	CS/CD
Healing Hands of Time	Liberty	30420	'94	CS/CD

Anthologies

Hello Walls	Sunset	5138	'66	†
	Pickwick	3504	'78	†
There'll Be No Teardrops	United Artists	930	'78	†
Face of a Fighter	Lone Star	4602	'78	†
Greatest Hits (and Some That Will Be)	Columbia	37542	'81	CS/CD
Willie Nelson	Columbia	38250	'83	†
Super Hits	Columbia	64184	'94	CS/CD
Revolutions of Time . . .	Columbia/Legacy	(3) 64796	'95	CS/CD
Super Hits, Volume 2	Columbia-Nashville	67295	'95	CS/CD
Country Winners	Pair	(2) 1007	'86	†
Once More with Feeling	Pair	(2) 1032	'86	†
Good Hearted Woman	Pair	(2) 1114	'86	†
The Legend Begins	Pair	1333	'94	CS/CD
The Legend Begins/Wild and Willie	Allegiance	72822	'87	CD†
Greatest Songs	Curb/CEMA	77366	'90	CS/CD
Super Hits	CSI	40022	'91	CD
Broken Promises	Intermedia	5048		LP/CS
Sings 28 Great Songs	Hollywood/IMG	405		CS/CD

Willie Nelson and Others

Willie Nelson and Friends	Plantation	24	'76	†

Waylon Jennings and Willie Nelson

Waylon and Willie	RCA	2686	'78	†
	RCA	5134	'84	†
	RCA	8401		CS
	RCA	58401	'95	CD
WW II	RCA	4455	'82	†
	RCA	5138	'84	†
	RCA	56329		CS/CD
Take It to the Limit	Columbia	38562	'83/'87	CD
Clean Shirt	Epic	47462	'91	CS/CD

Willie Nelson and Leon Russell

One for the Road	Columbia	(2) 36064	'79	†
	Columbia	36064		CS/CD

Willie Nelson and Danny Davis

With the Nashville Brass	RCA	3549	'80	†
	RCA	4301	'82	†

Willie Nelson and Ray Price

San Antonio Rose	Columbia	36476	'80	CS/CD

Willie Nelson and Roger Miller

Old Friends	Columbia	38013	'82	†

Willie Nelson and Webb Pierce

In the Jailhouse Now	Columbia	38095	'82	†

Willie Nelson, Kris Kristofferson, Dolly Parton, and Brenda Lee

The Winning Hand	Monument	(2) 38389	'83	†
	Sony	75067	'95	CS/CD

Willie Nelson and Merle Haggard

Pancho and Lefty	Epic	37958	'83	CD
Seashores of Old Mexico	Epic	40293	'87	CS/CD
Gospel's Best	MCA	20478	'94	CS/CD
The Best Of Gospel	MCA	20560	'94	CS/CD

Willie Nelson and Johnny Lee

Willie Nelson and Johnny Lee	Intermedia	5005	'83	LP/CD

Willie Nelson and Jackie King

Angel Eyes	Columbia	39363	'84	†

Willie Nelson and Billy Walker

Charlie's Shoes	DEC	02	'84	LP/CS

Willie Nelson and Faron Young

Funny How Time Slips Away	Columbia	39484		†

Willie Nelson and Kris Kristofferson

Music from *Songwriter*	Columbia	39531	'84	CS

Willie Nelson and Hank Snow

Brand on My Heart	Columbia	39977		†

The Highwaymen

Highwayman	Columbia	40056	'85	CS/CD
Highwayman 2	Columbia	45240	'90	CS/CD
The Road Goes on Forever	Liberty	28091	'95	CS/CD

Willie Nelson and Bobbie Nelson

Old Time Religion   LaserLight   12114   '92   CD

THE NEVILLE BROTHERS

Art Neville (b. Dec. 17, 1937, New Orleans, LA), kybd, voc; **Aaron Neville** (b. Jan. 24, 1941, New Orleans, LA), voc, perc; **Charles Neville** (b. Dec. 28, 1938, New Orleans, LA), sax, voc; **Cyril Neville** (b. Jan. 10, 1948, New Orleans, LA), perc, voc [Aaron's son **Ivan Neville** joined in 1979 for two years.]

THE METERS. Art Neville, kybd; **Leo Nocentelli** (b. June 15, 1946), gtr, voc; **George Porter**, bs; **Joe "Zigaboo" Modeliste** (b. Dec. 28, 1948), drm [**Cyril Neville** joined in 1975.]

The Neville brothers have been prime musical forces in the New Orleans community for more than 30 years. In the '60s and '70s Art Neville led the Meters, an influential band who appeared on many New Orleans recordings made at Allen Toussaint's famous studios. Meanwhile, brother Aaron had a major R&B hit with "Tell It Like It Is." Art and Aaron joined with brothers Charles and Cyril to form a family band in the late '70s. The band achieved critical acclaim, if limited commercial success. Meanwhile, Aaron Neville was befriended by pop star Linda Ronstadt, who recorded a successful duet ("Don't Know Much") with the singer in 1989 and helped launch his new solo career in the early '90s.

In the early '50s keyboardist Art Neville joined the New Orleans group the Hawketts. In 1955 they scored a local hit with "Mardi Gras Mambo" and the song became the theme to the city's annual celebration. By that time his saxophonist brother Charles had been touring with jazz artists Tiny Grimes and George Coleman and blues artists Bobby "Blue" Bland and B. B. King. Through arranger-producer Harold Battiste, Art was signed to Specialty Records in 1956, and he and his brother Aaron worked with Larry Williams and played on package tours with the Spaniels and Screamin' Jay Hawkins. When Art was drafted into the Army in 1958, Aaron took his place in the Hawketts. Upon Art's return, Aaron launched a solo career, soon managing an R&B hit in 1960 with "Over You." At the end of 1966 Aaron Neville scored a top R&B and smash pop hit with "Tell It Like It Is" on Parlo Records. Also in that year, Aaron joined with Art and brother Charles, along with saxophonist Gary Brown and future Meters guitarist Leo Nocentelli, bassist George Porter, and drummer Joseph "Zigaboo" Modeliste, to form the Neville Sounds.

Producer Allen Toussaint hired the entire band, minus vocalists Art and Charles and Brown, to be the house band for his studio. They backed virtually every New Orleans hit of the late '60s, including Ernie K-Doe's "Mother-in-Law," Betty Harris's "Cry to Me," and later Lee Dorsey's "Ride Your Pony," "Get Out My Life, Woman," and "Working in a Coal Mine." The Meters signed with Josie Records and recorded a number of instrumental albums, scoring smash R&B and major-to-moderate pop hits with "Sophisticated Cissy," "Cissy Strut," and "Look-Ka Py Py" in 1969. Meanwhile, Aaron, Cyril, and Brown played around New Orleans for seven years as the Soul Machine.

By 1972, with Art Neville and Leo Nocentelli taking up vocals, the Meters had signed with Reprise Records. However, their first two albums failed to sell, and it was not until 1975 that one of their albums, *Fire on the Bayou*, even charted. In the meantime, they backed Doctor John's *In the Right Place* album (which included the crossover hit "Right Place Wrong Time") and Labelle's *Nightbird* album (which included the top pop and R&B hit "Lady Marmalade"). Cyril Neville joined the Meters in 1975, and brothers Charles and Aaron contributed to the group from 1975 to 1977. The Meters opened shows for the Rolling Stones' 1975 American tour and summer 1976 European tour.

In 1976 the Meters and all four Neville brothers recorded an entire album of Mardi Gras music, backing uncle George "Big Chief Jolly" Landry and the Wild Tchoupitoulas, one of New Orleans's black Indian "tribes." In 1977 all four siblings left the Meters to form the Neville Brothers. They debuted to great acclaim with the Wild Tchoupitoulas at the 1977 Monterey Jazz Festival. They recorded one album for Capitol before switching to A&M for the excellent *Fiyo on the Bayou* album, which featured the Meters' "Hey Pocky Way" and "Fire on the Bayou," Jimmy Cliff's "Sitting in Limbo," the New Orleans classic medley "Brother John"/"Iko Iko," and "Mona Lisa," dedicated to Bette Midler.

In 1979 Aaron's son Ivan Neville joined the Neville brothers for two years. He later replaced Chaka Khan in Rufus for one album and toured with Bonnie Raitt for more than two years. He launched his solo career in 1988 with *If My Ancestors Could See Me Now*, which yielded a major hit with "Not Just Another Girl." In 1988 and again in 1992–1993 Ivan Neville toured and recorded with Keith Richards's X-Pensive Winos.

The Neville Brothers subsequently recorded the live set *Neville-ization* for the small Black Top label (reissued on Demon). In 1986 they played on the brief Amnesty International tour and opened for Huey Lewis and the News on tour. Recording *Uptown* for EMI with guests Jerry Garcia, Keith Richards, and Carlos Santana, the Neville brothers received a modicum of recognition with the 1987 compilation set *Treacherous*, released on Rhino. In 1988 they returned to A&M, where they recorded *Yellow Moon*, the best-selling album of their career, working with producer Daniel Lanois. It included Sam Cooke's "A Change Is Gonna Come," Cyril's "Sister Rosa," and "Voodoo."

In 1989–1990 Aaron Neville broke through into mass popularity thanks to Linda Ronstadt. He recorded four duets with her on her album *Cry Like a Rainstorm—Howl Like the Wind*. "Don't Know Much" and "All My Life" became smash pop and top easy-listening hits. Ronstadt coproduced Aaron's 1991 album *Warm Your Heart*, which yielded a near-smash pop and top easy-listening hit with "Everybody Plays the Fool." Meanwhile, the brothers released two other albums, 1990's *Brother's Keeper* and 1992's *Family Groove*.

After Aaron's solo career took off, Charles returned to jazz with the Diversity, while Cyril performed with his reggae band the Uptown All-Stars. Aaron reformed the Meters, replacing original member Modeliste with Russell Batiste in 1990; Nocentelli left the band in 1995, to be replaced by Brian Stoltz, who had previously toured with the Neville Brothers. In 1993 A&M Records issued Aaron Neville's *The Grand Tour*, and the Neville Brothers conducted an international tour that produced the excellent live set *Live on Planet Earth*.

Art Neville

His Specialty Recordings: 1956–1958	Specialty	7023	'93	CS/CD
Mardi Gras Rock 'n' Roll	Ace	188	'87	LP/CD

Aaron Neville

Like It Is	Minit	24007	'67	†
(reissued as) Tell It Like It Is	Curb/CEMA	77491	'91	CS/CD
Greatest Hits	Curb/CEMA	77303	'90	CS/CD
Golden Classics: Tell It Like It Is	Collectables	5132	'88	LP/CS/CD
Orchid in the Storm	Rhino (mini)	70956	'85/'90	CS/CD
The Classic: My Greatest Gift	Rounder	2102	'90	LP/CS/CD
Warm Your Heart	A&M	5354	'91	CS/CD
The Grand Tour	A&M	0086	'93	CS/CD
The Tattooed Heart	A&M	349	'95	CD

The Meters

The Meters	Josie	4010	'69	†
Look-Ka Py Py	Josie	4011	'70	†
	Rounder	2103	'90	LP/CS/CD

Struttin'	Josie	4012	'70	†
Good Old Funky Music	Rounder	2104	'90	LP/CS/CD
The Meters Jam	Rounder	2105	'92	CS/CD
Cabbage Alley	Reprise	2076	'72	†
Rejuvenation	Reprise	2200	'74	†
Fire on the Bayou	Reprise	2228	'75	†
Trick Bag	Reprise	2252	'76	†
New Directions	Warner Bros.	3042	'77	†
Uptown Rulers: The Meters Live on the Queen Mary	Rhino	70376	'92	CS/CD
Funkify Your Life: The Meters Anthology	Rhino	(2) 71869	'95	CD

The Wild Tchoupitoulas

The Wild Tchoupitoulas	Island	9360	'76	
	Antilles	7052		LP/CS/CD
	Mango	539908		LP/CS/CD

The Neville Brothers

The Neville Brothers	Capitol	11865	'78	†
Fiyo on the Bayou	A&M	4866	'81	CS/CD
	Demon	65		CD†
	Mobile Fidelity	602	'94	CD
Neville ization	Black Top	1031	'84	LP/CS
	Demon	31		CD†
Treacherous: A History of the Neville Brothers (1955–1985)	Rhino	(2) 71494	'87	CS/CD
Uptown	EMI America	17249	'87	LP/CS†
	EMI America	46754	'87	CD†
Treacherous Ioo: A History of the Neville Brothers (1955–1987)	Rhino	70776	'91	CS/CD
Yellow Moon	A&M	5240	'89	CS/CD
Brother's Keeper	A&M	5312	'90	CS/CD
	Mobile Fidelity	626	'95	CD
Family Groove	A&M	5384	'92	CS/CD
Live On Planet Earth	A&M	540225	'94	CS/CD

Ivan Neville

If My Ancestors Could See Me Now	Polydor	834896	'88	LP/CS/CD†

George Porter

Runnin' Partner	Rounder	2099	'90	LP/CS/CD

THE NEW YORK DOLLS

David Johansen (b. Jan. 9, 1950, Staten Island, NY), lead voc; **Johnny Thunders** (b. John Genzale, July 15, 1952, New York, NY; d. Apr. 23, 1991, New Orleans, LA), lead gtr, voc; **Sylvain Sylvain** (b. Syl Mizrahi), rhythm gtr, voc; **Arthur Kane**, bs; **Billy Murcia** (b. c. 1951, New York, NY; d. Nov. 6, 1972, London, England), drm [Billy Murcia was replaced by **Jerry Nolan** (b. May 7, 1946, New York, NY; d. Jan. 14, 1992, New York, NY).]

An early American glitter-rock group of the '70s, the New York Dolls sported makeup and flamboyant costumes that influenced groups such as Kiss and Aerosmith and helped open the way for the New York punk scene of the mid- to late '70s. Playing a crude, raw form of rock with lyrics preoccupied with the seamier side of New York life, the New York Dolls produced several punk classics, including "Personality Crisis" and "Jet Boy." However, their popularity was largely restricted to the New York area, and by the time they broke up they had been superseded by Patti Smith, the Ramones, and English punk groups such as the Sex Pistols and the Damned. Founder and lead singer David Johansen subsequently pursued a modest solo career before inventing the character of "Buster Poindexter" for a goofy yet endearing act as a lounge entertainer.

The New York Dolls were formed in New York City in 1971 by David Johansen, Johnny Thunders, Arthur Kane, Billy Murcia, and Rick Rivets, who was soon replaced by Sylvain Sylvain. Johansen had been vocalist for several Staten Island groups, whereas Thunders, Murcia, and Sylvain had constituted the trio Actress. Attracting attention in cheap, trashy Manhattan clubs with their brutal style of rock, their sexually ambiguous costumes, and their songs centered on drugs and lowlife concerns, the New York Dolls failed to extend their popularity beyond the city despite attempts at national touring and international publicity from a *Melody Maker* article. In November 1972 drummer Murcia died of a drug overdose during the group's first European tour and was replaced by Jerry Nolan.

The group signed with Mercury Records and their debut album, produced by Todd Rundgren, included punk "classics" such as "Jet Boy," "Personality Crisis," "Bad Girls," and "Looking for a Kiss," yet sold minimally. Their second, *Too Much Too Soon*, was produced by veteran George "Shadow" Morton and sold even less well, despite the inclusion of "Showdown" and "Who Are the Mystery Girls?" By summer 1974 the New York Dolls were relegated to the circuit of New York small clubs, yet their late-night performances at the Mercer Arts Center were well received and, some say, helped launch the local punk scene. The group broke up in April 1975, although Johansen and Sylvain continued to work together until 1978.

Sylvain Sylvain subsequently played for a time with the Criminals, and David Johansen eventually signed with Blue Sky Records for four solo albums. His recordings include "Wreckless Crazy," "Bohemian Love Pad," "Frenchette," "She Loves Strangers," and his own ballad "Heart of Gold." Sylvain left Johansen in December 1978, signing with RCA Records for two obscure albums. Johnny Thunders, who had left the New York Dolls in 1974, formed the Heartbreakers in 1977 with Jerry Nolan and bassist Richard Hell, formerly with Television, and guitarist Walter Lure. They were brought to England by punk impresario Malcolm McClaren, where they remained for more than a year, with Hell replaced by bassist Billy Rath. They recorded one album in England before the band fell apart, and then Thunders recorded a solo album, *So Alone*. The band reunited in New York in 1979, producing a live album, and then disintegrated yet again, only to reunite sporadically over the next decade or so. Thunders fled to Paris in 1981 and eventually returned in 1986. He died of an overdose of methadone and alcohol in New Orleans on April 23, 1991, at age 38.

By 1985 David Johansen had switched to Passport Records. He began hanging out at the New York City bar Tramps, where he developed the persona of Buster Poindexter, a sophisticated lounge singer. With the Banshees of Blue—keyboardist Joe Delia and drummer Tony Machine—he performed R&B and show tunes and devised an amusing onstage patter. He later appeared on MTV as a video jockey and correspondent, performed on television's *Saturday Night Live*, and acted in films such as *Married to the Mob* and *Freejack*. His eponymous debut as Buster Poindexter produced a moderate hit with the Caribbean song "Hot, Hot, Hot" and included the songs "Screwy Music," "Heart of Gold," and "Cannibal," which he wrote with Delia. He later recorded *Buster Goes Berserk* and *Buster's Happy Hour* for RCA.

The New York Dolls

Lipstick Killers (1972 studio demos)	ROIR	104		CS
New York Tapes 72–73 (recorded 1972–1973)	Skydog	62257	'95	CD
The New York Dolls	Mercury	675	'73	†
	Mercury	832752	'87	CD
Too Much Too Soon	Mercury	1001	'74	†
	Mercury	834230	'88	CD

Rock 'n' Roll	Mercury	522129	'94	CS/CD
Paris Burning (recorded 1974)	Skydog	62256	'94	CD
Live in NYC — 1975	Restless	72596	'92	CS/CD

Johnny Thunders and the Heartbreakers

Viva la Revolution!! (recorded 1977)	Skydog	62251	'94	CD
L.A.M.F.—The Lost Mixes	Cleopatra	044	'95	CS/CD

Johnny Thunders

So Alone	Sire	26982	'78/'92	CS/CD
Too Much Junkie Business (recorded 1982)	ROIR	118		CS
Stations of the Cross	ROIR	146		CS
Que Sera Sera	Jungle	49	'95	CD

Sylvain Sylvain

Sylvain Sylvain	RCA	3475	'79	†
Syl Sylvain and the Teardrops	RCA	3913	'81	†

David Johansen

David Johansen	Blue Sky	34926	'78	
	Razor & Tie	1989	'92	CS/CD
In Style	Blue Sky	36082	'79	†
	Razor & Tie	1990	'92	CS/CD
Here Comes the Night	Blue Sky	36589	'81	†
	Razor & Tie	1993	'92	CS/CD
Live It Up	Blue Sky	38004	'82	†
	Razor & Tie	1994	'92	CS/CD
From Pumps to Pompadours: The David Johansen Story	Rhino	71877	'95	CS/CD
Crucial Music: The David Johansen Collection	Relativity	1033		CS/CD

Buster Poindexter

Buster Poindexter	RCA	6633	'87	CS/CD
Buster Goes Berserk	RCA	9665	'89	CS/CD
Buster's Happy Hour	RCA	71680	'94	CS/CD

RANDY NEWMAN
(b Nov. 28, 1943, New Orleans, LA)

One of the most fascinating and distinctive singer-songwriters to emerge in the late '60s, Randy Newman achieved his first recognition when Judy Collins recorded his "I Think It's Gonna Rain Today" on her 1966 album *In My Life*. Recording his first album in 1968, Newman attracted the attention of musicians and critics and developed a cult following with his songs: alternately cynical, ironic, whimsical, and sarcastic but which nonetheless retained a deep-seated sense of humanity. Writing and recording classics such as "Living Without You," "Mama Told Me Not to Come," "Political Science," and "Sail Away," Randy Newman eventually broke through to a wider audience with 1974's *Good Old Boys*, and scored his biggest commercial success with 1977's *Little Criminals*, largely on the basis of the controversy stirred by its smash hit, "Short People." Never a prolific writer, Newman concentrated on film soundtracks through the '80s and '90s.

Randy Newman moved with his family to Los Angeles at age five. Highly influenced by uncles Emil, Alfred, and Lionel, who composed film scores, he began playing piano at age six and studied music theory as a child. By the age of 16, while still in high school, Newman worked as a songwriter at Metric Music, a subsidiary of Liberty Records, whose board chairman was the father of his boyhood friend Lenny Waronker (who would become president of Warner Bros. Records). In the early '60s Newman recorded demonstration tapes with session players such as Glen Campbell and Leon Russell while attendeding UCLA as a music major. He wrote songs for Schroeder Music; the Fleetwoods ("Come Softly to Me") recorded his "They Tell Me It's Summer" as the flip side of their moderate 1962 hit "Lovers by Night, Strangers by Day." In 1965 he scored the music for *Peyton Place*, television's first hit nighttime soap opera, and a year later Judy Collins included his tender "I Think It's Gonna Rain Today" on her *In My Life* album.

In 1967 Randy Newman began working as a session arranger at Warner Bros., and he signed his own record contract with the label's Reprise subsidiary by 1968. Recorded with an orchestra playing his arrangements under producers Lenny Waronker and Van Dyke Parks, his eponymous debut album featured "I Think It's Gonna Rain Today" and the touching "Living Without You," as well as the American profile "Beehive State" and the satirical "Davy, the Fat Boy." However, despite critical acclaim, the album sold so poorly that Reprise later gave away copies as a promotional gimmick. Newman's second album, *12 Songs*, also enjoyed critical success but commercial failure. Produced by Waronker and recorded with guitarists Ry Cooder and Clarence White, the album included the wry "Yellow Man" and "Mama Told Me Not to Come," a top hit for Three Dog Night in 1970. That year Newman began performing live occasionally, usually unaccompanied, and an engagement at New York's Bitter End resulted in 1971's *Live*. In 1970 Harry Nilsson released an entire album of Newman songs.

In 1972 Randy Newman debuted *Sail Away* with the New York Philharmonic. The album, generally regarded as his definitive work, includes the melodic title song, his satirical solution to the world's problems; "Political Science"; the sexual spoof "You Can Leave Your Hat On"; and the sarcastic "God's Song (That's Why I Love Mankind)." Newman's first modest album success came with *Good Old Boys*, which was debuted with the Atlanta Symphony Orchestra and supported by a 20-city tour. Concerned in a vaguely conceptual way with the American South, the album contained "Birmingham" and "Louisiana 1927" as well as his sly attack on southern lower-class morality, "Rednecks," plus "Naked Man" and "Back on My Feet Again." The song "Rednecks" sparked a minor controversy with its repeated use of the word "nigger."

Generally inactive for more than two years, Randy Newman reemerged in 1977 with *Little Criminals*. The album yielded a smash hit with "Short People," his satirical assault on prejudice that some myopic listeners misconstrued as an affront to small-statured people, resulting in the song's banishment by some radio stations. The album also featured "Rider in the Rain," a minor country hit recorded with Glenn Frey and Timothy Schmit of the Eagles. The success of *Little Criminals* was probably due more to the controversy over "Short People" than to anything else, as 1979's *Born Again* sold only modestly even though it featured more fine songs like "It's Money I Love," "The Story of a Rock and Roll Band," and "Mr. Sheep."

In 1981 Randy Newman composed and performed the score for the movie *Ragtime*, based on E. L. Doctorow's best-selling novel. He recorded his next album, *Trouble in Paradise*, with Bob Seger, Don Henley, Linda Ronstadt, and Paul Simon, and the album yielded a minor hit with the Newman-Simon duet "The Blues"; it also contained "I Love L.A." (later used as a commercial jingle by Nike shoes), "My Life Is Good," "Real Emotional Girl," and the scathing "Christmas in Capetown." Newman toured for the first time in three years in 1983 and played 40 concerts in 1984 with James Taylor. In 1985 he cowrote the script to the Steve Martin—Martin Short—Chevy Chase comedy western *Three Amigos* with Martin and Lorne Michaels (producer of *Saturday Night Live*), and he composed three songs for the movie.

His next album, 1988's *Land of Dreams*, was produced by and recorded with guitarist Mark Knopfler of Dire Straits. The album included "Follow the Flag" and "Roll with the

Punches," plus, for the first time, three autobiographical songs—"New Orleans Before the War," "Dixie Flyer," and "Four Eyes"—while yielding a minor hit with "It's Money that Matters." Newman toured in support of the album and subsequently composed and performed the scores to the movies *Parenthood*, *Avalon*, *Awakenings*, *The Paper*, and *Maverick*. In 1995 Reprise Records issued Randy Newman's full-length musical version of *Faust*, featuring performances by Linda Ronstadt, James Taylor, Bonnie Raitt, and Don Henley, with Newman himself portraying the Devil. Receiving critical accolades, the album did little on the commercial charts.

The Randy Newman Orchestra

Original Music from "Peyton Place"	Epic	26147	'65	†

Randy Newman

Randy Newman	Reprise	6286	'68	†
	Warner Bros.	26705	'95	CD
12 Songs	Reprise	6373	'70	CS/CD
Live	Reprise	6459	'71	†
	Warner Bros.	26706	'95	CD
Sail Away	Reprise	2064	'72	LP/CS/CD
Good Old Boys	Reprise	2193	'74	CS/CD
Little Criminals	Warner Bros.	3079	'77	CS/CD
Born Again	Warner Bros.	3346	'79	CD
Trouble in Paradise	Warner Bros.	23755	'83	CS/CD
The Natural (soundtrack)	Warner Bros.	25116	'84	LP/CS/CD
Land of Dreams	Reprise	25773	'88	CS/CD
Parenthood (soundtrack)	Reprise	26001	'89	CS/CD
Avalon (soundtrack)	Reprise	26437	'90	CS/CD
Awakenings (soundtrack)	Reprise	26466	'91	CS/CD
The Paper (soundtrack)	Reprise	45616	'94	CS/CD
Maverick (soundtrack)	Reprise	45816	'95	CS/CD
Faust	Reprise	45672	'95	CS/CD

HARRY NILSSON

(b. Harry Edward Nelson III, June 15, 1941, Brooklyn, NY; d. Jan. 15, 1994, Agoura Hills, CA)

Perhaps best remembered for his hit recordings of Fred Neil's "Everybody's Talkin'" (from the movie *Midnight Cowboy*) and Badfinger's "Without You," Brooklyn-born Harry Nilsson achieved success as a songwriter with Blood, Sweat and Tears' recording of his "Without Her" in 1968 and Three Dog Night's smash-hit recording of his "One" in 1969. Recording for RCA between 1967 and 1980, his output included an entire album of Randy Newman songs, the soundtrack to *The Point* (one of television's first full-length animated movies), and the best-selling album *Nilsson Schmilsson*, considered to be his finest work. Retaining the curious distinction of never having performed in public, Nilsson became known for his associations with Ringo Starr, Keith Moon, and John Lennon in the mid '70s. He also composed and performed the soundtracks to *Son of Dracula* and *Popeye*, but withdrew from recording in the '80s. Harry Nilsson eventually returned to the studio in 1993, but on January 15, 1994, he died at his home in the Agoura Hills above Los Angeles of a heart attack at age 52.

Nilsson

Spotlight	Tower	5095	'69	†

Early Tymes	Musicor	2505	'77	†
Pandemonium Shadow Show	RCA	3874	'67	†
	RCA	53874	'95	CS/CD
Aerial Ballet	RCA	3956	'68	†
	RCA	53956	'95	CS/CD
Skidoo (soundtrack)	RCA	1152	'68	†
Harry	RCA	4197	'69	†
Nilsson Sings Newman	RCA	4289	'70/'89	CD
	RCA	0203	'73	†
	RCA	54289	'95	CS/CD
The Point	RCA	1003	'71	†
	RCA	3811		†
	RCA	2593	'90	CS/CD
Aerial Pandemonium Ballet	RCA	4543	'71	†
Nilsson Schmilsson	RCA	4515	'71	CD
	RCA	3464		CS
	RCA	66599	'95	CD
	Mobile Fidelity	541	'90	CD
Son of Schmilsson	RCA	4717	'72	†
	RCA	3812		CS/CD
A Little Touch of Schmilsson in the Night	RCA	0197	'73	†
	RCA	3761		CS/CD
Son of Dracula (soundtrack)	Rapple/RCA	0220	'74	†
Pussycats	RCA	0570	'74	†
	RCA	50570	'95	CS/CD
Duit on Mon Dei	RCA	0817	'75	†
Sandman	RCA	1031	'76	†
. . . That's the Way It Is	RCA	1119	'76	†
Best	RCA	2257	'77	†
Knnillssonn	RCA	2276	'77	†
	RCA	66754	'95	CS/CD
World's Greatest Lover (soundtrack)	RCA	2709	'78	†
Greatest Hits	RCA	2798	'78	†
All Time Greatest Hits	RCA	9670	'89	CS/CD
Everybody's Talkin' and Other Hits	RCA	2089	'90	CS
Songwriter	RCA	61138	'92	CS/CD
	RCA	61155	'92	CD
Personal Best: The Harry Nilsson Anthology	RCA	(2) 66354	'95	CS/CD
Popeye (soundtrack)	Boardwalk	36880	'80	†
Rock 'n' Roll	Pickwick			†

Tribute Album

For the Love of Harry: Everybody Sings Harry	MusicMasters	65127		CS/CD

NIRVANA

Kurt Cobain (b. Feb. 20, 1967, Hoquiam, WA; d. Apr. 5, 1994, Seattle, WA), gtr, voc; **Krist Novoselic** (b. May 16, 1965, Los Angeles, CA), bs; **David Grohl** (b. Jan. 14, 1969, Warren, OH), drm

HOLE. Courtney Love (b. Courtney Harrison, July 9, 1964, San Francisco, CA), gtr, voc; **Eric Erlandson** (b. Jan. 9, 1963, Los Angeles, CA) gtr; **Melissa Auf der Maur** (b. Mar. 17,

1972, Montreal, Canada), bs; **Patty Schemel** (b. Apr. 24, 1967, Seattle, WA), drm [Bassist
Kristen Pfaff (b. c. 1968; d. June 16, 1994) joined in 1993; after Pfaff's death, Auf der Maur
returned to the band.]

Nirvana was the first grunge-rock band to achieve international popularity. They produced a surprisingly melodic yet deafeningly loud, guitar-based sound behind stark and unsettling lyrics that reflected a deep-seated sense of anger, alienation, and hopelessness regarding contemporary life and culture. Their success, along with that of rivals Pearl Jam, brought attention to Seattle as one of the most vital musical centers in the country, opening the door for similar acts such as Soundgarden, Stone Temple Pilots, Alice in Chains, and Green Day. The popularity of Nirvana inspired a fashion craze, favoring dirty, baggy jeans, flannel shirts, and combat boots.

Kurt Cobain and Krist Novoselic grew up in Aberdeen, Washington, where Cobain took up drums and fraternized with the local group the Melvins. Kicked out of his mother's house after quitting high school, Cobain experimented with guitar and formed Nirvana with Novoselic in 1987. They played club engagements in Olympia, Tacoma, and Seattle, and with Melvins' drummer Dale Crover recorded a 10-song demonstration tape that they submitted to Seattle's underground label, Sub Pop. Signed to the label, the two recorded *Bleach* with drummer Chad Channing and guitarist Jason Everman. The album featured their debut single, "Love Buzz," and "Negative Creep," and gained Nirvana their first underground following. They toured Europe as an opening act in 1989 and signed with DGC Records in 1990. With the departures of Everman and Channing, Nirvana recruited David Grohl as their drummer for *Nevermind*. An angry, raw, yet melodic work, the album yielded the band's barely intelligible theme song and first (smash) hit, the anthemic "Smells like Teen Spirit"; *Nevermind* became an instant best-seller. It also produced the moderate hit "Come as You Are" and the minor hit "Lithium."

The underground reputation won by Nirvana led to a major-label recording contract with DGC Records. The abrasive yet compelling album *In Utero* was banned by several major chain stores but nonetheless sold quite well, although not to the level of *Nevermind*. It featured the disconcerting "Rape Me," "Serve the Servants," "Dumb," and the surprisingly tender "All Apologies." In 1992 Cobain wed Courtney Love, singer-songwriter for the band Hole, and the two became tabloid darlings during their brief, stormy marriage.

During 1993 Nirvana performed a benefit in San Francisco for rape victims of the ongoing war in Bosnia and appeared on the MTV cable series *Unplugged*. By this time the band was one of rock's major attractions, an achievement that left Cobain feeling conflicted, at best. He fell into a coma in Rome after ingesting champagne and sedatives in March 1994, but he recovered. In less than a month he was found dead in his Seattle home, having shot himself in the head with a shotgun on April 5. Krist Novoselic and Dave Grohl called it quits as Nirvana and subsequently assembled Nirvana's recordings from *Unplugged* for 1995 release. Switching to lead vocals and rhythm guitar, Grohl formed Foo Fighters, recording much of the band's debut album by himself.

Courtney Love grew up in Eugene, Oregon, and moved to San Francisco in 1983, where she formed Sugar Baby Doll with Kathy Bjelland (now with Babes in Toyland) and Jennifer Finch (now with L7), and briefly sang with the band Faith No More. Subsequently moving to Los Angeles, she appeared in two Alex Cox movies, *Sid and Nancy* and *Straight to Hell*, but decided to concentrate on a career in rock music. She learned guitar and moved to Minneapolis, New York, and Seattle before returning to Los Angeles, where she formed Hole with Eric Erlandson, Melissa Auf der Maur, and Patty Schemel in 1989. Their debut album, *Pretty on the Inside*, on Caroline Records, won Love a reputation as an adamant, outspoken, and independent young woman vocalist and songwriter, and one of the first so-called riot grrrls. She became Kurt Cobain's companion in late 1991 and married him on February 24, 1992, giving birth to their child Frances Bean on August 18, 1992. She put her career on hold, eventually returning to touring in late 1993. With new bassist Kristen Pfaff, Hole recorded *Live Through This*, which featured "Miss World," "Doll Parts," "Asking for It," and "I Think that I Would Die." However, on June 16, 1994, Pfaff was found dead in Seattle of an apparent drug overdose at age 26. Melissa Auf der Maur subsequently rejoined Hole. Courtney Love served as executive music coordinator of the soundtrack to the 1995 cult movie *Tank Girl*, which featured performances by Hole, L7, Veruca Salt, Ice-T, and Joan Jett with Paul Westerberg. Later that year Hole toured as part of the Lollapalooza tour with Sonic Youth and Beck.

Nirvana

Bleach	Sub Pop	34	'89/'92	CS/CD
Nevermind	DGC	24425	'91	LP/CS/CD
Insecticide	DGC	24504	'93	LP/CS/CD
In Utero	DGC	24607	'93	LP/CS/CD
Unplugged in New York	DGC	24727	'94	LP/CS/CD

Kurt Cobain and William S. Burroughs

The "Priest" They Called Him	Tim/Kerr	44	'95	CD

Hole

Pretty on the Inside	Caroline	1710	'91	CS/CD
Live Through This	DGC	24631	'94	CS/CD
Ask For It (uncensored cover)	Caroline	1470	'95	LP
Ask For It (band photo cover)	Caroline	1481	'95	LP

Foo Fighters

Foo Fighters	Capitol	34027	'95	LP/CS/CD

THE NITTY GRITTY DIRT BAND

Jeff Hanna (b. Aug. 11, 1947, Detroit, MI), gtr, voc; **John McEuen** (b. Dec. 19, 1945, Long Beach, CA), bjo, mdln, gtr, pedal steel, voc; **Jimmie Fadden** (b. Mar. 9, 1948, Long Beach, CA), gtr, drm, har; **Ralph Barr** (b. Boston, MA), gtr, voc; **Les Thompson** (b. Long Beach, CA), bs, gtr, voc [Ralph Barr left in 1969, to be replaced by **Jimmy Ibbotson** (b. Jan. 21, 1947, Philadelphia, PA) on guitar, keyboards, drums, and vocals. Keyboardist-vocalist **Bob Carpenter** (b. Dec. 26, 1946, Philadelphia, PA) joined in 1976.]

A zany American country-rock band formed in Long Beach, California, in 1966, the Nitty Gritty Dirt Band performed an eclectic mélange of bluegrass, country, rock, and jug-band music while displaying remarkable instrumental virtuosity. Recording early versions of Jackson Browne's "Shadow Dream Song" and "These Days" (Browne was an early member), the group scored their first (moderate) hit in 1967 with "Buy for Me the Rain," followed by a near-smash version of Jerry Jeff Walker's "Mr. Bojangles" in late 1970 and minor hit versions of Kenny Loggins's "House at Pooh Corner" and Michael Nesmith's "Some of Shelley's Blues" in 1971. The group achieved their biggest album success with *Will the Circle Be Unbroken*, recorded in Nashville with country veterans such as Maybelle Carter, Roy Acuff, Earl Scruggs, Doc Watson, and Merle Travis. The album boosted the prestige of both the Nitty Gritty Dirt Band *and* the older country performers, and helped revive interest in country music. Les Thompson left in 1974, and Jim Ibbotson was out of the band from 1976 to 1982, during which time the group recorded as the Dirt Band.

Adding keyboardist Bob Carpenter in 1976, the Nitty Gritty Dirt Band became the first Western rock group to tour the Soviet Union in 1977. They scored major pop hits with Rodney Crowell's "An American Dream" and "Make a Little Magic" in 1979–1980 and began concentrating on a country-music career after Jim Ibbotson's return. Scoring a near-smash country hit with Ibbotson's "Dance Little Jean" in late 1983, the Nitty Gritty Dirt Band switched to Warner Bros. Records in 1984, where they achieved a string of country only smashes through 1989, including the top country hits "Long Hard Road," "Modern Day Romance," and "Fishin' in the Dark." John McEuen departed in 1987 and later recorded the all-instrumental album *String Wizards* with Vassar Clements, Jerry Douglas, and Earl Scruggs, as well as the score for the 10-hour TV miniseries *The Wild West*. The Nitty Gritty Dirt Band recorded *Will the Circle Be Unbroken, Volume 2* in 1989 with Emmylou Harris, Rosanne Cash, John Hiatt, John Prine, and others, and returned to their original label, Liberty, in the early '90s.

The Nitty Gritty Dirt Band

The Nitty Gritty Dirt Band	Liberty	7501	'67	†
Ricochet	Liberty	7516	'67	†
Rare Junk	Liberty	7540	'68	†
Alive	Liberty	7611	'69	†
Uncle Charlie and His Dog Teddy	Liberty	7642	'70	†
All the Good Times	United Artists	5553	'72	†
Will the Circle Be Unbroken	United Artists	(3) 9801	'72	†
	Capitol	(2) 51158	'86	†
	EMI	(2) 46589		CS/CD†
	Liberty	(2) 46589	'94	CS/CD
Stars and Stripes Forever	United Artists	184	'74	†
	Liberty	33828	'95	CD
Dream	United Artists	469	'75	†
Dirt, Silver and Gold	United Artists	(3) 670	'76	|
	Ono Way	(2) 18090	'04	CD

The Dirt Band

The Dirt Band	United Artists	854	'78	†
An American Dream	United Artists	974	'79	†
Make a Little Magic	United Artists	1042	'80	†
Jealousy	Liberty	1106	'81	†

Jimmy Ibbotson

Nitty Gritty	First American	7718	'80	†

The Nitty Gritty Dirt Band

Let's Go	Liberty	51146	'83	†
	Capitol	51146		†
Best	EMI America	10319	'87	†
	Capitol	46591	'87	CD†
	Liberty	46591	'94	CD
Plain Dirt Fashion	Warner Bros.	25113	'84	†
Partner, Brothers and Friends	Warner Bros.	25304	'85	†
Best: Twenty Years of Dirt	Warner Bros.	25382	'86	CS/CD
Hold On	Warner Bros.	25573	'87	CS/CD
Workin' Band	Warner Bros.	25722	'88	LP/CS/CD†
More Great Dirt: Best, Volume II	Warner Bros.	25830	'89	CS/CD
Will the Circle Be Unbroken, Volume 2	Universal	(2) 12500	'89	LP/CS
	Universal	12500	'89	CD
The Rest of the Dream	MCA	6407	'90	CS/CD
Greatest Hits	Curb/CEMA	77357	'90	CS/CD

Best	Curb/CEMA	77645	'93	CS/CD
Live Two Five Anniversary Package	Liberty	93128	'91	CS/CD
Not Fade Away	Liberty	98564	'92	CS/CD
Acoustic	Liberty	28169	'94	CS/CD

John McEuen

John McEuen	Warner Bros.	25266	'85	†
String Wizards	Vanguard	79462	'91	CS/CD
String Wizards II	Vanguard	79468	'93	CS/CD

TED NUGENT
(b. Dec. 13, 1948, Detroit, MI)

Scoring his first national hit with the psychedelic "Journey to the Center of the Mind" in 1968 as lead guitarist for the Amboy Dukes, Ted Nugent established the band in the American Midwest through years of heavy touring, despite numerous personnel changes. The Amboy Dukes continued to tour and record through 1974, but in 1975 Nugent went solo, establishing himself as a touring act and album artist with his bombastic, feedback-laden, high-decibel playing, blatantly sexist lyrics, and manic onstage antics. Recording heavy-metal favorites such as "Stranglehold," "Dog Eat Dog," "Free-for-All," "Death By Misadventure," and "Wang Dang Sweet Poontang," Nugent managed his only major hit with a live version of "Cat Scratch Fever" in 1977.

In 1989 Nugent formed Damn Yankees with bassist-vocalist Jack Blades of Night Ranger (1984's "Sister Christian") and guitarist-vocalist Tommy Shaw of Styx. The group scored a smash hit with "High Enough" in 1990 and a major hit with "Where Are You Goin' Now" in 1992. A rabid conservative, Nugent has spoken out in favor of bow-hunting and is a champion of the National Rifle Association, adding to his neanderthal image. By 1995 Nugent had returned to Atlantic for *Spirit of the Wild*, releasing independently a single from the record, "Fred Bear, The American Hunter's Theme Song," which sold more than 100,000 copies, primarily to Nugent's fringe fans.

The Amboy Dukes

The Amboy Dukes	Mainstream	6104	'68	†
	Mainstream	910	'92	CD†
Journey to the Center of the Mind	Mainstream	6112	'68	†
	Mainstream	911	'92	CD†
Migration	Mainstream	6118	'69	†
Best of the Original Amboy Dukes	Mainstream	6125	'71	
Journeys and Migrations	Mainstream	(2) 801		†
Dr. Slingshot	Mainstream	414		†

Ted Nugent and the Amboy Dukes

Survival of the Fittest/Live	Polydor	244035	'71	†
Call of the Wild	DiscReet	2181	'74	†
	Enigma/Retro	73392	'89	CS/CD†
	Bizarre/Straight	70353	'91	CS/CD
Tooth, Fang and Claw	DiscReet	2203	'74	†
	Enigma/Retro	73393	'89	CS/CD†
	Bizarre/Straight	70352	'91	CS/CD

Ted Nugent

Ted Nugent	Epic	33692	'75	CS/CD

Free-for-All	Epic	34121	'76	CS/CD
Ted Nugent/Free-for-All	Epic	38225	'86	CS
Cat Scratch Fever	Epic	34700	'77	CS/CD
Double Live Gonzo	Epic	(2) 35069	'78	†
	Epic Associated	(2) 35069		CS/CD
Weekend Warriors	Epic	35551	'78	CS/CD
State of Shock	Epic	36000	'79	CS/CD
Scream Dream	Epic	36404	'80	CS/CD
Intensities in Ten Cities	Epic	37084	'81	CS/CD
Great Gonzos! The Best of Ted Nugent	Epic	37667	'81	CS/CD
Out of Control	Epic/Legacy	(2) 47039	'93	CS/CD
Nugent	Atlantic	19365	'82	CS/CD
Penetrator	Atlantic	80125	'84	CS/CD
Little Miss Dangerous	Atlantic	81632	'86	CS/CD
If You Can't Lick 'Em . . . Lick 'Em	Atlantic	81812	'88	CS/CD
Spirit of the Wild	Atlantic	82611	'95	CS/CD
Damn Yankees				
Damn Yankees	Warner Bros.	26159	'90	CS/CD
Don't Tread	Warner Bros.	45025	'92	CS/CD

N.W.A.

Ice Cube (b. O'shea Jackson, June 15, c. 1969, Los Angeles, CA); **Dr. Dre** (b. Andre Young, Feb. 18, 1965, Los Angeles, CA); **Eazy-E** (b. Eric Wright, Sept. 7, 1963; d. Mar. 26, 1995, Los Angeles, CA); **MC Ren** (b. Lorenzo Patterson, June 16, year unknown, Los Angeles, CA); **DJ Yella** (b. Antoine Carraby, Dec. 11, year unknown, Los Angeles, CA)

N.W.A. (Niggaz Wit Attitude) was led by rappers Eazy-E, Ice Cube, and Dr. Dre. Although recording together only briefly, the group helped popularize gangsta rap and aroused widespread controversy with their brutal and cynical profanity-filled raps, particularly the anthemic "Fuck tha Police." Through his Ruthless Records label, group leader Eazy-E became one of the most important producers/promoters in rap before his tragically early death from AIDS. Ice Cube and Dr. Dre have both gone on to be successful solo artists.

Eric Wright dropped out of high school in the 10th grade and started Ruthless Records in 1986 with money earned selling drugs. In 1988, as Eazy-E, he recorded the trailblazing rap album *Eazy-Duz-It*, which included "Boyz-n-the Hood," written by O'shea Jackson and Andre Young. Jackson had begun writing his own raps at 14. Eazy-E formed N.W.A. (Niggaz Wit Attitude) with Jackson ("Ice Cube"), Young ("Dr. Dre"), Lorenzo Patterson ("MC Ren"), and disc jockey Antoine Carraby ("Yella") for recordings on his Ruthless label. The group recorded the landmark album *Straight Outta Compton*, which stirred controversy with the antiauthoritarian "Fuck tha Police" and included "Gangsta Gangsta" and "Dopeman." The album sold more than two million copies, but Ice Cube soon left the group amidst royalty disputes.

Ice Cube's debut album for Priority Records, *AmeriKKKa's Most Wanted*, included "Better Off Dead," "The Drive-By," and "It's a Man's World," stark portrayals of street life in South Central Los Angeles. In 1990 Ice Cube formed his own record label and production company, Street Knowledge, producing female rapper Yo Yo's *Make Way for the Motherlode*, issued on EastWest Records. Ice Cube recorded *Kill at Will*, which included "Dead Homiez" and "The Product," in 1991, and appeared in the film *Boyz n the Hood*. In the meantime, N.W.A. recorded the misogynist *Efil4zaggin* (backward: niggaz 4 life), which topped the album charts and sold more than one million copies. The album contained "Findum, Fuckum & Flee," "I'd Rather Fuck You," and "To Kill a Hooker," as well as an attack on Ice Cube, "Message to B.A." At the end of 1991 Ice Cube's album *Death Certificate* raised protests over the anti-Korean "Black Korea" and seemingly anti-Semitic "No Vaseline." *Billboard* magazine denounced the album as racist and hate-mongering, and Rabbi Abraham Cooper of the Simon Wiesenthal Center urged retailers to pull the record from their shelves.

In 1992 Ice Cube appeared with Ice-T in the film *Trespass*, participated in the Lollapalooza tour, and recorded *The Predator*, often regarded as his most powerful and cohesive album. It produced major pop hits with "It Was a Good Day" and "Check Yo Self" and included his response to the Los Angeles riots in the wake of the Rodney King verdict, "We Had to Tear This Mothafucka Up." In 1992 MC Ren recorded his solo debut album and Dr. Dre formed Death Row Records, launching his own solo career the following year with *The Chronic*. Dr. Dre scored two smash pop hits with "Nuthin' but a "G" Thang" and "Dre Day," which featured rapper Snoop Doggy Dogg. In 1994 Priority issued Ice Cube's *Bootlegs and B-Sides*, which included three new tracks, and Hitman released *Concrete Roots—Anthology*, a compilation of songs performed, produced, or written by Dr. Dre and recorded by acts such as N.W.A., Michel'le, and the World Class Wreckin' Cru. On March 26, 1995, Eazy-E died in Los Angeles at age 31 from complications brought on by AIDS. Ice Cube cowrote, coproduced, and costarred in the comedy film *Friday* and costarred in the drama *The Glass Shield*, both released in 1995.

Eazy-E

Eazy-Duz-It	Ruthless	57100	'88	CS/CD

N.W.A.

Straight Outta Compton	Ruthless	57102	'89	CS/CD
100 Miles and Runnin'	Ruthless (mini)	7224	'90	CS/CD
Efil4zaggin	Ruthless	57126	'91	CS/CD

Ice Cube

AmeriKKKa's Most Wanted	Priority	57120	'90	CS/CD
Kill at Will	Priority	7230	'91	CS/CD
Death Certificate	Priority	57155	'91	CS/CD
The Predator	Priority	57185	'92	CS/CD
Bootlegs and B-Sides	Priority	53921	'94	CS/CD

Dr. Dre

The Chronic	Interscope	57128	'93	CS/CD
Concrete Roots—Anthology	Hitman	51170	'94	CS/CD

MC Ren

Kizz My Black Azz	Ruthless	53802	'92	CS/CD

LAURA NYRO

(b. Laura Nigro, Oct. 18, 1947, Bronx, NY)

At the forefront of the female singer-songwriter movement beginning in the late '60s, Laura Nyro received widespread critical acclaim for her second album, *Eli and the Thirteenth Confession*, and its follow-up, *New York Tendaberry*. Nonetheless, she remained a cult favorite, as artists such as the Fifth Dimension, Blood, Sweat and Tears, Three Dog Night, and Barbra Streisand scored smash hits with pop-style renditions of her early compositions. Nyro retreated from the exigencies of the music business during the early '70s, reemerging between 1976 and 1978 and ultimately returning to touring in 1988 and recording in 1993.

Laura Nyro began playing piano at a very early age, ostensibly writing her first song at eight. After attending Manhattan's High School of Music and Art, she signed with Verve Records in 1966 and made her first extended professional appearance at San Francisco's hungry i in early 1967. Her debut album, *More Than a New Discovery* (reissued by Columbia as *The First Songs*), contained "Wedding Bell Blues," "And When I Die," "Stoney End," "Blowin' Away," and "He's a Runner" yet was sorely overlooked by the record-buying public. At 1967's celebrated Monterey Pop Festival she played with a trio of black female backup singers as a soul revue, but the experiment proved less than successful and she was nearly booed off the stage.

Switching to Columbia Records, Laura Nyro's debut for the label, *Eli and the Thirteenth Confession*, was greeted by highly favorable critical reviews but barely sold, despite the inclusion of "Sweet Blindness," "Eli's Coming," "Stoned Soul Picnic," and the overlooked "Woman's Blues." Although the public failed to recognize her exceptional songwriting, dynamic delivery, and fine piano accompaniment, a number of acts began recording her songs, with astounding success. In 1968 the Fifth Dimension scored a smash with her "Stoned Soul Picnic," followed through 1970 by "Sweet Blindness," the top hit "Wedding Bell Blues," and the major hits "Blowin' Away" and "Save the Country." Blood, Sweat and Tears had a smash hit with "And When I Die" in 1969 and recorded "He's a Runner" on their third album. Three Dog Night hit with "Eli's Coming," and Barbra Streisand scored a smash with "Stoney End" in late 1970.

Laura Nyro's second Columbia album, *New York Tendaberry*, became her best-selling album, yet the follow-up, *Christmas and the Beads of Sweat*, sold less well, despite yielding her only (minor) hit with a remake of Gerry Goffin and Carole King's "Up On the Roof." In 1971 Nyro recorded *It's Gonna Take a Miracle*, an album of soul/R&B classics, with Labelle, but then retired from the music business. She reemerged in 1976 with the jazz-flavored *Smile* and toured again, but again withdrew in 1979. She recorded the neglected (and since deleted) *Mother's Spiritual* for 1984 release, and later wrote "Broken Rainbow," used as the title song to an award-winning documentary about the Native Americans' loss of their land. Laura Nyro resumed touring in 1988, recorded *Live at the Bottom Line* for Cypress Records, and returned to Columbia Records for 1993's *Walk the Dog and Light the Light*.

Laura Nigro

More Than a New Discovery	Verve	3020	'67	†
(reissued as) The First Songs	Columbia	31410	'72	CD

Laura Nyro

Eli and the Thirteenth Confession	Columbia	9626	'68	CD
New York Tendaberry	Columbia	9737	'69	CD
Christmas and the Beads of Sweat	Columbia	30259	'70/'90	CD
It's Gonna Take a Miracle	Columbia	30987	'71	CD
Smile	Columbia	33912	'76/'91	CD
Season of Lights	Columbia	34331	'77	†
Nested	Columbia	35449	'78	†
Mother's Spiritual	Columbia	39215	'84	†
Live at the Bottom Line	Cypress	(2) 6430	'89	LP†
	Cypress	6430	'89	CS/CD†
Walk the Dog and Light the Light	Columbia	52411	'93	CS/CD

O

PHIL OCHS

(b. Dec. 19, 1940, El Paso, TX; d. April 9, 1976, Far Rockaway, NY)

Author of some of the most potent and clever topical and satirical songs of American folk music's protest era, Phil Ochs is best remembered for his songs "I Ain't a Marchin' Anymore," "There but for Fortune," and "Outside of a Small Circle of Friends."

The Texas-born singer was raised in Queens and attended military academy and journalism school. He first performed with a folk duo in Cleveland, originally provocatively named the Singing Socialists, but then taking the more conventional name of the Sundowners. Ochs came to Greenwich Village in 1961, meeting and befriending another young protest singer, Bob Dylan, and quickly becoming a leader of the folk-protest movement. He contributed to *Broadside* magazine, a popular journal devoted to topical song, and signed with the folk label Elektra, where he produced his first album, *All the News That's Fit to Sing*. His second, *I Ain't a Marchin' Anymore*, included the anti-Vietnam war song "Draft Dodger Rag," which was banned by many broadcast outlets. Joan Baez scored a (minor) hit with his "There but for Fortune" in 1965.

Ochs moved to California and switched to A&M Records in 1967 for *Pleasures of the Harbor*, often considered his finest album, featuring the black comedy of "Small Circle of Friends." He recorded *Tape from California* with producer Van Dyke Parks, followed by 1969's *Rehearsals for Retirement*, prophetically showing the singer pictured on a tombstone. His ironically titled *Greatest Hits* album followed, which actually contained none of his hits but all-new material. A controversial appearance with Ochs performing as a rock revivalist at Carnegie Hall in 1971 yielded the Canada-only release *Gunfight at Carnegie Hall*. Plagued by depression, Ochs relocated first to Africa and then to England, returning to the United States in late 1973. He became an outspoken critic of the repressive Chilean government, and organized a protest concert featuring Bob Dylan in New York. His last single released during his lifetime was "Here's to the State of Richard Nixon," a Watergate-era protest song. After years of suffering from bouts of writer's block and depression, Ochs committed suicide at his sister's home in Far Rockaway, New York, on April 9, 1976, at age 35.

Phil Ochs

Songs for Broadside (Broadside #10)	Folkways	5320	'76	†
Broadside Tapes #1 (Broadside #14)	Folkways	5362	'80	†
(reissued as) The Broadside Tapes, Volume 1 (recorded early '60s)	Smithsonian/ Folkways	40008	'94	CS/CD
A Toast to Those Who Are Gone (recorded before 1964)	Archives Alive	70080	'86/'89	CS/CD
All the News That's Fit to Sing	Elektra	7269	'64	†
	Hannibal	4427	'94	CD

I Ain't a Marchin' Anymore	Elektra	7287	'65	†
	Hannibal	4422	'94	CD
Phil Ochs Live in Concert	Elektra	7310	'66	†
There But for Fortune (recorded 1965–1966)	Elektra	60832	'89	CS/CD
Pleasures of the Harbor	A&M	4133	'67	†
Tape from California	A&M	4148	'68	†
Rehearsals for Retirement	A&M	4181	'69	†
Greatest Hits	A&M	4253	'70	†
Gunfight at Carnegie Hall	A&M	9010	'74	†
	Mobile Fidelity	794		CD
Chords of Fame	A&M	(2) 4599	'77	†
Greatest Hits	A&M	3125	'81	†
The War Is Over: The Best of Phil Ochs	A&M	5215	'88	CS/CD
There and Now: Live in Vancouver, 1968	Rhino	70778	'91	CS/CD

THE O'JAYS

Eddie Levert (b. June 16, 1942); **Walter Williams** (b. Aug. 25, 1942); **William Powell** (d. May 26, 1977); **Bobby Massey**; **Bill Isles**. [Bill Isles left in 1965. Bob Massey left in 1971. William Powell departed in late 1975, to be replaced by **Sammy Strain** (b. Dec. 9, 1941); in 1991 Strain was replaced by **Nathaniel Best** (b. Dec. 13, 1960, N. Miami Beach, FL).]

Long-lived American black vocal group the O'Jays eventually achieved widespread success during the '70s as the first major act on Philadelphia International Records, formed by songwriter-producers Kenny Gamble and Leon Huff. Established with their debut for the label, *Back Stabbers*, the O'Jays scored a number of pop and R&B crossover hits during the decade. Their landmark *Ship Ahoy* album featured sophisticated production and socially conscious lyrics, as evidenced by the nine-minute title cut. Reverting to strictly romantic material with 1978's *So Full of Love*, the O'Jays' popularity faded during the '80s, but they bounced back in the R&B field in the late '80s. In 1986 O'Jays mainstay Eddie Levert's sons Gerald and Sean formed Levert, achieving their biggest success with 1987's "Casanova."

The O'Jays initially formed in Canton, Ohio, in 1958 as the five-piece vocal group the Triumphs. Touring the so-called chitlin' circuit, the group recorded for King Records as the Mascots in 1961. They were renamed by Cleveland disc jockey Eddie O'Jay and signed to Imperial Records, for whom they recorded several modest hits, including 1965's "Lipstick Traces (On a Cigarette)." Bill Isles departed in 1965 while the O'Jays were working sessions for producer Phil Spector. They continued as a four-piece and switched to Bell Records, where they scored a near-smash R&B hit in late 1967 with "I'll Be Sweeter Tomorrow (Than I Was Today)." Subsequently recording for independent producer-songwriters Kenny Gamble and Leon Huff's short-lived Neptune label, the O'Jays managed major R&B hits with the duo's "One Night Affair," "Deeper (In Love with You)," and "Looky Looky (Look at Me Girl)" in 1969–1970.

In late 1971 Kenny Gamble and Leon Huff resurfaced with their newly formed Philadelphia International label, under the auspices of Columbia Records. As a trio (Bobby Massey had left in 1971 to become a record producer), the O'Jays were the label's first major act and ultimately its most successful act. Their debut for the label, *Back Stabbers*, featured Gamble and Huff's sophisticated production and socially aware lyrics; it remained on the album charts for nearly a year. The album yielded the top R&B and smash pop hits "Back Stabbers" and "Love Train," as well as the smash R&B and moderate pop hit "Time to Get Down." The group next recorded their landmark *Ship Ahoy* album, which contained more political-social "message" songs from Gamble and Huff. It remained on the album charts for nearly a year and produced the pop and R&B smashes "Put Your Hands Together" and "For the Love of Money."

The O'Jays's album *Survival* yielded the R&B smashes "Give People What They Want" and "Let Me Make Love to You" and was followed by the best-selling *Family Reunion*. In late 1975 William Powell retired from touring due to illness, and he eventually died on May 26, 1977. He was replaced by Sammy Strain, who had been a member of Little Anthony and the Imperials between 1960 and 1972. Subsequent R&B smashes for the O'Jays include "I Love Music (Part 1)" (a smash pop hit), "Livin' for the Weekend" (a major pop hit), "Message in Our Music," "Darlin' Darlin' Baby (Sweet, Tender, Love)," and "Work on Me." After "Use ta Be My Girl" became a top R&B and smash pop hit in 1978, the O'Jays scored R&B smashes with "Sing a Happy Song," "Forever Mine," and "Girl, Don't Let It Get You Down."

During the '80s the O'Jays' success was limited to the R&B field. Major R&B hits through 1985 included "I Just Want to Satisfy," "Your Body's Here with Me (But Your Mind's on the Other Side of Town)," "Extraordinary Girl," and "Just Another Lonely Night." In 1987 they scored the R&B smashes "Lovin' You" and "Let Me Touch You" for Philadelphia International, but they soon switched to EMI Records. By 1993 Sammy Strain had departed and was replaced by Nathaniel Best.

In 1985 Eddie Levert's sons Sean and Gerald formed Levert with Marc Goodman. Recording for Atlantic Records, the group scored R&B smashes with "(Pop, Pop, Pop, Pop) Goes My Mind," "Casanova" (a pop smash), "My Forever Love," and "Sweet Sensation" in the late-'80s. Gerald Levert achieved an R&B smash with Miki Howard on "That's What Love Is" in 1988, and later recorded *Private Line* for EastWest Records America, which yielded a moderate pop hit with "Baby Hold on to Me," recorded with his father Eddie. Gerald Levert scored a smash R&B and major pop hit with "I'd Give Anything" in 1994, and Sean Levert released his debut solo album in 1995.

The O'Jays

From the Beginning	Chess	91542		†
	MCA	22137	'94	CS/CD
Comin' Through	Imperial	12290	'65	†
Soul Sounds	Minit	24008	'67	†
Back on Top	Bell	6014	'68	†
(reissued as) The O'Jays	Bell	6082	'75	†
Full of Soul	Sunset	5222	'68	†
Greatest Hits	United Artists	5655	'72	†
	Liberty	10119		†
Back Stabbers	Philadelphia Int'l	31712	'72	†
In Philadelphia	Philadelphia Int'l	32120	'73	†
	Philadelphia Int'l	66115	'94	CS/CD
Ship Ahoy	Philadelphia Int'l	32408	'73	CS/CD
Live in London	Philadelphia Int'l	32953	'74	†
The O'Jays Meet the Moments	Stang	1024	'75	†
Survival	Philadelphia Int'l	33150	'75	CS
Family Reunion	Philadelphia Int'l	33807	'75	CS/CD
Message in the Music	Philadelphia Int'l	34245	'76	†
	The Right Stuff	66706	'93	CS/CD
Travelin' at the Speed of Thought	Philadelphia Int'l	34684	'77	†
Collectors's Items	Philadelphia Int'l	(2) 35024	'77	†
So Full of Love	Philadelphia Int'l	35355	'78	†
	The Right Stuff	27120	'93	CS/CD
Identify Yourself	Philadelphia Int'l	36027	'79	†

The Year 2000	TSOP	36416	'80	†
My Favorite Person	Philadelphia Int'l	37999	'82	†
When Will I See You Again	Philadelphia Int'l	38518	'83	†
Love and More	Philadelphia Int'l	39367	'84	†
Greatest Hits	Philadelphia Int'l	39251	'84	LP/CS/CD†
Love Train: The Best of the O'Jays	Philadelphia Int'l	66114	'94	CS/CD
Let Me Touch You	EMI Manhattan	53036	'87	LP/CS†
	EMI	46392	'87	CS/CD
Serious	EMI	90921	'89	CS/CD
Emotionally Yours	EMI	93390	'91	CS/CD
Home for Christmas	EMI	96420	'91	CS/CD
Heartbreaker	EMI	89740	'93	LP/CS/CD
Levert				
Bloodline	Atlantic	81669	'86	CS/CD
The Big Throwdown	Atlantic	81773	'87	CS/CD
Just Coolin'	Atlantic	81926	'88	CS/CD
Rope a Dope Style	Atlantic	82164	'90	CS/CD
For Real Tho'	Atlantic	82462	'93	CS/CD
Gerald Levert				
Private Line	EastWest	91777	'01	CS/CD
Groove On	EastWest	92416	'94	CS/CD
Eddie and Gerald Levert				
Father and Son	EastWest	61859	'95	
Sean Levert				
The Other Side	Atlantic	82663	'95	CS/CD

ROY ORBISON

(b. Apr. 23, 1936, Vernon, TX; d. Dec. 6, 1988, Madison, TN)

Beginning as a rockabilly singer in the mid-'50s, Roy Orbison achieved his first success on Sun Records, where he recorded along with artists Elvis Presley, Carl Perkins, Johnny Cash, and Jerry Lee Lewis. Nonetheless, his greatest success came between 1960 and 1965 as a singles artist on Monument Records through his dramatic and emotional renditions of his own ballads delivered in almost operatic fashion. Possessing a stunning tenor voice of extraordinary range and depth—certainly one of the most distinctive and engaging voices in the history of rock—Orbison scored more than 15 major hits in the first half of the '60s, including "Only the Lonely," "Running Scared," "Crying," and "Oh, Pretty Woman," his best-selling single and signature song. Orbison endured personal tragedies and diminished American popularity after switching to MGM Records in 1965, but he retained his superstar status in Britain through regular tours. Rarely performing and recording from the late '60s to the mid-'80s, he saw artists such as Linda Ronstadt, Don McLean, and Van Halen score smash hits with his songs between 1977 and 1982. He eventually reemerged in 1986 to record *Class of '55* with former Sun labelmates Johnny Cash, Carl Perkins, and Jerry Lee Lewis. Thereby inspired to write and record again, Orbison recorded with the supergroup the Traveling Wilburys, and produced the most successful album of his career, *Mystery Girl*, before dying of a heart attack on December 6, 1988, at age 52.

ROY ORBISON

Roy Orbison was raised in Wink, Texas, where he took up guitar at age six. He formed his own band, the Wink Westerners, in 1952. He subsequently attended North Texas University with Pat Boone, and first recorded in early 1956 as leader of the Teen Kings at Norman Petty's studio in Clovis, New Mexico. Signed to the Memphis-based Sun label, Orbison's soaring voice was hardly suited to the rockabilly he recorded there, yet "Ooby Dooby" became a minor hit in the summer of 1956. He toured and recorded for Sun until 1958 without achieving another hit.

Roy Orbison moved to Nashville to concentrate on his songwriting after the Everly Brothers had a major hit in 1958 with his "Claudette," written for his wife. Briefly recording for RCA Records, he switched to Fred Foster's Monument label in late 1959. After the minor hit "Uptown," Orbison scored a smash with "Only the Lonely," cowritten with his songwriting partner Joe Melson. The song initiated a string of powerful, almost operatic ballad hits that includes "Blue Angel," "I'm Hurtin'," and the top hit "Running Scared,"

recorded with a string section, male backing voices, and a driving bolerolike crescendo. The smash hit "Crying" was backed by the major hit "Candyman," written by Fred Neil, and Orbison's success continued with "Dream Baby," "Leah," "In Dreams," "Falling," and "Mean Woman Blues" (a near-smash R&B hit) backed with "Blue Bayou." In 1962 he first toured Great Britain, where he became a superstar, and in 1963 he toured that country as headliner act to the Beatles and Gerry and the Pacemakers. The hits continued with Willie Nelson's "Pretty Paper," "It's Over," and the top hit classic "Oh, Pretty Woman."

After hits with "Goodnight" and "(Say) You're My Girl," Roy Orbison switched to MGM Records, but only "Ride Away" proved to be a major hit and by 1968 he had dropped out of the charts. Dogged by personal problems (his wife was killed in a motorcycle accident on June 7, 1966; two of his three children died when his Nashville home burned in September 1968), Orbison appeared in the silly 1967 movie *The Fastest Guitar Alive* and recorded country-style material such as entire albums of songs by Don Gibson and Hank Williams and a duet effort with Hank Williams Jr. Seldom touring the United States after the late '60s and refusing to join rock-and-roll revival shows, Orbison eventually recorded new albums for Mercury, Monument, and Elektra in 1975, 1977, and 1979, respectively. In 1977 he returned to touring and saw Linda Ronstadt score a smash pop and country hit with his "Blue Bayou."

In early 1980 Roy Orbison opened several shows for the Eagles and achieved a minor pop and smash country hit in duet with Emmylou Harris on "That Lovin' You Feelin' Again" from the film *Roadie*. The following year Don McLean scored a smash hit with his rendition of Orbison's "Crying," and Van Halen achieved a near-smash with a remake of his "Oh,

Pretty Woman" in 1982. In 1986 he joined Sun Records alumni Johnny Cash, Carl Perkins, and Jerry Lee Lewis for *Class of '55*. The experience renewed his vigor for writing and recording, and he soon signed with Virgin Records and rerecorded 19 of his hits for *In Dreams*. His rerecording of "In Dreams" was featured in the 1986 movie *Blue Velvet*, and in late September he performed at an all-star tribute with Bruce Springsteen, Elvis Costello, Tom Waits, Bonnie Raitt, and others; it was aired on the Cinemax cable TV network in December 1988 and released as an album one year later, *A Black and White Night Live*. In 1987 Orbison was honored by the Rock and Roll Hall of Fame for his pioneering recordings. He also scored a moderate country hit with k. d. lang on a remake of his "Crying." That same year, Orbison joined George Harrison, Bob Dylan, Jeff Lynne, and Tom Petty as Lefty Wilbury for the Traveling Wilburys album *Volume One*, singing lead vocals on "Not Alone Any More."

During 1988 Roy Orbison recorded a new album for Virgin Records. However, on December 6, 1988, he died of a heart attack in Madison, Tennessee, at age 52. The album, *Mystery Girl*, was released in early 1989 and became the best-selling album of his career. It featured "Careless Heart," "She's a Mystery to Me" (written by the Edge and Bono of U2), "In the Real World," and "A Love So Beautiful" and yielded a near-smash hit with "You Got It," written by Orbison, Jeff Lynne, and Tom Petty. Virgin Records later assembled *King of Hearts* for 1992 release.

Roy Orbison

At the Rock House	Sun	1260		†
(reissued as) The Original Sound	Sun	113	'70	†
Sun Story, Volume 4	Sunnyvale	904	'77	†
The Sun Years	Rhino	70916	'89	CS/CD
Orbiting with Roy Orbison	Design	164		†
The RCA Days	RCA	9664		CS
Early Orbison	Monument	18023	'64	†
Lonely and Blue	Monument	14002	'61	†
	Monument	21427		CS/CD
Crying	Monument	14007	'62	†
	Monument	21428		CS/CD
In Dreams	Monument	18003	'63	†
	Monument	6620	'77	†
	Monument	21429		CS/CD
There Is Only One Roy Orbison	MGM	4308	'65	†
	Polydor	841153	'89	CS†
	Polydor	841153	'89	CS†
The Orbison Way	MGM	4322	'66	†
	Polydor	841154	'89	CS†
Classic Roy Orbison	MGM	4379	'66	†
	Polydor	841155	'89	CS†
Roy Orbison Sings Don Gibson	MGM	4424	'66	†
	Polydor	841156	'89	CS†
Fastest Guitar Alive (soundtrack)	MGM	4475	'67	†
	CBS	45405		CS/CD†
Cry Softly, Lonely One	MGM	4514	'67	†
Many Moods	MGM	4636	'69	†
Great Songs	MGM	4659	'70	†
Roy Orbison and Hank Williams, Junior	MGM	4683	'70	†
Hank Williams the Orbison Way	MGM	4835	'72	†

I'm Still In Love with You	Mercury	1045	'75	†
Regeneration	Monument	7600	'77	†
Laminar Flow	Elektra	198	'79/'89	CD
In Dreams	Virgin	(2) 90604	'87	LP/CS/CD†
	Virgin	(2) 86013		CS/CD
Mystery Girl	Virgin	91058	'89	LP/CS/CD†
	Virgin	86103		CS/CD
	Mobile Fidelity	555	'91	CD
A Black and White Night Live	Virgin	91295	'89	LP/CS/CD
	Virgin	86133		CS/CD
King of Hearts	Virgin	86520	'92	CS/CD

Anthologies

Greatest Hits	Monument	14009	'62	†
	Monument	6619	'77	†
More of Roy Orbison's Greatest Hits	Monument	18024	'64	†
Orbisongs	Monument	18035	'65	†
Very Best	Monument	18045	'66	†
	Monument	6622	'77	†
The All-Time Greatest Hits of Roy Orbison	Monument	(2) 31484	'72	†
	Monument	(2) 8600	'77	†
	Monument	44348	'88	CS/CD
The All-Time Greatest Hits of Roy Orbison, Volume 2	Monument	44349	'88	CS/CD
Our Love Song	Monument	45113	'89	CS/CD
Best-Loved Standards	Monument	45114	'89	CS/CD
Rare Orbison	Monument	45115	'89	CS/CD
The All-Time Greatest Hits of Roy Orbison, Volumes 1 and 2	Monument	45116	'89	CS/CD
For the Lonely: A Roy Orbison Anthology, 1956–1965	Rhino	(2) 1493	'88	CS
	Rhino	71493	'88	CD
The Classic Roy Orbison (1965–1968)	Rhino	70711	'89	CS/CD
The Singles Collection (1965–1973)	Polydor	839234	'89	LP/CS/CD†
Ride Away	Polygram	847983		CS/CD
Rare Orbison II	CBS	45404		†
	Sony	45404		CS/CD†
The Legendary Roy Orbison (1955–1985)	Sony	(4) 46809	'90	CS/CD
Crying	Sony	75050	'95	CS/CD
Best of His Rare Classics	Curb/CEMA	77481	'91	CS/CD
Roy Orbison Sings Lonely and Blue	Epic/Legacy	66219	'94	CD
Super Hits	Columbia-Nashville	67297	'95	CS/CD
Lonely and Blue	K-tel	75049	'95	CS/CD
In Dreams	K-tel	75031	'95	CS/CD
Go Go Go	Charly	27		CD†
The Legend	Hollywood/IMG	429		CS

Jerry Lee Lewis, Johnny Cash, Roy Orbison, and Carl Perkins

Class of '55	Columbia	830002	'86	LP/CS/CD

The Traveling Wilburys

Volume One	Wilbury	25796	'88	CS/CD
Volume 3	Wilbury	26324	'90	CS/CD

JOHNNY OTIS
(b. John Veliotes, Dec. 8, 1921, Vallejo, CA)

A pioneering figure in the development of rhythm-and-blues following the demise of the big bands in the late '40s, Johnny Otis made an indelible mark as bandleader, session musician, club owner, talent scout, record producer, tour leader, and songwriter. In the '50s he "discovered" Esther Phillips, Hank Ballard, Jackie Wilson, Little Willie John, and Etta James, among others, and organized and led perhaps the first and most enduring R&B revue. He composed "Wallflower (Dance with Me Henry)," "So Fine," "Every Beat of My Heart," and his own novelty hit "Willie and the Hand Jive." Largely inactive as a performer beginning in the mid-'60s, Johnny Otis revived his revue for a stunning performance at the Monterey Jazz Festival in 1970 and launched the career of his guitar-playing son Shuggie in the early '70s. After involvement with politics and his own nondenominational church during the '70s, Otis reemerged with new recordings in 1981 and resurrected his large-scale revue for tours in the '80s. In the '90s Johnny Otis moved to northern California, where he ran a grocery store and performed locally on weekends.

Raised in a black residential area of West Berkeley, California, Johnny Otis took up drums as a teenager, and later learned piano and vibraphone. Making his professional debut in 1939 with the West Oakland House Rockers, Otis left Berkeley in 1941 to tour with various "territory bands." He settled in Los Angeles in 1943, where he joined Harlan Leonard's big band as a drummer; he formed his own big band at Club Alabam for engagements and recordings from 1945 to 1947. The band hit with the original version of "Harlem Nocturne" in 1946, and Otis recorded with Illinois Jacquet, Lester Young, and Charles Brown ("Drifting Blues"). In 1948 he opened the Barrelhouse in Watts, California, as perhaps the first nightclub to exclusively feature black R&B performers. In the early '50s he served as "artists and repertoire" man for King Records, discovering talents such as Esther Phillips, Etta James, Jackie Wilson, Little Willie John, Hank Ballard, and the Robins (who became the Coasters). He also recorded a series of R&B hits in the early '50s as the Johnny Otis Orchestra with the Robins, "Little" Esther Phillips, and Mel Walker, including the top R&B hits "Double Crossing Blues," "Mistrustin' Blues," and "Cupid's Boogie." In addition, he conducted tours as the Rhythm and Blues Caravan, believed to be the first large "package" R&B revue to tour nationally, and he worked as a disc jockey beginning in 1954, subsequently hosting a weekly television show in Los Angeles.

Johnny Otis produced the top R&B hits "Hound Dog" for "Big Mama" Thornton in 1953, and the classic "Pledging My Love" for Johnny Ace in 1955. He formed Dig Records in 1955 and scored an R&B and pop smash with his own "Willie and the Hand Jive" on Capitol in 1958. Other hit compositions by Otis included "Wallflower (Dance with Me Henry)" for Etta James (1955), "So Fine" for the Fiestas (1959), and "Every Beat of My Heart" for the Pips (1961). Seldom touring after the mid-'60s, Otis worked as a producer-arranger, eventually returning to recording with 1969's *Cold Shot*, which introduced his guitar-playing son Shuggie (b. Johnny Otis Jr., Nov. 30, 1953, Los Angeles, CA). The album's success led to a contract with Epic Records that produced *Cuttin' Up*.

In 1970 Johnny Otis reassembled his revue with Joe Turner, Esther Phillips, Roy Milton, Roy Brown, and Eddie "Cleanhead" Vinson for an outstanding Saturday afternoon performance at the Monterey Jazz Festival; recordings from the show were released in 1971. During the '70s Johnny Otis became involved in Democratic Party politics as deputy chief of staff for Congressman Mervin Dymally. He was ordained a minister in 1975, and founded the nondenominational Landmark Community Church in Los Angeles in 1978. He also hosted a weekly radio show on KPFK in Los Angeles.

Otis's son Shuggie debuted in 1965 and was introduced by Al Kooper in 1970 with *Kooper Session*. Shuggie Otis later recorded several albums for Epic Records in the '70s, and was anthologized on *Shuggie's Boogie* in 1994.

In 1981 Bruce Iglauer of Alligator Records convinced Johnny Otis to record a new album. *The New Johnny Otis Show* was released the following year, and Otis soon returned to touring with his new revue, performing at supper clubs and the 1984 Monterey Jazz Festival. In the early '90s Otis moved to Sebastopol, California, where he opened the Johnny Otis Market. He hosted live revue-type music on weekend evenings, and broadcasts of the show began on KPFA radio in 1994. Sons Shuggie and Nick (on drums) continue to perform with their father.

Johnny Otis

The Spirit of the Black Territory Bands	Arhoolie	384	'92	CS/CD
The Original Johnny Otis Show (1945–1951)	Savoy Jazz	(2) 2230	'78	
The Original Johnny Otis Show, Volume 2 (1949–1951)	Savoy Jazz	(2) 2252	'78	LP
Rock and Roll Hit Parade	Dig	104	'57	†
Creepin' with the Cats: The Legendary Dig Masters	Ace	325		CD
The Johnny Otis Show	Capitol	490	'58	†
The Capitol Years (recorded 1957–1959)	Capitol	92858	'89	CS/CD†
Cold Shot	Kent	534	'68	†
Cuttin' Up	Epic	26524	'70	†
Live at Monterey	Epic	30473	'71	†
The New Johnny Otis Show	Alligator	4726	'81	LP/CS/CD

Shuggie Otis

Kooper Session: Al Kooper Otis Introduces Shuggie	Columbia	9951	'70	†
Here Comes Shuggie Otis	Epic	26511	'70	†
Freedom Flight	Epic	30752	'71	†
Inspiration Information	Epic	33059	'75	†
Shuggie's Boogie: Shuggie Otis Plays the Blues	Epic/Legacy	57903	'94	CS/CD

P

GRAHAM PARKER

(b. Nov. 18, 1950, East London, England)

THE RUMOUR. Graham Parker, voc, songwriter; **Brinsley Schwarz** (b. Mar 25, 1949, Woodbridge, England), gtr; **Martin Belmont**, gtr; **Bob Andrews** (b. June 20, 1949), kybd; **Andrew Bodnar**, bs; **Stephen Goulding**, drm

Originally accompanied by the Rumour, one of the finest rock bands involved in London's early-'70s pub scene, Graham Parker has been regarded, along with Elvis Costello, as one of the most compelling singer-songwriters of the British New Wave scene. By writing songs with a personalized vision that dealt with anger, frustration, and defiance in a variety of styles, from rockabilly to reggae, Graham Parker and the Rumour garnered critical praise for their early albums. Although they failed to sell, their albums presaged punk's rebellion against the pomposity of progressive rock and the slick, bland, complacent commercialism of many '70s groups. Achieving his biggest commercial and critical success with 1979's *Squeezing Out Sparks*, Parker eventually recorded for many labels with only modest success. His 1988 *The Mona Lisa's Sister* was hailed as a triumphant comeback, but he was unable to successfully follow it up.

Graham Parker grew up in Deep Cut, Surrey, a small town south of London, and formed his first band, the Deep Cut Three, at age 13. After a stint with the R&B-styled Blackrockers band, he dropped out of high school to travel around Europe by working a variety of mundane jobs and manning several bands. Years later, in 1975, Parker recorded a demonstration tape that led to a connection with the Rumour, an outstanding band comprised of veterans of England's declining pub-rock scene. Bob Andrews and Brinsley Schwarz had been members of the cult band Brinsley Schwarz, whereas Martin Belmont had been with Ducks Deluxe, and Andrew Bodnar and Stephen Goulding with Bontemps Roulez.

Signed to Mercury Records, Graham Parker and the Rumour recorded two well-received but poor-selling albums released in 1976. With Parker singing his songs in a gruff, raspy voice, *Howlin' Wind* featured such powerful and vituperative songs as "Between You and Me," "Back to School Days," and "Don't Ask Me Questions." *Heat Treatment*, which included "That's What They All Say," the excellent "Pourin' It All Out," and "Fool's Gold," became their first American album-chart entry, sparked by two American tours.

Scoring a minor hit with "Hold Back the Night" in spring 1977, Graham Parker and the Rumour recorded *Stick to Me* under producer Nick Lowe, another veteran of the band Brinsley Schwarz. However, the album was not well received, as Lowe's use of complex arrangements and a horn section was criticized, yet it contained a number of outstanding songs, including the title song as well as "Soul on Ice" and the ominous "Thunder and Rain." Their next album, the double-record set *The Parkerilla*, contained three live sides and one studio side. Switching to Arista Records, Parker and the group recorded *Squeezing Out Sparks* with veteran producer Jack Nitzche. Projecting a simpler, guitar-based sound unmuddled by horns, the album was critically lauded for containing Parker's best compositions and vocal performances to date. It included "Local Girls," "Nobody Hurts You," the passionate "You Can't Be Too Strong," and the potent "Passion Is No Ordinary Word," as well as "Mercury Poisoning" and "No Protection." Supported by a three-month American tour, the album sold far better than previous releases. In 1979 Dave Edmunds covered Parker's "Crawling from the Wreckage," while Parker recorded *The Up Escalator* with guest keyboardists Nicky Hopkins and Danny Federici. The album featured "Stupefaction," "No Holding Back," "Love Without Greed," and "Endless Night," with harmony vocals by Bruce Springsteen.

Graham Parker and the Rumour split company in 1981, and Parker recorded his next three albums as a solo artist while retaining guitarist Brinsley Schwarz. Moving in a softer direction, *Another Grey Area* included "Crying for Attention," "Temporary Beauty," and "No More Excuses," whereas *The Real Macaw* contained "Just Like a Man," "You Can't Take Love for Granted," and the minor hit "Life Gets Better." Switching to Elektra Records, Parker scored a moderate hit with "Wake Up (Next to You)" from *Steady Nerves*, which included the political "Break Them Down" and "Lunatic Fringe." He next signed with Atlantic Records, but no recordings were ever released. By 1988 Parker had moved to RCA Records, where his debut for the label, *The Mona Lisa's Sister*, was hailed as a brilliant return to form. The album contained his attack on Atlantic, "Success," plus "The Girl Isn't Ready," "Start a Fire," "Don't Let It Break You Down," "Back in Time," and the soothing "Blue Highways."

In 1990 Graham Parker joined Dave Edmunds, '60s rocker Dion, and Kim Wilson of the Fabulous Thunderbirds for a nine-week tour as Dave Edmunds's Rock and Roll Revue. Following two more modest-selling studio albums for RCA, Parker switched to Capitol for 1992's *Burning Questions*. Parker toured in support of the album, and in 1993 Rhino Records issued the stunning anthology set *Passion Is No Ordinary Word*. By 1995 Graham Parker had moved to the independent label Razor & Tie for *12 Haunted Episodes*.

Graham Parker and the Rumour

Howlin' Wind	Mercury	1095	'76	†
	Mercury	826273	'90	CD
Heat Treatment	Mercury	1117	'76	†
	Mercury	826274	'90	CD
Stick to Me	Mercury	3706	'77	†
	Mercury	824808	'90	CD
The Parkerilla	Mercury	(2) 100	'78	†
	Mercury	842263	'91	CD
Pourin' It All Out: The Mercury Years	Mercury	826097	'85	†
Squeezing Out Sparks	Arista	4223	'79	†
	Mercury	8075		CS/CD
The Up Escalator	Arista	9517	'80	†
	Razor & Tie	1980	'91	CD
Best	Philips	6360181	'82	†

The Rumour

Max	Mercury	1174	'77	†
Frogs, Sprouts, Clogs and Krauts	Arista	4235	'79	†
Purity of Essence	Hannibal	1305	'82	†

Graham Parker

Another Grey Area	Arista	9589	'82	†
	Razor & Tie	1982	'91	CD
The Real Macaw	Arista	8023	'83	†
	Razor & Tie	1983	'91	CD
Steady Nerves	Elektra	60388	'85	LP/CS/CD†

The Mona Lisa's Sister	RCA	8316	'88	CS/CD
Human Soul	RCA	9876	'90	CS/CD
Struck by Lightning	RCA	3013	'91	CS/CD
Best, 1988–1991	RCA	66097	'92	CS/CD
Burning Questions	Capitol	99003	'92	CS/CD
Passion Is No Ordinary Word: The Graham Parker Anthology, 1976–1991	Rhino	(2) 71425	'93	CS/CD
12 Haunted Episodes	Razor & Tie	2817	'95	CS/CD

PEARL JAM

Eddie Vedder (b. Dec. 23, 1964, Chicago, IL), lead voc; **Mike McCready** (b. Apr. 5, 1965, Seattle, WA), lead gtr; **Steve "Stone" Gossard** (b. July 20, 1966, Seattle, WA), rhythm gtr; **Jeff Ament** (b. Mar. 10, 1963, Big Sandy, MT), bs; **Dave Krusen**, drm [Dave Krusen was replaced by **Dave Abbruzzese** in 1992; Abbruzzese was replaced by **Jack Irons** in 1995.]

Along with Nirvana, Pearl Jam brought attention to the music of Seattle and launched grunge rock into mainstream popularity. Fronted by charismatic lead vocalist-songwriter Eddie Vedder, Pearl Jam tapped the rage and frustration of youth with a sense of longing and compassion missing from the songs of Nirvana. The band debuted in 1991 with the best-selling *Ten*, and have since been one of the most popular in all of rock. They have won fans by fighting what they consider to be the monopolistic practices of ticket-seller Ticketmaster, and have been outspoken in their support of lower ticket prices.

Formed in Seattle around 1990, Pearl Jam was initially comprised of Jeff Ament and Steve "Stone" Gossard, of Green River and Mother Love Bone; Eddie Vedder and Mike McCready of the one-shot Temple of the Dog; and Dave Krusen. Temple of the Dog was convened with Ament, Gossard, Vedder, and McCready and Soundgarden's Chris Connell and Matt Cameron to record a tribute album to Mother Love Bone lead vocalist Andrew Wood, who died of a drug overdose in 1990. Signed to Epic Records, Pearl Jam broke through with their debut album, *Ten*. Ultimately selling more than five million copies in the United States, the album featured highly melodic but aggressively played songs such as "Even Flow," the energetic ballads "Jeremy" and "Alive," and the plaintive "Release." In 1992 Pearl Jam became one of the most popular attractions on the second Lollapalooza tour.

Replacing drummer Dave Krusen with Dave Abbruzzese, Pearl Jam next recorded the softer *Vs.* album. Another instant best-seller, the album included the powerful "Leash," "Rear View Mirror," and "Blood," as well as the brooding "Dissident," the acoustic guitar–based "Daughter," and the introspective "Indifference." During 1993 Vedder sang three songs with the surviving Doors at the Rock and Roll Hall of Fame induction ceremony, and Pearl Jam appeared on MTV's *Unplugged*. The band toured Europe with Neil Young and collaborated with him on "Rockin' in the Free World" at the MTV Video Awards show.

One of the most populist and politically committed bands in contemporary rock, Pearl Jam sought to keep ticket prices reasonable for their planned summer tour of 1994, but they were thwarted by Ticketmaster, the only nationwide ticket-service agency. In May the band filed a complaint against Ticketmaster with the U.S. Justice Department, and Jeff Ament and Stone Gossard testified at Congressional hearings investigating monopolistic business practices in the ticket-distribution industry in June. In August 1994 Dave Abbruzzese left Pearl Jam after the group had completed recording *Vitalogy*, released on vinyl two weeks prior to its release on CD and cassette. The fastest-selling album of the year, *Vitalogy* returned to the ferocity of *Ten* with songs such as "Spin the Black Circle" (their first-ever single release) and "Last Exit"; it also contained "Not for You," "Satan's Bed," and "Nothingman." In a remarkably astute move, Pearl Jam bought three hours of satellite time in January 1995 to broadcast the three-hour show *Self-Pollution* on any radio station that availed itself of the band's free offer. The group eventually toured the United States in the summer of 1995 with new drummer Jack Irons, playing venues independent of Ticketmaster. However, the tour was beset with problems, including rain in Utah and Eddie Vedder's incapacitating illness after seven songs in San Francisco's Golden Gate Park. Neil Young completed the San Francisco show, and only days later Reprise issued Young's *Mirror Ball*, on which Pearl Jam served as his backing band—it is perhaps his best effort since his early days with Crazy Horse.

Temple of the Dog

Temple of the Dog	A&M	5350	'91	CS/CD

Pearl Jam

Ten	Epic Associated	47857	'91	LP/CS/CD
Vs.	Epic Associated	53136	'93	CS/CD
Vitalogy	Epic Associated	66900	'94	LP/CS/CD

Neil Young and Pearl Jam

Mirror Ball	Reprise	(2) 45934	'95	LP
	Reprise	45934	'95	CS/CD

TEDDY PENDERGRASS

(b. Mar. 26, 1950, Philadelphia, PA)

HAROLD MELVIN AND THE BLUE NOTES (TEDDY PENDERGRASS YEARS). Teddy Pendergrass, lead voc; **Harold Melvin** (b. June 25, 1939, Philadelphia, PA), voc; **Lawrence Brown**, voc; **Bernard Wilson**, voc; **Lloyd Parks**, voc

Teddy Pendergrass first achieved popularity when he took over the lead vocalist role for the veteran R&B vocal group Harold Melvin and the Blue Notes in 1970. They recorded a series of smash R&B hits into 1976, including the classic "If You Don't Know Me by Now," but the group suffered declining popularity with Pendergrass's departure that year. Quickly establishing himself as both a singles and album artist, Pendergrass gained recognition as one of the finest soul singers and most charismatic black sex symbols since Al Green. However, on March 18, 1982, he was involved in an auto accident that left him partially paralyzed, and his subsequent career never approached the enormity of his earlier successes.

The Blue Notes originated in Philadelphia in 1954 as a black R&B street-corner vocal group with Harold Melvin and Bernard Wilson. Making their first recordings for Josie Records in 1956, the Blue Notes toured the so-called chitlin' circuit for years, eventually scoring a major R&B hit with "My Hero" in 1960. Experiencing numerous personnel changes, the group pursued work in white supper clubs during the early and mid-'60s at the suggestion of Martha Reeves, with Melvin taking over as lead vocalist. As Harold Melvin and the Blue Notes, the group managed a moderate R&B hit with "Get Out" in 1965.

In 1969 Teddy Pendergrass joined Harold Melvin and the Blue Notes as drummer. During 1970 the group broke up briefly, and when they re-formed, Pendergrass was brought forward as lead singer. Pendergrass had been singing since age 2 and had taken up drums at 13. The group (which included vocalists Lawrence Brown and Lloyd Parks) signed with songwriter-producers Kenny Gamble and Leon Huff's newly formed Philadelphia International label in 1971. They achieved their first near-smash R&B hit with "I Miss You (Part 1)" in 1972; they then scored a top R&B and smash pop hit with "If You Don't Know Me by Now," followed in 1973 by the top R&B and near-smash pop hit "The Love I Lost (Part 1)." Smash R&B hits continued into 1975, with "Satisfaction Guaranteed," "Where Are All My Friends," "Bad Luck (Part 1)" (a major pop hit), and "Hope that We Can Be Together Soon," recorded with Sharon Paige. The group's best-selling album *Wake Up Everybody* from the same year yielded a major pop and top R&B hit with the title song and the near-smash R&B hit "Tell the World How I Feel About 'Cha Baby." Resenting his anonymous status in the group, Teddy Pendergrass subsequently left, and Melvin and the Blue Notes managed one last R&B smash with "Reaching for the World" in 1977.

Pendergrass wisely stayed with Philadelphia International Records. He did not perform for nearly a year, but finally reemerged in 1977 with the R&B smash "I Don't Love You Anymore." Quickly established as one of the most engaging soul singers of the '70s, Pendergrass was elevated to the status of sex symbol for his husky, sensual baritone voice and his natural and passionate stage demeanor. Scoring a top R&B and major pop hit with "Close the Door" in 1978, he performed several concerts that year. Although he never had another major pop hit, his string of R&B smashes continued with "Turn Off the Lights," "Can't We Try," "Two Hearts" (with Stephanie Mills), "I Can't Live Without Your Love," and "You're My Latest, My Greatest Inspiration."

On March 18, 1982, Teddy Pendergrass suffered severe neck injuries in a single-car accident in Philadelphia that left him partially paralyzed. He returned to recording in 1984 with Asylum Records, and introduced Whitney Houston with their smash R&B hit duet single "Hold Me." Pendergrass performed for the first time following his accident at the 1985 Live Aid concert in Philadelphia, and later achieved R&B smash hits with "Love 4/2" in 1986 and "Joy" in 1988. Subsequent albums failed to produce any major hits.

The Blue Notes

The Early Years	Collectables	5006		LP/CS

Harold Melvin and the Blue Notes

I Miss You	Philadelphia Int'l	31468	'72	†
Black and Blue	Philadelphia Int'l	32407	'73	†
To Be True	Philadelphia Int'l	33148	'75	†
Wake Up Everybody	Philadelphia Int'l	33808	'75/'86	CS/CD
Collector's Item	Philadelphia Int'l	34232	'76	CS/CD
Reaching for the World	ABC	969	'77	†
Now Is the Time	ABC	1041	'77	†
The Blue Album	Source	3197	'80	†
	Valley Vue	53091		CD
All Things Happen in Time	MCA	5261	'81	†
Talk It Up (Tell Everybody)	Philly World	90187	'84	†

Harold Melvin

The Trip Is Over	ABC	1093	'78	†

Teddy Pendergrass

Teddy Pendergrass	Philadelphia Int'l	34390	'77	CD†
	The Right Stuff	27630	'93	CS/CD
Life Is a Song Worth Singing	Philadelphia Int'l	35095	'78	CS/CD†
	The Right Stuff	27118	'93	CS/CD
Teddy	Philadelphia Int'l	36003	'79	†
	The Right Stuff	66707	'93	CS/CD
Teddy Live! Coast to Coast	Philadelphia Int'l	(2) 36294	'79	†
	The Right Stuff	(2) 29117	'94	CS/CD
TP	Philadelphia Int'l	36745	'80	†
	The Right Stuff	66691	'93	CS/CD
It's Time for Love	Philadelphia Int'l	37491	'81	†
This One's for You	Philadelphia Int'l	38118	'82	†

Heaven Only Knows	Philadelphia Int'l	38646	'83	†
Greatest Hits	Philadelphia Int'l	39252	'84	†
Love Language	Asylum	60317	'84	CS/CD
Working It Back	Asylum	60447	'85	CS/CD
Joy	Asylum	60775	'88	CS/CD
Truly Blessed	Elektra	60891	'91	CS/CD
A Little More Magic	Elektra	61497	'93	CS/CD

PENTANGLE

Bert Jansch (b. Nov. 3, 1943, Glasgow, Scotland), gtr, voc; **John Renbourn** (b. Aug. 8, 1944, London, England), gtr, sitar, voc; **Jacqui McShee** (b. Dec. 25, 1943, London, England), voc; **Danny Thompson** (b. Apr. 1939, Devon, England), standup bs; **Terry Cox** (b. Buckinghamshire, England), drm [The original group disbanded in 1973 and was reformed with various lineups in the '80s and '90s.]

Probably the first British folk-rock band, Pentangle continued to perform on acoustic instruments even after other British groups of the genre, most notably Fairport Convention, switched to electric instruments. Formed in 1967, Pentangle featured the crystalline soprano voice of Jacqui McShee and the virtuoso guitar playing of Bert Jansch and John Renbourn. Recording for Transatlantic in Great Britain (Reprise in the United States), Pentangle's eclectic music encompassed traditional British folk songs, jazz instrumentals, blues songs, and contemporary original compositions. One of the most popular folk-style British bands between 1968 and 1971, Pentangle attracted only a limited following in the United States, as virtually no British folk-rock band of the era achieved mass popularity in this country. Both Jansch and Renbourn recorded solo and duet albums during the existence of Pentangle, but the group disbanded in 1973.

Renbourn and Jansch later hooked up with blues guitarist Stefan Grossman (a veteran of the Even Dozen Band and the Fugs), recording for Grossman's Kicking Mule label in the '70s and '80s. At the beginning of the '90s, Pentangle reunited with McShee and Jansch for recordings on the Celtic label Green Linnet. In 1993 Flying Fish issued *Wheel of Fortune*, recorded by Renbourn and multi-instrumentalist Robin Williamson of the Incredible String Band.

Bert Jansch

Lucky Thirteen	Vanguard	79212	'66	†
Birthday Blues	Reprise	6343	'69	†
Rosemary Lane	Reprise	6455	'71	†
Moonshine	Reprise	2129	'73	†
Strolling Down the Highway	Transatlantic	604		CD†
A Rare Conundrum	Kicking Mule	302	'78	†
Conundrum	Kicking Mule	303		CS
Best	Kicking Mule	334	'79	†
	Shanachie	99004	'92	CS/CD
Thirteen Down	Kicking Mule	309	'80	LP
Heartbreak	Hannibal	1312	'83	CS/CD
Sketches	Temple	2035	'90	CS/CD

Pentangle

Pentangle	Reprise	6315	'68	†
Sweet Child	Reprise	(2) 6334	'69	†
Basket of Light	Reprise	6372	'70	†
	Transatlantic	205		CD†

Cruel Sister	Reprise	6430	'71	†
Reflection	Reprise	6463	'71	†
Solomon's Seal	Reprise	2100	'72	†
The Essential Pentangle, Volume 1	Transatlantic	602	'87	CD†
The Essential Pentangle, Volume 2	Transatlantic	606	'87	CD†
A Maid That's Deep in Love	Shanachie	79066		CS/CD
Early Classics	Shanachie	79078	'92	CS/CD
Open the Door	Varrick	017	'85	CS
In the Round	Varrick	026	'86	LP/CS/CD
So Early in the Spring	Green Linnet	3048	'90	CS/CD
Think of Tomorrow	Green Linnet	3057	'91	CS/CD

Bert Jansch and John Renbourn

Stepping Stones	Vanguard	6506	'69	†
Jack Orion	Vanguard	6544	'71	†
After the Dance	Shanachie	99006	'92	CS/CD

John Renbourn

The Soho Years	Transatlantic	603	'87	CD†
John Renbourn (recorded 1965–1966)	Reprise	(2) 6482	'73	†
Sir John Alot	Reprise	6344	'69	†
	Lost Lake	0084		†
	Shanachie	97021	'92	CS/CD
The Lady and the Unicorn	Reprise	6407	'71	†
	Lost Lake	0087		†
	Transatlantic	224		CD†
	Shanachie	97022	'92	CS/CD
Faro Annie	Reprise	2082	'72	†
A Maid in Bedlam	Shanachie	79004	'77	CS/CD
The Black Balloon	Kicking Mule	163	'79	†
	Shanachie	97009	'90	CS/CD
The Hermit	Transatlantic	336	'80	†
	Shanachie	97014	'91	CS/CD
The Enchanted Garden	Kicking Mule	312	'81	†
	Shanachie	79074	'90	CS/CD
Another Monday	Shanachie	95005		†
Live in America	Flying Fish	(2) 27103	'82	LP
The Nine Maidens	Flying Fish	378	'85	LP
	Flying Fish	90378	'85	CS
	Flying Fish	70378	'86	CD
Ship of Fools	Flying Fish	466	'88	LP
	Flying fish	90466	'88	CS
	Flying Fish	70466	'88	CD

John Renbourn and Stefan Grossman

Stefan Grossman and John Renbourn	Kicking Mule	152	'78	CS
Under the Volcano	Kicking Mule	162	'80	CS
Live	Shanachie	95001	'85	CS/CD
The Three Kingdoms	Shanachie	95006	'87	CS/CD
Snap a Little Owl	Shanachie	97003	'89	CS/CD

John Renbourn and Robin Williamson

Wheel of Fortune	Flying Fish	90626	'93	CS/CD

CARL PERKINS
(b. Apr. 9, 1932, near Tiptonville, TN)

With his smash-hit classic from 1956, "Blue Suede Shoes," Carl Perkins helped to define and establish rockabilly music. Like Chuck Berry and Buddy Holly (and unlike Elvis Presley), Perkins was one of the first rock-and-roll artists to write his own songs and play lead guitar. After leaving Sun in 1958 his success ended, although his career was briefly revived when the Beatles recorded three of his songs in 1964–1965. He then established himself as a country artist by touring with Johnny Cash for 10 years. Since leaving Cash in 1975, Carl Perkins has toured and recorded with his sons Stan and Greg.

Carl Perkins grew up in Lake County, Tennessee, and obtained his first guitar at age six. He formed a family band with his older brothers Jay and Clayton and drummer W. S. Holland to play local dances. The band signed with Flip Records in 1954 and recorded one single before moving to the Memphis-based Sun Records label in 1955. Their second Sun single, "Blue Suede Shoes," became a smash hit in the pop, country, *and* R&B fields and eventually sold two million copies. Booked to appear on the Ed Sullivan and Perry Como shows, the band was involved in a serious auto accident en route to New York near Dover, Delaware, on March 22, 1956. Jay later died of his injuries and Carl was hospitalized for months; due to this tragic accident Elvis Presley became the first rockabilly artist to appear on network television. Carl Perkins managed near-smash country hits later in 1956 with "Boppin' the Blues" and "Dixie Fried," but he was never able to reestablish his career's momentum.

On December 4, 1956, a Carl Perkins recording date attended by Sun labelmates Johnny Cash and Jerry Lee Lewis turned into an informal session of gospel singing when Elvis Presley dropped by. Unknown to the four, the session was recorded, and bootleg copies of the Million Dollar Quartet circulated for years until RCA finally issued the recordings in 1990.

In 1957 Carl Perkins had a major country hit with "Your True Love," but by 1958 he had switched to Columbia Records, where he scored a major country hit with "Pink Pedal Pushers." His career subsequently languished, but in 1964, while touring England with Chuck Berry, he met the Beatles, who soon recorded his songs "Slow Down," "Matchbox," and "Everybody's Trying to Be My Baby." His career was revived, particularly in Europe, and he soon joined Johnny Cash's road show, touring with him from 1965 to 1975. Perkins achieved country hits with "Country Boy's Dream" (on Dollie) in 1967 and "Restless" (on Columbia) in 1969, and provided Cash with his top country hit "Daddy Sang Bass."

In 1970 Carl Perkins recorded the sorely overlooked album *Boppin' the Blues* with NRBQ. He later recorded an album for Mercury, and left Johnny Cash in 1975 to form a performing band with sons Greg (bs) and Stan (drm). He recorded *Ol' Blue Suede's Back* in 1978 and joined Johnny Cash and Jerry Lee Lewis for 1982's *The Survivors*. Perkins sang on Paul McCartney's "Get It" from his *Tug of War* album and later performed for an HBO cable-television special that featured Eric Clapton, George Harrison, Dave Edmunds, and Ringo Starr. In 1986 he recorded *The Class of '55* with Johnny Cash, Jerry Lee Lewis, and Roy Orbison, contributing the autobiographical "Birth of Rock and Roll," which became a moderate country hit. A year later he was inducted into the Rock and Roll Hall of Fame. Carl Perkins has continued to record and tour into the '90s.

Carl Perkins on Sun

Dance Album	Sun	1225	'58	†
(reissued as) Teen Beat	Sun	1225	'61	†
Original Golden Hits	Sun	111		†
Blue Suede Shoes	Sun	112	'69	†

The Sun Story, Volume 3	Sunnyvale	903	'77	†
Dixie Fried	Charly	2		CD†
Original Sun Greatest Hits (1955–1957)	Rhino	70221	'86	CS
	Rhino	75890	'86	CD
Honky Tonk Gal: Rare and Unissued Sun Masters	Rounder	27	'89	LP/CS/CD
The Million Dollar Quartet				
The Million Dollar Quartet	RCA	2023	'90	LP/CS/CD
Carl Perkins				
Up Through the Years (1954–1957)	Bear Family	15246		CD
Whole Lotta Shakin'	Columbia	1234	'58	†
	Sony	1234		CS/CD†
	K-tel	75014	'95	CS/CD
On Top	Columbia	9931	'69	†
Restless: The Columbia Years	Legacy	48896	'92	CS/CD
Country Boy's Dream	Dollie	4001	'66	†
My Kind of Country	Mercury	691		†
Ol' Blue Suede's Back	Jet	35604	'78	†
Country Store	BMG	53	'88	†
Born to Rock	Universal	76001	'89	LP/CS/CD†
	Liberty	90079		CS/CD†
Family, Friends and Legends	Platinum		'92	†
Carl Perkins and Sons	RCA Nashville	66216	'93	CS/CD
Disciple in Blue Suede Shoes	RCA Nashville	66217	'93	CS/CD
Anthologies				
Greatest Hits	Columbia	9833	'69	†
Carl Perkins	Harmony	11385	'70	†
Brown-Eyed, Handsome Man	Harmony	31179	'72	†
Greatest Hits	Harmony	31792	'73	†
Jive After Five: The Best of Carl Perkins, 1958–1978	Rhino	70958	'90	CS/CD
Presenting Carl Perkins	Accord	7169	'82	†
Best	Sound	929	'91	CD
Best	Curb/CEMA	77598	'93	CS/CD
Introducing Carl Perkins	Boplicity	8		LP
Twenty Golden Pieces	Bulldog	2034		LP/CS
Carl Perkins and NRBQ				
Boppin' the Blues	Columbia	09981	'70/'90	CD
Carl Perkins, Johnny Cash, and Jerry Lee Lewis				
The Survivors	Columbia	37961	'82	LP/CS
Carl Perkins, Jerry Lee Lewis, Roy Orbison, and Johnny Cash				
Class of '55	Columbia	830002	'86	LP/CS/CD

PETER AND GORDON

Peter Asher (b. June 22, 1944, London, England), voc, gtr; **Gordon Waller** (b. June 4, 1945, Braemar, Scotland), voc, gtr

Perhaps the most popular British vocal duo of the '60s British Invasion, Peter and Gordon, like rivals Chad and Jeremy, experienced greater success in the United States than in Great

Britain. Initially aided by Beatles John Lennon and Paul McCartney, Peter and Gordon later hit with several novelty songs before disbanding in late 1967. Peter Asher subsequently became a noted producer, best known for his work with James Taylor and Linda Ronstadt.

Peter Asher was raised in London and became a child star in films along with his sister Jane. As a teenager he took piano lessons and attempted to learn oboe and double bass before joining a skiffle group at age 15. At 13 he had met Gordon Waller in public school, and the two teamed up in 1962. They played the coffeehouse circuit for nearly two years before signing with EMI Records (Capitol in the United States) around the beginning of 1964. At that time Jane Asher was dating Paul McCartney, and as a result of the relationship, McCartney contributed his previously unrecorded song "World Without Love" to Peter and Gordon. The single became a top British and American hit and the duo soon began touring the United States regularly. John Lennon and Paul McCartney subsequently gave Peter and Gordon the songs "Nobody I Know" and "I Don't Want to See You Again"; both became major American hits. Later hits for Peter and Gordon include the near-smash "I Go to Pieces" (written by Del Shannon), "True Love Ways" (cowritten by Buddy Holly), and "Woman" (written by McCartney). Their final major hits came in 1966–1967 with the novelty songs "Lady Godiva" and "Knight in Rusty Armour."

Near the end of 1967 Peter and Gordon split up. After producing three singles for former Manfred Mann vocalist Paul Jones, Peter Asher was asked by Paul McCartney to join Apple Records as a producer. He was soon elevated to head of A&R (Artists and Repertoire department) for the label. He signed James Taylor, who was then visiting London, to Apple and produced his overlooked debut album. In 1969 Asher resigned his position with Apple, moved to Los Angeles, and negotiated a new contract for Taylor with Warner Bros. Records. He subsequently produced Taylor's first three albums for the label, and produced albums by Tony Joe White and John Stewart. In 1973 Asher agreed to help Linda Ronstadt complete her *Don't Cry Now* album; he later limited himself to managing James Taylor and producing and managing Ronstadt. Largely on the strength of Asher's production, arrangements, and shrewd song selections, Ronstadt's *Heart Like a Wheel* album became a best-seller and established her as a popular recording artist. Asher continued to produce her albums into the '90s. He also produced James Taylor's *JT* and *Flag* albums and Bonnie Raitt's *The Glow*. In the late '80s Peter Asher produced the 10,000 Maniacs albums *In My Tribe* and *Blindman's Zoo*.

Peter and Gordon

A World Without Love	Capitol	2115	'64	†
I Don't Want to See You Again	Capitol	2220	'64	†
I Go to Pieces	Capitol	2324	'65	†
True Love Ways	Capitol	2368	'65	†
Sing and Play the Hits Of Nashville, Tennessee	Capitol	2430	'65	†
Woman	Capitol	2477	'66	†
Best	Capitol	2549	'66	†
	Capitol	16084		†
Lady Godiva	Capitol	2664	'67	†
Knight in Rusty Armour	Capitol	2729	'67	†
In London for Tea	Capitol	2747	'67	†
Hot, Cold and Custard	Capitol	2882	'68	†
Best	Rhino	70748	'91	CS/CD

Gordon Waller

And Gordon	ABC	749	'72	†

PETER, PAUL AND MARY

Peter Yarrow (b. May 31, 1938, New York, NY), gtr, ten voc; **Noel Paul Stookey** (b. Nov. 30, 1937, Baltimore, MD), gtr, bar voc; **Mary Travers** (b. Nov. 7, 1937, Louisville, KY), sop voc

Scoring a series of major hits between 1962 and 1969, Peter, Paul and Mary became the most popular and successful folk group of the '60s. They introduced and popularized the compositions of songwriters Bob Dylan, Gordon Lightfoot, and John Denver, among others. The trio's huge commercial success exposed both the folk and protest movements to a mass audience and opened the way for the later successes of Bob Dylan and folk-rock music. Disbanding in 1970, Peter, Paul and Mary pursued individual projects until reuniting in 1978. Expanding their touring schedule in 1983, Peter, Paul and Mary returned to recording in the late '80s as folk music enjoyed a renaissance with the likes of Tracy Chapman and Suzanne Vega.

Peter, Paul and Mary were brought together by manager Albert Grossman in New York City's Greenwich Village during 1961. Peter Yarrow was a Cornell University graduate in psychology who had worked for a time as a solo artist and appeared at the 1960 Newport Folk Festival. Noel Paul Stookey had led a high school rock band before pursuing a career around Greenwich Village as a stand-up comic. He encouraged former folk-group member Mary Travers to return to singing after her appearance in the flop Broadway show *The Next President*. Conducting intensive rehearsals for seven months, Peter, Paul and Mary debuted at the Bitter End in Greenwich Village and signed with Warner Bros. Records.

Peter, Paul and Mary's debut album became a top album hit, staying on the charts for more than three years. It included standard folk material such as Reverend Gary Davis's "If I Had My Way," Hedy West's "500 Miles," and Pete Seeger's "Where Have All the Flowers Gone," and original compositions by Yarrow and Stookey. It yielded a moderate hit with "Lemon Tree" and a near-smash hit with "If I Had a Hammer," coauthored by Seeger and Lee Hays. Quickly thrust into the forefront of the folk movement, Peter, Paul and Mary became favorites on the college circuit and frequently performed at political rallies and protest marches. Their second album, *(Moving)*, also became a best-seller, remaining on the album charts for nearly two years. It produced a smash hit with "Puff, The Magic Dragon," written by Yarrow and Leonard Lipton; moderate hits with "Stewball" and "Tell It on the Mountain"; and contained Woody Guthrie's "This Land Is Your Land."

With *In the Wind*, Peter, Paul and Mary began featuring songs by then-unknown contemporary songwriters, and the smash successes of "Blowin' in the Wind" and "Don't Think Twice, It's All Right" introduced Bob Dylan and bolstered the burgeoning folk-protest movement. Following the live double-record set *In Concert*, the trio recorded *A Song Will Rise*, which contained the first hit version of Gordon Lightfoot's "For Lovin' Me," and *See What Tomorrow Brings*, which included Lightfoot's "Early Morning Rain" and Tom Paxton's "Last Thing on My Mind."

Peter, Paul and Mary's *Album* remained on the charts for more than a year and was followed by perhaps their finest albums, *Album 1700* and *Late Again*. *Album 1700* yielded a near-smash hit with Stookey's collaborative tongue-in-cheek "I Dig Rock and Roll Music" and contained John Denver's "Leaving on a Jet Plane" (a top pop and easy-listening hit when released as a single two years later) and some of the group's most memorable compositions, including the touching "House Song," Yarrow's antiwar "The Great Mandella (The Wheel of Life)," and the classic "The Song Is Love." *Late Again* included "Hymn" and "Rich Man, Poor Man," coauthored by Stookey and Yarrow, respectively, as well as Tim Hardin's "Reason to Believe" and the moderate hit (Bob Dylan's) "Too Much of Nothing."

Following their children's album, *Peter, Paul and Mommy*, and the major hit "Day Is Done," the trio went their separate ways in 1970. Stookey fared the best of the three as a solo artist, scoring a major hit with "Wedding Song (There Is Love)" from the excellent *Paul And* album in 1971. By the mid-'70s Paul Stookey had retreated to Maine and Peter Yarrow had become involved in television and record production work, leaving Mary Travers as the only former member to perform extensively. In 1976 Yarrow produced Mary MacGregor's best-selling *Torn Between Two Lovers* album, coauthoring the top-hit title song. He also coproduced the 1978 CBS animated television special *Puff, The Magic Dragon*, based on the song. He later supervised the soundtracks to two more animated television specials based on the song.

In 1978 Peter, Paul and Mary reunited at the Survival Sunday benefit show in California, subsequently recording *Reunion* for Warner Bros. They performed 30 to 50 concerts a year until 1983, when they began playing around 100 engagements a year. Without a major label deal during most of the '80s, Peter, Paul and Mary eventually recorded *No Easy Walk to Freedom* for the small Gold Castle label, followed by the Christmas album *A Holiday Celebration*. Two Peter, Paul and Mary PBS television specials fared well in the late-'80s, and their Gold Castle recordings were reissued by Warner Bros. in 1992. By 1993 Peter, Paul and Mary returned to their original label, Warner Bros., for a second children's album, then released *Lifelines*, recorded with Holly Near, Judy Collins, Emmylou Harris, and John Sebastian two years later.

Peter, Paul and Mary

Peter, Paul and Mary	Warner Bros.	1449	'62	CS/CD
(Moving)	Warner Bros.	1473	'63	CD
In the Wind	Warner Bros.	1507	'63	†
	Warner Bros.	26224	'90	CD
In Concert	Warner Bros.	1555	'64	CS
	Warner Bros.	(2) 1555		CD
A Song Will Rise	Warner Bros.	1589	'65	†
	Warner Bros.	26225	'90	CD
See What Tomorrow Brings	Warner Bros.	1615	'65	†
	Warner Bros.	26654	'91	CD
Album	Warner Bros.	1648	'66	†
	Warner Bros.	26653	'91	CD
Album 1700	Warner Bros.	1700	'67	CS/CD
Late Again	Warner Bros.	1751	'68	†
	Warner Bros.	26666	'92	CD
Peter, Paul and Mommy	Warner Bros.	1785	'69	CS/CD
Best (Ten Years Together)	Warner Bros.	2552	'70	†
	Warner Bros.	3105		CS
(reissued as) 10 (Ten) Years Together	Warner Bros.	3105	'92	CD
Reunion	Warner Bros.	3231	'78	CS
No Easy Walk to Freedom	Gold Castle	71301	'87/'89	LP/CS/CD†
	Warner Bros.	45071	'92	CS/CD
A Holiday Celebration	Gold Castle	71316	'88/'89	LP/CS/CD†
	Warner Bros.	45070	'92	CS/CD
Flowers and Stones	Gold Castle			†
	Warner Bros.	45069	'92	CS/CD
Peter Paul and Mommy Too	Warner Bros.	45216	'93	CS/CD
Lifelines	Warner Bros.	45851	'95	CS/CD

Mary Travers

Mary	Warner Bros.	1907	'71	†
Morning Glory	Warner Bros.	2609	'72	†
All My Choices	Warner Bros.	2677	'73	†

Circles	Warner Bros.	2795	'74	†
It's in Every One of Us	Chrysalis	1168	'78	†
Paul Stookey				
Paul And	Warner Bros.	1912	'71	†
Noel-One Night Stand	Warner Bros.	2674	'73	†
Bodyworks	Gold Castle	71333	'90	CS/CD†
Peter Yarrow				
Peter	Warner Bros.	2599	'72	†
That's Enough for Me	Warner Bros.	2730	'73	†
Hard Times	Warner Bros.	2860	'75	†
Love Songs	Warner Bros.	2891	'75	†

TOM PETTY AND THE HEARTBREAKERS

Tom Petty (b. Oct. 20, 1953, Gainesville, FL), lead voc, 6- and 12-string gtr; **Benmont Tench** (b. Sept. 7, 1954, Gainesville, FL), kybd; **Mike Campbell** (b. Feb. 1, 1954, Gainesville, FL), lead gtr; **Ron Blair** (b. Sept. 16, 1952, Macon, GA), bs; **Stan Lynch** (b. May 21, 1955, Gainesville, FL), drm [**Howard Epstein** (b. July 21, 1955) replaced Ron Blair in 1982 and **Steve Ferrone** replaced Stan Lynch in 1994.]

TOM PETTY

One of the most consistently successful American rock bands of the '80s, Tom Petty and the Heartbreakers played engaging, unpretentious ensemble rock characterized by Petty's chiming guitar and accessible, perceptive songwriting. Achieving their first recognition in Great Britain, Tom Petty and the Heartbreakers were able to appeal to the New Wave crowd as well as mainstream rock fans. Since their breakthrough 1979 hit, "Refugee," the group has rarely been off the charts. Petty meanwhile has taken several sabbaticals from the group, first to perform with the supergroup the Traveling Wilburys, then to record two solo albums.

Taking up guitar at an early age, Tom Petty played around Gainesville, Florida, in various bands, including the Epics and Mudcrutch, between ages 14 and 17. He quit high school at 17 to tour with Mudcrutch, which included Mike Campbell and Benmont Tench. The three ended up in Los Angeles in the early '70s and recorded a demonstration tape that led to a recording contract with Shelter Records. The group ultimately stabilized around Petty, Campbell, Tench, and two other Gainesville-based musicians, Ron Blair and Stan Lynch. Their eponymous debut album, recorded in 1976, contained "Fooled Again (I Don't Like It)," the British hit "American Girl," and the moderate American hit "Breakdown." By the release of *You're Gonna Get It!*, Tom Petty and the Heartbreakers were well established as a club band in Los Angeles. The album included "Restless" and produced two minor hits with "I Need to Know" and "Listen to Her Heart."

Tom Petty and the Heartbreakers subsequently became embroiled in legal disputes when Shelter Records was taken over by ABC Records and ABC was sold to MCA. As the group pursued a new contract independent of MCA, they were enjoined from recording. Ultimately MCA agreed to create a new label, Backstreet, headed by Petty's friend Denny Bramson, for the group's recordings. Their debut for the label, *Damn the Torpedoes*, set the precedent for the group's subsequent success: midtempo ensemble rock songs with catchy melodies and hooks and accessible lyrics. The album contained "What Are You Doin' in My Life?" and "Here Comes My Girl" and yielded two major hits, "Don't Do Me Like That" and "Refugee."

Graduating from medium-size-hall to arena tours by 1981, Tom Petty and the Heartbreakers backed Stevie Nicks of Fleetwood Mac on her debut solo album, *Bella Donna*, which yielded the smash hit the Petty-Nicks duet "Stop Draggin' My Heart Around." Nicks reciprocated by recording "The Insider" for the group's *Hard Promises*, which produced a major hit with "The Waiting" and a minor hit with "A Woman in Love (It's Not Me)." In 1981 Petty was one of several contemporary artists to encourage Del Shannon to return to recording, producing his comeback album, *Drop Down and Get It*. During 1982 Howie Epstein replaced Ron Blair in the group, and their next album, *Long After Dark*, included the caustic "Same Old You" and yielded major hits with "You Got Lucky" and "Change of Heart."

After their lengthy tour of 1983, the members of Tom Petty and the Heartbreakers worked on outside projects. Stan Lynch toured with T-Bone Burnett, while Benmont Tench did shows with Stevie Nicks, and Howie Epstein backed John Hiatt on some dates. Mike Campbell later cowrote the smash hit "The Boys of Summer" with Don Henley. While completing work on the group's next album, Petty broke his left hand in a fit of pique in October 1984. Released in 1985 on MCA Records, *Southern Accents* was rather disjointed, with some songs revolving around Southern themes and some songs written with Dave Stewart of the Eurythmics, including the major hit "Don't Come Around Here No More."

During 1985 Tom Petty and the Heartbreakers resumed touring, appearing at both the Live Aid and Farm Aid benefits. Recordings from the tour were compiled for *Pack Up the Plantation*, which included cover versions of concert favorites such as "Shout," "Needles and Pins," and "So You Want to Be a Rock and Roll Star." The band backed Dylan at Farm Aid and later conducted a brief tour of Japan and Australia with Dylan. In 1986 Dylan, with Petty and the Heartbreakers as his supporting band, mounted a full-scale tour of America, his first in six years. With Petty and the Heartbreakers performing brief sets of their own between sets by Dylan, the tour introduced both acts to new audiences. The band also appeared on Dylan's *Knocked Out Loaded* album, which included "Got My Mind Made Up," cowritten by Petty and Dylan.

Tom Petty and the Heartbreakers' *Let Me Up (I've Had Enough)* includes "My Life"/"Your World" and produced hits with "Jammin' Me," cowritten by Petty and Dylan. In 1988 Petty joined George Harrison, Dylan, Roy Orbison, and Jeff Lynne in the supergroup the Traveling Wilburys, and their acoustic-based album *Volume One* yielded a moderate hit with "Handle with Care." Orbison's near-smash hit from *Mystery Girl*, "You Got It," was cowritten by Orbison, Lynne, and Petty. Petty's association with Lynne continued with *Full Moon Fever*, released as a solo Tom Petty album. Coproduced by Jeff Lynne and Mike Campbell, the album was recorded with Lynne, Harrison, and all the members of the Heartbreakers except Stan Lynch. It yielded a major hit with "I Won't Back Down," "Runnin' Down a Dream," and a near-smash with "Free Fallin'." In 1990 Petty rejoined Lynne, Harrison, and Dylan for a second album as the Traveling Wilburys, *Volume 3*.

Tom Petty and the Heartbreakers reassembled to record *Into the Great Wide Open* with Jeff Lynne as coproducer. The album, hailed as Petty's finest in years, included a number of songs cowritten with Lynne and yielded a major hit with "Learning to Fly." At the end of

1993 the group scored a major hit with "Mary Jane's Last Dance," one of two songs specifically created for Petty's Disney Channel cable-television special in January 1994. In October Stan Lynch left the group to work as an independent writer and producer. Switching to Warner Bros., Tom Petty recorded a second solo album, *Wildflowers*, which yielded a major hit with "You Don't Know How It Feels," then toured with the Heartbreakers in 1995.

Tom Petty and the Heartbreakers

Tom Petty and the Heartbreakers	Shelter	52006	'76	†
	MCA	52006		†
	MCA	10135	'91	CS/CD
You're Gonna Get It!	Shelter	52029	'78	†
	MCA	52029		†
	MCA	10134	'91	CS/CD
Damn the Torpedoes	Backstreet	5105	'79	†
	MCA	1486		CS
	MCA	31161	'85	CD
	Mobile Fidelity	551	'91	CD
Hard Promises	Backstreet	5160	'81	†
	MCA	1479		CS
	MCA	31066	'85	CD
	Mobile Fidelity	565	'92	CD
Long After Dark	Backstreet	5360	'82	†
	MCA	1571		CS
	MCA	31027	'85	CD
Southern Accents	MCA	39322		CS
	MCA	5486	'85	CD
Pack Up the Plantation-Live!	MCA	(2) 8021	'05	CS/CD
Let Me Up (I've Had Enough)	MCA	5836	'87	CS/CD
Into the Great Wide Open	MCA	10317	'91	CS/CD
Greatest Hits	MCA	10813	'93	CS/CD
Playback	MCA	(6) 11375	'95	CS/CD

The Traveling Wilburys

Volume One	Wilbury	25796	'88	CS/CD
Volume 3	Wilbury	26324	'90	CS/CD

Tom Petty

Full Moon Fever	MCA	6253	'89	CS/CD
Wildflowers	Warner Bros.	(2) 45759	'94	LP
	Warner Bros.	45759	'94	CS/CD

SAM PHILLIPS
(b. Jan. 5, 1923, Florence, AL)

Best remembered as the man who "discovered" and first recorded Elvis Presley, Sam Phillips was instrumental in the development and popularization of rockabilly music. Having previously made the initial recordings of bluesmen such as B. B. King, Howlin' Wolf, and Junior Parker, Phillips switched his attention to white Southern singers after the success of Presley, subsequently signing and recording the early works of Johnny Cash, Carl Perkins, Roy Orbison, and Jerry Lee Lewis. However, Sun Records eventually lost all of its major acts to larger labels, and its influence was in decline by the end of the '50s.

Sam Phillips was working as a disc jockey at Memphis's WRAC when he realized that few facilities existed to record local black performers. In 1950 he opened the Memphis Recording Service and made early recordings by B. B. King, Howlin' Wolf, and others, leasing them to established independent companies such as Modern/RPM and Chess/Checker. Forming the Sun label in late 1952, Phillips scored his first R&B hits the next year with Little Junior Parker's "Mystery Train" and Rufus Thomas's "Bear Cat."

In his search for a white singer who sounded black (his actual words were purportedly far less delicate), Sam Phillips found his man in Elvis Presley, who had first come to the Sun studio in July 1953 to make a private recording for his mother. Teamed with guitarist Scotty Moore and stand-up bassist Bill Black, Presley made his first recordings for Sun, Bill Monroe's "Blue Moon of Kentucky" backed with Arthur "Big Boy" Crudup's "That's All Right (Mama)," in July 1954. With some help from a local disc jockey, "That's All Right (Mama)" became a regional hit. Phillips subsequently recorded Presley's versions of songs written by black writers, backed by country-and-western standards. Country hits for Elvis on Sun in 1955 included "Baby Let's Play House," "I Forgot to Remember to Forget" (a top country hit), and "Mystery Train."

In November 1955 Sam Phillips sold Presley's Sun contract, as well as his master recordings, to RCA-Victor for an unprecedented $35,000. After Presley's departure Phillips began working with other white Southern singers, such as Johnny Cash and Carl Perkins. Perkins soon scored a smash country, R&B, and pop hit with his own "Blue Suede Shoes" in early 1956, launching rockabilly music in the mainstream. Cash achieved his first major pop hit for Sun (after several country hits) with "I Walk the Line" in fall 1956, followed by the sappy "Ballad of a Teenage Queen," "Guess Things Happen That Way," and "The Ways of a Woman in Love," the latter recorded under arranger-producer Bill Justis.

Issuing the early recordings of Roy Orbison in 1956 (including the minor pop hit "Ooby Dooby"), Sun Records next achieved smash three-way crossover hits in 1957–1958 with Jerry Lee Lewis's "Whole Lotta Shakin' Going On," "Great Balls of Fire," and "Breathless." In 1957 Phillips formed the subsidiary label Phillips International; hits on the label include Bill Justis's instrumental "Raunchy," Carl Mann's "Mona Lisa," and Charlie Rich's "Lonely Weekends." However, by 1958 Johnny Cash, Carl Perkins, and Roy Orbison had left Sun for major established labels, and Jerry Lee Lewis departed in 1962. Sun Records continued to operate in the '60s, but the label failed to produce any more significant hits or discover any important new acts. In 1968 Sam Phillips retired and sold the Sun masters to Nashville's Shelby Singleton. He was among the first inductees as a nonperformer into the Rock and Roll Hall of Fame in 1986.

WILSON PICKETT
(b. Mar. 18, 1941, Prattville, AL)

One of the most popular soul singers of the '60s, Wilson Pickett was aided immeasurably by the excellent studio bands backing him at the Stax Studio in Memphis, Tennessee, and the Fame Studios in Muscle Shoals, Alabama. Projecting a tough, aggressive, hard-driving emotionalism in his recordings, Pickett scored a series of R&B and pop hits on Atlantic Records between 1963 and 1972, including the classics "In the Midnight Hour," "Mustang Sally," and "Funky Broadway." Recording for a variety of labels since leaving Atlantic Records in 1972, Wilson Pickett failed to reestablish himself in the '80s and '90s.

Raised in rural Prattville, Alabama, Wilson Pickett moved to Detroit at age 16 and made his professional debut as lead singer of the gospel quartet the Violinaires in the late '50s. From 1961 to 1963 he manned the Detroit vocal group the Falcons, authoring and singing

WILSON PICKETT

lead on their smash 1962 R&B hit "I Found a Love." Pickett subsequently went solo, joining Lloyd Price's Double L label, where he wrote and recorded "If You Need Me" (a smash R&B hit for Solomon Burke in 1963) and scored a near-smash R&B hit with "It's Too Late."

Signing with Atlantic Records in 1964, Wilson Pickett began recording in Memphis, working with Booker T. Jones and Steve Cropper of the MGs. Cropper coauthored three of his early hits, the classic "In the Midnight Hour" (a major pop and top R&B hit), "Don't Fight It" (a smash R&B hit), and "634-5789" (another major pop and top R&B hit). Subsequently recording at the Fame Studios in Muscle Shoals, Alabama, Pickett scored major crossover hits with "Land of 1,000 Dances" (originally a minor hit for coauthor Chris Kenner in 1963), "Mustang Sally," a remake of "I Found a Love," "Funky Broadway," "She's Lookin' Good," and "I'm a Midnight Mover" through 1968. In 1969 he achieved a major pop hit with the Beatles' "Hey Jude," followed in 1970 by the crossover hit "Sugar Sugar." Later in 1970 Pickett worked with producers Kenny Gamble and Leon Huff at Sigma Sound Studios in Philadelphia, and the resulting album *In Philadelphia* yielded two major crossover hits with "Engine Number Nine" and "Don't Let the Green Grass Fool You."

After the crossover hits "Don't Knock My Love—Part 1" and "Fire and Water," Wilson Pickett left Atlantic Records. He recorded for a number of different labels during the '70s but failed to achieve another major pop or R&B hit. Pickett was arrested several times in the '80s and '90s and was sentenced to a year in jail in October 1993 for hitting a pedestrian while driving drunk. He was inducted into the Rock and Roll Hall of Fame in 1991.

Wilson Pickett

It's Too Late	Double L	8300	'64	†
In the Midnight Hour	Atlantic	8114	'65	†
	Rhino	71275	'93	CS/CD
The Exciting Wilson Pickett	Atlantic	8129	'66	†
	Rhino	71276	'93	CS/CD
Wicked Pickett	Atlantic	8138	'67	†
The Sound of Wilson Pickett	Atlantic	8145	'67	†
Best	Atlantic	8151	'67	†
I'm In Love	Atlantic	8175	'68	†
	Rhino	72218	'95	CD
Midnight Mover	Atlantic	8183	'68	†
Hey, Jude	Atlantic	8215	'69	†
Right On	Atlantic	8250	'70	†

In Philadelphia	Atlantic	8270	'70	†
	Rhino	72219	'95	CD
Best, Volume 2	Atlantic	8290	'71	†
Don't Knock My Love	Atlantic	8300	'71	†
Greatest Hits	Atlantic	(2) 501	'73	†
Best	Atlantic	81283	'85	LP/CS/CD†
	Rhino	81283		CS/CD
Greatest Hits	Atlantic	81737	'87	CD†
	Rhino	81737		CD
Great Wilson Pickett Hits	Wand	672	'66	†
Wickedness	Trip	8010	'71	†
Mr. Magic Man	RCA	4858	'73	†
Miz Lena's Boy	RCA	0312	'73	†
Pickett in the Pocket	RCA	0495	'74	†
Join Me and Let's Be Free	RCA	0856	'75	†
	RCA	2149	'77	†
Chocolate Mountain	Wicked	9001	'76	†
A Funky Situation	Big Tree	76011	'78	†
I Want You	EMI-America	17019	'79	†
Right Track	EMI-America	17043	'81	†
American Soul Man	Motown	6244		CD
A Man and a Half: The Best of Wilson Pickett	Rhino	(2) 70287	'92	CS/CD
Very Best	Rhino	71212		CS/CD

PINK FLOYD

Roger "Syd" Barrett (b. Jan. 6, 1946, Cambridge, England), lead gtr, voc; **Rick Wright** (b. July 28, 1945, London), kybd, voc; **Roger Waters** (b. Sept. 6, 1944, Great Bookham, England), bs, pno, voc; and **Nick Mason** (b. Jan. 27, 1945, Birmingham, England), drm [Syd Barrett was replaced in 1968 by **David Gilmour** (b. Mar. 6, 1944, Cambridge, England).]

Generally regarded as the first underground group to emerge from the London club scene of the '60s, Pink Floyd was probably the first British psychedelic band, due in large part to the lead-guitar playing and surrealistic, mystically obsessed lyrics of founder Syd Barrett. With Barrett's departure in 1968, the group became one of the first so-called progressive rock bands, featuring elaborate productions with choirs and sophisticated orchestrations and the keyboard-synthesizer playing of Rick Wright. Their 1973 concept album, *The Dark Side of the Moon*, established the band's reputation and continued to sell for years after its release.

Roger "Syd" Barrett attended school with Roger Waters and David Gilmour in the early '60s. Barrett moved to London after school, where he took up guitar and played in several groups, including a folk duo with Gilmour. Waters moved to London to study architecture and met Rick Wright and Nick Mason in an architecture class. Waters, Mason, and Wright formed Sigma 6, which later became the T-Set and the Abdabs. In 1965 the Abdabs broke up and Mason, Wright, and Waters recruited guitarists Bob Close and Syd Barrett and adopted the name Pink Floyd (after American bluesmen Pink Anderson and Floyd Collins). Close remained with the group only briefly. By February 1966 Pink Floyd had obtained their first regular engagement at the Marquee Club and won their first following. In October they moved to London's Sound/Light Workshop, where they were accompanied by a light show, the first of its kind in Great Britain. Becoming the house band at the UFO Club by year's end, Pink Floyd signed with EMI Records (the small, experimental Tower label in the United States).

PINK FLOYD

Pink Floyd's first single, Barrett's "Arnold Layne," concerned a perverted transvestite and proved so controversial that even underground Radio London banned the song, yet it became a moderate British hit. Barrett's "See Emily Play" became a smash British hit in the spring, and Pink Floyd's debut album was released in the United States near the end of 1967. Critically acclaimed, *The Piper at the Gates of Dawn* was dominated by Barrett's surreal, mystical songwriting. However, the group's next three British singles fared poorly as Pink Floyd toured America for the first time in October 1967. Barrett's behavior, erratic as it was, began to deteriorate by early 1968, and Dave Gilmour joined the group as second guitarist in February. By April Barrett had left amid rumors of drug abuse and bizarre stories of his unpredictable behavior. He inspired a devoted cult following that persists to this day, and recordings made by him with Gilmour and Wright during 1970 were eventually released in the United States in 1974. Syd Barrett remained a mysterious and enigmatic figure, seldom appearing in public.

With Barrett's departure, Roger Waters began assuming the role of chief songwriter. *A Saucerful of Secrets* contained his "Let There Be More Light" and "Set the Controls for the Heart of the Sun." In the summer of 1969 they first toured with a custom-built quadraphonic sound system, while their soundtrack to the film *More* was released. At the beginning of 1970 Pink Floyd's double-record set *Ummagumma* was issued on EMI's new "underground" label Harvest. Their first moderately successful album in the United States, *Ummagumma* was comprised of one live album and one studio album. *Atom Heart Mother* was debuted at the Bath Festival in England during June, and the album featured choirs, orchestras, and remarkably diverse sounds under the influence of electronics wizard Ron Geesin. Pink Floyd's stage shows became more elaborate, and in summer 1971 an outdoor concert in London utilized a 60 foot inflatable octopus. The group-produced *Meddle* included the instrumental "One of These Days" and the 23-minute-plus "Echoes," one of their most popular songs.

Following the soundtrack to the film *Le Vallee* entitled *Obscured by Clouds*, Pink Floyd spent nine months recording their next album. Premiered live in London in 1972 using more than nine tons of equipment, *The Dark Side of the Moon* was entirely comprised of songs written by Roger Waters and became an instant best-seller, establishing the group as superstars. Dealing with alienation and madness as caused by the pressures of contemporary society, the album yielded Pink Floyd's first major American hit, "Money," and included group favorites such as "Brain Damage" and "Time." The album sold millions of copies worldwide and remained on the American album charts for more than 14 years. Recorded for their new label Columbia, Pink Floyd's *Wish You Were Here* became a best-seller and featured the classic "Welcome to the Machine" as well as Gilmour's title song and Waters's tribute to Syd Barrett, "Shine on You Crazy Diamond."

Continuing to explore the themes of repression, alienation, and loneliness, Pink Floyd's *Animals* depicted society as divided into three castes—dogs, pigs, and sheep—and the album included songs for each. Their massive tour in support of the album utilized tons of musical and lighting equipment and, in performance, featured a huge flying pig. In late 1979 the group issued their next album, *The Wall*. Another bleak and gloomy view of modern society, the album was considered one of their most ambitious and personal works, and stayed on the album charts for more than two years, selling more than eight million copies in the United States alone. The album contained group favorites such as "Is There Anybody Out There?," "Nobody Home," and "Comfortably Numb," and produced a minor hit with "Run Like Hell" and a top hit with the controversial "Another Brick in the Wall (Part II)." The 1980 tour in support of *The Wall* was so massive that it was performed in only three cities, London, New York, and Los Angeles. It was one of the most elaborate rock productions ever mounted, utilizing a 30-foot-high, stage-wide wall of cardboard blocks that were toppled by the end of the shows. The production featured films, sophisticated lighting, and gigantic plastic inflatables in one of the most awesome and spectacular performances in rock history. The album later served as the basis for the grim, violent 1982 movie *The Wall*, starring Bob Geldof of the Boomtown Rats and directed by Alan Parker.

Following 1983's desultory *The Final Cut*, Pink Floyd dissolved. Dave Gilmour and Roger Waters each recorded solo albums for Columbia Records in 1984. In 1986 Waters sued for formal dissolution of Pink Floyd, but in 1987 Gilmour, Rick Wright, and Nick Mason reconstituted the group for *A Momentary Lapse of Reason*, entirely written by Gilmour. The album yielded a minor hit with "Learning to Fly" and remained on the album charts for more than a year. With eight-piece accompaniment, the three toured arenas in 1987 and stadiums in 1988. Waters countered with the concept album *Radio K.A.O.S.* and his own tour in 1987. Pink Floyd toured internationally in 1989, and in July 1990 *The Wall* was performed as a benefit for the Memorial Fund for Disaster Relief at the Berlin Wall by performers such as Paul Carrack, Van Morrison, Sinead O'Connor, Thomas Dolby, and Levon Helm and Rick Danko of the Band. In 1991 David Palmer and the Royal Philharmonic Orchestra recorded *The Music of Pink Floyd: Orchestral Maneuvers*, and in 1992 Waters recorded *Amused to Death*. In 1994 Pink Floyd issued the listless *The Division Bell* on Sony and toured once again. The tour produced the 1995 live set *Pulse*. A year later the group was inducted into the Rock and Roll Hall of Fame.

Syd Barrett

The Madcap Laughs and "Barrett"	Harvest	11314	'74	†
Barrett	Capitol	46606	'90	CS/CD
The Madcap Laughs	Capitol	46607	'90	CS/CD
Opel	Capitol	91206	'89	CS/CD
Crazy Diamond	Capitol	(3) 81412	'94	CD
Octopus (The Best Of)	Cleopatra	57712	'92	CD

Pink Floyd

The Piper at the Gates of Dawn	Tower	5093	'67	†
	Capitol	46384	'87	CS/CD
A Saucerful of Secrets	Tower	5131	'68	†
	Capitol	46383	'87	CS/CD
A Nice Pair (reissue of above two)	Harvest	(2) 11257	'73	†
	Capitol	11257		CS
More (soundtrack)	Tower	5169	'69	†
	Harvest	11198	'73	†
	Capitol	16230	'85	†
	Capitol	46386		CS/CD

Title	Label	Number	Year	Format
Relics (recorded 1967–1969)	Harvest	759	'71	†
	Capitol	16234	'83	CS
Ummagumma	Harvest	(2) 388	'69	†
	Capitol	46404		CS/CD
Atom Heart Mother	Harvest	382	'70	†
	Capitol	16337	'85	†
	Capitol	46381		CS/CD
	Mobile Fidelity	595	'94	CD
	Mobile Fidelity	202	'94	LP
Meddle	Harvest	832	'71	†
	Capitol	46034		CS/CD
	Mobile Fidelity	518		CD
Obscured by Clouds	Harvest	11078	'72	†
	Capitol	16330	'85	†
	Capitol	46385		CS/CD
The Dark Side of the Moon	Harvest	11163	'73	†
	Capitol	46001		LP/CS/CD
	Mobile Fidelity	517	'88	CD
The Dark Side of the Moon XX	Capitol	81479	'93	CD
Works (recorded 1968–1973)	Capitol	12276	'83	CS
	Capitol	46478		CD
Gift Set	Capitol	91340		CS/CD
Wish You Were Here	Columbia	33453	'75	LP/CS/CD
	Columbia/Legacy	53753	'93	CD
Animals	Columbia	34474	'77	LP/CS/CD
The Wall	Columbia	(2) 36183	'79	LP/CS/CD
	Mobile Fidelity	(2) 537	'90	CD
A Collection of Great Dance Songs (1975–1981)	Columbia	37680	'81	CS/CD
The Final Cut	Columbia	38243	'83	CS/CD
A Momentary Lapse of Reason	Columbia	40599	'87	CS/CD
Delicate Sound of Thunder	Columbia	(2) 44484	'88	CS/CD
The Division Bell	Columbia	64200	'94	LP/CS/CD
Pulse	Columbia	(2) 67065	'95	CS/CD

David Palmer and the Royal Philharmonic Orchestra

The Music of Pink Floyd: Orchestral Maneuvers	RCA	57960	'91	CS/CD

London Philharmonic Orchestra

Us and Them: Symphonic Pink Floyd	Point Music	446623	'95	CS/CD

Tribute Album

A Saucerful of Secrets: Tribute to Pink Floyd	Cleopatra	(2) 9551	'95	CD

David Gilmour

David Gilmour	Columbia	35388	'78	CS/CD
About Face	Columbia	39296	'84	CS/CD

Nick Mason

Fictitious Sports	Columbia	37307	'81	†

Nick Mason and Rick Fenn

Profiles	Columbia	40142	'85	†

Roger Waters

The Pros and Cons of Hitchhiking	Columbia	39290	'84	CS/CD

Radio K.A.O.S.	Columbia	40795	'87	CS/CD
Amused to Death	Columbia	47127	'92	CS/CD
	Columbia/Legacy	53196	'92	CD
	Columbia/Legacy	64426	'94	CD
The Wall: Berlin 1990	Mercury	(2) 846611	'90	CS/CD

GENE PITNEY
(b. Feb. 17, 1941, Hartford, CT)

Gene Pitney was a successful singles artist during the '60s, scoring numerous hits featuring his dramatic tenor voice. An accomplished songwriter, Pitney composed hits for many pop acts, and recorded a wide diversity of material. He was an early champion of the Rolling Stones, recording a Jagger-Richards composition, "That Girl Belongs to Yesterday," and made some of the earliest recordings of songs written by Randy Newman. Gene Pitney's popularity waned in the United States in the late '60s, yet he continued to tour Europe while becoming involved in the world of finance.

Gene Pitney grew up in Rockville, Connecticut, and studied piano, drums, and guitar as a teenager. He performed at high school dances with his group the Genials and made his first recordings for Decca in 1959 with Ginny Arnell as Jamie and Jane. He also recorded as Billy Bryan for Blaze Records and under his own name for Festival Records in 1960. His first major success came as a songwriter, composing the smash hits "Rubber Ball" for Bobby Vee, "Hello Mary Lou" for Ricky Nelson, and "He's a Rebel" for the Crystals.

Signed to Musicor Records, Pitney scored his first moderate hit in 1961 with his own "(I Wanna) Love My Life Away," followed by Carole King and Gerry Goffin's "Every Breath I Take," produced by Phil Spector. He soon achieved a major hit with "Town Without Pity" and smash hits with two Burt Bacharach–Hal David compositions, "(The Man Who Shot) Liberty Valance" and "Only Love Can Break a Heart," from his album of the same name, which also produced major hits with "Half Heaven-Half Heartache" and "True Love Never Runs Smooth." In 1963 he hit with "Mecca" and "Twenty-Four Hours from Tulsa," another Bacharach-David composition, and subsequently scored a moderate hit with Mick Jagger and Keith Richards's "That Girl Belongs to Yesterday." He assisted the Rolling Stones in the recording of their album *12 X 5*.

In 1964 Gene Pitney had near-smash hits with "It Hurts to Be in Love" and "I'm Gonna Be Strong," the latter written by Barry Mann and Cynthia Weil. He began recording albums in foreign languages. In 1965–1966 he recorded country albums with George Jones and Melba Montgomery, scoring major country hits with "I've Got Five Dollars and It's Saturday Night" and "Louisiana Mama" with Jones and "Baby, Ain't That Fine" with Montgomery. Major pop hits for Pitney through 1968 include "Last Chance to Turn Around" and "She's a Heartbreaker," and the Mann-Weil compositions "Looking Through the Eyes of Love" and "Backstage." He also recorded the Randy Newman songs "Nobody Needs Your Love," "Something's Gotten Hold of My Heart," and "Just One Smile," the latter a minor hit in 1966–1967.

Pitney never achieved another major pop hit, and his popularity faded in the United States in the late '60s. Nonetheless, he continued to tour Europe while avoiding oldies revival shows in this country. He became involved in real estate and stock market investments in the '70s and later scored a British near-smash hit in 1988 with a remake of "Something's Gotten Hold of My Heart" in duet with Marc Almond. In 1993 he performed for the first time in the United States in almost 20 years, giving a sold-out show at New York's Carnegie Hall.

Gene Pitney

Many Sides of Gene Pitney	Musicor	3001	'62	†
Only Love Can Break a Heart	Musicor	3003	'62	†
Sings Just for You	Musicor	3004	'63	†
Blue Gene	Musicor	3006	'63	†
Meets the Fair Young Ladies of Folkland	Musicor	3007	'64	†
Italiano	Musicor	3015	'64	†
It Hurts to Be In Love	Musicor	3019	'64	†
I Must Be Seeing Things	Musicor	3056	'65	†
Looking Through the Eyes of Love	Musicor	3069	'65	†
Espanol	Musicor	3072	'65	†
Backstage I'm Lonely	Musicor	3095	'66	†
Nessuno Mi Puo Giudicare	Musicor	3100	'66	†
The Gene Pitney Show	Musicor	3101	'66	†
Greatest Hits of All Time	Musicor	3102	'66	†
The Country Side of Gene	Musicor	3104	'66	†
Young and Warm and Wonderful	Musicor	3108	'66	†
Just One Smile	Musicor	3117	'67	†
Pitney Espanol	Musicor	3154		†
Sings Burt Bacharach	Musicor	3161	'68	†
She's a Heartbreaker	Musicor	3164	'68	†
This Is Gene Pitney (Singing the Platters' Golden Platters)	Musicor	3183	'70	†

Anthologies

World-Wide Winners	Musicor	3005	'63	†
Big 16	Musicor	3008	'64	†
More Big 16, Volume 2	Musicor	3043	'65	†
More Big 16, Volume 3	Musicor	3085	'66	†
Golden Greats	Musicor	3134	'67	†
The Gene Pitney Story	Musicor	(2) 3148	'68	†
Greatest Hits	Musicor	3174	'69	†
Superstar	Musicor	3193	'71		
Ten Years After	Musicor	3206	'71	†
Golden Hits	Musicor	3250	'71	†
A Golden Hour of Gene Pitney	Musicor	3233	'72	†
Gene Pitney	Springboard Int'l	4057	'76	†
The Best	Piccadilly	3321	'82	†
Anthology (1961–1968)	Rhino	(2) 1102	'84	†
	Rhino	5896		CS
Anthology (excerpts from above)	Rhino	75896	'87	CD
Best of Gene Pitney	K-tel	3028	'91	CS/CD
The Great Recordings	Tomato	(2) 71732	'95	CD
Greatest Hits	Curb/Atlantic	77758	'95	CS/CD
Best of Easy Listening	Richmond	2145		CS
Town Without Pity	Richmond	2306		CS
20 Greatest Hits	Fest	4410		CS/CD
The Best of Gene Pitney	Impact	004		LP

Gene Pitney and George Jones

Gene Pitney and George Jones	Musicor	3044	'65	†
It's Country Time Again	Musicor	3065	'65	†

Best of Country	Richmond	2223		CS
One Has My Name	Richmond	2239		CS
Gene Pitney and Melba Montgomery				
Being Together	Musicor	3077	'66	†
Gene Pitney, George Jones, and Melba Montgomery				
Famous Country Duets	Musicor	3079	'65	†

THE PLATTERS

Tony Williams (b. Apr. 5, 1928, Elizabeth, NJ; d. Aug. 14, 1992, New York, NY), lead ten voc; **David Lynch** (b. 1929, St. Louis, MO; d. Jan. 2, 1981), second ten voc; **Paul Robi** (b. 1931, New Orleans, LA; d. Feb. 1, 1989), bar voc; **Herb Reed** (b. 1931, Kansas City, MO), bs voc; **Zola Taylor** (b. 1934, Los Angeles, CA), contralto voc [Later members include **Sonny Turner** (b. c. 1939, Cleveland, OH); **Nate Nelson** (b. Apr. 10, 1932, New York, NY; d. June 1, 1984, Boston, MA); **Monroe Powell**; and **Gene Williams**. Mentor-manager-songwriter **Buck Ram** was born in 1908 in Chicago and died January 1, 1991, in Las Vegas, Nevada.]

Featuring a smooth, sophisticated sound and the superb lead tenor voice of Tony Williams, the Platters were the most successful black vocal group of the '50s. One of the first such groups to enjoy massive popularity with white audiences, the Platters helped launch doo-wop music and influenced a generation of groups with their inventive gospel-style harmonies. Masterminded by manager, producer, arranger, and chief songwriter Buck Ram, the Platters scored a series of smash pop and R&B hits between 1955 and 1960, including the classics "Only You," "The Great Pretender," and "The Magic Touch" (all written by Ram). Their recording success led to appearances on television and the cabaret circuit as well as rock-and-roll package shows. The Platters went into a decline with the 1960 departure of Tony Williams, yet a number of groups continued to tour as the Platters into the '90s.

In 1953 in Los Angeles, Tony Williams, David Lynch, Alex Hodge, and Herb Reed formed the Platters under the auspices of Buck Ram, a former writer and arranger for the big bands of the '30s and '40s. Contracted to the Cincinnati-based Federal/King label, the group unsuccessfully recorded Ram's "Only You" and other songs for the label. (These early recordings were later issued on King and Deluxe.) Ram subsequently replaced Hodge with Paul Robi and recruited female vocalist Zola Taylor, placing the group with Mercury Records. In fall 1955 the Platters scored a top R&B and smash pop hit with "Only You." During 1956 they achieved a top pop and R&B hit with Ram's "The Great Pretender," and pop/R&B smashes with Ram's "(You've Got) The Magic Touch" and the standard "My Prayer."

Crossover smashes for the Platters through 1957 include "You'll Never Never Know" (cowritten by Tony Williams and Paul Robi), "It Isn't Right," "On My Word of Honor," "One in a Million" (cowritten by Williams), "I'm Sorry" backed with "He's Mine," and Ram's "My Dream." Developing a wide audience among television viewers, rock-and-roll fans, and the larger pop audience, the Platters performed at rock-and-roll shows and supper clubs. In 1958 they scored top pop (and smash R&B) hits with the classic "Twilight Time" (coauthored by Ram) and the standard "Smoke Gets in Your Eyes." Subsequent crossover hits include "Enchanted" and "Harbor Lights," but in June 1960 Tony Williams left the Platters to pursue an inauspicious solo career. He was replaced by Sonny Turner, and the group managed major pop hits with the standards "To Each His Own" and "I'll Never Smile Again" through 1961. Zola Taylor left around 1963, and later Nate Nelson, lead singer of the Flamingos' 1959 crossover hit "I Only Have Eyes for You," replaced Paul Robi. The Platters' last major hits came in 1966–1967 with "I Love You 1,000 Times" and "With This Ring."

Sonny Turner left the Platters in the early '70s and Nate Nelson left in 1982. Buck Ram maintained the group with lead vocalist Monroe Powell and bass singer Gene Williams through the '80s. During this time former members Paul Robi and Herb Reed also toured with their own groups as the Platters. In 1990 the group was inducted into the Rock and Roll Hall of Fame

The Platters

The Platters	King	549	'55	†
	King	651	'59	LP/CS/CD
The Platters	Mercury	20146	'56	†
The Platters—Volume 2	Mercury	20216	'57	†
Rock All Night	Mercury	20293	'57	†
The Flying Platters	Mercury	20298	'57	†
Around the World with the Flying Platters	Mercury	20366	'58	†
		60043	'59	†
Remember When	Mercury	60087	'59	†
Reflections	Mercury	60160	'60	†
Life Is Just a Bowl of Cherries	Mercury	60245	'61	†
Sing for the Lonely	Mercury	60669	'62	†
Encore of Broadway Golden Hits	Mercury	60613	'62	†
Encore of Golden Hits of the Groups	Mercury	60693	'62	†
Moonlight Memories	Mercury	60759	'63	†
Sing All-Time Movie Hits	Mercury	60782	'63	†
Sing Latino	Mercury	60808	'63	†
Christmas with the Platters	Mercury	60841	'63	†
	Fontana	822742		†
	Polydor	822742			
	Mercury	822742	'94	CS/CD
10th Anniversary Album	Mercury	60933	'64	†
New Soul of the Platters	Mercury	60983	'65	†
I Love You 1,000 Times	Musicor	3091	'66	†
Have the Magic Touch	Musicor	3111	'66	†
Going Back to Detroit	Musicor	3125	'67	†
Sweet, Sweet Lovin'	Musicor	3156	'68	†
I Get the Sweetest Feeling	Musicor	3171	'68	†
Singing the Great Hits Our Way	Musicor	3185	'69	†
Greatest Hits, Featuring Paul Robi (recorded 1986)	Jango	775	'87	LP/CS/CD†

Anthologies

19 Hits	King	5002	'77	†
19 Original Hits	Deluxe	7835		CS
22 Greats	Deluxe	7862		CS
22 Gold	Deluxe	7884		CS
22 Hits	Deluxe	7895		CS
16 Greatest Hits	Deluxe	7900		CS/CD
Encore of Golden Hits	Mercury	20472	'60	†
	Mercury	60243	'61	†
	Mercury	826254		†
More Encore of Golden Hits	Mercury	20591	'60	†
	Mercury	60252	'61	†
	Mercury	8002	'79	†
	Mercury	826246		†

Encores	Mercury/Wing	12112	'60	†
The Flying Platters	Mercury/Wing	16226	'62	†
Reflections	Mercury/Wing	16272	'64	†
10th Anniversary Album	Mercury/Wing	16346	'67	†
Platterama	Mercury	4050	'82	†
Golden Hits	Mercury	826447	'86	CD†
More Golden Hits	Mercury	830773	'87	CD†
The Magic Touch: An Anthology	Mercury	(2) 510314	'91	CS/CD
The Very Best of the Platters	Mercury	510317	'91	CS/CD
New Golden Hits	Musicor	3141	'67	†
Golden Hour	Musicor	3231	'72	†
Only You	Music Disc	1002	'69	†
In the Still of the Night	Pickwick	3120	'69	†
Super Hits	Pickwick	3236		†
Only You	Pickwick	(2) 2083	'76	†
The Platters	Springboard Int'l	4059	'76	†
Attention	Phillips	6430046	'82	†
Anthology (1955–1967)	Rhino	71495	'86	CS
Red Sails in the Sunset	Allegiance	72913	'88	CD†
The Greatest Hits	Bella Musica	89903	'90	CD†
Golden Sides of the Platters	Pair	1130		CS
Only Their Best for You	Pair	1239	'91	CS/CD
All the Hits and More	Double Gold	(2) 53041	'95	CD
Pledging My Love	Richmond	2179		CS
With This Ring	Richmond	2184		CS
The Great Pretender	Richmond	2189		CS
Only You	Richmond	2210		CS
Twilight Time	Richmond	2218		CS
You'll Never, Never Know	Polygram	839693		CS
20 Greatest Hits	Fest	4415		CS/CD
Greatest Hits	Special Music	4802		CS/CD
Tony Williams				
A Girl Is a Girl Is a Girl	Mercury	60138	'59	†
Sings His Greatest Hits	Reprise	6006	'61	†
Magic Touch of Tony	Phillips	60051	'62	†

POCO

Jim Messina (b. Dec. 5, 1947, Maywood, CA), lead gtr, bs, voc; **Richie Furay** (b. May 9, 1944, Yellow Springs, OH), rhythm gtr, voc; **Randy Meisner** (b. Mar. 8, 1946, Scottsbluff, NE), bs, voc; **Rusty Young** (b. Feb. 23, 1946, Long Beach, CA), pedal steel, dobro, voc; **George Grantham** (b. Jan. 20, 1947, Cordell, OK), drm, voc [Bassist-vocalist **Timothy B. Schmit** (b. Oct. 30, 1947, Sacramento, CA) replaced Randy Meisner, and guitarist-vocalist **Paul Cotton** (b. Feb. 26, 1943, Los Angeles, CA) replaced Jim Messina, in 1970. Schmit and George Grantham left in 1979, to be replaced by **Steve Chapman** (b. England), drums, **Charlie Harrison** (b. England), bass, and **Kim Bullard** (b. Atlanta, GA), keyboards.]

Seminal West Coast country-rock band of the '70s, Poco did not attain the popularity of the Eagles, the first commercially successful band of the genre, until the late '70s. By that time founders Jim Messina and Richie Furay had moved on, as had founder Randy Meisner, who subsequently joined and departed the Eagles. Despite the personnel changes, Poco maintained a remarkably consistent sound, featuring group vocal harmonies and rock instrumentation. They recorded several outstanding albums, including 1973's *Crazy Eyes*, eventually breaking through with 1979's *Legend* and its two hit singles. The group disbanded in 1984 and reunited with the original members in 1989.

Jim Messina and Richie Furay, both former members of the Buffalo Springfield, formed Poco with Rusty Young, Randy Meisner, and George Grantham in August 1968. Debuting at the Troubadour in Los Angeles in November, Poco auditioned for Apple Records but signed with Epic. Given the chaotic career of the Buffalo Springfield, Poco's debut album was appropriately titled *Pickin' Up the Pieces*. The album sold only modestly and failed to yield a hit single. By the time of the album's release, Meisner had already departed to join Rick Nelson's Stone Canyon Band, later to help form the Eagles. Poco remained a quartet until February 1970, when Timothy B. Schmit joined the band. *Poco* and *Deliverin'* yielded minor hits with Messina's "You Better Think Twice" and Furay's "C'mon."

In November 1970 Jim Messina left Poco to form the successful Loggins and Messina duo with Kenny Loggins. He was replaced by Paul Cotton, the erstwhile leader of the Illinois Speed Press. This lineup—Furay, Young, Cotton, Schmit, and Grantham—recorded three albums and toured extensively, usually as a support act. *Crazy Eyes*, probably their finest album for Epic, sold moderately and included Furay's title song as well as excellent versions of Gram Parsons's "Brass Buttons" and J. J. Cale's "Magnolia."

Richie Furay left Poco in September 1973 to form the ill-fated Souther-Hillman-Furay Band, with singer-songwriter John David Souther and Chris Hillman, a former member of the Byrds and the Flying Burrito Brothers. An early associate of Jackson Browne and Glenn Frey, Souther had cowritten several songs for the Eagles and contributed three songs to Linda Ronstadt's album *Don't Cry Now*. Formed at the behest of Asylum Records president David Geffen as a prospective supergroup, they scored a major hit with Furay's "Fallin' in Love" from their debut album. However, the group encountered a credibility problem brought on by Asylum's massive hype campaign, and they disbanded in late 1975. Furay later recorded three solo albums for Asylum, managing a moderate hit with "I Still Have Dreams" in late 1979.

With Furay's departure, Poco continued as a four-piece, with Paul Cotton taking over as lead vocalist and Cotton and Young composing most of the material. They recorded two more albums for Epic before switching to ABC Records in 1975. They were able to achieve minor hits with "Keep On Tryin'" and the title songs to *Rose of Cimarron* and *Indian Summer*. However, by March 1978 Timothy B. Schmit had left to join the Eagles and George Grantham had left, to eventually join the Doobie Brothers. Rusty Young, the only remaining original member, and Paul Cotton reconstituted the group for their best-selling album *Legend*, which yielded the major hits "Crazy Love" and "Heart of the Night." Buoyed by the album's success (it stayed on the album charts for a year), Poco continued to tour and record until 1984, when they disbanded.

In 1989 the five original members of Poco—Jim Messina, Richie Furay, Randy Meisner, Rusty Young, and George Grantham—reunited to record *Legacy* for RCA. The album yielded a moderate hit with "Nothin' to Hide," cowritten by producer Richard Marx, and "Call It Love." They toured in 1990 with drummer Gary Mallaber, but the band soon disintegrated.

Poco

Pickin' Up the Pieces	Epic	26460	'69	†
	Epic/Legacy	66227	'95	CD
Poco	Epic	26522	'70/'90	CD
Deliverin'	Epic	30209	'71/'90	CD

From the Inside	Epic	30753	'71/'91	CD
A Good Feelin' to Know	Epic	31601	'72	CD
Crazy Eyes	Epic	32354	'73	†
	Epic/Legacy	66968	'95	CD
Seven	Epic	32895	'74	†
	Epic/Legacy	66985		CD
Cantamos	Epic	33192	'74	†
Live	Epic	33336	'76	†
Head Over Heels	ABC/MCA	890	'75	†
	MCA	37009		†
	MCA	31327	'88	CD
Rose of Cimarron	ABC/MCA	946	'76	†
	MCA	37010		†
	One Way	22076		CD
Indian Summer	ABC/MCA	989	'77	†
	MCA	37011		†
	MCA	31353	'89	CD
Legend	ABC/MCA	1099	'78	†
	MCA	1641		CS
	MCA	31019		CD
	MCA	11206	'95	CD
Under the Gun	ABC/MCA	5132	'80	†
	MCA	31334	'89	CD
Under the Gun/Legend	MCA	(2) 6907		CS
Blue and Gray	MCA	5227	'81	†
	One Way	22068		CD
Cowboys and Englishmen	MCA	5288	'82	†
	One Way	22067		CD
Ghost Town	Atlantic	80008	'82	†
Inamorata	Atlantic	80148	'84	†
Ghost Town/Inamorata	Rhino	72217	'95	CD
Legacy	RCA	9694	'89	CS/CD

Anthologies

The Very Best of Poco (1969–1974)	Epic	33537	'75	CS/CD
The Songs of Paul Cotton	Epic	36210	'79	†
The Songs of Richie Furay	Epic	36211	'79	†
Backtracks	Epic	1469		CS
The Forgotten Trail (1969–1974)	Epic	(2) 46162	'90	CS/CD
Backwards	MCA	5363	'83	†
Crazy Loving: The Best of Poco, 1975–1982	MCA	42323	'89	CD

The Souther-Hillman-Furay Band

The Souther-Hillman-Furay Band	Asylum	1006	'74	†
Trouble in Paradise	Asylum	1036	'75	†

Richie Furay

I've Got a Reason	Asylum	1067	'76	†
	Myrrh	6672	'81	†
Dance a Little Light	Asylum	115	'78	†
I Still Have a Dream	Asylum	231	'79	†

THE POINTER SISTERS

Ruth Pointer (b. Mar. 19, 1946, East Oakland, CA); **Anita Pointer** (b. Jan. 23, 1948, East
Oakland, CA); **Bonnie Pointer** (b. July 11, 1951, East Oakland, CA); **June Pointer** (b. Nov.
30, 1954, East Oakland, CA) [Bonnie Pointer left the group in 1978.]

The Pointer Sisters began their careers by creating a unique distillation of improvisatory jazz-style vocals, '40s-style dress, and campy onstage demeanor that established them as nostalgia entertainers more than recording artists in the mid-'70s. Performing a highly eclectic repertoire, from R&B to jazz classics and original compositions, they demonstrated remarkable vocal versatility and gained a large cult following. Discarding the old image and material in 1978, the Pointer Sisters enjoyed a revitalized career under producer Richard Perry, particularly with 1983's *Breakout*. They scored a series of pop and R&B smashes with contemporary material through 1985, but subsequently languished with RCA and Motown.

The Pointer sisters grew up as daughters of ministers. They first began singing together at the West Oakland Church of God in the early '60s. They discovered secular material during high school, and Bonnie and June began singing professionally in the late '60s as The Pointers—A Pair. They were members of Dorothy Morrison's Northern California State Youth Choir before forming the Pointer Sisters with Anita in December 1969. Stranded in Houston by their first manager, the three contacted San Francisco producer David Rubinson, who arranged their return to the Bay Area. He soon became their manager and found them session work with Cold Blood, Elvin Bishop, Taj Mahal, Boz Scaggs, and Grace Slick. In 1971 they recorded two singles for Atlantic Records, but neither proved successful.

Joined by sister Ruth in September 1972, the four Pointer sisters signed with Blue Thumb Records under David Rubinson, who produced their first three studio albums. Their debut album displayed a striking versatility of vocal talents and a diversity of musical styles and contained the originals "Sugar" and "Jada" as well as the Lambert, Hendricks and Ross classic "Cloudburst." It yielded a major pop and R&B hit with Allen Toussaint's "Yes We Can Can" and a minor crossover hit with Willie Dixon's "Wang Dang Doodle." Following a successful performance substituting for a canceled act at the Troubadour in Los Angeles in May 1973, the Pointer Sisters frequently appeared on the television shows of Helen Reddy and Flip Wilson.

The Pointer Sisters' second album, *That's a Plenty*, was even more jazz-oriented, containing vocal renditions of "Salt Peanuts" and "Black Coffee," jazz standards popularized by Dizzy Gillespie and Sarah Vaughan. The album produced a moderate country and major pop hit with Anita and Bonnie's "Fairytale," leading them to be the first black group to appear on the stage of the Grand Ole Opry, in 1976. *Steppin'* yielded a top R&B and major pop hit with their own "How Long (Betcha' Got a Chick on the Side)" and a major R&B hit with Allen Toussaint's "Going Down Slow"; it also contained Stevie Wonder's "Sleeping Alone" and "Easy Days," coauthored with Isaac Hayes. Subsequent releases fared poorly and the Blue Thumb label dissolved, leaving the sisters without a record label.

In 1978 Bonnie Pointer left the others to pursue a solo career on Motown Records. She scored a major R&B hit with "Free Me from My Freedom/Tie Me to a Tree (Handcuff Me)" and a major pop hit with Holland-Dozier-Holland's "Heaven Must Have Sent You" in 1978–1979. However, legal problems with Motown led to the end of her recording career until 1984, by which time her popularity had fizzled; she later recorded for Private Records.

In August 1978 Ruth and Anita Pointer signed with producer Richard Perry's newly formed Planet Records. They brought June back and recorded contemporary material for their debut on the label, *Energy*. The album yielded a smash pop hit with Bruce Springsteen's "Fire" and a moderate pop hit with "Happiness," and its success revived the Pointer

Sisters. Subsequent hits through 1982 included "He's So Shy" and "Slow Hand" (both smash pop and near-smash R&B hits), "Should I Do It," and "American Music."Their 1983 album, *Break Out*, remained on the album charts for two years and yielded six hits, including the pop and R&B smashes "Automatic" and "Jump (For My Love)," and the pop smashes "I'm So Excited" and "Neutron Dance," the latter featured in the movie *Beverly Hills Cop*.

The Pointer Sisters' next album, *Contact*, produced hits with "Dare Me" (an R&B smash), "Freedom," and "Twist My Arm." However, subsequent releases fared less well, and by 1988 the group had switched to Motown Records. June and Anita Pointer each issued solo albums in the late '80s. The group returned on SBK records in 1993.

The Pointer Sisters

The Pointer Sisters	Blue Thumb	48	'73	†
	MCA	31377	'90	CS/CD
That's a Plenty	Blue Thumb	6009	'74	†
Live at the Opera House	Blue Thumb	(2) 8002	'74	†
Steppin'	Blue Thumb	6021	'75	†
The Best of the Pointer Sisters	Blue Thumb	(2) 6026	'76	†
Having a Party	Blue Thumb	6023	'77	†
Retrospect	MCA	3275	'81	†
	MCA	27071		†
Yes We Can	MCA	20192	'85	†
Energy	Planet	1	'78	†
	RCA	5091	'84	†
Priority	Planet	9003	'79	†
	RCA	5089	'84	†
Special Things	Planet	9	'80	†
	RCA	5088	'84	†
Black and White	Planet	18	'81	†
	RCA	5092	'84	CS
	RCA	54125	'95	CS/CD
Best, 1978–1981	RCA	66198	'93	CS/CD
So Excited	Planet	4355	'82	†
	RCA	4355		CS
Greatest Hits	Planet	60203	'82	†
Break Out	Planet	4705	'83	†
	RCA	5410		CS
	RCA	4705	'84	CD
Contact	RCA	5487	'85	LP/CS/CD†
Hot Together	RCA	5609	'86	LP/CS/CD†
Serious Slammin'	RCA	6562	'88	LP/CS/CD†
Pointer Sisters's Greatest Hits	RCA	9816	'89	CS/CD
Sweet and Soulful	RCA	61135	'92	CS/CD
Right Rhythm	Motown	6287	'90	CS/CD†
Pointer Sisters	SBK	89553	'93	CS/CD

Bonnie Pointer

Bonnie Pointer	Motown	911	'78	†
Bonnie Pointer	Motown	929	'79	†
If the Price Is Right	Private	39406	'84	†

June Pointer

Baby Sister	Planet	4508	'83	†
June Pointer	Columbia	44315	'89	LP/CS/CD†

THE POLICE

Sting (b. Gordon Sumner, Oct. 2, 1951, Wallsend, Northumberland, England), lead voc, bs; **Andy Summers** (b. Andrew Somers, Dec. 31, 1942, Poulton-le-Fylde, Lancashire, England), lead gtr; **Stewart Copeland** (b. July 16, 1952, Alexandria, VA), drm, perc, voc

THE POLICE

Incorporating elements of reggae, pop, punk, and jazz, the Police featured the intelligently crafted songs and charismatic stage presence of lead singer Sting. The first British New Wave act to score a hit in America, with 1979's "Roxanne," the Police were initially rivaled by only Blondie in terms of commercial success for a New Wave act. After becoming one of the leading rock bands in the world, the Police dissolved in 1983. Sting became a highly successful solo artist and a somewhat less successful film actor. Guitarist Andy Summers became one of the pioneers in the development of guitar synthesizers, while drummer Stewart Copeland pursued soundtrack and television work in the '80s and '90s.

Stewart Copeland grew up in the Middle East as the son of the head of the Central Intelligence Agency's operations in the region. In 1966 the Copeland family moved to England, where Stewart attended the prestigious Millfield school in Somerset. In 1971 he returned to the United States to attend the University of California at Berkeley. He moved back to England at the behest of his promoter, brother Miles, in 1974 and joined the progressive-rock group Curved Air in the band's final years, as a percussionist. In late 1975 Copeland attended a performance in Newcastle by the local band Lost Exit, which included singer-bassist Sting. Born Gordon Sumner, Sting had been a semiprofessional musician around Newcastle since age 17 and had attempted music full-time in London in the early '70s. He returned to Newcastle in 1975 and taught school for two years. By late 1976 both Curved Air and Lost Exit had broken up, and Copeland and Sting formed the Police with guitarist Henry Padovani. The group recorded the song "Fall Out" for Miles Copeland's Illegal Records label, but the single failed to sell.

Andy Summers soon replaced Henry Padovani in the Police. Summers had taken up guitar at age 14 and started playing professionally at 16, in bands such as Soft Machine and the Animals in the late '60s. He studied classical composition and guitar at the University of California between 1969 and 1973 and returned to England to play with bands led by Kevin Coyne and Kevin Ayers. He met Stewart Copeland and Sting in 1977 while playing with the group Strontium 90. Signed to A&M Records, the Police recorded their debut album, *Outlandos d'Amour*, in 1978. The group financed their own tour of America in late 1978 before the record was released in this country. They achieved belated British hits with "Roxanne" and "Can't Stand Losing You," and "Roxanne" became a moderate American hit in early 1979. The album, which favored reggae rhythms and the catchy songwriting of Sting, stayed on the charts for more than a year.

The Police conducted their first British tour in summer 1979, and recorded *Regatta de Blanc* that year. It included "The Bed's Too Big Without You," "Bring on the Night," and the British top hits "Walking on the Moon" and "Message in a Bottle," the latter a minor American hit. The record stayed on the American album charts for nearly two years, securing their position in this country as one of the most exciting and creative bands in contemporary music.

Notorious for their unconventional business practices under Miles Copeland, the Police established themselves with an international audience by performing in Third World cities such as Cairo, Bangkok, Athens, and Bombay in 1980. Their diverse, engaging *Zenyatta Mondatta* album yielded two near-smash American hits, "Do Do Do Do, De Da Da Da" and "Don't Stand So Close to Me"; it also contained Summers's instrumental "Behind My Camel" and Sting's "Driven to Tears" and "Shadows in the Rain." Touring diligently to sustain their enormous popularity, the Police next recorded the concept album *Ghost in the Machine*, featuring Sting's most intelligent, incisive lyrics to date. It produced the smash hit "Every Little Thing She Does Is Magic," the near-smash "Spirits in the Material World," and the moderate hit "Secret Journey," as well as "Hungry for You" and "One World (Not Three)."

By the time the Police took a break from touring and recording in 1982, they had conducted 20 tours overall, including three major world tours. During the hiatus, Andy Summers explored the guitar synthesizer with former King Crimson guitarist and electronics wizard Robert Fripp on the *I Advance Masked* album for A&M. Sting starred in the disturbing movie *Brimstone and Treacle*, and Stewart Copeland composed the score for the Francis Ford Coppola movie *Rumblefish*.

Reconvening in 1983, the Police recorded the carefully crafted, compelling, and profound album *Synchronicity*, their masterpiece. The album includes "Walking in Your Footsteps" and yielded the top hit "Every Breath You Take," the smash hits "King of Pain" and "Wrapped Around Your Finger," and the major hit "Synchronicity II," all written by Sting. Following their stadium tour in support of *Synchronicity*, the Police announced they were taking a respite from touring and recording as the members pursued various outside projects.

Andy Summers rejoined Robert Fripp for another album of instrumentals, *Bewitched*, that contained a Dream Side and a Dance Side. He later recorded one side of the soundtrack to the 1986 movie *Down and Out in Beverly Hills* and the soundtrack to *My Weekend at Bernie's*. In the late '80s and '90s he recorded several solo albums.

Stewart Copeland was the most prolific former member of the Police. In 1984 he traveled to Africa to record traditional native music, assembling a film documentary and album, *The Rhythmatist*, that featured both authentic music and his own synthesizer compositions. Throughout the rest of the '80s and '90s he composed and performed for the movies and television; much of this work is unavailable in a recorded format. The film scores include *Out of Bounds* (1986), *Wall Street* (1987), *Talk Radio* (1988), *Men at Work* (1990), *Highlander II* (1991), and *Rappa Nui* (1994). For television, Copeland worked on the shows *The Ewoks* and *Droids* (1985), *The Equalizer* (1986), and *Babylon 5* (1993), among others. In 1988 he formed Animal Logic with jazz bassist Stanley Clarke and singer-songwriter Deborah Holland, recording two albums for I.R.S. His score for the half-hour ballet *King Lear*, featuring both orchestra and prerecorded music, was premiered by the San Francisco Ballet in 1985. In 1989 the Cleveland Opera performed Stewart Copeland's first operatic effort, the three-hour *Holy Blood and Crescent Moon*, as its season opener, but the performance was not well received by classical-music critics.

Sting continued to pursue his acting career during the '80s, securing roles in the film adaptation of Frank Herbert's *Dune* (1984), the remake of the 1935 horror classic *The Bride of Frankenstein* as *The Bride* (1985), and *Stormy Monday* (1988). Although Sting performed credibly, none of the films were well received by critics or audiences. By 1985 Sting had assembled several of New York's finest jazz musicians for recordings that confounded rock critics and disaffected jazz fans. With Sting playing guitar, not bass, *The Dream of the Blue Turtles* was recorded with saxophonist Branford Marsalis, keyboardist Kenny Kirkland, bassist Darryl Jones, and drummer Omar Hakim. Surprisingly, the album yielded four hits: the smash "If You Love Somebody Set Them Free," the near-smash "Fortress Around Your Heart," and the major hits "Love Is the Seventh Wave" and "Russians." In the latter half of 1985 Sting toured with his new band, and the film *Bring on the Night*, an account of his early rehearsals and first concert with the band, was released. He also appeared at the Live Aid concert in 1985, and toured for Amnesty International in 1986.

In 1987 Sting returned to bass to record the double-CD set . . . *Nothing Like the Sun* with Branford Marsalis and Kenny Kirkland. The album produced a near-smash hit with "We'll Be Together," a major hit with "Be Still My Beating Heart," and a minor hit with "Englishman in New York." It also included the gripping "They Dance Alone (Cueca Solo)," recorded with Andy Summers, Eric Clapton, and Mark Knopfler; the ballad "Sister Moon"; and "History Will Teach Us Nothing." In 1988 Sting toured early in the year, formed his own record company, Panagea, performed on the Amnesty International tour, and founded the environmental group Ark with David Bowie. He made his Broadway debut in the short-lived 1989 musical production *The Threepenny Opera* and created the Save the Rain Forest Foundation while enduring an extended period of writer's block.

Sting returned to recording in 1991 with the brooding *The Soul Cages*, scoring a smash hit with "All This Time"; he toured once again. Two years later he issued his most engaging work in years, *Ten Summoner's Tales*, which included "If I Ever Lose Faith in You" and "Fields of Gold," both major hits, as well as "She's Too Good for Me" and "Love Is Stranger than Justice." At the end of 1993 Sting scored a top hit in conjunction with Bryan Adams and Rod Stewart on "All for Love," from the movie *The Three Musketeers*. A 1994 best-of set, *Fields of Gold*, includes the odd "This Cowboy Song" and one other new track.

Curved Air

Live	BTM	5001	'75	†
Airborne	BTM		'76	†
Midnight Wire	RCA		'75	†

The Police

Outlandos d'Amour	A&M	4753	'79	†
	A&M	3311		CS/CD
Regatta de Blanc	A&M	4792	'79	†
	A&M	3312		CS/CD
Zenyatta Mondatta	A&M	4831	'80	†
	A&M	3720		CS/CD
Ghost in the Machine	A&M	3730	'81	CS/CD
Synchronicity	A&M	3735	'83	CS/CD
	Mobile Fidelity	511		CD
Live (recorded 1979–1983)	A&M	0222	'95	CS/CD
Every Breath You Take: The Singles	A&M	3902	'86	CS/CD
Message in a Box: The Complete Recordings	A&M	(4) 0150	'93	CS/CD
Every Breath You Take: The Classics	A&M	0380	'95	CS/CD

Andy Summers and Robert Fripp

I Advance Masked	A&M	4913	'82/'92	CD

Bewitched	A&M	5011	'84/'92	CD
Andy Summers				
Down and Out in Beverly Hills (one side of soundtrack)	MCA	6160	'86	†
XYZ	MCA	42007	'87	†
Mysterious Barricades	Private Music	2039	'88	LP/CS/CD
The Golden Wire	Private Music	2048	'89	CS/CD
Charming Snakes	Private Music	2069	'90	CS/CD
World Gone Strange	Private Music	82088	'91	CS/CD
Stewart Copeland				
The Rhythmatist	A&M	5084	'85	CD
Music from *The Equalizer* and Other Cliff Hangers	I.R.S./MCA	42099	'88	LP/CS/CD†
	I.R.S.	13184	'93	CD
Stewart Copeland Soundtracks				
Rumblefish	A&M	4983	'83/'92	CD
Out of Bounds	I.R.S./MCA	6180	'86	†
Wall Street/Talk Radio	Varese Sarabande	5215	'89	LP/CS/CD†
	Varese Sarabande	5459	'93	CD
Men at Work	Mesa	79025	'90	CS/CD
Animal Logic				
Animal Logic	I.R.S.	13020	'89	CS/CD
Animal Logic II	I.R.S.	13106	'91	CS/CD
Sting				
The Dream of the Blue Turtles	A&M	3750	'85	CS/CD
	Mobile Fidelity	528	'90	CD
Bring on the Night	A&M	(2) 6705	'85	CD
. . . Nothing Like the Sun	A&M	6402	'87	CS/CD
	Mobile Fidelity	546	'91	CD
Box Set (above 3 albums)	A&M	(4) 0019	'92	CD
Nada Como el Sol	A&M	3295		CS/CD
The Soul Cages	A&M	6405	'91	CS/CD
Ten Summoner's Tales	A&M	0070	'93	CS/CD
Fields of Gold	A&M	0030	'94	CS/CD
Mercury Falling	A&M	75021	'96	CS/CD

IGGY POP

(b. James Jewel Osterberg, Apr. 21, 1947, Ann Arbor, MI)

THE STOOGES. Iggy Pop, voc; **Ron Asheton** (b. Ronald Franklin Asheton Jr., July 17, 1948, Washington, D.C.), gtr; **Dave Alexander** (b. David Michael Alexander, June 3, 1947, Ann Arbor, MI; d. Feb. 10, 1975, Detroit, MI), bs; **Scott Asheton** (b. Scott Randolph Asheton, Aug. 16, 1949, Washington, D.C.), drm [Guitarist **James Williamson** (b. Birmingham, MI) joined in 1972; Ron Asheton switched to bass. In 1973 **Scott Thurston** joined on bass and keyboards.]

Often considered the forerunner of the punk groups of the late '70s, the Stooges featured minimalist music, chaotic guitar playing, and the vituperative and insolent lyrics of Iggy Pop. Leader Iggy Pop's spontaneously outrageous and sadomasochistic onstage behavior made him one of the first performance artists in rock, and as such he served as a precursor to the calculated theatrical excesses of Alice Cooper and Kiss. Enduring a chaotic period of drug and psychological problems, Iggy Pop reemerged as a solo act in the late '70s, eventually giving up his self-destructive onstage act while retaining his energetic, compelling image.

Iggy Pop played drums and sang lead with the Detroit-area high school band the Iguanas, and he later manned the Prime Movers. After a semester at the University of Michigan and as a drummer for a blues band in Chicago, he returned to Detroit, where he formed the Stooges in 1967 with Asheton brothers Ron and Scott and Dave Alexander. The Stooges performed loud, three-chord rock music fronted by the vocals and disturbing onstage antics of Iggy. Over the years his notoriety grew, with deeds such as threatening and vilifying audiences, cutting himself with broken bottles, pouring hot wax over his body, intentionally smashing his teeth, and vomiting, even urinating on audiences and allowing ardent fans to perform fellatio on him.

Signed to Elektra Records, the Stooges recorded their debut album under producer John Cale of the Velvet Underground. It featured Stooges favorites such as "No Fun" and "I Wanna Be Your Dog." However, their classic second album, *Funhouse*, failed to even make the album charts and the group experienced a period of disintegration. Taken to England by mentor David Bowie in 1972, Iggy Pop and new guitarist James Williamson were joined by the Asheton brothers for the Bowie-produced *Raw Power* on Columbia. An acknowledged early heavy-metal classic, the album included the title cut as well as "Search and Destroy," "Gimme Danger," "Death Trip," and "Your Pretty Face Is Going to Hell." The Stooges broke up in early 1974 and Pop ended up in Los Angeles, where he became addicted to heroin; he kicked the habit, then entered a mental hospital in 1975.

After moving to West Berlin in spring 1976, Iggy Pop again encountered David Bowie, who managed to secure him a recording contract with RCA Records. *The Idiot* contained "Sister Midnight" and the Bowie-Pop collaboration "China Girl" (a major hit for Bowie in 1983), and *Lust for Life* included "Fall in Love with Me," "Neighborhood Threat," and the title song. Pop returned to live performance, often accompanied by Bowie on keyboards, but the albums sold modestly at best, despite critical acclaim. Iggy Pop switched to Arista Records for 1979's *New Values* and another round of disturbing, if not outrageous, live performances later that year with former Sex Pistols bassist Glen Matlock and guitarist-keyboardist Ivan Kral from the Patti Smith Group.

During the '80s Iggy Pop abandoned his self-destructive onstage antics and recorded *Zombie Birdhouse* for Animal Records. He moved to New York City and recorded the theme song to the 1984 cult movie *Repo Man*, taking up acting and eventually securing minor roles in *Sid and Nancy* and *The Color of Money*. Pop cowrote five songs for David Bowie's *Tonight*, Bowie's last album to sell a million copies, and Bowie coproduced and coauthored five of the songs on Pop's *Blah Blah Blah* on A&M Records, hailed as his best recording in years. Former Sex Pistols guitarist Steve Jones cowrote three of the album's songs, including "Cry for Love," and the album otherwise featured "Isolation" and a remake of Johnny Kidd's "Real Wild Child." Pop conducted his first world tour in four years in 1986–1987, serving as the opening act for the Pretenders' 1987 tour. He later recorded *Instinct* with Steve Jones.

By 1990 Pop had moved to Virgin Records, where he recorded the best-selling album of his career, *Brick by Brick*. Produced by Don (Was) Fagenson, the album featured Slash and Duff McKagan from Guns N' Roses, included John Hiatt's "Something Wild," and yielded Pop's only (major) hit, "Candy," sung with Kate Pierson of the B-52's. He performed as one of the headline acts for 1990's Gathering of the Tribes festival (a precursor of the Lollapalooza tours) and toured again in 1993 in support of *American Caesar*. Skydog issued the live set *We Are Not Talking About Commercial Shit* in 1995, the year Iggy Pop recorded *Wild Animal* for New Rose Records.

The Stooges

The Stooges		Elektra	74051	'69	LP/CS/CD

Funhouse	Elektra	74071	'70	CS/CD
Iggy Pop and the Stooges				
Raw Power	Columbia	32111	'73	CS/CD
Metallic K.O. (recorded 1973)	Skydog	62232	'94	CD
Iggy Pop				
The Idiot	RCA	2275	'77	†
	Virgin	91342	'90	CS/CD†
	Virgin	86152		CS/CD
Lust for Life	RCA	2488	'77	†
	Virgin	91343	'90	CS/CD†
	Virgin	86153		CD
TV Eye—1977 Live	RCA	2796	'78	†
	Virgin	39628	'94	CD
Choice Cuts	RCA	4957	'84	†
New Values	Arista	4237	'79	†
Soldier	Arista	4259	'80	†
Party	Arista	9572	'81	†
Zombie Birdhouse	Animal	41399	'83	†
	I.R.S.	13063	'91	CS/CD
Blah Blah Blah	A&M	5145	'86	CS/CD
Instinct	A&M	5198	'88	CS/CD
Brick by Brick	Virgin	91381	'90	CS/CD†
	Virgin	86173		CS/CD
American Caesar	Virgin	39002	'93	CS/CD
We Are Not Talking About Commercial Shit	Skydog	62255	'95	CD
Wake Up Suckers	Skydog	62267	'95	CD
Wild Animal	New Rose	4050	'95	CD

ELVIS PRESLEY
(b. Jan. 8, 1935, East Tupelo, MS; d. Aug. 16, 1977, Memphis, TN)

The biggest single attraction in the history of popular music, Elvis Presley introduced rock and roll to an entire generation of white teenagers who were accustomed to passionless, banal ditties and unfamiliar with the ardent and intense black R&B music that had existed since at least the beginning of the '50s. In identifying a form of music and attendant lifestyle completely distinct from that of his fans' parents, Elvis Presley became the most important symbol of and idol within '50s rock and roll, enhancing its aura of teenage rebellion.

Although he retained the title of King of Rock and Roll and remained the music's most widely recognized figure, Elvis's primacy as a rock-and-roll artist quickly evaporated in the early '60s. He embarked on a dismal but lucrative career of inane movies (and soundtrack albums) that failed to provide him with the opportunity to test, much less prove, himself as an actor. Despite the fact that all of his movies were commercial successes, Elvis Presley's single and album sales were diminishing by the late '60s. With the advent of the rock-and-roll revival of the era, Presley unequivocally staged a successful comeback with a December 1968 NBC television special that revealed him to be a passionate, compelling, and unique performer. He returned to live performance in 1969 with his celebrated appearance in Las Vegas, where he quickly established himself as one of the most popular and highly paid cabaret artists in the world.

ELVIS PRESLEY

However, Elvis was unable to reestablish his popularity with the kind of youthful audience that had so ardently followed him during the '50s, and in a sense he devolved into a nostalgia act as his weight increased, health problems developed, and performances became sloppier and more perfunctory. Elvis Presley died in his Memphis mansion, Graceland, on August 16, 1977.

Elvis Presley began singing with his parents at the First Assembly of God Church in Tupelo, Mississippi, as a child and later accompanied them to camp meetings and revivals. He obtained his first guitar for his 11th birthday, and moved with his family to Memphis, Tennessee, in September 1948. He sang at a high school variety show in late 1952 and became a truck driver after graduating in June 1953. The next month, in the often told story, he went to the small local Sun Records studio to make a private recording of "My Happiness" for his mother. Noticed by secretary Marion Keisker, Presley was later teamed with guitarist Scotty Moore and stand-up bassist Bill Black by Sun Records president Sam Phillips, and the three rehearsed for several months. Returning to the Sun studios, the trio recorded Bill Monroe's "Blue Moon of Kentucky" and Arthur "Big Boy" Crudup's "That's All Right (Mama)" on July 6, 1954. Local disc jockey Dewey Phillips (no relation to Sam) played the latter song on his radio show and the single became a regional hit. Presley made his professional performing debut at Memphis's Overton Park on August 10, 1954, and was greeted ecstatically by an audience enthralled with his rough, passionate vocals and sexually charged persona. He soon began touring the South with Moore and Black, billed as the Hillbilly Cat, and his second and third Sun singles became regional hits. In October the three performed on Shreveport's *Louisiana Hayride* radio show (and would continue to do so until December 1956) and performed on the show's television version the following March. Released in April 1955, "Baby Let's Play House" became a smash country-and-western hit that summer, followed in September by the top country hit "I Forgot to Remember to Forget," backed with Junior Parker's "Mystery Train." Spotted by "Colonel" Tom Parker, a former carnival barker and erstwhile manager of Eddy Arnold and Hank Snow, Presley signed a new management deal with Parker in November 1955.

Elvis Presley's potent style and raw potential created a bidding war amongst major record labels, and RCA won out with an offer of $35,000, an astoundingly high figure for 1955. In January 1956, backed by guitarists Scotty Moore and Chet Atkins, bassist Bill Black, and drummer D. J. Fontana (who had joined the trio in July 1955), Elvis completed his first recording sessions in Nashville. Presley made his national television debut on the CBS network *Dorsey Brothers Show* on January 28, 1956, and within weeks his first RCA release, "Heartbreak Hotel," became a top country and pop and smash R&B hit. On June 5, as "I Want You, I Need You, I Love You" was becoming another three-way crossover smash, Presley appeared on *The Milton Berle Show* to an estimated audience of 40 million. Soon his first recording with the Jordanaires, "Don't Be Cruel"/"Hound Dog," became top hits in all three fields. Appearing on television's *Ed Sullivan Show* to an estimated audience of 54 million on September 9, Elvis was shown from the waist up only.

Elvis Presley's success was phenomenal, and the three-way crossover smashes continued with "Love Me Tender," "Love Me," "Too Much," and "All Shook Up." During 1956 his first movie, *Love Me Tender*, was released, followed in 1957 by *Loving You* and *Jailhouse Rock*. On December 4, 1956, Presley returned to the Memphis Sun studio to join Sun stalwarts Carl Perkins, Jerry Lee Lewis, and Johnny Cash in informally singing and playing a number of gospel songs. Unknown to them, the performance was recorded. Those recordings by the so-called Million Dollar Quartet were bootlegged and available in Europe for years before their eventual (1990) release in the United States. In January 1957 Elvis recorded the four-song gospel EP *Peace in the Valley*, later included on *Elvis's Christmas Album*, which also contained the secular "Blue Christmas," "Santa Bring My Baby Back to Me," and "Santa Claus Is Back in Town."

Elvis Presley's three-way crossover smashes continued with "Teddy Bear," "Jailhouse Rock"/"Treat Me Nice," and "Don't"/"I Beg of You." The army knocked on his door in early 1958, but he was allowed a two-month deferment to complete the movie *King Creole* before he was drafted, on March 24, 1958. Although he was to record only once during the next two years, the hits did not stop. However, after the three-way crossover smashes "Wear My Ring Around Your Neck" and "Hard Headed Woman," his subsequent crossover smashes were restricted to the pop and R&B fields. These included "One Night"/"I Got Stung," "(Now and Then There's) A Fool Such as I"/"I Need Your Love Tonight," and "Big Hunk of Love," the last four being his only new recordings during his army stint.

Discharged on March 5, 1960, Elvis Presley subsequently assembled the so-called Memphis Mafia entourage that served to protect and insulate him from the public until July 1976. He began recording far less exuberant and vital material with extra musicians to produce a fuller sound. Nonetheless, "Stuck on You," "It's Now or Never," and "Are You Lonesome Tonight" became smash pop and R&B hits. His ABC-TV show *Welcome Home Elvis*, aired on May 12, 1960, featured six minutes of Elvis, for which he was paid $125,000. The show was hosted by Frank Sinatra, a man who had earlier denounced rock and roll as "the most brutal, ugly, desperate, vicious form of expression," and into whose shoes Presley would later move.

After making his first full album of gospel material, *His Hand in Mine*, in 1960, Elvis appeared at his last public performance for eight years in Honolulu on March 25, 1961. He spent the '60s making a series of lucrative but mindless movies usually staged in exotic locations featuring numerous fleshy but virginal women and only the bare semblance of a plot. He also recorded a few nonsoundtrack albums as the pop-only smash hits continued: "Surrender," "I Feel So Bad," "(Marie's the Name) His Latest Flame"/"Little Sister," "Can't Help Falling In Love," "Good Luck Charm," and "She's Not You." "Return to Sender" and "(You're the) Devil in Disguise" became his final pop *and* R&B smashes, with the pop-only major hits "Bossa Nova Baby," "Kissin' Cousins," "Viva Las Vegas," and "Crying in the Chapel" (recorded in 1960) ensuing. To his credit, Elvis Presley recorded perhaps the finest gospel album of his career, *How Great Thou Art*, for 1967 release. He married Priscilla Beaulieu on May 1, 1967, and his only child, daughter Lisa Marie, was born on February 1, 1968.

In 1968, with the first inkling of a revival of interest in '50s rock and roll, Elvis Presley returned to television for an attempted comeback. Less than a week before the airing of his special, one of his finer later singles, "If I Can Dream," became a near-smash hit. The special, televised on NBC on December 3, 1968, featured large-scale production numbers and Presley performing in front of a small audience with old associates Scotty Moore and D. J. Fontana (Bill Black had died on October 21, 1965). The special was one of the five highest-rated shows of the television year and included both "If I Can Dream" and the haunting moderate hit "Memories." It represented, in many ways, the peak of Elvis Presley's later career.

Elvis returned to Memphis for the first time in 14 years to record his next album, *From Elvis in Memphis*, for which he personally chose the songs. Generally regarded as one of his finest later albums, it yielded a smash hit with Mac Davis's socially conscious "In the Ghetto" and included "Power of Love," "Any Day Now," and "Long Black Limousine." Elvis returned to live performance on July 31, 1969, with a monthlong engagement at the International Hotel (later the Hilton) in Las Vegas, backed by a 30-piece orchestra, chorus, and a five-man combo featuring guitarist James Burton and keyboardist Glen D. Hardin, two of the finest instrumentalists in the country. Recordings from the stand comprised the first record of *From Memphis to Vegas/From Vegas to Memphis*, while the second record (later issued as *Elvis Back in Memphis*) was taken from the Memphis sessions. The latter record included "Without Love (There Is Nothing)," "Do You Know Who I Am," and "Stranger in My Own Home." In the meantime, Presley scored a top hit with "Suspicious Minds," a smash hit with Mac Davis's "Don't Cry Daddy," and a major hit with Eddie Rabbit's "Kentucky Rain."

After another monthlong appearance at the International Hotel, in February 1970, Elvis Presley toured selected venues across the United States until his death in 1977, although he infrequently performed in Las Vegas after 1975. He scored a near-smash country hit with "There Goes My Everything" in 1971 and a smash pop hit with "Burning Love" in 1972. On January 14, 1973, Presley performed at a Honolulu benefit that produced his last major hit album, *Aloha from Hawaii*. Broadcast on NBC-TV and relayed via satellite to 40 countries, the special was viewed by an estimated audience of one billion.

Elvis Presley's fortunes again began to fade. He and Priscilla divorced on October 11, 1973, and his subsequent live performances became careless and mechanical, as rumors of drug abuse and erratic personal behavior began to circulate. Most of his subsequent successes came in the country field, where he had smash hits with "I've Got a Thing About You," "Help Me," "It's Midnight," "Hurt," "Moody Blue," and "Way Down." His last live performance took place in Indianapolis on June 26, 1977; on August 16, 1977, he died at age 42 in his Graceland mansion in Memphis of heart failure due to prescription-drug abuse.

Within three months of Elvis Presley's death, his rendition of "My Way," Frank Sinatra's theme song, became a major pop and smash country hit. Soon after, the cult of personality and exploitation of his recorded legacy began in earnest. RCA quickly reissued a number of his lesser movie soundtracks and continued to compile new albums into the '90s, the most noteworthy of which are *The Complete Sun Sessions*, *The Complete '50s Masters*, *The Top Ten Hits*, and *The Memphis Record*. Numerous books were written and published, including the vindictive *Elvis: What Happened?* (1977), Albert Goldman's mean-spirited *Elvis* (1980), ex-wife Priscilla's *Elvis and Me* (1985), and, most important, Peter Guralnick's *Last Train to Memphis* (1994). Television shows and documentaries are produced regularly, including *This Is Elvis* (1981), the excellent *Elvis '56* (1987), the top-rated *Elvis and Me* (1988), and the short-lived television series *Elvis* (1990). Sightings of Elvis are reported often in supermarket gossip papers, and scores of Elvis impersonators enjoy employment around the country. Graceland became the second most visited American home (after the White House) upon opening to the public in 1982, and Presley's image became the third most reproduced image in the world (after those of Jesus and Mickey Mouse). The U.S. Postal Service issue of a special Presley stamp in 1993 sold five hundred million copies, of which an estimated 60 percent were never used. Not surprisingly, Elvis was among the first inductees (1986) into the Rock and Roll Hall of Fame.

Elvis Presley's success was virtually unparalleled. Nearly 500 million copies of his records had been sold by the time of his death, and by 1995 total sales figures were estimated to top one billion. The record industry records he set were simply phenomenal. Although he was surpassed in several album and singles categories by the Beatles and Frank Sinatra, Elvis Presley holds the records for most charted albums, most charted hits, most consecutive top hits, most Top 10 hits, most consecutive Top 10 hits, most two-sided hits, most Top 40 hits, and most weeks at Number One.

Early Elvis Presley

The Sun Sessions	RCA	1675	'76	†
	RCA	3893		†
The Complete Sun Sessions	RCA	(2) 6414	'87	LP
	RCA	6414	'87	CS/CD
The First Live Recordings (recorded 1955–1956)	Music Works	3601	'84	†
Elvis Presley	RCA	1254	'56	†
	RCA	1254	'62	†
	RCA	5198	'84	CS/CD
	RCA	66659	'95	CD
Elvis	RCA	1382	'56	†
	RCA	1382	'62	†
	RCA	5199	'84	LP/CS/CD†
	RCA	50283	'94	CS/CD
The Million Dollar Quartet (recorded December 4, 1956)	RCA	2023	'90	LP/CS/CD
Stereo '57	RCA	9589	'89	CS/CD
The Elvis Tapes (interviews recorded 1957)	Ace	1		CD
Elvis's Christmas Album	RCA	1035	'57	†
	RCA	1951	'58	†
	Camden	2428	'70	CS/CD
	RCA	5486	'85	CS/CD
For LP Fans Only	RCA	1990	'59	CS/CD
A Date with Elvis	RCA	2011	'59	†
	RCA	2011	'89	CS/CD
The Complete '50s Masters	RCA	(5) 66050	'92	CS/CD
Elvis Is Back	RCA	2231	'60	†
	RCA	2231	'89	CD
I Was the One (recorded 1956–1960)	RCA	4678	'83	†

Scotty Moore

The Guitar That Changed the World	Epic	26103	'64	†

Soundtracks

Loving You	RCA	1515	'57	†
	RCA	1515	'88	CS/CD
Essential Elvis—The First Movies (*Love Me Tender*, *Jailhouse Rock*, and *Loving You*)	RCA	6738	'88	LP/CS/CD
King Creole	RCA	1884	'58	†
	RCA	3733		LP/CS/CD
G.I. Blues	RCA	2256	'60	†
	RCA	3735		CS/CD
Blue Hawaii	RCA	2426	'61	†
	RCA	3683		LP/CS/CD

Girls! Girls! Girls!	RCA	2621	'62	†
Girls! Girls! Girls!/Kid Galahad	RCA	66130	'93	CS/CD
It Happened at the World's Fair	RCA	2697	'63	†
	RCA	2568	'77	†
Fun in Acapulco	RCA	2756	'63	†
It Happened at the World's Fair/Fun in Acapulco	RCA	66131	'93	CS/CD
Kissin' Cousins	RCA	2894	'64	†
	RCA	4115	'82	†
Roustabout	RCA	2999	'64	†
Roustabout/Viva Las Vegas	RCA	66129	'93	CS/CD
Girl Happy	RCA	3338	'65	LP/CS
	RCA	1018		†
Harum Scarum	RCA	3468	'65	†
	RCA	2558	'77	†
	RCA	3734		†
Harum Scarum/Girl Happy	RCA	66128	'93	CS/CD
Frankie and Johnny	RCA	3553	'66	†
	RCA	2559	'77	†
Paradise Hawaiian Style	RCA	3643	'66	†
Frankie and Johnny/Paradise Hawaiian Style	RCA	66360	'94	CS/CD
Spinout	RCA	3702	'66	†
	RCA	2560	'77	†
	RCA	3676	'80	†
	RCA	3684		†
Double Trouble	RCA	3787	'67	|
	RCA	2564	'77	†
Spinout/Double Trouble	RCA	66361	'94	CS/CD
Clambake	RCA	3893	'67	†
	RCA	2565	'77	†
Kissin' Cousins/Clambake/Stay Away Joe	RCA	66362	'94	CS/CD
Speedway	RCA	3989	'68	†
Easy Come, Easy Go/Speedway	RCA	66558	'95	CS/CD
Flaming Star/Wild in the Country/Follow That Dream	RCA	66557	'95	CS/CD
Live a Little, Love a Little/Charro!/The Trouble with Girls/ Change of Habit	RCA	66559	'95	CS/CD
That's the Way It Is	RCA	4445	'70	†
	RCA	4114		CS
	RCA	54224		CD
	Mobile Fidelity	560	'92	CD
This Is Elvis (selections)	RCA	(2) 4031	'81	CS
Gospel Albums				
His Hand in Mine	RCA	2328	'60	†
	RCA	1319	'76	†
	RCA	3935		LP/CS
	RCA	1319	'88	CD
How Great Thou Art	RCA	3758	'67/'88	LP/CS/CD
He Touched Me	RCA	4690	'72	†
	RCA	1923		CS
	RCA	51923		CD
He Walks Beside Me	RCA	2772	'78	CS

You'll Never Walk Alone	Camden	2472	'71	†
	RCA-Camden	2472		CS/CD
Elvis Gospel, 1957–1971	RCA	9586	'89	CS/CD
Amazing Grace: His Greatest Sacred Performances	RCA	(2) 66421	'94	CS/CD
Other RCA Albums, 1960–1977				
Something for Everybody	RCA	2370	'61	CS/CD
Pot Luck	RCA	2523	'62/'88	CS/CD
Elvis for Everyone	RCA	3450	'65/'90	CS/CD
	RCA	4232	'82	†
	RCA	53450	'95	CS/CD
TV Special	RCA	3894		CS
Elvis (TV Special)	RCA	4088	'68	†
NBC TV Special	RCA	61021	'91	CS/CD
The Lost Album	RCA	61024	'91	CS/CD
From Elvis in Memphis	RCA	4155	'69	†
	RCA	1456		CS
	RCA	51456		CD
From Memphis to Vegas/From Vegas to Memphis	RCA	(2) 6020	'69	†
From Memphis to Vegas	RCA	(2) 2656		CS
The Memphis Record (reissue of *From Elvis in Memphis* and *From Vegas to Memphis*)	RCA	6221	'87	CS/CD
On Stage (February 1970)	RCA	4362	'70	CS
	RCA	54362		CD
At the International Hotel, Las Vegas	RCA	4428	'70	†
	RCA	3892		CS
	RCA	53892	'92	CD
Back in Memphis	RCA	4429	'70	†
	RCA	61081	'92	CS/CD
Elvis Country	RCA	4460	'71	†
	RCA	3956		†
	RCA Nashville	66405	'94	CD
I'm 10,000 Years Old/Elvis Country	RCA	66279	'93	CS/CD
Love Letters from Elvis	RCA	4530	'71	†
	RCA	54350	'92	CS/CD
Elvis Sings the Wonderful World of Christmas	RCA	4579	'71/'88	CD
	RCA	1936	'76	LP/CS
Elvis Now	RCA	4671	'72	†
	RCA	54671	'93	CS/CD
Live at Madison Square Garden	RCA	4776	'72	CS
	RCA	54776	'92	CD
Aloha from Hawaii	RCA	(2) 6089	'73	†
	RCA	2642		CS
	RCA	52642		CD
The Alternate Aloha	RCA	6985	'88	CS/CD
Elvis	RCA	0283	'73	†
Raised on Rock	RCA	0388	'73	
	RCA	50388	'94	CS/CD
Good Times	RCA	0475	'74	†
	RCA	50475	'94	CS/CD

Live On Stage in Memphis	RCA	0606	'74	CS
	RCA	50606	'94	CD
Having Fun with Elvis On Stage	RCA	0818	'74	†
Promised Land	RCA	0873	'75	CS/CD
Today	RCA	1039	'75	†
	RCA	51039	'92	CS/CD
From Elvis Presley Boulevard	RCA	1506	'76	CS/CD
Welcome to My World	RCA	2274	'77	CS
	RCA	52274	'92	CD
Moody Blue	RCA	2428	'77	CS/CD
In Concert	RCA	2587	'77	CS
	RCA	52587	'92	CD

Anthologies

Rocker (recorded 1956–1957)	RCA	5182	'84	CS/CD
Elvis's Golden Records, Volume 1	RCA	1707	'58	†
	RCA	1707	'62	†
	RCA	5196	'84	CS/CD
Elvis's Golden Records, Volume 2: 50,000,000 Elvis Fans Can't Be Wrong	RCA	2075	'59	†
	RCA	2075	'62	†
	RCA	5197	'84	CS/CD
Elvis's Golden Records, Volume 3	RCA	2765	'63	LP/CD
	RCA	1057		CS
Elvis's Golden Records, Volume 4	RCA	3921	'68	†
	RCA	1297		CS/CD
Elvis's Worldwide 50 Gold Award Hits, Volume 1	RCA	(4) 6401	'70	†
Elvis's Worldwide 50 Gold Award Hits, Volume 1, Parts 1 and 2	RCA	(2) 6401	'88	CD
Elvis's Worldwide 50 Gold Award Hits, Volume 1, No. 1	RCA	1773		CS
Elvis's Worldwide 50 Gold Award Hits, Volume 1, No. 2	RCA	1774		CS
Elvis's Worldwide 50 Gold Award Hits, Volume 1, No. 3	RCA	1775		CS
Elvis's Worldwide 50 Gold Award Hits, Volume 1, No. 4	RCA	1776		CS
Elvis—The Other Sides: Worldwide Gold Award Hits, Volume 2	RCA	(4) 6402	'71	†
A Legendary Performer, Volume 1	RCA	0341	'74	CS
Pure Gold	RCA	0971	'75	†
	RCA	3732		CS
	RCA	53732	'92	CD
A Legendary Performer, Volume 2	RCA	1349	'76	LP/CS
Elvis Sings for Children and Grownups, Too	RCA	2901	'78	†
A Canadian Tribute	RCA	7065	'78	†
A Legendary Performer, Volume 3	RCA	3082	'78	†
Our Memories of Elvis	RCA	3279	'79	†
Our Memories of Elvis, Volume 2	RCA	3448	'79	†
Elvis Aaron Presley: 1955–1980	rca	(8) 3699	'80	†
Guitar Man	RCA	3917	'81	†
Greatest Hits, Volume 1	RCA	2347	'81	†
The Elvis Medley	RCA	4530	'82	†
A Legendary Performer, Volume 4	RCA	4848	'84	CS
Elvis's Golden Records, Volume 5	RCA	4941	'84	CS/CD
A Golden Celebration	RCA	(6) 5172	'84	CS

A Valentine Gift for You	RCA	5353	'85	CS/CD
Reconsider Baby (Elvis Sings the Blues)	RCA	5418	'85	CS/CD
Always On My Mind	RCA	5430	'85	CS/CD
Return of the Rocker (recorded 1960–1963)	RCA	5600	'86	LP/CS/CD†
Elvis Country	RCA	6330		CS/CD†
The Number One Hits	RCA	6382	'87	LP/CS/CD
The Top Ten Hits	RCA	6383	'87	CS
	RCA	(2) 6383	'87	LP/CD
Memories of Christmas	RCA	4395	'87	CS/CD
Elvis in Nashville	RCA	8468	'88	CS/CD
Heartbreak Hotel, Hound Dog and Other Top Ten Hits	RCA	2079	'90	CS/CD
The Great Performances	RCA	2227	'90	LP/CS/CD
Hits Like Never Before	RCA	2229	'91	CS/CD
Elvis Sings Leiber and Stoller—Plus Missing Presley Duet	RCA	3026	'91	CS/CD
Collectors Gold	RCA	(3) 3114	'91	CS/CD
From Nashville to Memphis: The Essential '60s Masters 1	RCA	(5) 66160	'93	CS/CD
Heart and Soul	RCA	66532	'95	CS/CD
Command Performances: The Essential '60s Masters 2	RCA	66601	'95	CS/CD
Walk a Mile in My Shoes: The Essential '70s Masters	RCA	(5) 66670	'95	CS/CD
Elvis	Special Music	(4) 4695		CD
	Special Music	(4) 4965		CS/CD

Budget Albums

Elvis Sings "Flaming Star"	Camden	2304	'69	†
	RCA-Camden	2304		CS
Let's Be Friends	Camden	2408	'70	†
	RCA-Camden	2408		CS
Almost in Love	Camden	2440	'70	†
	RCA-Camden	2440		CS
C'mon Everybody	Camden	2518	'71	†
	RCA-Camden	2518		CS
I Got Lucky	Camden	2533	'71	†
	RCA-Camden	2533		CS
Elvis Sings Hits from His Movies	Camden	2567	'72	†
	RCA-Camden	2567		CS
Burning Love and Hits from His Movies, Volume II	Camden	2595		†
	RCA-Camden	2595		CS/CD
Separate Ways	Camden	2611	'73	†
	RCA-Camden	2611		CS
Love Me Tender	RCA-Camden	2650		CS
Double Dynamite	Camden	(2) 5001		†
Mahalo	Camden	7064		†
Sings for Children	RCA-Camden	2704		CS/CD
A Legendary Performer, Volume I	RCA-Camden	2705		CS/CD
A Legendary Performer, Volume II	RCA-Camden	2706		CS/CD
Blue Christmas	RCA	9800	'89	CS
Double Dynamite	Pair	1010	'86	CD
Remembering	Pair	1037	'86	CS/CD
Elvis Aaron Presley Forever	Pair	1185	'88	CD
Great Performances	Pair	1251		CS/CD
Elvis Country	K-tel	393		CS

THE PRETENDERS

Chrissie Hynde (b. Sept. 7, 1951, Akron, OH), lead voc, rhythm gtr; **James Honeyman-Scott** (b. Nov. 4, 1956, Hereford, England; d. June 16, 1982, London, England), lead gtr, kybd, voc; **Pete Farndon** (b. June 2, 1952, Hereford, England; d. Apr. 14, 1983, London, England), bs; **Martin Chambers** (b. Sept. 4, 1951, Hereford, England), drm [James Honeyman-Scott was replaced by **Robbie McIntosh** and Pete Farndon was replaced by **Malcolm Foster** in 1982. Foster and Martin Chambers left in 1984, to be replaced by bassist **T. M. Stevens** and drummer **Blair Cunningham**. Various musicians played with Hynde in different combinations between 1985 and 1993. In 1994 the entire group was reconstituted with Hynde, Chambers, **Adam Seymour** on guitar, and **Andy Hobson** on bass.]

THE PRETENDERS

One of the most successful groups to emerge from the British New Wave scene of the late '70s, the Pretenders were fronted by American-born singer-songwriter Chrissie Hynde. Building on the tradition started by Patti Smith, Hynde redefined the role of women vocalists in contemporary rock by offering provocative, aggressive songs of desire, defiance, and autonomy from a distinctly female perspective as well as traditional seductive songs of romance. One of the most compelling female singers in rock, Hynde served as an inspiration to the so-called riot grrrls of the '90s such as Courtney Love of Hole and Liz Phair.

Chrissie Hynde taught herself to sing and play guitar and wrote songs as a teenager. She studied art at Kent State University for a time, and performed on the Cleveland rock circuit before moving to London in 1973. There she worked as a rock critic for the *New Musical Express* while attempting to join various bands, including two with musicians who later formed the Clash and the Damned. Finally, in 1978 she formed the Pretenders with three Hereford-based musicians, James Honeyman-Scott, Pete Farndon, and Martin Chambers. The group recorded a demonstration tape, and Nick Lowe offered to produce their first single, "Stop Your Sobbing," written by the Kinks' Ray Davies. The song became a British hit, as did the follow-ups "Kid," written by Hynde, and "Brass in Pocket (I'm Special)," cowritten by Hynde and Honeyman-Scott.

The group toured extensively around Great Britain in 1979 and recorded their debut album under producer Chris Thomas. *The Pretenders* became an instant best-seller, staying on the charts for a year and a half while yielding a major American hit with "Brass in Pocket." The stunning debut, often regarded as one of the finest rock debut albums ever, included "Kid," "Stop Your Sobbing" (a minor hit), the aggressively autonomous "Precious," and the embittered "Up the Neck," as well as "The Wait" and the ballad "Lovers of Today."

Touring incessantly and becoming a major American concert attraction by 1980, the Pretenders issued a five-song minialbum before completing *Pretenders II*. The album included the British hits "Talk of the Town" and "Message of Love" as well as "The Adultress," "Bad Boys Get Spanked," and Ray Davies's "Go to Sleep." The group again toured America in 1981 and 1982, but Pete Farndon was dismissed from the band only days before James Honeyman-Scott was found dead in a friend's apartment on June 16, 1982. Hynde and Chambers recruited Bill Bremner and Tory Butler to record "Back on the Chain Gang," and the song became a smash hit in late 1982.

Shaken by the drug-related deaths of Honeyman-Scott and then Pete Farndon, Chrissie Hynde withdrew from music for a time after the birth of her daughter by Ray Davies. Hynde and Chambers reconstituted the Pretenders with guitarist Robbie McIntosh and bassist Malcolm Foster, yet their next album, *Learning to Crawl*, was largely recorded with session musicians. The album included four hits: "Back on the Chain Gang," "Middle of the Road," "Show Me," and a powerful remake of the Persuaders' 1972 hit "Thin Line Between Love and Hate."

The Pretenders resumed touring in 1984, but personnel changes continued with the departures of Martin Chambers and Malcolm Foster, and Hynde dismantled the band in 1985. She performed solo at Live Aid in 1985 and scored a major hit that summer with a remake of Sonny and Cher's "I Got You Babe," backed by UB40. In 1986 she reconstituted the Pretenders with Robbie McIntosh and Americans T. M. Stevens and Blair Cunningham for the rather mellow *Get Close*. Dominated by love songs, the album produced a major hit with "Don't Get Me Wrong" and a minor hit with "My Baby." Other tracks included "When I Change My Life," "Tradition of Love," and "How Much Did You Get for Your Soul," the album's only angry song. In 1987 Hynde again toured, this time with McIntosh, Foster, and keyboardist Rupert Black, with Iggy Pop as her opening act.

In 1990 Chrissie Hynde recorded the inconsequential *packed!* album. She eventually reconstituted the Pretenders in 1994 with guitarist Adam Seymour, bassist Andy Hobson, and former drummer Martin Chambers for *Last of the Independents* and her first tour in seven years. With the songs largely cowritten by Hynde and Seymour, the album, hailed as the Pretenders' most cohesive in years, featured the major hit "I'll Stand by You," "Night in My Veins," and the vehement "Money Talk" and "I'm a Mother."

The Pretenders

The Pretenders	Sire	6083	'80	CS/CD
The Pretenders (mini)	Sire	3563	'81	CS
Pretenders II	Sire	3572	'81	CS/CD
The Pretenders/Pretenders II	Sire	25137		CS
Learning to Crawl	Sire	23980	'84	CS/CD
Get Close	Sire	25488	'86	CS/CD
The Singles	Sire	25664	'87	CS/CD
packed!	Sire	26219	'90	CS/CD
Last of the Independents	Sire	45572	'94	CS/CD
Isle of View	Warner Bros.	46085	'95	CS/CD

PRINCE

(b. Prince Roger Nelson, June 7, 1958, Minneapolis, MN)

Along with Michael Jackson and Madonna, Prince was one of the most popular solo artists to emerge in the '80s. A hugely talented yet erratic and self-indulgent musician, Prince's work shows the strong influence of rock artist Jimi Hendrix and soul/funk artists such as James Brown, Sly Stone, and George Clinton. Prince fused elements of pop, rock, soul, and funk to produce some of the most influential and best-selling albums of the '80s. Drawing comparisons to Michael Jackson for his fusion of black and white musical styles, his shattering of racial barriers within the music industry, his ambiguous racial and sexual identity, and his reclusiveness, Prince gained his greatest success with 1984's film/album *Purple Rain*.

At age seven Prince took up piano as he was shuttled among relatives following his parents' separation. By 12 he had begun teaching himself guitar, subsequently mastering drums, bass, piano, and saxophone. While still in junior high school Prince formed with Andre Anderson the band Grand Central, which later evolved into Champagne with Anderson and Morris Day. Years later Anderson recorded as Andre Cymone, scoring a near-smash R&B hit with "The Dance Electric" in 1985. In 1976 Prince recorded demonstration tapes that led to a contract with Warner Bros. that allowed him total control over his recordings. He played all instruments and sang all vocals on his debut album, *For You*, which yielded a major R&B hit with the sexually suggestive "Soft and Wet." His penchant for puerile lyrics was confirmed with 1979's *Prince*, again self-recorded, which featured "I Wanna Be Your Lover," a top R&B and major pop hit. Despite receiving virtually no radio airplay of his songs, Prince quickly garnered a rabid following with black audiences and established his sexually explicit image with the appropriately titled *Dirty Mind*. Staying on the charts for a year, the album contained songs about oral sex ("Head") and incest ("Sister Sister") and sparked considerable controversy for its explicitness.

In 1981, under the influence of Sly Stone and Jimi Hendrix, Prince and Morris Day formed the black rock band the Time, with bassist Terry Lewis, keyboard players Jimmy "Jam" Harris and Monte Moir, guitarist Jesse Johnson, and drummer Jellybean Johnson. In the mid-'70s Lewis had formed and played bass for the funk band Flyte Tyme in Minneapolis, recruiting Harris for the band in the late '70s. Backed by the Time, Prince toured in 1981, but performances on the West Coast opening for the Rolling Stones were greeted with catcalls and hurled projectiles. During the year the Time released their debut album on Warner Bros., with Day singing lead vocals, writing all the lyrics, and coproducing the album. It yielded near-smash R&B hits with "Get It Up" and "Cool (Part 1)." In 1982 the Time's second album, *What Time Is It?*, yielded two R&B hits, the smash "777 9311" and "The Walk."

Meanwhile, in late 1981 Warner Bros. issued Prince's self-created *Controversy*, which effectively fused elements of funk and rock and produced R&B smashes with the title song and "Let's Work." His first crossover hits came from his next album, *1999*, which included the R&B smash title cut (a major pop hit) and the pop smashes "Little Red Corvette" and "Delirious" (both major R&B hits). The video to "Little Red Corvette" became the first by a black artist to be aired extensively on MTV and helped open the white-dominated cable-TV network to blacks. The album remained on the album charts for nearly three years and eventually sold more than three million copies, establishing Prince as one of the most exciting and popular new black performers of the decade. Prince toured again in 1982 with a show replete with stunning effects and grandiose staging, centered around Prince's provocative sexual persona. However, by 1983 Prince had dismissed the Time and formed the Revolution with guitarist Wendy Melvoin, keyboardists Lisa Coleman and Matt "Dr." Fink, saxophonist Eric Leeds, and bassist Brownmark.

The Time recorded one more album, *Ice Cream Castle*, before disbanding in 1984. The album yielded three R&B hits, including "Jungle Love," also a major pop hit. Jesse Johnson and Morris Day each pursued solo careers. Johnson scored three R&B smashes in 1985 with "Be Your Man," "Can You Help Me," and "I Want My Girl," followed by the R&B smashes "Crazay" (with Sly Stone) in 1986 and "Love Struck" in 1988. Day achieved an R&B smash with "The Oak Tree" in 1985 and a top R&B (and major pop) hit with "Fishnet" in 1988. The Time eventually regrouped in 1990, with Day, Johnson, Terry Lewis, Jimmy "Jam" Harris, Monte Moir, Jellybean Johnson, and 1984 member Jerome Benton, Lewis's half-brother. They scored a top R&B and near-smash pop hit with "Jerk-Out" that year. However, Day subsequently returned to solo recording with 1992's *Guaranteed*.

Terry Lewis and Jimmy "Jam" Harris formed their own production company, Flyte Tyme, in 1982, and wrote for and produced various acts beginning in 1983, including Klymaxx (1985's crossover smash "I Miss You"), the Human League (1986's crossover smash "Human"), and Robert Palmer (1986's pop smash "I Didn't Mean to Turn You On"). Their most conspicuous success came writing songs for and producing Janet Jackson. They wrote and produced her breakthrough 1986 *Control* album, 1989's *Rhythm Nation*, and 1993's *janet*. All three albums sold more than five million copies, and each produced at least five smash crossover hits. Jam and Lewis also produced Herb Alpert's 1987 comeback album *Keep Your Eyes On Me*, the New Edition's 1988 *Heart Break*, and the 1992 soundtrack to *Mo' Money*.

Prince scored his most spectacular success with the film and soundtrack *Purple Rain* in 1984. The film featured Patty "Apollonia" Kotero, the lead singer of Apollonia 6, and Morris Day as Prince's musical and romantic rival; it grossed more than $80 million at the box office. Primarily recorded with the Revolution, the soundtrack sold 11 million copies and produced five hits, including the top pop and R&B hits "When Doves Cry" and "Let's Go Crazy" and the crossover smashes "Purple Rain" and "I Would Die 4 U," both recorded "live" at the First Avenue Nightclub in Minneapolis. The film, soundtrack, and subsequent arena tour established Prince with white audiences, adolescents in particular, and made him a superstar.

Prince next announced his retirement from live performing and began building the Paisley Park recording studio near Minneapolis, which was completed in 1987. He also formed Paisley Park Records under the auspices of Warner Bros. His first album for the new label, the pretentious and insubstantial *Around the World in a Day*, yielded smash pop and R&B hits with "Raspberry Beret" and "Pop Life." His third album in less than two years, *Parade*, was issued on Paisley Park in 1986. The album was taken from the film *Under the Cherry Moon*, directed by Prince. A conspicuous failure after his popular ascension with *Purple Rain*, *Under the Cherry Moon* was lambasted as silly, vain, lifeless, and sexist. Nonetheless, *Parade* produced a top pop and R&B hit with "Kiss" (covered by Tom Jones in 1988), the major pop and R&B hit "Mountains," and the major R&B hit "Anotherloverholenyohead."

Prince had begun writing and producing for others beginning in 1982 with Vanity 6. The group scored a near-smash R&B-only hit with "Nasty Girl" and launched Vanity (Denise Matthews) on a marginally successful recording and film career. Apollonia 6's eponymous 1984 debut album contained the major R&B hit "Sex Shooter" from the film *Purple Rain*, and Chaka Khan scored a top R&B and smash pop hit with his "I Feel for You" that year. *The Family*, recorded by former Time members Jerome Benton and Jellybean Johnson, yielded a near-smash R&B hit with "The Screams of Passion" in 1985, the year Prince wrote and coproduced Sheena Easton's controversial smash pop hit "Sugar Walls" under the name of Alex Nevermind. Prince also wrote the Bangles' smash 1986 pop hit "Manic Monday" as Christopher. *Wendy and Lisa*, recorded by Wendy Melvoin and Lisa Coleman of the Revolution, produced a minor pop-only hit with "Waterfall" in 1987. Percussionist-vocalist Sheila Escovedo (as Sheila E.), who began touring and recording with Prince in 1986, recorded two modest-selling albums for Paisley Park Records in 1985 and 1987, scoring a major hit in 1986 with Prince's "A Love Bizarre" from the movie *Krush Groove*, in which she starred. Mavis Staples toured with Prince in 1988 and recorded *Time Waits for No One* for Paisley Park in 1989.

By 1987 Prince had dismissed the Revolution and recorded *Sign o' the Times* by himself. The album yielded a top R&B and smash pop hit with the title song as well as a pop smash and major R&B hit with "U Got the Look" and two major R&B hits, "If I Was Your Girlfriend" and "Hot Thing," the flip of the near-smash pop hit "I Could Never Take the Place of

Your Man." Several months later the concert film *Sign o' the Times* debuted to scathing reviews. Prince's next intended release, the so-called *Black Album*, was delayed and eventually withdrawn from release. Dark, sinister, and offensive, the album became quite popular as an illegal bootleg album, perhaps by design, and was eventually made available in limited release in late 1994.

Prince mounted his first full-scale American tour in four years in 1988, to support *Lovesexy*. The tour featured an eight-piece band that included Sheila E. and guitarist Levi Seacer Jr., but the album, his poorest-selling since his debut, produced only one pop hit, the smash "Alphabet Street." Prince's slide into commercial oblivion was arrested by 1989's *Batman*. Composed, arranged, performed, and produced by Prince, the album featured six songs included in the popular movie, plus three others: "The Arms of Orion," "Lemon Crush," and "Batdance." "Batdance" became a top pop and R&B hit, and "Partyman" became a major pop hit. In early 1990 Sinead O'Connor scored a top pop hit with Prince's "Nothing Compares 2 U," originally recorded by the Family in 1985. In 1991 Martika achieved a near-smash pop hit with "Love . . . Thy Will Be Done," written and produced by Prince.

In 1990 Prince and Morris Day reprised their roles from *Purple Rain* in the film *Graffiti Bridge*. The film was deemed another commercial and artistic failure, but the soundtrack album included Prince's top R&B and smash pop hit "Thieves in the Temple"; Tevin Campbell's near-smash pop hit "Round and Round" (written and produced by Prince); Mavis Staples's "Melody Cool"; the George Clinton–Prince duet "We Can Funk"; and four songs by the reunited Time. Prince subsequently formed the New Power Generation with Levi Seacer Jr., keyboardists Tommy Barbarella and Rosie Gaines, and rapper Tony M., among others. Prince and the New Power Generation's debut album, *Diamonds and Pearls*, yielded five pop hits, including the top pop hit "Cream," the top R&B and smash pop hit "Diamonds and Pearls," and two major pop hits, "Gett Off" and "Money Don't Matter 2 Night."

In 1992 Prince renewed his contract with Warner Bros. Records in a deal reportedly worth $100 million. His next album was issued with a combined male-female symbol as its title and yielded four hits but only one major pop hit, the smash "7," which "sampled" the '60s soul song "Tramp." Often referred to as Prince's "symbol" album or *TAFKAP* (for "the artist formerly known as Prince"), the album was primarily recorded with the New Power Generation and emphasized elements of rap music. Prince toured briefly in early 1993, but on April 27 he announced his "retirement" from recording and his intention to fulfill his contractual obligation to Warner Bros. with previously recorded material. Two months later, on his 35th birthday, he changed his name to the symbol used on his 1992 album and announced his separation from the New Power Generation. During the year, the renowned Joffrey Ballet utilized his music for its full-length rock ballet *Billboards*. He had never composed the music he had originally intended for the ballet.

Prince opened several Glam Slam nightclubs in 1993 and New Power Generation retail establishments in 1994. *Come*, his last album recorded with the New Power Generation and his last recorded before the name change, was issued in 1994, yielding a major R&B and moderate pop hit with "Letitgo." Dissolving Paisley Park Records, Prince subsequently recorded for NPG/Bellmark and a label using his symbol. "The Most Beautiful Girl in the World" became a smash R&B and pop and major easy-listening hit on NPG/Bellmark, and *The Beautiful Experience* contained seven different mixes of the song.

Early Prince

Prince for You	Warner Bros.	3150	'78	CS/CD
Prince	Warner Bros.	3366	'79	CS/CD
Dirty Mind	Warner Bros.	3478	'80/'85	CS/CD
Controversy	Warner Bros.	3601	'81	CS/CD
Dirty Mind/Controversy	Warner Bros.	23953		CS

1999	Warner Bros.	23720	'82/'85	CS/CD
The Time				
The Time	Warner Bros.	3598	'81	CS/CD
What Time Is It?	Warner Bros.	23701	'82	CS/CD
Ice Cream Castle	Warner Bros.	25109	'84	CS/CD
Pandemonium	Paisley Park	27490	'90	CS/CD
Jesse Johnson				
Jesse Johnson's Revue	A&M	5024	'85	LP/CS/CD†
Shockadelic	A&M	5122	'86	LP/CS/CD†
Every Shade of Love	A&M	5188	'88	LP/CS/CD†
Morris Day				
Color of Success	Warner Bros.	25320	'85	CS/CD
Daydreaming	Warner Bros.	25651	'88	CS/CD
Guaranteed	Reprise	45040	'92	CS/CD
Prince				
Sign o' the Times	Paisley Park	25577	'87	CS
	Paisley Park	(2) 25577	'87	CD
The Black Album	Warner Bros.	45793	'94	CS/CD
Lovesexy	Paisley Park	25720	'88	CS/CD
Batman (soundtrack)	Warner Bros.	25936	'89	CS/CD
	Warner Bros.	25978	'89	CD
Graffiti Bridge (soundtrack)	Paisley Park	(2) 27493	'90	LP
	Paisley Park	27493	'90	CS/CD
The Hits 1	Paisley Park	45431	'93	CS/CD
The Hits 2	Paisley Park	45435	'93	CS/CD
The Hits/The B-Sides	Paisley Park	(3) 45440	'93	CS/CD
The Gold Experience	Warner Bros.	45999	'95	CS/CD
The Beautiful Experience (mini)	NPG	71003	'94	CS/CD
Prince and the Revolution				
Purple Rain (soundtrack)	Warner Bros.	25110	'84	CS/CD
Around the World in a Day	Warner Bros.	25286	'85	CS/CD
Parade	Paisley Park	25395	'86	CS/CD
Prince and the New Power Generation				
Diamonds and Pearls	Paisley Park	25379	'91	CS/CD
("TAFKAP")	Paisley Park	45037	'92	CS/CD
	Paisley Park	45121	'92	CD
	Paisley Park	45123	'92	CS/CD
Come	Warner Bros.	45700	'94	CS/CD

JOHN PRINE

(b. Oct. 10, 1946, Chicago, IL)

Along with Steve Goodman, John Prine was one of the singer-songwriters to emerge from the Chicago folk scene in the '70s. He shared with Goodman and Loudon Wainwright III a predilection for clever and compassionate yet eccentric songwriting. Although his outstanding debut album contained the classic post–Vietnam War epic "Sam Stone" and the oft-covered "Angel from Montgomery" and "Hello in There," John Prine did not enjoy major success until 1991's *The Missing Years*.

Growing up on the outskirts of Chicago, in Maywood, Illinois, John Prine began playing guitar and writing songs at age 14. In 1970 he started performing at the Chicago folk club the Fifth Peg, where he and Steve Goodman were "discovered" by one of the oddest pairs in show business, Kris Kristofferson and Paul Anka. Signed to Atlantic Records, Prine's classic debut album included "Sam Stone," "Hello in There" (recorded by Bette Midler and Joan Baez in 1972 and 1975, respectively), and "Angel from Montgomery" (covered by Bonnie Raitt in 1974) as well as "Paradise," "Illegal Smile," and the humorous "Your Flag Decal Won't Get You into Heaven Anymore." However, the album sold marginally at best. It was followed by the country-flavored *Diamonds in the Rough* and *Sweet Revenge*, which featured the satirical "Dear Abby" and "Please Don't Bury Me." Following *Common Sense*, John Prine experienced a three-year recording hiatus; eventually he recorded the Steve Goodman–produced *Bruised Orange* for Asylum Records. However, neither this nor his following two Asylum albums sold particularly well, and he was dropped from the label in 1980.

Moving to Nashville, John Prine concentrated on touring and songwriting. He cowrote Don Williams's top country hit "Love Is On a Roll" with Roger Cook, Tammy Wynette's poignant minor country hit "Unwed Fathers" with Bobby Braddock, and "Jackie O" with John Mellencamp. In 1984 Prine formed his own independently distributed Oh Boy label for his first album in nearly five years, *Aimless Love*, which included "Unwed Fathers" and "Me, Myself and I." He experienced another hiatus in the late '80s, eventually reemerging in 1991 with *The Missing Years*, the fastest-selling album of his career. In 1992 John Prine appeared as a member of the Buzzin' Cousins in the film *Falling from Grace*, starring John Mellencamp.

John Prine

John Prine	Atlantic	8296	'71	†
	Atlantic	19156		CS/CD
Diamonds in the Rough	Atlantic	7240	'72	CS/CD
Sweet Revenge	Atlantic	7274	'73	CS/CD
	Atlantic	81430		CD†
Common Sense	Atlantic	18127	'75	CS/CD
Prime Prine: The Best of John Prine	Atlantic	18202	'76	CS/CD
Bruised Orange	Asylum	139	'78	CS
	Oh Boy	006	'89	CD
Pink Cadillac	Asylum	222	'79	CS
	Oh Boy	007	'89	CD
Storm Windows	Asylum	286	'80	CS
	Oh Boy	008	'89	CD
Aimless Love	Oh Boy	002	'84	CS/CD
German Afternoons	Oh Boy	003	'86	CS/CD
John Prine Live	Oh Boy	005		CS/CD
The Missing Years	Oh Boy	009	'91	CS/CD
Great Days: The John Prine Anthology	Rhino	(2) 71400	'93	CS/CD
Lost Dogs and Mixed Blessings	Oh Boy		'95	CS/CD

PROCOL HARUM

Gary Brooker (b. May 29, 1945, London, England), pno, voc; **Keith Reid** (b. Oct. 10, 1946, London, England), lyrics; **Matthew Fisher** (b. Mar. 7, 1946, London, England), org; **Ray Royer** (b. Oct. 8, 1945, England), gtr; **Dave Knights** (b. June 28, 1945, Islington, London, England), bs; **Bobby Harrison** (b. June 28, 1943, East Ham, London, England), drm [After the band's first single, Ray Royer and Bobby Harrison left, to be replaced by guitarist

Robin Trower (b. Mar. 9, 1945, London, England) and drummer **Barry J. "B. J." Wilson** (b. Mar. 18, 1947, Middlesex, England; d. 1989). Matthew Fisher and Dave Knights left in 1970, with **Chris Copping** (b. Aug. 29, 1945, England) joining on organ and bass; Trower left in 1971, to be replaced by guitarist **Dave Ball** (b. Mar. 30, 1950) and bassist **Alan Cartwright** (b. Oct. 10, 1945). Ball was replaced by guitarist **Mark Graham** in 1972. In 1976 Cartwright left, Copping switched to bass, and **Pete Solley** joined on organ. Disbanded in 1977, the group reunited in 1991 with Gary Brooker, Keith Reid, Fisher, and Trower, along with **Dave Bronze**, bass, and **Mark Brzezicki**, drums.]

One of the first late-'60s groups to regularly and prominently feature two keyboard instruments (piano and organ), the English group Procol Harum burst onto the scene with 1967's smash hit "A Whiter Shade of Pale," certainly one of the classic singles of the decade. Procol Harum's first albums were in the forefront of rock as literate, challenging music and encouraged the development of so-called progressive rock. Later emphasizing the powerful lead-guitar playing of Robin Trower, Procol Harum frequently toured the United States, where they became far more popular than they were in their native England. Trower left the group in 1971 and Procol Harum regrouped with several new members and enjoyed unexpected critical and commercial success with 1972's *Live with the Edmonton Symphony Orchestra*. Disbanding in 1977, Procol Harum reunited for an album and tour in 1991.

Procol Harum began their evolution as the Paramounts, an R&B group formed in southern England in 1962. The group was comprised of pianist Gary Brooker, guitarist Robin Trower, bassist Chris Copping, and drummer B. J. Wilson. Having recorded a series of unsuccessful British R&B singles, the Paramounts persevered until 1966, when Brooker left to form a group to record the songs he and lyricist Keith Reid had written. Thus was formed Procol Harum, with Brooker, Reid, organist Matthew Fisher, guitarist Ray Royer, bassist Dave Knights, and drummer Bobby Harrison. Their debut single on the Deram label, "A Whiter Shade of Pale," featured Reid's mythic and surreal lyrics and the ominous organ-playing of Fisher; the song became a smash British and American hit and launched Procol Harum into international prominence. However, both Royer and Harrison soon quit, and former Paramounts Robin Trower and B. J. Wilson were recruited for the completion of the debut album. *Procol Harum* served as an excellent first release, containing nine Brooker-Reid collaborations, including "A Whiter Shade of Pale," the foreboding "Something Following Me," the raunchy "Mabel," "Conquistador," and the powerful five-minute tour de force "(Outside the Gates of) Cerdes." Intellectually as well as emotionally stimulating, the album presented rock music unlike anything heard up until then.

Touring the United States for the first time in 1967–1968 as their song "Homburg" was becoming a moderate hit single, Procol Harum next recorded *Shine On Brightly*. Issued in the United States on A&M Records, the album included "Skip Softly (My Moonbeams)," "Rambling On," and the title song, as well as the 18-minute "In Held Twas in I," which depicted a stunning musical and lyrical journey from the depths of self-pity and depression to regal affirmation and faith. Their next album, *A Salty Dog*, explored a number of musical avenues enhanced by various dubbed-in sounds. It was filled with excellent songs, all with lyrics by Reid, such as "The Milk of Human Kindness," "Too Much Between Us," "All This and More," "Pilgrim's Progress," the title song, and the amusing but fateful "Boredom."

After producing *A Salty Dog*, Matthew Fisher left Procol Harum to become a producer and pursue a neglected solo career. Dave Knights also left, and he and Fisher were replaced by a single new member, bassist-organist Chris Copping, another former Paramount. Reduced to a performing quartet, Procol Harum emphasized the forceful guitar playing of Robin Trower on *Home* and *Broken Barricades*. *Home* included two Trower-Reid collaborations "Whisky Train" and "About to Die" as well as Brooker-Reid compositions such as "Still There'll Be More" and "Your Own Choice." *Broken Barricades* contained three more melodies provided by Trower, most significantly the tribute to Jimi Hendrix, "Song for a Dreamer," in addition to Brooker and Reid's "Simple Sister," "Power Failure," and the lurid "Luskus Delph."

In July 1971 Robin Trower departed from Procol Harum. The group realigned with Brooker, Wilson, Copping (who switched to organ), guitarist Dave Ball, and bassist Alan Cartwright. While touring North America in late 1971, Procol Harum was invited to record with the Edmonton Symphony Orchestra in Canada. Live recordings of the concert became an instant surprise success, garnering the group critical acclaim and an expanded audience. The album, which compiled several of the group's early songs and the "In Held Twas in I" suite in full orchestral and choral treatment, yielded the group's third and final hit, "Conquistador," originally included on their debut album. Procol Harum then switched to Chrysalis Records for *Grand Hotel*. However, their fortunes began to fade with *Exotic Birds and Fruit*, a decidedly hard-rock effort. *Procol's Ninth*, produced by legendary songwriters Jerry Leiber and Mike Stoller, included the favorite "Pandora's Box," but *Something Magic* fared poorly and Procol Harum disbanded in 1977.

Upon leaving Procol Harum, Robin Trower formed the short-lived group Jude with Scottish vocalist Frankie Miller, former Stone the Crows bassist Jim Dewar, and former Jethro Tull drummer Clive Bunker. Trower next formed his own powerhouse trio with Dewar (who sang vocals) and drummer Reg Isidore. Their debut album for Chrysalis, *Twice Removed from Yesterday*, sold marginally despite the stunning Jimi Hendrix–derived guitar playing of Trower on songs such as "Hannah" and "Man of the World." Nonetheless, *Bridge of Sighs* became a best-seller, at least in the United States, where Trower consciously concentrated his efforts. Former Sly and the Family Stone drummer Bill Lordan replaced Isidore for the best-selling *For Earth Below*. Subsequent Robin Trower albums through 1980 sold well, with *Long Misty Days* yielding Trower's only (minor) hit, "Caledonia." Dewar left in 1980 and Trower later recorded two albums with former Cream bassist Jack Bruce. Trower eventually returned to touring in 1986, recording *Passion* for GNP Crescendo Records. He later switched to Atlantic Records.

In 1991 Procol Harum reunited with Gary Brooker, Keith Reid, Matthew Fisher, and Robin Trower for *The Prodigal Stranger* and a new round of touring. In 1993 Windsong U.K. issued the live BBC Radio One concert *Robin Trower*, and in 1995 Procol Harum recorded *The Long Goodbye* for RCA and toured once again.

Procol Harum

Procol Harum	Deram	18008	'67	†
	A&M	2515	'87	CD
(reissued as) A Whiter Shade of Pale	A&M	4373	'73	†
	A&M	3136	'81	†
Shine On Brightly	A&M	4151	'68	CD†
A Salty Dog	A&M	4179	'69	†
	A&M	3123		CD
Home	A&M	4261	'70	†
	Mobile Fidelity	793	'89	CD
Broken Barricades	A&M	4294	'71	†
Live with the Edmonton Symphony Orchestra	A&M	4335	'72	†
	Mobile Fidelity	788	'90	CD
Best	A&M	4401	'73	†
	A&M	3259	'84	CS/CD
Grand Hotel	Chrysalis	1037	'73	†
	Chrysalis	21037	'85	CD†
Exotic Birds and Fruit	Chrysalis	1058	'74	†

Procol's Ninth	Chrysalis	1080	'75	†
Something Magic	Chrysalis	1130	'77	†
The Chrysalis Years (1973–1977)	Chrysalis	21705	'89	CS/CD†
The Prodigal Stranger	Zoo	11011	'91	CS/CD
The Long Goodbye	RCA	68029	'95	CS/CD

Matthew Fisher

Journey's End	RCA	0195	'73	†
I'll Be There	RCA	0325	'74	†
Matthew Fisher	A&M	4801	'80	†

Robin Trower

Twice Removed from Yesterday	Chrysalis	1039	'73	†
	Chrysalis	41039	'83	†
	Chrysalis	21039		CS/CD
Bridge of Sighs	Chrysalis	1057	'74	†
	Chrysalis	21057	'86	CS/CD
For Earth Below	Chrysalis	1073	'75	†
	Chrysalis	41073	'83	†
	Chrysalis	21073		CS/CD†
Live	Chrysalis	1089	'76	†
	Chrysalis	41089	'83	†
	Chrysalis	21089		CS/CD
Long Misty Days	Chrysalis	1107	'76	†
	Chrysalis	41107	'83	†
	Chrysalis	21107		CS/CD
In City Dreams	Chrysalis	1148	'77	†
	Chrysalis	41148	'83	†
	Chrysalis	21148		CS/CD†
Caravan to Midnight	Chrysalis	1189	'78	†
	Chrysalis	41189	'83	†
	Chrysalis	21189		CS/CD†
Victims of the Fury	Chrysalis	1215	'80	†
	Chrysalis	41215	'83	†
Back It Up	Chrysalis	41420	'83	†
	Chrysalis	21420	'86	CS/CD†
Essential	Chrysalis	21853	'91	CS/CD
Passion	GNP Crescendo	2187	'86	LP/CS/CD
Take What You Need	Atlantic	81838	'88	CS/CD†
In the Line of Fire	Atlantic	82080	'90	CS/CD†
Robin Trower	Windsong U.K.	013	'93	CD

Robin Trower, Jack Bruce, and Bill Lordan

B.L.T.	Chrysalis	1324	'81	†
	Chrysalis	41324	'83	†
	Chrysalis	21324	'91	CS/CD†

Robin Trower and Jack Bruce

Truce	Chrysalis	1352	'82	†
	Chrysalis	41352	'83	†
	Chrysalis	21352		CD†
	One Way	17609		CD

Robin Trower and Others

No Stopping Anytime (compilation of songs from above two albums) Chrysalis		21704	'89	CS/CD

Gary Brooker

No More Fear of Flying	Chrysalis	1224	'79	†
Lead Me to the Water	Mercury	4054	'82	†

PUBLIC ENEMY

Chuck D (b. Carlton Ridenhauer, Aug. 1, 1960, New York, NY); **MC Flavor Flav** (b. William Drayton, Mar. 16, 1959, New York, NY); **Professor Griff** (b. Richard Griffin); **Terminator X** (b. Norman Lee Rogers, Aug. 25, 1966, New York, NY) [Richard Griffin left in late 1989.]

One of the first rap groups to expand the music's concerns to that of self-education, self-determination, and black pride, Public Enemy broke through with 1990's *Fear of a Black Planet*, which included the controversial "Welcome to the Terrordome" and the anthemic "Fight the Power" and "Power to the People." Public Enemy stirred another round of controversy with "By the Time I Get to Arizona" from *Apocalypse 91*, perhaps their best-selling album.

The evolution of Public Enemy began in 1982 at Adelphi University on Long Island, when Chuck D and Hank Stocklee produced a collection of rap tracks, including "Public Enemy No. 1." Formed on Long Island, New York, in the mid-'80s, Public Enemy was comprised of Chuck D, Flavor Flav, Professor Griff, and disc jockey Terminator X. Signed to Rick Rubin's Def Jam label, with distribution by Columbia, the group's debut album, which included "Megablast" and "You're Gonna Get Yours," sold only modestly. However, their second, *It Takes a Nation of Millions to Hold Us Back*, remained on the album charts for nearly a year and proclaimed them "Prophets of Rage." The album featured "Bring the Noise," "Countdown to Armageddon," "Louder than a Bomb," "Party for Your Right to Fight," and "Don't Believe the Hype," in which they expressed their distrust of the media. In 1989 Professor Griff, as the group's Minister of Information, made anti-Semitic remarks that nearly broke up the group and led to his dismissal by year's end.

Public Enemy broke through as an album group with 1990's *Fear of a Black Planet*. Avoiding at least in part the sexism of some of the songs from their first two albums, *Fear of a Black Planet* contained "Brothers Gonna Work It Out," "Power to the People," "Revolutionary Generation," "Fight the Power" (featured in Spike Lee's film, *Do the Right Thing*), "Burn Hollywood Burn," and "Welcome to the Terrordome." *Apocalypse 91* became perhaps their best-selling and most controversial album. "By the Time I Get to Arizona" threatened violence against the state that refused to honor Martin Luther King Jr.'s nationally proclaimed holiday, and "How to Kill a Radio Consultant" denounced radio stations that refused to play rap songs. The album produced a minor pop hit with "Can't Truss It" and included a collaboration with the white thrash metal band Anthrax on "Bring the Noise." In 1992 *Greatest Misses* compiled many of their earlier favorites, and 1994's *Muse Sick-n-Hour Mess Age* produced a moderate pop and R&B hit with "Give It Up."

Public Enemy

Yo! Bum Rush the Show	Def Jam/Columbia	40658	'87	LP/CS/CD
It Takes a Nation of Millions to Hold Us Back	Def Jam/Columbia	44303	'88	CS/CD
Fear of a Black Planet	Def Jam/Columbia	45413	'90	CS/CD
Apocalypse 91 . . . The Enemy Strikes Black	Def Jam/Columbia	47374	'91	LP/CS/CD
Greatest Misses	Def Jam/Columbia	53014	'92	LP/CS/CD
	Def Jam/Columbia	53014	'92	CS/CD
Muse Sick-n-Hour Mess Age	Def Jam/Columbia	53362	'94	CS/CD

Q

QUEEN

Freddie Mercury (b. Frederick Bulsara, Sept. 5, 1946, Zanzibar, Africa; d. Nov. 24, 1991, Kensington, England), lead voc, kybd; **Brian May** (b. July 19, 1947, Twickenham, Middlesex, England), lead gtr; **John Deacon** (b. Aug. 19, 1951, Leicester, England), bs; **Roger Taylor** (b. July 26, 1949, Kings Lynn, Norfolk, England)

QUEEN

Perhaps the most consistently successful British group of the mid-'70s to mid-'80s despite critical hostility, Queen were one of the foremost glitter-rock bands of the era, thanks to the outlandish costumes and flamboyant and blatantly sexual on-stage behavior of lead singer Freddie Mercury. Eschewing synthesizers until 1980, Queen broke through into international popularity with 1976's near-smash hit single "Bohemian Rhapsody"; its video helped pioneer rock video in the days before MTV. Recording classics such as "We Will Rock You" and "Another One Bites the Dust," Queen suffered declining popularity in the United States after the mid-'80s. Discontinuing touring in 1986, Queen eventually recorded their most personal and emotionally accessible album, *The Miracle*, in 1989. After years of persistent rumors that he had contracted AIDS, Freddie Mercury died on November 24, 1991, one day after acknowledging the fact (the first rock star to do so). A 1992 tribute concert to Mercury, viewed by as many as one billion people, helped publicize the need to find a cure for the disease.

Queen was formed in 1971 by Brian May and Roger Taylor, former members of the group Smile, and Freddie Mercury from the group Wreckage. John Deacon was recruited through an advertisement, and the band rehearsed for 18 months before performing at showcase engagements in 1972, without playing any clubs or other small venues. Quickly signed to EMI Records (Elektra in the United States), Queen's debut album was accompanied by a massive promotional campaign that alienated many critics. It included the anthemic "Keep Yourself Alive" and yielded a major British hit with "Seven Seas of Rhye" yet failed to produce even a minor American hit. In 1973 Mercury covered the Beach Boys' classic "I Can Hear Music" as "Larry Lurex," and following *Queen II* the group toured Great Britain and America, opening for Mott the Hoople.

Queen broke through in 1975 with the major hit "Killer Queen" from *Sheer Heart Attack*. They subsequently toured the world and became international stars with 1976's *A Night at the Opera*. The album stayed on the charts for more than a year and contained Mercury's near-smash hit "Bohemian Rhapsody," Deacon's major hit "You're My Best Friend," and May's overlooked ballad "39." The promotional video for "Bohemian Rhapsody" helped pioneer rock videos long before the advent of MTV. The follow-up, *A Day at the Races*, produced a major hit with Mercury's "Somebody to Love," and their next album, *News of the World*, featured the smash hit "We Are the Champions" (by Mercury) and the classic "We Will Rock You" (by May). The diversified album *Jazz* produced a two-sided hit with the controversial "Bicycle Race"/"Fat Bottomed Girls."

One of the world's most popular touring bands by the late '70s, Queen recorded *The Game* after the live set *Queen Live Killers*. *The Game* topped the album charts and remained there for nearly a year, producing two top hits with Mercury's rockabilly-style "Crazy Little Thing Called Love" and Deacon's "Another One Bites the Dust," which surprisingly also became a smash R&B hit. The album yielded the moderate hits "Play the Game," which featured the group's first use of the synthesizer, and "Need Your Loving Tonight." Buoyed by the crossover success of "Another One Bites the Dust," Queen subsequently favored a dance-style sound through the mid-'80s. Major hits through 1984 included "Under Pressure," recorded with David Bowie; "Body Language"; and "Radio Ga-Ga," the last for their new label, Capitol.

Subsequent '80s recordings by Queen fared less well, as their American popularity faded. Nonetheless, their success grew across the world thanks to well-received international tours. During the decade the members of Queen began pursuing projects away from the group. May composed and recorded soundtracks, most notably for the films *Mad Max* and *The Road Warrior* (also known as *Mad Max 2*). He joined Eddie Van Halen and REO Speedwagon's Alan Gratzer for 1983's minialbum *Star Fleet Project*. Roger Taylor recorded two solo albums before forming his own band, the Cross, in 1987. In 1984 Freddie Mercury scored a minor hit with "Love Kills" from the movie *Metropolis*; he later recorded *Mr. Bad Guy* for Columbia Records.

The group's next album was the disjointed *A Kind of Magic*, which produced a moderate hit with the title song in 1986, the year the group stopped touring. In 1987 Freddie Mercury performed with Spanish opera singer Montserrat Caballé in Barcelona; recordings from the engagement were eventually released in 1992. Queen's next album, *The Miracle*, was perhaps the group's best work, with a surprisingly personal and honest tone. It includes "Invisible Man," "Rain Must Fall," "Was It All Worth It," and "I Want It All" (a minor hit). The foreboding *Innuendo*, Queen's final studio album, featured "These Are the Days of Our Lives" and "The Show Must Go On."

Badgered for years about reports that he had contracted AIDS through his legendary sexual exploits, Freddie Mercury maintained his stance of refusing to give interviews. On November 23, 1991, he publicly acknowledged that he did indeed have AIDS, and he died at his Kensington home in west London the next day. In April 1992 a tribute concert to Freddie Mercury was staged at Wembley Stadium in London, with performances by vocalists George Michael, Liza Minnelli, Elton John, and David Bowie backed by the surviving members of Queen, as well as Def Leppard, Metallica, and Guns N' Roses. The show, broadcast to more than 70 nations, reached upwards of one billion people.

Queen was introduced to an entirely new audience when the 1992 hit movie *Wayne's World* featured "Bohemian Rhapsody"; the song returned to MTV and reached Number Two on the pop charts. By 1993, with the dissolution of Queen, Brian May had formed his own band to record *Back to the Light* and tour in support of Guns N' Roses.

Queen

Queen	Elektra	75064	'73	†
	Hollywood	61064	'91	CS/CD
At the BBC (recorded 1973)	PGD	62005	'95	CS/CD
Queen II	Elektra	75082	'74	†
	Hollywood	61232	'91	CS/CD
Sheer Heart Attack	Elektra	1026	'74	†
	Hollywood	61036	'91	CS/CD
A Night at the Opera	Elektra	1053	'75	†
	Hollywood	61065	'91	CS/CD
	Mobile Fidelity	568	'92	CD
A Day at the Races	Elektra	101	'77	†
	Hollywood	61035	'91	CS/CD
News of the World	Elektra	112	'77	†
	Hollywood	61037	'91	CS/CD
	Mobile Fidelity	588	'93	CD
Jazz	Elektra	166	'78	†
	Hollywood	61062	'91	CS/CD
Queen Live Killers	Elektra	(2) 702	'79	†
	Hollywood	61066	'91	CS
	Hollywood	(2) 61066	'91	CD
The Game	Elektra	513	'80	†
	Hollywood	61063	'91	CS/CD
	Mobile Fidelity	610	'94	CD
	Mobile Fidelity	211	'95	LP
Flash Gordon (soundtrack)	Elektra	518	'80	†
	Hollywood	61203	'91	CS/CD
Greatest Hits	Elektra	564	'81	†
Hot Space	Elektra	60128	'82	†
	Hollywood	61038	'91	CS/CD
The Works	Capitol	12322	'84	†
	Capitol	46016		CD†
	Hollywood	61233	'91	CS/CD
A Kind of Magic	Capitol	12476	'86	†
	Capitol	46267	'86	CD†
	Hollywood	61152	'91	CS/CD
The Miracle	Capitol	92357	'89	LP/CS/CD†
	Hollywood	61234	'91	CS/CD
Innuendo	Hollywood	61020	'91	CS/CD
Live at Wembley	Hollywood	61104	'92	CS/CD
Classic Queen	Hollywood	61311	'92	CS/CD
Greatest Hits	Hollywood	61265	'92	CS/CD
Queen Collection	Hollywood	(3) 61407	'92	CD
Made in Heaven	Hollywood/PGD	62017	'95	CS/CD
Greatest Hits, I and II	Hollywood/PGD	(2) 62042	'95	CD

Queen and George Michael

Five Live	Hollywood	61479	'93	CS/CD

Brian May

Patrick (soundtrack)	Varese Sarabande	81107	'80	†
Patrick/Roadgames (soundtracks)	OnemOne	1014	'92	CD†
Mad Max (soundtrack)	Varese Sarabande	81144	'80	†
	Varese Sarabande	47144	'93	CD
The Road Warrior (soundtrack)	Varese Sarabande	81155	'83	†
(reissued as) Mad Max 2: The Road Warrior	Varese Sarabande	47262		CD
Death Before Dishonor (soundtrack)	Varese Sarabande		'88	†
	Prometheus	118	'93	CD
The Day After Halloween (soundtrack)	Citadel	7020	'81	†
The Day After Halloween/Harlequin (soundtracks)	OnemOne	1009	'92	CD†
Back to the Light	Hollywood	61404	'93	CS/CD

Brian May and Friends

Star Fleet Project (mini)	Capitol	15014	'83	†

Roger Taylor

Fun in Space	Elektra	522	'82	†
Strange Frontier			'84	†

The Cross

Shove It	Virgin	90857	'88	LP/CS/CD†

Freddie Mercury

Mr. Bad Guy	Columbia	40071	'85	CD
The Great Pretender	Hollywood	61402	'92	CS/CD

Freddie Mercury and Montserrat Caballé

Barcelona	Hollywood	61366	'92	CS/CD

QUICKSILVER MESSENGER SERVICE

John Cipollina (b. Aug. 24, 1943, Berkeley, CA; d. May 29, 1989, Greenbrae, CA), lead gtr, voc; **Gary Duncan** (b. Sept. 4, 1946, San Diego, CA), rhythm gtr, voc; **David Freiberg** (b. Aug. 24, 1938, Boston, MA); **Greg Elmore** (b. Sept. 4, 1946, Coronado, CA), drm [Songwriter-guitarist-vocalist **Dino Valenti** (b. Chester A. Powers, Nov. 7, 1943, Danbury, CT; d. Nov. 16, 1994, Santa Rosa, CA) was a member from 1970 to 1979. Various musicians came and went from 1971 to 1975, when the original band called it a day; the group re-formed for a 1987 reunion with Duncan and supporting musicians but quickly dissolved again.]

Along with the Grateful Dead, the Jefferson Airplane, and Big Brother and the Holding Company, the Quicksilver Messenger Service were pioneers of the psychedelic music scene in San Francisco during the second half of the '60s, although they didn't record their first album until 1968. The group endured a variety of personnel changes after their second album, remaining nominally intact through the '70s without ever achieving the national stature of other bands from the area.

Formed in late 1964 in San Francisco by John Cipollina, Gary Duncan, David Freiberg, and Greg Elmore, the Quicksilver Messenger Service debuted professionally in December 1965. The band had originally hoped to feature singer-guitarist-songwriter Dino Valenti as its lead vocalist, but he was jailed on a drug charge. Under his real name of Chester A. Powers, Valenti wrote "Hey Joe" (covered by numerous '60s stars, including the classic version by Jimi Hendrix) and "Let's Get Together" (the classic psychedelic-era song of fellowship that was covered by both the Youngbloods and Jefferson Airplane), and he recorded a solo album in 1968 under his own name. In the meantime, Quicksilver played locally and became fixtures of the burgeoning San Francisco music scene, eventually signing with Capitol Records in 1968. Their debut album contained the classic instrumentals "The Fool" and "Gold and Silver," featuring Cipollina's psychedelic lead guitar ruminations, Hamilton Camp's "Pride of Man," and Valenti's "Dino's Song." Their second album yielded a minor hit with Bo Diddley's "Who Do You Love" and included a campy version of Dale Evans's title song "Happy Trails."

Gary Duncan departed the Quicksilver Messenger Service in January 1969 but returned with Dino Valenti in December. Recording as simply Quicksilver, the group scored a near-moderate hit with "Fresh Air" in 1970 and a minor hit with "What About Me" in 1971. John Cipollina left in October 1970 and David Freiberg left in September 1971, to later join, tour, and record with the Jefferson Starship, from 1973 to 1985. In March 1975 Quicksilver reunited with Cipollina, Freiberg, Valenti, Duncan, and Elmore for the dismal *Solid Silver* album. The group remained nominally intact under Dino Valenti through 1979, as Cipollina pursued session work and various music projects around the Bay Area. In the '80s he formed a number of bands, including Thunder and Lightning, with Nick Gravenites, and the loosely structured Dinosaurs, with other Bay Area music veterans. Duncan led a re-formed Quicksilver in 1987 for a reunion album without the other original members, but it failed to attract even a nostalgia audience. John Cipollina died on May 29, 1989, in Marin County of emphysema at age 45, and Dino Valenti died on November 16, 1994, in Santa Rosa, California, after a brief illness, at age 51.

Quicksilver Messenger Service

Quicksilver Messenger Service	Capitol	2904	'68	†
	Capitol	16089		†
	Capitol	91146	'94	CD
Happy Trails	Capitol	120	'69	†
	Capitol	16090		†
	Capitol	91215	'94	CD
Shady Grove	Capitol	391	'70	†
	Capitol	16094		†
	One Way	57339		CD
Just for Love	Capitol	498	'70	†
	Capitol	16093		†
	One Way	57821		CD
What About Me	Capitol	630	'70	†
	Capitol	16092		†
	One Way	57820		CD
Quicksilver	Capitol	819	'71	†
	Capitol	16091		†
	One Way	17411		CD
Comin' Thru	Capitol	11002	'72	†
	One Way	17412		CD
Anthology	Capitol	(2) 11165	'73	†
Solid Silver	Capitol	11462	'75	†
	Capitol	11820	'78	†
Peace by Peace	Capitol		'86	†
Sons of Mercury (1968–1975)	Rhino	(2) 70747	'91	CS/CD

Dino Valenti

Dino	Epic	26335	'68	†

R

BONNIE RAITT

(b. Nov. 8, 1949, Burbank, CA)

One of the most talented female song interpreters and bottleneck-guitar stylists to emerge in the '70s, Bonnie Raitt often toured with the black blues artists that influenced her while recording the songs of obscure contemporary songwriters such as John Prine, Eric Kaz, and Karla Bonoff. Recording the definitive version of Kaz and Libby Titus's moving "Love Has No Pride" and Prine's "Angel from Montgomery," Raitt enjoyed modest success during the '70s. Neglected by her longtime record label Warner Bros., Bonnie Raitt finally broke through into mass popularity on Capitol Records with the 1989 album *Nick of Time*, and sustained that popularity with 1991's *Luck of the Draw* and 1994's *Longing in Their Hearts*, all produced by Don "Was" Fagenson.

The daughter of Broadway singer-actor John Raitt (*Carousel*, *The Pajama Game*, and *Oklahoma*), Bonnie Raitt moved with her family from New York to Los Angeles in 1957. Between ages 8 and 14 she was exposed to authentic blues and politicized folk music while attending Quaker summer camps in upstate New York. She took up guitar at age 9, and later learned piano. By her mid-teens she had mastered the bottleneck or slide-guitar technique that was to characterize her work. In 1967 she moved to Boston to attend Radcliffe College and met Dick Waterman (her manager until 1986), who introduced her to old blues performers such as John Hurt, Fred McDowell, and Sippie Wallace. She played Cambridge folk clubs such as Club 47 and enjoyed success in folk clubs around Boston, Philadelphia, and New York. By 1969 she had dropped out of Radcliffe and met bassist Freebo, a former member of the Edison Electric Band, who became a mainstay of her touring band of the '70s.

Signed to Warner Bros. Records in spring 1971, Bonnie Raitt's debut album contained two Sippie Wallace songs, "Mighty Tight Woman" and "Woman Be Wise," the originals "Thank You" and "Finest Lovin' Man," and Robert Johnson's "Walking Blues." Her second album, *Give It Up*, became her first album-chart entry and included "Give It Up or Let Me Go," "Love Me like a Man," Sippie Wallace's "You Got to Know How," and the definitive version of Eric Kaz and Libby Titus's "Love Has No Pride." Bonnie Raitt returned to the West Coast to record *Takin' My Time* under producer John Hall of Orleans. The album featured Eric Kaz's "Cry Like a Rainstorm," Chris Smither's "I Feel the Same," and Randy Newman's "Guilty." By 1974 Raitt's modest success had enabled her to assemble a touring band based around Freebo, and she toured tirelessly for years. She began playing electric lead guitar with *Streetlights*, recorded in New York under R&B producer Jerry Ragavoy. It included a stellar rendition of John Prine's "Angel from Montgomery" and the favorite "You Got to Be Ready for Love."

Bonnie Raitt moved to Los Angeles in 1975, where she recorded *Home Plate*, which included "Good Enough" and "Run Like a Thief." Her first major success came with 1977's *Sweet Forgiveness*, which produced a sluggish version of Del Shannon's "Runaway" (a minor hit) and contained Karla Bonoff's "Home" and Paul Siebel's oft-recorded "Louise." In 1979 Raitt became a founding member of MUSE (Musicians United for Safe Energy) with John Hall, Jackson Browne, and Graham Nash; she performed at five MUSE benefit shows staged at Madison Square Garden. *The Glow*, recorded under producer Peter Asher, included her own "Standin' by the Same Old Love" and Robert Palmer's "You're Gonna Get What's Coming," a minor hit. In 1980 Raitt scored a minor country hit with Rusty Wier's "Don't It Make You Wanna Dance" from the film *Urban Cowboy*. After 1982's *Green Light*, recorded with Texas guitarist Johnny Lee Schell and veteran keyboardist Ian McLagan, Warner Bros. refused to issue her next album, tentatively titled *Tongue and Groove*. She nonetheless continued to tour with a new band based around Schell and bassist James "Hutch" Hutchinson. She appeared at the Farm Aid and Amnesty International concerts and eventually assembled *Nine Lives* for release on Warner Bros. In 1987 Raitt participated in the joint Soviet/American Peace Concert, staged in Moscow.

Under new management, Bonnie Raitt eventually signed with Capitol Records. She recorded *Nick of Time* under producer Don "Was" Fagenson and the album became a surprise best-seller, eventually moving more than four million copies. The album yielded hits with John Hiatt's "Thing Called Love" (the first single and Raitt's first music video), the title track, and Bonnie Hayes's "Have a Heart"; it also included the self-affirming "I Ain't Gonna Let You Break My Heart Again," "I Will Not Be Denied," and her own "The Road's My Middle Name." In 1990 Raitt recorded duets with John Lee Hooker on "I'm in the Mood" and B. B. King on Doctor John's "Right Place Wrong Time." Raitt netted four Grammys in 1990, celebrating her newfound success and long career in the business. In 1991 she recorded *Luck of the Draw* with producer Don Was. The album yielded the smash hit "Something to Talk About," the major hit "I Can't Make You Love Me," and the moderate hit "Not the Only One" and eventually sold more than five million copies. That same year Raitt cofounded the Rhythm and Blues Foundation, to help aged (and often poverty-stricken) pioneers of that musical genre. Bonnie Raitt's perseverance had finally paid off, and her success continued with 1994's *Longing in Their Hearts*, again under producer Was. The album featured the major hit "Love Sneakin' Up on You," "Feeling of Falling," and Richard Thompson's "Dimming of the Day." In 1995 she scored a minor hit with a remake of Roy Orbison/Jeff Lynne/Tom Petty's "You Got It," which was used as a theme song for the film *Boys on the Side*; she also issued a two-CD live set, *Road Tested*, along with a video. Raitt was honored with a Bonnie Raitt–signature Fender guitar, with profits earmarked to encourage women to learn the instrument.

Bonnie Raitt

Bonnie Raitt	Warner Bros.	1953	'71	CS/CD
Give It Up	Warner Bros.	2643	'72	CS/CD
Takin' My Time	Warner Bros.	2729	'73	CS/CD
Streetlights	Warner Bros.	2818	'74	CS/CD
Home Plate	Warner Bros.	2864	'75	CS/CD
Sweet Forgiveness	Warner Bros.	2990	'77	CS/CD
The Glow	Warner Bros.	3369	'79	CS/CD
Green Light	Warner Bros.	3630	'82	CS/CD
Nine Lives	Warner Bros.	25486	'86	CS/CD
The Bonnie Raitt Collection	Warner Bros.	26242	'90	CS/CD
Nick of Time	Capitol	91268	'89	CS/CD
Luck of the Draw	Capitol	96111	'91	CS/CD
	Capitol	96860	'91	CD†

Longing in Their Hearts	Capitol	81427	'94	CS/CD
Road Tested	Capitol	(2) 33705	'95	CS/CD

THE RAMONES

Joey Ramone (b. Jeffrey Hyman, May 19, 1952, Forest Hills, NY), voc; **Johnny Ramone** (b. John Cummings, Oct. 8, 1951, Long Island, NY), gtr; **Dee Dee Ramone** (b. Douglas Colvin, Sept. 18, 1952, Vancouver, British Columbia, Canada), bs; **Tommy Ramone** (b. Tom Erdelyi, Jan. 29, 1952, Budapest, Hungary), drm [Later members include drummers **Marky Ramone** (b. Marc Bell, July 15, 1956, New York, NY) and **Richie Ramone** (b. Richard Reinhardt, aka Richard Beau) as well as bassist **C. J. Ramone** (b. Christopher Joseph Ward, Oct. 8, 1965, Long Island, NY).]

THE RAMONES

Credited with being New York City's leading proponents of punk rock in the mid-'70s, the Ramones proffered uncomplicated, furious rock featuring sarcastic, implacable, and wryly satirical lyrics that stood in staunch opposition to the overproduced and complacent contemporary musical styles—from progressive rock to disco to pop—then dominating popular music. Their first two albums, *The Ramones* and *The Ramones Leave Home*, became punk classics, and their headline engagements in London in July 1976 inspired a generation of young British musicians, including the Sex Pistols, the Clash, and dozens of other defiant, unconventional groups. However, while other punk groups either self-destructed, disappeared, or adopted more palatable musical textures and lyrical nuances to gain mainstream popularity, the Ramones remained stylistically intransigent and never attained more than a rabid cult following. Nonetheless, they have persevered into the '90s.

The Ramones formed in Forest Hills (Queens), New York, in August 1974 with high school dropouts Jeffrey Hyman, John Cummings, and Douglas Colvin. They debuted at New York's Performance Studio in March 1974; within two months, manager Tom Erdelyi joined on drums as Hyman switched to lead vocals. They began a residency at CBGB's, one of New York City's leading punk clubs (along with Max's Kansas City), in August and became one of the city's leading purveyors of frantic, unadorned, straight-ahead rock featuring vituperative, wryly satirical lyrics. Signed to Sire Records in November 1975, the Ramones' debut album contained punk favorites such as "Beat on the Brat," "Blitzkrieg Bop," "Judy Is a Punk," and "Now I Wanna Sniff Some Glue." Touring exhaustively, the group soon recorded *The Ramones Leave Home*, which included "Pinhead," "Commando," the classic "Gimme Gimme Shock Treatment," and their first minor hit, "Sheena Is a Punk Rocker."

The Ramones conducted their first tour of Great Britain in 1976, and their July 4th debut at London's Roadhouse caused a sensation that drew a number of musicians who would later form some of the country's most outrageous and popular punk bands. Their third album in 18 months, *Rocket to Russia*, produced minor hits with "Rockaway Beach" and "Do You Wanna Dance" and contained "Cretin Hop," "Teenage Lobotomy," and their first ballad, "Here Today, Gone Tomorrow." Tommy Ramone left the group in May 1978 to pursue a career in production, to be replaced by former Richard Hell and the Voidoids drummer Marc Bell, who became Marky Ramone. The group's next album, *Road to Ruin*, included the punk classic "I Wanna Be Sedated" as well as "I Just Want to Have Something to Do," the love song "Questioningly," and a cover of Sonny Bono's "Needles and Pins," a major hit for the Searchers in 1964.

In 1979 the Ramones appeared in the teenage movie *Rock 'n' Roll High School* and recorded *End of the Century*, their best-selling album, under legendary producer Phil Spector. The album featured "Rock 'n' Roll High School," the endearing "Do You Remember Rock 'n' Roll Radio?," and a remake of the Ronettes' "Baby I Love You." The group then recorded *Pleasant Dreams* under songwriter-producer Graham Gouldman, an erstwhile member of 10cc, which included "The KKK Took My Baby Away" and "We Want the Airwaves."

Despite the waning of punk's popularity in the '80s, the Ramones continued to record for Sire Records. However, Marc Bell left in 1983, to be replaced by Richie Ramone (Richard Beau). Bell returned in 1988, but Dee Dee Ramone departed in 1989 to pursue a solo career as Dee Dee King and was replaced by C. J. Ramone (Chris Ward). None of the group's '80s albums sold particularly well, although they did record occasional gems such as "Psycho Therapy," "Howling at the Moon," "Animal Boy," "My Brain Is Hanging Upside Down (Bonzo Goes to Bitburg)," "I Wanna Live," and "Merry Christmas (I Don't Want to Fight Tonight)." In 1990 the Ramones toured the world as part of the Escape from New York tour with Debbie Harry and the Tom Tom Club. By 1992 the Ramones had switched to the MCA-distributed Radioactive label for *Mondo Bizarro*, which included "Censorshit," "Cabbies on Crack," and "The Job that Ate My Brain." It was followed by an album of cover songs, *Acid Eaters*. In 1995 the band announced their retirement with the release of *Adios Amigos*, which features "I Don't Want to Grow Up," the ironic "Have a Nice Day," and "Born to Die in Berlin."

The Ramones

The Ramones	Sire	7520	'76	†
	Sire	6020		LP/CS
The Ramones Leave Home	Sire	7528	'77	†
	Sire	6031		LP/CS
Rocket to Russia	Sire	6042	'77	LP
Road to Ruin	Sire	6063	'78	LP
Rock 'n' Roll High School (soundtrack)	Sire	6070	'79	LP/CS/CD
End of the Century	Sire	6077	'80	LP/CS/CD
Pleasant Dreams	Sire	3571	'81	LP/CS/CD
Subterranean Jungle	Sire	23800	'83/'94	CD
Too Tough to Die	Sire	25187	'84	CS/CD
Animal Boy	Sire	25433	'86	CS/CD
Halfway to Sanity	Sire	25641	'87	CS/CD
Ramones Mania	Sire	(2) 25709	'88	LP
	Sire	25709	'88	CS/CD
Brain Drain	Sire	25905	'89	CS/CD
All the Stuff (and More), Volume I	Sire	26220	'90	CS/CD
All the Stuff (and More), Volume II	Sire	26618	'91	CS/CD
Loco Live	Sire	26650	'92	CS/CD

Mondo Bizarro	Radioactive	10615	'92	LP/CS/CD
Acid Eaters	Radioactive	10913	'93	CS/CD
Adios Amigos!	Radioactive	11273	'95	LP/CS/CD

Dee Dee King

Standing in the Spotlight	Sire	25884	'89	CS/CD†

THE [YOUNG] RASCALS

Felix Cavaliere (b. Nov. 29, 1943, Pelham, NY), org, voc; **Eddie Brigati** (b. Oct. 22, 1946, Garfield, NJ), voc; **Gene Cornish** (b. May 14, 1945, Ottawa, Canada), gtr; **Dino Danelli** (b. July 23, 1945, Jersey City, NJ), drm

An American singles band that achieved their greatest success from 1966 to 1968, the Young Rascals, as they were initially known, began as a white R&B group that appealed to both black and white audiences. One of the first white rock groups to record for Atlantic Records, the Young Rascals featured the amazingly soulful vocals of Felix Cavaliere. Shifting to pop-oriented material and a smoother sound with their smash hit "Groovin'," the Rascals continued to have major hits until 1969, eventually disbanding in 1972. After various solo and group projects, three of the four members reunited in 1988.

The Young Rascals were formed in the New York area in 1964 by Dino Danelli and three former members of Joey Dee's Starlighters: Felix Cavaliere, Gene Cornish, and Eddie Brigati. They started playing together at the Choo Choo Club in Garfield, New Jersey, in February 1965, then graduated to the Long Island discotheque the Barge and finally to various Manhattan clubs by fall 1965. Playing R&B-style music centered around the vocals and organ playing of Cavaliere, the group developed a reputation as an exciting live act and were signed to Atlantic Records by Ahmet Ertegun.

The Young Rascals' second single, "Good Lovin'," a cover version of the Olympics' minor 1965 hit, became a top pop hit in early 1966 and was followed by the major hits "You Better Run" (written by Cavaliere and Brigati) and "I've Been Lonely Too Long" (by Cavaliere). Their first two R&B-style albums became best-sellers, yet they adopted a lighter sound for *Groovin'*. The album yielded a top pop and smash R&B hit with the title song and smash hits with "A Girl Like You" and "How Can I Be Sure," all three written by Cavaliere and Brigati. After another major hit with the duo's "It's Wonderful," the group became simply the Rascals for the smash hit "A Beautiful Morning" and the top hit "People Got to Be Free" (also a major R&B hit), both by Cavaliere and Brigati. "A Ray of Hope," "See," and "Carry Me" became major hits for the Rascals through 1969, but by the time the group had switched to Columbia Records in 1971 only Cavaliere and Danelli remained. The group disbanded in 1972 after two poor-selling albums for the label.

Gene Cornish and Dino Danelli formed Bulldog and managed a moderate hit with "No" in 1972, later forming Fotomaker with Wally Bryson, former lead guitarist for the Raspberries. Felix Cavaliere surfaced as a solo artist in 1974, manned the group Treasure in 1977, and eventually scored a moderate solo hit with "Only a Lonely Heart Sees" in 1980. Eddie Brigati joined his brother David, another former member of Joey Dee's Starlighters, in 1976 for a neglected album on Elektra Records.

In 1988 Felix Cavaliere, Gene Cornish, and Dino Danelli reunited for the 40th anniversary concert of Atlantic Records and subsequently conducted a national tour. In 1994 Felix Cavaliere returned to recording with *Dreams in Motion* on Karambolage Records.

The Young Rascals

The Young Rascals	Atlantic	8123	'66	†
	Rhino	70237	'88	†
	Warner	27617		CD†

Collections	Atlantic	8134	'67	†
	Rhino	70238	'88	†
	Warner	27618		CD†
Groovin'	Atlantic	8148	'67	†
	Rhino	70239	'88	†
	Warner	27619		CD†

The Rascals

Once Upon a Dream	Atlantic	8169	'68	†
	Rhino	70240	'88	CS
Time Peace (The Rascals' Greatest Hits)	Atlantic	8190	'68	CS/CD
Freedom Suite	Atlantic	(2) 901	'69	†
	Rhino	70241	'88	CS
See	Atlantic	8246	'70	†
Search and Nearness	Atlantic	8276	'71	†
Peaceful World	Columbia	(2) 30462	'71	†
The Island of Real	Columbia	31103	'72	†
Rock and Roll Treasures	Pair	1106	'86	CS
Searching for Ecstasy: The Rest of the Rascals, 1969–1972	Rhino	70242	'86	CS
Anthology, 1965–1972	Rhino	(2) 71031	'92	CS/CD
Anthology	Rhino	71077		CS
Very Best	Rhino	71277	'93	CS/CD
The Ultimate Rascals	Warner	27605		CD

Bulldog

Bulldog	Decca	75370	'72	†
Smasher	Buddah	5600	'74	†

Fotomaker

Fotomaker	Atlantic	19165	'78	†

Felix Cavaliere

Felix Cavaliere	Bearsville	6955	'74	†
Destiny	Bearsville	6958	'75	†
Castles in the Air	Epic	35990	'80	†
Dreams in Motion	Karambolage	11062	'94	CS/CD

Treasure

Treasure	Epic	34890	'77	†

Brigati

Lost in the Wilderness	Elektra	1074	'76	†

OTIS REDDING
(b. Sept. 9, 1941, Dawson, GA; d. Dec. 10, 1967, near Madison, WI)

Generally regarded as the single most important and influential male soul artist of the '60s, Otis Redding was one of the first black artists to broaden his appeal to white audiences, with a raw, spontaneous style that bore a stark contrast to the smooth, sophisticated music of Motown. His intensely expressive yet gruff baritone, which was alternately seductive and agonized and exuded both gentleness and assertiveness, popularized the style and helped establish the Memphis-based Stax/Volt label. Largely unrecognized as a songwriter, Otis Redding authored or coauthored most of his own hits, including "These Arms of Mine," "I've Been Loving You Too Long (To Stop Now)," and "I Can't Turn You Loose," as well as "Respect"

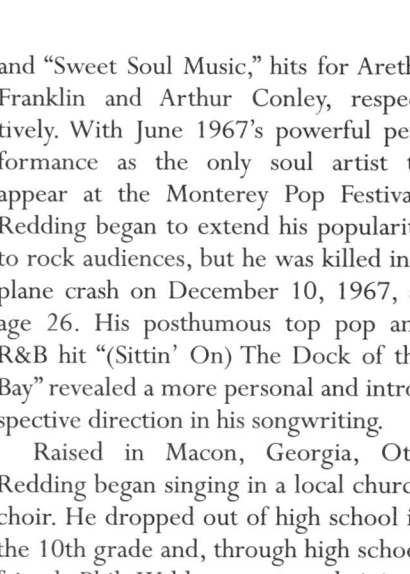

and "Sweet Soul Music," hits for Aretha Franklin and Arthur Conley, respectively. With June 1967's powerful performance as the only soul artist to appear at the Monterey Pop Festival, Redding began to extend his popularity to rock audiences, but he was killed in a plane crash on December 10, 1967, at age 26. His posthumous top pop and R&B hit "(Sittin' On) The Dock of the Bay" revealed a more personal and introspective direction in his songwriting.

Raised in Macon, Georgia, Otis Redding began singing in a local church choir. He dropped out of high school in the 10th grade and, through high school friend Phil Walden, met and joined Johnny Jenkins and the Pinetoppers. He toured the South with the group, and made his first recordings in 1960 as Otis and the Shooters. Relocating briefly to Los Angeles, he recorded "Shout Bamalama" there in 1961 in a vocal style reminiscent of Little Richard. The song was released nationally on the Bethlehem label.

In 1962 Otis Redding was allowed to record his own "These Arms of Mine" at a Johnny Jenkins session that was com-

OTIS REDDING

pleted early. Quickly signed to the newly formed Volt subsidiary of Stax Records, Redding's song became a major R&B and minor pop hit in early 1963. Through 1964 he recorded a number of modest crossover hits for Volt, including "That's What My Heart Needs," "Pain in My Heart," and "Chained and Bound," that established him in the R&B field. He scored his first moderate pop hit with the up-tempo "Mr. Pitiful" in early 1965. Recording with the Stax house band of Booker T. and the MGs and the Memphis Horns (often augmented by keyboardist Isaac Hayes), Redding toured regularly through 1967, accompanied by either Booker T. and the MGs or the Bar-Kays. Headlining the Stax/Volt European tour of 1965, he developed a greater initial following in Europe than at home for his raw, powerful music.

In spring 1965 Otis Redding achieved a major pop hit and smash R&B hit with the classic "I've Been Loving You Too Long (To Stop Now)," cowritten with Jerry Butler, and his emphatic "Respect" became a moderate pop and smash R&B hit. His *Otis Blue* album included two hits, Sam Cooke's "Shake" and "A Change Is Gonna Come," and the Rolling Stones' "Satisfaction," which later became a crossover hit and helped establish Redding with white fans. "I Can't Turn You Loose"/"Just One More Day" became a major two-sided R&B hit and was followed by the crossover hits "My Lover's Prayer" (by Redding), "Fa-Fa-Fa-Fa-Fa (Sad Song)" (cowritten by Redding and the MGs' Steve Cropper), and the classic "Try a Little Tenderness," all from his album *Dictionary of Soul*. In 1967 Arthur Conley scored a smash crossover hit with the Conley-Redding composition "Sweet Soul Music" and Aretha Franklin had a top pop and R&B hit with Redding's "Respect." Redding recorded *King and Queen* with Carla Thomas; the album yielded smash R&B and major pop hits with "Tramp" and "Knock on Wood."

Appearing as the only soul act at the June 1967 Monterey Pop Festival, Otis Redding attained widespread recognition with his incendiary performance and began firmly establishing himself with pop audiences. However, while touring, Redding's airplane crashed into Lake Monona near Madison, Wisconsin, on December 10, 1967, killing him and four members of the Bar-Kays: James King, Ronald Caldwell, Phalon Jones, and Carl Cunningham. In early 1968 Redding's recording of "(Sittin' On) The Dock of the Bay," cowritten with Steve Cropper, became a top pop and R&B hit. Posthumous crossover hits continued into 1969 with "The Happy Song (Dum Dum)," "Amen," "I've Got Dreams to Remember," "Papa's Got a Brand New Bag," and "Love Man." Otis Redding's recording legacy was largely ignored in the '70s and '80s, but virtually all his albums were reissued on CD in the early '90s, following his induction into the Rock and Roll Hall of Fame in 1989.

In the late '70s Otis Redding's sons Dexter and Otis III formed the Reddings with cousin Mark Locket for recordings on the Believe in a Dream label. They scored an R&B smash with "Remote Control" in 1980 and eventually switched to Polydor Records in the late '80s.

Otis Redding

Pain in My Heart	Atco	33161	'64	†
	Rhino	80253	'91	CS/CD
The Great Otis Redding Sings Soul Ballads	Volt	411	'65	†
	Atco	33248		†
	Rhino	91706	'91	CS/CD
Otis Blue/Otis Redding Sings Soul	Volt	412	'65	†
	Atco	33284		†
	Rhino	80318	'91	CS/CD
	Mobile Fidelity	575	'93	CD
The Soul Album	Volt	413	'66	†
	Atco	33285		†
	Rhino	91705	'91	CS/CD
Dictionary of Soul	Volt	415	'66	†
	Atco	33249		†
	Rhino	91707	'91	CS/CD
Live in Europe	Volt	416	'67	†
	Atco	33286		†
	Rhino	90395	'91	CS/CD
Dock of the Bay	Volt	419	'68	†
	Atco	33288		†
	Rhino	80254	'91	CS/CD
The Immortal Otis Redding	Atco	33252	'68	†
	Rhino	80270	'91	CS/CD
In Person at the Whisky a-Go-Go	Atco	33265	'68	†
	Rhino	70380	'92	CS/CD
Recorded Live	Atlantic	19346	'82	†
	Rhino	19346		CS
Love Man	Atco	33289	'69	†
	Rhino	70294	'92	CS/CD
Tell the Truth	Atco	33333	'70	†
	Rhino	70295	'92	CS/CD†
Good to Me: Live at the Whisky a-Go-Go, Volume 2	Stax	8579	'93	CS/CD

Anthologies

History	Volt	418	'67	†
	Atco	33261		†

Best	Atco	(2) 801	'72	†
Best of Otis Redding	Atlantic	81282	'85	†
The Otis Redding Story	Atlantic	(4) 81762	'87	CS†
	Atlantic	(3) 81762	'87	CD†
	Rhino	(2) 81762		CS
	Rhino	(3) 81762		CD
Very Best	Rhino	71147	'92	CS/CD
Otis! The Definitive Otis Redding	Rhino	(4) 71439	'93	CS/CD
Very Best, Volume 2	Rhino	71930	'95	CS/CD
Remember Me	Stax	8572	'92	CS/CD
The Ultimate Otis Redding	Warner	27608		CD
The Legend of Otis Redding	Pair	(2) 1062	'86	CS
Otis Redding and Carla Thomas				
King and Queen	Stax	716	'67	†
	Rhino	82256	'91	CS/CD
Otis Redding/Jimi Hendrix Experience				
Historic Performances at the Monterey International Pop Festival	Reprise	2029	'70	†
Otis Redding and Little Joe Curtis				
Here Comes Soul	Stereo Fidelity	29200	'68	†
The Reddings				
The Awakening	Believe in a Dream	36875	'80	†
Class	Believe in a Dream	37175	'81	†
Steamin' Hot	Believe in a Dream	37974	'82	†
If Looks Could Kill	Polydor	823324	'85	†
The Reddings	Polydor	835292	'88	LP/CS/CD†

R.E.M.

Michael Stipe (b. John Michael Stipe, Jan. 4, 1960, Decatur, GA), lead voc; **Peter Buck** (b. Peter Lawrence Buck, Dec. 6, 1956, Berkeley, CA), lead gtr, mdln; **Michael Mills** (b. Michael Edward Mills, Dec. 17, 1958, Orange, CA), bs, kybd, harmony voc; **Bill Berry** (b. William Thomas Berry, July 31, 1958, Duluth, MN), drm, harmony voc

The first American rock band of the '80s to prove the viability of both noncommercial college radio airplay and small, independent-label releases as means of popularizing a contemporary music group, R.E.M. was also an early favorite of rock critics. Maintaining both an anticommercial and anti—pop star stance in achieving their success, R.E.M. challenged listeners to comprehend their intelligent if surreal lyrics, written and initially sung in an almost unintelligible manner by lead vocalist Michael Stipe. Originally favoring a sound derived from '60s folk-rock, R.E.M. expanded their college following through four years of constant touring, eventually breaking through into the mainstream with *Document* and its near-smash hit single "The One I Love." Unable to extend their success on the I.R.S. label, R.E.M. switched to Warner Bros., scoring their biggest success with 1991's *Out of Time* and the hit single "Losing My Religion." R.E.M. eventually emphasized a harder-edged rock guitar sound with 1994's *Monster* and resumed touring in 1995 after a five-year absence.

R.E.M. was formed in early 1980 in Athens, Georgia, by four University of Georgia students. Bassist Michael Mills and drummer Bill Berry had played together in various groups since high school. With Michael Stipe serving as primary lyricist and lead singer and Peter Buck providing guitar, the group gained a local following and subsequently undertook tours of the Southeast. Their first single, "Radio Free Europe," was released on the small Hib-Tone label in 1981 and drew the attention of rock critics and college fans. Signed to the independent I.R.S. label, R.E.M. recorded a five-song EP, *Chronic Town*, in 1981. *Murmur*, their first full-length album, was released in 1982 and sold remarkably well, with A&M handling national distribution of the album. It contained "Radio Free Europe," a minor hit when rereleased in 1983, and "Talk About the Passion."

Quickly regarded as one of the more important purveyors of simple and unpretentious but effective and compelling rock music (at a time when the popularity of punk music was fading), R.E.M. conducted their first European tour in 1983 and soon recorded the exciting and engaging album *Reckoning*. It yielded a minor hit with "So. Central Rain (I'm Sorry)" and included the wry "(Don't Go Back To) Rockville." R.E.M. undertook a massive tour to support the rather existential *Fables of the Reconstruction/Reconstruction of the Fables*, recorded in London with veteran producer Joe Boyd. The album featured "Can't Get There from Here," "Driver 8," and "Feeling Gravity's Pull." They next recorded *Life's Rich Pageant* at John Mellencamp's Indiana studio. It contained "These Days" and "Superman" and produced a minor hit with "Fall on Me." *Dead Letter Office* compiled the *Chronic Town* EP and B-sides from their singles.

R.E.M. broke through into the pop mainstream with 1987's *Document*. Michael Stipe was enunciating more clearly, and the assured, provocative album yielded the near-smash hit "The One I Love" and the minor hit "It's the End of the World as We Know It (And I Feel Fine)"; the album also contained "Disturbance at the Heron House" and "Finest Worksong." In 1988 R.E.M. switched to the major label Warner Bros. Their debut for the label, *Green*, produced a smash hit with "Stand" and a minor hit with "Pop Song 89" and included "Orange Crush" and "World Leader Pretend."

R.E.M. subsequently suspended live performances after the tour in support of *Green*. In 1990 Peter Buck, Mike Mills, and Bill Berry recorded with singer-songwriter Warren Zevon as the Hindu Love Gods. R.E.M. reassembled for 1991's gentle acoustic album *Out of Time*, essentially comprised of love songs. Perhaps the most accessible album of the group's career, the album featured Buck on mandolin as well as a string section. It yielded a smash hit with the poignant "Losing My Religion" and the near-smash "Shiny Happy People" (with vocal backing by Kate Pierson of the B-52's); it also included the country-style "Country Feedback," "Half a World Away," and "Radio Song" (featuring rapper KRS-One). R.E.M. continued in an acoustic vein with the introspective *Automatic for the People*, which produced the three major hits "Drive," "Man on the Moon," and "Everybody Hurts."

R.E.M. returned to a brash, guitar-based rock sound for 1994's *Monster*. Another bestseller, the album featured a wide variety of material, from the sad country song "You" to the psychedelic guitar of the major hit "What's the Frequency, Kenneth?," from the imploring "Let Me In" and the anguished "I Don't Sleep, I Dream" to the raucous guitar duet with Sonic Youth's Thurston Moore on "Circus Envy" and the radio favorite "Bang and Blame." R.E.M. launched their first world tour in five years in 1995, but on March 1 drummer Bill Berry fell ill during a concert in Lausanne, Switzerland. He was operated on for a brain aneurysm and quickly recovered. Not to be outdone, Michael Stipe then underwent a hernia operation. Although their European tour was canceled, R.E.M. resumed their American tour in May.

R.E.M.

Chronic Town (mini)	I.R.S.		'81	†
	I.R.S./A&M	0502		CS
Murmur	I.R.S.	70604	'82	†
	I.R.S./A&M	0014	'84	CS/CD
	Mobile Fidelity	642	'95	CD

Reckoning	I.R.S.	70044	'84	†
	I.R.S./A&M	0044		CS/CD
Dead Letter Office	I.R.S.	70054	'87	†
	I.R.S./A&M	0054		CS/CD
Box Set	A&M	(3) 0020	'92	CD
Fables of the Reconstruction/Reconstruction of the Fables	I.R.S.	5592	'85	†
	I.R.S./MCA	5592		CS/CD
Life's Rich Pageant	I.R.S./MCA	5783	'86	CS/CD
R.E.M. No. 5: Document	I.R.S./MCA	42059	'87	CS/CD
Eponymous	I.R.S./MCA	6262	'88	LP/CS/CD
Green	Warner Bros.	25795	'88	CS/CD
Out of Time	Warner Bros.	26496	'91	CS/CD
	Warner Bros.	26527	'91	CD
Automatic for the People	Warner Bros.	45055	'92	LP/CS/CD
	Warner Bros.	45122	'92	CD
	Warner Bros.	45138	'92	CD
Monster	Warner Bros.	45740	'94	CS/CD
Tribute Album				
Surprise Your Pig: A Tribute To R.E.M.	Staple Gun	001	'92	LP/CS/CD
Hindu Love Gods				
Hindu Love Gods	Giant	24406	'90	LP/CS/CD

PAUL REVERE AND THE RAIDERS

Paul Revere (b. Jan 7, 1942, Boise, ID), kybd, **Mark Lindsay** (b. Mar. 9, 1942, Cambridge, ID), lead voc, sax; **Drake Levin**, gtr; **Mike Holliday**, bs; **Mike "Smitty" Smith**, drm [In 1964 **Phil "Fang" Volt** replaced Mike Holliday. Drake Levin was replaced by **Jim "Harpo" Valley** in 1966 and then **Freddie Weller** (b. Sept. 9, 1947, Atlanta, GA), who was with the group from 1967 to 1971. Mike Smith and Volt left in 1967 and were replaced by various musicians. The group was entirely reconstituted in 1971 around Mark Lindsay and Paul Revere.]

Popular Pacific Northwest band of the '60s that utilized Revolutionary War costumes and a silly stage act, Paul Revere and the Raiders were the first rock group to sign with Columbia Records. Scoring a series of smash-hit singles and best-selling albums in 1966 and 1967, Paul Revere and the Raiders faded from popularity in the '70s and established themselves on the oldies circuit under the directorship of Paul Revere. Mark Lindsay pursued a parallel solo career beginning in 1969, but he too quickly faded from view.

Starting out in Idaho with Paul Revere and Mark Lindsay as the Downbeats around 1958, Paul Revere and the Raiders achieved their first moderate hit with the instrumental "Like, Long Hair" on the Gardena label in 1961. Moving to Portland, Oregon, in 1962, the group enjoyed considerable regional success and secured a Columbia Records recording contract. The Raiders cut an early version of the raunchy Richard Berry classic "Louie, Louie," but it was another local group, the Kingsmen, who scored the national hit with the song in 1963. Lindsay left the band sometime in 1964, only to rejoin them after the group reestablished themselves in Southern California in 1965.

Paul Revere and the Raiders' first big break came in 1965, when they became regulars on the daily Dick Clark ABC television show *Where the Action Is*. That fall they had a moderate hit with "Steppin' Out," followed by the major hit "Just Like Me." In 1966 Drake Levin was drafted; upon his return from the army, he, Mike Smith, and Phil Volt departed to form

Brotherhood with keyboardist Ron Collins. With Revere and Lindsay as mainstays, Paul Revere and the Raiders scored smash hits with two Barry Mann and Cynthia Weil songs, "Kicks" and "Hungry," and "Him or Me—What's It Gonna Be?," written by Lindsay and producer Terry Melcher. "The Great Airplane Strike" and "Ups and Downs" became major hits. In 1967 Freddie Weller joined the group on lead guitar, and major hits continued through 1969 with "I Had a Dream," "Talk Too Much," "Mr. Sun, Mr. Moon," and "Let Me." Lindsay embarked on a parallel solo career at this time, producing major hits with "Arizona" and "Silver Bird."

Experiencing frequent personnel changes, the group became the Raiders in 1970 and managed a top hit with John D. Loudermilk's "Indian Reservation" and a major hit with "Birds of a Feather." Despite failing to chart after 1973, Paul Revere and the Raiders remained nominally intact under the direction of Paul Revere, establishing themselves on the state fair and oldies circuit and securing a long-standing engagement at Harrah's Reno (Nevada). Lindsay left permanently in 1976 and now works in A&R and commercials. In 1988 Paul Revere and erstwhile Righteous Brother Bill Medley opened the oldies dance club Kicks in Reno.

Paul Revere and the Raiders

Like, Long Hair	Gardena	1000		†
Paul Revere and the Raiders	Sande	1001		†
In the Beginning	Jerden	7004	'66	†
Here They Come	Columbia	09107	'65/'92	CD
Just Like Us!	Columbia	9251	'66	†
Midnight Ride	Columbia	09308	'66/'92	CD
The Spirit of '67	Columbia	9395	'66	†
Revolution!	Columbia	9521	'67	†
Two All-Time Great Selling LP's (reissue of above two albums)	Columbia	(2) 12	'69	†
Christmas Present . . . and Past	Columbia	9555	'67	†
Goin' to Memphis	Columbia	9605	'68	†
Something Happening	Columbia	9665	'68	†
Hard 'n' Heavy	Columbia	9753	'69	†
Alias Pink Puzz	Columbia	9905		†
Special Edition	Raider/America		'82	†

The Raiders

Collage	Columbia	9964	'70	†
Indian Reservation	Columbia	30768	'71	†
Country Wine	Columbia	31106	'72	†

Anthologies

Greatest Hits	Columbia	9462	'67	†
	Columbia	35593	'79	CS/CD
Greatest Hits, Volume II	Columbia	30386	'71	†
All-Time Greatest Hits	Columbia	(2) 31464	'72	†
The Legend of Paul Revere	Columbia	45311	'90	CS
	Columbia	45311	'90	CD
Paul Revere and the Raiders	Harmony	30089	'70	†
Good Thing	Harmony	30975		†
Movin' On	Harmony	31183	'72	†
Paul Revere and the Raiders	Pickwick	3176		†
Good Things	IMG	701		CS

The Brotherhood

The Brotherhood	RCA	4092	'68	†

Brotherhood, Brotherhood	RCA	4228	'69	†
Mark Lindsay				
Arizona	Columbia	9986	'70	†
Silverbird	Columbia	30111	'70	†
You've Got a Friend	Columbia	30735	'71	†

LIONEL RICHIE

(b. June 20, 1949, Tuskegee, AL)

THE COMMODORES. Lionel Richie, voc, kybd, sax; **Thomas McCiary** (b. Oct. 6, 1950, FL), gtr; **Milan Williams** (b. Mar. 28, 1949, MS), kybd; **William King** (b. Jan. 30, 1949, AL), trpt; **Ronald La Pread** (b. Sept. 4, 1950, AL), bs; **Walter "Clyde" Orange** (b. Dec. 10, 1947, FL), drm [**J. D. Nicholas** (b. Apr. 12, 1952, Watford, Hereford, England) replaced Lionel Richie in 1982.]

Starting out as a funk dance band, the Commodores evolved into a highly popular soul band of the late '70s, based on Lionel Richie's ingenuous romantic ballads. As Motown Records' first successful self-contained band, the Commodores rivaled the popularity of Stevie Wonder as a company act and Earth, Wind and Fire as a soul band. Beginning solo work in 1981 and leaving the band in 1982, Lionel Richie sustained his reputation as a consummate craftsman of mellow yet compelling love ballads, particularly with the 1983 album *Can't Slow Down*.

Formed in 1968 at Tuskegee Institute (now Tuskegee University) in Alabama by the merger of the Mystics and the Jays, the Commodores developed a regional reputation as a funk dance band before moving to New York in 1969. Signed to Atlantic Records for one unsuccessful album, the band switched to Motown in 1971 and toured for the next three years as opening act to the Jackson Five. They scored their first major pop and near-smash R&B hit with Milan Williams's instrumental "Machine Gun" in 1974.

After Thomas McClary's funky "Slippery When Wet" hit in 1975, the Commodores began featuring ballads written and sung by Richie, achieving smash pop hits with his "Sweet Love," "Just to Be Close to You," and "Easy." Although their next hits were the funky band compositions "Brick House" and "Too Hot to Handle," they quickly returned to the ballad format and scored the top pop hit "Three Times a Lady" and the smash pop hits "Sail On" and "Still." *In the Pocket* yielded "Lady (You Bring Me Up)" and "Oh No" in 1981, the year Richie began solo work. He wrote the top hit "Lady" and produced *Share Your Love* for Kenny Rogers; he also wrote and sang in duet with Diana Ross the top hit "Endless Love."

Lionel Richie left the Commodores in 1982, and was replaced by J. D. Nicholas. They eventually scored a smash hit with a tribute to Marvin Gaye and Jackie Wilson, "Nightshift," in 1985. Ron La Pread left after the hit, as had Thomas McClary in 1984. By 1986 the Commodores had switched to Polydor Records. In the '90s, with William King, J. D. Nicholas, and Walter Orange as mainstays, the Commodores recorded for Commodores Records.

In the meantime, Lionel Richie's debut album yielded the three smash hits "Truly," "You Are," and "My Love." His second album, *Can't Slow Down*, included the two top hits "All Night Long (All Night)" and "Hello," plus the smash hits "Running with the Night," "Stuck on You," and "Penny Lover." In early 1985 Richie cowrote with Michael Jackson the "We Are the World" single, recorded by scores of popular artists, which raised more than $50 million for famine relief in Africa. His next album produced *six* hits: the top "Say You, Say Me" (from the movie *White Nights*), the smashes "Dancing on the Ceiling," "Love Will Conquer All," and "Ballerina Girl," plus the major "Deep River Woman" (with the country group Alabama) and "Se La." Beset by personal problems, Richie withdrew from recording and performing in the late '80s, eventually reemerging with *Back to Front*, the hit "Do It to Me," and a world tour in 1992. However, he failed to produce a follow-up to this album as of 1995.

The Commodores

Machine Gun	Motown	798	'74	†
Caught in the Act	Motown	820	'75	†
	Motown	5240		CS/CD
Movin' On	Motown	848	'75	†
Hot on the Tracks	Motown	867	'76	†
	Motown	5257	'90	CS/CD†
The Commodores	Motown	884	'77	†
	Motown	5222	'90	CS/CD
Live!	Motown	(2) 894	'77	†
Natural High	Motown	902	'78	†
	Motown	5293		CS/CD
Greatest Hits	Motown	912	'78	CS/CD
Midnight Magic	Motown	926	'79	†
	Motown	5348		CS/CD
Natural High/Midnight Magic	Motown	8114	'86	CD†
Heroes	Motown	939	'80	†
	Motown	5353	'90	CS/CD
Heroes/The Commodores	Motown	8139	'86	CD†
In the Pocket	Motown	955	'81	†
	Motown	5438	'90	CS/CD†
Hot on the Tracks/In the Pocket	Motown	8144		CD†
All the Great Hits	Motown	6028	'82	CS/CD
Anthology	Motown	(2) 6044	'83	†
13	Motown	6054	'83	†
All the Great Love Songs	Motown	6107		CD
Nightshift	Motown	6124	'85	CD†
	Motown	5400		CS/CD
Compact Command Performances (14 Greatest Hits)	Motown	9039		CD†
Best	Motown	(2) 530358	'95	CS/CD
United	Mercury	831194	'86	LP/CS/CD†
Rock Solid	Polydor	835369	'88	LP/CS/CD†
Uprising	Intermedia	5047		LP/CS
Commodores Hits, Volume I	Commodores	011		CS/CD
Commodores Hits, Volume II	Commodores	012		CS/CD
Commodores Christmas	Commodores	020		CS/CD
XX—No Tricks	Commodores	030		CS/CD

Lionel Richie

Lionel Richie	Motown	6007	'82	CS/CD
Can't Slow Down	Motown	6059	'83	CS/CD
Dancing on the Ceiling	Motown	6158	'86	CS/CD
Back to Front	Motown	6338	'92	CS/CD

THE RIGHTEOUS BROTHERS

Bill Medley (b. Sept. 19, 1940, Santa Ana, CA), bs/bar voc; **Bobby Hatfield** (b. Aug. 10, 1940, Beaver Dam, WI), ten voc

Among the first to capitalize on what became known as blue-eyed soul, the Righteous Brothers achieved their greatest success in the mid-'60s under producer extraordinaire Phil Spector. His wall-of-sound technique, coupled with Bill Medley's booming bass vocals and Bobby Hatfield's soaring gospel-style tenor, yielded one of the finest singles of all time, 1964's "You've Lost That Lovin' Feelin'." The Righteous Brothers broke up for the first time in 1968, reuniting for 1974's maudlin smash hit "Rock and Roll Heaven." Medley subsequently pursued a prolific if neglected solo career, rejoining Hatfield occasionally into the '90s.

Bill Medley and Bobby Hatfield formed a vocal duo in 1961 and recorded for Smash Records as the Paramours. They ostensibly received the name the Righteous Brothers from fans attending performances during a six-month engagement at the Black Derby in Santa Ana, California. Switching to the small Hollywood label Moonglow, the duo scored their first moderate hit with Medley's "Little Latin Lupe Lu" in 1963. Building a regional following, the Righteous Brothers reached a national audience through regular appearances on television's *Hullabaloo* and *Shindig* shows beginning in 1964.

Later in 1964 Medley and Hatfield accepted an offer to record for producer Phil Spector, and before year's end they had scored a top pop and smash R&B hit with "You've Lost That Lovin' Feelin'," written by Spector, Barry Mann, and Cynthia Weil, on Spector's Philles label. A stunning recording featuring layers of orchestration and a near-orgasmic vocal performance by Medley and Hatfield, the single came to be regarded as one of the greatest ever recorded. Under Spector, the Righteous Brothers recorded three more smash crossover hits: "Just Once in My Life," written by Spector, Carole King, and Gerry Goffin; and the Tin Pan Alley standards "Unchained Melody" and "Ebb Tide."

By late 1965 the Righteous Brothers had switched to the Verve subsidiary of MGM Records, where they scored a top pop and major R&B hit with the Spector-style "(You're My) Soul and Inspiration," written by Barry Mann and Cynthia Weil. After the major hit "He," the Righteous Brothers managed only moderate to minor hits through 1967, and in July 1968 the duo broke up. Medley subsequently pursued a solo recording career with MGM, achieving the moderate hits "Brown Eyed Woman" and "Peace Brother Peace" in 1968. He recorded for MGM through 1970 and then switched to A&M Records. In the meantime, Hatfield recruited Jimmy Walker, a former member of the Knickerbockers, for a "new" Righteous Brothers album, then recorded a solo album.

The original duo reunited in 1974, recording for Dennis Lambert and Brian Potter's Haven label. Their album *Give It to the People* surprisingly yielded three hits: the smash rock-and-roll-death song "Rock and Roll Heaven," the major hit title song, and the moderate hit "Dream On." A second album for the label failed miserably, and Medley resumed his solo career in the late '70s with United Artists. He eventually achieved success in the country field on RCA Records in 1984 with "Till the Memory's Gone," "I Still Do," and "I've Always Got the Heart to Sing the Blues." During the '80s Medley opened two successful oldies dance clubs, the Hop in Orange County and, in 1988, Kicks in Reno, Nevada, with Paul Revere. In 1987 he scored a top pop and easy-listening hit in duet with Jennifer Warnes on "(I've Had) The Time of My Life" from the hit movie *Dirty Dancing*. With lead vocals by Bobby Hatfield, the Righteous Brothers' "Unchained Melody" became a major hit from the movie *Ghost* in 1990, and in 1991 the duo recorded *Reunion* and Bill Medley recorded *Blue Eyed Singer* for Curb/CEMA Records.

The Righteous Brothers

Right Now!	Moonglow	1001	'63	†

Some Blue-Eyed Soul	Moonglow	1002	'65	†
This Is New	Moonglow	1003	'65	†
Best	Moonglow	1004	'66	†
The Moonglow Years	Verve	511157	'91	CS/CD
You've Lost That Lovin' Feelin'	Philles	4007	'65	†
Just Once in My Life	Philles	4008	'65	†
Back to Back	Philles	4009	'65	†
Soul and Inspiration	Verve	65001	'66	†
Go Ahead and Cry	Verve	65004	'66	†
Sayin' Something	Verve	65010	'67	†
Greatest Hits	Verve	65020	'67	†
Souled Out	Verve	65031	'67	†
Standards	Verve	65051	'68	†
One for the Road	Verve	65058	'68	†
Greatest Hits, Volume 2	Verve	65071	'69	†
Greatest Hits	Verve	823662	'90	†
	Verve	823119	'90	CD†
The Very Best of the Righteous Brothers: Unchained Melody	Verve	847248	'91	CS/CD
The Righteous Brothers	MGM	102	'70	†
History	MGM	4885	'73	†
Give It to the People	Haven	9201	'74	†
The Sons of Mrs. Righteous	Haven	9203	'75	†
Anthology (1962–1974)	Rhino	(2) 71488	'89	CS/CD
Unchained Melody	Curb/CEMA	77381	'90	CS/CD
Reunion	Curb/CEMA	77423	'91	CS/CD
Best of the Righteous Brothers, Volume 2: Then and Now	Curb/CEMA	77522	'91	CS/CD
You've Lost That Lovin' Feelin'	Special Music	511078	'92	

Jimmy Walker and Bobby Hatfield as the Righteous Brothers

Re-birth	Verve	65076	'70	†

Bobby Hatfield

Messin' in Muscle	MGM	4727	'71	†

Bill Medley

100%	MGM	4583	'68	†
Soft and Soulful	MGM	4603	'69	†
Someone Is Standing Outside	MGM	4640	'70	†
Nobody Knows	MGM	4702	'70	†
Gone	MGM	4741	'71	†
A Song for You	A&M	3505	'71	†
Smile	A&M	3517	'73	†
Lay a Little Lovin' On Me	United Artists	929	'78	†
Sweet Thunder	United Artists	1024	'80	†
	Liberty	1097	'81	†
Right Here and Now	RCA	4434	'82	†
I Still Do	RCA	8519	'84	†
Still Hung Up on You	RCA	5352	'85	†
The Best of Bill Medley (rerecordings)	MCA/Curb	42257	'89	LP/CS/CD†
The Best of Bill Medley	Curb/CEMA	77307	'90	CS/CD
Blue Eyed Singer	Curb/CEMA	77409	'91	CS/CD

JOHNNY RIVERS

(b. John Ramistella, Nov. 7, 1942, New York, NY)

Popularizer of the mid-'60s discotheque scene through his live recordings at Los Angeles's Whisky a-Go-Go, Johnny Rivers successfully covered a number of rock and soul hits during the decade, achieving noteworthy hits with "Secret Agent Man," "Poor Side of Town," and, more than a decade later, "Swayin' to the Music (Slow Dancin')." He formed his own record label, Soul City, in 1966, and enjoyed considerable success recording the Fifth Dimension.

At age three Johnny Rivers moved with his family to Baton Rouge, Louisiana, where he grew up. He took up guitar at an early age and formed his first music group at 14. As a teenager he played on demonstration records in Nashville and New York. He took on the surname Rivers in 1958, at the prompting of disc jockey Alan Freed. He recorded for a variety of labels between 1958 and 1964, initially in a rockabilly style, and moved to Los Angeles in 1961. There he started playing regularly at local discotheques and won a long-running engagement at the newly opened Whisky a-Go-Go. Live albums recorded at the club sparked the discotheque craze and produced a number of hits beginning in 1964 with the smash hit "Memphis," written by Chuck Berry. In 1966 he scored a smash hit with P. F. Sloan and Steve Barri's television theme song "Secret Agent Man," and a top hit with his own "Poor Side of Town."

During 1966 Johnny Rivers formed Soul City Records, which employed the songwriting talents of Jimmy Webb for the initial hits of the Fifth Dimension. In 1968 Al Wilson had a major pop hit on the Soul City label with "The Snake." Johnny Rivers successfully covered several Motown classics in 1967 and achieved his final major hit for five years that year with James Hendricks's "Summer Rain." By the end of 1969 he had divested himself of interest in Soul City and ceased personal appearances. His biggest album success came with 1968's *Realization*, which stayed on the album charts for nearly a year. Johnny Rivers scored his final major hit in 1977 with "Swayin' to the Music (Slow Dancin')." In the early '80s he recorded the gospel album *Not a Through Street* for Priority Records. He remains active in the business end of the music industry.

Johnny Rivers

The Early Years	Sunset	5251	'69	†
The Sensational Johnny Rivers	Capitol	2161	'64	†
Go, Johnny, Go!	United Artists	6386	'64	†
At the Whisky a-Go-Go	Imperial	12264	'64	†
Here We a-Go-Go Again!	Imperial	12274	'64	†
In Action!	Imperial	12280	'65	†
Meanwhile, Back at the Whisky a-Go-Go	Imperial	12284	'65	†
Rocks the Folk	Imperial	12293	'65	†
And I Know You Wanna Dance	Imperial	12307	'66	†
Changes	Imperial	12334	'66	†
	Liberty	10121		†
Rewind	Imperial	12341	'67	†
Changes/Rewind	EMI	99900	'92	CS/CD
Realization	Imperial	12372	'68	†
Slim Slo Slider	Imperial	16001	'70	†
Totally Live at the Whisky a-Go-Go	EMI	32819	'95	CD
Home Grown	United Artists	5532	'71	†
L.A. Reggae	United Artists	5650	'72	†

Blue Suede Shoes	United Artists	075	'73	†
	Liberty	10154	'82	†
Wild Night	United Artists	486	'76	†
Last Boogie in Paris (recorded 1973)	Varese Sarabande	5580	95	CD
Road	Atlantic	7301	'74	†
New Lovers and Old Friends	Epic	33681	'75	†
Outside Help	Big Tree	76004	'77	†
Borrowed Time	RSO	3082	'81	†
Not a Through Street (religious)	Priority	38439	'83	†
	Epic	38439		LP/CS
Greatest Hits (rerecordings)	MCA	917	'85	†

Anthologies

Johnny Rivers	Pickwick	3022	'65	†
If You Want It, I Got It	Pickwick	3191		†
Golden Hits	Imperial	12324	'66	†
	Liberty	12324		†
A Touch of Gold	Imperial	12427	'69	†
	Liberty	12427		†
Best	Liberty	10120	'81	†
Whisky a-Go-Go Revisited	Sunset	5157	'67	†
Superpak	United Artists	(2) 93	'72	†
Very Best	United Artists	253	'74	†
	United Artists	444	'75	†
Best	EMI America	46594	'87	CD†
Best	EMI	90727		CS/CD
Best	EMI	92883		CS/CD
Anthology	Rhino	(2) 70793	'91	CS/CD

SMOKEY ROBINSON
(b. William Robinson, Feb. 19, 1940, Detroit, MI)

THE MIRACLES. William "Smokey" Robinson, lead voc; **Emerson Rogers**, ten voc; **Bobby Rogers** (b. Feb. 19, 1940, Detroit, MI), ten voc; **Ronnie White** (b. Apr. 5, 1939, Detroit, MI; d. Aug. 26. 1995, Detroit, MI), bar voc; **Warren "Pete" Moore** (b. Nov. 11, 1939, Detroit, MI), bs voc; **Marvin Tarplin**, gtr [**Claudette Rogers** (b. 1942, Detroit, MI) replaced Emerson Rogers in 1956 and retired in 1964. Smokey Robinson left in 1972 and was replaced by **William Griffin** (b. Aug. 15, 1950, Detroit, MI).]

Along with the Brian Holland–Lamont Dozier–Eddie Holland team, William "Smokey" Robinson was the songwriting and production mainstay of Berry Gordy's Detroit-based Tamla-Motown organization during the '60s. In fact, "Shop Around," written by Gordy and Robinson and recorded by Robinson's Miracles, effectively launched the company into national prominence. Robinson's emotion-laden tenor vocals, sung in a distinctive falsetto with impeccable phrasing and exquisite timing, were arguably the most expressive of any of the Motown singers. He was appointed Motown's vice-president in charge of artist development in 1967; the group became Smokey Robinson and the Miracles and continued to tour and record until early 1972, when Robinson left the Miracles and assumed full-time duties at Motown. He pursued a parallel solo recording career and resumed touring in 1975; he continued to be a hitmaker through 1987, when he was inducted into the Rock and Roll Hall of Fame. In 1990 Smokey Robinson left the Motown organization, after re-signing his vice-presidency post two years earlier.

William "Smokey" Robinson began writing songs as a child and formed the Matadors at Northern High School in Detroit with friends Bobby and Emerson Rogers, Ronnie White, and Warren "Pete" Moore in 1955. Emerson Rogers left the group for the U.S. Army in 1956 and was replaced by Bobby Rogers's sister Claudette. The group became the Miracles in 1957 and made their first recordings for End Records in 1958. While auditioning for a tour with Jackie Wilson, they were spotted by Berry Gordy Jr. Signed to Gordy's Tamla label in 1959, they recorded Gordy and Robinson's "Bad Girl." The song, leased to Chess Records, became a minor pop hit late in the year. The group's second nationally distributed release on Tamla, "Shop Around," written by Robinson and Gordy, became a top R&B and smash pop hit at the end of 1960 and effectively established the Motown organization in the pop mainstream.

Moderate pop and major R&B hits continued for the Miracles into 1962, when Mary Wells scored crossover smashes with three songs composed by Smokey Robinson: "The One Who Really Loves You," "You Beat Me to the Punch" (coauthored with Ronnie White), and "Two Lovers." In 1963 the Miracles achieved smash crossover hits with Robinson's "You've Really Got a Hold on Me" and Holland-Dozier-Holland's "Mickey's Monkey." Thereafter, the Miracles regularly placed singles in the middle level of the pop and R&B charts through 1964, as Robinson completed his first production with "The Way You Do the Things You Do" for the Temptations. Claudette Rogers, Smokey's wife since 1959, retired from the group in 1964; the couple divorced in 1985.

In early 1965 Smokey Robinson provided top pop and R&B hits to Mary Wells and the Temptations with "My Guy" and "My Girl," respectively. The Miracles' *Going to a Go-Go* album included four major pop and smash R&B hits, all coauthored by Robinson: "Ooo, Baby, Baby," the classic "The Tracks of My Tears," "My Girl Has Gone," and the title track. In 1965–1966 Robinson supplied Marvin Gaye with "I'll Be Doggone" and "Ain't That Pecu-liar"; the Temptations with "My Baby"; and the Marvelettes with "Don't Mess with Bill." Following another major pop and smash R&B hit with "(Come 'Round Here) I'm the One You Need," his group became Smokey Robinson and the Miracles in early 1967, the year he was appointed vice-president in charge of artist development at Motown. The group con-tinued to score crossover hits through 1968 with "The Love I Saw in You Was Just a Mirage," "More Love," the smash classic "I Second That Emotion," "If You Can Want," and "Special Oc-casion."

Although Smokey Robinson and the Miracles continued to achieve smash R&B hits, they had difficulty scoring major pop hits after early 1969's "Baby, Baby Don't Cry," perhaps due to the creative exhaustion of Robinson. The classic "Tears of a Clown," written with Stevie Wonder, became a belated top pop and R&B hit in late 1970 (it had been included on 1967's *Make It Happen* album) and was followed by the group's final major pop hit, "I Don't Blame You at All," in 1971. In January 1972 Motown announced the impending retirement of Smokey Robinson, and the group completed a six-month farewell tour, performing their final concert in Washington, D.C., on July 16.

Smokey Robinson subsequently assumed full-time duties as Motown vice-president, as the other Miracles sought out a new lead vocalist, eventually recruiting William Griffin. They managed R&B smashes with "Do It Baby" (a major pop hit) and "Don't Cha Love It" in 1974, and achieved their biggest latter-day success with 1975's top pop and smash R&B hit "Love Machine (Part 1)." By 1977 the Miracles had switched to Columbia Records. Griffin was replaced by his brother Donald, but the group disbanded in the late '70s, although they have had occasional reunions both on record and on the road, sometimes with Claudette Rogers Robinson.

Smokey Robinson's debut solo album, *Smokey*, yielded a major pop and smash R&B hit with "Baby Come Close" in late 1973. His next major pop hit came with "Baby That's Back-atcha," a top R&B hit from 1975, the year he resumed touring. Major R&B-only hits continued for Robinson until late 1979, when the sensuous "Cruisin'" became a smash pop and R&B hit. The similarly seductive "Being with You" became a crossover smash in 1981. During 1983 Robinson recorded with High Energy's Barbara Mitchell ("Blame It on Love") and Rick James ("Ebony Eyes"). He eventually achieved crossover smashes with 1987's "Just to See Her" and "One Heartbeat" from the album of the same name, his best-selling later album. Smokey Robinson left his position as Motown vice-president in 1988 and eventually returned to recording with 1991's *Double Good Everything* for SBK Records. Ronnie White, an original member of the Miracles, died in Detroit on August 26, 1995, of leukemia at age 57.

The Miracles

From the Beginning	Bell	1063		†
Hi, We're the Miracles	Tamla	220		†
	Motown	5160		CS/CD†
Cookin' with the Miracles	Tamla	223		†
	Motown	0368	'94	CS/CD
Shop Around	Tamla	224		†
I'll Try Something New	Tamla	230		†
Christmas with the Miracles	Tamla	236		†
	Motown	5254	'87	CD
The Fabulous Miracles	Tamla	238	'63	†
Miracles "Live" On Stage	Tamla	241	'63	†
Doin' Mickey's Monkey	Tamla	245	'63	†
	Motown	5439	'89	CD†
Tribute to the Great Nat King Cole	Tamla	261		†
Going to a Go-Go	Tamla	267	'65	†
	Motown	5269	'89	CS/CD
Away We a Go-Go	Tamla	271	'66	†
	Motown	5136	'89	CD†

Smokey Robinson and the Miracles

Make It Happen	Tamla	276	'67	†
(reissued as) The Tears of a Clown	Tamla	276	'70	†
	Motown	9092		CD†
	Motown	5156		CS/CD
Special Occasion	Tamla	290	'68	†
	Motown	5418	'89	CD
Live!	Tamla	289	'69	†
Time Out for Smokey Robinson and the Miracles	Tamla	295	'69	†
	Motown	5437	'89	CD†
Four in Blue	Tamla	297	'69	†
What Love Has Joined Together	Tamla	301	'70	†
A Pocket Full of Miracles	Tamla	306	'70	†
The Season for Miracles	Tamla	307	'70	†
	Motown	3762		CS
	Motown	5253	'91	CS/CD
One Dozen Roses	Tamla	312	'71	†
Flying High Together	Tamla	318	'72	†

Anthologies

Doin' Mickey's Monkey/Away We a Go-Go	Motown	8150		CD†
Going to a Go-Go/The Tears of a Clown	Motown	8004	'86	CD†
Time Out/Special Occasion	Motown	8143		CD†
Greatest Hits from the Beginning	Tamla	(2) 254	'65	†
	Motown	(2) 8238		†
Greatest Hits, Volume 2	Tamla	280	'68	†
	Motown	5210		CS/CD
1957–1972	Tamla	(2) 320	'72	†
Anthology	Motown	(3) 793	'74	†
	Motown	(2) 6196		CD†
	Motown	(2) 793		CD†
	Motown	(2) 0472	'95	CS/CD
Compact Command Performances (18 Greatest Hits)	Motown	9041		CD†
Compact Command Performances, Volume 2	Motown	6202	'86	CD†
What Love Has Joined Together	Motown	5282	'90	CS/CD†
Great Songs and Performances	Motown	5316		LP/CS/CD
Motown Legends	Motown	5360		†
The 35th Anniversary Collection	Motown	(4) 6334	'94	CD
Tears of a Clown	Pickwick	3389	'75	†
Whatever Makes You Happy: More of the Best (1961–1971)	Rhino	71181	'93	CS/CD
Motown Legends	Esx	8259	'95	CS/CD

Smokey Robinson

Smokey	Tamla	328	'73	†
	Motown	5134		CS/CD
Pure Smokey	Tamla	331	'74	†
A Quiet Storm	Tamla	337	'75	†
	Motown	5197	'89	CS/CD
Smokey/A Quiet Storm	Motown	8128	'86	CD†
Smokey's Family Robinson	Tamla	341	'76	†
Deep in My Soul	Tamla	350	'77	†
Love Breeze	Tamla	359	'78	†
Smokin'	Tamla	363	'79	†
Where There's Smoke	Tamla	366	'79	†
	Motown	5267	'89	CS/CD†
Warm Thoughts	Tamla	367	'80	†
Being with You	Motown	375	'81	†
	Motown	5349	'89	CS/CD
Being with You/Where There's Smoke	Motown	8101	'86	CD†
Yes It's You Lady	Tamla	6001	'82	†
Touch the Sky	Tamla	6030	'83	†
Blame It on Love and All the Great Hits	Tamla	6064	'83	†
	Motown	5401	'90	CS/CD
Essar	Tamla	6098	'84	†
Smoke Signals	Tamla	6156	'86	LP/CS/CD†
One Heartbeat	Motown	6226	'87	CS/CD
Love, Smokey	Motown	6268	'90	LP/CS/CD
Motown Superstar Series, Volume 18	Motown	5118		CS
Double Good Everything	SBK	97968	'91	CS/CD†

The Miracles

Renaissance	Tamla	325	'73	†
Do It Baby	Tamla	334	'74	†
Don't Cha Love It	Tamla	336	'75	†
City of Angels	Tamla	339	'75	†
The Power of Music	Tamla	344	'76	†
Greatest Hits	Tamla	357	'77	†
Love Crazy	Columbia	34460	'77	†
The Miracles	Columbia	34910	'78	†

ROCKPILE

Dave Edmunds (b. Apr. 15, 1944, Cardiff, Wales), gtr, kybd, voc; **Nick Lowe** (b. Mar. 25, 1949, Woolbridge, Suffolk, England), bs, voc; **Billy Bremner** (b. 1947, Scotland), gtr, voc; **Terry Williams** (b. 1948), drm

First working together in Brinsley Schwarz, one of the best-known London pub-rock bands of the mid-'70s, Dave Edmunds and Nick Lowe were two of the most important British producers of the late '70s and '80s. With both favoring the sound of music from the '50s and early '60s (in stark contrast to the vapid, overproduced progressive-rock and pop bands then so popular), Edmunds and Lowe formed Rockpile in 1977 for recordings and tours under each of their names before recording a sole album in 1980 as Rockpile. Dave Edmunds enjoyed considerable success on his own, particularly in the early '80s, but he largely withdrew from touring in 1987. Nick Lowe persevered with less acclaim, receiving a modicum of recognition in Little Village (with John Hiatt, Ry Cooder, and Jim Keltner) in 1992.

Dave Edmunds played in Welsh bands in the '60s and formed the trio Love Sculpture in 1967. The group scored a smash British hit with a frantic instrumental version of Khatchaturian's "Sabre Dance" in late 1968. After the group disbanded in 1969, Edmunds returned to rural Wales to build his own recording studio, Rockfield, where he developed and refined his talent for re-creating the sound and feel of music from the '50s and '60s—from sparse rockabilly and country to elaborate Phil Spector–styled epics. He performed all vocal and instrumental duties for his smash 1971 British and American hit, a remake of Smiley Lewis's 1955 R&B hit "I Hear You Knocking." He recorded his debut album, *Rockpile*, in 1972 and achieved smash British hits with remakes of the Ronettes' "Baby I Love You" and the Chordettes' "Born to Be with You" in 1973. He also produced albums by Shakin' Stevens and Ducks Deluxe in the early '70s and appeared in the 1974 David Essex film *Stardust*, writing several songs for the soundtrack.

Nick Lowe formed his first band, Sound 4 Plus 1, with guitarist Brinsley Schwarz at age 14, and later helped form Kippington Lodge with Schwarz in 1965. By late 1969 the group had evolved into Brinsley Schwarz, with Schwarz, Lowe, keyboardist Bob Andrews, and drummer Bill Rankin. Signed to British Liberty/United Artists (with early releases on Capitol in the United States), Brinsley Schwarz debuted at the Fillmore East, but their credibility was immediately brought into question when a planeload of British journalists were flown to New York to witness the event.

The group adopted an unobtrusive stance on the London pub and club circuit and developed a modest following as principals of so-called pub rock. Following their first two albums, the group added second guitarist Ian Gomm for *Silver Pistol*, generally regarded as their most consistent work. After *Nervous on the Road*, which included Lowe's "(What's So Funny 'Bout) Peace, Love and Understanding," Dave Edmunds produced their final British-only album *New Favourites*, but the group broke up in early 1975. Brinsley Schwarz and Bill

Rankin joined the pub-rock band Ducks Deluxe in their final days, and Schwarz and Bob Andrews later manned the Rumour, Graham Parker's backup band through 1980. The Rumour issued two albums of their own in the late '70s, while Ian Gomm pursued a solo career that produced a major hit with "Hold On" in 1979.

Nick Lowe began hanging around Stiff Records, a small independent label based in London, and assisted Dave Edmunds in the recording of *Subtle as a Flying Mallet*, issued on RCA Records in late 1975. Lowe produced Graham Parker and the Rumour's first and third albums, *Howlin Wind* and *Stick to Me*, while Edmunds produced the Flamin' Groovies' *Shake Some Action*. In 1977 Lowe and Edmunds formed the ad hoc group Rockpile with guitarist-vocalist Billy Bremner and drummer Terry Williams to accompany their solo recordings and tours. As one of the few signings to Led Zeppelin's Swan Song label, Edmunds recorded *Get It* with the group, augmented by Bob Andrews. The album featured Lowe's "I Knew the Bride," Edmunds and Lowe's "Here Comes the Weekend," Edmunds's country-style "Worn Out Shoes, Brand New Pockets," and Graham Parker's "Back to School Days." During 1977 Lowe produced the Damned's debut British album and Elvis Costello's stunning debut, *My Aim Is True*. Lowe and Edmunds took part in the first tour of Stiff artists before Lowe left the label to become an independent producer.

In 1978 both Dave Edmunds and Nick Lowe were busy with a variety of projects. Lowe recorded his solo debut, *Pure Pop for Now People* (titled *Jesus of Cool* in Great Britain), which included his own "Marie Provost," "Heart of the City," and "So It Goes" as well as the collaborative "(I Love the Sound of) Breaking Glass," a smash British hit. Edmunds recorded *Tracks on Wax 4*, which contained "Trouble Boys," Lowe's "Television," Lowe and Edmunds's "What Looks Best on You," and Lowe and Rockpile's "Never Been in Love." During the same year Edmunds produced the Flamin' Groovies' *Now* and Lowe produced Elvis Costello's *This Year's Model* and *Armed Forces*, which included a potent version of Lowe's "(What's So Funny 'Bout) Peace, Love and Understanding."

In 1979 Lowe produced the Pretenders' first single, "Stop Your Sobbing," and recorded *Labour of Lust*, his best-selling album. It included "Switchboard Susan," his own "Cracking Up," and the major pop hit "Cruel to Be Kind," written by Lowe and Ian Gomm. Lowe married Carlene Carter in August and later produced her albums *Musical Shapes* and *Blue Nun*. In the meantime, Edmunds recorded *Repeat When Necessary*, which featured Hank DeVito's "Sweet Little Lisa" and "Queen of Hearts," Graham Parker's "Crawling from the Wreckage," and Elvis Costello's "Girls Talk," a minor hit.

In 1980 Rockpile finally recorded an album under their own name, *Seconds of Pleasure*. It was dominated by songs written by Lowe, such as "Play That Fast Thing (One More Time)," "Pet You and Hold You," and "When I Write the Book," and yielded a moderate hit with "Teacher Teacher." Rockpile subsequently dissolved, and Terry Williams played with Dire Straits from 1983 to 1987. Dave Edmunds recorded *Twangin'*, which yielded a minor hit with John Fogerty's "Almost Saturday Night"; he also produced the Stray Cats hits "Rock This Town" and "Stray Cut Strut" as well as their albums *The Stray Cats* and *Rant and Rave*. In the meantime, Nick Lowe recorded *Nick the Knife* and *The Abominable Showman* and produced Paul Carrack's *Suburban Voodoo*, the Fabulous Thunderbirds' *T-Bird Rhythm*, and one side of John Hiatt's *Riding with the King*.

Dave Edmunds switched to Columbia Records for *D.E. 7th*, which featured "Me and the Boys" (by Terry Adams of NRBQ), Bruce Springsteen's "From Small Things (Big Things One Day Come)," and the country-style "Warmed Over Kisses (Left Over Love)." He later recorded *Information* under producer Jeff Lynne and scored a moderate hit with Lynne's "Slipping Away." During the mid-'80s Edmunds produced the Everly Brothers' two comeback albums, *EB '84* and *Born Yesterday*, as well as the Fabulous Thunderbirds' *Tuff Enuff* and k. d. lang's debut *Angel with a Lariat*. Nick Lowe assembled his Cowboy Outfit with Paul Carrack and Martin Belmont for two albums. Their eponymous debut included Lowe's

"Half a Boy and Half a Man," whereas *The Rose of England* included John Hiatt's "She Don't Love Nobody," Elvis Costello's "Indoor Fireworks," and a minor-hit version of "I Knew the Bride (When She Used to Rock and Roll)."

In 1987 Dave Edmunds toured in support of the live set *I Hear You Rockin'*, often regarded as his finest later album. It reprised his most popular recordings yet failed to sell in significant quantities. He subsequently withdrew from touring, although he served as concertmaster for the two-month 1990 tour by Graham Parker and Dion, whose comeback album *Yo Frankie* he produced; he also played with Ringo Starr's All-Starr Band in 1992. Edmunds recorded *Closer to the Flame*, which featured Al Anderson's "Never Take the Place of You" and John Hiatt and Anderson's "I Got Your Number," for Capitol in 1990.

In 1987 Nick Lowe, Ry Cooder, and Jim Keltner backed John Hiatt for the recording of Hiatt's breakthrough album *Bring the Family*. Dave Edmunds produced Nick Lowe's 1990 Warner Bros. album *Party of One*. In 1992 Lowe rejoined Hiatt, Cooder, and Keltner in the short-lived supergroup Little Village. In 1994 Lowe released *The Impossible Bird*, a collection of country-style songs that won critical praise though few sales; it was followed by a live album.

Love Sculpture

Blues Helping	Rare Earth	505	'70	†
	EMI America		'86	†
Forms and Feelings	Parrot	71035	'70	†

Brinsley Schwarz

Brinsley Schwarz	Capitol	589	'70	†
Despite It All	Capitol	744	'71	†
Silver Pistol	United Artists	5566	'72	†
	Liberty	10145	'81	†
Nervous on the Road	United Artists	5647	'72	†
	Liberty	10146	'81	†
Brinsley Schwarz	Capitol	(2) 11869	'78	†
Brinsley Schwarz	One Way	18464	'95	CD

The Rumour

Max	Mercury	1174	'77	†
Frogs, Sprouts, Clogs, and Krauts	Arista	4235	'79	†

Ian Gomm

Gomm with the Wind	Stiff/Epic	36103	'79	†
What a Blow	Stiff/Epic	36433	'80	†

Rockpile

Seconds of Pleasure	Columbia	36886	'80	LP/CS/CD

Dave Edmunds

Rockpile	MAM	3	'72	†
Subtle as a Flying Mallet	RCA	5003	'75	†
	RCA	4238	'82	†
Get It	Swan Song	8418	'77	CD
Tracks on Wax 4	Swan Song	8505	'78/'91	CD
Repeat When Necessary	Swan Song	8507	'79/'91	CD
Twangin'	Swan Song	16304	'81/'91	CD
Best	Swan Song	8510	'81	CS/CD
D.E. 7th	Columbia	37930	'82	†
	Columbia/Legacy	37930	'91	CD

Information	Columbia	38651	'83	†
	Columbia/Legacy	38651	'91	CD
Riff Raff	Columbia	39273	'84	†
I Hear You Rockin'	Columbia	40603	'87	CD
Closer to the Flame	Capitol	90372	'90	CD
Anthology (1968–1990)	Rhino	71191	'93	CS/CD
Nick Lowe				
Pure Pop for Now People	Columbia	35329	'78	CD†
Labour of Lust	Columbia	36087	'79	CD†
Nick the Knife	Columbia	37932	'82	†
	Columbia/Legacy	37932	'91	CD†
The Abominable Showman	Columbia	38589	'83	†
Nick Lowe and His Cowboy Outfit	Columbia	39371	'84	†
The Rose of England	Columbia	39958	'85	†
Basher: The Best of Nick Lowe	Columbia	45313	'89	CS/CD
Sixteen All-Time Lowes	Demon	20	'86	CD†
Nick's Knack	Demon	59		CD†
Party of One	Reprise	26132	'90	CS/CD
The Impossible Bird	Upstart	013	'94	CD
Nick Lowe and the Impossible Birds: Live! on the Battlefield	Upstart	021	'95	CD
Little Village				
Little Village	Reprise	26713	'92	CS/CD

THE ROLLING STONES

Michael "Mick" Jagger (b. July 26, 1943, Dartford, Kent, England), lead voc, har, gtr; **Keith Richards** (b. Dec. 18, 1943, Dartford, England), lead gtr; **Brian Jones** (b. Lewis Brian Hopkin-Jones, Feb. 28, 1942, Cheltenham, Gloucestershire, England; d. July 3, 1969, London, England), gtr, sitar, dulcimer, voc; **Bill Wyman** (b. William Perks, Oct. 24, 1936, Plumstead, London, England), bs; **Charlie Watts** (b. June 2, 1941, Islington, London, England), drm; **Ian Stewart** (b. 1938; d. Dec. 12, 1985, London, England), pno [Ian Stewart was phased out of the band in 1963, although he continued to tour and record with the group and became known as the sixth Rolling Stone. Brian Jones left the group in June 1969, to be replaced by guitarist **Michael "Mick" Taylor** (b. Jan. 17, 1948, Welwyn Garden City, Hereford, England). Taylor left in 1974 and was replaced by guitarist **Ron Wood** (b. June 1, 1947, Hillingdon, Middlesex, England). Bill Wyman left the group in 1992 and was replaced by bassist **Darryl Jones**.]

The first London-area R&B band to emerge in the wake of the more rock-and-roll oriented Beatles, the Rolling Stones initially interpreted American black R&B more effectively and sympathetically than any other group of white musicians to date. Cultivating an arrogant, rebellious, irreverent, and outrageous image, the Rolling Stones quickly became one of the most identifiable of the British groups. Writing their own songs beginning in 1964, Jagger and Richards developed into a powerful songwriting team that provided a number of classic '60s singles, including their breakthrough U.S. hit, "Satisfaction." In 1969, with the death of guitarist Brian Jones and the tragic concert at Altamont, California, the Stones reached a turning point in their careers. Jones was replaced by Mick Taylor, formerly of John Mayall's Bluesbreakers, who was perhaps the band's most gifted guitarist, although he did not fit in with their rowdy image. In the early '70s the band adopted the self-proclaimed position as the World's Greatest Rock and Roll Band; Mick Jagger became the world's best-known and

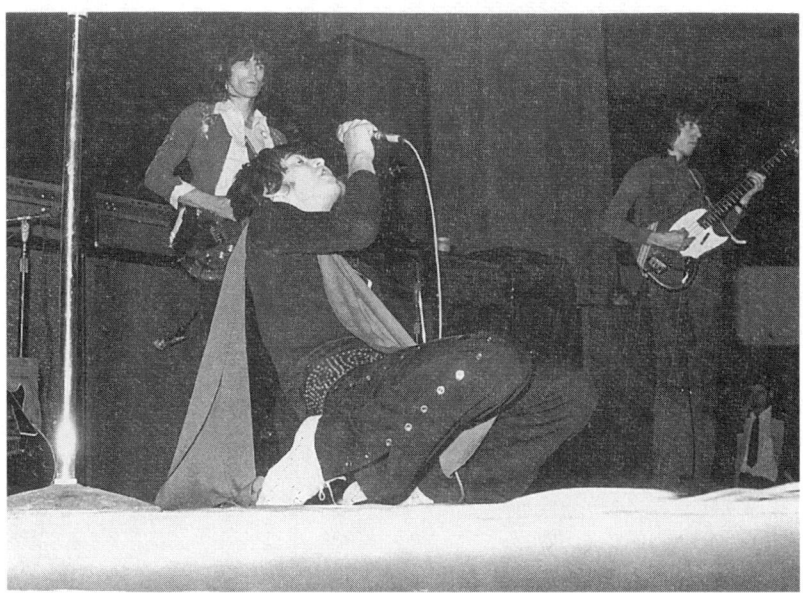

THE ROLLING STONES

most notorious rock performer, and Keith Richards garnered the reputation as the world's most infamous drug abuser. In 1974 Taylor left the group and was replaced by Ron Wood, formerly of the Faces. Although the Rolling Stones' popularity remained essentially undiminished, their reputation was brought into question in the late '70s through much of the '80s. Jagger and Richards had a much-publicized falling out, which was finally resolved for 1989's *Steel Wheels* album and tour. Longtime bassist Bill Wyman called it quits after the tour, but the band soldiered on, working with outside producer Don Was to produce *Voodoo Lounge* and the follow-up semiacoustic live album *Stripped*.

Mick Jagger and Keith Richards first met when they were six but did not encounter each other again until 1960, when they had a famous meeting on a suburban train platform. Jagger, a student at the London School of Economics, was playing with mutual friend Dick Taylor in Little Blues and the Blue Boys, who subsequently added Richards. Brian Jones had been playing as a jazz saxophonist before briefly joining Alexis Korner's Blues Incorporated. Wanting to form his own R&B band, Jones recruited pianist Ian Stewart and guitarist Jeff Bradford, among others. Jones first met Jagger, Richards, and Taylor at the Ealing club, where Blues Incorporated held residency. Jagger and Richards were soon jamming there with harmonica player Cyril Davies and Charlie Watts, Korner's drummer. By 1961 Jagger was rehearsing with Jones, Bradford, and Stewart; when Bradford dropped out, Richards and Taylor came on board. Jagger began singing with Blues Incorporated in late 1961, joining as permanent singer in early 1962, by which time the band had graduated to the Marquee Club in London. Jagger, Jones, and Richards began sharing an apartment and recorded a demonstration tape that was rejected by EMI Records. Taylor became the next departure, leaving to form the Pretty Things.

After debuting at the Marquee Club in spring 1962 as Brian Jones and Mick Jagger and the Rolling Stones, the group added bassist Bill Wyman through auditions in December 1962 and attempted to persuade drummer Charlie Watts to join. He eventually enlisted in January 1963, and the group (Jagger, Richards, Jones, Stewart, Watts, and Wyman) subsequently played the R&B club circuit and secured an eight-month residency at the Crawdaddy Club in Richmond, where they attracted a burgeoning following. In April Andrew Oldham became their manager and signed the group to Decca Records (London in the United States). Their first single, Chuck Berry's "Come On," became a minor British hit in June 1963, and Oldham began cultivating a rebellious image for the group. Ian Stewart was ousted from the band because he was too old to fit their scruffy image, although he continued to record and occasionally play with them and eventually became their tour manager.

After performing in a supporting role for a British tour of the Everly Brothers and Little Richard in September 1963, the Rolling Stones scored their first major British hit in December with "I Wanna Be Your Man," provided to them by Beatles songwriters John Lennon and Paul McCartney. They achieved a smash British hit with Buddy Holly's "Not Fade Away" in April 1964, and that single soon became the group's first moderate American hit. Their debut American album was pervaded with American R&B songs, such as "Walking the Dog," "I Just Want to Make Love to You," "Can I Get a Witness," and "Tell Me" (their first major American hit), and the group first toured the United States in June. Before the end of 1964, the Rolling Stones' *12 X 5* had yielded a major U.S. hit with "It's All Over Now" and a smash hit with "Time Is On My Side," but the group nonetheless remained a cult band during the early days of the British Invasion. With *Now!* Jagger and Richards began writing some of the group's songs, and the album produced a major American hit with "Heart of Stone" in early 1965.

Out of Our Heads, recorded primarily in Chicago's Chess studios, finally established the Rolling Stones in the United States. The album yielded a near-smash with Jagger and Richards's "The Last Time" (backed with "Play with Fire") and a top hit with their classic "(I Can't Get No) Satisfaction"; it also included "The Spider and the Fly" and the satirical "Under Assistant West Coast Promotion Man." The Rolling Stones toured the United States twice in 1965, achieving a top hit with "Get Off My Cloud" and a smash hit with the ballad "As Tears Go By" from their next album, *December's Children*. The psychedelic "19th Nervous Breakdown" became a smash hit. The group conducted their last tour of America for three years in 1966.

Aftermath, the first Rolling Stones' album comprised entirely of Jagger-Richards compositions, established the group as an album band. While yielding a top hit with the ominous "Paint It Black" (on which Brian Jones played sitar), the album contained the major hit "Lady Jane" (Jones on dulcimer), the chauvinistic "Stupid Girl" and "Under My Thumb," and the 11-minute "Going Home." During July "Mother's Little Helper" became a near-smash hit, as did "Have You Seen Your Mother, Baby, Standing in the Shadows" in November.

After the live album *Got Live, If You Want It*, the Rolling Stones issued the psychedelic-tinged *Between the Buttons*, which included the top hit "Ruby Tuesday" (backed by "Let's Spend the Night Together") and the overlooked "Yesterday's Papers," "Amanda Jones," and "Something Happened to Me Yesterday." Later Jagger and Richards, then Jones, were charged in the first big drug arrests in British rock, in response to which the stately *London Times* came to their defense. Their next album, *Flowers*, featured a number of their recent hits plus "Out of Time" and the country-style "Back Street Girl" and "Sittin' on a Fence." The Rolling Stones next attempted to capitalize on psychedelia and the success of the Beatles' *Sgt. Pepper's Lonely Hearts Club Band* with *Their Satanic Majesties Request*, but the album was not well received critically. Nonetheless, it yielded a major hit with "She's a Rainbow."

During 1967 Brian Jones had ostensibly played very little on the recordings of the Rolling Stones, due to his increasing dependence on drugs, becoming estranged from the rest of the group and even requiring hospitalization in December. He was arrested again in May 1968, shortly before the release of "Jumpin' Jack Flash," often regarded as the group's most potent single since "Satisfaction." The much-delayed *Beggar's Banquet*, undoubtedly their finest and most coherent album, included the classic "Sympathy for the Devil," the overlooked countrified "No Expectations," and "Stray Cat Blues," as well as "Street Fighting Man," oddly only a minor hit as a single. After participating in the legendary never-to-be-seen television special *Rock and Roll Circus*, Brian Jones quit the group in early July 1969, to be replaced by guitarist Mick Taylor from John Mayall's band. On July 3 Jones was found dead in his swimming pool at age 25, leading to later speculation that he was murdered. Two days later Taylor debuted with the Rolling Stones at a free concert at London's Hyde Park, attended by some 250,000 fans. Mick Jagger soon left for Australia, to perform the title role in the movie *Ned Kelly*, released in 1970.

During summer 1969 another Rolling Stones' classic single, "Honky Tonk Women," recorded with Mick Taylor, became a top hit. The group subsequently embarked on an

American tour in October. Concluding the tour, the group announced plans for a free concert in northern California, but the concert site was changed several times and eventually took place at Altamont Speedway. Held on December 6, the concert was a highly publicized tragedy. With the Hells Angels providing "security" in exchange for beer, the show was staged without adequate food services and health facilities. The Stones, demonstrating their aloofness from the audience, delayed more than an hour before appearing on the stage. Once they took the stage the group worked the crowd into hysteria, with unfortunate results. During "Sympathy for the Devil" a fan from near the front was stabbed to death by the Angels, as graphically captured on film, and the concert devolved into ugly chaos. Charges and countercharges by participants were later aired, and the leftist press denounced the event as the death of rock and roll and the "Woodstock spirit." The Rolling Stones did not perform "Sympathy for the Devil" for six years. A film recording of the 1969 tour and Altamont concert, *Gimme Shelter*, premiered in late 1970.

Also in late 1969 the Rolling Stones released *Let It Bleed*, which contained "Gimme Shelter" (ironic in the light of Altamont), the classic "You Can't Always Get What You Want," the sexist and racist "Midnight Rambler," and the title song. A period of inactivity ensued for the group, as Jagger appeared as the ambisexual star of Nicholas Roeg's film *Performance*. The soundtrack album included a Jagger solo single, "Memo from Turner." In March 1971 the Rolling Stones announced they were leaving England for tax purposes, yet they conducted their first British tour in five years, augmented by keyboardist Nicky Hopkins and saxophonist Bobby Keys. In April they issued the sexist and racist "Brown Sugar" (a top hit) on their newly formed record label, Rolling Stones Records, distributed by Atlantic in the United States. Their debut album for the label, *Sticky Fingers*, contained that hit, the countrified "Wild Horses" (a major hit), "Dead Flowers," the jam-style "Can't You Hear Me Knocking," and "Sister Morphine," the latter coauthored (without credit) by Marianne Faithfull. The famous cover art was designed by Andy Warhol, featuring a pair of jeans with a working zipper that (when lowered) revealed the equally famous Rolling Stones symbol, an extended, exaggerated tongue.

By the early '70s concerts by the Rolling Stones were attended more as cultural events than as musical performances. Mick Jagger, in particular, was adopted by the so-called jet set, especially after his much-publicized marriage to Bianca de Macias in May 1971. The double-record set *Exile on Main Street*, released to coincide with their massive 1972 tour (again accompanied by Nicky Hopkins and Bobby Keys), was greeted with equivocal reviews, although it produced a near-smash hit with "Tumbling Dice" and a major hit with "Happy." Conducting immensely successful tours of America and Europe in 1973, the Rolling Stones' next two albums, *Goat's Head Soup* and *It's Only Rock 'n' Roll*, were considered minor works compared to previous albums, yet each contained a few exceptional songs. *Goat's Head Soup* yielded a top hit with the ballad "Angie" and a minor hit with "Doo Doo Doo Doo Doo (Heartbreaker)"; it also contained the notorious "Star Star," perhaps better known as "Starfucker." *It's Only Rock 'n' Roll* produced major hits with the title song and "Ain't Too Proud to Beg" (originally a hit for the Temptations) and included "Time Waits for No One." In 1974 the in-concert film *Ladies and Gentlemen: The Rolling Stones*, filmed in Texas during the 1972 tour, was released.

During 1975 the Rolling Stones again mounted a huge, lavishly staged, and lucrative American tour, augmented by keyboard player Billy Preston. Mick Taylor had quit the group the previous December, to be replaced by "guest artist" Ron Wood, guitarist for the Faces, for the grandiose tour and subsequent recordings by the group. Their next album, *Black and Blue*, eventually appeared in 1976 to critical disapproval. The album's sexist promotional campaign later inspired a boycott by Women Against Violence Against Women (WAVAW) of the entire organization responsible for distribution of Rolling Stones Records. The album yielded only one major hit, "Fool to Cry." Ron Wood finally became an official member of the group in June 1977. In the meantime, Bill Wyman had recorded two solo albums, and Mick Taylor eventually resurfaced with a solo album on Columbia Records in 1979.

The Rolling Stones again toured the United States in 1978, this time without the elaborate staging and massive props of the 1975 tour, accompanied by keyboardist Ian McLagan (formerly of the Faces) and Ian Stewart. Performing at small and medium-size halls as well as at huge outdoor concerts, the group broke the rock-concert attendance record in July at the New Orleans Superdome, where more than 80,000 fans were present. *Some Girls* became the group's best-selling nonanthology album on the strength of the top hit disco-style single "Miss You," the near-smash hit "Beast of Burden," and the moderate hit "Shattered." The sexist and racist lyrics of the title song again stirred controversy, as did the jacket art.

In February 1977 Keith Richards was arrested in Toronto on charges of possession of heroin for sale, yet he got off lightly in October 1978, required only to continue drug rehabilitation and perform a benefit concert. For the concert, performed in April 1979, Richards and Ron Wood assembled the New Barbarians with keyboardist Ian McLagan, saxophonist Bobby Keys, jazz bassist Stanley Clarke, and Meters drummer Joe Modeliste. The concert and subsequent 14-city American tour neatly coincided with the release of Wood's third solo album, *Gimme Some Neck*, which included eight originals by Wood and Bob Dylan's "Seven Days." During 1979 the Rolling Stones were the subject of controversy as the result of former associate Tony Sanchez's ghastly and lurid account of his eight-year tenure with the band, entitled *Up and Down with the Rolling Stones*. Their reputation was also tarnished by a film made by Robert Frank during the group's 1972 tour, *Cocksucker Blues*. The movie, completed in 1973 and shown several times during 1975 and 1976, was legally suppressed by the group and was ultimately totally withdrawn from public viewing in 1988.

Finally, in 1980 another much-delayed Rolling Stones album was issued, *Emotional Rescue*, but it did little to dispel the allegation that the group was no longer the World's Greatest Rock-and-Roll Band (their self-proclaimed title). The album produced a smash hit with the title song and a major hit with "She's So Cold." In 1981 the Rolling Stones redeemed themselves with the unaffected album *Tattoo You*, the smash hit "Start Me Up," and the major hits "Waiting on a Friend" and "Hang Fire," as well as a massively successful tour conducted in the final four months of the year. However, Mick Jagger and Keith Richards became estranged from each other and the group devolved into solo projects and outside efforts. Despite signing a new distribution deal with Columbia Records in 1983, the Rolling Stones recorded only two studio albums, 1983's *Undercover* and 1986's *Dirty Work*, over the next seven years. During that time they scored a mere five hits, highlighted by the smashes "Undercover of the Night" and "Harlem Shuffle," a cover version of Bob and Earl's 1964 hit.

Much of the '80s was taken up by individual efforts. In 1983 Bill Wyman and Charlie Watts performed as part of Ronnie Lane's brief benefit tour for Appeal for Actions Research into Multiple Sclerosis. Mick Jagger recorded two lackluster solo albums, *She's the Boss* and *Primitive Cool*, managing major hits with "Just Another Night" and "Dancing in the Street" (recorded with David Bowie) and conducting a solo tour in 1988. Longtime associate Ian Stewart, who had recorded an album with his blues band Rocket 88 in 1980, died of a heart attack on December 12, 1985, at age 47. In 1986 Keith Richards served as music director and prime instigator for the Chuck Berry concert film *Hail! Hail! Rock 'n' Roll*. In 1987 Charlie Watts assembled the British jazz band the Charlie Watts Orchestra for one album, *Live at Fulham Town Hall*, and two brief American tours. In 1988 Keith Richards assembled a group that came to be known as the X-Pensive Winos, with drummer and songwriting partner Steve Jordan, guitarist Waddy Wachtel, keyboardist Ivan Neville, and bassist Charlie Drayton. They recorded *Talk Comes Cheap*, which featured the indictment of Jagger, "You Don't Move Me Anymore," and toured America in late 1988; their December 15 show was eventually released as *Live at the Hollywood Palladium*. In May 1989 Bill Wyman opened the restaurant Sticky Fingers Cafe in the fashionable Kensington district of London, featuring a lavish display of his Rolling Stones memorabilia.

Finally, in 1989 the Rolling Stones assembled to record the diverse *Steel Wheels* album and conduct an American stadium tour, their first tour in eight years. The album sold more than two million copies and produced the smash hit "Mixed Emotions" and the major hit "Rock and a Hard Place"; the tour was the highest-grossing rock tour to date. That same year the Rolling Stones were inducted into the Rock and Roll Hall of Fame. In 1990 they toured about a dozen European cities with their Urban Jungle tour. One of two studio cuts from the otherwise live album taken from the tours, *Flashpoint*, produced the minor hit "Highwire," which castigated international arms dealers. In late 1991 the Rolling Stones signed a new record deal with Virgin Records that was to commence in 1993, but Bill Wyman soon quit the group. Mick Jagger appeared in the 1992 science fiction thriller *Free-jack* and a year later recorded his third solo album, *Wandering Spirit*. In 1992 Ron Wood issued his solo album, *Slide On This*, and Keith Richards recorded a second solo album, *Main Offender*, and toured again with the X-Pensive Winos in 1993.

The Rolling Stones' debut on Virgin Records, *Voodoo Lounge*, was issued shortly before the group conducted a three-month tour of American stadiums. Recorded with bassist Darryl Jones, the album produced only the minor hits "Love Is Strong" and "Out of Tears," yet it sold more than two million copies and seemed to reestablish the group after a five-year lapse. The well-received tour grossed more than $120 million and appeared to confirm the band's reputation as World's Greatest, at least in live performance. An *MTV Unplugged*–style album was produced from live recordings cut in small concert halls in Europe, and cleverly titled *Stripped*; it featured a minor hit cover of Bob Dylan's "Like a Rolling Stone," along with remakes of many of the Stones' popular songs in semiacoustic settings.

Studio Albums

The Rolling Stones	London	375	'64	†
	Abkco	7375	'86	LP/CS/CD
12 X 5	London	402	'64	†
	Abkco	7402	'86	LP/CS/CD
Now!	London	420	'65	†
	Abkco	7420	'86	LP/CS/CD
Out of Our Heads	London	429	'65	†
	Abkco	7429	'86	LP/CS/CD
December's Children (and Everybody's)	London	451	'65	†
	Abkco	7451	'86	LP/CS/CD
Big Hits (High Tide and Green Grass)	London	1	'66	†
	Abkco	8001	'86	LP/CS/CD
Aftermath	London	476	'66	†
	Abkco	7476	'86	LP/CS/CD
Between the Buttons	London	499	'67	†
	Abkco	7499	'86	LP/CS/CD
Flowers	London	509	'67	†
	Abkco	7509	'86	LP/CS/CD
Their Satanic Majesties Request	London	2	'67	†
	Abkco	8002	'86	LP/CS/CD
Beggar's Banquet	London	539	'68	†
	Abkco	7539	'86	LP/CS/CD
Through the Past Darkly (Big Hits, Volume 2)	London	3	'69	†
	Abkco	8003	'86	LP/CS/CD

Let It Bleed	London	4	'69	†
	Abkco	8004	'86	LP/CS/CD
Hot Rocks: 1964–1971	London	(2) 606/7	'72	†
	Abkco	6667	'86	CS
	Abkco	(2) 6667	'86	LP/CD
More Hot Rocks (Big Hits and Fazed Cookies)	London	(2) 626/7	'72	†
	Abkco	6267	'86	CS
	Abkco	(2) 6267	'86	LP/CD
Metamorphosis	Abkco	1	'75	†
The Singles Collection: The London Years	Abkco	1218	'89	LP/CS/CD
The Singles Collection: The London Years	Abkco	(3) 1231	'91	CD
Sticky Fingers	Rolling Stones	59100	'71	†
	Rolling Stones	40488	'86	LP/CS/CD†
	Virgin	39504	'94	CD
	Virgin	39525	'94	CS/CD
Exile on Main Street	Rolling Stones	(2) 2900	'72	†
	Rolling Stones	40489		CS/CD†
	Virgin	39503	'94	CD
	Virgin	39524	'94	CS/CD
Goat's Head Soup	Rolling Stones	59101	'73	†
	Rolling Stones	39106		†
	Rolling Stones	40492	'86	CS/CD†
	Virgin	39498	'94	CD
	Virgin	39519	'94	CS/CD
It's Only Rock 'n' Roll	Rolling Stones	79101	'74	†
	Rolling Stones	40493	'86	CS/CD†
	Virgin	39500	'94	CD
	Virgin	39522	'94	CS/CD
Made in the Shade	Rolling Stones	79102	'75	†
	Rolling Stones	40495	'86	CD†
Black and Blue	Rolling Stones	79104	'76	†
	Rolling Stones	40495	'86	CS/CD†
	Virgin	39499	'94	CD
	Virgin	39520	'94	CS/CD
Some Girls	Rolling Stones	39108	'78	†
	Rolling Stones	40449	'86	CS/CD†
	Virgin	39505	'94	CD
	Virgin	39526	'94	CS/CD
Emotional Rescue	Rolling Stones	16015	'80	†
	Rolling Stones	40500	'88	CS/CD†
	Virgin	39501	'94	CD
	Virgin	39523	'94	CS/CD
Tattoo You	Rolling Stones	16052	'81	†
	Rolling Stones	40502	'88	CS/CD†
	Virgin	39502	'94	CD
	Virgin	39521	'94	CS/CD
Undercover	Rolling Stones	90120	'83	†
	Rolling Stones	40504	'86	†
	Virgin	39649	'94	CS/CD
Rewind (1971–1984)	Rolling Stones	90176	'84	†
	Rolling Stones	40505	'86	CD†

Dirty Work	Rolling Stones	40250	'86	CS/CD†
	Virgin	39648	'94	CS/CD
Steel Wheels	Rolling Stones	45333	'89	CS/CD†
	Virgin	39647	'94	CS/CD
Voodoo Lounge	Virgin	39782	'94	CS/CD

Live Albums

Got Live If You Want It	London	493	'66	†
	Abkco	7493	'87	LP/CS/CD
Get Yer Ya-Ya's Out	London	5	'70	†
	Abkco	8005	'86	LP/CS/CD
Love You Live	Rolling Stones	(2) 9001	'77	†
	Atco	(2) 9001		†
	Rolling Stones	40496		CS/CD†
Still Life (American concert recorded 1981)	Rolling Stones	39113	'82	†
	Rolling Stones	40503	'88	CS/CD†
Flashpoint	Rolling Stones	47456	'91	LP/CS/CD†
Stripped	Rolling Stones	41040	'95	CS/CD

Brian Jones

Brian Jones Presents the Pipes of Pan at Joujouka	Rolling Stones	49100	'71	†
	Point	446487	'95	CD

Wyman, Watts, Jagger, Ry Cooder, and Nicky Hopkins

Jammin' with Edward	Rolling Stones	39100	'72	†

Bill Wyman

Monkey Grip	Rolling Stones	79100	'74	†
Stone Alone	Rolling Stones	79103	'76	†
Drinkin' TNT 'n' Smokin' Dynamite	Blind Pig	1182	'82	†

Mick Taylor

Mick Taylor	Columbia	35076	'79/'92	CD

Ron Wood

I've Got Me Own Album To Do	Warner Bros.	2819	'74	†
	Warner Bros.	45692	'94	CD
Now Look	Warner Bros.	2872	'75	†
	Warner Bros.	45693	'94	CD
Gimme Some Neck	Columbia	35702	'79	CD
1234	Columbia	37473	'81	†
Slide On This	Continuum	19210	'92	CS/CD

Rocket 88 (with Ian Stewart)

Rocket 88	Atlantic	19293	'81	†

Mick Jagger

She's the Boss	Columbia	39940	'85	CS/CD†
	Atlantic	82553	'93	CS/CD
Primitive Cool	Columbia	40919	'87	LP/CS/CD†
	Atlantic	82554	'93	CS/CD
Wandering Spirit	Atlantic	82436	'93	CS/CD

Keith Richards

Talk Is Cheap	Virgin	90973	'88	CS/CD†
	Virgin	86079		CS/CD
(3 minis)	Virgin	91047	'89	CD†
	Mobile Fidelity	557	'92	CD
Keith Richards and the X-Pensive Winos at the Hollywood Palladium	Virgin	91808	'91	CS/CD†
	Virgin	86262		CS/CD
Main Offender	Virgin	86499	'92	CS/CD

THE RONETTES

Veronica "Ronnie" Bennett (b. Aug. 10, 1945, New York, NY); **Estelle Bennett** (b. July 22, 1944, New York, NY); **Nedra Talley** (b. Jan. 27, 1946, New York, NY)

Perhaps the best remembered of the so-called girl groups of the early '60s, the Ronettes achieved their biggest success under producer Phil Spector. Featuring his revolutionary wall-of-sound production technique, their classic "Be My Baby" became a smash R&B and pop hit in fall 1963. They followed up with several more hits but quickly faded from popularity with Spector's withdrawal from the music business in 1966 and the demise of his Philles label in 1967. Lead singer Ronnie Bennett was married to Spector from 1968 to 1974 and attempted several comebacks during the '70s and '80s.

Formed in New York City in 1958, the Ronettes were comprised of sisters Estelle and Veronica "Ronnie" Bennett and their cousin Nedra Talley. Performing as dancers at the opening of the Peppermint Lounge in New York City in 1961, the group signed with Don Kirshner's Colpix label, for whom they recorded several singles and an album's worth of material, later released in 1965. They attracted the attention of producer Phil Spector, who signed them to his Philles label. In 1963 they scored a smash pop and R&B hit with "Be My Baby," written by Spector, Jeff Barry, and Ellie Greenwich. Through 1964 they achieved major pop hits with "Baby, I Love You," written by Spector, Barry, and Greenwich, and "Walking in the Rain," written by Barry Mann and Cynthia Weil, and moderate pop hits with "Do I Love You?" and "(The Best Part of) Breaking Up."

The Ronettes continued to record for Philles Records with only minor success through 1966, when they broke up. In 1968 Ronnie Bennett married Phil Spector, and she spent the next four years with him ensconced in his Beverly Hills mansion. In 1969 he unsuccessfully attempted to revive the Ronettes on A&M Records with "You Came, You Saw, You Conquered." On her own, Ronnie Spector managed a minor hit with George Harrison's "Try Some, Buy Some" on Apple Records in 1971. She separated from Spector in 1972 and recorded two unsuccessful singles for Buddah Records with two new members as the Ronettes in 1973–1974. Late-'70s releases for Ronnie Spector include 1976's "Paradise," written by Phil Spector and Harry Nilsson and produced by Spector, and 1977's "Say Goodbye to Hollywood," written by Billy Joel and produced by "Miami" Steve Van Zandt. In 1980 Ronnie Spector recorded *Siren* for Genya Ravan's New York–based Polish Records; the album featured the Ramones' "Here Today, Gone Tomorrow" and "Happy Birthday, Rock and Roll," dedicated to Phil Spector. In 1986 she recorded a duet with Eddie Money on his "Take Me Home Tonight," achieving her greatest late-career success; the song's chorus reprised "Be My Baby" and Spector was prominently featured in the promotional video. Ronnie Spector recorded *Unfinished Business* for Columbia Records in 1987, and Harmony Books published her memoirs, *Be My Baby*, in 1990.

The Ronettes

The Ronettes Featuring Veronica	Colpix	486	†

The Early Years, 1961–1962	Rhino	70524	'92	CD
Presenting the Fabulous Ronettes	Philles	4006	'64	†
Best	Abkco	7212		CS/CD
Ronnie Spector				
Siren	Polish	808	'80	†
Unfinished Business	Columbia	40620	'87	†

LINDA RONSTADT

(b. July 15, 1946, Tucson, AZ)

LINDA RONSTADT

Linda Ronstadt combined folk, rock, and country music, along with the best material by young singer-songwriters and astutely chosen remakes of earlier pop hits, to become one of the most popular female rock vocalists of the second half of the '70s. Always an eclectic singer, she spent her second decade on the pop scene exploring various musical genres, including reviving earlier pop standards with noted arranger Nelson Riddle to surprising success and exploring her own Mexican-American heritage.

Raised in Tucson, Linda Ronstadt was inspired to sing by a musically talented father. By age 14 she was singing with brother Pete and sister Suzi in local pizza parlors and clubs, occasionally accompanied by bassist-guitarist Bob Kimmel. After one semester at the University of Arizona, she joined Kimmel in Los Angeles, where the two formed the Stone Poneys with local guitarist Kenny Edwards. Playing the region's club circuit, the group signed with Capitol Records in 1966 and recorded two albums largely comprised of material written by Kimmel and Edwards, although their only major hit was Mike Nesmith's "Different Drum." After a third album, recorded with studio musicians, Ronstadt pursued a solo career, initially as a country singer. In 1970 she achieved a major hit with "Long, Long Time." In 1971 her touring band coalesced around future Eagles Glenn Frey, Don Henley, and Randy Meisner, who accompanied her on her self-named solo album from that year, which produced a minor hit with Jackson Browne's "Rock Me on the Water."

Touring with Neil Young in early 1973, Linda Ronstadt reenlisted Kenny Edwards, who recruited songwriter-guitarist Andrew Gold for her new backup band. She recorded *Don't Cry Now* with three different producers. The album included three songs written by John David Souther—the title song, "I Can Almost See It," and "The Fast One"—and yielded minor hits with Eric Kaz and Libby Titus's "Love Has No Pride" and "Silver Threads and Golden Needles," a major hit for the Springfields in 1962. One of the album's producers, Peter Asher, became Ronstadt's sole producer and manager through the '70s; he produced the breakthrough *Heart Like a Wheel*, her final effort for Capitol Records. The album was an instant best-seller, yielding a top pop hit with "You're No Good" (a minor hit for Betty Everett in 1963), a smash country hit with Hank Williams's "I Can't Help It (If I'm Still in Love with You)," and a smash country and pop hit with Phil Everly's "When Will I Be Loved." The album also contained Souther's "Faithless Love," Anna McGarrigle's title song, and the Lowell George favorite "Willin'."

Linda Ronstadt's next album, *Prisoner in Disguise*, produced pop hits with covers of the Motown standards "Heat Wave" and "Tracks of My Tears" and a smash country hit with Neil Young's "Love Is a Rose"; it also included Lowell George's "Roll Um Easy" and Dolly Parton's "I Will Always Love You." *Hasten Down the Wind* contained the major pop hit "That'll Be the Day" (Buddy Holly's biggest hit), the smash country hit "Crazy" (Patsy Cline's biggest hit), and three compositions by Karla Bonoff, including the minor hits "Someone to Lay Down Beside Me" and "Lose Again." After completing a six-month tour of Europe and America in December 1976 and singing at President Carter's inaugural the following January, Linda Ronstadt recorded *Simple Dreams*. The album sold more than three million copies and produced five hit singles: "I Never Will Marry" (a near-smash country hit), Roy Orbison's "Blue Bayou" (a smash pop and country hit), Buddy Holly's "It's So Easy" (a smash pop hit), Warren Zevon's "Poor Poor Pitiful Me," and the Rolling Stones' "Tumblin' Dice."

During 1978 Linda Ronstadt attempted to record a trio album with Emmylou Harris and Dolly Parton, but the hastily made recordings proved unsatisfactory for release. Ronstadt's formula for success continued with *Living in the U.S.A.*, which produced hits with cover versions of "Back in the U.S.A." (Chuck Berry), "Ooh Baby Baby" (The Miracles), and "Just One Look" (Doris Troy). The album also contained J. D. Souther's "White Rhythm and Blues" and Elvis Costello's "Alison," Ronstadt's concession to the burgeoning New Wave movement. *Mad Love* was Ronstadt's attempt to record in a more contemporary vein; she included three songs by Costello and three by Mark Goldenburg of the Los Angeles-based Cretones, but the hits were "How Do I Make You" and covers of "Hurt So Bad" (Little Anthony and the Imperials) and "I Can't Let Go" (The Hollies). Her first album of new material in nearly 10 years to *not* sell a million copies, *Get Closer*, yielded moderate pop hits with the title cut and "I Knew You When," and a major country hit with "Sometimes You Just Can't Win."

Linda Ronstadt abandoned rock music for the rest of the '80s to pursue projects that helped establish her as an all-around entertainer. She appeared as Mabel in the Broadway production of Gilbert and Sullivan's *The Pirates of Penzance* and the subsequent movie version, in 1980 and 1983, respectively. In 1983, against the advice of then-boyfriend and former governor of California Jerry Brown, Ronstadt performed at the Sun City resort in South Africa. Later in the year, in a daring career move that defied conventional music-industry wisdom, she recorded an entire album of Tin Pan Alley ballads, *What's New*, with arranger-conductor Nelson Riddle, best known for his '50s work with Nat "King" Cole and Frank Sinatra, and his 46-piece orchestra. Although the album yielded only a minor pop hit, the title song, it eventually sold more than two million copies and encouraged Ronstadt to record two more albums with Riddle, *Lush Life* and *For Sentimental Reasons*. She made her big-band debut at Radio City Music Hall in New York with mixed results, and later played Las Vegas with the entire retinue. In late 1984 Linda Ronstadt performed the role of Mimi in a small-scale version of Puccini's opera *La Bohème* at the Public Theater in New York. Despite the improved power and discipline of her voice, the performance was judged lackluster and disappointing by critics. In late 1986 Ronstadt scored a smash pop hit with James Ingram on "Somewhere Out There" from the animated movie *An American Tail*.

Finally, in 1987 Linda Ronstadt's long-anticipated collaboration with Emmylou Harris and Dolly Parton was released on Warner Bros. Over the next year, *Trio* produced smash country hits with "To Know Him Is to Love Him" (a top pop hit for the Teddy Bears in 1958), "Those Memories of You," Linda Thompson's "Telling Me Lies," and Parton's "Wildflowers." Lauded for its rich harmonies, exquisite lead vocals, and sympathetic arrangements, the album sold more than a million copies. Ronstadt next pursued a reawakened fascination with traditional Mexican music, mariachi music in particular, performing in Luis Valdez's *Corridos! Tales of Passion and Revolution* for PBS television and recording the poignant *Canciones de Mi Padre* (Songs of My Father) for Elektra Records. The album sold astoundingly well for a foreign-language recording and inspired her to tour with mariachi bands in 1988 and 1992. The 1988 tour produced an award-winning PBS television show. She recorded two more albums of Mexican music, *Mas Canciones* (More Songs) and *Frenesi* (Frenzy), in the early '90s.

Linda Ronstadt returned to contemporary music with 1989's *Cry Like a Rainstorm—Howl Like the Wind*. The album included four songs written by Jimmy Webb and four duets with New Orleans vocalist Aaron Neville. Three of the duets became hits: the pop smash "Don't Know Much" and the near-smash "All My Life," both top easy-listening hits; and "When Something Is Wrong with My Baby." After nearly 40 years in the music business, Neville finally received widespread recognition as a result of the best-selling album. In the late-'80s and '90s Ronstadt became recognized as a producer by supervising albums by David Lindley, Neville, and Jimmy Webb. She returned to her country-rock sound with 1995's *Feels Like Home*, which featured Randy Newman's title song, Neil Young's "After the Goldrush," and Tom Petty's "The Waiting."

The Stone Poneys

The Stone Poneys	Capitol	2666	'67	†
	Capitol	80128	'95	CD
(reissued as) Beginnings	Capitol	11383	'75	†
	Capitol	16133		†
Evergreen, Volume 2	Capitol	2763	'67	†
	Capitol	80129	'95	CD
Stone Poneys and Friends, Volume III	Capitol	2863	'68	†
	Capitol	80130	'95	CD
Different Drum	Capitol	11269	'74	†
	Capitol	16299	'84	†
Stoney End	Pickwick	3298	'72	†

Linda Ronstadt

Hand Sown . . . Home Grown	Capitol	208	'69	†
	Capitol	16130		†
Silk Purse	Capitol	407	'70	†
	Capitol	16131		†
Linda Ronstadt	Capitol	635	'71	†
	Capitol	16132		
Heart Like a Wheel	Capitol	11358	'74	†
	Capitol	16332		†
	Capitol	46073		CS/CD
A Retrospective	Capitol	(2) 11629	'77	†
	Capitol	11629		CS
Rockfile (early Capitol material)	Pair	(2) 1125	'86	CS†
Don't Cry Now	Asylum	5064	'73	CD

Prisoner in Disguise	Asylum	1045	'75	†
	Elektra	1045		CS/CD
Hasten Down the Wind	Asylum	1072	'76	†
	Elektra	1072		CS/CD
Greatest Hits, Volume 1	Asylum	1092	'76	†
	Asylum	106		CS/CD
	DCC	1040		CD
Simple Dreams	Asylum	104	'77	†
	Elektra	104		CS/CD
Simple Dreams/Prisoner in Disguise	Elektra	60280		CS
Living in the U.S.A.	Asylum	155	'78	†
	Elektra	155		CS/CD
Mad Love	Asylum	510	'80	†
	Elektra	510		CS/CD
Greatest Hits, Volume 2	Elektra	516	'80	CS/CD
Keeping Out of Mischief	Asylum	540	'81	†
Get Closer	Asylum	60185	'82	CD
What's New	Asylum	60260	'83/'84	†
	Elektra	60260		CS/CD
Lush Life	Asylum	60387	'84	†
	Elektra	60387	'85	CS/CD
For Sentimental Reasons	Asylum	60474	'86	CS/CD
'Round Midnight: The Nelson Riddle Sessions	Asylum	(3) 60489	'86	CD
Prime of Life	Pair	(2) 1070	'86	†
Canciones de Mi Padre	Asylum	60765	'87	CS/CD
Cry Like a Rainstorm— Howl Like the Wind	Elektra	60872	'89	CS/CD
Mas Canciones	Elektra	61239	'91	CS/CD
Frenesi	Elektra	61383	'92	CS/CD
Winter Light	Elektra	61545	'93	CS/CD
Feels Like Home	Elektra	61703	'95	CS/CD
The Pirates Of Penzance				
Broadway Cast Album	Elektra	(2) 601	'81	CS
Linda Ronstadt, Dolly Parton, and Emmylou Harris				
Trio	Warner Bros.	25491	'87	CS/CD

ROXY MUSIC/BRYAN FERRY/BRIAN ENO

Bryan Ferry (b. Sept. 26, 1945, Washington, County Durham, England), lead voc, pno; **Brian Eno** (b. Brian Peter George St. John le Baptiste de la Salle Eno, May 15, 1948, Woodbridge, Suffolk, England), synth; **Phil Manzanera** (b. Philip Targett-Adams, Jan. 31, 1951, London, England), lead gtr; **Andy Mackay** (b. July 23, 1946, England), sax, oboe; **Graham Simpson**, bs; **Paul Thompson** (b. May 13, 1951, Jarrow, Northumberland, England), drm [Graham Simpson left in 1972, to be replaced by a quick succession of other bassists; Brian Eno left in 1973 and was replaced by **Eddie Jobson** (b. Apr. 28, 1955, Birmingham, England) on violin and synthesizer. The band was inactive from late 1976 to 1978, then regrouped with Ferry, Manzanera, Thompson, Mackay, and various supporting musicians; Paul Thompson left in 1980 and the band itself ended in 1983.]

One of the most experimental and provocative bands to emerge from the early-'70s British school of progressive rock, Roxy Music won immediate acceptance in Great Britain and

ROXY MUSIC

Europe yet never achieved more than cult status in the United States. Roxy Music featured two of the most influential British musicians of the era, lead guitarist Phil Manzanera and synthesizer player Brian Eno, as well as lead vocalist Bryan Ferry, who supplied the group's decadent, romantically nostalgic, and vaguely existentialist lyrics sung in a mechanical, colorless voice. Moving through a variety of eccentric images based in part on dress, Roxy Music dropped their initial glitter-rock stance and adopted a more musical approach with the departure of Brian Eno in 1973. Recording perhaps the finest album of their career with 1982's *Avalon*, Roxy Music endured until 1983, by which time their mechanistic, fashion-conscious, and synthesizer-based musical style had been adopted by Talking Heads, Blondie, Devo, and Duran Duran.

Bryan Ferry manned his first band, The Banshees, in summer 1964 and subsequently attended Newcastle University, from which he received a Fine Arts degree in 1968. During college he was a member of the white soul band Gas Board with bassist Graham Simpson. In November 1970 Ferry and Simpson formed Roxy Music with guitarist Roger Bunn, added saxophonist Andy Mackay the following January, and later enlisted keyboardist Brian Eno and drummer Dexter Lloyd. Eno had studied avant-garde music in England and Italy prior to his induction into the group by Mackay. Drummer Paul Thompson, a former member of Newcastle's Smokestack, replaced Lloyd in June 1971, and with the September departure of Bunn, former Nice guitarist David O'List manned Roxy Music through September 1972. Playing their first engagement in late 1971, Roxy Music added guitarist Phil Manzanera, a former member of Quiet Sun, when O'List left.

Signed to Island Records (Warner Bros./Reprise in the United States) and given early exposure through a *Melody Maker* article, Roxy Music recorded their debut album in spring 1972 with King Crimson lyricist Peter Sinfield as producer before embarking on their first tour of Great Britain that August. The album sold quite well in Great Britain and yielded a smash British hit with "Virginia Plain." First touring America in late 1972 and Europe in spring 1973, Roxy Music scored near-smash British hits with "Pyjamarama" and "Street Life" in 1973. Their album *For Your Pleasure*, also released in 1973, included the dance parody "Do the Strand," "Editions of You," and "In Every Dream Home a Heartache."

With Brian Eno's July 1973 departure, Bryan Ferry dropped his glitter garb in favor of white tuxedo and bow tie and adopted a more traditional approach to his music; the earlier complex arrangements were replaced by more straightforward rock and roll. Roxy Music's debut for their new label Atco, *Stranded*, included the British hit "Street Life" as well as "Song for Europe" and "Mother of Pearl." The group began to make inroads in the United States with several American tours between 1974 and 1976. *Country Life*, their best-selling album in America, included "All I Want Is You," "Out of the Blue," and "Thrill of It All." Their next, *Siren*, contained "Both Ends Burning" and "Sentimental Fool" and yielded their first moderate American hit with "Love Is the Drug."

Bryan Ferry launched his own parallel solo recording career in 1974 on Atlantic Records. He achieved his first minor American hit at the end of 1976 with "Heart on My Sleeve" from *Let's Stick Together*. By then Roxy Music had disbanded, with Phil Manzanera and Brian Eno recording with 801 and Ferry touring with his own band. The group reconvened in August 1978 with Ferry, Manzanera, Andy Mackay, and Paul Thompson, plus keyboardist Paul Carrack (Ace) and bassist Gary Tibbs. *Manifesto* yielded a moderate hit with "Dance Away," and the reunited group toured America in spring 1979 and recorded *Flesh and Blood* (and its minor hit "Over You") with Ferry, Manzanera, and Mackay as mainstays. The album yielded British hits with "Oh Yeah" and the title cut, a minor American hit. Following 1982's *Avalon*, often regarded as their masterpiece, Roxy Music disbanded.

Phil Manzanera subsequently recorded with Andy Mackay in the Explorers and later recorded several solo albums as well as albums with John Wetton and Sergio Dias. Ferry continued to pursue his modest solo career, scoring a moderate hit with "Kiss and Tell," from *Bete Noire* in 1988, the year he conducted his first American tour. In 1989 Reprise issued *Street Life*, comprised of Roxy Music hits and six solo hits by Ferry. Following an album of cover songs, *Taxi*, Ferry recorded perhaps the finest album of his career, *Mamouna*, with Robin Trower as coproducer; once again he toured the United States, with Trower as guest guitarist.

Between 1973 and 1977, Brian Eno recorded four albums for Island Records with which he demonstrated the concept of the recording studio as a compositional tool. Generally regarded as his most important solo works, these four albums—*Here Come the Warm Jets*, *Taking Tiger Mountain (By Strategy)*, *Another Green World*, and *Before and After Science*—were excerpted as *More Blank than Frank* in 1986. He also recorded two intriguing, highly influential all-instrumental albums with guitar synthesizer master Robert Fripp in the mid-'70s. Eno pursued his interest in the keyboard synthesizer through a series of albums in the '70s and '80s; he also recorded two albums with Phil Manzanera and others as 801 in 1976–1977.

Eno worked with David Bowie on his late-'70s electronic-music album *Low*, the song "Heroes," and *Lodger*, and produced the debut albums of Ultravox and Devo in 1977 and 1980, respectively. He produced three Talking Heads albums between 1978 and 1980, cowriting songs and singing on *Remain in Light*, and recorded *My Life in the Bush of Ghosts* with David Byrne in 1981. Later, with Canadian producer/engineer David Lanois, Eno coproduced U2's *Unforgettable Fire* (1984) and *The Joshua Tree* (1987). In the mid-'80s he began pursuing an interest in multimedia video installations, and he opened an art gallery in 1987. His video-audio-sculpture show *Latest Flame: Light and Sound Structures by Brian Eno* ran for two months at San Francisco's Exploratorium in 1988. In 1990 Eno released his first album of songs in 13 years, *Wrong Way Up*, with John Cale. Several other instrumental projects followed. In 1995 he collaborated again with David Bowie.

Roxy Music

Roxy Music	Reprise	2114	'72	†
	Atco	36133	'76	†
	Reprise	26039	'89	CS/CD
For Your Pleasure	Warner Bros.	2696	'73	†
	Atco	36134	'76	†
	Reprise	26040	'89	CS/CD
Stranded	Atco	7045	'74	†
	Reprise	26041	'89	CS/CD

Country Life	Atco	36106	'74	†
	Reprise	26042	'89	CS/CD
Siren	Atco	36127	'75	†
	Reprise	26043	'89	CS/CD
Viva! Roxy Music	Atco	36139	'76	†
	Reprise	26044	'89	CS/CD
Greatest Hits	Atco	38103	'77	†
Manifesto	Atco	38114	'79	†
	Reprise	26046	'89	CS/CD
Flesh and Blood	Atco	32102	'80	†
	Reprise	26075	'89	CS/CD
The Atlantic Years, 1973–1980	Atco	90122	'83	†
Avalon	Warner Bros.	23686	'82	CS/CD
The High Road (mini)	Warner Bros.	23808	'83	CS
Street Life: 20 Great Hits	Reprise	(2) 25857	'89	†
	Reprise	25857	'89	CS/CD
Heart Still Beating	Reprise	26402	'90	CS/CD

Brian Eno

Here Come the Warm Jets	Island	9268	'74	†
	Editions EG	1510		CS/CD
Taking Tiger Mountain (By Strategy)	Island	9309	'75	†
	Editions EG	1511		CS/CD
Another Green World	Island	9351	'76	†
	Editions EG	1512		CS/CD
Before and After Science	Island	9478	'78	†
	Editions EG	1513		CS/CD
Discreet Music	Antilles	7030	'77	†
	Editions EG	1520		CD
Music for Films	Antilles	7070	'79	†
	Editions EG	105	'81	†
	Editions EG	1515		CS/CD
Music for Airports	PVC	7908	'79	†
	Editions EG	1516		CS/CD
On Land	Editions EG	1517	'82	CS/CD
Apollo	Editions EG	1514	'83	CS/CD
Thursday Afternoon	Editions EG	1518	'85	CD
More Blank Than Frank	Editions EG	1519	'86	CS
Desert Island Selection	Editions EG	1519	'87	CD
My Squelchy Life	Opal/Warner Bros.	26504	'91	CS/CD
The Shutov Assembly	Opal/Warner Bros.	45010	'92	CS/CD
Nerve Net	Opal	45033	'92	CS/CD
Neroli	Gyroscope	6600	'93	CS/CD
Brian Eno I	Virgin	(3) 39110	'94	CD
Brian Eno II	Virgin	(3) 39114	'94	CD

Brian Eno And Robert Fripp

No Pussyfooting	Island	16	'75	†
	Antilles	7001		†
	Editions EG	1522		CD

Evening Star	Antilles	7018	'76	†
	Editions EG	103		†
	Editions EG	1560		CD
The Essential Fripp and Eno	Venture/Caroline	1886	'94	CS/CD
801				
801 Live	Editions EG	1553	'76/'87	CS/CD
Listen Now!	Editions EG	30	'77/'93	CD
Brian Eno and David Byrne				
My Life in the Bush of Ghosts	Sire	6093	'81	CS/CD
	Sire	45374	'93	CS/CD
Brian Eno and John Cale				
Wrong Way Up	Opal/Warner Bros.	26421	'90	CS/CD
Bryan Ferry				
These Foolish Things	Atlantic	7304	'74	†
	Reprise	26082	'90	CS/CD
Another Time, Another Place	Atlantic	18113	'74	†
	Reprise	26083	'90	CS/CD
Let's Stick Together	Atlantic	18187	'76	†
	Reprise	26084	'90	CS/CD
In Your Mind	Atlantic	18216	'77	†
	Reprise	26085	'90	CS/CD
The Bride Stripped Bare	Atlantic	19205	'78	†
	Reprise	26086	'90	CS/CD
Boys and Girls	Warner Bros.	25082	'85	CS/CD
Bete Noire	Reprise	25598	'87	CS/CD
Taxi	Reprise	45246	'93	CS/CD
Mamouna	Virgin	39838	'94	CS/CD
Phil Manzanera				
Diamond Head	Atco	36116	'75	†
	Editions EG	1576	'90	CD
K-Scope	Polydor	6178	'79	†
	EG	37	'93	CD
Guitarissmo	Editions EG	1552	'87	CD
Primitive Guitars	Editions EG	14	'87/'90	CD
Southern Cross	Agenda	74707	'91	CS/CD
Quiet Sun				
Mainstream	Antilles	7008	'76	†
The Explorers				
The Explorers			'85	†
Phil Manzanera and Andy Mackay				
Crack the Whip	Relativity	8263		LP/CS/CD†
Phil Manzanera and John Wetton				
Wetton/Manzanera	Geffen	24147	'87	CS
Phil Manzanera and Sergio Dias				
Mato Grosso	Black Sun	15010	'91	CS/CD

RUFUS

Chaka Khan (b. Yvette Marie Stevens, Mar. 23, 1953, Great Lakes, IL), voc; **Kevin Murphy**
and **Nate Morgan**, kybd; **Tony Maiden**, gtr; **Bobby Watson**, bs; **John Robinson**, drm
[Nate Morgan was replaced by **David Wolinski** in 1977.]

A Chicago-based multiracial funk and dance group of the '70s, Rufus scored a series of pop and R&B hits between 1974 and 1983. Featuring the powerful voice and erratic stage presence of Chaka Khan, Rufus achieved their first crossover smash with Stevie Wonder's "Tell Me Something Good" and persevered through 1983's "Ain't Nobody." Chaka Khan began a parallel solo career in 1978, and left Rufus for good in 1983, but she has enjoyed limited success.

Rufus evolved out of the American Breed (1968's "Bend Me, Shape Me") in the person of keyboardist Kevin Murphy. He formed Smoke, later known as Ask Rufus, with a variety of players. With the departure of vocalist Paulette McWilliams, Murphy recruited black vocalist Chaka Khan in 1972. Born Yvette Stevens, she had formed her first vocal group at age 11 and quit school to work with Chicago groups such as Lyfe and the Babysitters, changing her name to Chaka Khan in 1970. Signed to ABC Records, Rufus' debut album sold poorly. By 1974 the group was comprised of Khan, Murphy, keyboardist Nate Morgan, guitarist Tony Maiden, bassist Bobby Watson, and drummer John Robinson. During sessions for their second album, the group encountered Stevie Wonder, who offered his "Tell Me Something Good." The song became a smash pop and R&B hit in 1974, and the album, *Rags to Rufus*, later yielded crossover smashes with "You Got the Love" and "Once You Get Started," effectively launching the group's career.

Featuring infectious driving rhythms and the strong vocals of Chaka Khan, Rufus achieved smash R&B and moderate pop hits with "Please Pardon Me (You Remind Me of a Friend)," "Sweet Thing" (a pop smash), and "Dance Wit Me" from *Rufus Featuring Chaka Khan*, as well as "At Midnight (My Love Will Lift You Up)" and "Hollywood" from *Ask Rufus*. David Wolinski replaced Nate Morgan in 1977, and the crossover hits continued with "Stay," "Do You Love What You Feel," and "Sharing the Love" through 1981. Rufus recorded *Numbers* and *Party 'Til You're Broke* without Chaka Khan, but neither album sold well or produced a hit single. Chaka Khan's final two albums with Rufus, *Camouflage* and the live set *Stompin' at the Savoy*, produced Rufus' final R&B smashes with "Sharing the Love" and "Ain't Nobody" (a major pop hit), respectively.

Chaka Khan initiated her solo career in 1978, scoring an R&B smash and major pop hit with Nicholas Ashford and Valerie Simpson's "I'm Every Woman," and the R&B smashes "Clouds" and "What Cha' Gonna Do for Me." She next recorded an album of jazz standards, *Echoes of an Era*, with Chick Corea, Freddie Hubbard, Joe Henderson, and Lenny White, and the jazz-style *Chaka Khan*. Khan later scored the R&B smash "Got to Be There" and the top R&B and smash pop hit "I Feel for You," written by Prince and recorded with Grandmaster Mel and Stevie Wonder, but subsequent singles were essentially restricted to the R&B field. She managed a major pop hit in 1989 with "I'll Be Good for You," recorded with Quincy Jones and Ray Charles, from Jones's album *Back on the Block*, but 1993's "Feels Like Heaven," recorded with Peter Cetera, proved to be only a minor pop hit. She appeared on the video and recording of Whitney Houston's 1993 remake of "I'm Every Woman."

Rufus

Rufus				
Rufus	ABC	783	'73	†
	MCA	10663	'92	CD
Rags to Rufus	ABC	809	'74	†
	MCA	31365	'90	CD
Rufusized	ABC	837	'74	†
	MCA	10236	'91	CD

Rufus Featuring Chaka Khan	ABC	909	'75	†
	MCA	31373	'90	CD
Ask Rufus	ABC	975	'77	†
	MCA	10449	'92	CD
Street Player	ABC	1049	'78	†
	MCA	11031	'94	CD
Numbers	ABC	1098	'78	†
Masterjam	MCA	5103	'79	†
	MCA	10763	'93	CD
Party 'Til You're Broke	MCA	5159	'81	†
Camouflage	MCA	5270	'81	†
Very Best	MCA	5339	'82	†
Soul in Red	Warner Bros.	23753	'83	†
Live—Stompin' at the Savoy	Warner Bros.	(2) 23679	'83	CS/CD
Chaka Khan				
Chaka	Warner Bros.	3245	'78	†
Naughty	Warner Bros.	3385	'80	†
What Cha' Gonna Do for Me	Warner Bros.	3526	'81	†
Chaka Khan	Warner Bros.	23729	'82	†
I Feel for You	Warner Bros.	25162	'84	CS/CD
Destiny	Warner Bros.	25425	'86	LP/CS/CD†
C.K.	Warner Bros.	25707	'88	CS/CD
Life Is a Dance/The Remix Project	Warner Bros.	25946	'89	CS/CD
The Woman I Am	Warner Bros.	26296	'92	CS/CD
Chaka Khan/Chick Corea/Freddie Hubbard/Joe Henderson/Lenny White				
Echoes of an Era	Elektra	60021	'82	†

THE RUNAWAYS/JOAN JETT/LITA FORD

Cherie Currie (b. 1960, Los Angeles, CA), lead voc; **Joan Jett** (b. Joan Larkin, Sept. 22, 1960, Philadelphia, PA), gtr, voc; **Lita Ford** (b. Sept. 23, 1959, London, England), lead gtr, voc; **Micki Steele** (b. June 2, 1954), bs, voc; **Sandy West** (b. 1954), drm [Micki Steele left in 1975, to be replaced by several different bassists, including **Jackie Fox** (b. Jacqueline Fuchs, 1960).]

A teenage all-female rock band of the mid- and late '70s, the Runaways demonstrated that rock and roll was not the sole province of male bands. Showing minimal musical talent (in the spirit of punk musicians) and presenting a blatantly sexual show (years before Madonna), the Runaways were masterminded by eccentric Los Angeles producer Kim Fowley. Although they were dismissed critically and commercially in the United States, the Runaways nonetheless gained popularity in Japan and Europe. Producing three of rock music's top female players—Joan Jett, Lita Ford, and Micki Steele (later with the Bangles)— the group dissolved at the end of 1978. Jett emerged as one of the leading rock stars of the '80s, while Lita Ford emerged as rock's foremost female heavy-metal guitarist.

Joan Jett grew up in Rockville, Maryland, and moved to Southern California with her family in 1974, where she took up guitar. While hanging out at the Starwood Club on Hollywood's Sunset Strip, she met producer Kim Fowley, who put together the teenage all-female band the Runaways through local auditions in 1975. Initially comprised of Jett, bassist Micki Steele, and drummer Sandy West, the Runaways were soon joined by vocalist Cherie Currie and guitarist Lita Ford. Ford had emigrated to the United States from London as a child and had begun guitar lessons around age 12. Steele left the group after only a short time, to be replaced by a succession of bassists, including Jackie Fox.

Though the Runaways were musically crude, their debut album, for Mercury Records, includes the salutary "Cherry Bomb," a top hit in Japan. In performance they revealed the influence of both glitter and hard rock, yet they were dismissed for their musical deficiencies and their blatantly sexual presentation, highlighted by lead vocalist Cherie Currie's attire in lingerie. For their much-improved second album, *Queens of Noise*, Cherie Currie and Joan Jett shared lead vocals. The album featured the title song as well as "Born to Be Bad" and "I Love Playin' with Fire." Currie and Fox left in summer 1977 and, as a consequence, Jett took over on lead vocals. Following *Waitin' for the Night*, which included "Wasted" and "You're Too Possessive," the Runaways recorded their final album, eventually released in the United States as *Little Lost Girls*. They opened for the Ramones during their 1978 American tour and played their final engagement in San Francisco on New Year's Eve, 1978–1979. In 1985 Kim Fowley resurrected the group name with all new members for *Young and Fast*.

In 1978 Cherie Currie recorded a solo album in France; she recorded the dismal *Messin' with the Boys* a year later with her sister Marie. In spring 1979 Joan Jett traveled to England, where she recorded three songs with former Sex Pistols Paul Cook and Steve Jones. She later moved back to Los Angeles, where she produced the debut album of the punk group the Germs and met Kenny Laguna and Ritchie Cordell. They produced her solo debut album, but it was initially released in Europe only. Picked up by Boardwalk Records, the album was released as *Bad Reputation* in 1981. It featured the songs recorded with Cook and Jones as well as Gary Glitter's "Do You Wanna Touch Me (Oh Yeah)," a major hit when released in 1982.

Meanwhile, during 1980 Joan Jett assembled her backup band, The Blackhearts, with guitarist Ricky Byrd, bassist Gary Ryan, and drummer Lee Crystal. Their album *I Love Rock 'n' Roll* was released in 1981 and became a surprise best-seller, yielding a top hit with the title song, originally recorded by the British group the Arrows; a near-smash hit with a remake of Tommy James and the Shondells' "Crimson and Clover"; and a popular version of the Christmas song "Little Drummer Boy." Jett and manager Kenny Laguna formed Blackheart Records for subsequent recordings by Jett and the Blackhearts. The group's next release, *Album*, produced two moderate hits with "Fake Friends" and a cover of Sly and the Family Stone's "Everyday People"; it also contained "I Love Playin' with Fire." Following *Glorious Results of a Misspent Youth*, with "I Love You Love Me Love" and a new version of "Cherry Bomb," the band toured for most of 1985. Released in 1986, *Good Music* became the poorest-selling album of the group's career, despite the inclusion of the minor hit title song, which featured the Beach Boys on backing vocals.

In 1987 Joan Jett costarred with Michael J. Fox in the movie *Light of Day*. They played brother and sister members of a rock band called the Barbusters and, despite the film's commercial failure, her performance was generally praised. The soundtrack album produced a moderate hit with Bruce Springsteen's title song. For *Up Your Alley* Jett formed a new backup band, and the album became another best-seller thanks to the near-smash hit "I Hate Myself for Loving You," cowritten with Desmond Child; the major hit "Little Liar"; and Iggy Pop's "I Wanna Be Your Dog." Following her solo album of cover songs, *The Hit List*, and Jett and the Blackhearts' *Notorious*, which featured "Backlash," cowritten with Paul Westerberg of the Replacements, Jett withdrew from the music business in the early '90s. Cited along with the Pretenders' Chrissie Hynde as one of the inspirations for so-called riot grrrls such as Courtney Love (Hole), Kathleen Hanna (Bikini Kill), and Liz Phair, Jett finally reemerged in 1994 with *Pure and Simple*. The album included three songs cowritten with Hanna and featured "Spinster," "As I Am," "Eye to Eye," and "Go Home," inspired by the rape-murder of Mia Zapata, a member of the Seattle band the Gits.

Lita Ford returned to the music scene in 1983 as the singer–songwriter–lead guitarist of an otherwise all-male heavy-metal band. Recording two albums for Mercury, Ford's second, *Dancin' on the Edge*, included "Hit 'n' Run," "Ladykiller," "Dressed to Kill," and "Gotta Let Go." She eventually broke through in 1988 under producer Michael Chapman with *Lita*. The album included "Can't Catch Me," cowritten with Motörhead's Lemmy Kilmister, and the ballad "Falling In and Out of Love," written by Mötley Crüe's Nikki Sixx, and yielded the near-smash hits "Kiss Me Deadly" and "Close My Eyes Forever," the latter recorded with Ozzy Osbourne. Subsequent albums, however, sold progressively less well.

The Runaways

The Runaways	Mercury	1090	'76	†
Queens of Noise	Mercury	1126	'77	†
	Collector's Pipeline	015	'94	CD
Waitin' for the Night	Mercury	3705	'77	†
Little Lost Girls			'81	†
	Rhino	70861	'87	CS/CD
Best	Mercury	826279		CD
Neon Angels	Polygram	838583		CS/CD
Mama We're All Crazee Now	Rhino	602	'82	†
Young and Fast	Allegiance	72866	'87	LP/CS/CD†

Cherie and Marie Currie

Messin' with the Boys	Capitol	12022	'80	†

Joan Jett

Bad Reputation	Boardwalk	37065	'81	†
The Hit List	Blackheart	45473	'90	LP/CS/CD

Joan Jett and the Blackhearts

I Love Rock 'n' Roll	Boardwalk	33243	'81	†
Album	Blackheart	5437	'83	†
Glorious Results of a Misspent Youth	Blackheart	5476	'84	†
Good Music	Blackheart	40544	'86	†
	CBS Associated	40544		CS/CD
Up Your Alley	Blackheart	44146	'88	†
	CBS Associated	44146		CS/CD
Notorious	Blackheart	47488	'91	LP/CS/CD
Pure and Simple	Warner Bros.	45567	'94	LP/CS/CD

Lita Ford

Out for Blood	Mercury	810331	'83	CS/CD
Dancin' on the Edge	Mercury	818864	'84	CS/CD
Lita	RCA	6397	'88	CS/CD
Stiletto	RCA	2090	'90	CS/CD
Dangerous Curves	RCA	61025	'91	CS/CD
Best	RCA	66037	'92	CS/CD
Greatest Hits	RCA	66199	'93	CS/CD

TODD RUNDGREN

(b. June 22, 1948, Upper Darby, PA)

First recognized as the leader of the late-'60s Philadelphia group the Nazz, Todd Rundgren quickly established himself as one of America's studio geniuses with productions for the Band,

TODD RUNDGREN

Grand Funk Railroad, and the New York Dolls. Mastering a variety of instruments and musical styles, Rundgren performed all the musical chores on a number of his own albums. A compelling songwriter, he composed melodically and harmonically rich and demanding songs that were at once personal and intelligent. Playing and singing virtually all parts on 1972's *Something/Anything?* album, his biggest commercial and artistic success and generally regarded as his masterpiece, Rundgren formed Utopia in 1974 to explore new electronic musical devices and advanced technology on songs often cosmically obscure. He enjoyed modest success both on his own and with Utopia during the '70s, while producing albums for a variety of artists, including Hall and Oates, the Patti Smith Group, and Meatloaf (his multi-million-selling debut *Bat Out of Hell*). Rundgren began programming computers in the late '70s, an avocation that later led to pioneering efforts in video production and computer technology. Along with Thomas Dolby, Todd Rundgren was at the forefront of multimedia technology, issuing his 1993 *No World Order* as the first interactive music-only compact disc.

Growing up in the suburbs of Philadelphia, Todd Rundgren experimented with both guitar and flute during his high school years, joining the local blues band Woody's Truckstop after graduation. He left the group in 1967 to form the Nazz with vocalist Robert Antoni. Under the influence of the British groups of the mid-'60s, the Nazz concentrated on a careful mix of vocal harmonies and Rundgren's guitar playing, signing with Screen Gems/Columbia in 1968. With Rundgren writing most of the material and arranging the music, they managed a minor pop hit with "Hello It's Me" and recorded two overlooked albums before Rundgren's departure in 1970. He was replaced by Rick Nielsen and Tom Petersson, later members of Cheap Trick.

In the meantime, Todd Rundgren had learned engineering and production. He worked with the short-lived Ampex label, producing Ian and Sylvia's *Great Speckled Bird*, engineering Jesse Winchester's debut album, and performing all technical and musical chores save bass and drums for his own album *Runt*, which yielded a major hit with "We Gotta Get You a Woman." Word of his reputation as a studio master spread after he engineered the Band's *Stage Fright*, and in the next two years he engineered the Butterfield Blues Band's *Live* and coproduced Badfinger's *Straight Up* with George Harrison.

After *Runt*, Todd Rundgren switched to Albert Grossman's Bearsville label for the double record set *Something/Anything?*, his best-selling album. Largely played and sung by Rundgren on his own, the album demonstrated a diversity of styles. It included the favorites "It Wouldn't Have Made Any Difference" and "Black Maria" and yielded a major hit with "I Saw the Light," a minor hit with "Couldn't I Just Tell You," and a smash hit with a remake of "Hello It's Me." In contrast to the highly melodic and well-crafted songs of his previous albums, *A Wizard / A True Star* was rather esoteric and featured bold and loud synthe-sizer and guitar work. Essentially a creature of the studio, Rundgren produced Fanny's *Mother's Pride*, Grand Funk Railroad's best-selling *We're an American Band*, the debut album by the New York Dolls, and Daryl Hall and John Oates's experimental *War Babies* album.

By 1974 Todd Rundgren had formed Utopia with synthesizer player Roger Powell and drummer John "Willie" Wilcox to experiment with new technologies and sounds. Their de-but album sold modestly as Rundgren developed a devoted following in Great Britain and the United States. On his own, Rundgren recorded favorites such as "Just One Victory," "Sometimes I Don't Know What to Feel," "The Dream Goes on Forever," "Real Man," and "Love in Action." *Faithful* contained precise renditions of songs by Jimi Hendrix, the Beat-les, and the Beach Boys and included "Love of the Common Man." Utopia's lineup stabilized with Powell, Wilcox, and bassist Kasim Sulton by 1977. Their *Oops! Wrong Planet* featured "Love Is the Answer," and *Adventures in Utopia*, their best-selling album, produced hits with "Set Me Free" and "The Very Last Time." Rundgren's *Hermit of Mink Hollow*, which he wrote, arranged, produced, played, and sang in its entirety, yielded a major hit with "Can We Still Be Friends?" and helped establish him with the mainstream-rock audience.

In the late '70s Todd Rundgren continued to be active in the studio. He produced Meat-loaf's debut album, *Bat Out of Hell* (which sold more than 26 million copies worldwide), the Tubes' *Remote Control*, and the Patti Smith Group's *Wave*. He also began a career-long study of computer and multimedia technology, producing Holst's *The Planets* as RCA's first videodisc and creating the second video to be played on MTV, for "Time Heals." Utopia recorded its last albums in the early to mid-'80s, while Rundgren cut the all-solo effort *The Ever Popular Tortured Artist Effect*. He followed this with *A Cappella*, a curious album com-prised entirely of synthesized vocal recordings.

During the '80s Todd Rundgren produced albums for What Is This?, XTC, and the Pur-suit of Happiness. He moved to the San Francisco Bay Area in the mid-'80s and eventually released *Nearly Human* in 1989, the year Rhino Records issued anthology sets for both Utopia and Rundgren. In 1992 Rhino issued a set of his production efforts, and in 1993 Rundgren released *No World Order* as the first interactive compact disc, allowing listeners to choose from nearly a thousand four-bar music segments in various forms, directions, moods, tempos, and mixes. In 1995 Todd Rundgren announced his intention to become the first CD-ROM–only artist, signing with the interactive CD label ION. As TR-1 he has been an active voice on the Internet.

The Nazz

Introducing the Nazz	Screen Gems/ Columbia	5001	'68	†
(reissued as) The Nazz	Rhino	109	'83	†
	Rhino	70109		CD
Nazz Nazz	Screen Gems/ Columbia	5002	'69	†
	Rhino	110	'83	†
	Rhino	70110		CD
Nazz III	Screen Gems/ Columbia	5004	'71	†
	Rhino	111	'83	†
	Rhino	70111		CD
Best	Rhino	116	'84	†
	Rhino	70116		CD

Todd Rundgren

Runt	Ampex	10105	'70	†
	Bearsville	2046		†
	Rhino	70862	'87	CS/CD
The Ballad of Todd Rundgren	Ampex	10116	'71	†
	Bearsville	2047		†
	Rhino	70863	'87	CS/CD
Something/Anything?	Bearsville	(2) 2066	'72	†
	Rhino	71107	'87	CS/CD
	Mobile Fidelity	(2) 20591	'94	CD
A Wizard/A True Star	Bearsville	2133	'73	†
	Rhino	70864	'87	CS/CD
Todd	Bearsville	(2) 2169	'73	†
	Bearsville	(2) 6952		†
	Rhino	71108	'87	CS/CD
Initiation	Bearsville	6957	'75	†
	Rhino	70866	'87	CS/CD
Faithful	Bearsville	6963	'76	†
	Rhino	70868	'87	CS/CD
Hermit of Mink Hollow	Bearsville	6981	'78	†
	Rhino	70871	'88	CS/CD
Back to the Bars	Bearsville	(2) 6986	'78	†
	Rhino	71109	'87	CS/CD
Healing	Bearsville	3522	'81	†
	Rhino	70874	'87	CS/CD
The Ever Popular Tortured Artist Effect	Bearsville	23732	'83	†
	Rhino	70876	'88	CS/CD
A Cappella	Warner Bros.	25128	'85	†
	Rhino	75761		CD
Anthology (1968–1985)	Rhino	(2) 71491	'89	CS/CD
Undercover (soundtrack)	Enigma	73276	'87	LP/CS/CD
Nearly Human	Warner Bros.	25881	'89	CS/CD
2nd Wind	Warner Bros.	26478	'91	CS/CD
No World Order	Rhino	71266	'93	CS/CD
Best	Rhino	71029	'94	CS/CD
No World Order Lite	Forward	71744	'94	CS/CD

Todd Rundgren Productions

An Elpee's Worth of Productions	Rhino	70519	'92	CS/CD†

Utopia

Todd Rundgren's Utopia	Bearsville	6954	'74	†
	Rhino	70865	'87	CS/CD
Todd Rundgren's Utopia: Another Live	Bearsville	6961	'75	†
	Rhino	70867	'87	CS/CD
RA	Bearsville	6965	'77	†
	Rhino	70869	'87	CS/CD
Oops! Wrong Planet	Bearsville	6970	'77	†
	Rhino	70870	'87	CS/CD
	Mobile Fidelity	637	'95	CD
Adventures in Utopia	Bearsville	6991	'80	†
	Rhino	70872	'87	CS/CD

Deface the Music	Bearsville	3487	'80	†
	Rhino	70873	'87	CS/CD
Swing to the Right	Bearsville	3666	'82	†
	Rhino	70875	'87	CS/CD
Utopia	Network	(2) 60183	'82	†
	Rhino	70713	'89	CS/CD
Oblivion	Passport	6029	'84	†
POV	Passport	6044	'85	†
Anthology (1974–1985)	Rhino	70892	'89	CS/CD
Redux '92: Live in Japan	Rhino	71185	'93	CS/CD
Roger Powell				
Cosmic Furnace	Atlantic	7251	'73	†
Air Pocket	Bearsville	6994	'80	†
Kasim Sulton				
Kasim	EMI America	17063	'82	†

RUN-D.M.C.

Joseph "Run" Simmons (b. Nov. 14, 1964, Queens, NY); **Darryl "D.M.C." McDaniels** (b. May 31, 1964, Queens, NY); **Jason "Jam Master Jay" Mizell** (b. Jan. 21, 1965, Queens, NY)

The first rap group to enjoy mainstream pop success, thanks in large part to 1986's smash pop hit and video "Walk This Way," Run-D.M.C. was also the first rap group to have a video screened on MTV, to make the cover of *Rolling Stone*, and to perform on *American Bandstand* as well as the only rap group to appear at 1985's Live Aid concert. Although Run-D.M.C. projected a violent gangster image, their music concerned itself with peaceful messages advocating the avoidance of drugs and gangs. Nonetheless, their concerts, particularly those in 1986 in support of *Raising Hell*, were often accompanied by violence, drawing attention to the paradox between their good intentions and the violent outcome of their live music.

Joseph "Run" Simmons's brother Russell was instrumental in establishing rap artists such as Kurtis Blow and Grandmaster Flash and the Furious Five—pioneering rap acts—by booking them into Harlem clubs; he cofounded the pioneering rap label Def Jam, with Rick Rubin, and encouraged his younger brother to pursue a performing career. Joseph Simmons began composing and performing raps with Kurtis Blow in the late '70s and began collaborating with Darryl McDaniels in the early '80s to form Run-D.M.C. with disc jockey Jason Mizell. Scoring their first major R&B hit in 1983 with "It's Like That" on the small, independent label Profile, Run-D.M.C. continued to achieve major R&B hits through 1985 with "Hard Times," "Rock Box," and "30 Days" from their debut album; the title track and "You Talk Too Much" from *King of Rock*, regarded as one of rap's landmark albums; and "You Can't Rock It Like This" from the film *Krush Groove*. In 1985 they appeared at the Live Aid concert and later contributed to the recording of "Sun City" by Artists United Against Apartheid.

Run-D.M.C. scored an R&B smash with "My Adidas" in 1986 and soon established themselves with a larger audience with the pop and R&B smash "Walk This Way," featuring Aerosmith's Steve Tyler and Joe Perry (the song also revived Aerosmith's career). Both songs were included on their *Raising Hell* album, as was "You Be Illin'" (a major crossover hit) and "It's Tricky" (a major R&B hit); the album sold more than three million copies. They conducted a four-month, 62-city tour that year, but a number of their concerts were marred by violence. Their next album, *Tougher Than Leather*, sold quite well but not spectacularly and produced a major R&B hit with "Run's House." However, 1990's *Back from Hell* sold modestly at best; Simmons and McDaniels both admitted to drug and alcohol problems, and Simmons also had to defend himself against a charge of rape, later dropped. Run-D.M.C. did not score another major pop hit until 1993's "Down with the King." In 1992 MCA Music Entertainment, the distributor of Run-D.M.C.'s New York–based record label JDK Records, withdrew the misogynist "No Head, No Backstage Pass" by the group FU2 in the wake of the "Cop Killer" controversy that embroiled Ice-T.

Run-D.M.C.

Run-D.M.C.	Profile	1202	'84		CS/CD
King of Rock	Profile	1205	'85		CS/CD
Raising Hell	Profile	1217	'86		CS/CD
Tougher Than Leather	Profile	1265	'88		CS/CD
Back from Hell	Profile	1401	'90		LP/CS/CD
Together Forever: Greatest Hits 1983–1991	Profile	(2) 1419	'91		LP
	Profile	1419	'91		CS/CD
Down with the King	Profile	1140	'93		CS/CD

LEON RUSSELL

(b. Hank Wilson, Apr. 2, 1941, Lawton, OK)

With his gospel-style piano playing, raspy mumbling vocals, and compelling songwriting, Leon Russell established himself as one of rock's most unique figures. Initially a well-known session player and producer in Los Angeles during the mid-'60s, Russell first came to the public's attention in the late '60s with the Asylum Choir, in collaboration with songwriter-guitarist Marc Benno. He subsequently came to prominence as organizer and mastermind behind Joe Cocker's 1970 Mad Dogs and Englishmen tour, who later pursued a modestly successful solo recording career in the '70s. His popularity faded after the mid-'70s, although he made a remarkable comeback in the country field with his 1979 duet album with Willie Nelson. Continuing to tour in the '80s and '90s, Leon Russell returned to recording in 1992 after nearly a decade's absence.

Leon Russell started 10 years of classical piano lessons at age 3 and took up trumpet at 14, soon forming his first band. He later played briefly with Ronnie Hawkins and the Hawks and toured with Jerry Lee Lewis for six months. After moving to Los Angeles in 1959, he learned guitar from James Burton and became a session musician. He played on most of Phil Spector's hit productions through 1966, and on isolated hits by the Byrds, Herb Alpert, and Bob Lind. Russell also recorded with an astounding variety of artists, from Frank Sinatra to Gary Lewis and the Playboys, from Bobby Darin to Paul Revere and the Raiders.

In 1966 Leon Russell met songwriter-guitarist Marc Benno (b. July 1, 1947, Dallas, TX). By 1967 Russell had withdrawn from the studio scene to build his own elaborate home studio, although he occasionally appeared with friends Delaney and Bonnie Bramlett and played on infrequent sessions. Working briefly with the Bramlets, guitarist Don Preston, bassist Carl Radle, and others in the New Electric Horn Band, Russell formed the Asylum Choir with Benno in 1968, signing with the Smash subsidiary of Mercury Records. Their debut album sold poorly and their second, recorded in 1969, wasn't issued until the end of 1971, on Shelter Records. It included Russell's "Hello Little Friend" and Benno and Russell's "Sweet Home Chicago" and "Tryin' to Stay Alive."

In 1969 Leon Russell assisted Delaney and Bonnie on their album *Original—Accept No Substitute*, along with organist Bobby Whitlock, bassist Carl Radle, and vocalist Rita Coolidge. Later in the year he worked on Joe Cocker's second album, which contained Russell's "Delta Lady," written for Rita Coolidge. By the beginning of 1970, Russell and English producer Denny Cordell had formed Shelter Records, which soon released Russell's debut album. Recorded with Eric Clapton, George Harrison, and Stevie Winwood, among others, the modest-selling album included three classic Russell compositions, "Delta Lady," "Hummingbird," and "A Song for You," as well as two excellent collaborations, "Prince of Peace" and "Roll Away the Stone."

In a single day in March 1970 Leon Russell assembled the nucleus of the Mad Dogs and Englishmen aggregation for a two-month tour backing Joe Cocker. Consisting of more than 40 people, the entourage included Carl Radle, guitarists Chris Stainton and Don Preston, and backup singers Rita Coolidge and Claudia Lennear. The tour proved enormously successful, as did the subsequent live album and movie, but much to Cocker's chagrin, the spotlight frequently fell on Russell or Coolidge, who regularly performed Russell and Bonnie Bramlett's "Superstar." Shortly after the tour's conclusion in May, Russell assisted Eric Clapton with his debut solo album, coauthoring "Blues Power."

Leon Russell's next album, *Leon Russell and the Shelter People*, was recorded with four sets of accompanying musicians: The Shelter People, The Tulsa Tops, The Muscle Shoals Swampers, and Friends from England. The album included two Bob Dylan songs and excellent originals such as "Sweet Emily," "She Smiles Like a River," "The Ballad of Mad Dogs and Englishmen," and Russell and Don Preston's "Stranger in a Strange Land." In 1971 Russell produced the Bob Dylan singles "Watching the River Flow" and "George Jackson" and appeared at George Harrison's August Concert for Bangladesh. Finally, in 1972 Russell scored his first major hit with "Tight Rope" from *Carney*, his best-selling album; it also contained his own "If the Shoe Fits . . .," "Magic Mirror," the minor hit "Queen of the Roller Derby," and the engaging "This Masquerade," a smash pop and R&B hit for George Benson in 1976.

Following *Leon Live*, Leon Russell confounded critics with the unexpected album of country standards, *Hank Wilson's Back,* which yielded the minor hit "Roll in My Sweet Baby's Arms." In 1974 Russell ceased touring, appeared in the film biography *A Poem Is a Naked Person*, and issued *Stop All That Jazz*. His next album, *Will o' the Wisp*, produced a major hit with "Lady Blue" and a minor hit with "Back to the Island."

Russell subsequently severed his relationship with Shelter Records and recorded for his own label, Paradise, distributed by Warner Bros. In spring 1976 he announced his secret marriage the previous June to vocalist Mary McCreary, who had already recorded two solo albums and provided background vocals to Russell's *Will o' the Wisp*. The couple launched the Paradise label with the appropriately titled *Wedding Album*, which yielded the minor hit "Rainbow in Your Eyes," Russell's last. Subsequent albums by Mary alone, Leon alone, and the couple together fared poorly.

Russell bounced back with 1979's *One for the Road*, recorded with Willie Nelson, which included the top country hit "Heartbreak Hotel." He later recorded with the bluegrass-style New Grass Revival. Russell returned to touring in the mid-'80s, gigging with Edgar Winter in 1987 and 1989. In 1992 Leon Russell recorded *Anything Can Happen* for Virgin Records, and later played sessions for George Jones, Bela Fleck, and the Tractors.

Marc Benno briefly returned to Texas after the demise of Asylum Choir, but he was back in Los Angeles by 1969, where he signed with A&M Records as a solo act. Although he never rose from obscurity, he did write a number of excellent songs, including "Family Full of Soul," "Don't Let the Sun Go Down," and "Either Way It Happens." Benno traveled with Rita Coolidge's Dixie Flyers during her 1971 European tour, and contributed a number of songs to her first three albums, including "(I Always Called Them) Mountains," "Second Story Window," "Nice Feelin'," and "Inside of Me." After years off the concert and recording scene, Benno reemerged in 1979 with *Lost in Austin*, ably assisted by Eric Clapton. In the late '80s he composed "Rock 'n' Roll Me Again" for the best-selling *Beverly Hills Cop* soundtrack and moved to the San Francisco Bay Area. Marc Benno returned to recording with 1993's *Take It Back to Texas* on the Sky Ranch label.

The Asylum Choir

Look Inside the Asylum Choir	Smash	67107	'68	†
Asylum Choir II	Shelter	8910	'71	†
	Shelter	2120	'74	†
	Shelter	52010		†
	Shelter	8014		CS/CD

Marc Benno

Marc Benno	A&M	4273	'70	†
Minnows	A&M	4303	'71	†
Ambush	A&M	4364	'72	†
Lost in Austin	A&M	4767	'79	†
Take It Back to Texas	Sky Ranch	2303	'93	CD

Leon Russell

Looking Back	Olympic G.M.	7112	'74	†
Leon Russell	Shelter	1001	'70	†
	Shelter	8901		†
	Shelter	2118	'74	†
	Shelter	52007		†
	Shelter	8001	'89	CS/CD
	Shelter	1049		CD
Leon Russell and the Shelter People	Shelter	8903	'71	†
	Shelter	2119	'74	†
	Shelter	52008		†
	Shelter	8005	'89	CS/CD
Carney	Shelter	8911	'72	†
	Shelter	2121	'74	†
	Shelter	52011		†
	Shelter	8006	'89	CS/CD
Leon Live	Shelter	(3) 8917	'73	†
	DCC	(2) 8012		CS/CD
Hank Wilson's Back	Shelter	8923	'73	†
	Shelter	2131	'75	†
	Shelter	52014		†
	Shelter	8009		CS/CD
Stop All That Jazz	Shelter	2108	'74	†
	Shelter	52016		†
	Shelter	8011		CS/CD
Will o' the Wisp	Shelter	2138	'75	†
	Shelter	52020		†
	Shelter	8007		CS/CD
Best	Shelter	52004	'76	†
	Shelter	8017		CS/CD
Americana	Paradise	3172	'78	†
Live and Love	Paradise	3341	'79	†
Solid State	Paradise		'84	†
Hank Wilson, Volume II	Paradise		'84	†
Anything Can Happen	Virgin	91821	'92	CS/CD†
	Virgin	86265		CS/CD

Mary McCreary

Butterflies in Heaven	MCA	347	'73	†

Jezebel	Shelter	2110	'74	†
	Shelter	52027	'77	†
Heart of Fire	Paradise	3292	'79	†
Leon and Mary Russell				
Wedding Album	Paradise	2943	'76	†
Make Love to the Music	Paradise	3066	'77	†
Leon Russell and Willie Nelson				
One for the Road	Columbia	(2) 36064	'79	†
	Columbia	36064		CS/CD
Leon Russell and the New Grass Revival				
Live Album	Paradise	3532	'81	†

S

DOUG SAHM

THE SIR DOUGLAS QUINTET. Doug Sahm (b. Nov. 6, 1941, San Antonio, TX), gtr, fdl, voc;
Augie Meyer (b. May 31, 1940, San Antonio, TX), org; **Francisco "Frank" Morin** (b. Aug. 13,
1946), horns; **Harvey Kagan** (b. Apr. 18, 1946), bs; **John Perez** (b. Nov. 8, 1942), drm

In one of the stranger odysseys in the history of rock music, Doug Sahm started his career
as a country-music prodigy at age six, switched to rock and roll during the mid-'50s with
the Knights, and eventually formed the British-sounding Sir Douglas Quintet in 1964 with
organist Augie Meyer, hitting with "She's About a Mover" in 1965. He later introduced Tex-
Mex accordionist Flaco Jimenez to rock audiences, and he eventually formed the Texas Tornados in 1989 with Jimenez, vocalist Freddy Fender, and Augie Meyer. Along with Los
Lobos, the Texas Tornados helped popularize Tex-Mex music in the '90s, but Sahm left the
group in 1994 to re-form the Sir Douglas Quintet with two of his sons.

Doug Sahm began singing at age five and took up pedal steel guitar at six. He soon began making personal appearances with Webb Pierce and Faron Young, becoming a featured
player on the *Louisiana Hayride* country radio program by age eight. Making his first recordings around age 11, he switched to rock and roll in 1955 when he formed the Knights. The
group achieved several local hits through 1962.

In late 1964 Doug Sahm assembled the Sir Douglas Quintet with organist Augie Meyer.
Traveling to Houston to record for Huey Meaux, the group scored a major hit with Sahm's
"She's About a Mover" in 1965, followed by the moderate hit "The Rains Came" and the
oddly titled debut album *The Best of the Sir Douglas Quintet*. Meaux hoped to mask their
Texas identities by giving them a British-sounding name and obscuring their faces in a
dimly lit cover shot for the album! The band subsequently moved to San Francisco without
Meyer, recording *Honkey Blues* for Smash Records. Rejoined by Meyer, they recorded *Mendocino* for Smash, hitting with Sahm's title song. They then recorded two eclectic albums of
country, Tex-Mex, blues, and rock songs before Sahm disbanded the group and returned to
San Antonio.

Moving to Austin in late 1972, Doug Sahm switched to Atlantic Records for *Doug Sahm
and His Band* and *Texas Tornado*. Recorded with stellar backing musicians, including Bob Dylan, Doctor John, and Tex-Mex accordionist Flaco Jimenez, the sessions featured Sahm's
"Texas Tornado," Dylan's "Wallflower," and "(Is Anybody Going to) San Antone," released as
a single. Sahm switched to Warner Bros. for 1974's *Groover's Paradise*, recorded with Stu
Cook and Doug Clifford of Creedence Clearwater Revival. Sahm reunited the Sir Douglas
Quintet in 1977 to record *Live Love* for Meyer's Texas Re-Cord label, and he eventually
joined John Fahey's Takoma label at the beginning of the '80s. Sahm toured through the
decade both as a solo act and with various backup bands, often reviving the name of the
Quintet, even if no other original members were on board.

In 1989 Doug Sahm toured with blues singer Angela Strehli as Antone's Texas R&B Revue, with Flaco Jimenez as special guest. Later in the year he performed in San Francisco with Jimenez, Augie Meyer, and country singer Freddy Fender. Fender, although Mexican-American by birth, had scored top country and smash pop hits with "Before the Next Teardrop Falls" and "Wasted Days and Wasted Nights" in 1975 before his career faded. Jimenez had been playing Tex-Mex music on accordion for nearly 35 years. As the Texas Tornados, the group signed with Reprise Records and recorded three albums that sold quite well and helped popularize Tex-Mex music. However, in 1994 Doug Sahm re-formed the Sir Douglas Quintet with sons Shawn and Shandon to record *Day Dreaming at Midnight*.

Sir Douglas Quintet

The Best of the Sir Douglas Quintet	Tribe	47001	'66	†
Honkey Blues	Smash	67108	'68	†
Mendocino	Smash	67115	'69	†
Together After Five	Smash	67130	'70	†
1 + 1 + 1 = 4	Philips	600344	'70	†
Rough Edges	Mercury	655	'73	†
Texas Tornado	Atlantic	7287	'73	†
Live Love	Texas Re-Cord	1007	'78	†
Best	Takoma	7086	'80	†
Border Wave	Takoma	7088	'81	†
Quintessence	Varrick	004	'83	LP/CS
Day Dreaming at Midnight	Elektra/Nonesuch	61474	'94	CS/CD

Doug Sahm

The Return of Doug Saldana	Philips	600383	'71	†
Doug Sahm and His Band	Atlantic	7254	'73		
The Best of Doug Sahm's Atlantic Sessions	Rhino	71032	'92	CS/CD
Groover's Paradise	Warner Bros.	2810	'74	†
The Best of Doug Sahm and the Sir Douglas Quintet (1968–1975)	Mercury	846586	'90	CD
Hell of a Spell	Takoma	7075	'80	†
Juke Box Music	Antone's	0008	'89	LP/CS/CD

The Texas Tornados

The Texas Tornados	Reprise	26251	'90	CS/CD
Los Texas Tornados	Reprise	26472	'91	LP/CS/CD
Zone of Our Own	Reprise	26683	'91	CS/CD
Hangin' by a Thread	Reprise	45058	'92	CS/CD
Best	Reprise	45511	'94	CS/CD

SAM AND DAVE

Sam Moore (b. Oct. 12, 1935, Miami, FL); **Dave Prater** (b. May 9, 1937, Ocilla, GA; d. Apr. 9, 1988, near Sycamore, GA)

One of the most exciting live soul acts of the '60s, Sam and Dave scored hits with the soul classics "Hold On! I'm Comin'" and "Soul Man" in 1966–1967. Working with producer-songwriters Isaac Hayes and Dave Porter and backed by Booker T. and the MGs and the Memphis Horns, Sam and Dave provided a raw, dynamic sound that typified that of Stax Records. Sam and Dave broke up in 1969 and reunited from 1975 to 1981, enjoying renewed popularity as a result of the Blues Brothers' 1978 hit recording of "Soul Man."

SAM AND DAVE

Sam Moore was a member of the gospel group the Melionaires before pursuing a secular career in Miami, where he met Dave Prater around 1958. The two teamed up as a duet and recorded for Roulette Records in the early '60s, with little success. Switching to the Memphis-based Stax label in 1965, the duo was placed with songwriter-producers Isaac Hayes and Dave Porter, who wrote virtually all of their hits. Usually recording with Hayes on piano and backed by Booker T. and the MGs and the raw-sounding Memphis Horns, Sam and Dave scored a smash R&B hit with "You Don't Know Like I Know" at the beginning of 1966. Their Stax classic "Hold On! I'm Comin'" became a top R&B and major pop hit, followed by the R&B smashes "Said I Wasn't Gonna Tell Nobody," "You Got Me Hummin'," and "When Something Is Wrong with My Baby." They later scored pop and R&B smashes with the classic "Soul Man" and "Thank You," but in 1968 Stax/Volt Records was sold. The duo was as famous for their high-energy stage show, featuring a mixture of James Brown—like moves and gospelesque shouting, as they were for their recordings.

Sam and Dave moved to Atlantic Records in 1968, where their success was largely restricted to the R&B field, most notably with "You Don't Know What You Mean to Me" and "Soul Sister, Brown Sugar." They broke up acrimoniously in 1970 but reunited for 1975's *Back At 'Cha* and toured through 1981, inspired by the popularity of the Blues Brothers' film and recordings. However, they soon fell to squabbling again, and Dave took to touring with a new Sam, vocalist Sam Daniels. Dave Prater was killed in an automobile accident near Sycamore, Georgia, on April 9, 1988. Sam Moore appeared in the 1988 movie *Tapeheads* with Junior Walker. Sam and Dave were inducted into the Rock and Roll Hall of Fame in 1992.

Sam and Dave

Sam and Dave	Roulette	25323	'67	†
Hold On! I'm Comin'	Stax	708	'66	†
	Atlantic	80255	'91	CS/CD
Double Dynamite	Stax	712	'67	†
	Atlantic	80305	'91	CS/CD
Soul Men	Stax	725	'67	†
	Atlantic	81718	'87	CS†
	Rhino	70296	'92	CS/CD
I Thank You	Atlantic	8205	'68	†
	Rhino	71012	'92	CS/CD

Best	Atlantic	8218	'69	CS
Best	Atlantic	81279	'85	CS/CD
Greatest Songs	Curb/Atlantic	77740	'95	CS/CD
Back At 'Cha	United Artists	524	'75	†
The Best Soul	Sound	920	'91	CD
Soothe Me	Rhino	71232	'93	CS/CD
Sweat 'n' Soul: Anthology	Rhino	(2) 71253	'93	CS/CD
Very Best	Rhino	71871	'95	CS/CD
The Soul of Sam and Dave	Dominion	408		CS/CD
Sweet and Funky Gold	Hollywood/IMG	188		CS/CD

SANTANA

Carlos Santana (b. July 20, 1947, Autlán de Navarro, Jalisco, Mexico), lead gtr, voc; **Gregg Rolie** (b. June 17, 1947, Seattle, WA), kybd, voc; **David Brown** (b. Feb. 15, 1947, NY) bs; **Mike Carabello** (b. Nov. 18, 1947, San Francisco, CA), congas, perc; **Jose "Chepito" Areas** (b. July 25, 1946, Léon, Nicaragua), timbales, perc [Drummer **Michael Shrieve** (b. July 6, 1949, San Francisco, CA) added in 1969. Later members include guitarist **Neal Schon** (b. Feb. 27, 1954); **Armando Peraza** on timbales and percussion; keyboardists **Tom Coster** and **Chester Thompson**; drummers **Leon "Ndugu" Chancler** and **Graham Lear**; **Raul Rekow**, congas; bassists **Alphonso Johnson** and **Benny Reitveld**; and lead vocalists **Leon Patillo**, **Greg Walker**, **Alex Ligertwood**, and **Buddy Miles**. Gregg Rolie and Neal Schon formed Journey in 1973.]

One of the few unknown groups to appear at 1969's Woodstock Festival, Santana was immediately launched into international prominence with their landmark debut album. Showcasing the stunning lead-guitar playing of Carlos Santana, generally regarded as one of the most intensely emotional and technically disciplined rock guitarists, Santana prominently featured virtuoso Latin percussionists who propelled the group's sound. The success of Santana's first three albums spawned a number of less auspicious imitators and fostered the adoption of Latin, African, and exotic percussion instruments by soul, rock, and jazz groups. Touring more extensively than perhaps any other rock band, Santana became the most popular American band in the world by playing engagements on virtually every continent. However, beginning in 1972, Carlos Santana started recording outside the band, most notably with Buddy Miles and John McLaughlin, and with the 1975 departure of drummer Michael Shrieve, he became the only original member to still play in the band. With varying personnel, Santana continued to record best-selling albums of Latin-style rock through the '80s. In 1994 the most stellar lineup of Santana, minus bassist David Brown and guitarist Carlos Santana, regrouped to form Abraxas, while Carlos Santana recorded *The Santana Brothers* with brother Jorge.

Encouraged to learn violin by his father at age five, Carlos Santana moved with his family to Tijuana, Mexico, in 1952. He discovered guitar at age eight and emigrated with his family to San Francisco in 1962. After high school graduation, Santana moved back to Tijuana to play local bars and clubs for two years, then returned to San Francisco in 1966. He soon formed the Santana Blues Band with keyboardist Gregg Rolie and bassist David Brown to play local engagements, including the Fillmore Auditorium. He gained his first recognition as a guest guitarist on *The Live Adventures of Mike Bloomfield and Al Kooper*. Santana began exploring Latin and African rhythms in his music with the 1969 additions of conga player Mike Carabello, timbales player Jose "Chepito" Areas, and drummer Michael Shrieve. The group's name was subsequently shortened to Santana.

CARLOS SANTANA

At the Woodstock Festival in August 1969, Santana electrified the crowd with a stunning extended performance of the band's "Soul Sacrifice," featuring one of the most famous drum solos in the history of rock by Michael Shrieve. Signed to Columbia Records, Santana's debut album came out barely a month after Woodstock. It featured layers of exotic percussion and Carlos Santana's passionate lead-guitar playing (replete with his signature sustained-note style) and became an instant success, staying on the album charts for more than two years. The album included "Soul Sacrifice," a minor hit version of Olatunji's "Jingo," and the near-smash hit "Evil Ways." *Abraxas*, usually regarded as their finest work, yielded a smash hit with Peter Green's "Black Magic Woman" and a major hit with Tito Puente's "Oye Como Va," while containing Carlos's own "Samba Pa Ti." For their third album, variously referred to as *New Album* and *Santana III*, the group added guitarist Neal Schon. The album produced a major hit with "Everybody's Everything" and a moderate hit with "No One to Depend On."

Internal disputes within Santana had become rife in 1971 and the group disbanded for a time in 1972. In the meantime, Carlos Santana recorded a best-selling live album with powerhouse drummer-vocalist Buddy Miles from the Electric Flag. Santana formed a new edition of the group in fall 1972, by which time he had embraced the teachings of guru Sri Chinmoy and taken on the spiritual name Devadip. The new group's lineup included holdovers Neal Schon, Gregg Rolie, Chepito Areas, and Michael Shrieve, plus keyboardist Tom Coster and aging Latin percussionist Armando Peraza, among others. Shrieve had introduced Carlos Santana to the music of Miles Davis and John Coltrane, and this aggregation recorded Santana's first departure from Latin-style rock, *Caravanserai*, which revealed a decided jazz orientation. Gregg Rolie and Neal Schon subsequently departed to form Journey with bassist Ross Valory and well-traveled session drummer Aynsley Dunbar.

In 1973 Carlos Santana recorded *Love, Devotion, Surrender* and toured with guitarist "Mahavishnu" John McLaughlin, the man who had introduced him to the philosophy of Sri Chinmoy. Santana later recorded *Illuminations* with fellow devotee "Turiya" Alice Coltrane, the keyboard and harp-playing widow of jazz saxophonist John Coltrane. Santana the group's next album, *Welcome*, recorded with jazz vocalist Leon Thomas, continued to exhibit the group leader's spiritual bent and jazz orientation. Yet another edition of the band, with vocalist Leon Patillo and drummers Michael Shrieve and Leon "Ndugu" Chancler (Shrieve's subsequent replacement), recorded *Borboletta*. During 1975 Santana, rejoined by original bassist David Brown, toured the United States with Eric Clapton, and at midyear impresario Bill Graham became the group's manager.

Eventually, in 1976 Santana returned to its Latin-style sound with the highly acclaimed *Amigos* album, which featured "Europa," "Dance, Sister, Dance," and "Gitaro." The members included Tom Coster (utilizing synthesizer for the first time), vocalist Greg Walker, Armando Peraza, and Leon Chancler. Walker, Peraza, and Chancler left before the release of *Festival*, but Walker and Chepito Areas returned for the double-record set *Moonflower*, along with newcomers Raul Rekow (congas) and Graham Lear (drm). The live album yielded a major hit with a cover version of the Zombies' "She's Not There," and a follow-up studio work, *Inner Secrets*, provided hits with cover versions of Buddy Holly's "Well All Right" and the Classics IV's "Stormy." In 1979 Carlos Santana issued the solo album *Oneness: Silver Dreams—Golden Reality*, as Walker and Coster departed the group. *Marathon* featured new vocalist Alex Ligertwood and yielded a moderate hit with "You Know That I Love You." By early 1980 Santana included Ligertwood, Armando Peraza, Graham Lear, and Raul Rekow, among others. During the year Carlos Santana recorded *The Swing of Delight* with jazz musicians Herbie Hancock, Wayne Shorter, and Ron Carter.

Drummer Michael Shrieve left Santana in 1975 and formed Automatic Man with guitarist Pat Thrall (later with Asia), only to depart the group after a single album. He soon joined the multitalented Japanese artist Stomu Yamashta for his *Go* series of albums. Yamashta, a percussionist with the Osaka Philharmonic during the early '60s and composer of the score for Akira Kurosawa's movie *Yojimbo*, had led the extraordinary Red Buddha Theater troupe and the jazz-rock group East Wind. For the first album of the trilogy, Yamashta assembled Shrieve, Stevie Winwood, and electronics and synthesizer wizard Klaus Schulze to perform his original compositions. All three *Go* albums were astounding in their synthesis of rock, jazz, electronics, and Eastern music. During the '80s Shrieve formed Novo Combo, played in the short-lived group HSAS with Sammy Hagar, Neal Schon, and Kenny Aaronson, and recorded albums with synthesizer player Steve Roach and drummer David Beal, issuing his first album as a group leader, *Stiletto*, in 1989. The group included keyboardist Mark Isham and guitarists David Torn and Andy Summers (formerly of the Police).

Meanwhile, Santana the group scored a major hit with Russ Ballard's "Winning" and a minor hit with J. J. Cale's "The Sensitive Kind" from 1981's *Zebop!*, the band's last album to sell in mass quantities. They managed their final major hit in 1982 with "Hold On" from *Shango*. Carlos next recorded the diverse solo album *Havana Moon* with Booker T. Jones, the Fabulous Thunderbirds, and Willie Nelson, who sang lead vocals on "They All Went to Mexico." Santana began playing Nevada casinos in 1984, by which time the group included vocalist Greg Walker and Alex Ligertwood, drummer Graham Lear, and later mainstays Chester Thompson (kybd) and Alphonso Johnson (bs). Buddy Miles joined the group for the 1987 album *Freedom* and the subsequent tour. After the *Blues for Salvador* album and tour, Carlos Santana toured the United States and Europe with jazz saxophonist Wayne Shorter.

During 1988 veteran Santana members Carlos Santana, Gregg Rolie, Chepito Areas, and Michael Shrieve reunited, joined by Armando Peraza, Chester Thompson, and Alphonso Johnson, for a tour, but a promised reunion album was never recorded and they soon went their separate ways. During the '90s the group Santana recorded two more albums and toured with Bob Dylan, while Carlos Santana formed his own record label, Guts and Grace Records. In 1994 many of the original members of Santana reunited without Carlos Santana to form Abraxas, including Gregg Rolie, Neal Schon, Michael Carabello, Chepito Areas, and Michael Shrieve (augmented by bassist Ross Vallory). Also in 1994, Island Records issued *The Santana Brothers*, recorded by Carlos, his brother Jorge Santana, and his nephew Carlos Hernandez.

Santana

Santana				
	Columbia	9781	'69	CD
	Columbia	00692		CS
	Columbia/Legacy	64212	'94	CD

Abraxas	Columbia	30130	'70	†
	Columbia	30130	'85	CS/CD
	Mobile Fidelity	552	'91	CD
Santana III	Columbia	30595	'71	CS/CD
Caravanserai	Columbia	31610	'72	CS/CD
Welcome	Columbia	32445	'73	CS
Greatest Hits	Columbia	33050	'74/'84	CS/CD
Borboletta	Columbia	33135	'74	CS/CD
Amigos	Columbia	33576	'76	CS/CD
Festival	Columbia	34423	'76/'90	CS/CD
Moonflower	Columbia	(2) 34914	'77	†
	Columbia	34914		CS/CD
Inner Secrets	Columbia	35600	'78	CS/CD
Marathon	Columbia	36154	'79	CS/CD
Zebop!	Columbia	37158	'81/'84	CS/CD
Shango	Columbia	38122	'82	CS/CD
Beyond Appearances	Columbia	39527	'85	CS/CD
Freedom	Columbia	40272	'87	CS/CD
Viva Santana!	Columbia	(2) 44344	'88	CS/CD
Spirits Dancing in the Flesh	Columbia	46065	'90	CS/CD
Lotus	Columbia	(2) 46764	'91	CS/CD
Milagro	Polydor	513197	'92	CS/CD
Sacred Fire: Live in South America	Polydor	521082	'93	CS/CD
The Sound of Carlos Santana	Pair	1246		CS/CD
Doin' It	Pair	1286	'90	CS/CD
Early Magic!	Special Music	4809		CS/CD
Soul Sacrifice	Special Music	4821		CS/CD

Carlos Santana and Buddy Miles

Live!	Columbia	31308	'72	CS
	Columbia/Legacy	66416	'94	CD

Carlos Santana and Mahavishnu John McLaughlin

Love, Devotion, Surrender	Columbia	32034	'73	CS/CD

Devadip Carlos Santana and Turiya Alice Coltrane

Illuminations	Columbia	32900	'74	†

Carlos Santana

Oneness/Silver Dreams—Golden Reality	Columbia	35686	'79	†
The Swing of Delight	Columbia	(2) 36590	'80	†
	Columbia	36590	'90	CD
Havana Moon	Columbia	38642	'83	CS/CD
Blues for Salvador	Columbia	40875	'87	CS/CD

The Santana Brothers

Brothers	Island	523677	'94	CS/CD

Automatic Man (with Michael Shrieve)

Automatic Man	Island	9397	'76	†
	Antilles	7057		LP

Stomu Yamashta's Go (with Michael Shrieve)

Go	Island	9358	'76	†
	Island	9387		†

Go Too	Arista	4138	'77	†
	One Way	26785		CD
Go Live from Paris	Island	(2) 10	'78	

Novo Combo (with Michael Shrieve)

Novo Combo	Polydor	6331	'81	†
The Animation Generation	Polydor	6356	'82	†

Hagar, Schon, Aaronson, Shrieve

Through the Fire	Geffen	4023	'84	LP/CS/CD

Michael Shrieve

Transfer Station Blue	Fortuna	17023	'87	LP/CS/CD
Stiletto	Novus	3050	'89	CS/CD

Michael Shrieve and Steve Roach

The Leaving Time	Novus	3032	'88	LP/CS/CD†

Michael Shrieve and David Beal

The Big Picture	Fortuna	17060	'89	LP/CS/CD

BOZ SCAGGS
(b. William Royce Scaggs, June 8, 1944, OH)

Gaining his first recognition as guitarist and vocalist on Steve Miller's first two late-'60s albums, Boz Scaggs debuted solo in 1969 with his self-titled album, an overlooked blues classic recorded in Muscle Shoals, Alabama, with Duane Allman. Becoming a major star in his adopted hometown of San Francisco in the early '70s, Scaggs broke through as an album artist with 1974's *Slow Dancer*. Adopting a sophisticated soul-style sound, he was established nationally with 1976's *Silk Degrees* album and its four hit singles. Scoring four major hits again in 1980, Scaggs withdrew from recording and touring in 1981. Scaggs eventually issued new, modest-selling albums, in 1988 and 1994.

William "Boz" Scaggs grew up in Oklahoma and Texas, met Steve Miller at age 15 in a Dallas-area high school, and soon accepted Miller's offer to join his band, The Marksmen, as vocalist. He learned rhythm guitar from Miller, who moved to Wisconsin to attend the University of Wisconsin at Madison, a year before Scaggs's graduation. Scaggs followed Miller to the university the following year and joined Miller's band, The Ardells, before returning to Texas in 1963, where he formed his own band, The Wigs. In 1964 Scaggs traveled to England and decided to stay in Europe, singing on the streets of European cities and eventually establishing Stockholm as his base. Around 1966 he recorded a blues and folk-style album, *Boz*, that was issued in Europe only. Summoned by Steve Miller in 1967, Scaggs moved to San Francisco, where he joined Miller's band during the heyday of psychedelia and appeared on *Children of the Future* and *Sailor*, two of Miller's most highly regarded albums, before departing in August 1968.

Signed to Atlantic Records, Boz Scaggs's solo debut was arguably his finest work. Produced with engineer Marlin Greene and *Rolling Stone* editor Jann Wenner, the album was recorded in Muscle Shoals, Alabama, with the able assistance of keyboardist Barry Beckett and guitarist Duane Allman. It featured the 13-minute "Loan Me a Dime" and included "I'll Be Long Gone," "Sweet Release," and early country artist Jimmie Rodgers's "Waiting for a

Train." After returning to San Francisco permanently in 1970, Scaggs switched to Columbia Records for recordings in a less bluesy, more pop-oriented vein. *Moments*, recorded in San Francisco, yielded two minor hits with "We Were Always Sweethearts" and "Near You," but the follow-up, *Boz Scaggs and Band*, largely recorded in London, failed to produce a hit, although it did contain the favorite "Runnin' Blue." *My Time*, partially recorded in Muscle Shoals, produced the minor hit "Dinah Flo," but Scaggs was not to register another hit for four years.

Employing veteran Motown producer Johnny Bristol and utilizing studio musicians exclusively, Boz Scaggs recorded *Slow Dancer* in an orchestrated soul style. The album, often regarded as his finest later effort, includes "Angel Lady," "You Make It So Hard (To Say No)," and Bristol's "I've Got Your Number." Scaggs debuted the album in March 1974 at Oakland's Paramount Theater in a first-of-its-kind "black tie optional" setting, lavishly staging the event with a 27-piece orchestra and formally attired rock band, which included guitarist Les Dudek. Scaggs retained the format for Bay Area New Year's Eve shows in 1974, 1975, and 1976.

Boz Scaggs fully embraced a sophisticated soul and disco-tinged style for 1976's *Silk Degrees*. The album finally established him nationally, yielding the moderate hits "It's Over" and "What Can I Say" as well as the smash hit "Lowdown" and the near-smash "Lido Shuffle." It also included Scaggs's "We're All Alone Now," a top easy-listening and smash pop hit for Rita Coolidge in 1977. However, the album's phenomenal success overshadowed Scaggs's subsequent work. The equivocal *Down Two, Then Left* produced minor hits with "Hard Times" and "Hollywood," whereas *Middle Man* yielded major hits with "Breakdown Dead Ahead" and "Jojo," both cowritten with producer David Foster. In 1980 Scaggs scored major hits with "Look What You've Done to Me," from the movie *Urban Cowboy*, and "Miss Sun."

In 1981 Boz Scaggs ceased recording and began limiting live performances to Bay Area benefits and Japan, where his records had sold spectacularly. In 1984 he opened the restaurant Blue Light Cafe in San Francisco, later opening one of San Francisco's most daring and prominent nightclubs, Slim's, in 1988. He also released his first album of new material in eight years, but the sophisticated *Other Roads* produced only a moderate hit with the ballad "Heart of Mine." With the expiration of his Columbia contract, Boz Scaggs switched to Virgin Records for the rather sparse album *Some Change* in 1994, and conducted his first American concert tour in 14 years.

Boz Scaggs

Boz Scaggs	Atlantic	8239	'69	†
	Atlantic	19166	'78	CS/CD
Moments	Columbia	30454	'71	CS/CD†
Boz Scaggs and Band	Columbia	30796	'71	CD†
My Time	Columbia	31384	'72	CS/CD†
Slow Dancer	Columbia	32760	'74	CS/CD
Silk Degrees	Columbia	33920	'76/'85	CS/CD
	Columbia/Legacy	64420	'94	CD
	Mobile Fidelity	535	'90	CD
Silk Degrees/Slow Dancer	Columbia	38383	'86	CS
Down Two, Then Left	Columbia	34729	'77	CD
Middle Man	Columbia	36106	'80	CS/CD†
Hits!	Columbia	36841	'80	CS/CD
Other Roads	Columbia	40463	'88	CS/CD
Some Change	Virgin	39489	'94	CS/CD

NEIL SEDAKA

(b. March 13, 1939, Brooklyn, NY)

The composer of (at least) a thousand songs, Neil Sedaka scored a series of pop-style hit singles between 1959 and 1963 with songs coauthored with Howard Greenfield, his lyricist until 1973. The hits included "Oh! Carol," written for Carole King while working at New York's famed Brill Building under Don Kirshner, and "Breaking Up Is Hard to Do," perhaps his finest song. Sedaka ceased live performances after his popularity faded with the advent of the British Invasion, yet he continued to write songs. In the early '70s, encouraged by the enormous success of Carole King's *Tapestry*, Sedaka successfully made a comeback, first in Great Britain and then in the United States, on Elton John's Rocket label, scoring top pop hits with "Laughter in the Rain" and "Bad Blood." Although his careful mixture of early and recent material worked well on television and the cabaret circuit, Neil Sedaka has not had a major hit since 1980's "Should've Never Let You Go," recorded with his daughter Dara.

Extensively trained in the classics on piano from the age of eight, Neil Sedaka graduated from the famed Juilliard School of Music. He wrote his first song with 16-year-old Brooklyn buddy Howard "Howie" Greenfield when he was 13. Sedaka was a member of the Tokens from 1955 to 1958, years before the group scored a top hit with "The Lion Sleeps Tonight." He and Greenfield became professional songwriters at Al Nevins and Don Kirshner's Aldon Publishing Company, housed in New York's Brill Building, where Carole King, Gerry Goffin, Barry Mann, and Cynthia Weil also worked. Sedaka and Greenfield's first songwriting success came in summer 1958, when Connie Francis had a major hit with their "Stupid Cupid." They later provided her with "Where the Boys Are," and Greenfield coauthored her hits "Everybody's Somebody's Fool," "My Heart Has a Mind of Its Own," and "Breakin' in a Brand New Broken Heart."

Neil Sedaka signed his own recording contract with RCA Records and soon achieved a major hit with "The Diary" at the end of 1958. Over the next four years he regularly scored major hits with Greenfield collaborations such as "Oh! Carol," written for Carole King; "Stairway to Heaven" and "Calendar Girl" (both near-smash hits); "Little Devil"; "Happy Birthday, Sweet Sixteen"; the classic "Breaking Up Is Hard to Do" (a top hit); and "Next Door to an Angel." Sedaka achieved his last moderate hits for more than 10 years with "Alice in Wonderland," "Let's Go Steady Again," and "Bad Girl" in 1963. He subsequently ceased live performances, yet he continued to write hit songs, such as "Working on a Groovy Thing" and "Puppet Man" for the Fifth Dimension.

Neil Sedaka moved to England in 1970. Buoyed by the 1971 success of Carole King's *Tapestry*, he attempted a comeback on mentor Don Kirsher's Kirshner label with 1971's *Emergence*, which he regarded as his best album. It failed to sell in the United States, but he nonetheless encountered success in Great Britain, returning to live performance at London's Royal Albert Hall. After a second Kirshner album, *Solitaire*, Sedaka recorded the British-only album *The Tra-La Days Are Over*, with a group called Hot Legs, which later became 10cc. Unsigned to an American record company at the time, he recorded two more British albums and was signed by Elton John to his newly formed Rocket label. Sedaka's first Rocket album, *Sedaka's Back*, compiled songs from his three British albums and produced three American hits, the top "Laughter in the Rain," written with new lyricist Phil Cody, and the major "The Immigrant" (dedicated to John Lennon) and "That's When the Music Takes Me."

In 1975 the Captain and Tenille scored a top hit with Neil Sedaka and Howie Greenfield's "Love Will Keep Us Together," and the Carpenters achieved a major hit with Sedaka and Phil Cody's "Solitaire." Sedaka's *The Hungry Years* yielded a top hit with "Bad Blood," recorded with Elton John and cowritten with Cody, and a near-smash with an engaging, slowed-down version of "Breaking Up Is Hard to Do." Sedaka subsequently scored a major hit with "Love in the Shadows" and a moderate hit with "Steppin' Out" on Rocket and starred in his first American television special in 1976. However, he switched to Elektra Records in 1977 and managed his last (major) hit in 1980 with "Should've Never Let You Go," recorded with his daughter Dara. *My Friend* compiled recordings he made between 1974 and 1980.

Neil Sedaka has since been relegated to the oldies circuit; Howie Greenfield died in Los Angeles on March 4, 1986, at age 49.

Neil Sedaka

Neil Sedaka	RCA	2035	'59	†
Circulate	RCA	2317	'61	†
Little Devil and Other Hits	RCA	2421	'61	†
Italiano	RCA	10140	'64	†
Live in Australia	RCA	1540	'76	†
Emergence	Kirshner	111	'71	†
	RCA	1789	'76	†
Solitaire	Kirshner	117	'72	†
	RCA	1790	'76	†
Sedaka's Back	MCA/Rocket	463	'74	†
	Rocket	3046	'75	†
The Hungry Years	Rocket	2157	'75	†
Steppin' Out	Rocket	2195	'76	†
	Rocket	3049	'78	†
A Song	Elektra	102	'77	†
All You Need Is Music	Elektra	161	'78	†
In the Pocket	Elektra	259	'80	†
Now	Elektra	348	'81	†
Superbird	Quicksilver		'83	†
	Intermedia	5015		LP/CS
Come See About Me	MCA	5466	'84	†
Tuneweaver	Varese Sarabande	5549	'95	CD

Anthologies

Sings His Greatest Hits	RCA	2627	'62	†
	RCA	0928	'75	†
	RCA	3465		CS
	RCA	53465	'92	CD
Oh! Carol and Other Hits	RCA	0879	'75	†
	RCA	2088	'90	CS
Pure Gold	RCA	1314	'76	†
'50s and '60s	RCA	2254	'77	†
Many Sides	RCA	2524	'78	†
All Time Greatest Hits	RCA	6876	'88	CS/CD
All Time Greatest Hits, Volume 2	RCA	2406	'91	CS/CD
Oh! Carol and Other Big Hits	RCA-Camden	2701		CS/CD
My Friend (recorded 1974–1980)	Polydor	(2) 831235	'86	LP/CS/CD†
	Polydor	831235		CS
Singer, Songwriter, Melody Maker	Accord	7152	'81	†
Neil Sedaka's Diary	Pair	1283	'91	CS/CD†
Greatest Hits Live	K-tel	3083	'92	CS/CD
Laughter in the Rain: The Best of Neil Sedaka	Varese Sarabande	5539	'94	CS/CD

BOB SEGER

(b. May 6, 1945, Dearborn, MI)

THE SILVER BULLET BAND. Bob Seger, gtr, voc; **Andrew "Drew" Abbott**, gtr; **Robyn Robbins**, kybd; **Alto Reed**, sax; **Chris Campbell**, bs; **Charlie Allen Martin**, drm [Later members include keyboardist **Craig Frost** and drummers **Don Brewer** and **David Teegarden**.]

A regional star of the South and Midwest since the late '60s, Bob Seger labored for nearly a decade before gaining his first national recognition with 1976's *Live Bullet*, sometimes regarded as one of the finest live rock albums ever made. Established nationally with *Night Moves* and its three hit singles, Seger provided songs reflecting and celebrating the working-class American experience and served as model for later populists such as Bruce Springsteen and John Mellencamp, although he never enjoyed Springsteen's status as a critics's favorite. Like Springsteen, Seger remained committed to the idea that rock could function as a force to improve the quality of life. Astutely mixing original high-energy songs in the classic rock-and-roll mode and poignant, intelligent, and personal ballads, Seger's albums from 1976 to 1981 sold millions of copies. As a low-profile rock star, Bob Seger toured infrequently in the '80s and not at all in the '90s yet continued to record popular albums that maintained both his integrity and his artistry.

Bob Seger took up ukulele at age five and later learned guitar and piano. At age six he moved with his family to Ann Arbor, Michigan, where he grew up. While still in high school he began playing local lounges and teen clubs with the three-piece band the Decibels. After high school, Seger joined the Town Criers and met Eddie Andrews, recording his first single, "East Side Story," for Andrews's Hideout label in 1966. It was a local success, as were its follow-ups, "Persecution Smith" and "Heavy Music," which led to a Capitol Records recording contract in 1968. He assembled the Bob Seger System and scored a major national hit in 1970 with "Ramblin' Gamblin' Man." None of the group's three albums sold particularly well outside the Detroit region, so Seger disbanded the group and recorded the solo album *Brand New Morning* with acoustic instruments.

Subsequently recording for Eddie Andrews's Palladium label (distributed nationally by Reprise), Seger assembled the nucleus of his Silver Bullet Band around guitarist Andrew "Drew" Abbott and bassist Chris Campbell. With Abbott taking over on lead guitar, Seger was able to concentrate on his gruff, raspy style of singing. The album *Seven* revealed his developing talent as a songwriter and yielded a minor hit with the hard-driving "Get Out of Denver." Returning to Capitol Records, Seger and his band toured the nation extensively in 1974 and 1975 and recorded *Beautiful Loser*. The album included the powerful title song as well as the ballad "Jody Girl," "Travelin' Man," and the moderate hit "Katmandu," and sold more copies than the combined total sales of Seger's first seven albums.

Adding saxophonist Alto Reed and new keyboardist Robyn Robbins, Bob Seger and the Silver Bullet Band recorded *Live Bullet* in Detroit. The album included many of his regional hits, such as "Heavy Music" and "Lookin' Back," reprised his national hits "Ramblin' Gamblin' Man," "Get Out of Denver," and "Katmandu," and yielded a minor hit with a remake of Ike and Tina Turner's 1973 hit "Nutbush City Limits." It remained on the album charts for more than three years.

Finally, after 10 years of modest success, Bob Seger became established nationally with 1976's *Night Moves*, hailed as one of the finest albums of the '70s. The album yielded a smash hit with the title cut, a major hit with "Mainstreet," and a moderate hit with the hard-charging "Rock and Roll Never Forgets." In 1977 drummer David Teegarden, an associate of Seger's from the early '70s and a former member of Teegarden and Van Winkle, joined the Silver Bullet Band. Recorded with the Muscle Shoals Rhythm Section, *Stranger in Town* contained "Feel Like a Number" and produced a smash hit with "Still the Same" and major hits with "Hollywood Nights," "We've Got Tonite" (a smash pop and top country hit for Kenny Rogers and Sheena Easton in 1983), and "Old Time Rock & Roll." Seger subsequently cowrote the Eagles' top hit "Heartache Tonight" with Don Henley, Glenn Frey, and J. D. Souther. Keyboardist Robyn Robbins left Seger's band in 1979 and was replaced with Craig Frost, a former member of Grand Funk Railroad.

Bob Seger's next album, *Against the Wind*, included the favorite "Betty Lou's Gettin' Out Tonight" and yielded four hits, the smashes "Fire Lake" and the title cut, the major hit "You'll Accomp'ny Me," and the moderate hit "Horizontal Bop." Criticized as commercial, the album was Seger's last album to sell multimillion copies. The band toured extensively in 1980 and the tour produced the live double-record set *Nine Tonight*, producing a smash hit with "Tryin' to Live My Life Without You" and a moderate hit with "Feel Like a Number." Their next tour and album did not come until 1983, by which time Seger had dismissed guitarist Drew Abbott and drummer Dave Teegarden, the latter replaced by another former member of Grand Funk Railroad, Don Brewer. *The Distance* contained "Makin' Thunderbirds" and yielded a smash hit with Rodney Crowell's "Shame on the Money" and major hits with "Even Now" and "Roll Me Away."

During another three-year hiatus, Bob Seger scored a moderate hit with his earlier "Old Time Rock & Roll" from the movie *Risky Business* and a major hit with "Understanding" from the movie *Teachers*. *Like a Rock* produced two major hits, "American Storm" and the title track, and two minor hits, "It's You" and "Miami," in 1986. The tour in support of the album was conducted with Don Brewer, band veterans Alto Reed, Craig Frost, and Chris Campbell, and three newcomers, keyboardist Bill Payne (Little Feat) and guitarists Rick Vito and Fred Tackett. The following year Seger achieved a top hit with "Shakedown" from the movie *Beverly Hills Cop II* but then was inactive again for three years. He eventually returned to recording with 1991's *The Fire Inside*, produced by Don Was. The album produced a hit single, "The Real Love," but Bob Seger did not tour after its release and his next output, from 1994, was a greatest hits compilation.

The Bob Seger System

Ramblin' Gamblin' Man	Capitol	172	'69	†
	Capitol	16105		†
	Capitol	96261		CS/CD
Noah	Capitol	236	'69	†
Mongrel	Capitol	499	'70	†
	Capitol	16106		†
	Capitol	81240		CS/CD

Bob Seger

Brand New Morning	Capitol	731	'71	†
Smokin' O.P.'s	Palladium	1006	'72	†
	Reprise/Palladium	2109		†
	Reprise	2262	'77	†
	Capitol	11746	'78	†
	Capitol	16107		†
	Capitol	99077		CS/CD
Back in '72	Reprise/Palladium	2126	'73	†
	Reprise	2263	'77	†
Seven	Reprise/Palladium	2184	'74	†
	Reprise	2264	'77	†
	Capitol	11748	'78	†
	Capitol	16108		†
	Capitol	81241		CS/CD

Beautiful Loser	Capitol	11378	'75	†
	Capitol	16315	'84	†
	Capitol	91424		CS/CD
Bob Seger and the Silver Bullet Band				
Live Bullet	Capitol	(2) 11523	'76	CS
	Capitol	(2) 46085	CD	
Night Moves	Capitol	11557	'76	CS
	Capitol	46075		CD
	DCC	1028		CD
Stranger in Town	Capitol	11698	'78	CS
	Capitol	46074		CD
Against the Wind	Capitol	12041	'80	CS
	Capitol	46060		CD
Nine Tonight	Capitol	(2) 12182	'81	CS
	Capitol	(2) 46086		CD
The Distance	Capitol	12254	'83	CS
	Capitol	46005		CD
Like a Rock	Capitol	12398	'86	†
	Capitol	46195		CS/CD
The Fire Inside	Capitol	91134	'91	CS/CD
Greatest Hits	Capitol	30334	'94	CS/CD
	Capitol	30334	'95	LP

THE SEX PISTOLS

Johnny Rotten (b. John Lydon, Jan. 30, 1956, London, England), voc; **Steve Jones** (b. May 3, 1955, London, England), gtr, voc; **Glen Matlock** (b. Aug. 27, 1956, London, England), bs; **Paul Cook** (b. July 27, 1956, London, England), drm [Glen Matlock was replaced in February 1977 by **Sid Vicious** (b.John Simon Ritchie, May 10, 1957, London, England; d. Feb. 2, 1979, New York, NY).]

The archetypal punk rock band, the Sex Pistols quickly gained notoriety in Great Britain for their adamantly incompetent playing, cynically vituperative and anticommercial lyrics, and deliberate onstage vulgarity. Reacting to the complacency and blandness of established popular musicians and the policies of the music industry in general, the Sex Pistols intentionally sought to shock and agitate fans out of their musical apathy with tasteless acts of outrage, antagonism, and hostility. They were almost instantly transformed from unknowns to the most publicized and scrutinized rock band in the world in less than a year, without having even released an album. They scored their first recorded successes in Great Britain with "Anarchy in the U.K." and the controversial "God Save the Queen" in 1976–1977. Introducing the shocking, irreverent attitude and style of punk to America, the Sex Pistols essentially disintegrated after their overpublicized debut American tour of early 1978. Nonetheless, Sid Vicious continued to draw massive media attention for the alleged murder of his girlfriend in October 1978 and his drug-overdose death in February 1979, dramatized in the 1986 underground movie classic *Sid and Nancy*. Lead vocalist Johnny Rotten, one of the most acerbic and provocative figures in rock, persevered with Public Image Ltd. (PiL) after the demise of the Sex Pistols, but he never expanded his following beyond that of a cult.

The Sex Pistols were formed by entrepreneur Malcolm McLaren in August 1975 with vocalist Johnny Rotten and three former members of the Swankers, Steve Jones, Glen

Matlock, and Paul Cook. They played their first engagement in November and quickly generated outrage and havoc with their cynical and nihilistic songs and tastelessly hostile and abusive performances. The subject of rapidly spreading notoriety, the Sex Pistols signed with EMI Records in October 1976 and soon scored a smash British hit with the widely banned "Anarchy in the U.K.," written by Matlock. However, they were dropped by EMI in January after swearing on BBC-TV, an incident that won them front-page news coverage.

Disputes between Matlock and Rotten led to Matlock's departure from the Sex Pistols in February 1977, and he was replaced on bass by Sid Vicious, a former member of Siouxsie and the Banshees and Flowers of Romance. Picked up by A&M Records in March, the group was immediately dumped by the label and subsequently signed to Virgin Records in May. Their first release for the label, Matlock's sarcastic "God Save the Queen," became a smash British hit despite its banishment from radio. Their debut album, *Never Mind the Bullocks, Here's the Sex Pistols*, was issued in late 1977 (on Warner Bros. in the United States) and included "Pretty Vacant," "No Feelings," and the vitriolic tribute to their first label, "EMI."

In January 1978 the Sex Pistols made their first American tour, accompanied by media coverage unseen since the advent of the Beatles and the Rolling Stones. After the group's final engagement at Winterland in San Francisco on January 14, 1978, before the largest audience of their career, the Sex Pistols fell into disarray. Sid Vicious, Steve Jones, and Paul Cook later recorded a crude version of Frank Sinatra's theme song, "My Way," and by April Johnny Rotten (now using the name John Lydon) had formed Public Image Ltd. (PiL) with former Clash and Flowers of Romance guitarist Keith Levene. Recording their debut British album in 1978, the group released several albums though the early '90s. Drummer Martin Atkins joined PiL in 1979 and became a mainstay in the ever-changing group. Rotten published his autobiography in 1994. Steve Jones and Keith Levene later recorded solo albums, and Jones formed Havana 3 A.M. with guitarist Gary Myrick, singer Nigel Dixon, and former Clash bassist Paul Simonon in 1991.

Sid Vicious was charged with the October 21, 1978, stabbing death of his American girlfriend Nancy Spungen at New York's Chelsea Hotel, but he was found dead of a heroin overdose in a Greenwich Village apartment on February 2, 1979, at age 21, while out on bail. Their "romance" was dramatized in the gritty, raunchy, yet engaging 1986 movie *Sid and Nancy*, cowritten and directed by Alex Cox.

The Sex Pistols

Never Mind the Bullocks, Here's the Sex Pistols	Warner Bros.	3147	'77	CS/CD
The Great Rock 'n' Roll Swindle	Warner Bros.	45083	'92	CS/CD
Better Live Than Dead	Restless	72255		CS/CD
The Swindle Continues	Restless	72256		CS/CD
The Mini-Album	Restless	72257		CS/CD
Live at Chelmsford Top Security Prison	Restless	72511	'90	CS/CD

Public Image Ltd.

Second Edition	Island	(2) 3288	'79	†
	Warner Bros.	3288		CS/CD
The Flowers of Romance	Warner Bros.	3536	'81	CS/CD
This Is What You Want . . . This Is What You Get	Elektra	60365	'84	†
Public Image Ltd.	Elektra	60438	'86	CS/CD
Live	Elektra	60491		†
Happy?	Virgin	90642	'87	CS/CD†
	Virgin	86021		CS/CD
9	Virgin	91602	'89	CS/CD†
	Virgin	86105		CS/CD

Greatest Hits So Far	Virgin	91581	'90	CS/CD†
	Virgin	86196		CS/CD
That What Is Not	Virgin	91815	'92	CS/CD†
	Virgin	86263		CS/CD
Keith Levene				
Violent Opposition	Rykodisc	10049	'89	CD
Steve Jones				
Fire and Gasoline	MCA	6298	'89	†
Havana 3 A.M.				
Havana 3 A.M.	I.R.S.	13069	'91	CS/CD

SHA NA NA

John "Bowzer" Bauman (b. Sept. 14, 1947, Queens, NY), voc; **Henry Gross** (b. Apr. 1, 1951, Brooklyn, NY), gtr; **Donald York**, kybd, voc; **Lennie Baker** (b. Apr. 18, 1946, Whitman, MA), sax; **Johnny "Jocko" Marcellino**, drm [The above are original members. Keyboardist-vocalist **"Screamin'" Scott Simon** joined in 1969. Guitarist-vocalist **Dave "Chico" Ryan** joined in early '70s. Group mainstays since the mid-'80s: York, Baker, Marcellino, Simon, and Ryan.]

Performing amusing and lively recreations of the music, dress, and choreography of '50s rock and roll, Sha Na Na were launched into international prominence through their appearance at 1969's Woodstock Festival and the subsequent film. Featured at Ralph Nader's first rock-and-roll revival show several months later, Sha Na Na frequently upstaged the original '50s acts in concert during the early '70s. From 1977 to 1981 Sha Na Na appeared on their own syndicated television show that further expanded their audience.

Formed out of Columbia University glee club the Columbus Kingsmen in 1969, the group was initially comprised of John "Bowzer" Bauman, Johnny Contrado, Donald York, Frederick "Denny" Greene, Lennie Baker, Chris "Vinnie Taylor" Donald, Elliot Cahn, Bruce Clarke, Henry Gross, and Johnny "Jocko" Marcellino. Sha Na Na performed only their seventh engagement on Sunday morning, August 17, 1969, at the Woodstock Festival, preceding Jimi Hendrix. Henry Gross soon left to pursue a solo career that peaked with 1976's smash hit "Shannon," and keyboardist-vocalist "Screamin'" Scott Simon joined shortly after the Woodstock appearance. Signed to Kama Sutra Records, the group recorded a number of albums for the label through 1976, scoring their biggest success with 1973's *The Golden Age of Rock 'n' Roll*. Re-creating the sight and sound of '50s rock and roll, complete with split-second group choreography, gold lamé costumes, oily ducktail haircuts, and feigned "greaser" hostility, Sha Na Na became a fixture on the rock-and-roll revival circuit of the '70s. Bassist-vocalist Dave "Chico" Ryan joined the group around 1974.

Retaining a remarkably stable lineup during the '70s, Sha Na Na had their own syndicated television show that ran from 1977 to 1981. They also appeared in the 1978 movie musical *Grease*, starring John Travolta and Olivia Newton-John. By the mid-'80s John "Bowzer" Bauman, Frederick "Denny" Greene, and Johnny Contrado had left the group, which continued with Donald York, "Screamin'" Scott Simon, Lennie Baker, Dave "Chico" Ryan, and Johnny "Jocko" Marcellino as mainstays. More a musical revue than a rock band, Sha Na Na continue to play around 150 engagements a year at fairs, clubs, and private parties well into the '90s.

Sha Na Na

Rock 'n' Roll Is Here to Stay	Kama Sutra	2010	'69	†
	Kama Sutra	2077	'74	†
	Special Music	4910		CS/CD

Sha Na Na	Kama Sutra	2034	'71	†
The Night Is Still Young	Kama Sutra	2050	'72	†
The Golden Age of Rock 'n' Roll	Kama Sutra	(2) 2073	'73	†
From the Streets of New York	Kama Sutra	2075	'73	†
Hot Sox	Kama Sutra	2600	'74	†
Sha Na Now	Kama Sutra	2605	'75	†
The Best	Kama Sutra	(2) 2609	'76	†
Sha Na Na Is Here to Stay	Buddah	5692	'78	†
Remember Then	Accord	7115	'81	†
Sh-Boom	Accord	7146	'81	†
34th and Vine	Gold Castle		'90	†
Havin' an Oldies Party	K-tel	858	'91	CS/CD†
25th Anniversary Collection	Laurie	9003	'93	CS/CD
20 Greatest Hits	Fest	4401		CS
Sixteen Candles	Richmond	2347		CS/CD
Rock & Roll Is Here to Stay	Richmond	2351		CS
Heartbreak Hotel	Richmond	2354		CS/CD
The Best of Sha Na Na	Pair	1201		CS/CD
Henry Gross				
Henry Gross	ABC	747	'72	†
Henry Gross	A&M	4416	'74	†
Plug Me Into Something	A&M	4502	'75	†
Release	Lifesong	6002	'76	†
	Lifesong	34995		†
Release/Show Me to the Stage	Big Beat	104		CD
"Screamin'" Scott Simon				
Transmissions from Space	Rolling Rock	026	'82	†

DEL SHANNON

(b. Charles Westover, Dec. 30, 1934, Coopersville, MI; d. Feb. 8, 1990, Santa Clarita, CA)

One of the few early rock artists to write his own songs, Del Shannon was also noteworthy for his falsetto vocals. His biggest and best-remembered hit, 1961's "Runaway," featured an instrumental break by coauthor Max Crook performed on the Musitron, a keyboard instrument that preceded the synthesizer. Continuing to achieve major hits through 1964, Del Shannon enjoyed greater popularity in Great Britain than in the United States, a fate he shared with Gene Vincent. In fact he was the first American artist to record a Beatles song ("From Me to You") and wrote "I Go to Pieces" for Peter and Gordon. With his career in eclipse for nearly 15 years, Del Shannon attempted a comeback with 1981's *Drop Down and Get Me*, produced by Tom Petty. Unable to reestablish himself, Del Shannon committed suicide on February 8, 1990.

Charles Westover took up guitar and singing as a teenager and adopted his stage name, Del Shannon, after graduating from high school. He first performed on the Army's *Get Up and Go* radio show in Germany in 1958 while in the service. Following his discharge in 1959, he returned to Battle Creek, Michigan, and performed in local clubs with pianist Max Crook. In 1960 he signed with the Detroit-based Big Top label, achieving his most celebrated hit with "Runaway," cowritten with Crook, in 1961. He followed up with the smash hit "Hats Off to Larry" and the major hit "So Long Baby," and first toured Great Britain in 1962, meeting the Beatles and winning a devoted following. Scoring smash British hits with

"The Swiss Maid" and "Two Kinds of Teardrops," Shannon had a major American hit with "Little Town Flirt" in 1963, followed by a minor hit with his cover of "From Me to You," the first song written by John Lennon and Paul McCartney to make the American charts.

In late 1962 Del Shannon left Big Top amidst legal disputes with the label. He and his managers formed the short-lived label Berlee, on which he managed the minor hit "Sue's Gotta Be Mine" in late 1963. Switching to Amy Records in 1964, through 1965 he scored a major hit with "Handy Man," a near-smash with the classic "Keep Searchin' (We'll Follow the Sun)," and a moderate hit with "Stranger in Town." In early 1965 Peter and Gordon had a near-smash American hit with Shannon's "I Go to Pieces." By 1966 he had moved to Los Angeles and signed with Liberty Records. He enjoyed little success with the label and left it in 1969, arranging the Smith's smash hit "Baby It's You" that same year and producing Brian Hyland's smash hit "Gypsy Woman" a year later.

During the '70s Del Shannon recorded singles with Jeff Lynne and Dave Edmunds in England and successfully overcame an alcohol dependency. He met Tom Petty in 1978 and over the next three years recorded *Drop Down and Get Me*, with Petty as producer. The album produced a moderate hit with "Sea of Love," but Shannon was unable to sustain a career outside the oldies revival circuit. Del Shannon was nearing completion of a new album with Lynne and Petty when he shot himself to death on February 8, 1990.

Del Shannon

Runaway	Big Top	1303	'61	|
Little Town Flirt	Big Top	1308	'63	†
	Rhino	70983	'90	CS/CD
Handy Man	Amy	8003	'64	†
Sings Hank Williams	Amy	8004		†
	Rhino	70982	'90	CS/CD
1,661 Seconds	Amy	8006		†
This Is My Bag	Liberty	7453	'66	†
Total Commitment	Liberty	7479	'66	†
Further Adventures of Charles Westover	Liberty	7539	'68	†
The Liberty Years	EMI	95842	'91	CS/CD
Best	Dot	25824	'67	†
Del Shannon Sings	Post	9000		†
Live in England	United Artists	151	'74	†
Vintage Years	Sire	(2) 3708	'75	†
Best	Pickwick	3595	'78	†
Drop Down and Get Me	Elektra	568	'81	†
Runaway Hits	Rhino	71056	'86	†
Greatest Hits	Rhino	70977	'90	CS/CD
Rock On!	Gone Gator	10296	'91	CS/CD
Runaway	Pair	1293	'91	CS/CD
At His Best	Special Music	4823		CS/CD

THE SHIRELLES

Shirley Owens [Alston] (b. June 10, 1941, Passaic, NJ); **Beverly Lee** (b. Aug. 3, 1941, Passaic, NJ); **Doris Coley [Kenner]** (b. Aug. 2, 1941, Passaic, NJ); **Addie "Micki" Harris** (b. Jan. 22, 1940, Passaic, NJ; d. June 10, 1982, Atlanta, GA)

One of the earliest and most popular "girl groups" (preceded only by the Chantels), the Shirelles recorded excellent material in the early '60s provided by Carole King and Gerry

Goffin, Burt Bacharach and Hal David, and their producer Luther Dixon. They became stars with the smash crossover success of the classic "Will You Love Me Tomorrow" in late 1960. Scoring a series of hits with "Dedicated to the One I Love," "Baby It's You," and their best-remembered song, "Soldier Boy," the Shirelles enjoyed only modest success after the 1964 departure of Luther Dixon for Capitol Records.

Initially formed while Shirley Owens, Beverly Lee, Doris Coley, and Addie "Micki" Harris were in junior high school in Passaic, New Jersey, the Shirelles were singing at school and local parties, when schoolmate Mary Jane Greenberg heard them and introduced them to her mother, Florence, a music-industry veteran. She signed them to her tiny Tiara label, and their first recording, "I Met Him on a Sunday (Ronde, Ronde)," written by the four, became a moderate pop hit when leased to Decca Records in 1958. Florence Greenberg subsequently formed Scepter Records, and the Shirelles scored a minor hit in 1959 with "Dedicated to the One I Love." In 1960 "Tonight's the Night," cowritten by Owens and producer-arranger Luther Dixon, became a moderate pop and major R&B hit and was followed by the top pop and smash R&B hit classic "Will You Love Me Tomorrow," written by Carole King and Gerry Goffin. The song's success established the Scepter label and made the Shirelles one of the most popular "girl groups" of the early '60s.

THE SHIRELLES

In 1961 the Shirelles scored pop and R&B smashes with "Dedicated to the One I Love" (upon rerelease) and "Mama Said," coauthored by Dixon. After the major pop hit "Dear John" (a smash R&B hit), the group had crossover smash hits with "Baby It's You," written by Burt Bacharach, Hal David, and Bernie Williams, and the maudlin "Soldier Boy," cowritten by Dixon and Greenberg. "Welcome Home Baby" and "Everybody Loves a Lover" became major pop and R&B hits and were followed by the crossover smash "Foolish Little Girl," coauthored by Neil Sedaka's songwriting partner Howie Greenfield. After their final major hit, "Don't Say Goodnight and Mean Goodbye," the Shirelles worked on the movie *It's a Mad, Mad, Mad, Mad World*.

Luther Dixon subsequently left Scepter for Capitol Records, and the Shirelles never again scored a major hit. Doris Coley, by then Doris Kenner, left the group in 1968, and the remaining three attempted a comeback on RCA Records in the early '70s. In 1975 Kenner returned, but Shirley Owens, by then Shirley Alston, left for a solo career, recording two unsuccessful albums as Lady Rose. Micki Harris, Beverly Lee, and Doris Kenner toured as the Shirelles in the early '80s, but on June 10, 1982, Harris died of a heart attack at age 42 after a performance in Atlanta. The three surviving original members subsequently agreed that each could assemble groups using the name the Shirelles. The group was inducted into the Rock and Roll Hall of Fame in 1996.

The Shirelles

Tonight's the Night	Scepter	501	'60	†
Sing to Trumpets and Strings	Scepter	502	'61	†
	Sundazed	6016	'93	CD
Baby It's You	Scepter	504	'62	†
	Sundazed	6012	'93	CD
Greatest Hits	Scepter	507	'63	†
Foolish Little Girl	Scepter	511	'63	†
	Sundazed	6017	'93	CD
Sing Their Songs in the Great Movie "It's a Mad, Mad, Mad, Mad World" and Others	Scepter	514	'63	†
Sing Golden Oldies	Scepter	516	'64	†
Greatest Hits, Volume 2	Scepter	560	'66	†
Spontaneous Combustion	Scepter	562	'67	†
Remember When	Scepter	(2) 599	'72	†
Swing the Most	Pricewise	4001		†
Here and Now	Pricewise	4002		†
Happy and In Love	RCA	4581	'71	†
The Shirelles	RCA	4698	'72	†
Sing Their Best	Springboard Int'l	4006	'73	†
Very Best	United Artists	340	'75	†
	Rhino	71807	'94	CS/CD
To Know Him Is to Love Him	Piccadilly	3318	'82	†
Anthology, 1959–1967	Rhino	(2) 1101	'84	†
Anthology, 1959–1965	Rhino	5897	'80	CS
	Rhino	75897	'86	CD
Sha La La La La	Impact	003		LP
Lost and Found	Impact	010	'87	LP
Greatest Hits	Impact	011	'87	LP/CD
Dedicated to You	Pair	1241	'91	CS/CD
The World's Greatest Girl Group	Tomato	(2) 71731	'95	CD
Soulfully Yours	Kent	032		†
16 Greatest Hits	Deluxe	7904		CS
16 Greatest Hits	Fest	4414		CS/CD
Greatest Hits	Special Music	4805		CS/CD
Original Golden Hits	Hollywood/IMG	114		CS/CD
The Fabulous Shirelles	Ace	011		CS/CD
Best	Ace	356		CD

The Shirelles and King Curtis

Give a Twist Party	Scepter	507	'62	†
	Sundazed	6013	'93	CD

Lady Rose (Shirley Alston)

Lady Rose Sings the Shirelles's Greatest Hits	Strawberry	6004	'77	†
	Strawberry	6006	'77	†

CARLY SIMON

(b. June 25, 1945, New York, NY)

Achieving several pop and easy-listening hits during the '70s, Carly Simon cowrote many of her own songs, but her slick, sophisticated style and image bore stark contrast to that of most other '70s female singer-songwriters. Married to James Taylor from 1972 to 1983, Simon scored her best-remembered hit with late 1972's "You're So Vain" from her most successful album, *No Secrets*, produced by Richard Perry. Her popularity waned in the '80s, although she managed somewhat of a comeback with 1987's *Coming Around Again*.

Carly Simon was raised in affluence in Riverdale, New York, and Stamford, Connecticut, as the daughter of the cofounder of the Simon and Schuster publishing firm. While attending the exclusive Sarah Lawrence College, she began singing folk-style material with her older sister Lucy as the Simon Sisters. She dropped out of college after two years and performed with Lucy in area folk clubs during the early '60s, signing with Kapp Records in 1963. They scored a minor hit in 1964 with "Winkin', Blinkin' and Nod" and recorded two albums before Lucy's marriage broke up the duo. In 1966 Carly Simon met manager Albert Grossman, who envisioned her as a female Bob Dylan. She recorded with Al Kooper, Mike Bloomfield, and the Band's Rick Danko and Richard Manuel, but the material was never released. Simon served as colead vocalist of the New York–based rock band Elephant's Memory in 1969, and she wrote commercial jingles in 1969 and 1970.

In 1970 Carly Simon began cowriting songs with film critic and writer Jacob Brackman and signed with Elektra Records late in the year. Playing guitar and piano and singing in a powerful contralto voice, she scored a major pop and easy-listening hit with "That's the Way I've Always Heard It Should Be," cowritten with Brackman, from her debut album. A notoriously shy performer, Simon debuted in support of Cat Stevens at the Troubadour in Los Angeles in April 1971 and met singer-songwriter James Taylor, whom she married in November 1972. *Anticipation*, produced by Cat Stevens producer and former Yardbird Paul Samwell-Smith, yielded pop and easy-listening hits with her title song and "Legend in Your Own Time."

Carly Simon recorded her next three albums under producer Richard Perry. The first, *No Secrets*, included "We Have No Secrets" and yielded a top pop and easy-listening hit with "You're So Vain" and a major pop and smash easy-listening hit with "The Right Thing to Do," all of which she wrote. "You're So Vain," recorded with Mick Jagger as backup vocalist, was spurred into popularity by speculation about who inspired the lyric (she finally admitted that it was Warren Beatty). Simon abandoned touring in 1973 and retained a low public profile after the birth of her daughter in January 1974. Nonetheless, *Hotcakes* produced a smash hit with a horrendous remake of Charlie and Inez Foxx's "Mockingbird," recorded with husband James Taylor, and a major hit with "Haven't Got Time for the Pain," cowritten with Jacob Brackman. *Playing Possum*, her final album under Richard Perry, contained the major hit "Attitude Dancing" and the minor hits "Waterfall" and "More and More."

Appearing with James Taylor on his summer 1975 tour and singing backup on sister Lucy's debut album, Carly Simon's popularity began to wane. In 1977 she scored a smash pop and top easy-listening hit with "Nobody Does It Better" from the James Bond movie *The Spy Who Loved Me*, followed in 1978 by the near-smash "You Belong to Me," cowritten by Simon and Doobie Brother Michael McDonald. Later that year she managed a moderate pop and easy-listening hit with the Everly Brothers' "Devoted to You," in duet with James Taylor. "Jesse" became her final major hit for several years in 1980.

Carly Simon divorced James Taylor in 1983 and her career remained in eclipse until 1986, when "Coming Around Again," on her new label Arista Records, was featured in the movie *Heartburn*. Her first public performance in six years was given on Martha's Vineyard in 1987 and produced an HBO cable television special and live album. Simon next worked on the soundtrack to the movie *This Is My Life*, released on Quincy Jones's Qwest label. Since the mid-'80s she has authored four children's books and is said to be working on a fiction work for adults. In 1993 Carly Simon's opera *Romulus Hunt* premiered at the Kennedy Center in Washington, D.C. (years earlier, sister Joanne had become an opera singer). In 1991 sister Lucy received recognition as the composer of the musical *The Secret Garden*, a Broadway hit in 1991.

The Simon Sisters

Winkin', Blinkin' and Nod	Kapp	3359		†
Cuddlebug	Kapp	3397		†

Carly Simon

Carly Simon	Elektra	74082	'71	CS/CD
Anticipation	Elektra	75016	'71	CS/CD
No Secrets	Elektra	75049	'72	CS/CD
Hot Cakes	Elektra	1002	'74	'88 CD
Playing Possum	Elektra	1033	'75	CD
Best	Elektra	1048	'75	†
	Elektra	109		CS/CD
Another Passenger	Elektra	1064	'76	CD
Boys in the Trees	Elektra	128	'78	CS/CD
Spy	Elektra	506	'79	†
Come Upstairs	Warner Bros.	3443	'80	†
Torch	Warner Bros.	3592	'81	CS/CD
Hello Big Man	Warner Bros.	23886	'83/'00	CD
Spoiled Girl	Epic	39970	'85	CS/CD
Coming Around Again	Arista	8443	'87	CS/CD
Greatest Hits Live	Arista	8526	'88	LP/CS/CD
My Romance	Arista	8582	'90	CS/CD
Have You Seen Me Lately?	Arista	8650	'90	LP/CS/CD
Letters Never Sent	Arista	18752	'94	CS/CD
This Is My Life (soundtrack)	Qwest	26901	'92	CS/CD
Romulus Hunt	Angel	54915	'93	CS/CD

Lucy Simon

Lucy Simon	RCA	1074	'75	†
Stolen Time	RCA	1745	'77	†
The Secret Garden (music from Broadway original cast)	Columbia	48817	'91	CS/CD

SIMON AND GARFUNKEL/PAUL SIMON

Paul Simon (b. Nov. 5, 1941, Newark, NJ), gtr and voc; **Art Garfunkel** (b. Oct. 13, 1942, Queens, NY), voc

The most successful American vocal duo since the Everly Brothers, Simon and Garfunkel started out as a rock-and-roll duet in the late '50s but established themselves in the mid-'60s with Simon's folk-rock classic "The Sounds of Silence." Paul Simon's songs later became more personal, compassionate, and diversified, yet they were occasionally criticized as self-consciously "poetic." Nonetheless, he wrote some of the most literate, honest, and finely crafted songs of the second-half of the '60s. The duo's career culminated with the

SIMON (*r.*) AND GARFUNKEL (*l.*)

masterful *Bridge Over Troubled Water*, but at the height of their popularity Simon and Garfunkel parted company. Simon established a successful solo career in the '70s, then went through a period of career eclipse, only to return triumphantly with 1986's album *Graceland* and its subsequent tour; Garfunkel has been less fortunate in his attempts to establish himself as a solo artist.

Paul Simon grew up in Queens, New York, where he met Art Garfunkel at age 11. They began singing together around 1955, and in late 1957 they scored a moderate hit with "Hey, Schoolgirl" as Tom and Jerry on Big Records. They appeared on Dick Clark's *American Bandstand*, but subsequent singles proved failures and the two split up after high school to attend college. Garfunkel went to Columbia University and Simon attended Queens College, where he met Carole King. Simon began writing songs and working as a song promoter for E. B. Marks Publishing, while recording demonstration tapes (including one with Carole King, "Just to Be with You," that became a minor pop hit for the Passions in 1959). In the early '60s he worked as a songwriter-producer at Amy Records, where he recorded under a variety of pseudonyms, including Tico and the Triumphs ("Motorcycle") and Jerry Landis ("The Lone Teen Ranger") and, for Tribute Records, Paul Kane ("He Was My Brother"). Around the same time, Art Garfunkel was recording as Artie Garr on Octavia and Warwick Records.

After renewing his friendship with Art Garfunkel in 1962, Paul Simon pursued a career as a folk singer in Greenwich Village folk clubs and eventually won an audition with Tom Wilson of Columbia Records. The audition led to Simon and Garfunkel's debut album, *Wednesday Morning, 3 A.M.* Simon subsequently left for England, where he played folk clubs and recorded the British-only album *The Paul Simon Song Book*. After the first Simon and Garfunkel album failed, Wilson overdubbed rock instrumentation onto one of its tracks, "Sounds of Silence," without consulting the artists; it became a top hit in late 1965.

The duo reunited and recorded a new album featuring the reworked single. Pervaded by Simon's compositions and the duo's precise, close-harmony singing, the hits kept coming, with the smash "Homeward Bound" and the alienated "I Am a Rock." Strings were utilized for their third album, *Parsley, Sage, Rosemary and Thyme*, which included the self-consciously poetic major hit "The Dangling Conversation," the ditty "The 59th Street Bridge Song (Feelin' Groovy)" (a hit for the pop-rock group Harper's Bizarre), the satiric "A Simple Desultory Philippic," and the depressing but moving "7 O'Clock News/Silent Night."

Simon and Garfunkel subsequently scored major hits with "A Hazy Shade of Winter," "At the Zoo," and "Fakin' It" before working on the soundtrack to the hit Mike Nichols's movie *The Graduate.* The album included six instrumental songs by David Grusin, the hit "Scarborough Fair," based on a 17th-century folk ballad, and the top hit classic "Mrs. Robinson." *Bookends*, their first self-produced album, contained hits previously unreleased on an album, as well as "Save the Life of My Child" and "America." In 1969 Simon and Garfunkel achieved a near-smash hit with the classic "The Boxer," later included on *Bridge Over Troubled Water*. The album also yielded the smash title hit and "Cecilia," and the major hit "El Condor Pasa," recorded with the Peruvian group Los Incas; it also included "Keep the Customer Satisfied," "So Long, Frank Lloyd Wright," and "Baby Driver." The album, perhaps the finest of their career, ultimately sold more than five million copies in the United States. During 1970 the Simon and Garfunkel team separated. By then, Art Garfunkel had worked on the Mike Nichols's films *Catch-22* (1969) and *Carnal Knowledge* (1970).

By early 1972 Paul Simon was back with his debut solo album. Coproduced by Simon and engineer Roy Halee, *Paul Simon* confirmed his reputation as one of the consummate songwriting craftsmen of '70s rock with compositions such as "Duncan" and "Run That Body Down" and the hits "Mother and Child Reunion" (a smash recorded in Jamaica) and "Me and Julio Down by the Schoolyard." *There Goes Rhymin' Simon*, largely recorded in Muscle Shoals, Alabama, contained the smash hits "Loves Me Like a Rock" (recorded with the gospel group the Dixie Hummingbirds) and "Kodachrome" as well as "Something So Right" and "Take Me to the Mardi Gras." Touring America and Europe with the Jessy Dixon Singers and the South American band Urubamba in 1973, Simon recorded his next album on the tour.

Paul Simon coproduced his 1975 album *Still Crazy After All These Years*, which yielded the top pop and easy-listening hit "50 Ways to Leave Your Lover" and a moderate pop hit with the title song. It also included "I Do It for Your Love," "Have a Good Time," a duet with Phoebe Snow on "Gone at Last," and the near-smash pop and top easy-listening duet with Art Garfunkel "My Little Town." Simon toured again in 1975, with the Jessy Dixon Singers, and keyboardist Richard Tee and drummer Steve Gadd, among others. Simon appeared in Woody Allen's Academy Award–winning 1977 movie *Annie Hall* and issued *Greatest Hits, Etc.*, which compiled many of his hits and included the bonus songs "Slip Slidin' Away," a smash pop hit, and "Stranded in a Limousine."

In 1978, while still owing one album to Columbia, Paul Simon switched to Warner Bros. Records. He subsequently became involved in legal disputes with his former label while working on his first feature film, *One-Trick Pony*, for Warner. He wrote, scored, and starred in the movie as a musician seeking another hit record after years on the road. Eventually released in October 1980, the movie featured performances by the B-52's, Sam and Dave, and the reunited Lovin' Spoonful, with Lou Reed appearing as Simon's unsympathetic producer. The film proved a commercial failure, but the soundtrack album produced a near-smash hit for Simon with "Late in the Evening."

On September 19, 1981, Paul Simon and Art Garfunkel reunited for a free concert in New York's Central Park. The performance drew an estimated crowd of 500,000 and resulted in a live double-record set and HBO cable-television special. The two began recording an album together and toured for the first time in 13 years in 1983. However, fighting soon broke out again among the two, and Simon ultimately decided to erase Garfunkel's vocals and release the album as a solo album. Despite the inclusion of the moderate hit "Allergies" and excellent songs such as "Think Too Much" and "The Late Great Johnny Ace," *Hearts and Bones* (as the album was ultimately called) sold only moderately.

Simon became interested in the music of South Africa in summer 1984. In February 1985 he flew to Johannesburg to investigate the music of black South Africans. Using the recorded music of South African groups as a starting point, he began composing lyrics. He formed a basic group of musicians, with guitarist Chikapa "Ray" Phiri, bassist Baghiti Khumalo, and drummer Isaac Mthsli, and flew the trio to New York for recordings. Over the next year he recorded the material for *Graceland* with the trio, the vocal group Ladysmith Black Mambazo, and the band Stimela, among others. With the accordion as the common link, he also recorded "That Was Your Mother" with the zydeco band Rockin' Dopsie and the Twisters, and "All Around the World" with Los Lobos. The album produced a major hit with "You Can Call Me Al" and two minor hits with "Graceland" and "Boy in the Bubble"; amazingly, it sold spectacularly, eventually moving more than four million copies in the United States. It introduced America and the world to South African music and re-invigorated Simon's career. However, the album stirred controversy, inasmuch as Simon had recorded in South Africa during a United Nations cultural boycott of the country.

In 1987 Paul Simon toured internationally with Ladysmith Black Mambazo, Stimela, and South African expatriates Hugh Masekela and Miriam Makeba. Their concert in Zimbabwe, the country's biggest musical event since Bob Marley and the Wailers performed at that country's Independence Day celebration in 1980, resulted in a Showtime cable-TV special in May.

Paul Simon next immersed himself in the rhythms of Brazil and West Africa. As with *Graceland*, the rhythms preceded the songs for *The Rhythm of the Saints* in an inductive style of songwriting, with poet Derek Walcott as the lyrical inspiration. Regarded as even more ambitious than *Graceland*, *The Rhythm of the Saints* was recorded over a two-year period and featured "Born at the Right Time," "The Cool, Cool River," and "She Moves On," and yielded a minor hit with "The Obvious Child." Simon toured in support of the album and performed a free solo concert in New York's Central Park that drew 750,000 and was broadcast live on HBO. The concert also produced a live album that was issued in 1991. With the lifting of the cultural boycott of South Africa in late 1991, Simon became the first international star to perform in the country in early 1992, although one of the tour's offices was bombed and protesters picketed the concert. In June 1992 Paul Simon married Edie Brickell, vocalist for the New Bohemians from 1986 to 1991. In 1995 Simon was working on a Broadway musical with poet Walcott.

Art Garfunkel's solo career was launched with his 1973 debut album, *Angel Claire*, which featured easy-listening material such as Jimmy Webb's "All I Know" (a near-smash pop hit) and Van Morrison's "I Shall Sing" (a moderate hit). In 1974 he scored a moderate pop hit with "Second Avenue." In 1975 *Breakaway* yielded top easy-listening hits with "I Only Have Eyes for You," "Break Away," and the duet with Paul Simon "My Little Town." Garfunkel's 1977 *Watermark* album was comprised primarily of Jimmy Webb songs but yielded a major pop and top easy-listening hit with Sam Cooke's "(What a) Wonderful World," recorded with Paul Simon and James Taylor. Art Garfunkel conducted his only solo tour in 1977–1978; he later scored minor pop hits with "Since I Don't Have You" and "A Heart in New York," and costarred in the disconcerting and explicit Nicolas Roeg movie *Bad Timing—A Sexual Obsession*. He rejoined Simon for the much-ballyhooed concert in Central Park in 1981, and briefly resumed touring with Simon. However, a plan for a reunion album fell through, and Garfunkel's career has been more spotty in the '80s and '90s, with his occasional recordings producing no hits.

Simon and Garfunkel were inducted into the Rock and Roll Hall of Fame in 1990.

Simon and Garfunkel

Simon and Garfunkel	Pickwick	3059	'67	†
Wednesday Morning, 3 A.M.	Columbia	9049	'64	CS/CD
Sounds of Silence	Columbia	9269	'66	CS/CD
Parsley, Sage, Rosemary and Thyme	Columbia	9363	'66	CD
	Columbia	00132		CS
The Graduate (soundtrack)	Columbia	3180	'68	CD
	Columbia	20030		CS
Bookends	Columbia	9529	'68	CD
	Columbia	00420		CS

Bridge Over Troubled Water	Columbia	9914	'70	CS/CD
	Columbia/Legacy	53444	'93	CD
	Columbia/Legacy	64421	'94	CD
Greatest Hits	Columbia	31350	'72/'85	CS/CD
Collected Works	Columbia	(5) 37587	'81	†
	Columbia	(3) 45322	'90	CS/CD
The Concert in Central Park	Warner Bros.	(2) 3654	'82	CS
	Warner Bros.	3654		CD

Paul Simon

Paul Simon	Columbia	30750	'72	†
	Warner Bros.	25588	'88	CS/CD
There Goes Rhymin' Simon	Columbia	32280	'73	†
	Warner Bros.	25589	'88	CS/CD
Live Rhymin'	Columbia	32855	'74	†
	Warner Bros.	25590	'88	LP/CS/CD
Still Crazy After All These Years	Columbia	33540	'75	†
	Warner Bros.	25591	'88	CS/CD
Greatest Hits, Etc.	Columbia	35032	'77/'85	†
Collected Works	Columbia	(5) 37581	'81	†
One-Trick Pony (soundtrack)	Warner Bros.	3472	'80/'87	CS/CD
Hearts and Bones	Warner Bros.	23942	'83/'84	CS/CD
Graceland	Warner Bros.	25447	'86	LP/CS/CD
Negotiations and Love Songs, 1971–1986	Warner Bros.	(2) 25789	'88	CS
	Warner Bros.	25789	'88	CD
The Rhythm of the Saints	Warner Bros.	26098	'90	LP
	Warner Bros.	26091	'90	CS/CD
Paul Simon's Concert in the Park	Warner Bros.	(2) 26737	'91	CS/CD
1964–1993	Warner Bros.	(3) 45394	'93	CD

Art Garfunkel

Angel Claire	Columbia	31474	'73	CS/CD
Breakaway	Columbia	33700	'75	CS/CD
Watermark	Columbia	34975	'77	CD
Fate for Breakfast	Columbia	35780	'79/'90	CD
Scissors Cut	Columbia	37392	'81	CD
Lefty	Columbia	40942	'88	CD
Garfunkel	Columbia	45008	'89	CS/CD
Up Until Now	Columbia	47113	'93	CS/CD

Art Garfunkel and Amy Grant

The Animals' Christmas	Columbia	40212	'86/'90	CS/CD

SLY AND THE FAMILY STONE

Sly Stone (b. Sylvester Stewart, Mar. 15, 1944, Dallas, TX), lead voc, kybd, gtr; **Rose Stewart** (b. Mar. 21, 1945, Vallejo, CA), pno, voc; **Freddie Stewart** (b. June 5, 1946, Dallas, TX), gtr, voc; **Larry Graham** (b. Aug. 14, 1946, Beaumont, TX), bs, voc; **Jerry Martini** (b. Oct. 1, 1943, Boulder, CO), sax, clarinet, pno, accordion; **Cynthia Robinson** (b. Jan. 12, 1946, Sacramento, CA), trpt, voc; **Greg Errico** (b. Sept. 1, 1946, San Francisco, CA), drm

SLY STONE

In the late '60s and '70s, Sly and the Family Stone became one of the first groups to successfully combine elements of R&B and rock with self-affirming, socially optimistic lyrics to produce so-called psychedelic soul. A racially and sexually integrated group, Sly and the Family Stone featured psychedelic guitar, jazz-style horn arrangements, and the resounding funk bass of Larry Graham, all of which influenced later artists such as George Clinton, Rick James, and Prince. The group also utilized sophisticated vocal arrangements, often juxtaposing a woman's high voice and a man's low voice, with as many as three members sharing lead vocals. With Sly Stone providing classics such as "Dance to the Music," "I Want to Take You Higher," and "Everyday People," Sly and the Family Stone benefited from both AM and underground FM radio airplay and enjoyed popularity with both black and white audiences. Additionally, they performed an exciting stage act that was at once colorful, energetic, and spontaneous, in contrast to the carefully planned and executed routines of various Motown groups. Aided immeasurably by their outstanding performance at the Woodstock Festival in August 1969, Sly and the Family Stone were one of the most popular bands of the early '70s. However, their popularity diminished by the mid-'70s, as Sly became mired in concert cancellations, legal disputes, and, later, drug problems.

As a child, the Texas-born Sylvester Stewart moved to Vallejo, California, where he sang with siblings Rose and Freddie in the gospel group the Stewart Four, who recorded "On the Battlefield of My Lord" when Sylvester was four. By then he was already playing drums and guitar, and he eventually taught himself a number of other instruments, including piano and organ. In 1960 he scored a local hit with "Long Time Ago" and later manned the Stewart Brothers (with Freddie) and the Viscanes, who achieved another local hit with "Yellow River" when he was a high school senior. After graduation, he attended junior college and radio broadcasting school and secured disc jockey positions on San Francisco Bay Area black radio stations KSOL and KDIA. In 1964 Stewart met disc jockey Tom Donahue and soon became staff producer for Donahue's Autumn label. There he wrote and produced Bobby Freeman's smash crossover dance hit "C'mon and Swim" and produced the early hits of the Beau Brummels ("Laugh, Laugh," "Just a Little"), while recording local groups such as the Vejtables ("I Still Love You"), the Mojo Men ("Dance with Me"), and the Great Society (with Grace Slick). Brother Freddie formed the soul band the Stone Souls in the mid-'60s, while Sylvester led the Stoners, with trumpeter Cynthia Robinson.

Around 1966 the Stoners and the Stone Souls merged to form Sly and the Family Stone. Developing a regional reputation as a live act, the group was joined by the Stewarts' cousin Larry Graham, a veteran multi-instrumentalist, in 1967. The group's debut album, *A Whole New Thing* on Epic Records, featured shared and contrasted lead vocals, psychedelic lead guitar, complex horn arrangements, and a funky rhythm sound rooted in Graham's bass playing. *Dance to the Music* produced a near-smash pop and R&B hit with the title song, but the follow-up, *Life*, fared poorly. Early 1969's *Stand!*, sometimes labeled as soul music's first concept album, firmly established the group with black and white audiences. It included the classic "I Want to Take You Higher," "Don't Call Me Nigger, Whitey," the ominous "Somebody's Watching You," and "You Can Make It If You Try," and yielded a major crossover hit with the title cut and a top crossover hit with "Everyday People."

Sly and the Family Stone scored a smash pop and R&B hit with "Hot Fun in the Summertime" just days before their appearance at the Woodstock Festival in August 1969. Perhaps the most dynamic and electrifying act at the festival, the group next scored a top pop and R&B hit with "Thank You (Falettinme Be Mice Elf Agin)." However, Sly Stone became mired in legal and drug-related problems, and by 1971 the group had developed a reputation for failing to show up at scheduled concerts, a circumstance which occasionally led to riots, as it did in Chicago. Their next album of new material, the ironically titled *There's a Riot Goin' On*, came more than two years after the release of *Stand!* and revealed a softer and more personal feel to the music. The album yielded a top pop and R&B hit with "Family Affair" and a major crossover hit with "Runnin' Away." The group subsequently suffered the departures of several members, including bassist Larry Graham. Despite these problems, their next album, 1973's *Fresh*, produced a major pop and smash R&B hit with "If You Want Me to Stay." Sylvester Stewart married Kathy Silva in June 1974 during a concert at Madison Square Garden attended by 23,000 fans. Sly and the Family Stone achieved their last important hit soon thereafter with "Time for Livin'," a moderate pop and near-smash R&B hit.

Upon departure, Larry Graham formed Hot Chocolate and the group evolved into Graham Central Station. They scored a moderate pop and near-smash R&B hit with "Can You Handle It" in 1974. *Ain't No 'Bout-a-Doubt It*, the group's best-selling album, yielded a moderate pop and top R&B hit with "Your Love" and major R&B hits with "It's Alright" and "The Jam." Subsequent albums sold progressively less well as the group scored R&B hits with "Love," "Now Do U Wanta Dance," and "My Radio Sure Sounds Good to Me" through 1978. In 1980 Graham went solo, achieving his biggest success with his debut album *One in a Million You* and its two smash R&B hits "One in a Million You" (a near-smash pop hit) and "When We Get Married." After the 1981 R&B smash "Just Be My Lady," Graham's popularity waned.

By 1978 sax player Jerry Martini had left the band to join Rubicon with Jack Blades and Brad Gillis, scoring a major hit with "I'm Gonna Take Care of Everything." Blades and Gillis later formed Night Ranger for a modest career topped by their 1984 smash "Sister Christian." In the '90s Blades played in Damn Yankees with Ted Nugent and Tommy Shaw.

In the meantime, Sly Stone's career was in serious trouble. He recorded a solo album in 1979 and recorded his final Sly and the Family Stone album in 1983. During the '80s he was best known for his legal and drug problems; he unsuccessfully attempted a comeback with Bobby Womack in 1984, and again in 1987. He managed a minor pop and smash R&B hit in 1986 with "Crazay," recorded with Jesse Johnson of the Time. In 1993 the group was inducted into the Rock and Roll Hall of Fame.

Sly and the Family Stone

A Whole New Thing		Epic	26324	'67	†
		Epic	30335	'71	†
		Epic/Legacy	66424	'95	CD
Dance to the Music		Epic	26371	'68	†
		Epic	30334	'71	†
		Epic/Legacy	66427	'95	CD
Life		Epic	26397	'68	†
		Epic	30333	'71	†
		Epic/Legacy	66423	'95	CD

Stand!	Epic	26456	'69/'86	CS/CD
	Epic/Legacy	53410	'93	CD
	Epic/Legacy	64422	'94	CD
Greatest Hits	Epic	30325	'70	CS/CD
There's a Riot Goin' On	Epic	30986	'71	CS/CD
Fresh	Epic	32134	'73/'91	CD
Small Talk	Epic	32930	'74	†
High Energy	Epic	(2) 33462	'75	†
Heard Ya Missed Me, Well, I'm Back	Epic	34348	'76	†
Ten Years Too Soon	Epic	35974	'79	†
Anthology	Epic	(2) 37071	'81	†
	Epic	37071		CS/CD
Back on the Right Track	Warner Bros.	3303	'79	†
Ain't But the One Way	Warner Bros.	23942	'83	†
Best	IMG	717		CS
Sly Stone				
High on You	Epic	33835	'75	†
Graham Central Station				
Graham Central Station	Warner Bros.	2763	'73/'91	CD†
Release Yourself	Warner Bros.	2814	'74/'91	CD†
Ain't No 'Bout-a-Doubt It	Warner Bros.	2876	'75	†
Mirror	Warner Bros.	2937	'76	†
Now Do U Wanta Dance	Warner Bros.	3041	'77	†
My Radio Sure Sounds Good to Me	Warner Bros.	3175	'78	†
Star Walk	Warner Bros.	3322	'79	†
Larry Graham				
One in a Million You	Warner Bros.	3447	'80	†
Just Be My Lady	Warner Bros.	3554	'81	†
Sooner or Later	Warner Bros.	3668	'82	†
Victory	Warner Bros.	23878	'83	†
Fired Up	Warner Bros.	25307	'85	LP/CS†
Rubicon				
Rubicon	20th Century	552	'78	†

THE SMALL FACES

Steve Marriott (b. Jan. 30, 1947, Bow, London, England; d. Apr. 20, 1991, Saffron Walden, England), gtr, voc; **Ian McLagan** (b. May 12, 1946, Hounslown, England), kybd; **Ronnie Lane** (b. Apr. 1, 1946, Plaistow, London, England), bs, gtr; **Kenney Jones** (b. Sept. 16, 1948, East London, England), drm

THE FACES. Rod Stewart (b. Jan. 10, 1945, Highgate, London, England), voc; **Ron Wood** (b. June 1, 1947, Hillingdon, Middlesex, England), bs; **Ian McLagan**, **Ronnie Lane**, and **Kenney Jones**

HUMBLE PIE. Peter Frampton (b. Apr. 22, 1950, Beckenham, Kent, England), gtr, voc; **Greg Ridley** (b. Oct. 23, 1947, Carlisle, Cumbria, England), bs, voc; **Jerry Shirley** (b. Feb. 4, 1952, England), drm; **Steve Marriott** [Peter Frampton left in October 1971, to be replaced by **David "Clem" Clempson** (b. Sept. 5, 1949, England).]

Seminal British singles band of the latter half of the '60s, the Small Faces, along with the Who, were favorites of England's young mods, with their stylish dress and energetic performances. The band split in two when leader Steve Marriott left in 1969 to form Humble Pie with Peter Frampton. The remaining Small Faces regrouped as the Faces with Rod Stewart and Ron Wood from the Jeff Beck Group. Rod Stewart recorded both solo and with the Faces through 1975, after which he also pursued an hugely successful career as a solo artist. Steve Marriott re-formed the Small Faces in 1976, and Humble Pie re-formed in 1980. However, Ron Wood joined the Rolling Stones in 1975 and Kenney Jones joined the Who in 1978, while Ronnie Lane recorded with a variety of artists, including the Who's Pete Townshend. Steve Marriott had resumed recording with Peter Frampton in the early '90s, but he died in a home fire on April 20, 1991, at age 44.

Formed in 1965, the Small Faces recorded one major British-only hit single, "Whatcha Gonna Do About It," before early keyboardist Jimmy Winston was replaced by Ian McLagan. Effervescent and well dressed in performance, the Small Faces quickly became favorites of England's young mods, scoring major British-only hits written by Steve Marriott and Ronnie Lane through 1967, including the smashes "Sha La La La Lee," "All or Nothing," and "My Mind's Eye." They finally penetrated into the American market with 1967's "Itchycoo Park," made distinctive through the manipulation of phasing. Although Small Faces albums had been issued in Great Britain on Decca in 1966 and 1967, their first American release did not come until 1968. Following the second, *Ogden's Nut Gone Flake*, Steve Marriott quit the group to form Humble Pie with guitarist Peter Frampton, formerly with the Herd.

Humble Pie signed with Andrew Oldham's Immediate label, recording two albums and scoring the British-only hit "Natural Born Woman" for the label before switching to A&M Records in 1970. More effective live than on recordings, the group's first American success came with 1971's live double-record set *Rockin' the Fillmore*, which yielded a minor hit with "I Don't Need No Doctor." Marriott's hard-rock orientation had overwhelmed Frampton's more gentle, romantic leanings, and as a consequence Frampton left the group in October 1971. He went on to a solo career, climaxing with his 1976 megahit album, *Frampton Comes Alive*. Frampton was replaced by David "Clem" Clempson, previously with Colosseum; the group's first album with Clempson, *Smokin'*, became their best-seller, containing the favorite "30 Days in the Hole" and producing a minor hit with "Hot 'n' Nasty." Subsequent albums sold progressively less well, and the group disbanded in 1975.

With the dissolution of the first edition of the Small Faces, former members Ronnie Lane, Ian McLagan, and Kenney Jones recruited Ron Wood from the Jeff Beck Group in mid-1969. Encouraged to sit in with the group, former Beck vocalist Rod Stewart soon joined. They shortened their name to the Faces, although their debut album, *First Step*, was mistakenly credited to the Small Faces in the United States. Touring America successfully several times in 1970, the Faces broke through with late 1971's *A Nod Is as Good as a Wink . . . To a Blind Horse*. The album yielded a major hit with "Stay with Me" two months after "(I Know) I'm Losing You," recorded with the Faces, became a major hit from Stewart's solo album *Every Picture Tells a Story*.

Following his departure from the Jeff Beck Group, Rod Stewart had secured a solo recording contract with Mercury Records. Thus he recorded both solo and with the Faces, but his popularity as a solo artist became paramount with *Every Picture Tells a Story*. Stewart continued to record and tour through 1975 with the Faces, who became one of the most popular live bands of the time, but they managed only one more moderate hit, "Cindy Incidentally" in 1973. Ronnie Lane played his final engagement with the Faces that May, to be replaced on bass by Tetsu Yamauchi, formerly with Free. In 1974 Ron Wood recorded his first solo album, *I've Got My Own Album to Do*, with Ian McLagan and Rolling Stones guitarist Keith Richards. In the meantime, Lane formed Slim Chance, recording three British albums and scoring one British hit with "How Come?," but he released only one neglected album in the United States. During summer 1975 Wood toured with both the Rolling Stones (as Mick Taylor's replacement) and Rod Stewart and the Faces. Wood's second solo album was released that July. Given the apparent conflicts with Ian McLagan, Wood's increasing involvement with the Rolling Stones, and his own rising popularity, Rod Stewart announced his departure from the Faces in December 1975, effectively ending the band's career.

In 1976 Ronnie Lane reunited with Ron Wood for the soundtrack to the movie *Mahoney's Last Chance*, later recording *Rough Mix* with Pete Townshend of the Who. Wood, an official member of the Rolling Stones since July 1977, released another solo set, *Gimme Some Neck*, recorded with McLagan, Keith Richards, Charlie Watts, and Mick Fleetwood, in spring 1979. The album included eight Wood originals and "Seven Days," written for Wood by Bob Dylan. Wood later briefly toured with the New Barbarians, comprised of Richards, McLagan, and jazz bassist Stanley Clarke.

Steve Marriott recorded a solo album in 1976 and reconstituted the Small Faces in 1977–1978 with Ian McLagan, Kenney Jones, and bassist-vocalist Rick Wills for two overlooked albums on Atlantic. With the departures of Kenney Jones for the Who and Rick Wills for Foreigner, Steve Marriott folded the group. Marriott revived Humble Pie in the early '80s, working with ex–Jeff Beck vocalist Bobby Tench. The band recorded two albums and toured the United States, but fell into disarray when Marriott was hospitalized for treatment of an ulcer. On April 20, 1991, after returning from the United States where he had been working with Peter Frampton on a new Humble Pie project, Steve Marriott died in a house fire at his Saffron Walden cottage outside London at age 44.

In 1983 Ronnie Lane, the victim of multiple sclerosis since 1976, recruited Eric Clapton, Jeff Beck, Jimmy Page, Joe Cocker, Paul Rodgers, and others for a brief tour in support of his Appeal for Action Research into Multiple Sclerosis organization. He moved to Texas, and toured once again in 1987.

The Small Faces

There Are But Four Small Faces	Immediate	1252002	'68	†
	Immediate	47895	'91	CD
Ogden's Nut Gone Flake	Immediate	1252008	'68	
	ABKCO	4225	'73	†
	Compleat	675003	'85	†
	Immediate	46964	'91	CD
All or Nothing	Immediate	52427	'92	CD
Early Faces	Pride	0001	'72	†
History of the Small Faces	Pride	0014		†
Archetypes	MGM	4955	'74	†
Immediate Story, Volume 2	Sire	(2) 3709	'76	†
By Appointment	Accord	7157	'82	†
The Small Faces	Compleat	672004	'84	†
The Small Faces	Polydor	820572		CD†
From the Beginning	Polydor	820766		CD†
Playmates	Atlantic	19113	'77	†
78 in the Shade	Atlantic	19171	'78	†
20 Greatest Hits	Big Time		'88	CD†

Humble Pie

Town and Country	Immediate	207	'69	†
	Immediate	47349	'91	CS/CD†
As Safe as Yesterday	Immediate	101	'69	†
	Immediate	47899	'91	CS/CD†

Lost and Found—Town and Country/Safe as Yesterday	A&M	(2) 3513	'72	†
Humble Pie	A&M	4270	'70	†
	A&M	3127		†
	A&M	2512	'87	CD
Rock On	A&M	4301	'71	CD†
Rockin' the Fillmore	A&M	3506	'71	†
	A&M	6008		CS/CD
Smokin'	A&M	4342	'72	†
	A&M	3132		CS/CD
Eat It	A&M	(2) 3701	'73	†
Thunderbox	A&M	3611	'74	†
Street Rats	A&M	4514	'75	†
Best	A&M	3208		CS/CD
Hot 'n' Nasty: The Anthology	A&M	(2) 540164	'94	CS/CD
On to Victory	Atlantic	38122	'80	†
	Atco	38122	'91	CD
Go for the Throat	Atlantic	38131	'81	†
	Atco	38131	'91	CD
Steve Marriott				
Marriott	A&M	4572	'76	†
The Faces				
First Step	Warner Bros.	1851	'70	†
	Warner Bros.	26376	'93	CD
Long Player	Warner Bros.	1892	'71	†
	Warner Bros.	26191	'93	CD
A Nod Is as Good as a Wink . . . To a Blind Horse	Warner Bros.	2574	'71	†
	Warner Bros.	25929	'93	CD
Ooh La La	Warner Bros.	2665	'73	†
	Warner Bros.	26368	'93	CD
Snakes and Ladders: Best	Warner Bros.	2897	'76		
Rod Stewart and the Faces				
Live	Warner Bros.	2572		†
Coast to Coast: Overture and Beginners	Mercury	697	'73	†
	Mercury	832128		CD
Rod Stewart and the Faces	Springboard Int'l	4030	'75	†
Early Sessions	Richmond	2305		CS
Ron Wood				
I've Got My Own Album to Do	Warner Bros.	2819	'74	†
	Warner Bros.	45692	'94	CD
Now Look	Warner Bros.	2872	'75	†
	Warner Bros.	45693	'94	CD
Gimme Some Neck	Columbia	35702	'79	CD
1234	Columbia	37473	'81	†
Ronnie Lane and Slim Chance				
Ronnie Lane/Slim Chance	A&M	3638	'75	†
Ron Wood and Ronnie Lane				
Mahoney's Last Chance (soundtrack)	Atco	36126	'76	†

Ronnie Lane and Pete Townshend

Rough Mix	MCA	2295	'77	†
	Atco	90097	'83	CS/CD

Ian McLagan

Troublemaker	Mercury	3786	'80	†
Bump in the Night	Mercury	4007	'81	†

PATTI SMITH
(b. Dec. 31, 1946, Chicago, IL)

PATTI SMITH

A unique late-'70s female singer-songwriter, Patti Smith attempted to establish her literate and somewhat bizarre poetry as a rock art form when backed by minimalist, hard-driving music. In 1974 she began performing at New York clubs such as Max's Kansas City and CBGB's, serving as inspiration to the soon-to-burgeon punk-rock scene. Winning a cult following on both American coasts for her volatile and personal lyrics, erratic vocal style, and unusual stage antics, Smith finally broke nationally with the 1978 hit "Because the Night," cowritten by Smith and Bruce Springsteen. Recording two of the most striking albums of the late '70s, *Horses* and *Easter*, she retired after 1979's *Wave*, produced by Todd Rundgren. Patti Smith unsuccessfully attempted a comeback with husband Fred "Sonic" Smith of the MC5 in 1988; after his death, she resumed touring in 1995, opening for Bob Dylan on several dates, and she began recording a new album working with guitarist Lenny Kaye.

Patti Smith grew up in southern New Jersey, moving to New York City in 1967, where she frequented Pratt Art College. She later traveled to Paris with her sister, returning to New York in 1969. There she met playwright Sam Shepard, with whom she wrote the play *Cowboy Mouth*. In February 1971 she began reading her poetry at St. Mark's Church, accompanied by guitarist and rock critic Lenny Kaye. Attracting her initial following as a rock critic for *Creem* magazine, Smith subsequently published two volumes of writing, *Seventh Heaven* and *Witt*, in the early '70s. Encouraged to write songs and sing by Kaye and Blue Öyster Cult keyboardist Allen Lanier, she coauthored "Career of Evil," which the group included on their 1974 *Secret Treaties* album.

By 1974 Patti Smith was performing in Manhattan clubs such as Max's Kansas City and CBGB's backed by Lenny Kaye and pianist Richard Sohl. She recorded the single "Hey Joe"/"Piss Factory" for Kaye's Mer Records label, becoming one of the focal points of the emerging New York underground rock scene with her literate, passionate, and unusual lyrics, inconsistent vocal delivery, androgynous appearance, and ranting onstage antics. Late in the year, she signed with Arista Records, recording *Horses* under producer-artist John Cale, a former member of the Velvet Underground. Recorded with Lanier, Kaye, Sohl, Ivan Kral (bs, gtr, kybd), and Jay Dee Daugherty (drm), the album featured seven originals (she took sole credit for only the title song) and reworked versions of Van Morrison's "Gloria" and Chris Kenner's "Land of 1,000 Dances." The album sold modestly, and Smith made her first national tour in January 1976.

Forming the Patti Smith Group with Lenny Kaye, Ivan Kral, and Jay Dee Daugherty, Patti Smith next recorded *Radio Ethiopia*, but the album's heavy-metal sound overwhelmed her vocals. While on tour in January 1977 she fell off stage in Tampa, Florida, sustaining broken neck bones that necessitated a six-month period of recovery. In early 1978 she published a poetry collection, *Babel*, her first work released by a major publishing house (Putnam). The Patti Smith Group regrouped with Smith, Kaye, Kral, Daugherty, and keyboardist Bruce Brody for *Easter*. The album included "Rock 'n' Roll Nigger," "Privilege (Set Me Free)," "Till Victory," and "Space Monkey," and yielded a major hit with "Because the Night." *Wave*, produced by Todd Rundgren, featured "Revenge" and a version of the Byrds' "So You Want to Be a Rock 'n' Roll Star," and produced a minor hit with "Frederick." Later in 1979 Patti Smith retired from the music business and moved to Detroit, and in 1980 she married Fred "Sonic" Smith of the MC5.

Patti Smith reemerged in 1988 with *Dream of Life*, recorded with Richard Sohl, Jay Dee Daugherty, and Fred Smith. With Fred and Patti as cosongwriters, the album included "People Have the Power," "Up There Down There," the gentle "Paths That Cross," and the lullaby "The Jackson Song." However, it failed to sell in significant quantities. In late autumn 1995 Smith reemerged for a brief tour opening for Bob Dylan while preparing a new album of original compositions with Lenny Kaye.

Patti Smith

Horses	Arista	4066	'75	†
	Arista	8362		LP/CS/CD
Dream of Life	Arista	8453	'88	LP/CS/CD
Gone Again	Arista	7822	'96	CS/CD
The Patti Smith Group				
Radio Ethiopia	Arista	4097	'76	†
	Arista	8379	'87	LP/CS
	Arista	8161	'87	CD
Easter	Arista	4171	'78	†
	Arista	8349		LP/CS
	Arista	8166		CD
Wave	Arista	4221	'79	†
	Arista	8546		LP/CS/CD

SONNY AND CHER

Salvatore "Sonny" Bono (b. Feb. 16, 1935, Detroit, MI); **Cher** (b. Cherilyn Sarkisian, May 20, 1946, El Centro, CA)

Sonny and Cher were one of the most successful and famous couples in rock music in the mid-'60s, thanks to hits such as "I Got You Babe" and their biggest success, 1967's "The Beat Goes On." In the early '70s Cher established herself as a popular Las Vegas performer and easy-listening artist, while the couple enjoyed mainstream exposure with their CBS-TV variety show from 1971 to 1974. After they divorced in 1974, Cher returned to performing in Las Vegas, eventually becoming the city's highest-paid entertainer; she recorded for a number of different labels. During the '80s Sonny ran his own restaurant in Los Angeles, while Cher was becoming the only rock star to consistently demonstrate talent as an actor, as evidenced by the films *Silkwood*, *Mask*, *Suspect*, and *Moonstruck*. Sonny later entered Republican Party politics, serving as mayor of upscale Palm Springs from 1988 to 1992 and winning a seat in the House of Representatives from California in 1994. Cher's musical career blossomed in the late '80s, but both her music and acting careers seem to be in eclipse in the '90s.

Sonny Bono began writing songs during the early '50s, later holding a succession of different jobs to support his family. In 1957 Larry Williams recorded his "High School Dance" as the flip side of the smash hit "Short, Fat Fanny" on Specialty Records. As a consequence, Bono became an apprentice producer at Specialty while recording unsuccessfully as Don Christy and Ronny Sommers. With the demise of Specialty in 1959, Bono continued to write and record unsuccessfully, although his "Needles and Pins," cowritten with Jack Nitzche, became a major hit for the Searchers in 1964.

Born to Armenian and Cherokee Indian parents, Cher moved to Hollywood as a teenager to pursue an acting career, supplementing her income by singing background vocals on sessions for Phil Spector's Philles label. In 1963 she met Sonny Bono there, where he was working as Spector's assistant. The couple soon married, later recording as Sonny and Cher for Vault Records and as Caesar and Cleo for Reprise Records. Cher also recorded as Bonnie Jo Mason for Annette Records and as Cherilyn for Imperial Records.

Signed to Atco Records in 1965, Sonny and Cher scored a top pop hit with "I Got You Babe," produced and arranged by Sonny, and a major pop hit with "Just You" from their debut album, *Look at Us*. Sonny's "Laugh at Me" and the couple's "But You're Mine" became major hits on Atco, as Reprise reissued "Baby Don't Go" and it became a near-smash. Cher, recording solo for Imperial Records, scored major hits with Bob Dylan's "All I Really Want to Do" and "Where Do You Go" in 1965, followed by the smash "Bang Bang (My Baby Shot Me Down)" in spring 1966.

Sonny and Cher became prominent members of Los Angeles's elite hippie set and continued to achieve major hits with "What Now My Love," "Little Man," and Sonny's classic "The Beat Goes On." They appeared in the films *Good Times* (1966) and *Chastity* (1968). Cher scored a near-smash solo hit with "You Better Sit Down Kids" in late 1967, but the couple would not have another hit for four years. Cher switched to Atco Records in 1969, and Sonny and Cher moved to Kapp Records in 1971. In 1970 Cher began modeling for *Vogue*, becoming a fashion queen, an international celebrity, and the subject of gossip column reports.

Around 1970 Sonny and Cher moved on to the Las Vegas club circuit, later hosting their own variety show on CBS television from 1971 to 1974. Thereby leaving the rock audience behind in favor of the easy-listening crowd, Sonny and Cher scored near-smash pop and smash easy-listening hits with "All I Ever Need Is You" and "A Cowboy's Work Is Never Done." Cher achieved a succession of pop and easy-listening hits through 1974, including the top pop and smash easy-listening hits "Gypsys, Tramps and Thieves," "Half-Breed," and "Dark Lady." The couple divorced in 1974, and each had a television show that ran for only a short period of time. By 1975 Cher had switched to Warner Bros. Records for the Jimmy Webb–produced *Stars*, but the album and two subsequent productions for the label failed to yield any major hits. She married Gregg Allman in the summer of 1975, but the relationship lasted all of nine days, and the couple eventually divorced in 1977. The liaison produced one dismal album, *Two the Hard Way*. Sonny and Cher resumed their professional relationship from 1976 to 1977 for a revived *The Sonny and Cher Show* on CBS television.

Cher returned to performing in Las Vegas casinos and moved to Casablanca Records in 1979, scoring a near-smash pop hit with the disco-style "Take Me Home." Late in the year she formed the New Wave–style band Black Rose with guitarist Les Dudek, but their album failed to sell and the group soon disbanded.

In February 1982 Cher returned to her first career pursuit, acting, by appearing in the Broadway production of *Come Back to the Five and Dime, Jimmy Dean, Jimmy Dean*. She won praise for her straight dramatic role and later starred with Sandy Dennis and Karen Black in the film version. In late 1983 she garnered critical acclaim for her role in *Silkwood* with Meryl Streep and Kurt Russell, and in 1985 she enjoyed well-deserved recognition for her tough role in *Mask*, with Sam Elliott and Eric Stoltz. In 1986 she starred in the legal drama *Suspect* with Dennis Quaid, and in 1988 she achieved the pinnacle of any acting career, an Oscar, with her performance in the comedy *Moonstruck*, with Nicholas Cage, Vincent Gardenia, Danny Aiello, and Olympia Dukakis. In 1987 David Geffen convinced Cher to return to recording, and her debut for his label produced major hits with "I Found Someone," written and produced by Michael Bolton, and "We All Sleep Alone," cowritten and coproduced by Jon Bon Jovi. Her 1989 album, *Heart of Stone*, became the best-selling album of her career, moving more than two million copies. It yielded two smash pop and top easy-listening hits with "After All," sung in duet with Peter Cetera, and "If I Could Turn Back Time" (with its for-the-time-racy video, showing Cher cavorting in a skimpy, see-through bodysuit on the deck of a naval vessel), plus the near-smash "Just Like Jesse James" and the major title hit. However, the 1990 film *Mermaids*, which Cher starred in with Winona Ryder, was not well received, and her next album, 1991's *Love Hurts*, produced only one major hit, "Love and Understanding." In 1992 and 1994 Cher joined ensemble casts for the films *The Player* and *Ready to Wear*.

By 1980 Sonny had left show business to run his own restaurant in Los Angeles. After serving as mayor of Palm Springs from 1988 to 1992, Sonny unsuccessfully campaigned for the Republican Party nomination for the U.S. Senate seat vacated by the retiring Alan Cranston. In 1994 Sonny Bono won election as the Representative from California's 44th District.

In the '90s Sonny and Cher's daughter Chastity formed the pop band Ceremony with longtime friend Heidi Shink, who went by the name Chance for *Hang Out Your Poetry* on Geffen Records.

Sonny and Cher

Baby, Don't Go	Reprise	6177	'65	†
Look at Us	Atco	33-177	'65	†
The Wondrous World of Sonny and Cher	Atco	33-183	'66	†
At Their Best (compilation of above two albums)	Pair	(2) 1140	'86	CS
In Case You're In Love	Atco	33-203	'67	†
Good Times (soundtrack)	Atco	33-214	'67	†
Best	Atco	33-219	'67	†
The Two of Us	Atco	(2) 804	'72	†
The Beat Goes On	Atco	11000	'76	†
Sonny and Cher Live	Kapp	3654	'71	†
	Kapp	5554	'72	†
	MCA	2009		†
All I Ever Need Is You	Kapp	3660	'72	†
	Kapp	5560	'72	†
	MCA	2021		†
Mama Was a Rock 'n' Roll Singer, Papa Used to Write All Her Songs	MCA	2102	'73	†
Live in Las Vegas, Volume 2	MCA	(2) 8004	'73	†
Greatest Hits	MCA	2117	'74	†
All I Ever Need: The Kapp/MCA Anthology	MCA	(2) 11300	'95	CS/CD
The Beat Goes On — The Best of Sonny and Cher	Rhino	91796	'91	CS/CD
I Got You Babe	Rhino	71233	'93	CS/CD

Sonny

Inner Views	Atco	33-229	'67	†

Cher

All I Really Want to Do	Imperial	12292	'65	†
The Sonny Side of Cher	Imperial	12301	'66	†
All I Really Want to Do/The Sonny Side of Cher	EMI	80241	'92	CS/CD
Cher	Imperial	12320	'66	†
With Love	Imperial	12358	'67	†
Backstage	Imperial	12373	'68	†
Golden Greats	Imperial	12406	'68	†
This Is Cher	Sunset	5276	'70	†
Superpak	United Artists	(2) 88	'72	†
Superpak, Volume 2	United Artists	(2) 94	'72	†
Very Best	United Artists	237	'74	†
	United Artists	377	'75	†
Very Best, Volume 2	United Artists	435	'75	†
Best of Cher	EMI	91836	'89	CS/CD
Bang Bang: The Best of Cher	EMI	92773	'90	CS/CD
Best, Volume 1	Liberty	10110	'81	†
Best, Volume 2	Liberty	10111	'81	†
3614 Jackson Highway	Atco	33-298	'69	†
Chastity (soundtrack)	Atco	33-302	'69	†
Cher	Kapp	3649	'71	†
(reissued as) Gypsys, Tramps and Thieves	Kapp	5549	'72	†
	MCA	2020		†
	MCA	624		†
	MCA	31375	'90	CD
Foxy Lady	Kapp	5514	'72	†
Bittersweet White Light	MCA	2101	'73	†
Half-Breed	MCA	2104	'73	†
Dark Lady	MCA	2113	'74	†
Greatest Hits	MCA	2127	'74	†
	MCA	37028		
	MCA	922	'90	CS/CD
Cher Sings the Hits	Springboard Int'l	4029	'75	†
Stars	Warner Bros.	2850	'75	†
I'd Rather Believe in You	Warner Bros.	2898	'76	†
Cherished	Warner Bros.	3046	'77	†
Take Me Home	Casablanca	7133	'79	†
Prisoner	Casablanca	7184	'79	†
Outrageous	Polygram	838644		CS
I Paralyze	Columbia	38096	'82/'90	CS/CD
Cher	Geffen	24164	'87	CS/CD
Heart of Stone	Geffen	24239	'89	CS/CD
Love Hurts	Geffen	24369	'91	CS/CD
	Geffen	24421	'91	CD

Gregg Allman and Cher (Allman and Woman)

Two the Hard Way	Warner Bros.	3120	'77	†

Black Rose

Black Rose	Casablanca	7234	'80	†

Ceremony (with Chastity and Chance)					
Hang Out Your Poetry		Geffen	24523	'93	CS/CD

PHIL SPECTOR

(b. Dec. 26, 1940, Bronx, NY)

Undoubtedly the single most important and influential producer in the history of rock music, Phil Spector devised his trademark wall-of-sound technique in recording a series of smash hit records between 1962 and 1966 for the Crystals, the Ronettes, and the Righteous Brothers, among others, on his own label, Philles Records. Integrating numerous guitars, massive string and horn sections, and dozens of background voices to produce a dense, murky sound that emphasized only lead vocals and drums, Spector's production style brought an unprecedented level of sophistication and complexity to record production. He was the most successful independent producer in rock music when, in 1966, the dismal showing of Ike and Tina Turner's "River Deep—Mountain High" led to his withdrawal from the music business for several years. One of rock's most enigmatic and perplexing figures, Spector eventually reemerged with productions for the Beatles, John Lennon, and George Harrison in the early '70s, but these efforts paled in comparison to his earlier work, still acknowledged as classics some 30 years after their original release.

Phil Spector moved to Los Angeles at age 13 with his mother and sister. Having studied guitar and piano in high school, he formed the Teddy Bears in 1958 with Annette Kleinbard and Marshall Leib. Signed to Dore Records, the trio soon scored a top pop and near-smash R&B hit with Spector's own "To Know Him Is to Love Him" (the title line was drawn from Spector's father's tombstone!), but subsequent recordings for Imperial fared poorly and the group disbanded in 1959. Spector then worked on the West Coast under producers Lester Sill and Lee Hazlewood and subsequently served as understudy to Jerry Leiber and Mike Stoller in New York. He coauthored Ben E. King's solo debut pop and R&B hit "Spanish Harlem" with Leiber, and produced the hits "Corinna, Corinna" for Ray Peterson, "Pretty Little Angel Eyes" for Curtis Lee, and "I Love How You Love Me" for the Paris Sisters.

Phil Spector then returned to the West Coast, where he formed Philles Records with Lester Sill in late 1961. Spector was given total freedom in the studio, and he astutely utilized the services of some of the best songwriters of the day (Jeff Barry and Ellie Greenwich, Barry Mann and Cynthia Weil, Carole King and Gerry Goffin) and many of Los Angeles's finest session musicians (keyboardists Harold Battiste and Leon Russell; guitarists Barney Kessel, Herb Ellis, Tony Mottola, and Joe Pass; horn players Steve Douglas and Jim Horn; drummers Hal Blaine and Earl Palmer) to create his classic recordings. The Crystals were the label's first signing and they soon had pop and R&B hits with "There's No Other" and "Uptown." The so-called wall-of-sound technique devised by Spector was launched into international prominence with the Crystals' top pop and smash R&B hit "He's a Rebel," written by Gene Pitney. Following "He's Sure the Boy I Love," the Crystals had smash crossover hit classics with "Da Doo Ron Ron" and "Then He Kissed Me," both cowritten by Spector, Jeff Barry, and Ellie Greenwich.

In late 1962 Phil Spector bought out Lester Sill and assumed total control of Philles Records. In mid-1963 Spector signed the Ronettes to Philles Records and they soon had a smash pop and R&B hit with "Be My Baby," written by Spector, Barry, and Greenwich. Other major crossover hits for the Ronettes through 1964 were "Baby, I Love You" and

"Walking in the Rain." In late 1963 Spector issued the celebrated Christmas album *A Christmas Gift for You*, featuring Philles artists performing seasonal standards.

During 1964 Phil Spector signed the Righteous Brothers. At year's end the duo scored a top pop and smash R&B hit with "You've Lost That Lovin' Feelin'," written by Spector, Barry Mann, and Cynthia Weil; the song came to be regarded as one of rock's all-time classic singles. The Righteous Brothers subsequently achieved smash pop hits with "Just Once in My Life" (by Spector, Carole King, and Gerry Goffin), "Unchained Melody," and "Ebb Tide" before switching to Verve Records, where their top pop hit "(You're My) Soul and Inspiration" mimicked Spector's production style.

In spring 1966 Philles Records issued the Spector-Barry-Greenwich epic "River Deep—Mountain High" as recorded by Ike and Tina Turner, but the single failed to become anything more than a minor American pop hit (it was a smash hit in Great Britain), much to Spector's chagrin, as he ostensibly considered it his consummate production effort. Thus rebuffed by the American public, Spector withdrew from the record business and soon closed Philles Records, ending a stellar chapter in the history of rock music. He married Veronica "Ronnie" Bennett of the Ronettes in 1968 and retreated to his Hollywood mansion; the couple divorced in 1974.

During the rest of the '60s Phil Spector was largely inactive, although he did make a cameo appearance in the film *Easy Rider* and worked for a time at A&M Records, producing one album by the Checkmates. He was approached by John Lennon to help salvage the Beatles' *Let It Be* album, adding strings and vocal choruses to the original tracks, much to Paul McCartney's chagrin. Befriending Lennon and George Harrison, he produced Harrison's *All Things Must Pass* and four albums for John Lennon, including *Imagine*. Lennon and Spector worked together on the initial sessions for Lennon's album *Rock and Roll*, but the producer absconded with the tapes and Lennon had to complete the sessions on his own.

Spector formed Warner-Spector Records under the aegis of Warner Bros. Records in 1973. The label reissued his *Christmas Album* and issued the two-record set *Greatest Hits*, but productions for Cher ("A Woman's Story"), Cher and Nilsson ("A Love Like Yours Don't Come Knocking Every Day"), and Ronnie Spector (Spector and Nilsson's "Paradise") fared poorly. Forming Phil Spector International in Great Britain in conjunction with Polydor Records, Spector produced Dion's *Born to Be with You* (unreleased in the United States) for the label. Spector's later productions for Leonard Cohen (the disastrous *Death of a Ladies's Man*) and the Ramones (*End of the Century*) failed to reestablish him. Since coproducing Yoko Ono's *Season of Glass* in 1981, Phil Spector has remained largely in seclusion, emerging in 1991 to assemble the four-disc set *Back to Mono*, a celebration of his classic '60s recordings. He was inducted into the Rock and Roll Hall of Fame in 1989.

The Teddy Bears

The Teddy Bears	Imperial	9067	'59	†

Phil Spector

The Early Productions, 1958–1961	Rhino	203		LP
Today's Hits	Philles	4004	'63	†
A Christmas Gift for You	Philles	4005	'63	†
(reissued as) Phil Spector's Christmas Album	Apple	3400	'72	†
	Warner-Spector	9103	'75	†
	Pavillion	37686		†
(reissued as) A Christmas Gift for You	Rhino	70235		LP/CS/CD
Phil Spector's Greatest Hits	Warner-Spector	9104	'77	†
Phil Spector: Back to Mono (1958–1969)	ABKCO (4)	7118	'91	LP/CS/CD

THE SPINNERS

Robert Smith (b. Apr. 10, 1937, Detroit, MI), lead and ten voc; **George W. Dixon**, lead and ten voc; **Billy Henderson** (b. Aug. 9, 1939, Detroit, MI), ten voc; **Henry Fambrough** (b. May 10, 1935, Detroit, MI), bar voc; **Pervis Jackson**, bs voc [George Dixon was replaced in 1962 by **Edgar "Chico" Hamilton**; Robert Smith was replaced by **G. C. Cameron** in 1968, who was replaced in 1972 by **Philippe Wynne** (b. Apr. 3, 1941, Detroit, MI; d. July 14, 1984, Oakland, CA), who was replaced by **John Edwards** (b. St. Louis, MO) in 1977.]

A long-lived Detroit-based black vocal group, the Spinners first recorded in 1961 for Harvey Fuqua's Tri-Phi label before moving with Fuqua to Motown Records, where they languished for seven years. Switching to Atlantic Records in 1972 at the urging of Aretha Franklin, the Spinners were teamed with Philadelphia songwriter-producer Thom Bell. They scored a succession of smooth soul ballad crossover hits such as "I'll Be Around," "Could It Be I'm Falling in Love," and "(One of a Kind) Love Affair," featuring the distinctive lead vocals of Philippe Wynne. Rivaling the O'Jays as America's most popular black vocal group of the era, the Spinners were introduced to the Nevada cabaret circuit by Dionne Warwick. After Wynne's departure in 1977, neither the group nor Wynne as a soloist fared very well, although remarkably the Spinners persevered with lead vocalist John Edwards into the '90s without a personnel change.

The Spinners were initially formed around 1955 as an a cappella vocal group called the Domingos by five Detroit-area high school students: Robert Smith, George Dixon, Billy Henderson, Henry Fambrough, and Pervis Jackson. During the late '50s they performed locally, changing their name to the Spinners in 1961. The group signed with former Moonglow Harvey Fuqua's Tri-Phi label, scoring a smash R&B and major pop hit with "That's What Girls Are Made For." They switched to Motown Records when Fuqua joined the company in 1964. After achieving a moderate pop and near-smash R&B hit with "I'll Always Love You" in 1965, they replaced Smith with G. C. Cameron in 1968 and recorded for Motown's subsidiary label V.I.P., hitting in 1970 with "It's a Shame," written and produced by Stevie Wonder.

Leaving Motown in 1972, the Spinners replaced Cameron with charismatic singer Philippe Wynne and signed to Atlantic Records with the help of Aretha Franklin. Placed with Philadelphia soul songwriter-arranger-producer Thom Bell, they soon scored a top R&B and a smash pop hit with "I'll Be Around" and "Could It Be I'm Falling In Love" and an R&B smash with "Ghetto Child," all from their debut album for the label. *Mighty Love* produced three major pop and smash R&B hits with "Mighty Love—Pt. 1," "I'm Coming Home," and "Love Don't Love Nobody—Pt. 1."

Becoming one of the most popular soul groups of the mid-'70s, the Spinners included the top pop and smash R&B hit "Then Came You," recorded with Dionne Warwick, on their album *New and Improved*, which also produced near-smash R&B hits with "Living a Little, Laughing a Little" and "Sadie." *Pick of the Litter* yielded the top R&B and smash pop hit "They Just Can't Stop It (The Games People Play)" and an R&B near-smash with "Love or Leave." After a top R&B and smash pop hit with the disco-style "The Rubber Band Man" and the R&B smash "You're Throwing a Good Love Away," Philippe Wynne left the Spinners in 1977, to be replaced by John Edwards. Two years later producer-arranger Thom Bell also stopped working with the group. Still, the Spinners managed pop and R&B smashes with the oldies medleys "Working My Way Back to You"/"Forgive Me, Girl" and "Cupid"/"I've Loved You for a Long Time" in 1979–1980, though they never again achieved another major pop hit. Nonetheless, the Spinners remained intact into the '90s, recording *Down to Business* for Volt in 1989.

Wynne's solo debut, *Starting All Over*, fared dismally, and he soon joined George Clinton's Parliament-Funkadelic aggregation, recording *Jammin'* for Clinton's Uncle Jam label in 1980. While performing at the Oakland, California, nightclub Ivey's on July 14, 1984, Philippe Wynne collapsed and died of a heart attack at age 43.

The Spinners

The Original Spinners	Motown	639	'68	†
Second Time Around	V.I.P.	405	'70	†
Best	Motown	769	'73	†
	Motown	5199		CS/CD
Motown Superstar Series, Volume 9	Motown	109		†
	Motown	5109		†
The Spinners	Atlantic	7256	'73	†
	Rhino	71882	'95	CS/CD
Mighty Love	Atlantic	7296	'74	CS
	Rhino	71586	'95	CS/CD
New and Improved	Atlantic	18118	'74	†
	Rhino	71883	'95	CS/CD
Pick of the Litter	Atlantic	18141	'75	†
	Rhino	71884	'95	CS/CD
Live	Atlantic	(2) 910	'75	
Happiness Is Being with the Spinners	Atlantic	18181	'76	†
Yesterday, Today and Tomorrow	Atlantic	19100	'77	†
8	Atlantic	19146	'77	†
Best	Atlantic	19179	'78	†
	Rhino	19179		CS/CD
From Here to Eternally	Atlantic	19219	'79	†
Dancin' and Lovin'	Atlantic	19256	'79	†
	Rhino	71115	'92	CS/CD
Love Trippin'	Atlantic	19270	'80	†
Can't Shake This Feelin'	Atlantic	19318	'81	†
Grand Slam	Atlantic	80020	'83	†
Cross Fire	Atlantic	80150	'84	†
Lovin' Feelings	Mirage	90456	'85	†
A One of a Kind Love Affair — The Anthology	Atlantic	(2) 82332	'91	CS/CD
Down to Business	Volt	3403	'89	LP/CD
	Volt	53403	'89	CS
Very Best	Rhino	71213	'93	CS/CD

John Edwards

Life, Love and Living	Cotillion	9909	'76	†

Philippe Wynne

Starting All Over	Cotillion	9920	'77	†
Jammin'	Uncle Jam	36843	'80	†

SPIRIT

Jay Ferguson (b. May 10, 1947, Burbank, CA), lead voc; **Randy California** (b. Randolph Wolfe, Feb. 20, 1951, Los Angeles, CA), gtr; **John Locke** (b. Sept. 25, 1943, Los Angeles, CA), kybd; **Mark Andes** (b. Feb. 19, 1948, Philadelphia, PA), bs; **Ed Cassidy** (b. May 4, 1931, Chicago, IL), drm

Acclaimed as one of the West Coast's finest groups during the late '60s, Spirit never progressed beyond a cult status. Recording classics such as "Mechanical World" and "Nature's Way" and hitting with "I've Got a Line on You," Spirit fragmented after recording their masterpiece, *The Twelve Dreams of Dr. Sardonicus*. Lead vocalist–songwriter Jay Ferguson and bassist Mark Andes later formed Jo Jo Gunne, but the group scored only one hit, and Ferguson subsequently pursued a solo career that culminated in the pop-style near-smash "Thunder Island" in late 1977. Spirit reunited in 1976 and 1984 with little success and Ferguson's career faded in the early-'80s.

Jay Ferguson studied piano as a child and played music with bassist Mark Andes in high school. The two later formed the Red Roosters with Randy California, who picked up guitar at age five and frequented his uncle's folk club, the Ash Grove. The group evolved into Spirit in summer 1967 with the additions of keyboardist John Locke and drummer Ed Cassidy, then one of rock music's oldest drummers. Cassidy, a veteran jazz drummer, had previously worked with Julian "Cannonball" Adderley and Thelonious Monk. After developing a respectable following through engagements in West Coast clubs, Spirit signed with Lou Adler's Ode label. Their debut album featured Andes and Ferguson's neglected classic "Mechanical World," Ferguson's "Fresh-Garbage" and "Uncle Jack," and Locke's instrumental "Elijah." Their second album yielded the group's only major hit with Randy California's "I Got a Line on You," and *Clear Spirit* included the favorite "Dark Eyed Woman."

Spirit switched to Epic Records for their best-selling album, *The Twelve Dreams of Dr. Sardonicus*. The album yielded a minor hit with Ferguson's "Animal Zoo" and included Ferguson's "Mr. Skin" (a minor hit in 1973) and California's "Morning Will Come," "Nothin' to Hide," and his neglected classic "Nature's Way." However, in mid-1971 Jay Ferguson and Mark Andes left Spirit to form the hard-rock group Jo Jo Gunne with Mark's guitarist brother Matthew. One of the first signings to the newly formed Asylum label, Jo Jo Gunne recorded four albums for the label, yet they managed only one major hit, "Run Run Run," from their debut album. John Locke and Ed Cassidy persevered with brothers Al and Christian Staehly for *Feedback*, but by 1973 no original members remained in the group. Randy California eventually reemerged in 1972 with the experimental *Kaptain Kopter and the Fabulous Twirly Birds*; he later recorded *Spirit of '76* and *Son of Spirit* with Cassidy and bassist Barry Keene.

The original members, save Ferguson, reunited as Spirit in 1976, but Andes soon joined Firefall, while Ferguson initiated a solo career that produced a near-smash hit with "Thunder Island" in late 1977. In 1981 John Locke joined the hard-rock group Nazareth. In 1984 Ferguson, Locke, California, Andes, and Cassidy reunited briefly for *Spirit of '84*, but they soon went their separate ways. By the mid-'90s Spirit was comprised of Randy California, Ed Cassidy, and keyboardist Scott Monahan.

Spirit

Spirit	Ode	44004	'68	†
	Epic	31547	'92	CD
The Family That Plays Together	Ode	44014	'69	†
	Epic	31461	'72	†
Clear Spirit	Ode	44016	'69	†
Spirit/Clear Spirit	Epic	(2) 31457	'73	†
The Twelve Dreams of Dr. Sardonicus	Epic	30267	'70	CS/CD
	Mobile Fidelity	800		CD
Feedback	Epic	31175	'72	†
The Family That Plays Together/Feedback	Epic	(2) 33761	'75	†
Best	Epic	32271	'73	CS/CD
Time Circle (1968–1972)	Epic	(2) 47363	'91	CS/CD

Farther Along	Mercury	1094	'76	†
Future Games	Mercury	1133	'77	†
Spirit of '84	Mercury	818514	'84	†
Live Spirit	Potato	2001	'78	†
Potatoland	Rhino	303	'81	†
Rapture in the Chambers	IRS/MCA	82007		LP/CS/CD†
Jo Jo Gunne				
Jo Jo Gunne	Asylum	5053	'72	†
Bite Down Hard	Asylum	5063	'73	†
Jumpin' the Gunne	Asylum	5071	'73	†
So . . . Where's the Show?	Asylum	1022	'74	†
Randy California				
Kaptain Kopter and the Fabulous Twirly Birds	Epic	31755	'72	†
Randy California and Ed Cassidy				
Spirit of '76	Mercury	(2) 804	'75	†
Son of Spirit	Mercury	1053	'75	†
Jay Ferguson				
All Alone in the End Zone	Asylum	1063	'76	†
Thunder Island	Asylum	1115	'77	†
Real Life Ain't This Way	Asylum	158	'79	†
Terms and Conditions	Capitol	12083	'80	†
White Noise	Capitol	12196	'82	†

SPOOKY TOOTH

Gary Wright (b. Apr. 26, 1943, Creskill, NJ), kybd, voc; **Mike Harrison** (b. Sept. 3, 1945, Carlisle, Cumberland, England), kybd, voc; **Luther Grosvenor** (aka Ariel Bender, b. Dec. 23, 1949, Evesham, Worcester, England), gtr; **Greg Ridley** (b. Oct. 23, 1947, Carlisle, Cumberland, England), bs; **Mike Kellie** (b. Mar. 24, 1947, Birmingham, England), drm [Group disbanded in 1970 and re-formed in 1972 with Gary Wright, Mike Harrison, guitarist-vocalist **Mick Jones** (b. Dec. 27, 1944, London, England), bassist **Chris Stewart**, and drummer **Bryson Graham**; Harrison, Stewart, and Jones left in 1973 and re-formed in 1974 with keyboardist-vocalist **Mike Patto** (b. Sept. 22, 1946; d. Mar. 4, 1979, England) and bassist-vocalist **Val Burke**. The group disbanded for good in 1975.]

Formed by Briton Mike Harrison and American Gary Wright, Spooky Tooth was a seminal British underground band, although they never had a hit record. The group disbanded in 1970 and re-formed in 1972, as original bassist Greg Ridley joined Humble Pie and original guitarist Luther Grosvenor joined Mott the Hoople and later formed Widowmaker. Later member Mick Jones eventually founded Foreigner, and Harrison and Wright pursued solo careers, with Wright scoring the biggest success with *The Dream Weaver* in 1975.

Gary Wright performed as a child actor on television and Broadway, later playing keyboards in a number of high school bands. Graduating from New York University, he traveled to Berlin, Germany, to pursue graduate work, but musical interests prevailed and he formed a band called the New York Times. Invited to England by Traffic's manager, Chris Blackwell, Wright formed Spooky Tooth in 1968 with Mike Harrison, Luther Grosvenor, Greg Ridley, and Mike Kellie of the group Art. Spooky Tooth's debut album featured the contrasting vocal and songwriting styles of Wright and Harrison and was eventually released in the United States in 1971 as *Tobacco Road*. *Spooky Two* sold modestly, but Ridley left after its release to join Humble Pie, and the band's next album, *Ceremony*, was cocredited to French electronic-music wizard Pierre Henry. Wright left to pursue an inauspicious solo career in 1970, and Spooky Tooth disbanded after *The Last Puff*, recorded with Henry McCullough, Chris Stainton, and Alan Spenner from Joe Cocker's Grease Band.

Like Gary Wright, Luther Grosvenor and Mike Harrison unsuccessfully pursued solo careers, with Grosvenor joining Stealers Wheel, then Mott the Hoople, under the name of Ariel Bender. Wright and Harrison reconstituted Spooky Tooth with Mick Jones in 1972, but none of the new band's three albums sold significantly and the group disbanded in late 1974, with Jones going on to form Foreigner with Lou Gramm and Ian McDonald. In 1976 Grosvenor formed Widowmaker with vocalist John Butler, but the group proved unsuccessful.

Gary Wright's second attempt at a solo career succeeded with 1975's *The Dream Weaver*. He played virtually all parts on the album save drums and occasional guitar, and the album yielded belated smash American pop hits with the eerie title cut and "Love Is Alive." He toured as a major headline act in 1976, but after 1977's *The Light of Smiles* his popularity faded. He scored his last major hit in 1981 with "Really Wanna Know You." In 1995 Gary Wright returned to recording with *First Signs of Life* for the Worldly Music label.

Spooky Tooth

Tobacco Road	A&M	4300	'71	†
Spooky Two	A&M	4194	'69	†
	A&M	3124		CD
Ceremony	A&M	4225	'70	†
The Last Puff	A&M	4266	'70	†
You Broke My Heart . . . So I Busted Your Jaw	A&M	4385	'73	†
Witness	Island	9337	'73	†
The Mirror	Island	9292	'74	†
	Antilles	7046		LP
Hell or High Water	Accord	7168	'82	†

Gary Wright and Spooky Tooth

That Was Only Yesterday	A&M	(2) 3528	'76	†

Gary Wright

Extraction	A&M	4277	'71	†
Footprint	A&M	4296	'71	†
The Dream Weaver	Warner Bros.	2868	'75	CS/CD
The Light of Smiles	Warner Bros.	2951	'77	†
Touch and Gone	Warner Bros.	3137	'77	†
Headin' Home	Warner Bros.	3244	'79	†
The Right Place	Warner Bros.	3511	'81	†
Who I Am	Cypress	0111	'88	LP/CS/CD†
First Signs of Life	Worldly Music	7211	'95	CS/CD

Mike Harrison

Mike Harrison	Island	9313	'72	†
Smokestack Lightning	Island	9321	'72	†
Rainbow Rider	Island	9359	'76	†

Luther Grosvenor

Under Open Skies	Island	9312	'72	†

Widowmaker

Widowmaker	United Artists	642	'76	†
Too Late to Cry	United Artists	723	'77	†
Widowmaker	Esquire	74301	'92	CS/CD

BRUCE SPRINGSTEEN

(b. Sept. 23, 1949, Freehold, NJ)

THE E STREET BAND. Bruce Springsteen, gtr, voc; **Clarence Clemons** (b. Jan. 11, 1942), sax; **David Sancious**, kybd; **Danny Federici**, kybd; **Gary Tallent**, bs; **Vini Lopez**, drm [In 1974 David Sancious and Vini Lopez were replaced by **Roy Bittan** and **Max Weinberg**. Guitarist **"Miami" Steve Van Zandt** (b. Nov. 22, 1950, Boston, MA) joined in 1975 and left in 1984; he was replaced by guitarist **Nils Lofgren** (b. 1952, Chicago, IL). Vocalist **Patti Scialfa** joined in 1984.]

BRUCE SPRINGSTEEN

Bruce Springsteen burst upon the rock scene with his outstanding 1975 album *Born to Run*. Although the album became an instant best-seller, Springsteen's credibility was hurt by the bombastic hyperbole that proclaimed him the next Bob Dylan and the savior of rock and roll. He subsequently was embroiled in legal disputes that prevented him from recording, a situation that would have destroyed or at least crippled the career of an artist of lesser talent and fortitude. Springsteen returned to recording in 1978, but he did not achieve massive recognition for his talents until 1984's *Born in the U.S.A.* Suffused with engaging songs of celebration, hope, and disillusionment, the album established Springsteen as the most important rock artist of the '80s. After its huge success, Springsteen again withdrew from the rock scene and, much to the dismay of his fans, disbanded the E Street Band in 1989. Although his career has not reached its previous heights, he remains one of the most provocative songwriters and performers in rock.

Raised in New Jersey, Bruce Springsteen took up guitar at 13 and joined a local group, the Castiles, around 1963. In 1966 the band recorded several unreleased singles, later performing at the Cafe Wha in New York's Greenwich Village. Springsteen next formed a succession of bands (Steel Mill, Doctor Zoom and the Sonic Boom) with whom he performed around New Jersey clubs for years, most notably at the Stone Pony in Asbury Park. He turned down a contract offer from Bill Graham's Fillmore Records in 1969 and eventually signed a management contract with Mike Appel in May 1972. Appel arranged an audition with legendary record executive John Hammond, and Springsteen signed with Columbia Records in June. Recorded in both an acoustic and rock-band setting, his debut album, *Greetings from Asbury Park, New Jersey*, featured "Blinded by the Light" and "Spirit in the Night," hits for Manfred Mann in 1976, and "It's Hard to Be a Saint in the City." However, the album was generally ignored, except by rock critics and his cult following based in the Northeast. Released only months later, *The Wild, the Innocent and the E Street Shuffle* suffered similarly, even though it contained such excellent songs as "4th of July, Asbury Park (Sandy)," a minor hit for the Hollies in spring 1975; "Rosalita (Come Out Tonight)"; and "New York City Serenade."

By 1974 Bruce Springsteen had formed his permanent backup group, the E Street Band, with David Sancious, Gary Tallent, Clarence Clemons, and former Steel Mill members Danny Federici and Vini Lopez. They rigorously toured the East Coast during the year and were spotted by critic Jon Landau, who called Springsteen, in a famous quote, "the future of rock and roll." The band subsequently realigned with Tallent, Clemons, and Federici, plus Roy Bittan and Max Weinberg. In 1975 guitarist "Miami" Steve Van Zandt, a cofounder of Southside Johnny and the Asbury Jukes, joined. This aggregation recorded Springsteen's breakthrough album, *Born to Run*.

The album was launched with massive hype by Columbia; for a 5-day, 10-show run at New York's Bottom Line in August, a large number of tickets were reserved for so-called media tastemakers. Coproduced by Springsteen, Appel, and Landau, the album quickly produced a major hit with the title song. Springsteen was the first rock star to appear simultaneously on the covers of *Time* and *Newsweek* in October, attesting to his sudden popularity (and the power of Columbia's PR office), although ultimately damaging his credibility with hardcore rock fans. Nonetheless, *Born to Run* included standout songs such as "Tenth Avenue Freeze-Out," "Thunder Road," "Jungleland," and "She's the One." The album became a best-seller, remaining on the charts for more than two years, and it helped spur the sales of Springsteen's first two albums.

Bruce Springsteen soon became embroiled in legal disputes with manager Mike Appel that prevented him for more than a year from recording. He toured with the E Street Band in 1976 and 1977, establishing his reputation as a live performer with marathon three- and four-hour performances. Soon after the resolution of the legal problems in May 1977, Springsteen entered the studio to record a new album under mentor-producer-manager Jon Landau. Issued in mid-1978, *Darkness at the Edge of Town* revealed a growing maturity to Springsteen's songwriting, and aptly showcased the E Street Band. The album included "The Promised Land," "Racing in the Streets," and "Streets of Fire," and yielded moderate hits with "Prove It All Night" and "Badlands." During the year, Patti Smith scored her only major hit with "Because the Night," cowritten with Springsteen, and the Pointer Sisters achieved a smash hit with Springsteen's "Fire."

Touring tirelessly from July to September 1978 and again beginning in November, Springsteen performed at the September 1979 benefit concerts in New York for MUSE (Musicians United for Safe Energy), and his segment of the resulting movie and album came to be regarded as the highlight of the event. He spent more than a year recording his next album, ostensibly recording more than 50 songs, and upon release the two-record set *The River* was widely praised. Pervaded by songs using the automobile as its primary metaphor ("Stolen Car," "Drive All Night," "Wreck on the Highway," and "Cadillac Ranch"), the set also included Springsteen's first smash hit, "Hungry Heart," and the major hit "Fade Away," as well as "I'm a Rocker," "Independence Day," and "The Price You Pay." The release was accompanied by a three-month nationwide tour, his first in two years. In 1981 and 1982 Springsteen and Steve Van Zandt produced two comeback albums for Gary "U.S." Bonds. Each yielded a major hit: *Dedication* with "This Little Girl," and *On the Line* with "Out of Work."

Although Springsteen recorded the songs for his next album with the E Street Band, he ultimately decided to issue solo acoustic recordings he made as demonstration tapes for the work as *Nebraska* in 1982. A stark folk-style album somewhat reminiscent of a solo Bob Dylan, complete with honking harmonica, the album sold less well than previous albums but included such memorable songs as "Highway Patrolman," "Atlantic City," and the ominous "Johnny 99."

Meanwhile, various members of the E Street Band undertook solo projects. In 1982 Steve Van Zandt recorded *Men Without Women* with the 11-piece Disciples of Soul, as Springsteen worked on his next album. Van Zandt's solo album contained his "Under the Gun" and "Till the Good Is Gone" and sold modestly, yielding a minor hit with "Forever." Clarence Clemons formed the 10-piece soul band the Red Bank Rockers with vocalist John "J.T." Bowen for touring and the recording of *Rescue*, which featured Springsteen's "Savin' Up" and the single "A Woman's Got the Power."

In 1984 Columbia issued Bruce Springsteen's masterpiece, *Born in the U.S.A.* It is his most powerful musical statement, as it regards the promise and disappointment of the American dream. A tough but empassioned album, rooted in the belief that rock has the power to change and improve the quality of people's lives, *Born in the U.S.A.* yielded *seven* smash hits: the celebratory "Dancing in the Dark"; the desperate "Cover Me"; the rocking but disillusioned title cut; the gentle "I'm On Fire"; the nostalgic "Glory Days" and "My Hometown"; and the disillusioned "I'm Goin' Down." The album established Springsteen in the top rank of rock artists and ultimately sold 15 million copies in the United States. Between June 1984 and September 1985 he played more than 160 stadium concerts worldwide in support of *Born in the U.S.A.*, introducing new guitarist Nils Lofgren and backup vocalist Patti Scialfa. The tour solidified Springsteen's reputation as rock's most exciting and compelling live performer of the '80s.

"Miami" Steve Van Zandt had left the E Street Band following the recording of *Born in the U.S.A.* He trimmed the Disciples of Soul down to a five-piece band for the politically charged *Voice of America*. The album featured "I Am a Patriot" and "Undefeated (Everybody Goes Home)" and sold modestly. In 1985 Van Zandt assembled Artists United Against Apartheid to record his song "Sun City" as a protest against South Africa's racial policies. Recorded with 49 major contemporary-music stars, including Bob Dylan, Peter Gabriel, Jackson Browne, Lou Reed, Pete Townshend, Bonnie Raitt, Bono of U2, and Springsteen, the single proved only a moderate hit, although it did much to bring attention to the injustices suffered in South Africa. The single was soon followed by a six-song album, *Sun City*. In late 1985 Columbia issued Clarence Clemons's second album recorded with the Red Bank Rockers, *Hero*, which yielded a major hit with "You're a Friend of Mine," a duet with Jackson Browne.

Bruce Springsteen retained a low profile following the massive tour in support of *Born in the U.S.A.* He added vocals to the "We Are the World" superstar single, a smash pop, R&B, and easy-listening hit, and contributed his "Light of Day" composition, a moderate hit for Joan Jett and the Blackhearts, to the film of the same name. In May 1985 he married actress and model Julianne Phillips. In late 1986 Columbia issued *Live 1975–1985*, which compiled 40 songs recorded live over the past decade. The album yielded a near-smash hit with a cover version of Edwin Starr's "War" and a moderate hit with "Fire." The album sold spectacularly for a live, multirecord set.

Bruce Springsteen eventually reemerged in 1987 with *Tunnel of Love*. Leaving behind his angst-ridden songs of youth and disillusionment, the album investigated the exigencies and vagaries of interpersonal love. Recorded virtually solo by Springsteen, the album was a dark, intimate work, revealing not only his personal growth and maturity but also his leanings toward folk and even country music. It yielded the smash hit "Brilliant Disguise," the near-smash title cut, and the major hit "One Step Up." He briefly toured with the E Street Band in support of the album, performing standarized sets (as opposed to the free-form concerts of the past) in arenas rather than stadiums. His only other performances until 1992 were with the Amnesty International tour of 1988, and a benefit in Los Angeles for the Christic Institute in November 1990.

In 1987 Manhattan Records issued "Miami" Steve Van Zandt's *Freedom, No Compromise*, which included a duet with Springsteen, "I Am a Native American," and a duet with Ruben Blades, "Bitter Fruit." In 1989 Clarence Clemons toured with Ringo Starr's All-Starr Band and recorded *A Night with Mr. C*. Springsteen and Julianne Phillips divorced in March 1989, and that November he announced his dismissal of the E Street Band (retaining Roy Bittan and Patti Scialfa), much to the dismay of longtime fans. Bassist Gary Tallent became a Nashville producer, and guitarist Nils Lofgren returned to his solo career, touring with Ringo Starr's All-Starr Band in 1995. Drummer Max Weinberg founded his own record label, Hard Ticket, for recordings by his band Killer Joe, and later served as band leader for the house band on television's *Late Night with Conan O'Brien*. Keyboardist Danny Federici subsequently played with the house band at Los Angeles's House of Blues.

In July 1990 Patti Scialfa bore her and Springsteen's first son, Evan James. The couple married in June 1991. Springsteen released two albums of new material in 1992, *Human Touch* and *Lucky Town*. The energetic *Human Touch*, recorded in 1989–1990, yielded the major-hit title song and the minor hit "57 Channels (And Nothin' On)." The introspective *Lucky Town*, recorded in 1991, featured "Living Proof," the ballad "If I Should Fall Behind," and the autobiographical "Better Days" and "Local Hero." To promote the albums, Springsteen appeared on *Saturday Night Live*, his first-ever performance on network television, and gave an interview to *Rolling Stone* magazine. However, the albums sold only modestly, and he later toured with his new band, who were somewhat disappointing in light of the quality of his previous shows with the E Street Band. Springsteen and his new group performed on an MTV show called *Bruce Springsteen Plugged*.

Springsteen returned to the charts with the smash hit "Streets of Philadelphia," from the soundtrack to the 1993 film *Philadelphia*, the first major-studio effort to deal with the issue of AIDS. Springsteen won an Academy Award and four Grammys for this work. Patti Scialfa recorded her solo debut, *Rumble Doll*, for 1993 release, and Springsteen's *Greatest Hits* contained four previously unreleased songs, including the stark "Murder Incorporated," recorded during the *Born in the U.S.A.* sessions. The E Street Band reunited briefly to record a video for the song.

Springsteen returned to the solo semiacoustic format for his 1995 album *The Ghost of Tom Joad*. The title track referred directly to the legacy of social-protest music of singers like Woody Guthrie, who had written his own song based on the main character of John Steinbeck's *Grapes of Wrath*. These contemporary ballads focus on neglected Americans, such as immigrants and the inner-city homeless; the work was met by mixed critical reviews and sold modestly.

Bruce Springsteen

Greetings from Asbury Park, New Jersey	Columbia	31903	'73	CS/CD
The Wild, the Innocent and the E Street Shuffle	Columbia	32432	'73	CS/CD
Born to Run	Columbia	33795	'75	CS/CD
	Columbia	64406	'94	CD
Darkness at the Edge of Town	Columbia	35318	'78	CS/CD
The River	Columbia	(2) 36854	'80	CS/CD
Nebraska	Columbia	38358	'82	CS/CD
Born in the U.S.A.	Columbia	38653	'84	CS/CD
Bruce Springsteen and the E Street Band: Live, 1975–85	Columbia	(3) 40558	'86	CS/CD
Tunnel of Love	Columbia	40999	'87	CS/CD
Chimes of Freedom	Columbia	(4) 44445		CS
Human Touch	Columbia	53000	'92	LP/CS/CD
Lucky Town	Columbia	53001	'92	LP/CS/CD
Greatest Hits	Columbia	67060	'95	CS/CD
The Ghost of Tom Joad	Columbia	67484	'95	LP/CS/CD

Tribute Album

Cover Me: A Collection of Bruce Springsteen Songs	Rhino	70700	'86	CS/CD

Little Steven and the Disciples of Soul

Men Without Women	EMI America	17086	'82	†
	Razor & Tie	1981	'91	CD

Voice of America	EMI America	17120	'84	†
	Razor & Tie	1984	'91	CD
Artists United Against Apartheid				
Sun City	Manhattan	53019	'85	†
	EMI	91832	'89	CS/CD†
Little Steven				
Freedom, No Compromise	Manhattan	53048	'87	LP/CS†
	Manhattan	53048	'87	CD†
Clarence Clemons and the Red Bank Rockers				
Rescue	Columbia	38933	'83	†
Hero	Columbia	40010	'85	CS/CD†
Clarence Clemons				
A Night with Mr. C	Columbia	40917	'89	LP/CS/CD†
Killer Joe (with Max Weinberg)				
Scene of the Crime	Hard Ticket	65069	'91	CS/CD
Patti Scialfa				
Rumble Doll	Columbia	44223	'93	CS/CD

THE STAPLE SINGERS

Roebuck "Pops" Staples (b. Dec. 28, 1915, Winona, MS), gtr, voc; **Mavis Staples** (b. 1940, Chicago, IL), lead voc; **Cleotha Staples** (b. 1934, MS); **Pervis Staples** (b. 1935, MS); **Yvonne Staples** (b. 1939, Chicago, IL), voc

Perhaps the only American gospel group to achieve international popularity and widespread American recognition, the Staple Singers first developed a national reputation as a straightforward family gospel group in the '50s. They enjoyed success as a folk act in the '60s and eventually emerged as a soul group in the '70s on Stax Records, scoring smash pop and R&B hits with "I'll Take You There" and "If You're Ready (Come Go with Me)." Featuring the blues-style guitar playing of leader Roebuck "Pops" Staples and the astonishing contralto voice of lead singer Mavis Staples, the Staple Singers never abandoned gospel music, but rather expanded its boundary with pop-style songs of self-affirmation, international brotherhood, and interpersonal love. Mavis Staples launched her own solo recording career in 1970, and Pops Staples started his solo career in 1987.

Roebuck "Pops" Staples grew up in the rural Mississippi town of Drew and performed as a blues guitarist in his teens. Around 1931 he joined the local gospel group the Golden Trumpets and toured with them for two years. In 1935 he moved to Chicago, and he later sang with the Trumpet Jubilee. He organized a family gospel group with his son, Pervis, and daughters, Mavis and Cleo; they began performing as early as 1953. The Staple Singers developed a devoted local following and signed with United Records, switching to the larger independent label VeeJay in 1956. They became a national attraction on the gospel circuit after the success of 1957's *Uncloudy Day*, which featured traditional and original gospel material. Moving to Riverside Records in 1960 and Epic Records in 1964, the group played major folk and jazz festivals in the early '60s. By this time youngest daughter Yvonne had joined the group. Recording contemporary material, the Staple Singers scored minor pop hits in 1967 with Pops's "Why Am I Treated So Bad" and Stephen Stills's "For What It's Worth."

Switching to Stax Records in the summer of 1968, The Staple Singers began playing rock-concert halls and achieved their first major pop and smash R&B hit with "Heavy Makes You Happy (Sha-Na-Boom Boom)" in 1971. In 1970 Mavis Staples recorded her first solo album for the Stax subsidiary Volt, scoring a major R&B and minor pop hit with "I Have Learned to Do Without You"; however, her solo career never really took off. Pervis left the group in 1971.

The Staple Singers enjoyed their most widespread success with 1972's *Bealtitude: Respect Yourself*, which yielded the top pop and R&B hit "I'll Take You There" and the R&B smashes "Respect Yourself" (a major pop hit) and "This World." The group began touring internationally, and after the R&B smash "Oh La De Da," they achieved a top R&B and smash pop hit with "If You're Ready (Come Go with Me)" and a smash R&B and major pop hit with "Touch a Hand, Make a Friend" from *Be What You Are*. Following the R&B smash "City in the Sky," the Staple Singers collaborated with Curtis Mayfield on the soundtrack to the movie *Let's Do It Again*, scoring a top pop and R&B hit with the title song and a smash R&B hit with "New Orleans."

In 1976 the group moved to Warner Bros. Records to record as the Staples, yet their success was restricted to the R&B field with the major hits "Love Me, Love Me, Love Me" and "Unlock Your Mind." After three albums for Warner Bros. and one for 20th Century-Fox, the group resumed using the name the Staple Singers, eventually switching to Private I Records, where they managed a major R&B hit with "Slippery People" in 1984.

Mavis Staples recorded for at least three different labels in the '70s and '80s, eventually joining Prince's Paisley Park label in 1987. She toured with his band on his "Lovesexy" tour, and appeared in his movie *Graffiti Bridge* singing "Melody Cool"; Prince produced Mavis's 1994 album, *The Voice*. In 1987 Pops Staples launched his solo career on the Word label, while continuing to work with the family group. His 1992 album, *Peace to the Neighborhood*, was produced by veteran Memphis soul producer Willie Mitchell, while the follow-up *Father Father* won a Grammy for best contemporary blues album.

The Staple Singers

Uncloudy Day	VeeJay	5000	'57	†
Will the Circle Be Unbroken	VeeJay	5008	'61	†
Swing Low	VeeJay	5014	'62	†
Best	VeeJay	5019	'63	†
Best	VeeJay/Chameleon	74782	'88	†
Gospel Program	Gospel	3001	'62	†
Hammers and Nails	Riverside	93501	'62	†
The Twenty-Fifth Day of December	Riverside	93513		†
	Fantasy	9442	'73	†
This Land	Riverside	93524		†
This Little Light	Riverside	93527	'66	†
Use What You Got (recorded 1962–1964)	Fantasy	9423	'73	†
Great Day	Milestone	(2) 47028	'75	†
	Milestone	47028		CD
Amen	Epic	26132	'65	†
Freedom Highway	Epic	26163	'65	†
	Columbia/Legacy	47334	'91	CS/CD
Why	Epic	26196	'66	†
Pray On	Epic	26237		†
For What It's Worth	Epic	26332	'67	†
What the World Needs Now	Epic	26373		†
Heavy Makes You Happy	Epic	(2) 30635	'71	†
Pray On/Tell It Like It Is	Epic	(2) 33764	'75	†
Soul Folk in Action	Stax	2004		†
	Stax	8561	'91	CS/CD
We'll Get Over	Stax	2016		†
	Stax	8532	'95	LP/CS/CD

The Staple Singers	Stax	2034	'68	†
	Stax	8573	'92	CD
Bealtitude: Respect Yourself	Stax	3002	'72	†
	Stax	4116	'78	LP/CS/CD
Be What You Are	Stax	3015	'73	†
	Stax	8553	'90	LP/CS/CD
City in the Sky	Stax	5515	'74	†
Best	Stax	5523	'75	†
Chronicle	Stax	4119	'79	LP/CS
This Time Around	Stax	8511	'81	LP
Best	Stax	60007		CD
The Turning Point	Private I	39460	'84	†
The Staple Singers	Archive of Gospel Music	62		†
The Staple Singers, Volume 2	Archive of Gospel Music	72		†
Best	Buddah	2009	'69	†
Will the Circle Be Unbroken	Buddah	7508	'70	†
Tell It Like It Is	Harmony	31775	'72	†

The Staple Singers/Curtis Mayfield

Let's Do It Again (soundtrack)	Curtom	5005	'75	†

The Staples

Pass It On	Warner Bros.	2945	'76	†
Family Tree	Warner Bros.	3064	'77	†
Unlock Your Mind	Warner Bros.	3192	'78	†
Hold On to Your Dream	20th Century-Fox	636	'81	†

Mavis Staples

Only for the Lonely	Volt	6010	'70	†
	Stax	8539	'87	LP/CS
	Stax	88012	'87	CD
Mavis Staples	Volt	6007	'71	†
	Stax	4118	'78	LP/CS
A Piece of the Action (soundtrack)	Curtom	5017	'77	†
Oh, What a Feeling	Warner Bros.	3319	'79	†
Time Waits for No One	Paisley Park	25798	'89	CS/CD†
The Voice	Warner Bros.	25049	'93	CS/CD

"Pops" Staples/Albert King/Steve Cropper

Jammed Together	Stax	2020	'69	†
	Stax	8544	'90	LP/CS/CD

"Pops" Staples

Pops Staples	Word	8380	'87	†
Peace to the Neighborhood	Pointblank/Charisma	92147	'92	CS/CD†
	Pointblank/Charisma	86286	'92	CS/CD
Father Father	Pointblank/Charisma	39638	'94	CS/CD

RINGO STARR

(b. Richard Starkey, July 7, 1940, Dingle, Liverpool, England)

With his straightforward drumming, undistinguished voice, and infrequent songwriting, Ringo Starr was not expected to do much after the breakup of the Beatles, yet he managed a string of smash singles from 1971 to 1975 with cover songs, Hoyt Axton's "No No Song," and three originals—"It Don't Come Easy," "Back Off Boogaloo," and "Photograph." Enjoying his greatest album success with 1973's *Ringo*, Starr faded from public view in the '80s, only to return as leader of an all-star rock-and-roll revue, Ringo Starr and His All-Starr Band, for tours in 1989, 1992, and 1995.

Ringo Starr took up drums after high school, eventually joining Rory Storm and the Hurricanes. In 1961 he met Brian Epstein and subsequently joined the Beatles as Pete Best's replacement in August 1962. During the career of the Beatles, Starr was constantly overshadowed by the group's more talented members, developing the image of a cheerful, self-effacing buffoon in concerts and movies. He sang occasional lead vocals on songs such as "I Wanna Be Your Man," "Matchbox," "Honey Don't," "Boys," and the minor hits "Act Naturally" and "What Goes On," and contributed two songs to the group's catalog, "Don't Pass Me By" and "Octopus's Garden." His biggest success as a lead singer came with 1966's "Yellow Submarine" and the classic "With a Little Help from My Friends," perhaps the crowning achievement of his career with the Beatles.

After appearing in a cameo role in the 1969 film *Candy*, Ringo Starr costarred with Peter Sellers in 1970's *The Magic Christian*. His debut solo album, *Sentimental Journey*, was comprised of Tin Pan Alley standards, and his next, *Beaucoups of Blues*, featured country material. In 1971 he scored a smash hit with "It Don't Come Easy," performed at George Harrison's Concert for Bangladesh in August, and appeared in the role of Frank Zappa in Zappa's outlandish movie *200 Motels*. He had a near-smash hit with his own "Back Off Boogaloo" in 1972, and later appeared in the films *Son of Dracula* (with Harry Nilsson), the highly acclaimed *That'll Be the Day*, and the western *Blindman*. He also directed the film documentary of Marc Bolan, *Born to Boogie*.

Recorded under producer Richard Perry, Ringo Starr's first album in three years, *Ringo*, yielded the top hits "Photograph" (cowritten by Starr and George Harrison) and the rock classic "You're Sixteen" (a near-smash hit for Johnny Burnette in 1960) plus the smash "Oh, My, My"; it also contained one song written by each of the former Beatles, including John Lennon's ironic "I'm the Greatest." Perry also produced *Goodnight Vienna*, which included two smash hits, "Only You" (originally popularized by the Platters) and Hoyt Axton's humorous antidrug "No No Song" (backed as a single by Elton John and Bernie Taupin's "Snookero"). The album also produced a moderate hit with John Lennon's "It's All Down to Goodnight Vienna." The compilation set *Blast from Your Past* included "Early 1970," Starr's song about the breakup of the Beatles.

Ringo Starr switched to Atlantic Records for *Ringo's Rotogravure*, which yielded his last major hit, "A Dose of Rock 'n' Roll." After *Ringo the Fourth* he moved to Portrait Records for *Bad Boy* and Boardwalk Records for *Stop and Smell the Roses*, which produced his last moderate hit with George Harrison's "Wrack My Brain." In 1981 Starr costarred in the inane movie *Caveman* opposite Barbara Bach, whom he subsequently married. Joe Walsh produced Starr's 1983 album *Old Wave*, but it was never released in the United States. Starr appeared in Paul McCartney's disastrous 1984 movie *Give My Regards to Broad Street*, and legally prevented the release of recordings made in 1987 under Memphis producer Chips Moman.

Ringo Starr and his wife conquered their alcohol problem in 1988, and Ringo played the diminutive Mr. Conductor in the children's public television show *Shining Time Station* from 1989 to 1991. In 1989 Starr assembled a stellar cast for his first tour in 23 years. The All-Starr Band included guitarists Nils Lofgren and Joe Walsh, keyboardists Billy Preston and Dr. John, saxophonist Clarence Clemons, bassist Rick Danko, and drummers Jim Keltner and Levon Helm. The tour produced a live album on Rykodisc. Ringo's next tour, in 1992, featured holdovers Lofgren and Walsh, multi-instrumentalist Todd Rundgren, guitarist Dave Edmunds, vocalist Burton Cummings, bassist Timothy B. Schmit, and

Ringo's drummer son Zak Starkey. Earlier in the year Ringo had recorded *Time Takes Time*, but the album failed to sell despite favorable reviews, a stellar backing cast, and the inclusion of "Weight of the World" and "Don't Go Where the Road Don't Go." When Ringo Starr toured again in 1995, he was accompanied by vocalist Felix Cavaliere, guitarists Randy Bachman and Mark Farner, keyboardist Billy Preston, bassist John Entwistle, and Zak Starkey.

Starr appeared in the 1995 Beatles' TV documentary, and he drummed on the two new tracks recorded by Paul McCartney and George Harrison for the *Anthology* set of Beatles recordings. Always good-humored about his past role as part of the Fab Four, he satirized persistent reunion rumors earlier in the year by appearing in a commercial for Pizza Hut, where he is mistakenly reunited with the Pre–Fab Four, the Monkees!

Ringo Starr

Sentimental Journey	Apple/Capitol	3365	'70	†
	Capitol	16218		†
	Capitol	98615	'95	CD
Beaucoups of Blues	Apple/Capitol	3368	'70	†
	Capitol	16235	'81	†
	Capitol	32675	'95	CD
Ringo	Apple/Capitol	3413	'73	†
	Capitol	16114		†
	Capitol	95637	'91	CD
Goodnight Vienna	Apple/Capitol	3417	'74	†
	Capitol	16219		†
	Capitol	80378	'93	CS/CD
Blast from Your Past	Apple/Capitol	3422	'75	†
	Capitol	46663		CD
Ringo's Rotogravure	Atlantic	18193	'76	†
	Atlantic	82417	'92	CS/CD
Ringo the Fourth	Atlantic	19108	'77	†
	Atlantic	82416	'92	CS/CD
Bad Boy	Portrait	35378	'78	†
	Epic	35378	'91	CD
Stop and Smell the Roses	Boardwalk	33246	'81	†
	The Right Stuff	29676	'94	CS/CD
Old Wave	The Right Stuff	29675	'94	CS/CD
Starr Struck: Ringo's Best, Volume 2 (1976–1983)	Rhino	70135	'89	CS/CD
Ringo Starr and His All-Starr Band	Rykodisc	10190	'90	CS/CD
	Rykodisc	90190	'93	CD
Ringo Starr and His All-Starr Band, Volume 2: Live from Montreux	Rykodisc	20264		CS/CD
Time Takes Time	Private Music	82097	'92	CS/CD

STEELY DAN

Walter Becker (b. Feb. 20, 1950, New York, NY), bs, gtr, voc; **Donald Fagen** (b. Jan. 1, 1948, Passaic, NJ), kybd, voc

Although posing as a group, Steely Dan was essentially a studio duo comprised of songwriters Walter Becker and Donald Fagen. Composing musically sophisticated, lyrically erudite and oblique songs, Steely Dan immediately came to prominence with their excellent debut album, *Can't Buy a Thrill*, and its two hit singles, "Do It Again" and "Reeling in the Years." Admittedly more influenced by jazz than rock, Becker and Fagen persevered through 1980 as one of the most popular nontouring groups since the Beatles. They scored their biggest artistic and commercial success with their 1977 album, *Aja*, their acknowledged masterpiece. During the '80s the two pursued a variety of low-key independent endeavors, reuniting in 1993 for one of the most anticipated tours of the year.

Walter Becker and Donald Fagen met while attending Bard College in upstate New York in 1967. Fagen had studied jazz piano in high school, whereas Becker played bass and guitar. The two decided to form a composing team, and after Fagen's graduation and Becker's dismissal, the duo unsuccessfully attempted to sell their songs around New York. They formed a short-lived group on Long Island with guitarist Denny Dias and composed and performed the score to the obscure underground movie *You Gotta Walk It Like You Talk It*. Fagen and Becker next joined the backup group for Jay and the Americans and toured with them in 1970 and 1971. Through that group's producer, Gary Katz, they secured employment as staff songwriters for ABC-Dunhill in Los Angeles, but their failure to write hits led to the formation of Steely Dan as a vehicle for their songwriting.

Formed in 1972, Steely Dan was initially comprised of Becker, Fagen, Dias, lead vocalist David Palmer, guitarist Jeff "Skunk" Baxter, and drummer Jim Hodder. Their exceptional debut album, *Can't Buy a Thrill*, featured the disdainful "Dirty Work" and the vaguely political "Change of the Guard" and yielded near-smash hits with "Do It Again" and "Reeling in the Years." Touring infrequently, Steely Dan recorded their second jazz-inflected album without Palmer, as Fagen assumed the lead-vocalist role. *Pretzel Logic* produced a smash hit with "Rikki Don't Lose That Number," but following their 1974 tour, Becker and Fagen dismissed their band, with Baxter soon joining the Doobie Brothers. They retained Denny Dias while recording subsequent albums with session musicians. However, neither *Katy Lied* nor *The Royal Scam* yielded a major hit.

Released in late 1977, *Aja* became Steely Dan's best-selling and most highly regarded album. It ultimately yielded three major hits, with "Peg," "Deacon Blues," and "Josie." They also scored a major hit with "FM (No Static at All)" from the movie *FM* in 1978. The group's next album, *Gaucho*, did not come until 1980, yet it produced two major hits (their last) with "Hey Nineteen" and "Time Out of Mind."

By 1981, Walter Becker and Donald Fagen had parted company. Becker retreated to Hawaii, where he built his own recording studio, while Fagen recorded the autobiographical solo album *The Nightfly*, which yielded a major hit with "I.G.Y. (What a Beautiful World)" and a minor hit with the caustic "New Frontier." During the '80s Fagen composed songs, wrote a movie column for *Premiere* magazine, and contributed to the soundtrack of the movie *Bright Lights, Big City*. Around 1989 Fagen began performing in clubs around New York, later organizing and touring with the New York Rock and Soul Revue in 1991 and 1992. Becker and Fagen reunited to coproduce Fagen's second solo album, *Kamakiriad*, in 1993, and the duo assembled an 11-piece band for their first tour in 19 years. Although the tour sold out, the performances served more as cultural events than as music renaissance. In 1994 Walter Becker recorded his first solo album, *11 Tracks of Whack*, and Steely Dan toured once again.

Fagen/Becker/Dias

You Gotta Walk It Like You Talk It	Spark	02	'71	†

Steely Dan

Can't Buy a Thrill	ABC/MCA	758	'72	†
	MCA	37040		†
	MCA	1591		CS
	MCA	31192		CD

Countdown to Ecstasy	ABC/MCA	779	'73	†
	MCA	37041		†
	MCA	1592		CS
	MCA	31156		CD
Countdown to Ecstasy/Can't Buy a Thrill	MCA	(2) 6906		CS
Pretzel Logic	ABC/MCA	808	'74	†
	MCA	37042		†
	MCA	1593		CS
	MCA	31165		CD
Katy Lied	ABC/MCA	846	'75	†
	MCA	37043		†
	MCA	1594		CS
	MCA	31194		CD
The Royal Scam	ABC/MCA	931	'76	†
	MCA	37044		†
	MCA	1595		CS
	MCA	31193		CD
The Royal Scam/Katy Lied	MCA	(2) 6920		CS
Aja	ABC	1004	'77	†
	MCA	1004		†
	MCA	1688		CS
	MCA	37214	'84	CD
	Mobile Fidelity	515		CD
Greatest Hits	ABC/MCA	(2) 1107	'78	†
	MCA	(2) 6008		CS
Gaucho	MCA	6102	'80	†
	MCA	1693		CS
	MCA	37220	'84	CD
	Mobile Fidelity	545	'91	CD
Aja/Gaucho	MCA	(2) 6943		CS
Gold	MCA	5324	'82	†
	MCA	37243	'84	†
	MCA	1483		CS
Gold (expanded edition)	MCA	10387	'91	CS/CD
A Decade of Steely Dan	MCA	5570	'85	CD
	MCA	11214	'95	CD
Citizen Steely Dan: 1972–1980	MCA	(4) 10981	'93	CS/CD
Alive in America (recorded 1993–1994)	Giant	24634	'95	CS/CD
Donald Fagen				
The Nightfly	Warner Bros.	23696	'82/'84	CS/CD
Kamakiriad	Reprise	45230	'93	CS/CD
Walter Becker				
11 Tracks of Whack	Giant	22734	'94	CS/CD

STEPPENWOLF

John Kay (b. Joachim Krauledat, Apr. 12, 1944, Tilsit, East Germany), gtr, voc; **Goldy McJohn** (b. John Goadsby, May 2, 1945), kybd; **Michael Monarch** (b. July 5, 1950, Los Angeles, CA), gtr; **Nick St. Nicholas** (b. Klaus Karl Kassbaum, Sept. 28, 1943, Plön, Germany), bs; **Jerry Edmonton** (b. Jerry McCrohan, Oct. 24, 1946, Canada; d. Nov. 28, 1993, near Santa Ynez, CA), drm

Led by onetime folk singer John Kay, Steppenwolf scored two smash hits with the classics "Born to Be Wild" and "Magic Carpet Ride" in the late '60s, while recording Kay's decidedly existential and politically oriented songs, such as "Desperation," "The Ostrich," and "Don't Step on the Grass, Sam." Fading from popularity in the '70s, Steppenwolf disbanded for a time, only to be reconstituted in 1974 by Kay.

Born near-blind, John Kay fled East Germany with his mother in 1958, settling in Canada. He performed as a folk singer in Toronto's Yorkville district in the early '60s and toured the American folk-club circuit in 1964 before returning to Toronto, where he joined the Sparrow with brothers Jerry and Dennis Edmonton, Goldy McJohn, and Nick St. Nicholas. Traveling to New York, then Los Angeles, the Sparrow signed with Columbia Records, who eventually released their album after the success of Steppenwolf. In 1967 the Sparrow regrouped as Steppenwolf, replacing Dennis Edmonton (also known as Mars Bonfire) with guitarist Mike Monarch. Edmonton/Bonfire later recorded a neglected album for Columbia Records.

Developing a reputation as a live act on the West Coast, Steppenwolf signed with Dunhill Records. Their debut album yielded a smash hit with the classic biker song "Born to Be Wild," written by Edmonton/Bonfire, and included Hoyt Axton's "The Pusher" and Kay's existential "Desperation" and "The Ostrich." *Steppenwolf the Second* produced another smash hit with the psychedelic "Magic Carpet Ride"; it also contained Mars Bonfire's "Faster than the Speed of Life" and Kay's satirical "Don't Step on the Grass, Sam."

At Your Birthday Party yielded a near-smash hit with "Rock Me" and a minor hit with "It's Never Too Late," but subsequent singles by Steppenwolf proved moderate hits at best, and personnel defections began in 1969. Nick St. Nicholas formed T.I.M.E. with guitarist Larry Byrom, and remaining members Kay, McJohn, and Jerry Edmonton disbanded Steppenwolf in 1972. Kay recorded two overlooked albums for Dunhill and revived Steppenwolf with McJohn and Edmonton in 1974, scoring a major hit with "Straight Shootin' Woman" on Mums Records. The group disbanded again in 1976, with Kay reconstituting the group as its sole original member in 1980 for touring and recordings on DBX, Qwil, and I.R.S. Records. Kay continues to lead various permutations of the group, including appearances at Farm Aid II and III, and he authored his autobiography in 1994. McJohn settled in the Seattle area, where he continues to perform on the club circuit. St. Nicholas converted to Christianity, occasionally performs Christian rock, and is in the music management business; Monarch has become a country songwriter. Jerry Edmonton died in a car accident in the early '90s.

The Sparrow

The Sparrow	Columbia	9758	'69	†
Tighten Up Your Wig: The Best of John Kay and the Sparrow	Columbia/Legacy	53044	'93	CS/CD
Early Steppenwolf	Dunhill	50060	'69	†
	MCA	31356	'90	CD

Mars Bonfire

Faster than the Speed of Life	Columbia	9834	'69	†

Steppenwolf

Stepenwolf	Dunhill	50029	'68	†
	MCA	37045		†
	MCA	1596		CS
	MCA	31020		CD
Steppenwolf the Second	Dunhill	50037	'68	†
	MCA	37046		†
	MCA	1597		CS
	MCA	31021		CD

Steppenwolf/Steppenwolf the Second	MCA	(2) 6933		CS
At Your Birthday Party	Dunhill	50053	'69	†
	MCA	1668		CS/CD†
Monster	Dunhill	50066	'69	†
	MCA	31328	'88	CS/CD
Live	Dunhill	(2) 50075	'70	†
	MCA	(2) 6013	'89	CS
	MCA	6013	'89	CD
Seven	Dunhill	50090	'70	†
	MCA	37047		†
	MCA	1598	'89	CS/CD
Gold	Dunhill	50099	'71	†
For Ladies Only	Dunhill	50110	'71	†
	MCA	31354	'89	CD
Rest In Peace	Dunhill	50124	'72	†
16 Greatest Hits	Dunhill	50135	'73	†
	MCA	37049		†
	MCA	1599		CS
	MCA	37049		CD
16 Great Performances	ABC	4011	'75	†
	Pickwick	3603	'78	†
Born to Be Wild: A Retrospective	MCA	(2) 10389	'91	CS/CD
Slow Flux	Mums	33093	'74	†
Hour of the Wolf	Epic	33583	'75	†
Skullduggery	Epic	34120	'76	†
Reborn to Be Wild	Epic	34382	'76	CS
Wolftracks	DBX	1084	'84	†
	Allegiance	72854		LP/CS†

T.I.M.E.

12 Originals	Liberty	7558	'68	†
Smooth Ball	Liberty	7605	'69	†

John Kay

Forgotten Songs and Unsung Heroes	Dunhill	50120	'72	†
My Sportin' Life	Dunhill	50147	'73	†
Lone Steppenwolf	MCA	31178	'88	CD†
All in Good Time	Mercury	3715	'78	†

John Kay and Steppenwolf

Rock and Roll Rebels	Qwil	1560	'87	†
Rise and Shine	I.R.S./MCA	82046	'90	CS/CD
Live at Twenty-Five	ERA	5030	'94	CS/CD

CAT STEVENS

(b. Steven Georgiou, July 21, 1947, London, England)

A popular British singer-songwriter of the first half of the '70s, Cat Stevens utilizied a distinctive guitar sound backed by gentle rhythms for his engaging, mellow songs, such as "Wild World," "Peace Train," and "Oh Very Young." Scoring his last major hit at the end of 1974, Cat Stevens abandoned music and converted to the Muslim religion in 1979.

Cat Stevens began writing songs and playing folk music in the mid-'60s while at Hammersmith Art College. Signed to Deram Records on the strength of a demonstration tape, he scored major British-only hits with "Matthew and Son," "I'm Gonna Get Me a Gun," and "A Bad Night" in 1967. Restricting his touring to England, Belgium, and France, he worked tirelessly and contracted tuberculosis, resulting in his hospitalization in September 1968 and a protracted period of convalescence. Emerging in spring 1970, Cat Stevens returned to the studio with guitarist Alun Davies to record *Mona Bone Jakon*, his first album for A&M Records. The album produced a British-only hit with "Lady D'Arbanville" and gained him his first recognition in the United States.

Cat Stevens's next album, *Tea for the Tillerman*, included a number of exciting acoustic-guitar songs, such as "Where Do the Children Play," "Hard-Headed Woman," "Longer Boats," and "On the Road to Find Out," and yielded his first major American hit with "Wild World." The intriguing follow-up, *Teaser and the Firecat*, produced a moderate hit with "Moon Shadow" and the top easy-listening and near-smash pop hits "Peace Train" and "Morning Has Broken." Stevens later abandoned his guitar-dominated sound in favor of piano, and despite scoring only a single hit from his next three albums—*Catch Bull at Four*, *Foreigner*, and *Buddha and the Chocolate Box*—all sold quite well. His major hits through 1975 include the near-smash "Oh Very Young," a smash-hit version of Sam Cooke's "Another Saturday Night," and "Ready." Recording his final album in 1978, Cat Stevens converted to the Muslim religion in 1979, changing his name to Yusef Islam and establishing the relief organization Muslim Aid near London.

Cat Stevens

Matthew and Son	Deram	18005	'67	†
	Deram	820560		CD
New Masters	Deram	18010	'68	†
	Deram	820767		CD†
Very Young and Early Songs	Deram	18061	'71	†
Cat's Cradle	London	50010	'78	†
	Deram	820321		CS
Mona Bone Jakon	A&M	4260	'70	†
	A&M	3160		CS/CD
Tea for the Tillerman	A&M	4280	'70	CS/CD
	Mobile Fidelity	519		CD
Teaser and the Firecat	A&M	4313	'71	CS/CD
Catch Bull at Four	A&M	4365	'72	CS/CD
Foreigner	A&M	4391	'73/'95	CD
Buddah and the Chocolate Box	A&M	3623	'74	CS/CD
Greatest Hits	A&M	4519	'75	CS/CD
Numbers	A&M	4255	'75	†
Izitso	A&M	4702	'77	CD
Back to Earth	A&M	4735	'78	CD†
Footsteps in the Dark: Greatest Hits, Volume 2	A&M	3736	'84	†
	A&M	3285	'86	CS/CD
Cat Stevens	A&M	2522	'87	CD
Fan's Box Set	A&M	(3) 7103		CD†

ROD STEWART
(b. Jan. 10, 1945, Highgate, London, England)

A onetime member of several of the seminal British R&B-style bands of 1963–1966, Rod Stewart first gained recognition as the vocalist for the Jeff Beck Group in the late '60s.

Pursuing a solo recording career while performing and recording with the Faces, one of Britain's finest rock bands of the '70s, Stewart quickly eclipsed the group's popularity with his *Gasoline Alley* album, arguably his finest, followed by *Every Picture Tells a Story* and the smash hit "Maggie May." After four hitless years in the early '70s, Stewart became an international star, regaining his commercial success, if little critical acclaim, by recording middle-of-the-road pop and disco material. He has managed to maintain success on the charts through the '90s, despite his often uneven work on record and stage.

Rod Stewart, born to Scottish parents, attended the same secondary school as did Ray and Dave Davies (later of the Kinks), but dropped out of school at age 16. After working a variety of mundane jobs, he learned guitar and performed as a street singer in Spain and France for a number of months. Upon returning to England, he joined Jimmy Powell and the Five Dimensions as harmonica player; in 1963–1964 he led the group. In 1964 he recorded "Good Morning Little School Girl" for Decca on his own, and joined the R&B band the Hoochie Coochie Men, sharing lead vocals with British blues revivalist "Long" John Baldry. When the group disbanded in autumn 1965, Stewart joined Baldry's Steam-packet—which featured Brian Auger and Julie Driscoll—for a year before joining Shotgun Express, whose members included Peter Green and Mick Fleetwood (later of Fleetwood Mac).

In early 1967 Rod Stewart helped form the Jeff Beck Group with former Yardbirds lead guitarist Jeff Beck and bassist-guitarist Ron Wood. Their two albums, *Truth* and *Beck-ola*, served as foundations of the British blues movement and brought Stewart his first recognition. They became widely popular in the United States by means of numerous tours over the next two years, but the group fragmented in mid-1969.

Already signed as a solo artist to Mercury Records, Rod Stewart pursued a parallel career with the Faces, which evolved out of the Small Faces and whose leader, Steve Marriott, had left the group to form Humble Pie with Peter Frampton. Even before the Faces had recorded their debut album for Warner Bros., Mercury issued *The Rod Stewart Album*, which contained Mike D'Abo's "Handbags and Gladrags" and the Rolling Stones' "Street Fighting Man." Recording his early solo albums with Wood, Ian McLagan, guitarist Martin Quittenton, and drummer Mickey Waller, Stewart overshadowed the career of the Faces beginning with 1970's *Gasoline Alley*. The album included Elton John and Bernie Taupin's "Country Comfort," Stewart's own "Lady Day," and the title cut, by Stewart and Wood.

Developing an energetic and flashy stage act through successful American tours with the Faces beginning in 1970, Rod Stewart became an international star with *Every Picture Tells a Story* and its classic top-hit single, "Maggie May," written by Stewart and Quittenton. The album also included Stewart's beautiful "Mandolin Wind" and the major hit "(I Know) I'm Losing You," a near-smash hit for the Temptations in 1966–1967. After scoring a major hit with Wood and Stewart's "Stay with Me" by the Faces, Stewart's *Never a Dull Moment* yielded a major hit with Quittenton and Stewart's "You Wear It Well" and a moderate hit with Jimi Hendrix's "Angel"; it also contained "I'd Rather Go Blind." Stewart later became embroiled in legal disputes between Mercury and Warner Bros. that saw his next album, *Smiler*, delayed nearly a year. Ron Wood toured America with the Rolling Stones in 1975, and following the Faces' subsequent U.S. tour, Rod Stewart announced his departure from the group in December.

Signing with Warner Bros. in spring 1975 and moving to Los Angeles, Rod Stewart recorded *Atlantic Crossing* in Muscle Shoals, Alabama. The album seemed to mark a deterioration in the songwriting of Stewart. Nonetheless, his next album, *A Night on the Town*, yielded a top hit with "Tonight's the Night (Gonna Be Alright)" and major hits with Cat Stevens's "The First Cut Is the Deepest" and the poignant "The Killing of Georgie." Stewart conducted a massive worldwide tour in 1976–1977. His next album, *Foot Loose and Fancy Free*, produced the smash hit "You're in My Heart (The Final Acclaim)" and major hits with

"I Was Only Joking" and the disco-style "Hot Legs." By then an international celebrity, Stewart again mounted a marathon world tour in support of *Blondes Have More Fun*, which included the facile top pop and smash R&B hit "Do Ya Think I'm Sexy" and the major pop hit "Ain't Love a Bitch."

Foolish Behaviour continued Rod Stewart's reliance on formulaic songs and confirmed his artistic decline. Although his live performances devolved into self-parody, he nonetheless remained a popular concert attraction and singles artist. "Passion" and "Young Turks" beame smash hits, and "Tonight I'm Yours (Don't Hurt Me)" and "Baby Jane" became major hits. He seemed to pull out of his descent into mediocrity with 1984's *Camouflage* and resulting tour, thanks to his reunion with Jeff Beck, but the guitarist rescued only "Infatuation" from the album (it produced a second near-smash with the Persuaders' "Some Guys Have All the Luck"), and he left the tour after only seven shows. The banal love song "Love Touch" became a smash hit when used as the theme to the movie *Legal Eagles*. *Out of Order* (1988) yielded four major hits: "Lost in You," "Forever Young," "My Heart Can't Tell Her No" (a smash hit), and "Crazy About Her"; the album went on to sell two million copies.

The Rod Stewart anthology set *Storyteller* produced smash pop and top easy-listening hits with Tom Waits's "Downtown Train" and the Motown standard "This Old Heart of Mine," recorded with Ronnie Isley. He payed further tribute to Motown with the near-smash "The Motown Song" from *Vagabond Heart*, which also produced the smash hit "Rhythm of My Heart" and a major hit with Robbie Robertson's "Broken Arrow." In 1993 Stewart toured with a large string section and performed on the MTV series *Unplugged*, re-uniting with ex-bandmate Ron Wood. The album derived from the MTV performance, *Unplugged . . . and Seated*, yielded a smash pop and top easy-listening hit with Van Morrison's "Have I Told You Lately" and a major pop hit with Tim Hardin's "Reason to Believe," a song he originally recorded in 1971. In 1994 he was inducted into the Rock and Roll Hall of Fame. Stewart's free 1994–1995 New Year's concert at Copacabana Beach in Rio de Janeiro, Brazil, drew an estimated 3.5 million fans, establishing an attendance record for an open-air concert. *A Spanner in the Works* (1995) followed the semiacoustic style of the MTV show and was his final album for Warner Bros.

Rod Stewart and Steampacket

Rod Stewart and Steampacket	Springboard Int'l	4063	'76	†

The Jeff Beck Group

Truth	Epic	26413	'68	†
	Epic	47412		CD
Beck-ola	Epic	26478	'69	†
	Epic	47411		CD
Truth/Beck-ola	Epic	(2) 33779	'75	†
	Epic	33779		CS

The Faces

First Step	Warner Bros.	1851	'70	†
	Warner Bros.	26376	'93	CD
Long Player	Warner Bros.	1892	'71	†
A Nod Is as Good as a Wink . . . To a Blind Horse	Warner Bros.	2574	'71	†
	Warner Bros.	25929	'93	CD
Ooh La La	Warner Bros.	2665	'73	†
	Warner Bros.	26368	'93	CD
Snakes and Ladders: Best	Warner Bros.	2897	'76	†

Rod Stewart and the Faces

Live	Warner Bros.	2572		†

Coast to Coast: Overture and Beginners	Mercury	697	'73	†
	Mercury	832128		CD
Rod Stewart and the Faces	Springboard Int'l	4030	'75	†
Early Sessions	Richmond	2305		CS†
Rod Stewart				
The Rod Stewart Album	Mercury	61237	'69	†
	Mercury	8001		†
	Mercury	830572		CS/CD
Gasoline Alley	Mercury	61264	'70	†
	Mercury	824881		CS/CD
Every Picture Tells a Story	Mercury	609	'71	†
	Mercury	822385	'84	CS/CD
	Polygram	846495		CS/CD
	Mobile Fidelity	532	'90	CD
Never a Dull Moment	Mercury	646	'72	†
	Mercury	826263		CS/CD
Sing It Again, Rod	Mercury	680	'73	†
	Mercury	824882		CS/CD
Smiler	Mercury	1017	'74	†
	Mercury	832056		CS/CD
Best	Mercury	7507	'76	†
	Mercury	826287		CS
Best, Volume 2	Mercury	7509	'77	†
	Mercury	822791		CS
The Mercury Anthology	Mercury	(2) 512805	'92	CD
Vintage	Mercury	518097	'93	CS/CD
You Wear It Well	Polygram	836739	'92	CS/CD
Atlantic Crossing	Warner Bros.	2875	'75	†
	Warner Bros.	3108		CS/CD
A Night on the Town	Warner Bros.	2938	'76	†
	Warner Bros.	3116		CS/CD
Foot Loose and Fancy Free	Warner Bros.	3092	'77	CS/CD
Blondes Have More Fun	Warner Bros.	3261	'78	CS/CD
Greatest Hits	Warner Bros.	3373	'79/'84	CS/CD
Foolish Behaviour	Warner Bros.	3485	'80	†
Tonight I'm Yours	Warner Bros.	3602	'81	CS/CD
Absolutely Live	Warner Bros.	23743	'82	CS/CD
Body Wishes	Warner Bros.	23877	'83	†
Camouflage	Warner Bros.	25095	'84	CS/CD
Rod Stewart	Warner Bros.	25446	'86	LP/CS/CD†
Out of Order	Warner Bros.	25684	'88	CS/CD
Storyteller: The Complete Anthology, 1964–1990	Warner Bros.	(4) 25987	'89	CS/CD
Downtown Train: Selections from the "Storyteller" Anthology	Warner Bros.	26158	'90	CS/CD
Vagabond Heart	Warner Bros.	26300	'91	CS/CD
Once in a Blue Moon	Warner Bros.	45117		CS/CD
Unplugged . . . and Seated	Warner Bros.	45289	'93	CS/CD
A Spanner in the Works	Warner Bros.	45867	'95	CS/CD
A Shot of Rhythm and Blues	Private Stock	2021	'76	†
Rod the Mod	Accord	7142	'81	†
Back on the Street Again	Intermedia	5054		LP/CS

Ridin' High	Intermedia	5080		LP/CS
Twice as Much Rod	Pair	1135		CS
Maggie May	RCA-Camden	5000		CS

THE STYLISTICS

Russell Tompkins Jr. (b. Mar. 21, 1951, Philadelphia, PA), lead ten voc; **Airron Love** (b. Aug. 8, 1949, Philadelphia, PA), ten voc; **Herbert Murrell** (b. Apr. 27, 1949, Lane, SC), lead bar voc; **James Dunn** (b. Feb. 4, 1950, Philadelphia, PA), bar voc; **James Smith** (b. June 16, 1950, New York, NY), bs voc

One of the leading exponents of the lush, mellow sound of Philadelphia soul under producer Thom Bell, the Stylistics scored a series of pop, R&B, and easy-listening hits in the first half of the '70s with songs written by Bell and Linda Creed, such as "Betcha By Golly, Wow," "Break Up to Make Up," and "You Make Me Feel Brand New." Sustaining their success under producers Hugo and Luigi for several years after the departure of Bell, the Stylistics continued to score R&B hits through 1986, despite several personnel changes.

The Stylistics formed in 1968 with the merger of two Philadelphia vocal groups, the Percussions and the Monarchs. The group was comprised of Monarchs Russell Tompkins Jr., Airron Love, and James Smith and Percussions James Dunn and Herbert Murrell. They first recorded for Sebring Records in 1969, and their song "You're a Big Girl Now" was later picked up by Avco Embassy (later simply Avco), where it became a smash R&B hit. Teamed with producer Thom Bell and the songwriting team of Bell and Linda Creed, the Stylistics scored a series of smash R&B hits through spring 1974, two of which, "Betcha By Golly, Wow" and "You Make Me Feel Brand New," also became smash pop and easy-listening hits. Burt Bacharach and Hal David's "You'll Never Get to Heaven (If You Break My Heart)" was a smash R&B and easy-listening hit in 1973. Bell-Creed pop and R&B smashes for the Stylistics include "You Are Everything," "I'm Stone in Love with You," and "Break Up to Make Up," all major easy-listening hits. The team's "Stop, Look, Listen (To Your Heart)," "People Make the World Go Round," and "Rockin' Roll Baby" became smash R&B and major pop hits for the Stylistics.

When Thom Bell began working with the Spinners, the Stylistics were placed with the songwriting-production team of Hugo and Luigi under arranger-conductor Van McCoy for 1974's *Let's Put It All Together*. The album's title song was a major pop and easy-listening and smash R&B hit, but the Stylistics never again scored a major pop hit. "Heavy Fallin' Out" and "Thank You Baby" became R&B smashes, but even their popularity in that field began to fade after their switch to H&L Records in 1976. In 1978 James Dunn retired due to ill health and the Stylistics switched to Mercury and then TSOP records for the major R&B hits "First Impressions" and "Hurry Up This Way Again," respectively. James Smith left the group in 1981, and the Stylistics scored their final minor R&B hits on Streetwise Records from 1984 to 1986.

The Stylistics

The Stylistics	Avco Embassy	33023	'71	†
	Amherst	748	'95	CS/CD
Round 2	Avco Embassy	11006	'72	†
	Amherst	747		CS/CD
Rockin' Roll Baby	Avco	11010	'73	†
Let's Put It All Together	Avco	69001	'74	†
Heavy from the Mountain	Avco	69004	'74	†

Best	Avco	69005	'75	†
	Amherst	743	'86	LP
	Amherst	5743	'86	CS
	Amherst	9743	'86	CD
Thank You Baby	Acco	69008	'75	†
You Are Beautiful	Avco	69010	'75	†
Fabulous	H & L	69013	'76	†
Once Upon a Jukebox	H & L	69015	'77	†
In Fashion	Mercury	3727	'78	†
Love Spell	Mercury	3753	'79	†
Hurry Up This Way Again	TSOP	36470	'80	†
All-Time Classics	Amherst	744	'86	LP
	Amherst	5744	'86	CS
	Amherst	9744	'86	CD
Best, Volume 2	Amherst	745	'86	LP
	Amherst	5745	'86	CS
	Amherst	9745	'86	CD
Greatest Love Hits	Amherst	5746	'86	CS
	Amherst	9746	'86	CD
Love Talk	Amherst	4404		LP
	Amherst	54404		CS
	Amherst	94404		CD

DONNA SUMMER

(b. LaDonna Gaines, Dec. 31, 1948, Boston, MA)

The biggest and most enduring female recording star to emerge from the disco scene of the late '70s, Donna Summer scored one of the first disco hits with the erotic "Love to Love You Baby" in late 1975 and became disco's most recognized and popular solo artist. Ably supported by European songwriter-producers Pete Bellotte and Giorgio Moroder, Summer diversified into funk and synthesizer-dominated pop, and blossomed as a songwriter with 1979's *Bad Girl* album, which eventually sold more than six million copies. Switching to Geffen Records in 1980 for several equivocal rock-oriented albums, Summer scored her biggest later success with the 1983 album *She Works Hard for the Money*.

Donna Summer grew up in Dorcester, Massachusetts, and began singing in a church choir as a child. She worked sessions and recorded demonstration records as a teenager, and quit school two months short of high school graduation to join the otherwise all-white group Crow, debuting with them at Boston's Psychedelic Supermarket in 1967. Later in the year she won a role in the Munich, Germany, production of *Hair* and moved to Europe. She performed in the musical for over a year, then joined the Vienna Folk Opera in 1969, performing in productions of *Porgy and Bess* and *Showboat*. In Germany she appeared in *Godspell* and *The Me Nobody Knows* and worked sessions for producer-songwriters Pete Bellotte and Giorgio Moroder. From 1973 to 1975 Summer recorded for the team's Oasis Records, scoring European hits with "Hostage" and "Lady of the Night." In 1975 Moroder brought her recording of "Je T'Aime" to Neil Bogart of Casablanca Records. The song was re-recorded in a 17-minute version with the sound of Summer's simulated orgasms surrounded by electronic keyboards and a disco-style rhythm as "Love to Love You Baby." The song was picked up by New York discos and became a smash American pop and R&B hit in an abbreviated four-minute version.

Summer returned to the United States in late 1975 and toured the country in early 1976 in support of her second album, *Love Trilogy*, which solidified her popularity with the disco crowd. Later in the year she recorded the concept love album *Four Seasons of Love*, which produced major R&B and minor pop hits with "Spring Affair" and "Winter Melody." Scoring a near-smash pop and R&B hit with the synthesizer-dominated "I Feel Love" from *I Remember Yesterday*, Summer appeared in the 1978 disco-comedy movie *Thank God It's Friday* and contributed four songs to the soundtrack album, including the smash crossover hit "Last Dance," essentially her last disco hit.

The two-record set *Live and More* compiled live and studio recordings, including a top pop and near-smash R&B hit version of Jimmy Webb's "MacArthur Park" and the crossover smash "Heaven Knows," recorded with Brooklyn Dreams. The album remained on the album charts for more than a year and expanded Summer's popularity into the pop mainstream. Donna Summer began exploring funk with her masterful *Bad Girls* album in 1979. The album produced the top pop and smash R&B hit "Hot Stuff," the top pop and R&B hit title track, and the pop smash "Dim All the Lights." Before year's end she scored a top pop hit in duet with Barbra Streisand on "No More Tears (Enough Is Enough)," and the anthology set *On the Radio* yielded a crossover smash with the title song.

In 1980 Donna Summer switched to Geffen Records and married Bruce Sudano of Brooklyn Dreams, with whom she wrote Dolly Parton's top country hit "Starting Over Again." Pete Bellotte and Giorgio Moroder produced her debut for the label, *The Wanderer*. The decidedly rock-oriented album yielded a pop smash with the title song and moderate pop hits with "Cold Love" and "Who Do You Think You're Foolin'." The album also revealed her born-again Christianity with songs such as "I Believe in Jesus." However, subsequent albums for Geffen sold progressively less well and all were later deleted by the label. Her next album, *Donna Summer*, produced by Quincy Jones, includes the smash crossover hit "Love Is In Control" and the moderate pop hits "The Woman in Me" and "State of Independence," the latter recorded with an all-star choir that included Michael Jackson, Lionel Richie, Dionne Warwick, and Stevie Wonder.

Summer's social conscious came to the fore with the title song to 1983's *She Works Hard for the Money*, recorded for Mercury Records as part of her legal settlement with Casablanca Records; the song became a smash crossover hit. The album also yielded a near-smash R&B hit with "Unconditional Love." Brenda Russell's "Dinner with Gershwin" became a near-smash R&B hit from 1987's *All Systems Go*, her first album in three years and her final album for Geffen Records. In 1989 Donna Summer moved to Atlantic Records, where she soon had a near-smash pop hit with "This Time I Know It's for Real," but subsequent recordings have fared far less well.

Donna Summer

Love to Love You Baby	Oasis	5003	'75	†
	Casablanca	822792	'92	CS/CD
A Love Trilogy	Oasis	5004	'76	†
	Casablanca	5004	'80	†
	Casablanca	822793	'92	CS/CD
Four Seasons of Love	Oasis	7038	'76	†
	Casablanca	826236	'91	CS/CD
I Remember Yesterday	Casablanca	7056	'77	†
	Casablanca	826237	'91	CS/CD
The Deep (soundtrack)	Casablanca	7060	'77	†
Once Upon a Time	Casablanca	(2) 7078	'77	†
	Casablanca	826238	'87	CD

Live and More	Casablanca	(2) 7119	'78	†
	Casablanca	811123		CS/CD
Bad Girls	Casablanca	(2) 7150	'79	†
	Casablanca	822557		CS/CD
On the Radio—Greatest Hits, Volumes 1 and 2	Casablanca	(2) 7191	'79	†
	Casablanca	822558		CS/CD
Greatest Hits, Volume 1	Casablanca	7201	'80	†
Greatest Hits, Volume 2	Casablanca	7202	'80	†
Walk Away—Collector's Edition (The Best of 1977–1980)	Casablanca	7244	'80	†
	Casablanca	810011		CD
	Casablanca	822560		CS
Greatest Hits	Casablance	822559		CS
The Dance Collection	Casablanca	830534	'87	CS/CD
The Wanderer	Geffen	2000	'80	†
	Casablanca	522942	'94	CS/CD
Donna Summer	Geffen	2005	'82	†
	Casablanca	522943	'94	CS/CD
Cats Without Claws	Geffen	24040	'84	†
	Casablanca	522944	'94	CS/CD
All Systems Go	Geffen	24102	'87	CS/CD†
	Casablanca	522945	'94	CS/CD
Anthology	Casablanca	(2) 518144	'93	CS/CD
She Works Hard for the Money	Mercury	812265	'83	CS/CD
The Summer Collection	Mercury	826144	'85	CS/CD
Endless Summer: Donna	Mercury	516917	'94	CS/CD
Another Place and Time	Atlantic	81987	'89	CS/CD
Mistaken Identity	Atlantic	82285	'91	CD

THE SUPREMES

Diana Ross (b. Mar. 26, 1944, Detroit, MI); **Florence Ballard** (b. June 30, 1943, Detroit, MI; d. Feb. 22, 1976, Detroit, MI); **Mary Wilson** (b. Mar. 6, 1944, Greenville, MS); **Barbara Martin** [Barbara Martin left in 1962; Florence Ballard departed in 1967 and was replaced by **Cindy Birdsong** (b. Dec. 15, 1939, Camden, NJ).]

Undoubtedly Motown's most successful female group, scoring ten top pop hits between 1964 and 1967, the Supremes were certainly one of the most popular vocal groups of all time. Prime purveyors of the sophisticated, highly commercial, and sometimes bland black vocal group sound of Motown, the Supremes were one of the first black groups to achieve massive popularity with both black and white audiences. Carefully groomed and promoted by legendary Motown founder Berry Gordy Jr., the group made a star out of lead singer Diana Ross, who left in 1969 to pursue a solo singing and acting career. The reconstituted Supremes managed several crossover smashes through 1972, and endured until 1977.

Diana Ross, Florence Ballard, Mary Wilson, and Betty McGlown began singing together while still in high school in 1959 as the Primettes, the companion group to the Primes, whose members Otis Williams and Eddie Kendricks later formed the Temptations. In 1960 Barbara Martin replaced Betty McGlown and the group made their first recording for Lupine Records. They auditioned for Berry Gordy Jr. while still in high school, but he insisted they finish school before he would sign them.

Signed to Gordy's Tamla Records by 1961, the group changed their name to the Supremes and recorded two unsuccessful singles for the label before switching to Motown in 1962. Barbara Martin left the group in 1962, and they continued as a trio, working as backup vocalists for other Motown artists until 1964. The Supremes scored their first minor pop hit in 1962 with Smokey Robinson's "Your Heart Belongs to Me," and they were subsequently placed with songwriter-producers Brian Holland, Lamont Dozier, and Eddie Holland. They eventually achieved their first major pop and R&B hit with "When Your Lovelight Starts Shining Through His Eyes" in late 1963.

In summer 1964 the Supremes' "Where Did Our Love Go" initiated a string of five top pop hits: "Baby Love," "Come See About Me," "Stop! In the Name of Love," and "Back in My Arms Again." Other Holland-Dozier-Holland songs to become top pop and R&B hits for the Supremes through spring 1967 are "You Can't Hurry Love," "You Keep Me Hangin' On," and "Love Is Here and Now You're Gone." "I Hear a Symphony" and the psychedelic-sounding "The Happening" became top pop and smash R&B hits, and "Nothing but Heartaches," "My World Is Empty Without You," and "Love Is Like an Itching in My Heart" were smash pop and R&B hits.

In 1967 Florence Ballard quit (or was forced out of, depending on whose version of the event is to be believed) the Supremes, to be replaced by Cindy Birdsong, a former member of Patti Labelle and the Blue Belles. Ballard briefly attempted a solo career on ABC Records and eventually died impoverished of cardiac arrest on February 22, 1976, at age 32. The group was subsequently billed as Diana Ross and the Supremes, scoring a pop and R&B smash with another pyschedelic soul song, "Reflections."

After the near-smash pop and major R&B hit "In and Out of Love," the Holland-Dozier-Holland team left Motown Records. In 1968 Diana Ross and the Supremes scored a top pop and smash R&B hit with "Love Child," one of Motown's few attempts at socially conscious lyrics, followed by the crossover smash "I'm Gonna Make You Love Me," recorded with the Temptations. In 1969 "I'm Livin' in Shame" became a crossover smash and "I'll Try Something New," recorded with the Temptations, became a major pop and R&B hit, as did "The Composer." Diana Ross's final hit with the Supremes, "Someday We'll Be Together," was a top crossover hit.

At the end of 1969 Diana Ross left the Supremes for a solo career. Mary Wilson and Cindy Birdsong persevered with new member Jean Terrell. Over the next two years they scored major pop and smash R&B hits with "Up the Ladder to the Roof," "River Deep—Mountain High" (with the Four Tops), "Nathan Jones," and "Floy Joy," with the smash pop and top R&B hit "Stoned Love" intervening. Birdsong left the group in 1972, then returned and left again in 1976. Terrell left in 1973. By 1976 the Supremes were comprised of Wilson, Scherrie Payne, and Susaye Greene. The group essentially disbanded in 1977, although Wilson toured England with two new members in 1978. Mary Wilson recorded a solo album for Motown in 1979 and subsequently sustained her own career, largely in Europe. In 1982 the musical *Dreamgirls*, seemingly based on the career of the Supremes, began a successful run on Broadway. In 1983 the Supremes (Ross, Wilson, and Cindy Birdsong) reunited for the 25th anniversary Motown television special, but tales of Ross's untoward behavior at the ceremony were confirmed in Wilson's best-selling book *Dreamgirl: My Life As a Supreme*, published in 1986. The Supremes were inducted into the Rock and Roll Hall of Fame in 1988.

Through early 1971 Diana Ross scored a top pop and R&B hit with "Ain't No Mountain High Enough" and major crossover hits with "Reach Out and Touch (Somebody's Hand)" and "Remember Me," all written by Nick Ashford and Valerie Simpson. But Ross didn't have another major pop hit until 1973's top pop and smash R&B hit "Touch Me in the Morning." In the meantime she had begun regularly appearing on television and made the movie *Lady Sings the Blues*, portraying Billie Holiday. The soundtrack album became a best-seller and temporarily reinvigorated Ross's career.

In 1973 Diana Ross teamed with Marvin Gaye for *Diana and Marvin*. The album yielded three hits, including the major pop hits "You're a Special Part of Me" (an R&B smash) and "My Mistake (Was to Love You)." In 1975 Ross starred in the film *Mahogany*, and the movie's theme, also known as "Do You Know Where You're Going To," became a top pop and major R&B hit. A year later her most successful album in years, *Diana Ross*, produced a top pop and R&B hit, the disco-sounding "Love Hangover," and a major pop and R&B hit, "One Love in My Lifetime."

In June 1976 she brought her *Evening with Diana Ross* stage show to Broadway, later touring the country with the show and appearing in the first one-woman, prime-time television special in March 1977. After the crossover hit "Gettin' Ready for Love," Ross appeared in the film version of the hit play *The Wiz* with Michael Jackson, Nipsey Russell, and Richard Pryor. Probably the most expensive all-black film ever made till then ($20 million), the film was visually spectacular, utilizing stunning costuming, elaborate special effects, and massive production numbers, but despite a $6 million promotional campaign, it proved a relative failure.

Ross's musical career was revitalized with her 1980 album *Diana*, which yielded a top crossover hit with "Upside Down" and a crossover smash with "I'm Coming Out." "It's My Turn," from the movie of the same name, became a major crossover hit that year, and in 1981 her collaboration with Lionel Richie, "Endless Love" (again from the movie with the same title), became a top pop, easy-listening, and R&B hit. In 1981 Ross switched to RCA Records for a reported $20 million, recording six albums for the label through 1987. Smash R&B and major pop hits through 1985 include a remake of Frankie Lymon and the Teenagers's "Why Do Fools Fall in Love," "Mirror Mirror," "Muscles" (written and produced by Michael Jackson), "Swept Away" (written and produced by Daryl Hall), and "Missing You" (written and produced by Lionel Richie and dedicated to Marvin Gaye). However, after the major R&B hits "Telephone," "Eaten Alive," and "Dirty Looks," Diana Ross never again scored another major hit. In 1989 she returned to Motown Records, but Berry Gordy Jr. was by then no longer involved with the company and her albums sold poorly. In 1993 Villard Books published Diana Ross's evasive, self-serving autobiography, *Secrets of a Sparrow*.

The Supremes

Meet the Supremes	Motown	606	'63	†
	Motown	5253		CS/CD†
Where Did Our Love Go	Motown	621	'64	†
	Motown	5270		CS/CD†
A Bit of Liverpool	Motown	623	'64	†
	Motown	5249	'89	CD†
Country, Western and Pop	Motown	625	'65	†
	Motown	530327	'94	CS/CD
More Hits	Motown	627	'65	†
	Motown	5440	'89	CS/CD†
We Remember Sam Cooke	Motown	629	'65	†
	Motown	5495	'91	CS/CD†
At the Copa	Motown	636	'65	†
	Motown	5162	'90	CS/CD†
Merry Christmas	Motown	638	'65	†
	Motown	5252		CS/CD
I Hear a Symphony	Motown	643	'66	†
	Motown	5147		CS/CD

Where Did Our Love Go/I Hear a Symphony	Motown	5270	'86	CD†
Supremes a Go-Go	Motown	649	'66	†
	Motown	5138	'89	CS/CD
Sing Holland-Dozier-Holland	Motown	650	'67	†
	Motown	5182	'89	CS/CD†
Sing Rodgers and Hart	Motown	659	'67	†
The Supremes Sing Rodgers and Hart	Motown	9074	'87	CD†
Greatest Hits	Motown	(2) 663	'67	†
Greatest Hits, Volumes 1 and 2	Motown	(2) 237		CS†
	Motown	237		CD†
Greatest Hits, Volume 1	Motown	5357	'89	CS/CD
Greatest Hits, Volume 2	Motown	5358		CS/CD
Diana Ross and the Supremes				
Reflections	Motown	665	'68	†
	Motown	5494	'91	CS/CD
Love Child	Motown	670	'68	†
	Motown	5245	'89	CS/CD†
Love Child/Supremes a Go-Go	Motown	8121	'86	CD†
Funny Girl	Motown	672	'68	†
Live at London's Talk of the Town	Motown	676	'68	†
	Motown	530328	'94	CS/CD
Let the Sunshine In	Motown	689	'69	†
	Motown	5305		CS/CD
Cream of the Crop	Motown	694	'69	†
	Motown	5435	'89	CS/CD†
Let the Sunshine In/Cream of the Crop	Motown	8132	'86	CD†
Greatest Hits, Volume 3	Motown	702	'70	†
	Motown	5203		CS/CD
Farewell	Motown	708	'70	†
Anthology	Motown	(3) 794	'74	LP/CS
	Motown	(2) 794		CD
Motown Superstar Series, Volume 1	Motown	101		†
	Motown	5101		CS
Compact Command Performance (18 Greatest Hits)	Motown	6073		CD†
Great Songs and Performances	Motown	5313		CS/CD
Supremes Sing Motown	Motown	5371		†
25th Anniversary	Motown	(3) 5381	'86	CS†
	Motown	(2) 5381	'86	CD†
Every Great No. 1 Hit	Motown	9038	'87	CD†
	Motown	5498		CS/CD
Never-Before-Released Masters	Motown	9075	'87	CD†
More Hits by the Supremes	Motown	5440	'89	CS/CD†
More Hits by the Supremes/Sing Holland-Dozier-Holland	Motown	8151		CD†
Captured Live On Stage	Motown	(2) 5278		CS/CD
Motown Legends	Esx	8520	'95	CS/CD
The Supremes and the Temptations				
The Supremes Join the Temptations	Motown	679	'68	†
	Motown	5139		CS/CD
T.C.B.	Motown	682	'68	†
	Motown	5171		CS/CD

Together	Motown	692	'69	†
	Motown	5436	'89	CS/CD†
The Supremes Join the Temptations/Together	Motown	8138		CD†
On Broadway	Motown	699	'69	†
Motown Legends	Motown	5368		†
The Supremes and the Four Tops				
The Magnificent Seven	Motown	717	'70	†
	Motown	5123		CS/CD†
The Return of the Magnificent Seven	Motown	736	'71	†
Dynamite	Motown	745	'71	†
Best	Motown	5491	'91	CS/CD
The Supremes (without Diana Ross)				
Right On	Motown	705	'70	†
	Motown	5442	'89	CS/CD†
New Ways, But Love Stays	Motown	720	'70	†
	Motown	5497	'91	CS/CD†
Touch	Motown	737	'71	†
	Motown	5447		CS/CD†
Floy Joy	Motown	751	'72	†
	Motown	5441	'89	CS/CD†
The Supremes	Motown	756	'72	†
The Supremes	Motown	828	'75	†
High Energy	Motown	863	'76	†
Mary, Scherrie and Susaye	Motown	873	'77	†
At Their Best (1973–1978)	Motown	904	'78	†
Greatest Hits and Rare Classics	Motown	5487	'91	CS/CD
Mary Wilson				
Mary Wilson	Motown	927	'79	†
Scherrie Payne and Susaye Greene				
Partners	Motown	920	'79	†
Diana Ross				
Diana Ross	Motown	711	'70	†
Diana!	Motown	719	'71	†
	Motown	5155		CS/CD†
Everything Is Everything	Motown	724	'70	†
Surrender	Motown	723	'71	†
	Motown	5423	'89	CD†
Lady Sings the Blues	Motown	(2) 758	'72	CS
	Motown	758		CD
Touch Me in the Morning	Motown	772	'73	†
	Motown	5163		CS/CD
The Last Time I Saw Him	Motown	812	'73	†
Live at Caesar's Palace	Motown	801	'74	†
	Motown	5169		CS/CD
Mahogany (soundtrack)	Motown	858	'75	†
Diana Ross	Motown	861	'76	†
	Motown	5294	'89	CS/CD
Greatest Hits	Motown	869	'76	CS
	Motown	896	'91	CD

An Evening with Diana Ross	Motown	(2) 877	'77	†
	Motown	(2) 5268		CS
	Motown	5268		CD
Baby, It's Me	Motown	890	'77	†
	Motown	5434		CD
Ross	Motown	907		†
The Boss	Motown	923	'79	†
	Motown	5198		CS/CD
Diana	Motown	936	'80	†
	Motown	5383	'87	CS/CD
Diana/The Boss	Motown	8102	'86	CD†
To Love Again	Motown	951	'81	†
All the Great Hits	Motown	(2) 960	'81	†
	Motown	960		CS/CD
Ain't No Mountain High Enough	Motown	5135	'89	CS/CD
Ain't No Mountain High Enough/Surrender	Motown	8142		CD†
Anthology	Motown	(2) 6049	'83	LP/CS/CD
Diana's Duets	Motown	5214	'87	CS/CD
Compact Command Performance (14 Greatest Hits)	Motown	6072		CD†
All the Great Love Songs	Motown	6105		CD†
Why Do Fools Fall In Love	RCA	4153	'81	†
	RCA	5162	'84	CS
Silk Electric	RCA	4384	'82/'90	CS/CD
Ross	RCA	4677	'83	LP/CS/CD†
Swept Away	RCA	5009	'84	CS/CD
Eaten Alive	RCA	5422	'85	CD
Red Hot Rhythm and Blues	RCA	6388	'87	LP/CS/CD†
Endless Love	RCA	61154	'92	CS/CD
Workin' Overtime	Motown	6274	'89	CS/CD	
The Force Behind the Power	Motown	6316	'91	CS/CD
Stolen Moments: The Lady Sings . . . Jazz and Blues	Motown	6340	'93	CS/CD
Musical Memoirs, Forever	Motown	(4) 6357	'93	CS/CD
The Remixes	Motown	6377	'94	LP/CS/CD
Diana Extended/The Remixes	Motown	6377	'94	CD
One Woman: The Ultimate	Motown	0428	'94	CS/CD
Take Me Higher	Motown	0586	'95	CS/CD

Diana Ross and Marvin Gaye

Diana and Marvin	Motown	803	'73	†
	Motown	5124	'87	CS/CD

Diana Ross and Others

The Wiz (soundtrack)	MCA	(2) 14000	'78	†
	MCA	(2) 6010		†

T

TALKING HEADS

David Byrne (b. May 14, 1952, Dumbarton, Scotland), voc, gtr; **Jerry Harrison** (b. Feb. 21, 1949, Milwaukee, WI), kybd, gtr; **Tina Weymouth** (b. Nov. 22, 1950, Coronado, CA), bs, synth; **Chris Frantz** (b. May 8, 1951, Fort Campbell, KY), drm

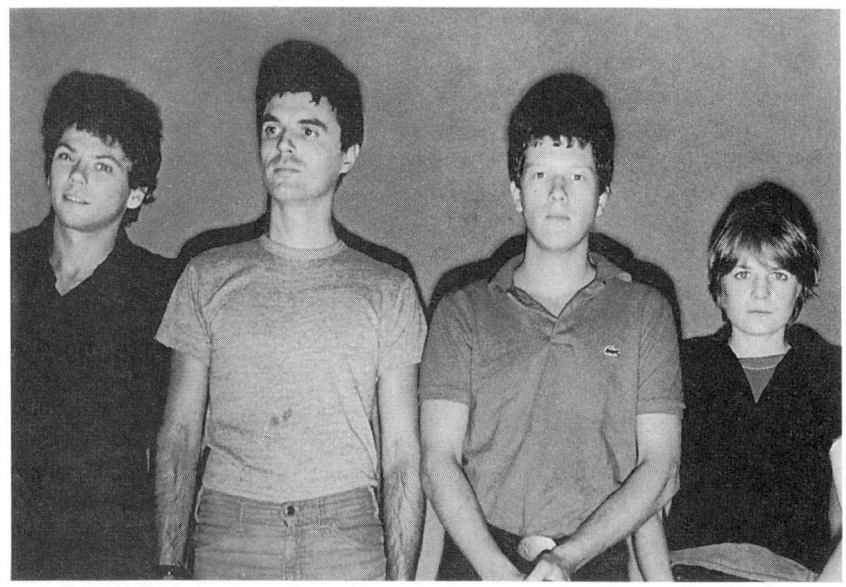

<small>TALKING HEADS</small>

One of the first important bands to emerge from the mid-'70s New York City punk and New Wave scenes, Talking Heads initially featured minimalist instrumentation on leader David Byrne's neurotic yet intelligent and often surreal dance songs of alienation and estrangement. Finding favor with the college audience as well as the New Wave crowd, Talking Heads eventually left behind their minimalist roots to develop a layered, highly percussive, and funk-based sound. The group broke through commercially with *Speaking in Tongues* and its near-smash hit "Burning Down the House," as well as the hit art-house film *Stop Making Sense*. Always open to side projects, Talking Heads officially disbanded in late 1991. David Byrne remained the most conspicuous and productive of the former members, ultimately returning to the basic rock band format for 1994's *David Byrne*.

David Byrne grew up in Baltimore and later attended the Rhode Island School of Design, where he met Chris Frantz and Tina Weymouth. Byrne and Frantz played with a quintet variously known as the Artistics and the Autistics, and the three moved to New York in early 1975 and formed Talking Heads as a trio. Frantz and Weymouth married, and the three rehearsed for five months, debuting at CBGB's in June 1975. Harvard graduate Jerry Harrison, a member of Jonathan Richman's Modern Lovers until 1974, joined the group in 1976, and the quartet toured Europe with the Ramones. Signed by Sire Records, Talking Heads' debut album won quick acclaim for its stark instrumentation and Byrne's unique vocal and songwriting style. The album included the favorite "Don't Worry About the Government" and produced a minor hit with the bizarre "Psycho Killer."

Talking Heads subsequently toured Europe and America regularly to establish themselves as a live band, and enlisted producer Brian Eno for their next three albums. The first, *More Songs About Buildings and Food*, yielded a major hit with a cover of Syl Johnson's "Take Me to the River" while including "Big Country" and "Found a Job." The rather dense and ominous *Fear of Music* included the African-sounding "I Zimbra," "Heaven," "Memories Can't Wait," and the paranoid anthem minor hit "Life During Wartime (This Ain't No Party . . . This Ain't No Disco . . . This Ain't No Fooling Around)."

Talking Heads put their minimalist sound behind them for *Remain in Light*, Brian Eno's final production for the band. Recorded with guitarist Adrian Belew (who had played with Frank Zappa and David Bowie), synthesizer player Bernie Worrell (from Parliament-Funkadelic), and percussionist Steve Scales, the album fused funk and African rhythms, the electronic and synthesizer sound favored by Eno and Worrell, and layered vocals and solos to produce a demanding and intricate series of song constructions. It includes "Crosseyed and Painless" and "Houses in Motion" and yielded a minor hit with "Once in a Lifetime." The group toured the world with an expanded band that included the additional musicians used on the record, with live recordings from this tour eventually released in 1982.

However, Talking Heads were not to record another studio album for almost three years, as the members pursued a variety of outside projects. David Byrne collaborated with Brian Eno on the instrumental album *My Life in the Bush of Ghosts*, which featured the rhythms of Africa and the Middle East; he also composed the score for the Twyla Tharp ballet *The Catherine Wheel*. He later produced the B-52's *Mesopotamia* EP and Fun Boy Three's *Waiting*. Jerry Harrison recorded a solo album, and Chris Frantz and Tina Weymouth assembled the Tom Tom Club with Tina's sisters Loric, Lani, and Laura, guitarists Adrian Belew and Monte Brown, and keyboardist-producer Steven Stanley. The album produced a British smash with the rap-style "Wordy Rappinghood" and a moderate American hit with "Genius of Love."

With Brian Eno's departure as producer, Talking Heads returned to their basic sound for 1983's *Speaking in Tongues*. The album remained on the charts for nearly a year and contained the near-smash hit "Burning Down the House," the minor hit "This Must Be the Place (Naive Melody)," plus "Girlfriend Is Better" and "Swamp." In December 1983 Talking Heads, as part of their American tour, performed four nights at the Pantages Theater in Los Angeles. The songs were performed in approximate chronologic order, thus providing a historic perspective, and built from Byrne's solo performance (accompanied by a percussion part prerecorded and played on a boom box) of "Psycho Killer" as additional members joined him on stage. Weymouth entered to play "Heaven," then Frantz came on for "Thank You for Sending Me an Angel." By the sixth song the entire entourage, including percussionist Steve Scales, keyboardist Bernie Worrell, and guitarist Alex Weir, was on stage. Filmed under the direction of Jonathan Demme, the performances were assembled into the film *Stop Making Sense*, acclaimed as one of the finest rock concert documentaries ever made upon its release in 1984. The soundtrack album remained on the charts for more than two years and later yielded a minor hit with the new version of "Once in a Lifetime."

In 1984 David Byrne scored and recorded the music for avant-garde artist Robert Wilson's *The Knee Plays*, derived from Wilson's ambitious opera *the CIVIL warS*. Talking Heads recorded the rather accessible *Little Creatures* album, which contained "Road to Nowhere" and "Stay Up Late," yielded a minor hit with "And She Was," and became a best-seller. In 1985 Byrne cowrote, directed, and starred in the movie *True Stories*, an oddly entertaining and droll satire on American life set in the fictional town of Virgil, Texas. Talking Heads' recording of the album's music was remarkably diverse, incorporating country, Tex-Mex, and zydeco musics, while producing a major hit with "Wild Wild Life."

Over the next few years the members of Talking Heads pursued a variety of outside projects. Jerry Harrison played sessions for the Violent Femmes and the BoDeans, among others, while Tina Weymouth and Chris Frantz produced Ziggy Marley's breakthrough album *Conscious Party*. David Byrne collaborated with Ryuichi Sakamoto and Cong Su on the award-winning soundtrack to the film *The Last Emperor*. In 1988 Talking Heads reunited to record *Naked*, which featured "Blind," "Mr. Jones," and "(Nothing But) Flowers," but the group members soon went their separate ways, coming back together only in late 1991 to record four uncompleted tracks for the anthology set *Sand in the Vaseline*.

In 1988 David Byrne established his own record company, Luaka Bop, for various world music recordings. In 1989 he recorded *Rei Momo* with Latin and Brazilian musicians and released two albums of Brazilian music, *Beleza Tropical* and *O Samba*, on Luaka Bop. He toured with a large band of Brazilian musicians in support of *Rei Momo*, and later recorded orchestral music for *The Forest*, a theatrical piece by Robert Wilson. Jerry Harrison assembled the large band the Casual Gods for recordings on Sire Records, and Chris Frantz and Tina Weymouth reassembled the Tom Tom Club, with Weymouth as lead vocalist, for recordings and a 1989 tour. With the demise of Talking Heads in 1991, Byrne utilized many of the musicians from *Rei Momo* to record *Uh-Oh*, but then returned to a basic rock band setup for 1994's *David Byrne*. However, he failed to achieve any hits as a solo artist.

Talking Heads

Talking Heads: 77	Sire	6036	'77	CS/CD
More Songs About Buildings and Food	Sire	6058	'78	CS/CD
Talking Heads: 77/More Songs About Buildings and Food	Warner Bros.	23712		CS
Fear of Music	Sire	6076	'79	CS/CD
Remain in Light	Sire	6095	'80	CS/CD
The Name of the Band Is Talking Heads	Sire	(2) 3590	'82	CS
Speaking in Tongues	Sire	23883	'83	CS/CD
Stop Making Sense (soundtrack)	Sire	25121	'84	CS
	Sire	25186		CS/CD
Little Creatures	Sire	25305	'85	CS/CD
True Stories	Sire	25512	'86	CS/CD
Naked	Sire	25654	'88	CS/CD
Popular Favorites, 1976–1991/Sand in the Vaseline	Sire	(2) 26760	'92	CS/CD

David Byrne and Brian Eno

My Life in the Bush of Ghosts	Sire	6093	'81	CS/CD
	Sire	45374	'93	CS/CD

David Byrne

The Catherine Wheel	Sire	3645	'81	CS/CD
Music for "The Knee Plays"	ECM	25022	'85	†
Rei Momo	Sire	25990	'89	CS/CD
The Forest	Luaka Bop/ Warner Bros.	26584	'91	CS/CD
Uh-Oh	Luaka Bop/ Warner Bros.	26799	'92	CS/CD
David Byrne	Luaka Bop/ Warner Bros.	45558	'94	CS/CD

David Byrne/Ryuichi Sakamoto/Cong Su

The Last Emperor (soundtrack)	Virgin	86029	'88	CD

Tom Tom Club

Tom Tom Club	Sire	3628	'81	CS/CD

Close to the Bone	Sire	23916	'83	CS
Boom Boom Chi Boom Boom	Sire	25888	'89	CS/CD†
Dark Sneak Love Action	Sire	26951	'92	CS/CD

Jerry Harrison

The Red and the Black	Sire	3631	'81	†

Jerry Harrison and the Casual Gods

Casual Gods	Sire	25663	'88	CS/CD†
Walk on Water	Sire	25943	'90	CS/CD

JAMES TAYLOR
(b. Mar. 12, 1948, Boston, MA)

James Taylor established himself in the forefront of the '70s singer-songwriter movement with the desperately personal "Fire and Rain" single and *Sweet Baby James* album. Finding an audience with both pop and easy-listening fans, Taylor continued to be a best-selling album artist through the '70s, as his songs came to reflect less personal anguish and more gentle compassion. Married to Carly Simon from 1972 to 1983, Taylor continued to record albums of substantial popularity into the '90s.

James Taylor and his siblings Alex, Kate, and Livingston were raised in affluence and moved with their parents to Chapel Hill, North Carolina, after Livingston's birth in 1950. They spent summers on exclusive Martha's Vineyard beginning in 1953. From an early age, Alex studied violin, Livingston and Kate learned piano, and James took cello lessons. After meeting guitarist Danny "Kootch" Kortchmar on Martha's Vineyard in 1963, James formed the Fabulous Corsairs with brother Alex and three friends in North Carolina in 1964. While later attending boarding school near Boston, James began to suffer bouts of depression, which led him to commit himself voluntarily to a psychiatric hospital in 1965, where he began writing songs. After discharging himself nine months later, he went to New York in summer 1966 and formed the Flying Machine with Kortchmar, bassist Zach Weisner, and drummer Joel O'Brien. The group debuted at the Cafe Bizarre that fall and later moved up to the Night Owl, where they played regularly for seven months. Before disintegrating in spring 1967, they made some recordings that were later issued after the success of *Sweet Baby James*.

James Taylor next moved to London, where he made a demonstration tape that so impressed Paul McCartney and Apple A&R chief Peter Asher that he was signed to the Beatles' record label. His debut solo album, which contained odd orchestral segues between songs, included the ominous "The Blues Is Just a Bad Dream," "Knocking 'Round the Zoo," "Something in the Way She Moves" (which provided an opening line for George Harrison's "Something"), and the excellent "Carolina on My Mind" and "Rainy Day Man." However, the album went generally unnoticed, and with affairs in disarray at Apple, Peter Asher negotiated a contract for Taylor with Warner Bros. Records.

After debuting at Los Angeles's Troubadour Club in summer 1969, James Taylor recorded his next album in California with Peter Asher, now his manager, producing. *Sweet Baby James* established him in the vanguard of the emerging singer-songwriter movement with its anguished smash hit single "Fire and Rain." Recorded with Danny Kortchmar, Carole King, and drummer Russ Kunkel, among others, the album also featured the moderate hit "Country Road" and the gentle "Sunny Skies" and "Blossom." Taylor next recorded *Mud Slide Slim and the Blue Horizon* with Kortchmar, King, Kunkel, and bassist Leland Sklar under producer Asher. The album yielded a top pop and easy-listening hit with King's "You've Got a Friend" and a moderate hit with "Long Ago and Far Away," while including "Love Has Brought Me Around," "You Can Close Your Eyes," and the classic "Hey Mister, That's Me Up on the Jukebox." Taylor's then-girlfriend, Joni Mitchell, provided backing vocals on the record.

In the wake of James Taylor's enormous success, siblings Livingston, Kate, and Alex launched their own recording careers. Livingston's modest-selling debut for Atco produced a minor hit with "Carolina Day," but subsequent albums for Capricorn sold poorly. He later recorded for Epic, Critique, and Vanguard. Kate recorded her first album with James, Carole King, and Linda Ronstadt, and the album sold moderately without yielding a hit single. In the late '70s she recorded two albums for Columbia. Alex fared the least well of the three, and he died of a heart attack in Sanford, Florida, on March 12, 1993, at age 47.

In 1972 Danny Kortchmar, already a veteran of the band Jo Mama, formed the Section with keyboardist Craig Doerge, bassist Leland Sklar, and drummer Russ Kunkel to back James Taylor on tour and record independently. Kortchmar also recorded a solo album, and the Section later served as Peter Asher's "house band" and toured with Jackson Browne on his Running on Empty tour.

On November 3, 1972, James Taylor married songstress Carly Simon, shortly before the release of *One Man Dog*. Recorded with Simon, Carole King, Linda Ronstadt, and the Section, the album produced a major hit with "Don't Let Me Be Lonely Tonight" and a minor hit with "One Man Parade." In 1973 Taylor costarred with Beach Boy Dennis Wilson in the miserable film *Two-Lane Blacktop*, and scored a smash hit with Carly Simon on a deplorable off-key version of "Mockingbird." Taylor's next album, *Walking Man*, the first not produced by Peter Asher, failed to produce a hit single, but 1975's *Gorilla* yielded a smash pop and top easy-listening hit with Holland-Dozier-Holland's "How Sweet It Is (To Be Loved by You)" and a moderate hit with "Mexico." Taylor toured again in 1975, and his final album for Warner Bros., *In the Pocket*, includes the major pop and top easy-listening hit "Shower the People."

Switching to Columbia Records, James Taylor's debut for the label, *JT*, reunited him with producer Peter Asher and furnished a smash hit with a remake of Jimmy Jones's "Handy Man," a major hit with "Your Smiling Face," and a minor country hit with "Bartender's Blues," a smash country hit for George Jones in 1978. Early that year Taylor had a major pop and top easy-listening hit with Sam Cooke's "Wonderful World," recorded with Paul Simon and Art Garfunkel for Garfunkel's album *Watermark*. After scoring a major hit with Carole King and Gerry Goffin's "Up on the Roof" from *Flag*, Taylor scored his last major pop hit, in 1981 with "Her Town Too," recorded with J. D. Souther.

Taylor continued to tour and record through the '90s, although he ceased placing hits on the top of the charts. He had a minor hit in 1985 with a cover of Buddy Holly's "Everyday," and another with 1988's "Never Die Young." Taylor's *New Moon Shine* (1991) presented him with a more country-style accompaniment, although it failed to perform well in either country or pop markets.

James Taylor

James Taylor and the Original Flying Machine—1967	Euphoria	2	'71	†
	Springboard Int'l	4023	'75	†
James Taylor	Apple	3352	'68	†
	Apple	97577	'91	CS/CD
Sweet Baby James	Warner Bros.	1843	'70/'84	CS/CD
Mud Slide Slim	Warner Bros.	2561	'71	CS/CD
Sweet Baby James/Mud Slide Slim	Warner Bros.	23709		CS
One Man Dog	Warner Bros.	2660	'72	†
	Warner Bros.	25933	'91	CD
Walking Man	Warner Bros.	2794	'74	CS/CD
Gorilla	Warner Bros.	2866	'75	CS/CD
In the Pocket	Warner Bros.	2912	'76	CS/CD

Greatest Hits	Warner Bros.	2979	'76	†
	Warner Bros.	3113		CS/CD
JT	Columbia	34811	'77	CS/CD
	Columbia	53787	'93	CD
Flag	Columbia	36058	'79	CS/CD
Dad Lives His Work	Columbia	37009	'81	CS/CD
That's Why I'm Here	Columbia	40052	'85	CS/CD
Never Die Young	Columbia	40851	'88	CS/CD
New Moon Shine	Columbia	46038	'91	CS/CD
Live	Columbia	(2) 47056	'93	CS/CD
Best Live	Columbia	66235	'94	CS/CD
Livingston Taylor				
Livingston Taylor	Atco	33-334	'70	†
Liv	Capricorn	863	'71	†
Over the Rainbow	Capricorn	0114	'73	†
3-Way Mirror	Epic	35540	LP/CS/CD†	
	Epic/Legacy	57312	'94	CS/CD
Man's Best Friend	Epic	36153		LP/CS/CD†
Life Is Good	Critique	90941	'88	LP/CS/CD†
Our Turn to Dance	Vanguard	9469	'93	CS/CD
Kate Taylor				
Sister Kate	Cotillion	9045	'71	†
Kate Taylor	Columbia	35089	'78	†
It's in There and It's Got to Come Out	Columbia	36034	'79	†
Alex Taylor				
With Friends and Neighbors	Capricorn	860	'71	†
Dinnertime	Capricorn	0101	'72	†
The Third Time's for Music	Dunhill	50151	'74	†
Dancing with the Devil	Wild Dog Blues	9007	'91	LP/CS/CD

THE TEMPTATIONS

Eddie Kendricks (b. Dec. 17, 1939, Birmingham, AL; d. Oct. 5, 1992, Birmingham, AL), ten voc; **Otis Williams** (b. Otis Miles, Oct. 30, 1941, Texarkana, TX), bar voc; **Melvin Franklin** (b. David English, Oct. 12, 1942, Montgomery, AL; d. Feb. 23, 1995, Los Angeles, CA), bs voc; **Paul Williams** (b. July 2, 1939, Birmingham, AL; d. Aug. 17, 1973, Detroit, MI), bar voc; **Elbridge Bryant**. [Elbridge Bryant left in late 1963, to be replaced by baritone **David Ruffin** (b. Davis Elis Ruffin, Jan. 18, 1941, Meridian, MS; d. June 1, 1991, Philadelphia, PA). Ruffin left the group in 1968, to be replaced by **Dennis Edwards** (b. Feb. 3, 1943, Birmingham, AL). Eddie Kendricks and Paul Williams left in 1971. Later members include **Damon Harris** (b. July 3, 1950, Baltimore, MD), **Glenn Leonard** (b. Washington, D.C.), **Louis Price**, **Richard Street** (b. Oct. 5, 1942, Detroit, MI), **Ricky Owens**, **Ali Ollie Woodson**, **Richard Tyson**, **Theo Peoples**, and **Ray Davis** (b. Mar. 29, 1940, Sumter, SC). David Ruffin's brother **Jimmy Ruffin** (b. May 7, 1939, Collinsville, MS) was a solo artist for Motown.]

Motown's longest enduring and most popular male vocal group, the Temptations were the most successful male vocal group of the '60s and early '70s. One of the first groups to feature two lead singers, baritone David Ruffin and tenor Eddie Kendricks, they achieved their initial success under the aegis of songwriter-producer Smokey Robinson, who cowrote

THE TEMPTATIONS

most of their early hits, including the classic "My Girl." Working primarily with songwriter-producer Norman Whitfield beginning in 1966, the Temptations scored a dozen major crossover hits featuring the brilliant combination of Ruffin's rich, earthy voice and Kendricks's plaintive near-falsetto voice.

With Ruffin's departure in 1968, Whitfield changed the group's sound to psychedelic soul, providing the group with the smash hits "Cloud Nine," "Psychedelic Shack," "Ball of Confusion," and the classic "Papa Was a Rolling Stone," in conjunction with songwriter Barrett Strong. Enduring numerous personnel changes over the course of their career, including the departures of Ruffin and Kendricks for modest solo careers, the Temptations reunited in 1982 for a tour and album. By 1995 only Otis Williams remained from the original group, and Ruffin, Kendricks, Paul Williams, and Melvin Franklin had died.

The evolution of the Temptations began during the late '50s with two Detroit-based groups, the Primes and the Distants. The Distants, with Otis Williams, Melvin Franklin, Richard Street, and Elbridge Bryant, had been formed by members of the Questions and the Elegants; the Primes (whose companion group the Primettes later became the Supremes) included Eddie Kendricks and Paul Williams. In 1960 Kendricks and Paul Williams joined Bryant, Franklin, and Otis Williams to become the Elgins, signing with Berry Gordy's Miracle label. They changed their name to the Temptations in 1961 and switched to the Gordy label in 1962, scoring their first R&B hit with "Dream Come Home." In late 1963 Bryant quit the group and was replaced by David Ruffin.

In early 1964 the Temptations achieved their first major pop hit with "The Way You Do the Things You Do," cowritten and produced by Smokey Robinson and featuring the lead vocals of Eddie Kendricks. After two moderate hits, the group scored a top pop and R&B hit with the classic "My Girl," written and produced by Robinson and Ronald White, with Ruffin on lead vocals. Subsequent major pop and smash R&B hits produced and cowritten by Robinson include "It's Growing," "Since I Lost My Baby," "My Baby," and "Get Ready." The group next recorded primarily under songwriter-producer Norman Whitfield, who produced and coauthored the top R&B and smash pop hits "Ain't Too Proud to Beg," "Beauty Is Only Skin Deep," and "(I Know) I'm Losing You." Frank Wilson produced the crossover smash "All I Need," and Whitfield provided the crossover smashes "You're My Everything," "(Loneliness Made Me Realize) It's You That I Need," the classic "I Wish It Would Rain," and "I Could Never Love Another (After Loving You)." In July 1968 David Ruffin left the group for a solo career and was replaced by Dennis Edwards of the Contours. By then, former Distant and Monitor member Richard Street had begun filling in for an ailing Paul Williams. The reconstituted Temptations were teamed with the Supremes in 1968 and 1969, scoring a smash crossover hit with "I'm Gonna Make You Love Me" and a major crossover hit with "I'll Try Something New."

David Ruffin's brother Jimmy had been recording for Berry Gordy's Soul label since 1964. He scored a near-smash pop and R&B hit with "What Becomes of the Broken-hearted" in 1966 and subsequent major crossover hits with "I've Passed This Way Before" and "Gonna Give Her All the Love I've Got." David Ruffin managed a smash pop and R&B hit with "My Whole World Ended (The Moment You Left Me)" in 1969, followed by the major R&B hits "I've Lost Everything I Ever Loved" and "I'm So Glad I Fell for You." The brothers cut a duet album in 1970, yielding a major R&B hit with "Stand By Me," but by 1972 Jimmy Ruffin had left the Motown organization. David Ruffin stayed on, eventually scoring a top R&B and near-smash pop hit with "Walk Away from Love" and near-smash R&B hits with "Heavy Love" and "Everything's Coming Up Love" in 1975–1976. In 1980 Jimmy Ruffin scored a near-smash pop hit with "Hold On to My Love," cowritten and produced by Bee Gee Robin Gibb.

Beginning in late 1968, Norman Whitfield began experimenting with psychedelic soul and social consciousness for the Temptations. With this new style the Temptations scored a top pop and R&B hit with the classic "I Can't Get Next to You" and smash R&B and pop hits with "Cloud Nine," "Run Away Child, Running Wild," "Psychedelic Shack," and "Ball of Confusion," all cowritten by Whitfield and Barrett Strong. The Temptations returned to their mellow ballad style in 1971 for the top pop and R&B hit classic "Just My Imagination (Running Away with Me)" with Eddie Kendricks on lead vocals, but that summer Kendricks left the group for a solo career and was permanently replaced by Damon Harris. Around the same time, Paul Williams retired from touring due to illness and was replaced by stand-in Richard Street. On August 17, 1973, Paul Williams was found dead in his car in Detroit, an apparent suicide at age 34.

In 1973 Eddie Kendricks's solo career took off. The disco-style songs "Keep On Truckin' (Part 1)" and "Boogie Down" became top R&B and pop hits and were followed by seven R&B smashes, including the major pop hits "Son of Sagittarius" and "Shoeshine Boy." In 1978 he switched to Arista Records, where he managed one major R&B hit, "Ain't No Smoke Without Fire."

Through 1976 the Temptations scored 13 smash R&B hits. Of these, "Superstar (Remember How You Got Where You Are)," "Let Your Hair Down," and "Shakey Ground" became major pop hits; the classic "Papa Was a Rolling Stone" became a top pop hit; and "Masterpiece" became a near-smash pop hit. Damon Harris left in 1975 and was replaced by Glenn Leonard. Harris returned to his prior group, which later became Impact, before attempting a solo career in late 1978. Edwards left the group from 1977 to 1979, replaced by Louis Price. The Temptations switched to Atlantic Records in May 1977 but were back at Gordy by 1980, by which time Edwards had returned to replace Price.

In 1982 the Temptations reunited with David Ruffin and Eddie Kendricks for one album and tour. The reunion album yielded an R&B smash with "Standing on the Top—Part 1," featuring Rick James. The group managed another R&B smash with "Treat Her Like a Lady" in 1984, but they would not achieve another major pop hit until 1991. Edwards left again, from 1984 to 1987, and was replaced by Ali Ollie Woodson. In 1986–1987 the Temptations had smash R&B hits with "Lady Soul," "I Wonder Who She's Seeing Now," and "Look What You Started."

In 1985 David Ruffin and Eddie Kendrick (he had shortened his name) joined white soul singers Daryl Hall and John Oates for the reopening of the Apollo Theater in Harlem. The four scored a major pop hit with "The Apollo Medley," comprised of "The Way You Do the Things You Do" and "My Girl." Two years later Ruffin and Kendrick recorded a duet album that yielded the major R&B hit "I Couldn't Believe It." On June 1, 1991, David Ruffin died of a drug overdose in Philadelphia at age 50. On October 5, 1992, Eddie Kendricks died of lung cancer in Birmingham, Alabama, at age 52.

In 1989 the Temptations scored a smash R&B hit with "Special"; that same year the group was inducted into the Rock and Roll Hall of Fame. In 1991 they accompanied Rod Stewart on the near-smash pop hit "The Motown Song," from his *Vagabond Heart* album. The group continued to record for Motown in the '90s, but on February 23, 1995, Melvin Franklin died of heart failure in Los Angeles at age 52. For subsequent appearances the Temptations have been comprised of Otis Williams, Richard Tyson, Ali Ollie Woodson, Theo Peoples, and Ray Davis.

The Temptations

Meet the Temptations	Gordy	911	'64	†
	Motown	5140	'89	CS/CD
The Temptations Sing Smokey	Gordy	912	'65	†
	Motown	5205	'89	CS/CD
Temptin' Temptations	Gordy	914	'65	†
	Motown	5374	'90	CS/CD
Gettin' Ready	Gordy	918	'66	†
	Motown	5373	'89	CS/CD
Live!	Gordy	921	'67	†
With a Lot o' Soul	Gordy	922	'67	†
	Motown	5299	'89	CS/CD†
In a Mellow Mood	Gordy	924	'67	†
	Motown	5235	'89	CS/CD
I Wish It Would Rain	Gordy	927	'68	†
	Motown	5276	'89	CS/CD
Live at the Copa	Gordy	938	'68	†
	Motown	5306	'89	CS/CD†
Cloud Nine	Gordy	939	'69	†
	Motown	5159		CS/CD
The Temptations Show (TV)	Gordy	933	'69	†
Puzzle People	Gordy	949	'69	†
	Motown	5172	'89	CS/CD
Christmas Card	Gordy	951	'69	†
	Motown	5251		CS/CD
Psychedelic Shack	Gordy	947	'70	†
	Motown	5164		CS/CD
At London's Talk of the Town	Gordy	953	'70	†
Sky's the Limit	Gordy	957	'71	†
	Motown	5474	'90	CS/CD
Solid Rock	Gordy	961	'72	†
	Motown	5480	'90	CS/CD
All Directions	Gordy	962	'72	†
	Motown	5417	'89	CD
Masterpiece	Gordy	965	'73	†
	Motown	5144	'89	CS/CD
1990	Gordy	966	'73	†
The Temptations	Gordy	967	'74	†
A Song for You	Gordy	969	'75	†
	Motown	5272	'89	CS/CD
House Party	Gordy	973	'75	†

Wings of Love	Gordy	971	'76	†
The Temptations Do The Temptations	Gordy	975	'76	†
Hear to Tempt You	Atlantic	19143	'77	†
Bare Back	Atlantic	19188	'78	†
Power	Gordy	994	'80	†
Give Love at Christmas	Gordy	998	'80	†
	Motown	5279		CS/CD
The Temptations	Gordy	1006	'81	†
Reunion	Gordy	6008	'82	†
	Motown	0304	'94	CS/CD
Surface Thrills	Gordy	6032	'83	†
Back to Basics	Gordy	6085	'83	†
Truly for You	Gordy	6119	'84	†
	Motown	6119	'88	CS/CD
Touch Me	Gordy	6164	'86	†
To Be Continued . . .	Gordy	6207	'86	†
	Motown	6207		CS/CD
Together Again	Motown	6246	'87	LP/CS/CD
Special	Motown	6275	'89	LP/CS/CD
Milestone	Motown	6331	'91	CS/CD

Reissues

Cloud Nine/Puzzle People	Motown	8116	'86	CD†
Psychedelic Shack/All Directions	Motown	8122	'86	CD†
A Song for You/Masterpiece	Motown	8135	'86	CD
Live at the Copa/With a Lot o' Soul	Motown	8137	'86	CD†
I Wish It Would Rain/In a Mellow Mood	Motown	8154		CD†
Meet the Temptations/The Temptations Sing Smokey	Motown	8160		CD†

Anthologies

Greatest Hits, Volume 1	Gordy	919	'66	†
	Motown	5411	'88	CS/CD
Greatest Hits, Volume 2	Gordy	954		†
	Motown	5412	'88	CS/CD
Anthology	Motown	(3) 782	'73	LP/CS
	Motown	(2) 782		CD
Compact Command Performance (15 Greatest Hits)	Motown	6125	'85	CD†
25th Anniversary	Motown	(2) 5389	'86	CS/CD†
All the Million Sellers	Motown	5212		LP/CS/CD
Great Songs and Performances	Motown	5315		CS/CD
Emperors of Soul	Motown	(5) 0338	'94	CS/CD
Anthology: The Best of	Motown	(2) 0524	'95	CS/CD
For Lovers Only	Motown	0568	'95	CS/CD
Puzzle People	Pickwick	3396		†
Hum Along and Dance: More of the Best (1963–1974)	Rhino	71180	'93	CS/CD
Motown Legends	Esx	8524	'95	CS/CD
Motown Legends	Esx	8525	'95	CS/CD

The Temptations and the Supremes

The Supremes Join the Temptations	Motown	679	'68	†
	Motown	5139	'89	CS/CD
T.C.B.	Motown	682	'68	†
	Motown	5171	'89	CS/CD†

Together	Motown	692	'69	†
	Motown	5436	'89	CS/CD†
The Supremes Join the Temptations/Together	Motown	8138		CD†
On Broadway	Motown	699	'69	†
Motown Legends	Motown	5368		CS†

Jimmy Ruffin

Top Ten	Soul	704	'67	†
	Motown	5445		CS/CD
Ruff 'n Ready	Soul	708	'69	†
	Motown	5459	'90	CS/CD†
Groove Governor	Soul	727	'70	†
Sunrise	RSO	3078	'80	†

David and Jimmy Ruffin

I Am My Brother's Keeper	Soul	728	'70	†
Motown Superstar Series, Volume 8	Motown	108		†
	Motown	5108		CS†

David Ruffin

My Whole World Ended	Motown	685	'69	†
Doin' His Thing—Feelin' Good	Motown	696	'69	†
David Ruffin	Motown	762	'73	†
Me 'n' Rock 'n' Roll Are Here to Stay	Motown	818	'74	†
Who I Am	Motown	849	'75	†
Everything's Coming Up Love	Motown	866	'76	†
In My Stride	Motown	885	'77	†
At His Best	Motown	895	'78	†
	Motown	5211		CS/CD
So Soon We Change	Warner Bros.	3306	'79	†
Gentleman Ruffin	Warner Bros.	3416	'80	†

Daryl Hall and John Oates with David Ruffin and Eddie Kendricks

Live at the Apollo	RCA	7035	'85	CS/CD

David Ruffin And Eddie Kendricks

Family	RCA	6765	'87	CS/CD

Eddie Kendricks

All By Myself	Tamla	309	'71	†
People . . . Hold On	Tamla	315	'72	†
	Motown	5280		CS/CD
Eddie Kendricks	Tamla	327	'73	†
Boogie Down	Tamla	330	'74	†
For You	Tamla	335	'74	†
The Hit Man	Tamla	338	'75	†
He's a Friend	Tamla	343	'75	†
Goin' Up in Smoke	Tamla	346	'76	†
Slick	Tamla	356	'77	†
At His Best	Tamla	354	'78	†
	Motown	5481	'90	CS/CD
Motown Superstar Series, Volume 19	Motown	5119		CS†
Vintage '78	Arista	4170	'78	†
Something More	Arista	4250	'79	†
Love Keys	Atlantic	19294	'81	†

Monitors (with Richard Street)				
Greetings! We're The Monitors	Soul	714	'69	†
True Reflection (with Glenn Leonard)				
Where I'm Coming From	Atco	7031	'73	†
Impact (with Damon Harris)				
Impact	Atco	36-135	'76	†
The 'Pac Is Back	Fantasy	9359	'77	†
Damon Harris				
Damon	Fantasy	9567	'78	†
Dennis Edwards				
Don't Look Any Further	Gordy	6057	'84	†
	Motown	5404		CS/CD†
Coolin' Out	Gordy	6148	'85	†

10cc

Eric Stewart (b. Jan. 20, 1945, Manchester, England), gtr, voc; **Graham Gouldman** (b. May 10, 1946, Manchester, England), bs, voc; **Lawrence "Lol" Creme** (b. Sept. 19, 1947, Manchester, England), gtr, kybd, voc; **Kevin Godley** (b. Oct. 7, 1945, Manchester), drm [Kevin Godley and Lol Creme left in 1977. Godley was replaced by vocalist-guitarist **Rick Fenn**, and keyboardist **Tony O'Malley**; Creme was replaced first by **Paul Burgess**, then **Stuart Tosh**. The group disbanded in 1980, with Eric Stewart and Graham Gouldmam leading various revived versions of the band into the '90s.]

Formed by highly experienced English musicians, 10cc was one of the most popular British bands of the '70s, managing American smash hits with "I'm Not in Love" and "The Things We Do for Love." With its roots in the pop-rock group Wayne Fontana and the Mindbenders and the short-lived rock outfit Hotlegs, the group developed into one of the leading purveyors of British pop.

Formed in Manchester, England, in 1963, Wayne Fontana and the Mindbenders included lead vocalist Wayne Fontana (b. Glynn Ellis, Oct. 28, 1945, Manchester, England) and lead guitarist Eric Stewart. The group scored a British only hit with "Um Um Um Um Um Um" in 1964 and a top American and smash British hit with "Game of Love" in 1965. After "It's Just a Little Bit Too Late," Fontana left the group in October 1965 for a solo career that produced British-only hits with "Come On Home" and "Pamela Pamela." The Mindbenders persevered, scoring a smash British and American hit with "A Groovy Kind of Love" and a British-only hit with "Ashes to Ashes" in 1966. The group added bassist Graham Gouldman in 1968 but soon disintegrated. By then, Gouldman had written a number of pop-style hits for several different English groups, including "For Your Love" and "Heart Full of Soul" for the Yardbirds; "Look Through Any Window," "Bus Stop," and "Stop Stop Stop" for the Hollies; and "Listen People" and "No Milk Today" for Herman's Hermits. Gouldman also recorded a solo album for RCA in 1968.

With the demise of the Mindbenders, Graham Gouldman joined the Kasenetz-Katz organization as a songwriter, while Eric Stewart set up Strawberry Studios in Stockport, where he rehearsed with guitarist-keyboardist Lol Creme and drummer Kevin Godley. The three scored a smash British hit with "Neanderthal Man" in 1970 and quickly formed Hotlegs to tour in support of the hit. Later adding Gouldman, the group backed Neil Sedaka on his comeback British-only albums *Solitaire* and *The Tra La La Days Are Over* in 1971 and 1972.

In 1972 Creme, Godley, Stewart, and Gouldman took their recording of Creme and Godley's '50s parody "Donna" to producer Jonathon King, who issued it as a single on his newly formed UK label as performed by 10cc. It became a smash British-only hit and was followed by the top British hit "Rubber Bullets" and the major British hits "The Dean and I," "Wall Street Shuffle," and "Silly Love" through 1974. Debuting in August 1973, 10cc made their first American tour the following February. Switching to Phonogram Records (Mercury in the United States) in February 1975, they soon achieved a smash British and American hit with the aurally layered Gouldman-Stewart composition "I'm Not in Love." However, subsequent American hits eluded them, as they scored major British hits with "Art for Art's Sake," "Life Is a Minestrone," and "I'm Mandy Fly Me."

In October 1976 Lol Creme and Kevin Godley announced their departure from 10cc. The group's first album produced by Eric Stewart and Graham Gouldman, 1977's *Deceptive Bends*, yielded a smash British and American hit with "The Things We Do for Love" and a smash British hit with "Good Morning Judge." 10cc managed their last British hit with "Dreadlock Holiday" in 1978 and their last (minor) American hit with "For You and Me" in 1979. Gouldman and Stewart persevered with 10cc into the '80s. Later member Rick Fenn recorded a mostly instrumental album with Nick Mason of Pink Floyd in 1985. Eric Stewart cowrote six of the ten songs on Paul McCartney's 1986 album *Press to Play*, and Gouldman formed Wax (later Wax U.K.) with American studio musician Andrew Gold, scoring a moderate hit with "Right Between the Eyes" in 1986.

In 1977 Lol Creme and Kevin Godley recorded *Consequences* to showcase their own invention, the Gizmo, a guitar attachment that enabled the instrument to create synthesizer effects. Neither the Gizmo nor the album proved successful, yet Creme and Godley continued to record into the late '80s, scoring a major hit with "Cry" in 1985. Beginning in 1980, Creme and Godley diversified their careers, producing videos for Asia ("In the Heat of the Moment"), The Police ("Wrapped Around Your Finger" and "Every Breath You Take"), Sting ("Set Them Free"), Duran Duran ("A View to a Kill"), Wang Chung ("Everybody Have Fun Tonight"), and Huey Lewis and the News ("Hip to Be Square"). Lol Creme directed the 1992 Jamaican comedy movie *The Lunatic*. Graham Gouldman and Eric Stewart reunited as 10cc for 1995's *Mirror Mirror*, recorded with the assistance of Paul McCartney.

Wayne Fontana and the Mindbenders

Game of Love	Fontana	67542	'65	†
Best	Fontana	522666	'94	CS/CD

The Mindbenders

A Groovy Kind of Love	Fontana	67554	'66	†

Wayne Fontana

Wayne Fontana	MGM	4459	'67	†

Graham Gouldman

The Graham Gouldman Thing	RCA	3954	'68	†
Animalympics	A&M	4810	'80	†

Hotlegs

Thinks School Stinks	Capitol	587	'71	†
	One Way	17961	'94	CD

10cc

10cc	UK	53105	'73	†
Sheet Music	UK	53107	'74	†
Two Classic Albums by 10cc: 10cc and Sheet Music	DCC	053	'90	CS/CD
100 cc	UK	53110	'75	†
The Original Soundtrack	Mercury	1029	'75	†
	Mercury	830776	'90	CS†

How Dare You!	Mercury	1061	'76	†
	Mercury	836949	'90	CD†
Deceptive Bends	Mercury	3702	'77	†
	Mercury	836948	'90	CD†
Live and Let Live	Mercury	(2) 8600	'77	†
Bloody Tourists	Polydor	6161	'78	†
Greatest Hits, 1972–1978	Polydor	6244	'79	†
Look, Hear?	Warner Bros.	3442	'80	†
Ten Out of Ten	Warner Bros.	3575	'82	†
Mirror Mirror	Critique	15430	'95	CS/CD

Kevin Godley and Lol Creme

Consequences	Mercury	(3) 1700	'77	†
L	Polydor	6177	'78	†
Freeze Frame	Polydor	6257	'80	†
	Polydor	831555	'87	CD†
The History Mix, Volume 1	Polydor	825981	'85	†
Goodbye Blue Sky	Polydor	835348	'88	LP/CS/CD†

Rick Fenn and Nick Mason

Profiles	Columbia	40142	'85	†

Wax U.K.

Magnetic Heaven	RCA	9546	'86	LP/CS/CD†
American English	RCA	6770	'88	LP/CS/CD†

THREE DOG NIGHT

Danny Hutton (b. Sept. 10, 1942, Buncrana, Ireland), voc; **Cory Wells** (b. Feb. 5, 1942, Buffalo, NY), voc; **Chuck Negron** (b. June 8, 1942, Bronx, NY), voc; **Mike Allsup** (b. Mar. 8, 1947, Modesto, CA), lead gtr; **Jimmy Greenspoon** (b. Feb. 7, 1948, Los Angeles, CA), kybd; **Joe Schermie** (b. Feb. 12, 1948, Madison, WI), bs; **Floyd Sneed** (b. Nov. 22, 1943, Calgary, Alberta, Canada), drm

One of the most popular American rock bands of the early '70s, Three Dog Night featured three lead vocalists who provided tight three-part harmony. Scoring ten smash hits between 1969 and 1974, Three Dog Night was responsible for exposing the compositions of once-neglected songwriters such as Harry Nilsson, Laura Nyro, Randy Newman, and Hoyt Axton to widespread attention.

Danny Hutton was raised in the United States and began his musical career at 19 as a producer, songwriter, and eventually vocalist. In 1965 he had a minor hit with "Roses and Rainbows" on the HBR (Hanna-Barbera) label. Envisioning a group fronted by three singers who would share lead vocals and perform three-part harmony, Hutton recruited Cory Wells from a group he was producing, the Enemys, and Chuck Negron. Wells had manned a Texas band called the Satellites before moving to Los Angeles with The Enemys, while Negron was a solo artist for Columbia Records. The three assembled a band and took the name Three Dog Night in 1968. After successful engagements in West Coast clubs and a long-term stand at Los Angeles's Whisky a-Go-Go, the group signed with Dunhill Records.

Recording under producer Gabriel Mekler, Three Dog Night scored a major hit with the Otis Redding classic "Try a Little Tenderness" and a smash hit with Harry Nilsson's "One" from their debut album. Their second album, also released in 1969, yielded the smash hit "Easy to Be Hard" (from the rock musical *Hair*) and major hits with "Celebrate" and Laura Nyro's "Eli's Coming"; it also contained Elton John and Bernie Taupin's obscure

"Lady Samantha." Subsequently recording under producer Richard Podolor, Three Dog Night next recorded a best-selling live album. *It Ain't Easy* (1970) included the top hit "Mama Told Me Not to Come," written by Randy Newman, and the major hit "Out in the Country," written by Paul Williams and Roger Nichols. That same year their next studio album, *Naturally*, produced the three hits "One Man Band," Hoyt Axton's "Joy to the World" (a top hit), and Russ Ballard's "Liar" (a near-smash hit).

Following the anthology set *Golden Biscuits*, Three Dog Night issued *Harmony* in 1971, which yielded smash hits with Paul Williams's "An Old Fashioned Love Song" (a top easy-listening hit) and Hoyt Axton's "Never Been to Spain," and a major hit with "The Family of Man." *Seven Separate Fools* (1972) produced the top pop and easy-listening hit "Black & White" and the major hit "Pieces of April," whereas *Cyan* included the smash hit "Shambala" and the major hit "Let Me Serenade You." The Jimmy Ienner–produced *Hard Labor* yielded a smash hit with Leo Sayer's "The Show Must Go On" and a major hit with John Hiatt's "Sure As I'm Sittin' Here" in 1974.

Personnel changes in the band began for Three Dog Night in 1973. They scored their final moderate hits with Allen Toussaint's "Play Something Sweet (Brickyard Blues)" in 1974 and "Til The World Ends" in 1975. After 1976's *American Pastime*, Three Dog Night disbanded. Cory Wells recorded a solo album for A&M in 1978, and Three Dog Night reunited for 1983's *It's a Jungle* under Richard Podolor. They toured into the late '80s, replacing Chuck Negron with guitarist-vocalist Paul Kingery at the beginning of 1986. With Danny Hutton and Cory Wells as mainstays, Three Dog Night continued touring into the '90s. Chuck Negron returned to recording with 1995's *Am I Still in Your Heart*.

Danny Hutton

Pre-Dog Night	MGM	4664	'70	†

Three Dog Night

Three Dog Night	Dunhill	50048	'69	†
Suitable for Framing	Dunhill	50058	'69	†
Captured Live at the Forum	Dunhill	50068	'69	†
	MCA	31342	'89	CD
It Ain't Easy	Dunhill	50078	'70	†
Naturally	Dunhill	50088	'70	†
Golden Biscuits	Dunhill	50098	'71	†
Harmony	Dunhill	50108	'71	†
Seven Separate Fools	Dunhill	50118	'72	†
Around the World	Dunhill	(2) 50138	'73	†
Cyan	Dunhill	50158	'73	†
	MCA	31366	'90	CD
Hard Labor	Dunhill	50168	'74	†
	MCA	31362	'90	CD
Joy to the World—Their Greatest Hits	Dunhill	50178	'74	†
	MCA	1466		CS/CD
Dog Style	Dunhill	50198	'74	†
Coming Down Your Way	ABC	888	'75	†
American Pastime	ABC	928	'76	†
Best	MCA	(2) 6018	'82	LP/CS
	MCA	6018		CD
Celebrate: The Three Dog Night Story	MCA	(2) 10956	'93	CS/CD
It's a Jungle	Passport	5001	'83	†

Cory Wells

Touch Me	A&M	4673	'78	†

Chuck Negron

Am I Still in Your Heart   Viceroy   8024   '95   CS/CD

TRAFFIC/STEVE WINWOOD

Steve Winwood (b. May 12, 1948, Birmingham, England), kybd, gtr, voc; **Chris Wood** (b. June 24, 1944, Birmingham, England; d. July 12, 1983, London, England), flt, sax; **Jim Capaldi** (b. Aug. 24, 1944, Evesham, Worchestershire, England), drm, kybd, voc [Multi-instrumentalist **Dave Mason** (b. May 10, 1946, Worcester, England) was in and out of the group from spring 1967 to fall 1968, and returned again briefly in 1971. Bassist **Rick Grech** (b. Nov. 1, 1946; d. Mar. 17, 1990, England) joined in 1970 and was replaced first by **David Hood** in 1971 and then by **Rosco Gee** in 1973. Drummer **Jim Gordon** and percussionist **Reebop Kwaku Baah** (b. Konongo, Ghana, d. ca. mid-'80s) joined in 1971, although Gordon was soon gone and replaced by **Roger Hawkins**, who remained with the band until 1973.]

TRAFFIC

Steve Winwood gained his first recognition with the Spencer Davis Group as a teenager, singing, playing on, and cowriting the group's near-smash hits. Joining drummer-songwriter Jim Capaldi, reed player Chris Wood (one of the first horn players to be an integral part of a major British rock band), and intermittent member Dave Mason, Winwood recorded three fascinating albums with Traffic, characterized by surreal lyrics, a jazz-style sound, and his distinctive, compelling voice. After enduring a chaotic history of breakups, reformations, and personnel changes, Traffic regrouped (following Winwood's brief experience with the supergroup Blind Faith) to record the best-selling folk-style *John Barleycorn Must Die* album. Never achieving a major American hit, Traffic nonetheless established themselves as a popular album band, particularly with the classic jazz-style *Low Spark of High Heeled Boys*, perhaps the group's finest album and Winwood's most lyrically incisive. Following two more studio albums, Traffic disbanded in 1974. Winwood reemerged in 1981 with the smash hit "While You See a Chance," and fully established himself as a solo artist with the 1986 album *Back in the High Life* and its four hit singles. Solidifying his position with 1988's *Roll With It*, Winwood rejoined Capaldi as Traffic for a 1994 tour and album.

Steve Winwood gained his first musical experience with a skiffle band at age 11. An accomplished multi-instrumentalist, he performed with his brother, Miff, in a traditional-style jazz band in their native Birmingham. They met University of Birmingham lecturer and part-time musician Spencer Davis, who enticed them into his group. Winwood became the focal point for the band's high-energy R&B, remaining with them from 1963 to 1967 and coauthoring the group's two near-smash hits, "Gimme Some Lovin'" and "I'm a Man." Wanting to form his own group, Winwood left Davis in spring 1967 and retreated to a Berkshire cottage for six months of rehearsals with Dave Mason, Chris Wood, and Jim Capaldi. Capaldi and Mason had played in the Birmingham-based group Deep Feeling, and Chris Wood had jammed with the other three in Birmingham clubs before Winwood's departure from the Spencer Davis Group.

Traffic's debut album for Island (United Artists in the United States), *Mr. Fantasy*, featured Winwood and Capaldi's "Paper Sun," with Mason on sitar, and Mason's "Hole in My Shoe," both smash British hits. The remarkably diverse and experimental album also contained "Coloured Rain," "Heaven Is in Your Mind," "Dear Mr. Fantasy," and "Smiling Phases," all cowritten by Winwood, Capaldi, and Wood. Dave Mason's penchant for pop-style melodies conflicted with the jazz orientation of the others, and he left the group in December 1967. Nonetheless, he was back for their second album, *Traffic*, which included his "You Can All Join In" and classic "Feelin' Alright?" as well as Winwood and Capaldi's "Pearly Queen" and their surreal "Forty Thousand Headmen." Traffic first toured America in 1968, but by October Mason had left again. *Last Exit* featured one live side and one studio side, which inlcuded "Medicated Goo" and "Shanghai Noodle Factory."

Traffic subsequently fell into disarray. Steve Winwood joined Ginger Baker, Eric Clapton, and bassist Rick Grech for Blind Faith. The group conducted one American tour and recorded one best-selling album, which contained three Winwood songs, including "Sea of Joy" and the classic "Can't Find My Way Back Home." Winwood subsequently joined Ginger Baker's Air Force, with Baker, Grech, Chris Wood, and Denny Laine, for one live album.

Steve Winwood began work on a solo album in January 1970, and Capaldi and Wood worked on some of the sessions. This work evolved into Traffic's best-selling album to date, *John Barleycorn Must Die*. The album combined elements of jazz, rock, and folk and served as a fine testament to Winwood's versatility. In addition to the title song, the album included the instrumental "Glad," Winwood and Capaldi's "Freedom Rider" and "Stranger to Himself," and the minor hit "Empty Pages." The group toured again in 1970, augmented by Rick Grech, and their brief British tour in the summer of 1971 with Dave Mason resulted in the live set *Welcome to the Canteen*. Mason returned to his solo career as Winwood, Wood, and Capaldi recorded *The Low Spark of High Heeled Boys*, perhaps the crowning achievement of their career. In addition to the 12-minute title song, the album contained "Many a Mile to Freedom," Grech and drummer Jim Gordon's "Rock and Rock Stew," and Capaldi's "Light Up or Leave Me Alone."

Jim Capaldi next recorded his debut solo album for Island Records at Muscle Shoals, Alabama, with Steve Winwood, Dave Mason, and studio veterans David Hood (bs) and Roger Hawkins (drm). Hood and Hawkins joined Traffic in Jamaica to record *Shoot Out at the Fantasy Factory*, which featured Winwood and Capaldi's "(Sometimes I Feel So) Uninspired." Joined by Muscle Shoals associate Barry Beckett (kybd), the aggregation conducted a 1973 world tour and recorded the live *On the Road* album. The Muscle Shoals recruits departed after the tour, and Traffic completed their final British and American tours in 1974 and recorded their last studio album, the keyboard-dominated *When the Eagle Flies*.

Traffic disbanded, and Capaldi resumed his solo recording career for Island and later RSO Records. Steve Winwood recorded a jam album for Antilles before joining Japanese percussionist-keyboardist Stomu Yamashta in the ambitious Go group. Winwood recorded his debut solo album for Island in 1977, and began collaborating with songwriter Will Jennings in the '80s. Winwood's 1981 *Arc of a Diver* album, recorded entirely on his own, yielded a near-smash hit with "While You See a Chance," but after 1982's *Talking Back to the Night* he was not to record another album for four years. In the meantime, Capaldi scored a major hit in 1983 with "That's Love" on his new label, Atlantic Records. Chris Wood died of liver failure on July 12, 1983.

Steve Winwood eventually reemerged in 1986 with the best-selling *Back in the High Life* album. It yielded four hits, the top hit "Higher Life," the near smash "The Finer Things," and the major pop and top easy-listening hits "Freedom Overspill" and "Back in the High Life Again." Reestablished as a solo artist, Winwood toured in 1986 and scored a near-smash with "Valerie" from the compilation set *Chronicles*. Jim Capaldi returned to Island Records in 1988 and assisted Winwood on his next two albums. Winwood's 1988 *Roll With It* album, on his new label Virgin Records, produced a top pop and easy-listening hit with the title track, a smash hit with "Don't You Know What the Night Can Do?," and a major pop and top easy-listening hit with "Holding On." Winwood toured again in 1988, and next recorded *Refugees of the Heart*, which yielded a major hit with "One and Only Man," cowritten with Capaldi.

In 1994 Steve Winwood and Jim Capaldi revived Traffic for *Far from Home*, with Winwood singing and playing guitar, keyboards, bass, and synthesized reeds. The album featured "Here Comes a Man" and "Nowhere Is Their Freedom." Recruiting four backup musicians, Winwood and Capaldi toured extensively in the United States as Traffic in 1994.

Spencer Davis Group

Gimme Some Lovin'	United Artists	6578	'67	†
I'm a Man	United Artists	6589	'67	†
Greatest Hits	United Artists	6641	'68	†
Best	EMI	91834	'89	CS/CD†
	EMI	46598		CS/CD
Best (1964–1967)	Rhino	70172	'87	CS
Greatest and Latest (rerecordings)	Pro Acoustic	701	'86	CS/CD

Traffic

Mr. Fantasy	United Artists	6651	'68	†
	Island	90060		LP/CS/CD†
	Island	842783		CS/CD
	Mobile Fidelity	572	'93	CD
Traffic	United Artists	6676	'68	†
	Island	90059		LP/CS/CD†
	Island	842590		CS/CD
Last Exit	United Artists	6702	'69	†
	Island	90925	'88	LP/CS/CD†
	Island	842787	'88	CS/CD
Best	United Artists	5500	'69	†
John Barleycorn Must Die	United Artists	5504	'70	†
	Island	90058		LP/CS/CD†
	Island	842780		CS/CD
Welcome to the Canteen	United Artists	5550	'71	†
	Island	90924	'88	LP/CS/CD†
	Island	842417	'88	CS/CD
Heavy Traffic	United Artists	421	'75	†
More Heavy Traffic	United Artists	526	'75	†
The Low Spark of High Heeled Boys	Island	9306	'71	†
	Island	9180		†
	Island	90026		LP/CS/CD†
	Island	842779		LP/CS/CD
	Mobile Fidelity	209	'94	LP
	Mobile Fidelity	609	'94	CD

Shoot Out at the Fantasy Factory	Island	9323	'73	†
	Island	9224		†
	Island	90027		LP/CS/CD†
	Island	842781		CS/CD
On the Road	Island	(2) 9336	'73	†
	Island	(2) 2		†
	Island	(2) 90028		LP†
	Island	90028		CS/CD†
	Island	842893		CS/CD
Smiling Phases	Island	(2) 510553	'91	CD
When the Eagle Flies	Asylum	1020	'74	†
Far from Home	Virgin	39490	'94	CS/CD
Blind Faith				
Blind Faith	Atco	33-304	'69	†
	RSO	3016	'77	†
	RSO	825094	'86	LP/CS/CD†
	Polydor	825094		CS/CD
	Mobile Fidelity	507	'89	CD
Ginger Baker's Air Force				
Ginger Baker's Air Force	Atco	(2) 703	'70	†
	Polydor	837349	'89	CD†
Jim Capaldi				
Oh, How We Danced	Island	9314	'72	†
	Island	9187		†
Whale Meat Again	Island	9254	'74	†
Short Cut Draw Blood	Island	9336	'76	†
	Antilles	7050		LP
Daughter of the Night	RSO	3037	'78	†
Fierce Heart	Atlantic	80059	'83	†
One Man Mission	Atlantic	80182	'84	†
Some Come Running	Island	91024	'88	LP/CS/CD†
	Island	842606		CS/CD†
Steve Winwood				
Winwood	United Artists	(2) 9950	'71	†
	United Artists	(2) 9964	'72	†
Steve Winwood	Island	9494	'77	†
	Island	842774	'89	CS/CD
Arc of a Diver	Island	9576	'81	†
	Island	842365	'90	CS/CD
	Mobile Fidelity	579	'93	CD
Talking Back to the Night	Island	9777	'82	†
	Island	842366	'90	CS/CD
Back in the High Life	Island	25448	'86	LP/CS/CD†
	Island	830148	'90	CS/CD
	Mobile Fidelity	611	'94	CD
Chronicles	Island	25660	'87	LP/CS/CD†
	Island	842364	'90	CS/CD
The Finer Things	Island	(4) 516870	'95	CS/CD

Roll With It	Virgin	90946	'88	CS/CD†
	Virgin	86069		CS/CD
Refugees of the Heart	Virgin	91405	'90	LP/CS/CD†
	Virgin	86189		CS/CD

Steve Winwood/Remi Kabaka/Abdul Lasisi Amao

| Mdash-Aiye-Keta | Antilles | 7005 | '76 | † |

Stomu Yamashta's Go (with Steve Winwood)

Go	Island	9358	'76	†
	Island	9387		†
Go Live from Paris	Island	(2) 10	'78	†

THE TUBES

Fee Waybill (b. John Waldo, Sept. 17, 1950, Omaha, NE), lead voc; **Bill Spooner** (b. Apr. 16, 1949, Phoenix, AZ) and **Roger Steen** (b. Nov. 13, 1949, Pipestone, MN), gtrs; **Michael Cotten** (b. Jan. 25, 1950, Kansas City, MO), synth; **Vince Welnick** (b. Feb. 21, 1951, Phoenix, AZ), kybd; **Rick Anderson** (b. Aug. 1, 1947, St. Paul, MN), bs; **Prairie Prince** (b. May 7, 1950, Charlotte, NC), drm

A '70s and '80s rock-satire band, the Tubes achieved notoriety and a cult following in the San Francisco Bay Area with their outlandish blend of rock music and irreverent lyrics, costume changes and characters, choreography, and theatrical presentation in live performance. The Tubes' satirical and iconoclastic bent often resulted in humorous self-parody, including the hilarious heavy-metal takeoff, "White Punks on Dope," with lead singer Waybill taking the fanciful name of Quay Lewd. Scoring their first minor hit with the classic girl-group send-up "Don't Touch Me There" in 1976, the Tubes endured five years without another hit record. In the meantime, they recorded several commercially successful albums, including *Remote Control*, produced by Todd Rundgren, and *The Completion Backward Principle*. Beginning in 1978, the Tubes began eliminating some of the more elaborate aspects of their stage act, and by 1982 they had transformed themselves into a straightforward rock band. They had a near-smash hit with the uncharacteristic ballad "She's a Beauty" in 1983 from *Outside/Inside*, and endured into the late '80s even as Fee Waybill pursued an unsuccessful solo career. By 1991 Vince Welnick joined the Grateful Dead as keyboardist. The group reunited for a tour of the United States and Europe in 1993.

The Tubes

The Tubes	A&M	4534	'75	†
	A&M	3161		CD
	Mobile Fidelity	822		CD†
Young and Rich	A&M	4580	'76	†
	A&M	3222	'84	CD†
Now	A&M	4632	'77	†
	A&M	3243	'84	†
What Do You Want from Live	A&M	(2) 6003	'78	†
Remote Control	A&M	4751	'79	†
	A&M	3242	'84	CD
T.R.A.S.H. (Tubes Rarities and Smash Hits)	A&M	4870	'81	†
	A&M	3244	'84	CD
The Completion Backward Principle	Capitol	12151	'81	†
	Capitol	48454	'86	CS/CD

Outside/Inside	Capitol	12260	'83	†
	Capitol	48453	'88	CD†
Love Bomb	Capitol	12381	'85	†
	Capitol	16446	'87	CD†
Best	Capitol	98539	'92	CS/CD
Fee Waybill				
Read My Lips	Capitol	12369	'84	†

IKE AND TINA TURNER

Ike Turner (b. Izear Turner, Nov. 5, 1931, Clarksdale, MS); **Tina Turner** (b. Anna Mae Bullock, Nov. 26, 1938, Brownsville, TN)

Bandleader, songwriter, arranger, producer, and multi-instrumentalist Ike Turner achieved his first success in 1951 accompanying Jackie Brenston's top R&B hit "Rocket 88," often regarded as the first rock-and-roll record. Devising a revue format for his Kings of Rhythm in St. Louis, Turner added vocalist and wife-to-be Tina in 1956, who became the show's focal point, thanks to her gospel-style vocals and energetic dancing (accompanied by the provocatively dressed Ikettes). Their 1966 recording of "River Deep—Mountain High," produced by the legendary Phil Spector, established their popularity in Britain, leading to an invitation to open the Rolling Stones' 1969 American tour. They subsequently attracted a new following among the rock audience with their smash crossover hit "Proud Mary" in 1971.

Tina Turner, long abused by Ike physically and psychologically, walked out on him in 1976 and subsequently spent nearly a decade trying to establish herself as a solo recording and performing artist, while retaining her fierce, flamboyant style. She finally achieved her breakthrough with 1984's *Private Dancer*, an album that sold six million copies, and its three smash crossover hits. Her popularity was enhanced by her performance in the 1985 film *Mad Max: Beyond Thunderdome*; the 1986 publication of her autobiography *I, Tina*; and the subsequent film biography *What's Love Got to Do with It*, released in 1993.

Ike Turner started playing piano at age 5 and initiated his musical career at age 11 as piano accompanist to blues guitarists Sonny Boy Williamson (Aleck Ford) and Robert Nighthawk. Mastering guitar, he formed the Rhythm Kings, who later backed Jackie Brenston's top R&B hit "Rocket 88" in 1951. Turner was hired as a songwriter and talent scout by Modern Records, ostensibly "discovering" B. B. King and Howlin' Wolf and playing sessions for King, Wolf, Elmore James, and Johnny Ace. Around 1954 he moved to St. Louis, where he became an R&B star with the Rhythm Kings.

Tina Turner grew up in Knoxville, Tennessee, and sang in a local church choir as a child. She moved to St. Louis around 1954 and met Ike Turner at age 17, joining his revue in 1956. The couple later married and Ike developed an exciting stage act known as the Ike and Tina Turner Revue in 1960, based around Tina as lead vocalist and accompanied by his Kings of Rhythm and a female backing vocal group, dubbed the Ikettes. Recording for the Midwestern R&B label Sue, Ike and Tina Turner scored a series of R&B smashes in the early '60s with "A Fool in Love" (a major pop hit), "I Idolize You," "It's Gonna Work Out Fine" (another major pop hit), "Poor Fool," and "Tra La La La La." In 1962 the Ikettes had a smash R&B and major pop hit with "I'm Blue (The Gong-Gong Song)" on Atco Records.

During the '60s the Ike and Tina Turner Revue toured the chitlin' circuit of R&B clubs with their raunchy and overtly sexual stage act and recorded for a variety of labels, including Warner Bros., Loma, Pompeii, Blue Thumb, and Minit. They met songwriter-producer

Phil Spector while working on the film *The T'N'T Show*, and he coauthored and produced their "River Deep—Mountain High," regarded as one of the finest singles of all time, in 1966. Although the song became a smash hit in Great Britain, it fared dismally in the United States and led to Spector's temporary withdrawal from the music business.

In 1969 the Ike and Tina Turner Revue received their first massive exposure to a white audience during the Rolling Stones' tour of the United States. They soon began recording contemporary material such as the Beatles' "Come Together," the Rolling Stones' "Honky Tonk Women," and Sly Stone's "I Want to Take You Higher." They finally broke through with the mainstream audience with a dynamic reworking of Creedence Clearwater Revival's "Proud Mary," a smash pop and R&B hit from *Workin' Together*, the best-selling album of their career. They scored their last major pop hit together in 1973, with Tina's autobiographical "Nutbush City Limits." In 1974 Ike Turner disbanded the Ike and Tina Turner Revue, and a year later Tina appeared in the equivocal film *Tommy* as the Acid Queen, singing the Who song of the same name.

In July 1976, in the face of contractual obligations for albums and tours, Tina Turner walked out on her abusive husband Ike. Over the next eight years she struggled to survive and establish herself in a solo career. She divorced Ike and developed a slick but ribald lounge act for Las Vegas casinos and later the Fairmont hotel chain. She recorded a final album for United Artists in 1978, and eventually signed with Capitol Records in 1983. In the meantime, Ike Turner became mired in legal and drug-related problems that led to his incarceration for two years, from 1989 to 1991.

Tina Turner finally broke through with 1984's *Private Dancer*. The album produced five hits, including a smash R&B and major pop hit with her version of Al Green's "Let's Stay Together"; the top pop and smash R&B hit "What's Love Got to Do with It"; and the pop and R&B smashes "Better Be Good to Me" and the title track, which was written by Mark Knopfler. The album stayed on the charts for more than two years and sold six million copies. Tina conducted a tour of more than a hundred cities in 1985, as the third *Mad Max* film, *Beyond Thunderdome*, costarring Turner, became one of the year's hit movies. The soundtrack album included the crossover smash "We Don't Need Another Hero" and the major pop hit "One of the Living." In 1986 Turner recorded the best-selling *Break Every Rule* album and published her autobiography, *I, Tina*. Although not as consistent as *Private Dancer*, *Break Every Rule* yielded four hits, including the crossover smash "Typical Male" and the major pop hit "What You Get Is What You See."

Although Tina Turner did not tour the United States for six years, she continued to tour Europe and record. Her live album included Robert Palmer's "Addicted to Love" and her own "Nutbush City Limits," and 1989's *Foreign Affair* produced a major pop hit with "The Best." In 1991 she and husband Ike were inducted into the Rock and Roll Hall of Fame. She again toured the United States in 1993, as the movie *What's Love Got to Do with It*, based on her autobiography, became one of the year's most highly acclaimed hits. Celebrated by feminists for her successful struggle to escape an abusive relationship and establish herself independently, Tina Turner saw her success wane in the United States in the mid '90s, although she retained an enormous following in Europe and around the world.

Ike and Tina Turner

The Sound of Ike and Tina Turner	Sue	2001	†
Dance With Ike and Tina Turner	Sue	2003	†
Dynamite	Sue	2004	†
Don't Play Me Cheap	Sue	2005	†
It's Gonna Work Out Fine	Sue	2007	†

Greatest Hits	Sue	1038		†
The Soul of Ike and Tina Turner	Kent	519		†
	Kent	014		†
	United	7740		†
Festival of Live Performances	Kent	538		†
	United	7755		†
Please, Please, Please	Kent	550		†
	United	7765		†
Revue Live	Kent	5014		†
	United	7735		†
The Ike and Tina Sessions	Kent	065	'87	LP/CS/CD†
The Dynamic Duo	Crown	004		†
The Ike and Tina Show Live	Warner Bros.	1579	'65	†
Live	Loma	5904	'67	†
Greatest Hits	Warner Bros.	1810	'69	†
River Deep—Mountain High	Philles	4011	'66	†
	A&M	4178	'69	†
	A&M	3179	'82	LP/CS/CD†
So Fine	Pompeii	6000	'68	†
Cussin', Cryin' and Carryin' On	Pompeii	6004	'69	†
Outta Season	Blue Thumb	5	'69	†
The Hunter	Blue Thumb	11	'69	†
The Hunter/Outta Season	Blue Moon	4001	'93	CD
Best	Blue Thumb	49		†
In Person	Minit	24018	'69	†
Come Together	Liberty	7637	'70	†
Workin' Together	Liberty	7650	'70	†
Get Back	Liberty	51156	'85	†
Her Man . . . His Woman	Capitol	571	'70	†
What You Hear Is What You Get	United Artists	(2) 9953	'71	†
'Nuff Said	United Artists	5530	'71	†
Feel Good	United Artists	5598	'72	†
Let Me Touch Your Mind	United Artists	5660	'72	†
Greatest Hits	United Artists	5667	'73	†
World of Ike and Tina Turner	United Artists	(2) 064	'73	†
Nutbush City Limits	United Artists	180	'73	†
The Gospel According to Ike and Tina Turner	United Artists	203	'74	†
Greatest Hits	United Artists	592	'76	†
Airwaves	United Artists	917	'78	†
Workin' Together	EMI America	10311	'86	CS†
Best	EMI America	46599	'87	CD†
Proud Mary: The Best of Ike and Tina Turner	EMI	95846	'91	CS/CD

Anthologies

16 Great Performances	ABC	4014		†
Too Hot to Hold	Springboard Int'l	4011		†
	Pickwick	3284		†
Workin' Together	Pickwick	3032	'78	†
	Pickwick	3606	'79	†
Get It—Get It!	Pickwick	3328		†
Hot 'n' Sassy	Accord	7147	'81	†

Golden Empire	Striped Horse	2001	'86	†
Golden Classics	Collectables	5107	'88	LP/CS/CD
It's Gonna Work Out Fine	Collectables	5137		LP/CS/CD
Greatest Hits, Volume 1	Saja	91223	'89	CS/CD
Greatest Hits, Volume 2	Saja	91224	'89	CS/CD
Greatest Hits, Volume 3	Saja	91228	'89	CS/CD
Greatest Hits	Curb/CEMA	77332	'90	CS/CD
The Great Rhythm and Blues Sessions	Tomato	70382	'91	CD
Workin' It Out	Pair	1292	'91	CS/CD
The Ike and Tina Turner Collection	Mogull	35830	'93	CS/CD
Legendary Superstars: Ike and Tina Turner Featuring the Ikettes	Original Sound	9323	'94	CS/CD
Rock and Roll	Richmond	2233		CS
So Fine!	Special Music	4826		CS/CD

Ike Turner and His Kings of Rhythm

Volume 1	Ace	22	'88	†
Volume 2	Ace	146		†

Ike Turner

Rocks the Blues	Crown	367		†
A Black Man's Soul	Pompeii	6003	'69	†
Blues Roots	United Artists	5576	'72	†
Confined to Soul	United Artists	051	'73	†
The Edge	Fantasy	9597	'80	†
I Like Ike: Best	Rhino	71819	'94	CS/CD

The Ikettes

Soul Hits	Modern	102	'65	†
(G)Old and New	United Artists	190	'74	†
Fine, Fine, Fine	Kent	063	'87	LP/CD

Tina Turner

Turns the Country On	United Artists	200	'74	†
Acid Queen	United Artists	495	'75	†
	Razor & Tie	1985	'91	CD
Rough	United Artists	919	'78	†
Private Dancer	Capitol	12330	'84	†
	Capitol	46041		CS/CD
Break Every Rule	Capitol	12530	'86	†
	Capitol	46323		CS/CD
Tina Live in Europe	Capitol	(2) 90126	'88	CS/CD
Foreign Affair	Capitol	91873	'89	CS/CD
	Capitol	91329		CD†
Simply the Best	Capitol	97152	'91	CS/CD
The Collected Recordings	Capitol	(3) 29724	'94	CD

Soundtrack

What's Love Got to Do with It	Virgin	88189	'93	CS/CD

Compilations

Tina Turner	Bella Musica	89926	'90	CD†
Tina Turner, Volume 2	Bella Musica	89941	'91	CD†
Tina Turner Goes Country	Playback	12331		CS

THE TURTLES

Mark Volman (b. Apr. 19. 1947, Los Angeles, CA), voc; **Howard Kaylan** (b. Howard Kaplan, June 22, 1947, New York, NY), kybd, voc; **Al Nichol** (b. Mar. 31, 1946, Winston-Salem, NC), kybd, gtr, bs, voc; **Jim Tucker** (b. Oct. 17, 1946, Los Angeles, CA), gtr; **Chuck Portz** (b. Mar. 28, 1945, Santa Monica, CA), bs; **Don Murray** (b. Nov. 8, 1945, Los Angeles, CA), drm

Mistakenly identified with the folk-rock movement as a result of their near-smash hit version of Bob Dylan's "It Ain't Me, Babe" in 1965, the Turtles evolved from a surf band and enjoyed their greatest success with pop-style songs, such as "Happy Together," "She'd Rather Be with Me," and "Elenore." As the band developed, principals Howard Kaylan and Mark Volman moved into more sophisticated, satirical material, leading to the band's eventual dissolution. With the demise of the Turtles in 1970, the two joined Frank Zappa's Mothers of Invention as Phlorescent Leech and Eddie, later shorted to Flo and Eddie. Touring extensively and recording four albums with Zappa, including the movie soundtrack *200 Motels*, Flo and Eddie later recorded four brilliant yet overlooked albums of rock parody and satire. In the '80s they pursued session work, wrote commercials, and scored and recorded the soundtracks for the children's cartoons *Strawberry Shortcake* and *The Care Bears*. In the latter half of the '80s, Volman and Kaylan reconstituted the Turtles for national tours and club appearances.

Mark Volman and Howard Kaylan met at Westchester High School in Los Angeles in 1961 and manned the surf groups the Nightriders and the Crossfires with Al Nichol and Chuck Portz between 1962 and 1965. Adopting the name the Turtles under a new manager and signing with White Whale Records, the group added guitarist Jim Tucker and drummer Don Murray. During the burgeoning days of folk-rock, the Turtles scored a near-smash hit with Bob Dylan's "It Ain't Me, Babe," followed by the major hit "Let Me Be" from their debut, folk-oriented album. After the major hit "You Baby," John Barbata replaced Murray on drums. The Turtles subsequently achieved their most successful year in 1967, with the top pop hit "Happy Together," the smash hit "She'd Rather Be with Me," and the major hits "You Know What I Mean" and "She's My Girl." With Volman, Kaylan, and Nichol as mainstays, the Turtles recorded 1968's *The Turtles Present the Battle of the Bands*, which yielded smash hits with "Elenore" and "You Showed Me," written by Gene Clark and Jim McGuinn. For this unusual album the group recorded under a variety of different names in different styles, showcasing a developing satirical bent with songs such as "Surfer Dan," "I'm Chief Kamanananalea (We're the Royal Macadamia Nuts)," and "Chicken Little Was Right." After 1969's highly uncommercial *Turtle Soup*, with Ray Davies of the Kinks serving as producer, the Turtles disbanded.

Volman and Kaylan subsequently joined Frank Zappa's Mothers of Invention, taking the stage names of Phlorescent Leech and Eddie. Touring Europe and America extensively with Zappa, Mark "Flo" Volman and Howard "Eddie" Kaylan performed their own feature spot in concert and recorded four albums with the group, including the soundtrack to the movie *200 Motels*. Also appearing in the film, Volman and Kaylan easily eclipsed the performances of Zappa and Ringo Starr. Volman and Kaylan also recorded as background vocalists for Marc Bolan/T. Rex in 1971–1972 (including the major hit "Bang a Gong"). Flo and Eddie left the Mothers of Invention in 1972 and recorded two outstanding yet neglected albums of rock satire for Reprise Records. They toured in support of Alice Cooper's *Billion Dollar Babies* in 1973.

Kaylan and Volman next wrote the screenplay to the X-rated animated movie *Cheap*, wrote satirical articles for the American rock press, and hosted their own successful syndicated radio show, originating from Los Angeles's KROQ. Signed to Columbia Records in 1975, the duo recorded two more excellent yet overlooked albums of rock parody and satire before moving into session and television work. They recorded a silly reggae album in 1981, and later wrote radio and television commercials (including all of the commercials for David Bowie's RCA albums). They also wrote and recorded music for the children's cartoons *Stawberry Shortcake* and *The Care Bears*.

Thanks to the reissue of classic Turtles material by revival label Rhino Records, the band enjoyed renewed popularity in the early '80s, leading Volman and Kaylan to revive the band. In 1984 and 1985, with a reconstituted Turtles, they headlined two Happy Together tours with other '60s groups, and subsequently toured independently as the Turtles.

The Crossfires

Out of Control	Rhino	019	'81	†
	Sundazed	6062	'95	CD

The Turtles

It Ain't Me Babe	White Whale	7111	'65	†
	Rhino	151	'82	CS
You, Baby	White Whale	7112	'66	†
	Rhino	153	'83	†
Happy Together	White Whale	7114	'67	†
	Rhino	152	'83	CS
Golden Hits	White Whale	7115	'67	†
The Turtles Present the Battle of the Bands	White Whale	7118	'68	†
Turtle Soup	White Whale	7124	'69	†
More Golden Hits	White Whale	7127	'70	†
Wooden Head	White Whale	7133	'70	†
	Rhino	154	'84	†
Happy Together Again—Greatest Hits	Sire	(2) 3703	'74	†
Greatest Hits	Rhino	160	'82	†
Best (1965–1969)	Rhino	70177	'87	CS
Turtle Wax: Bcst, Volume 2	Rhino	70159	'88	CS/CD
Captured Live	Rhino	71153	'92	CS/CD
Best	Rhino	71027	'94	CS/CD
Love Songs	Rhino	71873	'95	CS/CD
20 Greatest Hits	Rhino	5160		CD

Flo and Eddie with Frank Zappa and the Mothers of Invention

Chunga's Revenge	Bizarre/Reprise	2030	'70	†
	Rykodisc	10164	'90	CD†
	Rykodisc	10511	'95	CD
Fillmore East, June 1971	Bizarre/Reprise	2042	'71	†
	Rykodisc	10167	'90	CD†
	Rykodisc	10512	'95	CS/CD
Just Another Band from L.A.	Bizarre/Reprise	2075	'72	†
	Rykodisc	10161	'90	CD†
	Rykodisc	10515	'95	CD
200 Motels (soundtrack)	United Artists	(2) 9956	'71	†
	MCA	(2) 4183	'86	LP/CS

Flo and Eddie

The Phlorescent Leech and Eddie	Reprise	2099	'72	†
Flo and Eddie	Reprise	2141	'73	†

Illegal, Immoral and Fattening	Columbia	33554	'75	†
	One Way	22673		CD
Moving Targets	Columbia	34262	'76	†
Best (from four above albums)	Rhino	70134	'86	CS
Rock Steady with Flo and Eddie	Epiphany	4010	'81	†
Best	Rhino	71097	'92	CD

U

U2

Paul "Bono" Hewson (b. May 10, 1960, Dublin, Ireland), lead voc, gtr; **David "The Edge" Evans** (b. Aug. 8, 1961, Barking, Essex, England), lead gtr, kybd, voc; **Adam Clayton** (b. Mar. 13, 1960, Chinnor, Oxfordshire, England), bs; **Larry Mullen** (b. Oct. 21, 1960, Dublin, Ireland), drm

Perhaps the most engaging and influential rock band of the '80s, U2 quickly progressed to become one of the most politically and spiritually concerned rock acts of the era, comparable to only Bruce Springsteen in their ability to fuse social and existential commentary with rock music in a manner both profound and entertaining. Starting out as an unpretentious people's band, U2's success served to restore some sense of compassion and humanity to a rock scene bludgeoned by punk and heavy-metal music. With lead vocalist and principal songwriter Bono emerging as one of the most charismatic front men for a rock band, U2's greatest commercial and critical success came with 1987's *The Joshua Tree*, a remarkable work in the depth and breadth of its moving spiritual and existential concerns. Since then, the band has been criticized for being both overly self-indulgent and humorless, leading to a reevaluation of their message and sound.

Formed in Dublin, Ireland, in 1976 as Feedback, the group toured locally as the Hype and changed their name to U2 in 1977. Signed to CBS Ireland, they scored Irish-only hits with "Another Day" and "Stones for Boys," and made their first foray into London in 1979. They returned successfully in 1980 and signed with Island Records. Their debut album, *Boy*, explored the issue of maturation from adolescence and included the anthemic "I Will Follow" and "Into the Heart." U2 made a brief tour of East Coast American clubs and later conducted their first major American tour in 1981, to support their next album, *October*, which produced the minor British hits "Fire" and "Gloria." The group took a break from touring and recording of more than a year before recording *War*, which established them in Great Britain and yielded a British smash with "New Year's Day"; it also included the political "Sunday Bloody Sunday," concerned with the hostilities gripping Ireland. The album became a best-seller in the United States, remaining on the charts for more than three years. U2 subsequently toured during summer 1983, with live recordings from that tour later issued on *Under a Blood Red Sky*.

Winning the praise of rock stalwarts such as Pete Townshend and Bruce Springsteen, U2 vaulted into the top echelon of rock acts with their tour in support of 1984's *The Unforgettable Fire*. The album produced their first moderate American hit, "Pride (In the Name of Love)," a tribute to Martin Luther King Jr., and included "4th of July." Lead vocalist Bono and bassist Adam Clayton assisted in recording the Band Aid single "Do They Know It's Christmas?" and U2 was the highlight of the Live Aid concert in 1985. Later in the year they released another live mini-LP, *Wide Awake in America*, and toured the world in 1986, joining that year's Amnesty International tour.

In 1987 U2 issued their masterpiece *The Joshua Tree*. The album yielded four hits, including the top "With or Without You" and "I Still Haven't Found What I'm Looking For." It also contained the major hit "Where the Streets Have No Name," the powerful "Bullet the Blue Sky," the poignant "Running to Stand Still," and the tragic "Mothers of the Disappeared." The album remained on the album charts for nearly two years and sold more than 5 million copies in the United States and more than 14 million worldwide. For 18 months in 1987 and 1988, U2 toured the world, playing arenas in the first round and stadiums in the second. The tour produced a documentary concert movie and best-selling double-record album that contained nine studio tracks, including "Love Rescue Me," cowritten with Bob Dylan, "When Love Comes to Town," recorded with B. B. King, the smash hit "Desire," and the major hit "Angel of Harlem."

However, some American critics reacted negatively to the album and film, accusing the band of being self-absorbed. As an apparent consequence, U2 withdrew from the music scene for several years, emerging triumphantly with 1991's *Achtung Baby*. Featuring shorter, more danceable songs concerned not with social issues but with interpersonal relationships and love, the album produced five hits, including the near-smashes "Mysterious Ways" and "One." The group toured again in 1992, again playing arenas, and then stadiums. The stadium segment of the tour was the most spectacuar tour of the year, with the production featuring a massive stage, hundreds of tons of equipment, and multiple video screens. It set the technological standard for stadium-rock shows, and the tour was the highest-grossing tour of the year, more than double the revenues of either the Grateful Dead or Guns N' Roses/Metallica.

In 1993 U2 extended their contract with Island Records. The contract gave Island worldwide distribution rights to their next six albums and was reportedly worth $200 million, far exceeding recent contracts given to Prince, Michael Jackson, and Madonna. However, their next album, *Zooropa*, failed to yield any major hit single and was largely experimental, pervaded by slow, long songs that evinced longtime producer Brian Eno's penchant for electronic processing and synthesizers.

U2

Boy	Island	9646	'81	†
	Island	90040		LP/CS/CD†
	Island	842296		LP/CS/CD
October	Island	9680	'81	†
	Island	90092		LP/CS/CD†
	Island	842297		LP/CS/CD
War	Island	90067	'83	LP/CS/CD†
	Island	811148		LP/CS/CD
	Mobile Fidelity	571	'93	CD
Under the Blood Red Sky (mini)	Island	90127	'83	LP/CS/CD†
	Island	818008		LP/CS/CD
The Unforgettable Fire	Island	90231	'84	LP/CS/CD†
	Island	822898		LP/CS/CD
	Mobile Fidelity	624	'95	CD
Wide Awake in America (mini)	Island	90279	'85	LP/CS/CD†
	Island	842479		LP/CS/CD
The Joshua Tree	Island	90581	'85	LP/CS/CD†
	Island	842298		LP/CS/CD
Rattle and Hum	Island	(2) 91003	'88	LP†
	Island	91003	'88	CS/CD†
	Island	(2) 842299		LP/CS/CD
Achtung Baby	Island	510347	'91	LP/CS/CD
Zooropa	Island	518047	'93	LP/CS/CD

VAN HALEN

David Lee Roth (b. Oct. 10, 1955, Bloomington, IN), lead voc, gtr; **Edward Van Halen** (b. Jan. 26, 1957, Nijmegen, Netherlands), lead gtr; **Michael Anthony** (b. June 20, 1955, Chicago), bs, voc; **Alex Van Halen** (b. May 8, 1955, Nijmegen), drm [David Lee Roth left in 1985, to be replaced by **Sammy Hagar** (b. Oct. 13, 1947, Monterey, CA).]

VAN HALEN

Mainstays of heavy-metal music since the late '70s, Van Halen featured the bombastic, narcissistic, debauched personality of vocalist David Lee Roth until 1985. Garnering a huge following among American male youth for their live shows, Van Halen was propelled by the inventive, rapid-fire playing of lead guitarist Eddie Van Halen, often regarded as the most influential guitarist since Jimmy Page. Van Halen continued their hit-making and best-selling ways after Roth's departure with new vocalist Sammy Hagar, who brought a mellower and more commercial sound to the group with his songwriting. Maintaining a low profile after 1988's Monsters of Rock tour, one of the most successful tours of the year and one of the most expensive ever mounted, Van Halen were challenged in the heavy-metal field by upstarts Metallica and Guns N' Roses by the late '80s. Nonetheless, their success continued unabated as Roth struggled to establish himself in a solo career.

Edward and Alex Van Halen took classical piano lessons as children, moving with their family to the United States in 1965 and settling in Pasadena, California, in 1968. Eddie took up guitar at age 12, and the brothers formed Broken Crumbs with bassist Michael

Anthony in the early '70s. They later recruited vocalist David Lee Roth, a onetime student of Pasadena City College, from the Red Ball Jets for the group Mammoth. Spotted by Gene Simmons of Kiss, who produced a demonstration tape for the band, Mammoth changed their name to Van Halen in 1974 and began several years of playing the Southern California bar circuit. The band eventually signed with Warner Bros. Records, with Ted Templeman producing all their albums through 1993.

Van Halen's debut album remained on the album charts for more than three years, yielded a moderate hit with a remake of the Kinks' "You Really Got Me," and eventually sold more than six million copies. The group quickly became established as a hugely popular live act in the United States, particulalry among male white youth, with David Lee Roth's sex, drugs, and alcohol party-persona and Eddie Van Halen's outstanding guitar playing, characterized by extended solos and his unique technique of hammering on the guitar strings with both hands. Their second album became an instant best-seller and produced their first major hit, "Dance the Night Away." Despite scoring only one more major hit through 1983—1982's cover version of Roy Orbison's "Oh, Pretty Woman"—Van Halen's albums sold in the millions, save 1981's *Fair Warning*. They reaffirmed their position as the leading purveyor of pop-style heavy-metal music with *1984*, which yielded the top hit "Jump" and major hits "I'll Wait" and "Panama."

By early 1985 David Lee Roth had recorded a minialbum that produced a smash hit with a remake of the Beach Boys' "California Girls" and a major hit with his copy of Louis Prima's rendition of the medley "Just a Gigolo/I Ain't Got Nobody." Bouyed by the success, Roth left Van Halen for a solo career. Recruiting guitarist Steve Vai and bassist Billy Sheehan, Roth toured in support of the best-selling *Eat 'Em and Smile* (1986) and *Skyscraper* (1988) albums. The first album yielded the major hit "Yankee Rose" and the second produced the smash "Just Like Paradise," but Roth never scored another major hit. In the '90s Roth retired his boisterous and self-serving persona, eventually reemerging for a club tour in support of the eclectic *Your Filthy Little Mouth*, which included a duet with Travis Tritt on "Cheatin' Heart Cafe."

Despite dire predictions that Van Halen would never be the same without David Lee Roth, the band not only survived but maintained their astounding level of popularity with new vocalist Sammy Hagar, a veteran of Montrose and a successful solo recording artist (1982–1983's "Your Love Is Driving Me Crazy" and 1984's "I Can't Drive 55."). Hagar favored harmony vocals, perhaps to cover his limited vocal range, and brought a pop sensibility to the band's basic heavy-metal sound. His debut with Van Halen, *5150*, sold more than four million copies and yielded a smash hit with the ballad "Why Can't This Be Love" and the major hits "Dreams" and "Love Walks In." In 1987 Sammy Hagar recorded a solo album that yielded a major hit with "Give to Live."

In 1988 Van Halen recorded the formulaic *OU812*, which produced the smash hit "When It's Love" and major hit "Finish What Ya Started." They toured with Metallica and the Scorpions, among others, on the heavily attended Monsters of Rock tour. Overshadowed by Metallica on tour and challenged in the heavy-metal field by Metallica and Guns N' Roses, Van Halen withdrew for several years, reemerging in 1991 with *For Unlawful Carnal Knowledge*, its major hit "Top of the World," and a new round of touring. Their 1993 tour yielded the live set *Right Here, Right Now*. In 1994 Van Halen recorded their first album without producer Ted Templeman, *Balance*, touring once again in 1995. *Unboxed*, issued in 1994, compiled Sammy Hagar's greatest hits of the '80s, along with two newly recorded songs.

Van Halen

Van Halen	Warner Bros.	3075	'78	CS/CD
Van Halen II	Warner Bros.	3312	'79	CS/CD
Women and Children First	Warner Bros.	3415	'80	CS/CD
Fair Warning	Warner Bros.	3450	'81	CS/CD
Women and Children First/Fair Warning	Warner Bros.	25140		CS

Diver Down	Warner Bros.	3677	'82	CS/CD
1984 (MCMLXXXIV)	Warner Bros.	23985	'84	CS/CD
5150	Warner Bros.	25394	'86	CS/CD
OU812	Warner Bros.	25732	'88	CS/CD
For Unlawful Carnal Knowledge	Warner Bros.	26594	'91	CS/CD
Van Halen Live: Right Here, Right Now	Warner Bros.	(2) 45198	'93	CS/CD
Balance	Warner Bros.	45760	'95	LP/CS/CD
David Lee Roth				
Crazy from the Heat (mini)	Warner Bros.	25222	'85	CS/CD
Eat 'Em and Smile	Warner Bros.	25470	'86	CS/CD
Skyscraper	Warner Bros.	25671	'88	CS/CD
A Little Ain't Enough	Warner Bros.	26477	'91	LP/CS/CD
Your Filthy Little Mouth	Reprise	45391	'94	CS/CD
Sammy Hagar				
Sammy Hagar (reissued as "I Never Said Goodbye")	Geffen	24144	'87	CS/CD
Unboxed	Geffen	24702	'94	CS/CD

THE VAUGHAN BROTHERS

Jimmie Vaughan (b. Mar. 20, 1951, Dallas, TX); **Stevie Ray Vaughan** (b. Oct. 3, 1954, Dallas, TX; d. Aug. 27, 1990, East Troy, WI)

THE FABULOUS THUNDERBIRDS. Jimmie Vaughan, gtr, **Kim Wilson** (b. Jan. 6, 1951, Detroit, MI), voc, har; **Keith Ferguson** (b. July 23, 1946, Houston, TX); **Mike Buck** (b. June 17, 1952). [Mike Buck left in 1980, to be replaced by **Fran Christina** (b. Feb. 1, 1951, Westerly, RI). In 1984 Keith Ferguson departed and was replaced by **Preston Hubbard** (b. Mar. 15, 1953, Providence, RI). Group reorganized in 1991 with Wilson, Christina, Hubbard, and guitarists **Duke Robillard** and **Kid Bangham**.]

STEVIE RAY VAUGHAN AND DOUBLE TROUBLE. Stevie Ray Vaughan, gtr; **Tommy Shannon**, bs; **Chris Layton**, drm [**Reese Wynans** joined as keyboardist in 1985.]

As lead guitarists with the Fabulous Thunderbirds and Double Trouble, respectively, Jimmie and Stevie Ray Vaughan helped foster the blues revival of the '80s, along with artists such as George Thorogood and Robert Cray. While the Fabulous Thunderbirds favored a more R&B style, scoring their biggest hit with 1986's "Tuff Enuff," Stevie Ray Vaughan and Double Trouble played under the influence of Texas and Chicago blues guitarists, as well as Jimi Hendrix. Jimmie Vaughan left the Fabulous Thunderbirds in 1990 and recorded *Family Style* with his brother, but on August 27, 1990, Stevie Ray was killed in a helicopter crash in East Troy, Wisconsin. Jimmie Vaughan has since recorded a solo album, while the Fabulous Thunderbirds continue to tour with new guitarist Duke Robillard. The remaining members of Double Trouble have recorded an album with two new guitarists as Arc Angel.

Stevie Ray Vaughan began playing guitar in 1963, by which time his brother Jimmie was playing with such Dallas groups as the Swinging Pendulums. Stevie Ray began playing Dallas clubs at 14, with such bands as Blackbird and Cracker Jack. Jimmie moved to Austin in 1970, where he formed Storm with guitarist Denny Freeman. After a brief stay in California, Jimmie returned to Austin, forming Jimmie Vaughan and the Fabulous Thunderbirds with vocalist Lou Ann Barton and drummer Otis Lewis. Barton and Lewis left in late 1974, and Keith Ferguson, a veteran of both Storm and the Nightcrawlers (with Stevie Ray), joined, as did Kim Wilson, who became the group's chief songwriter and musical director as well as lead singer and harmonica player.

With the addition of drummer Mike Buck, the Fabulous Thunderbirds became the house band at the recently opened Austin club Antone's; they subsequently won a reputation as one of the most engaging blues bands in the state. Their first recognition outside Texas came at the 1978 San Francisco Blues Festival, and they signed with Takoma Records. In 1980 Fran Christina replaced Mike Buck during the recording of *What's the Word* on Takoma's parent label Chrysalis. The Fabulous Thunderbirds played up to three hundred engagements a year, yet their albums failed to sell and they were dropped by Chrysalis in 1982.

Stevie Ray Vaughan followed his brother to Austin in 1973, where he played with the Nightcrawlers and the Cobras. Around 1977 he formed Triple Threat with Lou Ann Barton and guitarist W. C. Clark. By 1978 Barton had left and the band evolved into Double Trouble, with Vaughan, bassist Tommy Shannon from Blackbird and Cracker Jack, and drummer Chris Layton. In April 1982 the band auditioned in New York City for the Rolling Stones, and in July Atlantic Records producer Jerry Wexler convinced the promoters of Switzerland's Montreux Jazz Festival to book Vaughan and the band. Among those in the audience were Jackson Browne and David Bowie. Vaughan subsequently played guitar on six songs for Bowie's *Let's Dance* album, including the hits "Let's Dance," "China Girl," and "Modern Love."

Jackson Browne offered the group free studio time at his studio in Los Angeles, and John Hammond Jr., the blues-playing son of Columbia executive John Hammond, submitted a tape recording of the group's performance at Montreux to his father. Signed to the Columbia subsidiary Epic, Stevie Ray Vaughan and Double Trouble used the studio time to record their debut album, 1983's *Texas Flood*, generally considered the group's finest album. The follow-up *Couldn't Stand the Weather* featured Vaughan's stunning rendition of Jimi Hendrix's "Voodoo Chile (Slight Return)," and 1985's *Soul to Soul* saw the permanent addition of keyboardist Reese Wynans.

The Fabulous Thunderbirds continued to tour arduously following the expiration of their Chrysalis contract. Keith Ferguson left in 1984 and was replaced by Preston Hubbard. They then recorded *Tuff Enuff* in London in 1985 with Dave Edmunds producing, and the album became a best-seller when released on CBS Associated, producing a major hit with the title song and a moderate hit with "Wrap It Up." The band began playing concert halls rather than clubs, but subsequent albums sold progressively less well. Jimmie Vaughan left the group in 1990 and recorded *Family Style* with his brother Stevie Ray. However, before the album's release, Stevie Ray Vaughan was killed in a helicopter crash on August 27, 1990, in East Troy, Wisconsin, after performing at a concert with his brother, Eric Clapton, Robert Cray, and Buddy Guy.

With Kim Wilson and Fran Christina as mainstays, the Fabulous Thunderbirds regrouped with guitarists Duke Robillard and Kid Bangham, and, later, pianist Gene Taylor, but by 1993 the band was again without a recording contract. Double Trouble musicians Tommy Shannon and Chris Layton formed Arc Angels with guitarists Charlie Sexton and Doyle Bramhall II, recording an album for DGC Records in 1992. Jimmie Vaughan recorded his solo debut album in 1994.

The Fabulous Thunderbirds

The Fabulous Thunderbirds	Takoma	7068	'79	†
	Chrysalis	21250	'85	CS/CD†
What's the Word	Chrysalis	1287	'80	†
	Chrysalis	21287	'87	CS/CD†
Butt Rockin'	Chrysalis	1319	'81	†
	Chrysalis	21319		CS/CD†
T-Bird Rhythm	Chrysalis	1395	'82	†
	Chrysalis	21395	'86	CS/CD†

The Essential Fabulous Thunderbirds	Chrysalis	21851	'91	CS/CD
Tuff Enuff	CBS Associated	40304	'86	CS/CD
Hot Number	CBS Associated	40818	'87	CS/CD
Powerful Stuff	CBS Associated	45094	'89	CS/CD
Walk That Walk, Talk	Epic Associated	47878	'91	CS/CD
Hot Stuff: The Greatest	Epic Associated	53007	'92	CS/CD
Roll of the Dice	Private Music	82130	'95	CS/CD
Stevie Ray Vaughan and Double Trouble				
In the Beginning	Epic	53168	'92	CS/CD
Texas Flood	Epic	38734	'83	CS/CD
Couldn't Stand the Weather	Epic	39304	'84	CS/CD
	Epic/Legacy	64425	'94	CD
Soul to Soul	Epic	40036	'85	LP/CS/CD
Live Alive	Epic	40511	'86	CS/CD
In Step	Epic	45024	'89	LP/CS/CD
The Sky Is Crying	Epic	47390	'91	LP/CS/CD
The Vaughan Brothers				
Family Style	Epic Associated	46225	'90	LP/CS/CD
Jimmie Vaughan				
Strange Pleasure	Epic	57202	'94	CS/CD
Arc Angels				
Arc Angels	DGC	24465	'92	CS/CD

THE VELVET UNDERGROUND/LOU REED

Lou Reed (b. Mar. 2, 1944, Freeport, Long Island, NY), voc, kybd, gtr; **John Cale** (b. Dec. 4, 1940, Granant, South Wales), viola, kybd, bs; **Sterling Morrison** (b. Aug. 29, 1942, East Meadow, Long Island, NY; d. Aug. 30, 1995, Poughkeepsie, NY); **Nico** (b. Christa Paffgen, Oct. 16, 1939, Cologne, West Germany; d. July 18, 1988, Ibiza, Spain), voc; **Maureen "Mo" Tucker** (b. 1945, NJ), drm [Nico left after the first album. John Cale left in 1968 and was replaced by multi-instrumentalist **Doug Yule**. Reed left in 1970, and the group disbanded by 1971. The original lineup reunited in 1993.]

Seminal late-'60s New York band whose influence was not recognized until years after their disbandment, the Velvet Underground featured the stark, sinister, and real-life songs of Lou Reed, the avant-garde musical innovations of John Cale, the thin but sensual voice of Nico, and the drumming of Maureen Tucker, one of the few female drummers in rock music. Launched in association with artist Andy Warhol, the Velvet Underground toured with his total environment show, the Exploding Plastic Inevitable, perhaps the first multimedia show complete with music, dancers, films, lights, and projections. The Velvet Underground became the vehicle for Reed's eerie visions of life after the departures of Nico (after the first album) and Cale (after the second album), yet the group was essentially defunct by 1970. Serving as an inspiration to the late-'70s punk and New Wave movements, the influence of the Velvet Underground can be seen to this day with groups like R.E.M. and Sonic Youth.

While Nico's solo career remained relatively undistinguished and John Cale retained a limited following among critics and avant-garde fans, Lou Reed became the most successful, if erratic, of the former members as a solo artist. While Cale produced two of Nico's albums, the Stooges' debut, and, later, Patti Smith's *Horses*, Reed broke through with his

David Bowie—produced album, *Transformer*, which produced a surprise major hit with "Walk on the Wild Side." Scoring his biggest album success with the live *Rock 'n' Roll Animal*, with its classic "Rock 'n' Roll" song, Lou Reed followed up with the best-selling *Sally Can't Dance* album. During the early '80s Reed recorded mellower rock for adults, returning to his harsher thematic styles with 1989's *New York*. In 1990 he teamed with John Cale for *Songs for Drella*, a tribute album to their onetime mentor Andy Warhol, and later recorded the moody examination of life and the spirit, *Magic and Loss*.

Lou Reed initiated five years of classical piano training at the age of five and first played professionally while in his early teens with Long Island bands such as Pasha and the Prophets and the Jades. A published poet, he worked as a journalist and as a songwriter for Pickwick Records. He met violist John Cale in 1964. Cale had studied classical viola and piano in London, and his compositions had been broadcast by the BBC when he was eight years old. Cale came to the United States in 1963 on a Leonard Bernstein fellowship, but abandoned his classical studies to pursue his interest in avant-garde music, joining LaMonte Young's experimental group on electric viola.

Reed teamed with Cale and classically trained guitarist Sterling Morrison in bands such as the Ostriches and the Primitives, adding female drummer Maureen Tucker in 1965. The group became the Velvet Underground, debuted at Cafe Bizarre in Greenwich Village in winter 1966, and immediately sparked controversy for their unorthodox music and stage demeanor. They came to the attention of pop artist Andy Warhol, who was looking for a rock group to add to his multimedia outfit, the Factory. Among the members of the Factory was Nico, who had been a European model since age 16. She had moved to New York in 1959 and studied acting with Lee Strasberg before appearing in Warhol's 1966 film *Chelsea Girls*. Augmented by Nico, the Velvet Underground joined Warhol's total environment show, the Exploding Plastic Inevitable, which opened in New York and subsequently toured Canada and the United States.

Signed to MGM/Verve Records, the Velvet Underground recorded their debut album with Andy Warhol as nominal producer. Packaged in a jacket that featured Warhol's famous peelable banana cover, *The Velvet Underground and Nico* was comprised of music and lyrics the likes of which had not yet appeared in rock music. Propelled by John Cale's innovative musical experimentation and Lou Reed's disarmingly realistic and sinister lyrics, the album included the startling "Heroin," with its screeching, electronic, drugged-out crescendo, the sadomasochistic "Venus in Furs," the gritty "I'm Waiting for the Man," "There She Goes Again," and the gentle "Sunday Morning" and "I'll Be Your Mirror," the latter sung by Nico. Garnering virtually no radio airplay, the album failed to sell, yet it was eventually recognized as one of the most influential albums of the late '60s.

Nico subsequently left the Velvet Underground to pursue a solo career, and with the attendant loss of interest by Warhol and the press, the group's next album, *White Light/White Heat*, was largely ignored by the public, yet it contained the lurid 17-minute classic "Sister Ray." The group toured to diminishing audiences, and Cale left in March 1968. He was replaced by multi-instrumentalist Doug Yule for *The Velvet Underground*, which featured the ballad "Pale Blue Eyes." The group switched to Cotillion Records for their final studio album, *Loaded*, which included "Rock 'n' Roll" and "Sweet Jane." Following a summer's residency at Max's Kansas City in New York, Reed left the Velvet Underground in August 1970, after which the group maintained with new members through 1971.

Nico was the first former member of the Velvet Underground to record a solo album, but *Chelsea Girl* failed to sell despite the inclusion of Jackson Browne's "These Days" and Bob Dylan's "I'll Keep It with Mine." It was followed by *The Marble Index*, featuring her own songs, and two subsequent albums that were produced by John Cale. In the meantime, Cale had produced the Stooges' debut album, launched his own recording career with *Vintage Violence*; he recorded *Church of Anthrax* with minimalist musician Terry Riley. Cale switched to

Reprise for 1972's *The Academy in Peril* and the critically acclaimed *Paris 1919*, released a year later, but by 1974 he had returned to England.

In 1974 Nico and John Cale performed a concert at London's Rainbow Theater with synthesizer player Brian Eno (of Roxy Music) and bassist Kevin Ayers and percussionist Robert Wyatt (of Soft Machine) that produced the live album *June 1, 1974*. Cale recorded *Fear* and *Slow Dazzle* with Eno and guitarist Phil Manzanera, another veteran of Roxy Music, and toured Europe in spring 1975. He produced Patti Smith's stunning debut *Horses*, and switched to A&M Records for his next album, 1980's *Sabotage*. Nico, meanwhile, continued to tour sporadically in Europe, becoming a sad shadow of herself due to heroin addiction. She died after sustaining a cerebral hemorrhage following a fall off a bicycle on the island of Ibiza in Spain on July 18, 1988. Her life story was celebrated in the acclaimed 1995 documentary film *Nico Icon*.

Lou Reed was the most successful of the ex-bandmembers in his solo career. By 1972 he had signed a solo contract with RCA Records, and he recorded his debut album in London. His second, *Transformer*, was produced by David Bowie and yielded a major hit with "Walk on the Wild Side," which served as his breakthrough. However, the follow-up, *Berlin*, sold poorly. Reed next assembled a touring band to record *Rock 'n' Roll Animal* at New York's Academy of Music. The album became the best-selling of his career and included remakes of his Velvet Underground songs "Heroin" and "Sweet Jane" as well as the classic "Rock 'n' Roll." *Sally Can't Dance* also sold quite well, despite its air of parody, but Reed's career reached its nadir with 1975's *Metal Machine Music*, which consisted of little more than electronic beeps and tape hiss.

Following *Coney Island Baby*, Reed switched to Arista Records for a number of poor-selling, mediocre albums through 1980. Moving to RCA Records, he recorded more accessible and mature albums, beginning with 1982's acclaimed *The Blue Mask*. He toured with the first Amnesty Internationl tour and performed a number of benefits for the homeless. Reed returned to his anxious style of songwriting in 1989 with the politicized *New York* album, hailed as his most vital in 15 years. In 1990 Reed joined John Cale for the first time in 20 years to compose and perform the tribute album to the late Andy Warhol, *Songs for Drella*. Cale had recently assisted Brian Eno in the recording of *Wrong Way Up*, and Reed subsequently recorded the moving yet demanding *Magic and Loss*. In January 1993 Lou Reed performed at President Bill Clinton's inaugural ball.

In 1993 the original lineup reunited as the Velvet Underground for a European tour and *Live MCMXCIII*, but bickering soon erupted between Cale and Reed and the tour fizzled. On August 30, 1995, Sterling Morrison died of non-Hodgkins lymphoma in Poughkeepsie, New York. The Velvet Underground was inducted into the Rock and Roll Hall of Fame in 1996.

The Velvet Underground

The Velvet Underground and Nico	Verve	65008	'67	†
	Verve/Polydor	823290	'85	CS/CD
White Light/White Heat	Verve	65046	'68	†
	Verve	825119	'85	CS/CD
VU	Verve	823721	'85	CS/CD
Another View	Verve	829405	'86	CS/CD
Live with Lou Reed, Volume I	Verve/Polydor	834823	'88	CD
Live With Lou Reed, Volume II	Verve/Polydor	834824	'88	CD
The Best of the Velvet Underground: Words and Music of Lou Reed	Verve	841164	'89	CS/CD
The Velvet Underground	MGM	4617	'69	†
	Verve/Polydor	815454	'85	CS/CD
The Velvet Underground	MGM	131	'71	†
Archetype	MGM	4950	'74	†

1969 Live	Mercury	(2) 7504	'74	†
	Mercury	826284		CS
Loaded	Cotillion	9034	'70	†
	Warner	27613		CD
Live at Max's Kansas City	Cotillion	9500	'72	CS/CD
Lou Reed with the Velvet Underground	Pride	0022	'73	†
Live MCMXCIII	Sire	(2) 45464	'93	CS/CD
	Sire	45465	'93	CS/CD
	Sire	45434	'93	CD

Nico

Chelsea Girl	Verve	65032	'67	†
	Polydor	835209	'88	CD
The Marble Index	Elektra	74029	'68/'91	CD
Desertshore	Reprise	6424	'72	†
	Warner Archives	6424	'93	LP/CS/CD
The End	Island	9311	'75	†
Drama of Exile	Cleopatra	1079	'93	CS/CD
Chelsea Girl Live (recorded 1982)	Cleopatra	6108	'95	CD
Hanging Gardens	Restless	72383		CS/CD
Do or Die	ROIR	117		CS/CD
Live Heroes	Performance	385		LP/CS/CD

John Cale

Vintage Violence	Columbia	1037	'70	†
	Columbia/Legacy	01037	'91	CD
The Academy in Peril	Reprise	2079	'72	†
	Warner Archives	2079	'93	LP/CD
Paris 1919	Reprise	2131	'73	†
	Reprise	25926	'93	CD
Fear	Island	9301	'75	†
Slow Dazzle	Island	9317	'75	†
Guts	Island	9459	'77	†
	Antilles	7063		LP
Sabotage	A&M	7063	'80	†
Honi Soit	A&M	4849	'81	†
Caribbean Sunset	Antilles	8401	'84	LP
John Cale Comes Alive	Antilles	8402		LP
Words for the Dying	Opal/Warner Bros.	26024	'89	CS/CD†
Even Cowgirls Get the Blues	ROIR	196	'91	CS/CD
Fragments of a Rainy Season	Hannibal	1372	'92	CS/CD
Music for a New Society	Rhino	71743	'94	CD

John Cale and Terry Riley

| Church of Anthrax | Columbia | 30131 | '71 | † |

John Cale, Kevin Ayers, Brian Eno, and Nico

| June 1, 1974 | Island | 9291 | '74 | † |

John Cale and Brian Eno

| Wrong Way Up | Opal/Warner Bros. | 26421 | '90 | CS/CD |

John Cale and Bob Neuwirth

| Last Day on Earth | MCA | 11037 | '94 | CS/CD |

Lou Reed

Lou Reed	RCA	4701	'72	†
Transformer	RCA	4807	'72	CD
	RCA	3806		LP/CS
	RCA	66600	'95	CD
Berlin	RCA	0207	'73/'89	CS/CD
	RCA	4388		†
Rock 'n' Roll Animal	RCA	0472	'74	†
	RCA	3664	'80	CS/CD
Sally Can't Dance	RCA	0611	'74/'89	CS/CD
Live	RCA	0959	'75	†
	RCA	3752		CS/CD
Metal Music Machine: The Amine Beta Ring	RCA	(2) 1101	'75	†
Coney Island Baby	RCA	0915	'76/'89	CS/CD
	RCA	2480	'77	†
Walk on the Wild Side: The Best of Lou Reed	RCA	2001	'77	†
	RCA	7653	'88	CS
	RCA	3753	'88	CD
Rock and Roll Heart	Arista	4100	'76	†
Street Hassle	Arista	4169	'78	†
	Arista	18499	'87	CS/CD
Live . . . Take No Prisoners	Arista	(2) 8502	'78	†
The Bells	Arista	4229	'79	†
Growing Up in Public	Arista	9522	'80	†
Rock 'n' Roll Diary, 1967–1980	Arista	8603	'80	†
	Arista	8434		CS
The Blue Mask	RCA	4221	'82	†
Legendary Hearts	RCA	4568	'83/'90	CS/CD
New Sensations	RCA	4998	'84	CS/CD
Mistrial	RCA	7190	'86	CS/CD
Walk on the Wild Side and Other Hits	RCA	52162	'90	CS/CD
Between Thought and Expression: The Lou Reed Anthology	RCA	(3) 2356	'92	CS/CD
Wild Child	Pair	1024	'86	CD
New York	Sire	25829	'89	CS/CD
Magic and Loss	Sire	26662	'92	CS/CD

Lou Reed and John Cale

Songs for Drella	Sire	26140	'90	CS/CD
	Sire	26205	'90	CD

Maureen Tucker

Life in Exile After Abdication	50 Skidillion Watts	7	'89	LP/CS/CD
Dogs Under Stress	Sky	3103	'94	CD
I Spent a Week There the Other Night	Sky	3104	'94	CD

GENE VINCENT

(b. Vincent Eugene Craddock, Feb. 11, 1935, Norfolk, VA; d. Oct. 12, 1971, Newhall, CA)

In one of the most tragic and depressing episodes in the history of rock, Gene Vincent rose to prominence with the 1956 smash hit "Be-Bop-a-Lula," only to be discounted as a major artist in the United States by 1958. Recording further hits with "Lotta Lovin'" and "Dance to the Bop," Vincent also recorded the rockabilly classics "Race with the Devil," "Bluejean Bop," and "Crazy Legs." Lacking Elvis Presley's charisma and sporting a lower-class image unlike that of rising stars such as Ricky Nelson and Fabian, Vincent withdrew to England at the end of 1959, only to be injured in the car crash that killed Eddie Cochran. He became immensely popular in England and remained there until 1967. He unsuccessfully attempted an American comeback in the early '70s, but he died of an ulcer hemorrhage on October 12, 1971, destitute and neglected.

Gene Vincent and the Blue Caps

Blue Jean Bop	Capitol	764	'56	†
Gene Vincent and the Blue Caps	Capitol	811	'57	†
Gene Vincent Rocks and the Blue Caps Roll	Capitol	970	'58	†
A Gene Vincent Record Date	Capitol	1059	'58	†
The Bop that Just Won't Stop	Capitol	11287	'74	†
	Capitol	11826	'78	†
	Capitol	16209		†
Gene Vincent and His Blue Caps	Curb/CEMA	77623	'93	CS/CD

Gene Vincent

Sounds Like Gene Vincent	Capitol	1207	'59	†
Crazy Times	Capitol	1342	'60	†
Gene Vincent's Greatest	Capitol	380	'69	†
	Capitol	16208		†
Gene Vincent	Capitol	94074	'90	CS/CD
I'm Back and I'm Proud	Dandelion	102	'70	†
Slow Times Comin'/Sunshine	Kama Sutra	2019	'70	†
The Day the World Turned Blue	Kama Sutra	2027	'71	†
Forever	Rolling Rock	022	'82	†
Rockabilly Fever	Intermedia	5074		LP/CS
Ain't That Too Much	Sundazed	12004	'93	CD

TOM WAITS
(b. Dec. 7, 1949, Pomona, CA)

One of the authentic characters of rock music to emerge in the '70s, Tom Waits wrote compassionate songs concerned with the tawdry side of urban life, delivered in a stream-of-consciousness style reminiscent of the Beat poets of the '50s. Cultivating the image of an inebriated yet discerning denizen of the streets, Waits interspersed his repertoire with humorous and often bawdy monologues in performance. Best remembered for his early compositions "Ol' 55" and "(Looking for) The Heart of Saturday Night," Waits achieved his breakthrough with 1976's *Small Change* and later became a character actor in a wide variety of movies. He composed and shared vocal duties with Crystal Gayle on the critically acclaimed soundtrack to the film *One from the Heart*, and in the late '80s cowrote and performed *Frank's Wild Years*.

Tom Waits grew up in Whittier, California, and dropped out of high school during his junior year. He taught himself piano and guitar and began writing songs at 19 under the influence of the Beat poets and Tin Pan Alley writers. Waits first played at the Troubadour in Los Angeles in 1969, where he was spotted by former Frank Zappa manager Herb Cohen, who signed him to a songwriting contract. In performance, he developed a cult following for his free-verse monologues and incisive songs uttered in a gruff, gravelly, mumbling voice. Eventually signed to Elektra/Asylum Records in 1972, Tom Waits's first two albums failed to sell, yet the first featured the favorite "Ol' 55," later covered by the Eagles, and the second included the oft-recorded "(Looking for) The Heart of Saturday Night," "Semi-Suite," and "Diamonds on My Windshield." He made the charts with his third album, *Small Change*, which included "A Bad Liver and a Broken Heart" and "The Piano Has Been Drinking (Not Me)." He continued to record for Asylum, with minimal success, through 1980, eventually switching to Island Records for the acclaimed *Swordfishtrombones* in 1983.

Tom Waits launched his career as a character actor in 1979's *Paradise Alley*. He finally achieved mainstream recognition with the soundtrack to 1982's *One from the Heart*, performed with Crystal Gayle. At the end of 1981 he married Irish playwright and poet Kathleen Brennan, and the couple later wrote the musical *Frank's Wild Years*, produced by the esteemed Steppenwolf Company of Chicago in 1986. His tour of the show in 1987 produced the live set *Big Time*. Over the years, Waits appeared in a number of movies, including *Rumblefish*, *Down by Law*, *Ironweed*, *The Two Jakes*, and *Bram Stoker's Dracula*. After composing and recording the soundtrack to the film *Night on Earth*, he recorded 1992's adventurous *Bone Machine* with David Hidalgo (of Los Lobos) and Keith Richards, which garnered a Grammy for best alternative music album. Waits next wrote and recorded the songs for avant-garde opera director Robert Wilson's *The Black Rider*, which featured famed Beat author William S. Burroughs.

Tom Waits

The Early Years	Rhino	70557	'91	CS/CD
	Bizarre/Planet	40601	'95	CD
The Early Years, Volume 2	Bizarre/Straight	71089	'93	CS/CD
Closing Time	Asylum	5061	'73	CD†
	Elektra	5061	'90	CD
The Heart of Saturday Night	Asylum	1015	'74	CS/CD
Nighthawks at the Diner	Asylum	(2) 2008	'75	CS
	Asylum	2008		CD
Small Change	Asylum	1078	'76	CS/CD
Foreign Affairs	Asylum	1117	'77	CD
Blue Valentine	Asylum	162	'78	CS/CD
Heartattack and Vine	Asylum	295	'80	†
	Elektra	295	'90	CS/CD
Anthology	Elektra	60416	'85	CS
One from the Heart (soundtrack, with Crystal Gayle)	Columbia	37703	'82/'85	CD
Swordfishtrombones	Island	90095	'83	LP/CS/CD†
	Island	842469		CS/CD
Rain Dogs	Island	90299	'85	LP/CS/CD†
	Island	826382		CS/CD
Frank's Wild Years	Island	90572	'87	LP/CS/CD†
	Island	842357		LP/CS
Big Time	Island	90987	'88	LP/CS/CD†
	Island	842470		LP/CS
Night on Earth (soundtrack)	Island	510725	'92	CS/CD
Bone Machine	Island	512580	'92	CS/CD
The Black Rider	Island	518559	'93	CD

JERRY JEFF WALKER

(b. Ronald Clyde Crosby, Mar. 14, 1942, Oneonta, NY)

In a diverse '60s career, Jerry Jeff Walker started as a folk-style artist, manned a rock band called Circus Maximus, and recorded several neglected solo albums before scoring his most conspicuous success as the author of the classic "Mr. Bojangles," a near-smash hit for the Nitty Gritty Dirt Band in late 1970. Moving to Austin, Texas, in 1971, Walker became intimately involved with the area's burgeoning country-music scene, later labeled the outlaw movement. Although he never attained the success of fellow outlaws Waylon Jennings and Willie Nelson, Walker regularly recorded the compositions of Texas songwriters such as Guy Clark and Rodney Crowell.

Jerry Jeff Walker obtained his first guitar at 13 and left home at 16 to drift around the country, eventually playing coffeehouses in the early '60s. In 1966 he helped form Circus Maximus, which Vanguard Records promoted as a psychedelic group. Their debut album included the underground favorite "Wind" and Walker's "Fading Lady." After their second album, Walker left the group and recorded a solo album for Vanguard that was released after the modest success of his classic "Mr. Bojangles" on Atco in the summer of 1968. Popularized by New York's underground FM radio station WBAI, the song was written about a street dancer whom Walker met in a New Orleans jail. "Mr. Bojangles" ultimately became a hit for the Nitty Gritty Dirt band in late 1970 and has since been recorded by dozens of artists.

With the profits from "Mr. Bojangles," Jerry Jeff Walker retreated to Austin, Texas, in 1971. Signed to MCA Records and given artistic control over his recordings, Walker recorded his debut for the label largely in Austin, employing musicians who became the Lost Gonzo Band, his touring band until 1977. The album included his own "Hairy Ass Hillbillies" and "David and Me" and Guy Clark's "That Old Time Feeling" and "L.A. Freeway," the latter a minor hit. Becoming an integral part of the developing Austin music scene, Walker recorded *Viva Teralingua* live in 1973 in an abandoned saloon in the near-ghost town of Luckenback (immortalized by Waylon Jennings in 1977). The best-selling album of his career, it contained his own "Gettin' By" and "Sangria Wine," plus Ray Wylie Hubbard's barroom classic "Up Against the Wall Red Neck," Guy Clark's "Desperados," and Lost Gonzo Band leader Gary P. Nunn's "London Homesick Blues," later used as the theme for the public-television music show *Austin City Limits*. After *Collectibles* (with "I Like to Sleep Late in the Morning") and *Ridin' High* (with Willie Nelson's "Pick Up the Tempo"), Walker recorded the excellent *It's a Good Night for Singin'*, which featured Tom Waits's "(Lookin' for) The Heart of Saturday Night," Billy Joe Shaver's "Old Five and Dimers," "Couldn't Do Nothin' Right" (coauthored by Walker and Nunn), and "Some Day I'll Get Out of These Bars."

Beginning in 1975, the Lost Gonzo Band attempted their own recording career, as Jerry Jeff Walker continued to record for MCA until 1978. Featuring Rodney Crowell's "Song for the Life," Rusty Wier's "Don't It Make You Wanna Dance," and "Railroad Lady," cowritten by Walker and Jimmy Buffett, Walker's *A Man Must Carry On* sold quite well. However, subsequent albums sold progressively less well, and by 1978 Walker had switched to Elektra Records, only to return to MCA in 1981.

By the late '80s Jerry Jeff Walker was touring as a solo act. In 1986 he formed the record label Tried and True Music, with manufacture and distribution handled by Rykodisc. Walker scored three minor country hits in 1989 with "I Feel Like Hank Williams Tonight," "The Pickup Truck Song," and "Trashy Women" and enjoyed a revitalization of his career with *Live at Gruene Hall*. He played the inaugurals of Texas Governor Ann Richards in 1991 and President Bill Clinton in 1993, and in the early '90s hosted the music show *Texas Connection* on the Nashville cable network (TNN). In 1993 Jerry Jeff Walker recorded the sequel to *Viva Teralingua*, *Viva Luckenback!*

Circus Maximus

Circus Maximus	Vanguard	79260	'67/'90	CS/CD
Neverland Revisited	Vanguard	79274	'68	†

Jerry Jeff Walker

Driftin' Way of Life	Vanguard	6521	'69	†
	Vanguard	73124	'85	CS/CD
Mr. Bojangles	Atco	33-259	'68	†
	Rhino	71518	'93	CD
Five Years Gone	Atco	33-297	'69	†
Bein' Free	Atco	33-336	'70	†
Jerry Jeff Walker	MCA	75384	'73	†
	MCA	510		†
	MCA	2358		†
	MCA	37004		†
	MCA	918		CS
Viva Teralingua	MCA	382	'73	†
	MCA	2350		†
	MCA	37005		†
	MCA	919		CS/CD
Walker's Collectibles	MCA	450	'74	†
	MCA	2355		†
	MCA	27027	'84	†

Ridin' High	MCA	2156	'75	†
	MCA	37006		†
	MCA	920		CS/CD
Viva Teralingua/Ridin' High	MCA	(2) 6932		CS
It's a Good Night for Singin'	MCA	2202	'76	†
	MCA	27026	'84	†
A Man Must Carry On	MCA	(2) 6003	'77	CS
	MCA	(2) 8013		†
Contrary to Ordinary	MCA	3041	'78	†
Best	MCA	5128	'80	†
	MCA	27075		CS
Jerry Jeff	Elektra	163	'78	†
Too Old to Change	Elektra	239	'79	†
Reunion	MCA	5199	'81	†
Cowjazz	MCA	5355	'82	†
Great Gonzos	MCA	10381	'91	CS/CD
Mr. Bojangles	Bainbridge	6222	'82	LP/CS
Gypsy Songman	Rykodisc	20071	'88	CS/CD
Live at Gruene Hall	Rykodisc	10123	'89	CS/CD
Navajo Rug	Rykodisc	10175	'91	CS/CD
Hill Country Rain	Rykodisc	10241	'92	CS/CD
Viva Luckenback!	Rykodisc	10268	'93	CD
The Lost Gonzo Band				
The Lost Gonzo Band	MCA	487	'75	†
Thrills	MCA	2232	'76	†
Signs of Life	Capitol	11788	'78	†
Rendezvous	Amazing	1028	'92	CS/CD

JUNIOR WALKER AND THE ALL STARS

Junior Walker (b. Autry DeWalt II, 1942, Blytheville, AR; d. Nov. 23, 1995, Battle Creek, MI), sax, voc; **Willie Woods**, gtr; **Vic Thomas**, org; **James Graves**, drm

Featuring the saxophone playing of leader Junior Walker, Junior Walker and the All Stars scored top R&B and pop smashes with 1965's "Shotgun" and 1969's "What Does It Take (To Win Your Love)."

In the mid-'50s Walker met guitarist Willie Woods, and the two moved to Battle Creek, Michigan, by the decade's end. Originally formed in 1961, Junior Walker and the All Stars initially recorded for Harvey Fuqua's Harvey label, later recording for the Soul subsidiary of Motown Records. Achieving major crossover hits in the second half of the '60s with "(I'm a) Roadrunner," "How Sweet It Is (To Be Loved by You)," "Come See About Me," and "These Eyes," Junior Walker and the All Stars managed their last major R&B hit with the instrumental "Walk in the Night" in 1972. Junior Walker also recorded as a solo act for Soul Records in the late '70s, and he continued to tour into the '90s. Walker died of cancer on November 23, 1995, in Battle Creek, Michigan.

Junior Walker and the All Stars

Shotgun	Soul	701	'65	†
	Motown	5141	'89	CS/CD
Soul Session	Soul	702	'66	†

Roadrunner	Soul	703	'66	†
	Motown	5427	'89	CD†
Shotgun/Road Runner	Motown	8123	'86	CD†
Live!	Soul	705	'67	†
	Motown	5465	'90	CS/CD†
Home Cookin'	Soul	710	'69	†
	Motown	530402	'94	CS/CD
Greatest Hits	Soul	718	'69	†
	Motown	5208		CS/CD
What Does It Take to Win Your Love	Soul	721	'70	†
Live	Soul	725	'70	†
A Gasssss	Soul	726	'70	†
Rainbow Funk	Soul	732	'71	†
Moody Jr.	Soul	733	'72	†
Hot Shot	Soul	745	'76	†
Anthology	Motown	(2) 786	'74	LP/CS
Motown Superstar Series, Volume 5	Motown	5105		†
All the Great Hits	Motown	9012		CD†
	Motown	5297		CS/CD
Compact Command Performances	Motown	6203	'86	CD†
Gotta Hold On to This Feeling	Motown	5460	'90	CS/CD†
Nothing But Soul: The Singles, 1962–1983	Motown	(2) 6270	'94	CS/CD
Shotgun	Pickwick	3391	'75	†
Junior Walker				
Sax Appeal	Soul	747	'76	|
Whopper Bopper Show Stopper	Soul	748	'76	†
Smooth	Soul	750	'78	†
Back Street Boogie	Whitfield	3331	'79	|
Blow the House Down	Motown	6053	'83	†

JOE WALSH/THE JAMES GANG

Original lineup, 1967: **Jim Fox**, drms; **Tom Kriss**, bs; **Glen Schwartz**, gtr [Glen Schwartz left in 1969 and was replaced by **Joe Walsh** (b. Nov. 20, 1947, Wichita, KS); Tom Kriss left and was replaced by **Dale Peters**. Walsh left in 1971 and was replaced by guitarist **Dominic Troiano** and vocalist **Roy Kenner**. Troiano left in 1973 and was replaced by guitarist **Tommy Bolin** (b. 1951, Sioux City, IA; d. Dec. 4, 1976, Miami, FL). The group disbanded in 1974 and re-formed in 1975 with Fox, Peters, guitarist **Richard Shack**, and guitarist-vocalist **Bubba Keith**; it ended again in 1976.]

Acknowledged as one of the finest lead guitarists in rock, Joe Walsh manned the James Gang during their greatest hit-making period before forming his own band and scoring a major hit with "Rocky Mountain Way" from his best-selling 1973 album, *The Smoker You Drink, the Player You Get*. Walsh was a member of the Eagles from 1975 to 1982, and he continued to record solo albums during his tenure with the group and after the group's breakup. He rejoined the Eagles for their reunion album and tour in 1994.

Joe Walsh was raised in New Jersey, took up clarinet and oboe in junior high school, and later switched to rhythm guitar with the duo the G-Clefs. After playing bass for the Nomads during his senior year of high school, he enrolled at Kent State University in Ohio in fall 1965, later playing lead guitar for the Measles for three years. Recruited for the hard-rock Ohio-based group the James Gang in April 1969, Walsh sang and played lead guitar with the power trio through their most successful period. Authoring their hit "Walk Away" and coauthoring "Funk #49," Walsh recorded four albums with the group before leaving in November 1971. Walsh was replaced by Dominic Troiano, who in turn left in 1973 to join the Guess Who and was replaced by Tommy Bolin, but the group never again achieved their previous popularity.

After moving to Boulder, Colorado, Walsh formed Barnstorm with bassist Kenny Passarelli and drummer Joe Vitale. Their second album, *The Smoker You Drink, the Player You Get*, yielded a major hit with "Rocky Mountain Way" and remained on the album charts for more than a year. Walsh next recorded 1974's *So What* with the assistance of Eagles Glenn Frey, Don Henley, and Randy Meisner, retaining Henley and Frey for *You Can't Argue with a Sick Mind* from a year later, and the best-selling *But Seriously Folks*, released in 1978, which produced a major hit about his sardonic view of stardom, "Life's Been Good."

Meanwhile, at the end of 1975 Walsh joined the Eagles as Bernie Leadon's replacement, adding a much-needed instrumental punch to the group's mellow sound, as evidenced by 1977's "Life in the Fast Lane," which he cowrote. Walsh scored a major hit on his own with "All Night Long" from the soundtrack to the movie *Urban Cowboy*. His '80s solo outings were less successful, and by the early '90s he was touring with Ringo Starr's All-Starr Band as well as a reunited James Gang. Walsh rejoined the Eagles for their 1994 *Hell Freezes Over* album and tour.

The James Gang (with Joe Walsh)

Yer Album	Bluesway	6034	'69	†
	ABC	688	'71	†
	One Way	22052		CD
The James Gang Rides Again	ABC	711	'70	†
	MCA	1636		CS
	MCA	31145		CD
Thirds	ABC	721	'71	†
	One Way	22031		CD
Live in Concert	ABC	733	'71	†
	Mobile Fidelity	789		CD
Best	ABC	774	'73	†
	MCA	1637		CS
16 Greatest Hits	ABC	(2) 801	'74	†
	MCA	(2) 6012		CS
	MCA	6012		CD

Joe Walsh

Barnstorm	Dunhill	50130	'72	†
	MCA	37053		†
	Mobile Fidelity	777	'90	CD
The Smoker You Drink, the Player You Get	Dunhill	50140	'73	†
	MCA	37054		†
	MCA	1602		CS
	MCA	31121		CD
	MCA	11170	'94	CD
So What	Dunhill	50171	'74	†
	MCA	37055		†
	MCA	10761	'93	CD

You Can't Argue with a Sick Mind	ABC/MCA	932	'76	†
	MCA	37051		†
	MCA	1600		CS
	MCA	31120		CD
Best	ABC/MCA	1083	'78	†
	MCA	37052		†
	MCA	1601		CS/CD
Look What I Did: The Joe Walsh Anthology	MCA	(2) 11233	'95	CD
But Seriously Folks	Elektra/Asylum	141	'78/'91	CS/CD
There Goes the Neighborhood	Elektra/Asylum	523	'81/'91	CS/CD
You Bought It, You Name It	Warner Bros.	23884	'83	†
	Full Moon/Asylum	23884		CS
The Confessor	Warner Bros.	25281	'85	CS/CD
Got Any Gum	Warner Bros.	25606	'87	LP/CS/CD†
Ordinary Average Guy	Epic Associated/ Pyramid	47384	'91	CS/CD
Songs for a Dying Planet	Epic Associated	48916	'92	CS/CD

WAR

Howard Scott (b. Mar. 15, 1946, San Pedro, CA), gtr, perc; **Leroy "Lonnie" Jordan** (b. Nov. 21, 1948, San Diego, CA), kybd; **Charles Miller** (b. June 2, 1939, Olathe, KS; d. 1980, Los Angeles, CA), rds; **Morris "B. B." Dickerson** (b. Aug. 3, 1949, Torrance, CA), bs, perc; **Lee Oskar** (b. Oskar Hansen, Mar. 24, 1948, Copenhagen, Denmark), har; **Thomas Sylvester "Papa Dee" Allen** (b. July 18, 1931, Wilmington, DE), perc; **Harold Brown** (b. Mar. 17, 1946, Long Beach, CA), drm

WAR

An all-black Southern California band of 10 years experience with varying personnel, War took their name and stabilized their membership with the addition of Danish-born white harmonica player Lee Oskar under former Animals vocalist Eric Burdon. Scoring a pop smash with Burdon on "Spill the Wine," War left Burdon and initiated their own career in 1971 and became popular with white AM radio listeners while retaining an avid black following. Achieving crossover smashes with "The World Is a Ghetto," "The Cisco Kid," "Why Can't We Be Friends," and "Low Rider," War was alternately mellow and percussive in their sound, distinctly fusing elements of jazz and funk with harmonious singing on catchy, melodic tunes. Overwhelmed by the rise of disco in the late '70s, War served as an inspiration to rap acts of the '80s and '90s and returned to recording in 1994.

Ostensibly started as as group by Howard Scott, Charles Miller, and Harold Brown around 1959, the three were joined by B. B. Dickerson and Lonnie Jordan in the formation of the Creators during the early '60s. Enduring frequent personnel changes, the group persevered on the Southern California club circuit under a variety of names. Around 1966, Brown, Miller, and Scott got together with Jordan, Dickerson, and "Papa Dee" Allen as Night Shift. Introduced to former Animals vocalist Eric Burdon and his harmonica-playing friend Lee Oskar, Night Shift began working with the two as War.

Eric Burdon and War recorded two albums for MGM, and scored a smash pop hit with "Spill the Wine" in 1970. The band toured with, then without, Burdon, and signed with United Artists Records as an act in their own right. Their debut album was largely overlooked, but their second, *All Day Music*, yielded a moderate hit with the title song and a major pop and R&B hit with "Slippin' into Darkness." War was established with both black and white audiences with their late 1972 album, *The World Is a Ghetto*, which stayed on the album charts for more than a year. It yielded crossover smashes with the title song and "Cisco Kid." After *Deliver the Word*, which produced the crossover smash "Gypsy Man" and the major crossover hit "Me and Baby Brother," War became entangled in legal disputes with United Artists for two years, returning with the new studio album *Why Can't We Be Friends?* in 1975. The album produced R&B and pop smash hits with the title song and "Low Rider" and was soon followed by the crossover smash "Summer."

After *Platinum Jazz* on United Artists's Blue Note label, War switched to MCA Records, while Lee Oskar recorded several solo albums. However, the group never scored another major pop hit, as personnel changes began to affect the group. War managed major R&B hits with "Youngblood (Livin' in the Streets)" on United Artists and "Good, Good Feelin'" on MCA, eventually moving to RCA in the early '80s for the R&B hits "You Got the Power" and "Outlaw." The group continued to record into the late '80s, with Howard Scott and Lonnie Jordan as mainstays. In 1992 Avenue Records issued *Rap Declares War*, recorded by artists such as De La Soul, Ice-T, and the Beastie Boys in homage to the group's work. The following year, War re-formed with Jordan, Scott, Lee Oskar, and latter-day drummer Ronnie Hammon. Joined by Harold Brown, who had set up a recording studio in New Orleans, War recorded a new album for Avenue Records, who have reissued many of their earlier recordings.

Eric Burdon and War

Eric Burdon Declares "War"	MGM	4663	'70	†
	Avenue	71050	'92	CS/CD
(reissued as) Spill the Wine	Lax	37109	'81	†
Black Man's Burdon	MGM	(2) 4710	'70	†
	Rhino	(2) 71193	'93	CS/CD
Love Is All Around	ABC	966	'76	†
	Rhino	71218	'93	CS/CD
Best (recorded 1969–1971)	Avenue	71954	'95	CD

War

War	United Artists	5508	'71	†
	Avenue	71041	'92	CS/CD
All Day Music	United Artists	5546	'71	†
	Lax	37111	'81	†
	Avenue	71042	'92	CS/CD
The World Is a Ghetto	United Artists	5652	'72	†
	Lax	37112	'81	†
	Avenue	71043	'92	CS/CD

Deliver the Word	United Artists	128	'73	†
	Avenue	71044	'92	CS/CD
War Live	United Artists	(2) 193	'74	†
	Avenue	(2) 71052	'92	CS/CD
Why Can't We Be Friends?	United Artists	441	'75	†
	Lax	37113	'81	†
	Avenue	71051	'92	CS/CD
Greatest Hits	United Artists	648	'76	†
Youngblood (soundtrack)	United Artists	904	'78	†
Platinum Jazz	Blue Note	690	'77	†
	Rhino	71259	'93	CS/CD
Galaxy	MCA	3030	'77	†
	Avenue	71192	'93	CS/CD
The Music Band	MCA	3085	'79	†
The Music Band—2	MCA	3193	'79	†
The Music Band Live	MCA	5156	'80	†
Best of the Music Band	MCA	5362	'82	†
Music Band Jazz	MCA	5411	'83	†
Outlaw	RCA	4208	'82	†
	Avenue	71956	'95	CD
Life (Is So Strange)	RCA	4598	'83	†
Best of War . . . and More	Priority	9467	'87	†
	Avenue	70072	'91	CS/CD
War	Avenue	71706	'94	LP/CS/CD
Anthology (1970–1994)	Avenue	(2) 71774	'94	CS/CD

Lee Oskar

Lee Oskar	United Artists	594	'76	†
	Avenue	71719	'95	CD
Before the Rain	Elektra	150	'78	†
	Avenue	71721	'95	CD
My Road Our Road	Elektra	526	'81	†
	Avenue	71720	'95	CD

Lonnie Jordan

Different Moods of Me	MCA	2329	'78	†

Tribute Album

Rap Declares War	Avenue	71040	'92	CS/CD

DIONNE WARWICK

(b. Marie Dionne Warwick, Dec. 12, 1940, East Orange, NJ)

In perhaps the most successful hit-making partnership of the '60s, singer Dionne Warwick, lyricist Hal David, and producer-arranger-composer Burt Bacharach achieved more than 35 hits, including a number of smashes, between 1962 and 1971. Featuring Warwick's svelte, light, and perfectly phrased vocals, Bacharach's precise orchestral arrangements, and David's pop-style lyrics, their songs brought a new level of sophistication to soul music. However, by 1967 Bacharach and David's material had become geared to easy-listening and cabaret audiences, and Warwick's most consistent success occurred in the easy-listening arena. Warwick managed to retain her popularity despite label changes in 1971 and 1979 and the loss of the Bacharach-David team in 1972, scoring '70s and '80s hits and making a comeback with 1985's "That's What Friends Are For," the profits from which went to AIDS research.

Dionne Warwick was born into a family of gospel singers and began singing in church choirs and gospel groups at age six. She was a member of the Drinkard Singers and later the trio the Gospelaires with sister Dee Dee and aunt Cissy Houston (Whitney's mother). Warwick graduated from Hart Music College in Connecticut and began singing sessions in New York in the late '50s. During the sessions for the Drifters' "Mexican Divorce" in 1960, she met songwriter-producer-arranger Burt Bacharach, who helped secure her a recording contract with Scepter Records.

With Bacharach arranging and providing the music and collaborator Hal David supplying the lyrics, Dionne Warwick scored her first major pop and smash R&B hit with her first single, "Don't Make Me Over," at the end of 1962. Through 1966, with the compositions of Bacharach and David, she scored smash pop, R&B, and easy-listening hits with "Anyone Who Had a Heart," "Walk On By," and "Message to Michael," and major pop and R&B hits with "Reach Out for Me," "Trains and Boats and Planes," and "I Just Don't Know What to Do with Myself."

Fully established as an international recording star and cabaret performer, Dionne Warwick began recording less dynamic Bacharach-David songs as the duo started working on movie scores and stage musicals. Through 1968 she scored a smash pop and R&B hit with "I Say a Little Prayer," a pop and easy-listening smash with "(Theme from) The Valley of the Dolls," a major pop and R&B hit with "Alfie," a major pop and easy-listening hit with "Promises, Promises," and a three-way crossover hit with "Do You Know the Way to San Jose." The rest of her hits through 1972, save the pop and R&B smash "This Girl's In Love with You" and the pop smash "I'll Never Fall In Love Again," were in the easy-listening field.

By 1972 Dionne Warwick had switched to Warner Bros. Records, but after a single album with Burt Bacharach and Hal David, the duo and the singer parted company. She didn't achieve another major hit until 1974, when "Then Came You," recorded with the Spinners and produced by Thom Bell, became a top pop and smash R&B and easy-listening hit. Bell supervised her *Track of the Cat* album, which produced an R&B smash with "Once You Hit the Road." She next recorded *A Man and a Woman* with producer—keyboard player Isaac Hayes.

In 1979 Warwick switched to Arista Records, where her debut, simply *Dionne*, was produced by Barry Manilow. It yielded a smash pop hit with "I'll Never Love This Way Again" and a major pop hit with "Deja Vu" and became her best-selling album in 10 years. "No Night So Long" became a major pop and R&B hit in 1980. Bee Gee Barry Gibb produced her 1982 *Heartbreaker* album, which yielded a major pop and R&B hit with the title tune. Luther Vandross produced Warwick's *How Many Times Can We Say Goodbye*, and the title song, sung as a duet, became a smash R&B and major pop hit in 1983.

Dionne Warwick did not have another major hit for two more years. In late 1985 "That's What Friends Are For," written by Burt Bacharach and Carole Bayer Sager and recorded by Warwick and "friends" Elton John, Gladys Knight, and Stevie Wonder, became a top pop and R&B hit. At the request of Elizabeth Taylor, profits from the song were donated to the cause of AIDS research, eventually totalling more than $1.5 million. In 1980–1981 and again in 1985 and 1986, Dionne Warwick hosted the syndicated variety series *Solid Gold*. She managed her last major pop and R&B hit with "Love Power," in duet with Jeffrey Osborne, in 1987. Warwick became notorious for hosting a series of infomercials for the Psychic Friends Network in the late '80s. She continued to record for Artista into the '90s, recording *Celebration in Vienna* with opera singer Placido Domingo for Sony Classical in 1994.

Dionne Warwick

Presenting Dionne Warwick	Scepter	508	†

Title	Label	Number	Year	Format
Anyone Who Had a Heart	Scepter	517		†
Make Way for Dionne Warwick	Scepter	523	'64	†
The Sensitive Sound of Dionne Warwick	Scepter	528	'65	†
Here I Am	Scepter	531	'65	†
In Paris	Scepter	534	'66	†
Here, Where There Is Love	Scepter	555	'66	†
On Stage and At the Movies	Scepter	559	'67	†
The Windows of the World	Scepter	563	'67	†
Golden Hits, Volume 1	Scepter	565	'67	†
Magic of Believing	Scepter	567		†
Valley of the Dolls	Scepter	568	'68	†
Promises, Pomises	Scepter	571	'68	†
Soulful	Scepter	573	'69	†
Greatest Motion Picture Hits	Scepter	575	'69	†
Golden Hits, Volume 2	Scepter	577	'69	†
I'll Never Fall In Love Again	Scepter	581	'70	†
Very Dionne	Scepter	587	'70	†
The Dionne Warwick Story—A Decade of Gold	Scepter	(2) 596	'71	†
From Within	Scepter	598	'72	†
Anthology, 1962–1971	Rhino	(2) 1100	'84/'89	†
Anthology	Rhino	75898	'86	CD†
Dionne	Warner Bros.	2585	'71	†
Just Being Myself	Warner Bros.	2658	'73	†
Then Came You	Warner Bros.	2846	'75	†
Track of the Cat	Warner Bros.	2893	'75	†
Love at First Sight	Warner Bros.	3119	'77	†
Dionne	Arista	4230	'79	†
	Arista	9512		†
No Night So Long	Arista	9526	'80	†
Hot! Live and Otherwise	Arista	(2) 8605	'81	†
	Arista	(2) 8111		CS/CD†
Friends to Love	Arista	9585	'82	†
Heartbreaker	Arista	9609	'82	†
How Many Times Can We Say Goodbye	Arista	8104	'83	†
Finder of Lost Loves	Arista	8262	'84'85	†
Dionne Warwick and Friends	Arista	8398	'85	CS/CD
Reservations for Two	Arista	8446	'87	†
Greatest Hits, 1979–1990	Arista	8540	'89	CS/CD
Sings Cole Porter	Arista	8573	'90	LP/CS/CD
Friends Can Be Lovers	Arista	18682	'93	CS/CD
Aquarela Do Brasil	Arista	18777	'94	CS/CD

Anthologies

Title	Label	Number	Year	Format
Golden Voice	Springboard Int'l	4001	'73	†
Sings Her Very Best	Springboard Int'l	4002	'73	†
One Hit After Another	Springboard Int'l	4003	'73	†
Greatest Hits, Volume 2	Springboard Int'l	4032	'75	†
Dionne Warwick	Pickwick	(2) 2056	'73	†
Make It Easy on Yourself	Pickwick	3338		†
Very Best	United Artists	337	'75	†
	United Artists	388	'75	†

Only Love Can Break a Heart	Musicor	2501	'77	†
The Dynamic Dionne Warwick (Greatest Hits)	Pair	(2) 1043	'86	†
Masterpieces	Pair	(2) 1098	'86	†
At Her Very Best	Pair	1243		CS/CD
Collection	Rhino	71100	'89	CS/CD
Hidden Gems: The Best of Dionne Warwick, Volume 2	Rhino	70329	'92	CS/CD
From the Vaults	Soul Classics	2104	'95	CS/CD
Her Greatest Hits	Special Music	4929		CS/CD
Her Greatest Hits, Volume 2	Special Music	4930		CS

Dionne Warwick and Isaac Hayes

A Man and a Woman	ABC	(2) 996	'77	†
	MCA	(2) 10012	'83	†

Dionne Warwick and Placido Domingo

Celebration in Vienna	Sony Classical	64304	'94	CS/CD

MUDDY WATERS

(b. McKinley Morganfield, Apr. 4, 1915, Rolling Fork, MS; d. Apr. 30, 1983, Westmont, IL)

One of the few black blues artists to gain widespread recognition and admiration from white audiences, Muddy Waters was instrumental in establishing the sound and style of Chicago blues that influenced a whole generation of black blues musicians in the late-'40s and '50s and the white blues revival of the late '60s. His first release on Chess Records, "Rollin' Stone," was later adopted as the name of both the heavily R&B-influenced English group and the underground rock music–oriented publication. During the '50s and '60s virtually every practitioner of the Chicago style of blues populated his band at one time or another, including Otis Spann, Buddy Guy, Little Walter Jacobs, and James Cotton, making it a proving ground for younger blues musicians. Along with Willie Dixon, Muddy Waters was one of the premier composers of classic and enduring blues songs, including "I Got My Mojo Working" and "Baby Please Don't Go." Waters was overwhelmed by the rise of rock and roll in the late '50s. Nonetheless, he became one of the few black blues artists to bene-fit from both the folk boom of the early '60s and the British and American blues revival of the late '60s. Subjected to unsympathetic musical treatment with Chess Records during the '70s, Waters finally found a compatible setting in the late '70s with Blue Sky Records and producer Johnny Winter. Muddy Waters died on April 30, 1983, in a Chicago suburb, leaving a potent legacy for blues musicians that served to inspire another blues revival in the '80s.

At an early age, Muddy Waters moved to Clarksdale, Mississippi, where he grew up on the Stovall plantation. He started playing harmonica at age 7 and switched to guitar at 17. Strongly influenced by blues guitarists Son House and Robert Johnson, Waters developed a distinctive style of acoustic-guitar playing, using a bottleneck that produced a remarkable biting, stinging sound. Becoming one of the area's best-known and most popular blues per-formers through engagements at picnics, dances, and small clubs, he was sought out by folklorist Alan Lomax, who first recorded Waters during the summers of 1941 and 1942. These classic recordings stand as a monument to the artistry of Muddy Waters and alone represent a major accomplishment in a career that lasted 40 years.

In May 1943 Muddy Waters permanently left Mississippi for Chicago, where he played in local clubs and obtained his first electric guitar in 1945. Around 1946 he made his first commercial recordings for Columbia Records, but they were not released until years later. Signing with Aristocrat Records (which became Chess Records in 1949), Waters recorded the blues classics "(I Feel Like) Going Home" and "I Can't Be Satisfied" in early 1948, and the record became Aristocrat's biggest seller. He began playing larger clubs and scored a local hit with "Rollin' Stone," his first release on Chess.

Around 1950 Muddy Waters began recording with harmonica players Little Walter Jacobs and Walter Horton. Waters soon scored the national R&B hits "Louisiana Blues" with Jacobs and "Long Distance Call" with Horton in 1951. Forming his own band with Jacobs and second guitarist Jimmy Rogers, Waters hit with "Honey Bee," "Still a Fool," and "She Moves Me." Augmented by pianist Otis Spann, this legendary blues band, the prototype of all subsequent Chicago blues bands, defined the style of modern electric blues. Jacobs left the band in 1952 and later recordings featured Horton or Jacobs sitting in. Smash R&B hits for Waters through 1956 include "Mad Love," the Willie Dixon–composed classics "I'm Your Hoochie Coochie Man," "I Just Want to Make Love to You," and "I'm Ready," "Manish Boy" (a reworking of Bo Diddley's "I'm a Man"), "Trouble No More," "Forty Days and Forty Nights," and "Don't Go No Further." Jimmy Rogers left the band around 1956, but Otis Spann stayed on until his death in 1968.

In 1955 Muddy Waters brought Chuck Berry to Chess Records, where he was quickly signed. However, by 1956 Waters was being overwhelmed by the rise of rock and roll as practiced by Berry, Bill Haley, Elvis Presley, and others. Waters's last rhythm-and-blues hit came in 1958 with "Close to You," recorded with harmonica player James Cotton, bassist Willie Dixon, and Otis Spann. Muddy Waters's first album, issued as *The Best of Muddy Waters* in 1958, contained most of his best-remembered recordings made between 1948 and 1954. However, the album failed to sell in significant quantities, as rock and roll became *the* music of young blacks and whites.

Nonetheless, Muddy Waters was able to maintain some of his popularity in conjunction with the folk movement of the late '50s and early '60s. He appeared at the 1960 Newport Folk Festival, and played acoustic guitar on *Folk Singer*, which included "Feel Like Going Home" and the Sonny Boy Williamson classic "Good Morning, Little School Girl." An early '60s tour of England featured Waters on acoustic guitar, much to the chagrin of his British fans who expected to hear the electric blues band of his earlier recordings. Despite the eclipse in his popularity on the American charts, Muddy Waters was receiving the praise of a number of British and American artists strongly influenced by his work, including Mike Bloomfield, Eric Clapton, and Mick Jagger. Their praise brought renewed opportunities to record and tour, and Waters began gaining a rock audience. He also recorded with younger blues and rock musicians, most notably on *Fathers and Sons*, featuring Waters and Otis Spann with white blues musicians such as Bloomfield and Paul Butterfield, and on *London Muddy Waters Sessions*. Other late-'60s/early-'70s Chess recordings featured less interesting rock-styled accompaniments.

Finally, in 1976 Muddy Waters moved to Blue Sky Records. Since the label's roster included white blues artists Johnny and Edgar Winter, Waters again received sympathetic treatment from his record label, with Johnny Winter producing his work. Waters recorded *Hard Again* with Winter and James Cotton, while *I'm Ready* featured Winter and old associates Walter Horton and Jimmy Rogers. Waters again toured the country in 1978, concluding the year as opening act to Eric Clapton in Europe. *Live* compiled recordings made during the 1977 and 1978 tours. Waters's final Blue Sky album was issued in 1981. On April 30, 1983, Muddy Waters died in the Chicago suburb of Westmont of a heart attack at age 68. His popularity remained undiminished, as Chess reissued many of his recordings beginning in 1987, the year he was inducted into the Rock and Roll Hall of Fame. The mammoth *Chess Box* was issued in 1989, followed by 1994's *One More Mile*.

Muddy Waters

Down at Stovall's Plantation (recorded 1941–1942)	Testament	2210	'69	†

The Complete Plantation Recordings/The Historic 1941–1942 Library of Congress Field Recordings	Chess	9344	'93	CS/CD
Chicago Blues: In the Beginning	Testament	2207		†
More Real Folk Blues (recorded 1948–1952)	Chess	1511	'67	†
	Chess	9278	'88	CS/CD
Best (recorded 1948–1954)	Chess	1427	'58	†
	Chess	9255	'87	CS
	Chess	31268	'87	CD
(reissued as) Sail On	Chess	1539	'69	†
Trouble No More: Singles (1955–1959)	Chess	9291	'89	LP/CS/CD
Sings Big Bill Broonzy (recorded 1959–1960)	Chess	1444		†
	Chess	9197	'87	CS
At Newport, 1960	Chess	1449	'61	†
	Chess	9198	'87	LP/CS
	Chess	31269	'87	CD
Folk Singer	Chess	1483	'64	†
	Chess	9261	'87	LP/CS
	Mobile Fidelity	593	'93	CD
	Mobile Fidelity	201	'94	LP
Folk Singer/Sings Big Big Bill Broonzy	Chess	5907		CD
The Real Folk Blues (recorded 1949–1964)	Chess	1501	'66	†
	Chess	9274	'88	LP/CS/CD
Muddy, Brass and the Blues	Chess	1507	'66	†
	Chess	9286	'89	CS/CD
They Call Me Muddy Waters	Chess	1553	'71	†
	Chess	9299		CS/CD
AKA McKinley Morganfield	Chess	(2) 60006	'71	†
Live at Mr. Kelly's	Chess	50012	'71	†
	Chess	9338	'92	CS/CD
London Muddy Waters Sessions	Chess	60013	'72	†
	Chess	9298	'89	CS/CD
Can't Get No Grindin'	Chess	50023	'73	†
	Chess	9319	'90	LP/CS/CD
"Unk" In Funk	Chess	60031	'74	†
	Chess	91513		CS/CD
At Woodstock	Chess	60035	'75	†
Muddy Waters	Chess	(2) 203	'77	†
Rolling Stone	Chess	9101		CS/CD
Rare and Unissued	Chess	9180		LP/CS/CD
The Chess Box	Chess	(6) 80002	'89	CS
	Chess	(3) 80002	'89	CD
One More Mile: Chess Collectibles, Volume One (recorded 1948–1972)	Chess	(2) 9348	'94	CS/CD
Muddy Waters, Bo Diddley, and Little Walter				
Super Blues	Checker	3008	'67	†
	Chess	9168		CS/CD
Muddy Waters, Howlin' Wolf, and Bo Diddley				
The Super Super Blues Band	Checker	3010	'68	†
	Chess	9169		CS

Muddy Waters, Otis Spann, Mike Bloomfield, Paul Butterfield

Fathers and Sons	Chess	(2) 127	'69	†
	Chess	(2) 50033		†
	Chess	(2) 92522	'89	LP/CS
	Chess	92522	'89	CD

Muddy Waters and Otis Spann

Collaboration	Tomato	71661	'95	CD

Muddy Waters and Howlin' Wolf

London Revisited	Chess	60026	'74	†

Muddy Waters and Memphis Slim

Chicago Blues Master, Volume 1	Capitol	29375	'95	CD

Muddy Waters

Electric Mud	Cadet	314	'68	†
After the Rain	Cadet	320	'69	†
Goin' Home Live in Paris, 1970	New Rose	5099	'93	CD
Mud in Your Ear	Muse	5008	'73	LP/CS
	Muse	6004		CD
Live in Switzerland, 1976	Landscape	908	'91	CD†
Muddy Waters Chicago Blues Band:	Landscape	921	'93	CD
Live in Switzerland 1976, Volume 2				
Unreleased in the West (live 1976)	Moon/FTC	8507	'92	CD
	Moon	007		CD
Unreleased in the West, Volume 2	Moon/FTC	8517	'92	CD
	Moon	017		CD
Hard Again	Blue Sky	34449	'77	CS/CD
I'm Ready	Blue Sky	34928	'78	CS/CD
Muddy "Mississippi" Waters Live	Blue Sky	35712	'79	CS/CD
King Bee	Blue Sky	37064	'81	CS/CD
Blue Skys	Epic Associated/	46172	'92	CS/CD
	Legacy			
Muddy Waters	Bella Musica	89930	'90	CD†
Mean Mistreater	CSI	75112	'92	CD
Baby Please Don't Go	Vogue	670410		CD|
Sweet Home Chicago	Intermedia	5071		LP/CS
The Warsaw Sessions	Kicking Mule	79		LP
The Warsaw Sessions, Volume 2	Kicking Mule	80		LP

Paul Rodgers and Others

A Tribute to Muddy Waters	Victory	480013	'93	CS/CD

JANN WENNER/ROLLING STONE MAGAZINE

(b. 1946, New York, NY)

With *Rolling Stone* magazine, editor and mastermind Jann Wenner created a viable alternative to trade and fan magazines in the coverage of contemporary popular music in the late '60s. *Rolling Stone* employed some of the finest music writers in the business, notably Jon Landau, probably the first rock critic to gain a legitimate reputation, as well as more idiosyncratic social commentators, including "Doctor" Hunter S. Thompson, the creator of the so-called gonzo style of journalism, most notably with his highly-acclaimed two-part article "Fear and Loathing in Las Vegas" and his astute coverage of the 1972 presidential campaign. By the mid-'70s *Rolling Stone* began emphasizing investigative reporting and coverage of popular culture to the detriment of rock music coverage, while expanding its circulation and obtaining advertising from cigarette, liquor, and automobile manufacturers. Wenner abandoned San Francisco for New York in 1977 and began ingratiating himself to movie stars and celebrities in his magazine articles. Broadening the magazine's popularity with writers such as Dave Marsh, Tom Wolfe, and Joe Eszterhaus, and photographers Annie Leibovitz and Richard Avedon, *Rolling Stone* again started emphasizing music coverage in the mid-'80s. Launching an expensive two-year advertising campaign to entice upscale readership in 1985, *Rolling Stone* lost its already faltering position as a cutting-edge music publication with the rise of *Spin* magazine in the '90s.

Jann Wenner was raised in suburban Marin County, north of San Francisco. He attended the University of California at Berkeley during the free speech movement, which he covered for the campus publication the *Daily California*. He met *San Francisco Chronicle* music critic Ralph J. Gleason in 1965 and dropped out of college in 1966 to work as a freelance writer and arts editor for the local radical magazine *Sunday Ramparts*. In 1967 Wenner and Gleason formulated a plan to publish a professional, journalistic periodical that would serve as an alternative to music trade magazines, fan magazines, and underground journals in its coverage of contemporary popular music and the youth culture.

By borrowing $7,500 from friends and relatives, persuading a printer to provide credit and free office space, and employing a part-time volunteer staff, Jann Wenner published the first issue of *Rolling Stone* with a cover date of November 9, 1967. Although most of the issue's press run was returned, the publication was remarkably professional. However, Wenner's mercurial management style soon led to the departure of early staff members and the recruitment of Jon Landau. Eschewing psychedelic art and obtaining newsstand distribution (rather than having it sold on the streets by vendors), *Rolling Stone* was a financial success by 1969. Increased revenues allowed Wenner to expand and professionalize his staff. Supported by record-company advertising since its eighth issue, *Rolling Stone* moved to a new, expensive location in 1970, opened offices in Los Angeles and New York, and unsuccessfully attempted to launch a British edition in conjunction with Mick Jagger.

From the start, *Rolling Stone* sought to treat rock music seriously. One of the first, and most popular, repeated features was the so-called Rolling Stone Interview, modeled in length and scope on the famous *Playboy* interviews. Pete Townshend was among the first to give a lengthy interview in 1968, establishing him as an important spokesperson for the new rock music. John Lennon spoke extensively with Jann Wenner in 1970, shortly after the breakup of the Beatles, setting the standard for the candor and range of these pieces. Other noteworthy rock artists were soon demanding equal treatment, and the interviews have been collected in published form in several volumes.

As *Rolling Stone* expanded rapidly, Jann Wenner spent money extravagantly and failed at establishing two new magazines, *New York Scenes* and the environmentally minded *Earth Times*. On the verge of financial collapse, the magazine was ostensibly bailed out by record companies. A 1970 cover article on American politics, published in Wenner's absence, led to the dismissal of many staff members—including managing editor John Burks, who was largely responsible for the magazine's success—and the end of political coverage. Nonetheless, award-winning articles on the Altamont concert disaster and the Charles Manson family brought *Rolling Stone* respectability with the straight press, and the publication's heretofore chaotic front-office operation was stabilized under self-made millionaire-investor Max Palevsky.

With *Rolling Stone* at perhaps the height of its fame in 1970, Jann Wenner employed writer Hunter S. Thompson, a cult figure largely on the basis of his book, *The Hell's Angels*.

Practicing a writing style that became known as gonzo journalism, a careful and precise yet rambling stream-of-consciousness style complete with accounts of fortifying drug use, Thompson soon made an impact with the critically acclaimed two-part article "Fear and Loathing in Las Vegas." He subsequently produced perhaps the most discerning coverage of the 1972 presidential campaign, which encouraged Wenner to expand the magazine's political coverage and hire first-rate reporters such as Joe Klein and Richard Goodwin while extending the provinces of cultural critic Jonathon Cott and investigative reporter Joe Eszterhaus. In 1975 *Rolling Stone* eliminated nudity and four-letter words from its editorial content and actively sought mainstream advertisers of cigarettes, cameras, liquor, and automobiles.

The decline of Hunter Thompson's writing and the death of Ralph Gleason in June 1975 marked a difficult period for *Rolling Stone*. Celebrities such as Truman Capote, Andy Warhol, and John Dean were hired to write articles. Jon Landau departed and the quality of the magazine's music coverage began to suffer, as the magazine presented long, in-depth articles primarily concerned with established artists. Although *Rolling Stone* gained notoriety for its investigative reporting, as evidenced by articles on Karen Silkwood and Patty Hearst, the magazine was scooped by the straight press on reports of music industry "drugola" and endured a declining reputation for its music coverage.

In September 1976 Jann Wenner announced that he was moving *Rolling Stone* to New York City, where he sought to shake the magazine's counterculture image and establish a new legitimacy as a general interest magazine with cover stories on personalities such as Jane Fonda, Johnny Carson, and Robert Redford. In 1977 Wenner bought *Outside* magazine, selling it in 1979 during a difficult financial period. In 1981 he expanded *Rolling Stone*'s coverage of motion pictures and signed a film deal with Paramount Pictures that produced the facile and self-aggrandizing *Perfect* in 1985. In late 1981 Wenner launched the magazine *Record* to exclusively cover contemporary rock music, but the venture ended in 1986.

Rolling Stone adopted a slick-paper format in 1983, and the magazine began again emphasizing music coverage in 1984. In 1985 Wenner and his wife bought up the outstanding shares of Straight Arrow Press, the parent company of *Rolling Stone*, thus securing total control of the magazine. That year Wenner also bought 50 percent interest in *Us* magazine and launched an offensive two-year advertising campaign to divorce *Rolling Stone* from its hippie origins. By the '90s *Rolling Stone* had been superceded by *Spin* magazine as the most daring and adventurous periodical covering contemporary popular music. In 1992 Jann Wenner launched the outdoor magazine *Men's Journal*, inaugurating the family magazine *Family Life* in 1993.

THE WHO

Pete Townshend (b. May 19, 1945, Chiswick, London, England), lead and rhythm gtr, voc; **Roger Daltrey** (b. Mar. 1, 1944, Hammersmith, London, England), lead voc; **John Entwistle** (b. Oct. 9, 1944, Chiswick, England), bs, French horn, voc; **Keith Moon** (b. Aug. 23, 1947, Wembley, London, England; d. Sept. 7, 1978, London, England), drm [Keith Moon was replaced by **Kenney Jones** (b. Sept. 16, 1948, Stepney, East London, England) in 1979.]

Hugely popular in their native England by 1966 largely on the basis of their wildly exciting and visually arresting live performances, the Who, like the Beatles and perhaps the Rolling Stones, were comprised of distinct and immediately recognizable personalities. Pete Townshend, primary composer and one of rock music's all-time great guitarists and showmen, provided the group's powerful guitar riffs and performed feats such as rapid windmill guitar strokes, acrobatic leaps, and knee drops on stage, often ending shows in the early days by smashing his guitar. Keith Moon, one of rock music's most flamboyant and maniacally

THE WHO'S PETE TOWNSHEND

colorful figures, played drums with incredible energy and melodic style, influencing an entire generation of rock drummers. Roger Daltrey, one of rock music's most distinctive voices, melodic even at high volumes, added his own touches by madly twirling his microphone and vigorously prancing on stage. John Entwistle played his bass with a rapid virtuoso technique largely overlooked by critics, performing unmoved and stock-still, as the group's apparent center of gravity. Influential to the mod, heavy-metal, and punk movements, one of the first groups to develop large-scale concept albums, and one of the greatest performing bands of all time, the Who are perhaps the most underappreciated of all of the first-generation British Invasion groups.

Around 1959 Pete Townshend and classically trained John Entwistle were members of a Dixieland jazz group, with Townshend on banjo and Entwistle on trumpet. By the early '60s the two had formed the Detours with Roger Daltrey and drummer Doug Sanden. Daltrey functioned as the leader, lead guitarist, and lead singer with the group, but eventually assumed the sole role of lead vocalist. Under manager Peter Meaden, the group adopted a colorful mod image, became the High Numbers, and issued their first single, "I'm the Face," in mid-1964. By October 1964 they had replaced their original drummer with Keith Moon from the surf band the Beachcombers. The group became the Who under new managers Kit Lambert and Chris Stamp, who encouraged Townshend to develop his writing. The two urged the group to display open aggression on stage, and cultivated the group's mod image with flashy clothes, including Townshend's renowned Union Jack jacket. In 1965, during a performance at the Railway Tavern, Pete Townshend inadvertently broke the neck of his guitar on a low ceiling. This led to the first instance of Townshend and Keith Moon's onstage destruction of their equipment, an expensive practice the group reenacted at virtually every performance for the next four years.

Signed to American Decca (Brunswick and later Reaction and Track in Great Britain) on the recommendation of producer Shel Talmy, the Who scored four consecutive smash hits in Britain through spring 1966, with Talmy as producer: "I Can't Explain," the archetypal heavy-metal song "Anyway, Anyhow, Anywhere," the classic pre-punk anthem "My Generation," and "Substitute." "I Can't Explain" and "My Generation" became minor American hits. The Who's debut album contained "My Generation," "The Kids Are Alright," and the satiric "A Legal Matter," all by Townshend, plus the manic instrumental "The Ox," but it failed to sell in the United States. Their second album, *Happy Jack*, yielded their first American hit with the title song, and included Entwistle's "Boris the Spider" and "Whiskey Man" as well as Townshend's first attempt at a multiple-theme extended piece, "A Quick One While He's Away."

Launched in America with their frenetic performance at the Monterey Pop Festival in June 1967 (later chronicled in the D. A. Pennebaker film) and subsequent late-summer tour in support of Herman's Hermits, the Who issued one of the earliest concept albums, *The Who Sell Out*, at year's end. Featuring an album cover satirizing print advertisements and mock radio-station commercials between songs, the album contained the near-smash hit "I Can See for Miles," "Armenia City in the Sky," and the gentle "Rael." The Who quickly became a major concert attraction in the United States, and next released the anthology set *Magic Bus*, which included Townshend's "Call Me Lightning," the title cut (a major American hit), "Pictures of Lily," and a remake of the surf song "Bucket T.," featuring Entwistle's humorous French horn solo.

The Who's next album was the highly influential rock opera *Tommy*. Although not the first work of its kind, the album proved hugely successful, remaining on the album charts for more than two years and yielding a major hit with "Pinball Wizard." An odd and elaborate tale of lost innocence, redemption, and contrition, *Tommy* featured a number of instrumental interludes and Sonny Boy Williamson's "Eyesight to the Blind," as well as the psychedelic "Acid Queen," the inspiring "Sensation," the liberating "I'm Free," and Tommy's final rejection and plea for acceptance, "We're Not Gonna Take It/See Me, Feel Me." Performed in its entirety only twice—once in London and once in New York—*Tommy* drew the attention and praise of serious drama, opera, and classical-music critics, as well as fans and rock critics. Ultimately, despite its flaws, *Tommy* may be judged as one of the most fully realized and important musical productions of the 20th century.

Tommy was performed in excerpted form by the Who for nearly two years and inspired both an all-star London stage production and an excessive and frankly unfortunate film. The stage production, released on album in late 1972, featured the London Symphony Orchestra and Chamber Choir and performances by Rod Stewart, Merry Clayton, Stevie Winwood, Sandy Denny, Richie Havens, Ringo Starr, and the Who. Director, screenwriter, and coproducer Ken Russell's 1975 film version, an extravagant and bizarre production replete with repulsive, inane, and tedious scenes, featured Roger Daltrey as Tommy and performances by Eric Clapton, Tina Turner, Elton John, and the members of the Who. It also contained the decidedly shallow acting and poor musical performances of Ann-Margaret, Oliver Reed, and Jack Nicholson.

Seriously challenging the Rolling Stones' claim to being the world's greatest rock-and-roll band, particularly after their celebrated appearance at the Woodstock Festival (and subsequent film), the Who next released *Live at Leeds*, one of the most exciting live albums ever recorded. The album produced a major hit with Eddie Cochran's "Summertime Blues" and contained extended versions of both "My Generation" and "Magic Bus."

Who's Next, their first studio album in two years, was another milestone in the history of rock, showcasing Townshend's outstanding and innovative use of synthesizers. The album included several finely crafted and brilliantly performed extended pieces such as "Baba O'Riley," "Song Is Over," and the disillusioned "Won't Get Fooled Again" (a major hit), as well as the menacing "Behind Blue Eyes" (a moderate hit) and Entwistle's "My Wife." The Who soon issued the anthology set *Meaty, Beaty, Big and Bouncy*, which Townshend reviewed in *Rolling Stone*. The album successfully collected the singles of the Who through "Pinball Wizard" and "The Magic Bus," and included Townshend's overlooked "The Seeker." In summer 1972 the Who scored a major hit with "Join Together."

The Who's next album of new material was the double-record set *Quadrophenia*. Although greeted by equivocal reviews, the album was perhaps even more ambitious and personal than *Tommy* and every bit its equal in musical and dramatic terms. Concerned with the early history of the Who and the mod movement through its protagonist, Jimmy, *Quadrophenia*'s title referred to Jimmy's double schizophrenia, the four members of the Who as representatives of the four sides of his personality, and the four recurrent musical themes of the album. Oddly criticized for its lack of unity, the album was heavily orchestrated and lavishly produced. It included "I'm the One," "5:15," "Is It In My Head," and "Drowned," plus the minor hits "Love, Reign O'er Me" and "The Real Me." For the first time in two years, the Who toured in support of the album.

In the meantime, the members of the Who pursued individual projects. John Entwistle recorded three solo albums through 1973, and Pete Townshend, a convert to the philosophy of Meher Baba, recorded his solo debut for devotees of the guru, *Who Came First*. It proved so popular that it was issued as a regular commercial release in 1972. With Townshend handling virtually every musical instrument and engineering chore, the album included "Pure and Easy," "Nothing Is Everything (Let's See Action)," and an adaptation of Meher Baba's Universal Prayer, "Parvardigar." Roger Daltrey's debut solo album proved the most successful of the group members' releases. Produced by David Courtney and former pop star Adam Faith, *Daltrey* featured the collaborative compositions of Courtney, Faith, and Leo Sayer. The album yielded a minor hit with "Giving It All Away" and contained outstanding existential songs such as "The Way of the World," "You Are Yourself," and "Hard Life," plus "One Man Band."

During 1974 John Entwistle assembled a remarkable collection of mostly unreleased Who material as *Odds and Sods*. An excellent summation of the career of the Who, the album included their first single release, "I'm the Face," a dynamic and superior version of "Pure and Easy," the menacing and moving "Naked Eye," and the neglected rock anthem "Long Live Rock." During this time, Keith Moon intitiated an acting career with appearances in Frank Zappa's *200 Motels* (1971) as well as the David Essex films *That'll Be the Day* (1973) and *Stardust* (1974). John Entwistle toured and recorded with the band Ox in 1975, while Keith Moon issued his first solo album and Daltrey his second. Daltrey's *Ride a Rock Horse* included "Oceans Away" and yielded a minor hit with Russ Ballard's "Come and Get Your Love."

The Who's next album, *The Who By Numbers*, was recorded during a relatively inactive period that lasted until 1977. It was perhaps the group's weakest effort to date, although it produced a major hit with "Squeeze Box." The Who conducted a major American tour in 1975–1976, but Townshend, suffering a permanent hearing loss from prolonged exposure to loud noise and desirous of spending more time with his family, withdrew from the public eye soon after. Daltrey appeared in Ken Russell's equivocal *Lisztomania* movie as composer Franz Liszt in 1975, and Moon moved to Los Angeles in 1976. Daltrey recorded his third solo album in 1977, and Townshend reemerged triumphantly with *Rough Mix*, recorded with Ronnie Lane of the Faces.

In 1978 the Who returned with their first album in nearly three years, *Who Are You*. It contained "Had Enough," "Sister Disco," and "Music Must Change," and produced a major hit with the title song. However, on September 7, 1978, Keith Moon was found dead in his London flat at age 31, the victim of a drug overdose. By the beginning of 1979, former Small Faces drummer Kenney Jones had replaced Moon. The group toured in summer 1979, augmented by keyboardist John "Rabbit" Bundrick, a former member of Free. During the year, the Who released two feature-length films and double-record soundtrack albums, the excellent documentary *The Kids Are Alright* and the fictional *Quadrophenia*, based on their 1973 album. *The Kids Are Alright* included the first official release of footage from the legendary 1968 television special *The Rolling Stones Rock and Roll Circus*, and the soundtrack yielded a minor hit with "Long Live Rock." Perhaps due to American audiences unfamiliarity with the mod movement, *Quadrophenia* failed at the box office. The soundtrack album featured remixes from the original album, three new songs, and an entire side of oldies, including James Brown's "Night Train" and the Ronettes' "Be My Baby."

The Who toured America again in late 1979, but at a performance at Cincinnati's Riverfront Stadium on December 3, 11 people were killed in the crush of fans outside the stadium, marring what was otherwise a successful series of concerts. By 1980 the Who had switched to Warner Bros. for their American releases, and Townshend had recorded *Empty Glass*, with its near-smash hit "Let My Love Open the Door," as his debut for his new label, Atco. Roger Daltrey starred in the title role of the film *McVicar*, based on the life of bank robber John McVicar, widely known in Great Britain for his repeated escapes from prison. The soundtrack album, credited to Daltrey and Russ Ballard, featured all the members of the Who and produced a major hit with "Without Your Love." In 1981 the Who toured again and released *Face Dances*, which yielded a major hit with "You Better You Bet."

In 1982 the Who conducted their farewell tour of stadiums, with the Clash as their opening act. The tour produced the live set *Who's Last*. During the year, Atco issued Townshend's *All the Best Cowboys Have Chinese Eyes*, and Townshend joined the prestigious publishing firm Faber and Faber as an editor the following year. Townshend's *Scoop* compiled his demo recordings, as would *Another Scoop* in 1987. In 1983 Roger Daltrey appeared in the BBC production of *The Beggar's Opera* as McHeath, and the following year he costarred in the BBC–Time-Life production of Shakespeare's *Comedy of Errors*. He switched to Atlantic for *Parting Should Be Painless*, followed in 1985 by *Under the Raging Moon*. During 1985, Pete Townshend published his first book, *Horse's Neck*, and recorded the brilliant *White City—A Novel* with Pink Floyd guitarist David Gilmour, among others. The album yielded a major hit with "Face the Face."

The Who reunited for the Live Aid concert in 1985, but immediately after went their separate ways. Townshend toured England with Deep End, which included David Gilmour, and the tour produced both a concert video and an album, released in 1986. John Entwistle toured on his own in 1988, while Townshend composed and recorded songs for the musical *The Iron Man*, based on a story by Ted Hughes. The album included the Who's "Dig" and "Fire" and John Lee Hooker's "Over the Top" and "I Eat Heavy Metal."

Townshend, Daltrey, and Entwistle reunited for a 25th anniversary Who stadium tour in 1989, sponsored by Budweiser and Miller Lite beers. For the tour, the three were augmented by guitarist Steve Bolton, keyboardist John "Rabbit" Bundrick, drummer Simon Phillips, a five-piece horn section, and three backup vocalists. The tour included two full performances of *Tommy*, one in New York and one in Los Angeles. The Los Angeles show, the highlight of the tour, was offered as a pay-per-view cable televison show and featured guest performances by Stevie Winwood, Elton John, Billy Idol, Phil Collins, and Patti Labelle. However, the tour was viewed cynically by critics. In 1990 the group was inducted into the Rock and Roll Hall of Fame.

In November 1991 Pete Townshend began working with Des McAnuff, the artistic director of the La Jolla (California) Playhouse, to transform *Tommy* into a stage musical. The setting was changed, connecting dialogue was added, and Townshend composed one new song, "I Believe My Own Eyes." The show opened at the La Jolla Playhouse in July 1992, debuted on Broadway in May 1993, and won five Tony Awards the next month. The show went on national tour in October.

In the meantime, Roger Daltrey starred in the 1990 film *Mack the Knife*, with Raul Julia, and recorded *Rocks in the Head* for 1992 release. In 1994 he conducted a Daltrey Sings Townshend tour with 32-piece orchestra. Pete Townshend composed and recorded the ambitious rock opera *PsychoDerelict* and toured the show with three actors and an eight-piece band in 1993. The August performance at the Brooklyn Academy of Music was later broadcast as part of PBS television's *Great Performances* series. In 1995 John Entwistle toured as a member of Ringo Starr's All-Starr Band.

Early Albums

The Who Sings My Generation	Decca	74664	'66	†
	MCA	2044		†
	MCA	31330		CD
Happy Jack	Decca	74892	'67	†
	MCA	2045		†
(reissued as) A Quick One	MCA	31331		CD
The Who Sell Out	Decca	74950	'67	†
	MCA	2046		†
	MCA	31332		CD

Tommy

Tommy	Decca	(2) 7205	'69	†
	MCA	(2) 10005		†
	MCA	10801	'93	CS/CD
	Mobile Fidelity	533	'90	CD
Tommy (1972 studio cast)	Ode	(2) 99001	'72	†
Tommy (with London Symphony Orchestra and Chamber Choir)	Rhino	71113	'89	CS/CD
Tommy (studio cast excerpts)	Pickwick	3339		†
Tommy (movie soundtrack)	Polydor	(2) 9502	'75	
	Polydor	(2) 841121	'94	CD
The Who's Tommy (excerpts from 1993 Broadway original cast musical)	RCA	(2) 61874	'93	CS/CD
The Who's Tommy (excerpts from original cast musical)	RCA	62522	'94	CS/CD

The Who

Live at Leeds	Decca	79175	'70	†
	MCA	2022		†
	MCA	3023		†
	MCA	37000		†
	MCA	11215	'95	CS/CD
	MCA	11230	'95	CD
Who's Next	Decca	79182	'71	†
	MCA	2023		†
	MCA	3024		†
	MCA	1691		CS
	MCA	37217		CD
Quadrophenia	MCA	(2) 10004	'73	†
	MCA	(2) 6895		CS/CD
	Mobile Fidelity	(2) 20550	'91	CD
The Who by Numbers	MCA	2161	'75	†
	MCA	3026		†
	MCA	37002		†
	MCA	1579		CS
	MCA	31197		CD
Who Are You	MCA	3050	'78	†
	MCA	1580		CS
	MCA	37003		CD
	Mobile Fidelity	561	'92	CD
The Kids Are Alright (soundtrack)	MCA	(2) 11005	'79	†
	MCA	(2) 6899		CS
	MCA	6899		CD

Face Dances	Warner Bros.	3516	'81	†
	MCA	25987	'89	CS/CD
It's Hard	Warner Bros.	23731	'82	†
	MCA	25986	'89	CS/CD
Who's Last	MCA	(2) 8018	'84	CS/CD
Join Together	MCA	(2) 19501	'90	CS/CD

Anthologies

Magic Bus	Decca	75064	'68	†
	MCA	2047		†
	MCA	31333		CD
Meaty, Beaty, Big and Bouncy	Decca	79184	'71	†
	MCA	2025		†
	MCA	3025		†
	MCA	1578		CS
	MCA	37001		CD
Odds and Sods	MCA	2126	'74	†
	MCA	37169	'82	†
	MCA	1659		CS/CD
Hooligans	MCA	(2) 12001	'81	CS/CD
Greatest Hits	MCA	5408	'83	†
	MCA	1496		CS/CD
Who's Missing (recorded 1965–1972)	MCA	25982	'86	CS
	MCA	31221	'86	CD
Two's Missing (recorded 1964–1973)	MCA	5712	'87	CS
	MCA	3122?	'87	CD
Who's Better Who's Best	MCA	(2) 8031	'89	CS
	MCA	8031	'89	CD
30 Years of Maximum R&B: The Gift Set	MCA	(4) 11150	'94	CD

Reissues

A Quick One/The Who Sell Out	MCA	(2) 4067	'74	CS
Magic Bus/The Who Sings My Generation	MCA	(2) 4068	'74	CS
Who Are You/Live at Leeds	MCA	(2) 6913		CS
Meaty, Beaty, Big and Bouncy/The Who By Numbers	MCA	(2) 6914		CS
Who's Next/Odds and Sods	MCA	(2) 6939		CD

The Who and Various Artists

Quadrophenia (soundtrack)	Polydor	(2) 6235	'79	†
	Polydor	519999	'94	CD

John Entwistle

Smash Your Head Against the Wall	Decca	79183	'71	†
	MCA	2024		†
Whistle Rhymes	Decca	79190	'72	†
	MCA	2027		†
Rigor Mortis Sets In	MCA	321	'73	†
Mad Dog (with Ox)	MCA	2129	'75	†
Too Late the Hero	Atco	38-142	'81	†

Roger Daltrey

Daltrey	MCA	328	'73	†
	MCA	2349		†
	MCA	37032		†

Ride a Rock Horse	MCA	2147	'75	†
	MCA	37030		†
One of the Boys	MCA	2271	'77	†
	MCA	37031		†
Best Bits	MCA	5301	'82	†
Parting Should Be Painless	Atlantic	80128	'84	†
Under a Raging Moon	Atlantic	81269	'85	CS/CD
Rocks in the Head	Atlantic	82359	'92	CS/CD
Roger Daltrey/Rick Wakeman				
Lisztomania (soundtrack)	A&M	4546	'75	†
	Saga	9042	'92	CD
Roger Daltrey/Russ Ballard				
McVicar (soundtrack)	Polydor	6284	'80	†
Pete Townshend				
Who Came First	Decca	79189	'72	†
	MCA	2026		†
	Rykodisc	10246	'92	CS/CD
Empty Glass	Atco	32100	'80	CS/CD
	Atlantic	82544	'94	CD
All the Best Cowboys Have Chinese Eyes	Atco	38149	'82	CS/CD
Scoop	Atco	(2) 90063	'83	†
	Atco	90063		CS/CD
White City: A Novel	Atco	90473	'85	CS/CD
Another Scoop (recorded 1964–1984)	Atco	(2) 90539	'86	CD
Pete Townshend's Deep End Live	Atco	90553	'86	CD
The Iron Man (A Musical by Pete Townshend)	Atlantic	81996	'89	CD
PsychoDerelict	Atlantic	82494	'93	CS/CD
PsychoDerelict (edited version)	Atlantic	82535	'93	CS/CD
Pete Townshend and Ronnie Lane				
Rough Mix	MCA	2295	'77	†
	Atco	90097	'83	CS/CD

JACKIE WILSON

(b. June 9, 1934, Detroit, MI; d. Jan. 21, 1984, Mount Holly, NJ)

Clyde McPhatter's 1953 replacement in the Dominoes, Jackie Wilson launched his solo career in 1957 with songs cowritten by Berry Gordy Jr. and became one of the first R&B vocalists to enjoy success in the early rock-and-roll era. A masterful live performer and stupendous dancer (Michael Jackson later incorporated many of his stage moves), Wilson sang both rockers and ballads passionately with his astonishingly wide-ranging voice. He scored a dozen smash R&B and major pop hits between 1958 and 1961, including "Lonely Teardrops," "I'll Be Satisfied," "Night," and "I'm Comin' On Back to You." However, after the smash crossover hit "Baby Workout," Wilson was overwhelmed by the emergence of soul music in the '60s. He managed to return to the charts with a smash pop and top R&B hit with the classic "(Your Love Keeps Lifting Me) Higher and Higher" in 1967. Relegated to the oldies circuit, Jackie Wilson suffered a massive heart attack on stage in Cherry Hill, New Jersey, on September 29, 1975, and eventually died on January 21, 1984. He was inducted into the Rock and Roll Hall of Fame in 1987.

Billy Ward and the Dominoes

14 Hits (1951–1965)	King	5005	'77	†
14 Original Greatest Hits	Deluxe	7838		CS
21 Hits	King	5008	'77	†
21 Original Greatest Hits	Deluxe	7841		CS
Featuring Clyde McPhatter and Jackie Wilson	King	733		LP/CS/CD
Sixty Minute Man: The Best of Billy Ward and the Dominoes	Rhino	71509	'93	CD

The Dominoes

Have Mercy Baby	Charly	44		CD†

Jackie Wilson and the Dominoes

14 Hits	King	5007	'77	†

Jackie Wilson

14 Hits	Deluxe	7840		CS
He's So Fine	Brunswick	54042	'58	†
Lonely Teardrops	Brunswick	54045	'59	†
So Much	Brunswick	754050	'60	†
Sings the Blues	Brunswick	754055	'60	†
My Golden Favorites	Brunswick	754058	'60	†
A Woman, a Lover, a Friend	Brunswick	754059	'60	†
You Ain't Heard Nothin' Yet	Brunswick	754100	'61	†
By Special Request	Brunswick	754101	'61	†
Body and Soul	Brunswick	754105	'62	†
At the Copa	Brunswick	754108	'62	†
Sings the World's Greatest Melodies	Brunswick	754106	'63	†
Baby Workout	Brunswick	754110	'63	†
Merry Christmas	Brunswick	754112	'63	†
My Golden Favorites, Volume 2	Brunswick	754115	'64	†
Somethin' Else	Brunswick	754117	'64	†
Soul Time	Brunswick	754118	'65	†
Spotlight On Jackie Wilson	Brunswick	754119	'65	†
Soul Galore	Brunswick	754120	'66	†
Whispers	Brunswick	754122	'67	†
Higher and Higher	Brunswick	754130	'67	†
	Rhino	71850	'95	CS/CD
I Get the Sweetest Feeling	Brunswick	754138	'68	†
Greatest Hits	Brunswick	754140	'69	†
Do Your Thing	Brunswick	754154	'69	†
It's All a Part of Love	Brunswick	754158	'70	†
This Love Is Real	Brunswick	754167	'73	†
Nowstalgia	Brunswick	754199	'74	†
The Jackie Wilson Story	Epic	(2) 38623	'83	†
	Epic	38623		CD†
The Jackie Wilson Story, Volume 2	Epic	39408	'85	†
The Soul Years	Kent	027		LP/CS†
Higher and Higher	Kent	901	'86	CD†
Reet Petite	Ace	125		LP/CS†
	Ace	902		CD
Very Best	Ace	913	'87	CD
Through the Years: A Collection of Rare Album Tracks and Single Sides	Rhino	70230	'87	†

Mr. Excitement	Rhino	(3) 70775	'92	CS/CD
Very Best	Rhino	71559	'94	CS/CD
My Way	CSP	(2) 18815		†
Jackie Wilson and Linda Hopkins				
Shake a Hand	Brunswick	754113	'63	†
Jackie Wilson and Count Basie				
Manufacturers of Soul	Brunswick	754134	'68	†

JOHNNY WINTER/EDGAR WINTER

Johnny Winter (b. Feb. 23, 1944, Leland, MS), gtr, voc; **Edgar Winter** (b. Dec. 28, 1946, Beaumont, TX), kybd, sax, voc

JOHNNY WINTER (*r.*) AND B. B. KING (*l.*)

Offered a lucrative contract by Columbia Records in 1969, blues guitarist Johnny Winter was initially hailed as rock music's next superstar, yet he failed to live up to his record company's publicity. Nonetheless, he recorded several best-selling albums with producer-guitarist Rick Derringer, including 1973's *Still Alive and Well*. Johnny's keyboardist-saxophonist brother Edgar Winter fared better commercially, first with White Trash, then later with the Edgar Winter Group. That group included guitarists Ronnie Montrose and Rick Derringer for their best-selling *They Only Come Out at Night* album and top hit single "Frankenstein." In the late '70s Johnny Winter brought blues legend Muddy Waters a modicum of recognition by producing his albums for Blue Sky Records. However, neither Johnny nor Edgar Winter were able to reestablish their '70s popularity in the '80s or '90s.

Johnny and Edgar Winter, born albinos, grew up in Beaumont, Texas, where Johnny took up clarinet at age 6, later graduating to ukelele then guitar by age 11. Edgar learned keyboards and saxophone, and the brothers formed Johnny and the Jammers around 1959. The brothers toured the Southern club circuit in a group called Black Plague in the early '60s. Johnny briefly traveled to Chicago in 1962, subsequently manning Edgar's band from 1964 to 1966. Johnny ended up in Houston and began backing local bluesmen and recording for regional labels. In April 1968 Johnny formed Winter with bassist Tommy Shannon and drummer John "Red" Turner for various Texas engagements, and the group was briefly praised in a *Rolling Stone* article about the Texas music scene in its December 2, 1968, issue, which led to a flurry of interest in the artist.

Johnny Winter was sought out by New York entrepreneur Steve Paul, who booked Winter into his New York club, The Scene. Graduating to the Fillmore East, Winter was signed to Columbia Records for hundreds of thousands of dollars in 1969, an unprecedented amount for an unproved artist. Accompanied by a massive publicity campaign, Winter's debut Columbia album sold quite well without yielding a hit single. He recorded *Second Winter* in Nashville with brother Edgar, who signed with Epic Records and recorded his debut, *Entrance*, virtually by himself. In 1970 Johnny Winter formed Johnny Winter And with former McCoys Rick and Randy Zehringer, but their debut album sold poorly, despite the inclusion of the original version of "Rock and Roll Hoochie Koo," written by Rick Zehringer, now using the last name Derringer. The live follow-up became the best-selling album of Johnny Winter's career, but he soon went into semi-retirement, suffering from exhaustion, depression, and heroin addiction.

By 1971 Edgar Winter had formed White Trash with guitarist Floyd Radford and vocalist Jerry LaCroix, scoring a minor hit with "Keep Playin' That Rock 'n' Roll." Rick Derringer supplanted Radford for the best-selling live set *Roadwork*, which featured Derringer's "Still Alive and Well" and a new version of "Rock and Roll Hoochie Koo." Winter subsequently formed the Edgar Winter Band with guitarist Ronnie Montrose and multi-instrumentalist Dan Hartman. With Derringer producing, *They Only Come Out at Night* became the best-selling album of Edgar's career, yielding a top hit with the instrumental "Frankenstein" and a major hit with "Free Ride." With Derringer replacing Montrose, *Shock Treatment* produced the moderate hit "River's Risin'."

Johnny Winter reemerged in 1973 with *Still Alive and Well*, his most critically successful album. It included Derringer's title song as well as the Winter originals "Rock and Roll" and "Too Much Seconal," and "Silver Train," written for him by Rolling Stones Mick Jagger and Keith Richards. After *Saints and Sinners*, Johnny Winter switched to Steve Paul's Blue Sky label, where he recorded four albums and produced four albums for blues legend Muddy Waters. In 1975 Edgar Winter recorded the solo jazz-style *Jasmine Nightdreams* for Blue Sky and a final album with the Edgar Winter Group. In 1976 Johnny and Edgar Winter recorded the modest-selling album *Together*.

Edgar recorded two final albums for Blue Sky through the early '80s, reemerging in the late '80s to tour with Leon Russell. Johnny Winter continued to record into the '90s, first for the Chicago-based Alligator label, then one album for MCA/Voyager, and three albums for Pointblank and Relix in the '90s.

Johnny Winter

Raw to the Bone (1967)	Sky Ranch	2334	'93	CD
Austin, Texas	United Artists	139		†
The Johnny Winter Story	GRT	10010		†
First Winter	Buddah	7513		†
About Blues	Janus	3008		†
Before the Storm	Janus	3056		†
Early Times	Jansco	3023	'70	†
The Progressive Blues Experiment	Imperial	12431	'69	†
	One Way	57340		CD
Johnny Winter	Columbia	9826	'69	CS/CD
Second Winter	Columbia	(2) 9947	'69	†
	Columbia	9947		CS/CD
Johnny Winter And	Columbia	30221	'70	CS
Johnny Winter And—Live	Columbia	30475	'71	CS/CD
Johnny Winter And/Live	Columbia	(2) 33651		CS
Still Alive and Well	Columbia	32188	'73	CS
	Columbia/Legacy	66421	'94	CD
Saints and Sinners	Columbia	32715	'74	†

Scorchin' Blues	Columbia/Legacy	52466	'92	CS/CD
A Rock 'n' Roll Collection	Columbia/	46985	'94	CS/CD
Ready for Winter	Accord	7135	'81	†
John Dawson Winter III	Blue Sky	33292	'74	†
Captured Live	Blue Sky	33944	'76	CS/CD
Nothin' but the Blues	Blue Sky	34813	'77	CS/CD
White, Hot and Blue	Blue Sky	35475	'78	†
Raisin' Cain	Blue Sky	36343	'80	†
Guitar Slinger	Alligator	4735	'84	LP/CS/CD
Serious Business	Alligator	4742	'85	LP/CS/CD
3rd Degree	Alligator	4748	'86	LP/CS/CD
The Winter of '88	MCA/Voyager	42241	'88	CS/CD
Let Me In	Pointblank/Charisma	91744	'91	CS/CD†
	Pointblank/Charisma	86244		CS/CD
Hey, Where's Your Brother	Pointblank	86512	'92	CS/CD
Birds Can't Row Boats	Relix	2034		CS/CD
Lone Star Kind of Day	Relix	2042		CS/CD
Walking By Myself	Relix	2048		CS/CD
The Winter Scene	Pair	1273	'90	CD
Early Heat	Special Music	4816		CS/CD
Best	IMG	716		CS

Johnny and Edgar Winter

Together Live	Blue Sky	34033	'76	CS

Johnny Winter/Sonny Terry/Willie Dixon

Whoopin'	Alligator	4734	'84	LP/CS/CD

Edgar Winter

Entrance	Epic	26503	'70	†
	Epic	48536	'92	CD
Jasmine Nightdreams	Blue Sky	33483	'75	†
The Edgar Winter Album	Blue Sky	35989	'79	†
Standing on Rock	Blue Sky	36494	'81	†
Mission Earth	Rhino	70709	'89	CS/CD
The Edgar Winter Collection	Rhino	70895	'89	CS/CD

Edgar Winter's White Trash

White Trash	Epic	30512	'71	CS/CD
Road Work	Epic	(2) 31249	'72	†
	Epic	31249	'87	CS/CD
Recycled	Blue Sky	34858	'77	†

The Edgar Winter Group

They Only Come Out at Night	Epic	31584	'72	CS/CD
Shock Treatment	Epic	32461	'74/'90	CD
The Edgar Winter Group with Rick Derringer	Blue Sky	33798	'75	†

STEVIE WONDER

(b. Steveland Morris, May 13, 1950, Saginaw, MI)

Achieving his first recognition as a child prodigy with the top hit instrumental "Fingertips—Part 2" in 1963, Stevie Wonder languished for several years at Motown before establishing himself as a singles artist in the mid-'60s with "Uptight (Everything's Alright)." A multital-ented musician who had mastered harmonica, drums, and keyboards as a child, Wonder's first self-produced album, *Signed Sealed and Delivered*, initiated a series of albums he performed, recorded, and produced entirely by himself. Wonder broke through to the mass white audi-ence without abandoning his black fans with 1972's *Talking Book* album, yielding two top-hit classics, "Superstition" and "You Are the Sunshine of My Life." Stevie Wonder's productivity has been sporadic since the late '70s, although he continued to score smash crossover hits well into the '80s, including the best-selling single of his career, 1984's "I Just Called to Say I Love You."

Afflicted by blindness as a newborn, Stevie Wonder moved with his family to Detroit as an infant. Playing harmonica by age five, he started piano lessons at six and took up drums at eight. Writing his first song at age 10, Wonder was spotted by the Miracles' Ronnie White, who took him to Brian Holland. Holland arranged an audition with Motown Records' Berry Gordy Jr., and Wonder was immediately signed to the Tamla label and as-signed the name "Little" Stevie Wonder. In 1963 he scored a surprising top pop and R&B hit with the raucous harmonica instrumental "Fingertips—Part 2," recorded live, complete with mistakes, musical puns, and a shouting stage manager. The following year he enrolled in the Michigan School for the Blind, studied classical piano, and managed moderate hits with the harmonica-based songs "Workout, Stevie, Workout" and "Harmonica Man."

Dropping the "Little" appellation, Stevie Wonder emerged in 1965–1966 with the ener-getic dance-style smash hit "Up-Tight (Everything's Alright)," which he cowrote; the major hit "Nothing's Too Good for My Baby"; and a near-smash-hit version of Bob Dylan's "Blowin' in the Wind" from *Up-Tight*. While recording a wide variety of material on his al-bums, Wonder quickly established himself as a popular crossover singles artist with such ro-mantic ballads and up-tempo pop-style songs as "A Place in the Sun," "Trav'lin' Man," the top R&B and pop smash "I Was Made to Love Her," and "I'm Wondering." Following an al-bum of Christmas material and an instrumental album released under the name Eivets Red-now, Wonder's *For Once in My Life* yielded five hits, including the top R&B and smash pop hit "Shoo-Be-Doo-Be-Doo-Da-Day" and the crossover smash title song. *My Cherie Amour* pro-duced two smash hits, with the title song and "Yester Me, Yester-You, Yesterday."

Stevie Wonder's first self-produced album, *Signed Sealed and Delivered*, contained four hits, including the top R&B and smash pop hit title song and the crossover smash "Heaven Help Us All." Wonder began experimenting with various rhythmic and musical textures and different electric keyboard instruments, including the synthesizer, with *Where I'm Coming From*. The al-bum included the crossover smash "If You Really Love Me" and the neglected ballad "Never Dreamed You'd Leave in Summer," both written by Wonder and then-wife Syreeta Wright.

In 1971, at age 21, Stevie Wonder negotiated a new contract with Motown that gained him artistic control over his recordings and provided for the unprecedented formation of his own music-publishing company, Black Bull Music, and production company, Taurus Productions. For his first album under the new contract, *Music of My Mind*, he played every instrument and coauthored the songs with Syreeta Wright. The album sold remarkably well despite yielding only one hit, "Superwoman (Where Were You When I Needed You)." The al-bum began to establish Wonder as an album artist, and as a consequence of a well-received summer 1972 tour with the Rolling Stones, he attracted a huge following among the white rock audience while retaining his black fans.

Stevie Wonder's growing popularity and recognition was immeasurably bolstered by the exceptional *Talking Book* album, one of the finest albums of the '70s. In addition to produc-ing two top pop hits with the mellow "You Are the Sunshine of My Life" (a smash R&B hit) and the seminal "Superstition" (a top R&B hit), the album contained three other excellent songs: "You've Got It Bad Girl," "Blame It on the Sun," and "I Believe (When I Fall In Love It Will Be Forever)." For his next album Wonder performed virtually all the instrumental chores and solely composed all the songs. The monumental *Innervisions* yielded two top

R&B and pop smash hits, the socially conscious "Higher Ground" and "Living for the City," and the smash R&B and major pop hit "Don't Worry 'Bout a Thing." The album also included favorites such as "Too High," "Golden Lady," and "All in Love Is Fair."

Involved in record production beginning with the Spinners' 1970 hit "It's a Shame," Stevie Wonder produced Syreeta Wright's first and second albums and Minnie Riperton's *Perfect Angel*. However, on August 6, 1973, he was involved in a serious auto accident near Durham, North Carolina, that left him in a coma for several days. He staged a remarkable recovery and recorded yet another outstanding album, *Fulfillingness' First Finale*. It debuted at the top of the album charts and produced the top pop and R&B hit "You Haven't Done Nothin'" (ostensibly an indictment of Richard Nixon) and the seminal crossover smash "Boogie On, Reggae Woman," while including the religious "Heaven Is 10 Million Years Away." Following a tour in winter 1974, Wonder essentially retired from the road to work on his epic, *Songs in the Key of Life*. Eventually issued in fall 1976 accompanied by a four-song EP, the album included two top crossover hits, "I Wish" and the tribute to Duke Ellington, "Sir Duke." The album also contained the moderate crossover hits "Another Star" and "As," as well as "Isn't She Lovely" and other captivating songs.

Film producer Michael Braun subsequently approached Stevie Wonder about composing a song for a documentary on plant life. Wonder ultimately composed and recorded an entire score, later returning to the studio to add more songs and lyrics and overdub the sounds of nature. Eventually issued in 1979 as *Journey Through the Secret Life of Plants*, the album was criticized as esoteric, inaccessible, and tedious, yet it yielded a crossover smash with "Send One Your Love." Wonder toured in 1980 and recorded *Hotter Than July*, which produced a top R&B and smash pop hit with "Master Blaster (Jammin')," inspired by Bob Marley, and the smash R&B and major pop hit "I Ain't Gonna Stand for It." The album also contained his tribute to Martin Luther King Jr., "Happy Birthday," as well as the ballad "Lately" and up-tempo songs such as "Let's Get Serious" and "Always."

Stevie Wonder has maintained a low profile since the early '80s. In 1982 he scored a top R&B and smash pop hit with "That Girl" from his anthology set *Original Musiquarium*, which also provided the hits "Do I Do" and "Ribbon in the Sky." His duet with Paul McCartney on "Ebony and Ivory" became a top R&B and smash pop hit. He participated in the campaign to establish Martin Luther King Jr.'s birthday as a national holiday and hosted a 1986 television special marking its first celebration. He provided seven original songs to the soundtrack to the 1984 film *Woman in Red*, including the top pop and R&B hit "I Just Called to Say I Love You" and the major crossover hit "Love Light in Flight." The soundtrack album also included the didactic "Don't Drive Drunk," but the song did not appear in the movie.

Touring in 1983 and 1986, Stevie Wonder issued his first album of new material in five years, *In Square Circle*, in 1985. The album yielded four hits, including the top pop and R&B hit "Part-Time Lover" and the crossover smash "Go Home." Along with Elton John and Gladys Knight, Wonder was one of Dionne Warwick's "friends" on the top pop and R&B hit "That's What Friends Are For," which helped raise money for AIDS research. *Characters*, from 1987, produced two top R&B hits, "Skeletons" (a major pop hit) and "You Will Know," and an R&B smash duet with Michael Jackson, "Get It." In 1989 Stevie Wonder was inducted into the Rock and Roll Hall of Fame. He composed and recorded 11 songs for the soundtrack to Spike Lee's provocative film *Jungle Fever*, released in 1991, and eventually toured in support of 1995's *Conversation Piece*. However, his recent work has neither produced hits nor attracted much critical acclaim.

Stevie Wonder

Tribute to Uncle Ray	Tamla	232	†
The Jazz Soul of Little Stevie Wonder	Tamla	233	†
	Motown	5219	CS/CD

The 12-Year-Old Genius	Tamla	240	'63	†
Workout, Stevie, Workout	Tamla	248		†
With a Song in My Heart	Tamla	250		†
	Motown	5150		CS/CD
Stevie at the Beach	Tamla	255		†
Up-Tight (Everything's Alright)	Tamla	268	'66	†
	Motown	5183		CS/CD
Down to Earth	Tamla	272	'66	†
	Motown	5166	'89	CS/CD
I Was Made to Love Her	Tamla	279	'67	†
	Motown	5273	'89	CS/CD
Someday at Christmas	Tamla	281	'67	†
	Tamla	362	'78	†
	Motown	9081		CD†
	Motown	5255		CS/CD
Eivets Rednow	Gordy	932	'68	†
For Once in My Life	Tamla	291	'69	†
	Motown	9032		CD†
	Motown	5234		CS/CD
My Cherie Amour	Tamla	296	'69	†
	Motown	9083		CD†
	Motown	5179		CS/CD
Live	Tamla	298	'70	†
Signed Sealed and Delivered	Tamla	304	'70	†
	Motown	9029		CD|
	Motown	5176		CS/CD
Where I'm Coming From	Tamla	308	'71	†
	Motown	5247	'90	CS/CD
Music of My Mind	Tamla	314	'72	†
	Motown	9076	'87	CD†
	Motown	314		CS/CD
Talking Book	Tamla	319	'72	†
	Motown	9051		CD†
	Motown	319		CS/CD
Innervisions	Tamla	326	'73	†
	Motown	9052	'87	CD†
	Motown	326		CS/CD
	Mobile Fidelity	554	'91	CD
Fulfillingness' First Finale	Tamla	332	'74	†
	Motown	9077	'87	CD†
	Motown	332		CS/CD
Songs in the Key of Life	Tamla	(2) 340	'76	†
	Tamla	6115		CD†
	Motown	(2) 340		LP/CS/CD
Journey Through the Secret Life of Plants	Tamla	(2) 371	'79	†
	Tamla	(2) 6127		CD†
	Motown	(2) 6127		CD
Hotter Than July	Tamla	373	'80	†
	Tamla	6205	'86	CD†
	Motown	9064	'87	CD†
	Motown	6205		CS/CD

The Woman in Red (soundtrack)	Motown	6108	'84	CS/CD
In Square Circle	Tamla	6134	'85	LP/CS/CD†
	Motown	6134		CS/CD
Characters	Motown	6248	'87	LP/CS/CD
Jungle Fever (soundtrack)	Motown	6291	'91	LP/CS/CD
Conversation Piece	Motown	0238	'95	CS/CD
Reissues				
My Cherie Amour/Signed Sealed and Delivered	Tamla	8106	'86	CD†
For Once in My Life/Up-Tight	Tamla	8125	'86	CD†
Down to Earth/I Was Made to Love Her	Tamla	8153		CD†
Anthologies				
Greatest Hits	Tamla	282	'68	†
	Motown	282		CS/CD
Greatest Hits, Volume 2	Tamla	313	'71	†
	Motown	313		CS/CD
Love Songs: 20 Classic Hits	Tamla	6144		CD†
	Motown	9050		CD†
Looking Back	Motown	(3) 804	'77	†
Original Musiquarium I (Greatest Hits)	Tamla	(2) 6002	'82	†
	Motown	6002		LP/CS/CD
Motown Legends	Motown	5362		†
Motown Legends	Esx	8527	'95	CS/CD

X

John Doe (b. John Nommensen, Feb. 25, 1954, Decatur, IL), bs, voc; **Exene Cervenka** (b. Christine Cervenka, Feb. 1, 1956, IL), voc; **Billy Zoom** (b. Feb. 20, ca. 1949, IL), lead gtr; and **D[on]. J. Bonebrake** (b. Dec. 8, 1955, Burbank, CA), drm [Billy Zoom departed in 1985, to be replaced by guitarists **Dave Alvin** (b. Nov. 11, 1955) and **Tony Gilkyson** (b. Aug. 6, 1952, Los Angeles, CA). Alvin left in 1987, and the band ended in 1988; Doe, Cervenka, Gilkyson, and Bonebrake reunited in 1993.]

One of the most challenging groups to emerge from the Los Angeles punk scene of the late '70s, X garnered critical adulation for their stunning debut album *Los Angeles*, on Slash Records. Featuring the ragged, oblique harmonies and demanding, pessimistic songwriting of John Doe and Exene Cervenka, X's first four albums were produced by former Doors keyboardist Ray Manzarek. Retaining artistic control over their recordings with their switch to the major label Elektra in 1982, X achieved their biggest-seller with 1983's *More Fun in the New World*. However, X never achieved the commercial success envisioned by critics. Recording and performing in an acoustic folk and country style in the mid-'80s with the Knitters, augmented by Dave Alvin, X endured until 1988, and reunited in 1993.

John Doe grew up in Baltimore and manned local rock bands until moving to Los Angeles in 1976. In 1977 he met guitarist Billy Zoom, ostensibly a veteran of the bands of Gene Vincent and Ray Campi, and met Exene Cervenka at a poetry workshop in Venice, California. They played at Hollywood's seminal punk club the Masque, and added drummer D. J. Bonebrake, who debuted with X in February 1978. They began winning a rabid following by regularly playing at underground Los Angeles clubs, and released their debut single, "Adult Books"/"We're Desperate," on the Dangerous label in April 1978.

Spotted by former Doors keyboardist Ray Manzarek in 1979, X eventually signed with the independent label Slash. With Manzarek producing, their debut album, *Los Angeles*, depicted the seamy underside of the city and its punk subculture in such songs as "Johnny Hit and Run Paulene," "Sex and Dying in High Society," and the classic title song. The album drew praise from critics on both coasts. Doe and Cervenka married, and X appeared in the classic punk documentary film *The Decline of Western Civilization*, and later *Urgh! A Music War*. Their second album, *Wild Gift*, was also critically lauded and included "In This House That I Call a Home," "When Our Love Passed Out on the Couch," and "It's Who You Know."

Switching to the major label Elektra, retaining producer Ray Manzarek and winning artistic control over their recordings, X scored their first significant success with 1983's *Under the Big Black Sun*. The album contained favorites such as "Motel Room in My Bed," "Riding with Mary," and the haunting "Come Back to Me," but it failed to produce a hit single. *More Fun in the New World*, their final album with producer Manzarek, became their best-selling album, featuring the explosive "Devil Doll," the countrified "New World," and the funky "True Love." In 1985 X employed heavy-metal producer Michael Wagener for the equivocal *Ain't Love Grand*, which includes "Burning House of Love," "Around My Heart," and "Little Honey," cowritten by Doe and the Blasters' Dave Alvin. At the end of 1985 John Doe and Exene Cervenka divorced, and Doe left the band.

Beginning in 1984, various members of X and the Blasters assembled to play local benefit concerts. The loosely assembled aggregation became known as the Knitters and played acoustic-based folk and country-style music. In 1986 the Knitters, with John Doe, Exene Cervenka, Dave Alvin, D. J. Bonebrake, and stand-up bassist Johnny Ray Bartel, toured and recorded *Poor Little Critter on the Road*. The album includes Alvin's "4th of July," "Cryin' But My Tears Are Far Away," and a remake of X's "The New World."

After Zoom left X, guitarists Dave Alvin and Tony Gilkyson from the band Lone Justice took his place. Alvin stayed on for one album, *See How We Are*, which included his "4th of July" as well as "In the Time It Takes" and and the ballad "When It Rains . . . ," before leaving for a solo career. X maintained through 1988 with Doe, Cervenka, Gilkyson, and Bonebrake.

Following X's breakup, Exene Cervenka retreated to Idaho, taught herself guitar, and recorded two solo albums produced by Tony Gilkyson, while Doe recorded a single solo album and appeared in the movies *Roadside Prophets* and *Pure Country*. In 1993 John Doe, Exene Cervenka, Tony Gilkyson, and D. J. Bonebrake reunited as X for *Hey Zeus* on Mercury Records; they issued the live acoustic set *Unclogged* on their own independent label, Infidelity, two years later.

X

Los Angeles	Slash	104	'80	†
	Slash	23930		CS/CD
Wild Gift	Slash	107	'81	†
	Slash	23931		CS/CD
Los Angeles/Wild Gift	Slash	25771	'88	CD
Under the Big Black Sun	Elektra	60150	'82	CS/CD
More Fun in the New World	Elektra	60283	'83	CS/CD
Ain't Love Grand	Elektra	60430	'85	CS/CD
See How We Are	Elektra	60492	'87	CS/CD
Live at the Whisky a-Go-Go on the Fabulous Sunset Strip	Elektra	(2) 60788	'88	CS/CD
Hey Zeus	Mercury	519261	'93	CS/CD
Unclogged	Infidelity	10812	'95	CS/CD

The Knitters

Poor Little Critter on the Road	Slash	25310	'86	CS/CD

Exene Cervenka

Old Wives' Tales	Rhino	70913	'89	CS/CD
Running Sacred	RNA	70757	'90	CS/CD

John Doe

Meet John Doe	DGC	24291	'90	CS/CD†

Y

THE YARDBIRDS

Keith Relf (b. Mar. 22, 1943, Richmond, Surrey, England; d. May 14, 1976, West London, England), voc, har; **Chris Dreja** (b. Nov. 11, 1946, Surbiton, Surrey, England), rhythm gtr; **Paul Samwell-Smith** (b. May 8, 1943, London, England), bs; **Jim McCarty** (b. July 25, 1943, Liverpool, England), drm; **Anthony "Top" Topham**, lead gtr [Anthony Topham was replaced by **Eric Clapton** (b. Eric Clapp, Mar. 30, 1945, Ripley, Surrey, England) in October 1963. Clapton was replaced by **Jeff Beck** (b. June 24, 1944, Surrey, England) in March 1965. Paul Samwell-Smith was replaced by **Jimmy Page** (b. Jan. 9, 1944, Middlesex, England) on bass and guitar in June 1966.]

The Yardbirds are best remembered as the British group that introduced three of rock music's most outstanding lead guitar players, Eric Clapton, Jeff Beck, and Jimmy Page. Nonetheless, the Yardbirds were one of England's most influential groups, comparable in significance (but not popularity) to the Beatles, the Rolling Stones, and the Who. Despite the fact that they were more proficient and innovative musicians than the Rolling Stones, the Yardbirds failed to become superstars, perhaps because the Stones were better performers and lead vocalist Keith Relf lacked Mick Jagger's charisma. Certainly the Yardbirds' chaotic career of personnel and managerial hassles interfered with their success.

Under Eric Clapton, the Yardbirds developed what they termed the rave-up, an extended improvisational passage that could last 30 minutes, which was later termed psychedelic when employed by emerging San Francisco bands. With Clapton as a member, the Yardbirds were one of the finest British R&B-style bands, but they adopted a more innovative yet commercial pop style under Jeff Beck. Along with the Who's Pete Townshend, Jeff Beck was one of the first electric guitarists to effectively and creatively use feedback in his playing, thus reinforcing the group's psychedelic reputation and presaging the development of heavy-metal music. After session guitarist Jimmy Page joined in June 1966, the Yardbirds briefly utilized twin lead guitars, a format later popularized by the Allman Brothers and others. Although Page's arrival marked the beginning of the end for the Yardbirds, the group did record one prototypical heavy-metal hit with Beck and Page on lead guitars, "Happenings 10 Years Time Ago" (which was actually predated by the Who's "Anyway, Anyhow, Anywhere"). With Beck's departure in November 1966, the Yardbirds endured a dismal period under producer Mickie Most and evolved into Led Zeppelin, the first group specifically described as heavy metal, in October 1968.

Formed in 1963 as the Metropolis Blues Quartet by Keith Relf, Chris Dreja, Paul Samwell-Smith, and Jim McCarty, the group became the Yardbirds in June 1963 with the addition of lead guitarist Anthony "Top" Topham. He was replaced by Eric Clapton, a former member of the Roosters and Casey Jones and the Engineers, in October. After developing a devoted following on the London-area R&B club circuit with their dynamic rave-ups of blues material, the Yardbirds took over residency of the Crawdaddy Club in Richmond, in place of the Rolling Stones. They first recorded behind bluesman Sonny Boy Williamson and later moved to London's Marquee Club, where they recorded their debut album, *Five Live Yardbirds*, for Britain's Columbia Records. Their debut American album for Epic Records, *For Your Love*, produced a smash hit with Graham Gouldman's title song. However, Clapton, disillusioned by the seemingly commercial and pop direction the group was taking, had already left in March 1965, in favor of John Mayall's Bluesbreakers, and was replaced by Jeff Beck.

The Yardbirds enjoyed their most creative and successful period during the tenure of Jeff Beck. Their second American album, *Having a Rave Up*, contained one live side of blues material, including Howlin' Wolf's "Smokestack Lightning" and Bo Diddley's "I'm a Man," recorded with Eric Clapton, and a studio side featuring Jeff Beck. The studio side was comprised of two Graham Gouldman songs, "Heart Full of Soul" (a near-smash hit) and "Evil-Hearted You"; the socially conscious "You're a Better Man than I"; the Gregorian chant–like "Still I'm Sad"; Johnny Burnette and the Rock 'n' Roll Trio's "The Train Kept a-Rollin'"; and the hit version of "I'm a Man." Gaining an enhanced reputation for their experimentation with exotic instrumentation and Beck's creative use of feedback, the Yardbirds scored major hits with "Shapes of Things" and the title song to *Over Under Sideways Down*. The album also included the exotic-sounding "Hot-House of Omagarashid" and "Ever Since the World Began," as well as the favorites "Lost Woman" and "Jeff's Boogie."

In 1966 Chris Dreja recorded two unsuccessful solo singles; in June, Paul Samwell-Smith departed the Yardbirds to become a producer, most notably for Cat Stevens. Session guitarist Jimmy Page was recruited to take up bass, but he switched to lead guitar when Jeff Beck became ill in September. With Dreja moving to bass upon Beck's return, Beck and Page played twin lead guitars until November, when Beck quit the group. This lineup recorded only two songs, "Happenings 10 Years time Ago" (a moderate hit) and "Stroll On," performed in the movie *Blow-Up*. With Beck's departure, the remaining four continued to perform and record as the Yardbirds under producer Mickie Most. Achieving minor hits with "Little Games," "Ha Ha Said the Clown," and Nilsson's "Ten Little Indians," the aggregation released one American album, *Little Games*.

In summer 1968 Keith Relf and Jim McCarty dropped out to form the short-lived duo Together, and Page and Dreja unsuccessfully attempted to recruit guitarist Terry Reid for the New Yardbirds. With Dreja's departure to become a photographer, Page enlisted three new members to meet their contractual obligations that fall, and in October the group changed its name to Led Zeppelin.

Relf and McCarty subsequently formed the progressive-rock group Renaissance with Relf's vocalist sister Jane in 1969, but after one album—produced by Paul Samwell-Smith—Relf and McCarty left. Relf later played with Medicine Head, featuring vocalist John Fiddler, and eventually formed Armageddon around 1975. The group recorded one album for A&M Records, but on May 14, 1976, Relf was found dead at age 33 in his West London house, apparently electrocuted while playing guitar. McCarty was a member of Shoot in 1973 and later formed Illusion with Jane Relf. In the mid-'80s Dreja, Samwell-Smith, and McCarty recorded two albums as Box of Frogs with former Medicine Head vocalist John Fiddler.

The Yardbirds were inducted into the Rock and Roll Hall of Fame in 1992.

The Yardbirds

Five Live Yardbirds (recorded 1964)	Rhino	70189	'88	CS/CD
Live with Sonny Boy Williamson	Mercury	61071	'66	†
For Your Love	Epic	26167	'65	†
Having a Rave Up	Epic	26177	'65	†
Over Under Sideways Down	Epic	26210	'66	†
(reissued as) The Yardbirds	Epic	38455	'83	†

Greatest Hits	Epic	26246	'67	†
Little Games	Epic	26313	'67	†
Little Games Sessions and More	EMI	(2) 98213	'92	CD
The Yardbirds Featuring Performances by Beck, Clapton and Page	Epic	(2) 30135	'70	†
The Yardbirds with Jimmy Page—Live!	Epic	30615	'71	†
Favorites	Epic	34490	'77	†
Great Hits	Epic	34491	'77	†
Eric Clapton and the Yardbirds	Springboard Int'l	4036	'75	†
Jeff Beck and the Yardbirds	Springboard Int'l	4039	'75	†
For Your Love	Accord	7143	'81	†
Afternoon Tea	Rhino	253	'82	†
Greatest Hits, Volume 1	Rhino	70128	'86	CS
	Rhino	75895	'88	CD
Best of the Yardbirds	Rhino	71025	'94	CS/CD
Compleat Collection	Compleat	(2) 2002	'84	†
Volume 1: Smokestack Lightning	Sony	(2) 48655	'91	CD
Volume 2: Blues, Backtrack's and Shapes of Things	Sony	(2) 48658	'91	CD
Clapton's Cradle: The Early Yardbirds Recordings	Evidence	26072	'95	CD
Greatest Hits	Charly	8		CD†
The Best of British Rock	Pair	1151		CD
The Best of British Rock	Special Music	4902		CS
The Yardbirds Featuring Eric Clapton and Jeff Beck	Special Music	4928		CD

Eric Clapton, Jeff Beck, and Jimmy Page

Guitar Boogie	RCA	4624	'72	†
	RCA	3768		†

Renaissance (with Keith Relf)

Renaissance	Elektra	74068	'70	†

Armageddon (with Keith Relf)

Armageddon	A&M	4513	'75	†

Shoot (with Jim McCarty)

On the Frontier	EMI	11229	'73	†

Illusion (with Jim McCarty)

Out of the Mist	Island	9489	'77	†
Illusion	Island	9519	'78	†

Box of Frogs

Box of Frogs	Epic	39327	'84	†
Strange Land	Epic	39923	'86	†

YES

Jon Anderson (b. Oct. 25, 1944, Accrington, Lancashire, England), voc; **Tony Kaye** (b. Jan. 11, 1946, Leicester, England), kybd; **Peter Banks** (b. Apr. 8, 1947, Barnet, Hereford, England), gtr; **Chris Squire** (b. Mar. 4, 1948, London, England), bs; **Bill Bruford** (b. William Scott Bruford, May 17, 1949, Sevenoaks, Kent, England), drm [Peter Banks departed in 1970, to be replaced by **Steve Howe** (b. Apr. 8, 1947, London, England). Tony Kaye left in 1971, to be replaced by **Rick Wakeman** (b. May 18, 1949, West London, England). Bill Bruford left in 1972, to be replaced by **Alan White** (b. June 14, 1949, Pelton,

County Durham, England). Wakeman left in 1974, to be replaced by **Patrick Moraz** (b. June 24, 1948, Morges, Switzerland). Wakeman returned when Moraz left in 1976. Jon Anderson and Wakeman left in 1980, to be replaced by vocalist **Trevor Horn** (b. July 15, 1949, Hertfordshire, England) and keyboardist **Geoff Downes**. Yes disbanded later in 1980, re-grouping in 1983 with Anderson, Kaye, Squire, and White, adding guitarist **Trevor Rabin** (b. Jan. 13, 1954, Johannesburg, South Africa). Anderson left in 1988, and then Anderson, Kaye, Squire, White, Rabin, Bruford, Wakeman, and Howe reunited in 1991 as Yes; the band returned to its 1983–1987 lineup in 1994.]

A seminal British band of the '70s, Yes, along with the Moody Blues and the Nice/Emerson, Lake and Palmer, was an early progressive-rock band, prominently featuring keyboards, orchestral-style arrangements, and classical-style music. Gaining their first recognition as the opening act for Cream's farewell London performance in late 1968, Yes's success was based largely on thick vocal harmonies, astounding but uninspired instrumental technique, and regular use of sophisticated electronic gear. Propelled into American popularity with *The Yes Album*, which featured all original material and introduced the synthesizer to the group sound, Yes was fronted by songwriter-vocalist Jon Anderson, whose work was frequently criticized as obtuse, pretentious, and inaccessible. After scoring their first album and singles success under classically trained keyboardist Rick Wakeman, Yes recorded *Fragile* and *Close to the Edge*, hailed as classics for their textural and melodic richness. Wakeman left in 1974 and quickly established himself as a purveyor of orchestrated rock-instrumental versions of classic tales. In the mid-'70s the various members began recording albums on their own, and Wakeman returned to Yes in 1976. He left again in 1980 and the group disbanded for a time, reuniting for the biggest hit of their career, "Owner of a Lonely Heart," in late 1983. Enduring a protracted period of legal disputes in the late '80s, Yes reunited again in 1991.

Yes was formed in 1968 after the meeting of vocalist Jon Anderson and bassist Chris Squire. Anderson had been touring and performing with bands such as the Warriors for a decade, whereas the classically trained Squire had formed his own band at 16 and joined Syn (whose guitarist was Peter Banks) in 1965 for two years of engagements. Seeking to form a group that emphasized vocal harmonies backed by dense, structured music, Anderson and Squire recruited Banks, keyboardist Tony Kaye, and drummer Bill Bruford. After substituting for an absent Sly and the Family Stone at the Speakeasy Club in October 1968, Yes secured a residency at the Marquee Club and subsequently opened for Cream's farewell concerts at the Royal Albert Hall in December.

Signed to Atlantic Records, Yes released the classically influenced debut album *Time and a Word*, recorded with full orchestra, which began to establish the group's British reputation as a technically proficient progressive-rock band. In 1970 Banks departed to form his own band, Flash, and was replaced by classically trained guitarist Steve Howe, a veteran of bands such as the Syndicate, Bodast, and Tomorrow. Howe's instrumental talents extended from guitar to pedal steel guitar and, later, guitar synthesizer.

With Anderson providing most of the group's material and Kaye introducing the synthesizer to the group sound, Yes broke through in the United States with *The Yes Album* and its moderate hit "Your Move." Containing six pieces, three of which were nine minutes in length, the instrumentally complex album was hailed as an early example of symphonic rock. Yes first toured America in a support role in 1971, but soon suffered the departure of Tony Kaye for his own group Badger. He was replaced by Rick Wakeman, a former member of the Strawbs. Wakeman had entered the prestigious Royal Academy of Music at 16 for more than a year's study of piano and clarinet before leaving to teach music and record with T. Rex, Cat Stevens, and David Bowie. Wakeman introduced multiple keyboards, such as the mellotron, clavinet, and harpsichord, to Yes and became the group's focal point in concert.

The next Yes album, *Fragile*, with cover art by Roger Dean, featured four group pieces and five individual works, yielding a major hit with an edited version of "Roundabout."

After touring the United States as a headline act in 1972, Yes recorded *Close to the Edge*, which contained only three songs, the side-long title track, the moderate hit "And You and I," and "Siberian Khatru." However, shortly after the album was recorded, Bill Bruford left to join King Crimson and was replaced by classically trained drummer Alan White, a session player for Gary Wright, George Harrison, and Joe Cocker and a former member of John Lennon's Plastic Ono Band. Following the live three-record set *Yessongs*, Jon Anderson and Steve Howe composed the lyrics to *Tales from Topographic Oceans*, based on guru Paramhansa Yoganada's Shastic Scriptures. An elaborately experimental work, the album explored a variety of musical textures, themes, and instrumentation and received mixed reviews.

In June 1974 Rick Wakeman departed Yes to pursue a solo career already initiated on A&M Records with the instrumental *Six Wives of Henry VIII* album. His *Journey to the Centre of the Earth*, based on the Jules Verne story and narrated by actor David Hemmings, was recorded live with 45-piece orchestra and 48-person choir at the London Royal Festival Hall in January 1974. Wakeman soon became recognized as a purveyor of contemporary light orchestral music, and he next recorded the ambitious *Myths and Legends of King Arthur and the Knights of the Round Table*. The work was premiered as a pageant on ice at the London Empire Pool in May 1975 with massive orchestral and choral support. Wakeman toured America with a hundred-person-plus entourage of singers and musicians in early 1975, and returned late in the year with a trimmed-down English Rock Ensemble. He also wrote the score to the Ken Russell film *Lisztomania*, recorded *No Earthly Connection* with the English Rock Ensemble, and performed the soundtrack to the movie *White Rock*.

In the meantime, classically trained Swiss keyboardist Patrick Moraz, a former member of Refugee and the composer of numerous film scores, joined Yes in August 1974. His debut with Yes, *Relayer*, contained only three pieces, including the side-long "Gates of Delirium." The various members of Yes began recording solo albums in 1975. Yes mounted its most massive tour of America in summer 1976, and Wakeman rejoined the group late in the year following the departure of Moraz, who joined the Moody Blues, staying for 14 years. Yes embarked on a massive world tour in 1977 in support of *Going for the One*, then moved toward shorter songs for 1978's *Tormato*.

In the summer of 1980 Jon Anderson and Rick Wakeman left Yes to pursue solo projects. They were replaced by vocalist Trevor Horn and keyboardist Geoff Downes, who had scored a moderate hit in 1979–1980 with "Video Killed the Radio Star" as the Buggles. By fall the new edition of Yes was touring in support of *Drama*, but the group subsequently broke up. Jon Anderson collaborated with Greek keyboardist Vangelis (Evangelos Papathanassiou), achieving minor hits with "I Hear You Now" and "I'll Find My Way Home." He also recorded three solo album for three different labels during the '80s. Steve Howe and Geoff Downes formed Asia with vocalist-bassist John Wetton and drummer Carl Palmer. Asia scored a smash hit with "Heat of the Moment" and a near-smash with "Don't Cry," but Howe left in 1985 to form the short-lived GTR with vocalist Max Bacon and guitarist Steve Hackett, achieving a major hit with "When the Heart Rules the Mind."

In 1983 Yes regrouped with original members Jon Anderson, Tony Kaye, Chris Squire, and Alan White, adding South African guitarist Trevor Rabin. *90125* yielded a top hit with Rabin's "Owner of a Lonely Heart" and a major hit with "Leave It." *Big Generator*, from 1987, produced two moderate hits, "Love Will Find a Way" and "Rhythm of Love." Anderson left again in 1988, recording *Anderson, Bruford, Wakeman, Howe*, as Squire and Rabin laid claim to the Yes name. Trevor Rabin recorded a solo album in 1989, and Yes ultimately reunited with Anderson, Kaye, Squire, White, Rabin, Bruford, Wakeman, and Howe for 1991's dismal *Union* album and a new round of touring. In the '90s Wakeman also recorded for Relativity Records.

By 1994 Howe, Wakeman, and Bruford had left Yes again, with Rabin taking over control of the group. Yes recorded *Talk* for Victory Records, while Howe recorded for Relativity and Herald and Anderson recorded for Windham Hill and Angel.

Yes

Yes	Atlantic	8243	'69	CS/CD†
	Atlantic	82680	'94	CD
Time and a Word	Atlantic	8273	'70	†
	Atlantic	81473		CD†
	Atlantic	82681	'94	CD
Yesterdays (songs from above two albums)	Atlantic	18103	'75	†
	Atlantic	19134		†
	Atlantic	81533		CD†
	Atlantic	82684	'94	CD
The Yes Album	Atlantic	8283	'71	†
	Atlantic	19131		CS/CD†
	Atlantic	82665	'94	CS/CD
Fragile	Atlantic	7211	'72	†
	Atlantic	19132		CS/CD†
	Atlantic	82667	'94	CS/CD
	Atlantic	82524	'94	CD
Close to the Edge	Atlantic	7244	'72	†
	Atlantic	19133		CS/CD†
	Atlantic	82666	'94	CS/CD
Fragile/Close to the Edge	Atlantic	80002		CS
Yessongs	Atlantic	(3) 100	'73	CS/CD†
	Atlantic	(3) 82682	'94	CS/CD
Tales from Topographic Oceans	Atlantic	(2) 908	'74	CS/CD†
	Atlantic	(2) 82683	'94	CS/CD
Relayer	Atlantic	18122	'74	†
	Atlantic	19135		CS/CD†
	Atlantic	82664	'94	CS/CD
Going for the One	Atlantic	19106	'77	CS/CD†
	Atlantic	82670	'94	CS/CD
Tormato	Atlantic	19202	'78	†
	Atlantic	82277	'91	CS/CD†
	Atlantic	82671	'94	CS/CD
Drama	Atlantic	16019	'80	†
	Atlantic	81473		CD†
	Atlantic	82685	'94	CD
Yesshows	Atlantic	(2) 510	'80	†
	Atlantic	82686	'94	CD
Classic Yes	Atlantic	19320	'81	CS/CD†
	Atlantic	82687	'94	CS/CD
"90125"	Atco	90125	'83	CS/CD
90125 Live: The Solos	Atco	90474	'85	CS
Big Generator	Atco	90522	'87	CS/CD
Yesyears	Atco	(4) 91644	'91	CS/CD
Yestory	Atco	92202	'92	CS/CD
Union	Arista	8643	'91	CS/CD
An Evening of Yes Music Plus	Herald	(2) 006	'94	CD

Talk	Victory	480033	'94	CS/CD
Anderson, Bruford, Wakeman, Howe				
Anderson, Bruford, Wakeman, Howe	Arista	90126	'89	LP/CS/CD†
	Arista	8590	'90	CS/CD
Flash (with Peter Banks)				
Flash	Capitol	11040	'72	†
	One Way	17796		CD
Flash in the Can	Capitol	11115	'72	†
	One Way	56841		CD
Out of Our Heads	Capitol	11218	'73	†
	One Way	17414		CD
Peter Banks				
The Two Sides of Peter Banks	Capitol/Sovereign	11217	'73	†
Badger (with Tony Kaye)				
One Live Badger	Atco	7022	'73	†
White Lady	Epic	32831	'74	†
Rick Wakeman				
The Six Wives of Henry VIII	A&M	4361	'73	†
	A&M	3229	'84	CD
Journey to the Centre of the Earth	A&M	3621	'74	†
	A&M	3156		CS/CD
	Mobile Fidelity	848		CD
The Myths and Legends of King Arthur	A&M	4515	'75	†
	A&M	3230	'84	CD
No Earthly Connection	A&M	4583	'76	†
White Rock (soundtrack)	A&M	4614	'77	†
Criminal Record	A&M	4660	'77	†
Rhapsodies	A&M	(2) 6501	'79	†
Greatest Hits	Herald	(2) 007	'94	CD
Zodiaque	Relativity	1024		CD
The Family Album	Relativity	1025		CD
A Suite of Gods	Relativity	1026		CD
Rick Wakeman/Roger Daltrey				
Lisztomania (soundtrack)	A&M	4546	'75	†
Refugee (with Patrick Moraz)				
Refugee	Charisma	6066	'74	†
Patrick Moraz				
i	Atlantic	18175	'76	†
Human Interface	Cinema/Capitol	12558		†
	Cinema/Capitol	46872		CD†
Patrick Moraz and Bill Bruford				
Flags	EG	1565	'90	CD
Steve Howe				
Beginnings	Atlantic	18154	'75	†
	Atlantic	80319	'94	CD
The Steve Howe Album	Atlantic	19243	'80	†
	Atlantic	81559	'94	CD

Not Necessarily Acoustic	Herald	12	'94	CS/CD
Turbulence	Relativity	1061		CS/CD
Asia				
Asia	Geffen	2008	'82	CS/CD
Alpha	Geffen	4008	'83	CS/CD
Astra	Geffen	24072	'85	LP/CS/CD†
	MCA	20851	'95	CS/CD
GTR				
GTR	Arista	8400	'86	CS/CD†
Chris Squire				
Fish Out of Water	Atlantic	18159	'75	†
Alan White				
Ramshackled	Atlantic	18167		†
Cinema (with Alan White)				
Wrong House	A&M	5184	'88	LP/CS/CD†
Jon Anderson				
Olias of Sunhollow	Atlantic	18180	'76	†
Song of Seven	Atlantic	16021	'80	†
Animation	Atlantic	19355	'82	†
(reissued as) Jon Anderson	Atlantic	19355		CS
3 Ships	Elektra	60469	'85	†
In the City of Angels	Columbia	40910	'88	CD
Deseo	Windham Hill	11140	'94	CS/CD
Change We Must	Angel	55088	'94	CS/CD
Jon and Vangelis				
Short Stories	Polydor	6272	'80	†
	Polydor	800027		CD
Friends of Mr. Cairo	Polydor	6326	'81	†
	Polydor	800021		CD
Private Collection	Polydor	813174	'83	CD
Best	Polydor	821929	'84	CS/CD
Trevor Rabin				
Trevor Rabin	Chrysalis	1196	'78	†
Face to Face	Chrysalis	1221		†
Can't Look Away	Elektra	60781	'89	CS/CD

NEIL YOUNG

(b. Nov. 12, 1945, Toronto, Ontario, Canada)

CRAZY HORSE. Danny Whitten (d. Nov. 29, 1972, Los Angeles, CA), gtr, voc; **Billy Talbot**, bs; **Ralph Molina**, drm [After the tenures of guitarist-vocalists **Nils Lofgren** and **Greg Leroy**, **Frank Sampedro** became the group's permanent guitarist, in 1975.]

An exceptional songwriter, the author of lyrically beautiful love songs, hard-edged rockers, potent sociopolitical pieces, and evocative songs sometimes reflectively melancholic, sometimes brooding and desperate, Neil Young scored his biggest early success with *After the Goldrush* and *Harvest*. Recognized as a potent lead guitarist, Young subsequently embarked on an erratic solo career that gained him the reputation as one of the most enigmatic and elusive

NEIL YOUNG

artists to emerge from the '60s. He has often worked with the backup band Crazy Horse, who have inspired him to some of his best work on album and on stage. Often changing styles, Young has continued to record with Crazy Horse while also rejoining Crosby, Stills, and Nash from time to time, as well as working with other accompanists, including a 1995 collaboration with Pearl Jam.

Neil Young grew up in Winnipeg, Manitoba, where he formed Neil Young and the Squires while in high school. He later returned to his birthplace, Toronto, to play folk music at clubs in the city's Yorkville district, where he met Stephen Stills, Richie Furay, and Joni Mitchell. After joining the Mynah Birds, which included bassist Bruce Palmer and later funk star Rick James, Young traveled with Palmer to Los Angeles, where he again encountered Furay and Stills and subsequently formed the Buffalo Springfield in March 1966 with them. The group became known for the exciting lead guitar duels between Stills and Young in concert, and for their involvement in the developing folk-rock movement. Although the group disbanded in May 1968, Young contributed some of their best-remembered songs, including "Flying on the Ground Is Wrong," the psychedelic "Mr. Soul," the major production effort "Broken Arrow," and the lyrical "On the Way Home" and "I Am a Child."

Subsequently pursuing a solo career, Young released his debut album, largely overlooked, which included two of his typical, brooding songs, "The Loner" and "I've Been Waiting for You," as well as the poignant "Old Laughing Lady" and the bizarre "Last Trip to Tulsa." His second album, *Everybody Knows This Is Nowhere*, was recorded with Crazy Horse, whom Young had met in 1968. Previously known as the Rockets, Crazy Horse was comprised of Danny Whitten, Billy Talbot, and Ralph Molina. During the mid-'60s the three had been members of the vocal group Danny and the Memories in the Los Angeles area before they moved to San Francisco in 1966 and took up instruments. They returned to Los Angeles and added violinist Bobby Notkoff and guitarists Leon and George Whitsell, becoming the Rockets for local engagements and one album on White Whale Records. Young's *Everybody Knows This Is Nowhere*, often regarded as one of his finest albums, yielded the minor hit "Cinnamon Girl" and included the title song as well as "The Losing End" and the classics "Cowgirl in the Sand" and "Down by the River."

In June 1969 Neil Young joined David Crosby, Stephen Stills, and Graham Nash for touring, including their celebrated appearance at the Woodstock Festival, and the recording of *Déjà Vu*. Adding cohesion and instrumental vitality to the otherwise remarkably subdued group, Young contributed "Helpless" and the three-part "Country Girl" to the best-selling album.

Having fired Crazy Horse because of Danny Whitten's increasing dependence on heroin, Young reluctantly rehired the band for his next solo album, *After the Goldrush*, which featured Crazy Horse's newest member, guitarist Nils Lofgren, and keyboardist-producer Jack Nitzsche. The album produced a moderate hit with "Only Love Can Break Your Heart" and contained the potent classic "Southern Man" as well as "Tell Me Why," "When You Dance I Can Really Love," and Young obscurities "Birds" and "I Believe in You."

Between May and August 1970 Young rejoined Crosby, Stills and Nash on tour. His response to the murder of four students at Kent State University by National Guardsmen, "Ohio," became a major hit at the end of June. The tour's subsequent live album, *Four Way Street*, included a number of Young favorites. Young then embarked on a solo tour, but retreated into inactivity soon after to recover from a slipped disc.

Crazy Horse, comprised of Whitten, Talbot, Molina, Lofgren, and Jack Nitzsche, recorded their debut album for Reprise. Released in 1971, the album included Lofgren's "Beggar's Day," Young's "Dance, Dance, Dance," and Whitten's "I Don't Want to Talk About It" and "Come On Baby, Let's Go Downtown." However, by the end of 1971 Lofgren had left the group and Whitten had become useless. With Talbot and Molina as mainstays, neither *Loose* nor *At Crooked Lake* fared well for Crazy Horse. Danny Whitten died of a heroin overdose on November 29, 1972, in Los Angeles. That, coupled with the overdose death of road crew member Bruce Berry, severely affected Neil Young.

Neil Young's next album, 1972's *Harvest*, featured a new backup group, the Stray Gators, with pedal steel guitarist Ben Keith, pianist Nitzsche, bassist Tim Drummond, and drummer Kenneth Buttrey. It became Young's best-selling album, yielding a top hit with "Heart of Gold" and a moderate hit with the reflective "Old Man" while containing the resigned "Out on the Weekend," "A Man Needs a Maid" (recorded with the London Symphony Orchestra), and the ironically prophetic "The Needle and the Damage Done." After touring again in fall 1972 with the Stray Gators, Young issued *Journey Through the Past* as the soundtrack to the retrospective film premiered five months later. The album, an odd collection of performances by Young, the Buffalo Springfield, and Crosby, Stills, Nash and Young, and the frankly incoherent movie were not well received.

Mounting a massive American tour in early 1973, Neil Young recorded his next album, *Time Fades Away*, on tour. The album featured "Journey Through the Past," "Last Dance," and "Don't Be Denied," and sold modestly. Young reassembled Crazy Horse with Ralph Molina, Billy Talbot, Nils Lofgren, and Ben Keith for extensive touring in 1973–1974, with recordings from the tour eventually issued in 1975 as *Tonight's the Night*. Dedicated to Danny Whitten and Bruce Berry, the album was a highly personal, starkly harrowing, and decidedly anti–music business album. It included Whitten's "Come On Baby, Let's Go Downtown" and Young's own antidrug title song as the album's opening and closing tracks. The rather somber and restrained studio album *On the Beach* had intervened. It contained several surreal songs, such as "Vampire Blues" and "Ambulance Blues," as well as "See the Sky About to Rain" and the minor hit "Walk On By."

Neil Young toured extensively with Crosby, Stills and Nash in 1974–1975, subsequently recording *Zuma* with Crazy Horse, now comprised of Ralph Molina, Billy Talbot, and new guitarist Frank Sampedro. Without yielding a hit single, the album marked the beginning of Young's return to public favor. It contained the seven-minute "Cortez the Killer" and "Pardon My Heart." Young and Stephen Stills reunited for *Long May You Run*, which included Young's title song and "Midnight on the Bay," but the concurrent tour was aborted when Young developed throat problems. Young next planned to release the three-record-set anthology *Decade*, but it was deferred in favor of *American Stars 'n' Bars*, which featured Crazy Horse on one side and the vocal assistance of Linda Ronstadt, Emmylou Harris, and Nicolette Larson. The album contained the potent "Like a Hurricane" and the humorous "Homegrown." *Decade* followed in 1978, compiling material from Young's days with both the Buffalo Springfield and Crosby, Stills and Nash, as well as Young solo material and five previously unreleased songs, including "Love Is a Rose," later popularized by Linda Ronstadt.

Neil Young mounted his first major tour in nearly two years with Crazy Horse in fall 1978 in support of *Comes a Time*, his most accessible album since *Harvest*, and Crazy Horse's *Crazy Moon* on RCA Records. The tour, filmed and recorded, yielded the flawed 1979 movie *Rust Never Sleeps* and the double-record set *Live Rust*, which includes Young's "Lotta Love," a near-smash hit for Nicolette Larson in 1978–1979. The studio album *Rust Never Sleeps* contains one acoustic side and one side recorded with Crazy Horse. It yielded a minor hit with the anthemic "Hey Hey, My My (Into the Black)," reprised in "My My, Hey Hey (Out of the Blue)" as a tribute to the Sex Pistols' Johnny Rotten, while containing "Thrasher," "Powderfinger," and the unusual social commentary "Welfare Mothers." *Hawks and Doves*, recorded with session musicians, was followed by Neil Young and Crazy Horse's *re-ac-tor* in late 1981.

Neil Young subsequently switched to Geffen Records for the strange, synthesizer-dominated *Trans* and rockabilly-style *Everybody's Rockin'*, recorded with a band called the Shocking Pinks. Touring regularly in the '80s, he next recorded the country-style *Old Ways* with Bela Fleck and Nashville studio veterans Ralph Mooney and Hargus "Pig" Robbins. He co-founded the Farm Aid benefit concert in 1985 with Willie Nelson, and he performed at it. Young mounted the most ambitious tour of his career with Crazy Horse in support of 1986's *Landing on Water*. In 1987 Young began hosting annual benefits in the San Francisco Bay Area for the Bridge School, a program for physically disabled, nonspeaking children that regularly drew top-name performers.

After *Life*, Neil Young returned to Reprise Records for the big-band, blues-style *This Note's for You* in 1987, which featured the satirical title song, a parody of the Budweiser beer commercial. The video for the song was at first rejected by MTV because it attacked the increasing commercialism in rock music. Two years later, his *Freedom* album, with "Wrecking Ball" and the anthemic "Rockin' in the Free World," became his best-selling album in years. In 1990 Crazy Horse recorded their first album in more than 10 years, *Left for Dead*, and accompanied Young on *Ragged Glory*, which includes "F*!#in' Up," "Mansion on the Hill," and "Love and Only Love."

Freedom and *Ragged Glory* helped reestablish Young as a contemporary recording artist, drawing comparisons to his finest previous work. Dubbed the Godfather of Grunge, he demonstrated his interest in current music by booking Sonic Youth as his opening act during his 1991 tour with Crazy Horse. Late that year Young issued *Weld*, recorded on tour, and *Arc*, a 35-minute set comprised of feedback and electronic shrieks. The two sets were released simultaneously with a third set, *ArcWeld*, that combined both albums.

Neil Young enjoyed his greatest acclaim in years during the '90s. He returned to the acoustic sound of folk rock with 1992's *Harvest Moon*, inappropriately labeled the follow-up to 1972's *Harvest*. Recorded with the Stray Gators, the band who helped record *Harvest*, the album failed to produce a hit single, although the video for the title track received wide play on both MTV and VH-1, and the album proved to be his most popular since 1979's *Live Rust*. Young's performance on the MTV show *Unplugged* was recorded and issued in 1993, followed a year later by *Sleeps with Angels*, recorded with Crazy Horse, which included his title song lament to Kurt Cobain. Young substituted for an ill Eddie Vedder at a Pearl Jam concert in San Francisco in June 1995. Only days later, Reprise isssued *Mirror Ball*, recorded with Pearl Jam as his backing band. The album featured Vedder sharing vocals with Young on the title song, "Peace and Love," cowritten by Vedder, and "Throw Your Hatred Down," "Act of Love," and "I'm the Ocean."

Neil Young

Neil Young	Reprise	6317	'69	LP/CS/CD
After the Goldrush	Reprise	6383	'70	†
	Reprise	2283		LP/CS/CD

Harvest	Reprise	2032	'72	†
	Reprise	2277		LP/CS/CD
After the Gold Rush/Harvest	Reprise	23715		CS
Journey Through the Past (soundtrack)	Reprise	(2) 6480	'72/'95	CD
Time Fades Away	Reprise	2151	'73/'95	CD
On the Beach	Reprise	2180	'74	†
Tonight's the Night	Reprise	2221	'75	LP/CS/CD
Decade	Reprise	(3) 2257	'77	LP/CS
	Reprise	(2) 2257		CD
Comes a Time	Reprise	2266	'78	CS/CD
Hawks and Doves	Reprise	2297	'80	†
Trans	Geffen	2018	'83	†
Old Ways	Geffen	24068	'85	†
Landing on Water	Geffen	24109	'86	CS/CD
Lucky Thirteen	Geffen	24452	'93	CS/CD
Freedom	Reprise	25899	'89	CS/CD
Arc	Reprise	26769	'91	CD
Harvest Moon	Reprise	45057	'92	CS/CD
Unplugged	Reprise	45310	'93	CS/CD
Mirror Ball	Reprise	(2) 45934	'95	LP
	Reprise	45934	'95	CS/CD

The Rockets

The Rockets	White Whale	7116	'68	†

Neil Young and Crazy Horse

Everybody Knows This Is Nowhere	Reprise	6349	'69	†
	Reprise	2282		CS/CD
Zuma	Reprise	2242	'75	CS/CD
Rust Never Sleeps	Reprise	2295	'79	LP/CS/CD
Live Rust	Reprise	(2) 2296	'79	CS
	Reprise	2296		CD
re-ac-tor	Reprise	2304	'81/'95	CD
Life	Reprise	24154	'87	LP/CS/CD†
Ragged Glory	Reprise	26315	'90	CS/CD
Weld	Reprise	(2) 26671	'91	CS/CD
Arc Weld	Reprise	(3) 26746	'91	CD
Sleeps with Angels	Reprise	(2) 45749	'94	LP
	Reprise	45749	'94	CS/CD
Broken Arrow	Reprise		'96	CS/CD

Neil Young, Crazy Horse, and the Bullets

American Stars 'n' Bars	Reprise	2261	'77	CS

Crazy Horse

Crazy Horse	Reprise	6438	'71/'94	CD
Loose	Reprise	2059	'72	†
At Crooked Lake	Epic	34710	'72	†
Crazy Moon	RCA	3054	'78	†
Left for Dead	Sisapa	77707	'90	CS/CD†

The Stills-Young Band

Long May You Run	Reprise	2253	'76	CS/CD

Neil Young and the Shocking Pinks				
Everybody's Rockin'	Geffen	4013	'83	†
Neil Young and the Bluenotes				
This Note's for You	Reprise	25719	'88	CS/CD

THE YOUNGBLOODS

Jesse Colin Young (b. Perry Miller, Nov. 11, 1944, New York, NY), voc, gtr, bs; **Jerry Corbitt** (b. 1946, Tifton, GA), gtr, bs, voc; **Lowell "Banana" Levinger** (b. 1946, Cambridge, MA), kybd, gtr, bjo, mdln, pno; **Joe Bauer** (b. Sept. 26, 1941, Memphis, TN), drm [Jerry Corbitt left in 1969 and was not replaced until 1971, by bassist **Michael Kane**. The group disbanded in 1972.]

Favorably compared to the Lovin' Spoonful as purveyors of good-time music in the late '60s, the Youngbloods helped popularize Dino Valenti's anthemic "Get Together." Fronted by singer-songwriter-guitarist Jesse Colin Young, the Youngbloods recorded their finest album, *Elephant Mountain*, as a trio before disbanding in 1972. Jesse Colin Young established himself as a purveyor of mellow, folk-style songs for RCA Records, particularly with *Song for Juli* and *Light Shine*, but he subsequently enjoyed only limited success.

Jesse Colin Young assumed his stage name in 1963 when he was working East Coast folk clubs. He recorded one album for Capitol before switching to Mercury, where he recorded *Jesse Colin Young and the Youngbloods* with Peter Childs and John Sebastian. During 1965 he formed a duet with Jerry Corbitt, adding Lowell "Banana" Levinger and Joe Bauer at year's end. Initial recordings as the Youngbloods were eventually released on Mercury Records in 1970, but their first minor hit, the silly dance ditty "Grizzly Bear" (by Corbitt), was issued on RCA Records. Their RCA debut album included "Get Together" by Chester Powers (aka Dino Valenti), a minor hit in 1967 and a smash hit upon rerelease in 1969. *Earth Music*, recorded in New York City, contained Young's "All My Dreams Are Blue" and "The Wine Song," and the ditty "Euphoria."

In late 1967 the group moved to the San Francisco Bay Area and endured the departure of Corbitt. As a trio, the Youngbloods recorded *Elephant Mountain*, regarded as their finest album. It includes "Rain Song," several gentle Young songs, such as "Sunlight," "Beautiful," and "Ride the Wind," and two rather ominous Young songs, "Darkness, Darkness" and "Quicksand."

The Youngbloods switched to Warner Bros. Records, where they recorded for the subsidiary label Raccoon. However, none of their albums sold particularly well, and by 1972 the group had broken up. Young's first solo album for Warner Bros., *Song for Juli*, contained idyllic compositions such as "Morning Sun," "High on a Ridgetop," and "Country Home," as well as the title song, written for his daughter. It became the best-selling album of Young's solo career, although he continued to record for Warner Bros. through 1977. He switched to Elektra for 1978's *American Dreams*, but did not record again until 1987. In the '90s Jesse Colin Young reemerged with *Swept Away* on his own Ridgetop label.

Jesse Colin Young				
The Soul of a City Boy	Capitol	2070	'64	†
	Capitol	11267	'74	†
	Capitol	16129		†
	One Way	17526	'95	CD
Jesse Colin Young and the Youngbloods	Mercury	61005	'65	†
Together	Raccoon	2588	'72	†
Song for Juli	Warner Bros.	2734	'73	†

Light Shine	Warner Bros.	2790	'74	†
Songbird	Warner Bros.	2845	'75	†
On the Road	Warner Bros.	2913	'76	†
Love on the Wing	Warner Bros.	3033	'77	†
American Dreams	Elektra	157	'78	†
The Highway Is for Heroes	Cypress	0103	'87	LP/CS/CD†
Best: The Solo Years	Rhino	70767	'91	CS/CD
Swept Away	Ridgetop	1035		CD

The Youngbloods

Two Trips with Jesse Colin Young	Mercury	61273	'70	†
The Youngbloods	RCA	3724	'67	†
Earth Music	RCA	3865	'67	†
Elephant Mountain	RCA	4150	'69	†
	Mobile Fidelity	792	'89	CD
Best	RCA	4399	'70	†
	RCA	3680	'80	CS/CD
Ride the Wind	RCA	4465		†
	Raccoon	2563	'71	†
Sunlight	RCA	4561	'71	†
This Is the Youngbloods	RCA	(2) 6051	'72	†
Rock Festival	Raccoon	1878	'70	†
Good and Dusty	Raccoon	2566	'71	†
High on a Ridgetop	Raccoon	2653	'72	†

Jerry Corbitt

Corbitt	Polydor	244003	'69	†
Jerry Corbitt	Capitol	771	'71	†

Joe Bauer

Moonset	Raccoon	1901	'71	†

Bauer, Banana, and Kane

Crab Tunes/Noggins	Raccoon	1944		†

Banana and the Bunch

Mid-Mountain Ranch	Raccoon	2626	'72	†

Z

FRANK ZAPPA

(b. Dec. 21, 1940, Baltimore, MD; d. Dec. 4, 1993, Los Angeles, CA)

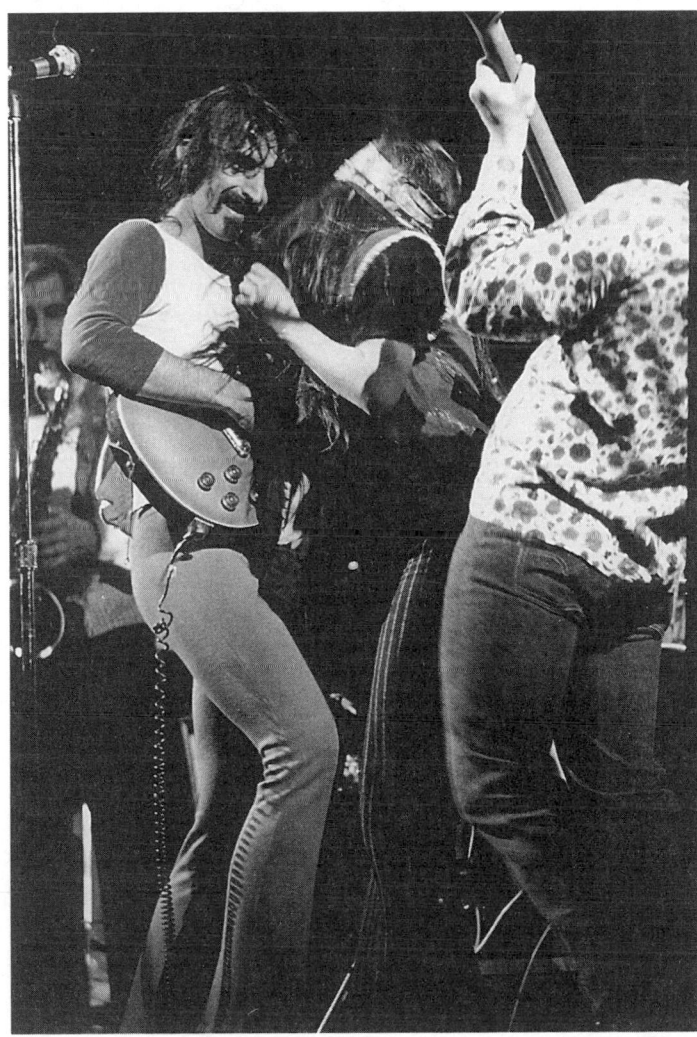

FRANK ZAPPA

Probably the single most iconoclastic, innovative, and adventurous artist in the development of contemporary popular music since the mid-'60s, Frank Zappa pursued a singular musical vision with total disregard for critical and commercial considerations. He first came to prominence as the mastermind of the Mothers of Invention, perhaps the first and only rock group to establish *and* sustain themselves as a strictly underground phenomenon. Zappa pushed the boundaries of rock music, combining elements of jazz, avant-garde, classical, and historic rock while always pursuing his own unique vision.

Frank Zappa moved with his family to California at age 10, and eventually they settled in Lancaster by 1956. Taking up drums at 12, he became a member of the Blackouts while still in high school. Switching to guitar at 18, Zappa then studied harmony in college, and manned groups such as the Omens, with Don Van Vliet (later known as Captain Beefheart), and Captain Glasspack and His Magic Mufflers. After composing the score to the film *The World's Greatest Sinner*, he bought a recording studio in Cucamonga, California, with the profits from a second soundtrack, *Run Home Slow*, in 1963. There he recorded unsuccessfully for a variety of obscure labels under a variety of names, and wrote the

'50s parody/tribute pastiche "Memories of El Monte" for the Penguins with Ray Collins. In early 1965 Zappa began working with the R&B band the Soul Giants, whose members included vocalist Ray Collins, bassist Roy Estrada, and drummer Jim Black (aka Jimmy Carl Black). Becoming the Mothers under Zappa's direction, the group included as its early members guitarists Alice Stuart, Henry Vestine (later with Canned Heat), and Jim Guercio (later the producer-manager of Chicago).

Spotted by producer Tom Wilson, the group was signed to the Verve subsidiary of MGM Records as the Mothers of Invention, with members Zappa, Collins, Estrada, Black, and guitarist Elliott Ingber. Their debut album, *Freak Out!*, came to be regarded as the first concept album and was probably the first double-record set in rock, certainly the first for a new, unknown group. It contained a wondrous mixture of '50s parodies ("How Could I Be Such a Fool," "You Didn't Try to Call Me"), social commentary ("Trouble Every Day," Zappa's response to the Watts riots, and "Who Are the Brain Police"), songs about the group ("Hungry Freaks, Daddy," "Motherly Love"), and bizarre and complex extended pieces ("Help, I'm a Rock," "The Return of the Son of Monster Magnet"), as well as the pop-style "Any Way the Wind Blows."

When Elliott Ingber left the group, the Mothers of Invention added keyboardist Don Preston, saxophonists Bunk Gardner and Jim "Motorhead" Sherwood, and drummer Billy Mundi for *Absolutely Free*. The album included the socially conscious satires "Plastic People," "Brown Shoes Don't Make It," and "America Drinks and Goes Home," the classic "Call Any Vegetable," and the jam "Invocation and Ritual Dance of the Young Pumpkin." In late November 1966 the Mothers began a six-month residency at the Garrick Theater in New York's Greenwich Village, where their shows had a decidedly theatrical bent, utilizing props and choreography and inviting crazy participation by audience members. Eschewing the standard path to popularity involving the contrivance of a palatable image and the manipulation of the mass media, Zappa and the Mothers intentionally projected a group aura of flagrantly indelicate and contemptuous onstage behavior that can be seen as the first instance of calculated theatrics in rock.

Despite the seemingly chaotic and deranged nature of their onstage spectacle, Frank Zappa and the Mothers of Invention performed (and recorded) remarkably disciplined, precise, and technically demanding music, complete with intricate and complex changes of time and key signatures and unusual and difficult phrasings, directed by Zappa as composer, arranger, conductor, and lead guitarist. The group's third album, recorded with new member keyboardist–woodwind player Ian Underwood, was *We're Only in It for the Money*. It effectively parodied the Beatles' *Sgt. Pepper's Lonely Hearts Club Band* in its packaging and sound, while deriding the hippie movement as well as the group's growing contingent of fans. Jim Black returned to drums and Art Tripp was added on percussion with the departure of Billy Mundi, for their next album, *Cruising with Ruben and the Jets*. Zappa satirized '50s rock and roll a full year before the advent of Richard Nader's "Rock-and-Roll Revival" and Sha Na Na, whose recreations served more as commercial and nostalgic products than as amusing parody.

On his own Frank Zappa debuted in 1968 with *Lumpy Gravy*. The album explored techniques from classical music, featured 50 instrumentalists, and revealed Zappa's ongoing proclivity for the unique fusion of modern classical and rock music, a penchant that may ultimately lead to Zappa's recognition as one of the most important composers of serious music in the 20th century. *Uncle Meat* further revealed his compositional and improvisational talents, and *Hot Rats* showed his exceptional skills as both a melodist and guitarist. *Hot Rats* was recorded with the assistance of Ian Underwood, violinist Jean-Luc Ponty, and Captain Beefheart. Sometimes regarded as an early jazz-rock fusion album and usually considered to be one of Zappa's finest early solo albums, *Hot Rats* featured heavy use of synthesizers and included the classic "Willie the Pimp" (with vocals by Beefheart), plus "Peaches en Regalia" and "The Gumbo Variations." It also features extensive use of the synthesizer, an instrument some claim Zappa introduced to live performance with the Mothers. Nonetheless, Zappa was never lumped with the progressive-rock groups of the late '60s, since he composed and performed as a true devotee of classical music (and Edgar Varèse, in particular), and not as a dilettante and usurper of the tradition.

During 1968 and 1969 Zappa also produced albums for the GTOs and Wild Man Fischer and Captain Beefheart's *Trout Mask Replica*. He formed Straight and Bizarre Records in conjunction with manager Herb Cohen under the aegis of Warner Bros./Reprise Records. Alice Cooper's debut album was issued on Straight, and Bizarre releases included the Mothers' *Uncle Meat* and Zappa's *Hot Rats*. In late 1969 Zappa announced that the Mothers would no longer tour. Subsequent releases for the early incarnation of the group were *Burnt Weenie Sandwich*, a testament to Zappa's experiments with dissonance, free-form jazz, and complex compositions, and *Weasels Ripped My Flesh*.

Frank Zappa composed and arranged *King Kong: Jean-Luc Ponty Plays the Music of Frank Zappa* for the violinist before forming a new edition of the Mothers in 1970 with Underwood, keyboardist George Duke, drummer Aynsley Dunbar, and former Turtles vocalists Mark Volman and Howard Kaylan, initially billed as the Phlorescent Leech and Eddie (later shortened to Flo and Eddie). Already having revealed a preoccupation with scatalogical and pucrile themes, in the tradition of satirist Lenny Bruce, Frank Zappa and the Mothers became even more surrealistically humorous and outrageous with the addition of Flo and Eddie. Moreover, during Flo and Eddie's tenure, Zappa conducted video explorations with his *200 Motels* movie that were later adopted by MTV. The film contained several of Zappa's puerile songs, such as "Shove It Right In" and "Penis Dimension," and featured performances by Ringo Starr and Keith Moon. During 1970 and 1971 the Mothers toured extensively, producing the live albums *Fillmore East, June 1971*, and *Just Another Band from L.A.*, which included the mini-opera "Billy the Mountain" and Flo and Eddie's "Eddie, Are You Kidding?"

Seriously injured when pushed from the stage of the Rainbow Theatre in London in December 1971, Frank Zappa reemerged in 1972 with the solo album *Waka Jawaka—Hot Rats*, with its side-long "Big Swifty." With Don Preston, George Duke, Aynsley Dunbar, and additional horns and percussionists, Zappa next recorded *The Grand Wazoo* as the Mothers. A new edition of the Mothers, with Bruce Fowler and Ian Underwood, recorded *Over-Nite Sensation* with Duke and Jean-Luc Ponty for Zappa's newly formed DiscReet label. The live set *Roxy and Elsewhere*, with "Penguin in Bondage" and the instrumental "Don't You Ever Wash That Thing," and *One Size Fits All* were the final albums for the Mothers.

Frank Zappa's solo debut on DiscReet, *Apostrophe (')*, was recorded with a variety of former Mothers plus former Cream bassist Jack Bruce, and yielded a minor hit with the lyrically juvenile "Don't Eat the Yellow Snow." During May 1975 Zappa and old associate Captain Beefheart performed at the Armadillo World Headquarters in Austin, Texas, and live recordings from the shows were issued as *Bongo Fury*. Following *Zoot Allures*, Zappa ended his relationship with manager Herb Cohen and Warner Bros./Reprise, although the label continued to issue new material for several years.

After touring in 1978 with a band that included guitarist Adrian Belew, keyboardist Peter Wolf, and drummer Terry Bozzio, Frank Zappa eventually signed with Phonogram/Mercury, who issued his albums on Zappa Records. His debut for the label, *Sheik Yerbouti*, was his most accessible album in years and served to introduce a new generation to his unique vision. While containing more puerile material such as "Broken Hearts Are for Assholes" and the Peter Frampton parody "I Have Been in You," the album included the moderate hit "Dancin' Fool" (a parody of disco music) and the controversial "Jewish Princess."

Originally intended as a triple-record set, the elaborate tale *Joe's Garage* from 1979 was ultimately issued as a single record, *Act I*, and double-record, *Acts II and III*. *Act I* included more Zappa scatology, such as "Crew Slut" and "Wet T-Shirt Nite," as well as the potentially controversial "Catholic Girls," whereas *Acts II and III* were viewed as dreary and boring. Zappa's film *Baby Snakes* was premiered in early 1980, and after Mercury refused to issue his single "I Don't Wanna Get Drafted," he severed relations with the company. Subsequent Zappa albums were released on the Barking Pumpkin subsidiary of Capitol Records, later transferred to Rhino Records.

Zappa was amazingly prolific in the '80s and utlimately established himself as a true classical composer. Although largely ignored by critics and pop-music fans, Zappa scored a surprise hit in 1981 with "Valley Girl," featuring his daughter Moon Unit's amusing cameo appearance. In 1982 he demonstrated his facility as a guitarist and melodist with *Shut Up 'n' Play Yer Guitar*. He sued his former label Warner Bros. in 1983 and was awarded the ownership of his master recordings for the label in an out-of-court settlement. Conductor Pierre Boulez commissioned Zappa to compose a symphonic work, which was issued on Angel Records in 1984. Zappa also discovered the work of an obscure 18th-century classical composer named Francesco Zappa and recorded an album of his work. In the meantime, Frank Zappa had formed a merchandising company, a music publishing house, and a video company, all run by his wife, Gail.

In 1985 Frank Zappa took center stage at Senate subcommittee hearings considering the recommendations of the Parents' Music Resource Center, staunchly opposing censorship in the recording industry and vociferously advocating the right of freedom of speech. His *Frank Zappa Meets the Mothers of Prevention* lampooned the PMRC and includes the biting "Porn Wars." He reached a licensing agreement with the small Rykodisc label in 1986, and many of his earlier recordings were rereleased by the company. In 1986 and 1987 Rykodisc issued recordings of Zappa's symphonic compositions recorded by the 102-piece London Symphony Orchestra, conducted by Kent Nagano. Having studied and used the synthesizer for years, Zappa composed and performed the Grammy Award–winning *Jazz from Hell* on the synclavier, a sophisticated instrument that was both synthesizer and computer.

In 1988 Frank Zappa conducted his final four-month tour, the Broadway the Hard Way tour, of the United States and Europe. During the American portion of the tour, fans were encouraged to register to vote at facilities provided at concert sites. The tour produced two albums, *The Best Band You Never Heard in Your Life* and *Make a Jazz Noise Here*. That same year, Zappa anthologized his concert career with the 12-CD set *You Can't Do that On Stage Anymore*, also available as six separate two-CD sets. Later, to circumvent the bootlegging of recordings of his live concerts, he issued the eight-CD set *Beat the Boots* in 1991 (also available as single CDs), followed by *Beat the Boots # 2* in 1992. In 1990 Zappa met with new Czechoslovakian president Václav Havel and briefly served as that country's cultural and trade emissary to the West. Zappa later formed the company So What? to link businesses in the Soviet Union and Eastern Europe with those in the West.

Diagnosed with prostate cancer in 1990, Frank Zappa died of complications from the disease on December 4, 1993, in his Laurel Canyon home. His final works include *Playground Psychotics*; *The Yellow Shark*, performed by the German classical group Ensemble Modern; and *Zappa's Universe*, performed by a large stage cast that included Steve Vai, son Dweezil Zappa, and the Persuasions. His last and perhaps most ambitious work, *Civilization, Phaze III*, was initially available only by mail order through Barking Pumpkin Records. In 1994 Rykodisc acquired the rights to Frank Zappa's entire catalog, reissuing virtually all of his recordings in 1995.

Dweezil Zappa launched his own recording career in 1987. In 1993 Dweezil and his brother Ahmet formed Z and recorded for Barking Pumpkin.

The Mothers of Invention

Freak Out!	Verve	(2) 65005	'66	†
	Barking Pumpkin/ Rhino	74208	'88	CS
	Rykodisc	40062	'88	CD†
	Rykodisc	10501	'95	CS/CD

Absolutely Free	Verve	65013	'67	†
	Barking Pumpkin/ Rhino	74214		CS
	Rykodisc	10093		CD†
	Rykodisc	10502	'95	CS/CD
We're Only in It for the Money	Verve	65045	'67	†
	Rykodisc	10503	'95	LP/CS/CD
Cruising with Ruben and the Jets	Verve	65055	'68	†
	Barking Pumpkin/ Rhino	74209	'88	CS
	Rykodisc	10063	'88	CD†
	Rykodisc	10505	'95	CD
Mothermania—The Best of the Mothers	Verve	65068	'69	†
The &?X! of the Mothers	Verve	65074	'69	†
The Mothers of Invention	MGM	112	'70	†
The Worst of the Mothers	MGM	4754	'71	†
Weasels Ripped My Flesh (recorded 1967–1969)	Bizarre/Reprise	2028	'70	†
	Rykodisc	10163	'90	CD†
	Rykodisc	10510	'95	CD
Uncle Meat	Bizarre/Reprise	(2) 2024	'69	†
	Barking Pumpkin/ Rhino	74210	'88	CS
	Rykodisc	(2) 10064/65	'88	CD†
	Rykodisc	10506	'95	CS
	Rykodisc	(2) 10506/07	'95	CD
Burnt Weenie Sandwich	Reprise	6370	'70	†
	Barking Pumpkin	74239	'91	CS/CD
	Rykodisc	10509	'95	CD
Ahead of Their Time	Barking Pumpkin/ Rhino	74246	'93	CD
	Rykodisc	10559	'95	CD

Jean-Luc Ponty

King Kong/Ponty Plays Zappa	World Pacific	20172	'70	†
	Pacific Jazz	89539	'93	CD

Ruben and the Jets (with Jim Sherwood)

For Real	Mercury	659	'73	†
Con Safos	Mercury	694	'73	†

The Grandmothers

The Grandmothers	Rhino	302	'81	†

Frank Zappa and the Mothers

Fillmore East, June 1971	Reprise	2042	'71	†
	Rykodisc	10167	'90	CD†
	Rykodisc	10512	'95	CS/CD
200 Motels (soundtrack)	United Artists	(2) 9956	'71	†
Just Another Band from L.A.	Bizarre/Reprise	2075	'72	†
	Rykodisc	10161	'90	CD†
	Rykodisc	10515	'95	CD
The Grand Wazoo	Bizarre/Reprise	2093	'72	†
	Rykodisc	10026	'86	CD†
	Rykodisc	10517	'95	CD

Over-Nite Sensation	DiscReet/Reprise	2149	'73	†
	DiscReet	2288		†
	Barking Pumpkin/ Rhino	74221	'89	CS
	Rykodisc	10518	'95	CS/CD
Roxy and Elsewhere	DiscReet	(2) 2202	'74	†
	Barking Pumpkin/ Rhino	74241	'92	CS/CD
	Rykodisc	10520	'95	CS/CD
One Size Fits All	DiscReet	2216	'75	†
	Barking Pumpkin/ Rhino	74216	'88	CS
	Rykodisc	10063		CD†
	Rykodisc	10521	'95	CD

Frank Zappa/Captain Beefheart/The Mothers

Bongo Fury	DiscReet	2234	'75	†
	Barking Pumpkin/ Rhino	74220		CS
	Rykodisc	10097	'89	CD†
	Rykodisc	10522	'95	CD

Frank Zappa

Lumpy Gravy	Verve	68741	'68	†
	Rykodisc	10504	'95	CD
Hot Rats	Bizarre/Reprise	6356	'69	†
	Barking Pumpkin/ Rhino	74211	'88	CS
	Rykodisc	10066	'88	CD†
	Rykodisc	10508	'95	CS/CD
Chunga's Revenge	Bizarre/Reprise	2030	'70	†
	Rykodisc	10164	'90	CD†
	Rykodisc	10511	'95	CD
Waka Jawaka—Hot Rats	Bizarre/Reprise	2094	'72	†
	Barking Pumpkin/ Rhino	74215	'88	CS
	Rykodisc	10094		CD†
	Rykodisc	10516	'95	CD
Apostrophe (')	DiscReet	2175	'74	†
	DiscReet	2289		†
	Barking Pumpkin/ Rhino	74222	'89	CS
	Rykodisc	10519	'95	CS/CD
Zoot Allures	Warner Bros.	2970	'76	†
	Rykodisc	10160	'90	CD†
	Rykodisc	10523	'95	CD
Zappa in New York	DiscReet	(2) 2290	'78	†
	Barking Pumpkin/ Rhino	(2) 74240	'91	CS/CD
	Rykodisc	(2) 10524/25	'95	CD

Studio Tan	DiscReet	2291	'78	†
	Barking Pumpkin/ Rhino	74237	'91	CS/CD
	Rykodisc	10526	'95	CD
Sleep Dirt	DiscReet	2292	'79	†
	Barking Pumpkin/ Rhino	74238	'91	CS/CD
	Rykodisc	10527	'95	CD
Orchestral Favorites	DiscReet	2294	'79	†
	Barking Pumpkin/ Rhino	74236	'91	CS/CD
	Rykodisc	10529	'95	CD
Sheik Yerbouti	Zappa	(2) 1501	'79	†
	Barking Pumpkin/ Rhino	74225	'91	CS
	Rykodisc	40162	'90	CD†
	Rykodisc	10528	'95	CS/CD
Joe's Garage, Act I	Zappa	1603	'79	†
	Rykodisc	10530	'95	CS
Joe's Garage, Acts II and III	Zappa	(2) 1502	'79	†
	Rykodisc	10531	'95	CS
Joe's Garage	Barking Pumpkin/ Rhino	(2) 74206	'87	CS
Joe's Garage, Acts I, II, and III	Rykodisc	(2) 10060/61		CD†
	Rykodisc	(2) 10530/31	'95	CD
Tinsel Town Rebellion	Barking Pumpkin	(2) 37336	'81	†
	Rykodisc	40166	'90	CD†
	Rykodisc	10532	'95	CD
You Are What You Is	Barking Pumpkin	(2) 37537	'81	†
	Rykodisc	40165	'90	CD†
	Rykodisc	10536	'95	CD
Ship Arriving Too Late to Save a Drowning Witch	Barking Pumpkin	38066	'82	†
	Barking Pumpkin/ Rhino	74235	'91	CS/CD
	Rykodisc	10537	'95	CD
Shut Up 'n' Play Yer Guitar	Barking Pumpkin	(3) 38289	'82	†
	Rykodisc	(2) 10028/29	'86	CD†
	Rykodisc	(3) 10533-35	'95	CD
The Man from Utopia	Barking Pumpkin	38403	'83	†
	Barking Pumpkin/ Rhino	74245	'93	CD
	Rykodisc	10538	'95	CD
Them or Us	Barking Pumpkin/ Rhino	(2) 74200		CS
	Rykodisc	40027	'86	CD†
	Rykodisc	10543	'95	CD

Thing Fish	Barking Pumpkin	(3) 74201	'84	†
	Barking Pumpkin/ Rhino	(3) 74201		CS
	Rykodisc	(2) 10020/21	'86	CD†
	Rykodisc	(2) 10544/45	'95	CD
Frank Zappa Meets the Mothers of Prevention	Barking Pumpkin	74203	'86	†
	Barking Pumpkin/ Rhino	74203		CS
	Rykodisc	10023	'86	CD†
	Rykodisc	10547	'95	CD
Does Humor Belong in Music	Rykodisc	10548	'95	CD
Jazz from Hell	Barking Pumpkin/ Rhino	74205	'87	CS
	Rykodisc	10030		CD†
	Rykodisc	10549	'95	CD
Guitar	Barking Pumpkin/ Rhino	(2) 74212	'88	CS
	Rykodisc	(2) 10079/80	'88	CD†
	Rykodisc	(2) 10550/51	'95	CD
Broadway the Hard Way	Barking Pumpkin/ Rhino	74218	'88	CS
	Rykodisc	40096	'89	CD†
	Rykodisc	10552	'95	CD
Baby Snakes (soundtrack)	Barking Pumpkin/ Rhino	74219	'88	CS/CD
	Rykodisc	10539	'95	CS/CD
The Best Band You Never Heard in Your Life	Barking Pumpkin/ Rhino	(2) 74233	'91	CS/CD
	Rykodisc	(2) 10553/54	'95	CD
Make a Jazz Noise Here	Barking Pumpkin/ Rhino	(2) 74234	'91	CS/CD
	Rykodisc	(2) 10555/56	'95	CD
Playground Psychotics	Barking Pumpkin/ Rhino	(2) 74244	'92	CD
	Rykodisc	(2) 10557/58	'95	CD
Strictly Commercial: The Best of Frank Zappa	Rykodisc	40500	'95	LP/CS/CD
Reissues				
We're Only in It for the Money/Lumpy Gravy	Rykodisc	40024	'86	CD
Apostrophe/Over-Nite Sensation	Rykodisc	40025	'86	CD
Classical Recordings				
The Perfect Stranger: Boulez Conducts Zappa	Angel	38170	'84	†
	Barking Pumpkin/ Rhino	74242	'92	CS/CD
	Rykodisc	10542	'95	CD
Francesco Zappa	Barking Pumpkin	74202	'84	†
	Barking Pumpkin/ Rhino	74202		CS/CD
	Rykodisc	10546	'95	CD
London Symphony Orchestra	Rykodisc	10022	'86	CD

London Symphony Orchestra, Volume 2	Barking Pumpkin/ Rhino	74207	'87	CS
London Symphony Orhcestra, Volume I and II	Rykodisc	(2) 10540/41	'95	CD
The Yellow Shark	Barking Pumpkin/ Rhino	71600	'93	CS/CD
	Rykodisc	40560	'95	CS/CD

You Can't Do That On Stage Anymore

(in a box)	Rykodisc	(12) 10092		CD
Sampler	Barking Pumpkin/ Rhino	(2) 74213	'88	CS
Volume 1	Rykodisc	(2) 10081/82	'88	CD†
	Rykodisc	10561/62	'95	CD
Volume 2	Barking Pumpkin/ Rhino	(3) 74217	'88	CS
	Rykodisc	(2) 10083/84		CD†
	Rykodisc	(2) 10563/64	'95	CD
Volume 3	Rykodisc	(2) 10085/86		CD
	Rykodisc	(2) 10065/66	'95	CD
Volume 4	Barking Pumpkin/ Rhino	(2) 74231		CS
	Rykodisc	(2) 10087/88		CD
	Rykodisc	(2) 10567/68	'95	CD
Volume 5	Rykodisc	(2) 10089/90	'92	CD†
	Rykodisc	10569/70	'95	CD
Volume 6	Rykodisc	(2) 10091/92	'92	CD†
	Rykodisc	(2) 10571/72	'95	CD

Beat The Boots

Beat the Boots	Foo-Eee	(8) 70907	'91	CS
As An Am Zappa, New York, 10/31/81	Foo-Eee	70537	'91	CD
The Ark: The Mothers of Invention, Boston 7/68	Foo-Eee	70538	'91	CD
Freaks and Motherfu*%!!@#: Fillmore East 5/11/70	Foo-Eee	70539	'91	CD
Unmitigated Audacity: Zappa (Mothers), Notre Dame University, 5/12/74	Foo-Eee	70540	'91	CD
Anyway the Wind Blows: Zappa, Paris, 2/24/79	Foo-Eee	70541	'91	CD
'Tis the Season to Be Jelly: Zappa (Mothers), Sweden, 9/30/67	Foo-Eee	70542	'91	CD
Saarbrucken 1979: Zappa, Saarbrucken, 9/3/78	Foo-Eee	70543	'91	CD
Piquantique: Zappa, Stockholm, 8/21/73, and Sydney, 1973	Foo-Eee	70544	'91	CD
Beat the Boots # 2	Foo-Eee	(11) 70372	'92	LP
	Foo-Eee	(7) 70372	'92	CS
	Foo-Eee	(0) 70372	'92	CD

Tribute Album

Zappa's Universe	Verve	513575	'93	CS/CD

Dweezil Zappa

Havin' a Bad Day	Rykodisc	10057	'87	CD†
My Guitar Want to Kill Your Mama	Rykodisc		'88	†
Confessions	Barking Pumpkin	74232	'91	CS/CD†

Z

Shampoohorn	Barking Pumpkin/ Rhino	71760	'94	CS/CD

ZZ TOP

Billy Gibbons (b. Dec. 12, 1949, Houston, TX), gtr, voc; **Dusty Hill** (b. 1949, Dallas, TX), bs, voc; **Frank Beard** (b. Dec. 10, 1949, Houston, TX), drm

The long-lived Texas-based blues and boogie band ZZ Top established themselves through years of rigorous touring and best-selling albums, beginning with 1973's *Tres Hombres*. Playing fundamental three-chord rock, ZZ Top recorded songs preoccupied with women, alcohol, and cars, in the power-trio format pioneered by Cream. Scoring their first major hit with "Tush" in 1975, ZZ Top were established as a touring band. Visually unmistakable in the '80s (Gibbons and Hill sported foot-long beards), they eventually achieved their second major hit in 1984 with the near-smash hit "Legs," from *Eliminator*, which remained on the album charts for more than three years. They have continued to record and tour, although with less popularity, into the '90s.

ZZ Top formed in 1969 in Houston, Texas. Billy Gibbons had played lead guitar in the Houston psychedelic band Moving Sidewalks, while Dusty Hill and Frank Beard had played in the Dallas-based band American Blues. Signed to London Records, ZZ Top's first album failed to sell, yet they embarked on a series of near-constant tours that ultimately established them in the United States. *Rio Grande Mud* (1972) yielded their first minor hit, "Francene," and the follow-up *Tres Hombres* became a best-seller, remaining on the album charts for more than a year. *Fandango!*, comprised of one live side and one studio side, included their tribute to Texas border radio stations, "Heard It on the X," and produced their first major hit with "Tush." For their Worldwide Texas tour of 1976–1977, ZZ Top was accompanied by a retinue that included longhorn cattle, bison, snakes, cactus, and a vulture. The tour was the most successful of the year and established the group nationally as a touring band.

Exhausted from years of constant touring (around three hundred engagements a year), ZZ Top took three years off, eventually switching to Warner Bros. for *Deguello*. The album yielded a moderate hit with "I Thank You" and a minor hit with the favorite "Cheap Sunglasses." They conducted a yearlong tour in 1981–1982, in support of *El Loco*. They scored their first near-smash hit with the sexist "Legs" from 1983's *Eliminator*, and their tour in support of the album lasted more than two years. ZZ Top finally established themselves as a popular recording band with late 1985's *Afterburner*. Benefiting from frequent showings of their videos on MTV, the album yielded four hits: the near-smash "Sleeping Bags," the major hits "Stages" and "Rough Boy," and the minor hit favorite "Sharp Dressed Man." They toured again in 1986 and eventually recorded *Recycler*, touring once again, this time with an elaborate show that included lasers and fireworks.

In 1993 ZZ Top signed a $30-million, five-album contract with RCA. Their debut for RCA, *Antenna*, included the radio favorites "Pincushion" and "Breakaway," and their tour in support of the album featured barely clothed female dancers, which substantiated their raunchy and superficial image.

ZZ Top

First Album	London	584	'70	†
	Warner Bros.	3268		LP/CS/CD
Rio Grande Mud	London	612	'72	†
	Warner Bros.	3269		LP/CS/CD
Tres Hombres	London	631	'73	†
	Warner Bros.	3270		LP/CS/CD
Fandango!	London	656	'75	†
	Warner Bros.	3271		LP/CS/CD
Tres Hombres/Fandango!	Warner Bros.	23710		CS

Tejas	London	680	'77	†
	Warner Bros.	3272		LP/CS/CD
Best	London	706	'77	†
	Warner Bros.	3273		LP/CS/CD
Deguello	Warner Bros.	3361	'79	LP/CS/CD
El Loco	Warner Bros.	3593	'81	LP/CS/CD
El Loco/Deguello	Warner Bros.	23957		CS
Eliminator	Warner Bros.	23774	'83	LP/CS/CD
Afterburner	Warner Bros.	25342	'85	LP/CS/CD
The ZZ Top Six Pack (reissue of first six albums, through *El Loco*)	Warner Bros.	(6) 25661	'88	CD
Recycler	Warner Bros.	26265	'90	CD
Greatest Hits	Warner Bros.	26846	'92	CS/CD
One Foot in the Blues	Warner Bros.	45815	'94	CS/CD
Antenna	RCA	66317	'93	CS/CD

BIBLIOGRAPHY

BOOKS AND ARTICLES ABOUT ARTISTS

References under each artist's name are in chronological order.

ABBA
Lindvall, Marianne. *ABBA: The Ultimate Pop Group*. Edmonton: Hurtig, 1977.
Edington, Harry, and Himmelstrand, Peter. *ABBA*. Magnum, 1978.
Tobler, John. *ABBA for the Record: The Authorized Story in Words and Pictures*. Stafford, England: Pemberton, 1980.
York, Rosemary. *ABBA in Their Own Words*. London: Omnibus, 1981.

AC/DC
Bunton, Richard. *AC/DC: Hell Ain't No Bad Place to Be*. London: Omnibus, 1982.
Dome, Malcolm. *AC/DC*. London: Proteus, 1982.
Ezra, Paul. *The AC/DC Story*. London: Babylon Books, 1982.
Putterford, Mark. *AC/DC Illustrated Biography*. London: Omnibus, 1992.

Aerosmith
Putterford, Mark. *The Fall and Rise of Aerosmith*. London: Omnibus, 1991.

The Allman Brothers Band
Crowe, Cameron. "The Allman Brothers Story." *Rolling Stone*, no. 149 (December 6, 1973), pp. 46–50, 52, 54.
Nolan, Tom. *The Allman Brothers Band: A Biography in Words and Music*. New York: Chappell Music, 1976.
Freeman, Scott. *Midnight Riders: The Story of the Allman Brothers Band*. Boston: Little Brown, 1995.

The Animals
Blackford, Andy. *Wild Animals*. London: Sidgwick & Jackson, 1986.
Kent, Jeff. *The Last Poet: The Story of Eric Burdon*. Witan Creations, 1989.

Bachman-Turner Overdrive
Melhuish, Martin. *Bachman-Turner Overdrive: Rock Is My Life, This Is My Story, This Is My Song: The Authorized Biography*. Toronto: Two Continents, 1976.

Joan Baez
Swanekamp, Joan. *Diamonds and Rust: A Bibliography and Discography of Joan Baez*. Ann Arbor, MI: Pierian Press, 1982.

The Band
Marcus, Greil. "The Band's Last Waltz—That Train Don't Stop Here Anymore." *Rolling Stone*, no. 229 (December 30, 1976), pp. 38–42.

The Beach Boys
Barnes, Ken. *The Beach Boys: A Biography in Words and Pictures*. New York: Sire Books, 1976.

Leaf, David. *The Beach Boys and the California Myth.* New York: Grosset & Dunlap, 1978.

Tobler, John. *The Beach Boys.* London: Hamlyn, 1978.

Preiss, Byron. *The Beach Boys.* New York: Ballantine Books, 1979.

Gaines, Steve. *Heroes and Villains: The True Story of the Beach Boys.* New York: Macmillan, 1978.

Elliott, Brad. *Surf's Up: The Beach Boys on Record, 1961–1981.* Ann Arbor, MI: Pierian Press, 1982.

Milward, John. *The Beach Boys: Silver Anniversary.* New York: Doubleday/Dolphin, 1986.

The Beatles

Braun, Michael. *Love Me Do: The Beatles' Progress.* London: Penguin Books, 1964.

Epstein, Brian. *A Cellarful of Noise.* Garden City, NY: Doubleday, 1964.

Shepherd, Billy. *The True Story of the Beatles.* New York: Bantam Books, 1964.

Davies, Hunter. *The Beatles.* New York: McGraw-Hill, 1968.

Davis, Edward E. *The Beatles Book.* New York: Cowles, 1968.

Fast, Julius. *The Beatles: The Real Story.* New York: Putnam, 1968.

Scaduto, Anthony. *The Beatles.* New York: Signet Books, 1968.

Cott, Jonathan, and Dalton, David. *The Beatles Get Back.* London: Apple, 1970.

Dilello, Richard. *The Longest Cocktail Party: A Personal History of Apple.* Chicago: Playboy Press, 1972.

McCabe, Peter, and Schonfeld, Robert. *Apple to the Core: The Unmaking of the Beatles.* New York: Pocket Books, 1972.

Mellers, Wilfrid. *Twilight of the Gods.* London: Faber and Faber, 1973.

Taylor, Derek. *As Time Goes By.* San Francisco: Straight Arrow Books, 1973.

Burt, Robert, and Pascall, Jeremy. *The Beatles: The Fabulous Story of John, Paul, George and Ringo.* London: Octopus Books, 1975.

Carr, Roy, and Tyler, Tony. *The Beatles: An Illustrated Record.* New York: Harmony Books, 1975.

Williams, Allan, and Marshall, William. *The Man Who Gave the Beatles Away.* New York: Macmillan, 1975.

Castleman, Harry, and Podrazik, Walter J. *All Together Now: The First Complete Beatles Discography, 1961–1975.* Ann Arbor, MI: Pierian Press, 1976.

———. *The Beatles Again?* Ann Arbor, MI: Pierian Press, 1977.

Schaffner, Nicholas. *The Beatles Forever.* New York: McGraw-Hill, 1977.

DiFranco, J. Philip (editor). *The Beatles: A Hard Day's Night.* London: Penguin, 1978.

Miles (compiler). *Beatles in Their Own Words.* New York: Quick Fox, 1978.

Shipper, Mark. *Paperback Writer: The Life and Times of the Beatles: The Spurious Chronicle.* New York: Grosset & Dunlap, 1978.

Friede, Goldie; Titone, Robin; and Weiner, Sue. *The Beatles, A to Z.* New York: Methuen, 1980.

Martin, George, with Hornsby, Jeremy. *All You Need Is Ears.* New York: St. Martin's Press, 1980.

Schaffner, Nicholas. *The Boys from Liverpool: John, Paul, George, Ringo.* Toronto: Methuen, 1980.

Stokes, Geoffrey. *The Beatles.* New York: Times Books/A Rolling Stone Book, 1980.

Blake, John. *All You Needed Was Love: The Beatles After the Beatles.* London: Hamlyn, 1981.

Doney, Malcolm. *Lennon and McCartney.* Midas Books, 1981.

Norman, Philip. *Shout! The True Story of the Beatles.* Elm Tree Books, 1981.

Schultheiss, Tom (compiler). *The Beatles: A Day in the Life.* New York: Quick Fox. 1981.

Woffinden, Bob. *The Beatles Apart.* London: Proteus, 1981.

Stannard, Neville. *The Long and Winding Road: A History of the Beatles on Record.* London: Virgin Books, 1982.

———. *Working Class Heroes: The History of the Beatles' Solo Recordings.* London: Virgin Books, 1983.

Brown, Peter, and Gaines, Steven. *The Love You Make: An Insider's Story of the Beatles.* New York: McGraw-Hill, 1983.

Harry, Bill. *Paperback Writers: An Illustrated Bibliography.* London: Omnibus, 1984.

Castleman, Harry, and Podrazik, Wally. *The End of the Beatles.* Ann Arbor, MI: Pierian Press, 1985.

Taylor, Derek. *It Was Twenty Years Ago.* New York: Bantam Books, 1987.

Wiener, Allen J. *The Beatles: A Recording History.* Bailey Brothers and Swinfen, 1987.

Lewisohn, Mark. *The Beatles: 25 Years in the Life.* London: Sidgwick & Jackson, 1988.

Coleman, Ray. *The Man Who Made the Beatles: An Intimate Biography of Brian Epstein.* New York: McGraw-Hill, 1989.

McKeen, William. *The Beatles: A Bio-Bibliography.* New York: Greenwood Press, 1989.

Russell, Jeff. *The Beatles Album File and Complete Discography.* Dorset, England: Blandford Press, 1989.

Lewisohn, Mark. *Complete Beatles Recording Sessions: The Official Story of the Abbey Road Years.* London: Hamlyn, 1990.

Pawlowski, Gareth L. *How They Became the Beatles: A Definitive History of the Early Years, 1960–1964.* Macdonald, 1990.

Lewisohn, Mark. *The Complete Beatles Chronicle.* New York: Harmony Books, 1992.

Jeff Beck

Rohter, Larry. "Jeff Beck: The Progression of a True Progressive." *Downbeat*, vol. 44, no. 12 (June 16, 1977), pp. 13, 14, 53.

The Bee Gees

Stevens, Kim. *The Bee Gees: A Photo Bio.* New York: Jove, 1978.

Chuck Berry

Marcus, Greil. "Chuck Berry Interview." *Rolling Stone*, no. 35 (June 14, 1969), pp. 15–17.

Salvo, Patrick William. "A Conversation with Chuck Berry." *Rolling Stone*, no. 122 (November 23, 1972), pp. 35, 36, 38, 42.

DeWitt, Howard A. *Chuck Berry: Rock 'n' Roll Music.* Fremont, CA: Horizon Books, 1981.

Black Sabbath

Welch, Chris. *Black Sabbath.* London: Proteus, 1982.

Johnson, Gary. *Ozzy Osbourne.* London: Proteus, 1985.

Wall, Mick. *Diary of a Madman: The Uncensored Memoirs of Rock's Greatest Rogue.* London: Zomba, 1986.

Blondie

Bangs, Lester. *Blondie.* New York: Fireside Books, 1980.

Mike Bloomfield

Ward, E. *Michael Bloomfield: The Rise and Fall of an American Guitar Hero.* Port Chester, NY: Cherry Lane Books, 1983.

Booker T. and the MGs

Schneckloth, Tim. "Booker T. and the MGs: Time, Soul and One Magic River." *Downbeat*, vol. 44, no. 16 (October 6, 1977), pp. 18, 19, 46.

David Bowie

Tremlett, George. *The David Bowie Story.* London: Futura, 1974.

Douglas, David. *Presenting David Bowie.* New York: Pinnacle Books, 1975.

Claire, Vivian. *David Bowie! The King of Glitter Rock.* New York: Flash Books, 1977.

Fletcher, David Jeffrey. *David Robert Jones Bowie: The Discography of a Generalist, 1962–1979.* Chicago: F. Fergeson Productions, 1979.

Fletcher, David Jeffrey. "A Decade of Changes." *Goldmine*, no. 46 (March 1980), pp. 12–16.

Miles, and Charlesworth, Chris. *David Bowie Black Book: The Illustrated Biography.* London: Omnibus, 1980.

Carr, Roy, and Murray, Charles Shaar. *Bowie: An Illustrated Record.* New York: Avon Books, 1981.

Charlesworth, Chris. *David Bowie: Profile.* New York: Proteus, 1981.

Cann, Kevin. *David Bowie: A Chronology.* London: Vermilion Books, 1983.

Lynch, Kate. *David Bowie: A Rock 'n' Roll Odyssey.* London: Proteus, 1984.

Hopkins, Jerry. *Bowie.* Elm Tree Books, 1985.

Gillman, Peter and Leni. *Alias David Bowie.* Hodder, 1990.

Bowie, Angela, with Carr, Patrick. *Backstage Passes: Life on the Wild Side with David Bowie.* New York: Putnam, 1993.

James Brown

Rose, Cynthia. *Living in America: The Soul Saga of James Brown.* London: Serpent's Tail, 1990.

Jackson Browne

Crowe, Cameron. "A Child's Garden of Jackson Browne." *Rolling Stone,* no. 161 (May 23, 1974), pp 38–40.

The Byrds

Scoppa, Bud. *The Byrds.* New York: Scholastic Book Services, 1971.

Captain Beefheart

Winner, Langdon. "The Odyssey of Captain Beefheart." *Rolling Stone,* no. 58 (May 14, 1970), pp. 36–40.

Keepnews, Peter. "Captain Beefheart." *Downbeat,* vol. 48, no. 4 (April 1981), pp. 19–22, 63, 64.

Webb, Colin David. *Captain Beefheart: The Man and His Music.* Kawabata Press, 1990.

The Carpenters

Coleman, Ray. *The Carpenters: The Untold Story.* New York: HarperCollins, 1994.

Johnny Cash

Govoni, Albert. *A Boy Named Cash.* New York: Lancer Books, 1970.

Hudson, James A. *Johnny Cash Close-Up.* New York: Scholastic Book Services, 1971.

Wren, Christopher. *Winners Got Scars, Too: The Life and Legends of Johnny Cash.* New York: Dial Press, 1971.

Conn, Charles P. *The New Johnny Cash.* New York: Family Library, 1973.

Ray Charles

Fong-Torres, Ben. "The *Rolling Stone* Interview: Ray Charles." *Rolling Stone,* no. 126 (January 18, 1973), pp. 29–36.

Cher

Taraborelli, J. Randy. *Cher.* New York: St. Martin's Press, 1989.

Quirk, Lawrence J. *Totally Uninhibited: The Life and Wild Times of Cher.* New York: William Morrow, 1991.

Eric Clapton

Turner, Steven. "The *Rolling Stone* Interview: Eric Clapton." *Rolling Stone,* no. 65 (July 18, 1974), pp. 53–58.

Pidgeon, John. *Eric Clapton: A Biography.* Panther/Granada, 1976.

Shapiro, Harry. *Slowhand: The Story of Eric Clapton.* London: Proteus, 1984.

Coleman, Ray. *Survivor: The Authorized Biography of Eric Clapton.* London: Sidgwick & Jackson, 1986.

Roberty, Marc. *Clapton: The Complete Chronicle.* Pyramid Books, 1991.

Shapiro, Harry. *Eric Clapton: Lost in the Blues.* Guinness, 1992.

Dick Clark

Uslan, Michael, and Solomon, Bruce. *Dick Clark's the First 25 Years of Rock & Roll*. New York: Dell, 1981.

The Clash

Miles, and Tobler, John. *The Clash*. London: Omnibus, 1981.

The Coasters

Millar, Bill. *The Coasters*. Star/W. H. Allen, 1975.

Joe Cocker

Bean, J. P. *Joe Cocker: With a Little Help from My Friends*. London: Omnibus, 1991.

Leonard Cohen

Dorman, L. S., and Rawlins, C. L. *Leonard Cohen: Prophet of the Heart*. London: Omnibus, 1990.

Judy Collins

Claire, Vivian. *Judy Collins*. New York: Flash Books, 1978.

Commander Cody and His Lost Planet Airmen

Stokes, Geoffrey. *Starmaking Machinery: The Odyssey of an Album*. New York: Bobbs-Merrill, 1976.

Sam Cooke

McEwen, Joe. *Sam Cooke: A Biography in Words and Pictures*. New York: Sire Books, 1977.
Wolff, Daniel, with Crain, S. R.; White, Clifton; and Tenenbaun, G. David. *You Send Me: The Life and Times of Sam Cooke*. New York: William Morrow, 1995.

Alice Cooper

Demorest, Steve. *Alice Cooper*. New York: Popular Library, 1974.
Greene, Bob. *Billion Dollar Baby*. New York: Atheneum, 1974.

Elvis Costello

Reese, Krista. *Elvis Costello*. New York: Proteus/Charles Scribner's, 1981.
St. Michael, Mick. *Elvis Costello*. London: Omnibus, 1986.
Gouldstone, David. *Elvis Costello: A Man Out of Time*. London: Sidgwick & Jackson, 1989.
Thomas, Bruce. *The Big Wheel*. New York: Viking Press, 1990.

Cream

Hall, Stanley. "Jack Bruce: Low-Key Eclectic." *Downbeat*, vol. 45, no. 2 (January 26, 1978), pp. 17, 18, 39.

Creedence Clearwater Revival

Gleason, Ralph J. "The *Rolling Stone* Interview: John Fogerty." *Rolling Stone*, no. 52 (February 21, 1970), pp. 17–22, 24.
Hallowell, John. *Inside Creedence*. New York: Bantam Books, 1971.

Crosby, Stills and Nash

Fong-Torres, Ben. "The *Rolling Stone* Interview: David Crosby." *Rolling Stone*, no. 63 (July 23, 1970), pp. 21–27.
Crowe, Cameron. "The Actual Honest-to-Goodness Reunion of Crosby, Stills and Nash." *Rolling Stone*, no. 240 (June 2, 1977), pp. 54–61.
Zimmer, Dave. *Crosby, Stills and Nash: The Authorized Biography*. London: Omnibus, 1984.

Bobby Darin

Diorio, Al. *Borrowed Time: The 37 Years of Bobby Darin*. Philadelphia: Running Press, 1981.
Darin, Dodd. *Dream Lovers*. New York: Warner Books, 1994.

Deep Purple

Charlesworth, Chris. *Deep Purple: The Illustrated Biography.* London: Omnibus, 1984.

Neil Diamond

Fong-Torres, Ben. "The Frog Who Would Be King: The Importance of Being Neil Diamond." *Rolling Stone*, no. 222 (September 23, 1976), pp. 100–106, 109.

Dion

Price, Richard. "Hey, Dion, My Man! Wandering Back to the Mean Street Music of Arthur Avenue." *Rolling Stone*, no. 218 (July 29, 1976), pp. 34–37.

Dire Straits

Oldfields, Michael. *Dire Straits.* London: Sidgwick & Jackson, 1984.

Palmer, Myles. *Mark Knopfler: The Unauthorized Biography.* London: Sidgwick & Jackson, 1992.

Doctor John

Hohman, Marv. "Roots Conquer All: Dr. John." *Downbeat*, vol. 42, no. 10 (May 22, 1975), pp. 13–16, 40, 41.

The Doobie Brothers

White, Timothy. "The Doobie Brothers: The Road Goes On Forever." *Rolling Stone*, no. 300 (September 20, 1979), pp. 9, 10, 14, 16, 39.

The Doors

Hopkins, Jerry. "The *Rolling Stone* Interview: Jim Morrison." *Rolling Stone*, no. 38 (July 26, 1969), pp. 15–18, 22, 24.

Jahn, Mike. *Jim Morrison and the Doors.* New York: Grosset & Dunlap, 1969.

Jackson, Blair. "The Second Coming of Jim Morrison." *BAM*, no. 45 (December 1, 1978), pp. 26–29.

Hopkins, Jerry, and Sugerman, Danny. *No One Here Gets Out Alive.* New York: Warner Books, 1980.

Sugerman, Danny. *The Doors: An Illustrated History.* New York: Quill Books, 1983.

Tobler, John, and Doe, Andrew. *The Doors.* London: Proteus, 1984.

Lisciandro, Frank. *Morrison: A Feast of Friends.* London: Omnibus, 1991.

Seymore, Bob. *Jim Morrison: The End.* London: Omnibus, 1991.

Riordan, James, and Prochnicky, Jerry. *Break On Through: The Life and Death of Jim Morrison.* London: Plexus, 1992.

The Drifters

Millar, Bill. *The Drifters: The Rise and Fall of the Black Vocal Group.* London: Studio Vista, 1971.

Bob Dylan

Ribakove, Sly, and Ribakove, Barbara. *Folk Rock—The Bob Dylan Story.* New York: Dell, 1966.

Kramer, Daniel. *Bob Dylan.* New Jersey: Castle Books, 1967.

Pennebaker, D. A. *Bob Dylan: Don't Look Back.* New York: Ballantine Books, 1968.

Pickering, Steve (editor). *A Commemoration.* Berkeley, CA: Book People, 1971.

Scaduto, Anthony. *Bob Dylan: An Intimate Biography.* New York: Grosset & Dunlap, 1971.

Thompson, Toby. *Positively Main Street: An Unorthodox View of Bob Dylan.* New York: Coward-McCann, 1971.

Gray, Michael. *Song and Dance Man: The Art of Bob Dylan.* London: Hart-Davis, MacGibbon, 1972.

McGregor, Craig. *Bob Dylan: A Retrospective.* Garden City, NY: Doubleday, 1972.

Rolling Stone. Knockin' on Heaven's Door: On the Road in '74. New York: Pocket Books, 1974.

Pickering, Steve. *Bob Dylan Approximately.* New York: David McKay, 1975.

Shepard, Sam. *Rolling Thunder Logbook.* New York: Viking Press, 1977.

Gross, Michael. *Bob Dylan: An Illustrated History.* New York: Grosset & Dunlap, 1978.

Marchbank, Pearce (editor). *Bob Dylan in His Own Words.* New York: Quick Fox, 1978.

Rinzler, Alan. *Bob Dylan: An Illustrated Record.* New York: Harmony Books, 1978.

Sloman, Larry. *On the Road with Bob Dylan.* New York: Bantam Books, 1978.

Cable, Paul. *Bob Dylan: His Unreleased Recordings.* New York: Schirmer Books, 1980.

Williams, Paul. *Dylan: What Happened?* Encinitas, CA: Entwhistle Books, 1980.

Shelton, Robert. *No Direction Home: The Life and Music of Bob Dylan.* New York: William Morrow, 1986.

Wolliver, Robbie. *Bringing It All Back Home.* New York: Pantheon, 1987.

Spitz, Bob. *Dylan: A Biography.* Michael Joseph, 1989.

Thomson, Elizabeth M., and Gutman, David. *Dylan Companion.* New York: Macmillan, 1990.

Heylin, Clinton. *Dylan — Behind the Shades.* New York: Viking Press, 1991.

The Eagles

Swenson, John. *The Eagles.* New York: Ace Books, 1981.

Brian Eno

Tamm, Eric. *Brian Eno: His Music and the Vertical Colour of Sound.* London: Faber & Faber, 1989.

Everly Brothers

Karpp, Phyllis. *Ike's Boys.* Ann Arbor, MI: Pierian Press, 1988.

Fairport Convention

Humphries, Patrick. *Meet on the Ledge: A History of Fairport Convention.* Eel Pie, 1982.

Fleetwood Mac

Carr, Roy, and Tyler, Tony. *Fleetwood Mac: Rumours 'n' Fax.* New York: Harmony Books, 1978.

Graham, Samuel. *Fleetwood Mac: The Authorized History.* New York: Warner Books, 1978.

Clarke, Steve. *Fleetwood Mac.* London: Proteus, 1985.

The Flying Burrito Brothers

Griffin, Sid. *Gram Parsons: A Musical Biography.* Pasadena: Sierra Books, 1985.

Fong-Torres, Ben. *Hickory Wind: The Life and Times of Gram Parsons.* New York: Pocket Books, 1991.

Peter Frampton

Daly, Marsha. *Peter Frampton.* New York: Tempo Books, 1978.

Adler, Irene. *Peter Frampton.* New York: Quick Fox, 1979.

Aretha Franklin

Bego, Mark. *Aretha Franklin.* New York: St Martin's Press, 1990.

Alan Freed

Jackson, John A. *Big Beat Heat: Alan Freed and the Early Years of Rock 'n' Roll.* New York: Schirmer Books, 1991.

Marvin Gaye

Ritz, David. *Divided Soul: The Life of Marvin Gaye.* New York: McGraw-Hill, 1985.

Davis, Sharon. *I Heard It Through the Grapevine: Marvin Gaye, the Biography.* Edinburgh: Mainstream, 1991.

Genesis

Gallo, Armando. *Genesis: The Evolution of a Rock Band.* London: Sidgwick & Jackson, 1978.

Clarke, Steve. *Genesis: Turn It On Again.* London: Omnibus, 1984.

Waller, Johnny. *Phil Collins.* Zomba, 1986.

Bright, Spencer. *Peter Gabriel: An Authorized Biography.* London: Sidgwick & Jackson, 1988.

Berry Gordy

Morse, David. *Motown and the Arrival of Black Music.* London: Studio Vista, 1971.

Benjaminson, Peter. *The Story of Motown.* New York: Grove Press, 1979.

George, Nelson. *Where Did Our Love Go? The Rise and Fall of the Motown Sound.* New York: St. Martin's Press, 1986.

Singleton, Raymona Gordy. *Berry, Me and Motown.* Chicago: Contemporary Books, 1990.

Bill Graham

Glatt, John. *Rage and Roll: Bill Graham and the Selling of Rock.* New York: Birch Lane Press, 1994.

The Grateful Dead

Reich, Charles, and Wenner, Jann. *Garcia: A Signpost to New Space.* San Francisco: Straight Arrow Books, 1972.

Harrison, Hank. *The Dead Book: A Social History of the Grateful Dead.* New York: Link Books, 1973.

Grushkin, Paul; Bassett, Cynthia; and Grushkin, Jonas. *Grateful Dead: The Official Book of the Dead Heads.* New York: William Morrow, 1983.

Gans, David, and Simon, Peter. *Playing in the Band: An Oral and Visual Portrait of the Grateful Dead.* New York: St. Martin's Press, 1985.

Jensen, Jamie. *Built to Last: Twenty-Five Years of the Grateful Dead.* London: Penguin, 1990.

Troy, Sandy. *One More Saturday Night: Reflections with the Grateful Dead, Dead Family and Dead.* New York: St. Martin's Press, 1992.

Guns N' Roses

Elliot, Paul. *Guns N' Roses: The World's Most Outrageous Hard Rock Band.* London: Hamlyn, 1990.

Sugerman, Danny. *Appetite for Destruction: The Days of Guns N' Roses.* New York: St. Martin's Press, 1992.

Bill Haley

Swenson, John. *Bill Haley: The Daddy of Rock and Roll.* New York: Stein and Day, 1983.

George Harrison

Michaels, Ross. *George Harrison: Yesterday and Today.* New York: Flash Books, 1977.

Clayson, Alan. *The Quiet One: A Life of George Harrison.* London: Sidgwick & Jackson, 1990.

Jimi Hendrix

Welch, Chris. *Hendrix: A Biography.* New York: Flash Books, 1973.

Knight, Curtis. *Jimi.* New York: Praeger, 1974.

Carey, Gary. *Lenny, Janis and Jimi.* New York: Pocket Books, 1975.

Henderson, David. *Jimi Hendrix: Voodoo Child of the Aquarian Age.* Garden City, NY: Doubleday, 1978.

Hopkins, Jerry. *Hit and Run: The Jimi Hendrix Story.* New York: Perigee, 1983.

Henderson, David. *'Scuse Me While I Kiss the Sky.* New York: Doubleday/Dolphin, 1983.

Sampson, Victor. *Hendrix: An Illustrated Biography.* London: Proteus, 1984.

Shapiro, Harry, and Glebbeek, Caesar. *Electric Gypsy.* London: Heinemann, 1990.

Potash, Chris (editor). *The Jimi Hendrix Companion: Three Decades of Commentary.* New York: Schirmer Books, 1996.

Buddy Holly

Laing, Dave. *Buddy Holly.* London: Studio Vista, 1971.

Goldrosen, John. *Buddy Holly: His Life and Music.* Bowling Green, OH: Popular Press, 1975.

———. *The Buddy Holly Story.* New York: Quick Fox, 1979.

Flippo, Chet. "The Buddy Holly Story: Friends Say Movie's Not Cricket." *Rolling Stone*, no. 274 (September 21, 1978), pp. 49–51.

Janet Jackson
Taraborrelli, J. Randy. *Out of the Madness: The Strictly Unauthorized Biography of Janet Jackson.* New York: Harper, 1994.

Michael Jackson
Brown, Geoff. *Michael Jackson: Body and Soul: An Illustrated Biography.* London: Virgin Books, 1984.
Magee, Doug. *Michael Jackson.* London: Proteus, 1984.
Nelson, George. *Michael Jackson.* New York: Dell, 1984.
————. *The Michael Jackson Story.* London: New English Library, 1984.
Taraborrelli, J. Randy. *Michael Jackson: The Magic and the Madness.* New York: Birch Lane Press, 1991.

The Jackson Five
Manning, Steve. *The Jacksons.* New York: Bobbs-Merrill, 1977.

The Jefferson Airplane/Starship
Gleason, Ralph J. *The Jefferson Airplane and the San Francisco Sound.* New York: Ballantine Books, 1969.
Rowes, Barbara. *Grace Slick: The Biography.* Garden City, NY: Doubleday, 1980.

Waylon Jennings
Allen, Bob. *Waylon and Willie.* New York: Quick Fox, 1979.

Billy Joel
Gambaccini, Peter. *Billy Joel: A Photo-Bio.* New York: Quick Fox, 1979.

Elton John
Gambaccini, Paul. *A Conversation with Elton John and Bernie Taupin.* New York: Flash Books, 1975.
Stein, Cathi. *Elton John.* London: Futura, 1975.
Tatham, Dick, and Jasper, Tony. *Elton John.* London: Octopus Books, 1976.
Newman, Gerald. *Elton John.* New York: Signet Books, 1976.
Shaw, Greg. *Elton John: A Biography in Words and Pictures.* New York: Sire Books, 1976.
Nutter, David. *Elton: It's a Little Bit Funny.* New York: Viking Press, 1977.
Finch, Alan. *Elton John: The Illustrated Discography.* London: Omnibus, 1981.
Charlesworth, Chris. *Elton John, "Only the Piano Player": The Illustrated Elton John.* London: Omnibus, 1984.

Janis Joplin
Dalton, David. *Janis.* New York: Simon and Schuster, 1971.
Landau, Deborah. *Janis Joplin: Her Life and Times.* New York: Paperback Library, 1971.
Caserta, Peggy. *Going Down with Janis.* New York: Dell, 1973.
Friedman, Myra. *Buried Alive: The Biography of Janis Joplin.* New York: William Morrow, 1973.
Carey, Gary. *Lenny, Janis and Jimi.* New York: Pocket Books, 1975.
Amburn, Ellis. *Pearl: The Obsessions and Passions of Janis Joplin.* New York: Warner Books, 1992.

B. B. King
Sawyer, Charles. *The Arrival of B. B. King.* Garden City, NY: Doubleday, 1980.

Carole King
Cohen, Mitchell S. *Carole King: A Biography in Words and Pictures.* New York: Sire Books, 1976.

King Crimson

Tamm, Eric. *Robert Fripp: From King Crimson to Guitar Craft.* London: Faber & Faber, 1991.

The Kinks

Rogan, Johnny. *The Kinks: The Sound and the Fury.* Elm Tree Books, 1984.
Savage, Jon. *The Kinks: The Official Biography.* London: Faber & Faber, 1985.

Kiss

Swenson, John. *Kiss.* New York: Ace Books, 1978.

Kris Kristofferson

Kalet, Beth. *Kris Kristofferson.* New York: Quick Fox, 1979.

Led Zeppelin

Gross, Michael. *Robert Plant.* New York: Popular Library, 1975.
Yorke, Ritchie. *The Led Zeppelin Biography.* Toronto: Methuen, 1976.
Myletts, Howard, and Bunton, Richard. *Led Zeppelin: In the Light, 1968–1980.* London: Proteus, 1981.
Burston, Jeremy. *Led Zeppelin: The Book.* London: Proteus, 1982.
Myletts, Howard. *Jimmy Page: Tangents Within a Framework.* London: Omnibus, 1983.
Davis, Stephen. *Hammer of the Gods: The Led Zeppelin Saga.* London: Sidgwick & Jackson, 1985.
Lewis, Dave. *Led Zeppelin: A Celebration.* London: Omnibus, 1991.

Jerry Leiber and Mike Stoller

Palmer, Robert. *That Was Rock & Roll: The Legendary Leiber and Stoller.* New York: Harvest/HBJ Books, 1978.

John Lennon

Lennon Remembers: The Rolling Stone Interviews by Jann Wenner. San Francisco: Straight Arrow Books, 1971.
Young, Paul. *The Lennon Factor.* New York: Stein & Day, 1972.
Fawcett, Anthony. *John Lennon: One Day at a Time; A Personal Biography of the Seventies.* New York: Grove Press, 1976.
Tremlett, George. *The John Lennon Story.* London: Futura, 1976.
Lennon, Cynthia. *A Twist of Lennon.* Star/W. H. Allen, 1978.
Garbarini, Vic, and Cullman, Brian, with Graustark, Barbara. *Strawberry Fields Forever: John Lennon Remembered.* New York: Bantam/Delilah Books, 1980.
Connolly, Ray. *John Lennon, 1940–1980: A Biography.* London: Fontana, 1981.
Cott, Jonathan, and Doudna, Christine. *The Ballad of John and Yoko.* Garden City, NY: Doubleday Dolphin/Rolling Stone, 1982.
Green, John. *Dakota Days: The Untold Story of John Lennon's Final Years.* New York: St. Martin's Press, 1983.
Coleman, Ray. *Lennon.* New York: McGraw-Hill, 1985.
McCabe, Peter, and Schonfeld, Robert D. *John Lennon: For the Record.* New York: Bantam Books, 1985.
Wiener, Jon. *Come Together: John Lennon in His Own Time.* London: Faber and Faber, 1985.
Goldman, Albert. *The Lives of John Lennon.* New York: William Morrow, 1988.
Solt, Andrew, and Egan, Sam. *Imagine: John Lennon.* New York: Macmillan, 1988.
Thomson, Elizabeth, and Gutman, David (editors). *The Lennon Companion: 25 Years of Comment.* New York: Schirmer Books, 1988.

Jerry Lee Lewis

Palmer, Robert. "The Devil and Jerry Lee Lewis." *Rolling Stone*, no. 306 (December 13, 1979), pp. 57–61.

Cain, Robert. *Whole Lotta Shakin' Goin' On.* New York: Dial Press, 1981.

Palmer, Robert. *Jerry Lee Lewis Rocks.* New York: Delilah Books, 1982.

Lewis, Myra. *Great Balls of Fire: The True Story of Jerry Lee Lewis.* London: Virgin Books, 1982.

Tosches, Nick. *Hellfire: The Jerry Lee Lewis Story.* New York: Dell, 1982.

Gordon Lightfoot

Gabiou, Alfrieda. *Gordon Lightfoot.* New York: Quick Fox, 1979.

Little Richard

White, Charles. *The Life and Times of Little Richard.* New York: Harmony Books, 1984.

Madonna

Voller, Debbi. *Madonna: The New Illustrated Biography.* London: Omnibus, 1990.

Cahill, Marie. *Madonna.* London: Omnibus, 1991.

Anderson, Christopher. *Madonna Unauthorized.* New York: Simon and Schuster, 1991.

Thompson, Douglas. *Like a Virgin: Madonna Revealed.* London: Sidgwick & Jackson, 1992.

The Mamas and the Papas

Johnson, John. "Michelle Phillips Talks About . . . The Mamas and the Papas." *Goldmine,* no. 52 (September 1980), pp. 12, 13, 15.

Bob Marley

Boot, Adrian, and Goldman, Vivien. *Bob Marley: Soul Rebel—Natural Mystic.* New York: St. Martin's Press, 1982.

White, Timothy. *Catch a Fire: The Life of Bob Marley.* New York: Holt, Rinehart and Winston, 1983.

Davis, Stephen. *Bob Marley.* Garden City, NY: Doubleday, 1985.

Paul McCartney

Gambaccini, Paul. "The *Rolling Stone* Interview: Paul McCartney." *Rolling Stone,* no. 153 (January 31, 1974), pp. 32–34, 38–40, 42, 44, 46.

Tremlett, George. *The Paul McCartney Story.* New York: Popular Library, 1975.

Mendelsohn, John. *Paul McCartney: A Biography in Words and Pictures.* New York: Sire Books, 1977.

Welch, Chris. *Paul McCartney: The Definitive Biography.* London: Proteus, 1984.

Salewicz, Chris. *McCartney.* London: Futura, 1987.

Flippo, Chet. *Yesterday: The Unauthorized Biography of Paul McCartney.* Garden City, NY: Doubleday, 1988.

Bette Midler

Baker, Robb. *Bette Midler.* New York: Popular Library, 1975.

Joni Mitchell

Fleischer, Leonore. *Joni Mitchell.* New York: Flash Books, 1976.

Crowe, Cameron. "The *Rolling Stone* Interview: Joni Mitchell." *Rolling Stone,* no. 296 (July 26, 1979), pp. 46–53.

The Monkees

Lefcowitz, Eric. *The Monkees' Tale.* San Francisco: Last Gasp, 1985.

Reilly, Ed; McMannus, Maggie; and Chadwick, Bill. *The Monkees: A Manufactured Image.* Ann Arbor, MI: Pierian Press, 1988.

Van Morrison

Yorke, Ritchie. *Van Morrison: Into the Music.* London: Charisma/Futura, 1975.

Rogan, Johnny. *Van Morrison: The Great Deception.* London: Proteus, 1982.

DeWitt, Howard A. *Van Morrison: The Mystic's Music.* Fremont, CA: Horizon Books, 1983.

Rick Nelson

Callahan, Mike; Buschardt, Bud; and Goddard, Steve. "Both Sides Now: Rick Nelson." *Goldmine*, no. 51 (August 1980), pp. 17–20.

Selvin, Joel. *Ricky Nelson: Idol for a Generation.* Chicago: Contemporary Books, 1990.

Willie Nelson

Flippo, Chet. "The Saga of Willie Nelson: From the Night Life to the Good Life." *Rolling Stone*, no. 269 (July 13, 1978), pp. 45–49.

Allen, Bob. *Waylon and Willie.* New York: Quick Fox, 1979.

Randy Newman

White, Timothy. "Bet No One Ever Hurt This Bad." *Rolling Stone*, no. 303 (November 1, 1979), pp. 40–44.

Harvey, Steve. "Randy Newman." *Goldmine*, no. 66 (November 1981), pp. 16–19, 21.

The New York Dolls

Morrisey, Steven. *New York Dolls.* London: Babylon Books, 1981.

Nirvana

Arnold, Gina. *Route 666: On the Road to Nirvana.* New York: St. Martin's Press, 1993.

Ted Nugent

Holland, Robert. *The Legendary Ted Nugent.* London: Omnibus, 1982.

Phil Ochs

Eliot, Marc. *Death of a Rebel—Starring Phil Ochs.* Garden City, NY: Anchor Press/Doubleday, 1979.

Yoko Ono

Hopkins, Jerry. *Yoko Ono: A Biography.* London: Sidgwick & Jackson, 1987.

Roy Orbison

Amburn, Ellis. *Dark Star.* New York: Lyle Stuart, 1990.

Johnny Otis

Welding, Pete. "The *Rolling Stone* Interview: Johnny Otis." *Rolling Stone*, no. 97 (December 9, 1971), pp. 48–52.

Sam Phillips/Sun Records

Vernon, Paul. *The Sun Legend.* London: Steve Lane, 1969.

Escott, Colin, and Hawkins, Martin. *Catalyst: The Story of Sun Records.* London: Aquarius Books, 1975.

Pink Floyd

Miles. *Pink Floyd: Another Brick.* London: Omnibus, 1981.

Watkinson, Mike, and Anderson, Pete. *Crazy Diamond: Syd Barrett and the Dawn of Pink Floyd.* London: Omnibus, 1990.

Schaffner, Nicholas. *Saucerful of Secrets: The Pink Floyd Odyssey.* London: Sidgwick & Jackson, 1991.

The Police

Woolf, Rosetta. *Message in a Bottle.* London: Virgin Books, 1981.

Goldsmith, Lynn. *The Police.* London: Vermilion, 1983.

Iggy Pop

Nilsen, Per, and Sherman, Dorothy. *Iggy Pop: The Wild One.* London: Omnibus, 1988.

Elvis Presley

Friedman, Favius. *Meet Elvis Presley.* New York: Scholastic Book Services, 1971.

Hopkins, Jerry. *Elvis: A Biography.* New York: Simon and Schuster, 1971.

Mann, May. *Elvis and the Colonel: From the Intimate Diaries of May Mann.* New York: Drake Publishers, 1975.

Harbinson, William Allen. *The Illustrated Elvis.* New York: Grosset and Dunlap, 1976.

Jones, Peter. *Elvis.* London: Octopus Books, 1976.

Zmijewsky, Steve. *Elvis: The Films and Career of Elvis Presley.* Secaucus, NJ: Citadel Press, 1976.

Mann, Richard. *Elvis.* Van Nuys, CA: Bible Voice, 1977.

West, Red; West, Sonny; and Hebler, Dave. *Elvis: What Happened?* New York: Ballantine Books, 1977.

Lichter, Paul. *The Boy Who Dared to Rock: The Definitive Elvis.* New York: Dolphin Books, 1978.

Reggero, John. *Elvis in Concert.* New York: Delta/Lorelei, 1979.

Hopkins, Jerry. *Elvis: The Final Years.* New York: St. Martin's Press, 1980.

Crumbaker, Marge, with Tucker, Gabe. *Up and Down with Elvis Presley.* New York: Putnam, 1981.

Goldman, Albert. *Elvis.* New York: McGraw-Hill, 1981.

Hawkins, Martin, and Escott, Colin. *The Illustrated Discography.* London: Omnibus, 1981.

Dundy, Elaine. *Elvis and Gladys.* New York: Macmillan, 1985.

Presley, Priscilla, with Harmon, Sandra. *Elvis and Me.* New York: Putnam, 1985.

Cotton, Lee. *The Elvis Catalog.* New York: Dolphin/Doubleday, 1987.

————. "Elvis on Disc." *Pulse.* August 1987, pp. 48, 49, 51, 58, 59.

de Barbin, Lucy, and Matera, Davy. *Are You Lonesome Tonight?* New York: Villard, 1987.

Hawkins, Martin, and Escott, Colin. *Elvis Presley.* London: Omnibus, 1987.

Marcus, Greil. *Dead Elvis: A Chronicle of a Cultural Obsession.* New York: Viking Press, 1992.

Esposito, Joe, and Oumano, Elena. *Good Rockin' Tonight: Twenty Years on the Road and on the Town with Elvis.* New York: Simon and Schuster, 1994.

Guralnick, Peter. *Last Train to Memphis: The Rise of Elvis Presley.* Boston: Little, Brown, 1994.

The Pretenders

Miles. *Pretenders.* London: Omnibus, 1981.

Salewicz, Chris. *The Pretenders.* London: Proteus, 1982.

Prince

Hoskyns, Barney. *Prince: Imp of the Perverse.* London: Virgin Books, 1988.

Hill, Dave. *Prince: A Pop Life.* London: Faber & Faber, 1989.

Nilsen, Per. *Prince: A Documentary.* London: Omnibus, 1990.

Procol Harum

Smith, Ronald L. "The Complete Procol Harum." *Goldmine,* no. 45 (February 1980), pp. 12, 13.

Public Image Ltd.

Heylin, Clinton. *Public Image Limited: Rise Fall.* London: Omnibus, 1989.

Queen

Tremlett, George. *The Queen Story.* London: Futura, 1978.

Davis, Judith. *Queen: An Illustrated Biography.* London: Proteus, 1981.

Clarke, Ross. *A Kind of Magic: A Tribute to Freddie Mercury.* London: Kingsfleet, 1992.

Sky, Rick. *The Show Must Go On: The Life of Freddie Mercury.* London: Fontana, 1992.

Rainbow

Makowski, Peter. *Rainbow.* London: Omnibus, 1981.

The Ramones

Miles. *The Ramones: An Illustrated Biography.* London: Omnibus, 1981.

R.E.M.
Gary, Marcus. *An R.E.M. Companion——It Crawled from the South*. London: Guinness, 1992.

Otis Redding
Schiesel, Jane. *The Otis Redding Story*. Garden City, NY: Doubleday, 1973.

Lou Reed
Clapton, Diana. *Lou Reed*. London: Proteus, 1982.
Doggett, Peter. *Lou Reed: Growing Up in Public*. London: Omnibus, 1992.

Lionel Richie
Nathan, David. *Lionel Richie: An Illustrated Biography*. London: Virgin Books, 1985.

The Rolling Stones
Goodman, Pete. *Our Own Story by the Rolling Stones*. New York: Bantam Books, 1965.
Luce, Philip C. *The Stones*. London: Howard Baker, 1970.
Dalton, David. *Rolling Stones: An Unauthorized Biography in Words, Pictures and Music*. New York: Amsco Music Publishing, 1972.
Dimmick, Mary Laverne. *The Rolling Stones: An Annotated Bibliography*. Pittsburgh, PA: University of Pittsburgh, Graduate School of Library and Information Sciences, 1972.
Elman, Richard. *Uptight with the Stones: A Novelist's Report*. New York: Charles Scribner's, 1973.
Marks-Highwater, J. *Mick Jagger: The Singer, Not the Song*. New York: Popular Library, 1973.
Greenfield, Robert. *A Journey Through America with the Rolling Stones*. New York: Dutton, 1974.
Scaduto, Anthony. *Mick Jagger: Everybody's Lucifer*. New York: David McKay, 1974.
Tremlett, George. *The Rolling Stones*. New York: Warner Books, 1974.
Rolling Stone. The Rolling Stones. San Francisco: Straight Arrow Books, 1975.
Carr, Roy. *Rolling Stones: An Illustrated Record*. New York: Harmony Books, 1976.
Jasper, Tony. *The Rolling Stones*. London: Octopus Books, 1976.
Southern, Terry. *The Rolling Stones on Tour*. France: Dragon Dream, 1978.
Dalton, David. *Rolling Stones*. New York: Quick Fox, 1979.
Sanchez, Tony. *Up and Down with the Rolling Stones: The Inside Story*. New York: William Morrow, 1979.
Flippo, Chet. "Nothing Lasts Forever." *Rolling Stone*, no. 324 (August 21, 1980), pp. 38–42, 52.
Dalton, David. *The Rolling Stones: The First Twenty Years*. New York: Alfred A. Knopf, 1981.
Dowley, Tim. *Mick Jagger and the Stones*. Midas Books, 1982.
Palmer, Robert. *The Rolling Stones*. Garden City, NY: Doubleday, 1983.
Booth, Stanley. *Dance with the Devil: The Rolling Stones and Their Times*. New York: Random House, 1984.
Norman, Philip. *Sympathy for the Devil: The Rolling Stone Story*. New York: Simon and Schuster, 1984.
Fitzgerald, Nicholas. *Brian Jones: The Inside Story of the Original Rolling Stones*. New York: Putnam, 1985.
Hotchner, A. E. *Blown Away: The Rolling Stones and the Death of the Sixties*. New York: Simon and Schuster, 1990.
Andersen, Christopher. *Jagger Unauthorized*. New York: Delacorte, 1993.

Linda Ronstadt
Kanakaris, Richard. *Linda Ronstadt: A Portrait*. Los Angeles: Los Angeles Pop, 1977.
Claire, Vivian. *Linda Ronstadt*. New York: Flash Books, 1978.
Moore, Maury Ellen. *The Linda Ronstadt Scrapbook*. New York: Sunridge, 1978.
Berman, Connie. *Linda Ronstadt*. Carson City, NV: Proteus, 1980.

Roxy Music

Lazell, Barry, and Rees, Dafydd. *Bryan Ferry and Roxy Music.* London: Proteus, 1982.

Run-D.M.C.

Adler, B. *Run-D.M.C.* New American Library, 1987.

Doug Sahm

Flippo, Chet. "Like to Send This Out to Everybody: Sir Douglas of the Quintet Is Back (In Texas)." *Rolling Stone*, no. 86 (July 8, 1971), pp. 26–29.

Bob Seger

Marsh, Dave. "Bob Seger: Not a Stranger Anymore." *Rolling Stone*, no. 267 (June 15, 1978), pp. 67–71.

The Sex Pistols

Gruen, Bob. *Chaos: The Sex Pistols.* London: Omnibus, 1990.

Savage, Jon. *England's Dreaming: Sex Pistols and Punk Rock.* London: Faber & Faber, 1991.

Paul Simon

Alterman, Loraine. "The *Rolling Stone* Interview: Paul Simon." *Rolling Stone*, no. 59 (May 28, 1970), pp. 36–39.

Landau, Jon. "The *Rolling Stone* Interview: Paul Simon." *Rolling Stone*, no. 113 (July 20, 1972), pp. 32–38.

Leigh, Spencer. *Paul Simon: Now and Then.* Liverpool, England: Raven Books, 1973.

Marsh, Dave. *Paul Simon.* New York: Quick Fox, 1978.

Humphries, Patrick. *Paul Simon.* Garden City, NY: Doubleday, 1990.

Sly and the Family Stone

Fong-Torres, Ben. "Everybody Is a Star: The Travels of Sylvester Stewart." *Rolling Stone*, no. 54 (March 19, 1970), pp. 28–34.

Patti Smith

Roach, Dusty. *Patti Smith: Rock & Roll Madonna.* South Bend, IN: and books, 1979.

Sonny and Cher

Pellegrino, Vicki. *Cher!* New York: Ballantine Books, 1975.

Phil Spector

Wenner, Jann. "The *Rolling Stone* Interview: Phil Spector." *Rolling Stone*, no. 45 (November 1, 1969), pp. 23–29.

Williams, Richard. *Out of His Head: The Sound of Phil Spector.* New York: Outerbridge and Lazard, 1972.

Beach, Keith A. "Phil Spector: An Overview." *Goldmine*, no. 55 (December 1980), pp. 11–15.

Ribowsky, Mark. *He's a Rebel.* New York: Dutton, 1989.

Bruce Springsteen

Gambaccini, Paul. *Bruce Springsteen: A Photo-Bio.* New York: Jove, 1979.

Marsh, Dave. *Born to Run: The Bruce Springsteen Story.* Garden City, NY: Doubleday, 1979.

Marsh, Dave. *Glory Days.* New York: Pantheon, 1987.

Cat Stevens

Charlesworth, Chris. *Cat Stevens.* London: Proteus, 1985.

John Stewart

Leviton, Mark. "John Stewart: Wheels of Thunder." *BAM*, no. 77 (April 18, 1980), pp. 20–22.

Rod Stewart

Cromelin, Richard. *Rod Stewart*. New York: Chappell Music, 1976.

Pidgeon, John. *Rod Stewart and the Changing Faces*. St. Albans: Panther, 1976.

Tremlett, George. *The Rod Stewart Story*. London: Futura, 1976.

Jasper, Tony. *Rod Stewart*. London: Octopus Books, 1977.

Donna Summer

Haskins, James. *Donna Summer: An Unauthorized Biography*. Boston: Little, Brown, 1983.

The Supremes

Itzkowitz, Leonore K. *Diana Ross*. New York: Random House, 1974.

Berman, Connie. *Diana Ross: Supreme Lady*. New York: Popular Library, 1978.

Haskins, James. *I'm Gonna Make You Love Me: The Story of Diana Ross*. New York: Dial Press, 1980.

Taraborrelli, J. Randy. *Call Her Miss Ross*. New York: Birch Lane Press, 1989.

Talking Heads

Reese, Krista. *The Name of the Band Is Talking Heads*. London: Proteus, 1983.

Gans, David. *Talking Heads — The Band and Their Music*. London: Omnibus, 1986.

James Taylor

Crouse, Timothy. "The First Family of the New Rock." *Rolling Stone*, no. 76 (February 18, 1971), pp. 34–37.

The Temptations

Sbarbori, Jack. "The Way They Do the Things They Do: The Story of the Temptations." *Goldmine*, no. 53 (October 1980), pp. 11–17.

10cc

Tremlett, George. *The 10cc Story*. London: Futura, 1976.

Three Dog Night

Cohen, Joel. *Three Dog Night and Me*. Pasadena, CA: Open Horizon, 1971.

Ike and Tina Turner

Fong-Torres, Ben. "The World's Greatest Heartbreaker." *Rolling Stone*, no. 93 (October 14, 1971), pp. 36–40.

U2

Dunphy, Eamon. *Unforgettable Fire — The Story of U2*. New York: Viking Press, 1988.

Williams, Peter, and Turner, Steve. *U2: Rattle and Hum*. Pyramid, 1988.

Stokes, Niall. *U2: Three Chords and the Truth*. London: Omnibus, 1990.

The Velvet Underground

Thompson, Dave. *Beyond the Velvet Underground*. London: Omnibus, 1989.

Gene Vincent

Hagerty, Britt. *The Day the World Turned Blue*. Dorset, England: Blandford Press, 1985.

Tom Waits

Humphries, Patrick. *Small Change: A Life of Tom Waits*. London: Omnibus, 1989.

Muddy Waters

Guralnick, Peter. "Muddy Waters: A Man of the Blues." *Rolling Stone*, no. 91 (September 16, 1971), pp. 36–39.

Obrecht, Jas. "Muddy Waters: Bluesman, 1915–1983." *Guitar Player*, August 1983, pp. 48, 52-54, 57, 67–70.

Jann Wenner

Anson, Robert Sam. *Gone Crazy and Back Again*. Garden City, NY: Doubleday, 1981.

Draper, Robert. *Rolling Stone Magazine: The Uncensored History.* Garden City, NY: Doubleday, 1990.

The Who
Wenner, Jann. "The *Rolling Stone* Interview: Pete Townshend." *Rolling Stone*, no. 17 (September 14, 1968), pp. 1, 10–15; and no. 18 (September 28, 1968).

Herman, Gary. *The Who.* London: Studio Vista, 1971.

Stein, Jeff, and Johnston, Chris. *The Who.* New York: Stein and Day, 1973.

Rolling Stone. The Who. San Francisco: Straight Arrow Books, 1975.

Tremlett, George. *The Who.* New York: Warner Books, 1975.

Swenson, John. *The Who: Britain's Greatest Rock Group.* New York: Tempo, 1979.

Marcus, Greil. "The *Rolling Stone* Interview: Pete Townshend." *Rolling Stone*, no. 320 (June 26, 1980), pp. 34–39.

Butler, Dougal, with Trengrove, Chris, and Lawrence, Peter. *Full Moon: The Amazing Rock & Roll Life of Keith Moon.* New York: William Morrow, 1981.

Barnes, Richard. *The Who: Maximum R&B.* New York: St. Martin's Press, 1982.

Marsh, Dave. *Before I Get Old: The Story of the Who.* London: Plexus, 1983.

Stevie Wonder
Haskins, James. *The Story of Stevie Wonder.* New York: Dell, 1976.

Elsner, Constance. *Stevie Wonder.* New York: Popular Library, 1977.

Haskins, James. *The Stevie Wonder Scrapbook.* New York: Grosset and Dunlap, 1978.

Wilson, Beth P. *Stevie Wonder.* New York: Putnam, 1978.

Neil Young
Crowe, Cameron. "The *Rolling Stone* Interview: Neil Young." *Rolling Stone*, no. 193 (August 14, 1975), pp. 36–38, 40, 51.

Dufrechou, Carole. *Neil Young.* New York: Quick Fox, 1978.

Crowe, Cameron. "Neil Young: The Last American Hero." *Rolling Stone*, no. 284 (February 8, 1979), pp. 41–46.

Rogan, Johnny. *Neil Young: The Definitive Story of His Musical Career.* London: Proteus, 1982.

Frank Zappa
Walley, David. *No Commercial Potential: The Saga of Frank Zappa and the Mothers of Invention.* New York: Outerbridge and Lazard, 1972.

Snyder, Michael, and Jackson, Blair. "Frank Zappa: Revel Without Applause." *BAM*, no. 26 (January 1978), pp. 30, 31, 33, 35–37.

Occhiogrosso, Peter. *The Real Frank Zappa Book.* New York: Poseidon Press, 1989.

ZZ Top
Thomas, Dave. *Elimination: The ZZ Top Story.* London: Omnibus, 1986.

BOOKS AND ARTICLES BY ARTISTS

References under each artist's name are in chronological order.

Joan Baez
Daybreak. New York: Dial Press, 1968.

And a Voice to Sing With. New York: Summit Books, 1987.

Joan Baez (Harris) and David Harris
Coming Out. New York: Pocket Books, 1971.

Chuck Berry
Chuck Berry: The Autobiography. New York: Harmony Books, 1987.

Pete Best and Patrick Doncaster
Beatle: The Pete Best Story. London: Plexus, 1985.

Sonny Bono
And the Beat Goes On. New York: Pocket Books, 1991.

James Brown with Bruce Tucker
James Brown: The Godfather of Soul. New York: Macmillan, 1987.

Jack Bruce
Quiet Man. London: Sidgwick & Jackson, 1990.

Jimmy Buffett
"Where Is Joe Merchant?" New York: Harcourt, Brace, Jovanovich, 1992.

Eric Burdon
I Used to Be an Animal, But I'm All Right Now. London: Faber and Faber, 1986.

Johnny Cash
Man in Black. Grand Rapids, MI: Zondervan Publishing, 1975.
Man in White. San Francisco: Harper and Row, 1986.

Ray Charles and David Ritz
Brother Ray: Ray Charles' Own Story. New York: Dial Press, 1978.

Dick Clark and Richard Robinson
Rock, Roll & Remember. New York: Popular Library, 1976.

Leonard Cohen
The Favorite Game. New York: Viking Press, 1963.
The Spice Box of Earth. New York: Viking Press, 1965.
Let Us Compare Mythologies. Toronto: McClelland and Stewart, 1966.
Beautiful Losers. New York: Viking Press, 1966.
Selected Poems, 1956–1968. New York: Viking Press, 1968.
The Energy of Slaves. New York: Viking Press, 1972.

Judy Collins
Shameless: A Novel. New York: Paperbooks, 1995.

Alice Cooper (Group)
Me, Alice: The Autobiography of Alice Cooper. New York: Putnam, 1975.

David Crosby
Long Time Gone. Garden City, NY: Doubleday, 1990.

John Densmore
Riders on the Storm: My Life with Jim Morrison and the Doors. London: Bloomsbury, 1991.

Donovan
Dry Songs and Scribbles. Garden City, NY: Doubleday, 1971.

Bob Dylan
Tarantula. New York: Macmillan, 1971.
Bob Dylan: Writings and Drawings. New York: Alfred Knopf, 1973.
Lyrics: 1962–1985. New York: Alfred A. Knopf, 1985.

Richard Fariña
Been Down So Long It Looks Like Up to Me. New York: Random House, 1969.
Long Time Coming and a Long Time Gone. New York: Random House, 1969.

Mick Fleetwood and Stephen Davis
Fleetwood: My Life and Adventures with Fleetwood Mac. New York: William Morrow, 1990.

Connie Francis
Who's Sorry Now? New York: St. Martin's Press, 1984.

Bob Geldof
Is That It? London: Penguin, 1986.

Berry Gordy
To Be Loved. New York: Warner Books, 1994.

Bill Graham and Robert Greenfield
Bill Graham Presents: My Life Inside Rock and Out. Garden City, NY: Doubleday, 1992.

George Harrison
I Me Mine. London: W. H. Allen, 1980.

Mickey Hart
Drumming at the Edge of Magic: A Journey into the Spirit of Percussion. San Francisco: Harper and Row, 1990
Planet Drum: A Celebration of Percussion and Rhythm. New York: HarperCollins, 1992.

Levon Helm with Stephen Davis
This Wheel's On Fire: Levon Helm and the Story of the Band. New York: William Morrow, 1994.

Ian Hunter
Diary of a Rock and Roll Star. St. Albans: Panther, 1974.

Janis Ian
Who Really Cares? New York: Dial Press, 1969.

Michael Jackson
Moonwalk. Garden City, NY: Doubleday, 1988.

Davy Jones
They Made a Monkee Out of Me. Studio City, CA: Dove Books on Tape, 1988.

John Kay with John Einarson
Magic Carpet Ride: The Story of John Kay and Steppenwolf. East Haven, CT: InBook, 1994.

Al Kooper
Backstage Passes: Rock 'n' Roll Life in the Sixties. New York: Stein and Day, 1977.

Tuli Kupferberg
Snow Job: 1946–1959. New York: Pup Press, 1959.

Tuli Kupferberg and Robert Bashlow
1001 Ways to Beat the Draft. New York: G. Layton, 1965.

Tuli Kupferberg and Sylvia Topp
As They Were. New York: Links, 1973.

John Lennon
In His Own Write. New York: Simon and Schuster, 1964.
A Spaniard in the Works. New York: Simon and Schuster, 1965.
Skywriting by Word of Mouth. New York: Harper and Row, 1986.

John Lydon and Keith and Kent Zimmerman
Rotten: No Irish, No Blacks, No Dogs. New York: St. Martin's Press, 1994.

Bette Midler
A View from a Broad. New York: Simon and Schuster, 1980.
The Saga of Baby Divine. New York: Crown, 1983.

Mitch Mitchell and John Platt
Jimi Hendrix: Inside the Experience. New York: Harmony Books, 1990.

Jim Morrison
The Lords and the New Creatures. New York: Simon & Schuster, 1970.
The American Night: The Writings of Jim Morrison. New York: Viking Press, 1991.
The American Night, Volume 2. New York: Viking Press, 1991.

Willie Nelson and Bud Shrake
Willie: An Autobiography. New York: Simon and Schuster, 1988.

John Phillips
Papa John: An Autobiography. Garden City, NY: Doubleday, 1986.

Michelle Phillips
California Dreamin': The True Story of the Mamas and the Papas. New York: Warner Books, 1986.

Noel Redding and Carole Appleby
Are You Experienced? London: Fourth Estate, 1990.

Martha Reeves and Mark Bego
Dancing in the Street: Confessions of a Motown Diva. New York: Hyperion, 1994.

Smokey Robinson and David Ritz
Smokey: Inside My Life. Headline, 1989.

Diana Ross
Secrets of a Sparrow. New York: Villard Books, 1993.

Ed Sanders
Peace Eye. Cleveland, OH: Frontier Press, 1965.
Shards of God. New York: Grove Press, 1970.
The Family: The Story of Charles Manson's Dune Buggy Attack Battalion. New York: Dutton, 1971.
Tales of Beatnik Glory. New York: Stonehill, 1975.

Patti Smith
Seventh Heaven. Boston: Telegraph Books, 1972.
Witt. New York: Gotham, 1973.
Ha! Ha! Houdini. New York: Gotham, 1977.
Babel. New York: Putnam, 1978.

Ronnie Spector with Vince Waldron
Be My Baby: How I Survived Mascara, Miniskirts and Madness; Or My Life as a Fabulous Ronette. New York: Harmony Books, 1990.

Pete Townshend
"Meaty, Beaty, Big and Bouncy." *Rolling Stone*, no. 97 (December 9, 1971), pp. 36–37.
"The Punk Meets the Godfather." *Rolling Stone*, no. 252 (November 17, 1977), pp. 54–59.

Tina Turner and Kurt Loder
I, Tina. New York: Penguin, 1987.

Roger Waters and David Appleby
Pink Floyd: The Wall. New York: Avon, 1982.

Otis Williams
Temptations. New York: Putnam, 1988.

Brian Wilson and Todd Gold
Wouldn't It Be Nice—My Own Story. San Francisco: HarperCollins, 1991.

Mary Wilson
Dream Girl: My Life as a Supreme. New York: St. Martin's Press, 1986.
Supreme Faith: Someday We'll Be Together. San Francisco: HarperCollins, 1990.

Bill Wyman and Ray Coleman
Stone Alone: The Story of a Rock 'n' Roll Band. New York: Viking Press, 1990.

DISCOGRAPHIES, RECORD CHARTS, AND RECORD GUIDES

Christgau, Robert. *Christgau's Record Guide: Rock Albums of the '70s.* New Haven, CT: Ticknor and Fields, 1981.

————. *Christgau's Record Guide: The '80s.* New York: Pantheon, 1990.

Emerson, Lucy. *The Gold Record.* New York: Fountain, 1978.

Gambaccini, Paul. *Rock Critics Choice: The Top 200 Albums.* New York: Quick Fox, 1978.

Gillett, Charlie, and Nugent, Stephen. *Rock Almanac: Top Twenty Singles, 1955–1973, and Top Twenty Albums, 1964–1973.* Garden City, NY: Doubleday, 1976.

————. *Rock Almanac: Top Twenty American and British Singles and Albums of the 50's, 60's and 70's.* Garden City, NY: Anchor Press, 1978.

Goldstein, Stewart, and Jacobson, Alan. *Oldies but Goodies: The Rock 'n' Roll Years.* New York: Mason/Charter, 1977.

Gonzalez, Fernando L. *Disco-File: The Discographical Catalog of American Rock and Roll and Rhythm and Blues.* Flushing, NY: Gonzalez, 1977.

Hill, Randall C. *The Official Price Guide to Collectible Rock Records.* Orlando, FL: House of Collectibles, 1980.

Hounsome, Terry, and Chambre, Tim. *Rock Record.* New York: Facts on File, 1981.

Leadbitter, Mike, and Slaven, Neil. *Blues Records: 1943–1966.* New York: Oak Publications, 1968.

Leibowitz, Alan. *The Record Collector's Handbook.* New York: Everest House, 1980.

Marsh, Dave (editor). *The Rolling Stone Record Guide.* New York: Random House/Rolling Stone Press, 1979.

Miron, Charles. *Rock Gold: All the Hit Charts from 1955 to 1976.* New York: Drake Publishers, 1977.

Murrels, Joseph (compiler). *The Book of Golden Discs.* London: Barrie and Jenkins, 1974.

Osborne, Jerry. *Record Album Price Guide.* Phoenix, AZ: O'Sullivan, Woodside, 1977.

Propes, Steve. *Those Oldies but Goodies: A Guide to 50's Record Collecting.* New York: Macmillan, 1973.

————. *Golden Oldies: A Guide to 60's Record Collecting.* Philadelphia: Chilton, 1974.

————. *Golden Goodies: A Guide to 50's and 60's Popular Rock and Roll Record Collecting.* Philadelphia: Chilton, 1975.

Robbins, Ira (editor). *The Trouser Press Guide to New Wave Records.* Charles Scribner's, 1983.

Rohde, H. Kandy. *The Gold of Rock and Roll: 1955–1967.* New York: Arbor House, 1970.

Rolling Stone. *The Rolling Stone Record Review.* San Francisco: Straight Arrow Books, 1971.

————. *The Rolling Stone Record Review, Volume II.* New York: Pocket Books, 1974.

Roxon, Lillian. *Rock Encyclopedia.* New York: Grosset and Dunlap, 1969.

Lillian Roxon's Rock Encyclopedia. Compiled by Ed Naha. New York: Grosset and Dunlap, 1978.

Schwann Spectrum. Published quarterly. Santa Fe, NM: Stereophile, Inc.

Tudor, Dean, and Tudor, Nancy. *Contemporary Popular Music.* Littleton, CO: Libraries Unlimited, 1979.

————. *Grass Roots Music.* Littleton, CO: Libraries Unlimited, 1979.

————. *Black Music.* Littleton, CO: Libraries Unlimited, 1979.

Umphred, Neal. *Goldmine's Price Guide to Collectible Record Albums 1949–1989*. Iola, WI: Krause Publications, 1991.

————. *Goldmine's Rock 'n' Roll 45 RPM Record Price Guide*. Iola, WI: Krause Publications, 1992.

Whitburn, Joel. Record Research Collection (includes *Top Pop: Singles, 1955–1993*; *Top Albums, 1955–1992*; *Top R&B Singles, 1942–1988*; *Top Country Singles, 1944–1993*; *Top Adult Contemporary, 1961–1993*; *Pop Memories, 1890–1954*; *Pop Annual, 1955–1994*; plus yearly supplements entitled *Music Yearbook*). Menomenee Falls, WI: Record Research, 1988, 1992, 1993.

ENCYCLOPEDIAS, DICTIONARIES, AND GENERAL REFERENCE

Baker, Glenn A., and Cope, Stuart. *The New Music*. New York: Harmony Books, 1981.

Bane, Michael. *The Outlaws: Revolution in Country Music*. New York: Country Music Magazine Press, 1978.

————. *White Boy Singin' the Blues: The Black Roots of White Rock*. New York: Penguin Books, 1982.

Beckman, Jeanette, and Adler, Bill. *Rap: Portraits and Lyrics of a Generation of Black Rockers*. London: Omnibus, 1991.

Belz, Carl. *The Story of Rock*. Second Edition. New York: Oxford University Press, 1972.

Benjaminson, Peter. *The Story of Motown*. New York: Grove Press, 1979.

Benson, Dennis C. *The Rock Generation*. Nashville: Abingdon, 1976.

Berry, Peter E. *". . . And the Hits Just Keep on Comin'."* Syracuse, NY: Syracuse University Press, 1977.

Betrock, Alan. *Girl Groups: The Story of a Sound*. New York: Delilah Books, 1982.

Boeckman, Charles. *And the Beat Goes On: A Survey of Pop Music in America*. Washington, D.C.: Robert B. Luce, Inc., 1972.

Brown, Len, and Friederich, Gary. *Encyclopedia of Rock and Roll*. New York: Tower Publications, 1970.

Burchill, Julie, and Parsons, Tony. *The Boy Looked at Johnny: The Obituary of Rock and Roll*. London: Pluto Press, 1978.

Busnar, Gene. *It's Rock 'n' Roll*. New York: Wanderer Books, 1979.

Cash, Anthony. *Anatomy of Pop*. London: British Broadcasting Corporation, 1970.

Chapple, Steve, and Garofalo, Reebee. *Rock 'n' Roll Is Here to Pay: The History and Politics of the Music Industry*. Chicago: Nelson-Hall, 1977.

Christgau, Robert. *Any Old Way You Choose It: Rock and Other Pop Musics, 1967–1973*. Baltimore: Penguin Books, 1973.

Clark, Al (editor). *The Rock Yearbook, 1982*. New York: St. Martin's Press, 1981.

————. *The Rock Yearbook, 1983*. New York: St. Martin's Press, 1982.

————. *The Rock Yearbook, 1984*. New York: St. Martin's Press, 1984.

Clarke, Donald (editor). *Penguin Encyclopedia of Popular Music*. New York: Viking Press, 1990.

Cohn, Nik. *Rock from the Beginning*. New York: Stein and Day, 1969.

Coon, Caroline. *1988: The New Wave Punk Rock Explosion*. London: Orbach and Chambers, 1977.

Cranna, Ian (editor). *Rock Yearbook 1986*. New York: St. Martin's Press, 1985.

Cummings, Tony. *The Sound of Philadelphia*. London: Methuen, 1975.

Dachs, David. *Anything Goes: The World of Popular Music*. New York: Bobbs-Merrill, 1964.

————. *Inside Pop: America's Top Ten Groups*. New York: Scholastic Book Services. 1968.

————. *American Pop*. New York: Scholastic Book Services, 1969.

————. *Inside Pop 2*. New York: Scholastic Book Services, 1970.

————. *Encyclopedia of Pop / Rock*. New York: Scholastic Book Services, 1972.

Dalton, David, and Kaye, Lenny. *Rock 100*. New York: Grosset & Dunlap, 1977.

David, Andrew. *Rock Stars: People at the Top of the Charts*. Northbrook, IL: Domus, 1979.

Davis, Clive. *Clive: Inside the Record Business*. New York: William Morrow, 1975.

Davis, Julie. *Punk*. Ridgewood, NJ: Davidson Publishing, 1977.

Davis, Stephen. *Reggae Bloodlines: In Search of the Music and Culture of Jamaica*. Garden City, NY: Anchor Press, 1977.

Denisoff, R. Serge. *Solid Gold: The Record Industry, Its Friends and Enemies*. New York: Transaction Books, 1975.

DeTurk, David A., and Poulin Jr., A. (editors). *The American Folk Scene*. New York: Dell, 1967.

Doukas, James N. *Electric Tibet*. Hollywood: Dominican Publishing Company, 1969.

Eisen, Jonathon (editor). *The Age of Rock*. New York: Random House, 1969.

————. *The Age of Rock 2*. New York: Random House, 1970.

————. *Twenty Minute Fandangos and Forever Changes*. New York: Random House, 1971.

Elmlark, Walli, and Beckley, Timothy G. *Rock Raps of the 70's*. New York: Drake Publishers, 1972.

Elson, Howard. *Early Rockers*. London: Proteus, 1982.

Field, James J. *American Popular Music, 1950–1975*. Philadelphia: Musical Americana, 1976.

Flattery, Paul. *The Illustrated History of British Pop*. New York: Drake Publishers, 1975.

Fong-Torres, Ben (editor). *The Rolling Stone Rock 'n' Roll Reader*. New York: Bantam Books, 1975.

————. *What's That Sound? The Contemporary Music Scene from the Pages of Rolling Stone*. Garden City, NY: Anchor Press, 1976.

Frame, Peter. *Rock Family Trees*. New York: Quick Fox, 1980.

————. *Rock Family Trees 2*. New York: Quick Fox, 1983.

Fredericks, Vic (editor). *Who's Who in Rock 'n' Roll*. New York: Frederick Fell, 1968.

Gabree, John. *The World of Rock*. New York: Fawcett Publications, 1968.

Gaines, Steve. *Who's Who in Rock 'n' Roll*. New York: Popular Library, 1975.

Garland, Phyl. *The Sound of Soul*. Chicago: Henry Regnery Company, 1969.

Gillett, Charlie. *The Sound of the City: The Rise of Rock 'n' Roll*. New York: Dell, 1972.

————. *The Sound of the City: The Rise of Rock and Roll*. New York: Pantheon, 1983.

————. *Making Tracks: The Story of Atlantic Records*. New York: Outerbridge and Lazard, 1973.

———— (editor). *Rock File*. London: New English Library, 1972.

————, and Nugent, Stephen. *Rock Almanac*. Garden City, NY: Anchor Press/Doubleday, 1976.

Goldman, Albert H. *Freakshow*. New York: Atheneum, 1971.

Goldstein, Richard. *Goldstein's Greatest Hits*. Englewood Cliffs, NJ: Prentice-Hall, 1970.

Goldsworthy, Jay (editor). *Casey Kasem's American Top 40 Yearbook*. New York: Target Books, 1979.

Gray, Andy. *Great Pop Stars*. London: Hamlyn, 1973.

Green, Jonathon (editor). *The Book of Rock Quotes*. London: Omnibus, 1978.

Groia, Philip. *They All Sang on the Street Corner: New York City's Rhythm and Blues Vocal Groups of the 1950's*. Setauket, NY: Edmond, 1974.

Gross, Michael, and Jakubowski, Maxim (editors). *The Rock Yearbook, 1981*. London: Virgin Books, 1980.

Grossman, Lloyd. *A Social History of Rock Music: From the Greasers to Glitter Rock*. New York: McKay, 1976.

Guitar Player. *Rock Guitarists.* Saratoga, CA: Guitar Player Productions, 1974.

————. *Rock Guitarists, Volume II.* Saratoga, CA: Guitar Player Productions, 1977.

Guralnick, Peter. *Feel Like Going Home: Portraits in Blues and Rock 'n' Roll.* New York: Outerbridge and Dienstfrey, 1971.

————. *Sweet Soul Music.* Harper and Row, 1986.

Hall, Douglas K., and Clark, Sue C. *Rock: A World as Bold as Love.* New York: Cowles, 1970.

Haralambos, Michael. *From Blues to Soul in Black America.* New York: Drake Publishers, 1975.

Hardy, Phil. *Encyclopedia of Rock.* New York: Schirmer Books, 1988.

Hardy, Phil, and Laing, Dave (editors). *The Encyclopedia of Rock, Volume 1: The Age of Rock 'n' Roll.* St. Albans: Aquarius, 1976.

————. *The Encyclopedia of Rock, Volume 2: From Liverpool to San Francisco.* St. Albans: Aquarius, 1976.

————. *The Encyclopedia of Rock, Volume 3: The Sounds of the Seventies.* St. Albans: Aquarius, 1976.

The Harmony Illustrated History of Rock. New York: Harmony Books, 1982.

Helander, Brock. *The Rock Who's Who.* New York: Schirmer Books, 1982.

Heylin, Clinton (editor). *Penguin Book of Rock 'n' Roll Writing.* New York: Viking Press, 1992.

Hibbert, Tom (editor). *Rock Yearbook, 1987.* New York: St. Martin's Press, 1987.

Hirshey, Gerri. *Nowhere to Run: The Story of Soul Music.* New York: Times Books, 1984.

Hoare, Ian (editor). *The Soul Book.* New York: Delta Books, 1976.

Hodenfield, Chris. *Rock '70.* New York: Pyramid Publications, 1970.

Hopkins, Jerry. *Rock: From Elvis to the Rolling Stones.* New York: Quadrangle / New York Times Book Company, 1973.

Jasper, Tony. *Understanding Pop.* London: S.C.M. Press, 1972.

Jenkinson, Philip, and Warner, Alan. *Celluloid Rock: Twenty Years of Movie Rock.* London: Lorrimer, 1974.

Laing, Dave. *The Sound of Our Time.* Chicago: Quadrangle Books, 1970.

————. *The Electric Muse: The Story of Folk into Rock.* London: Methuen, 1975.

Landau, Jon. *It's Too Late to Stop Now: A Rock 'n' Roll Journal.* San Francisco: Straight Arrow Books, 1972.

Larkin, Rochelle. *Soul Music.* New York: Lancer Books, 1970.

Logan, Nick, and Woffinden, Bob. *The Illustrated Encyclopedia of Rock.* New York: Harmony Books, 1977.

Lydon, Michael. *Rock Folk: Portraits from the Rock 'n' Roll Pantheon.* New York: Dial Pres, 1971.

————. *Boogie Lightnin'.* New York: Dial Press, 1974.

Mabey, Richard. *Behind the Scene.* London: Penguin Books, 1968.

————. *The Pop Process.* London: Hutchinson, 1969.

Macken, Bob; Fornatale, Peter; and Ayres, Bill. *The Rock Music Source Book.* Garden City, NY: Anchor Press, 1980.

Marchbank, Pearce, and Miles. *The Illustrated Rock Almanac.* New York: Paddington Press, 1977.

Marcus, Greil. *Rock and Roll Will Stand.* Boston: Beacon Press, 1969.

————. *Mystery Train: Images of America in Rock 'n' Roll Music.* New York: Dutton, 1975.

Marsh, Dave. *The Heart of Rock and Soul.* Penguin, 1989.

————, and Swenson, John (editors). *The Rolling Stone Record Guide.* New York: Random House / Rolling Stone Press, 1979.

————, and Stein, Kevin. *The Book of Rock Lists.* Garden City, NY: Dell / A Rolling Stones Book, 1981.

May, Chris. *Rock 'n' Roll*. London: Socion Books, n.d.

————, and Phillips, Tim. *British Beat*. London: Socion Books, n.d.

McDonough, Jack. *San Francisco Rock*. San Francisco: Chronicle Books, 1985.

Meltzer, Richard. *The Aesthetics of Rock*. New York: Something Press, 1970.

Miller, Jim (editor). *Rolling Stone Illustrated History of Rock & Roll*. New York: Rolling Stone Press/Random House, 1976, 1980.

Morse, David. *Motown and the Arrival of Black Music*. New York: Macmillan, 1971.

Muirhead, Bert. *The Record Producers File: A Directory of Rock Album Record Producers, 1962–1984*. Dorset, England: Blandford Press, 1984.

Nanry, Charles (editor). *American Music: From Storyville to Woodstock*. New Brunswick, NJ: Transaction Books, 1972.

Nelson, George. *The Death of Rhythm & Blues*. New York: Pantheon, 1988.

Nite, Norm N. *Rock On: The Illustrated Encyclopedia of Rock 'n' Roll: The Solid Gold Years*. New York: Thomas Y. Crowell, 1974.

————. *Rock On: The Illustrated Encyclopedia of Rock 'n' Roll, Volume II: The Modern Years, 1964–Present*. New York: Thomas Y. Crowell, 1978.

————. *Rock On: The Illustrated Encyclopedia of Rock 'n' Roll, Volume 3: The Video Revolution, 1978–Present*. New York: Harper and Row, 1985.

————. *Rock On Almanac: First Four Decades of Rock 'n' Roll—A Chronology*. New York: HarperCollins, 1991.

Ochs, Michael. *Rock Archives*. New York: Doubleday/Dolphin, 1984.

O'Donnell, Jim. *The Rock Book*. New York: Pinnacle Books, 1975.

Orloff, Katherine. *Rock 'n' Roll Woman*. Los Angeles: Nash Publishing, 1974.

Palmer, Robert. *Rock & Roll. An Unruly History*. New York: Crown, 1995.

Palmer, Tony. *All You Need Is Love: The Story of Popular Music*. New York: Grossman Publishers, 1976.

Pareles, Jon, and Romanowski, Patricia (editors). *The Rolling Stone Encyclopedia of Rock & Roll*. New York: Simon and Schuster, 1983.

Pascall, Jeremy. *The Illustrated History of Rock Music*. New York: Galahad Books, 1978.

Passman, Arnold. *The Dee Jays*. New York: Macmillan, 1971.

Petrie, Gavin (editor). *Black Music*. London: Hamlyn, 1974.

————. *Rock Life*. London: Hamlyn, 1974.

Phoebus. *The Stars and Superstars of Rock*. London: Phoebus Publishing/Octopus Books, 1974.

————. *Country Music*. London: Phoebus Publishing, 1976.

————. *The Stars and Superstars of Black Music*. London: Phoebus Publishing, 1977.

————. *West Coast Story*. London: Phoebus Publishing, 1977.

Pollock, Bruce. *In Their Own Words*. New York: Macmillan, 1975.

————. *When Rock Was Young*. New York: Holt, Rinehart and Winston, 1981.

Redd, Lawrence N. *Rock Is Rhythm and Blues: The Impact of Mass Media*. East Lansing, MI: Michigan University Press, 1974.

Reid, Jan. *The Improbable Rise of Redneck Rock*. Austin, TX: Heidelberg Publishers, 1974.

Rivelli, Pauline, and Levin, Robert (editors). *The Rock Giants*. New York: World, 1970.

Robinson, Richard (editor). *Rock Revolution*. New York: Popular Library, 1976.

————, and Zwerling, Andy. *The Rock Scene*. New York: Popular Library, 1971.

Rolling Stone. *The Rolling Stone Interviews*. New York: Paperback Library, 1971.

————. *The Rolling Stone Interviews, Volume 2*. New York: Paperback Library, 1973.

————. *The Rolling Stone Reader*. New York: Warner Paperback Library, 1974.

————. *Rolling Stone's Illustrated History of Rock 'n' Roll*. New York: Random House, 1993.

Romanowski, Patricia, and George-Warren, Holly (editors). *The New Rolling Stone Encyclopedia of Rock & Roll.* New York: Fireside Books, 1995.

Roxon, Lillian. *Rock Encyclopedia.* New York: Grosset and Dunlap, 1969.

Sander, Ellen. *Trips: Rock Life in the Sixties.* New York: Charles Scribner's, 1973.

Sarlin, Bob. *Turn It Up! (I Can't Hear the Words): The Best of the New Singer/Songwriters.* New York: Simon and Schuster, 1974.

Schafer, William J. *Rock Music: Where It's Been, What It Means, Where It's Going.* Minneapolis, MN: Augsburg Publishing, 1972.

Schicke, C. A. *Revolution in Sound: A Biography of the Recording Industry.* Boston: Little, Brown, 1974.

Scoppa, Bud. *The Rock People.* New York: Scholastic Book Services, 1973.

Selvin, Joel. *Monterey Pop.* London: Plexus, 1992.

Shaw, Arnold. *The Rock Revolution.* New York: Crowell-Collier, 1969.

————. *The World of Soul.* New York: Cowles, 1970.

————. *The Rockin' 50's.* New York: Hawthorn Books, 1974.

————. *Honkers and Shouters: The Golden Years of Rhythm and Blues.* New York: Macmillan, 1978.

————. *Black Popular Music in America.* New York: Schirmer, 1990.

Sia, Joseph J. *Woodstock '69: Summer Pop Festivals.* New York: Scholastic Book Services, 1970.

Silver, Caroline. *The Pop Makers.* New York: Scholastic Book Services, 1966.

Somma, Robert (editor). *No One Waved Goodbye: A Casualty Report on Rock and Roll.* New York: Outerbridge and Dientsfrey, 1971.

Spitz, Robert Stephen. *The Making of Superstars: Artists and Executives of the Rock Music Business.* Garden City, NY: Anchor Press, 1978.

Stambler, Irwin. *Encyclopedia of Popular Music.* New York: St. Martin's Press, 1965.

————. *Guitar Years: Pop Music from Country and Western to Hard Rock.* Garden City, NY: Doubleday, 1970.

————. *Encyclopedia of Pop, Rock, and Soul.* New York: St. Martin's Press, 1975; New York: Macmillan, 1989.

————, and Landon, Grelun. *Encyclopedia of Folk, Country, and Western Music.* New York: St. Martin's Press, 1969.

Suter, Paul. *HM A–Z.* London: Omnibus, 1985.

Thomson, Liz (editor). *New Women in Rock.* New York: Delilah/Putnam, 1984.

Tobler, John. *Guitar Heroes.* New York: St. Martin's Press, 1978.

Tosches, Nick. *Unsung Heroes of Rock 'n' Roll.* Charles Scribner's, 1984.

Van Der Horst, Brian. *Rock Music.* New York: Watts, 1973.

Vassal, Jacques. *Electric Children: Roots and Branches of Modern Folk-Rock.* Trans. Paul Barnett. New York: Taplinger, 1975.

Vinson, Lee. *Encyclopedia of Rock.* New York: Drake Publishers, 1976.

von Schmidt, Eric, and Rooney, Jim. *Baby, Let Me Follow You Down: The Illustrated Story of the Cambridge Folk Years.* Garden City, NY: Anchor Books, 1979.

Ward, Ed; Stokes, Geoffrey; and Tucker, Ken. *Rock of Ages: The Rolling Stone History of Rock and Roll.* Penguin, 1988.

White, Timothy. *Rock Lives.* New York: Henry Holt, 1989.

Williams, Paul. *Outlaw Blues: A Book of Rock Music.* New York: Dutton, 1969.

Wood, Graham. *An A–Z of Rock and Roll.* London: Studio Vista, 1971.

York, William (editor). *Who's Who in Rock Music.* Seattle: Atomic Press, 1978.

Young, Jean, and Lang, Michael. *Woodstock Music Festival Remembered.* New York: Ballantine Books, 1979.

Zalkind, Ronald (editor). *Contemporary Music Almanac 1980/81.* New York: Schirmer Books, 1980.

INDEX

Anthem of the Sun, 262
Anthology (Beatles film), 37
Anthology (Beatles), 283, 654
Anthony, Michael, 701–703
Anthony, Mike, 408
Anthrax, 359, 543
Anticipation, 622
Antoni, Robert, 594
Any Day Now, 20
"Any Day Now," 527
"Any Way the Wind Blows," 146, 179, 760
Any Which Way You Can, 173
"Anyday," 107
Anything Can Happen, 599
"Anything Can Happen," 72
Anytime . . . Anywhere, 133
"Anytime, Anyplace," 311
"Anyway, Anyhow, Anywhere," 728, 745
"Anyway You Want It," 109
"Apeman," 356
Apocalypse, 430
Apocalypse 91, 543
Apocalypse Now, 181, 264
"Apollo Medley, The," 679
Apollonia 6, 536
Apostrophe ('), 761
Appel, Mike, 646, 647
Appetite for Destruction, 274
Appice, Carmine, 39, 40, 54
Appice, Vinnie, 48
"Apple Scruffs," 282
"Approaching Lavender," 385
Aqua Boogie, 115
Aqualung, 326
"Aqualung," 326
"Aquarius/Let the Sun Shine In," 213
Arc, 755
Arc Angels, 703, 704, 705
Arc of a Diver, 688
Archies, The, 27
Archives to '80s, 419
ArcWeld, 755
Ardells, The, 439, 609
Are You Experienced?, 287
"Are You Lonesome Tonight," 526
"Are You Man Enough," 230
"Are You Sure Hank Done It This Way," 323
Areas, Jose "Chepito," 605–609
Aretha Gospel, 235
Aretha Now, 236
"Arizona," 560
Ark, 11
Armageddon, 746, 747
Armchair Theatre, 200
Armed Forces, 136, 571
"Armenia City in the Sky," 729
"Arms of Orion, The," 537
"Armstrong," 352
Arnell, Ginny, 510
Arnold, Eddy, 525
Arnold, Jerome, 79
Arnold, Pat, 201

"Arnold Layne," 507
Aronoff, Kenny, 319
"Around My Heart," 744
Around the Next Dream, 143
Around the World in a Day, 536
"Arrow Through Me," 427
Arrows, The, 592
Ars Longa Vita Brevis, 201
Art, 644
"Art for Art's Sake," 684
Art of Noise, The, 197
Arthur, 18
Arthur (or the Decline and Fall of the British Empire), 356
"Artificial Flowers," 156–57
Artistics, The, 672
Artwoods, The, 158
"As," 740
"As I Am," 592
"As Long As I'm Moving," 70
"As Tears Go By," 575
"As Usual," 375
Asbury Jukes, The, 647
Asher, Jane, 498
Asher, Peter, 497–99, 550, 583, 675, 676
"Ashes by Now," 152
"Ashes of Love," 223
"Ashes to Ashes," 63, 683
Asheton, Ron, 522–24
Asheton, Scott, 522–24
Ashford, Nicholas, 213, 243, 300, 362, 590, 667
Ashford, Rosalind, 417–18
Ashley, Bob, 271
Asia, 202, 203, 250, 346, 347, 349, 607, 684, 749, 752
Ask Rufus, 590
Ask Rufus, 590
"Ask the Lonely," 230
"Asking for It," 474
Association, The, 15–16
Astral Weeks, 451
Asylum Choir, The, 598, 599, 600
At Crooked Lake, 754
At Fillmore East, 7, 8
"At Midnight (My Love Will Lift You Up)," 590
"At Seventeen," 302
"At the Zoo," 624
At Your Birthday Party, 657
Atkins, Chet, 170, 171, 204, 322, 575
Atkins, Cholly, 360
Atkins, Martin, 616
"Atlanta Lady," 318
"Atlantic City," 647
Atlantic Crossing, 660
"Atlantis," 176
Atom Heart Mother, 507
"Atomic," 52
"Atomic Dog," 116
Atomic Rooster, 201, 419
Attila, 329, 330
"Attitude Dancing," 622
Attractions, The, 136, 137
Au Go Go Singers, 73
Aucoin, Bill, 359

Auf der Maur, Melissa, 472–74
Auger, Brian, 11, 429, 660
August, 140
Austin City Limits, 713
Autistics, The, 672
Autoamerican, 52
"Automatic," 518
Automatic for the People, 558
Automatic Man, 607, 608
"Autumn Almanac," 356
Avalon, 471, 586, 587
Avalon, Frankie, 111, 456
Avedon, Richard, 726
Average White Band, 183, 184, 427
Avory, Mick, 355–58
Awakenings, 471
Axis: Bold as Love, 287
Axton, Hoyt, 20, 178, 352, 653, 657, 685, 686
Ayers, Kevin, 519, 707, 708
Aykroyd, Dan, 59

B

B-52's, 523, 558, 625, 673
Baah, Reebop Kwaku, 687–91
Baba, Meher, 730
"Baba O'Riley," 729
Babes in Toyland, 92, 473
"B-A-B-Y," 284
"Baby (You've Got What It Takes)," 43
"Baby, Ain't That Fine," 510
"Baby, Baby Don't Cry," 567
"Baby, Don't Do It," 243
"(You're So Square) Baby, I Don't Care," 442
"Baby, I Love You," 27, 236, 552, 570, 581, 639
"Baby, I Love Your Way," 232
"Baby, It's You," 17, 619, 620
"Baby, Let Me Follow You Down," 185
"Baby, Please Don't Go," 371, 450, 722
"Baby, What a Big Surprise," 105
"Baby, You're Right," 66
"Baby Baby Baby," 236
"Baby Come Close," 568
"Baby Don't Change Your Mind," 362
"Baby Don't Go," 636
"Baby Driver," 625
"Baby Grand," 330
"Baby Hold on to Me," 482
"Baby I Need Your Loving," 230, 294
"Baby Jane," 661
"Baby Let Me Hold Your Hand," 99
"Baby Let's Play House," 504, 525
"Baby Love," 294, 667
"Baby Plays Around," 137
Baby Snakes, 761
"Baby Talk," 314
"Baby That's Backatcha," 568

Babylon 5, 520
"Baby's Callin' Me Home," 439
Babysitters, The, 590
Bach, Johann Sebastian, 326
Bacharach, Burt, 17–18, 77, 91, 163, 213, 236, 396, 510, 620, 663, 719–20
Bachman, Randy, 271–73, 654
Bachman, Robbie, 271–73
Bachman, Tim, 271–73
Bachman-Turner Overdrive, 271–73
Back At 'Cha, 604
"Back Door Man," 180
Back from Hell, 597
Back from Rio, 84
Back in Black, 5
"Back in My Arms Again," 294, 667
Back in the High Life, 687, 689
"Back in the High Life Again," 689
"Back in the Saddle," 6
"Back in the U.S.A.," 583
"Back in the U.S.S.R.," 36
"Back in Time," 490
"Back Off Boogaloo," 653
"Back on My Feet Again," 470
Back on the Block, 590
"Back on the Chain Gang," 534
Back Stabbers, 481
"Back Stabbers," 481
Back Street Crawler, 18
"Back Street Girl," 575
"Back Street Slide," 209
Back to Avalon, 393
"Back to Front," 562
Back to Mono, 640
"Back to School Days," 489, 571
Back to the Egg, 427
"Back to the Island," 599
Back to the Light, 546
Back to the Roots, 419
Back to the World, 423
"Back Together Again," 277
"Back Up Train," 269
Backbeat, 37
"Backlash," 592
"Backstage," 510
Bacon, Max, 250, 749
Bad, 310
"Bad," 310
"Bad, Bad Leroy Brown," 148
"Bad Blood," 332, 611
Bad Boy, 653
"Bad Boys Get Spanked," 534
Bad Company, 18–20, 226, 346, 347, 372, 453
"Bad Company," 19
"Bad Girl," 404, 567, 611
Bad Girls, 664, 665
"Bad Girls," 468
Bad Influence, 140
"Bad Influence," 140
"Bad Luck," 339
"Bad Luck (Part 1)," 492
"Bad Moon Rising," 146
Bad Reputation, 592
"Bad Time," 260
"Bad to Me," 35